American Voices

American Voices

An Encyclopedia of Contemporary Orators

Edited by Bernard K. Duffy
and Richard W. Leeman

Greenwood Press
Westport, Connecticut • London

Library of Congress Cataloging-in-Publication Data

American voices : an encyclopedia of contemporary orators / edited by Bernard K. Duffy and Richard W. Leeman.
    p. cm.
  Includes bibliographical references and index.
  ISBN 0–313–32790–4 (alk. paper)
    1. American prose literature—20th century—Dictionaries.
2. Political oratory—United States—History—20th century—Dictionaries.
3. Orators—United States—Biography—Dictionaries. 4. Speeches, addresses, etc.,
American—Dictionaries. I. Duffy, Bernard K. II. Leeman, Richard W.
PS408.A47   2005
815'.5409358—dc22   2005006187

British Library Cataloguing in Publication Data is available.

Library of Congress Catalog Card Number: 2005006187
ISBN 0–313–32790–4

First published in 2005

Greenwood Press, 88 Post Road West, Westport, CT 06881
An imprint of Greenwood Publishing Group, Inc.
www.greenwood.com

Printed in the United States of America

The paper used in this book complies with the
Permanent Paper Standard issued by the National
Information Standards Organization (Z39.48–1984).

10 9 8 7 6 5 4 3 2 1

Contents

Preface   ix

Introduction   xi

John D. Ashcroft   1
Harry Hellenbrand

Elizabeth M. Birch   8
Shawn Parry-Giles and Jason Edward Black

Patrick J. Buchanan   16
C. Brant Short

George Herbert Walker Bush   22
Craig R. Smith

George Walker Bush   31
Richard E. Vatz

Robert Carlyle Byrd   39
William D. Pederson and Sina K. Nazemi

Stokely Carmichael (Kwame Touré)   46
Robert E. Terrill

James Earl "Jimmy" Carter   53
Richard W. Leeman

Cesar Estrada Chavez   61
John C. Hammerback and Richard J. Jensen

Ward L. Churchill   70
Catherine H. Palczewski and Randall A. Lake

Hillary Diane Rodham Clinton   77
Karrin Vasby Anderson

William Jefferson Clinton   84
Stephen A. Smith

Mario Matthew Cuomo   97
Mary Anne Trasciatti

Thomas Andrew Daschle   104
Troy A. Murphy

Angela Yvonne Davis   111
Cindy L. Griffin

Alan Dershowitz   119
R. John DeSanto and Daniel A. Grano

Elizabeth Hanford Dole   126
Nichola Gutgold

Marian Wright Edelman   133
Beth Waggenspack

Joycelyn Elders   141
Lorraine D. Jackson

Jerry Falwell   149
Paul Stob and Charles Conrad

Louis Abdul Farrakhan   155
Mark Lawrence McPhail

Gerald Rudolph Ford   164
Hermann G. Stelzner, revised by Charles F. Ottinger

Albert Arnold Gore, Jr.   169
David Hoffman

William Franklin (Billy) Graham, Jr.   177
*Hal W. Fulmer and Jennifer Young
Abbott*

Anita Faye Hill   187
Vanessa B. Beasley

Jesse Louis Jackson   192
David B. McLennan

Lyndon Baines Johnson   203
David Zarefsky

Sonia Johnson   211
Karen A. Foss

Barbara Charline Jordan   217
Carl R. Burgchardt

Edward Moore Kennedy   224
William D. Pederson

John Fitzgerald Kennedy   231
*Theodore O. Windt, Jr., revised by
Steven R. Goldzwig*

Robert Francis Kennedy   238
*Steven R. Goldzwig and Patricia A.
Sullivan*

John F. Kerry   247
*Bernard K. Duffy and Marilyn
DeLaure*

Martin Luther King, Jr.   258
*Marilyn DeLaure and Bernard K.
Duffy*

Larry Kramer   270
Charles E. Morris

Winona LaDuke   277
*Dayle C. Hardy-Short and C. Brant
Short*

Audre Geraldine Lorde   285
Lester C. Olson

Wilma Mankiller   293
Christopher J. Skiles

Thurgood Marshall   299
Stephen A. Smith

William (Bill) Paul McCartney   307
Jennifer Young Abbott

Russell Means   316
*Randall A. Lake and Catherine H.
Palczewski*

Harvey Bernard Milk   324
Karen A. Foss

Ralph Nader   330
*Patricia A. Sullivan and Steven R.
Goldzwig*

Richard Milhous Nixon   338
*Celeste M. Condit and Shannon
Holland*

Samuel Augustus Nunn   346
Edward M. Panetta

Sandra Day O'Connor   353
Janice Schuetz

H. Ross Perot   360
*Valerie A. Endress and Mari Boor
Tonn*

Colin Luther Powell   368
Richard W. Leeman

Ronald Wilson Reagan   378
*Ronald H. Carpenter and Windy Y.
Lawrence*

Janet Reno   390
Janice Schuetz

Donald H. Rumsfeld   398
Gordon Stables

Antonin Scalia   407
Catherine Langford

Al Sharpton   414
Daniel A. Grano

Gloria Steinem   422
Lisa Shawn Hogan

George Corley Wallace   429
Andrew King

Alyce Faye Wattleton   434
Lorraine D. Jackson

Christine Todd Whitman   440
Kristina Horn Sheeler

Malcolm X   449
Thomas W. Benson

Bibliographic Essay   455
Alan Razee

Index   465

About the Editors and Contributors   477

Preface

Sixteen years have passed since the publication of *American Orators of the Twentieth Century* and *American Orators Before 1900*. Although unnumbered, the present work is effectively a third volume that dovetails with the twentieth-century volume. We decided that a new book on contemporary speakers must include all American presidents since 1960 and the most recognized speakers from the 1960s to the present day. Thus, there are essays on legendary speakers such as Martin Luther King Jr., Malcolm X, John Kennedy, and Ronald Reagan, but the broad majority of essays in this book are about quite recent speakers.

With all such books, difficult choices arise. As editors we have tried to be as inclusive as possible, and the selection of speakers represented is varied. Most are politicians, activists, and jurists. Some speak to national audiences, some to much smaller groups united by common interest. One of our primary aims in this work was to cast a broad net and include figures who are important in their communities but who may not be as well known to the general public. The list of speakers we wanted to cover exemplifies contemporary American oratory but is by no means exhaustive.

In editing, there are too many matters that are beyond control for us to hope for perfection, from finding authors willing to break new ground in writing about figures heretofore unexamined to the difficulties of corralling errant essays. We do not presume that we will please everyone in our selection of speakers. Although we began with a list that pleased us, the general guidance of the Greenwood editorial board and the specific interests of scholars in the field also helped to shape the book. Scholars proposed several figures whom we had not contemplated including.

In this undertaking we were always buoyed by confidence in the professionalism, competence, and imagination of the chapter authors. Colleagues who agreed to write essays about figures on whom little or no scholarly literature exists had difficult tasks. The first furrow in untilled soil is sometimes the hardest, although the reconsideration of extensively studied figures clearly presents its own challenges.

Web addresses listed in the references have been checked for accuracy. However, even material available from the most stable Web sites, such as those of government agencies and large non-profit organizations, can be relocated or deleted completely. If a specific Web page cannot be accessed, it is often possible to find the same page by searching the Web site where the document was stored. For example, a speech that had been in a current events file is sometimes archived to a different place on the Web site, but is still available. Because Web pages are less stable than Web sites, we have often listed only the Web site, such as www.pbs.org or www.cnn.com, in the hope that the desired material is researchable through the Web site. Web sites are less vulnerable to elimination, although this also occurs when, for example, a public official loses an election or when an organization changes its name or loses funding. Although Web research can often be frustrating, we believe it better to include Web materials rather than to omit them, but realize that accessing such material is an imperfect process. We apologize for any inconvenience this may cause readers.

From proposal to finished work, this project has taken four years. As always, the Greenwood editors and staff have been supportive and encouraging. They understand the complexities of a project requiring cooperation from a host of people. We appreciate the assistance of acquisitions editors Douglas Goldenberg-Hart and Sarah Colwell, copyeditor Beth Wilson, permissions editor Marcia Goldstein, and production editor Deborah Masi. We also thank the Greenwood consultants for their enthusiastic support of this project. Our mentors, emeritus professors Robert P. Newman and Trevor Melia, and professors Kathleen Jamieson and Chuck Kaufman, deserve our gratitude for personifying scholarship and teaching of the highest caliber.

Our respective institutions provided sabbaticals and staff support, which we gratefully acknowledge. Professors Ronald Carpenter of the University of Florida, and Marilyn DeLaure and Susan Duffy of Cal Poly, graciously read and offered very useful suggestions for the introduction. Deron Nardo helped procure permissions. We were greatly encouraged by students at our respective institutions who responded to our ideas and, through their expressions of interest, affirmed the inherent value of the project. Appreciation is affectionately owed to our spouses, Susan Duffy and Carol Leeman, and our children, Elizabeth Duffy and Christopher and Gregory Leeman, for their patience when occasionally the exigencies of writing and editing distracted us from the attention they deserve.

Bernard K. Duffy, San Luis Obispo, California
Richard W. Leeman, Charlotte, North Carolina

Introduction

This book defines the higher role of oratory in an era of sound bites and image politics. In many discussions of formal speeches, pundits routinely attempt to forecast which phrases will be highlighted in the news, discussed in Internet chat rooms, and used in political advertisements. Considering the dominance of the electronic media in American life, civic oratory might seem atavistic, an obligatory performance in a media spectacle where the scenic backdrop and visual symbolism dominate. Oratory today differs stylistically from anything Demosthenes, Edmund Burke, or Daniel Webster could have anticipated, and differs radically in the media through which most people hear and see speeches delivered, but still persists as vital to democratic decision-making, to supporting traditional values, and to dissenting from them.

Since the study of rhetoric began in the fifth and fourth centuries B.C., philosophers and rhetoricians have debated the cultural and social role of the orator. Among the Sophists, Gorgias declared that rhetoric is the "master art." The fifty-eight studies in this book confirm the undiminished role of public speaking in contemporary American political life. The focus of the book is upon what Aristotle described as "civic discourse," speech concerning issues affecting the public. While oratory flourished in the city-state of Athens, where there was widespread and intimate participation in political life, one might assume that it is less useful in a mass society wherein political participation is more often vicarious than direct. Many events in recent history have been successfully addressed by rhetoric, but response to the terrorist attack of September 11, 2001, is illustrative. International political leaders immediately spoke to mourn those who died, to praise rescue workers and volunteers who risked their lives, to comfort the families of the dead and injured, to condemn terrorists and terrorism, to relieve public anxiety, and to affirm the democratic institutions the terrorists sought to undermine. Though physically devastating, the attack was also a symbolic act that needed to be countered symbolically. American entry into World War II was marked by Franklin Roosevelt's "War Address" with an opening phrase crystallizing American sentiments toward the Japanese attack on Pearl Harbor: "Yesterday, December 7, 1941—a date which will live in infamy." George W. Bush looked for the same note of solemnity with his declaration on September 11: "Today, our fellow citizens, our way of life, our very freedom came under attack." Although monumental attacks on America have been few, American speeches frequently respond to recurrent circumstances and contain repeated appeals to civic virtues and values.

The terrorist attacks on New York and Washington called for affirmations of the nation's unwavering commitment to a free and open society. Orators in those fateful days could have cribbed from Pericles, the democratic ruler of Athens, who said in 430 B.C.: "[T]here is a great difference between us and our opponents, in our attitude toward military security. . . . Our city is open to the world, and we have no periodical deportations in order to prevent people from observing or finding out secrets which might be of military advantage to our enemy. This is because we rely, not on secret weapons, but on our own real courage and loyalty."[1] Uttered 2400 years ago to eulogize those who had died in the first year of the Peloponnesian War, such sentiments also were expressed in the wake of the World Trade Center attack. Public oratory remains the means by which democratic societies renew their values and create solidarity. Even if trained as specialists, orators, when speaking to the public, must speak as citizens joined in deliberations about policies that concern all. In a democracy, public judgments are predicated upon the values of the community or nation. Guiding audiences in making such judgments is the virtuous orator's role.

The term "oratory" kindles thoughts not only of classical antiquity but also of an era in the United States when political speeches were delivered by an orator standing on a stump, hay wagon, or makeshift wooden platform; when public lectures were delivered on a Chautauqua or Lyceum stage, and formal ceremonial speeches were declaimed at a monument or the site of a battle. With their broad learning, linguistic mastery, dramatic delivery, and elastic, sonorous voices, public lecturers such as suffragist Susan B. Anthony and philosopher Ralph Waldo Emerson, and ceremonial speakers such as Senators Edward Everett and Daniel Webster, performed as virtuosos an art that many appreciated but few mastered. In the school system, oral reading and recitation were the norm.[2] Students fortunate enough to study Latin in high school and college eventually read and translated the orations of Cicero. At that time, "oratory," defined by its ideal, suggested not only eloquence but grandiloquence. Now, the luster of nineteenth-century speeches seems all but lost in the informal utterances of modern politicians and social activists.

Much was expected of the old orator. Following Cicero's prescriptions for the creation of a perfect orator in *De Oratore*, illustrious speakers were not merely wordsmiths and phrase makers but community leaders of prudence and erudition as well. They knew how to harmonize their eloquence with the sentiments of their audiences. The culturally conservative rhetorical critic Richard Weaver idealized oratory in nineteenth-century America, arguing that it appealed to a collection of settled beliefs less likely to exist in a more discordant, heterogeneous modern society. The bond created by received truths about religion and government in agrarian society elevated orators to positions of moral authority and civic stature. According to Weaver's sympathetic account, these notable public voices reminded audiences of what they already believed, of ideas and deeply held convictions, made effective by eloquent oratorical embodiment.[3] This is not to say, of course, that there were not deeply dividing issues, such as secession, abolition, and suffrage.

Another influential critic, Edwin Black, provocatively sees entirely different tendencies in even the most celebrated nineteenth-century oratory, which he believes created complacency and prevented needed change. He regards as presumptuous, and even dangerous, the ceremonial discourses of silver-tongued speakers such as Daniel Webster. Black objects that Daniel Webster and other popular speakers of his day presumed to direct audience sentiment, to tell audiences precisely how they should feel, with little or no room left for individual response. When he was eulogizing the Battle of Bunker Hill before its veterans, for example, Webster's rhetorical invention unfolded a detailed description of how the veterans should respond emotionally to the memory the battle; for example: "I perceive that a tumult of contending feelings rushes upon you. The images of the dead as well as the persons of the living, present themselves to you. The scene overwhelms you, and I turn from it." Sentimental old oratory, according to Black, was a species of escapism; it distracted attention from the social problems of the nineteenth century, the most glaring of which, slavery, would eventuate in civil war. In Black's negative reading of "old oratory," public speakers celebrated the nation's successful experiment in democracy by appealing to the smug self-satisfaction of its citizens. They obscured social problems with reaffirmations of received truths and an inflated, overly ornamented style. Black allows that not all nineteenth-century oratory suffered from these tendencies. Lincoln as president spoke with the terseness of one who respected words too much to waste them and, while appealing to sentiment and values, also permitted his audiences room for individual emotional and intellectual response.[4] No matter whether one accepts Black's liberal or Weaver's conservative interpretation, the difference between the common fare of nineteenth-century speeches and Lincoln's Gettysburg Address can be likened to that between a modern romance novel and a Shakespearean sonnet.

The appraisal of old oratory obviously has much to do with whether one trusts not only appeals to collective sentiment but collective sentiment itself. Unquestioned social agreements can lead to decision-making pathologies such as "group think," wherein problems are sublimated or go unnoticed. Public sentimentalism can mask what might be discerned in the cool light of individual reason. The orator's appeal to strongly felt emotions evinced by nationalism and patriotism can threaten healthy self-criticism and social progress. Weaver's warning concerns an excess in the other direction. As Black fears the irrational effects of sentimentalism, Weaver fears the wholesale rejection of both sentiment and rhetoric as legitimate forces in shaping public judgments. Logic without rhetoric, he concludes, is "among the most subversive enemies of society and culture."[5]

Societies that applaud rhetoric also implicitly applaud social cohesion, since no speaker can persuade in the absence of shared values and beliefs. Rhetoric develops "a meditative relationship" between past and present, and without traditional rhetoric, society is trapped in the present moment, neither remembering its history nor envisioning its future.[6] Traditionally, orators brought cultural and philosophical perspective to the present by exploiting their sentiments toward well remembered historical events and by creating prophetic visions of the future. But in modern times, image politics, an endless stream of information, and the remorseless focus of broadcasters on news events predicted to stimulate visceral responses make it well-nigh impossible for the orator to convert audiences to contemplation. Consequently, the contemporary orator's invocations of history are far more superficial and far less educational. Television, Neil Postman says pithily, "is a speed-of-light medium, a present centered medium."[7] There is little wonder, then, that modern orators seek neither to teach history nor to help audiences recall the history easily forgotten in the quick succession of news stories bombarding them daily.

If nineteenth-century citizens could congratulate themselves on their capacity to share an appreciation for the past and to agree on fundamental questions of democracy and religious morality, twenty-first-century citizens should equally value the capacity of the nation to incorporate diverse perspectives, opinions, and voices. The ablest modern orators do not necessarily ascend from the ranks of the best educated or the best situated. Today, as in the Athenian democracy that Pericles extolled: "What counts [in choosing leaders] is not membership of a particular class, but the actual ability which the man possesses."[8] Neither, of course, were all nineteenth-century speakers born to the purple, although until recently anthologists and critics focused on leaders of the establishment rather than on protesters such as abolitionists, suffragists, and populist labor leaders. Particularly in presenting modern speeches, recent anthologists have broadened the canon of oratory. Nineteenth-century orators earned acclaim by celebrating the nation's ideals and accomplishments. Since the 1950s, many of the most effective orators have been those who helped transform the nation through social protest. While orators in the nineteenth century often wore the mantle of political power, orators in the modern era as frequently speak from the perspective of the disenfranchised. Contemporary orators are not only presidents, legislators, and jurists, but also civil rights leaders, war protesters, gay and lesbian activists, unionists, and feminists. Yet, modern orators, whether criticizing or supporting the status quo, appeal no less to the heartfelt beliefs of their audiences. Oratory may not be the performance art it was in the nineteenth and early twentieth centuries, but it is no less important socially, and certainly no less in evidence.

In every election season, candidates for public office accuse each other of using "mere rhetoric" to obscure reality, although rhetoric as an art is conceived by Aristotle as amoral (that is, morally neutral). A charismatic speaker such as Democratic vice-presidential candidate John Edwards, who made his living persuading juries, nevertheless recently accused President George W. Bush of using "rhetoric." Labeling speeches *rhetoric* in its pejorative sense is the ultimate dismissal. Politicians and pundits encourage the public to regard rhetoric as an instrument of obfuscation rather than of persuasion, and to view as propaganda the persuasive efforts of contrary-minded politicians and pundits. The French theologian and social critic Jacques Ellul explains that propaganda short-circuits reason by appeals to strong collective emotions, such as hatred and fear.[9] Students are rightly taught to be wary of the demagoguery of Joseph McCarthy and Huey Long and the dissembling of Richard Nixon. It is easy to see why good speakers do not admit to being rhetorically skillful and why the self-described "plain speaking" of Harry Truman and George W. Bush is advertised as a virtue. "I am not the eloquent speaker that my opponent is" has been a commonplace appeal since rhetoric first became a subject of study. In fact, "plain speaking" is not any less rhetorical than the refined oral prose of John F. Kennedy, whose eloquence helped to define the nature of his leadership.

American presidents have varied greatly in their oratorical abilities. George W. Bush is no Ronald Reagan, and Jimmy Carter is no Bill Clinton. The retiring Calvin Coolidge did not hold a candle to the garrulous Theodore Roosevelt.[10] George Washington was not the equal of John Adams. Nor are successful activists equally adept at speaking. Cesar Chavez did much to advance the cause of farmworkers, but his acumen as an orator did not remotely approach that of Martin Luther King, Jr. or Malcolm X. While the ability to communicate orally is vital to political and social leaders, the quality and character of their speaking can vary greatly and still be effective. Although the public might identify oratory with polished style and delivery, the perceived ethos of the orator is often more determinative of success than either text or performance. In an egalitarian society perhaps the most grievous rhetorical mistake is to attempt to adopt a style of speaking that sounds contrived or out of character.

The hallmark of a professional speechwriter is the acquired ability to write plausibly in the voice of the person who will deliver the message. In political life, good speeches must always portray character and personality, but political rhetoric invariably trades on oversimplification. Complex private personalities must somehow be distilled to create public personas. The public responds to memorable markers of character and personality. A photograph showing presidential candidate Michael Dukakis in a tank with a comically cocked helmet was used to cast doubt on his leadership ability, and Howard Dean's raucous speech to his campaign supporters in Iowa, the "I Have a Scream" speech, was endlessly replayed on television and helped to derail his candidacy. Dean later noted that had the microphone amplified audience noise as much as his voice, the shouting would have made more sense. Politically it did not matter if the portrayals were accurate. As with verbal allegations, meaningful images are made to appear credible by repetition alone.

Memorable words also adhere to visual images.[11] Ronald Reagan's angry and adamant, staccato demand, "Mr. Gorbachev, open this gate. Mr. Gorbachev, tear down this wall," required the Brandenburg Gate and the Berlin Wall as scenic elements. In the television age, pictures are often remembered far beyond the words accompanying them. The visual representation of George W. Bush landing in a navy plane on the deck of the U.S.S. *Abraham Lincoln* at the professed conclusion of the active phase of the Iraq War made what he said afterward anticlimactic. John Kerry, accepting the nomination of the Democratic Party beneath an enormous American flag, and with his swift boat crew seated close by, needed to utter words that fulfilled the scene, but the pictures linger longer than the utterances. In image-driven politics, issues are subordinated to personality. Few people remember the arguments made in the Reagan/Carter presidential debates, but most television viewers remember Reagan's bemused facial response and disarming quip to Carter, "There you go again," because they believed they had had a glimpse into Reagan's character. To some viewers, Reagan's apparently impromptu comment was symbolic of his bemused frustration with Carter's persistent challenges.

Where there is image, there is also the possibility of being duped by a guileful misrepresentation. Even among a public that believes it can read character in facial expression and tone of voice, the politics of image threatens to create cynicism. The boast of the Greek Sophists remains true—it *is* possible to make vice appear to be virtue and virtue appear to be vice. But truth also needs to be presented effectively. Honest and competent politicians do not succeed unless they can make themselves appear so. Good causes often languish for want of words that represent them as good causes.

The Greek Sophist Gorgias observed that if one truly understood the past, present, and future, one would not "take opinion as counselor to the soul."[12] Oratory is less about what is known than what is believed, and less about reality than about appearance. Despite the disclosures of modern science, political judgments are still based upon fallible opinion. The esoteric science of stem cell research is tethered to political judgments based upon common opinion. Supporters of stem cell research such as Ronald Reagan Jr., whose father died of Alzheimer's disease—for which the morally controversial research might be a boon—appeal not to scientific minds but to public sensibilities.

The domination of the visual electronic media has made the shaping of public opinion more, not less, important than when ideas were conveyed from mouth to ear. Although direct public participation in the political process is limited in modern, centralized democracies, the need for governmental administrations to form public opinion is, if anything, greater, as Jacques Ellul notes. Leadership in a modern democracy requires that public officials appear to be following public opinion, which is assessed regularly through efforts of pollsters. In the interests of creating and coalescing opinion, politicians unleash all of the resources of public relations, advertising, and public speaking based as much as possible upon social scientific principles of effectiveness.[13] Campaigns on behalf of compulsory health insurance or tax reduction measures must be waged effectively before politicians can act in accordance with the wishes of their constituencies.

In fact, since the early twentieth century, American presidents have increasingly taken their messages directly to the people, whose opinions could then be used to influence Congress. According to Jeffrey Tulis, the "rhetorical presidency" began with Theodore Roosevelt, who regarded the presidency as a "bully pulpit," a concept which was developed more fully by Woodrow Wilson. Wilson, Tulis notes, believed that the public could determine which politicians were prepared to lead by listening to their oratory. The demagogue could be distinguished from the true leader, who was not, in Wilson's words, simply "clever and engaging" but "equipped [for] the high duties of statesmanship." Wilson described the orator in much the same terms that Cicero used to characterize the ideal orator in *De Oratore* (*The Making of the Orator*). To summarize Wilson, that orator had to be a person of "character," "resource," "vision," "intellect," "conviction," "earnestness of purpose," and "capacity for leadership." His or her role was not to mouth existing opinions of the public, but to help create and shape these opinions, so that government then could respond to them. Although some, including Ellul, might view this role of rhetoric as guileful manipulation, Wilson had boundless faith in the discernment of the people to differentiate oratory from mere speaking, and in the ability of genuine orator–statesmen not merely to state personal views but also to educate and persuade.[14]

The use of the presidency to coalesce public support would not be possible without the existence of national audiences forged first by newspapers; later by newsreels, radio, and television; and most recently by the Internet. Richard Auletta reported in *The New Yorker* that the Bush campaign could reach six million voters via the Internet with one computer keystroke.[15] Recordings and videos of speeches by political candidates, legislators, the judiciary, and public advocates are readily available online, through media network organizations such as C-SPAN. Those who use the mass media for persuasion create large, though often segmented, mass audiences composed of individuals eager to feel part of a collective whole. While reading books tends to individualize, listening to radio or watching television tends to erode individuality and to create a group mentality. When his voice was carried via radio, Calvin Coolidge spoke directly to more Americans than all of his predecessors combined. Forging broad alliances with audiences in a culture dominated by the mass media comes at a price; audiences are often so large that speakers can do little more than appeal to emotion, the lowest common denominator. Conversely, many speakers appeal not to the largest audience possible, but to a segmented audience united by a common cause. Social conservatives, environmentalists, feminists, and Native Americans draw cohesive audiences from across geographic regions. Formed through the Internet, radio, or television, these are fertile audiences that speakers readily cultivate.

Speakers who use television to appeal to the broadest range of audiences require the skills of one speaking to a large crowd; they learn to speak in the same way that muralists paint. Just as muralists use broad brushes and swaths of color to create images best viewed from a distance, so orators who rely on the mass media use words that evoke the most basic emotions but lose in subtlety what they gain in immediate effect. These communicators thereby can more reliably engender unalloyed anger, hatred, or national pride than more subtle or complex emotions such as compassion, contentment, or love. As Isocrates said: "[W]hile we call eloquent those who are able to speak before a crowd, we regard as sage those who most skillfully debate their problems in their own minds."[16] The task of these orators often is not to convince audiences with data and closely reasoned arguments, but to persuade them with broad appeals to a cultural fabric of values and sentiments. Because the media in 1960 dramatized the "shameful conditions" of blacks in America, Martin Luther King, Jr.'s speeches are not chiefly about the fact of overt racism, but more about developing the emotional and moral fervor necessary to overcome it. Along with their adaptation to "the crowd," orators today also realize that television draws audiences closer to the visual image, inviting consideration of nonverbal cues to personality such as posture and facial expression. In a televised town hall debate with Bill Clinton, the sense that George H. W. Bush was not taking his challenger seriously was underscored by a visual moment when Bush checked his watch for the time.

American oratory in today's electronic media age differs from that during an era when speeches were delivered to relatively small audiences within range of the speaker's voice and were further disseminated in print—sometimes in advance of their delivery. That difference is well illustrated by considering examples of effective images used by American presidents in their inaugural addresses. American political oratory, particularly that which has a national audience, trades on words that create lingering images and stimulate the resurgence of feelings that run deep in the collective consciousness of the people.

Politicians or their speechwriters have a great store of images to adapt and re-deploy, and these images often sound vaguely or uncannily alike, although some of the new phrasings are undoubtedly accidental replications. Lincoln, a master of political prose, closed his First Inaugural Address with a literary image: "Though passion may have strained, it must not break our bonds of affection. The mystic chords of memory stretching from every battlefield and patriot grave to every living heart and hearthstone all over this broad land, will yet swell the chorus of the Union, when again touched, as surely they will be, by the better angels of our nature." Woodrow Wilson certainly had filed away this archetypal image. In his First Inaugural Address he said: "The feelings with which we face this new age of right and opportunity sweep across our heartstrings like some air out of God's own presence, where justice and mercy are reconciled and judge and the brother are one."[17] George H. W. Bush's Inaugural Address invoked the same sorts of images, but in a new vernacular style: "We live in a peaceful, prosperous time, but we can make it better. For a new breeze is blowing, and a world refreshed in freedom seems reborn. For in man's heart, if not in fact, the day of the dictator is over. The totalitarian era is passing, its old ideas blown away like leaves from an ancient lifeless tree. A new breeze is blowing and a nation refreshed in freedom stands ready to push on."

Lincoln's image requires a bit of reflection to be completely appreciated. No less subtle is Wilson's image, which requires some sensitivity to both religion and literature. These were speeches meant first for the ear and then for print. In a print culture, the standards of formal oratory are literary. Bush's image, on the other hand, was intellectually available to virtually all Americans who heard it, at the moment they heard it, but its goal was the same—to tell Americans what is "in man's heart, if not in fact," as Bush revealingly said.[18] Civic oratory speaks to emotional and moral sensibilities bordering upon, if not the same as, those that religion addresses. An evil genius at the art of oratory, and the sort of demagogue that Wilson feared, Huey Long told a national audience that American government is "almost a religion."[19] Like all demagogues, Long knew that focusing upon appeals to faith averted the risks inherent in making rational arguments.

In a society dominated by science, technology, and business enterprise, ruled by objectivity and pragmatic effectiveness, contemporary orators still seek in their verbal embodiments of national ideals what the calculus of science, engineering, and business cannot: emotional responses and values shared by the speaker and the mass audience. The difference today is that these images are expressed in a vernacular style necessitated by the ability of the mass media to reach not only those physically present or those who read, but anyone who owns a television set. The images are retained *because* television allows them to persist in memory, as part phrase and part picture.[20]

The vernacular style of contemporary American oratory is pervasive. This mode of speech is not, however, identified only with populist politicians, activists, or social reformers, those speakers most likely to have the ear of the common citizen.

To be understood, perhaps even to be heard, virtually all public orators today need to speak in a language understandable by the least educated members of their audiences. In their usual speaking style, even the best-educated speakers, such as Janet Reno, Sandra Day O'Connor, and Alan Dershowitz, are no less plain-spoken than Cesar Chavez, Winona LaDuke, or Sonia Johnson. Ronald Reagan wooed his audiences with a vernacular style that included the ubiquitous "well" as the verbalized herald of his thoughts. In the same vein, wags have suggested that George W. Bush might make the word "and" acceptable as the way to begin a sentence, and Michael Gourevitch calls him "a master of the American vernacular, that form of expression which eschews slickness and makes a virtue of the speaker's limitations—an artfulness that depends on artlessness."[21] Politicians, who are the frequent subjects of personal interviews and the attention once reserved for actors and athletes, have learned to disclose their feelings in their speeches; they, after all, are what interests the public.[22] Indeed, Kathleen Hall Jamieson has argued that Reagan's style favored the feminine in its heavy use of narrative and personal disclosure.[23] Television brings even the most distant and powerful orators into our living rooms. The spoken word thus ceases to live autonomously, as it did in the print age; in the media age it is married to the speaker who utters it.

Modern political orators from all walks of life place themselves at the foreground of their speeches. The modest rhetorical stance taken by Abraham Lincoln in his presidential addresses often perplexes modern readers. Remote and seemingly impersonal, the introduction to Lincoln's Second Inaugural Address draws attention to words conspicuous for their absence. The first three sentences of the address contain not a single personal pronoun. Studiously avoiding personal reference, Lincoln begins: "Fellow Countrymen: At this second appearing to take the oath of the Presidential office there is less occasion for an extended address than there was at the first." George W. Bush's First Inaugural Address contains no fewer than seven uses of "I" or "me" in the first ten lines. The first ten lines of Bill Clinton's inaugural addresses show a corresponding propensity toward the use of "us," "our," and "we." Stylistically, this is consistent with the informality that predominates in today's oral prose, but it also reflects the sense of intimacy such informality projects.

If it were not for television, vernacular speech and self-reference might be less prominent. Television has created what has been called a "secondary orality," wherein the spoken message, together with its visual context, dominates in the creation of public opinion.[24] Once, citizens hoping to become voices of the people could speak without downplaying their erudition, education, or literary ability; in fact, orators were once acclaimed precisely for their ability to frame thoughts in phrases that the ordinary person could not summon. That is less true today, although formal occasions do still call forth sustained eloquence. There are contemporary speakers, such as Martin Luther King Jr., John F. Kennedy, and Jesse Jackson, who are prominently known for their eloquence, but most contemporary orators rise to eloquence only as the situation demands. Ronald Reagan's *Challenger* speech, George W. Bush's address to Congress after 9/11, and Barbara Jordan's speech to the House Judiciary Committee are examples of modern speeches in which the speaker sought and achieved eloquence. Such eloquence might be defined less by literary style than by meeting conspicuously well the rhetorical need created by historical events. Wisdom, as Cicero noted, is the first requirement for eloquence. Most contemporary orators, like their predecessors, perform at levels of rhetorical ability far surpassing that of their audiences, but today the orator's linguistic choices generally must be drawn from words commonly heard in conversation rather than from words commonly read in literature. Speakers have always been well advised to "compose without being noticed," using "words from ordinary language," as Aristotle noted.[25] To be understood is the first requirement of persuasion; thus, refusing to speak in the idiom courts rhetorical failure.

Today's vernacular style goes far beyond the exploitation of the popular idiom, however. Modern speeches meant for television audiences sometimes sound as if they are cobbled together from bits of narrative, affirmations, images, and arguments. Reading a television speech manuscript side by side with a fastidious literary example of classical oratory, one is struck by the brevity of paragraphs, often composed of one or two sentences, and the inattention to structural elements once necessary to integrate long discourses, of a pre-television era. Reading the script of a news broadcast, rather than seeing it telecast, creates the same perception. The truncations and disjunctions in modern political speaking seem to mirror the shortened attention spans conditioned by television with its quick succession of visual and auditory stimuli. Ironically, though it mimics the style of conversational phrases, oratory in the vernacular does not come naturally to all speakers. For those speakers who have difficulty sounding other than formal, the adaptation to vernacular prose must seem effortless and natural. Critics complained that in his debates against George W. Bush, Al Gore, already known as a wooden speaker, committed the sin of talking down to his audience, which in a new world of personality politics made him even more vulnerable to parodies and satirizing. He violated Aristotle's admonition to "seem to speak not artificially but naturally," although the standards by which naturalness is judged have changed greatly.[26]

The vernacular style is only one aspect of media politics, and even if they do not seek or hold office, orators who seek national audiences must follow the norms governing electronically broadcast oral advocacy. All speakers come to realize that audiences watching and hearing messages on television are often as interested in their quirks and mannerisms, their habits, lifestyles, and personal narratives and confessions, as they are in their message. Because of media exposure that creates celebrity status, politicians and activists play a secondary role as entertainers. They can, therefore, move fluidly between stumping for legislation or social causes and appearing on television as actors, talk show guests or hosts, and endorsers of products. Postman may be correct: "Entertainment is the supra-ideology of all discourse on television. No matter what is depicted or from what point of view, the overarching presumption is that it is there for our amusement and pleasure."[27]

Reporters encourage television viewers to interpret speakers as characters within unfolding historical dramas, and to assess their emotional states, characters, and personalities through cues such as facial expression, gestures, and tone of voice. Speakers, therefore, must be good performers or at least have qualities that viewers find interesting. What sounds eloquent and wise when presented with an expressive face and evocative delivery can seem hollow and insipid when scrutinized in print. Although this is not unique to televised speeches, television so privileges the visual over the verbal that audiences are doubly distracted from noticing faults of reasoning, if not the very absence of reasoning. At the same time, the audiences perceive the subtlest facial response. Satirists convincingly capture media personalities by emulating telling gestures, expressions, and body movements. Voice and words seem proportionally less important in creating a convincing impression because the television medium so emphasizes visual stimuli. As Postman also notes, in a media age, " 'political knowledge' means having pictures in your head more than having words."[28]

Not all contemporary speeches meant for broadcast are equal; some are better adaptations to television than others. The best television speeches manage to say something important, wise, and true that can be understood instantly by a mass audience. Truman, whose political reputation was based upon plain speaking, and Reagan, who understood the medium of television through having been a professional entertainer, adapted easily to televised political speaking. Many of the speakers included in this volume, particularly those who speak to small gatherings, without the gaze of the television lens, speak with a gravity of thought and a richness of style admirable by any measure of literate discourse. Difficult to compare with speeches before small gatherings, broadcast speeches strive to develop a sense of intimacy where geographic distances deny intimacy.

Roderick Hart speaks persuasively of media audiences' need to feel intimate with politicians. The desire for intimacy accounts for the peculiar importance of portraying the lives of public advocates through personal interviews, biographical films, and candid video representations of formerly private moments with family. To be successful, public advocates must cultivate in their audiences a sense of familiarity and kinship. Hart claims that only the artificial feeling of intimacy created by television can explain the outrage felt when public figures violate expectations. Omnipresent and omniscient with its close-up shots and focus on facial reactions, television invites the belief that celebrities, politicians, and public advocates are known personally and intimately.[29] Television has made intimacy, narrative, and self-reference the unchallenged norms of political discourse.

The potent effect televised images can have was anticipated by George Orwell's conception of the hypnotic, omnipresent close-up of "Big Brother." In reality, political leaders and social advocates, whose voices and faces become familiar to the public through the electronic media, neither frighten nor tyrannize but, rather, frequently appeal to the public need for a hero or an ego ideal. Effectiveness thus lies increasingly in creating a sense of familiarity with the people being addressed. Ellul points out that, paradoxically, the mass media speak both to the individual personally and to the individual as part of a mass society; television creates a "purely illusory and fallacious" satisfaction of the need for true friendship and intimacy with "a leader, a hero, a movie star, or a TV personality."[30] When viewed from armchairs and sofas in American homes, speakers able to unify media audiences relieve feelings of alienation, uprootedness, and social isolation that attend urbanization, specialized work, and the complexities of modern life.[31] Hart perceptively expresses this psychological engagement with television: "When television brings the faces of politicians close to us, it makes us forget that it is a medium (a device that comes between). Instead, it presents itself as window first; then open window; then no window. The candidate sits on *our* sofa. And we chat."[32] The sense of viewing a speech with many others, even though they are not physically present, creates the possibility of what psychologists refer to as "social facilitation," the behavior of people in a crowd who have lost the inhibitions that attend solitary action and individual responsibility. Although watching a speech on television does not seem to demand action, Ellul maintains that in forming strong responses to what they see and hear, viewers are acting, even if only vicariously.[33] The Internet affords somewhat different opportunities to overcome social isolation and feel an active participant in worldly affairs. Individuals can listen to clips and complete audio and video texts of speeches, detached from their place and time, or read immediate commentary by pundits on speeches as they are being delivered. Online discussions in chat rooms, whether contributed to or simply read; invitations to complete polls and record opinions; and encouragements to follow Web links create a sense of interactive participation not available through television.

Listening to oratory helps satisfy the public need to participate in civic affairs. The televised town hall meeting debates used in presidential campaigns attempt to re-create the community interactions of a bygone era. They invite a feeling of presence by viewers among the small group of the electorate who actually experience face-to-face interaction with candidates during the debate. With their remarkably large viewerships, the debates serve their purpose exceedingly well, although they are more like paired interviews than anything that might be heard at the Oxford Union debating society or at the nineteenth-century debates between Abraham Lincoln and Stephen Douglas.

The criticisms of modern presidential debates are familiar. Candidates strain to answer questions with stock material, and repeat words and phrases tested by focus groups and made familiar by salvos of political advertisements. Commentators create audience interest by focusing on the suspenseful possibility that a decisive gaffe of phrase, gesture, or untoward response will turn the tide of the campaign. Because of the restrictive format, candidates have time to affirm positions and make promises, but not to express detailed plans. Plans are consigned to print and campaign Web sites, not to televised speeches. Despite their limitations, modern presidential debates do make television audiences better informed decision-makers. Studies conducted in 1992 and 1996 showed that presidential debate audiences became 30 percent better informed on the issues.[34] However critical one might be of the debates, they do approach the lofty ideal of participatory democracy.

From this vantage point one can see more clearly the shadowy abyss of thirty-second political ads, where omission, diversion, innuendo, false association, repetition, and downright lying are so common as to seem appropriate. Dirty tricks and negative advertisements, the paltry substitutes for oratory in political decision-making, are the poison of an oratory-reliant democracy in a media age.[35] Civic speaking must remain the anchor of democratic decision-making. Without speakers, speeches, and audiences, one is left with questionable television advertisements that ideally should not work, but often do. Decision-making shortcuts, such as political advertisements, lead ineluctably downward to a place where words and images are merely repeated stimuli meant to create response without the benefit of thoughtful reflection.

Cicero said that in rhetoric everything important to society eventually passes in review. That is not less so than it was twenty-two centuries ago. Issues related to war, terrorism, environment, economics, rights, respect, and morality are brought to the public forum in the guise of oratory. Rhetorical discourse appeals to the living attitudes, sentiments, values, and ideals of the citizenry. Reading historic speeches helps one to re-create the past while considering how that past informs the present. While some speeches transcendentally attain the status of eloquent literature, others respond to historical events and fade into obscurity. To understand a speech, therefore, is to understand its historical context, the speaker's motivations, and the nature of the audience to which the speaker appealed.

While television, radio, and the Internet have affected the style of public discourse, at the core its function is the same. Communities require the affirmation of their values and the deliberate discussion of their problems. Remarkable in both their differences and their similarities to their historical forerunners, modern political speeches, as Woodrow Wilson realized, are the surest tests of leadership in a democracy, and no substitute should prevail. As the speakers discussed in these pages personify, speaking is so basic to democracy that neither pyrotechnic chat rooms nor captious political advertising can or should take the place of catalyzing and eloquent speeches. What oxygen is to the living body, speaking is to the body politic: an essential and irreplaceable element. Only in its study can one hope for the improvement of American public address in the new century. The contemporary American orators included in this volume illustrate the diligence with which community leaders voice the concerns of their audiences, and the critical role that speaking shall always play in the discourse and decision-making of the American polity. That American civic oratory persists despite the welter of media noise provides confidence in a system of government that has made free speech both process and product.

NOTES

1. Pericles, "Funeral Oration," in Synoptic History of Classical Rhetoric, ed. James J. Murphy and Richard A. Katula, 3rd ed. (Mahwah, N.J.: Hermagoras Press, 2003), 242–43.

2. Karl Wallace, ed., A History of Speech Education in America (New York: Appleton-Century-Crofts, 1954), 282–97.

3. Richard M. Weaver, "The Spaciousness of Old Oratory," in his The Ethics of Rhetoric (Chicago: Henry Regnery, 1953).

4. Edwin Black, "The Sentimental Style," in his Rhetorical Questions (Chicago: University of Chicago Press, 1992), 100–105.

5. Richard M. Weaver, Visions of Order (Baton Rouge: Louisiana State University Press, 1964), 70.

6. Richard M. Weaver, Ethics of Rhetoric, 178. See also Weaver, Visions of Order, 55–56.

7. Neil Postman, Amusing Ourselves to Death: Public Discourse in the Age of Show Business (New York: Viking, 1985), 136–38.

8. Pericles, "Funeral Oration," 242.

9. Jacques Ellul, *Propaganda: The Formation of Men's Attitudes* (New York: Knopf, 1965), 73, 153.

10. Bruce Gronbeck maintains, nevertheless, that "Silent Cal's" voice and New England accent played well enough on the radio to launch him as a "media personality." "The Presidency in the Age of Secondary Orality," in *Beyond the Rhetorical Presidency*, ed. Martin J. Medhurst (College Station: Texas A&M University Press, 1996), 32.

11. See Kathleen Jamieson, "The Memorable Phrase, the Memorable Picture," in her *Eloquence in an Electronic Age* (Oxford: Oxford University Press, 1988), 90–91ff.

12. Gorgias, "Encomium of Helen," in *On Rhetoric: A Theory of Civic Discourse*, trans. George Kennedy (Oxford: Oxford University Press, 1991), 286.

13. Ellul, *Propaganda*, 122–28.

14. Jeffrey K. Tulis, *The Rhetorical Presidency* (Princeton, N.J.: Princeton University Press, 1987), 125, 130–32.

15. Richard Auletta, "Kerry's Brain," *The New Yorker*, September 22, 2004, p. 74.

16. Isocrates, "Antidosis," 256, in *Isocrates*, vol. 2, trans. George Norlin (Cambridge, Mass.: Harvard University Press, 1929), 327–29.

17. Quoted in Dante Germino, *The Inaugural Addresses of American Presidents: The Public Philosophy and Rhetoric* (Lanham, Md.: University Press of America, 1984), 9.

18. See Bernard K. Duffy, "George Bush's Inaugural Address," in *The Inaugural Addresses of Twentieth-century American Presidents*, ed. Halford Ross Ryan (Westport, Conn.: Praeger, 1993), 292–94. I commented therein that the lyricism of George H. W. Bush's images were like those of country music. Gourevitch says similarly that the current President Bush's "speeches rely on the same stagger-stacking of phrases and refrains that characterize popular songs and phrases." Michael Gourevitch, "Bushspeak: The President's Vernacular Style," *The New Yorker*, September 13, 2004, p. 38.

19. Huey Long, "Every Man a King," in *Contemporary American Public Discourse*, ed. Halford Ross Ryan, 3rd ed. (Prospect Heights, Ill.: Waveland Press, 1992), 37.

20. Jamieson calls this a "synoptic visual-verbal statement," "The Memorable Phrase," 115.

21. M. Gourevitch, "Bushspeak," p. 38.

22. Postman, *Amusing Ourselves to Death*, 132–35; Roderick P. Hart, *Seducing America: How Television Charms the Modern Voter*, rev. ed. (Thousand Oaks, Calif.: Sage, 1999), 24–32.

23. Jamieson, 165–200.

24. Gronbeck, *Beyond the Rhetorical Presidency*, 30–49.

25. Aristotle, *Rhetoric*, 1404b.

26. Ibid.

27. Postman, *Amusing Ourselves to Death*, 87, 132–33.

28. Ibid., 130.

29. Hart, *Seducing America*, 27, 34. This is not to say that politicians have not always felt a need to close the psychological distance between themselves and their constituents. In a day when presidential candidates did not campaign after nomination, Lincoln still understood the value of having a plentiful supply of photographs to circulate to the newspapers, often showing him with deliberately tousled hair. Franklin Roosevelt hoped that his Fireside Chats would replicate the quality of conversations he had with his neighbors in rural Hyde Park, New York. He and Harry Truman also very successfully broke down geographic barriers to communication with their "whistlestop" tours, during which brief, informal speeches were presented from the backs of trains to small assemblages. In a sense, every public speaker confronts the challenge of speaking to an audience while making individuals feel they are being spoken to directly.

30. Ellul, *Propaganda*, 90–99, 171, 175.

31. Ibid., 138–60.

32. Hart, *Seducing America*, 35.

33. Ellul, *Propaganda*, 90–99, 127–32.

34. Kathleen Hall Jamieson, *Everything You Think You Know About Politics—and Why You're Wrong* (New York: Basic Books, 2000), 163–64.

35. See Kathleen Hall Jamieson, *Dirty Politics: Deception, Distraction, and Democracy* (Oxford: Oxford University Press, 1992).

JOHN D. ASHCROFT (1942–)
Missouri Governor, U.S. Senator, U.S. Attorney General

HARRY HELLENBRAND

"We have no king but Jesus." In 1999, John Ashcroft told an audience at Bob Jones University that the American colonists turned away British tax collectors with this slogan. The quotation assured his listeners at this evangelical Christian school that tithe was more righteous than tax and that faith inspired the republic, even if church and state were separate. But Ashroft's speech outraged his critics. They viewed it as proof of his partisan zealotry. Had he not said at other times, "There are two things you find in the middle of the road, a moderate and a dead skunk"?

As Ashcroft averred in his 1998 U.S. Senate speech on Iraq, he prefers words that "draw a bright line, "and the moral repute of the speaker highlights that line." Thus, he mocked President Clinton's verbal dodges and sordid deeds in an address to the Conservative Political Action Committee in 1998. In contrast, Ashcroft praised President Reagan. Reagan's words—"evil empire," for instance—distilled complexity into a symbol "that led the world to . . . [his] point of view," Ashcroft told the *Southern Partisan* in 1999. Persuasion, he believes, especially when reinforced by reputation, reforms people and thereby minimizes the need for government to act for them.

Civil speech, in other words, can limit the need for civil service. But a leader's speech also must be convincingly martial. According to Ashcroft, a politician can become a heroic orator in the war on terror by conveying "the calling of our time," as presidents Lincoln and Kennedy did in their eras. In November 2002, Ashcroft said to a meeting of U.S. attorneys that American leaders who rallied the people against terrorism recalled Henry V at Agincourt. Henry inspired his "band of brothers" so eloquently that Shakespeare immortalized him. The war on terror challenged today's speakers to be inspirational as well. At stake were "the values of democracy" and "vital public interests." Of course, speakers in a modern democracy face a challenge that Henry did not. They have to preserve "traditional [civil] law" while defeating threats to "national security."

Ashcroft's belief that words can inspire derives from his family. His father and grandfather were Pentecostal ministers; he is active in the Assemblies of God. Nonetheless, he pursued law and then politics after attending Yale College and the University of Chicago for his J.D. He taught law at Southwestern University in Missouri, and with his wife, Janet, wrote three business law textbooks. His two memoirs, which he composed with a professional writer, recount how he applied his father's calling to politics. In politics he, the son, could speak the good beyond a congregation and then make it public policy.

What constitutes this good? In *On My Honor: The Beliefs That Shape My Life*, Ashcroft attributed his conservative Republican beliefs to his father's emphasis on self-reliance and personal responsibility. Free "the prisoners of the war on poverty" from welfare; free the people from welfare bureaucrats by funding "charitable and even faith-based-organizations" to help the poor, as he said in his Senate speech "Personal Responsibility" (1996). Restrain the branches of government to a strict construction of their limits. Improve education while requiring institutional accountability. Eliminate prejudice and affirmative action by treating each person as an

for unequal expenditures in black schools. In a speech to the Conservative Political Action Committee in 1997, Ashcroft lashed out at Judge Clark. The judge personified "a robed contemptuous intellectual elite" who usurped the powers of the state legislature and governor. Ever on guard against the temptation of judges to make law and policy, Ashcroft told the *Southern Partisan* in 1999 that the Supreme Court vindicated him in *Gregory v. Ashcroft*. The Court upheld his decision as governor to retire state judges at age seventy, despite charges of age discrimination. A governor, aided by the Tenth Amendment, prevailed over the legal aristocracy.

As governor, Ashcroft boosted spending on education, while in his 1990 "State of the State Address" he distinguished between those social programs that were "safety nets" for the industrious and those that were "mattresses" for the

---

As governor of Missouri and a U.S. senator, Ashcroft attacked the Washington bureaucrats who built big government. But when he became George W. Bush's attorney general and the war on terror began, he defended the PATRIOT Act as the best way to preempt terrorists, even if this meant breaking down the wall between domestic law enforcement and foreign intelligence.

---

individual, not a member of an ethnic group. Balance government budgets, just as families balance accounts. Protect the unborn by banning—or at least curtailing—abortion. Protect life and property by enforcing capital punishment and not infringing on the constitutional right to bear arms. Strengthen the military to safeguard freedom.

Religion taught Ashcroft how to deal with electoral defeat. "For every crucifixion," he wrote in *On My Honor*, "there is a resurrection." Elected as Missouri's state auditor in 1973, he served as attorney general from 1975 until 1986. Then Ashcroft won two terms as governor. As attorney general and governor, he fought the meddling of the federal bench—and especially Judge Russell Clark—in Missouri's affairs. The courts ruled that schools in St. Louis and Kansas City were segregated. As a result, the state was liable

lazy. Other governors elected him chairman of the National Governors' Association because he was a strong voice for consolidating federal programs into block grants that were accountable to the states.

In 1994, Ashcroft won a Senate seat. The Senate, ironically, provided him with a pulpit for decrying the "distant elite" in Washington. The elite "colonized" Americans through disproportionate taxation, he said to the Northeastern Leadership Conference in 1995. They surrendered sovereignty to the United Nations. They ignored the opposition of the American people to abortion. They shackled new technology with limits on encryption so that government could peer into codes and patents.

In 2000, Senator Ashcroft lost his bid for reelection to Governor Mel Carnahan, who died in a plane crash before the election although the seat was filled by Carnahan's wife. Many voters, especially blacks, resented that Ashcroft had "Borked"—that is, assailed—President Clinton's nominee for the Eighth Circuit, Judge Ronnie White, an African American. On the Senate floor in 1999, Ashcroft had labeled White "pro-criminal." Against this backdrop, President-elect Bush nominated Ashcroft for attorney general. In a withering confirmation hearing, Democrats portrayed Ashcroft as an extremist. He was a racist, they suggested, because he had distorted Judge White's record, opposed fairness in the schools of St. Louis and Kansas City, and disagreed with affirmative action. Ashcroft tried to cripple *Roe v. Wade*, they charged; he even supported a constitutional amendment to ban abortion.

Ashcroft held his temper at the hearing. He attributed his political views to strict interpretations of the law. As attorney general of Missouri, he said, he was bound to defend his state against meddling judges. As for abortion, he regarded *Roe v. Wade* as the precedent in force. Only a constitutional amendment, which he supported, could overturn it. The full Senate confirmed him. After September 11, 2001, this opponent of federal power would refocus the Department of Justice. Prevention of terror preempted prosecution of crime. He championed the USA PATRIOT Act (Uniting and Strengthening America by Providing Appropriate Tools Required to Intercept and Obstruct Terrorism), which amalgamated—and expanded—federal agencies.

WE BAND OF BROTHERS

Ashcroft's opposition to Judge White, as detailed in his Senate speech, and his defense against charges of racism showed how, as befit a lawyer and a son of a preacher, he argued from first principles. His indictment of White's character and decisions was a legal syllogism. The major premise was clear: *Federalist 78* and the Constitution directed judges not to substitute their will for "that of the legislative body." The minor premise combined facts into a charge: White's "pro-criminal and activist" opinions "redirect[ed] the law" with "a slant toward criminals." Even his character was questionable. His favoring of affirmative action biased him, Ashcroft charged; it led Judge White to overturn

the opinion of a lower court judge who opposed racial preferences. The conclusion was indubitable: White was unsuitable for the Eighth Circuit because he bent the law.

In effect, the minor premise and conclusion reversed Jefferson's adage about reconciliation in his First Inaugural Address. For Ashcroft, every "difference of opinion" was a "difference of principle." As a result, White's dissents in several death penalty cases were intolerable. White's explanation that he had been concerned about a lower court justice's prejudgment of a case and a defendant's competence to stand trial was not credible.

In January 2001, during his confirmation hearing for attorney general, Ashcroft fended off White's apologists. He implied that his opponents crucified him for his faith. He said, "[E]very person is a special creation of God." Ashcroft saw White as a man, he said, not as a member of a race. He even invoked Martin Luther King's dream that one day people would be judged by the "contents of their characters" [*sic*], not "the color of their skin" The conclusion was clear: White, not he, sullied King's legacy. Ashcroft regretted that White's own bias inspired him to overturn a ruling by a lower court because that judge had sneered publicly at affirmative action.

Ashcroft's delivery is imposing because of his voice; it is accessible because of his diction and order. His baritone rumbles toward the end of long phases. In Congress, he was a member of a singing quartet. As attorney general, he regaled audiences by singing "Let the Eagle Soar," which he wrote. Although he rarely gestures, his eyes fix upon his listeners. Generally, he avoids colloquialisms, jargon, and even sectarian expressions. He steers toward plain words and prose syntax, which he punctuates with repetition, opposition, and parallelism. In 1989, for instance, his State of the State address relied on a triple parallel to highlight the metaphysics behind his policy: "God is all that he wills to be . . . animals are all that they will ever be . . . man is only part of what he wholly hopes to be." Policy developed out of man's yearning to rise above his middle rung on the great chain of being. The gap between God's "will" and man's "hopes" revealed the latter's deficiency. Unlike animals, humans progressed by praying to God and enacting policy.

By the time Ashcroft arrived in the Senate in 1994, he had whetted the weapons of a Washington outsider (Republican governor) fighting elitist power (the Clinton administration). His speeches turned on polarizing images that were emphasized by the order of the sentences. In "Independence Means Risk," delivered to the Northeastern Leadership Conference in 1995, he prefaced a tightly arranged attack on the welfare policies of the Great Society with a phrase from the American Revolution. Like king and Parliament long ago, the national government in Washington, D.C., exercised the tyrannical "rule of a distant elite." Ashcroft charged, "It created an underclass. . . . It rewards [immoral] behavior. . . . It thwarts . . . charitable organizations. . . ." In the Declaration of Independence in 1776, Jefferson had similarly listed the charges against King George: "He has. . . . He has. . . . He has. . . ." Jefferson had ended his bill of particulars, "He [the King] has waged cruel war against human nature." Echoing Jefferson, Ashcroft concluded his indictment, "It [the national government] has waged war against the American spirit." Ashcroft had delivered his declaration of independence— from the welfare state.

Four years later, the infamous speech at Bob Jones University was constructed on a spiritual antithesis: "There is a difference between a culture that has no King but Caesar, no standard but the civil authority, and a culture that has no king but Jesus, no standard but the eternal authority." "[A] culture" began both phrases; "authority" ended them. Ashcroft twice omitted the conjunction "and" in the sentence: between "Caesar" and "no" and between "Jesus" and "no." This effect—asyndeton—made the only "and" the balance point of the sentence. Ashcroft weighed Caesar against Jesus.

Opposing views square off across a "bright line" in many of Ashcroft's speeches. Often, as in one of his last Senate speeches—against the desecration of the flag in 2000—he establishes empathy by characterizing his view as American, not "academic and elitist." His 1997 speech in the Senate on banning partial-birth abortions took this tack. Speaking for "virtually every American," he pegged these abortions as a "clear-cut wrong." The speech pivoted on a gruesome analogy with "a mother [found] guilty of second-degree murder." She killed her newborn with "a single blow to the back of the head." "Location," he argued—a baby viable in the womb vs. a newborn outside of it—should not fix "the value of human life." His opponents, he chided, hung their "reasoning on a thin, irrational thread of support."

As Ashcroft's career has changed, so have his public and his rhetoric. His speech against partial-birth abortions in 1997 and his 1982 oral argument in *Planned Parenthood v. John Ashcroft*, when he was Missouri attorney general, illustrate the evolution from lawyer to policy-maker. The forum was forensic, not deliberative. He avoided put-downs. Plain image and precedent appealed to the judges' hearts and minds, so Ashcroft directly defended Missouri's "compelling state interest" to impose medical requirements on second-trimester abortions by invoking the legal "bright line" after twelve weeks in *Roe v. Wade*. If the Supreme Court limited the state's authority after twelve weeks, he argued, it would erode its own precedent in *Roe*; it also would gut the power of "the elected representatives of the people" to make abortions safe.

In *The Paranoid Style in American Politics*, Richard Hofstadter foresaw the main features of Ashcroft's rhetoric. Especially in deliberative, ceremonial, and policy speeches, Ashcroft has often interpreted "secular politics" as a spiritual struggle "with the minions of absolute evil." Hofstadter explained that this view has colored the political rhetoric of "ascetic Protestantism" for over a century. "Exaggeration, suspiciousness, and conspiratorial fantasy" accentuated the fiendishness of the enemy. However, one morning changed forever Ashcroft's understanding of "absolute evil": September 11, 2001.

Before 9/11—in Hofstadter's words— Ashcroft regretted "that the worst enemy of American liberty is to be found in Washington." After 9/11, he knew that the "enemy that threatens" America was terrorism. Testifying to the Senate Judiciary Committee in December 2001 on the need for greater national security, Attorney General Ashcroft held up an "al Qaeda training manual." He described it as a " 'how-to' guide for terrorists." Terrorists "infiltrate our communities—plotting, planning, waiting to kill again," he warned. "They exploit our openness . . . by deliberate, premeditated design." Groups like al-Qaeda opened an onslaught against "civilization," not just a war against the United States.

September 11, 2001, inspired the attorney general and his chief speechwriter, Jessica Gavora, to recast his rhetoric. Gavora is the author of *Tilting The Playing Field*, an analysis of Title IX's effect on college sports, particularly men's athletics. In July, Ashcroft's installation speech sounded familiar oppositions: "Main Street" over "Wall Street" and "our culture" over "our government." Echoing Emma Lazarus, as he had before, he declared that the "alchemy of freedom," not government programs, converted tired and poor immigrants into industrious Americans. But after 9/11, his topics became stopping foreign evil and increasing executive

maintained without religion." The reasoning and narration in the middle sections confirmed terrorism as a threat that was virtually a supernatural conspiracy, "both immediate and vast." Its "supporters, patrons, and sympathizers" constituted a "multinational empire of evil"—rivaling, he implied, the "evil empire" of the Cold War.

Contrast ordered the middle sections. Terrorists followed "the voice of evil disguised as freedom." Civil people hearkened to "the voice of God" that described freedom in a "society of laws." Terrorists celebrated "imposition"; civil people honored "inspiration." In the conflict between good and evil, Ashcroft was like a minister, a vessel for the Word. "Civilized people of all faiths are called to the defense of his Creation," he declaimed. He sounded God's call to arms. The battle against terror was spiritual—uniting the righteous of voluntaristic faiths—more than it was national.

President Ronald Reagan labeled the Soviet Union and its satellites the "evil empire." President George W. Bush called rogue dictatorships like Korea and Iraq the "axis of evil." Attorney General John D. Ashcroft upped the ante of evil. After 9/11, he described terrorists as a "multinational empire of evil."

---

authority to do so. Quickly, Ashcroft became the spokesperson for the Bush administration's broad interpretations of executive power in the PATRIOT Act. In his December 6, 2001, testimony to Congress, he also asserted, on behalf of the president, a strong claim to executive privilege to withhold information about national security from Congress. Here his rhetoric again called upon his religious background as much as upon his legal training.

Ashcroft's speech to the National Religious Broadcasters Convention in February 2002, for example, defended strong government to a conservative, religious audience. As he had at Bob Jones University in 1999, he stressed a spiritual approach to policy in order to gain empathy. The beginning of the speech focused on his morning devotionals. The conclusion quoted Washington's Farewell Address: "Morality cannot be

The language of good against evil did not necessarily reassure secular audiences. Would the campaign against terror inadvertently throttle liberty? Setting up military tribunals for terrorists, sharing information between law enforcement and intelligence agencies, and shifting the Department of Justice from prosecution toward prevention could themselves be threats. Ashcroft's testimony before the Senate Judiciary Committee in December 2001 bypassed a problem in this strategy. He funneled a narrative of the administration's policy of prevention toward a crucial definition. Terrorists were a "narrow class" of persons who committed political violence. The government would pursue these obvious lawbreakers. But in fact, "the preventative campaign" focused on potential and probable, not just actual, perpetrators.

How does a nation reconcile security with liberty? This was the question that Ashcroft often had to address with secular audiences after September 11, 2001. His speech to the Eighth Circuit Judges Conference in August 2002 invoked not the "voice of God" but, suitably for this audience, the words of Ben Franklin, Justice Robert H. Jackson, George Washington, and Edmund Burke. On the one hand, Franklin cautioned not to trade "essential liberty" for "temporary safety." On the other hand, Jackson had warned that the Bill of Rights was not a "suicide pact" to protect liberty at the cost of life.

The solution was a synthesis, but it was also a paradox. Washington called it "ordered liberty." Burke described it as "liberty connected with order." Ashcroft defined this paradox first with opposing negatives and then with a metaphor that stirred the audience's feelings. Liberty did not legitimate the "unbridled will" of anyone to do anything. Nor did order authorize the government to become "Big Brother." Rather, order and liberty intertwined like the structure and pathways in "a tall office building—a skyscraper." They enabled people to work together.

The tenor of this metaphor—"ordered liberty"—faded before the audience's memory of the vehicle: the crumbling Twin Towers. The speech then moved to a litany of the terrorists' intentions ("they seek . . . they seek . . . they seek") that required extirpation without the extinction of liberty. Ashcroft ended with an analogy that reinforced the precedent for tribunals outside ordinary courts. Like Nazis, terrorists attacked civilization itself. In effect, image and pathos—the skyscraper and Nazis at Nuremberg—carried the argument that liberty depended on order to defeat terror.

"[T]he tall office building" was an affecting symbol, like a red cape before a bull. It forced an American audience to react emotionally. National consciousness had converted the Twin Towers into a crucifixion for almost three thousand dead and the regeneration of the American spirit. The Towers had achieved an iconic status that transcended argument and compelled assent to what they now stood for: faith in "ordered liberty"—or patriotism that defended liberty by preempting absolute evil.

Such an icon had appealed to Ashcroft be-

fore. He supported a constitutional amendment against the desecration of the flag, in the Senate in 2000, because Americans needed "a symbol beyond reproach" to galvanize them into action as a nation. This symbol—the flag—was not an act of speech. Were it an act of speech, then negative responses like defacing it would be protected by the First Amendment. No, the flag was different. It joined object with spirit outside of speech. In a literal way it incarnated "loved ones lost, and . . . the American way of life."

For John D. Ashcroft, a speaker should anchor his words on icons that, in turn, rest on immutable belief. A nation also should anchor its policies on such icons and belief. After all, belief surpasses debate and dissent. Belief—unquestioned belief—inspires individual persons to act as one people.

INFORMATION SOURCES

Research Collections and Collected Speeches

Ashcroft's "State of the State" addresses, 1988–93, are available in the University of Missouri–Columbia Library. Beginning on May 8, 1994, the *Kansas City Star* ran a series on the desegregation suits in St. Louis and Kansas City on p. A1. The suits embroiled Ashcroft as attorney general and then governor. The *Congressional Record—Senate: 1994–2000.* Washington, D.C.: Government Printing Office, 1994–2000. Contains Ashcroft's speeches and remarks in the Senate. His speeches and testimony as U.S. attorney general are archived at the U.S. Department of Justice, Office of the Attorney General.

Ashcroft, John. "Chairman's Agenda for 1991–92." In *Redefining the Possible:Achieving the National Education Goals.* Washington, D.C.: National Governors' Association, 1991.

———. "A Clear and Present Danger." In *Rights vs. Public Safety.* Washington, D.C.: Center for Policy Research, 2001.

———. "Culture of Responsibility." In *Reclaiming America for Christ: Seventeen Powerful Messages from the 1996 Reclaiming America for Christ Conference.* Fort Lauderdale, Fla.: Coral Ridges Ministries, 1996.

———. "The Government Should Fund Faith-Based Social Services." In *Religion in America: Opposing Viewpoints,* ed. William Dudley et al. San Diego: Greenhaven Press, 2002.

———. "Government Welfare Corrupts the Poor."

In *Welfare Reform: The Politics of Wealth and Poverty*, ed. Gary E. McCuen. Hudson, Wis.: Gary E. McCuen Publications, 1996.

————. "Leadership: The Art of Redefining the Possible." In *Governors on Governing*, ed. Robert D. Behn. Washington, D.C.: National Governors' Association Lanham, Md.: University Press of America, 1991.

————, with Gary Thomas. *Lessons from a Father to His Son*. Nashville, Tenn.: Thomas Nelson, 1998.

————. *On My Honor: The Beliefs That Shape My Life*. Nashville, Tenn.: Thomas Nelson, 2001.

Web Sites

Congressional Record Web site [*CRS*]. Contains transcripts of Ashcroft's remarks and statements delivered at congressional hearings. http://www.gpoaccess.gov/crecord/index.html

Department of Justice Web site [*DOJ*]. Archives Ashcroft's speeches and testimony as attorney general. http://www.usdoj.gov/ag/index.html

Kansas City Star Web site includes texts of speeches and remarks surrounding the desegregation lawsuits filed in Missouri. Use "Color of Class" as the keyword. http://www.kansascity.com/mld/kansascity/archives/

Selected Critical Studies

Baker, Nancy V. "The Law: The Impact of Antiterrorism Policies on Separation of Powers. Assessing John Ashcroft's Role." *Presidential Studies Quarterly* (December 2002): 765–79.

Brown, Cynthia, ed. *Lost Liberties: Ashcroft and the Assault on Personal Freedom*. New York: New Press, 2003.

Burnet, Robyn, and Nick Decker. *A Working Missouri: The Ashcroft Years, 1985–1993*. Jefferson City, Mo., 1992.

Doherty, John. "Ashcroft's Power Grab." *reasonline*, June 2002. http://www.reason.com/0206/fe.bd.john.shtml

Eastland, Terry. "General Ashcroft: Justice Goes to War." *The Weekly Standard*, December 17, 2001. http://www.weeklystandard.com/content/public/articles/000/000/000/661wkzqt.asp

Hofstadter, Richard. *The Paranoid Style in American Politics and Other Essays*. New York: Knopf, Vintage Books, 1967.

Lewis, Neil A. "A Nation Challenged: The Senate Hearing: Ashcroft Defends Antiterror Plan; Says Criticism May Aid U.S. Foes." *New York Times* (late ed.—final), December 7, 2001, p. A1.

Rosen, Jeffrey. "How to Stop Big Brother." *The New Republic ONLINE*, December 16, 2002 http://www.tnr.com/

Selected Biographies

"Attorney General John D. Ashcroft." Archived at U.S. Department of Justice, Office of the Attorney General.

"John Ashcroft." *On the ISSUES: Every Political Leader on Every Issue*. http://www.issues2000.org/Senate/John_Ashcroft.htm

"John Ashcroft: Timeline." *St. Louis Post Dispatch* (five-star lift), December 24, 2000, News, p. A5.

Fineman, Howard. "The Gospel of St. John." *Newsweek*, June 1, 1998, p. 29.

Klaidman, Daniel. "Holy Warrior in the Hot Seat." *Newsweek*, December 10, 1998, pp. 44–48.

"Missouri's Champion of States' Rights and Traditional Values." *Southern Partisan* (second quarter 1998): 4–7. http://www.talkingpointsmemo.com/docs/ashcroft.sp.1.html

CHRONOLOGY OF MAJOR SPEECHES

See "Research Collections and Collected Speeches" for source codes.

"Oral Argument" (*Planned Parenthood v. Ashcroft*). November 30, 1982. *Supreme Court of the United States: no. 81-1255, no. 81-163*. Washington, D.C., June 15, 1983.

"Commitment to Progress" ("State of the State address"). Jefferson City, Mo., 1989. Archived at University of Missouri–Columbia Library.

"Nine Resolutions for the 1990's" ("State of the State address"). Jefferson City, Mo., 1990. Archived at University of Missouri–Columbia Library.

"Independence Means Risk" (speech to the Northeastern Leadership Conference). Atlantic City, N.J., May 21, 1995. *Vital Speeches of the Day*, July 17, 1995, pp. 600–3.

"Personal Responsibility" (speech in the Senate). *CRS*, August 1, 1996, pp. S9322–34.

"Judicial Despotism in the Age of Russell Clark" (speech at Conservative Political Action Committee Annual Meeting). Washington, D.C., March 7, 1997. http://www.lermanet.com/cos/senashcroft.htm

"Partial-Birth Abortion Ban Act of 1997" (speech in the Senate). *CRS*, May 19, 1997, pp. S4664–65.

"Great Necessities, Great Virtues" (speech at Conservative Political Action Committee Conference). Arlington, Va., January 30, 1998. http://www.chuckbaldwinlive.com/ashcroft.html

"Iraq" (speech in the Senate). *CRS*, February 27, 1998, p. S1134.

"We Have No King but Jesus" (commencement address at Bob Jones University). Greenville, S.C.,

May 8, 1999. *ABCNEWS.com*, January 12, 2001. http://abcnews.go.com/

"Opposition to Judge Ronnie White" (speech in the Senate). *CRS*, October 4, 1999, pp. S11867–75.

"Flag Desecration Constitutional Amendment" (speech in the Senate). *CRS*, March 28, 2000, p. S1765.

"Racism Corrupts the Mind and Poisons the Spirit" (self-defense against charges of racism). January 9, 2001. *Concerned Women for America: Library*. http://www.cwfa.org/articles/1715/CWA/misc/index.htm

Confirmation Hearing on John Ashcroft to Be Attorney General of the United States (January 16–19, 2001). Committee on the Judiciary, United States Senate, 117th Congress, serial no. J-107-1. Washington, D.C.: Government Printing Office, 2002.

"Installation" (inaugural speech as attorney general). Washington, D.C., July 16, 2001. Available at *DOJ*.

"Testimony of Attorney General John Ashcroft." Senate Committee on the Judiciary. Washington, D.C., December 6, 2001. Available at *DOJ*.

"Speech" (National Religious Broadcasters Convention). Nashville, Tenn., February 9, 2002. Available at *DOJ*.

"Speech" (Eighth Circuit Judges Conference). Duluth, Minn., August 7, 2002. Available at *DOJ*.

"Remarks at the Executive Office of United States Attorneys Awards." Washington, D.C., November 6, 2002. Available at *DOJ*.

"Speech" (White House Faith-Based and Community Initiatives Conference). Denver, Colo., January 13, 2003. Available at *DOJ*.

"Speech" (Council on Foreign Relations). Washington, D.C., February 10, 2003. Available at *DOJ*.

"Leadership in the Cause of Liberty" (Robert H. Krieble Lecture, Heritage Foundation). New Orleans, April 24, 2003. Available at *DOJ*.

ELIZABETH M. BIRCH (1957–)
Executive Director, Human Rights Campaign

SHAWN PARRY-GILES AND JASON EDWARD BLACK

The public address of Elizabeth M. Birch, though varying in circumstance and content, generally focuses on the concept of equality. To Birch—and the lesbian, gay, bisexual, and transgender (LGBT) rights movement of which she is a national leader—equality demands that American institutions and society accept as *whole citizens* all people, regardless of race, class, gender, religion, or sexual preference. This notion of equality remains predicated on the Declaration of Independence. Though early conceptions of the Declaration offered equality in terms of voting rights, property privileges, and protection under the law to Euro-American men, movements throughout U.S. history have agitated to change the meaning of equality. Over time, the abolitionist, suffragist, women's rights, civil rights, Red Power, and Chicano movements have worked to ensure equality for their constituent groups. Birch and the LGBT rights organization she leads, the Human Rights Cam-

paign (HRC), seek to add citizens leading alternative lifestyles to the list of beneficiaries enjoying the fruits of the Declaration.

Birch moved to the United States from Canada in the 1970s, during the height of the gay liberation movement coalescing in San Francisco and New York. She remembers reading about the 1969 Stonewall riots in New York, an event that piqued the interest of several closeted and open LGBT individuals. Stonewall was a gay bar in Greenwich Village that the New York Police Department raided to halt so-called lewd behavior. The raid and subsequent rebellion lasted four nights, with violent battles between the police and LGBT activists. Stonewall solidified the LGBT movement by providing it an exigence against which to mobilize. Birch also recollects the assassination of openly gay San Francisco councilman Harvey Milk. Milk's murder was seen by the LGBT community as a hate crime directed against a gay man—not a city official. By the time she graduated from college, Birch knew she had to do something about the inequalities perpetrated against the LGBT community. With an infectious passion for American equality, she decided to attend law school.

After graduating from Santa Clara School of Law in 1980, Birch clerked for the California Supreme Court, where she helped draft rulings related to equality issues such as employment discrimination and affirmative action. She next worked as a commercial litigator at a San Francisco law firm and as worldwide director of litigation for Apple Computers, where, again, she explored issues of equality and discrimination. Importantly, during her time in corporate law Birch worked pro bono to effect social change to the benefit of the LGBT community. For instance, she wrote myriad HIV/AIDS antidiscrimination laws that currently remain in effect in California.

munity. Further, it supports a multitude of programs designed to promote equality, such as the National Coming Out Project, the HRC WorkNet, the HRC FamilyNet, and Equality Rocks, a concert sustained by artists ranging from Garth Brooks to Melissa Etheridge.

As an activist and leader, Birch has made several media appearances. For example, she has represented the LGBT community on *Good Morning America*, *The Today Show*, *20/20*, *This Week*, *Face the Nation*, *Nightline*, *Crossfire*, *Larry King Live*, the *NewsHour with Jim Lehrer*, *Politically Incorrect*, and many more network and cable programs. She also has worked as a consultant for the popular prime-time shows *Ellen*, *Will & Grace*, and *The West Wing* concerning issues of LGBT identity, equality, and family issues. In 2002 Birch was honored for her appearances with one of the highest accolades bestowed upon America ac-

> "I believe in the power of the word and the value of honest communication. During my years as a litigator at a major corporation, I was often amazed at what simple, fresh, and truthful conversation could accomplish."
>
> *Elizabeth Birch's "Open Letter and Speech to the Christian Coalition," 1995*

As her interest in LGBT issues intensified, Birch began representing homosexuals in California and drafting equal-employment policies covering those leading alternative lifestyles. For her successful endeavors in bolstering equality Birch received the Ninth Circuit's Pro Bono Lawyer of the Year Award in 1987.

In 1995, Birch accepted the post of executive director at the HRC—the nation's largest LGBT advocacy organization in the United States. Under her leadership, the institution has grown from 100,000 members when she arrived to a present total of 500,000 LGBT and non-LGBT members. Since Birch joined the organization, HRC has built a reputation as both an educational agency and a political advocacy group. Regarding education, the HRC counsels the American public, the media, corporate America, and families on issues related to the LGBT com-

tivists: the Leadership Conference on Civil Rights Award.

ELIZABETH BIRCH: TAKING RISKS AND FIGHTING INEQUALITY

Elizabeth Birch's greatest speeches have originated in the wake of grave exigencies. A strong-willed activist, Birch repeatedly takes risks in her speech events, whether addressing hostile audiences such as the Christian Coalition, orating as the first openly gay speaker at the 2000 Democratic National Convention, or daring to get back to the business of equality mere weeks following the September 11 tragedy. To Birch, equality waits for no opponent or obstacle. Her rhetoric is charged with an alchemy of patience and immediacy that coalesces into speeches endearing the LGBT cause to the audience and concluding with concrete lists of anaphoric demands. Moreover, Birch's discourse remains infused with familial language and the construction of common ground.

Birch's 1995 "Open Letter and Speech to the Christian Coalition" exemplifies her willingness to take chances in order to connect with non-LGBT groups and to promote LGBT equality. In the fall of 1995, the Christian Coalition held its annual convention in Washington, D.C. House Speaker Newt Gingrich and the "Republican Revolution" were at the peak of their power, having swept the 1994 congressional election. The Republican bloc refused to include LGBT issues in their legislative plans for reform. The Christian Coalition, a right-wing group, persuaded Gingrich and his peers to exclude LGBT issues from the new plans. At the pinnacle of the Coalition's anti-LGBT rhetoric, the Christian group released a scathing, nationwide letter denigrating the LGBT community.

Not one to sit idly by, Birch decided to storm the Coalition's annual convention. She had been executive director of the HRC for just three months, and was intent on ensuring an HRC presence in the national debate over LGBT equality. Birch contacted Ralph Reed, then head of the Christian Coalition, asking for time to address the convention to talk about ways to humanize the issue of gay equality. Reed declined, so Birch rented a ballroom in an adjacent hotel and publicized her speech by distributing handbills to the general public. Her use of the image event was important for a number of reasons. First, Birch employed the news media to cover what was seen as a radical move: battling the Coalition convention by holding a counterconvention. Second, she produced her speech in written form—through an open letter—that allowed the media and Coalition members a preview of what she would discuss. The open letter also provided a transcript of her later talk, which could be replicated in print and on the Internet. Thus, Birch's words were not only quipped and quoted in the following day's papers; a full record was available to the American public to peruse at its leisure.

Birch stepped to the podium on September 8, 1995, before an audience of several hundred Coalition members. They constituted her oppositional, target, and empirical audience. Also, however, Birch appealed to the American news media and public as target audiences by widely disseminating the speech's transcript.

Birch's first rhetorical move linked the LGBT community with the Christian Coalition. This bridge constructed a "common ground" between the two adversarial groups. She opened the 1995 address with a tribute to open communication:

> I believe in the power of the word and the value of honest communication. During my years as a litigator at a major corporation, I was often amazed at what simple, fresh, and truthful conversation could accomplish. And what is true in the corporate setting is also true, I am convinced, in our communities. If we could learn to speak and listen to each other with integrity, the consequences might shock us.

Cognizant that her audience would rebuke her before hearing her words, Birch convinced them that she was not speaking to proselytize. She did not want to lecture, but wished to dialogue. Clearly, Birch would have liked them to grant blanket equality to LGBT people, but she would be content if the Coalition would "hear her words." Importantly, she criticized the Coalition's recent editorial campaign against the LGBT community by appealing to one of America's greatest democratic tools: dialogue and compromise.

But why should the Coalition members listen to Birch? And, if they listened, why should the group care about equality for the LGBT community—a group it found despicable, unnatural, and sinful? Birch anticipated these questions and arranged her answers in a "we are you and you are us" fashion. Ostensibly, Birch's arrangement here united the HRC and the Coalition into a human family: "Although the stereotype would have us believe otherwise, there are many conservative Americans within the nation's gay and lesbian communities. What's more, there are hundreds of thousands of Christians among us . . . including those represented in the Christian Coalition." Birch argued that in denying equality, or at least respect, to LGBT people, the Coalition would similarly deny other conservatives, Coalition members, and Christians. Such a denial of rights would violate the basic tenets of Christianity, from the Golden Rule to the "love thy neighbor" doctrine.

Birch further connected the groups by moving spatially closer to Coalition members. That members might violate God's laws in denying equality to "conservatives" or "Christians" was one thing. Birch then moved the possible closeted LGBT person from the general to the specific: "Like it or not, we are a part of your family. And we are a part of your community." She began to offer specific examples of the conflation of LGBT and Coalition groups: "We are your neighbors and colleagues, business associates and friends. More intimately, you are fathers of sons who are gay and mothers of daughters who are lesbians. I know many of your children very, very well. I work with them. I worry with them. And I rejoice that they are part of our community." Basically, Birch brought the gay community home to the Coalition. In particular, her use of pronouns crafted identification with those countering LGBT equality. In Birch's discourse we see the following arrangements: "We" are "your" neighbors and colleagues. "You" are our parents, and have created "us." Hence, we all belong in "our" community. The "our" construction unites "we" and "you" into a common community—one that intertwines more than it diverges. The arrangement of LGBT and non-LGBT subjects assists in linking the two opponents as one *people* in Birch's discourse.

Birch continued exhorting the Coalition to dialogue with the HRC. "By taking away respectability, rhetorically as well as legally, we justify the belief that they [LGBT] are not quite human, not quite worthy, not quite deserving of our time, our attention, or our concern." Here, Birch developed a repetitive rhetoric, broken into units of three. This rapid and successive approach demonstrated the callous attitude of the Christian Coalition in not listening to what the HRC had to say. By denying the LGBT community a voice, the religious right articulated that gays and lesbians were not human, worthy, or deserving; that time, attention, and concern should not be afforded LGBT people. Would "good Christians" and "good parents" deny even a voice to those in their spiritual or human family? Birch urged, "No . . . it would be not only highly regrettable, but terribly hypocritical; it would not be worthy of the true ideals and val-

ues based in love at the core of what we call Christian." Birch challenged the Coalition members to rethink their commitment to Christian and American tenets. Are we not, she asked, "all God's children? Are we not all created equal" in the eyes of our fellow citizens?

Next, Birch moved away from the familial and common ground petitions to concentrate on her demands for social change. Having connected with her audience through appeals to pathos, or emotionality, she arrived at her arguments for LGBT equality. First, she asked the Christian Coalition to "please make integrity a watchword for the campaigns you launch." Ostensibly, Birch contended that name-calling and perpetuating falsehoods and negative caricatures of the LGBT community did nothing to secure the equality of gays and lesbians, nor was it congruent with the Coalition:

> We could express our convictions in words that are, if not affectionate, and if not even kind, then at least decent, civil, humane. We need not demonize each other simply because we disagree. . . . If we, in the name of civil rights, slander you, we have failed our ideals, as surely as any Christian who slanders us in the name of God has failed the ideals of scripture.

At the least, she argued, be true to your Christian philosophy. In exchange, the HRC and LGBT communities would keep the lines of communication open, never reverting to ad hominem or personal attacks, or relying on negative media campaigns to ruin the Christian Coalition's public image. To Birch, in the 1995 address this joint respect "commits the groups to a higher moral ground" in order to foster the equality of LGBT persons, as well as of Christian Coalition members.

In addition to creating community, Birch's "open letter" called on the Christian Coalition to approach gays and lesbians not as tainted sinners, but as human beings and American neighbors. Birch even reminded members that many LGBT members are Christians and remain excommunicated by the very church communities that helped raise them: "[T]he deepest agony of life is not that they risk physical abuse or that they will never gain their civil rights, but that they have felt the judgment of an institution on which they stake their lives: the church." Birch's appeal to ethos asked Coalition members to welcome their children back into the Christian home, the church. Her discourse subordinated social and political equality to the simple right to life and liberty. Such appeals to Christianity connected with the Coalition's values of spirituality and community inspired by the word of Christ.

It remains difficult to judge the effect of Birch's speech to the Christian Coalition. No exit polls were taken, and her requests for social change were long-term in nature, not immediate and concrete. The demands were behavioral, social, and institutional, and not narrowly defined policy changes. Birch's subsequent appearance in LGBT publications such as *Out*, *Advocate*, and *Gay Parent* magazines as a leader of the new gay liberation movement, however, may have resulted from her newsworthy open letter/speech to the Christian Coalition. According to an interview with Birch on March 23, 2003, the Coalition speech was "her first major speech" as HRC director. She believes her Coalition speech helped move her into the public and political eye as an LGBT leader; such a claim can be measured, perhaps, by viewing the explosion of public appearances Birch made following the 1995 address.

Elizabeth Birch's risky public address also found a home in 2000, when she requested time to speak before the Democratic National Convention (DNC). The speech she delivered on August 15, 2000, illustrates the fashion in which Birch and the HRC employ specific examples as logos and pathos in bringing to light the need for LGBT policy reform. Birch's DNC oratory represented the first time an openly gay person addressed a national political convention on prime-time television.

Birch's appeals for LGBT equality came at an interesting time in gay and lesbian social history. In the wake of the brutal murder of Matthew Shepard—an openly gay college student tortured and left to die in Laramie, Wyoming—the media had been fishing for an LGBT platform from either the Democratic or the Republican presidential campaign. Despite appeals from Shepard's mother and the Laramie Project movement, the Republican National Convention (RNC) refused to allow LGBT equality a place on its platform.

The Democrats, however, allowed America's gay and lesbian citizenry a voice at their convention through Birch. At the convention, her immediate audience was the DNC, but her television appearance allowed her to address the larger audience of the American public, and the oppositional audience of the Republican Party. Republicans were closely monitoring both the rhetoric of the DNC and the media's interpretation of the Democrats' inclusion of LGBT equality on its political agenda.

Birch's speech hearkened back to a sense of American family. Her words defined the wounds dividing the populace, and suggested ways they could heal. The speech began, "[T]onight, we celebrate the American family. But we know that America's family is not yet whole." Birch then articulated a list, employing anaphora (the repetition of a word or phrase), noting the recent fractures in American equality.

> Because of the color of his skin, James Byrd, Jr. was dragged behind a truck in Jasper, Texas, until his body was shattered on a drainage ditch. Because of her faith, 14-year-old Kristi Beckel was gunned down as she worshiped in a Texas Baptist Church. Because Matthew Shepard was gay, he was driven into the countryside on a freezing Wyoming night, beaten, and hung on a fence to die.

This anaphoric construction served two primary purposes. First, Birch criticized the RNC by illuminating hate crimes committed in Texas, home of Republican nominee George W. Bush, as examples. The image of Texas as a breeding ground for hate crimes, combined with the Republican Party's denial of LGBT issues on its platform, associated the opposition with a disdain for American equality. In a strategic rhetorical move, Birch reminded her audience that Texas was, perhaps not inconsequently, the home state of presidential hopeful George W. Bush. Second, Birch linked the atrocities against race and religion with violent acts against an alternative lifestyle. In this way, she included LGBT persons under the label "American equality" and dismissed the proposition that equality rests solely on race, religion, gender, and class.

Moreover, Birch's 2000 DNC speech reconstructed "America's gay children" as worthy of equality. Having placed LGBT persons under the aegis of equality through anaphora, she then discussed the importance of considering the rights of those "left on the margins of family life and out of the vision of America."

> I want you to know that your gay children are gifted and strong. All are heroic in the way they have conquered barriers to their own self-respect. Many have suffered cruelty or violence. Some serve their communities with leadership and grace. . . . All were created by God. And, you have a right to be proud of each and every one of them.

Here, Birch's rhetoric takes on a spatial arrangement as it skips from "many" to "some" to "all," referring to both the accomplishments and the plights of the LGBT community. Though many have suffered and have lost their livelihood, and some have served patriotically, *all* "were created by God" and "are heroic in the way they have conquered barriers to their own self respect."

Birch's rhetoric succeeded in pointing out the social and political achievements of some or most gays and lesbians. Indeed, this arrangement united the LGBT community with the population at large. The power of the discourse, however, lay in articulating the familial presence of the LGBT citizenry. These people, she insinuated, are part of the American family. Hence, "leaders must love all its [*sic*] children and safeguard the family called America." Like non-LGBTs, "all" gays and lesbians demand respect and equality, if for no other reason than that they are the children of God and America.

The healing nation, Birch concluded, must understand that equality exists regardless of a person's physical or spiritual characteristics. Instead, equality must be applied unconditionally. And such an application cannot be achieved until certain inequities and hate crimes gain remedy. Again, Birch created an anaphoric narrative questioning the healing and unity of the American family:

> As long as a young man can be left on a fence to die, our American family will be fractured. As long as gay parents live in fear that their children might be taken from them, our family is torn. As long as hardworking Americans can be fired in 30 states simply for being gay, our

family is not whole. As long as gay people are barred from serving openly and [with] dignity in the armed forces of the United States, our family is not just. As long as gay, lesbian, bisexual, and transgender youth are at risk . . . then the American family we celebrate tonight is not yet healed.

Birch arranged her rhetoric in a juxtaposed fashion, conveying to her audiences a particular injustice followed by a reminder of how the American family remains disjointed. Birch then asked the American public to engage in empathy, to place themselves in an LGBT individual's place. What would life be like if one could be brutalized or killed? What if someone could take away another's children or job? How do such realities fulfill the American essence of equality?

According to Birch, her 2000 speech to the DNC helped the Democratic Party carve out a unique issue that the Republican Party could not address due to its religious ties and conservative worldview of family values. Ostensibly, her remarks had the effect of providing the DNC a position on LGBT rights, thus conveying to the American Left and the news media the party's desire to seek social change for citizens leading alternative lifestyles. At the same time, her address—aired on prime-time television—elevated the Human Rights Campaign as a notable force in the LGBT community.

Elizabeth Birch's emphasis on "healing" occupied a third speech: her October 6, 2001, oratory at the HRC's fifth annual National Dinner. Delivering the speech only a few weeks following the tragedies of September 11, Birch took a risk in moving forward with both the HRC dinner and the quest for LGBT equality. Given before 2,500 pro-LGBT activists and community members, the speech came at a time when many organizations around the nation were canceling events. Birch believed that coming together as a community would assist HRC members in reconciling what occurred at the World Trade Center and the Pentagon. From a political standpoint, the LGBT community was still unsure of how they would be treated in the wake of the tragedies. Many of the Americans who perished were gays and lesbians who left behind not only life partners but also monetary resources and property holdings. A national question still lingered: Could LGBT domestic partners share in the rights to their deceased's assets? Moreover, for those suffering in hospitals, could their life partners remain with them as they healed or slipped away? For pragmatic reasons as well as healing purposes, Birch decided to speak on equality as a way to bring the LGBT community closer together in the time of national crisis.

She started by reminding her audience that many of America's fallen heroes were gays and lesbians. Surely, she said, "as [the LGBT community] mourns the loss of every life," it should also be "inspired and lifted by the stories of unmatched courage from members of our community." Through rhetorical example, she detailed the actions of Mark Bingham, a gay man, in helping thwart the terrorists' goal of crashing United Flight 93 into the Capitol. In addition, she delivered an encomium on the family of Ronald Gamboa and Dan Brandhorst, gay men who held "their 3-year-old son, David, as close as they could—as any loving parent would" as United Flight 175 hurtled into the second Trade Center tower. Finally, she paid tribute to gay pilot David Charlebois, lesbian nurse and American Flight 11 passenger Carol Flyzik, and gay rescue worker John Keohane. These examples inspired the sort of pride Birch hoped her organization would bear in mind as it moved forward following the crisis.

Next, Birch elevated the LGBT community as a beacon of light for America to follow in its suffering. As she noted throughout the speech, "our work and dreams are lived always in the sunlight—and never in the shadows." The metaphors of light and shadow retained significance in Birch's community-building. The metaphor of "shadows" evokes a sense of fear. For the LGBT community, fear could represent anything from fear of losing one's job in a homophobic workplace to the fear of losing one's life in the Wyoming, countryside. The notion of shadow also correlates with a second metaphor commonly associated with the LGBT community—that of the "closet." Birch hearkened back to a time of "shadows" most LGBT persons faced when they were locked within their own bodies and minds, fearful of stepping out of a

lonely and frightening place. In contrast, the metaphor of "sunshine" referred to the moment of clarity when gays and lesbians escaped the dark solitude of self and "came out" to the world openly and unashamedly.

The imagery of "light" and "beacon" assisted Birch in discussing how America should follow the path of the LGBT community. The LGBT community, she argued, had survived despite suffering prejudice and hatred. Its bravery should be emulated, she said:

> Our community knows all too well the devastating effects of hate. As gay, lesbian, bisexual and transgender Americans, many of us have known from a young age what it is to be teased or taunted, brutalized or killed—simply for who we are. . . . I suspect the gay community of our nation has a thing or two to share with America about facing down fear and safeguarding cherished values of honesty, integrity, strength . . . and equality.

As America faced its darkest hour, Birch said, it could learn from the HRC and its constituents. The parallel between America and the LGBT community represented a key pathos appeal.

Finally, in the speech Birch argued for the strengthening of the HRC and its goal of equality despite the national crisis. "I say this now," she exhorted her audience, "our goals have never been so vital and relevant. Our goals are no less important after September 11 than before." In patriotic fashion, Birch united American equality in the wake of September 11 with LGBT equality in the wake of Stonewall, Harvey Milk's assassination, and Matthew Shepard's torture. This arrangement moved the terrorist crisis in line with past crises: "At this moment of national crisis, our quest is not beside the point. It is the point. And this burning within us to make America that much better is not just America's gift to us; it is our gift to America. We must not let this unity—this sacred quest for an equal nation— . . . drift to any distant place in our lives." For Birch, LGBT equality was not moot, because America was now forced to reconstruct its identity. Indeed, gay and lesbian rights could play a key role in this reconstruction. Birch appealed to the HRC to let its struggle "be [its] gift to America." For in the American family's greatest catastrophe, the LGBT community "can make America stronger at its broken places."

The effects of Birch's 2001 speech remain difficult to ascertain. According to Birch, her speech ignited a wholesale revival of Human Rights Campaign members. Every local HRC convention went as planned, based on Birch's exhortation to the group to demonstrate its bravery in a time of extreme crisis. In this way, the speech most likely supported an internally based effect rather than a wider impact on the American community at large.

Though it is difficult to gauge the success of Birch's discourse, one might look to external factors such as the growing membership of the HRC. The burgeoning number of antidiscrimination LGBT laws being passed throughout state and local jurisdictions also indicates the rhetorical appeal of Elizabeth Birch and the many activists like her. Her oratory reflects the lifework of a social activist intent on strengthening the focus of American equality. Her words encourage all Americans to heed the natural law tenet proffered by the Declaration of Independence— that all people are created equal—and to welcome people of all persuasions as members of the same American family.

INFORMATION SOURCES

Research Collections and Collected Speeches

There are no archival collections or published collections of Birch's speeches at this time.

Audiovisual Materials

There are no readily available video or audio versions of Elizabeth Birch's speeches.

Web Sites

Transcripts of speeches delivered by Elizabeth Birch are occasionally published as news releases and can be found by accessing the Human Rights Campaign's Web site, www.hrc.org. Researchers can also find HRC white papers, policy initiatives, and LGBT narratives at that site.

Selected Biographies

Bull, Chris, ed. *Come Out Fighting: A Century of Essential Writing on Gay and Lesbian Liberation.* New York: Thunder's Mouth Press/Nation Books, 2001.

Marcus, Eric. *Making Gay History: The Half-Century Fight for Gay and Lesbian Equal Rights.* New York: Perennial, 2002.

Williams, Walter L., and Yolanda Retter, eds. *Gay and Lesbian Rights in the United States: A Documentary History.* Westport, Conn.: Greenwood, 2003.

CHRONOLOGY OF MAJOR SPEECHES

"Speech at the Ninth Circuit's Lawyer of the Year Award Ceremony." Winter 1987.

"Open Letter and Speech to Christian Coalition." Washington, D.C., September 8, 1995.

"Address at the Democratic National Convention." Los Angeles, August 15, 2000. Available at http://www.civilrights.org/issues/hate/details.cfm?id=5440.

"Address at HRC's Fifth Annual National Dinner." Washington, D.C., October 6, 2001.

"Open Letter on Ideology of the HRC." Washington, D.C., Spring 2002.

"Address to the North Carolina HRC." Raleigh, N.C., May 6, 2002.

"Speech to the Leadership Conference on Civil Rights Award Ceremony." Washington, D.C., November 13, 2002.

"Address at HRC's Sixth Annual National Dinner." Washington, D.C., December 9, 2002.

PATRICK J. BUCHANAN (1938–)
Presidential Speechwriter, Political Commentator, U.S. Presidential Candidate

C. BRANT SHORT

Patrick J. Buchanan is one of the few presidential speechwriters in American history to wage a serious campaign for the presidency. Although many speechwriters have remained involved in politics, few have made the transition to seeking any elected office, let alone the highest political position in the United States. Buchanan speaks with ideological fervor, distinguishing himself from other politicians by his commitment to a political/cultural worldview that resists compromise and negotiation. In many ways, Buchanan is a throwback to the nineteenth century, when fiery oratory and vigorous public debate dominated American politics. Eschewing moderation in his campaign oratory, he articulated a vision that some observers considered politically unwise. In one review of Buchanan's 1992 address to the Republican National Convention, political observer Richard Brookhiser aptly summarized Buchanan's reputation among fellow conservatives: "He's the kind of person democracies want to have on call, not making the calls."

Patrick Joseph Buchanan was born on November 2, 1938—"All Soul's Day," he reports in his autobiography—in Washington, D.C., the third son in an Irish-Scots Catholic family that included seven boys and two girls. Buchanan's father, William, demanded much of his sons, and his political views reflected deep devotion to the Catholic Church and an absolute rejection of communism and FDR liberalism. Buchanan's description of his father mirrors the image that many apply to the son: "My father was given to explosions—of laughter, applause, anger, and delight. . . . Called 'Wild Bill' as a young man, for his forensic encounters over religion, politics, and sports, he loved debating and had a distinctly Irish side, which enjoyed jokes (only clean ones), loved funny stories, and appreci-

ated powerful rhetoric and good language." The Catholic Church defined his father's life. "My father's religious beliefs permeated everything," Buchanan recalled. "Abandoned at eleven by a father whom he idolized, my father transferred his total loyalty to the Church, to the nuns and Jesuit priests who had instructed him in the Faith."

Buchanan's oratory in large measure reflects the values he learned while growing up in a devout Catholic family in the 1940s and 1950s. Writing that his childhood in the Church gave him a "code of conduct, a sure knowledge of right and wrong," Buchanan concluded, "We had a hierarchy of values . . . we were not confused. We had certitude." He credits Gonzaga High School as a major influence in his life, even more important than his college years at Georgetown University. Buchanan, whose family lived in Georgetown, commuted to campus and felt that the "day students" were not as welcome as the out-of-town boarders living in the dormitories. Moreover, he was unimpressed with many of the priests teaching at the university; they lacked the spiritual commitment and certainty about the world that Buchanan found appealing in his high school teachers.

Although Buchanan liked to debate the issues of the day with family and friends, and displayed both intelligence and self-confidence, he found public speaking problematic. His training in speech and debate left much to be desired; in high school and college he had adverse experiences that fostered the stage fright he continues to experience. While he was participating in a high school debate, Buchanan's mind went blank: "As my sweating hand gripped the lectern, I stared, paralyzed, for what seemed an eternity into the impassive faces in that audience of two hundred men." Humiliated after the experience, Buchanan concluded that there "were some things that came naturally for some people, and public speaking did not come naturally to me." For years he avoided giving speeches, and when he was forced to speak, Buchanan memorized his oration and kept a written text nearby. "Even today," he wrote in his autobiography, "my stomach churns more when I have to address a hundred people than when I have to appear on television before a million." Buchanan noted that the "most painful" course he took at Georgetown University was public speaking, although he acknowledged that the university "was wise to force us through a semester of it." The class was taught

as a graduate student at the Columbia School of Journalism, where he received the M.A. degree in journalism in 1962.

In June 1962 Buchanan joined the *St. Louis Globe Democrat* as a reporter, then quickly moved to writing editorials for the newspaper. Although in his early twenties, he was preparing editorials for the paper on a regular basis. While employed at the newspaper, he met Richard Nixon and sought employment with the former vice president, who was considering another presidential campaign. In 1966 Buchanan became Nixon's first full-time aide and earned his annual salary of $10,000 by handling Nixon's correspondence and helping him write a nationally syndicated newspaper column. Nixon used

---

Pat Buchanan is justifiably famous for his use of sharp, biting language. He wrote Vice President Spiro Agnew's 1969 speech that vigorously attacked the media's coverage of Vietnam, student demonstrations, and the Nixon administration. In that speech Buchanan castigated news commentators who, he said, "enjoy a right of instant rebuttal to every presidential address, but more importantly, wield a free hand in selecting, presenting and interpreting the great issues in our nation." In his 1992 speech delivered at the Republican National Convention, Buchanan called that summer's Democratic National Convention, which had nominated Bill Clinton as a centrist "New Democrat," "the greatest single exhibition of cross-dressing in American political history."

---

in an especially challenging manner: as each student presented a speech, the audience members were instructed to hold up signs with constructive comments on delivery and gestures ("slow down," for example). Unfortunately, some of Buchanan's classmates also held up signs with messages he recalled being unprintable, making him lose his composure and, in his view, dropping his final grade from an A to a C.

Buchanan majored in English as an undergraduate, and took courses in literature, language, religion, history, and philosophy. He did not take a single course in government, politics, economics, biology, or chemistry. He received his B.A. degree in 1961 and continued his work

him in a variety of roles in the 1968 presidential campaign and brought him to the White House in 1969. Buchanan's major role entailed preparing Nixon for press conferences, and he also served as a principal presidential speechwriter from 1969 to 1974. From 1966 on, he was a personal and political adviser to President Nixon and was one of those closest to the president until he resigned in 1974, maintaining an intimate relationship with the president that was shared by a select few. Buchanan served as an adviser to Gerald Ford and later joined the Reagan administration as director of communication from 1985 to 1987.

Buchanan moved back to journalism after

Nixon's resignation, writing columns for two national press syndicates between 1975 and 1985 as well as preparing radio commentaries for NBC for five years. He appeared on television on a regular basis, cohosting a political talk show on CNN in the 1980s and 1990s between his three presidential campaigns (1992, 1996, and 2000). After his last campaign in 2000, he joined MSNBC as a television host, and continues to write a nationally syndicated column. During the 1990s, Buchanan also wrote several controversial books, including *A Republic, Not an Empire: Reclaiming America's Destiny* (1999) and *The Death of the West: How Dying Populations and Immigrant Invasions Imperil Our Country and Civilization* (2002).

Buchanan's political oratory owes much to his work as a speechwriter, where he learned to craft a compelling rhetorical message. Preparing speeches for President Nixon, Buchanan found that years of reading poetry and literature had developed in him an "excellent ear" for creating a sense of rhythm and cadence in a speech manuscript. The great orations in history, Buchanan observed, "all have about them that musical quality, as though the words are actually marching in cadence." Nixon utilized three primary speechwriters in his first term: Buchanan, William Safire, and Raymond Price. Significantly, Nixon rejected the committee approach and used each man for a particular kind of speech. According to Safire, "Price was the liberal, Buchanan the conservative, Safire the centrist; Price a WASP, Buchanan a Catholic." Buchanan was called upon for conservative speeches, usually on domestic topics, and would sometimes be asked for conservative punch lines to enhance Nixon's style.

Scholars credit Buchanan for his work in preparing three of the most notable political speeches of the twentieth century: Nixon's "Silent Majority" and "Cambodia Incursion" speeches and Vice President Spiro Agnew's "Television News Coverage" speech. Although several persons, including Nixon himself, claimed that the president wrote the "Silent Majority" speech entirely on his own, Buchanan has stated that he assisted in the preparation of this address, considered by many to be Nixon's finest rhetorical effort as president. There is no doubt that Buchanan served as the principal writer of the other two speeches, both of which required

the language and logic of the most conservative speechwriter in the administration. Nixon's April 1970 "Cambodia Incursion" speech articulated in clear and powerful prose the administration's policy of widening the Vietnam War. While many observers assumed Nixon would attempt to appease his critics and reduce the scope of the war, especially in light of massive antiwar demonstrations, the president called upon Buchanan, who prepared a speech that was called "patriotic, angry, stick-with-me-or-else, alternately pious and strident" by Nixon speechwriter William Safire. Vice President Agnew's "Television News Coverage" speech reflected Buchanan at his best. Angered by negative news analysis of Nixon's "Silent Majority" speech, Buchanan prepared a powerful indictment of "elite media" coverage and gave the speech text to Nixon, who agreed that the vice president should find a forum and deliver it. The speech polarized the nation, with liberal voices decrying the message while conservatives felt it struck a chord with America's "silent majority." For at least a decade, observed Safire, the speech killed television's "instant analysis" of presidential speeches.

Buchanan's political oratory centers upon his three campaigns for the presidency. In 1992, disappointed with the Bush administration's failure to embrace conservative political values and eager to have a platform from which to express his views, Buchanan challenged the incumbent president for the Republican nomination. In 1996 he ran again for the Republican presidential nomination, losing to Kansas Senator Robert Dole. Frustrated by the ideological timidity of the Republican Party, Buchanan sought and received the presidential nomination of the Reform Party in 2000. In these campaigns he articulated what were, in his view, "true" conservative values.

Buchanan's most notable political speech, experts conclude, was delivered at the 1992 Republican National Convention, a reflection of his importance in influencing the Republican political agenda. The setting was important symbolically for several reasons. On this day of the convention, President George H. W. Bush accepted the Republican nomination for a second time, overcoming a significant challenge from Buchanan, who in primary elections had received over three million votes from disgruntled Republicans. More-over, the convention took place in Bush's home-town of Houston, Texas, a place hostile to Buchanan's attacks on its favorite son. Most im-portant, the convention heard Ronald Reagan de-liver his last major political address, the last hur-rah of the Reagan era in American politics. In this highly charged atmosphere, Patrick Buchanan spoke for his principles, reaffirmed his commit-ment to the conservative ideology of the Reagan Revolution, and, being loyal to his party, endorsed George H. W. Bush for the presidency. Commu-nication scholars Robert C. Rowland and John Jones conducted a comparative analysis of Buchanan's and Reagan's convention addresses, noting that Buchanan's speech became one of the "most discussed" speeches of the 1990s. They concluded that the two speeches presented two competing visions of American conservatism, Buchanan promoting "extremism" and Reagan leading the party back to "traditional liberalism." Moreover, Buchanan utilized "we" and "they" throughout the speech to distinguish between the believers in his crusade and those on the outside. In this manner he claimed success in the cam-paign by carrying a message of true conservatism to the American people, even though he lost the nomination. The speech represented the culmina-tion of a presidential bid that challenged the lead-ership of his own political party. Feeling betrayed by the Bush administration, especially its global economic policies, Buchanan based his primary campaign on an "America First" platform, calling for a fence on the Mexican/American border, adoption of a trade policy that protected Ameri-can jobs, and elimination of foreign aid. He also assailed the Bush administration for its failure to defend the values of Western culture in a climate of multicultural excess.

The speech began by acknowledging Bush's victory and Buchanan's pledge to support the president in the fall campaign. Then Buchanan turned to his campaign and the values he deemed important in the election. Drawing on his background as a journalist and speech-writer, he utilized suggestive and evocative lan-guage as a major element in his effort to inspire his audience. Calling the Democratic National Convention that nominated Bill Clinton as a centrist "New Democrat" "the greatest single

exhibition of cross-dressing in American polit-ical history," Buchanan attacked the "prophets of doom" at the convention who attacked the Reagan decade. Indeed, he continued, the Rea-gan years were not "terrible years in America. They were great years. . . . And everyone knows it except for the carping critics who sat on the sidelines of history, jeering at one of the great statesmen of the modern time, Ronald Reagan." After attacking the Democratic oppo-sition, Buchanan enlarged the context of the speech, claiming that the election represented a "religious war" for the "soul of America. It is a cultural war as critical to the kind of nation we shall become as the Cold War itself, for this war is for the soul of America." In this way, Buchanan positioned himself as an ideologue who refused to compromise for political expe-diency. This stance paved the way for his books, his political commentary, and his two subsequent attempts at the presidency.

Buchanan's political oratory is defined by a number of characteristics. Buchanan regularly weaves logical, emotional, and ethical appeals into a unified persuasive message. His logical appeals typically are grounded in contrasting his beliefs and values with those of his opposition. In the 1992 Republican Convention speech, for example, Buchanan listed the Clinton cam-paign's agenda on issues such as abortion, ho-mosexual rights, women in combat, litmus tests for Supreme Court appointments, and school vouchers. He did not need to build the case for his positions, since his convention audience al-ready embraced his stands. Some observers be-lieve that Buchanan's oratory draws upon the themes established by American populists such as William Jennings Bryan and Huey Long, and uses that populist style of argumentation, de-manding justice for the common person in light of the collusion of big business and big govern-ment. His use of pathos (or emotional appeals) often explores the plight of the common person abused by the prevailing political powers. In his "Den of Thieves" speech, Buchanan identified those who suffer most from high energy costs: the college student who delivers pizzas; the truck drivers who bring the products essential to the economy; and the independent taxi drivers who are facing a "collapse in take-home pay that could force their families onto food stamps. These are the American[s] who are paying the price of their own government's past neglect and present cowardice."

Buchanan enhances his ethos by using such techniques as identifying himself with notable leaders such as Ronald Reagan, illustrating his consistent stand on particular issues, and explaining the political risks he takes for his commitment. He also utilizes a form of mythical appeal, affirming the guiding principles of American institutions and praising the vision of the Founding Fathers. In announcing his 1996 presidential candidacy, Buchanan called for Americans to "recapture our lost national sovereignty." American patriots who stood at Lexington and Concord Bridge and Bunker Hill gave "all they had, that the land they loved might be a free, independent, sovereign nation." Yet, in today's world, American sovereignty, "purchased with the blood of patriots, is being traded away for foreign money, handed over to faceless foreign bureaucrats at places like the IMF, the World Bank, the World Trade Organization and the U.N."

Buchanan's persuasive appeals develop from his views of history, literature, and Judeo-Christian values. His devout Roman Catholic faith guides his critiques of modern culture and provides the foundation for his vision of how government should function in a democracy. For example, Buchanan charged that America's children are being "robbed of their innocence" and being "poisoned against their Judeo-Christian heritage." If elected president, Buchanan pledged to use the fullest extent of his power to "defend American traditions and the values of faith, family, and country."

As a former speechwriter and journalist, Buchanan is careful in the way he uses language. He skillfully attacks his opponents with biting sarcasm and ridicule. In his Houston speech, for example, he chastised a number of Democrats, including Senator Edward Kennedy: "How many 60-year-olds do you know who still go to Florida for spring break?" Buchanan uses vivid verbal images to support his positions, as in his acceptance speech at the 2000 Reform Party Convention, in which he proclaimed: "As for those homeless conservatives, who were locked up in the basement at the big Bush Family Reunion in Philadelphia," the Reform Party offered

plenty of room. Moreover, the two major political parties had failed the voters: "My friends, it is time to pick up the pitchforks and go down and clean out the pigpen. If you want real reform, vote Reform."

Some critics have charged that Buchanan conveys hostile messages through strategic choices of language, using code words to make disparaging comments about religious and ethnic groups. In an analysis of his 1996 campaign speaking, *New York Times* reporter James Bennet wrote:

> Criticism of Mr. Buchanan's language has swirled around him for years, and it is a testament either to his innocence or to his oratorical nimbleness that the debate still rages. His critics acknowledge their charges can be hard to prove, arising as they sometimes do from inferences drawn from inflection, context, and juxtaposition of ideas in his speeches, rather than flat out assertions.

Buchanan defended himself by calling such charges "ridiculous" and said that he did not need to use "code" language to convey his message to the voters.

Buchanan's delivery is serviceable, although at times it presents problems. In his autobiography, Buchanan noted that he lacked a strong delivery early his public speaking career. Remembering being called upon to speak on significant issues while working at the *St. Louis Globe Democrat* in the mid-1960s, Buchanan noted, "A mediocre speaker, who did not enjoy it, I did not look forward to these appearances. I drafted my speeches at work at night and read them to the audience." Not only was Buchanan reading his speeches but they sounded like editorials and not, as he wished, like oral arguments in a trial. Moreover, he found that his voice was "unsuited to the podium; when [I am] excited, it has a tendency to rise so high that only the dogs can understand me." Buchanan has improved upon his delivery since those early days. Novelist Norman Mailer, in an analysis of the various speakers at the 1992 Republican National Convention for *The New Republic*, was taken with Buchanan's delivery. Calling Buchanan "pleasant-faced" and "mild-voiced," Mailer noted that the audience appeared to hang on each of Buchanan's words as the speech began in a deliberate and restrained manner. But as the speech continued, and Buchanan offered his vision of the culture war and the "fight for the soul of America," Mailer found Buchanan's delivery symbolic of the deeper message of his address: "The fact that his voice had begun to wear down into a hoarse whisper made him only more effective in his peroration. Each of his words now seemed to insist on a private physical toll; so suffering, he spoke to a sentiment that no other politician of either party would have dared to come close to uttering in public."

Buchanan's speech structure typically follows a classical format. He uses introductions effectively to greet his audience, build his credibility, and introduce his speaking purpose. Humor is often a part of his introductions, helping to ease the transition to the political message of the body of the speech. Buchanan uses rhetorical questions as a convenient transitional device in the body of his speech and, often, a standard problem/solution framework. His conclusions are designed to inspire action, and often he recounts a heroic act or calls upon God's help. In his "Reform Party Nomination Acceptance Speech," Buchanan ended with this charge:

> What are we fighting for? To save our country from being sold down the river into some godless New World Order, and to hand down to our children a nation as good, as great, as the one our parents gave to us—forever independent, forever free. That's what this Gideon's Army is fighting for; and we will fight on and on and on and on—until God Himself calls us home.

When asked to identify the speeches he considers most representative of his work, Buchanan listed two orations: the 1969 speech he wrote for Vice President Agnew that attacked the news media's liberal bias and, likely a surprise to some observers, the eulogy for his father, who died in 1988. In this speech, the private and the public sides of Buchanan are revealed, and though not a political address, it conveys Buchanan's view of citizenship as well as of family. Buchanan opened with a powerful statement, summarizing the goal of the eulogy: "Large men leave an emptiness, a void when they pass on, and Pop leaves an immense void."

He recalled his father's intense devotion to family and church and his love of life: "He lived the life he wanted to live; and he loved every minute of it." Most important for Buchanan, the political crusader, was his father's demand for loyalty: "Pop was the personification of loyalty; loyalty to friends, loyalty to family, loyalty to faith; he was a living embodiment of what used to be called manly values." In his conclusion, Buchanan asked his father to say a prayer for the living, "because we need them now." In a short but powerful statement of what a father meant to a son, he said, "Pop was, quite simply, the best man I ever knew."

Pat Buchanan uses oratory, both as a candidate and as a commentator, to persuade audiences to join his crusade. Although he has never held elected office, he moved from a presidential speechwriter and adviser to a major figure in American politics in the last three decades of the twentieth century. In this way, his political speaking deserves attention from anyone interested in evaluating contemporary American politics.

INFORMATION SOURCES

Research Collections and Collected Speeches

There are no archival collections or published collections of Buchanan's speeches at this time. Three of the speeches he wrote during the Nixon administration appear on the "*One Hundred Greatest Political Speeches of the Twentieth Century*" Web site. A number of Buchanan's essays, public statements, and public speeches, including audio and video clips, are available at www.buchanan.org, a Web site that emerged as part of his presidential campaigns. Buchanan's journalistic columns are widely available.

Web Sites

American Cause Web site. Buchanan is founder and chairman of The American Cause, an organization devoted to furthering the conservative movement in the United States. Columns by Buchanan are on its Web site. www.theamericancause.org

The Official Pat Buchanan for President 2000 Campaign Archive [BFP]. Still maintained, this Web site includes essays, statements, and speeches delivered during Buchanan's presidential campaigns. Audio and video clips are included. www.buchanan.org

One Hundred Greatest Political Speeches of the Twentieth Century. This list includes three speeches for which Buchanan was lead author: Richard Nixon's

"Silent Majority" and "Cambodia Incursion," and Spiro Agnew's "Television News Coverage." www.news.wisc.edu/misc/speeches

Audiovisual Material

The Official Pat Buchanan for President 2000 Campaign Archive. Speech clips (audio and audiovisual) can be found at this website maintained by the Internet Brigade. www.buchanan.org

Selected Critical Studies

Bennet, James. "Candidate's Speech Is Called Code for Controversy." *New York Times*, February 25, 1996, p. 22.

Brookhiser, Richard. "Party in Search of a Theme." *National Review*, September 14, 1992, pp. 32–35.

Courtaway, Kyle R. " 'Don't You Know Me? I'm Your Nativist Son': The Rhetorical Construction of Enemies in Patrick Buchanan's 1996 Presidential Campaign." M.A. thesis, Illinois State University, 1998.

Hartnett, Stephen, and Eric Ramsey. " 'A Plain Public Road': Evaluating Arguments for Democracy in a Post-Metaphysical World." *Argumentation and Advocacy* 35 (1999): 95–115.

Jarman, Jeffrey W. "Pat Buchanan and the Rhetoric of Authoritarianism." Ph.D. dissertation, University of Kansas, 1998.

Mailer, Norman. "Republican Convention Revisited: By Heaven Inspired." *The New Republic*, October 12, 1992, pp. 22–32.

Rowland, Robert C., and John Jones. "Entelechial and Reformative Symbolic Trajectories in Contemporary Conservatism: A Case Study of Reagan and Buchanan in Houston and Beyond." *Rhetoric & Public Affairs* 4 (2001): 55–84.

Safire, William. *Before the Fall: An Inside View of the Pre-Watergate White House.* Garden City, N.Y.: Doubleday, 1975.

Smith, Craig R. "Richard M. Nixon and Gerald R. Ford: Lessons on Speechwriting." In *Presidential Speechwriting: From the New Deal to the Reagan Revolution and Beyond*, ed. Kurt Ritter and Martin Medhurst. College Station: Texas A&M University Press, 2003.

Selected Biographies

Buchanan, Patrick. *Right from the Beginning.* Washington, D.C.: Regnery Gateway, 1990.

CHRONOLOGY OF MAJOR SPEECHES

See "Research Collections and Collected Speeches" for source codes.

"The Best Man I Ever Knew" (eulogy for William Baldwin Buchanan). January 7, 1988. In *Right from the Beginning*, 385–90.

"This Election Is About Who We Are" (speech to the Republican National Convention). Houston, Tex., August 17, 1992. *Vital Speeches of the Day*, September 15, 1992, pp. 712–16.

"Republican Candidate for President" (speech at the Manchester Institute of Arts and Sciences). Manchester, N.H., March 20, 1995. *Vital Speeches of the Day*, May 5, 1995, pp. 461–64.

"Toward a More Moral Foreign Policy" (speech at the Center for Strategic and International Studies). Washington, D.C., December 16, 1999. *BFP.*

"To Reunite a Nation" (speech at the President Richard M. Nixon Library). Yorba Linda, Calif., January 18, 2000. *BFP.*

"A Den of Thieves" (speech at Boston University). March 31, 2000. *BFP.*

"Trouble in the Neighborhood" (speech to the San Diego World Affairs Council). April 28, 2000. *BFP.*

"Reform Party Nomination Acceptance Speech." Long Beach, Calif., August 12, 2000. *BFP.*

GEORGE HERBERT WALKER BUSH (1924–)
Forty-first President of the United States

CRAIG R. SMITH

On the third day of the 1980 Republican National Convention in Detroit, George H. W. Bush came forward to address the assembled delegates, his candidacy for the nomination ended. In a well-delivered address, Bush called for party unity. Unknown to Bush, Ronald Reagan, the nominee, was watching from his hotel room because he had become disenchanted with the recommendation that he take Gerald Ford on the ticket. When Bush completed his address, Reagan told his advisers he wanted Bush. The next night Bush delivered one of the shortest acceptance speeches in convention history. In it, he compared Reagan to "Dwight Eisenhower, a man of decency, compassion, and strength."

Bush embraced the progressive agenda within the Republican Party that is traceable to Teddy Roosevelt. In his autobiography, *Looking Forward*, Bush writes that his father had "a powerful impact on the way" he came to view the world. Prescott Bush retired from the Senate in 1962, the year his son George began his political life as Republican chairman of Harris County, Texas. Bush's character development can be traced to his education at Phillips Academy in Andover, Massachusetts. Once Bush received his diploma, he signed up to become the Navy's youngest fighter pilot in World War II, distinguishing himself in battle and being rescued by a U.S. submarine after his plane was shot down by the Japanese. After the war, Bush enrolled at Yale, where he served as captain of the baseball team (which twice lost the NCAA finals) and graduated in three years, Phi Beta Kappa.

Bush also has credentials as a successful businessman. In the summer of 1948, he went to work for Dresser Industries, first as an equipment clerk in Odessa, Texas, then as a salesman in California until 1950, when Dresser transferred him to Midland, Texas. Bush left Dresser to set up Bush-Overby Oil Development Company, which bought prospective royalties on oil prospects. At twenty-seven, Bush was an entrepreneur meeting a payroll, an experience he would not let audiences forget. By 1952, he was partners with Hugh Liedtke, who eventually ran Pennzoil. Their company, Zapata Petroleum, made large profits in the new enterprise of offshore oil drilling, and Bush moved to Houston, where the operation was headquartered.

In 1964, Bush won the U.S. Senate nomination to oppose incumbent Ralph Yarborough, a liberal Democrat. He lost the election but kept the race close despite Lyndon Johnson's landslide at the top of the ticket. Two years later, he was elected to Congress and became the first freshman to be named to the House Ways and Means Committee since Thaddeus Stevens. Bush experienced his first political crisis when he decided to support the Open Housing Act of 1968. When he returned to Houston to explain his vote, he was roundly booed. In response, he paraphrased the sentiments Edmund Burke had expressed at Bristol: "Your representative owes you not only his industry, but his judgment and he betrays instead of serving you, if he sacrifices it to your opinion." Bush's speech converted many in the all-white audience and was responsible in part for his unopposed reelection later that year in a district that in 1970 was represented by Barbara Jordan after Bush decided to run for the Senate again.

By 1970, Yarborough was an unpopular senator ripe for the picking. Sensing that, the Democratic Party nominated Lloyd Bentsen, a wealthy, conservative business executive, in place of Yarborough. Bush lost a very close race to Bentsen, but was rewarded when President Nixon nominated him to be ambassador to the United Nations. In that position, he faced several Middle Eastern crises, the expulsion of Taiwan from the United Nations, and the invasion of East Pakistan by India.

When Nixon won his forty-nine-state landslide in 1972, he shook up his administration and asked Bush to chair the Republican Party. A year later the Watergate crisis broke, and in 1974, Bush was one of those who asked Nixon to resign. The new president, Gerald Ford, returned Bush to the world of foreign affairs, naming him ambassador to China.

While Bush served in China, the Watergate crisis claimed another victim: William Colby, head of the Central Intelligence Agency. The president nominated Bush to replace Colby. Because he was seen as a politician and not from the CIA, Senate Democrats complained that appointing Bush would further damage the Agency, which had been kept out of politics. During the hearings on his nomination, Bush promised not to seek or accept the vice presidential nomination should he be approved. Once at the CIA, he developed a loyal following that would serve him in subsequent political campaigns. Ford's loss of the presidency to Jimmy Carter meant the end of Bush's tenure at the CIA.

GEORGE BUSH AS PRESIDENTIAL PERSUADER

Out of public office for the first time in years, Bush began to assess his chances of winning the Republican nomination for president in 1980, accepting speaking engagements across the country starting in 1977. In January 1978, I met with Bush at his home in Houston and became one of his speechwriters. The remainder of this study is supported by my personal experiences with Bush, for whom I continued to consult until his failure to win reelection in 1992. He also relied on Raymond Price, who wrote Nixon's very effective acceptance speech in 1968; Peggy Noonan, a successful stylist for Reagan; and Victor Gold, who had written for Agnew. While each of us did entire speeches independent of the others, we had diverse strengths that were sometimes

mat; he preferred speaking extemporaneously from notes. Ironically, the speeches for which he received the most plaudits were delivered from texts and heavily rehearsed. Nonetheless, Bush took a hand in his speeches to a much greater degree than had Gerald Ford or Ronald Reagan.

In 1978, I traveled with Bush to craft a standard stump speech. We began in Harris County, Texas, and continued on to Tulsa, Beloit (Wisconsin), Chicago, and Pittsburgh. By the time he reached Pittsburgh, where he was to address the World Affairs Council on June 13, Bush had honed the material and agreed to more than the usual amount of signposting. In the introduction, for example, he said, "I will address three subjects: relations with the People's Republic of China, the future of the Western alliance, and the current situation in the American intelligence community." He used parallel structure to great

---

Before being elected president, George Bush had compiled one of the longest political résumés of any president. He had been U.S. congressman, ambassador to China, ambassador to the United Nations, director of the Central Intelligence Agency, head of the Republican National Committee, and vice president of the United States. He had also been the youngest Navy fighter pilot in World War II.

---

combined for major speeches. My charge was to take researched issue positions and craft them into the body of the speeches; Price, and later Noonan, worked on style; Gold worked on humor and political "zingers." Occasionally others contributed lines. For example, in a speech Bush delivered during the Pennsylvania primary that I had helped to write, Pete Teely, Bush's press secretary, inserted a line that dubbed Reagan's budget proposals "voodoo economics." The term would cost Bush later.

By 1980, Bush emerged as a competent if not charismatic political orator as the result of a number of practices. First, Bush resisted organizational language. Second, he abjured rehearsal, which meant that he was less fluent than he could have been, and sometimes wandered from his text. Third, texts were not Bush's favorite for-

effect, and the complex material was leavened with simple sentences and a direct style: "The crucifixion of the CIA must stop. . . . If we continue to serve up tasty dishes of CIA revelations to famished journalists and self-proclaimed whistleblowers, the consequences will be simple: We shall not be able to attract talented people to the agency." Bush also wanted to make certain his audience understood that he was an expert on his topic: "There are 6,000 NATO tanks facing 16,000 Warsaw Pact tanks across the Elbe. . . . We have 1,700 war planes in Western Europe, while the Warsaw Pact has 2,900."

These rhetorical tactics succeeded in projecting the persona of a strong, intelligent presidential candidate. In early 1980, Bush won the Iowa caucuses. His decision to abandon issues to talk about his momentum ("the big mo") in

New Hampshire hurt his candidacy. However, a worse blow was delivered when just before a one-on-one debate with Reagan, the aged movie star grabbed a microphone and upstaged Bush by arguing that all GOP candidates should participate in the debate. The move revived Reagan's flagging campaign. On May 20, despite Bush's win in Michigan, Reagan clinched the nomination with wins in Nebraska and Oregon.

Bush was an active vice president thrust to the fore when Reagan was shot on March 30, 1981. The vice president worked behind the scenes as president of the Senate to pass the Reagan budget package and tax reform bills. He played a major role in developing foreign policy and eliminating government regulations. He headed major antidrug efforts. He traveled to over seventy-five countries to represent the president. He spent much time at political fund-raisers for Republican candidates. In 1984 he performed above press expectations in a vice presidential debate with Representative Geraldine Ferraro. Bush had been advised that the debate would be difficult to win because if he attacked Ferraro, he would appear ungentlemanly, but if he treated Ferraro with deference, talk would resurface that he was a preppy wimp. Bush's depth of knowledge on foreign policy and domestic issues served him well in the debate.

In 1988, in his announcement of candidacy, Bush claimed that records were made to be broken and that he hoped to become the first sitting vice president to win the presidency since Martin Van Buren. He enlarged his rhetorical stable by adding Roger Ailes, who advised Bush to "counterpunch" in debates, interviews, and press conferences. The results of this policy were mainly effective, as in the Republican candidates' debate in Houston, when Bush turned to former Governor DuPont and said, "Let me help you with that, Pierre." DuPont, who prefers to be called "Pete," had lectured Bush on giving peace a chance.

However, in one significant instance the results were mixed. On the night of Reagan's last State of the Union address, Dan Rather interviewed Bush live on *CBS Evening News*. CBS had led Bush to believe the interview would cover many issues. Instead, Rather ran a prepared story on the Iran-Contra scandal that implicated Bush, then peppered Bush with questions about his role. Bush defended himself and then asked that Rather move on. The anchorman refused, and Bush insulted Rather by bringing up an incident in which Rather had walked off the network set. The anchorman then cut off the interview, offending many viewers. Some critics believe that Bush's poor showing in the ensuing Iowa caucuses was due to the fact that many voters thought he had engaged in unpresidential behavior.

Bush revived his presidential candidacy in New Hampshire by running negative advertising against the leader in the polls, Senator Bob Dole, and by appealing to voters in a more down-to-earth manner. The next primaries came in the South on "Super Tuesday"; Bush won the biggest single victory in terms of delegates that any candidate had ever achieved. Nonetheless, his difficulties with the public continued into the summer of 1988. When Michael Dukakis finished his acceptance speech at the Democratic National Convention in July, he led Bush by ten to seventeen percentage points in opinion polls. Republican strategists believed that Bush's only hope for victory was to deliver "the speech of his life" in accepting the Republican nomination. Bush and his writers did not disappoint them. After his acceptance speech, he led Dukakis by more than seven percentage points in most polls and never looked back.

The success of Bush's acceptance speech can be explained by several factors. First, Dukakis' more general speech left him open to redefinition by Bush. In one of the most effective passages in his acceptance speech, Bush compared himself and Dukakis on the issues, in an effort to coalesce a majority of support: "Should public school teachers be required to lead our children in the Pledge of Allegiance? My opponent says no—but I say yes. Should society be allowed to impose the death penalty on those who commit crimes of extraordinary cruelty and violence? My opponent says no—but I say yes." Identification also proved effective in personal terms as Bush for the first time spoke about himself and his approach to government with emotion: "I want a kinder, gentler nation." He then specifically identified with segments of his audience: "This is America: the Knights of Columbus, the Grange, Hadassah, the Disabled American Veterans, the Order of Ahepa, the Business and Professional Women of America, the union hall, the Bible study group, LULAC, Holy Name—a brilliant diversity spread like stars, like a thousand points of light in a broad and peaceful sky."

The speech also contained humor that was both self-deprecating and effective in poking fun at the Democrats. He referred to a liberal Senate trio as "three blind mice." He reinforced the humor by using Dirty Harry-like phrasing, particularly when it came to domestic issues. "Read my lips, no new taxes" brought cheers from the audience, but would later compromise Bush's presidency. The style of the speech not only suited Bush, it demonstrated the importance of tropes and figures in modern rhetoric. Repetition, periodic structure, antithesis, alliteration, metaphor, and allegory provided subliminal support for the message. Repetition and alliteration marked this passage: "I seek the presidency for a single purpose, a purpose that has motivated millions of Americans across the years." Antithesis, balance, and metaphor distinguished the following: "The stakes are high and the choice is crucial, for the differences between the two candidates are as deep and wide as they have ever been in our long history." The speech retained Bush's penchant for facts, which enhance his ethos, and a new concern for "compassion" that would be carried on by his son a few campaigns later. Finally, the speech was unified around the theme of "mission," from Bush's first mission as a pilot to his final mission as president.

Poll data demonstrated that Bush retained his lead through Election Day because his stump oratory reinforced the themes he had initiated in the acceptance speech. For example, on September 19, 1988, Bush visited the oldest flag company in America, in Bloomfield, New Jersey, to stress military preparedness, patriotism, and arms control, issues where his lead in the polls was large. There, he linked his audience to his presidency: "Since 1849, a flag [from your company] has flown on January 20th every four years, presiding over the swearing in of the president of the United States. That's a ceremony I hope to be a part of next year." Bush had criticized Dukakis' stand against the Pledge of Al-

legiance's "under God" phrase; this appearance reinforced the difference between the two men. Bush then appealed across party lines and further adapted to his New Jersey audience by quoting Woodrow Wilson, who had been governor of New Jersey, on the value of the flag. Most important, Bush stuck to his "mission" theme throughout the address: "My mission is simple. To build a better America."

A month later in Xenia, Ohio, Bush demonstrated that he would make sure that the crime issue, on which he also led Dukakis, was paramount in the minds of his audience and the press. Committees advertising on behalf of Bush had severely criticized Dukakis for being lenient and pardoning felons. In Xenia, Bush reinforced these efforts by consistently contrasting himself with Dukakis: "It is my belief, that of the two of us, I am the one who shares the hopes and beliefs and values of the American people." Bush then narrowed his focus to "the peace of our neighborhoods and the safety of ordinary, law-abiding citizens." He emphasized the dialectic by associating Dukakis with "liberalism" and those who blame society instead of criminals for the crime. Bush also refuted the charge that his campaign had become too negative: "I do not believe it is negative to try to clarify the distinctions with one's opponent." Reinforcing the advertising campaign, Bush then told the "story of Willie Horton."

The two presidential campaign debates gave Bush another chance to contrast himself with his opponent. Bush, unlike Dukakis, was warm and humorous. Though Dukakis was more specific, Bush was effective in listing the accomplishments of the Reagan/Bush administration and in labeling Dukakis a liberal. As Halford Ryan points out, "Bush would spend as much time in defining what he was not, which was Dukakis, as in defining what he was." When Dukakis failed to show any emotion in a response to a hypothetical question about his wife being raped, Bush promptly labeled him the "ice man." On Election Night, Bush won by 7 million votes, capturing 426 electoral votes to only 111 for Dukakis.

Bush assembled a youthful speechwriting staff at the White House that consisted of approximately five full-time writers and a dozen researchers. But more than most presidents, Bush was often dissatisfied with the results of the in-house writing. Jennifer Grossman, one of his writers, reports that meetings were "brief and distracted." Outside consultants were often used for major speeches. They made a conscious effort to make Bush sound Lincolnesque, particularly regarding the Gulf War. During that conflict, speeches emphasized Bush as the transcendent statesman with noble war goals.

The main problem with Bush's presidential rhetoric was Bush himself. He disdained rehearsal. His love of substance often caused him to neglect style, particularly in televised speeches he delivered from the Oval Office. One of the most serious mistakes Bush made was to insist that his press conferences occur during the day. These extemporaneous dialogues showcased his sagacity, humor, and humanity. Unfortunately, only a small segment of the public saw this kinder, gentler Bush. Not wanting to appear to be imitating Reagan, Bush refused to hold his press conferences at night, when a much larger audience could have seen them. This strategic error contributed to bringing down his presidency.

One final note on Bush's speech preparation and rhetorical sensitivity comes from Wynton Hall's thorough study of Bush's use of poll data. Bush was much less reliant on poll data than Nixon or Reagan had been—less, indeed, than any president since Dwight Eisenhower. Bush's pollster, Robert Teeter, conducted only six national polls during the first two years of his presidency, and only one in 1991. Reagan had sixteen conducted during his first year in office. Nixon had maintained an ongoing polling operation, as had Jimmy Carter. Perhaps this phenomenon contributed to Bush's appearing to be out of touch with the American public in 1992.

When George Bush began his Inaugural Address on January 20, 1989, he saluted George Washington, who had delivered the first inaugural address two hundred years earlier. Bush then uttered a prayer of his own composition. The tone was somber, and the rest of the address was traditional. It called for an end to the bitter divisions in Congress. In its most original moment, Bush claimed that "The final lesson of Vietnam is that no great nation can long afford to be sundered by a memory." The Inaugural

Address echoed the 1988 acceptance speech: "It is to make kinder the face of the nation and gentler the face of the world," and he revisited the "thousand points of lights."

The style of the speech was appropriate and often moving. For example, Bush framed a unifying metaphor of a "new breeze"; at the end he said, "The new breeze blows, a page turns, the story unfolds. . . ." Alliteration was wisely used: "A president is neither prince nor pope." And some antitheses proved effective: "We need compromise; we have had dissension." For the most part, however, the Inaugural Address was a simple speech that set the administration's goals in clear, plain English.

Like many inaugurals, it eschewed specific policy recommendations. The address was more about challenges than solutions, more about values than options. Thus, it was reflective and general rather than policy-oriented and specific. As Bernard Duffy remarks, "The address is strong in imagery and weak in intimations of policy." Bush faced a Democrat-controlled Congress, a situation that required him to be conciliatory, particularly in his domestic policy: "Good will begets good will. Good faith can be a spiral that endlessly moves on." However, Bush tempered his appeal to Democrats with a call for more reliance on voluntarism and less focus on material possessions.

On the other hand, his foreign policy expertise allowed Bush to outline his new view of the world: "[T]he day of the dictator is over." Like other presidents, he portrayed America as a model of democratic values for the rest of the world, but he went beyond that passive paradigm by asserting that America had a leading role to play in a new world order: "Destiny has laid upon our country the responsibility of the free world's leadership." Bush would bring this conception to fruition when the United States led a coalition of nations into Iraq.

Close textual analysis of the inaugural reveals the influence of previous ones. Duffy points to the grand goals of Wilson's foreign policy, the anti-material moment in Franklin Roosevelt's first inaugural, and even Lyndon Johnson's concern for the poor. Yet, Bush's rejection of the "old way" is a clear indication that he not only sought to reduce the size of government and increase reliance on volunteers; he also wanted to move away from the culture of greed bred in the Reagan years.

He would be given a chance in his State of the Union addresses. He seemed to feel more at home in the House chamber, before a joint session of Congress, than in the White House. His delivery in each of his State of the Union addresses was up to the standard of his 1988 acceptance speech. He used the teleprompters well, and seemed genuinely buoyed by the cheering from the Congress and the galleries. Only three weeks after his Inaugural Address, Bush presented his "budget plan" to Congress: it purported to set out "a realistic plan for tackling" the deficit. Other proposals in the speech were drawn from the Republican credo, including a call for a presidential line item veto, a balanced budget amendment, and reliance on the free enterprise system. After an appeal to "family and faith," Bush turned to his specific agenda. He proposed increasing funds for scientific and technological research, creating enterprise zones and a council on competitiveness headed by the vice president, and cutting the minimum tax on capital gains. Next, Bush took up education by proposing "merit schools" for students and rewards for excellent teachers. The president then called for a "war against drugs," to be led by a "drug czar."

Bush defended the Strategic Defense Initiative, then called for a ban on chemical weapons, an end to nuclear proliferation, self-determination in Central America, and a strengthening of our European defensive ties. In conclusion, he appealed to young Americans to "hold fast to your dreams" and quoted Churchill's famous lines: "We shall not fail or falter. . . . Give us the tools and we will finish the job."

The State of the Union address of January 31, 1990, is important because it began the process by which Bush became enmeshed in a plan to raise taxes, thereby breaking his strongly worded acceptance speech pledge, "No new taxes." Bush signaled that he knew the workings of Congress when he reminded his audience that he had served in the House and had been president of the Senate. He then reviewed the changes in the world and enhanced his credibility by associating

with them: "Panama is free. . . . a free Poland. . . . [the Berlin] wall is history. . . ."

After a transition to the domestic scene, Bush set forth his agenda, which differed little from that of the 1989 speech. The first hint at compromise came in the line "In the spirit of cooperation, I offer my hand to all of you." Senator George Mitchell, the majority leader, would take that hand, with dire consequences for the president. In April, on national television, first Bush and then Mitchell endorsed a budget plan that included new taxes. Bush was deserted by 126 members of his own party in the House. The debacle severely damaged his chances of re-election.

President Bush was more successful with his "war on drugs," begun on September 5, 1989. After the speech, polls showed that the number of people who believed the drug crisis was the most important problem facing this country had risen from 27 percent to 63 percent. Bush used rhetorical strategies ranging from simple, inartistic proofs to sophisticated stylistic devices. For example, statistics on the number of drug users magnified the problem while enhancing the president's expertise.

On September 26, 1989, Bush returned to the United Nations to praise U.N. peacekeeping forces. He singled out Lt. Col. William Higgins, who had been hanged by terrorists in the Middle East. Bush went on to declare Marxism dead, and identified democracy with individualism and capitalism, but resisted criticism of Soviet leader Mikhail Gorbachev. He surveyed the setbacks for totalitarianism around the world. In an awkward antithesis, he said, "Advocates of the totalitarian idea saw its triumph written in the laws of history. They failed to see the love of freedom that was written in the human heart."

Bush then called for the elimination of chemical weapons worldwide by proposing a three-part treaty that already had the tacit agreement of the Soviet Union. He praised the new "openness" (*glasnost*) in the Soviet Union as a prelude to his call for replacing "conflict with consensus." Bush declared, "The new world of freedom is not a world where a few nations live in comfort while others live in want."

On December 20, 1989, the president announced a military incursion into Panama to capture its "dictator," Manuel Noriega. Panama was a prelude to Bush's moves against the aggression of Iraq. In August 1990, Iraq invaded Kuwait, threatening oil supplies from the region. In response, Bush organized a grand alliance of more than twenty nations that protected the Saudi frontier, and on September 12, 1990, he addressed a joint session of Congress to discuss the situation. In what would become two commonplaces for speeches on the war, Bush read a letter from a soldier and then acknowledged the teamwork of Generals Colin Powell and Norman Schwarzkopf. Then the president presented his conditions to Iraq: "Kuwait's legitimate government must be restored. The security and stability of the Persian Gulf must be assured."

Only through a series of speeches did the rationale for the Gulf War evolve. By January 16, 1991, when he asked for congressional support, Bush declared that what Saddam Hussein had done "shall not stand." He justified American action by comparing Saddam Hussein to Hitler, and his tank attack to a "blitzkrieg." In this equation, "one small country" became the Poland of 1939, and the public, according to poll data, finally got the message. That call for war was enhanced by the fact that Bush had put together a coalition of allies that included Arab as well as European nations. In this way, he demonstrated that world opinion was on America's side and that a "new world order" had been established.

In March 1991, the president appeared before a joint session of Congress to declare that the "war is over." House Speaker Tom Foley departed from tradition by extending to the commander in chief his "warmest congratulations on a brilliant victory." Bush was humble in victory, praising his team of advisers and "all who served in the field." He then extended the themes he had initiated in earlier speeches into vindication for his policy: "We went halfway around the world to do what is moral and just and right. . . . We lifted the yoke of aggression. . . ." At the end of the speech, he was one of the most popular presidents in American history.

In *Looking Forward*, Bush recounts a prophetic conversation with Jim Rhodes, governor of Ohio. After Bush had listed everything he would do if he became president, Rhodes pulled out his wallet and slapped it on the table. "That's it right there. . . . Who can put money in people's pockets. . . . That's what it's all about, George—jobs, jobs, jobs." The anecdote haunted Bush throughout 1992. In his State of the Union Address, he prayed for an economic recovery, but it never came. Thus, in the summer of 1992, he found himself behind his Democratic opponent in all the polls.

The acceptance speech at the Republican National Convention in Houston in August failed for a number of reasons. First, Bush had failed to deliver on some of his promises, and had clearly broken the one concerning "no new taxes." Second, he had failed to contextualize America's economic difficulties in terms of the world picture. That the United States was doing well during a worldwide economic slowdown was not sufficient to overcome people's immediate economic difficulties. Third, the media framed Bush's speech in terms of those who had spoken earlier in the convention, including a rabidly right-wing Pat Buchanan who drowned out Reagan's marvelous swan song with a mean-spirited attack on Hillary Clinton and a declaration of a "cultural war." A religiously intolerant Pat Robertson, and a remarkably divisive Marilyn Quayle, identified the Republican Party with a prudish social agenda.

Despite this environment, Bush's speech did have its strong points. It was delivered well and with an uncharacteristic amount of emotion. On foreign policy, he scored heavily with the delegates, the guests, and the national audience by articulating a litany of successes running from the fall of the Berlin Wall to "the last breath of Communism." The new world order was defined in a way the average American could understand. As in 1988, Bush tried to depict his opponent dialectically: "I want to talk about the sharp choice I intend to offer Americans this fall, a choice between different agendas, different directions, and yes, a choice about the character of the man you want to lead this nation." The character attack on Bill Clinton failed to resonate with a public preoccupied with economic conditions. Later in the address, Bush extended the counterpoint to the Democratic Party: "In the '70s, they wanted a hollow army; we wanted a strong fighting force. In the '80s, they wanted a nuclear freeze, and we insisted on peace through strength." He then invoked the memories of Richard Nixon, Gerald Ford, and Ronald Reagan, tipping the audience off that the speech was taking a stridently partisan tone. Joking about Clinton's not inhaling and attacking his lack of military service—"I bit the bullet and he bit his nails"—would have been better left to others. The second half of the speech continued the partisan tone by articulating proposals that failed to come together in a unified way. The gun-toting, tough-on-crime Bush did not mesh with the kinder, gentler nobleman.

Much worse for Bush were the three presidential debates that followed in the fall. Bush is not a natural debater: he speaks too elliptically for the public; he disdains the anecdotes that served Reagan so well; attacking is not part of his personality, as was apparent in the acceptance speech. Worse, in the debates Bush could not control the focus of issues. Try as he might, the economy would remain the focus. Ross Perot would aim most of his verbal bullets at Bush, whom he truly despised, much to the delight of the smooth-talking Clinton. Bush's diffident performance was particularly evident in the second debate, where he was caught glancing at his watch. Furthermore, he undermined his credibility on economic issues when he did not pay attention to a question from an African American woman, and said he "didn't get" what she meant. The public didn't think he got their message either, and he was defeated in the general election.

INFORMATION SOURCES

Research Collections and Collected Speeches

The George H. W. Bush Presidential Library is housed at Texas A&M University and has an excellent Web site (see below). Bush's speeches prior to becoming president can be found in *Vital Speeches of the Day* and other standard sources (see below).

Annenberg/Pew Archive of Presidential Campaign Discourse [*AP*]. Philadelphia: Annenberg School for Communications, 2000. (Computer file.)

Public Papers of the Presidents of the United States: George Bush, 1989–93 [*PP*]. Washington, D.C.: Government Printing Office, 1989–93.

Smith, Craig. *Private Collection of Bush Campaign Speeches* [*PC*]. Long Beach, Calif.: 1978–92.

Smith, Curt. ed. *Chronological Files: Presidential Remarks* [*CF*]. College Station, Tex.: George Bush Library, 1989–92.

Vital Speeches of the Day [*VSD*]. Mount Pleasant, S.C.: City News Publishing Co., 1980–93.

Web Sites

George Bush Presidential Library. http://bushlibrary. tamu.edu/research.html

Unofficial Web site of President George Bush. This site includes audio clips of presidential speeches. www.chez.com/georgebush

Audiovisual Material

Commander in Chief: George Bush. Bethesda, Md.: Discovery Channel School, 2001.

C-SPAN, 444 North Capitol St. NW, Washington, D.C., 2001.

University of Michigan President Visual Material Series. Ann Arbor: University of Michigan, 1967– .

Vanderbilt Television News Archive, Vanderbilt University Library, Nashville, Tenn. 37240.

Selected Critical Studies

Clayman, Steven E. "Caveat Orator: Audience Disaffiliation in the 1988 Presidential Debates." *Quarterly Journal of Speech* 78 (1992): 33–60.

Denton, Robert E. Jr., ed. *The 1992 Presidential Campaign.* Westport, Conn.: Praeger, 1994.

Downs, Valerie C., Lynda L. Kaid, and Sandra Ragan. "The Impact of Argumentativeness and Verbal Aggression on Communicator Image: The Exchange Between George Bush and Dan Rather." *Western Journal of Speech Communication* 54 (1990): 99–112.

Drew, Elizabeth. *Election Journal: Political Events of 1987–1988.* New York: William Morrow, 1989.

Duffy, Bernard K. "President Bush's Inaugural Address, 1989." In *The Inaugural Addresses of Twentieth-Century American Presidents*, ed. Halford Ross Ryan. Westport, Conn.: Praeger, 1993.

Grossman, Jennifer. "Why Bush Will Connect with Us Tonight." *Los Angeles Times*, January 28, 2003, p. B13.

Hall, Winton C. "'Reflections of Yesterday': George H. W. Bush's Instrumental Use of Public Opinion Research in Presidential Discourse." *Presidential Studies Quarterly* (September 2002): 531–58.

Ryan, Halford Ross. "The 1988 Bush–Dukakis Presidential Debates." In *Rhetorical Studies of Na-*

tional Political Debates, 1960–1988, ed. Robert Friedenberg. Westport, Conn.: Praeger, 1990.

Trent, Judith S. "The 1984 Bush–Ferraro Vice Presidential Debate." In Rhetorical Studies of National Political Debates, 1960–1988, ed. Robert Friedenberg. Westport, Conn.: Praeger, 1990.

Selected Biographies

Bush, George. Looking Forward. New York: Bantam, 1988.

Parmet, Herbert S. George Bush: The Life of a Lone Star Yankee. New York: Scribner, 1997.

CHRONOLOGY OF MAJOR SPEECHES

See "Research Collections and Collected Speeches" for source codes.

"Pittsburgh World Affairs Council." Pittsburgh, Pa., June 13, 1978. PC.

"Vice Presidential Nomination Acceptance." Detroit, Mich., July 17, 1980. VSD 46 (1980–81): 646–47.

"Acceptance of Nomination." New Orleans, La., August 18, 1988. VSD 55 (1988–89): 3–5.

"Stump Speech." Bloomfield, N.J., September 19, 1988. AP.

"Law Enforcement." Xenia, Ohio, October 7, 1988. AP.

"Inaugural Address: A New Breeze Is Blowing."

Washington, D.C., January 20, 1989. VSD 55 (1988–89): 258–60.

"President's Budget Message." Washington, D.C., February 9, 1989. VSD 55 (1988–89): 290–94.

"War on Drugs." Washington, D.C., September 5, 1989. VSD 55 (1988–89): 738–40.

"New World Freedom." New York, September 26, 1989. PP, p. 4, October 2, 1989–January 1, 1990, pp. 1435–40.

"Address to the Nation Announcing U.S. Military Action in Panama." Washington, D.C., December 20, 1989. VSD 56 (1989–90): 194–95.

"State of the Union Address." Washington, D.C., January 31, 1990. VSD 56 (1989–90): 258–61.

"Iraq's Invasion of Kuwait." Washington, D.C., September 11, 1990. VSD 56 (1989–90): 674–75.

"War with Iraq." Washington, D.C., January 16, 1991. VSD 57 (1990–91): 226–27.

"State of the Union Address." Washington, D.C., January 29, 1991. VSD 57 (1990–91): 258–61.

"The War Is Over." Washington, D.C., March 6, 1991. VSD 57 (1990–91): 354–56.

"State of the Union Address." Washington, D.C., January 28, 1992. VSD 58 (1991–92): 258–63.

"Acceptance of Nomination: A New Crusade to Reap the Rewards of Our Global Victory." Houston, Tex., August 20, 1992. VSD 58 (1991–92): 706–17.

GEORGE WALKER BUSH (1946–)
Forty-third President of the United States

RICHARD E. VATZ

George Walker Bush, whose middle initial serves as his nickname (pronounced "Dubya") for both his admirers and his detractors, is the forty-third president of the United States. Since his father, the forty-first president, is also George Bush, if not George W. Bush, another reference to the president is 43, while his father is often referred to as 41.

Bush was sworn into office January 20, 2001, after one of the most contested presidential elections in our nation's history. His victory was not established immediately following Election Night of 2000 because the Florida vote had been

successfully challenged. After the Supreme Court of the United States—by a margin of one vote—reversed the judgment of the Florida Supreme Court, which had ordered a recount, on December 12, 2000, George W. Bush was determined to have won the presidential contest and was inaugurated.

Born on July 6, 1946, in New Haven, Connecticut, George W. Bush spent his youth in Texas. He comes from one of America's most prominent political dynasties. His father served as president from January 1989 until January 1993, and before that was a political jack-of-all-trades:

ambassador to the United Nations, director of the Central Intelligence Agency, and vice president before reaching the presidency. W's grandfather was a senator from Connecticut, and his brother Jeb has served as governor of Florida.

Bush's reputation stems from a label that distinguished him from his Republican opponents early in the presidential race: he was the "compassionate conservative." This label, supporters claim, dates back to his years as the forty-sixth governor of Texas, which he claims as the source of his operative values, among them limited government, personal responsibility, the importance of family, and a governing philosophy that emphasizes a federalism with support for local control of government.

THE BIRTH OF THE "WAR ON TERROR" RHETORICIAN

In the presidential campaign of 2000, George Bush failed to impress very many people with his speeches or his performance in the presidential debates. Vice President Gore seemed more conversant with the issues. In contrast, Bush relied on and relished the perception that he was the "Ingenuous One," the antithesis of President Bill Clinton, who was seen by many as brilliant and eloquent, but also a rogue and a fraud. Bush capitalized on Clinton's indiscretions in much the same way that Jimmy Carter capitalized on the albatross of Watergate that hung around the neck of Gerald Ford. Counterbalancing Bush's claim to innocence and ingenuousness was the fact that he was a president elected by fewer popular votes than Vice President Gore received. His potential for leadership was also undermined by persistent doubts that he had the intellect and focus to be president.

In his Inaugural Address on January 20, 2001, Bush had planned to center on domestic issues, emphasizing, as one of his senior aides informed the press, "education reform, tax cuts, prescription drug benefits for seniors, a military pay raise, and boosting the role of religious charities in administering social services." In fact, the new president gave a slightly meandering speech that reiterated his claim to being a conservative, but a "compassionate" conservative who is reflected in his vision, articulated in that speech, of "America at its best."

The speech, written by chief speechwriter Mike Gerson, was a eulogy to America that began with some healing words: an encomium to President Clinton and Vice President Gore following the difficult election of 2000 and the sexual scandals of the Clinton administration. Liberal historian Arthur M. Schlesinger, Jr. memorably characterized the composition of presidential inaugural addresses as "an inferior art form [with a high] platitude quotient" and "few surprises," and his assessment hit close to the mark with Bush's Inaugural Address. There were precious few specifics, even for an inaugural address, and critics could not be faulted for finding the speech overly general and even, perhaps, unfocused. The only reference to "weapons of mass destruction" was a promise in a single sentence that the United States would "confront" them "so that a new century is spared new horrors."

There was no prescient mention of terrorism. The most significant speech the president made in the ensuing seven months was on August 9, 2001, an address to the nation on stem cell research funding. In this speech devoted to the complicated issue of whether federal funds should be used to support "scientific research on stem cells derived from human embryos," Bush gave a surprisingly complex analysis of the issue, but he seemed to lack a clear commitment, except to "oppose human cloning." His decision was to allow federal funding of research using existing stem cell lines "where the life and death decision has already been made." Thus, he appeared to be Solomonic, said his supporters, or weak, said his detractors, in finding middle ground between scientists who wanted such research to combat horrific diseases and conservative groups who, because of the unavoidable destruction of embryos in harvesting stem cells, wanted no support whatsoever for stem cell research. The speech yielded an image of a tortured president—at least on this issue—who closed his speech by saying, "I have made this decision with great care, and I pray it is the right one." In the weeks that followed, Bush was at the center of the growing controversy regarding whether he was already vacationing too much for a president, as he took a one-month break, one of the longest such breaks in presidential history. Then the terror attacks of September 11, 2001, occurred.

There is a consensus among political observers that the attacks on New York and Washington on September 11, 2001, almost nine months following his inauguration, focused Bush both personally and with respect to his public speaking. In fact, it would not be inaccurate to portray his rhetorical style as one summarized by the word "focus." Both his supporters and his detractors argue that Bush's style, for better or worse, has not permitted deviation from script or purpose when addressing terrorism and foreign policy throughout his presidency since the attacks of September 11.

The transformation of George Bush—rhetorically and psychologically—resulting from the events of September 11 is described thoroughly

rorist attack on America. Using his father's locution "This will not stand," referring to Iraq's attack on Kuwait in 1991, Bush stated: "Terrorism against our nation will not stand," a statement that he has said reflects his lack of calculation in framing his public utterances: "What you saw was my gut reaction coming out."

This self-appraisal is consistent with Woodward's description of the post-9/11 President Bush as confident and as one who talks often of "instincts," almost as a "second religion." Moreover, as he prepared to speak to Congress nine days later, Bush further reinforced Woodward's characterization: "I know exactly what I need to say, and how to say it, and what to do . . . I have never felt more comfortable in my life." Unless this was an epiphany, it belied the popular conception of Bush as confused and substantially

---

"We are not deceived by [the terrorists'] pretenses to piety. We have seen their kind before. They are the heirs of all the murderous ideologies of the 20th century. By sacrificing human life to serve their radical visions—by abandoning every value except the will to power—they follow in the path of fascism, and Nazism, and totalitarianism. And they will follow that path all the way, to where it ends: in history's unmarked grave of discarded lies."

George Bush, "Freedom from Fear"

---

in Bob Woodward's *Bush at War*, a work informed by extraordinary access given to Woodward by many of the principals of the Bush administration. The information is made credible by the lack of disputes of the major sources following the book's publication; the information is made less credible by Woodward's admitted time-honored (or time-dishonored) attribution of, as he puts it, "thoughts, conclusions and feelings to the participants." Woodward and his colleague Dan Balz also interviewed the president at length twice in 2002, as Woodward did George H. W. Bush after the invasion of Panama and in the time leading up to the Gulf War.

At 9:30 A.M. on September 11, Bush issued a four-paragraph statement from the Emma E. Booker Elementary School in Sarasota, Florida, where he had been told by Karl Rove of the ter-

dependent on Vice President Cheney, a view popularly and humorously depicted on shows such as *Saturday Night Live.*

On September 20, 2001, at 9:00 P.M., Bush spoke to a joint session of Congress, a speech that was broadcast to the nation on all major radio and television networks. In that address the president gave an upbeat appraisal of the strength of the country in the face of the attacks of September 11, nine days earlier. The public witnessed a new George W. Bush that evening, one who was strong, sure-footed, confident, and focused. The president referred to the ceremonial responses of "all of America," citing "Republicans and Democrats joined together on the steps of this Capitol singing 'God Bless America.'" Then he thanked Republican *and* Democratic leaders for allocating funds to deal with the terrorist actions and threat, and praised their "friendship," "leadership," and "courage." The theme of political unity was reinforced by the Democrats, who did not ask for air time for a response (which is usually the case with presidential addresses).

The president also avoided the mistake, characteristic of Lyndon Johnson's presidency, of promising too much too soon, warning that the war against terrorism would be neither short, like 1990's war against Iraq, nor casualty-free, like the war in Kosovo. An interesting question concerning Bush's speeches leading up to the invasion of Iraq is whether he violated this strategy by implying that the United States would find weapons of mass destruction in Iraq.

The speech abjured diplomatic ambiguity, similar to President Franklin Delano Roosevelt's address to Congress following Pearl Harbor. The president clearly pointed to the enemy terrorists and named the "murderers" as Al-Qaeda, with whom "our war on terror begins," and its leader, Osama bin Laden. He then detailed their history of "terrorism." The president was equally unambiguous in citing complicity as the equal of murder, as in the case of the Taliban, who aided and abetted Al-Qaeda. It was a war, Bush said, which "will not end until every terrorist group of global reach has been found, stopped and defeated." The president did not compromise his rhetorical attack. He cast the enemy as "evil"; analogized their beliefs to "fascism, Nazism and totalitarianism"; and promised that their destiny would be the same.

Bush prepared Americans for their new war, describing the differences inherent in fighting an enemy that does not emanate from specific territory: "Americans should not expect one battle, but a lengthy campaign unlike any other we have ever seen." The speech included this preeminently critical and memorable component: "We will pursue nations that provide aid or safe haven to terrorism. Every nation in every region now has a decision to make: *Either you are with us or you are with the terrorists.*" And yet, despite its forcefulness, the speech was thoughtful and measured—Bush stressed that he was not condemning "our many Muslim friends." Near the end of the speech was a paragraph that conveyed clearly the new demeanor of this president: "I will not forget the wound to our country and those who inflicted it. I will not yield. I will not rest. I will not relent in waging this struggle for freedom and security for the American people."

Bush's new confidence and focus were evident in his State of the Union address on January 29, 2002. He stated that although the "nation is at war, our economy is in recession, and the civilized world faces unprecedented dangers . . . the state of our Union has never been stronger." He celebrated the American military victories in Afghanistan and the recovery in New York and the Pentagon, yet he avoided—again—specific promises of an end to terrorism that ran the risk of raising expectations. In one key line he warned that "our war against terrorism is only beginning." This State of the Union address portrayed an active and assertive president, as least insofar as the war on terrorism was concerned: "I will not wait on events, while danger gathers. . . . The United States of America will not permit the world's most dangerous regimes to threaten us with the world's most destructive weapons." The "axis of evil" phrase (penned by speechwriter David Frum as the "axis of hatred") received its first public use here and referred to North Korea, Iran, Iraq, "and their terrorist allies." Bush's rhetoric became continuous with the historically nondiplomatic rhetoric of "evil," an unambiguous word that had not been used prominently by a president since Ronald Reagan's "evil empire" reference to the Soviet Union.

In this speech the president complimented Congress on their response to 9/11, and there was a generalized encomium of economic security and "good jobs," a phrase repeated several times. Most of the economic section was general, however; terrorism and foreign policy were clearly the new focus of the new president. Apropos of Bush's new focus, confidence and ingenuousness were imputed to the president with few exceptions, but the exceptions were significant. Emblematic of them was an event that was atypical of the president, but that threatened his perceived sincerity as well as the perception of a newly "focused" president. In the first week of August 2002, Bush quipped to reporters concerning the threat from Iraq: "I call upon all nations to do everything they can to stop these terrorist killers. Thank you. Now watch this [golf] drive." Aired that evening on the news, Bush's apparently impromptu remark was cited by *New York Times* columnist, Thomas Friedman on August 22, 2002, as demonstrating a "real contempt for the world, and a real lack of seriousness." Even some of Bush's supporters expressed concern that his flippant remark might reveal a lack of authentic commitment on the most critical issue of our time, international terrorism. It would not be an exaggeration to call Bush's remarks "reckless," threatening as they did—along with similar prior remarks cited by Friedman—the critical assumption of his new seriousness on this issue.

On January 28, 2003, Bush delivered his State of the Union address from the U.S. Capitol. Part of the president's charm—which opponents would call obstinacy and/or rhetorical inadequacy—is his persistent pronunciation of "nuclear" as "new-cue-lar." There is no record of his answering a question on why he does this, nor did the self-described "new-cue-lar" engineer Jimmy Carter explain his identical pronunciation of the vexatious word. Bush's pronunciation of "nuclear," as well as his frequent syntactical errors, may simply result from a staunch refusal to accept prescriptive norms of English speech or a preference for the vernacular speech of Texas. As liberal pundit E. J. Dionne once opined, "Casting Bush as a dummy also plays into his strategy of casting himself as a Texas common man." Pronunciations aside, this speech has become controversial because of the alleged certitude of his references to weapons of mass destruction in Iraq. In his speech the president called the state of the Union "strong," and promised that the country would face its problems with "focus and clarity and courage." He praised his tax cut proposals, which he saw as critical to bringing "our economy out of recession." But the emphasis of the speech, not unexpectedly, was on the war on terrorism, for which the Department of Homeland Security, praised in the speech, had been created.

The first half of the speech was on domestic issues, but the pundits generally believed that the second half of the speech—on terrorism and Iraq—would occupy most of the president's attention. Bush argued that the war against terror was linked inextricably to the need to disarm Iraq. He praised the "calm unity" which allowed the country to press its war against terrorism "with confidence, because this call of history has come to the right country." Bush painted a picture of a dangerous Saddam Hussein who was uncooperative in the search for weapons of mass destruction and who had flouted the Gulf War armistice for twelve years. He cited source after source, some named and some not, who believed that Saddam had weapons of mass destruction that had not been accounted for or verifiably destroyed. As of the writing of this essay, Bush's critics are still making accusations ranging from alleged misrepresentation of the Iraqi threat to Bush's misreading of that threat.

Sixteen words from that speech have been focused on in particular: "The British government has learned that Saddam Hussein recently sought significant quantities of uranium from Africa." The criticisms constituted and constitute a direct attack on President Bush's credibility, and charges of the statement's falsity have been the one specified example cited of the president's alleged "lying," although that has subsequently been a general charge by his opponents. As conservative columnist William Safire describes it: "The he-lied-to-us charge was led by Joseph Wilson, a former diplomat sent in early 2002 by the C.I.A. to Niger to check out reports by several European intelligence services that Iraq had secretly tried to buy that African nation's only major export, 'yellowcake' uranium ore." While Wilson claimed that the story of Iraq's attempt to buy the yellowcake was false, his claim became intertwined with the issues of the motives and "outing" of his C.I.A. wife, Valerie Plame. Conservatives claim that the literal truth of the president's claim is validated by the panel headed by Britain's eminently respected Lord Butler, which in its examination of British intelligence during the war, said, "the statement in President Bush's State of the Union address of 28 January 2003 that 'The British Government has learned that Saddam Hussein recently sought significant quantities of uranium from Africa' was well-founded." Regardless, there has been no evidence of intentional, knowing falsehoods in Bush's rhetoric on the war. Yet, as the president's first term came to an end, the animus toward him among Democrats and liberals grew significantly.

As is frequently the case with Bush, there is a reference in the 2003 State of the Union address to religion as a source of strength—more than the perfunctory closing reference to the Almighty: "We do not claim to know all the ways of Providence, yet we can trust in them, placing our confidence in the loving God behind all of life and all of history."

In his State of the Union address on January 20, 2004, Bush presented a defense of his war on terrorism as well as of his invasion of Iraq. This time he reversed the order of his 2003 State of the Union address by placing terrorism and Iraq policies first and ending with domestic concerns. Clearly the emphasis was on Iraq and terrorism. In this address the president's rhetoric made particularly salient the linkage of his policies on terrorism and Iraq to success in Libya; "the leader of Libya voluntarily pledged to disclose and dismantle all of his regime's weapons of mass destruction programs," effecting the world's "changing for the better." Also in this speech is a critical tenet of the Bush administration's foreign policy, repeated often in ensuing speeches: the crucial importance of instilling democracy in Iraq and in the Middle East more generally.

One of the major criticisms by opponents of the president has been his conducting of press conferences. In these press conferences he often provides a list of reporters on whom he calls in order, dismissing the spontaneity that has characterized especially certain Democratic presidents, such as Clinton and Kennedy. Moreover, there has been criticism regarding the choices of reporters he calls on and the unimportance of tradition, or at least what the press corps has regarded as tradition. For example, in response to her public and generally known personal criticism of Bush, the president chose on occasion not only not to call on first, but at times not to call on at all, Helen Thomas, who wrote for United Press International and then Hearst News Service. Ms. Thomas had been more and more vocal in her opposition to the president and to the war in general. In one of her speeches she complained that "Bush has held only six

press conferences, the only forum in our society where a president can be questioned. I'm on the phone to [press secretary] Ari Fleischer every day, asking will he ever hold another one? The international world is wondering what happened to America's great heart and soul."

On March 6, 2003, Bush held a major prime-time press conference to address the issue of Iraq. By the time of this second prime-time press conference, his eighth altogether, critics were pointing out that Bill Clinton had held thirty press conferences and George H. W. Bush had held fifty-eight. Bush defenders countered that while the president had not had many prime-time news conferences, the number of times he had made himself available for questions exceeded two hundred. Howard Kurtz, media critic for the *Washington Post* and host of television's only show on media criticism, *Reliable Sources*, observed on May 25, 2003, that Bush is on television a "substantial amount." In this forty-five-minute appearance on March 6 in the East Room of the White House, the president focused on one message consistently, and his style was somber, resolute, and subdued. The message was that the United States was not going to back off from its demand that Saddam disarm and, echoing John F. Kennedy's message regarding the Cuban missile crisis more than forty years earlier, *the greatest risk of all would be to do nothing.*

On May 1, 2003, the president delivered one of his most controversial speeches from the aircraft carrier USS *Abraham Lincoln*. His plane made a "tailhook" landing, traveling at 150 mph and hooking onto a steel wire across the flight deck, coming to a complete stop in about 350 feet. Critics were appalled. This speech, pursuant to America's and its allies' victory in Iraq, showed the continuing confidence and focus of the president's rhetorical style. It celebrated—too much, critics said—that the allies had prevailed, and depicted the "battle of Iraq" as "one victory in a war on terror that began on September 11th, 2001, and still goes on." It reiterated the points argued since September 11, 2001: that American action against terrorism had been "focused" and unrelenting; that while "force . . . remains our last resort," we shall remain proactive in our war against terrorism: "The enemies of freedom are not idle, and neither are we . . . we will continue to hunt down the enemy before he can strike." The tone of this speech, like many of the Bush speeches on terrorism, was reminiscent of John F. Kennedy's inauguration and missile crisis speeches.

Adding to Bush's persuasiveness, at least with respect to the "war on terrorism," has been his credibility. As the well-known liberal columnist Richard Cohen put it in the *Washington Post* on June 3, 2003: "[Bush] has shown he means what he says. When he said he wouldn't deal with Arafat, he didn't deal with him. When he said he would whack Iraq, he whacked it. When he said he would get involved in the peace process, he did. He not only can bang heads together, he will. His record so far says so." The confidence—indeed, overconfidence—of this speech has been the object of virulent criticism, perhaps because the succeeding months have witnessed a deadly resistance that has been difficult to quell. Particularly irritating to Bush critics was the "Mission Accomplished" banner that was located behind Bush aboard the *Abraham Lincoln* when he gave this speech. Cited as evidencing the bravado and swagger that has been prevalent in Bush's rhetoric, opponents of the administration have focused on this event as synecdoche for the misleading optimism that they claim is characteristic of him. In a widely repeated statement at his news conference on October 28, 2003, Bush claimed that the sign was not erected by the White House but was put up by the Navy, adding, "I know it was attributed somehow to some ingenious advance man from my staff—they weren't that ingenious, by the way."

Dovetailing with this apparent ability to rely—positively or negatively—on Bush's words is the rhetorical/political necessity of seeing a policy through, irrespective of the ebbs and flows of short-term success which surround it. In a speech in Alabama in early November 2003, Bush said, "The enemy in Iraq believes America will run. That's why they're willing to kill innocent civilians, relief workers, coalition troops. America will never run." The reaction was, according to the *Washington Post*, a standing ovation.

Bush's acceptance speech at the 2004 Republican National Convention in New York City, written by Michael Gerson, earned him, by vary-

ing accounts, a 4–11 percent bump in his race with Democratic presidential nominee John Kerry. This speech—and the theme of the convention in general—highlighted the president's then three-year self-description as "focused" and emphasized the campaign's depiction of Senator John Kerry as "flip-flopping" (a charge heightened by the use of flip-flop shoes at the convention as a visual metaphor) and inconsistent.

The speech was not a "barn burner"—it was sixty-five minutes long and laid out a lengthy domestic agenda, partly in an effort to show the president as "forward-looking," in contrast to Senator Kerry, who, Republicans argued, had still not indicated an agenda and was focused on the Vietnam War of thirty years earlier. The speech, which is best seen in the context of tremendously supportive speeches by Senator John McCain (whose support had seemed reluctant at times), Rudy Giuliani, Governor Arnold Schwarzenegger of California, Laura Bush, and Vice President Cheney. Perhaps the most representative lines of the president's address were "I will never relent in defending America—whatever it takes" and "In the last four years, you and I have come to know each other. Even when we don't agree, at least you know what I believe and where I stand." The former emphasized the focus on fighting terrorism and, by implication, the inextricable link to the Iraqi War, stated and restated in speech after speech at this convention. The latter was an attempt to say that if at times Bush's "compassionate conservatism"—also referenced in this speech—seemed more conservative than compassionate, small disagreements paled in contrast with the president's reliability in his relentless attention to the dangers of terrorism.

In assessing Bush's rhetoric the honest writer must also bring up a rhetorical/political phenomenon that has enveloped this president: a personal animus, often dubbed frankly as a "hatred," felt by his detractors that is perhaps comparable only with that felt by opponents of Bill Clinton and Richard Nixon in the last generation of presidents. Typified by an article by Jonathan Chait in the September 29, 2003, *New Republic*, this personal hostility is a result of Bush's rhetorical style, his controversial victory over Vice President Gore in the electoral college, and his often referred-to "lack of self-doubt," as well as policy differences. The possible primacy of a *rhetorical* cause of this personal dislike of Bush is articulated in the same issue of the *New Republic* by Ramesh Ponnuru, who states that the cause of Bush hatred is not his being born into privilege: "It's that Bush seems to lack the kind of extemporaneous verbal intelligence that is rated highly by people who possess it."

George W. Bush's oratory should cause reconsideration of the assumption that only grandiloquence can lead people to conclude that a president is an impressive and motivating speaker. Certainly powerful, even bombastic, delivery helped cement the oratorical reputations of presidents in the television age—John F. Kennedy, Ronald Reagan, and Bill Clinton—as excellent speech givers. Bush's lack of flair as a speaker can be attributed to a multitude of purposes, including his likely desire to counter the "reckless cowboy" image that many had imputed—and continue to impute—to him. But W's increased focus and resoluteness since the events of September 11, 2001, save a few exceptions of mistaken flippancy, have demonstrated that the substance and seriousness of the message can confer the reputation of being a strong and persuasive, if not uniquely gifted, public speaker.

INFORMATION SOURCES

Research Collections and Collected Speeches

George Bush's speeches, press conferences, and extemporaneous remarks are in the *Public Papers of the President* as well as the *Weekly Compilation of Presidential Documents*. Many speech texts and audio and video clips are available through the official White House site and through C-SPAN's Web site.

Web Sites

C-SPAN. Includes video clips of presidential speeches, statements, and press conferences. www.c-span.org

White House official Web site [*WHW*]. Includes texts of speeches, statements, and press conferences, as well as audio and video clips. www.whitehouse.gov

Selected Critical Studies

Chait, Jonathan. "Mad About You: The Case for Bush Hatred." *New Republic*, September 29, 2003, pp. 20–22.

Cohen, Richard. "The Warrior Tackles Peace." *Washington Post*, June 3, 2003, p. A23.

Friedman, Thomas L. "Because We Could." *New York Times*, June 4, 2003, p. A31.

Hatfield, James H. *Fortunate Son: George W. Bush and the Making of an American President.* Berkeley, Calif.: Omega Publishing Endeavors, 2001.

Kaplan, David A. *The Accidental President.* New York: William Morrow, 2001.

Miller, Mark Crispin. *The Bush Dyslexicon: Observations on a National Disorder.* New York: Norton, 2002.

Ponnuru, Ramesh. "Hate Crimes: The Case Against Bush Hatred." *New Republic*, September 29, 2003, pp. 24–25.

Safire, William. "Sixteen Truthful Words." *New York Times*, July 19, 2004, p. 7.

Selected Biographies

Frum, David. *The Right Man: The Surprise Presidency of George W. Bush.* New York: Random House, 2003.

Woodward, Bob. *Bush at War.* New York: Simon and Schuster, 2002.

CHRONOLOGY OF MAJOR SPEECHES

See "Research Collections and Collected Speeches" for source code.

"President Bush's Inaugural Address." Washington, D.C., January 20, 2001. *WHW.*

"Remarks by the President on Stem Cell Research." Midland, Tex., August 9, 2001. *WHW.*

"Freedom from Fear" (address to a joint session of Congress). Washington, D.C., September 20, 2001. *WHW.*

"Remarks by the President at Signing of the PATRIOT Act." Washington, D.C., October 26, 2001. *WHW.*

"Address to the Nation on Terrorism." Atlanta, Ga., November 8, 2001. *WHW.*

"The State of the Union Address." Washington, D.C., January 29, 2002. *WHW.*

"President's Remarks to the Nation." New York City, September 11, 2002. *WHW.*

"President's Remarks at the United Nations General Assembly." New York City, September 12, 2002. *WHW.*

"President Bush Outlines Iraqi Threat." Cincinnati, Ohio, October 7, 2002. *WHW.*

"President Bush Signs Homeland Security Act." Washington, D.C., November 25, 2002. *WHW.*

"President Bush Taking Action to Strengthen America's Economy." Chicago, January 7, 2003. *WHW.*

"President Bush Celebrates First Anniversary of No Child Left Behind." Washington, D.C., January 8, 2003. *WHW.*

"The State of the Union Address." Washington, D.C., January 28, 2003. *WHW*.

"President George Bush Discusses Iraq in National Press Conference." Washington, D.C., March 6, 2003. *WHW*.

"President Bush Announces Combat Operations in Iraq Have Ended" (remarks by the president from the U.S.S. *Abraham Lincoln*). Persian Gulf, May 1, 2003. *WHW*.

"The State of the Union Address." Washington, D.C., January 20, 2004. *WHW*.

"Acceptance Speech at the Republican National Convention." New York City, September 2, 2004. Available at *WHW*.

ROBERT CARLYLE BYRD (1917–)
U.S. *Senator from West Virginia*

WILLIAM D. PEDERSON AND SINA K. NAZEMI

Huey P. Long, Louisiana's "Kingfish" populist governor–senator and stump orator who used the Great Depression as his stepping-stone to power, referred to himself as "sui generis," a term more accurately applied to Senator Robert C. Byrd, given his outstanding legislative and oratorical legacy. From modest beginnings, the self-taught Byrd has emerged as one of the foremost orators of his era, spanning the twentieth and twenty-first centuries. With virtuoso political talent, he has mastered each of the three positions that yield power in the U.S. Congress: "the godfather" (party leader); "the warlord" (committee chair); and "the maverick," a legislator who opposes what Alexis de Tocqueville aptly called "the tyranny of the majority" in a democratic political system. Most congressional leaders master only one of these positions to gain the power associated with it. Byrd's ability is such that he possesses the flexibility and versatility to have mastered all three concurrently, not only in his legislative pursuits but also in his compelling oratory that started pianissimo but built to a resonating crescendo as he found his full political voice.

As is true of many talented political leaders, Robert Byrd's origins branded him as a psychological outsider, but he displayed an unusual determination to repeatedly prove his worth. He was born Cornel Calvin Sales, Jr. on November 20, 1917, in North Wilkesboro, North Carolina. When his mother died in the great influenza pandemic of 1918, her last wish was for her fifth and final child to be reared by the boy's paternal aunt and her husband, whose only child had died. The couple renamed their nephew Robert, and three years later they moved to West Virginia, whose origins as a state would become a metaphor for the political life of the man who would become its most famous son. West Virginia was the by-product of a polity that had undergone a major civil war; Byrd was the by-product of personal upheaval precipitated by his mother's death. It was not until he graduated from high school at age sixteen, during the Great Depression, that he learned his origins and real name.

Meanwhile, he had been reared in extremely humble circumstances. His uncle–father worked at subsistence-level jobs, including coal mining. Poverty prevented Byrd from attending college until he was almost twice as old as most students beginning their undergraduate studies. Thus a pattern was established of belated attempt and accomplishment that has been reflected throughout Byrd's life. He did not own his first car until he was older. He entered law school as an older student. He was in his late thirties before he traveled abroad. And he developed his gift for oration belatedly. Byrd went through a "postponed identity crisis," not by choice but because of circumstances caused by his humble start in life. He had to concentrate on "catching up" just to get even. He started as a gas station attendant, then became a produce salesman, a self-taught butcher, and a shipyard worker. In June 1948 he bought a small grocery store. The only facet of his life that was not postponed was his emotional development. In 1937, he married his high school sweetheart, Erma Ora James, also from a coal miner's family. Their sixty-seven-year marriage produced two daughters.

EMERGENCE OF A SELF-TAUGHT ORATOR

Robert Byrd's entry into the political arena occurred immediately after World War II when he ran for the West Virginia House of Delegates in 1946. His oratorical skills in that campaign were modest, consisting primarily of the ability to speak in a straightforward style. A man of few words, but with the ability to learn on the campaign trail, he heeded the recommendation of a veteran politician who discovered Byrd could play the fiddle. He advised the neophyte politi-

voting record on economic issues and a conservative stance on most other issues.

Always ambitious and energetic, Byrd began his formal undergraduate education while serving in the state legislature. He eventually attended four West Virginia colleges: Beckley College, Concord College in Athens, Morris Harvey College (now Charleston University), and Marshall College (now Marshall University in Huntington). He earned only seventy undergraduate academic credit hours, but in 1994 Marshall University bestowed an honorary B.A. summa cum laude on the autodidact with a reputation for intensity. The intensity that drove Byrd to learn was blamed for the stomach ulcer he developed while in the West Virginia Senate.

His formal undergraduate education was episodic and revolved around his political career, which was propelling him upward. In 1952, while still in the state senate, he withdrew from Marshall College and ran for the U.S. House of

Robert Byrd is the only member of Congress to have started, and completed, his law degree while holding office. A 1963 graduate of the American University School of Law, he received his diploma from President John F. Kennedy, that year's commencement speaker.

cian to make his fiddle case his campaign briefcase. It became an enduring campaign symbol for the "down-home" politician who also began wearing a trademark red vest. It worked. He found his niche and his identity. Byrd was reelected to the House of Delegates in 1948, and to the West Virginia Senate in 1950.

His first and only speech in the West Virginia legislature during his freshman term came in 1947 and dealt with a bill designed to liberalize workmen's compensation, aimed especially at coal miners. Byrd had introduced the bill and had been advised not to talk too much or too often, but to be prepared when he did. It was an effective debut, for Byrd's colleagues gave unanimous consent to include his remarks in the house *Journal.* The topic of the speech ultimately summarized his entire legislative career—a liberal

Representatives. During the primary campaign, the news story broke that Byrd was a member of the Ku Klux Klan. As a result, he was shunned by the Democratic Party and had to run without party backing. It was a twist of irony that Byrd had joined the Klan in the early 1940s at the suggestion of a Grand Dragon, the retired minister who was the first to suggest he seek a political career. Byrd won his first election to Congress during the McCarthy era, a period when the Klan was an anticommunist organization. Like his fellow Southern autodidact Hugo L. Black, who joined the Klan in Alabama to help win election to the U.S. Senate and went on to become one of the greatest justices in U.S. Supreme Court history, Byrd would always regret his Klan membership. In Congress, he compiled a record at odds with the Klan.

Byrd's six years in the U.S. House of Representatives was a period in which his political education was still continuing. In the "old Congress," before reforms of the mid-1970s, the path to power was summarized by Speaker Sam Rayburn's sage advice to freshman congressmen: "To get along, go along." Byrd complied. During his second congressional term, he was a member of the Foreign Affairs Committee, which gave him the opportunity to travel overseas for the first time in his life. In 1955, he would visit more than twenty countries.

The ever serious and energetic Byrd began his law school education in January 1953, enrolling for night classes at George Washington University Law School. After completing twenty hours, he learned that because he did not have an undergraduate degree, George Washington would not award him a law degree. He transferred to American University's Washington College of Law after its dean agreed to allow him to earn his law degree if he maintained at least a "B" overall average. Byrd had no interest in practicing law, but he did have the classic autodidact's drive to receive such a degree. His perseverance was rewarded in 1963 when he graduated cum laude and accepted his diploma from President John F. Kennedy, the commencement speaker. It took him a decade, but Byrd became the first member to begin and complete law school while serving in Congress.

In 1958, Byrd was elected to the U.S. Senate, where he set multiple records. Having never lost a political election, he served longer in the U.S. Senate than any other West Virginia senator, and in 1970 he became the first candidate to carry every county in the state, a feat he would repeat several times. In fact, he has served more consecutive Senate terms and has cast more roll call votes than anyone in U.S. Senate history.

Byrd began his new political role by learning the invisible ropes that bound members of the "Gentlemen's Club," as the U.S. Senate has been called. As a freshman senator, he was appointed to a coveted seat on the Appropriations Committee for his support of Senate Majority Leader Lyndon B. Johnson. By the beginning of his second term, he had become a full member of the club, on track to become one of its "godfathers," a party leader. From 1967 to 1971,

Byrd was chief assistant to Senate Majority Leader Mike Mansfield (D.-Montana), serving as the Senate Democratic Conference secretary with backing of the Southern bloc. As a consequence, he began remaining on the Senate floor and studying parliamentary procedure. He soon was expert on Senate rules and prerogatives, and eventually had a Senate rule named for him. As might be expected from a "godfather," Byrd supported the Gulf of Tonkin resolution—opposed by only two senators—that gave President Lyndon B. Johnson carte blanche to operate militarily in Southeast Asia. Byrd later regretted his stance, but as a strong presidential supporter he had obtained Johnson's old seat on the Armed Services Committee when Johnson became vice president. Earlier blights on his record were his participation in the filibuster by Southern senators against the 1964 Civil Rights Act and his opposition to the nomination of Thurgood Marshall, the first African American named to the U.S. Supreme Court.

Through it all, Byrd continued to amass power in the Senate and, to the amazement of many, became the Senate Democratic whip in 1971 by defeating the incumbent, Edward M. Kennedy (D-Mass.). Byrd had backing from the Southern bloc, including the deathbed help of Richard Russell (D-Ga.), and he became an instant dragon slayer, to the dismay of liberals. In 1969, Byrd had moved from the Armed Services Committee to the Judiciary Committee, and in 1971 President Richard Nixon considered him for the U.S. Supreme Court until Byrd concluded he was not interested in a seat on the High Court. Byrd's voting record began to moderate; the National Association for the Advancement of Colored People (NAACP) eventually would give him a 78 percent approval rating.

In January 1977, Byrd advanced from the Senate's "godfather" understudy seat to the lead role when Mike Mansfield retired. He defeated Hubert Humphrey (D-Minn.) to become Senate majority leader. It was the Senate's most powerful leadership post, but he did not enjoy it. During the television age, the position required more of a "show horse" politician who could play to audiences than the traditional "workhorse" who got the job done. Byrd was more of the latter than the former, although he had by then recorded an album, *Mountain Fiddler*, and appeared on the popular television show *Hee Haw*. Later, to the consternation of some, Byrd would appear in a minor role in the 2003 Civil War film *Gods and Generals*, playing Confederate Brigadier General Paul J. Semmes, who had owned more than a dozen slaves. Byrd, despite his early Ku Klux Klan ties, viewed the film as a way to make history come alive for contemporary audiences, not as propaganda for a lost cause.

After wielding power as the top Democratic "godfather" for a dozen years, Byrd relinquished that role to don the mantle of "warlord" as chair of the Senate Appropriations Committee. He eschewed vacations and other absences from the Senate, and became the workhorse warlord on Appropriations, bringing millions of dollars in pork to his state. To many, he was the "King of Pork," funneling jobs and a tidal wave of federal dollars to West Virginia.

Although he had opposed the nomination of Thurgood Marshall, years later Byrd at first supported the nomination of Judge Clarence Thomas. One of Byrd's most powerful addresses, delivered before the Senate on October 15, 1991, concerned the nomination of Clarence Thomas to the Supreme Court. Initially, Byrd had planned to vote in favor of President George H. W. Bush's nominee to succeed Marshall, who was retiring from the Supreme Court. Two days before the Senate vote, the news media sensationally reported that Anita F. Hill, a law professor at the University of Oklahoma, had been sexually harassed by Thomas during the 1980s, while she worked for him at the Department of Education and the Equal Employment Opportunity Commission. As was his style, Byrd delivered the riveting speech from only a few notes.

Byrd began his address by recognizing that despite the remarks he would make, Thomas would likely be confirmed. However, he wanted his reasons for changing his mind—he now opposed the confirmation—on the record. He showed his seriousness about the confirmation by stating that except for fifteen minutes, he had watched the three days of televised hearings. Byrd also stated that for several years he had been a member of the Judiciary Committee (but did not mention that Richard Nixon had once considered him for an opening on the Supreme

Court). It was his belief that "the courts should be conservative," and he had not agreed with the Earl Warren Court (1953–69) because, as he had repeatedly charged at that time, the Court was acting like a legislature. Byrd went on to say that he considered Judge Thomas's stated jurisprudence to be consistent with his own. However, the Hill–Thomas confrontation had made him reconsider, and conclude that Judge Thomas should not be confirmed.

In his speech, Byrd discussed the five primary reasons that he had changed his mind. First, he said, he simply "believes Anita Hill." He based his belief in her veracity, in part, on the fact that she was brought up in the church attended by her poor Southern family, which struck a responsive chord with the devout, churchgoing Byrd. In addition, he said he had watched her family at the hearings and observed how they interacted with one another. Second, she was a reluctant witness whose public testimony was consistent with what she had confided privately on many prior occasions. He dismissed those who charged Hill with poor judgment because she had not filed an earlier complaint against Thomas. Perhaps thinking of his own flawed judgment in joining the KKK years before, Byrd rhetorically asked who in the Senate had never used poor judgment at some time. And, typically, he cited an example from Roman history to justify why it is best sometimes not to reveal secrets.

Byrd then articulated his view that Judge Thomas stonewalled and circumvented the purpose of the hearings by his refusal even to listen to Professor Hill's sworn testimony against him, which precluded committee members from being able to question him about it. To Byrd, it revealed a flaw in Judge Thomas's judicial temperament, for he believed that it is incumbent on judges to be willing to hear both sides of a case. Fourth, Byrd charged that Judge Thomas was raising the specter of racism in an attempt to divert attention from the real issue through his allegation that the committee hearings constituted "high-tech lynchings of uppity blacks."

Finally, Byrd rejected the notion that senators should give Judge Thomas "the benefit of the doubt." A student of the Constitution, Byrd drew the distinction between the legislative confirmation process and the judicial process in a court of law. Thomas, he asserted, had "no particular right" to a seat on the Court. In fact, Byrd argued, any benefit of the doubt should accrue "to the Court" or "to the country." In his view, "a more exemplary nominee" than Judge Thomas was needed. In his conclusion, Byrd quoted Shakespeare to refute Judge Thomas's effort to divert blame from himself to "the process."

As Byrd predicted, his speech did not prevent the appointment of Judge Thomas to the Supreme Court, but Byrd's compelling oratory demonstrated his formidable intelligence and reasoning ability without even a hint of prejudice.

Although Byrd's oratorical legacy is thoughtful, powerful speeches, he occasionally made an attempt at humor. On one such occasion, he took the floor to poke fun at the popular American habit of liberally sprinkling "you know" throughout conversations. On July 10, 1998, in a tongue-in-cheek presentation titled "The Spoken Word" before the Senate, he took issue with the cliché. In his critique, he applauded both the Great Emancipator for his "Gettysburg Address" and Martin Luther King, Jr. for his "I Have a Dream," calling both great speeches even if they didn't—you know—include that ubiquitous expression. Despite his status as a delayed college and law school graduate, Byrd proved that he had mastered the King's English and could use it as a precision political tool to help achieve his goals and retain his leadership.

At his pinnacle of power, Byrd assumed yet another leadership role in the Senate: zealous defender of the legislative branch against encroachment by the executive branch. C-SPAN brought his oratory to the American home, showcasing his speeches that are laced with quotes from American presidents, the U.S. Constitution, the Bible, and, increasingly, Roman history. Byrd used his powerful oration to link the U.S. Senate with the Roman Senate, stressing the importance of upholding the separation of powers between the legislative and executive branches of government if America's noble experiment in democracy were to succeed.

Byrd's rhetorical approach is well illustrated in his 1993 series of addresses that oppose empowerment of the chief executive of the United States with the line item veto. On May 5, 1993, Byrd launched his series of fourteen one-hour

addresses against presidential line-item veto power. His final presentation, on October 18, 1993, which served to summarize his oratorical marathon, opens by citing Montesquieu's classic *The Spirit of the Laws* (1748), which had influenced the framers of the Constitution to divide the functions and the powers of government among three discrete branches. He commended Montesquieu's wisdom to his twentieth-century audience, urging them to heed Montesquieu's advice and gain insight from Roman history, for human nature does not change.

The bulk of the speech contrasted Roman and American history. It briefly notes that overexpansion (territorial and otherwise) contributed to major political and personal corruption in Rome, and draws a parallel to President Eisenhower's warning about the threat of the military-industrial complex in the United States. In the longest section of the address, Byrd focuses on the experiences of Polybius, the Greek historian who witnessed the Roman Republic at its pinnacle. Byrd asserts that the longevity of the Roman Republic is attributable to the Roman Senate's control over the public purse. America's constitutional system is similar to Rome's with its checks and balances and separation of powers, and by extension of logic the United States Senate should retain control of the purse strings. Byrd urges his colleagues to maintain the constitutional equilibrium intended by the framers.

He then turns to the fall of Rome, rejecting Edward Gibbon's *Decline and Fall of the Roman Empire* in favor of Will Durant's twentieth-century perspective asserted in *The Story of Civilization*, which attributes the fall to "increasing despotism." The Roman Senate lost its will to govern and too eagerly abrogated its responsibility to a "one-man government." Byrd concludes by observing that the American public is impatient with federal deficits, but that "quack remedies" such as the line-item veto are deceptive panaceas, and implored Congress to retain the power of the purse.

His position as the chairman of the Senate Appropriations Committee and his reputation as "the King of Pork" may have contributed to the failure of Byrd's rhetoric to persuade his fellow senators. Ironically, the U.S. Supreme Court eventually declared, in effect, that Byrd was right: the line-item veto violated the Constitution's separation of powers.

Byrd's final role, as a maverick, was one that only someone working from an enormous base of institutional knowledge and personal power could hope to undertake successfully. During debate on the Gulf of Tonkin resolution, Byrd supported the president and classic maverick Wayne L. Morse (D.-Ore.) used his oratorical repertoire as a former speech professor and law school dean to become the only senator to take the floor and plead eloquently against approval. Although he was the educational inverse of Morse, Byrd would years later reprise Morse's role as the maverick, using his own unique oratorical skills to challenge America's intervention in Iraq and the doctrine of preemption.

His "Rush to War Ignores U.S. Constitution" address on October 3, 2002, illustrates this. Byrd begins his speech by quoting the Roman historian Titus Livius as he argues against haste in authorizing presidential use of "whatever force he deems necessary in Iraq or elsewhere." He then charges that the president exhibits the flaw that was the source of Greek tragedies: hubris. Byrd cites both Abraham Lincoln's critique of James Polk's behavior that provoked the Mexican–American War and a Congressional Research Service study showing that historically the United States had never engaged in a "preemptive" military attack abroad.

In addition, Byrd cites not only constitutional restrictions against the proposed "preemptive strike" doctrine but also court precedent (*Myers v. United States*, 1926) against the exercise of arbitrary power. He warns that America's use of a "preemptive" strike will set a precedent for other nations to justify military adventures. Byrd also questions the timing of the proposed legislation—just thirty-three days before a national election—and warns about a possible long-term occupation. He concludes by urging restraint and allowing time to build an international coalition, as the United States did before the 1991 Persian Gulf War.

Despite Byrd's rhetorical pleas, the resolution passed 296–133 in the House and 72–23 in the Senate. Nonetheless, Byrd continues to speak out for the legislative prerogative and public debate, and has encouraged the latter with his latest book, *Losing America: Confronting a Reckless and Arrogant President* (2004), which includes eight of his recent speeches.

Byrd wants the Senate to abandon its rubber-stamp approach to approving administration-made foreign policy and assert its constitutional authority as full partner with the executive branch in making foreign policy. In what may be his final and greatest role in his half-century in the Congress, the maverick veteran senator has assumed center stage as a hero to those who once questioned him.

INFORMATION SOURCES

Research Collections and Collected Speeches

No archival collection of Senator Robert C. Byrd's speeches is available. However, many of his addresses and comments are available in a variety of published sources: *Congressional Digest* (*CD*), *Congressional Record*, *Vital Speeches of the Day*, and the *New York Times*, as well as at the senator's official Web site.

Byrd, Robert. *The Senate. 1789–1989,* vol. 3, *Classic Speeches. 1830–1993,* [*TSCS*], ed. Wendy Wolff. Washington, D.C.: Government Printing Office, 1994.

———. *The Senate of the Roman Republic: Addresses on the History of Roman Constitutionalism.* Washington, D.C.: Government Printing Office, 1995.

———. *Losing America: Confronting a Reckless and Arrogant Presidency.* New York: Norton, 2004.

Web Site

The senator's official Senate Web site includes some speech texts. http://byrd.senate.gov/

Selected Critical Studies

Bucher, Gregory S. "Book Review of Robert C. Byrd, *The Senate of the Roman Republic: Addresses on the History of Roman Constitutionalism.*" *Classical World* 90 (1997): 369.

Carlson, Peter. "The Senator Votes Nay." *Washington Post*, May 24, 2003, p. C1.

Crowley, Michael. "Inside Job." *New Republic*, November 11, 2002, pp. 15–17.

Haas, Lawrence J. "Byrd's Big Stick." *National Journal*, February 9, 1991, pp. 316–20.

Plotz, David. "Byrd Brain." *New Republic*, January 18, 1999, pp. 15–16.

Rogers, David. "Byrd Unleashes Oratorical Fury." *Wall Street Journal*, May 21, 2003, p. A4.

Tierney, John. "Byrd, at 85, Fills the Forum with Romans and Wrath." *New York Times*, November 20, 2002, p. A1.

Selected Biographies

Byrd, Robert C. "Education of a Senator. 1917–1958." In *The Senate. 1789–1989. Addresses on the History of the United States Senate*, Volume II, ed. Wendy Wolff. Washington, D.C.: Government Printing Office, 1991.

———. "Reflections of a Party Leader." In *The Senate, 1789–1989*. Washington, D.C.: Government Printing Office, 1991.

———. "Rise to Leadership. 1959–1977." In *The Senate. 1789–1989. Addresses on the History of the United States Senate*, Volume II, ed. Wendy Wolff. Washington, D.C.: Government Printing Office, 1991.

———. "The Democratic Leader and Foreign Policy. 1977–1989." In *The Senate, 1789–1989. Addresses on the History of the United States Senate*, Volume II, ed. Wendy Wolff. Washington, D.C.: Government Printing Office, 1991.

Unger, Stanford J. "The Man Who Runs the Senate." *Atlantic*, September 1975, pp. 29–35.

CHRONOLOGY OF MAJOR SPEECHES

See "Research Collections and Collected Speeches" for source code.

"Russia's New War Against Free Nations Can Threaten the Welfare of Workers in Any Country" (address to the Ravenswood Junior Chamber of Commerce). Ravenswood, W. Va., January 26, 1961. *Vital Speeches of the Day*, March 1, 1961, pp. 297–98.

"School Busing and Forced Integration, a Dissenting Opinion." Washington, D.C., September 8, 1971. *Vital Speeches of the Day*, October 15, 1971, pp. 7–11.

"Everyday Life in Communist China. United States Relations with the People's Republic of China" (address to the U.S. Senate). Washington, D.C., September 4, 1975. *Vital Speeches of the Day*, October 1, 1975, pp. 738–45.

"Should the U.S. Proceed with Procurement of the MX Missile?" Washington, D.C., March 19, 1985. *CD*, June/July 1985, pp. 170ff.

"Should the Boren Amendment to Curtailing PACs Be Adopted?" Washington, D.C., August 11, 1986. *CD*, February 1987, p. 40.

"Should Congress Grant Line-Item Veto Authority to the President?" Washington, D.C., April 11, 1989. *CD*, June/July 1990, pp. 175ff.

"Should the Senate-Passed Immigration Act of 1989 Be Approved?" Washington, D.C., July 13, 1989. *CD*, October 1989, p. 237.

"On the Budget Reconciliation Bill" (address to the U.S. Senate). Washington, D.C., October 13, 1989. In his *The Senate. 1789–1989*, vol. 2. Washington, D.C.: Government Printing Office, 1991.

"Should Semiautomatic Assault-Style Weapons Be Banned by Congress?" Washington, D.C., May 23, 1990. *CD*, November 1990, pp. 266–68.

"On the Persian Gulf War" (address to the U.S. Senate). Washington, D.C., January 12, 1991. *TSCS*, pp. 747–55.

"On the Nomination of Clarence Thomas to the Supreme Court" (address to the U.S. Senate). Washington, D.C., October 15, 1991. *TSCS*, pp. 759–68.

"Should the Freedom Support Act of 1992 Be Approved?" Washington, D.C., July 2, 1992. *CD*, August/September 1992, pp. 217ff.

"Line-Item Veto XIV" (address to the U.S. Senate). Washington, D.C., October 18, 1993. *TSCS*, pp. 771–79.

"The Spoken Weed" (address to the U.S. Senate). Washington, D.C., July 10, 1998. *Harper's*, November 1998, pp. 26–27.

"Rush to War Ignores U.S. Constitution" (address to the U.S. Senate). Washington, D.C., October 3, 2002. http://www.senate.gov/-gov/byrd/speech.htm

"Should the Senate Authorize the Use of Force Against Iraq?" (address to the U.S. Senate). Washington, D.C., October 8, 2002. *CD*, December 2002, pp. 301, 303, 305.

STOKELY CARMICHAEL (KWAME TOURÉ) (1941–1998)
African American Civil Rights Leader

ROBERT E. TERRILL

It has often been noted that the life of Stokely Carmichael closely parallels the history of the 1960s civil rights movement in the United States. His own evolution from nonviolent resister to Pan-Africanist revolutionary matches one arc of development within the movement as a whole. His rhetoric, of course, had much to do with both his presence at many of the crucial moments in the movement's history and his influence at those moments. Well-educated, articulate, attractive, and apparently fearless, Carmichael rose to prominence within the civil rights movement in part because of his ability to speak effectively to a wide range of audiences, from illiterate Black sharecroppers to privileged white college students. And he was willing to say things that his Black audiences might be thinking but would not have said out loud, things certain to enrage or frighten his white audiences.

Carmichael was born on June 29, 1941, in Port of Spain, Trinidad. His parents immigrated to New York when he was a toddler; Stokely and other members of his family followed in 1952. Although Carmichael would gain his notoriety in part through his willingness to denounce the "American dream" as an instrument of racist oppression, his father strongly believed in it, even though his hard work was never able to lift his family out of poverty. As Carmichael put it in a 1967 interview with Gordon Parks in *Life* magazine:

> My old man believed in this work-and-overcome stuff. He was religious, never lied, never cheated or stole. He did carpentry all day and drove taxis all night.... May Charles [Stokely's mother] had to bribe an official with 50 bucks and a bottle [of] perfume to get him into the union. *He didn't know.* "See," he said, "have patience and things will come to you." The next thing that came to that poor black

man was death—from working too hard. And he was only in his 40s.

Carmichael became a naturalized American citizen in 1954, and his family moved to an Italian American neighborhood in the Bronx where he was the only Black member of a street gang called the Morris Park Avenue Dukes.

His life changed dramatically in 1956, when he was accepted by the elite Bronx High School of Science. He felt awkward among his new white friends as the son of a Black maid attending Park Avenue parties where Black maids handed around refreshments, but he excelled in school. During this time Carmichael saw his first sit-in on television. He became active in the Congress of Racial Equality (CORE), picketing a Woolworth's in New York and participating in sit-ins in Virginia and South Carolina. Because of his outstanding academic record, he was offered several scholarships to white universities, but chose to attend Howard University. At Howard, Carmichael became involved with the Nonviolent Action Group (NAG) as well as the Student Nonviolent Coordinating Committee (SNCC), one of the two organizations with which he would forever be associated in the public mind. (The other, years later, would be the Black Panthers.) Carmichael majored in philosophy, becoming interested in the works of Albert Camus, Jean-Paul Sartre, and George Santayana, and began to mine the works of these thinkers for theoretical insights and frameworks that he applied to the struggle for civil rights.

During his freshman year, in 1961, Carmichael joined his first Freedom Ride, taking an integrated bus through the South to challenge segregated interstate travel. He was arrested in Jackson, Mississippi, for entering the "whites only" bus station waiting room, and was held for over forty days at Parchman Penitentiary; while there, he turned twenty-two. Carmichael remained active in the civil rights movement throughout college, participating in a hospital workers' strike in New York, Freedom Rides in Maryland, and mass demonstrations in Albany, Georgia. Carmichael was graduated with honors from Howard in 1964, just in time for "Freedom Summer." Hundreds of white Northern students, recruited and organized by SNCC, descended into the South to register Black voters.

Tensions were beginning to appear within the movement as some of the veterans of previous Mississippi summer voter registration campaigns began to question the continued viability of nonviolent resistance. Predictably, Carmichael was at the epicenter of this rift. For example, Carmichael, now the project coordinator for the Delta region, argued at a SNCC training camp that nonviolent self-sacrifice was an unnatural philosophy and an ineffective tactic. When the bodies of three civil rights workers—James Chaney, Mickey Schwerner, and Andrew Goodman—were pulled from the Olen Burrage Dam on August 4, Carmichael was tempted to abandon nonviolence altogether in favor of joining some members of the Council of Federated Organizations (COFO) in armed retaliation.

In the summer of 1965, SNCC ran a voter registration drive centered in Lowndes County, Alabama, and Carmichael was instrumental in organizing the Lowndes County Freedom Organization (LCFO). Alabama state law required all political parties to have a symbol, and the LCFO chose a black panther, which was later to serve as the inspiration for the Black Panther Party. In May 1966, Carmichael was elected chairman of SNCC, replacing John Lewis. The election signaled a significant change in policy for the organization, for the twenty-four-year-old Carmichael had become an increasingly vocal critic of nonviolence. Under Carmichael, SNCC began to make it clear that its white members were no longer welcome.

A few weeks after being installed as SNCC chairman, perhaps the most significant event of Carmichael's life occurred. James Meredith, who in 1961 had been the first Black person to attend the University of Mississippi, had decided to march from Nashville, Tennessee, to Jackson, Mississippi, in an attempt to help

Blacks overcome their fear of registering to vote. Approximately twenty miles after he entered Mississippi, he was shot. He was too badly injured to go on, and black leaders met to discuss how to continue. Disagreements arose, but Carmichael was among those who chose to continue the march. On June 17, when the Meredith march reached Greenwood, Mississippi, Carmichael introduced the world to "Black Power." Though the phrase had been used before, it was Carmichael who popularized the term and who articulated a flexible and adaptive ideology to accompany it. It was a watershed moment, marking and giving voice to the rising frustration and shifting demographics within the civil rights movement.

Over the next three years, Carmichael was frequently invited to address students at both white and Black colleges; he spoke at rallies and marches; he published essays in *The New York Review of Books* and *The Massachusetts Review*; and, with Charles V. Hamilton, he wrote the book *Black Power: The Politics of Liberation*. In 1967, Carmichael took a controversial trip outside the United States, visiting and talking with government leaders in Cuba, North Vietnam, China, and Guinea. While in Guinea he stayed at the home of Head of State Sékou Touré and was befriended by Kwame Nkrumah, the deposed leader of Ghana. Returning to the United States, he relinquished ties with SNCC and accepted an invitation to become prime minister of the Black Panther Party; he remained affiliated with the group until 1969, even though his Pan-Africanist and Black separatist stances often brought his ideas into conflict with other Panther leaders, such as Eldridge Cleaver and Huey Newton, who considered themselves Marxists.

In 1968, Carmichael married well-known South African singer Miriam Makeba, and eventually moved with her to Guinea, where he took up permanent residence in Conakry. He began to refer to himself as Kwame Touré, in homage to his two African mentors. He continued to travel around the globe as a spokesperson for the All African Peoples Revolutionary Party, often speaking at college campuses in the United States. Twice divorced, Carmichael died on November 15, 1998, at the age of fifty-seven, in Conakry. The cause of death was prostate cancer, which he insisted was given to him by the FBI. To the end, he answered his telephone with the phrase "Ready for the revolution!"

CARMICHAEL'S RHETORIC: DEFINITION, DISTINCTION, AND DIFFERENCE

Stokely Carmichael was active in the civil rights movement for many years before he rose to prominence during the 1966 Meredith march, and then his most active time as an orator in the United States lasted only until 1968, when he moved to Guinea. In 1971, with the editorial assistance of Ethel N. Minor, Carmichael published fourteen of his addresses in a volume titled *Stokely Speaks*. This volume, and *Black Power: The Politics of Liberation*, published in 1967, constitute Carmichael's most significant rhetorical efforts. Because all of these speeches, and the book, were produced in a short span of time, they are more profitably considered as the constituent elements of a single sustained rhetorical project.

Some of the variation in Carmichael's rhetoric may stem from his often noted ability to adapt his delivery, tone, and style to his immediate audience. Before Black audiences he was animated, usually speaking extempore, mocking and mimicking white leaders, emphasizing his points with flamboyant gestures, and sounding his voice across its entire range from a high falsetto to a booming bass. Before white audiences he generally was more subdued, often reading verbatim from his published essays. Before both audiences he would punctuate his speeches with allusions to philosophers such as Albert Camus and Jean-Paul Sartre as well as with quotations from Frantz Fanon and Malcolm X. He generally wore a coat and tie when speaking, but removed the coat and loosened the tie soon after he began.

Carmichael's speeches and *Black Power* are rich texts that would reward far more study than they have received. Three characteristics of these texts are especially important. The first of these is the recurring strategy of *definition*, in which Carmichael redefines key terms, such as "integration," often in startling ways, and then proceeds to use these redefined terms as the

starting points for further argument. A second and closely related pattern that emerges in his rhetoric is Carmichael's tendency to set two terms in *distinct opposition* to one another and then elevate one—generally the term suppressed in white American culture—over the other. Both of these patterns, to varying degrees, occur in *Black Power* as well as in Carmichael's oratory. However, it also is important to note the difference in tone and purpose between *Black Power* and the speeches in *Stokely Speaks*.

Carmichael's speeches were loosely structured, but often followed a general pattern of development from abstract to specific. He would begin by providing a theoretical or conceptual framework, then flesh out that framework with detailed examples from history, from his reading, or from his own experiences, then sometimes conclude with an emotional call to action. In this way the structure of his speeches reinforced his argument—just as his speeches were built on a foundation of self-defined terms, so African Americans should build their own identities and coalitions.

A rhetoric of definition has great persuasive potential, for if a speaker can invite an audience to share her or his definitions of key terms, these terms can become the building blocks of successive argument. Furthermore, people who share definitions of key terms may more easily identify themselves as members of a single group. For a minority audience, accepting definitions that differ from those adhered to by the dominant culture can become an attractive and empowering source of differentiation and identity.

Carmichael seemed aware of the potential power of the rhetoric of definition; indeed, in his speech at the University of California at Berkeley in October 1966, he defined the civil rights movement in general, and the controversy over Black Power in particular, as a struggle over the need for African Americans to be able to define themselves: "We must wage a psychological battle on the right for black people to define themselves as they see fit, and organize themselves as they see fit." Carmichael also repeatedly urged his audiences, both Black and white, to understand how important it was for African Americans to invent terms that were free of the constraints imposed by the dominant white culture. In *The New York Review of Books*, in September 1966, he wrote: "An organization which claims to speak for the needs of a community—as does the Student Nonviolent Coordinating Committee—must speak in the tone of that community, not as somebody else's buffer zone." "We are now engaged," he declared in the Berkeley speech, "in a psychological struggle in this country about whether or not black people have the right to use the words they want to use without white people giving their sanction." At Morgan State College in January 1967, he diagnosed a weakness of the nonviolent integration campaign as stemming from Black leaders being caught up in "reacting to a definition by a white man." He then reminded his listeners that "the first need of a free people is to be able to define their own terms and have those terms recognized by their oppressors." This idea was

decent house or education, blacks must move into a white neighborhood or send their children to a white school." Ghetto riots were defined by Carmichael as "rebellions," justified retribution for the conditions imposed upon ghetto residents by the dominant culture. At Morgan State, he went so far as to suggest that such retribution was overdue because "Anytime a man has been charging us all that money for fifteen years, his store should have been bombed five years ago." This brief review suggests that a subtle progression might be discerned as Carmichael's definitions became more radical and more challenging over time. The procedural critique implied in the redefinition of what constitutes a "qualified" panel of experts is not as incendiary as the later redefinition of ghetto violence as a justified rebellion. Focusing too narrowly on such a progression, however, may distract us from the significance of

---

Many African American speakers in the 1960s, and especially those advocating Black Pride and Black Power, emphasized the need for African Americans to control the language that was used to talk about them. As Carmichael argued, "the first need of a free people is to be able to define their own terms and have those terms recognized by their oppressors."

---

reiterated in *Black Power* when the authors observed: "Those who have the right to define are the masters of the situation."

If Carmichael had merely observed the need for self-definition, then his rhetoric might not have been so controversial. But the definitions that he offered to his audiences often challenged the status quo. Examples of these redefinitions occur frequently in Carmichael's public address. Writing in *The New Republic* in January 1966, Carmichael critiqued the common practice of appointing committees of "qualified" experts to study the causes of riots or poverty, because such tactics separated the "qualified" from the "unqualified" and then silenced the latter. In *The New York Review of Books*, Carmichael redefined "integration," declaring that "integration is a subterfuge for the maintenance of white supremacy" because it entails a belief "that in order to have a

this rhetorical strategy itself: Carmichael attempted to redefine the civil rights struggle from the ground up.

The rhetoric of redefinition is evident in *Black Power*. The book begins, for example, with a careful definition of "racism" as "the predication of decisions and policies on considerations of race for the purpose of *subordinating* a racial group and maintaining control over that group." Such a definition might not seem out of place in a scholarly treatise, but as it is developed, its more radical tinge becomes evident. The authors distinguish between two types of racism, *individual* and *institutional*, and then introduce perhaps the most controversial definition of the book: "institutional racism has another name: colonialism." This definition is developed through an extended analogy in which Carmichael and Hamilton list multiple points of comparison between the Black ghettos in the heart of American cities and colonies in Africa and elsewhere. "It is more than a figure of speech," they conclude, "to say that the Negro community in America is the victim of white imperialism and colonial exploitation."

The distinction between individual and institutional racism is an example of a second important element that characterized Carmichael's rhetoric. Often, in his speeches, Carmichael presented two opposed terms which he argued were essential to understanding a given issue or controversy; then he defined each term carefully and often in fine detail; and finally he demonstrated how using these two terms as an analytical lens reveals one course of action as singularly desirable. In this way, Carmichael presented to his audiences a well-ordered view of the world in which there exist stark choices among distinct options. This is a rhetoric of great potential power, able perhaps to appeal both to black audiences growing increasingly suspicious about the degree of collusion between the government and the civil rights movement, and to white audiences facing confusing upheavals in the social order.

Writing in *The New Republic* in January 1966, Carmichael argued that "our [American] society is *exclusive* while maintaining that it is *inclusive.*" By this he meant that we like to believe that everyone can "make it," but in reality the only three ways to do so are "by having money, by knowing the right people, and by education." The implication, of course, is that to understand American culture, we need to suppress our urge to describe the nation as inclusive, and instead elevate the truth that our nation is exclusive. In his Berkeley speech, he critiqued a differentiation that he believed characterized the dominant ideology: "Their one rationalization is that the rest of the world is uncivilized and they are in fact civilized. But the West is un-civ-i-lized." (The hyphens show how Carmichael drew this word out for emphasis.) Again, the implication is that to understand and resist the ideology of the dominant white culture, we need to reverse our understanding of "civilized" and "uncivilized." In a speech delivered on February 17, 1968, at a benefit birthday party for Black Panther Huey Newton, Carmichael argued that "there are two types of oppression. One is exploitation, and the other is colonization. And we

have to understand the difference between them." Poor whites are exploited, Carmichael explained, but "*We* are colonized." In an address to the Organization of Arab Students, titled "The Black American and Palestinian Revolutions," Carmichael offered a differentiation with particularly radical implications, between "the Black militant" and "the Black revolutionary": "The black militant is one who yells and screams about the evils of the American system, himself trying to become a part of that system. The Black revolutionary's cry is not that he is excluded, but that he wants to destroy, overturn, and completely demolish the American system and start with a new one that allows humanity to flow." For Carmichael, of course, the day of the Black militant had passed and the day of the Black revolutionary had arrived. In a speech to the student body at the historically Black North Carolina A&T University in Greensboro, North Carolina, he made it plain: "We need more black revolutionaries and less militants."

This strategy of differentiation recurs throughout Carmichael's speeches and reinforces a central theme of his oratory: that a broad and flexible approach, and a willingness to entertain even radical options as live possibilities, present the best prospects for success. In his speech at North Carolina A&T, he carefully differentiated between "metaphysical philosophy" and "dialectical philosophy," and declared metaphysical philosophy "archaic" because it is dialectical philosophy "that deals with opposites." Such a philosophy is needed, Carmichael argued, in order to account for and enlist a broader range of human emotion—"if you love you must at least have the capacity to hate." A philosophy that opens onto the whole gamut of human emotion has the potential to empower the people most fully. In a pamphlet titled *The Pitfalls of Liberalism*, published in 1969, he differentiated between *legaliz-ing* and *legitimating* violence. Though the United States possessed the power to legalize violence in Vietnam, for example, "I may never legitimize it in my own mind." Similarly, though Carmichael did not have the power to legalize violence against "white policemen who terrorize black communities," he had legitimated it in his mind. And the implication, as always, is that Black people should invest less energy in attempting to alter the legalization of things, and more energy in legitimating actions that might lead toward freedom. In that same pamphlet, Carmichael criticized liberals for not understanding "the difference between influence and power," so that they mistakenly seek "influence rather than power." He used the example of the labor movement, saying that it was able to *influence* the passage of various acts of legislation, but lacked the *power* needed to implement and enforce that legislation. The present crisis, for Carmichael, required power rather than mere influence.

And in a speech delivered at Morehouse College, after he had moved to Guinea, Carmichael set *attitude* and *ideology* in distinction. He credited Martin Luther King with developing an "attitude . . . of confrontation," which was well-suited to his historical circumstances. As an example of ideology, on the other hand, he presented the Black Muslims. "They have discipline because they have the same ideology. . . . An ideology is merely a cohesive force, a set of principles, a set of beliefs that tell us where we're going, what our goals are, and what we hope to achieve." For Carmichael, the time for mere attitudes had passed, and the time for ideology had arrived.

Interestingly, this recurrent rhetorical strategy of distinguishing between opposites is not strongly evident in *Black Power*. Its most significant occurrence has already been noted; Carmichael differentiates individual and institutional racisms so that institutional racism can be aligned with colonialism. Why antithetical pairings are not as much in evidence in *Black Power* is not clear. It might be because the rhetorical strategy of distinct opposition is more useful or appropriate to an oral medium, since it provides an audience hearing a speech with clear organizational categories. Or perhaps this strategy, so characteristic of Carmichael's oral rhetoric, was muted through the collaborative process of writing a two-author book. Most likely, *Black Power* is a more scholarly coloration of Carmichael's chameleon-like style, and stark distinctions would be jarring within this stylistic context. The book lacks much of the radical attitude and revolutionary energy of Carmichael's oratory.

Black Power consists of eight chapters and an afterword; recent editions also contain a preface and additional afterword written in 1992 by Carmichael and Hamilton. It seems to follow, in its structure, an outline very much like many of Carmichael's speeches: the first three chapters develop a theoretical framework; the next four chapters present detailed case studies intended to illustrate that framework; and the last chapter and original afterword lay out a plan of action and an emotional motivational appeal. The case studies detailed in chapters 4 through 7 include discussions of the Mississippi Freedom Democratic Party; the voter registration drive in Lowndes County, Alabama; the problematic history of the Tuskegee Civic Association; and, finally, the volatility of the Black ghettos. All of these topics, along with many of the specific arguments and examples, are familiar from Carmichael's speeches—with the exception of the chapter on Tuskegee, which is based on Hamilton's experiences and research.

On closer inspection, however, a significant difference between *Black Power* and Carmichael's oratory becomes evident. The last chapter of the book in particular takes the argument in a novel direction. This chapter supplies a list of specific actions, all of which involve working within the existing system rather than radically reconstructing it. For example, the authors urge tenement residents to "form cohesive organizations—unions—to act in their common interest vis-à-vis the absentee slumlord." They suggest a "community rebate plan" in which Black people would refuse to do business with any business owners "who did not agree to 'reinvest,' say, forty to fifty percent of his net profit in the indigenous community." And the Black people in the ghettos should "form independent party groups to elect their own choices to office when and where they can." It is true that significant social and cultural effects would follow, in 1967 as in the present, from successfully organizing African American ghetto residents, from boycotting exploitative ghetto businesses, and from electing more African Americans to political office. But it must also be recognized that these goals are far removed from Carmichael's justification of violence against ghetto shop owners and his declaration, in the very last sentence of *Stokely Speaks*, that "We are not afraid of the inevitable bloodshed, for beyond it we see victory in the air." In his 1992 afterword,

Carmichael acknowledges the reformist nature of *Black Power*: "A great deal of hostility greeted the book upon its publication," he remembers. "This was most surprising. The book does not advocate Revolution. It preaches reform."

When the book is read against Carmichael's oratory, the more scholarly and reformist tone of *Black Power* is clear. Depending on one's point of view, it may be disappointing. But it may also have been strategic. *Black Power* was intended for an audience different from that which came to hear Carmichael speak. While those who sought out his public oratorical performances might be assumed to be largely sympathetic, no parallel presumption could be made regarding the audience for the book. Also, further differences between a written and an oral medium may be partially responsible. While oratory traditionally is crafted to address a specific and time-bound situation, written treatises more commonly address larger and more persistent issues. In either case, Stokely Carmichael continues to have much to say to us today.

Despite the fact that he was influential in the United States for only a few years, Carmichael was one of the most important African American rhetors of the American civil rights era. He was present at, and an active participant in, several of the most significant developments within the movement. He participated in nonviolent resistance in the form of sit-ins, Freedom Rides, voter registration drives, and marches. He was beaten and jailed as a part of the great effort to awaken the moral conscience of white America. Then he became an eloquent and representative voice for those who, like him, slowly evolved from endorsing nonviolent efforts to achieve integration to sympathizing with a more militant separatism. As the war in Vietnam wore on, and it became clear that young African Americans were fighting and dying there in disproportionate numbers, he helped to articulate the connection between racism and war. He was coauthor of one of the most widely read books on race relations published during the era; although it lacked the revolutionary fervor of much of his oratory, it still provoked tremendous reaction, and its meaning and impact are still debated today. And as African American consciousness began to encompass a solidarity with people of African descent the world over, Pan-African ideals began to permeate his discourse. Truly, to study the rhetoric of Stokely Carmichael is to study the discourse of an era.

INFORMATION SOURCES

Research Collections and Collected Speeches

The most important and widely available collection of Stokely Carmichael's speeches is *Stokely Speaks*. There has been no other major attempt to collect and publish Carmichael's oratory or to gather it at a single location. Other anthologies listed below each include one speech delivered by Carmichael, and the videotape is widely available. The book *Black Power* is an essential component of Carmichael's rhetorical project.

Andrews, James R., and David Zarefsky. *Contemporary American Voices: Significant Speeches in American History, 1945–Present* [*CAV*]. New York: Longman, 1992.

Carmichael, Stokely. *Stokely Speaks* [*SS*], ed. Ethel N. Minor. New York: Random House, 1971.

Carmichael, Stokely, and Charles V. Hamilton. *Black Power: The Politics of Liberation* [*BP*]. New York: Random House, 1967. Republished, with additional preface and afterwords by the authors. New York: Vintage Books, 1992.

Rohler, Lloyd E., and Roger Cook, comps. *Great Speeches for Criticism and Analysis* [*GSCA*], 2nd ed. Greenwood, Ind.: Alistair Press, 1993.

Audiovisual Materials

Great Speeches [*GS*], vol. 8. Greenwood, Ind.: Educational Video Group, 1992.

Selected Critical Studies

Brockriede, Wayne, and Robert L. Scott. "Stokely Carmichael: Two Speeches on Black Power." *Central States Speech Journal* 19 (1968): 3–13.

Gallagher, Victoria J. "Black Power in Berkeley: Postmodern Constructions in the Rhetoric of Stokely Carmichael." *Quarterly Journal of Speech* 87 (2001): 144–57.

Gregg, Richard B., A. Jackson McCormack, and Douglas J. Pedersen. "The Rhetoric of Black Power: A Street-Level Interpretation." *Quarterly Journal of Speech* 55 (1969): 151–60.

Scott, Robert L., and Wayne Brockriede. *The Rhetoric of Black Power*. New York: Harper & Row, 1969.

Stewart, Charles J. "The Evolution of a Revolution: Stokely Carmichael and the Rhetoric of Black Power." *Quarterly Journal of Speech* 83 (1997): 429–46.

Biography

Carmichael, Stokely, and Ekwueme Michael Thelwell. *Ready for Revolution: The Life and Struggles of Stokely Carmichael.* New York: Scribner's, 2003.

CHRONOLOGY OF MAJOR SPEECHES

See "Research Collections and Collected Speeches" for source codes.

"Who Is Qualified?" (delivered at several times and locations as an address). *New Republic*, January 8, 1966. *SS*, pp. 9–16.

"Power and Racism" (delivered at several times and locations as an address). *New York Review of Books*, September 1966. *SS*, pp. 17–30.

"Toward Black Liberation" (delivered at several times and locations as an address). *The Massachusetts Review*, September 1966. *SS*, pp. 31–43.

"Berkeley Speech." Berkeley, Calif., October 1966. *SS*, pp. 45–60; *CAV*, pp. 100–7.

"At Morgan State." Baltimore, Md., January 28, 1967. *SS*, pp. 61–76.

"We Ain't Going" (address at Tougaloo College). Jackson, Miss., April 11, 1967. *GSCA*, pp. 58–62.

"The Dialectics of Liberation" (address to the Congress on the Dialectics of Liberation). London, July 18, 1967. *SS*, pp. 77–100.

"Free Huey" (address to the benefit birthday party for Huey P. Newton). Oakland, Calif., February 17, 1968. *SS*, pp. 111–30.

"The Black American and Palestinian Revolutions" (address to the Organization of Arab Students convention). Ann Arbor, Mich., August 25–31, 1968. *SS*, pp. 131–43.

"A New World to Build" (address at North Carolina A&T University). Greensboro, N.C., December 9, 1968. *SS*, pp. 145–64.

"The Pitfalls of Liberalism." *SS*, pp. 165–73.

"Pan-Africanism" (address at Morehouse College). Atlanta, Ga., April 1970. *SS*, pp. 183–220.

JAMES EARL "JIMMY" CARTER (1924–)
Thirty-ninth President of the United States

RICHARD W. LEEMAN

Jimmy Carter has always been considered more a communicator than an orator; someone who speaks publicly but not eloquently. Still, his public speaking career has been an enigma. In 1976 he was perceived as an extremely effective campaigner, a presidential candidate who came out of nowhere to win the Democratic nomination and then the presidency. His strategic use of organization, early campaigning, and focus on the early primaries to become the early favorite has remained a model for little-known presidential hopefuls. Yet the rhetorical style that served him so well in the campaign, failed as presidential oratory, and Carter remains characterized as one of the least effective modern presidents, with a substantial portion of the blame laid at his oratorical door. His public speaking regularly failed to move the public, emotionally or politically. Yet his postpresiden-

tial career has been luminous, and he is generally considered one of the finest former presidents we have had. His speaking has again played a central role in framing the public's appreciation of Jimmy Carter.

Carter came to the presidency with a background quite different from other modern presidents and presidential aspirants. Jimmy Carter was born in Plains, Georgia, and raised in nearby Archer. His father, James Earl Carter Sr., was a peanut farmer and a small businessman. His mother, Lillian Carter, was a registered nurse who in 1966, at the age of sixty-eight, joined the Peace Corps and served in India. Carter graduated from the U.S. Naval Academy in 1946, just after the close of World War II. He served as a submariner, and in the early 1950s he was assigned to help develop the Navy's nuclear-powered submarine fleet. Upon the death of his father in 1953, Carter resigned his commission as a lieutenant and took over the family farm and warehouse business. Active in community affairs, Carter ran for and was elected to the Georgia state senate in 1962. He lost his first gubernatorial campaign in 1966, but was elected governor in 1970. He based his campaign on the principles of clean government and the need for racial equality. Limited by state law to a single term as governor, in 1974 Carter became chairman of the Democratic National Congressional Campaign Committee. That December, he declared his candidacy for president of the United States. In a crowded field of Democratic contenders, Carter emerged early as the front runner and won the Democratic nomination in 1976. Attacking the Ford presidency as lackluster and the post-Watergate Republican Party as the party of corporations and corruption, Carter defeated Gerald Ford for the presidency by 297 electoral votes to 240. In his presidential campaign, he billed himself as a farmer, businessman, nuclear engineer, and former governor. He had neither Washington political experience nor a legal background. His campaign slogan, "Why Not the Best?," was taken from the title of his autobiography, and created high expectations for the first U.S. president from the Deep South since the Civil War.

THE PLAIN, MORAL SPEAKING OF JIMMY CARTER

Carter's oratorical roots lay in his background as an engineer, his extensive campaigning for governor and then president, and his religious faith. In *A Government as Good as Its People*, Carter estimated that he gave some 3,300 speeches as governor and presidential candidate. Missing from that total are the numerous speeches he delivered as a two-time campaigner for the governorship. According to his autobiographical accounts, Carter campaigned for governor just as he later did for president: by extensive and exhaustive traveling, speaking primarily to small and medium-sized audiences. Even as president, Carter felt more comfortable addressing small audiences; he particularly enjoyed question-and-answer periods. He did best when discussing specific policies; with more formal,

stylized speeches given to larger audiences or in front of a television camera, he was ill at ease. He also had difficulty articulating broad, cohesive political philosophy.

As a campaigner, Carter employed a plain style of rhetoric that suggested a man of sincerity, honesty, and quiet competence. His soft-spoken style complemented his direct promises and statements, such as "I will never lie to you" and "Why not the best?" Carter demonstrated his sincerity by incorporating references to his religious faith into his political rhetoric, startling many of his campaign audiences with straightforward pronouncements such as "I'm a devout Christian" and "The most important thing in my life is Jesus Christ." Carter confirmed his sincerity with unanticipated and often out-of-place smiles, as well as by a grammar marred by extended complex sentences, sentence fragments, and fractured syntax.

Carter's plain style was appropriate to the substance of his campaign message. His speeches developed two recurring themes: pragmatic realism and the idea that the people are a source of national strength. In the first, he frequently declared that choices are difficult, the world is complex, and success often is limited. This theme often led to unusual oratorical claims. For example, his 1976 acceptance speech, delivered July 15 in New York City, included the statement "Our party's not been perfect," hardly typical of convention rhetoric. Clearly, Carter borrowed some of this rhetoric of limits from Jerry Brown's "small is beautiful/less is more" campaign, but the general themes of limitation and pragmatic realism are also evident in his gubernatorial oratory.

The second theme in Carter's campaign was an almost mystical evocation of the *Volk* (the people), in which Carter portrayed Americans as the wellspring of goodness and morality. If only the Central Intelligence Agency had reflected the American people, he argued in his acceptance speech, it would not have marched down its foolish and immoral path. He had found his two years of campaigning a "humbling experience," for he had come to realize that power rests with the people, not the "power brokers." This concept of the people culminated in his claims that "it's time for the people to run the government and not the other way around" and that as president, he would try to form "a government as good as its people." Carter's rhetoric treated these dual themes of the world's complexity and the people's basic goodness and strength as complementary. As a presidential candidate, he claimed, "I recognize the difficulty," but "with your help" the difficulties could be met. When he said that "as president I want you to help me," he was not simply using a rhetorical trope. He was in fact calling upon the people to be the solution.

In 1976 this rhetoric worked well. After an era in which a "pay any price" approach had led to Vietnam and an imperial presidency had culminated in Watergate, Americans were willing to listen to an orator who talked of limits, honesty, basic morality, and quiet strength. Carter also enjoyed the advantage of running against a similarly plain-styled speaker.

To be sure, Carter's rhetoric did not meet with universal acclaim. He won in 1976 by a very close margin, and even during the campaign certain questions about him had been raised by the press and the public. Some people voiced concern about his religion and how it might affect his work as president. Some critics thought him overly moral and preachy, and others wondered what Carter really believed. The claim that he was trying to be all things to all people received extended play in the media. Still others complained that he made exaggerated claims. The media particularly criticized Carter's assertion that he would never lie and his biographical claim that he had been a nuclear physicist. Despite these reservations, the public accepted Carter as a sincere, honest, compassionate person who would guide the ship of state with a steady hand.

Carter's Inaugural Address, given in Washington, D.C., on January 20, 1977, and written almost entirely by him, pursued the theme of pragmatic realism. He argued that "even our great nation has its recognized limits and . . . we can neither answer all questions nor solve all problems." Instead, "we must simply do our best." Dramatically, and unexpectedly, Carter also proclaimed his limits as president. "I have no new dream," he said, "but rather urge a fresh faith in the old dream." These presidential lim-

its held a critical place in Carter's rhetoric because they underscored the importance of the people. "A President may sense and proclaim that new spirit, but only a people can provide it," Carter stated. Furthermore, he suggested that "your strength can compensate for my weakness, and your wisdom can help to minimize my mistakes." Critics noted not only the pronounced theme of limitations but also the awkwardness of the formulation. Strict parallel structure would change "help minimize my mistakes" to "compensate for my stupidity."

Both the domestic and the foreign press noted the brevity and spiritual flavor of the Inaugural Address. The speech was "notably lacking in the kind of idealistic fervor and self-certainty one associates with the 1960's and early 1970's," wrote the *Washington Post*. Contrasting Carter's and Kennedy's inaugural addresses, the *Times* of London judged that although Carter's speech lacked idealism, it was widely perceived to be a "moralistic speech," "spiritual in tone," one granting almost "mystical properties" to the "American people." In general, the U.S. and European press reacted in much the same fashion as the *New York Times*, which noted that there was "nothing memorable" in the speech, but "we liked the melody"; Americans would have to wait and see how his presidency performed. Interestingly, these commentaries echoed those of Georgia's press on his gubernatorial Inaugural Address six years earlier. In 1971, a leading columnist for the *Atlanta Constitution* wrote, "Frankly, the state will not know for several months which is the real Carter. There are clues leading in all directions."

Throughout his four years as president, Carter pursued his major theme of pragmatic realism, which emphasized the complexity of the world and the resulting limits on what can be accomplished. He cautioned repeatedly that "these measures will not be easy, nor will they be popular"; "there are no easy answers"; and "to be secure we must face the world as it is." Even the January 23, 1980, announcement of the Carter Doctrine, which emphatically drew the line against further Soviet expansion, included a caveat: "Our material resources, great as they are, are limited. Our problems are too complex for simple slogans or for quick solutions. We cannot solve them without effort and sacrifice." His penchant for realism led Carter to make unexpected admissions while president, just as he had as campaigner. As a presidential contender, he revealed that he had lusted in his heart. As president, in his April 18, 1977, speech "The Moral Equivalent of War," nationally televised form Washington, D.C., he offered candidly that "many of you have suspected that some supplies of oil and gas are being withheld. . . . You may be right, but suspicions about the oil companies cannot change the fact that we are running out of petroleum." For a president to admit that he did not know something as significant as the withholding of oil supplies—in a prepared speech, not an extemporaneous press conference—speaks tellingly of Carter's candor: it was a kind of painful honesty. In his "New Foreign Policy" address, a commencement speech at Notre Dame on May 22, 1977, he reported, "We are trying to get other nations, both free and otherwise, to join us in this effort." A rhetor less concerned with accuracy and more attentive to the image of leadership would have reworded that sentence, perhaps saying "We call on all nations to join us in this effort," as John Kennedy had in his Inaugural Address.

Carter's theme of realism reached its apex in his August 14, 1980, acceptance speech in New York, in which he noted, "I'm wiser tonight than I was four years ago. . . . I think I'll be a better president in the next four years just continuing what we are doing." He left to the electorate the task of deciphering what it was we were "continuing" that would make us better, and to wonder whether perhaps there was not a better method for educating a person to be president. Yet Carter's declaration of being wiser echoed a similar claim in his 1976 acceptance speech—that he had learned much while campaigning. What sounded impressive coming from a campaigner, however, raised eyebrows when enunciated by a president.

Similarly, Carter continued to place his faith in the *Volk*. His energy speeches called for sacrifice and effort by the ordinary person. His foreign policy was "rooted in our moral values, which never change." The Panama Canal treaties should be passed, he argued from the Oval Office on February 1, 1978, because they were fair and Americans were essentially a great, generous, strong, and fair people. "We have profound moral commitments," he told the Congress, "which are deeply rooted in our values as a people." Although most politicians and all presidents pay lip service to the myth of the people, Carter seems to have had a deep and abiding faith in it. Both the pervasiveness of the myth in his rhetoric and the substantive ways in which the myth was involved in his speeches suggest this conclusion. Additionally, his faith in the people seemed to resonate with his Christian belief in basic human goodness.

If, however, people are created in God's image, they also sin. In his "Moral Equivalent of War" speech, Carter argued that Americans must change their energy consumption habits. "We must not be selfish or timid," he argued, implying quite clearly that Americans had been both. Indeed, later in the speech he declared that to continue present policy would be simply to "drift along." His "Crisis of Confidence" speech exemplifies this predicament in which Carter placed himself. When he argued that the solution would be discovered within the people themselves, he implied logically that the root of the problem could be found there as well. When Carter said that his successes would be the people's successes, he invited them to consider his failures as their failures. In the summer of 1979, Carter went to Camp David to revitalize his energy program but ended up contemplating his presidency. Upon his return to Washington, he delivered his July 15 "Crisis of Confidence" speech, in which he not only apologized for his own failures but also told the public that as a moral community they had failed, too. One of the problems, Carter claimed, was that they were not confident enough. A second problem was that "too many of us now tend to worship self-indulgence and consumption." "Why," he wondered, "have we not been able to get together as a nation to resolve our serious energy problem?" This dualistic view of the people was not new in the Carter presidency. His celebrated "Law Day" speech, delivered in Athens, Georgia, at the University of Georgia Law School on May 4, 1974, inveighed against the special interests and warned of the selfishness of the people. It also contained the seeds of his "Crisis of Confidence" speech. Even his 1976 acceptance speech cautioned that "all of us must be careful not to cheat each other," and he used his Farewell Address to issue, once more, a warning against such selfishness.

Carter combined the themes of selfishness and limits to suggest a kind of minimalism: for example, "Because this is not a mandatory control plan, I cannot stop irresponsible corporations from raising . . . prices or a selfish group of employees from using its power to demand excessive wages." Addressing U.S. energy policy, Carter insisted that "once again, the selfishness of the few will block action which is badly needed to help our entire nation . . . unless you speak out." Repeatedly, Carter's speeches sprang from a native dislike, or distrust, of rhetoric. James Fallows, Carter's leading speechwriter for the first two years of his administration, claimed that Carter "didn't think it was important to give effective speeches." He apparently thought that sincerity was sufficient, that rhetoric was simply embellishment which at its worst obscured reality. As a result, he spurned many of the rhetorical practices that other presidents had used faithfully. For example, he generally avoided extensive speech rehearsal. He first read the speech into a cassette, played it back, and then read it once more. Reportedly he bristled when his speaking style was criticized. While he practiced extensively for his debates with Gerald Ford, he was too busy with presidential duties to do the same for the debate against Ronald Reagan.

James Fallows made famous the claim that "Carter thinks in lists, not arguments." According to Fallows, when Carter edited a speech, he generally cut the explanatory and argumentative material and replaced it with what he considered "meat," which was presented in a list of topics. Carter's speeches were in fact often a compilation of lists. The "Moral Equivalent of War" laid out six guidelines for foreign policy; the speech for the Panama Canal treaties unfolded in a question-and-answer format. The problem with this style was not simply that Carter had many lists, but that his method of arranging the lists often seemed haphazard. In "New Foreign Policy," he appended three minor goals regarding China, Latin America, and South Africa after he presented his six guidelines—almost as if those goals were afterthoughts. The Panama Canal

speech revealed similar problems. Carter appeared to have given no thought to the order of the questions and answers. In his speech following the failed mission to rescue the U.S. hostages in Iran, Carter accurately identified the major arguments, criticisms, and questions that would arise, and answered them. To hear the speech, however, was to listen to a series of responses answering a set of implied questions. The speech lacked an overall vision of the United States, the hostages, and Iran. Where other rhetors would have more dramatically focused attention toward a "criminal Iran," Carter merely declared that the United States would "continue to hold . . . Iran responsible." The lack of an overall vision was endemic to Carter's oratory. According to Fallows, for a major address that was to clarify the U.S. foreign policy direction, Carter essentially coupled together two memos: one by his hawkish foreign policy adviser Zbigniew Brzezinski and one by the far more conciliatory Secretary of State Cyrus Vance. The resulting speech sounded almost schizophrenic.

Carter's language reflected his concern with reality and limitations and his lack of concern with rhetoric. His speeches were written in complex sentences, many beginning with conjunctions. By using the passive voice, Carter divorced himself linguistically from events that, he thus implied, were beyond his control. For example, in his Panama Canal treaties speech, he equivocated: "What they regard as the last vestige of alleged American colonialism is being removed." Carter also strove for a rhetoric of realism through an informality of expression. He frequently used commonplaces such as "the first thing I would like to do," "I'm glad to announce to you," "you can see this is a vital and continuing process," and "these efforts will cost money, a lot of money." His Inauguration Day walk down Pennsylvania Avenue, his wearing a cardigan sweaters while delivering speeches, and his softball games manifested his informality. At times his inclination to express ideas colloquially worked effectively in his speeches. In the speech on the Panama Canal Treaty, he rejected the "we bought it, it's ours" argument on the ground that the United States had been making annual payments to Panama since the canal's opening. As Carter phrased it, "You do not pay rent on your own land." On other occasions his taste for the informal resulted in problems. Hamilton Jordan notes that before his debate with Reagan, Carter discussed using the "Amy and nuclear war" anecdote about a conversation in which his twelve-year-old daughter, Amy, had discussed her concerns about nuclear war. Carter felt that the conversation illustrated the poignancy of the issue; his advisers correctly predicted that the public would perceive it as trite and preachy.

This is not to say that Carter never used figures of speech or attempted formal diction; however, his syntactical and semantic proclivities frequently made the trope or scheme less than effective. Carter's use of hyperbole was particularly unfortunate. Scarcely two hours after his advisers had discussed with him his tendency to exaggerate, Carter said, "I want to thank Chancellor Schmidt [of West Germany] for the superb welcome they've given us. I've never met any other world leader who has been of more assistance." On New Year's Eve in 1978, Carter toasted the Shah of Iran, saying, "And there is no leader with whom I have a deeper sense of personal gratitude and personal friendship." One year later the Shah had been deposed, and the Iranian people remembered well the "devil Carter's" friendliness with him. Carter also used hyperbole to heighten the public's perception of a problem. The energy crisis was therefore the "greatest challenge our country will face during our lifetime"; the Soviet invasion of Afghanistan was the "most serious threat to peace since the Second World War." His use of exaggeration to draw distinctions between himself and Reagan led to charges of meanness in the 1980 campaign.

Carter's delivery also reinforced his theme of pragmatic realism. Observations in the press almost universally recognized this characteristic. They repeatedly noted that he was somber and soft-spoken, avoided histrionics with a reflective tone, was serious and unsmiling, and spoke in a determined fashion, attempting to convince more by persuasion than by exhortation. While generally content with his delivery, however, the press almost invariably asked whether Carter would be able to accomplish what his oratory had set on the table.

In most regards, Jimmy Carter's postpresiden-

tial public speaking has been strikingly similar to his presidential oratory. As it had during his presidential campaign, that style of discourse has served him well enough. The man who is widely regarded as one of the least effective presidents in modern times is just as widely considered a model former president. Primarily, Jimmy Carter's postpresidential reputation rests upon his deeds rather than his oratory. Since his defeat in 1980, the former president has established the Carter Center in Atlanta, Georgia; become the best-known spokesman for Habitat for Humanity; acted as a presidential emissary for peace to Haiti; and received the Nobel Peace Prize. The Carter Center, especially, has come to be recognized as a potent vehicle for the advocacy of peace and health issues in the developing countries, and as a nonpartisan oversight agency for certifying the democratic legitimacy of elections.

Jimmy Carter's public speaking on behalf of these causes has, like his presidential speaking, been marked by strong moral commitments and forthright honesty. He candidly pointed out to his Nobel Lecture audience in Oslo, Norway, that "I worship Jesus Christ," and he concluded a 1999 speech to the Global Health Council with the declaration "That's my prayer." When appropriate, Carter does not explicitly reference his Christianity. No specific reference is made to his particular religious beliefs in his speech accepting the Distinguished Graduate Award from the U.S. Naval Academy, nor is one found in his "Address to the People of Cuba," delivered in Havana on May 14, 2002. Seeking to forge common ground between Cuba and the United States, the latter speech contains the strong moral overtones and the confessional appeals that often marked his presidential speaking. "The hard truth," he told his television audience, "is that neither the United States nor Cuba has managed to define a positive and beneficial relationship." After discussing the U.S. embargo and the issue of Cuban refugees, Carter grounded his major appeal in morality, but without overt Christian references. Cuba, he argued, needed to embrace democracy and human rights. "My nation is hardly perfect in human rights," he confessed, to the consternation of many moderate and conservative critics. But he also lectured the Cubans: "Cuba has adopted a socialist government where one political party dominates, and people are not permitted to organize any opposition movements. Your constitution recognizes freedom of speech and association, but other laws deny these freedoms to those who disagree with the government." Only a Cuban commitment to democracy, he concluded, would permit full normalization of relations.

As president, Jimmy Carter included frequent autobiographical references in his oratory. His speeches since 1981 have accentuated that practice, replete with personal references to both his presidential and postpresidential years. "When I was involuntarily retired in 1980 as a result of election," he told his Global Health Council audience, "I went back home as one of the youngest survivors of the White House office. . . . [My wife and I have] now visited more than 115 nations in the world since we've left the White

individual, a child, a mother, who suffers from a completely curable or preventable disease, or who suffers from malnutrition when the means of producing food is available.

Other personal references are only slightly less autobiographical, such as remembering Anwar Sadat and Yitzak Rabin in the opening of his Nobel Lecture, or discussing his recent visit to China in his speech celebrating Habitat for Humanity's twenty-fifth anniversary. Carter has always presented his vision to the audience through the prism of his own life, and he continues to do so as former president.

Carter has remained relatively plain-spoken in his oratory, even in those situations where eloquence might be expected or at least excused. His Nobel Lecture, for example, is a series of observations regarding peace in our world. In

---

Only three U.S. presidents have received the Nobel Peace Prize: Theodore Roosevelt, for negotiating the Russian–Japanese Peace Treaty; Woodrow Wilson, for his work establishing the League of Nations; and Jimmy Carter, for his international efforts to promote peace, democracy, and human rights. Of those three presidents, only Jimmy Carter received the award for his postpresidential work.

House, concentrating mostly on the poorest nations on Earth where people are still deprived of things that we daily take for granted." He often contrasts his presidential life with his life as a former president. As he described it later in his Global Health Council speech:

I have changed my total life's commitment from being the president of a great nation, even a superpower, to working in the Carter Center, where half, more than half, of our total personnel and funding goes into health. And this is not an accident. I'm still deeply committed to peace. I'm still deeply committed to human rights. I'm still deeply committed to freedom and democracy, and environmental quality like I always was, but now I've learned that the key to all these major challenges to the human race depends to a great degree on the health of an

that speech he addresses the weapons race, democracy, the role of the United Nations in pursuing peace, the "scourge of racism," and the importance of reducing the "growing chasm between the richest and the poorest people on earth." In the style typical of Carter, it is an earnest speech, but not a moving one. Other ceremonial speeches, such as the one when he accepted the U.S. Naval Academy Distinguished Graduate Award or the speech marking Habitat's anniversary, presented similar invitations to eloquence. The former, however, was a brief, personal reminiscence of association with the Navy, and the latter, although unified around a theme of confronting crisis, was unable to settle upon a single, elegant message.

Jimmy Carter's rhetoric has typically demonstrated the honesty, sincerity, and compassion that led to his election in 1976. By the end of his presidency, however, his rhetoric of morality and reality was describing a continuing energy problem, a painful hostage crisis, and a weak economy. Rather than creating an image of leadership, his rhetoric of the people and his message that the people were the solution came to imply that the people were the cause of the nation's problems. His plain style of rhetoric, with its accompanying informality and realism, gave a clearer sense of the present than a vision for the future. That same blend of realism with virtue that seemed to incapacitate him as a president, however, has stood him well since 1981. As a man of conscience confronting a world with its shortcomings, challenging it to do better, and leading by his own example, Jimmy Carter has used simple and direct public speaking that has fit the man and his mission.

INFORMATION SOURCES

Research Collections and Collected Speeches

The Jimmy Carter Presidential Library and Museum in Atlanta, Georgia, contains a variety of relevant materials and speeches. Archival holdings of speech drafts had not been fully cataloged as of this writing.

Carter, Jimmy. *A Government as Good as Its People* [*GGP*]. New York: Simon and Schuster, 1977.

———. *Public Papers of the President: Jimmy Carter* [*PP*]. 4 vols. Washington, D.C.: Government Printing Office, 1977–81.

Windt, Theodore. "Jimmy Carter." In *Presidential Rhetoric (1961–1980)* [*PR*], ed. Theodore Windt, 2nd ed. Dubuque, Iowa: Kendall/Hunt, 1980.

Web Site

The Jimmy Carter Presidential Library and Museum [*JCL*]. This Web site contains a sampling of important presidential speeches, as well as his "Law Day" speech in 1974 and his Nobel Lecture in 2002. http://www.jimmycarterlibrary.org

Audiovisual Material

There are no major audiovisual collections of Jimmy Carter's speeches. Some audio recordings can be accessed from the Jimmy Carter Presidential Library and Museum Web site.

Selected Critical Studies

Bitzer, Lloyd, and Theodore Rueter. *Carter vs. Ford: The Counterfeit Debates of 1976.* Madison: University of Wisconsin Press, 1980.

Hahn, Dan F. "Flailing the Profligate: Carter's Energy Sermon of 1979." *Presidential Studies Quarterly* 10 (1980): 583–87.

———. "The Rhetoric of Jimmy Carter, 1976–1980." *Presidential Studies Quarterly* 14 (1984): 265–88.

Hahn, Dan F., and J. Justin Gustainis. "Anatomy of an Enigma: Jimmy Carter's State of the Union Address." *Communication Quarterly* 33 (1985): 43–49.

Jamieson, Kathleen Hall. *Packaging the Presidency.* New York: Oxford University Press, 1984.

Patton, John H. "A Government as Good as Its People: Jimmy Carter and the Restoration of Transcendence to Politics." *Quarterly Journal of Speech* 63 (1977): 249–57.

Sudol, Ronald A. "The Rhetoric of Strategic Retreat: Carter and the Panama Canal Debate." *Quarterly Journal of Speech* 65 (1979): 379–91.

Selected Biographies

Carter, Jimmy. *Keeping Faith: Memoirs of a President.* New York: Bantam Books, 1982.

———. *Why Not the Best?* Nashville, Tenn.: Broadman Press, 1975.

Fallows, James. "A Passionless Presidency." *Atlantic Monthly*, May 1979, pp. 33–48, and June 1979, pp. 75–81.

Johnson, Haynes Bonner. *In the Absence of Power.* New York: Viking Press, 1980.

Jordan, Hamilton. *Crisis: The Last Year of the Carter Presidency.* New York: Putnam, 1982.

Powell, Jody. *The Other Side of the Story.* New York: Morrow, 1984.

CHRONOLOGY OF MAJOR SPEECHES

See "Research Collections and Collected Speeches" for source codes.

"Law Day Speech." Athens, Ga., May 4, 1974. *GGP*, pp. 30–42 (edited); *JCL*.

"Announcement Speech." Washington, D.C., December 12, 1974. *Atlanta Constitution*, December 13, 1974, p. 18A; *GGP*, pp. 43–50 (edited).

"Acceptance Speech." New York City, July 15, 1976. *GGP*, pp. 125–34.

"Inaugural Address." Washington, D.C., January 20, 1977. *PP*, vol. I, pp. 1–4; *JCL*.

"Report to the American People" (first fireside chat). Washington, D.C., February 2, 1977. *PP*, vol. I, pp. 69–77.

"The Energy Problem" ("The Moral Equivalent of War"). Washington, D.C., April 18, 1977. *PP*, vol. I, pp. 656–62; *PR*, pp. 238–42.

"A New Foreign Policy." South Bend, Ind., May 22, 1977. *PP*, vol. I, pp. 954–62; *PR*, pp. 242–47.

"The Panama Canal Treaties." Washington, D.C., February 1, 1978. *PP*, vol. II, pp. 258–63; *PR*, pp. 248–53.

"Address on the Camp David Agreement." Washington, D.C., September 18, 1978. *PP*, vol. II, pp. 1533–37; *PR*, pp. 254–58.

"Salt II." Washington, D.C., June 18, 1979. *PP*, vol. III, pp. 1087–92; *PR*, pp. 258–63.

"Energy and National Goals" ("A Crisis of Confidence"). Washington, D.C., July 15, 1979. *PP*, vol. III, pp. 1235–41; *PR*, pp. 264–70.

"State of the Union" (Carter Doctrine), Washington, D.C., January 23, 1980. *PP*, vol. IV, pp. 194–200; *PR*, pp. 270–76; *JCL*.

"Address on the Iranian Rescue Attempt." Washington, D.C., April 25, 1980. *PP*, vol. IV, pp. 772–73; *PR*, pp. 276–78.

"Acceptance Speech." New York City, August 14, 1980. *PP*, vol. IV, pp. 1532–40.

"Farewell Address." Washington, D.C., January 14, 1981. *PP*, vol. IV, pp. 2889–93; *JCL*.

"Speech to the Global Health Council." June 20–22, 1999. Available at http://www.globalhealth.org/

"Speech at Habitat's 25th Anniversary Celebration." Indianapolis, Ind., September 15, 2001. Available at http://www.habitat.org/how/25th/carterindy.html

"Address to the HIV/AIDS Summit 2002." Abuja, Nigeria, March 9, 2002. Available at http://www.gatesfoundation.org/

"Faith-Based Groups Confronting HIV/AIDS." Abuja, Nigeria, March 10, 2002. Available at http://www.gatesfoundation.org/

"Address to the People of Cuba." Havana, May 14, 2002. Available at http://www.amaericanrhetoric.com/speeches/jimmycartercubaspeech.htm

"Acceptance Speech" (for Distinguished Graduate of the U.S. Naval Academy Award). October 12, 2002. Available at http://www.usna.com/

"Nobel Lecture." Oslo, Norway, December 10, 2002. *JCL*. Available at http://www.nobel.se/peace/laureates/2002/carter-lecture.html

CESAR ESTRADA CHAVEZ (1927–1993)
Labor Leader and Civil Rights Activist

JOHN C. HAMMERBACK AND RICHARD J. JENSEN

By the time of his death in 1993, Cesar Chavez had achieved stature matched by few in recent American history. President Clinton eulogized him as "an authentic hero to millions of people throughout the world," while newspaper reports of his death described a "charismatic 1960s hero," "a folk legend," and "a symbol of social justice." Such praise seemed fitting for a man who accomplished what almost all knowledgeable observers had predicted would be impossible: establishing the first permanent union of farmworkers, then achieving a startling string of victories including contracts with major growers, collective-bargaining legislation for farmworkers, and a 70 percent increase in real wages for farmworkers from 1964 to 1980, with such benefits as health and disability insurance and a credit union. California immortalized Chavez by bestowing the rare honor of a state holiday to honor him and his life's work.

Cesar Chavez's early life prepared him well for the daunting challenges he would face as a leader and a rhetor. He was born on March 31, 1927, in Yuma, Arizona, near his family's farm. The enterprising Chavezes, who operated several businesses, lost their land and businesses during the Great Depression and became migrant workers following the crops in the Southwest. As wandering crop pickers, the family sometimes lived barely above subsistence level and often suffered the humiliation of racial discrimination.

The Chavez children had few opportunities for an adequate formal education, but young Cesar's informal education taught him much that would be indispensable in later years. Various family members spoke out against growers who mistreated their workers, provided personal aid and support to workers, and joined associations and unions of workers—organizations neither permanent nor successful until decades later, when Cesar made his indelible mark on labor history. From his early experiences, Chavez learned many important lessons—including the value of assertively confronting injustice, the mistakes to avoid when attempting to organize agricultural workers, and the ways of farmworkers and migrant workers.

After a variety of uninspiring and dead-end jobs, Chavez served in the Navy in World War II and married. Lacking focus in his life, he drifted into San Jose, California, and settled in a barrio called "Sal Si Puedes," an expression that translates roughly as "escape if you can." In the 1950s his apparently ordinary life began its transformation into the extraordinary when he discovered his purpose for being. Direction came from Father Donald McDonnell and Fred Ross, his two mentors in life as well as in labor organizing. Father McDonnell taught Chavez about social justice and the history of labor movements among farmworkers, and tutored him regarding the Roman Catholic Church's teachings on the need for supporting workers and promoting moral causes. Fred Ross, a long-time activist and organizer, enlisted Chavez in the Community Services Organization (CSO), a community organizing group for Mexican Americans that was sponsored by Saul Alinsky's Chicago-based Industrial Areas Foundation. While rising to a leadership position in the CSO, Chavez grew increasingly frustrated that the group would not organize farmworkers. In 1962 he left the CSO to take up the monumental challenge of establishing the nation's first permanent union of farmworkers.

In the early spring of 1962, Chavez moved to Delano, in California's fertile San Joaquin Valley, to begin a quest that almost every labor leader considered impossible. Their reasons seemed sound: California farmworkers typically had been illiterate, indigent, and migratory; and the multibillion-dollar agribusiness industry, possessing formidable political, economic, and social power, had easily broken all previous unions. Further diminishing Chavez's prospects was his lack of coworkers, personal wealth, political influence, or formal education past the eighth grade. Yet, through preparation, perseverance, public address, and perhaps prayer, the quiet and unassuming Chavez would succeed where others had failed.

Chavez's reading of St. Thomas Aquinas, St. Paul, Gandhi, books on Mexican American history, and biographies of prominent labor leaders stimulated his intellectual growth and taught him means to move people to action. Winthrop Yinger, in *Cesar Chavez: The Rhetoric of Nonviolence*, reported that from St. Paul, Chavez learned the importance of face-to-face communication. As Chavez put it: "St. Paul must have been a terrific organizer, as he would go and talk with the people right in their homes, sit with them and be one of them."

Although Chavez was convinced that his unionizing career depended heavily upon his oratorical skills, the quiet and shy organizer felt awkward and nervous when speaking before groups. To overcome this weakness, he resolutely forced himself to speak at meetings and carefully identified avenues to rhetorical success and pitfalls of oratorical failure. In an interview published in the July 1966 issue of *Ramparts* magazine, he recalled often lying awake at night after a meeting, "going over the whole thing, playing the tape back, trying to see why people laugh at one point, or why they were for one thing or against another." Jacques Levy, in *Cesar Chavez: Autobiography of La Causa*, quotes Chavez as saying that "there are some very simple things that have to be done, certain key things that nobody can do without, like talking to people." As a CSO speaker, he also learned that clear illustrations and examples were more effective in communicating ideas than was philosophizing. According to biographer Peter Matthiessen, Chavez felt that to reach listeners, "you have to draw a simple picture and color it in."

The young labor leader's difficult and time-consuming work quickly bore fruit. In 1962 the National Farm Workers Association was founded in Fresno, California, with Chavez as president. From its beginning, the association, later to grow into a union named the United Farm Workers

(UFW), was closely identified with the civil rights movement and its techniques of aggressive nonviolence. As Chavez attracted national attention, the initially inept public speaker gained a reputation as the most persuasive union leader in a generation.

Chavez believed that his union was not yet ready for a major strike in 1965. Despite his conviction, however, he and his association of crop pickers joined a group of Filipino farmworkers in a bitter strike that would last for five years. That strike made Chavez a national figure, helped him create close relationships with powerful allies such as Senator Robert Kennedy and Walter Reuther of the United Auto Workers, and converted his union into a worthy cause for many student and liberal organizations throughout the country. During the strike he originated many innovative tactics, including a nationwide boycott of grapes, new methods of picketing, a well-publicized march from Delano to Sacramento, and the use of the fast as a means to solidify union members and their supporters behind a commitment to nonviolence.

In 1970, the UFW signed a series of contracts with grape growers. The crop pickers' euphoria soon gave way to fears of defeat by an unexpected antagonist. Reneging on its agreement not to organize field workers, the powerful Teamsters Union joined with the growers to challenge the UFW for workers in the lettuce, strawberry, and vegetable fields of the Salinas Valley. Chavez responded by extending the boycott to lettuce, and again sought help from outside allies. Eventually he signed contracts with growers and defeated the Teamsters, ending the first of many major battles with that union. That victory led to an increase in the UFW's membership. By 1972, the union had more than 30,000 workers and had formally affiliated with the AFL–CIO, thus increasing its prominence in American labor.

Chavez relied on his skills as a manager as well as a rhetor. He successfully consolidated the union's victories by building an infrastructure to implement contracts and initiating administrative changes, including moving UFW headquarters from Delano to La Paz, a former tuberculosis sanatorium in the mountains south of Bakersfield. Yet his primary commitment seemed to be his rhetorical discourse. The period from 1973 to 1983 placed Chavez and the UFW on a roller coaster of heady highs and demoralizing lows. In 1973, after the Teamsters again leagued with growers in undemocratic processes and occasionally violent means to wrest UFW contracts from grape growers, Chavez and his followers turned to politics to reach their goals. Fortunately, UFW ally Jerry Brown had become governor of California; in 1975 he helped in passing the California Agricultural Labor Relations Act (ALRA) that granted workers rights to conduct elections to choose their union and to boycott. The UFW, always more popular than the Teamsters with those who worked the fields, won local union elections and by 1976 had regained many contracts with the growers.

The nation turned more conservative in the 1980s, marked by the elections of presidents Ronald Reagan, Chavez's longtime opponent, and George H. W. Bush. In California, Chavez's foes fought to undercut provisions of the ALRA and rejoiced when George Deukmejian became governor. The new governor and his allies weakened the ALRA, causing Chavez to return to many of his standard organizing tactics, including the boycott. He also expanded his rhetorical reach by hiring public relations experts who helped him purchase computerized mailing equipment that could send out millions of messages each year. While he fought threatening forces outside the union, internal battles badly divided his union—and revealed Chavez's shortcomings as a bureaucrat. Between 1978 and 1981, many of Chavez's early and valuable coworkers resigned because of disagreements with his leadership.

The last decade of Chavez's life was especially difficult for him. He continued to rely on the boycott, though it lacked its impact of earlier decades, and he remained steadfast in his incessant rhetorical crusade, adding themes such as the dangers of pesticides and their effects on consumers as well as on crop pickers. The union was battling attacks from various opponents when Chavez died suddenly in April 1993 at Yuma, Arizona, near his birthplace. His funeral drew 35,000 mourners ranging from farmworkers to national celebrities.

CHAVEZ AS RHETOR

Chavez's extraordinary commitment to and perseverance with public address flowed organically from his worldview. He possessed a millennial interpretation of contemporary history, a view based on his beliefs in God, the injustices suffered by the poor, the need to organize workers, and the power of public address. A devout Roman Catholic, he accepted the orthodox position that the church is a powerful moral and spiritual force in the world and that Christ's model of nonviolence is admirable. As the 1960s ended, he shared his understanding of contemporary reforms: "People are not going to turn back now. The poor are on the march: black, brown, red, everyone, whites included. We are now in the world will respond to a cause that involves injustice." As Hammerback and Jensen argue in *The Rhetorical Career of Cesar Chavez*, in his public speaking Chavez created his rhetorical appeal by merging three rhetorical dynamics: his substantive message of justice, the first-person image of Chavez as one committed to the ideal of justice, and his second-person image of the audience as a body of fair-minded individuals who, like Chavez, could become fully committed to the worldview he espoused. By so closely aligning his message with himself and his audience, Chavez created identification with his audience and thus generated significant persuasive appeal.

A brief examination of representative samples of Chavez's extensive public communication, which included speeches, letters, interviews, fasts, marches, boycotts, proclamations, and religious and ethnic icons, will illustrate his rhetorical

---

"It is how we use our lives that determines what kind of men we are. . . . I am convinced that the truest act of courage, the strongest act of manliness is to sacrifice ourselves for others in a totally non-violent struggle for justice. To be a man is to suffer for others. God help us to be men."

—*Cesar Chavez, "Statement on Conclusion of a Fast for Nonviolence"*

---

midst of the biggest revolution this country has ever known." Consisting primarily of disadvantaged members of racial minorities, the UFW was unlike other unions in that it sought to alter the conditions of human life. In "Letter from Delano" (1969), Chavez stated his conviction that "our cause is just, that history is a story of social revolution, and that the poor shall inherit the land." Interviewed in *Look* (April 1, 1969), he announced with assurance: "We will win, we are winning, because ours is a revolution of mind and heart, not just economics."

Just as irreconcilable labor–management disputes can often be settled by an impartial third-party arbiter, so he envisioned a human arbiter of his struggle for justice: public opinion. In the *Christian Century* (February 18, 1970), he confidently forecast: "I contend that not only the American public but people in general throughout the characteristics and substantive themes. The qualities and tactics reflect his understanding of reform rhetoric in the will of God. To explain Chavez's rhetorical transformation of audiences into committed supporters, some of whom would give material aid to the UFW and others of whom would work tirelessly and sacrifice and suffer for his cause, we developed a model of the rhetorical workings of changing the character of audiences. This rhetorical dynamic, which results from a synergistic merging of Chavez's substantive message (his themes, arguments, explanations) with the picture of Chavez that his audiences received and the picture of these audiences as communicated by Chavez, produced identification that drew audiences to adopt qualities of Chavez himself. We explain and illustrate this process in detail in our book *The Rhetorical Career of Cesar Chavez*.

In March 1966 Chavez and a group of coworkers issued "El Plan de Delano" (the Plan of Delano), referring to the plan as a blueprint "for the liberation of farm workers of the United States of North America, affiliated with the unique and true union of farm workers . . . seeking social justice in farm labor with those reforms that they believe necessary for their well-being as workers." Because farmworkers must be granted their "basic God-given rights as human beings," the Plan requested allegiance and assistance from all groups, particularly the Christian church. The Plan announced that farmworkers "across the country—the Mexicans, Filipinos, Blacks and poor whites; the Puerto Ricans, the Japanese, the Indians, the Portuguese and the Arabs" would unite in a nonviolent movement to improve their lives. The document echoed Chavez's belief that ultimately the farmworkers would prevail, that their victory over the growers was inevitable.

On February 14, 1968, in response to potential violence in the fields, Chavez began a twenty-five-day fast as an act of penance, redirecting farmworkers to the nonviolent roots of their movement. During the fast he prepared a document, "The Mexican-American and the Church," that was presented at the Second Annual Mexican-American Conference in Sacramento, California, March 8–10, 1968. He noted that Protestant ministers worked in his "moral" movement at its beginning, while the Catholic Church initially either ignored the workers or stood against them. In characteristically clear and simple language arranged in his signature pattern of anaphora, he pleaded for the Catholic Church to use its tremendous power to improve human lives: "We don't ask for more cathedrals. We don't ask for bigger churches or fine gifts. We ask for its presence with us, beside us, as Christ among us. We ask the Church to sacrifice with the people for social change, for justice, and for love of brother. We don't ask for words. We ask for deeds. We don't ask for paternalism. We ask for servanthood."

The fast ended on March 10, 1968, with a religious service and fiesta. Some 8,000 to 10,000 people assembled to hear a speech written by Chavez, who was too weak to talk, read in both English and Spanish. Described by Winthrop Yinger in *Cesar Chavez: The Rhetoric of Nonviolence* as "a compilation or model of the strategy and mind of Cesar Chavez," the brief statement began by thanking people for their support during the fast. The speech depicted those gathered to end the fast: "We are a family bound together in a common struggle for justice. We are a Union family celebrating our unity and the nonviolent nature of our movement." He had fasted because his "heart was filled with grief and pain for the suffering of farm workers. The Fast was first for me and then for all of us in this Union. It was a Fast for nonviolence and a call to sacrifice." The antagonists of this union family were strong but not invincible: "We have something the rich do not own. We have our own bodies and spirits and the justice of our cause as our weapons." The conclusion contained one of Chavez's most memorable statements: "It is how we use our lives that determines what kind of men we are. . . . I am convinced that the truest act of courage, the strongest act of manliness is to sacrifice ourselves for others in a totally nonviolent struggle for justice. To be a man is to suffer for others. God help us to be men."

Chavez also used public letters to spread his message. In a widely anthologized letter to E. L. Barr Jr., president of the California Grape and Free Fruit League, he quoted from Martin Luther King Jr.'s "Letter from Birmingham Jail" to explain why farmworkers resorted to strikes: "Injustice must be exposed, with all the tension its exposure creates, to the light of human conscience and the air of national opinion before it can be cured." Elevating his campaign to a high moral level, Chavez declared that farmworkers' suffering locked them "in a death struggle against man's inhumanity to man in the industry that you represent. And this struggle itself gives meaning to our life and ennobles our dying."

Chavez's speech at the Montopolis Community Center in Austin, Texas, on February 6, 1971, illustrated his ability to speak movingly in both English and Spanish. Some 5,000 listeners, including supporters of La Raza and strikers against the Economy Furniture Company, heard opening words that set his persuasive tone of graciousness: "Friends, sisters, honored guests, I'm extremely pleased to be here in Austin and in Texas. I've heard so much of the warm Texas hospitality, and let me tell you that I really know what you mean when you say, when you hear in California about Texas hospitality. . . . I think that everyone that I have come in contact with in this day and a half has been extremely gracious and courteous and friendly." Later in the speech he generously acknowledged that "there's so many good people that must be thanked"—Texas legislators, county commissioners, people who met him at the airport. Former U.S. Senator Ralph Yarborough, listening in the audience, was a longtime friend of the farmworkers and "a great man."

Chavez briefly examined the Economy strike and then urged a boycott of Montgomery Ward until the store discontinued its line of Economy furniture. Discussion of immediate issues preceded a lengthy explanation of broader questions of what, how, and why nonviolent tactics succeeded in a right cause. Maintaining that workers possess an "inherent" right to join unions in order to reach "their rightful place in society," he argued that the boycott would triumph because it was an "extension of love from one human being to the other," and therefore a "powerful weapon of the poor people and people who struggle for justice." This expression of love "creates a chain reaction that has tremendous consequences for good." To chart the influence of the boycott, he used detailed anecdotes to show that children recognized his name and had heard of the farmworkers' sanctions against grapes and lettuce. Once Mexican Americans were treated as "human beings," they would obtain political power as well as union contracts. His concern for justice extended far beyond his race, however, and he called for mutual assistance for all needy people.

A section in English emphasized moral questions. "The thing that all of us want—and here we're concerned for one another—is to build and not destroy," he related, "and really be concerned, really for the dignity of men" in order to "change things so we can get justice and dignity for our people." Nonviolence was essential, he added, to effect these changes. Chavez's conclusion in Spanish consisted almost exclusively of a series of anecdotes and sayings. He urged Mexican Americans to help each other and to stress education of the young. After telling a lengthy story that ended with one Mexican cowboy telling another that he would not cut off the head of a bee because a bee is "very organized; if I harm it, I'll have thousands of its kind on me soon," he made his point: "That is how we ought to think: a wrong against any one of us is a wrong against us all."

Chavez addressed students at Santa Clara University on October 26, 1972. Throughout his career he spoke on many campuses, addressing sympathetic students and recruiting volunteer workers. He opened by noting a dispute between the university and many of its employees, comparing the university's workers' concerns with those of farmworkers. Members of the audience were entreated to "understand what the grievance is, take a little time and find out. Find out what the grievance is." In the speech's body he reviewed the campaign against Proposition 22, a proposition that the agricultural industry had put on the ballot. "The employers have come to the conclusion that they can no longer stop the forward thrust of the farm workers movement by the traditional method that they have used for many years," he charged, "one of ridiculing the movement, trying to make the movement illegal, trying to say the movement is comprised of communists and trying to ignore us." Growers now had chosen a very potent method of supporting and enacting legislation that stops farmworkers from organizing. He pointed to the disreputable tactics used by the growers to qualify the proposition for the ballot. Proposition 22 was defeated, and political action by both the growers and the union would continue to increase.

Chavez's growing national reputation led to an invitation to nominate Governor Jerry Brown for president at the Democratic National Convention on July 14, 1976. His speech violated many of the expectations for a nominating speech. Instead of centering on Brown or the Democratic Party, he concentrated on what he called "social justice and civil rights." After pointing out many problems in the country, he concluded by saying, "People are the best answer to solving their own problems. Until our government hears the voices of those with problems, all the people, we will never be able to solve those problems and more and more people will be turned off."

Some of the most personally draining speeches for Chavez were his eulogies for farmworkers killed while working to build the union. On February 14, 1979, Chavez spoke at a ceremony honoring Rufino Contreras, who was murdered while talking to a group of strikebreakers in a field. Chavez began with a haunting image: "February 10, 1979, was a day of infamy for farm workers. It was a day without joy. The sun didn't shine. The birds didn't sing. The rain didn't fall. Why was this such a day of evil? Because on this day greed and injustice struck down our brother Rufino Contreras." Listeners heard how Contreras and other family members had worked for twenty years to amass wealth for the company that killed him. To his own question of how the company thanked Contreras for his service, Chavez answered: "When they spoke out against the injustice they endured, the company answered them with bullets; the company sent hired guns to quiet Rufino Contreras." Typical of the eulogistic form, he praised Contreras for his acts and promised that his brother in the fields was not dead, because his spirit would live as long as farmworkers met and organized. He concluded with a plea for workers to keep alive their comrade's memory: "It is our mission to finish the work Rufino has begun among us, knowing that true justice for ourselves and our opponents is only possible before God, who is the final judge." Thus, even when honoring the dead, Chavez presented his vision of a life spent following the will of God by diligently working for justice. For Chavez, such a life required that he speak to audiences wherever they might be found.

In September 1984 Chavez delivered a lengthy address to the UFW's Seventh Constitutional Convention in Fresno, California. He began ominously: "There is a shadow falling over the land, brothers and sisters, and the dark forces of reaction threaten us now as never before. The enemies of the poor and the working classes hold power in the White House and the governor's office." He then recited a litany of harmful actions that the union's enemies were inflicting against poor people, specifically arguing against Proposition 39, which attempted to redraw boundaries of legislative and congressional districts so that Mexican Americans

would be divided and lose much of their power. With characteristic faith, he promised that anti-UFW efforts would fail because "history and inevitability are on our side." The increase in the number of Hispanics, with a corresponding growth in their political, social, and economic power, formed part of that "inevitability." He concluded by telling union members: "Now it is our turn to fight back; it's our turn to strike a blow for all Hispanics in California by defeating Proposition 39."

Chavez's address at the Commonwealth Club of San Francisco, on November 9, 1984, presented his case in its most polished form. He carefully composed the speech and read it to his urban audience, word for word, from a typed text. Following a stark introduction that featured an example of braceros who died when their substandard bus crashed and a verbal picture of the harsh life endured by farmworkers, he uncharacteristically confided details about his own difficult life and high aspirations. The body of the speech focused on pesticides and their terrible effects on crop pickers, faulting growers for not changing their practices even though they were poisoning people and the land. The final section emphasized the growing power of Mexican Americans and predicted that California's future belonged to brown people. To illustrate his claim that social change, once begun, cannot be reversed, he again employed anaphora in these simple examples: "You cannot uneducate the person who has learned to read. You cannot humiliate the person who feels pride. You cannot oppress the people who are not afraid anymore." When Mexican Americans seized that power they deserved, he concluded, "we shall see the fulfillment of that passage from the book of Matthew in the New Testament, 'The last shall be first and the first shall be last.' And on that day, our nation shall fulfill its creed and that fulfillment shall enrich us all."

In 1986 Chavez continued to teach audiences about the dangers of pesticides in a series of renditions of his "Wrath of Grapes Speech." These speeches typically began with a review of the extensive use and effects of pesticides on crops and offered specific examples, including that of Juan Chaboya, who was "murdered by deadly chemicals in the freshly sprayed fields outside San

Diego, his dead body dumped by the growers forty-five miles away in a Tijuana clinic." "What excuse for justice will we offer his four children and his widow," Chavez challenged his listeners, "if we do nothing?" He methodically chronicled the campaign to outlaw the most commonly used pesticides and proposed a renewed boycott of grapes as a centerpiece of UFW protest.

In March 1989 Chavez spoke at Pacific Lutheran University, his first public appearance after one of his lengthy fasts. He again focused on pesticides and personalized their evils, this time with the story of Johnnie Rodriguez, "who was a five-year-old boy when he died after a painful two-year battle against cancer." Johnnie's parents were exposed to pesticides as they worked in the fields, Chavez related, and sadly even children were constantly exposed to these poisons in agricultural areas such as McFarland. "I keep a picture of Johnnie Rodriguez," Chavez disclosed. "He is sitting on his bed, hugging his teddy bears. His sad eyes and cherubic face stare out at you. The photo was taken four days before he died." Chavez's ensuing lengthy description of the use of pesticides and the scientific studies of their harmful effects as well as their misuse by growers ended on a personal note when he expressed frustration that he had not done enough—a frustration that motivated him to undertake a thirty-six-day fast in order to purify himself and serve as a penance for those who misused pesticides. He concluded by linking religious imperatives with his call to boycott grapes: "Our cause goes on in hundreds of distant places. It multiplies among thousands and then millions of caring people who heed through a multitude of simple deeds the commandment set out in the book of the Prophet Micah in the Old Testament: 'What does the Lord require of you, but to do justice, to love kindness, and to walk humbly with your God.' Thank you. And boycott grapes."

Throughout Chavez's rhetorical career his delivery—his use of voice and body—reinforced his persona as a reasonable advocate who placed content over personality, and thus shifted attention from himself to his ideas and information. Levy reported that his speeches were "soft, sweetened by a Spanish accent," and Matthiessen, that "what is striking in his gentle voice is his lack of man-

nerisms." The September 2, 1973, *Times of London* noted that he "over-whelmed the listener with his gentleness." Yinger, who heard Chavez speak three or four dozen times between 1965 and 1976, recounted his "conversational tone of delivery. He does not punctuate his ideas with shouts, indeed, he seldom raises his voice at all." In 1974, Dorothy Rensenbrink caught much of Chavez's essence as a speaker. "I have heard Cesar Chavez speak many times," she reported, and "I am puzzled at the power of such an uncommanding person to command so much loyalty from so many." He "speaks as though he is resuming a friendly conversation with his audience," she continued, and after hearing his quiet appeal she reacted as did many in his audiences: "I am finally hooked by recognition. It is hard to describe why. It is not self-recognition, just a kind of kindred recognition; as it is with thee, so it is with me." Another member of Chavez's audience described the same mysterious charisma: "You sit there and wonder where he's going and after a while his personality sneaks up on you."

Cesar Chavez's deepest beliefs and strongest feelings resulted in large part from his early experiences and heritage as well as from his later study of labor leaders and Catholic writings on social justice. His worldview not only motivated him to communicate his righteous case unceasingly in his thirty years as a union and civil rights leader, it also directed him to the rhetorical qualities that characterized his discourse for more than three decades. Convinced that a God omnipresent in human affairs would bring victory to a righteous cause, and that his case for supporting his union fit into his broader argument that racial minorities were being swept toward the economic, social, and political justice they deserved, Chavez and his coworkers had only to craft and present the arguments and evidence to educate audiences. As an essential part of God's plan to improve workers' lives, Chavez found the appropriate rhetorical profile: he relied on lucid explanations and arguments, illustrated with plentiful facts, simple anecdotes, and concrete examples; featuring plentiful previews, reviews, signposts, and transitions; and expressed in simple, personal, and sometimes repetitive language. Elevating his message and himself above purely practical, pragmatic, or selfish interests, he stressed moral issues and treated opponents generously. His relatively quiet and always controlled delivery further focused attention on his message rather than on himself.

Not neglecting rhetorical concerns, the savvy communicator adapted his topics to his immediate audiences and pressing issues. Addressing Mexican Americans, for example, he employed conventionally powerful patterns, forms, and appeals: folk sayings and *dichos* (maxims); anecdotes and stories (*cuentos*); Spanish formality, graciousness, and respect, as illustrated by his warm and respectful acknowledgments in introductions; and familial and religious themes and images, which surfaced in his references to God and his examples of and quotes about Mexican, Mexican American, and Southwestern families. To Anglo idealists in the idealistic 1960s, he was also an ideal spokesman—one with a case built on abundant facts and high moral principles. That well reasoned and amply proven case, presented so calmly and clearly, appeared to trust the good judgment of all listeners.

INFORMATION SOURCES

Research Collections and Collected Speeches

Many collections contain samples of Chavez's speeches and writings. The two most extensive are the United Farm Workers Papers in the Archives of Labor and Urban Affairs at Wayne State University in Detroit, and the Jacques Levy Papers in the Beinecke Rare Book and Manuscript Library at Yale University. Among others are the San Joaquin Valley Farm Labor Collection, Special Collections Department, Fresno State University; the Chicano Studies Library, Arizona State University; and those at other colleges and libraries. Speeches and interviews also appear in *Catholic Worker*, *El Grito*, *El Malcriado*, the *Fresno Bee*, the *Los Angeles Free Press*, *Movement*, *National Catholic Reporter*, *Playboy*, *Ramparts*, *Christian Century*, and *Look*. The only published collection of a comprehensive sample of Chavez's speeches is Jensen and Hammerback's *The Words of Cesar Chavez*. Some primary documents are reprinted in Richard W. Etulain, *Cesar Chavez: A Brief Biography with Documents* (New York: Palgrave, 2002).

Cortes, Carlos E., Arlin I. Ginsburg, Allan W. Green, and James A. Joseph, eds. *Three Perspectives on Ethnicity* [*TPE*]. New York: Putnam, 1976.

Garcia, F. Chris, ed. *Causa Politica: A Chicano Politics Reader* [*LCP*]. Notre Dame, Ind.: University of Notre Dame Press, 1974.

Jensen, Richard J., and John C. Hammerback, eds. *The Words of Cesar Chavez* [*WCC*]. College Station: Texas A&M University Press, 2002.

Simmen, Edward, ed. *Pain and Promise: The Chicano Today* [*PPCT*]. New York: New American Library, 1972.

Tice, Robert, ed. "The Rhetoric of La Raza" [*RLA*]. Unpublished manuscript, Chicano Studies Collection, Hayden Library, Arizona State University.

Valdez, Luis, and Stan Steiner, eds. *Aztlan: An Anthology of Mexican American Literature* [*AAM*]. New York: Vintage Books, 1972.

Yinger, Winthrop, ed. *Cesar Chavez: The Rhetoric of Nonviolence* [*CCRN*]. Hicksville, N.Y.: Exposition Press, 1975.

Web Sites

There are several major Web sites that include copies of speeches and other resource materials. The most useful is the site maintained by the Cesar E. Chavez Institute for Public Policy, currently housed at the University of San Francisco. The UFW website has some limited materials useful for researchers, including a movie on Cesar Chavez that can be downloaded.

Cesar E. Chavez Institute for Public Policy. http://www.sfu.edu/~cci

United Farm Workers. http://www.ufw.org

Audiovisual Materials

With the exception of the UFW's Web site movie, there are no audiovisual materials related to Chavez currently available. The Cesar E. Chavez Institute for Public Policy has several audio clips that can be downloaded. A documentary, *The Fight in the Fields*, has been produced and aired on PBS, but is not currently available on video.

Selected Critical Studies

Hammerback, J. C., and Richard J. Jensen. "Ethnic Heritage as Rhetorical Legacy: The Plan of Delano." *Quarterly Journal of Speech* 80 (1994): 53–70.

———. *The Rhetorical Career of Cesar Chavez*. College Station: Texas A&M University Press, 1998.

Hammerback, J.C., and Richard J. Jensen. "The Rhetorical Worlds of Cesar Chavez and Reies Tijerina." *Western Journal of Speech Communication* 44 (1980): 166–76.

Hammerback, John C., Richard J. Jensen, and Jose Angel Gutierrez. "Teaching the 'Truth': The Righteous Rhetoric of Cesar Chavez." In *A War of Words: Chicano Protest in the 1960s and 1970s*, ed. Hammerback, Jensen, and Gutierrez. Westport, Conn.: Greenwood Press, 1985.

Selected Biographies

Day, Mark. *Forty Acres: Cesar Chavez and the Farm Workers*. New York: Praeger, 1971.

Dunne, John Gregory. *Delano*, rev. and updated ed. New York: Farrar, Straus & Giroux, 1971.

Ferriss, Susan, and Ricardo Sandoval. *The Fight in the Fields: Cesar Chavez and the Farmworkers Movement*, ed. Diana Hembree. New York: Harcourt Brace, 1997.

Griswold de Castillo, Richard, and Richard A. Garcia. *Cesar Chavez: A Triumph of Spirit*. Norman: University of Oklahoma Press, 1995.

Levy, Jacques E. *Cesar Chavez: Autobiography of La Causa*. New York: Norton, 1975.

Matthiessen, Peter. *Sal si Puedes: Cesar Chavez and the New American Revolution*. New York: Random House, 1969.

Ross, Fred. *Conquering Goliath: Cesar Chavez at the Beginning*. Keene, Calif.: United Farm Workers, 1989.

Taylor, Ronald B. *Chavez and the Farm Workers*. Boston: Beacon Press, 1975.

CHRONOLOGY OF MAJOR SPEECHES

See "Research Collections and Collected Speeches" for source codes.

"The Plan of Delano." Delano, Calif., March 1966. *TPE*, pp. 379–82.

"The Organizer's Tale." Delano, Calif., July 1966. *AAM*, pp. 297–302.

"The Mexican-American and the Church." Sacramento, Calif., March 8–10, 1968. *CP*, pp. 143–46.

"Statement by Cesar Chavez on the Conclusion of a Fast for Nonviolence." Delano, Calif., March 10, 1968. *CCRN*, pp. 46–47.

"Speech in Austin, Texas." February 6, 1971. *RLA*, pp. 1–18.

"Speech at Santa Clara University." October 26, 1972. *WCC*, pp. 73–78.

"Nomination Address for Governor Jerry Brown at the Democratic National Convention." New York City, July 14, 1976. *WCC*, pp. 91–92.

"Eulogy for Rufino Contreras." Calexico, Calif., February 14, 1979. *WCC*, pp. 181–82.

"Address to the UFW's 7th Constitutional Convention." Fresno, Calif., September 1984. *WCC*, pp. 117–22.

"Address to Commonwealth Club of San Francisco." November 9, 1984. *WCC*, pp. 122–29.

"Wrath of Grapes Speech." Delivered at various times and locations, 1986. *WCC*, pp. 132–35.

"Speech at Pacific Lutheran University." Tacoma, Wash., March 1989. *WCC*, pp. 140–50.

WARD L. CHURCHILL (1947–)
Native American Activist, Professor

CATHERINE H. PALCZEWSKI AND RANDALL A. LAKE

Ward Churchill, an enrolled Keetoowah Band Cherokee, is an associate professor of ethnic studies, communications, and American Indian studies at the University of Colorado–Boulder. He is a member of the Governing Council of the Colorado Chapter of the American Indian Movement. He has been the national spokesperson for the Leonard Peltier Defense Committee, a delegate to the United Nations Working Group on Indigenous Populations, and a jurist with the International People's Tribunal.

His roles as a professor and as an indigenous people's activist provide Churchill with numerous opportunities for public, often unorthodox, oratory. As a vigorous opponent of state power, traditional political platforms are often denied him. Consequently, Churchill is one of many contemporary activists who seek out diverse avenues for advocacy that range from public oratory to the Internet, from online publications such as *Z* magazine to alternative publication houses such as AK Press. Churchill challenges audiences to be skeptical of state power by focusing on two forms of abuse: COINTEL-PRO—the U.S. government's "counterintelligence program"—and the ways in which Native Americans have experienced, and continue to experience, genocide. Specific themes in his rhetoric include media images of Native Americans; environmental destruction of Native lands; American Indian law; the September 11 attacks; and the well-known plight of Leonard Peltier. Since 1985, Churchill has delivered more than four hundred speeches at political rallies, academic conferences, and college campuses in the United States and Canada, as well as the United Nations.

In his autobiographical statement distributed by Speakout!, the speakers' bureau through which his events are organized, Churchill dates his political activism from 1969. After returning from a combat tour in Vietnam, he became a downstate organizer for Students for a Democratic Society (SDS) in Illinois, joined its Weather Underground faction, and became liaison to the Peoria chapter of the Black Panther Party. In 1972, Clyde Bellecourt recruited him to the American Indian Movement (AIM); he moved to South Dakota in 1975 and to Denver in 1976. From 1981 to 1983, he participated in the Dakota AIM occupation of the Yellow Thunder Camp in the Black Hills and was director of the Colorado AIM chapter. For the next decade, with Russell Means and Glenn T. Morris, Churchill was coordinator of Colorado AIM; following a reorganization, he served on the Colorado AIM Governing Council from 1993 to 1994.

Churchill's international activism began in 1983, when he was a delegate to AIM's International Indian Treaty Council. He was credentialed for three years with the United Nations Working Group on Indigenous Populations, during which time he was an observer at the Ninth Inter-American Indian Congress. In 1993, he was member/rapporteur of the presiding panel of the People's International Tribunal, Hawaii. Churchill has appeared as an expert witness at numerous tribunals and trials. Most recently he was named to the permanent advisory board of the Institute on the Holocaust and Genocide at Hebrew University in Jerusalem.

THE NEW INDIAN WAR AND ITS WARRIOR

Churchill is a controversial advocate in both Native American and Euramerican communities. Opposition to him in the former can be explained in part by a split between the Bellecourt-supported National American Indian Movement and the Autonomous Confederation—American Indian Movement. Churchill explicitly dissociates himself from Minneapolis-based National AIM, calling it "a basically social service-oriented—and that's it's [*sic*] best side—technically criminal organization." In his book *Indians Are Us?* he derides those affiliated with National AIM as "a whole herd of hang-around-the-forts, sell-outs and 'nickel' Indians." In contrast, as he told Shawn Setaro in an online interview, he believes that the autonomous AIM chapters are "still trying to adhere to a [*sic*] agenda of being a national liberation movement." For its part, at its Web site National AIM condemns Churchill as a "provocateur/disrupter who intentionally disrupts the activities and integrity of American Indian organizations and communities for his own personal megalomania and gratification." In particular, Churchill's "usage of words is intended to inflame, and disrupt activities of indigenous rights and liberation organizations." Indeed, Churchill's very claim to native ancestry is contested by some opposition Native Americans.

Among Euramericans, Churchill most recently sparked controversy with comments made following the September 11, 2001, attacks on the World Trade Center (WTC) and the Pentagon. He had been scheduled to speak at the University of Vermont and at a rally in Burlington, opposing the bombing of Afghanistan. A reporter uncovered an online essay by Churchill titled "'Some People Push Back': On the Justice of Roosting Chickens," in which he analogized the WTC workers to the Nazis, referring to them as "little Eichmanns inhabiting the sterile sanctuary of the twin towers." Although Churchill later qualified this statement, some rally organizers wanted to revoke his invitation to speak and one group withdrew its sponsorship in protest. The controversy reemerged in January 2005 when the essay garnered national media attention and sparked a university review of his tenure.

Churchill's primary technique of persuasion derives from his early association with the Black Panthers. In his speech "In a Pig's Eye," given on May 16, 2001, in San Francisco, he embraced Huey P. Newton's definition of politics:

> And Huey had the ability to encapsulate relatively complex ideas in a couple of sentences and make them accessible to people. . . . "*Politics*," [Newton] said, "*is the ability to define a phenomena* [*sic*] *and cause it to act in a desired manner*" Simple as that. Heavy statement actually. . . . Heavy in terms of what it is that goes into causing the phenomena we are up against to act in the desired manner. Usually to go away. . . . And how to make them go away becomes something worthy of some serious consideration. But, what gets glossed over in placing the emphasis there is . . . in order to cause it to act in a desired manner, you first have to be able to define the phenomena. If you can't define what it is you are up against, you are just sort of throwing darts with a blindfold on and hoping you will at least hit the wall where the board is hanging. . . . You need something more than luck on your side if you are going to go up against phenomena like the FBI. Like the aggregate power of the United States in its statist construction. (Emphasis in the original)

Accordingly, Churchill repeatedly names the native experience strategically: it is "genocide" perpetrated on indigenous peoples by a "colonialist" power. As he claims in his 1993 speech "Life in Occupied America," delivered in Berkeley, California, "Every time you see on a map an American Indian reservation, you're seeing a U.S. internal colony. It is as simple as that."

Although he attempts to define phenomena in such a way that they act as he desires, Churchill also understands the limits of this strategy. When asked by Shawn Setaro why he himself has not been targeted for COINTELPRO-like "counterintelligence neutralization," he emphasized the difficulty of convincing audiences, remarking: "Well. I've been public, but how public is that actually, do you think? See, you're free to say anything you want to say in this country so long as nobody, or at least very few people, are actually listening."

Moreover, Churchill believes that even when people are listening, too much public advocacy has promoted ineffective forms of action. In his speech "Pacifism and Pathology in the American Left," given in Oakland, California, on November 26, 2001, he argues that U.S. policies have inflicted untold death and suffering around the world, in response to which, he says, opponents have petitioned, marched, held rallies, and written books. Yet, these actions have failed to stop the carnage because those who perform them presume, wrongly, that evil is a matter of ignorance or error: "Defy logic by announcing that we are speaking truth to power, as though power didn't know what it was doing, somehow. We might wish to consider, perhaps, speaking to people once in a while. But, to what purpose?" Advocacy's goal, he argues, should not be to modify diets, or create bicycle paths, or bear moral witness, or feel better about ourselves by attending a rally that leaves power untouched. The experiment with "non-violence," in which pacifism is merely the avoidance of risk, has failed. To be effective, Churchill believes, advocacy must confront and overturn the imbalance of power between citizens and their government; if people are serious about stopping the carnage, they must seize the power necessary to do so. In pursuit of this goal, he holds that no tactical option should be foreclosed.

Some activists and scholars view Churchill as a prominent and important contemporary public advocate on American Indian issues. Bell hooks comments, "Churchill's is insurgent intellectual work—breaking new ground, forging new paths, engaging us in critical resistance." Russell Means has been similarly positive: "What Ward says is important. I want you to listen to him." Dr. Betty Parent, coordinator of the American Indian Studies Program at San Francisco State University, records that "Ward Churchill's talk on genocide and the American Indian was positively spellbinding, and I speak as one who was initially skeptical of his thesis."

Because only a few of his more than four hundred speeches are extant, identifying Churchill's most significant addresses is difficult. However, those that have been preserved appear to be representative of the general form and content of his rhetoric. To begin, Churchill's speeches are intimately connected to his written discourse. "Pacifism and Pathology in the American Left," which responds to the September 11 attacks, draws heavily from his book *Pacifism as Pathology* as well as the online essay "Some People Push Back." His speeches "Life in Occupied America" and "Native America: A Little Matter of Genocide" echo *A Little Matter of Genocide*. "In a Pig's Eye" has its rhetorical roots in *Agents of Repression*. Churchill's strategic redundancy enables him routinely to speak without a prepared script, and often without any notes whatsoever. As a result, his oral style is informal, sometimes even ungrammatical, yet laced with a comparatively sophisticated vocabulary not typical of impromptu conversation. This means that an adequate understanding of Churchill's public advocacy requires attention to his writing as well as his speaking.

Rather than attempting to describe his most significant speeches, a more appropriate approach is to discuss the substantive and stylistic features that characterize his advocacy. Churchill advances two fundamental claims: first, that the state, particularly through abuse of its police power, is an agent of repression, and second, that government policy toward Native Americans was and is genocidal. His arguments in support of these claims are marked by emotional intensity and intellectual rigor. Both his writings and his speeches are documented extensively. In fact, he often employs the government's own documents to prove his harshest accusations against it. Examples include citing COINTELPRO documents to demonstrate the prevalence and nastiness of government repression, and citing federal vital statistics regarding life expectancy, for instance, to prove that Native Americans are the victims of genocide.

COINTELPRO is a powerful example of the abuse of police powers because in this operation the U.S. government targeted its own citizens:

> Cointelpro—this counterintelligence program was not aimed at agents of foreign powers, spies, saboteurs, or otherwise. It was aimed at the citizens of the United States—those citizens who have politically objectionable point of views [*sic*]. And who determined what was politically objectionable? The people in the driver's seat of the counterintelligence program. It

wasn't subject to any check; it wasn't subject to any scrutiny; it wasn't subject to anything at all, because it was illegal and secret. And in a secret operation, you don't exactly send it over to the Attorney General to ask whether your take on the political propriety of the Socialist Workers Party is exactly correct or not. You don't send it off to a think tank at Harvard University to see if your take on the minutes posed by the communist party USA, or Martin Luther King's Southern Christian Leadership Conference, or whatever organization or individuals you are targeting, would be correct. You simply make the decision as to what is politically objectionable and you set in motion the machinery that is necessary to neutralize the activity by which that objectionable political expression occurs.

Detailing actions against the Black Panthers and the American Indian Movement, Churchill tries to generate a critical consciousness in his audiences that enables them to question governmental actions. More recently, he has suggested that the expanded police powers given the government in the wake of September 11 are a more recent manifestation of the COINTELPRO mentality.

Almost all of Churchill's rhetoric eventually addresses the topic of genocide. Treatments range from short essays critical of Thanksgiving (e.g., "A Day to Give Thanks?"), to lengthy legal briefs defending Columbus Day protesters (e.g., "Bringing the Law Home"), to speeches detailing the history of genocide (e.g., "Native America: A Little Matter of Genocide" and "Life in Occupied America"). Churchill marshals a wide range of examples, historical and contemporary, to prove his claim. Lord Jeffrey Amherst's distribution of smallpox-infected blankets to Indians—arguably the first documented case of biological warfare—is a favorite. Another is the "scalp bounty," which, he argues in "Native America, Genocide and the Scalp Bounty," represents state-sanctioned murder:

> What's a "Scalp Bounty?" It's a matter of official policy, promulgated in every antecedent East Coast colony of the European powers, every state of the union after the decolonization of the 13 Atlantic Coast colonies creating the United States, every single territory and

subsequent state of the United States, with the exceptions of Alaska and Hawaii, at some point in their history. Promulgation, that is of a policy that said that a citizen producing the scalp, in some cases, the bloody red skin of an adult male Indian, would be paid, if you take Pennsylvania colony in say the 1740s as example, the equivalent of the annual wage of your average farmer. . . . Forty pounds Sterling, that is the equivalency of the annual wage. Adult . . . female Indian, 20 pounds Sterling. Kill two women, annual wage. Ten pounds Sterling for a child. Child being defined as any human being, of either sex, under 12 years of age, down to and including fetus. And there are cases on record where professional scalp hunters did kill pregnant women, open their bellies, scalp the fetus and collect twice. This was a profession. And the Indians were being hunted and killed as a matter of

to be able to understand the nature of the process in order to recognize when it presents itself in concrete terms and only in the recognition, can you devise ways and means of heading it off. And it is in everybody's interest to head it off because it is like a cancer. ("Native America: A Little Matter of Genocide")

This strategy of defining genocide has achieved some notable successes. For example, this appeal led a Denver jury to acquit Churchill and others of charges stemming from protests against that city's Columbus Day parade in 1991. However, these successes have been sporadic; Churchill's definitional claim is not generally accepted among Euramerican audiences. As Lilian Friedberg has noted, although *A Little Matter of Genocide* makes claims as powerful as Daniel Jonah Goldhagen's *Hitler's Willing*

"Leonard [Peltier] is a prisoner of war. He is a prisoner of the longest on-going war in this hemisphere. . . . the struggle at this point having lasted a little over 500 years. That is 500 years of conquest, colonization and genocide. It is also 500 years of consistent resistance on the part of those who were targeted for that."

—*Ward Churchill, "In a Pig's Eye"*

---

policy throughout the Anglo-American portion of North America for several centuries.

These historical examples are intended to disrupt the cultural amnesia that attends celebrations of Thanksgiving (in which the Pilgrims' eventual slaughter of the very peoples who had helped them is forgotten) or of Columbus' "discovery" of America (in which his enslavement and destruction of the Taino people is forgotten), and that rationalizes the obliteration of first nations as the Euramericans' "manifest destiny." But, important as historical examples may be in reshaping audience understandings of the past, Churchill never stops here. Instead, contemporary examples of the mistreatment of Native Americans make clear that

> Genocide is not something relegated to the past. Genocide is an ongoing reality. You've got

Executioners, "Churchill's stellar and seminal piece of scholarship on Holocaust and denial in the Americas . . . did not meet with the same degree of public success."

Churchill's speeches on COINTELPRO and genocide consistently retell history, reminding audiences of that which often is ignored or forgotten. Thus, when decrying FBI repression, he is certain to discuss the FBI's genesis in the Pinkerton Agency, whose founding purpose was to suppress the labor movement. When condemning contemporary genocide, he invariably invokes Columbus' colonization of the Americas. This constant situating of contemporary wrongs in a forgotten historical context has several purposes. First, it reeducates audiences about the past from a subaltern perspective. Second, it makes his accusations about current evils more plausible. Third, by suggesting that he has "done his homework" and is aware of facts not generally known, it enhances Churchill's ethos as an informed, comparatively "expert" advocate.

Churchill consistently strives to instill in audiences a sense of obligation to act, not so much out of guilt as out of privilege. As he explains in his 1993 speech "Life in Occupied America": "But you are responsible for the fact that you enjoy benefits that obtain from the outcome. That's one hand, a motivation for you to take stock of what the situation is of Native People in occupied America today and set yourself about doing something about it."

What kind of action is entailed by this obligation? In the final analysis, Churchill's advocacy encourages not decorous participation in politics-as-usual, but social revolution. Skeptical of gun laws that prevent dispossessed groups from defending themselves, of antismoking laws that misdirect attention, and of "speaking truth to power" when power doesn't care about truth, he advocates radical action. When asked, following his "In a Pig's Eye" address in 2001, how the government can be made accountable, he responded:

> You are not going to make a moral argument that is going to convince these people to obey their own law. You are not going to make a logical argument, because you are gentle and polite and persuasive and all of that. You probably are not going to get it through petition campaigns. I doubt that lighting an infinite number of candles and chanting chants and bearing moral witness is going to have much effect. Speaking truth to power isn't going to do it because power knows everything you are saying and frankly, power don't care. You know? You have to speak to people and galvanize people, not on the basis of some altruistic understanding of what is right and what they should do or "sympathy for the Indians," but an understanding that it is in their own self-interest to compel by whatever means are available and necessary for the government to adhere to the rule of law or be abolished. I favor the latter myself. . . .

Abolition of the state is his ultimate goal. In "Doing Time" he exhorts:

> In abolishing the state, you resolve all. How do you do that? . . . you recognize the monster for what it is and you withdraw your consent and

participation unilaterally and absolutely from participation in any way it is not coerced. Make that conscious leap and you've taken the first step. And if you have taken the first step, you've just empowered yourself to take the second, the third, the fourth.

Abolition is appropriate because the state apparatus is intrinsically self-contradictory; Churchill confronts European America with its own hypocrisy. Describing COINTELPRO activities in 2000, for example, he comments: "They change the name from time to time, but the one most commonly used was Key Agitator Index. They basically went about the business of, in the process of surveilling and monitoring the activities of the organizations they determined had un-American goals, you know like blacks having the right to vote in Mississippi, there's an un-American goal for you." Similarly, "Life in Occupied America" notes bitterly that Native Americans are simultaneously the most land-rich and economically poorest people in the United States and, with palpable outrage, observes that lands held collectively by Native Americans were stolen in a campaign to "civilize" them, and then turned into national parks, held collectively by Euramericans as testimony to the latter's "advanced state of civilization."

By juxtaposing facts in a way that suggests inconsistency in a logical sense and hypocrisy in a moral sense, Churchill strives to render his audience's unexamined perspective incongruous; incongruity in turn is a wedge that makes possible an alternative perspective, the perspective of the dispossessed. Churchill's attempt to shift his audience's perspective is, perhaps, most notable—and most controversial—in his commentaries on the events of September 11, 2001. His essay "'Some People Push Back' opens by recalling Malcolm X's infamous comment about John F. Kennedy's assassination: that the assassination was an instance of the "chickens coming home to roost." Then Churchill remarks: "On the morning of September 11, 2001, a few more chickens—along with some half-million dead Iraqi children—came home to roost in a very big way at the twin towers of New York's World Trade Center. Well, actually, a few of them seem to have nestled in at the Pentagon as well." He challenges the popular belief that those who commandeered the airplanes were cowardly, fanatical, even insane "terrorists" who initiated a war against innocent civilians, arguing to the contrary that "America's indiscriminately lethal arrogance and psychotic sense of self-entitlement have long since given the great majority of the world's peoples ample cause to be at war with it." Compared with the impact of U.S. economic sanctions and military strikes on Iraq, he contends that the United States "will have gotten off very, very cheap."

Churchill's November 16, 2001, speech at the AK Press warehouse, "Pacifism and Pathology in the American Left," elaborates. Churchill argues that for many people, the issue of violence versus nonviolence is not a question of principle but, rather, is a matter of tactics, "a question of what works." He concedes that crashing jetliners into the WTC and Pentagon failed to end American imperialism; nonetheless, he argues, this was the most effective tactic available to Al-Qaeda and its supporters in Afghanistan and Iraq:

> On 9/11, nineteen guys equipped with $30.00 worth of box cutters did one hundred billion, and the count is increasing, dollars worth of damage structurally to the economy of the United States. . . . In other words, nineteen guys did more bleeding of the system, in terms of values that it understands, than every boycott and every march and every campaign that we have undertaken since Vietnam. And they did it in about 20 minutes.

Most Americans abhor this moral calculus. Nonetheless, in a nation that often seems to operate in a state of political amnesia, dissenting voices such as Ward Churchill perform an invaluable service by holding us, and our government, accountable for the past, articulating alternative ways of comprehending the present, and envisioning a future in which the privileges enjoyed by some are not purchased with the repression of others.

INFORMATION SOURCES

Research Collections and Collected Speeches

Because no speeches are available in print form, and only a few in audio, reliance on Churchill's writings is essential to understanding his rhetoric. The books listed below often are referred to with differ-

ences in the titles, some attributable to changes when the books were reprinted, and others attributable to simple mistakes.

Churchill, Ward. *Acts of Rebellion: The Ward Churchill Reader*. New York: Routledge, 2003.

———. *Agents of Repression: The FBI's Secret Wars Against the Black Panther Party and the American Indian Movement*. Written with Jim Vander Wall. Boston: South End Press, 1988.

———. "A Day to Give Thanks?" *The Progressive Media Project*. November 15, 2000. www.progressive.org/pmpdvwc0.htm

———. *Fantasies of the Master Race: Literature, Cinema, and the Colonization of American Indians*, ed. M. Annette Jaimes. Monroe, Me.: Common Courage Press, 1992; San Francisco: City Lights Books, 1998.

———. *From a Native Son: Selected Essays on Indigenism, 1985–1995*. Boston: South End Press, 1996.

———. *Indians Are Us? Culture and Genocide in Native North America*. Monroe, Me.: Common Courage Press, 1994.

———. *A Little Matter of Genocide: Holocaust and Denial in the Americas, 1492 to the Present*. San Francisco: City Lights Books, 1997.

———. *Pacifism as Pathology: Reflections on the Role of Armed Struggle in North America*. Written with Mike Ryan. Winnipeg, Canada: Arbeiter Ring, 1998.

———. *Perversions of Justice: Indigenous Peoples and Angloamerican Law*. San Francisco: City Lights Books, 2003.

———. *Since Predator Came: Notes from the Struggle for American Indian Liberation*. Littleton, Colo.: Aigis Press, 1995.

———. " 'Some People Push Back': On the Justice of Roosting Chickens." *Pockets of Resistance* no. 11 (September 2001). Available at http://www.darknightpress.org/index.php?i=news&c=recent&view=9&long=1

———. *Struggle for the Land: Indigenous Resistance to Genocide, Ecocide and Expropriation in Contemporary North America*. Monroe, Me.: Common Courage Press, 1993; San Francisco: City Lights Books 2002.

Web Site

While some materials may be found at a variety of Web sites, there is no central site that provides a wide range of documents.

Audiovisual Materials

AK Press, 674-A 23rd Street, Oakland, Calif., 94612-1163 [*AKP*]. www.akpress.org. To date, AK Press has issued three CDs and one VHS cassette of Churchill's speaking.

Government Repression of Political Movements. Scholars Forum Series. Mount Union College, 1994.

Institutional Racism in Higher Education. Convocation Series. Finger Lakes Community College, 1994.

The Tribunal: The People's International Tribunal, 1993. Honolulu: Na Maka o ka Aina, 1994.

USA on Trial: The International Tribunal of Indigenous Peoples and Oppressed Nations in the USA. San Francisco: Mission Creek Video, 1993.

Selected Critical Study

Friedberg, Lilian. "Dare to Compare." *American Indian Quarterly* 24 (Summer 2000): 353–80. Expanded Academic ASAP. August 15, 2001.

Selected Biographies

"Curriculum Vitae." Available by mail from *Speakout!* www.speakoutnow.org

Lee Lew-Lee. "Interview with Ward Churchill." *Prevailing Winds Magazine* 4 (1996): 35–38.

Philion, Stephen E. "Peace Activists Disagree with Ward Churchill's Comments." December 3, 2001. http://archives.econ.utah.edu/archives/pen-1/2001 m12/msg0059.htm

Setaro, Shawn. "Ward Churchill Interview." Available at zena.secureforum.com/Znet/setaro_Churchill. htm

CHRONOLOGY OF MAJOR SPEECHES

See "Research Collections and Collected Speeches" for source code.

"Life in Occupied America." Berkeley, Calif., April 23, 1993. *AKP.*

"WBAI Interview with Ward Churchill." August 20, 1995. Available at www.refuseandresist.org/mumia/1995/churchill.html

"Native America: A Little Matter of Genocide." Colorado Springs, Colo., April 2, 1998. *AKP.*

"Doing Time: The Politics of Imprisonment." Winnipeg, Canada, September 15, 2000. *AKP.*

"Native America, Genocide and the Scalp Bounty." Medford, Mass., March 12, 2001. *AKP.*

"In a Pig's Eye: Reflections on the Police State, Repression, and Native America." San Francisco, May 16, 2001. *AKP.*

"Pacifism and Pathology in the American Left." Oakland, Calif., November 16, 2001. *AKP.*

"Meet the New Boss, Same as the Old Boss: Globalisation, Genocide, and Resistance." Toronto, Canada, January 17, 2002. Excerpted in *Community Action Notes* 6 (February 2, 2002): 3–4; full speech available at http://www.radio4all.org/unwelcome/archive76-100.html (follow link to show #93).

HILLARY DIANE RODHAM CLINTON (1947–)
First Lady of the United States, U.S. Senator

KARRIN VASBY ANDERSON

Hillary Rodham Clinton is a complex and controversial figure in the history of American oratory. As U.S. first lady she spoke to domestic and international audiences, promoting universal health care, children's welfare, women's rights, and historic preservation. She weathered controversy as an accomplished political spouse active in her husband's administration, and steeled herself through a series of public scandals. Influenced by the diverse forces of Methodism, political liberalism, feminism, and legal studies, Rodham Clinton's rhetoric illustrates the ways in which an orator can respond strategically to even the most daunting constraints.

Hillary Diane Rodham was born on October 26, 1947, to Dorothy and Hugh Rodham. Raised with her two brothers in Park Ridge, Illinois, she grew up in a stable, middle-class environment. Her childhood was active, with Hillary involved in her church youth group, Girl Scouts, National Honor Society, and student government. Conservative values and her parents' emphasis on self-sufficiency shaped her early years. The Rodhams were involved in the Methodist Church, and Hillary reflected her father's Republican politics when in 1964 she campaigned for Barry Goldwater as a "Goldwater Girl."

An accomplished student and ambitious individual, Hillary Rodham entered Wellesley College after graduating from high school in 1965. The liberal campus environment exposed her to new political perspectives, and by 1968 she shed her conservative political roots, campaigning for Eugene McCarthy in that year's presidential campaign. She continued to excel academically and involve herself in campus government, winning the office of president of the Wellesley College Government Association her senior year. The year 1969 was an important year for Hillary Rodham as orator. She was the first Wellesley student invited to give a commencement address on behalf of the student body, and her speech was excerpted in the June 20, 1969, issue of *Life* magazine. This gave her some prominence when she entered Yale Law School as one of only twenty-seven women students. At Yale, she served on the Board of Editors of the *Yale Law Review* and interned with Marian Wright Edelman, who was instrumental in Rodham's involvement with the Children's Defense Fund. Yale also was the place where she met her future husband, Bill Clinton.

After graduating from Yale Law in 1973, Rodham worked on the House Judiciary Committee inquiry into impeachment of President Richard Nixon. Her relationship with Bill Clinton continued, and she followed him to Arkansas, supporting his unsuccessful bid for the U.S. Congress in 1974. The two married in 1975 and Hillary Rodham, who retained her maiden name, became the breadwinner for the family while her husband pursued political ambitions. Bill Clinton was elected Arkansas state attorney general in 1976. Rodham was recruited by the prestigious Rose law firm in Little Rock in 1977. In 1978, Bill Clinton was elected state governor and Hillary Rodham was named a partner at Rose. In 1980, she gave birth to their daughter, Chelsea.

As the first lady of Arkansas, Rodham had a bully pulpit from which to advocate for change. She turned her concern for children and families into a campaign for educational reform in

Arkansas. In 1979, President Jimmy Carter appointed Rodham to the independent Legal Services Corporation, an activist lawyers' group she would later chair, the first woman to serve in that capacity. Bill Clinton lost his reelection bid in 1980. Prompted by concerns that her public persona as an independent feminist hurt him with the Arkansas electorate, Hillary Rodham changed her name and helped her husband regain the Arkansas governorship in 1982. He remained in that office for the next ten years.

The Clintons emerged on the national stage during the 1992 presidential campaign. Rodham Clinton was a key supporter of her husband in the face of controversy about past marital indiscretions, and her status as an accomplished, professional woman triggered speculation about the extent to which she would be involved in governing decisions should her husband win the election. Bill Clinton did win the 1992 election, and served two consecutive terms as U.S. president.

Rodham Clinton assumed a high profile as U.S. first lady when she was appointed chair of the President's Task Force on Health-Care Reform in 1993. A sweeping attempt to provide universal health-care coverage to all Americans, Clinton's key domestic initiative was an ambitious and controversial piece of legislation. Rodham Clinton's role as task force chair put her at the center of a major public policy debate. She stumped for health-care reform to audiences nationwide and testified on behalf of the president's bill before Congress. The legislation ultimately was defeated, and Rodham Clinton's credibility was damaged as a result. When the Republican Party swept the 1994 elections, many blamed Rodham Clinton and the failed health-care reform efforts for the Democratic Party's loss of support.

After the 1994 elections, Rodham Clinton shifted her energies to the international stage, traveling abroad and speaking out for the welfare of women and children. These speeches were well received and garnered positive press for the first lady. Her popularity was tested when, in 1998, allegations surfaced that Bill Clinton had had an affair with a White House intern, Monica Lewinsky. The charges were part of the much larger Whitewater investigation. Although the so-called Whitewater scandal began with questions about a real estate investment deal the Clintons made during the 1980s, the special counsel's investigation ballooned to include a variety of controversies that plagued the Clinton White House. Rodham Clinton initially denounced the charges about her husband and Monica Lewinsky as evidence that a "vast, right-wing conspiracy" was out to destroy the Clinton presidency. After physical evidence of the affair surfaced, however, Bill Clinton admitted to misconduct and Rodham Clinton was once again in the spotlight because of her husband's indiscretions. Her decision to remain in the marriage drew both criticism and praise, though her poll numbers during that period remained positive, and many credited her with once again salvaging her husband's political career.

As Bill Clinton's presidency was coming to a close, Rodham Clinton embarked on her own political career, running for the U.S. Senate from New York in the 2000 election. In November 2000 she became the first U.S. first lady to seek and win elective office. She pledged to serve her entire first term, but immediately upon her election, pundits began to speculate about a possible presidential bid of her own in 2004 or 2008.

HILLARY RODHAM CLINTON: FROM SPOUSE TO SENATOR

When Hillary Rodham gave the commencement address on behalf of Wellesley's class of 1969, she articulated a sentiment that would become a recurring theme in her rhetoric. Chastising the speaker who preceded her, Rodham stated, "For too long our leaders have used politics as the art of the possible. And the challenge now is to practice politics as the art of making what appears to be impossible, possible." Whether it be educating children more effectively, providing universal health-care coverage to all Americans, or promoting women's rights internationally, Rodham Clinton has used her rhetoric to promote seemingly impossible political goals. In some cases, her efforts have produced historic victories. In others, she has suffered bitter defeat. The extent to which she has treaded new symbolic ground in U.S. political culture makes her an important figure in the history of U.S. oratory.

Hillary Rodham Clinton's rhetoric reflects the diverse forces that have shaped her identity: Methodism, political liberalism, feminism, and the law. Early in her public career, her oratorical style was rooted in her professional training as a lawyer. In "The Discursive Performance of Femininity," rhetorical critic Karlyn Kohrs Campbell describes her health-care reform speeches as follows:

> Her tone is usually impersonal, disclosing minimal information about herself; her ideas unfold deductively in the fashion of a lawyer's brief; all kinds of evidence are used, but personal examples rarely, if ever, appear.... [S]he is impassioned but very rarely emotional.... [S]he may say that she speaks "as a mother, a wife, a daughter, a sister, a woman," but she does not assume those roles in speaking. Instead, she plays the roles for which she has been professionally trained, the roles of lawyer, advocate, and expert. She confronts her adversaries and debates positions as she has done in the courtroom; she even attacks her opponents. In other words, she speaks forcefully and effectively, manifesting her competence in meeting rhetorical norms, but with few of the discursive markers that signal femininity.

Campbell notes that failure to conform to norms of femininity may have contributed to the negative responses Rodham Clinton received during the health-care reform campaign. She contends, however, that such a reaction is a sign not of Rodham Clinton's failings as a rhetor, but of the American public's hesitation to accept the U.S. first lady as expert and advocate.

Thematically, Rodham Clinton's health-care reform rhetoric touted five key principles: universal access to health care, primary and preventive health care, choice, cost control, and quality. Though the notion that the government should be responsible for insuring the nation's health is politically liberal, Rodham Clinton invoked her conservative roots in order to suggest that governmental involvement would serve the interests of self-sufficiency. In her June 1993 speech to the American Medical Association "Health Care: We Can Make A Difference," she stated that caring for children is "our primary responsibility as adults" as well as "our primary responsibility as a government," claiming that by "stand[ing] behind families, teachers, and others who work with the young," we "enable them to meet their own needs by becoming self sufficient and responsible so that they, in turn, will be able to meet their families' and their own children's needs." She continued the argument by reminiscing about her own childhood, in which "there seemed to be more strong families" and "more safer neighborhoods." There seemed to be an outlook of caring and cooperation among adults that stood for and behind children." The linking of health-care reform to the well-being of children illustrates Rodham Clinton's characteristic emphasis on children's welfare, a theme that permeates her public advocacy.

The pairing of governmental responsibilities and self-sufficiency was also illustrated in her 1993 commencement address at the University of Michigan. She told the graduates that

In April 1993, speaking at the University of Texas in Austin, she delivered what became known as the "Politics of Meaning" speech, in which she asserted, "We need a new politics of meaning. We need a new ethos of individual responsibility and caring. We need a new definition of civil society which answers the unanswerable questions posed by both the market forces and the governmental ones, as to how we can have a society that fills us up again and makes us feel that we are part of something bigger than ourselves." At the time, the speech was treated as a departure from her typical political advocacy, but it revealed an impulse to conflate politics and morality. The spiritual influences on Rodham Clinton's rhetoric affected her ethos as well. One newspaper report suggested that the Clinton marriage survived scandal and infidelity, in part, because Bill and Hillary Clinton

---

"If there is one message that echoes forth . . . let it be that human rights are women's rights and women's rights are human rights, once and for all."

—*Hillary Rodham Clinton, Address to the United Nations Fourth World Conference on Women, 1995*

---

an exaggerated emphasis on "me" as opposed to "we" has accentuated the gaps between us and has resulted in the problems that I have referred to. And so what we now have an opportunity to do is work to right that balance again, to develop shared goals and to be part of reaching them. It does not mean sacrificing individual rights. It does not mean stifling the spirit of any of us. But it does mean that promoting the common good in our democratic system requires us to work together to provide each other with certain rights and opportunities. And in return, it requires each individual to be responsible to themselves, for themselves, and on behalf of their families.

Despite the lawyerly tone present in many health-care reform speeches, a few addresses illustrate a more philosophic side to Rodham Clinton's rhetoric, informed by her spirituality.

"see themselves in almost Messianic terms, as great leaders who have a mission to fulfill."

The congressional defeat of the Clinton health-care reform bill caused Rodham Clinton to retreat from domestic policy-making, but she did not relinquish her role as public advocate. She embarked on an international tour, often accompanied by daughter Chelsea, during which she gave speeches touting women's rights and promoting the welfare of children and families. Perhaps the most significant address given during this period was her September 5, 1995, speech to the United Nations Fourth World Conference on Women in Beijing, China. Rodham Clinton's presence at the conference was initially controversial because of China's record of human-rights violations. Some charged that the first lady's attendance would bring the Chinese government positive press that it did not deserve. In her memoir, *Living History*,

Rodham Clinton stated that her goal for the speech was to "push the envelope as far as I [could] on behalf of women and girls." After valorizing women's ability to achieve community and touting the centrality of women to the world economy, the first lady concluded her speech with a powerful indictment:

> It is a violation of human rights when babies are denied food, or drowned, or suffocated, or their spines broken, simply because they are born girls. It is a violation of human rights when women and girls are sold into the slavery of prostitution. It is a violation of human rights when women are doused with gasoline, set on fire and burned to death because their marriage dowries are deemed too small.

After reciting a long list of gendered human-rights violations, Rodham Clinton exhorted, "If there is one message that echoes forth from this conference, let it be that human rights are women's rights and women's rights are human rights, once and for all." That message, although blacked out of the closed-circuit television the Chinese government was using to broadcast conference highlights, garnered praise from Rodham Clinton's U.S. audience. U.S. newspapers heralded the speech as both a tough critique of China's poor human-rights record and an impassioned appeal for the welfare of women and children worldwide. Rodham Clinton may have fared better in the press after this speech than she did after some of her hard-hitting health-care reform speeches because she was acting within traditional boundaries set for the U.S. first lady. Rather than delivering domestic policy speeches to male-dominated groups such as the American Medical Association or Congress, she addressed groups of women and promoted virtues such as democracy, capitalism, and human rights.

Rodham Clinton's speech to the Fourth World Conference on Women typified many of the trends that could be observed in her rhetoric during the period that followed her health-care reform campaign and preceded her bid in 2000 for the U.S. Senate. Her speeches were often more ceremonial than deliberative in tone, so the mode of speaking matched her role as first lady. Although her health-care reform speeches had employed war metaphors and combative

language, rhetoric from this period invoked images of the family, nurturance, and cooperation.

This shift toward a more traditional, feminine persona was incorporated into both her rhetorical style and her public persona. In 1996, Rodham Clinton published *It Takes a Village: And Other Lessons Children Teach Us*. The book outlined many policy proposals to promote and protect the welfare of children, but the publicity for the book cast Rodham Clinton as a traditional first lady. She donned pastel outfits, and chose a Jackie-Kennedy bouffant hairdo for the book's dust jacket photograph. The description of the author inside the book stated, "Hillary Rodham Clinton is America's First Lady. A longtime child advocate, she lives in the White House with the President and their daughter, Chelsea. This is her first book." That brief narrative emphasized Rodham Clinton's role as wife and mother, and ignored her professional accomplishments and qualifications. Rodham Clinton invoked the title of the book repeatedly in her speeches. Her domestic speeches echoed the style she developed on the international stage, emphasizing the welfare of children and employing familial metaphors. For example, in her speech to the 1996 Democratic National Convention, she stated her intention to "talk about what matters most in our lives and in our nation—children and families." She continued, "I wish we could be sitting around a kitchen table, just us, talking about our hopes and fears, about our children's futures. For Bill and me, family has been the center of our lives."

In July 1998, Rodham Clinton embarked on another domestic political campaign, which her office called "Save America's Treasures." The explicit purpose of the campaign, according to the first lady's page on the White House Web site, was to "preserve those aspects of our shared heritage . . . which define our nation and transcend the generations." Rodham Clinton played up the seemingly innocuous nature of this campaign, saying, "No one is going to stand up against The Star-Spangled Banner and its need for preservation." Her initial speaking tour took place in the northeastern United States, where she visited sites in need of historic preservation. The highlight of this tour was her address at Seneca Falls, New York, commemorating the 150th anniversary of the first women's rights convention. Although the Save America's Treasures tour fit within the traditional bounds of the first lady's role, Rodham Clinton's rhetoric employed an explicitly feminist tone. She heralded women activists, inventors, and entrepreneurs. She used historical commemoration as a vehicle for advancing arguments in favor of women's rights and women's empowerment. Perhaps most interesting was the strategic advantage this tour would provide insofar as it allowed her to travel through the state of New York, garnering positive press and connecting with New York voters. Just one year after the kickoff of the Save America's Treasures tour, Rodham Clinton entered the race for the U.S. Senate seat open in New York— a race she won in 2000.

Although Hillary Rodham Clinton is a versatile and accomplished orator, her public rhetoric has shaped much more than opinions about the causes she champions. Rodham Clinton has been studied as an exemplar for a generation of women who came of age during the women's movement and who have struggled with the multiple roles they inhabit. Author Betty Friedan described media coverage of Rodham Clinton as a "massive Rorschach test of the evolution of women in our society." Scholars in the fields of communication, political science, women's studies, and media studies have written extensively on Rodham Clinton, using her public career as a case study in gender, power, and publicity in U.S. political culture. Controversies surrounding her public role have spawned debates in the popular press about the nature of the U.S. first ladyship and, more broadly, about women's roles in U.S. society.

Rodham Clinton remains a polarizing and controversial figure, in part because she is linked to a polarizing and controversial presidential administration. Her husband was one of only two U.S. presidents to be impeached, and the Clinton name invokes a long string of scandals: Whitewater, Nannygate, Travelgate, Filegate, Gennifer Flowers, Paula Jones, and Monica Lewinsky. Hillary Rodham Clinton's political identity was shaped by controversy, and her responses, especially to her husband's sex scandals, have contributed to her credibility as a rhetor. Although some find her unflagging support of an unfaithful husband to be inconsonant with the feminist principles she espouses,

Rodham Clinton's defense of her husband during the 1992 presidential campaign and following the 1998 Lewinsky revelations benefited her husband and resulted in positive poll ratings for her, as well. Rodham Clinton was credited with saving her husband's political career in 1992 when she attested to the strength of her marriage on *60 Minutes*, despite revelations about Bill Clinton's possible infidelity. The positive press Rodham Clinton gained in 1998, after handling revelations about the Lewinsky affair with what many press reports described as "grace" and "dignity," benefited her when she later ran for the U.S. Senate. The public's interest in her was illustrated by the staggering sales of her memoir, *Living History*, published in June 2003. Though many doubted that publisher Simon and Schuster would recoup the $8 million advance it gave Rodham Clinton for the book, first-day sales topped 200,000 copies.

Hillary Rodham Clinton made history in 2000 when she was elected to the U.S. Senate. Early committee assignments in the Senate included the Armed Services, Public Works, Health, Education, Labor, and Pensions committees. During her first two years as a U.S. senator, she was praised for keeping a low profile, deferring to more senior colleagues, and working hard on committee assignments. Her rhetoric assumed a more centrist political tone, and the publicity she gained promoting *Living History* provided her with a high national profile. In 2003 reporters repeatedly asked her about possible presidential aspirations. She said that she had none, but pundits suggested that she may be poised for a run at the White House in 2008. Whether or not Rodham Clinton tackles that particular challenge, she appears to be trying to fulfill the goal she espoused in 1969, of pursuing politics as "the art of making what appears to be impossible, possible."

INFORMATION SOURCES

Research Collections and Collected Speeches

Addresses given by Rodham Clinton as U.S. first lady are available online at the National Archives Clinton Presidential Materials Project and in print form in *Remarks and Commentary by First Lady Hillary Rodham Clinton: Vital Voices, 1997–1999.*

Washington, D.C.: Government Printing Office, 1999. Archival materials of this period will be available upon completion of the William Jefferson Clinton Presidential Library in Little Rock, Arkansas. Senator Clinton's speeches and addresses are available in the *Congressional Record*, both in print and online, and on her U.S. Senate home page

Clinton, Hillary. *Remarks and Commentary by First Lady Hillary Rodham Clinton—Vital Voices, 1997–1999 [VV]*. Washington, D.C.: Office of the President of the United States, 1999.

Web Sites

Congressional Record [CR]. http://thomas.loc.gov

The National Archives Clinton Presidential Materials Project [*CPM*]. This site contains archives of complete White House Web sites from 1993 to 2000, including full texts of selected speeches and texts of her weekly newspaper column, "Talking It Over." http://clinton.archives.gov/sitemap.html

National First Ladies' Library Web site. This site contains a bibliography of primary texts by Rodham Clinton, newspaper articles about her, and scholarly books, essays, and studies about her. http://www.firstladies.org

Senator Clinton's page on the U.S. Senate Web site [*USS*]. This site contains full texts of selected speeches and information about her legislative activities. http://clinton.senate.gov/

Audiovisual Materials

A Conversation with Hillary Rodham Clinton. Lexington: Kentucky Author Forum, University of Louisville, 1997.

Drawing Conclusions: Editorial Cartoonists Consider Hillary Rodham Clinton. New York: First Run/Icarus Films, 1998.

The Governor and Mrs. Clinton. Talk with David Frost. PBS Video, 1992.

"Hillary Rodham Clinton: Changing the Rules." *Biography.* New York: Arts and Entertainment Network, 1994.

"They Don't Bake Cookies." *Democracy in America.* CNN, 1996. Transcript available at http://www.cqi.cnn.comm/ALLPOLITICS/1966/resources/democracy/cookies/

Selected Critical Studies

Anderson, Karrin Vasby. "From Spouses to Candidates: Hillary Rodham Clinton, Elizabeth Dole, and the Gendered Office of U.S. President." *Rhetoric & Public Affairs* 5 (2002): 105–32.

———. "Hillary Rodham Clinton as 'Madonna':

The Role of Metaphor and Oxymoron in Image Restoration." *Women's Studies in Communication* 25 (2002): 1–24.

———. " 'Rhymes with Rich': 'Bitch' as a Tool of Containment in Contemporary American Politics." *Rhetoric & Public Affairs* 2 (1999): 599–623.

Bostdorff, Denise M. "Hillary Rodham Clinton and Elizabeth Dole as Running 'Mates' in the 1996 Campaign: Parallels in the Rhetorical Constraints of First Ladies and Vice Presidents." In *The 1996 Presidential Campaign: A Communication Perspective*, ed. Robert E. Denton, Jr. Westport, Conn.: Praeger, 1998.

Campbell, Karlyn Kohrs. "The Discursive Performance of Femininity: Hating Hillary." *Rhetoric & Public Affairs* 1 (1998): 1–19.

———. "The Rhetorical Presidency: A Two-Person Career." In *Beyond the Rhetorical Presidency*, ed. Martin J. Medhurst. College Station: Texas A&M University Press, 1996.

———. "Shadowboxing with Stereotypes: The Press, the Public, and the Candidates' Wives," Research paper R-9, pp. 1–19. Cambridge, Mass.: President and Fellows of Harvard College, 1993.

Jamieson, Kathleen Hall. "Hillary Clinton as Rorschach Test." In her *Beyond the Double Bind: Women and Leadership*. New York: Oxford University Press, 1995.

Kelley, Colleen Elizabeth. *The Rhetoric of First Lady Hillary Rodham Clinton: Crisis Management Discourse*. Westport, Conn.: Praeger, 2001.

Mattina, Anne F. "Hillary Rodham Clinton: Using Her Vital Voice." In *Inventing a Voice: The Rhetoric of American First Ladies of the Twentieth Century*, ed. Molly Wertheimer. Lanham, Md.: Rowman & Littlefield, 2004.

Muir, Janette Kenner, and Lisa M. Benitez. "Redefining the Role of the First Lady: The Rhetorical Style of Hillary Rodham Clinton." In *The Clinton Presidency: Images, Issues, and Communication Strategies*, ed. Robert E. Denton, Jr. and Rachel L. Holloway. Westport, Conn.: Praeger, 1996.

Parry-Giles, Shawn J. "Mediating Hillary Rodham Clinton: Television News Practices and Image-Making in the Postmodern Age." *Critical Studies in Media Communication* 17 (2000): 205–26.

Sullivan, Patricia A., and Lynn H. Turner. "Power and Politics: A Case Study of Hillary Rodham Clinton." In their *From the Margins to the Center: Contemporary Women and Political Communication*. Westport, Conn.: Praeger, 1996.

Winfield, Betty Houchin. " 'Madame President': Understanding a New Kind of First Lady." *Media Studies Journal* 8 (1994): 59–71.

Selected Biographies

Brock, David. *The Seduction of Hillary Rodham.* New York: Free Press, 1996.

Clinton, Hillary Rodham. *Living History.* New York: Simon and Schuster, 2003.

Milton, Joyce. *The First Partner—Hillary Rodham Clinton, A Biography.* New York: Perennial, 2000.

Radcliffe, Donnie. *Hillary Rodham Clinton: A First Lady for Our Time.* New York: Warner Books, 1993.

Sheehy, Gail. *Hillary's Choice.* New York: Ballantine Books, 2000.

CHRONOLOGY OF MAJOR SPEECHES

See "Research Collections and Collected Speeches" for source codes.

"Remarks of Hillary D. Rodham, President of the Wellesley College Government Association and Member of the Class of 1969" (Wellesley commencement address). May 31, 1969. Available at http://www.feminist.com/resources/artspeech/poli/hillary.htm and at http://www.wellesley.edu/Public/Affairs/Commencement/1969/053169hillary.html

"Remarks by First Lady Hillary Rodham Clinton at the Liz Carpenter Lecture Series on Civil Society" ("Politics of Meaning" speech). University of Texas, Austin, April 7, 1993. *CPM* and *Tikkun* (May 1993).

"Remarks by the First Lady in Commencement Address to the University of Michigan." Ann Arbor, Mich., May 1, 1993. *CPM.*

"Health Care: We Can Make a Difference." *CPM*; *Vital Speeches of the Day,* July 15, 1993, pp. 580–85.

Address to the United Nations Fourth World Conference on Women. Beijing, China, September 5, 1995. *CPM.*

Address to the 1996 Democratic National Convention. Chicago, August 27, 1996. Available at http://www.pbs.org/newshour/convention96/floor_speeches/hillary_clinton.html

Address at the 150th Anniversary of the First Woman's Rights Convention. Seneca Falls, N.Y., July 16, 1998. *CPM.*

Announcement for Senate candidacy. Purchase, N.Y., February 6, 2000. Retrieved from www.nytimes.com, February 7, 2000.

Address to the 2000 Democratic National Convention. Los Angeles, August 14, 2000. Available at http://www.pbs.org/newshour/election2000/demconvention/video.html; http://www.npr.org/news/nationalelection2000/demconvention/democrat.mon.eve.html. *Vital Speeches of the Day,* September 1, 2000.

WILLIAM JEFFERSON CLINTON (1946–)
Forty-second President of the United States

STEPHEN A. SMITH

Bill Clinton was born William Jefferson Blythe III on August 19, 1946, in Hope, Arkansas, to Virginia Cassidy Blythe, and named for his father, who had recently died in an auto accident. After his mother obtained a nursing degree, she married an automobile salesman named Roger Clinton, and when Bill was seven years old, the family moved to Hot Springs, Arkansas.

While attending public school in Hot Springs, Clinton never took a class in public speaking, but he was in school plays, memorized speeches in the Masonic youth organization De Molay, was successful in class elections, and, in an exercise for his Latin class, assumed the role of defense counsel for Catiline in the Senate trial for conspiracy in which Cicero was his accuser. In addition, he "grew up in a family of great bullshitters, always telling stories around meals," which probably "accounts for whatever speaking ability I have," he said in an interview for this essay.

In 1963, before his senior year in high school, Clinton was elected to Boys Nation and invited to the White House to meet President Kennedy. That experience and a memorable photograph of the event strengthened Clinton's inclination toward a career in public service. That same summer, Dr. Martin Luther King, Jr. gave his historic "I Have a Dream" speech at the Lincoln Memorial. Clinton watched the speech on television and later memorized the words. No question about it, he said forty years later, "it was the best speech I've ever heard." During his senior year, he gave several speeches to local civic clubs about his experience at Boys Nation and meeting Kennedy, a topic of much local interest after Kennedy's assassination that fall.

Entering Georgetown University in 1964 and majoring in international affairs, Clinton had no academic courses in communication or public speaking, although he continued to win class elections and began participating in public affairs beyond campus. During his last two years at Georgetown, he held a part-time clerk position on the Senate Foreign Relations Committee, chaired by Senator J. William Fulbright (D-Ark.), during a period when the senator and his committee were engaging the national debate on the Vietnam War.

Spending his summers at home in Arkansas, Clinton gained his first experience in political campaigns. In 1966, he was on the campaign staff of Frank Holt, an unsuccessful candidate for governor in the Democratic primary, mostly doing the necessary grunt work but also appearing with other student leaders supporting Holt in a paid political program on statewide television. He also gave his first campaign speeches, speaking as a surrogate for the candidate at rallies in his old hometown of Hope and at the Mt. Nebo Chicken Fry, traditionally the most important stump speech venue in Arkansas primary elections. Following graduation from Georgetown in 1968, Clinton joined Senator Fulbright's reelection campaign staff, working in the headquarters and often as a driver, observing Fulbright's local speeches and the personal campaigning demanded of candidates.

As a Rhodes Scholar at Oxford University from 1968 to 1970, Clinton continued his reading in politics, philosophy, and economics, and he frequently attended the speakers and the weekly debates of the Oxford Union Society. Upon returning to the United States to begin classes at Yale Law School, he spent considerable time during his first semester as a congressional district coordinator for Joseph Duffey's 1970 campaign for the U.S. Senate, and

his senior year on the staff of Senator George McGovern's 1972 presidential campaign. He also met his future wife, Hillary Rodham, at Yale, where as a team they reached the final round in the Barristers' Union Prize Trial competition.

After graduating from Yale in 1973, Clinton accepted a position that fall on the faculty of the University of Arkansas Law School at Fayetteville. In February 1974, at the age of twenty-seven, he announced his candidacy for Congress from the Third Congressional District. Handily defeating three opponents in the primary, he ran a close but unsuccessful race against Republican incumbent John Paul Hammerschmidt. Clinton gave countless speeches during the campaign and became a compelling orator on the stump, almost always speaking extemporaneously.

Hillary Rodham had joined the law faculty at Arkansas in 1974, and she and Clinton were married in 1975. Drawing from his experience in the congressional race and having gained favorable statewide recognition among the Democratic Party and the media, Clinton ran for, and was elected, attorney general of Arkansas in 1976. While attorney general, he delivered an average of four speeches a week, mostly dealing with utility rate regulations and consumer protection, official functions of the office with which he had considerable legislative and legal success. He was also a popular speaker with civic groups on other social and political issues.

Two years later, at age thirty-two, Clinton became the youngest governor in the United States and gave what can be considered the best inaugural address of his career. As governor of Arkansas, he concentrated on the stock issues of state government: improving the state's educational system, building better roads, energy rates and conservation, economic development, environmental protection, and quality of life for senior citizens. At the Democratic National Convention in 1980, Clinton delivered an important message about the party's need to reach out to disaffected citizens, but he became one of the more surprising victims of the Reagan landslide, losing his bid for reelection to political novice Frank White.

Clinton was elected governor again in November 1982, having adopted a somewhat less ambitious and more pragmatic style and agenda, and, served four additional terms in office. Despite a disastrous nominating speech for Michael Dukakis at the 1988 Democratic National Convention, Clinton built political networks and rebuilt his national image as chair of the National Governors Association and a leading voice in the centrist Democratic Leadership Council, positioning himself for a shot at the Democratic nomination for president in 1992. He was rated the most effective governor in the country by his colleagues.

Announcing his campaign for president in October 1991, Clinton stressed the issues of health care, education, and the economy, challenging the popular incumbent, George H. W. Bush. Overcoming accusations of marital infidelity and draft evasion during the primaries, Clinton went on to claim the nomination and to defeat Bush and H. Ross Perot in the 1992 elec-

"Building a Bridge to the 21st Century." He defeated Republican Bob Dole and H. Ross Perot with 49 percent of the popular vote and an electoral landslide of 379 to 159. Much of Clinton's second term was dominated by media coverage of an investigation by Special Prosecutor Kenneth Starr and Clinton's impeachment and acquittal on charges of perjury and obstruction of justice. Nonetheless, in major speeches he continued his arguments for increased opportunity, personal responsibility, and coming together as One America, initiating a national "conversation on race" that had been a consistent theme throughout his career. At the close of his second term in 2001, Clinton touted his presidency as "eight years of peace, progress and prosperity."

After leaving office, Clinton remained in demand as a speaker and Democratic fund-raiser, with his speeches netting as high as $150,000 on the national and international lecture circuit, and

> Although generally regarded as one of the more effective presidential communicators of recent times, Clinton eschewed traditional eloquence. For a president to succeed, he said "sending right signals is more important than giving a great speech."

tion. In addition to casting himself as "the Man from Hope" and focusing campaign speeches on his plans to revive the economy with a theme of "Putting People First," Clinton campaigned with a nationwide bus tour, did well in the televised debates, connected with people in town hall meetings, and appeared on talk shows.

After taking office in January 1993, Clinton proposed an ambitious but somewhat unfocused agenda, securing a budget reduction plan that fueled a sustained economic recovery but failing to convince Congress to reform the health-care system. After the Republicans captured majorities in both the House and the Senate in 1994, Clinton was forced to develop new strategies in rhetorically leading a divided government.

Though he was unopposed for the Democratic nomination in 1996, Clinton ran a cautious campaign and premised his reelection on the theme

wrote an account of his life in politics. Working through the William J. Clinton Foundation, with offices in Harlem in New York City and the Clinton Library in Little Rock, he continued to participate in the public dialogue on the worldwide battle against AIDS/HIV; racial, ethnic, and religious reconciliation; economic empowerment; and citizen service.

OPPORTUNITY, RESPONSIBILITY, AND COMMUNITY

It seems that at the age of 27, Bill Clinton sprang rhetorically full-grown onto the political scene in Arkansas, making his first political race as a candidate for Congress in 1974. Governor Dale Bumpers, then running for the U.S. Senate against Fulbright in the Democratic primary, recalled in his autobiography, almost thirty years later, the first time he heard Clinton speak that March, at the River Valley campaign kickoff rally in Russellville. "In four minutes he delivered one of the most beautiful, eloquent speeches I ever heard, pushing every emotional button on every value Americans cherish. He spoke of our solemn duty to our children and the peace, education, and economic security to which they were entitled," Bumpers said. "He spoke without a note and without a single hesitation or grammatical error, which I found remarkable." Then, Bumpers added, "I especially remember that as my staff and I drove the seventy miles back to Little Rock, I said, 'I hope that guy never runs against me.' "

Clinton has always been at his best when speaking extemporaneously on the campaign trail. In Arkansas, he never used notes or a text for speeches at campaign rallies, and he was equally adept at one-take political campaign spots that compressed a message to twenty-eight seconds. During his political career in Arkansas, as attorney general and five terms as

from staff, old friends, political supporters, and an occasional academic, but the crafting was fundamentally his own; he was always revising until the last minute with a felt-tip pen, even when one legislative address was being typed in final draft for the media after he had reached the podium and begun his remarks. Of these, his first gubernatorial Inaugural Address in 1979, was the most elegant, speaking of "pride and hope" and calling for "a new era of achievement and excellence" with an innocence and enthusiasm that would later be tempered by the political realities of the 1980s. That speech also contains the rudimentary themes of opportunity, responsibility, and community that would continue to be at the center of his public rhetoric, and Clinton said in a recent interview that he considers it among the best speeches he ever delivered.

In his first nationally televised speech, Clin-

The *Los Angeles Times* called Clinton's 1988 DNC speech nominating Michael Dukakis "the speech that ate Atlanta." With many other critics, the paper thought that the up-and-coming Clinton had committed "nationally televised political suicide." Four years later he was the Democratic Party's presidential nominee.

---

governor, Clinton sometimes used briefing notes provided by his staff or an outline of key words and main points that he hurriedly sketched out on the way to speaking engagements before civic clubs and professional associations, but these were only to order the main points. The important facts and statistics he could remember, and the specific rhetorical choices were always effortless and his own. He was a master of detail with a down-home delivery that connected with his audience, able to fluently tailor his metaphors and his message to his immediate audience.

On more formal occasions of state, such as his five inaugural addresses or the presentation of his legislative program to the General Assembly in the State of the State speeches, Clinton relied on a prepared text. In these instances, he would seek suggestions for issues and themes

ton spoke on behalf of the Democratic Governors Association to the 1980 Democratic National Convention, and he did well with a prepared text. Here, too, he offered a preview of a recurring rhetorical theme when he called for new solutions to old problems and demanded that the party reach out to the millions of Americans who do not care and do not watch political conventions on television, who "cannot be moved by the symbols and accomplishments of the Democratic Party of the past."

Perhaps the worst speech of Clinton's career was his nominating speech for Michael Dukakis at the 1988 Democratic National Convention, doomed from the start when he stepped to the podium for a fifteen-minute speech with a nineteen-page text, one that had expanded with each revision by Clinton and the Dukakis staff and was slowed by orchestrated applause on the convention floor. Clinton realized, only a few minutes into his delivery, that it was not the speech demanded by the situation, but he felt compelled to follow the approved text rather than break into an energizing, extemporaneous alternative. A bored and annoyed audience on the floor let Clinton know he was sinking, network commentators expressed disbelief at the effort, cameras showed the flashing red light on the lectern and the faces of delegates chanting "get the hook." The loudest applause came when Clinton said "In conclusion," and ended the speech at thirty-two minutes. The *Los Angeles Times* dubbed it "the speech that ate Atlanta," and mused that the Democratic Party's rising star had committed "nationally televised political suicide."

Memories of the Atlanta convention speech still lingered in 1991 when Clinton announced his candidacy for president on October 3, but his rhetorical performance was now his to own and much improved. Calling for change and offering himself as the agent, he said, "Together I believe we can provide leadership that will restore the American dream, that will fight for the forgotten middle class, that will provide more opportunity, insist on more responsibility, and create a greater sense of community for this great country." Calling Clinton a "compelling orator," Morton Kondracke wrote in *The New Republic*, "Clinton's message has every sign of being the right one, and his oratory suggests the messenger may be the right one, too."

With a series of three thoughtful, carefully written, and well received major speeches delivered at Georgetown University in October, November, and December, Clinton sought to elaborate on his political principles and worked to establish his credentials to be the next president. The first elaborated his vision of the basic social compact: "a New Covenant, a solemn agreement between the people and their government, to provide opportunity for everybody, inspire responsibility throughout our society, and restore a sense of community to this great nation." Those would be the enduring themes not only of the campaign but also of his presidency. The remaining two speeches dealt with the idea of the New Covenant for economic change and for national security, serving to demonstrate that Clin-

ton, governor of a small state, had a command of national issues and the competence to deal with them.

"Clinton is a man of many words, most of them his own," noted David Maraness of the *Washington Post* during the campaign. Although at times he relied on staff speechwriters, for drafts, "Clinton is a better speechwriter than any of us," admitted Bruce Reed, who contributed to the policy message. "The best thing about writing for him is that he does most of the work. He cares a lot about ideas and words and rhythms, which makes him harder to write for, but in an ideal world there would be more politicians like him and fewer of us."

Most of Clinton's 1992 campaign speeches were extemporaneous, with fewer than a dozen delivered from prepared texts, and were sometimes thought to be overly complex policy discussions that lost his audience. Even if he was criticized for talking "too long about certain issues," Clinton believed that "it was really important for me to establish a feeling that I was competent." More often it worked, and David Von Drehle, writing in the *Washington Post*, concluded, "He's Elvis Presley with a calculator on his belt, an outsized candidate with a drawl as big as his brain, a would-be president of both pie charts and Moon Pies." Yet, when hit with charges of infidelity and draft-dodging during the crucial New Hampshire primary, Clinton ignored the policy minutiae and spoke without notes, exhorting a packed crowd at the Elks Club in Dover on February 12. "They tell me I'm on the ropes . . . because other people have questioned my life after years of public service," Clinton said. "You give me this election, and I won't be like George Bush and forget who gave me a second chance, and I'll be there for you until the last dog dies." It saved his candidacy and was, Clinton still thinks, the most important stump speech he ever gave in any campaign.

The 1992 campaign speech that has received the most national attention was his acceptance speech at the Democratic National Convention, introduced by a video biography, *The Man from Hope*. Clinton understood the importance of the opportunity, and had prepared for the speech by reviewing previous convention acceptance speeches and a large stack of staff memos suggesting what needed to be said, going through numerous drafts and practicing his presentation. Speaking not only to the convention delegates but also to a prime-time television audience, Clinton presented his personal story and his political vision of opportunity, responsibility, and community in a tone more appropriate for the living room than for the passionate partisan audience in Madison Square Garden. While he most admired the examples of Martin Luther King and John Kennedy, he saw them as transitional public speakers for the electronic age and thought that Ronald Reagan was the first master of the stylistic requirements for communicating in the era dominated by television. Clinton, understanding the dimensions of the rhetorical presidency, said he learned: "I had to work hard to try to modulate my style to retain whatever passion and rhythm I had in my speeches—from growing up in Arkansas and that stump oratory—so that I could still keep what was good about it without losing the television audience."

While Clinton's acceptance speech was fifty-four minutes long, his First Inaugural Address ran only fourteen minutes. There were threads of historical and philosophical continuity with mentions of Washington, Jefferson, and Roosevelt, and his words made allusions to Kennedy's Inaugural and King's dream. To signal the change of administrations, Clinton chose for his theme "Forcing the Spring," which he said came from a four-page draft found in the typewriter of his late friend Timothy Healy. The changes Clinton advocated were not unexpected. "We must do what America does best: offer more opportunity to all and demand more responsibility from all," he said in an echo of the recent campaign. "Let us all take more responsibility, not only for ourselves and our families but for our communities and our country."

Clinton's first State of the Union speech focused on explaining and promoting his economic plan, and the process for its execution revealed a familiar pattern of merging information from policy staff with evolving drafts from speechwriters. Finding the text unimpressive, Clinton ordered another rewrite on the morning of the speech that involved both staff and the first lady, who thought the draft "just not good enough." That evening, Clinton began his remarks with the quip that it was "nice to have a fresh excuse for giving a long speech," then implored Congress to join him "on a great national journey" to revive the economy. Although he called for setting the nation on a new course, he suggested that the new direction would be found in the old values of a commitment to opportunity, to individual responsibility, and to community. As he moved to specifics of the plan and encountered audible disagreement from the Republicans, Clinton departed from the prepared text and responded extemporaneously on two separate points with arguments appealing to, and reminding them of, their joint obligations to the American people.

Clinton's ability to adapt and extemporize was again demonstrated when he presented his health-care proposals in a televised address before a joint session of Congress that October. As usual, the speech text had gone through numerous drafts and last-minute revisions. As he reached the podium and looked at the teleprompter, Clinton saw not the health-care speech he was to deliver that evening but the text from his economic policy speech of February. Calmly turning to Vice President Gore, he asked that the staff load the appropriate speech text and then began the speech, continuing for seven minutes before the problem was corrected. It was unnoticed by the audience, but it was a rhetorical performance that would have been daunting for other recent presidents.

What many consider the best speech of Clinton's presidential tenure was not an official one required by tradition, nor was it one primarily about a government program or a call to pass specific legislation. It was the call for personal responsibility and social action, delivered in November to the convocation of the Church of God in Christ at Memphis, from the same pulpit where Martin Luther King had delivered his last sermonic speech in 1968. Clinton reviewed the progress toward King's dream, reaffirmed his commitment to those ideals, and said: "I have tried to keep the faith." Weaving his continuing theme of opportunity, responsibility, and community with examples that resonated with the African American audience, Clinton spoke in the pace, cadence, and timbre of the pulpit that gave the message an emotional force and display of political passion that is not evident in the transcribed text. Although he had sounded the same themes before, this time the rhetoric captured the imagination of a wider audience.

Michael Putzel of the *Boston Globe* complained that "Clinton rarely finishes working on a speech before delivering it, advance texts are rare, and little effort is devoted to presenting the president at his best." That even this important speech "came as a complete surprise to the president's own communications staff and the reporters who regularly cover him, most of whom remained in Washington that Saturday morning covering the NAFTA battle, having been assured by aides the president would not make news on his brief outing." Clinton, too, was somewhat surprised at the response to the Memphis speech. "I think I underestimated the importance of the president's voice, just being able to speak about those issues in a coherent, clear, forceful way," he said, having realized, as a result of the moving letters he received, that "the words of a president count" and that "the opportunity to speak turned out to be action in itself, because it seemed to galvanize the energy and concentration of a nation."

As his first year in office came to an end, Clinton reflected on the unanticipated problems and opportunities for presidential leadership from the bully pulpit. "It's not as easy to reach out directly to the people and cut through the cacophony of noise and rhetoric. Sure, the President can give an address to the nation, but you can only do that every so often. You can't just abuse the networks or the privilege. And sure you can do press conferences, but it's not quite the same," he confessed in an interview with the *Los Angeles Times*. Yet, David Broder of the *Washington Post* concluded, "The most encouraging thing about President Clinton . . . is the serious reflection he is doing about the use of the rhetorical powers of his office. It has taken awhile, but he now seems to understand that of the many roles he must play, none is more important to the nation than being communicator-in-chief, using the White House forum to mobilize and focus public opinion."

Clinton's concerns about the state of genuine democratic dialogue became more evident during 1994 as the congressional Republicans aggressively opposed his plans for health-care reform and his legislative program generally. In his remarks at the Jefferson-Jackson Democratic Governors Association luncheon on May 14, Clinton complained that "our national debate is so shrouded in this shrill, uncivil, diversionary rhetoric" and challenged his audience to "change the dimensions of our conversation away from all this division, destruction, the shouting, this uncivil, this often outright dishonest talk, to a calm and more hospitable and more open and more respectful tone." Concluding that the oppositional rhetoric was often more personal attack than policy disagreement, he added, "Of those little words—opportunity, responsibility, and community—I believe with all my heart, by far the most important is community."

Nonetheless, the 1994 congressional elections resulted in a Republican majority in both houses and a divided government. Clinton faced a new and different audience when he delivered his 1995 State of the Union address. While his speechwriters were crafting drafts, Clinton was meeting privately with Dick Morris, who was urging a very different message. In the end, Clinton merged significant parts of both speeches and held forth for eighty-two minutes. Tracy Lee Simmons, writing for the *National Review*, found the speech exhausting: "Clinton's oratory suffers a far deeper ill than prolixity. Namely, it hardly qualifies as oratory at all. . . . Good oratory depends on several virtues, few of which Clinton practices: concentration of phrase, clarity of purpose, force, gravity."

Similar criticism came from Walter Shapiro writing in *Esquire*. "After two years in the White House, the president has yet to deliver a speech on global policy that anyone who is not a card-carrying member of the Council on Foreign Relations remembers." Clinton too often allowed the State Department to "muffle his foreign policy speeches with diplomatic code," Shapiro added, and most voters "do not walk around with foreign-policy decoder rings. They hunger for rhetorical power."

Michael Waldman, formerly Clinton's chief speechwriter, explained that while Clinton "is a very good speaker and a gifted communicator . . . he doesn't go in for the kind of high-blown rhetoric, chiseled phrases. When we [would] hand him a speech that had a lot of fancy rhetoric in it, he would cross it out and mutter, "Words, words, words." Waldman said that with Clinton "the eloquence came from policy. Where he was most effective as a speaker and most animated was when he was up there arguing Social Security or health care, on the bread and butter of policy." Strangely, for a man who held Kennedy and King as models of eloquence and who excelled as an exciting stump speaker, Clinton seemed to agree, saying in a recent interview that he thought, for a president trying to enact legislation and advance policies, "sending the right signals is more important than giving a great speech."

An example that reflected the philosophy of signaling prosaic policies instead of stimulating political passions was Clinton's acceptance speech at the 1996 Democratic National Convention in Chicago. Constrained by the usual rhetorical limitations of incumbents seeking reelection, Clinton's speech rehearsed the past successes of his administration, identified problems remaining to be resolved, and offered his continued leadership as the solution. Using the effective theme of a "Bridge to the 21st Century," the speech went on for sixty-six minutes, far more pedestrian prose than political poetry, earnestly enumerating some thirty different policy goals more appropriate for a State of the Union speech and losing the attention and enthusiasm of many in the audience. It was a safe speech for a campaign that was hardly in doubt, but with only a few exceptions, it was not a particularly memorable performance.

Second inaugural addresses lack the excitement and tension reflecting a change in executive leadership, and are more tempered with realism than are first inaugurals. Clinton's speech fit this pattern established by the previous thirteen in that genre. Nonetheless, as he stood at the west front of the Capitol and looked toward the Lincoln Memorial and the scene of Martin Luther King's 1963 speech, it also reflected his continued hope for creating opportunity and building community. In preparation for drafting the address, Clinton had reread King's optimistic "A Testament of Hope" and Lincoln's Second Inaugural Address, delivered when the nation faced a far greater challenge than the political partisanship and petty bickering of the 1990s.

Appropriately for the first inaugural address ever to be streamed live on the World Wide Web, Clinton looked at the future challenges facing the nation and began the twenty-two-minute speech by noting that at "the dawn of the 21st century, a free people must choose to shape the forces of the information age and the global society to unleash the limitless potential of all our people and form a more perfect Union." Signaling another philosophical break with the past by recalling the political stance of Ronald Reagan's First Inaugural declaration that "government is not the solution to our problem; government is the problem," Clinton said, "Today we can declare: Government is not the problem, and government is not the solution. We, the American people, we are the solution. . . . With a new vision of government, a new sense of responsibility, a new spirit of community, we will sustain America's journey."

The speech was also significant in giving more attention to the issue of racial conflict and harmony than any previous presidential inaugural address. The issue of racial reconciliation addressed here is the rhetorical theme that has dominated Clinton's political career, and it is the one on which his position has always been clear, consistent, and predictable. "The divide of race has been America's constant curse," Clinton said, crippling "both those who are hated and, of course, those who hate, robbing both of what they might become. . . . We cannot—we will not—succumb to the dark impulses that lurk in the far regions of the soul, everywhere. We shall overcome them."

Invoking King's memorable speech that had inspired him as a teenager, Clinton said: "Thirty-four years ago the man whose life we celebrate today spoke to us down there at the other end of this Mall in words that moved the conscience of a nation. Like a prophet of old, he told of his dream that one day America would rise up and treat all its citizens as equals before the law and in the heart. . . . Martin Luther King's dream was the American dream. His quest is our quest: the ceaseless striving to live out our true creed." Closing the inaugural speech with a refrain from the recent election campaign, Clinton called upon the American people to "build our bridge . . . to a blessed land of new promise."

Although Peggy Noonan, a former Reagan

speechwriter who reflected the immediate oppositional spin, told the *New York Times* that she
found the speech "vapid" and "banal," Clinton
still counts the Second Inaugural Address
among the best speeches of his presidency. It
was, he said in a recent interview, "a coherent
statement of what I believe and what we were
trying to do."

In his 1997 State of the Union speech, Clinton laid out what he wanted to accomplish during the four years of his second term, devoting
almost one-fourth of it to education; however,
he had to compete for the nation's attention with
the verdict in the O.J. Simpson civil case. Even
the PBS coverage could not wait for the president to leave the House chamber before reporting on the Simpson verdict, and the Simpson
story led on the front pages of many of the
major newspapers the following day.

There was no such lack of attention focused
on the 1998 State of the Union address. After
four years of unsuccessful pursuit in the Whitewater investigation by Independent Counsel
Kenneth Starr, the previous week brought allegations that Clinton had sexual relations with
former intern Monica Lewinsky and that he encouraged her to lie about it under oath. In a
speech that was more about the state of the president than about the state of the union, every
word was sure to be closely analyzed, and an
unusually large audience of 120 million viewers
watched the speech on television. Clinton was
up to the task, and gave a performance that signaled business as usual in a seventy-two-minute
speech that effectively communicated an agenda
of forty-nine new policy initiatives.

Clinton told the Congress that "the state of
our Union is strong," but quickly added that this
"is not a time to rest. It is a time to build," leaving no doubt that he planned to continue in office. Touting the first projected budget surplus
in a generation, he asked rhetorically, "What
should we do with this surplus? I have a simple
four-word answer: Save Social Security first,"
an answer that was met with prolonged applause
in the chamber and deftly settled a potential political confrontation over taxes and spending.

Then, Clinton moved through other issues before closing with a return to his continuing
theme of community. "Our Founders set Amer-

ica on a permanent course toward a more perfect
Union. To all of you I say, it is a journey we can
only make together, living as one community."
Leaving no doubt that he intended to remain in
office and pursue the building of community,
Clinton added: "We, in this Chamber and in this
Government, must do all we can to address the
continuing American challenge to build one
America. But we'll only move forward if all our
fellow citizens, including every one of you at
home watching tonight, is also committed to this
cause. We must work together, learn together,
live together, serve together."

Michael Waldman considered the speech the
most significant one of his time on the speechwriting staff. "He found a way to convey optimism, and personal buoyancy and positive
movement for the country in the middle of the
most withering controversy. And where he will
be remembered in his speeches is not so much
for the chiseled words on the wall, but by appropriately using language, moving billions and
trillions of dollars in the budget," Waldman suggested. A Gallup poll indicated that Clinton had
also succeeded in addressing his immediate
problems, at least for that especially tense political moment, with 67 percent of viewers saying they had watched to see how Clinton would
handle the situation and 84 percent having a
positive reaction to the speech.

Clinton's relationship with the intern, however, remained the focus of Kenneth Starr's investigation and the fascination of the media. On
August 17, after testifying before Starr's grand
jury, Clinton went on television to offer an apology to the nation. "I must take complete responsibility for all my actions, both public and
private," he said. "I know that my public comments and my silence about this matter gave a
false impression. I misled people, including even
my wife. I deeply regret that." Many pundits and
political communication scholars thought the
apology ineffective, because Clinton went on to
question the motives and actions of Starr and argued, "This has gone on too long, cost too much,
and hurt too many innocent people. . . . It is time
to stop the pursuit of personal destruction and
the prying into private lives and get on with our
national life." At the White House prayer breakfast on September 15, Clinton continued his

apology in an effort to satisfy those who wanted more. "I agree with those who have said that in my first statement after I testified I was not contrite enough. I don't think there is a fancy way to say that I have sinned," he said. "It is important to me that everybody who has been hurt know that the sorrow I feel is genuine: first and most important, my family, also my friends, my staff, my Cabinet, Monica Lewinsky and her family, and the American people. I have asked all for their forgiveness."

No apology, however, would have stopped Kenneth Starr from sending a titillating report to Congress recommending impeachment, nor would it have prevented the House of Representatives from adopting articles of impeachment in a party-line vote. Clinton's 1999 State of the Union speech was delivered during the U.S. Senate trial on his impeachment, presenting an extraordinary rhetorical challenge. David Kusnet, a former speechwriter, advised a strategy that avoided "pious platitudes, happy-talk, and focus-group-tested mini-initiatives" and reminded "voters that the challenges they face are more important than the charges he faces."

Clinton began his address with disarming remarks to Speaker Hastert. "Mr. Speaker, at your swearing-in, you asked us all to work together in a spirit of civility and bipartisanship. Mr. Speaker, let's do exactly that." Then, reviewing the success of his administration's first six years, Clinton delivered a seventy-seven-minute speech that contained sixty-seven new initiatives and was interrupted ninety-eight times by applause. While his personal political predicament muted calls for personal responsibility, the speech was strong on opportunity and community, including an assessment of the national dialogue on race and the introduction of Rosa Parks in the gallery.

Skillfully arguing by implication and shifting the focus away from his immediate political difficulties, Clinton expressed optimism about the nation's future and his own. "A hundred years from tonight, another American President will stand in this place and report on the State of the Union. He—or she— . . . will look back on a 21st century shaped in so many ways by the decisions we make here and now," he told an audience that included his jurors. "So let it be said

of us then that we were thinking not only of our time, but of their time; that we reached as high as our ideals; that we put aside our divisions and found a new hour of healing and hopefulness; that we joined together to serve and strengthen the land we love."

Although the *Wall Street Journal* editorialized that it "was the most shameless State of the Union speech any president has ever delivered," the speech allowed Clinton to accomplish rhetorically all of his political objectives. Jonathan Freedland, writing in *The Guardian*, called the speech "an act of sheer political chutzpah," and Arianna Huffington's syndicated column expressed "a sense of amazement, even awe, at the fact that a defendant in a Senate impeachment trial could still convey with his body language, his exuberant smile and his wonkish text that he was in control—if not of himself, then at least of the country and his adversaries." Even Pat Robertson, during a broadcast of *The 700 Club*, said that Clinton "hit a home run," and added, "From a public relations standpoint, he's won. They might as well dismiss this impeachment hearing and get on with something else, because it's over as far as I'm concerned." The American public seemed to agree, giving Clinton a 76 percent overall job approval in an NBC survey after the speech. In an interview four years later, Clinton recalled it as "a good speech under adverse conditions" and noted that, politically, it was probably the most important speech of his presidency.

In an era when few presidents contributed as much to the drafting of their own speeches, even fewer seem to have given much thought to the nature and function of rhetoric, which Clinton defines as "speaking, the purpose of which is to persuade, either through reason or emotion." Most national politicians use the term only as shorthand to dismiss the arguments of their opponents, and Clinton, too, sometimes complained about the negative rhetoric of national politics. As an example, he said the list of sixty-four negative words distributed to Republican candidates by Newt Gingrich's political action committee in 1990 to help their party define Democrat opponents—by using such words as traitor, bizarre, sick, radical, pathetic, and disgrace—undermined democratic dialogue by demonizing the political opposition, obscuring the realities of the policy debate, and limiting an audience's ability to seriously consider the issues. "Rhetoric is not, by definition, a bad thing," he added. "It can be a wonderful thing."

Although national political communication is dominated by television and media consultants, and high political oratory is a vanishing art, Clinton believes that public speaking "still matters" in public life, especially for the president or a governor, because one must "sell attributes as well as issues, and the way you speak, regardless of what you say, either does or doesn't communicate strength, confidence, and optimism," qualities that are important in gaining votes, whether in election campaigns or persuading Congress to enact legislation.

No other modern president has demonstrated Clinton's rhetorical ability to connect with audiences of different races and at every level of age, class, and education. His passionate campaign stump speeches and his easy command of the unscripted town hall format were models of effective political communication. While less inspiring, perhaps, his formal presidential addresses also revealed a coherent and complex understanding of public policy and an effective use of language to explain it.

Since leaving office in January 2001, Clinton has continued to live a life of words. In 2001, his first year out of office, he was paid $9.2 million for fifty-nine speaking appearances. Each year since, he has made hundreds of speeches to raise funds for Democratic candidates, nonprofit institutions, his foundation's public policy projects, and the Clinton Presidential Library. About 40 percent of his appearances are paid speeches, with fees ranging from $28,000 to as much as $350,000 for international venues. Clinton won a Grammy for a recording of *Peter and the Wolf* with Mikhail Gorbachev and Sophia Loren, and he wrote a best-selling 957-page autobiography, *My Life*.

Bill Clinton remains an international figure and is, perhaps, even more highly regarded abroad than in the United States. After his address to the British Labour Party conference at Blackpool in October 2002, the British press was effusive. "Over-endowed with the priceless gift of making everyone in the hall feel as if he was talking directly to them," wrote Paul Waugh, deputy political editor of *The Independent*, "Mr Clinton worked the room with intimate eye contact." Ruth Wishart of the *Glasgow Herald* observed, "Listening to him as he shaped his arguments, bringing them full circle to the need to recognise the importance of celebrating our differences and harmonising our aspirations rather than succumbing to the dangerous world of fundamentalists, you couldn't stifle a fervent wish he was still calling America's shots."

"There is no single definition of what makes a great political speech. Probably the accolade is handed out too readily. Yet no one who was present at Blackpool yesterday afternoon was in any doubt that they had just heard one. In an intimate, almost conversational tone, speaking only from notes, Bill Clinton delivered the speech of a true political master," said an editorial in *The Guardian*. "For this was the speech of a truly serious political leader, and if it went on five minutes longer than it needed to do, it was still a performance of the highest possible class. If one were reviewing it, five stars would not be enough. . . . What a speech. What a pro. And what a loss to the leadership of America and the world."

While contemporary assessments of Bill Clinton and his rhetoric have often tended to reflect the critic's political or ideological stance, it appears that time will be kind to Clinton's image as a public speaker. He proved to be an especially popular and effective speaker as a party elder at the 2004 Democratic National Convention, where a partisan crowd of delegates gave the speech glowing reviews and the speaker a more enthusiastic welcome than he had received at the 2000 convention. With more than 2,589 speech texts available online from his eight years as president and more speeches being delivered weekly since leaving office, it is certain that future scholars will have an opportunity to provide additional rhetorical analyses and a more thorough critical assessment.

INFORMATION SOURCES

Research Collections and Collected Speeches
Arkansas Archives of Public Communication [*AAPC*]. Manuscript Collection 942, Special Collections,

Mullins Library, University of Arkansas, Fayetteville. The Arkansas Archives holds thirty-six folders, sixty-five audiotapes, and twenty-nine videotapes related to the prepresidential career of Bill Clinton, including typescript speech texts and audiotapes of official and campaign speeches from his 1974 campaign for Congress, the 1976 race for attorney general, and his years as governor. Additional materials related to Clinton are commissioned polls, campaign literature, political correspondence, and radio and television political commercials and programs. There are also several student research papers on Clinton's Arkansas campaigns, based primarily on interviews with campaign staff members. An online finding aid for the collection is available at http://libinfo.uark.edu/specialcollections/findingaids/aapc.html

Clinton Presidential Center [*CPC*]. The William J. Clinton Presidential Foundation seeks to strengthen the capacity of people in the United States and throughout the world to meet the challenges of global interdependence. To accomplish this mission, the Foundation currently focuses its work in five critical areas: the battle against HIV/AIDS; racial, ethnic, and religious reconciliation; citizen service; economic empowerment of poor people; and leadership development. The Center has online materials from Clinton's years as president, including photographs, 2,589 speech texts, streaming video of eight State of the Union speeches, and 467 radio address texts, as well as texts of selected speeches delivered after Clinton left office in 2001. A searchable Web site is available at http://www.clintonpresidentialcenter.org

The Clinton Presidential Materials Project [*CPMP*]. Administered by the National Archive and Records Administration at the Clinton Presidential Library in Little Rock, its primary mission is the preservation of the presidential records, personal and donated papers, and memorabilia of the Clinton administration. The Clinton Project has begun processing the presidential records to ensure that a wide variety of presidential records will be readily available at the Clinton Library on January 20, 2006. Records not yet processed and opened may be requested by filing a Freedom of Information Act request. Personal papers and other donated historical materials from President and Mrs. Clinton, their families, friends, staff, and associates will be available to researchers according to the terms of the donor's deed of gift. Research sessions are available by appointment only. For more information about research availability, contact the Clinton Presidential Materials Project staff by E-mail at clinton.library@nara.gov

or by telephone at (501) 244-9756. A searchable Web site is available at http://clinton.archives.gov

Gubernatorial Papers of Bill Clinton, 1979–1992 [*GPBC*]. The personal, political, and public papers related to Clinton's years as governor of Arkansas are presently (2004) held in storage at the Central Arkansas Library System/Little Rock Public Library. The collection is unprocessed and cannot be accessed by scholars without special authorization.

Smith, Stephen A., comp. and ed. *Preface to the Presidency: Selected Speeches of Bill Clinton, 1974–1992* [*PTP*]. Fayetteville: University of Arkansas Press, 1996. A collection of fifty speech texts from Clinton's prepresidential career, thirty-six of which are from his 1991–92 campaign for president. Also included are political speeches from his campaigns for Congress, attorney general, and governor; speeches at the Democratic National Convention (1980, 1984, 1988, 1992); and his five gubernatorial Inaugural Addresses (1979, 1983, 1985, 1987, and 1991).

The Public Papers of the Presidents of the United States [*PPP*]. Washington, D.C.: Government Printing Office, 1993–2001. *The Public Papers of the Presidents of the United States* is compiled and published by the Office of the Federal Register and the National Archives and Records Administration. It constitutes an official record series in which Clinton's presidential writings, addresses, and remarks of a public nature are made available. It is also available online at http://www.gpoaccess.gov/pubpapers/search.html

Weekly Compilation of Presidential Documents [*WCPD*]. Washington, D.C.: Government Printing Office, 1993–2001. The *Weekly Compilation of Presidential Documents* is the official publication of presidential statements, messages, remarks, interviews, press conferences, and other materials released by the Clinton White House press secretary, and it is the most complete textual record of Clinton's public remarks during his two terms in office. Published by the Office of the Federal Register and the National Archives and Records Administration, the *Weekly Compilation of Presidential Documents* is also available on *GPO Access* from 1993 on: http://www.gpoaccess.gov/wcomp/search.html

Web Sites

The Clinton Years. A joint project of ABC News *Nightline* and PBS *Frontline*, based on extensive interviews with twenty campaign advisers, White House staffers, and cabinet members. http://www.pbs.org/wgbh/pages/frontline/shows/clinton

The Clinton Years. A retrospective series of *Washington Post* articles looking at Bill Clinton's impact and legacy as president. Provides analysis of politics and policies of the Clinton administration, as well as an archive of postpresidential articles dealing with the Clinton legacy. http://www.washingtonpost.com/wp_dyn/politics/news/postseries/clintonyears

Audiovisual Material

C-SPAN Archives. The Public Affairs Video Archives at Purdue University holds the collection of speeches and programs cablecast during the years of the Clinton presidency. Tapes may be purchased by individuals for research and education purposes. Contact Public Affairs Video Archives, Purdue Research Park, P.O. Box 2909, West Lafayette IN 47996-2909. E-mail: info@c-span.archives.org

Selected Critical Studies

Blaney, Joseph Richard, and William L. Benoit. *The Clinton Scandals and the Politics of Image Restoration.* Westport, Conn.: Praeger, 2001.

Denton, Robert E., ed. *The 1992 Presidential Campaign: A Communication Perspective.* Westport, Conn.: Praeger, 1994.

Denton, Robert E., and Rachel L. Holloway, eds. *The Clinton Presidency: Images, Issues, and Communication Strategies.* Westport, Conn.: Praeger, 1996.

————. *Images, Scandal, and Communication Strategies of the Clinton Presidency.* Westport, Conn.: Praeger, 2003.

Murphy, John M. "Inventing Authority: Bill Clinton, Martin Luther King, Jr., and the Orchestration of Rhetorical Traditions." *Quarterly Journal of Speech* 83 (1997): 71–89.

————. "Rhetoric and the Presidency of William Jefferson Clinton." In *The Presidency and Rhetorical Leadership,* ed. Leroy G. Dorsey. College Station: Texas A&M University Press, 2002.

Parry-Giles, Shawn J., and Trevor Parry-Giles. "Collective Memory, Political Nostalgia, and the Rhetorical Presidency: Bill Clinton's Commemoration of the March on Washington, August 28, 1998." *Quarterly Journal of Speech* 86 (2002): 417–37.

Simons, Herbert W. "A Dilemma-Centered Analysis of Clinton's August 17th Apologia: Implications for Rhetorical Theory and Method." *Quarterly Journal of Speech* 86 (2000): 438–53.

Smith, Stephen A., ed. *Bill Clinton on Stump, State, and Stage: The Rhetorical Road to the White House.* Fayetteville: University of Arkansas Press, 1994.

Waldman, Michael. *POTUS Speaks: Finding the Words That Defined the Clinton Presidency.* New York: Simon and Schuster, 2000.

Selected Biographies

Allen, Charles, and Jonathan Portis. *The Comeback Kid: The Life and Career of Bill Clinton.* New York: Carol Publishing Group, 1992.

Clinton, Bill. *My Life.* New York: Alfred A. Knopf, 2004.

Dumas, Ernest, comp. and ed. *The Clintons of Arkansas: An Introduction by Those Who Know Them Best.* Fayetteville: University of Arkansas Press, 1993.

Klein, Joe. *The Natural: The Misunderstood Presidency of Bill Clinton.* New York: Doubleday, 2002.

Maraniss, David. *First in His Class: A Biography of Bill Clinton.* New York: Simon and Schuster, 1995.

Walker, Martin. *The President We Deserve: Bill Clinton, His Rise, Falls, and Comebacks.* New York: Crown, 1996.

CHRONOLOGY OF MAJOR SPEECHES

See "Research Collections and Collected Speeches" for source codes.

"The Fight for Fairness and Justice." Hot Springs, Ark., September 13, 1974. *PTP,* pp. 1–5.

"A New Era of Achievement and Excellence" (first gubernatorial inaugural). Little Rock, Ark., January 9, 1979. *PTP,* pp. 10–13.

"We Must Speak to America." New York City, August 14, 1980. *PTP,* pp. 23–27.

"Nomination of Michael Dukakis." Atlanta, Ga., July 20, 1988. *PTP,* pp. 59–68.

"A Campaign for the Future." Little Rock, Ark., October 3, 1991. *PTP,* pp. 79–86.

"A New Covenant: Responsibility and Rebuilding the American Community." Washington, D.C., October 23, 1991. *PTP,* pp. 87–97.

"A New Covenant for Economic Change." Washington, D.C., November 20, 1991. *PTP,* pp. 98–110.

"A New Covenant for American Security." Washington, D.C., December 12, 1991. *PTP,* pp. 111–24.

"A Vision for America: A New Covenant." New York City, July 16, 1992. *PTP,* pp. 212–22.

"First Inaugural Address." Washington, D.C., January 20, 1993. *WCPD* 29, no. 3 (1993): 75–77.

"Address Before a Joint Session of Congress on Administration Goals." Washington, D.C., February 17, 1993. *WCPD* 29, no. 7 (1993): 215–24.

"Address to a Joint Session of the Congress on Health Care Reform." Washington, D.C., September 22, 1993. *WCPD* 29, no. 38 (1993): 1836–46.

"Remarks to the Convocation of the Church of God

in Christ." Memphis, Tenn., November 13, 1993. *WCPD* 29, no. 46 (1993): 2357–62.

"Address Before a Joint Session of the Congress on the State of the Union." Washington, D.C., January 25, 1994. *WCPD* 30, no. 4 (1994): 148–57.

"Address Before a Joint Session of the Congress on the State of the Union." Washington, D.C., January 24, 1995. *WCPD* 31, no. 4 (1995): 96–108.

"Remarks at the University of Texas." Austin, October 16, 1995. *WCPD* 31, no. 42 (1995): 1847–53.

"Address Before a Joint Session of the Congress on the State of the Union." Washington, D.C., January 23, 1996. *WCPD* 32, no. 4 (1996): 90–98.

"Remarks Accepting the Presidential Nomination at the Democratic National Convention." Chicago, August 29, 1996. *WCPD* 32, no. 35 (1996): 1577–86.

"Second Inaugural Address." Washington, D.C., January 20, 1997. *WCPD* 33, no. 4 (1997): 60–63.

"Address Before a Joint Session of the Congress on the State of the Union." Washington, D.C., February 4, 1997. *WCPD* 33, no. 6 (1997): 136–45.

"Remarks at the University of California San Diego Commencement Ceremony" ("Call for a Conversation on Race"). La Jolla, Calif., June 14, 1997. *WCPD* 33, no. 25 (1997): 876–82.

"Address Before a Joint Session of the Congress on the State of the Union." Washington, D.C., January 27, 1998. *WCPD* 34, no. 5 (1998): 129–39.

"Address to the Nation on Testimony Before the Independent Counsel's Grand Jury." Washington, D.C., August 17, 1998. *WCPD* 34, no. 34 (1998): 1638–39.

"Remarks at a Breakfast with Religious Leaders" ("The Second Apology"). Washington, D.C., September 11, 1998. *WCPD* 34, no. 37 (1998): 1762–63.

"Address Before a Joint Session of the Congress on the State of the Union." Washington, D.C., January 19, 1999. *WCPD* 35, no. 3 (1999): 78–88.

"Address Before a Joint Session of the Congress on the State of the Union." Washington, D.C., January 27, 2000. *WCPD* 36, no. 4 (2000): 160–72.

"Speech to British Labour Party Conference." Blackpool, U.K., October 2, 2002. *CPC*, http://www.clintonpresidentialcenter.org/100202-sp-labour.htm

"Reflections on the 50th Anniversary of *Brown v. Board of Education.*" New York City, February 10, 2004. http://www.columbia.edu/acis/networks/advanced/brown/

MARIO MATTHEW CUOMO (1932–)
Governor of New York

MARY ANNE TRASCIATTI

Mario Matthew Cuomo was born June 15, 1932, to Italian immigrant parents. For most of his childhood, he lived behind the small grocery store owned by his family in the working-class immigrant community of South Jamaica, Queens, in New York City. In 1949, the Cuomo family moved to a more comfortable residence in the middle-class community of Holliswood, Queens.

Reared in an Italian-language home, Cuomo spoke little English when he began public grammar school. By the time he entered middle school, he had mastered the language and developed into an avid reader and high-achieving student. A devout Catholic, Cuomo served as an altar boy in his youth. He attended Catholic high school in Brooklyn, earning an academic scholarship in his sophomore year. Upon graduation from high school, he was offered, and accepted, an academic scholarship to St. John's College, also in Brooklyn. In addition to being a talented student, Cuomo was also a skilled athlete; he excelled at baseball and played in a number of local leagues. Although he was not a member of the St. John's baseball team, he was offered a contract with the Pittsburgh Pirates' organization after his sophomore year of college. His career with the Pirates lasted only one season; Cuomo left the organization after he was hit on the head, knocked unconscious, and hospitalized. Cuomo's competitive activities were largely confined to the playing field during his high school and college years; he was not a debater, nor did he show particular interest in politics. However, he did begin to develop his social conscience as a college student, taking a full complement of religion and philosophy courses.

While still a student at St. John's, Cuomo met his future wife, Matilda Raffa. The two were married soon after his graduation in the spring of 1954, and they eventually had five children. In the fall of 1954, Cuomo entered St. John's law school. He graduated two years later, tied for first in his class, and subsequently landed a prestigious clerkship at the New York State Court of Appeals. Despite his high class standing and the prestigious clerkship, none of the Manhattan law firms to which he applied would hire him. Cuomo eventually secured a position with a Brooklyn law firm, where in addition to representing corporate clients he did pro bono work, primarily for poor defendants in criminal cases. Cuomo built a promising legal career on his skill as a mediator. By the early 1960s, the young attorney was being asked to speak on a variety of issues as a representative of local organizations such as the Catholic Interracial Council, the Committee on Catholic-Jewish Relations of Brooklyn and Queens, and the Legal Aid Society, on whose board of directors he served. These early speeches were well received, and he was soon writing speeches for Congressman (and future governor) Hugh Carey.

Cuomo's political career was launched with his involvement in three high-profile legal "crusades" in his home borough of Queens in the 1960s. In the first of these battles, he successfully challenged a powerful real estate developer, Robert Moses, on behalf of a group of scrap metal dealers in Willets Point who would be put out of business if Moses secured city approval to build a park in their neighborhood. Soon after, in 1967, he helped residents of Corona resist a plan to tear down houses in their community as part of a plan for building a new high school. From 1971 to 1972, he worked with city officials and residents of Forest Hills to broker a compromise plan for a controversial low-income housing project in that neighborhood.

Cuomo's efforts on behalf of his clients brought him to the attention of New Yorkers statewide and whetted his appetite for public service; however, the promising young attorney did not easily make the move from law to politics. On the contrary, Cuomo's early political career was marked by a series of unsuccessful runs for public office. He entered and then withdrew from the race for mayor of New York City in 1973; the next year, he sought and lost the Democratic nomination for lieutenant governor; he ran again for mayor in 1977, this time on the Liberal Party ticket, and was defeated. Despite his defeat at the polls, however, Cuomo matured as a political candidate during the 1977 mayoral race, particularly with regard to his political oratory. His speeches became less legalistic and technical, and he developed a more conciliatory and engaging style. An experienced campaigner by 1978, Cuomo sought and won the office of lieutenant governor that year. Having gained stature in the Democratic Party, he was tapped to run Jimmy Carter's New York primary reelection campaign, and then to cochair the 1980 New York Carter-Mondale campaign.

By the 1980s, Cuomo was emerging as a significant figure in New York politics. In 1982, he successfully challenged the well-known mayor of New York City, Ed Koch, for the Democratic nomination for governor. Cuomo's strategy for the primary and general elections was to package traditional Democratic values in family rhetoric. It was a successful strategy, and he won the election, becoming the first Italian American governor in New York history. The family theme reverberated in his First Inaugural Address, which earned him accolades from prominent national politicians in both the Democratic and the Republican parties. An obviously gifted speaker, Cuomo was invited to deliver the 1984 keynote address at the Democratic National Convention in San Francisco, at which Walter Mondale and Geraldine Ferraro were to be nominated for the presidency and vice presidency, respectively. Although he was Mondale's first choice for keynote speaker, Cuomo did not readily embrace the opportunity, thinking that Senator Edward Kennedy of Massachusetts, who had been Mondale's principal rival in the primaries, was a more appropriate choice. After he spoke with Kennedy, however, Cuomo accepted the invitation. In preparation for his first significant appearance on national television, he wrote his own text, which he revised after consultation with some of his advisers. Cuomo's strategy for capturing the audience's attention at the convention was a novel one. He was introduced via a six-minute movie about his growing up in New York. The houselights were then turned off, and a spotlight focused on him as he walked to the podium. "A Tale of Two Cities" was an expanded version of his gubernatorial Inaugural Address, lambasting Ronald Reagan and the Republican Party for having abandoned all but the richest and most successful Americans. The speech met with thunderous applause at its conclusion, and Cuomo, who was hailed as an extraordinary political orator, was catapulted into the national spotlight.

Two months after his resounding success at the Democratic National Convention, Cuomo delivered another career-making speech at Notre Dame University. When he accepted the invitation to speak at Notre Dame, he was embroiled in a much-publicized conflict with New York City's highest-ranking cleric, James Cardinal O'Connor. O'Connor claimed that Cuomo's pro-choice position on abortion was untenable in terms of Catholic doctrine. Cuomo seized upon the Notre Dame invitation as an opportunity to rebut O'Connor's argument. The speech, which he researched and wrote himself, offered a cogent analysis of the relationship between a Catholic politician's religious beliefs and his stand on issues pertaining to public morality, such as abortion, euthanasia, and the death penalty. It earned him high marks from Catholics and non-Catholics alike.

By now a national political figure, Cuomo was reelected governor of New York in 1986, defeating his Republican challenger, Andrew O'Rourke, by a historically wide 65–32 percent margin. After much speculation, he announced that he would not seek the Democratic nomination for the presidency in 1988 and again in 1992. Cuomo successfully sought a third term as governor 1990, but he lost his bid for a fourth consecutive term to George Pataki in 1994; despite this defeat, he remained an important figure in the Democratic Party. He has since worked as a behind-the-scenes political adviser to his son Andrew, and returned to practicing law.

MARIO CUOMO: AN ORATOR IN PURSUIT OF THE COMMON GOOD

After his 1984 keynote address, Cuomo was perceived as having the potential to usher in a new version of Roosevelt's New Deal coalition, uniting middle-class whites, European ethnics, liberal intellectuals, unionized workers, and African Americans under the Democratic Party umbrella. Since he had never held elected office outside New York State, Cuomo's political promise was in no small measure attributable to his oratorical skill.

Cuomo's appeal to diverse constituencies inhered in his ability to confront thorny political issues head-on without alienating his audience. Adapting mediation skills he honed as an attorney, Cuomo structured his political speeches so as to point out tension between competing ideas or forces and then to suggest a way of resolving that tension in the interest of the common good. His July 16, 1984, keynote address, "A Tale of Two Cities," epitomizes this structure.

Cuomo began the speech with a pointed criticism of President Ronald Reagan's lack of un-

---

"I'm glad they didn't ask my father if he could speak English, because he couldn't. I'm glad they didn't ask my mother if she could count, because she couldn't. They didn't go to school a day in Italy. . . . And so the revival of anti-immigrant sentiment in America, however motivated, is sad to me personally. And millions like me."

—Mario Cuomo, "Immigration Address at the Urban Research Institute," 1992

---

derstanding of the financial hardships suffered by many Americans during his administration.

> Ten days ago, President Reagan admitted that although some people in this country seemed to be doing well nowadays, others were unhappy, and even worried, about themselves, their families, and their futures. The president said he didn't understand that fear. He said, "Why, this country is a shining city on a hill." . . . But the hard truth is that not everyone is sharing in this city's splendor and glory. . . . In fact, Mr. President, this nation is more a "Tale of Two Cities" than it is a "shining city on a hill."

Juxtaposed against the Puritan ideal of America as the "shining city on the hill," Cuomo's literary allusion to Dickens's classic novel underscored extremes of affluence and poverty characteristic of the United States economy in the early 1980s. From here, Cuomo argued to the inexorable conclusion that extremes of affluence and poverty should not coexist in a humane society. He used a series of examples to build this argument inductively. Addressing Ronald Reagan directly, he admonished:

> Maybe if you went to Appalachia, where some people still live in sheds, and to Lackawanna, where thousands of unemployed steel workers wonder why we subsidize foreign steel while we surrender their dignity to unemployment and to welfare checks; maybe if you stepped into a shelter in Chicago and talked with some of the homeless there . . . maybe then you'd understand.

The crux of his argument was that economic disparities should be resolved in the political arena and, further, that the Democratic Party was committed to that task. Using religious language and imagery to convey his party's commitment to the American public, Cuomo described the Democrats as a party with "a *credo*," a party that was committed to the ideals of St. Francis of Assisi, patron saint of San Francisco and "the world's most sincere democrat."

> We believe, as Democrats, that a society as blessed as ours, the most affluent democracy in the world's history, that can spend trillions on instruments of destruction, ought to be able to help the middle class in its struggle, ought

> to be able to find work for all who can do it, room at the table, shelter for the homeless, care for the elderly, the infirm, hope for the destitute.

Thus enumerating a range of economic positions, from affluence to middle-class to destitute, Cuomo conveyed his party's sympathy for the fortunes of all Americans, rich as well as poor. In so doing, he shielded the party and himself from allegations of class warfare or, worse, irresponsible "tax and spend" liberalism, and thus reclaimed the middle class as the "heart" of the Democratic constituency. In fact, Cuomo appealed so strongly to working-class voters in this speech that Ronald Reagan changed his campaign strategy so as to reclaim his hold on that group.

Cuomo addressed a different set of issues in his September 13, 1984, speech at the University of Notre Dame. Having taken a stand on abortion that differed from the official Catholic position, and having been publicly chastised by a Catholic bishop for his stand, Cuomo responded at Notre Dame with an apologia, or speech of self-defense. The foundation of this speech comprised key questions about the extent to which his religious beliefs should constrain his political decisions.

> As a Catholic, I respect the teaching authority of the bishops. But must I agree with everything in the bishops' pastoral letter on peace and fight to include it in party platforms?
>
> And will I have to do the same for the forthcoming pastoral on economics even if I am an unrepentant supply-sider?
>
> Must I, having heard the pope renew the church's ban on birth control devices, veto the funding of contraceptive programs for non-Catholics or dissenting Catholics in my state?

After acknowledging Americans as "a religious people," albeit with different beliefs and "no established church," Cuomo proceeded to answer the questions he had posed in the negative. Using his own case as the exemplar, he built an argument for the separation of private (religious) and public (political) morality as necessary for protecting the political rights and religious freedom of believers and nonbelievers. This separation depended on the exclusion of religious arguments from political deliberation, including debate on laws to regulate abortion, euthanasia, and other controversial issues. Although it removed religion from any active role in the public sphere, Cuomo maintained that this separation was not inconsistent with the Church's own teachings: "There is no Church teaching that mandates the best political course for making our belief everyone's rule. . . . There is neither an encyclical nor a catechism that spells out a political strategy for achieving legislative goals." Thus Cuomo resolved the tension between church and state in favor of the state, but under the aegis of Catholic doctrine.

In addition to being a skilled arguer, Cuomo has a keen understanding of the power of words. From his first campaign for lieutenant governor in 1974, he acknowledged a distinction between the business of campaigning and that of governing. He summarized this distinction most aptly in his February 1, 1985, Chubb Fellowship lecture at Yale University: "We campaign in poetry. But when we're elected we're forced to govern in prose." To infuse his campaign oratory, and indeed all of his political speeches, with a poetic sensibility, Cuomo employed a number of stylistic devices.

Often he used antithesis, which is natural, given his tendency to address competing ideas within a speech. For example, in his Second Inaugural Address, delivered January 1, 1987, Cuomo enumerated his administration's accomplishments, followed by a list of social problems still to be resolved. He then added, "we can dismiss it *all*, on the assumption that *the price of comfort for most of us is that government must forget the rest of us*." In a November 16, 1991, speech to the Fortune 500 Forum, he skillfully combined antithesis with anaphora, the repetition of a word or phrase:

> We've won the Gulf War, but we have not overcome the gulf crisis in our own country. There is still a gulf between us and our competitors. Between those assured of healthcare and those who must beg for it. Between our ability to build smart bombs and our ability to produce smart students. Between America as it is and America as it should be.

With a play on the word "gulf" and repetition of the word "between," Cuomo conveyed the shortcomings of the Bush administration in no uncertain terms.

Perhaps the most notable of Cuomo's stylistic devices is his use of the "family" metaphor to convey his vision of compassionate, competent government. He used it in reference to New York State in his First Inaugural Address, January 1, 1983:

> We must be the family of New York, feeling one another's pain, sharing one another's blessings, reasonably, equitably, honestly, fairly, without respect to geography or race or political affiliation.

He expanded the boundaries of the metaphor to include the entire nation in his 1984 keynote address:

> We believe we must be the family of America, recognizing that at the heart of the matter we are bound one to another, that the problems of a retired school teacher in Duluth are *our* problems. That the future of a child in Buffalo is *our* future. The struggle of a disabled man in Boston to survive, to live decently, is *our* struggle. . . .

The family metaphor provided a basis for contrast between the Democratic platform and what Cuomo called the "social Darwinism" of the Republican Party. As Cuomo described it in his 1984 keynote address: "President Reagan told us from the beginning that he believed in a kind of social Darwinism. Survival of the fittest. . . . The strong will inherit the land!" Against this competitive, individualistic ideal, the family metaphor emphasized cooperation and mutual self-interest. Thus, it offered Cuomo a way to advocate on behalf of programs for the poor, children, immigrants, the elderly, and other relatively powerless segments of the population without alienating middle-class voters who might see such programs as coming at their own expense. Still, he was careful to point out that family was not a cover for wasteful government programs. In his Yale speech, for example, Cuomo described the family ideal as "intelligent self interest." Rather than being "an excuse for fiscal waste in government," he maintained, family is "a simple affirmation . . . of what we are capable of when we draw on all our strengths to deal with all of our vulnerabilities." Cuomo continued to use the family metaphor in his speeches into the 1990s, including his speech nominating Bill Clinton as the Democratic candidate for the presidency at the 1992 Democratic National Convention. Alluding to his keynote address eight years earlier, he asserted that Clinton would make Americans "not a collection of competing special interests, but one great, special family—the family of America!"

Another stylistic staple of Cuomo's oratory is his inclusion of autobiographical information. In his early speeches, when he was still a relatively unknown political commodity, he regularly recounted various aspects of his growing up the child of hardworking Italian immigrants in one of New York City's poorer neighborhoods as a way to identify with his audience. Thus, for example, in an August 16, 1982, speech to the Black Ministers Association during his first gubernatorial campaign, Cuomo cultivated rapport with his audience by noting that he, too, was born "outside the 'majority grouping' of Americans—a grouping that looked down upon me and my parents, saw us as different." In his First Inaugural Address, he likewise drew upon the shared immigrant experience to ingratiate himself with his new constituents:

> Like all of us in this room today—and all of us in New York State except for our Native American brothers and sisters—I am the offspring of immigrants. My parents came some sixty years ago from another part of the world, driven by deprivation, without funds, education, or skill.

By the 1990s, when Cuomo had firmly established his political reputation, he included biographical information primarily in speeches focusing on ethnicity or immigration. The following excerpt from a June 11, 1992, address at the Urban Research Center at New York University, in which he argued against a rising tide of attitudes and policies that discriminated against immigrants, is illustrative:

> I was born just a few miles from here, across the river, in South Jamaica, Queens, of immigrant parents. Everyone in that neighborhood came from somewhere else. I thank God this country didn't say to them, "We can't afford you. You might take someone else's job, or cost us too much."

> I'm glad they didn't ask my father if he could speak English, because he couldn't. I'm glad they didn't ask my mother if she could count, because she couldn't. They didn't go to school a day in Italy. . . . And so the revival of anti-immigrant sentiment in America, however motivated, is sad to me personally. And millions like me.

These vignettes contributed to Cuomo's ethos on two levels. At the most basic level, they enhanced his credibility among Italian Americans and other southeastern European ethnics in New York State who saw their experiences mirrored in his own. At the same time, the appeal of Cuomo's narrative extended beyond the ethnic enclaves of New York. The story of his growing up the child of immigrants in a poor neighborhood to become governor of his home state had universal appeal because it cast Cuomo as the quintessential achiever of the American dream. But Cuomo's use of the immigrant story was far from self-congratulatory. He observed in his First Inaugural Address: "The achievement of our past imposes upon us the obligation to do as much for those who come after us." In other words, the struggles of their immigrant forebears imposed a moral obligation on contemporary Americans, including himself, to enact compassionate social and economic policies for the well-being of all.

Cuomo is one of the most acclaimed political orators of the late twentieth century. In particular, his two 1984 speeches, the keynote address to the Democratic National Convention and the speech at Notre Dame, are considered masterworks of political discourse. With the keynote address, Cuomo became the Democratic spokesman for ethnic and working-class Americans; with the Notre Dame speech, he established himself as a key figure in the debate over the proper role of religion in the public sphere. In both cases, and in his prior and subsequent speeches as well, Cuomo demonstrated a rare ability to address complex issues in an informative, engaging manner.

Even before the 1984 election was fully underway, Cuomo was being mentioned as the next Democratic candidate for the presidency. But Democrats who comforted themselves in the aftermath of the Mondale-Ferraro defeat with thoughts of a future Cuomo candidacy were to be disappointed, for the governor chose not to run for the nation's highest elective office in 1988 and 1992. Cuomo remains, nonetheless, an important figure in the Democratic Party, and his collected speeches are an eloquent reminder of the power of oratory to unite disparate interests in pursuit of the common good.

INFORMATION SOURCES

Research Collections and Collected Speeches

At present, there are some archival holdings of Cuomo's papers, including transcripts of press conferences and remarks, at the New York State Library. His 1984 speech to the Democratic National Convention is widely accessible on the Internet, in both written and video form. Cuomo has also reprinted selected speeches from his gubernatorial campaign in his published diaries and has published one volume of selected speeches spanning the years 1974–93.

Cuomo, Mario M. *More Than Words: The Speeches of Mario Cuomo* [*MTW*]. New York: St. Martin's, 1993.

Cuomo, Mario M. "Selected Speeches." In *Diaries of Mario M. Cuomo. The Campaign for Governor* [*DMC*]. New York: Random House, 1984.

Web Site

New York State Library. Archival holdings include transcripts of press conferences, speaking schedules, and remarks. http://nysl.nysed.gov

Audiovisual Material

Great Speeches Videos. Educational Video Group. www.evgonline.com. Videos in this series include Cuomo's 1984 and 1992 Democratic National Convention speeches.

Selected Critical Studies

Henry, David. "The Rhetorical Dynamics of Mario Cuomo's 1984 Keynote Address: Situation, Speaker, Metaphor." *Southern Speech Communication Journal* 53 (1988): 105–20.

Troup, Calvin L. "Cuomo at Notre Dame: Rhetoric Without Religion." *Communication Quarterly* 43 (1995): 167–81.

Selected Biographies

Cuomo, Mario M. *Diaries of Mario M. Cuomo. The Campaign for Governor*. New York: Random House, 1984.

McElvaine, Robert S. *Mario Cuomo: A Biography*. New York: Scribner's, 1988.

CHRONOLOGY OF MAJOR SPEECHES

See "Research Collections and Collected Speeches" for source codes.

"Address to the New Democratic Coalition." New York City, May 11, 1974. *MTW*.

"Address to New York State Democratic Coalition." Syracuse, N.Y., June 22, 1982. *DMC*.

"Address to Black Ministers Association." Rochester, N.Y., August 16, 1982. *DMC*.

"First Inaugural Address." Albany, N.Y., January 1, 1983. *MTW*.

"Democratic National Convention Keynote Address" ("A Tale of Two Cities"). San Francisco, July 16, 1984. *MTW*.

"Religious Belief and Public Morality: A Catholic Governor's Perspective" (speech at the University of Notre Dame). South Bend, Ind., September 13, 1984. *MTW*.

"*E Pur Si Muove*: Chubb Fellowship Lecture." New Haven, Conn., February 1, 1985. *MTW*.

"Second Inaugural Address." Albany, N.Y., January 1, 1987. *MTW*.

"Fortieth Anniversary of Israel." New York City, May 10, 1988.

"United Auto Workers Convention." Anaheim, Calif., June 22, 1989. *MTW*.

"National Italian American Foundation Dinner." Washington, D.C., October 20, 1990. *MTW*.

"Who Is God?" (speech at the 92nd Street Y). New York City, October 15, 1991. *MTW*.

"Fortune 500 Forum." Charleston, S.C., November 16, 1991. *MTW*.

"NAACP Address." New York City, December 11, 1991. *MTW*.

"Immigration Address at the Urban Research Center." New York City, June 11, 1992. *MTW*.

"Nominating Speech, Democratic National Convention." New York City, July 15, 1992. *MTW*.

"Robert Kennedy Memorial." New York City, March 9, 1993. *MTW*.

THOMAS ANDREW DASCHLE (1947–)
U.S. Senator, Democratic Party Leader

TROY A. MURPHY

Scarcely a profile of former Senate minority leader Tom Daschle (D-S.D.) exists that does not in some way describe the senator from South Dakota as "softspoken," "mild-mannered," or "low-key." Indeed, the communication skill most often mentioned as central to Daschle's leadership is not rousing oratory or rhetorical prowess, but a talent not traditionally associated with political leaders: he listens well. As leader of Senate Democrats, Daschle called to mind not the arm-twisting or aggressive posturing of Lyndon Johnson, but the modesty of Mike Mansfield.

Despite his relatively quiet demeanor and uncommon propensity to listen rather than speak, a review of Daschle's oratory nonetheless reveals a successful communicator, both in the caucus cloakroom and in more traditional forums of political oratory. His rhetorical style is direct, organized, and plainspoken, commonly invoking themes that illustrate a populist strain of rhetoric befitting his rural constituency of South Dakota. This rural population, while fast eroding as a power base in electoral politics, retains a special place in American mythology because it symbolically calls forth and identifies romantic traditions of Jefferson's yeoman farmer and the agrarian roots of American democracy. Daschle's rhetorical style weaves together emotional and logical appeals, combining an agrarian populism that extols the virtues of rural America and ordinary citizens with a simple, direct, and tightly organized message that clearly defines and elucidates public policy options for his audience. In so doing, Daschle managed to successfully blend the often disparate rhetorical demands placed upon him as a rhetor who simultaneously represented a small, generally Republican state and the national Democratic Party.

Thomas Andrew Daschle was born on December 9, 1947, in Aberdeen, South Dakota, the eldest child of Betty and Sebastian "Dash"

Daschle's four sons. His father was a bookkeeper for a local auto parts store and a decorated veteran of World War II. After attending Aberdeen Central High, where he first satisfied his thirst for politics through Boys' State, a leadership conference sponsored by the American Legion, Daschle attended South Dakota State University (SDSU) in Brookings. In his sophomore year he ran for class president, a campaign noteworthy as one of Daschle's only election defeats. Later that year, he was elected treasurer of the SDSU College Democrats, a victory he would later jokingly credit with salvaging his political career. Daschle was the first of his siblings to graduate from college, obtaining a B.A. in political science from SDSU in 1969.

Having enrolled in the ROTC program at SDSU, Daschle spent the three years after graduation stationed in Colorado as an intelligence officer in the U.S. Air Force. In 1973, he returned to South Dakota politics as a legislative assistant for Senator James Abourezk, working in the senator's Washington office. Two years later, Daschle became Abourezk's field director in South Dakota, organizing the state outreach office, overseeing constituent services, and, as it would turn out, preparing for a run for the House of Representatives.

When Abourezk decided against seeking a second term in the Senate in 1978, Congressman Larry Pressler ran for the Senate seat, opening up one of the two positions in South Dakota's House delegation. At thirty-one, Daschle ran for the open House seat. When the original count indicated just fourteen votes separated Daschle and his opponent, Leo Thorsness, each candidate set up an office in Washington during the lengthy recount. Daschle was eventually declared the victor by 139 votes. He spent four terms in the House, concentrating primarily on agricultural issues and leading the fight for compensating

Vietnam veterans exposed to the chemical defoliant Agent Orange. In the House, Daschle was elected Rocky Mountain regional whip in 1979 and was whip-at-large from 1982 to 1986.

In 1986, near the height of the farm crisis that gave rise to national media attention and "Farm Aid" concerts, Daschle became one of the most recognized critics of Ronald Reagan's farm policy. The 1986 Senate race in South Dakota was one of the most closely watched races in the nation, seen by many as a referendum on Reagan's policy for rural America. Daschle defeated Republican Jim Abnor, garnering 52 percent of the statewide vote. Once in the Senate, Daschle secured a position on the influential Finance Committee, and almost immediately began working in Senate leadership positions. In 1988, majority Leader George Mitchell named Daschle cochair of the Democratic Policy Committee (DPC), a position that was historically reserved for the majority leader. He served in this unprecedented leadership position until Mitchell's retirement in 1994, when Daschle made his own bid for the majority leader position. In a close election reminiscent of his first election to the House, Daschle was elected Senate Democratic leader by a single vote. Other than Lyndon Johnson, Daschle was the most junior senator ever to hold the position of majority leader, having served in the Senate for only eight years when he became leader. He served as Democratic leader from 1994–2004. He was widely considered to be a leading candidate for the Democratic presidential nomination in 2004 before dropping out of consideration on January 7, 2003, declaring that "my heart is in the Senate." Daschle lost his Senate seat in a hotly contested race with former Republican Congressman, John Jhune, in 2004.

TOM DASCHLE: "PRAIRIE POPULIST" AND PARTY LEADER

In assessing common strategies and recurring patterns evident in Daschle's oratory, four areas suggest themselves for closer examination. First, Daschle consistently invoked themes that exemplified the agrarian myth. He used narratives of rural America and agrarian life to speak effectively to issues affecting both South Dakota and the nation. Second, Daschle relied on emotionally powerful anecdotes to complement this agrarian populism. His speeches combined praise of ordinary citizens and rural America with a detailed, deliberative message that advanced preferred public policy options. Third, the arrangement of Daschle's speeches was consistent with a plainspoken ethos, employing clear disposition and orderly construction. Speeches were tightly organized in a simple, direct style that effectively utilized internal summaries and clear transitions. Finally, Daschle's persona and rhetorical style exemplified characteristics that confirmed Kathleen Hall Jamieson's thesis concerning a modern "transformation of political speechmaking." Although Daschle occasionally exhibited the fiery language and passionate delivery traditionally associated with rhetorical eloquence, he typically utilized oratory that was more conversational and personal in both delivery and narrative style, and thus better suited for the television era.

Students of American political discourse have long noted the persistence of appeals to an "agrarian myth." This myth, often explicitly or implicitly tied to Jeffersonian ideals, holds the simple yeoman farmer as the exemplar of effective self-governance and democratic virtue, and the small towns and farming communities throughout the land as the bedrock of democracy. Like all mythological constructs, the resonant themes of the agrarian myth have both historical legacies and contemporary continuities. Daschle's use of the agrarian myth enhanced and renewed the populist themes of orators such as William Jennings Bryan. In the watershed election of 1896, Bryan spoke to an era of rapid industrialization by pitting a populist agrarian myth against William McKinley's myth of the "self-made man." While Daschle's style was markedly different from the firebrand oratory of Bryan, populist themes remained a significant feature of his discourse. These themes recurred in Daschle's role as both a rural state senator representing the needs of the agricultural community and as a leader of the Democratic Party whose basic tenets were in many ways set in motion by Bryan's insurgent campaign of 1896.

Daschle commonly described the family farm as the "backbone of America," intimating that the values of American democracy are best illustrated through the self-reliant family farmer and the rural communities throughout America. In a speech to the Democratic Leadership Council in July 2001, he renewed the agrarian myth for the contemporary context, recalling a populist distinction between community and individualism: "For a long time and up until today, people have seen the world in terms of separate, competing entities . . . on one side are those who see America as a land built solely on the strength of rugged individualism. On the other side, there are those who ascribe our strength as a call to collective action." By situating a historically resonant, yet largely untenable, dichotomy between these two positions, Daschle utilized a narrative of South Dakota rural communities to position the American creed as a synthesis rather than a dichotomy. He stated: ". . . I come from a place where people know that those views of America are not mutually exclusive. . . . My own grandparents were German

Democratic Party: "This awareness that we must all work together to create a better future defines me as a South Dakotan, but it also defines us, I believe, as Democrats." He utilized a personalized narrative of agrarian community to define his values and the values of the party for which he was a principal spokesperson. Like all congressional orators who hold dual rhetorical positions through leadership responsibilities, Daschle had to balance, through discourse, his national leadership position with a rhetoric persuasive to his home constituency. Given the elasticity of the agrarian myth as a broad-based and resonant expression of American ideals, the narratives of rural America, central to Daschle's rhetoric, are effective in bridging the distance between rural state senator and national party leader.

Throughout the 2000 campaign season, Daschle often told an anecdote based upon the same agrarian myth and the rustic wisdom of the

> Daschle usually delivered plainspoken speeches, typical of our mediated age in which orators come into our living rooms to "talk" to us. His speeches reflected an introductory public speaking class, in which students are encouraged to "tell them what you are going to tell them, tell them, and tell them what you told them."

farmers who immigrated to South Dakota because of the promise of free land. My grandparents and those who undertook that journey with them worked very hard. . . . But they understood that no matter how hard they worked, there were still some essential things they couldn't do by themselves." Daschle illustrated the importance of community and collective action by relying on agrarian themes that were consistent with his humble persona as a rural state senator, yet transferable across regional and ideological differences: "It took neighbors working together to raise the barns, to clear the land, to plant the crops. It took communities to build schools and to hire teachers. It took everyone in small towns working together to weather storms and clean up after the floods."

Daschle made explicit the connection between the values of rural America and the values of the

American farmer. Rather than using a personal narrative, however, Daschle drew from popular culture to identify these values for his audience. In a speech to the 2000 Democratic National Convention in Los Angeles, he recalled a scene from one of his favorite films, *The Straight Story*. He described the movie: "It's about an old farmer named Alvin Straight. He wants to see his brother one last time to make peace before one of them dies—only Alvin can't drive anymore because his eyes are bad and his hips are worse. So he rides his John Deere lawn mower nearly 300 miles." Setting up the quaint image portrayed in the film, Daschle continued: "On the road, he meets a young woman who's in a lot of trouble. He tells her that when his children were little, he would hand them a stick, and tell them to break it. And they would, just like that. Then, he'd put the sticks in a bundle and ask his kids to break it. They couldn't. He gave them some advice: 'That bundle is family.'" Daschle suggested that whatever "troubles" exist within contemporary society, the simple lesson from the farmer might serve as a basic philosophy for how to address those problems. He reminded his fellow Democrats and a national audience, "That bundle is our community. We are stronger together than we are alone. That is the simplest description I know of our party's belief."

Daschle used the wisdom of the common farmer, and values inspired through the agrarian community, to define the Democratic Party and the values of a democratic society. Here again, he blended the need to define the party's core beliefs with an image central to his ethos as a farm state senator and a voice consistent with his South Dakota constituency. This strategy allowed Daschle to define the Democratic Party with an appealing image of family and community, an expression with which all American citizens could identify. At the same time, the narrative was important in maintaining an ethos appropriate to South Dakota. This demand was especially acute for Daschle, given the generally conservative voting patterns of his home state and an enduring memory of South Dakota voters rejecting fellow liberal Democratic Senator George McGovern after McGovern rose to national prominence in 1972. Daschle appeared to be constantly aware of this unique rhetorical demand, consistently placing South Dakota values and anecdotes in the forefront as he sought to rhetorically define Jeffersonian ideals and the principles of the modern Democratic Party.

In addition to anecdotes that grow out of personal experience and popular culture, another category of narratives common to Daschle's oratory is worthy of special attention. If Daschle rose to the U.S. Senate and to national prominence as one of the strongest critics of Ronald Reagan's farm policy in the mid-1980s, he nevertheless appropriated some of Reagan's rhetorical tactics. He often utilized a rhetorical device popularized by and commonly associated with Reagan: the employment of ordinary citizens as the personification of American ideals and the "heroes" of American democracy. Reagan was particularly adept at civic epideictic oratory, that

genre of speaking used when lauding public virtues and condemning public evils. The image of the ordinary citizen as hero has been described as a central theme of Reagan's presidency because the dramatic yet simple narratives fulfilled an epideictic function central to Reagan's appeal as an orator. For Daschle, however, the narratives of ordinary citizens fulfilled both an epideictic and a deliberative function.

In classic terms, Aristotle recognized the importance of the epideictic speech as a way of celebrating the values and principles of the state. In the aftermath of the September 11, 2001, terrorist attacks, recognizing the heroism of firefighters, police officers, and ordinary citizens became a common theme for precisely this reason: the optimistic narratives of sacrifice and honor served as a means of expressing and defining American identity in the context of perhaps unprecedented national anxiety.

Senator Daschle and his staff were particularly attuned to the terrorist threat when a letter containing anthrax was sent to Daschle's office on October 15, 2001. Two weeks later, Daschle spoke about the meaning of September 11 to the Sioux Falls, South Dakota, Chamber of Commerce. He described the heroism he saw in his staff, and the examples of other heroes throughout South Dakota and the nation. Recognizing specific individuals, Daschle highlighted constituent Glenn Spencer, who "loaded up his pickup in Sioux Falls and drove to New York with all the steel-toed boots, tube socks, and work gloves he could get his hands on." Similarly, Nicole North and her second grade class in Dell Rapids raised money for a relief fund, "showing us that small acts of kindness do, indeed, add up." Daschle linked narratives of personal heroism with South Dakota's ranching community, a constituency central to the agrarian myth: "If anyone's known hard times in the past few years, it's ranch families. But when disaster struck on September 11, Don and Adeline Hight of Murdo sold 100 calves and donated the proceeds—more than $40,000—to help the victims of the attacks." Daschle agreed with the manager of the local Livestock Association, who called their donation "an act of true Americanism."

The discourse of heroic, yet ordinary, citizens

is a common theme that melds dramatic narratives of success and sacrifice with a populist image recognizing the power and virtue of ordinary citizens. In the context of September 11, Daschle utilized the strategy of highlighting ordinary citizens in a manner similar to President Reagan, rehearsing national ideals and enhancing national identity. Yet, Daschle's speeches consistently complemented an epideictic narrative of praise with a more deliberative message intended to advocate specific actions the government can take to partner effectively with and assist these citizens.

In his position as cochair of the DPC shortly before becoming majority leader, Daschle was the "point man" in the U.S. Senate for President Bill Clinton's 1992 health-care reform initiative. In this post, Daschle was influential in a series of floor statements made by Democratic senators titled "Faces of the Health-Care Crisis." In a speech on the Senate floor in September 1993, Daschle provided the reason for the series of speeches. He stated: "For this is not simply a debate about arcane principles of health-care financing . . . this is a debate about people—Americans whose lives have been deeply affected by our health system's failings. They are real people, not just numbers." Daschle proceeded to highlight a constituent, DeAnn Thomas, from Flandreau, South Dakota. Thomas' diabetes caused her to live "in constant fear that one illness or accident could wipe her out financially." After illustrating her case as all too common, Daschle declared: "DeAnn Thomas is just one of the millions of reasons why we must remain committed to reform of our health-care system." He reminded Senate colleagues that the debate was not about the "percentage of GNP we spend on health care. It is not just about controlling the deficit. It is about people, people like DeAnn Thomas, people who long for the day when they have security, who long for the day when they, too, can look to their future with some degree of confidence that the problems they are experiencing in health care will not keep them from being employed, will not keep them from being mothers and fathers, will not keep them from being the Americans they know they can be." The strategy of highlighting ordinary citizens created an image that resonated with an American public

who could more readily identify with the plight of a fellow citizen than with the statistical vagaries of a complicated health-care system. The emotional resonance of this identification was furthered by Daschle's use of stylistic devices such as repetition and parallel construction, illustrating how citizens "long for the day" when health-care concerns "will not keep them" from enjoying the financial and emotional security they deserve.

Daschle's narratives of ordinary citizens were not used simply to symbolize individual success, but also to personify and exemplify policy needs, in the arena of health care and elsewhere. Daschle again blended the epideictic and deliberative functions in a 2000 speech titled "Federal Government in the Indian Nation: Indian Education." In addition to highlighting several heroic citizens who were helping to solve the many social and economic problems that plague reservation life, he recalled for his largely Native American audience an anecdote involving Environmental Protection Agency (EPA) officials who sought to destroy two tons of dynamite that had been buried on the reservation for sixty years. Despite months of unsuccessful attempts to locate the dynamite, including a false alarm that necessitated the evacuation of the entire town, the EPA refused to listen to one of the town's elders who had worked on the original road crew and had been involved in burying the dynamite. Daschle highlighted the wisdom of this ordinary citizen, Nathan Thompson, saying: "When they finally did listen, they found the dynamite: just where Nathan Thompson told them they would—and detonated it safely." Daschle made explicit the meaning of the anecdote: "Now, some people might look at that story as a sort of dark comedy. I see it differently. I see it as a metaphor for what happens when non-tribal governments fail to listen to Indian people on matters affecting Indian communities. There is a long history of that—here in South Dakota, and across this nation." Daschle's use of Nathan Thompson in this speech was representative of how ordinary citizens were rhetorically highlighted as worthy of praise and honor, but not simply to eulogize America's greatness. Rather, Daschle followed up their stories by speaking explicitly of the ways in which collective action could and must be taken in the legislative arena. Whether the citizens highlighted were family farmers, ranchers, Native Americans, or other ordinary citizens, they personified the values of democracy while simultaneously highlighting exigent issues that framed the policy agenda of Daschle's party.

While Daschle's speeches were often filled with the pathos of personal stories of sacrifice, honor, and heroism, the deliberative goal of his rhetoric was achieved further through a plain style that was well organized and easy for listeners to follow. He employed a clear, simple arrangement, almost always punctuating his speeches with organizational cues that enumerated the main points of his message in clear terms. Speeches often began and ended in a traditional arrangement almost reflective of an introductory-level speech class in which students are encouraged to "tell them what you are going to tell them, tell them, and tell them what you told them."

Daschle's 1997 speech opening the 105th Congress was representative. He tightly organized his message of what Senate Democrats hoped to accomplish in the coming legislative session. Outlining the "Families First Agenda," Daschle enumerated the most important aspects of the legislative agenda, listed each important bill central to that agenda in parallel fashion—"our first bill," "our second bill"—provided strong evidence and cogent reasons illustrating the need for legislative action in each area, and closed the speech by saying, "These are our top six priorities," effectively summarizing and reviewing the agenda and legislative proposals outlined. In a much publicized speech on the state of the American economy in January 2002, Daschle followed the same strategy, developing a clearly organized message of "steps" that must be taken to revive the economy. Once again enumerating the steps in a clear arrangement, he developed evidence to suggest that these steps were the fairest and most balanced way to achieve economic growth, and described the benefits that would accrue from their being followed. The messages in these and other speeches followed a clearly organized pattern that made Daschle's speeches internally coherent, well developed, and easy to follow.

The simplicity and orderliness of Daschle's speeches were further advanced through his engaging and personable delivery style. In contrast to a traditional style of political discourse that emphasizes contentious debate and fiery rhetoric, Daschle more closely represented what some have called an "intimate" style of discourse that captures ideas in brief, emotional narratives and is often more personal and conversational in both tone and delivery. Even the strongest partisan opponents of Daschle have at times been forced to recognize the effectiveness of his rhetorical style. Following President George W. Bush's election in 2000, noted GOP pollster Frank Luntz advised Republican Party elders to "demonize" Daschle as an "obstructionist" on President Bush's legislative agenda. The national Republican strategy to concentrate efforts and campaign funds to label Daschle an obstructionist of Bush's agenda along with Bush's popularity in South Dakota, ultimately led to Daschle's defeat in 2004. Nonetheless, even Luntz's polling indicated that while the effort to demonize Daschle had indeed driven up the senator's "negatives," there was something else: Daschle "consistently scores well" with voters on explaining issues such as the economy. Luntz described Daschle's success: "He's very calm. It's like he's telling a bedtime story."

Whether the stories Daschle employed were about farmers, rural America, or ordinary citizens, the recurrent patterns of his discourse worked together to enhance Daschle's credibility as both senator and Senate minority leader. He utilized the myth of agrarian communities to rehearse and renew national ideals, the narratives of ordinary citizens as an emotional appeal symbolizing both hope and exigency, and clear rhetorical arrangement that was well reasoned and logically organized. Daschle employed the classical forms of proof: he created ethos through an appeal to his own rural background and the identification of rural values; he engendered pathos through dramatic narratives and anecdotes that invited his audiences to identify with the plight of those similar to themselves; and he incorporated ample evidence and well-reasoned warrants that increased the logical appeal of his message. Accepting, as some contemporary rhetorical scholars have, that "mythos" may itself be a separate and distinct category of proof, Daschle clearly utilized an important cultural heritage of Jeffersonian democracy and the myth of agrarian community.

Tom Daschle identified himself as a "prairie populist," but did not go against his personality to try to emulate a style of populist oratory appropriate to an earlier age. Rather, this "mild-mannered" and "soft-spoken" Midwesterner articulated populist themes in a style appropriate to his personal ethos and the demands of an electronic age. The themes he identified helped Daschle define his party in a way that remained true to his background and primary constituency. He complemented resonant epideictic expressions with clear and concise deliberative arguments on public policy. Finally, Daschle's effectiveness as a communicator was often as interpersonal as it was formal, relying on a personality that even his strongest opponents described as engaging and likable. His credibility as an orator stemmed not from attempting to emulate a formal model but from a blending of personal attributes, audience values, and rhetorical telos to yield a rhetorical style that was effective for both a farm state senator and a national party leader.

INFORMATION SOURCES

Research Collections and Collected Speeches

There are no archival collections or published collections of speeches at this time. His speeches concerning national issues are available through the Democratic Policy Committee's Web site, and speeches delivered in the Senate may be located in the *Congressional Record* or Thomas, the Library of Congress's official Web site for legislative affairs. Senator Tom Daschle Senate Office, United States Senate, Washington, DC 20510. Transcripts of several of Daschle's speeches are available from the author, Troy A. Murphy. [*TAM*]

Congressional Record [*CR*]. University of Michigan, Dearborn, MI.

Web Sites

Democratic Policy Committee's Web site [*DPC*]. This site includes speeches by Daschle on national issues. www.democrats.senate.gov or http:/democrats.senate.gov/dpc/

Library of Congress [*LC*]. The Library's Web site includes transcripts of speeches delivered in the Senate. www.thomas.loc.gov

Audiovisual Materials

There are no readily accessible audiovisual materials.

Critical Studies

No critical studies examining Daschle's oratory have been published.

Selected Biography

Daschle, Tom. *Like No Other Time: The 107th Congress and the Two Years That Changed America Forever.* Written with Michael D'Orso. New York: Crown, 2003.

CHRONOLOGY OF MAJOR SPEECHES

See "Research Collections and Collected Speeches" for source codes.

"Remarks at Mt. Rushmore on Fourth of July." Keystone, S.D., July 4, 1985. *TAM.*

"Faces of the Health-Care Crisis: DeAnn Thomas." Washington, D.C., September 8, 1993. *CR*, September 8, 1993, PS11073; *LC.*

"Putting a Value on the Contract. Remarks by Senate Democratic Leader Tom Daschle to the Center for National Policy." Washington, D.C., April 5, 1995. *TAM.*

"Remarks to Democratic Convention." Chicago, August 26, 1996. Audio and transcript available at www.pbs.org/newshour/convention96/floor_speeches/daschle.html

"Remarks by Senate Democratic Leader Tom Daschle on the Opening of 105th Congress." Washington, D.C., January 21, 1997. *TAM*; *LC.*

"Remarks to Democratic Convention." Los Angeles, August 15, 2000. Audio and transcript available at www.pbs.org/newshour/election2000/demconvention/daschle.html

"Federal Government in the Indian Nation: Indian Education." Washington, D.C., November 15, 2000. *Vital Speeches of the Day*, November 15, 2000, pp. 74–78.

"Remarks of Senate Majority Leader Daschle at the Fifth Annual DLC National Convention." Indianapolis, Ind., July 16, 2001. *TAM.*

"Remarks by Senate Majority Leader Tom Daschle, Rainbow/PUSH Annual Conference." Chicago, August 8, 2001. *TAM.*

"A New Century of American Leadership: Meeting Our Global Obligations" (address to the Woodrow Wilson International Center for Scholars). Washington, D.C., August 9, 2001. *Vital Speeches of the Day*, September 1, 2001, pp. 676–81.

"Remarks by Senator Tom Daschle, Sioux Falls

Chamber of Commerce Annual Dinner." Sioux Falls, S.D., October 29, 2001. *TAM*.

"America's Economy: Rising to Our New Challenges: Remarks by Senate Majority Leader Tom Daschle at the Center for National Policy." Washington, D.C., January 4, 2002. Available at www.cnponline.org/Press%20Releases/Transcripts/Daschle%20Speech.htm

"Speech at Columbia University." New York City, April 21, 2002. Available at http://www.dashpac.com/home/agenda/speeches.cfm?SpeechID=13

"Making a Difference: America and the Senate One Year After the Jeffords Switch" (address to the National Press Club). Washington, D.C., May 22, 2002. *DPC*.

"Remarks by Senate Majority Leader Daschle at the Hispanic Leadership Summit." Washington, D.C., June 20, 2002. *DPC*.

"Remarks by Senate Majority Leader Tom Daschle, League of Conservation Voters Annual Dinner." Washington, D.C., September 19, 2002. *TAM*.

"Remarks by Daschle on Democratic Civil Rights Agenda." Detroit, Mich., January 20, 2003. *DPC*.

"Prebuttal to State of the Union" (address to National Press Club). Washington, D.C., January 27, 2003. *DPC*.

ANGELA YVONNE DAVIS (1944–)
Professor, History of Consciousness, University of California, Santa Cruz

CINDY L. GRIFFIN

Although Angela Y. Davis was once labeled a dangerous, hardened criminal, she describes herself as a Black woman who is a Communist, a woman who has dedicated her "life to the struggle for the life of Black people," the struggle against racism and sexism ("Angela Davis Speaks," 1973). Her rhetoric is both radical and revolutionary, and as an orator she captures the devastating impacts of both immediate and long-term oppression. In her speeches, Davis identifies and examines the myriad interconnections between past and present; she explores the connections between racism and sexism, economic oppression and violence, and the impending nuclear annihilation brought about by the government's domestic and foreign policies. Throughout her speeches, she presents a vision of a world without any of these foes: a world in which African American women and men live in health, safety, and respect; a world in which children are free to grow, play, and learn without physical or mental harassment and harm; and a world in which the human spirit is strong not because it refuses to be broken but because

it is nurtured, valued, and encouraged. Davis's skill and contribution as an orator rest on her ability to call attention to the subtle and the overt oppression that occurs in the present and has occurred in the past while simultaneously building a vision of a safer and healthier future.

Born January 27, 1944, Davis grew up in Birmingham, Alabama, in the neighborhood known as "Dynamite Hill." The nickname Dynamite Hill was given to the area because of the numerous bombings that took place there—bombings designed to keep African Americans from moving and living there. As a young child, Davis learned the lessons of racism and poverty well and vowed to herself that she would never wish she were white, regardless of the privileges afforded to those with the "right" skin color. In her autobiography she explains that in elementary school she learned more than the mechanics of reading, writing, and arithmetic; she learned "that just because one is hungry, one does not have the right to a good meal; or when one is cold, to warm clothing, or when one is sick, to medical care."

Davis attended high school in Birmingham

until her junior year and then, looking for greater academic challenges, she entered Elizabeth Irwin High School in New York City. In her history classes there, Davis was exposed to communism, and the theories in *The Communist Manifesto* hit her "like a bolt of lightning" (*Autobiography*, p. 109). In the *Manifesto* she found answers to the dilemmas of racial oppression with which she had struggled as a young child and began to get a sense of how emancipation for Black people might become a reality. In 1961, Davis entered Brandeis University to study French literature and spent her junior year in France. From an American newspaper in France, she learned of the murder of the four young girls in the bombing of the 16th Street Baptist Church in Birmingham, Alabama—three were friends of her family. She describes her grief and fury over these brutal and senseless killings: "No matter how much I talked, the people around me were simply incapable of grasping it. They could not understand why the whole society was guilty of this murder—why their beloved Kennedy was also to blame, why the whole ruling stratum in their country, by being guilty of racism, was also guilty of this murder" (*Autobiography*, p. 131).

Committed to social change and possessing a burning desire to study philosophy, Davis, after her return to Brandeis, scheduled a meeting with Herbert Marcuse, who was teaching there. This first meeting grew into weekly discussions of her readings of the philosophers he suggested. In her last year at Brandeis, Davis applied for and received a scholarship to study philosophy in Frankfurt. After graduating Phi Beta Kappa and magna cum laude from Brandeis, she left to study in Germany. The civil rights struggle in America and her intense desire to be a part of it brought her home from Germany in 1967, before she completed her graduate studies but not before Marcuse had agreed to direct her dissertation at the University of California at San Diego. Davis took her first teaching job at the University of California at Los Angeles in 1969, before completing her degree. Engaged in the civil rights movement in southern California, a member of the Black Panthers, and a member of the Communist Party, she apparently was more than the Board of Regents could handle. Fired from her teaching position at UCLA be-

cause of her political views, reinstated, and then fired again, Davis saw her life becoming more dramatic, public, and revolutionary. In 1970, the FBI placed Davis on their "Ten Most Wanted" list on charges of murder, kidnapping, and conspiracy after guns registered in her name were used in a failed attempt to take hostages from a Marin County courthouse who were to be exchanged for several Black political prisoners. Incarcerated without bail for twenty months, Davis finally was acquitted of all charges in 1972. Since the 1970s, Davis has been a lecturer at Claremont College in California, Stanford University, and San Francisco State University. She is currently a professor in the History of Consciousness Program at the University of California at Santa Cruz. She explains her life of public activism and struggle as follows: "For me revolution was never an interim 'thing-to-do' before settling down; it was no fashionable club with newly minted jargon, or new kind of social life—made thrilling by risk and confrontation. Revolution is a serious thing. . . . When one commits oneself to the struggle, it must be for a lifetime" (*Autobiography*, p. 162).

ANGELA DAVIS: REVOLUTIONARY POLITICS, RADICAL CONNECTIONS

Throughout her career as a speaker, Davis has relied on her revolutionary politics and her Communist perspective to weave together seemingly disparate and disconnected themes. At the core of her rhetoric is her powerful and relentless argument for the end of racism and sexism, as well as a recognition of the interconnections between both forms of oppression. Each of her speeches contains, in some form, a call for the recognition of the relationships among racism, sexism, economic oppression, and violence against women and all people of color. Her speeches reflect her vision of a world without racism—a world without the daily reality of danger, harassment, and death for African Americans. Davis asks her audiences to recognize and resist racism in its most subtle and blatant forms, to speak out against sexism, and to protest economic oppression in as many ways as they are able.

Although texts of Davis's speeches prior to 1983 are not available, her work from the 1980s and beyond is marked by a consistency that likely characterizes her earlier oratory. From her prison cell in 1971, for example, Davis issued a tribute to be read at the funeral of George Jackson, one of the Soledad Brothers killed by guards at San Quentin Prison in 1971. A close friend of Davis, Jackson wrote the militant book *Soledad Brother* (1970), and offered a powerful voice in the fight against racism in the late 1960s and early 1970s. This early text is similar to Davis's later rhetoric; Davis made connections across themes and between experiences in ways that foreshadowed her published speeches of the 1980s. In her eulogy of Jackson, Davis linked the imprisonment of Black and Third World people to racism and classism, using the prison sentence of one year to life given to Jackson at the age of eighteen for a robbery involving seventy dollars—and the eleven years served until his murder—as her example. Jackson's imprisonment and death, she explained, was a sign of

not have invited a woman who is a Communist and activist in radical political struggles" to be their commencement speaker. Rather than continuing to doubt their abilities, Davis placed her faith in these young women and men and encouraged them to engage in the struggle for political and personal freedom. She asked them to imagine a world in which they could live with dignity and to imagine a future of justice, equality, and peace.

The future, Davis explained, belonged to these graduating seniors—young people who certainly could run the country much more efficiently and peacefully than it currently was being run. She asked them to envision a world in which everyone had a home, enough food to eat, a well-paying job, and respect. She asked her audience to imagine a shorter workweek, free education, equal opportunities for women and men, no homophobia, no sexism, and no Ku Klux Klan. She

"[If] . . . we are not afraid to adopt a revolutionary stance—if, indeed, we wish to be radical in our quest for change—then we must get to the root of our oppression. After all, *radical* simply means 'grasping things at the root.'"

Angela Davis, "Let Us All Rise Together"

the intense need to strengthen the mass movement against oppression, and his memory and legacy must fuel the fires of resistance within the African American community. While not as intricate as her later speeches, this early text suggests Davis's recognition of interconnections and her ability to locate individual experiences within the larger issues of race and class.

In one of her earliest published speeches, "Imagining the Future" (1983), addressed to the graduating seniors of Berkeley High School, Davis created a vision of a world free from oppression for her audience. Having once believed that the youth of the 1980s were more concerned with MTV than with political issues, she apologized for uncritically accepting the "propagandistic notions" that caused her to misjudge her audience. Davis surmised that "unconcerned and apolitical young people obviously would

asked them to dream a world without the draft, without war, without capital punishment, without prisons, and without the "oppression of people of color." Imagining a future was not enough, however, and she explained that "we must do more than engage in such flights of imagination." The future depended on her audience's willingness to "march, protest, petition, and pursue whatever other avenues of collective resistance will guarantee that one day all people will live together in total peace." They must do this, she explained, because each person is responsible for the future; "[a]ll of us, the young and the old alike, women as well as men, must stand up, speak out, and fight for a better world."

As she addressed the graduating Black students at the University of California at Los Angeles two years later, Davis reminded her audience that while they might have a vision for their own futures, they also must recognize their role in creating change and must never forget the relationship between the past and the future. In her speech, "Reaping Fruit and Throwing Seed" (1985), she asked her audience to link themselves to their history and to remember "that people marched and organized, were arrested and lost their jobs— some even lost their lives—in order to clear the way for this victorious moment" of graduation: "I urge you to reflect not only on your own time and efforts, but on the struggles of our forebears as well, which made it possible for you to attend this university, to gain an education, and to collect your diplomas here today." While the struggles before them would be daunting at times, and oppression and discrimination surely awaited them, connections to other oppressed peoples must remain at the center of their visions. Just as the people of South Africa would prevail, so, too, would these students. They must remember, however, the poverty of others, the oppression and violence leveled against their children and people of color, Reagan's racist policies, and the marginalization of their own communities. By highlighting these particular issues and experiences, Davis reminded her audience of the connections among the past, the present, and the future, as well as of oppression in other parts of the world. She concluded, "[as] you reap the fruit of past struggles, you must also throw the seed for future battles."

Regardless of her topic, Davis's speeches brought to the forefront the centuries-long struggle against oppression and the violence and harassment African American people had endured. In her 1984 address to the conference on Women and the Struggle Against Racism, "Facing Our Common Foe: Women and the Struggle Against Racism," Davis not only identified the marginalization Black women experienced as a result of the insensitivity of many of the white women involved in the women's movement, but she also expressed the need to unify struggles against sexism and to place Black women's experiences at the center of this struggle. Historically as well as currently, white leaders of the women's movement had ignored the needs of their Black sisters, considering the "triple oppression" felt and voiced by Black women as "at best of marginal relevance to their experiences." What women of all colors needed to recognize, Davis argued,

was that in the "pyramid" of oppression, Black women resided at the bottom, while white women, depending on their economic status, resided at or near the top. Changes at the top of the pyramid affected only those who resided at the top, but changes at the bottom of the pyramid affected all who resided within this structure. "The forward movement of women of color almost always initiates progressive change for all women," she explained.

Davis linked advances made today to African American women and men of the recent past. The national political campaigns of Shirley Chisholm, Charlene Mitchell (the Communist Party's 1968 presidential candidate), Charlotta Bass (the Progressive Party's 1952 vice presidential candidate), Davis herself (who was the vice presidential candidate of the Communist Party in the 1980 and 1984), and Jesse Jackson had all pushed the boundaries of racism and oppression, she asserted, making the path that others would follow a little easier. Jesse Jackson may have "opened the door," Davis reminded her audience, but Geraldine Ferarro "walked through!" While advances had been made, she cautioned, Black women still remained discredited and marginalized. "If it was necessary for Sojourner Truth to exclaim, 'Ain't I a woman?' in 1851, Black women are still compelled to expose the invisibility to which we have been relegated, in both theory and practice, within large sectors of the established women's movement."

Davis did more than recognize the interconnections of past and present; she offered solutions to the oppressive conditions she saw. Rather than continue to perpetuate this marginalization, she argued, the women's movement must place the concerns and experiences of African American women at the very core of their agenda: "In order for the women's movement to meet the challenges of our time, the special problems of racially oppressed women must be given strategic priority." Women of color and working-class women "confront sexist oppression in a way that reflects the real and complex objective interconnections between economic, racial, and sexual oppression." For these reasons, issues of women's poverty, welfare benefits, teen pregnancy, safe contraception, abortion, child care, education, affirmative action, and well-paying jobs "must be given strategic priority" within the women's movement. Although these issues might be faced by women of all colors, Davis explained, the recognition that these were issues that Black women faced in a more devastating way would facilitate the elimination of racist structures within the women's movement. The "process of exorcising racism from our ranks," she argued, "will determine whether the women's movement will ultimately have a part in bringing about radical changes in the socioeconomic structures of this country."

Not only must white women recognize the oppression perpetuated by marginalizing African American women, but they must eradicate the racist structures within their own movement by being especially clear about the sexist and racist structures embedded in society as a whole. In her speech "We Do Not Consent: Violence Against Women in a Racist Society" (1985), presented at Florida State University, Davis identified these structures by arguing that a web of interconnection existed between the past and the present, between global violence and localized racist actions. With sexual assault as her focus, Davis carefully identified the interconnections between global and local violence. Sexual assault, she explained, must be situated "within its larger sociopolitical context. If we wish to comprehend the nature of sexual violence as it is experienced by women as individuals, we must be cognizant of its social mediations" at the global level.

Davis reminded her audience that the "imperialist violence imposed on the people of Nicaragua, the violence of South African apartheid, and the racist-inspired violence inflicted on Afro-Americans and other racially oppressed people here in the United States" are linked to "[r]ape, sexual extortion, battering, spousal rape, sexual abuse of children, and incest." Citing June Jordan's poem *Passion* (1980), Davis suggested that Black women were considered "the wrong people of the wrong skin on the wrong continent." The violence that occurred against women of color in South Africa, Namibia, Angola, Zimbabwe, and numerous other countries meant that, for the Black woman, the message was still "I was wrong I was wrong again to be me being me where I was/wrong to be who I am." For Davis, "sexual violence against individual women and

neocolonial violence against people and nations" had clear parallels.

In her speech, Davis brought her argument from this global level to the local, domestic level and then moved back out again to the question of global violence. She explained that at the local level, "one out of three women will be sexually assaulted in her life time." In addition, "one out of four girls will be raped before she reaches the age of eighteen. Despite these startling statistics, there is only a 4 percent conviction rate of rapists—and these convictions reflect only the minute percentage of rapes that are actually reported." More rapes are committed by white men than Black men, but "there are a disproportionately large number of Black men in prison on rape convictions"—a testament to our racist penal system. The myth of the Black man raping the white woman, Davis continued, was simply that—a myth. Davis reminded her audience that "proportionately more white men rape Black women than Black men rape white women." The final irony of this oppressive situation lay in history because "Black women's bodies were considered to be accessible at all times to the slave master as well as to his surrogates" during slavery. White men rape Black and white women, but Black men go to jail.

Leaving this local level and returning to the global political arena, Davis argued that as imperialist aggression increased, so did domestic and racist violence against women. As violence around the world became more widespread, women could "expect that individual men will be more prone to commit acts of sexual violence against the women around them." Men are socialized to rape, she argued, and the level of violence inflicted on women is often a result of official policy. Her audience need only consider the atrocities of Vietnam to be reminded of this. In Vietnam, she argued, "U.S. soldiers often received instructions for their search and destroy missions that involved 'searching' Vietnamese women's vaginas with their penises." Sexual assault, she argued, "bears a direct relationship to all of the existing power structures in a given society. This relationship is not a simple, mechanical one, but rather involves complex structures reflecting the interconnectedness of the race, gender, and class oppression that characterize the society." Foreign policy condoned and even encouraged sexual assault, and domestic actions followed in kind.

Davis continued to develop the theme of interconnectedness by relating global violence to local violence. She argued that the "explosion of sexual violence" in the United States was happening at a time when the government had "developed the means with which to annihilate human life itself." The government spent millions and millions of dollars an hour on "the most devastating instruments of violence" the human race has ever known, taking that money from programs that assisted people living in or near poverty; just five hours of military spending—$200 million—"could provide annual support for sixteen hundred rape crisis centers and battered women's shelters." Davis' strategy was not only to expose the myth of sexual assault but also to link military destruction and spending to women's abuse and oppression. Violence against women occurred at the local and the global levels, and activists must contextualize the rape epidemic in order to dismantle the structures that perpetuated this atrocity. From police violence against African American women in the United States to the policies of Vietnam, South Africa, and Central America, "sexual violence can never be completely eradicated until we have successfully effected a whole range of radical social transformations in our country."

In 1987, Davis turned her attention from sexual violence to violence against African American women's health. In a speech delivered to the North Carolina Black Women's Health Project at Bennett College in Greensboro, North Carolina, "Sick and Tired of Being Sick and Tired: The Politics of Black Women's Health," Davis drew interconnections not only between global and local issues but between health and poverty. Never fond of Ronald Reagan, in this address Davis used statistic after statistic and example after example to illustrate the damage that Reagan's policies had done to African American women, revealing the absurdity of Reagan's domestic cutbacks and the impossible situation those reductions created for African American women and children.

Davis began by explaining that politics "do not stand in polar opposition to our lives. Whether we desire it or not, they permeate our existence, insinuating themselves into the most private spaces of our lives." As an example she cited cases of Black women being turned away from doctors and hospitals because they were assumed not to have insurance coverage when they actually did. She noted that although Black women were less likely to get breast cancer, they were more likely to die from it. Fewer Black women received prenatal care, and more Black infants than white infants died as a result. Violence against Black women's health was the result of racism, for which much of the blame lay with Reagan. She attacked his domestic policies, his racist stance, and his willingness to eliminate the small amount of financial assistance Black women received: "[H]ealth ought to be universally recognized as a basic human right. Yet in this society, dominated as it is by the profit seeking ventures of monopoly corporations, health has been callously transformed into a commodity—a commodity that those with means are able to afford."

She presented a string of statistics in order to make her point: Black women are twice as likely as white women to die of hypertensive cardiovascular disease; they have three times the rate of high blood pressure; Black women are twelve times more likely to contract the AIDS virus than white women; where usually there is one doctor per fifteen hundred people, in "Central Harlem, there is only one doctor per forty-five hundred people"; infant mortality for Black children is twice that of white infants; lupus is "three times more common among Black women than white"; and Black women are far more likely to die of diabetes and cancer than their white counterparts. As numbers and comparisons continued, Davis painted a graphic picture of the obstacles Black women faced under the Reagan administration.

In this speech, Davis again intertwined the global with the local, explaining that while Reagan's policies funneled millions of dollars into military spending, few Black people—especially women—were employed in this arena. Returning to an earlier theme from her speaking career, Davis stated that "[s]ince 1980, the military budget has more than doubled, taking approximately $100 billion from social programs that were underfunded to begin with." She concluded by suggesting that, once again, the larger social and political context of racism and sexism must be recognized if poverty, sickness, and joblessness are to be challenged and eliminated. Reagan's global focus on military spending and defense had been devastating locally and had left Black women in very difficult situations. Subsidized programs must be reinstated, Davis concluded—programs that "emphasize prevention, self-help, and empowerment."

Speaking earlier in 1987, this time to the National Women's Studies Association annual conference at Spellman College, Davis returned to the themes of unity and the necessity of recognizing the interconnectedness of racism and sexism. In her speech, "Let Us All Rise Together: Radical Perspectives on Empowerment for Afro-American Women," Davis brought together each of the issues on which she had touched throughout her speaking career. Empowerment for African American women, she argued, would come only when individuals recognized the connection of human dignity with global responsibility. Citing Gerda Lerner's *Black Women in White America*, Davis explained: "We are not drawing the color line; we are women, American women, as intensely interested in all that pertains to us as such as all other American women."

In this speech, Davis argued that empowerment for African American women should be linked to their history and guided by the principle called for by the National Association of Colored Women's Clubs of the early 1900s: "Lifting as we climb." African American women, Davis argued, brought to the women's movement "a strong tradition of struggle around issues that politically link women to the most crucial progressive causes." African American women brought a concern for homelessness, joblessness, repressive legislation, "homophobia, ageism, and discrimination against the physically challenged." Davis explained that while these were the issues with which Black women had concerned themselves, these were also the issues that "should be integrated into the overall struggle for women's rights," and these were the issues that united individuals on both local and global levels. To break the "historical pattern" of oppression meant that individuals must merge the local with the global, recognize the links between racism

and sexism, and move toward a "revolutionary, multiracial women's movement."

Davis argued that "Lifting as we climb" meant that Reagan and his administration—"the most racist, antiworking class, sexist" administration in our recent past—must be stopped. "Lifting as we climb" meant that "sexist-inspired violence—in particular, terrorist attacks on abortion clinics"—must be stopped. "Lifting as we climb" meant jobs, union organizing, affirmative action, pay equity, an end to sexual harassment, paid maternity leave, and funding for AIDS research. "Lifting as we climb" meant "grass-roots organizing" and the "transformation of the socioeconomic conditions that generate and persistently nourish the various forms of oppression we suffer." "Lifting as we climb" meant that we "learn from the strategies of our sisters in South Africa and Nicaragua," that we "forge a new socialist order—an order which will reestablish socioeconomic priorities so that the quest for monetary profit will never be permitted to take precedence over the real interests of human beings."

For Davis, an orator with radical politics and a revolutionary commitment to eliminating oppression, "Lifting as we climb" meant that we "who are women of color must be willing to appeal for multiracial unity in the spirit of our sister-ancestors. Like them, we must proclaim: We do not draw the color line. The only line we draw is one based on our political principles." She explained that if "we are not afraid to adopt a revolutionary stance—if, indeed, we wish to be radical in our quest for change—then we must get to the root of our oppression. After all, *radical* simply means 'grasping things at the root.'" African American women must take the lead in the movement against racial oppression and violence, they must call attention to the issues that affect women at all levels, they must make the connections between the global and the local, and, as their sisters-ancestors did generations ago, they "must lift as we climb."

During the 1990s, Davis carried her theme of "Lifting as we climb" into her speeches about issues related to Black women in higher education, affirmative action, and the prison system, addressing the intricacies of racism in new ways. In Davis's 1994 speech "Black Women in the

Academy: Defending Our Name 1894–1994," her radical connections came in the form of four charges to her audience. First, she argued, as Black women continued to advance in higher education—as students, teachers, and staff—they no longer could look to "a single monolithic force against which we position ourselves to defend our name—i.e., the white establishment. We have to defend our names in those places we consider home as well." Second, "we can no longer ignore the ways in which we sometimes end up reproducing the very forms of domination" we like to "attribute to something or somebody else." Third, Davis charged, "we have to rid ourselves of the habit of assuming that the masses of Black women are to be defined in accordance with their status as victims." Finally, Davis urged her audience not to position themselves against other women of color as they "so fervently" defended their names.

Speaking in 1996 at the Feminist Family Values Forum, Davis restated her commitment to radical and revolutionary ideas: "I want to begin by suggesting that particularly at this time in the history of our country and the history of the globe, radical activism is needed more than ever before." As women from across the country, and internationally, addressed issues of racism, sexism, the chipping away of affirmative action, immigrant-bashing, the explosion of the "punishment industry," and the "overruling of the educational system by the prison system," they must act radically. "As a matter of fact," Davis explained, "I don't think we can move forward if young women and young people are not at the forefront of our struggles. You have to be a little young and crazy to get out there and do the things that are necessary in order to try to change the world."

In the fall of 2000, Davis delivered the keynote address to participants at the Color of Violence Conference in Santa Cruz, California. Davis described the event, the first of its kind, as historic, and continued to draw connections between the sexism and racism of the past and of the present. She urged her audience to pay tribute to activists and scholars of the past who had made it possible to see the "concealed layers of aggression systematically directed at women," honoring those who helped us see that domestic violence is not normal. However, Davis admonished her audience to focus on a present contradiction, once again highlighting her talent for connecting the global to the local and the past to the present. How can a state, she asked, "infused with racism, male dominance, class-bias, and homophobia act to minimize violence in the lives of women of color?" The answer to this question is vexing, Davis acknowledged. Undaunted, she called for a coming together of individuals working on the issue of domestic violence coupled with "political mobilization" that attended to past efforts as well as present solutions, and that focused on global as well as state and local "forces that shape violence against women of color."

Although her life and her rhetoric have been revolutionary, Davis sees herself as belonging to a "community of humans—a community of struggle against poverty and racism" (*Autobiography*, p. ix). While some might disagree, Davis also views her life as quite unexceptional. She explains that the "forces that have made my life what it is are the very same forces that have shaped and misshaped the lives of millions of my people. . . . I am convinced that my response to these forces has been unexceptional as well, that my political involvement, ultimately as a member of the Communist Party, has been a natural, logical way to defend our embattled humanity" (p. x). This commitment to relationship, interconnection, confrontation, and vision informs Davis's rhetoric and her life. As a rhetor in a sexist and racist society, Davis uses her life and words to present the global through the lens of the local, the past through the lens of the present and the future, and the humanness and dignity of African American individuals through the harshness of a racist society.

INFORMATION SOURCES

Research Collections and Collected Speeches

Davis's major speeches have been published in several anthologies and histories. There are neither archival collections or research collections at this writing.

Bright, Susan, ed. *Feminist Family Values Forum* [*FFV*]. Austin, Tex.: Plain View Press, 1996.

Davis, Angela Y. *Women, Culture, and Politics* [*WCP*]. New York: Random House, 1989.

Foner, Philip S., ed. *The Voice of Black America:*

Major Speeches by Negroes in the United States, 1797–1971 [*VBA*]. New York: Simon and Schuster, 1972.

James, Joy, ed. *The Angela Y. Davis Reader* [*ADR*]. Malden, Mass.: Blackwell, 1998.

Web Site

Applied Research Center, Race and Public Policy Program [*CL*]. Oakland, Calif. This Web site's archived material includes a variety of articles and speeches by Angela Davis. www.arc.org

Selected Critical Studies

"Angela Davis Speaks: An Interview with the Controversial Marxist Leader in the Black Movement." In *Today Like It Is*. North Hollywood, Calif: Center for Cassette Studies, 1973.

Aptheker, Bettina. *The Morning Breaks: The Trial of Angela Davis.* New York: International Publishers, 1975.

Davis, Angela Y. *If They Come in the Morning: Voices of Resistance*. New York: Third Press, 1971.

Ginger, Ann F., ed. *Angela Davis Case Collection: Annotated Procedural Guide and Index.* Berkeley, Calif.: Meiklejohn Civil Liberties Institute, 1974.

Major, Reginald. *Justice in the Round: The Trial of Angela Davis.* New York: Third Press, 1973.

Parker, J. A. *Angela Davis: The Making of a Revolutionary.* New Rochelle, N.Y.: Arlington House, 1973.

Timothy, Mary. *Jury Woman.* San Francisco: Glide Publications, 1975.

Biography

Davis, Angela Y. *Angela Davis—An Autobiography.* New York: Random House, 1974, 1988.

CHRONOLOGY OF MAJOR SPEECHES

See "Research Collections and Collected Speeches" for source codes.

"The Legacy of George Jackson." Marin, Calif., August 25, 1971. *VBA*, pp. 1191–94.

"Imagining the Future." Berkeley, Calif., June 16, 1983. *WCP*, pp. 171–78.

"Facing Our Common Foe: Women and the Struggle Against Racism." Minnesota Coalition for Battered Women, November 15, 1984. *WCP*, pp. 16–34.

"Reaping Fruit and Throwing Seed." University of California, Los Angeles, June 15, 1985. *WCP*, pp. 179–85.

"We Do Not Consent: Violence Against Women in a Racist Society." Florida State University, Tallahassee, Fla., October 16, 1985. *WCP*, pp. 35–52.

"Peace Is a Sisters' Issue Too: Afro-American Women and the Campaign Against Nuclear Arms." Los Angeles, November 16, 1985. *WCP*, pp. 66–72.

"Let Us All Rise Together: Radical Perspectives on Empowerment for Afro-American Women." Spellman College, June 25, 1987. *WCP*, pp. 3–15.

"Sick and Tired of Being Sick and Tired: The Politics of Black Women's Health." Bennett College, Greensboro, N.C., August 29, 1987. *WCP*, pp. 51–65.

"Children First: The Campaign for a Free South Africa." Harare, Zimbabwe, September 27, 1987. *WCP*, pp. 104–8.

"The Politics of Black Women's Health." *Vital Signs* 5 (February 1988): 53–65.

"Black Women in the Academy: Defending Our Name 1894–1994." Cambridge, Mass., January 15, 1994. *ADR*, pp. 222–31.

"Keynote." Austin, Tex., May 12, 1994. *FFV*, pp. 56–63.

"The Color of Violence Against Women." Santa Cruz, Calif., Fall 2000. *CL*, pp. 1–7.

ALAN DERSHOWITZ (1938–)
Harvard Law Professor

R. JOHN DeSANTO AND DANIEL A. GRANO

Renowned Harvard Law School professor, criminal defense lawyer, and best-selling author Alan Dershowitz is known for his advocacy of civil liberties in a rapidly changing world of international terrorism and business corruption. In addition to teaching the lawyers of tomorrow through his speeches, interviews, and writings, he has defended many high-profile, controversial clients, including kidnap victim-terrorist Patty Hearst, junk bond ace Michael Milken, televangelist Jim Bakker, boxer Mike Tyson, high society's Claus von Bulow, hotelier Leona Helmsley, automaker John DeLorean, and football star O. J. Simpson. Additionally, he has represented death row inmates, as well as many lawyers, including F. Lee Bailey. Dershowitz's ability to agitate public consciousness about fundamental legal and ethical issues in a common way makes him an important speaker and writer.

Dershowitz was born in Brooklyn, New York, and graduated with a bachelor's degree from Brooklyn College in 1959; three years later he earned an LLB from Yale Law School. He clerked for Chief Judge of the U.S. Court of Appeals of the District of Columbia David Bazelon and later for Supreme Court Justice Arthur Goldberg, and then was hired by Harvard Law School at age twenty-five. He became a full professor at age twenty-eight, the youngest in the school's history. He currently teaches courses in criminal law, psychiatry and the law, constitutional litigation, civil liberties, and violence. Famous for defending controversial clients and taking unpopular positions, he is considered one of America's top commentators on legal issues. His well-known controversial arguments, often grounded in the First Amendment, have earned him notoriety as well as several distinguished awards. For example, in 1983 Dershowitz received the William O. Douglas First Amendment Award from the Anti-Defamation League of B'nai B'rith for his leadership and advocacy in human rights struggles. Dershowitz has also received honorary degrees from Yeshiva University and the Hebrew Union Haifa University, and the New York Criminal Bar Association has honored him for his outstanding defense of human rights.

Dershowitz frequently appears as a guest on network and cable TV talk shows, often taking controversial positions on issues relating to the criminal justice system. Many popular magazines have contributed to his iconic status. *Time* magazine, for example, described him as "the top lawyer of last resort in the country . . . a sort of judicial St. Jude." *Business Week* wrote that he is "a feisty civil libertarian and one of the nation's most prominent legal scholars." He frequently writes columns for the *New York Times*, and more than one hundred of his articles have appeared in magazines and newspapers including the *Washington Post*, *The New Republic*, the *Los Angeles Times*, and the *San Francisco Chronicle*. Dershowitz has articulated his controversial positions in numerous books devoted to examining important contemporary legal and ethical issues. Important recent volumes include *Why Terrorism Works: Understanding the Threat, Responding to the Challenge*; *Shouting Fire: Civil Liberties in a Turbulent Age*; *Supreme Injustice: How the High Court Hijacked Election 2000*; and *Sexual McCarthyism: Clinton, Starr, and the Emerging Constitutional Crisis*.

DEFENDING RIGHTS AND CHALLENGING CONVENTION

As a speaker on publicly relevant issues such as the First Amendment and constitutional rights, Dershowitz, who has a penchant for the limelight, is one of the most recognized legal figures of the day. His written and oral arguments challenge legal truisms, question commonly held legal and ethical positions, and contribute to the public dialogue on American society and the law.

As one might expect, Dershowitz has his critics. A letter to the editor in the *Wall Street Journal* by Washington attorneys Michael F. Armstrong, Robert S. Bennett, and Ronald P. Fischetti illustrates the controversy that Dershowitz's positions often create. Dershowitz had publicly criticized Robert Morvillo, lead counsel in the trial of Martha Stewart, for not introducing testimony by additional witnesses who might have strengthened Stewart's case. He also criticized Morvillo for not putting Stewart on the stand to testify, although he could not in fact ascertain whether that was Morvillo's or Stewart's decision. Armstrong et al. characterized Dershowitz's critique as "superficial and scurrilous." Dershowitz's technique—attacking another lawyer, knowing that the lawyer cannot defend himself or herself without revealing privileged communications—is, Armstrong et al. argued, "the same tactic he has employed to garner press coverage for his Monday-morning quarterbacking in other high profile cases." Going further, they pointed out that "Professor Dershowitz is an academic who doesn't try cases" and that his arguments demonstrate "his lack of trial experience"; they concluded that Dershowitz should "stick to what he knows and resist the urge to view every guilty verdict in a high profile case as just another opportunity for further self-aggrandizement." Dershowitz's harsh criticism of fellow lawyers is a hallmark of his writings, interviews, and speeches. Hostile reactions like the *Wall Street Journal* letter illustrate one of the effects of Dershowitz's tactics. Speakers who want to increase social consciousness of constitutional and civil liberties issues often resort to agitation as a way to get their message across; to that purpose Dershowitz agitates by attacking others and thereby publicizing his own controversial stands.

As a speaker and writer, Dershowitz commonly attempts to reeducate audiences by challenging common knowledge and core beliefs about legal issues. In *Shouting Fire: Civil Liberties in a Turbulent Age*, for example, he argued that portrayed Falwell having sex with his dead mother in an outhouse. Falwell had received a $200,000 judgment against *Hustler* and Flynt, but the Supreme Court reversed it. Falwell paraphrased Justice Holmes in response to the reversal: "Just as no person may scream 'fire' in a crowded theater when there is no fire, and find cover under the First Amendment, likewise, no sleazy merchant like Larry Flynt should be able to use the First Amendment as an excuse for maliciously and dishonestly attacking public figures, as he has so often done." In this case, Falwell utilized the Holmes argument as an item of common knowledge; the role of an advocate such as Dershowitz is to agitate a different understanding of that argument, creating controversy around its meaning and usefulness.

Dershowitz critiqued Falwell's response, and the Holmes argument, by appealing to people's common knowledge that analogies and their sub-

---

"This is a sad day for America. The man who got the most votes throughout the United States and also in Florida has lost because he was short one vote in the United States Supreme Court."

Alan Dershowitz commenting on Court TV regarding the 2000 presidential election

---

that many people misinterpret Justice Oliver Wendell Holmes's commonly known example of unprotected speech: falsely shouting "fire!" in a crowded theater. He was concerned that the public's formulation of Holmes's dictum simply supports attempts to censor all manner of speech. Famous arguments such as Holmes's become items of common knowledge that people can use to interpret legal issues such as censorship. To confront public knowledge of this sort, speakers and writers must issue challenges in common ways, using examples, stories, and, especially in legal contexts, precedent. This is how Dershowitz used the *Hustler* v. *Falwell* decision by the Supreme Court to illustrate the weakness of the Holmes argument for censoring speech. The Reverend Jerry Falwell had originally sued *Hustler* magazine and its publisher, Larry Flynt, for libel and emotional distress because the magazine had published a satirical parody of a Campari liquor ad jects are never perfect fits. As he wrote in *Shouting Fire*, "Analogies are, by their nature, matters of degree. Some are closer to the case example than others. But any attempt to analogize political ideas in a pamphlet, ugly parody in a magazine, offensive movies in a theater, controversial newspaper articles, or any of the other expressions and actions catalogued above to the very different act of shouting "Fire!" in a crowded theater is either self-deceptive or self-serving." The examples in this statement outline actual cases in which applying the "fire in a crowded theater" analogy would be unreliable. Dershowitz reinforced the point by using the humorous example of 1960s activist Abbie Hoffman, who referred to a time when he was near a fire with a crowd of people and got in trouble for shouting, "Theater, Theater!" That, argued Dershowitz, was as clever and productive a use of Holmes's flawed analogy as anyone has ever made: "So let us hear no more nonsensical analogies to shouting in a crowded theater." Here, Dershowitz demonstrated an ability to challenge a typical mode of public reasoning—argument from analogy. In addition, he was able to work that challenge into an accessible criticism of legal and ethical issues having to do with First Amendment rights and censorship.

As much as speakers and writers must challenge commonly held beliefs about subjects such as law and ethics in order to encourage social change, they must also speak and write in ways that confirm what people find valuable. Arguments that are completely dissonant will often fail. As an effective agitator for social change, Dershowitz displays an ability to confirm major societal values as he challenges others. In *Supreme Injustice*, for example, he built the case that it was a partisan Supreme Court that stole the 2000 presidential election from Al Gore. He had developed the basic argument for the book on December 13, 2000, when he spoke on Court TV: "This is a sad day for America. The man who got the most votes throughout the United States and also in Florida has lost because he was short one vote in the United States Supreme Court." The five justices who voted for Bush simply preferred that he be president, said Dershowitz. In his book, he detailed the background, politics, and history of each of the nine Supreme Court justices, and described how the five majority judges relied upon the Equal Protection clause of the Constitution to stop the Florida recount. Such an application of the clause, Dershowitz noted, was not at all consistent with previous decisions that relied upon that legal principle. History, he concluded in *Supreme Injustice*, would be extremely critical of the judges who stole the election of 2000 from the people. Employing characteristically graphic language, he wrote that "their places in history have been irrevocably established by their corrupt decision in this most important of cases . . . the self-inflicted wound by the majority in *Gore vs. Bush* will fester so long as any of these justices remain on the Court."

Dershowitz made a compelling argument in this legal context by calling upon precedent, a mode of reasoning that people generally understand should hold sway in legal cases. He also took advantage of commonly held beliefs and values concerning the electoral process, especially the idea that voters should have a major-

ity voice that cannot be taken away by a smaller group making a decision based on faulty legal precedent. In this example, Dershowitz was able to fit complex legal and ethical matters into an accessible, dramatic form that included the decision of a powerful few overruling the voice of "the people." As he rendered a controversial opinion on the Supreme Court's decision, Dershowitz was at the same time confirming major societal values about voters' rights and the democratic process.

Sexual McCarthyism, a book examining the impeachment and Senate trial of President Clinton, is yet another example of Dershowitz's ability to publicly "teach" legal and ethical issues through the discussion of current contexts. On January 15, 1999, Dershowitz testified before the House Judiciary Committee when it was considering the articles of impeachment against President Clinton. He stated that the central point about the proceedings was "whether the allegations, if true, constitute treason, bribery or high crimes and misdemeanors." We need to focus on the intent of the framers of the constitutional system and the criteria for removal of the president, he argued; not on who was touched by whom and where. He pointed out that in the 1950s Senator Joseph McCarthy, J. Edgar Hoover, and Roy Cohn had used their government power to pry into the lives of public figures. "The key to sexual McCarthyism is the use of government power," he argued. "That's why the Starr Report is an example of Sexual McCarthyism." Dershowitz effectively packed the legal dangers of the Clinton case into the phrase "sexual McCarthyism," reminding his hearers of the unreasonable tactics and harmfulness of McCarthy era discourse, and forming an association between that negative period and the present case. Coining the phrase in this way offered audiences a "shorthand" criticism of a complex legal and constitutional matter. Dershowitz added an appeal to the reasonability of precedent when he advised that we discern what the framers of the Constitution originally intended as reasons for impeachment, then apply that understanding to the Clinton case. These strategies again illustrate Dershowitz's talents in agitating an awareness of important legal matters in a common way.

Dershowitz's speeches before various groups

emphasize the same controversial themes, purposes, and strategies as his written arguments. Typically, Dershowitz expresses core constitutional values as a means for commenting on particular social issues. In his commencement address at Rice University on May 10, 1997, for example, he argued that the diversity of the United States is the root of our strength and mission as a national community. Typically in a ceremonial address, including a commencement address, speakers will praise or blame people, ideas, or values. Dershowitz used this address as an opportunity to praise diversity and blame problems common to his other criticisms. Speaking about his own graduation from public school in New York City, he described the education he had received as an attempt to "Americanize us, to assimilate us, and to homogenize us. It was as if the Eleventh Commandment and the Twenty-Fifth Amendment read 'thou shalt melt into the great melting pot called America and become more like real Americans who founded this great nation.' " Many did melt, he noted, as the censorship and political correctness of the 1950s permeated the collegiate atmosphere. Soon, however, college campuses seemed like an academic version of Beirut or Sarajevo, where people were no longer content to be judged by their skin, national origin, religion, gender, sexual preference, or ethnicity. Today, the debate continues to swirl around questions of race, ethnicity, gender, and other such factors in admissions and hiring practices.

Blaming forces of pressure toward homogeneity such as political correctness allowed Dershowitz to attack a favorite target—censorship—using accessible historical and cultural examples. This also allowed him to praise Rice University as "a microcosm of the best of America. It is so diverse a place that there is no room for censorship." Commencement addresses are typically advisory, and Dershowitz's advice to this particular audience rang familiar with his advice on legal and cultural matters at large: "The Marketplace of Ideas must be kept open. I urge you to look back to the history of the 1950s when political correctness prevailed on campuses, but the people with the power to define what was correct came from the right rather than from the left. McCarthyism was the 1950s

version of today's political correctness. We must resist censorship of both the right and the left. We must have faith in the Marketplace of Ideas, especially on college campuses." The Rice University commencement address illustrated Dershowitz's ability to adjust the message of his books and popular commentaries to a particular audience; in this way he met the expectations of the situation and the type of speech he was giving even as he advocated his view of the Constitution and the proper application of its principles.

Dershowitz has also drawn public attention by commenting on the role of religion in constitutional politics and law through debates and speeches. In debates, he has demonstrated an ability to fashion overarching constitutional principles into attacks on his opponents. An example case is a debate Dershowitz had with conservative statesman Alan Keyes on the potential for organized religion to solve social problems. Dershowitz established the basic grounds for his disagreement with Keyes as constitutional: "You'll notice that the Constitution . . . particularly the Declaration of Independence, never mentions Christianity. Yes, it mentions 'nature's God,' but it never mentions Christianity. It was a document designed as a document of revolution, a document of consensus." As in other contexts, Dershowitz offered what he viewed as an accurate and applicable understanding of constitutional law and ethics; he turned this understanding into criticism directed at Keyes. Dershowitz accused Keyes, for example, of stating that he would disqualify an atheist from being selected for the Supreme Court, "thereby violating the text of the Constitution which says that no religious test shall ever be required for holding public office in the United States." After Keyes's counterarguments concerning his true intent, Dershowitz stated, "You love citing the Declaration of Independence, but you hate citing the Constitution." Dershowitz implied by his attack that Keyes was finding the evidence for his arguments not in actual constitutional law, but rather in the Declaration of Independence and the preamble to the Constitution, where the law does not actually reside. This strategy exemplifies Dershowitz's overall approach of offering a revised understanding of constitutional, legal, and ethical generalities and turning these into particular criticisms of social values, ideas, and figures. By repeatedly appealing to the Constitution in attacking Keyes, Dershowitz appealed to core values that his audience would likely find favorable. But he also issued a challenge by privileging legality over the value-based language of the Declaration of Independence and Preamble to the Constitution, through which so many people understand the meaning of the Constitution. This tactic of both confirming and challenging public understandings of constitutional law and ethics is central to Dershowitz's efforts at agitation.

In Dershowitz's most controversial speeches, however, the emphasis is decidedly on challenging core values. His October 15, 2003, speech at the national convention of the Freedom from Religion Foundation, in which he addressed the separation of church and state, is representative. In the speech, Dershowitz praised Jefferson's belief in a "God in nature" as proper for the sake of protecting civil liberties: "Jefferson's God did not endanger our liberties. Jefferson's God did not try to impose anything on the rest of us. Jefferson's God was a god of choice, and belief in whom had no consequences at all." Dershowitz worked this last statement into a criticism of Christian morality as conditional, based on a desired reward in heaven. In the speech Dershowitz pointed to "organized exclusivist religions, particularly those that believe there is only one right way, and want either by subtle or overt means [to] impose that right way on us," as "institutions which pose the greatest dangers to our liberty." Following this warning, Dershowitz maintained that "the concept of freedom *from* religion" was more important than any other right in the Constitution, because "freedom from religion entails freedom of religion. It entails freedom of conscience, it entails freedom of speech and freedom of assembly."

Dershowitz arrived at this general constitutional point through a series of aggressive criticisms of Christianity, including a review of the full text of the Ten Commandments, where he cited language that would justify what people would commonly consider today to be legal injustices. By challenging common knowledge on the language and meaning of the Ten Commandments, as well as the bases of Christian charity and morality, Dershowitz employed the same strategies detailed above. His speech at the Freedom from Religion Foundation may be somewhat different from others in the severity of its claims, but not in its tactics. Consistent with his other public comments, Dershowitz offered his view on what "freedom from religion" meant as a key legal and ethical idea bound up in the separation of church and state: "Freedom from religion doesn't mean that you are obliged not to have religion, it means you are free from having religion imposed on you in the public sphere, free from having to take an oath of religion, free from having to say 'Under God' in the Pledge of Allegiance. . . ." Once again, Dershowitz used this speech to agitate controversy on the meaning of fundamental legal and ethical values bound up in the Constitution.

As a final example of Dershowitz's ability to publicize his own controversial stands, his comments on the constitutionality of torture following the 9/11 terrorist attacks on the United States are illustrative. In a January 18, 2002, interview, CBS news commentator Mike Wallace asked Dershowitz if torture of terrorism suspects by the FBI would be constitutional. Dershowitz offered an equivocal answer, saying that while torture was not strictly prohibited by the Fifth Amendment, "it may be a violation of due process. But what is due process? *Due process is the process you are due under the circumstances of the case.* And the process our alleged terrorist who was planning to kill thousands of people may be 'due' is very different than the process that an ordinary criminal may be due" (emphasis added). Again, on March 3, 2003, CNN's Wolf Blitzer posed the same question to Dershowitz, as well as to Ken Roth, the executive director of Human Rights Watch. Dershowitz attempted to elaborate on his earlier answer, saying that "my basic point, though, is we should never, under any circumstances allow low-level people to administer torture. If torture is going to be administered as a last resort in a ticking bomb case, to save enormous numbers of lives, it ought to be done openly, with accountability, with the approval by the President of the United States or the Supreme Court." By defining "due process" Dershowitz attempted to provide a reasonable foundation for his controversial argument. His recommendation was also qualified when he noted the specific and special circumstances under which torture should be allowed. As a concluding example, Dershowitz's comments on open, state-supported torture demonstrate that the premises for even his most controversial arguments are constitutional. By choosing constitutional premises, Dershowitz is able to ground his claims in notions of law and ethics that audiences find reasonable. The Constitution in this way serves as a location of common values and beliefs where Dershowitz can discover arguments. Dershowitz's claims, like the one above on torture, have drawn popular criticism. But Dershowitz has succeeded as a public agitator, and this can be attributed in large part to his skill in adding reasonability to controversial claims by applying fundamental legal premises.

The consistent theme of Dershowitz's spoken and written arguments is that a sound understanding of legal principles must be applied to particular cases that arise in the public sphere so that constitutional, legal, and ethical foundations will continue to ensure our civil liberties. Dershowitz's ability to teach ideas of legal and constitutional precedent in a common way points to his importance as a public figure. Whether audiences agree or disagree with his particular arguments, Dershowitz has contributed to the public dialogue on core cultural values and their legal implications.

INFORMATION SOURCES

Research Collections and Major Speeches

Although no archival collection is available at this writing, Alan Dershowitz is a prolific writer and frequent speaker on TV and radio news and talk shows; many of his speeches are on audiotapes as well as in texts. He has written eighteen books, many of them best-sellers, that reflect his liberal philosophy concerning legal justice.

Dershowitz, Alan. *The Advocate's Devil*. New York: Warner Books, 1994.
———. *The Best Defense*. New York: Random House, 1982.
———. *Contrary to Popular Opinion*. New York: Pharos Books, 1992.
———. *Reasonable Doubts: The O.J. Simpson Case and the Criminal Justice System*. New York: Simon and Schuster, 1996.

———. *Sexual McCarthyism: Clinton, Starr, and the Emerging Constitutional Crisis*. New York: Basic Books, 1998.
———. *Shouting Fire: Civil Liberties in a Turbulent Age*. Boston: Little, Brown, 2002.
———. *Supreme Injustice: How the High Court Hijacked Election 2000*. New York: Oxford University Press, 2001.
———. *Why Terrorism Works: Understanding the Threat, Responding to the Challenge*. New Haven, Conn.: Yale University Press, 2002.

Web Sites

Court TV. Alan Dershowitz has been a frequent guest on *Court TV Talk*. This Web site contains transcripts of his appearances. http://www.courttv.com

Harry Walker Agency. The Harry Walker Agency represents Dershowitz as a lecturer. The Web site includes lecture titles. http://www.harrywalker.com

Nizkor Project. This site includes commentary by Dershowitz on the debates concerning historical revisionists and the Holocaust. His writings on this subject also appeared in the *Washington Times*, February 14, 1992. http://www.nizkor.org/ftp.cgi/ orgs/american/codoh/press

Audiovisual Materials

Court TV Talk. Many of Alan Dershowitz's appearances on *"Court TV Talk"* are available online in audio and video format. www.courttv.com

"Criminal Justice After the O.J. Simpson Case." This audio program of one hour and nineteen minutes features Dershowitz using examples from the O.J. Simpson case in discussing America's justice system. The program was recorded on May 23, 1996, at the Smithsonian Institution. http://smithsonian associates.org/

Critical Study

Armstrong, Michael, et al. "Letter to the Editor." *Wall Street Journal*, March 7, 2004.

Selected Biographies

Dershowitz, Alan. *Chutzpah*. Boston: Little, Brown, 1991.
———. *The Story of My Life*. Boston: Little, Brown, 1996.

CHRONOLOGY OF MAJOR SPEECHES

See "Research Collections and Collected Speeches" for source codes.

"Commencement Speech at Rice University." Houston, Tex., May 10, 1997. Available at http://www. rice.edu/projects/reno/speeches/19970510_Der showitz.html

"Testimony Before House Judiciary Committee." Washington, D.C., December 1, 1998. Available at http://www.house.gov/judiciary/101308.htm

"Debate on Organized Religion Between Alan Keyes and Alan Dershowitz." Franklin & Marshall College, September, 27, 2000. Available at www.renewamerica.us/archives/speeches/00_09_27debate.htm

"Televised Interview and Comments on the Suit Representing Palm Beach, Florida, Voters." November 15, 2000. Available at http://www.courttv.com/talk/chat_transcripts/111500electiondershowitz.html

"Interview with Wolf Blitzer." Atlanta, Ga., March 3, 2003. Available at http://www.cnn.com/

"Keynote Speech to Australia/Israel and Jewish Affairs Council." Sydney, Australia, March 31, 2004. Available at www.aijac.org.au/resources/speeches/dershowitz_speech.html

"Acceptance Speech (speech at the Freedom from Religion Foundation Conference). Washington, D.C., October 15, 2003. Available at www.ffrf.org

"Speech in Support of Israel" (speech at University of California at Berkeley). April 29, 2004. Available at www.frontpagemag.com/Articles/readarticle.asp?ID=13590

ELIZABETH HANFORD DOLE (1936–)
Republican Senator from North Carolina

NICHOLA GUTGOLD

When Elizabeth Dole spoke about her husband at the Republican National Convention in August 1996, she broke with tradition by stepping down the podium steps and moving around the audience. At first, she moved around freely, a lavalier microphone clipped to her suit, and then, when the sound malfunctioned, she held a microphone and continued her sprightly speech. Her style, widely compared with that of talk show hostess Oprah Winfrey, impressed journalists and the public, even though she represented herself not as a political insider, but as a traditional wife of a candidate. Dole's speech offered personal revelations and relied on storytelling throughout as she repeatedly described why Bob Dole was the "strongest, most compassionate man" she had ever known. This attention-getting speech seemed like the grand finale for Elizabeth Dole, who had been a visible, high-ranking Republican woman for over a quarter of a century in Washington, D.C. Her career took a dramatic turn, however, when she ran for elected political office, first as a presidential candidate in 1999, and then when she ran for, and won, a Senate seat from her home state of North Carolina in 2002.

Dole's rhetoric makes heavy use of narrative and self-disclosure. When addressing small gatherings, she likes to depart from the podium, move around within the audience, and use her hands and face expressively. She is fond of telling stories of her Washington career, and several of her speeches repeat the same stories—which, together with her precise diction and polished platform presence—have led many commentators to remark that she sounds scripted. Her formal, letter-perfect public speaking style undoubtedly stems from her penchant for excellence, rooted deeply in the work ethic she learned as a child, the same work ethic that has helped her to achieve many important positions throughout her notable career.

Mary Elizabeth Alexander Hanford was born on July 29, 1936, the only daughter of John and Mary Hanford. Another child, John, had been born thirteen years earlier. By the time she was two, Elizabeth had given herself the nickname "Liddy," a name that stuck with her throughout her childhood and early Washington career. She grew up in Salisbury, North Carolina, where her father built considerable family wealth as a floral wholesaler and her mother volunteered for many church and community activities. In many ways, the life of Elizabeth Hanford Dole would read well as fiction: an archetypal modern woman with Old World manners and refinement gone to Washington to make a difference for herself, for women, and for the nation. For a woman reared in her region and her generation, the most important quality she could learn was graciousness. Through all the stresses of political life, she has never abandoned this lesson, for graciousness remains a hallmark of Elizabeth Dole's rhetoric.

Hanford entered Duke University, in Durham, North Carolina, to study government. At Duke she also ran for every office she could, winning the election for president of the Women's Student Government. During her senior year she was selected 1958 Leader of the Year for the women's and men's campuses, and received glowing reviews in the campus newspaper for sparking change at Duke. She was also elected May Queen, since for her feminism did not mean forsaking her femininity. After graduating from Duke, Hanford went to Oxford for a summer of study and sightseeing, and also traveled to Russia. Curious to see that country and learn what it was like, she prepared a five-point argument to win her parent's approval for the trip. Upon her return Hanford enrolled in a dual degree program at Harvard to continue her study of government, her passion, and teaching, her practical plan for the future. She was a talented, innovative teacher, but she felt that teaching was not the field in which she was most interested in serving. During her second summer at Harvard, she landed a secretarial position in the Washington, D.C., office of Senator Everett Jordon (DNC). While there, she visited high-powered women to ask them for advice about entering a career in government. Senator Margaret Chase Smith advised her that she should obtain a law degree. After earning her master's degree in education from Harvard, she continued to work at the law library. She also spent the next two summers as a tour guide at the United Nations. In 1962, she decided to take Senator Smith's advice, and applied to Harvard Law School. After graduation, she moved from Cambridge, Massachusetts, to Washington, D.C., and there found a position with the Department of Health, Education, and Welfare (HEW), organizing a conference on deaf education. She then learned to be a public advocate in night court.

When Lyndon Johnson assumed the presidency after John F. Kennedy's assassination, Hanford accepted an appointment as a consumer advocate. When Johnson decided not to run for reelection in 1968 and Richard Nixon defeated Hubert Humphrey, she was able to keep her position at HEW even though her boss, Betty Furness, left the agency. Furness was replaced by Virginia Knauer, and Hanford was promoted to deputy of the agency, renamed the President's Committee on Consumer Interests. The agency had labels affixed to food and other products to reveal their contents, and "sell by" dates printed on food and drug packages. Hanford honed her skills as an advocate for consumer protection in frequent speaking engagements that her boss was unable to fulfill. In 1973, she was nominated, and confirmed by the Senate, to fill a vacancy on the Federal Trade Commission. Her rise in Washington was well underway.

In 1975 Hanford married Robert Dole, a Kansas senator and chairman of the Republican Party. Soon thereafter, Gerald Ford asked Robert Dole to be his running mate in the 1976 presidential election. After her husband accepted, Elizabeth Dole switched her party affiliation to Republican, and became a full-time campaign wife. As the years went by, she gained a reputation as a copious underliner of briefing books and a scrupulously prepared speech-giver. When Bob Dole ran for president in 1980, Elizabeth Dole was a popular and impressive campaigner on his behalf.

After Ronald Reagan won the presidency, Bob Dole became head of the powerful Senate Finance Committee, and Elizabeth Dole secured a White House post as head of the Office of Public Liaison. In 1983, Reagan asked her to lead the Department of Transportation, a cabinet position responsible for 100,000 employees nationwide and a budget of $27 billion. In 1987, she resigned as secretary of transportation to join her husband's campaign for the Republican presidential nomination.

In 1988 newly elected President George Bush asked Elizabeth to serve as secretary of labor.

She served for a year and a half, then left to become president of the American Red Cross. In 1995, she took a fourteen-month unpaid leave of absence to join her husband's campaign for president. She stepped down from the American Red Cross on January 4, 1999, and on March 10, 1999, announced that she was creating an exploratory committee to determine whether she should seek the Republican presidential nomination in 2000. She made a six-month bid for the presidency and then withdrew from the race due to a lack of funds. On September 11, 2001, Elizabeth Dole was scheduled to announce her candidacy for the U.S. Senate from her hometown of Salisbury, North Carolina, but after the terrorist attacks on that day, she postponed her announcement until February 23, 2002. She won the Senate race on November 5, 2002, and at age sixty-six became the first woman elected to the Senate from North Carolina.

ELIZABETH DOLE: THE ORATORY OF A FEMININE FEMINIST

Elizabeth Dole's oratorical style is always gracious, precise, and laden with narrative. It is the embodiment of her penchant for preparation, her Southern upbringing, and her warm and loquacious nature. Dole prepares fully for each speaking event, and she always considers her audience very carefully, tailoring her speech to meet the specific needs of the event. She takes an active role in the speechwriting process, working closely with her speechwriters. Over the years, her speechwriters have included Rick Smith, Kerry Tymchuk, and Mari Maseng Will. Broadly, three categories of speeches constitute Elizabeth Dole's speaking career: administrator speeches, as a cabinet member and Red Cross president; campaign speeches, delivered as a spouse of a candidate and as a candidate; and ceremonial speeches, delivered in these other roles.

A typically autobiographical speech that Elizabeth Dole gave was at the National Prayer Breakfast in 1987. The National Prayer Breakfast Organization annually selects a well-known Christian to serve as keynote speaker for its renowned prayer breakfast. Held at the very ornate and regal Washington, D.C. Hilton Hotel, the National Prayer Breakfast started as a Senate event. It has grown to include an audience of approximately four thousand, consisting of members of Congress, the president and first lady, the vice president and his wife, other political and business leaders, ambassadors, and foreign dignitaries.

Dole accepted the invitation with the knowledge that she was to speak about her relationship with God. She was a well-known Republican woman and the only woman serving in President Reagan's cabinet at that time. She opened her speech by stating her speaking objectives: "I consider it one of the greatest possible privileges to be invited to share this morning with fellow travelers a little of my own spiritual journey. Like most of us, I am just one person struggling to relate faith to life, but I am grateful that members of the congressional prayer groups have asked me to speak from the heart, about the difference Jesus Christ has made in my life." This speech came at a time in her life after Elizabeth had experienced a "reordering of priorities" that brought her closer to God. As she told the story in this speech:

> My grandmother, Mom Cathey, who lived within two weeks of her 100th birthday, was my role model. I remember many Sunday afternoons with other neighborhood children in her home—the lemonade and cookies—I think that's what enticed us—the Bible games, listening to Mom Cathey as she read from this Bible—now one of my most cherished possessions. She practiced what she preached, and lived her life for others. In a tragic accident, Mom Cathey lost a son at the hands of a drunk driver. The insurance policy on his life built a wing in a far-off church mission in Pakistan. Although Mom was not at all a wealthy woman, almost anything she could spare went to the ministers at home and missions abroad. When it became necessary in her 90's, to go into a nursing home, she welcomed the opportunity. I can still hear her saying, "Elizabeth, there might be some people there who don't know the Lord, and I can read the Bible to them."

Dole went on to tell the audience that her religious upbringing had been pushed aside because of the frantic pace of her career. She compared the story of Esther, the Old Testament heroine confronted with a difficult choice, to her own struggle to stand for her beliefs.

Dole's use of self-disclosing narrative is well exemplified in the prayer breakfast speech, as it also is in her fourth annual "State of the Workforce" address delivered on October 24, 1990, in Washington, D.C. She began the speech by announcing that she would leave the Labor Department to head the Red Cross. She introduced her self-disclosing narrative in the third paragraph: "Almost two years ago, I stood before you in this very hall to take the oath of office and begin my tenure as Secretary. It was one of my proudest moments in my twenty-five year career in public service. I truly believed this— the people's department—would be my mission field, a place where I would have been dedicated to making a difference—a positive difference in people's lives." In this speech Dole discussed her three main goals as labor secretary. She concluded with additional narrative about her mo-

nesses, ensuring full compliance with our child labor laws; and in far flung corners of the world where people needed help. The opportunity to devote myself to these causes on a full-time basis is what led me to the Red Cross." She continued her narrative with this personal connection to the Red Cross: "I found myself remembering the many ways in which the Red Cross has touched my life. When my brother was stationed in the Pacific in World War II, his load was made lighter by the presence of Red Cross volunteers. Back in Salisbury, North Carolina, my mother was a Red Cross volunteer, telling me that 'she couldn't remember when she felt so important.'" Significantly, Dole justified her decision to work at the Red Cross through her mother's approval. Similarly, she connected the values her family placed on religion to her decision to return to the church in the prayer breakfast speech.

In her public speaking, Elizabeth Dole is best known for her ability to deliver a highly choreographed speech in an intimate, conversational manner. Her most famous speech was given at the 1996 Republican National Convention, where she broke with tradition and walked on the convention floor amid the audience while delivering a compelling testimonial on behalf of the presidential nominee, her husband, Robert.

---

tive: "as I leave one organization dedicated to serving people [the Labor Department] for another dedicated to the same purpose."

Dole's narrative self-revelations were also represented in a speech she gave on February 4, 1991, when she introduced herself to her staff as she took over as the president of the Red Cross. She realized that she needed to secure the trust of the organization and convince the staff that she was "one of them." She attempted to do that by stating: "For me, the most rewarding times in my public service career were not spent in smoke-filled rooms exchanging political gossip. Rather, they were in classrooms, listening to at-risk youth and teen mothers who were turning their lives around; in fields, meeting with migrant workers who needed a voice; deep in coal mines, meeting with miners concerned about safety; in busi-

Another speech that looms large in Dole's career, one entirely cast in narrative, was the 1996 Republican National Convention speech, for which she received effusive praise. Upon hearing her speech, Robert Dole reported thinking that he should have withdrawn his acceptance of the Republican presidential nomination and nominated her instead. After this speech, a journalist writing for *USA Today* described Elizabeth Dole as "likely to be the most agile TV campaigner of the new Republican ticket," while a headline in the *New York Daily News* described the aftermath of her performance as a "Liddy Lovefest." After she was introduced by California governor Pete Wilson, Dole emerged in a mustard yellow silk suit, looking at least a decade younger than her sixty years. Slim and well coiffed, she said:

Thank you, Thank you so much. [APPLAUSE] Oh, my. [APPLAUSE] Thank you, ladies and gentlemen. Thank you so much, ladies and gentlemen, for that wonderful warm welcome. And thank you, Governor Wilson, for your very kind words of introduction. Now, you know, tradition is that speakers at the Republican National Convention remain at this very imposing podium. But tonight, I'd like to break with tradition for two reasons—one, I'm going to be speaking to friends, and—secondly, I'm going to be speaking about the man I love. And it's just a lot more—comfortable for me to do that down here with you.

[APPLAUSE] Thank you. [APPLAUSE] Governor, how are you doing tonight?

In this public oration, Elizabeth Dole interjected interpersonal communication. She mimicked conversation with her intimate delivery and colloquial explanation about what she was going to do in the speech. She continued to explain to the audience the approach that she would be taking with the unique presentation. "Now for the last several days, a number of men and women have been painting a remarkable portrait of a remarkable man, a man who is the strongest and the most compassionate, most tender person that I've ever known—the man who quite simply, is my own personal Rock of Gibraltar." She signaled the importance of her remarks by describing the election as "a defining moment in our nation's history." She said, "This election is about the vision and the values that will shape America as we move into the next century, and it's about the character of the man who will lead us there." She then began a long series of vignettes from Bob Dole's life, starting with his birth.

At the time of this convention speech, Bob Dole trailed Bill Clinton dramatically in the polls and his image for many outside the convention hall was that of a pragmatic and often acerbic politician who had frequently served others as a hatchet man. His wife's chief objective was to rehabilitate his image as a leader with tender qualities hidden from the public. She told story after story about Bob Dole's generosity, leadership, and kindness. Her speech approached hagiography as she recounted his life through his innumerable good deeds. She told of charity birthday celebrations, the formation of the Dole Foundation, and even Bob Dole's selection by his colleagues as the nicest, friendliest senator! She read part of a letter from Democratic Senator Dianne Feinstein to further elaborate on her husband's exemplary character. This speech is Dole's most memorable speaking moment, and may have done the most to bring her to the attention of the press and public as an effective orator and a staunch Republican spokesperson.

The next time the American public heard from Elizabeth Dole was when she stepped down as president of the American Red Cross. Characteristic of her rhetoric, Dole confided in the third paragraph of her resignation speech: "I spent a lot of time over the holidays thinking about the future. And I have a great feeling about this year. Some people say our country is in a crisis. But I believe that America is equal to today's challenges. I know 1999 will be a good year—for the American Red Cross and for the American people—because I know the strength and goodness of those of you in this room and around the country." Further on in the speech, Dole again used inclusive language and disclosure: "We've spent most of this decade together, you and I. And together we've remade our world. For we have not been resistant to change, we have welcomed it." She teased that crowd as well as the media with her next comment, which hinted at a presidential bid: "The years I've spent at the Red Cross, with you, have been the most fulfilling of my career, and I thank you. I love the American Red Cross. But the Red Cross is now as solid as a rock. And at this important time in our national life, I believe there may be another way for me to serve our country. The Red Cross has been a glorious mission field, but I believe there may be other duties yet to fulfill."

Here Dole spoke as a leader, ending one career and subtly suggesting a similar future of leadership, but at the same time using an inbred graciousness to identify with her audience. Her resignation drew significant print and electronic media coverage, televised on both CNN and C-SPAN, as well as every major network's evening news. This speech could be described as a bridge between Dole's nonpolitical career life as president of the American Red Cross and her possible political life as a candidate. It illustrates her ability to create a positive image for herself while fulfilling the purpose that the speech needed to serve—in this case, to announce her Red Cross resignation. Dole did seek the presidency in an exploratory bid that lasted six months, but she dropped out, claiming that a lack of funds made the continuance of her quest futile.

During her exploratory bid, Elizabeth Dole returned to Melrose High School in Melrose, Massachusetts, where she had been a student teacher during the 1959–1960 academic year while a master's degree student at Harvard University. She accepted an open invitation by school administrators to "come back anytime" as an opportunity to present a potent campaign speech that outlined her philosophy for education reform in America. As part of her campaign to win the Republican nomination for president, Dole walked a fine line. In effect, she was criticizing the American educational system inside the American educational system. So, she made the distinction that the difficulties in the system were not within Melrose. She drew upon her experience as a teacher to acquire ethos for her proposed education initiatives. Faced with a different rhetorical task, she did not spend as much time telling a story. She presumed that the audience had prior knowledge of her and that in this situation she needed to establish a different kind of credibility. She relied more heavily on evidence in the form of statistics and specific examples. She used the prop of a heavy stack of papers, stating: "Take a look at the unwieldy stack of paper. These are just a few of the federal rules and regulations that affect your school and others. In this stack is the Clinton-Gore Elementary and Secondary Reauthorization Bill. It's more than 600 pages long. I think somebody wasn't listening to the teacher about keeping his work short and to the point." The last sentence was the quintessence of Dole's ability to envelop harsh criticism in polite and charming discourse. She included herself as an educator in America: "we educators," "our classrooms," "our teachers," and "our kids." She understood her purpose as a candidate, and this speech showed that sensitivity.

On May 14, 2000, Dole returned to her alma matter, Duke University, as the commencement speaker. She made light of her now defunct candidacy in the presidential race with this remark early in the speech: "Thank you, Madam President, for that more than generous introduction. We're all so grateful for your strong and able leadership. Madam President—that does have a nice ring to it, doesn't it? Oh, well. When the Class of 2000 invited me to be a part of this special day, I was both touched and flattered. After all, I come before you as a recent dropout from the Electoral College!" Then, true to her speaking style, she recounted several stories. "Today is the latest, but by no means the last chapter in a story that began in room 304 of Alspaugh House in the autumn of 1954." The speech progressed with stories about her experiences at Duke and also disclosed Dole's spiritual beliefs. She observed: "Meanwhile, we are told that change is the only constant. Yet, amidst so much change, it is critically important that we cling to what is changeless—to love and honor and reverence for things seen and unseen. In this age of satellite dishes, automated tellers and 500 channels on which to watch infomercials for the Ab Flex, may I suggest that we frazzled humans have need of inspiration as well as information, and a faith to match our facts? You don't have to be a missionary to have a sense of mission."

Dole's sense of mission manifested itself in her bid for the North Carolina Senate seat vacated by longtime Republican senator Jesse Helms. On February 23, 2002, in her hometown of Salisbury, North Carolina, Dole announced her Senate candidacy. This announcement speech combined storytelling and campaign statements that both endeared her to the audience and explained her position on a number of important campaign issues. She introduced herself: "I am Mary and John Hanford's daughter, raised to believe that there are no limits to individual achievement and no excuses to justify indifference. From an early age I was taught that success is measured, not in material accumulations, but in service to others. I was encouraged to join causes larger than myself, to pursue positive change through a sense of mission, and to stand up for what I believe. I am Bob Dole's wife, blessed with the love of a great and decent man, whose quiet acts of generosity are on par with his wartime heroism. And I am a daughter of North Carolina, a proud Tarheel who's always cherished my roots here in Salisbury."

On November 5, 2002, Election Night, Dole was declared the winner, the first female senator ever from North Carolina. She announced her victory with these remarks in Salisbury: "Oh, wow! What a night! Oh my word, thank you so much. What a wonderful, warm welcome. I'm thrilled to see you all. Well, I am just as thrilled as you are. We'll never forget this night, will we? And I want to tell you that just a few moments ago, I had a call from Erskine Bowles and he was congratulating me. He was very gracious. And he had a strong campaign, and certainly he cares about the people of North Carolina. And obviously, I'd like to thank each person individually, but we can't do that tonight. But I do want to mention a few people who must be thanked. First of all, my husband, Bob Dole. Let me tell you, he's the best surrogate a candidate could have. And he was hoping to get to all of the 100 counties, and he got darn near close. He did real well. Also he was on the phone calling all the hundred county coordinators and cheering people on, you know. So he's been a great surrogate. And then I want to thank my precious mother and my brother and sister-in-law, John and Bunny Hanford, my family."

On November 13, 2002, just one week after her victory in North Carolina, Dole was welcomed as a new senator by Senator Bill Frist of Tennessee. In her first official remarks as a newly elected senator, Dole said, "Thank you so much, Senator Frist, and let me say it's a great privilege to be here today, with this tremendous class. As far as North Carolina is concerned, it's jobs, jobs, jobs. We're going through a very painful economic transition in North Carolina right now." She continued to list her priorities as a new senator, which included regulatory reform and tobacco-quota buyout. And then, as always, she summed up graciously: "I look forward to seeing a lot of you all, and certainly working with this tremendous class that I'm privileged to belong to." On June 5, 2003, Senator Dole delivered her maiden speech on the Senate floor. Focusing her remarks on the issue of hunger in North Carolina, across America, and around the world, she spoke about her plan to help build a model gleaning program in North Carolina that could be expanded to help eradicate hunger across the country. Drawing upon her previous work in humanitarian efforts, Dole's oratory sounded familiar themes:

> There is a very special tradition in America when it comes to fighting hunger. Perhaps it is a function of our agricultural bounty, the famines in Europe that led to early migration, or the teachings of all major religions, but Americans are intolerant of hunger in our land of plenty. The gleaning system in North Carolina works because of the cooperative efforts of so many groups . . . from the Society of St. Andrew and its volunteers that gather and deliver the food to the dozens of churches and humanitarian organizations that help distribute this food to the hungry. . . . Indeed, gleaning is, at its best, a public-private partnership.

Continuing her work in the Senate, on Wednesday, June 10, 2003, Dole pushed a key housing initiative that was part of the final economic growth package approved by the Senate. The Jobs and Economic Growth Bill included a provision to make mortgage insurance tax deductible. Dole voted for the final package, which was passed by a vote of 51–49. "Today's low interest rates in the mortgage market, coupled with this deduction, will benefit many Americans," she said. "It's an innovative way to help make the American dream of owning a home more affordable."

Elizabeth Dole is well received as a speaker and has earned a reputation as a well prepared, yet adaptable, public speaker. Her varied career as an administrator, the spouse of a candidate, and now a Republican senator has required her to present different kinds of speeches, and she has met the those oratorical challenges with intelligence, charm, and graciousness.

INFORMATION SOURCES

Research Collections and Collected Sources

At the present time there are no archival holdings of Dole's papers. Some of Dole's Senate speeches are available through her Senate Web site.

Wertheimer, Molly and Nichola D. Gutgold. *Elizabeth Hanford Dole: Speaking from the Heart.* Westport: Praeger, 2004.

Web Site

Dole's official Web site is http:/dole.senate.gov/

Audiovisual Material

There are no major audiovisual resources available, although there are some audio clips available at Dole's Senate Web site, and some public speaking tapes feature her 1996 Republican National Convention address.

Selected Critical Studies

Campbell, Karlyn Kohrs. "Shadowboxing with the Stereotypes: The Press, the Public and the Candidates' Wives." Research Paper R-9. Harvard University, John F. Kennedy School of Government. July 1993.

————. "The Discursive Performance of Hating Hillary." *Rhetoric and Public Affairs* 1, no. 1 (1998): 1–17.

Gutgold, Nichola. "Managing Rhetorical Role: Elizabeth Dole from Spouse to Candidate 1996–1999." *Women and Language* 24 (Spring 2001): 29–36.

Selected Biographies

Dole, Bob, and Elizabeth Dole, with Richard Norton Smith and Kerry Tymchuk. *Unlimited Partners: Our American Story*. New York: Simon and Schuster, 1996.

Kozar, Richard. *Elizabeth Dole*. Philadelphia: Chelsea House, 2000.

Lucas, Eileen. *Elizabeth Dole: A Leader in Washington*. Brookfield, Conn.: Millbrook Press, 1998.

Mulford, Carolyn. *Elizabeth Dole: Public Servant*. Hillside, N.J.: Enslow, 1992.

CHRONOLOGY OF MAJOR SPEECHES

"National Prayer Breakfast." Washington, D.C., February 5, 1987.

"University of Virginia Commencement." Charlottesville, Va., May 17, 1987.

"Department of Transportation Awards Ceremony." Washington, D.C., September 16, 1987.

"Address at the Republican National Convention." New Orleans, La., August 16, 1988.

"AFL–CIO Constitutional Convention." Washington, D.C., November 13, 1989.

"International Labor Conference." Geneva, Switzerland, June 11, 1990.

"Women's Bureau 70th Anniversary." Washington, D.C., October 23, 1990.

"Everybody Counts" (fourth annual State of the Workforce address). Washington, D.C., October 24, 1990.

"A Tradition of Trust" (American Red Cross inaugural address). Washington, D.C., February 4, 1991.

"Address to the Republican National Convention." San Diego, August 14, 1996.

"Redbook Mothers Against Drunk Driving." Washington, D.C., May 9, 1997.

"Economic Summit for Women." Albany, N.Y.: May 20, 1997.

"An America We Can Be" (Lancaster County Chamber of Commerce). Hershey, Pa., April 7, 1998.

"American Red Cross Resignation." Washington, D.C., January 4, 1999.

"Duke University Commencement Address." Durham, N.C., May 14, 2000.

"Address to the Republican National Convention." Philadelphia, August 1, 2000.

"North Carolina Senate Race Kickoff Rally." Salisbury, N.C., February 23, 2002.

"North Carolina Senate Election Night Victory Speech." Salisbury, N.C., November 5, 2002.

"Republican Senate Conference Welcome Remarks." Washington, D.C., November 13, 2002.

"Senate Maiden Speech." Washington, D.C., June 5, 2003.

MARIAN WRIGHT EDELMAN (1939–)
Children's Advocate, Lawyer, Author

BETH WAGGENSPACK

An impassioned and relentless champion of needy children and families, Marian Wright Edelman has exemplified her parents' teachings, dedicating her life to helping others as a vocal child advocate. Edelman recalled in her book *The Measure of Our Success* that "the legacies that parents and church and teachers left to my generation of Black children were priceless but not material: a living faith reflected in daily service, the discipline of hard work and stick-to-it-ness, and a capacity to struggle in the face of adversity." Today, she crusades for children with the passionate advocacy skills she developed while an attorney on the front lines of the tumultuous civil rights movement in Mississippi in the 1970s. Then, the goals were minority freedom and recognition. Her goals are the same now, but her focus has shifted to a new list of needs, including health care for all children, full funding for the Head Start program, and other progressive legislation emphasizing social reform, family preservation, and government intervention.

Marian Wright grew up in segregated South Carolina, with service to others an essential part of her upbringing; she described that public service legacy to *Parade* magazine as "the rent we pay for living." Named after Marian Anderson, the world-famous contralto who, with the help of Eleanor Roosevelt, overcame racism to deliver a memorable rendition of "America" at the Lincoln Memorial in 1939, Edelman, too, would raise her impassioned voice in the struggle for civil rights. She credits her parents for providing her with strong values, high expectations, and steady support. Her father, Arthur J. Wright, a Baptist minister in Bennettsville, South Carolina, was the strong family head who provided out-front community leadership. Today, Edelman remembers her father as someone who lived his faith every day and whose church was the hub of her childhood social life. In the segregated South, Black children could not play in public playgrounds or sit at lunch counters to get a drink, so Arthur Wright built a playground and a canteen behind his church. There were no nursing homes for the Black elderly, so he founded the Wright Home for the Aged, which is still in existence. Her mother, Maggie Bowen Wright, reared five children, of whom Marian was the youngest. When Arthur Wright died in 1954, she extended the family tradition of service by opening her home to twelve foster children and took charge of the operation of the Wright Home for the Aged. In Marian Wright's youth, child-rearing and parental work were inseparable, and children were taught not by exhortation but by

personal example. Those values permeate Edelman's rhetoric.

Marian Wright grew up on a regimen of study, discipline, self-development, service to others, and community support. She told reporter Norman Atkins that when she went off to predominantly Black Spelman College, neighbors sent her shoe boxes stuffed with biscuits, chicken, and greasy dollar bills. As a student she was at the center of the sit-ins and the early civil rights movement, as well as president of the student body. Her education concentrated on international relations; during her junior year at Spelman, she received a Merrill Scholarship to study at the University of Paris and in Geneva, Switzerland. That summer, she participated in a student exchange study tour of East Germany, Poland, Czechoslovakia, and the USSR. Following her graduation in 1960, Wright entered Yale University, where she received her law degree in 1963. During the summer of 1962, she worked in Crossroads Africa, a work project in Ivory Coast in West Africa.

In 1963 Wright's civil rights involvement increased when she joined the NAACP Legal Defense and Education Fund as a staff attorney. She worked in the Mississippi race war in 1964, a few months before the Neshoba County killings of three civil rights activists by Ku Klux Klan members. She drew national attention to and obtained relief for the starving children of the Mississippi Delta by taking Senator Robert Kennedy on a personal tour. She later recalled this excursion to Norman Atkins:

> I'll never forget. He walked into this really dark, dank shack with dirt floors in Cleveland, Mississippi. And there were no television cameras there. In the back room, the mother was washing the tub. And sitting on the ground was this baby with a bloated belly. I remember him sitting there, stooping down with the baby and really trying to get a response. He was just visibly shaken. He said he had not realized that there was anything like this in this country. I'm ashamed to say that it took me so long to realize the importance of simply personalizing suffering.

This method of personalizing the crisis of children would later become a hallmark of Edelman's rhetoric. A year later she established the NAACP

Legal Defense and Education Fund in Jackson, Mississippi, serving as its director until 1968. In 1965 she was the first Black woman admitted to the Mississippi bar. While working for the NAACP's Legal Defense and Educational Fund she met Peter Edelman, a Harvard-educated Jewish lawyer who was a legislative assistant to Senator Robert Kennedy. Their 1968 wedding was one of Virginia's first interracial marriages.

Founded by Edelman in 1973, the Children's Defense Fund (CDF), a private, nonprofit organization, owes its birth to the disturbances in Mississippi during the summer of 1964 and the Head Start battles of 1965, where both the great need for and the limits of local action were apparent. In *The Measure of Our Success*, Edelman noted: "As a private civil rights lawyer, I learned that I could have only limited, albeit important impact on meeting epidemic family and child needs without a coherent national policy and investment strategies to complement community empowerment strategies. The goal of the CDF is to educate the nation about the needs of children in order to encourage investment before they get sick, drop out of school, suffer due to breakdowns in the family structure or get involved in criminal activity." CDF collects and analyzes data; produces reports on issues that affect children; disseminates information on key issues that affect children; provides information, technical assistance, and support to state and local child advocates; lobbies Congress; monitors the development and implementation of federal and state policies that affect children; and litigates cases significant to children's rights.

As director of the CDF, Edelman has forged an almost legendary reputation as a tenacious lobbyist. Her detractors accuse her of bullheadedness, an inability to compromise, and a shortsighted perspective on political realities. Others charge that she is an old-fashioned 1960s liberal, loyal to the out-of-date premise that government money solves social problems. Edelman illustrates her persistence and determination with a story about one of her self-professed role models, Sojourner Truth. Truth retorted to a heckler who announced that he "cared no more for her anti-slavery talk than for a flea bite," "Maybe not, but the Lord willing, I'll keep you scratching." Edelman learned in childhood that one

should never back down in the face of perceived injustice.

Edelman's political focus continued with the advent of the Clinton administration. Hillary Clinton made her first postelection appearance at a CDF fund-raiser, and she is a former CDF staff attorney and chairperson. Former Atlanta mayor Andrew Young suggested at the 1992 CDF annual conference that the close friendship between Edelman and the Clintons was an appealing reason to vote for Bill Clinton. Just as Mary McLeod Bethune focused Eleanor Roosevelt's eyes on the plight of Blacks and the poor, which in turn influenced Franklin Delano Roosevelt's social legislation, so Young suggested that one might hope for Marian Wright Edelman's profound impact on a Clinton administration. Despite her preferential status, Edelman did not moderate her challenges to the president. On November 3, 1995, she published an open letter to President Clinton in the *Washington Post*, calling for him to "Protect Children from Unjust Policies." In part, she asked for his "unwavering moral leadership for children" to oppose welfare and Medicaid block grants, which she called unjust policies that are "fatally flawed, callous, anti-child assaults; that "eviscerate the moral compact between the nation and its children and its poor." The letter asserted that the historical lessons of the "immoral abandonment of structures of law and equity led to decades of setbacks," and suggested that the regressive attacks on children would be a "defining moral litmus test" of the Clinton presidency.

More recently, the Bush administration's welfare reform plans have been taken to task. In a commentary for the Religion News Service, Edelman asserted that Bush's new welfare reform plan of child care block grants requires states to increase the work requirements for families moving from welfare to work, raises the number of hours that mothers must work to receive benefits, and does it without any additional federal funds for child care. Edelman says that this position contradicts Bush's 2000 campaign of compassionate conservatism, when he co-opted the CDF's motto to "Leave No Child Behind." As a result, she asserts that Bush's true commitment to "profligate tax cuts—which leaves no millionaire behind while leaving millions of children behind without safe child care, health care, and in poverty—is unwavering." In a CDF press statement issued on April 10, 2001, Edelman said: "We must not let the words 'Leave No Child Behind' become a fig leaf for unjust political and policy choices that, in fact, will leave millions of children and the poor behind. The litmus test of caring for children is what is done, not just what is said. Children are not fed or housed by words."

Edelman is the author of countless articles and seven books, including *Families in Peril: An Agenda for Social Change*, a series of lectures she delivered for Harvard's 1986 W.E.B. Du Bois lecture series, and her autobiographical *The Measure of Our Success*, a volume that shares her commitment to service and the values she used while raising her three sons. From 1976 to 1987, Edelman chaired the board of trustees of Spelman College, and in 1971 she was the first

and unwilling to compromise too easily. When reporter Gayle Pollard Terry asked in a 1993 interview, "Are you tough?," Edelman answered, "I'm tough in the sense that I believe as strongly in what I'm doing as anybody else believes in what they are doing. I reject that description; I don't see them talking about men being tough if they fight hard for a tax loophole or fight hard for a special interest. I believe deeply in children and families." Calling herself "a determined optimist" in *Families in Peril*, she believes that effective action "requires thorough fact-finding and analysis, a capacity to see a problem whole and then to break it into manageable pieces for action, to delineate clear long-term, intermediate, and short-term goals; and to pursue those goals through a range of strategies that must be constantly evaluated and adapted to changing political and community

---

"We pray to accept responsibility for children who steal Popsicles before supper, erase holes in the math notebooks and can never find their shoes. We're also going to pray to accept responsibility for children who don't have any rooms to clean up, whose pictures aren't on anybody's dresser, and whose monsters are real."

Marian Wright Edelman's "Prayer"

---

woman elected by alumni as a member of the Yale University Corporation. She has received numerous honorary degrees and awards, including the Albert Schweitzer Humanitarian Prize, a MacArthur Foundation Prize, the Heinz Award for the Human Condition, the Dale Richmond Award, and the Robert F. Kennedy Lifetime Achievement Award. In 2000, she received the Presidential Medal of Freedom, the nation's highest civilian award, given to persons who have made especially meritorious contributions to the security or national interests of the United States, to world peace, or to cultural or other significant public or private endeavors.

EDELMAN'S RHETORIC OF SERVICE

Edelman's character as a rhetor is marked by a personality that is both spiritually optimistic

needs." Reflecting these standards, Edelman's speeches, essays, and books are marked by a staggering compilation of statistics, homey aphorisms, startling challenges, fear-provoking images, religious allusions, tenacity, and value statements learned in her youth. She has statistics at her fingertips to demonstrate the extent of problems and the effectiveness of every dollar spent in reacting to those problems. She employs catchy sayings, condensed thoughts, signposts for life, and common sense in her attempts to put a face on her constituents. Examples from speeches, interviews, and printed works illustrate the tenor of Edelman's rhetoric.

Edelman's basic message does not vary much from medium to medium. Her issues are framed as a "children's approach" to politics, with the recurring theme that children are not being treated fairly or equally. Relying heavily on the values she was taught as a child, Edelman regularly voices the belief, as phrased in *The State of America's Children 1992*, that we must "struggle to live our national and family values in our private and public lives and insist that our leaders do so." Too often, she insists, they have failed to do so. At the CDF conference in March 1993, Edelman noted, in a speech titled "The Forgotten Children," "Over the past ten years we have witnessed the American dream shifting into reverse." She pointed out that nutrition, immunization, and quality day care were urgent needs, and the outlook for America's children was grim. The inequities between the public, political system and private, family life resonate throughout her messages.

Edelman's rhetoric is laced with the values of public service that her parents taught her. In her 1992 interview with Eleanor Clift, Edelman noted that one should teach by precept and example; that family values and family rituals are old traditions that need to be revived in America; and that family values and family disintegration are reflected by the millions of divorces and by the two million mothers of childbearing age who use cocaine. Edelman explained her zeal to Norman Atkins by noting: "I happen to come out of a family that values self-help as well as being somebody who believes in public justice and a positive role for government, which is the way communities solve their problems." This clash of values and actions is often the source of drama in Edelman's oratory. In a speech to the United Methodist Women's Assembly in 2002, she exclaimed, "It's time to build a massive movement with the same power and spirit and sweeping changes as the civil rights, women's rights, anti-war and environmental movements." In a 2001 commencement address at Tulane University, she pleaded: "It's time! It's time to build a mighty movement to Leave No Child Behind in the richest and most powerful nation on earth. I hope you will be part of it." Her appeals to righteousness and her tendency to cast the poverty debates as a conflict between good people and those who are callous in their neglect and greed parallel the rhetorical strategies of the civil rights movement from which Edelman emerged. In the Atkins interview, she directly compared the two crusades: "The struggle of the Nineties is to re-

frame the civil rights agenda to be about economic empowerment. It's clear that whatever project you label 'black and poor' is going to get a smaller constituency. Which is why we focused on children and into prevention." In her speech "The Forgotten Children," she pointed out the economic disparity that exists for children in poverty: "We can either pay now to prepare our children to be healthy, well-educated, and employable or pay a great deal more later to cover the costs of their ailments and diseases, unemployment and homelessness. We need to make a down payment on the nation's economic future by investing in our children and families today."

Edelman frequently uses the images of battle, crusade, and imminent crisis. In several of her 1991 commencement addresses, she noted that twelve million children lack the basic amenities of life, and she challenged the United States to work as hard to overcome poverty as it did to win the Gulf War. In a keynote speech at a youth health conference sponsored by the Columbia School of Public Health in 1995, she asserted: "I don't use the word 'evil' very often, but I tell you it is evil what is happening in Washington today. And I tell you, we must stand up with all our might and fight this." This urgency permeates Edelman's rhetoric as she expresses an unwillingness to await gradual change in the face of an enemy that she believes is consuming the souls of the nation's children.

Edelman's use of statistics exhibits the extent of the problems to audiences who might not appreciate their urgency. Her 1986 Du Bois lecture "The Black Family in America" is representative. To support her claim that "black children in young female-headed households are the poorest in the nation," Edelman noted that "while a black child born in the United States has a one in two chance of being born poor, a black child in a female-headed household has a two in three chance of being poor. If that household is headed by a mother under twenty-five years of age, that baby has a four in five chance of being poor." In her 1999 Colorado College address, Edelman employed statistics to challenge the audience about what they think they know. "From 1968 through 1996," she said, "when one and a quarter million Americans died violently here at home, fewer than 32,000 American soldiers died in military conflicts in other countries. We were 44 times more likely to kill each other than to be killed by any external enemy."

In an introduction to the 2001 CDF national convention, she noted that "more than 14 million American children (nearly one in five) live in poverty even though the economy continues to expand, and more and more millionaires are created each day. The number of children living in families with incomes below one-half of the federal poverty line increased in 1997 for the second year in a row. The number of these children has increased by 20 percent since 1995." Her keynote speech in 2002 to the Texas CDF spoke of the "90,000 children" lost to gunfire since 1979, "eight every day." She noted that "only 44% of children in families with incomes below $15,000 a year who are ages 3–5 and not yet in kindergarten are enrolled in preschool programs, compared with 71% of children from families with incomes over $75,000." She lamented that "children in welfare families have one-fourth as many words as children in more affluent families by the time they reach first grade." Then she asked: "What is wrong with us that we would spend 10, 20, 30, 40 thousand dollars to lock a kid up but refuse to give them a good head start in child care and start in life? We simply have to change these priorities." The wealth of data Edelman employs is sometimes overwhelming. She presents data on reported abuse cases, children born into poverty, children lost to gunfire, children who can't read proficiently, inequities in preschool programs for low-income families, money spent on defense projects versus teacher salaries, and a litany of others social problems.

The religion of Edelman's youth plays a foundational role in much of her oratory, but it is a religious value system that promotes self-sufficiency and public service. Edelman told Atkins: "My reading of Christ is that you help people, not judge them—the judgment doesn't belong to us. . . . I believe very much in the Gospel that says you help people who are hungry and you help people who are suffering and you help people who need help. And I believe very deeply in private charity and in personal service, but I also understand that those are not substitutes for public justice." In a 1986 Du Bois lecture titled "Leadership and Social Change,"

she reminded listeners that "the Bible is replete with the images and power of small things which achieve great ends when they are grounded in faith; a mustard seed, a jawbone, a stick, a slingshot, a widow's mite." Edelman's religious theme is often combined with prophecies of doom, as in the 1992 Atkins interview, in which she expressed a series of biting antitheses: "It is evil to let children die when you have the capacity to save them. It is wrong, for example, not to immunize children and to have them dying of measles in the richest nation on earth. . . . I cannot believe for a moment that God's not going to punish a nation that has the capacity to save young lives and chooses not to." In her 1999 commencement address at Colorado College, she told a fictional narrative of a child whose life was changed by one caring person. Edelman concluded with a quote from Mark 8:36: " 'For what shall it profit a man or a woman if we shall gain the whole world and lose our soul?' We must not lose our soul in America." In *The State of America's Children 1996*, she noted that "the prodigal son returned home before it was too late. The rich man did not. Can America come home before it's too late to its founding creed of God-given human equality and act to leave no child behind?" While Edelman might not profess to judge others, she clearly envisions a higher power that does sit in judgment.

If she is assigning ultimate judgment to God, Edelman does explicitly condemn what she perceives as evil. In "Leadership and Social Change," for example, she identified the "weasels" in public life, including the greedy military weasel, the unfairness weasel, the bystander weasel, and the ineffectiveness weasel, all of whom have gnawed away at the rights of children and the moral underpinnings of our democracy. In the 1992 Scott interview, she regretted that "over the past 10 years we have witnessed the American dream shifting into reverse. Every American needs to ask why there are more poor children in rich America than there are citizens in famine-stricken Somalia." In her 1999 Colorado College commencement address, she censured the escalating violence by and against children, calling it a "cumulative, convergent, and heightened manifestation of a range of serious and too-long-neglected problems." She explored a litany of causes: "Epidemic child and family poverty, increasing economic inequality, racial intolerance and hate crimes, rampant drug and alcohol abuse, pervasive violence in our homes and popular culture, growing numbers of out-of-wedlock births and divorces, and overly busy and stressed-out parents have all contributed to the disintegration of the family, community, and spiritual values and support all children need." In the same address, she called for people to open their eyes and see what is going on; to stop adult hypocrisy and double standards, such as putting unwed celebrity mothers on magazine covers; to stop pornography; and to act like adults.

Edelman frequently binds her audience through vows, prayers, or pledges; a practice that probably reflects her early legacy of church and service. Reporter Mary Ann French wrote that in a speech delivered to an academic seminar at Georgetown University, Edelman abruptly suggested to the audience of "sociological sightseers" that they join her in her version of a schoolteacher's appeal to a higher power:

> We pray to accept responsibility for children who steal Popsicles before supper, erase holes in the math notebooks and can never find their shoes. We're also going to pray to accept responsibility for children who don't have any rooms to clean up, whose pictures aren't on anybody's dresser and whose monsters are real . . . in 1992 let's decide to vote for and pray for and speak for those children in America whose nightmares come in the daytime, who'll eat anything, who have never seen a dentist, who aren't spoiled by anybody, who go to bed hungry and cry themselves to sleep. . . . Let's commit this year to starting a movement that cares and votes and organizes for those children whom we smother, but also for those children who will grab the hand of anybody kind enough to offer it. Every American is going to have to offer that hand if your future is going to be preserved, if our children are going to be protected. Every American is going to have to commit to leave no child behind, struggling to change the priorities of a nation so that our children can get what we got and want to pass on in the future.

Similarly, in her 2001 Tulane University commencement address, Edelman exhorted the audience to action, stressing the moral urgency to act now rather than hear her speech as contemplative listeners.

> It's time! It's time to build a mighty movement to Leave No Child Behind in the richest and most powerful nation on earth. I hope you will be part of it. . . . It's time for idealism and not ideology, time for greatness, not greed. . . . Child poverty, neglect, health care, illiteracy, and gun deaths are not acts of God. They are our moral and political choices as a nation. What can you do to help build a nation that values each child? Redefine the measure of success in our power and money crazed culture. Never work just for money and power. . . . Assign yourself to make a difference in building a just America where no child is left behind.

Perhaps Edelman's greatest rhetorical strength is in putting a face on the poverty, disease, and inherent underlying unfairness of the state of children today, as she did with Robert Kennedy in 1964. As she told Atkins, Edelman likes to relate to her audience the outcomes of the Child Watch Visitation Program, one of CDF's attempts to make the extent of the problems known to the larger community.

> One distinguished woman was very upset when she went to see the boarder-baby ward at DC General and realized that there was no place for these children to play. Her response was to raise money and build a play area. Union members were taken to some of the homeless shelters and decided to start a clothing drive. We took a bunch of Atlanta ministers to a neonatal intensive-care unit. After their visit, we asked the hospital what it wanted. It turned out that it was very hard to get pauper's burials at the time that babies died, so they wanted the ministers to bury the babies so that the mothers didn't have to go through two bouts of grief. It became very practical and immediate.

Edelman's ability to make the never imagined real, whether through word or deed, encourages others to contribute their service.

Marian Wright Edelman's oratory is legendary for two additional factors: her soft-spokenness and the fountain of facts that she spurts out with disarming ease. She tends to speak primarily from note cards, and her remarks often ignore any time constraints. French described Edelman as a woman who manages to peer down her nose at people even though she's shorter than most. Journalists are warned to bring a tape recorder because no one on the face of the earth "can write as fast as Edelman can talk." According to French, Edelman delivers facts with devastating speed: "Sometimes her speech takes a geographic turn, but it's hard to tell whether you're hearing the south of her youth or the New England of her early married years. If the audience is lucky, they follow about every third line she delivers. The rest of the time they look stunned, both by the velocity of the delivery and by the content of what words they can catch."

Marian Wright Edelman has spent her entire life calling for public justice for those whom society treats unfairly. She successfully uses challenges and entreaties to a public that is apathetic or ignorant, rather than unfeeling. She employs homey aphorisms, "Daddy's frequent words and Mama's stories," and religious allusions that call to mind a simpler time when "family values" was more than just a political phrase. Her command of startling and staggering statistics, as well as realistic portrayals of the face of poverty, illustrates the exigency of civil rights violations maintained by society in its treatment of children. Her rhetoric is neither gentle nor inflammatory, but infused with an absolute certainty in the rightness of her cause. In her public speaking as in her leadership of the CDF, Marian Wright Edelman has exemplified the legacy of service and the spirit of social responsibility that was passed on to her in childhood.

INFORMATION SOURCES

Research Collections and Collected speeches

Although no research collection of Edelman's work now exists, her seven books include volumes of her political advocacy, inspirational works, and an autobiography. Many of Edelman's remarks and press releases are on the Children's Defense Fund Web site, http://www.childrensdefense.org/

Edelman, Marian Wright. *Families in Peril: An Agenda for Social Change* [*FIP*]. Cambridge, Mass.: Harvard University Press, 1987.

Web Site

Children's Defense Fund Web site [*CDF*]. http://www.childrensdefense.org

Audiovisual Materials

Sound recordings and videotapes of Edelman's speeches are available from a variety of sources, most often produced by the organization to which she delivered the recorded speech. Historical videotapes are also available.

The Leaders: James P. Comer; Marian Wright Edelman; Lawrence Douglas Wilder. Chicago: Public Media, 1991. (Video.)

Selected Critical Studies

Atkins, Norman. "Marian Wright Edelman: On the Front Lines of the Battle to Save America's Children." *Rolling Stone*, December 10–24, 1992, pp. 127–29+.

Clift, Eleanor. "A Mother's Guiding Message." *Newsweek*, June 8, 1992, p. 27.

"The Forgotten Children." *The Progressive*, April 1993, p. 9.

French, Mary Ann. "The Measure of Her Success: Marian Wright Edelman's Lessons on Raising Kids and on Raising Consciousness." *Washington Post*, May 10, 1992, pp. F1+.

Moore, Yvette. "Edelman: Time for Children's Movement." United Methodist Women's Assembly, 2002. Available at http://gbgm-umc.org/umw/assembly/responsedaily/edelman.stm

Scott, Matthew S. "The Great Defender." *Black Enterprise*, May 1992, pp. 67–69.

Shapiro, Joseph P. "The Unraveling Kids' Crusade." *U.S. News & World Report*, March 26, 1990, pp. 22–24.

Soloman, Sheneka T. "The Educational Theory of Marian Wright Edelman." Available at http://womenshistory.about.com/gi/dynamic/offsite.htm?site=http://www.newfoundations.com/GALLERY/Edelman.html

Terry, Gayle Pollard. "Marian Wright Edelman: Crusading for Children with This Aggressive Defense Fund." *Los Angeles Times*, November 21, 1993, p. M3.

Selected Biographies

Bakhtiar, Ruth. "Never for a Moment Lacked a Purpose: Marian Wright Edelman, Crusader for Civil and Children's Rights." March 12, 2001. Available at http://www.cnn.com/2001/fyi/teachers.newsroom/03/12/edelman/ Women's History Month

Edelman, Marian Wright. *Lanterns: A Memoir of Mentors.* Boston: Beacon Press, 1999.

———. *The Measure of Our Success: A Letter to my Children and Yours.* Boston: Beacon Press, 1992.

"A Life Full of Accomplishments." CNN Newsroom Archive, March 12, 2001.

CHRONOLOGY OF MAJOR SPEECHES

See "Research Collections and Collected Speeches" for source codes.

"Children's Legislative Issues" (address to the National Education Association's Twenty-third Conference on Human and Civil Rights in Education) February 22, 1985.

"The W.E.B. Du Bois Lectures." Cambridge, Mass., 1986. *FIP.*

"Address to the National Association for the Education of Young Children." Washington, D.C., 1990. Sound recording available from National Association for the Education of Young Children.

"Children in Their Families." Chautauqua, N.Y., 1991. Sound recording available from Chautauqua Institution.

"Families in Peril: Agenda for Social Change." Chautauqua, N.Y., 1991. Sound recording available from Chautauqua Institution.

"Commencement Speech at Duke University." Durham, N.C., May 17, 1992.

"The A.B.C.'s of Commitment." Charlotte, N.C., June 27, 1993. Sound recording available from Pacifica Radio.

"Leave No Children Behind" (address to National Association for the Education of Young Children annual meeting). Washington, D.C., 1993. Videotape available from National Association for the Education of Young Children.

"Commencement Speech at Gallaudet University." Washington, D.C., 1995. Videotape available from Gallaudet University.

"Keynote Address" (Columbia School of Public Health). New York City, 1995.

"Hope for America's Children: The Dream or the Nightmare?" Washington, D.C., 1996. Videotape available from the National Association for the Education of Young Children.

"Priorities for America's Children" (Ford Hall Forum). Boston, 1996. Sound recording available from Ford Hall Forum.

"Standing Up for the World's Children: Leave No Child Behind" (State of the World Forum). San Francisco, 1996. Available at http://womenshistory.about.com/library/bio/bblio_marian_wright_edelman.html

"Standing Strong & Together for Children, Leave No Child Behind" (CDF keynote address). Washington, D.C., 1997. Videotape available through Children's Defense Fund.

"Commencement Speech at UNC Chapel Hill." Chapel Hill, N.C., May 17, 1998. Available at http://www.unc.edu/news/archives/may98/marian2.htm

"Stand for Children, the Power of Collaboration" (Charlemae Rollins President Program). Chicago, 1998. Sound recording available from American Library Association.

"Colorado College Baccalaurete Address." Colorado Springs, Colo., May 16, 1999. Available at http://gos.sbc.edu/e/edelman2.html

"Commencement Speech at Tulane University." New Orleans, La., May 19, 2001. Available at http://www.grads.tulane.edu/edu/edepse.shtml

"Children CARE: Because We All Do!" (keynote address to the Texas CDF). San Antonio, Tex., October 23, 2002. Available at http://www.cdftexas.org/MWE_10_3_02KeynoteSpeech.htm

"Introduction to CDF Presidential Candidates Forum on Children." Washington, D.C.: April 9, 2003. *CDF.*

JOYCELYN ELDERS (1933–)
Pediatric Endocrinologist, U.S. Surgeon General

LORRAINE D. JACKSON

Joycelyn Elders's oratory is a reflection of her multifaceted background and all that these life experiences have taught her. Her discourse focuses primarily on themes of prevention over treatment, openness over censorship, and community involvement over complacency. A prolific speaker, she confronts numerous societal health problems. She is a fervent advocate for comprehensive sex education, school-based clinics, health-care reform, providing health access to the poor, and the prevention of abuse and interpersonal violence. While discussing complex health policy topics, she is able to maintain a frank and down-to-earth tone capable of reaching diverse audiences. She is principled, pragmatic, resilient, and always looking toward the future with hope and vision.

Born Minnie Lee Jones on August 13, 1933, Elders was the first of eight children of Haller and Curtis Jones in the small rural town of Schaal, Arkansas. In her autobiography, Elders recounts the family of ten living in a succession of leaky wooden shacks, each without electricity or indoor plumbing. She spent her childhood laboring alongside her family, tending the cotton fields and livestock and, of course, helping with her seven younger siblings. She kept "farm hours," rising at 4 A.M. and working until the end of the day, when she could bathe in a round tin tub on the porch, scrubbing hard to get the ticks off. Her father hunted raccoons and possums on the side, selling the pelts to Sears and Montgomery Ward. For many years the family lived hand-to-mouth, sharecropping on other people's land. Young Joycelyn would assist her father in skinning and stretching the pelts on drying racks, and also helped her mother make stew with the carcasses. In addition to hard work, Joycelyn's mother valued learning. She taught Joycelyn her alphabet and numbers, telling her, "You've got to get a good start." At the time, Elders did not really know what the good start might be for, but nonetheless she studied the only two books in the house, a reading primer and the Bible. Later, when she attended Bright Star Elementary School, she was delighted to be able to take books home for enjoyment after chores were done. As a child, she had little exposure to the medical field. She recalls her father taking her brother on a twelve-mile mule ride to see the doctor after his appendix ruptured. Joycelyn never visited a doctor as a child.

In 1944, the family moved west when Curtis and Haller took jobs at the Richmond shipyards in California. Joycelyn took a placement test for the Richmond school system and was accelerated two years, which placed her in the eighth grade. The family returned to Arkansas after a couple of years to resume farming and be near family. With the demands of farming and the tendency to marry young, finishing high school in Howard County, Arkansas, was an uncommon and celebrated event. Joycelyn was one of only nine students to graduate high school that year. Her valedictorian address was about "doing your absolute best wherever you find yourself and whatever the circumstances." After her speech, a professor representing Philander Smith College made a short announcement: the college was awarding a full tuition scholarship to the class valedictorian. Despite this exciting news, it was initially unclear whether Joycelyn would go to college—the family had to pick cotton that had ripened early in order to afford the $3.83 bus fare to Little Rock.

It was only after Joycelyn entered college at age fifteen that she saw a doctor for the first time. She also met Edith Irby, the first Black woman to attend the University of Arkansas Medical School. The meeting prompted her to strive to become a physician. "You can't be what you can't see," Joycelyn later observed. She worked as a maid throughout college while simultaneously keeping up with her studies, and graduated with her B.A. degree in 1952.

After a brief marriage ended, she joined the U.S. Army to become a physical therapist. This made her eligible for the G.I. Bill, enabling her to attend the University of Arkansas Medical School. As one of only three Black students and the only Black female in the entering class of 1956, she could not eat lunch in the "whites only" cafeteria. Nonetheless, she disregarded incidents of racism and segregation, and remained focused on her goal. At one point she was sent to give physical examinations to the local high school basketball players. Oliver Elders, the basketball coach, had never seen a "lady doctor," nor had his players. He offered her a season pass to the basketball games, and she soon became a basketball fan. Within two months the couple married. They have two sons, Eric, born in 1963, and Kevin, born in 1965.

After serving her internship at the University of Minnesota Hospital, Elders returned to the University of Arkansas Medical Center, where she rose to the position of chief pediatric resident. In 1967, she earned an M.S. degree in biochemistry and joined the faculty as an assistant professor of pediatrics. She attracted mentors who cultivated her interest in research, and successfully applied for National Institutes of Health (NIH) grants. She was promoted to associate professor in 1971 and to full professor in 1976, and was among the first to be board certified in the new specialization of pediatric endocrinology.

In the 1970s Elders crossed paths with Arkansas governor Bill Clinton when he appointed her to the Industrial Development Commission to oversee health issues. Clinton also attended the funeral of her brother Bernard, a prominent veterinarian, after a man who had an obsession with Bernard's wife murdered him. This meant a great deal to Elders and her family, and when Clinton later asked her to become Arkansas's chief public health director in 1987, she agreed, on the condition that she could retain

one point she was asked at a press conference whether or not condoms would be distributed in the school clinics. She replied, "We aren't going to put them on their lunch trays. But yes, we intend to distribute condoms." Although many, including the governor supported her position, Elders was taken aback by the swell of immediate outrage from vocal opponents. Elders, who is pro-choice, initially tried to address their concerns by explaining that rather than encouraging immorality or abortion, sex education ultimately prevents abortions and unplanned pregnancies. But she discovered that a zealous group, whom she calls "very religious non-Christians," opposes both reproductive choice *and* sex education, something she feels is irrational and hypocritical.

Despite the controversy, Elders's health-care successes did not go unnoticed. President-elect

---

"We have buried our heads in the sand for far too long. While we have been sitting on the beach sipping lemonade saying "Just say No," our children have been drowning in an ocean of sharks—alcohol, drugs, violence, teen pregnancy, STDs and AIDS. We have got to get in the lifeboats known as "common sense" and throw out the lifeline or we are going to lose an entire generation of young people."

Joycelyn Elders, "Speech to the Association of Reproductive Health Professionals," 1993

---

her academic appointment. Between 1988 and 1992 Elders visited the 106 clinics under her care and studied the health-care needs of the state. She increased the availability of childhood screenings, immunizations, breast cancer screenings, and HIV testing. Under her leadership, the rate of early childhood screenings rose from just four thousand to forty-five thousand in four years. Many of the children she saw were born to adolescents, and some of them were the product of sexual abuse. Some teens believed that babies came from storks or from swallowing watermelon seeds. Elders became convinced that the cycle of poverty, sexual ignorance, teenage pregnancy, and STD rates needed to be addressed, and saw comprehensive health education, including school-based clinics, as an important solution. At

Clinton wanted her "to do for the whole country" what she had done for Arkansas, and she was offered the position of surgeon general in 1992. Despite attempts to thwart her confirmation with a series of hollow charges of ethical misconduct and criticism from conservative groups, the Senate confirmed her by a vote of 65–34.

One of the main responsibilities of the surgeon general is to publicize preventive information about pervasive health problems. During her term she advocated prevention regarding traditional topics such as smoking, as well as more contentious issues such as comprehensive sex education and condom availability. She also spoke about adolescent health care, interpersonal violence, women's and minority health issues, and health-care reform. When a conservative lobbying group dubbed her "the Condom Queen," she was unfazed and did not regard the moniker as demeaning. She remarked that if she could get every young male who engaged in sex to use a condom, she would gladly wear a Condom Queen crown.

With a background as a medical researcher, it was not uncommon for Elders to say that a topic merited further study. Her 1993 remark that the potential impact of the legalization of drugs should be studied was rebuked by the Clinton administration. During a panel discussion on World AIDS Day, and later on *Nightline*, Elders was asked if masturbation should be discussed in sex education. As an advocate for comprehensive and age-appropriate health education, Elders stated, "That is part of human sexuality, and perhaps it should be taught." Of course, she was saying it should be discussed as a part of human sexuality. But her remark that perhaps masturbation should be "taught" caught the attention of detractors in the administration. It also provided fodder for comedians. One *Saturday Night Live* skit portrayed the surgeon general's stand-in issuing a warning that high school students were masturbating at only a fifth grade level. David Letterman's Top Ten list of fictitious movies included *Home Alone with Joycelyn Elders*. The Clinton administration did not find the situation amusing, however, and in December 1994, Elders was asked to resign. She left the post and returned to her academic work. She is the author of over 150 articles in pediatric endocrinology, and holds numerous honorary doctorates and prestigious awards. She is currently a distinguished professor of public health at the University of Arkansas, and maintains a busy schedule as a public speaker.

JOYCELYN ELDERS: ADVOCATING PREVENTION THROUGH EDUCATION

In her 1993 statement before the U.S. Senate Labor and Human Resource Committee, Joycelyn Elders stated:

> Mr. Chairman, and members of this committee, I want to change the way we think about health—by putting prevention first. . . . I want to be the voice and the vision for the poor and the powerless. I want to change concern about

social problems that affect health into commitment. And I would like to make every child born in America a planned, wanted child. . . . Should I be confirmed, I would like to work with you and all America to develop an action plan to improve the health of our country. . . . I am a hard worker. I am willing to give my time and my talent. . . . We have a big task before us, and I hope you will see fit to make me part of your team.

Elders was indeed a hardworking surgeon general. During her fifteen-month tenure she delivered over three hundred speeches across the United States. Although speechwriters contributed background information and data, her speeches were largely her own. The themes of her speeches are consistent with her values. Although Elders adapted her messages to suit different audiences and occasions, she consistently emphasized the role of education in prevention.

Her messages were typically organized using a problem-solution format wherein she developed startling statistics or examples and followed these with detailed and multipronged solutions. Often, the solutions prescribed specific actions her audience could take to ameliorate problems. Thus, many of her speeches were persuasive and designed to actuate her audience into community involvement, leadership, and prevention efforts. Her 1993 speech "Physician Activism: Prevention, Prevention, Prevention," delivered to over two thousand medical students in Philadelphia, is representative. Initially, Elders established her credibility by noting her experience in all facets of the health profession—first as a medical student, then as a clinician, a researcher, a state health director, and surgeon general. This background, she stated, "leads me to one fundamental conclusion: we must put prevention first." She developed this idea by highlighting five areas that concerned her: teen pregnancy ("Every 64 seconds an infant is born to a teenage mother"), STDs ("One in four sexually active teens will contract an STD before graduating from high school"), violence ("Every five hours, a 15–19 year old is murdered"), alcohol and other drugs ("Over 40% of recent high school graduates said they have used an illicit drug"), and poverty ("Each night, 3.5 million or 12.3% of children under age 12 go to bed hungry").

Elders then outlined her prescriptions for improving the nation's health and well-being. These included comprehensive school-based health education from kindergarten through high school, family planning and sex education, support for parents in rearing children, reinforcement of male responsibility, school-linked clinics to provide medical care to teens, and opportunities for higher education to combat poverty. She asked her audience to do three things. First, she encouraged the medical students to learn about the needs and problems of their community. Second, she promoted volunteerism and suggested that the audience members speak at local schools and find other outlets for educating and helping the community. Third, she discussed the importance of exhibiting leadership. This could be accomplished, she asserted, by educating others about problems, advocating sound solutions, enabling others to find solutions, and taking risks. She concluded with an appeal for involvement:

> As health care providers, as part of our communities, it is our responsibility to reach out, to lead—and that involves risks. You embody our Nation's best hope for a healthy future. You are the health professionals who can make prevention our national watchword, and who can ensure our children's future.

In several speeches, Elders stated that no subjects were dearer to her heart than those of childhood and adolescent prevention efforts. In her 1993 speech before the Association of Reproductive Health Professionals, she again illuminated the health concerns of young people. After doing so, she asked:

> What does all of this mean? It means we have buried our heads in the sand for far too long. While we have been sitting on the beach sipping lemonade saying "Just say No," our children have been drowning in an ocean of sharks—alcohol, drugs, violence, teen pregnancy, STDs and AIDS. We have got to get in the lifeboats known as "common sense" and throw out the lifeline or we are going to lose an entire generation of young people.

Elders subscribes to the philosophy that too often our health-care efforts are made after problems arise. On many occasions, she referred to the health-care system as a "sick-care sys-

tem" because of the emphasis on treatment rather than prevention. She expounded on this point in an address to the National Family Planning and Reproductive Health Association on February 25, 1994:

> It breaks my heart that the time and money devoted to preventive efforts pales in comparison to what we spend on care and treatment for sick babies, premature parenthood, welfare dependency, and sexually transmitted diseases. These are debts that we indeed must pay, but they are avoidable debts. It's time we took our intellectual understanding that prevention pays and translate it into funding and access and delivery strategies that emphasize prevention spending as smart spending.

Speaking at Planned Parenthood in New York City on May 2, 1994, Elders used alliteration to reiterate this theme:

> The opponents of full choice like to talk accusingly about the "A" word. I know that all of you at Planned Parenthood hear that daily. But we need to talk more loudly and more clearly about many other "A" words, including *access, affordability* and the *array* of reproductive health-care services.

Elders's concern about ineffectual prevention policies and losing the talents of young people extended to the topic of violence. In her speech "Violence as a Public Health Issue," delivered on January 6, 1994, she said, "I am worried that one-quarter of all young African American males ages 20–29 are incarcerated, on probation or on parole, while only one-fifth are enrolled in higher education." She believes violence is a public health problem, amenable to scientific study and prevention efforts, rather than under the exclusive domain of the criminal justice system. To illustrate this point, Elders offered an analogy between traffic crashes and violence:

> Twenty-some years ago, when the toll of traffic crashes skyrocketed, we went into the schools and strengthened driver's education; we went to the auto manufacturers to make cars safer, adding seat belts and child safety seats; and we worked with the highway designers to make highways safer. . . . Just as we reduced the number of deadly traffic crashes, we can engage in a similar process with respect to black on black crime and youth violence.

Near the end of this speech Elders made a plea for community involvement, asking the audience to "help me change the way our communities think about violence—by making it a matter of public health and prevention. I want all of us in this room to be the voice and the vision for the poor and the powerless."

In a March 13, 1994, speech to the American Medical Association's National Conference on Family Violence, Elders again expressed concern about the epidemic of violence. She noted that "The average child sees 8,000 murders and 100,000 acts of violence on television before finishing elementary school," and "over three million young children witness parental violence every year." The consequences of violence in media and families are staggering. She asserted that "thirty percent of all emergency room visits by women result from domestic assaults." In 1992, she stated, the average cost of a violent injury was $44,000, and the total medical cost of violence in the United States was $13.5 billion. Using apt imagery, Elders elucidated her point that "violence begets violence" by stating that "the long term or cyclical effects of violence in the home are like ripples from a rock thrown in the water—they don't subside, they just get bigger and bigger." She then offered prescriptions for violence prevention in school curricula, including guidance in conflict management, impulse control, and problem-solving skills. She also described parent education, including knowledge about the risks of child abuse, and family support programs as possible solutions. The speech closed with a favorite simile. Knowing that activists sometimes become weary from their ongoing involvement in a cause, Elders related some advice she had received when she wanted to give up: "When you're dancing with a bear, you can't get tired and sit down. You have to wait until the bear gets tired."

A seemingly tireless promoter of the needs of children and adolescents, Elders did not limit her speaking to health professionals in medical forums. She also recognized, for example, the important role of the church in the community. A speech delivered on July 31, 1994, at the First Baptist Church in Warrenton, Virginia, illustrates her ability to adapt her message to her audience. Early in this speech, she established common ground with her listeners by mentioning her brother, a preacher. She also used audience-oriented language by citing a biblical verse:

> Too many of our children are not growing up. The Bible says, and I have heard my brother, the Rev. Chester Jones, preach on the verse in Proverbs 22:6 that says "Train up a child in the way he should go; and when he is old, he will not depart from it." I am here to tell you that many of our children are not being trained up in the way they should go and therefore are not growing old.

Elders's speech at the Black Methodists for Church Renewal (BMCR) national meeting, delivered on March 25, 1994, also focused on the church's role in overcoming the dysfunctional environments that many children endure. This speech differed from those given in academic and medical forums in several respects. Namely, she made use of more stylistic devices and relied less on statistical evidence to outline the problems. In particular, she used more imagery and metaphors to make her points: "Today in our cities children are killing children, peddlers are killing non-paying junkies, and the fear of gunshots that deliver more than ten children's corpses every day imprison entire neighborhoods." As in the organization of her other persuasive speeches, she developed a solution. For this audience, the solution lay in "giving our time, talents and resources."

> BMCR, we as the church, as parents, as preachers, as teachers, as doctors, as lawyers, as social workers, as law enforcement officials, must be better than the criminal. It is a real tragedy when it is easier for our children to find a handgun, a drug dealer, a way to become pregnant, a way to get expelled from school, a way to curse older people, a way to steal, kill and die, than it is to find a good parent, a good preacher, or a good friend. . . . BMCR, we must work together—block by block—to revive damaged lives, looted and burned out homes and businesses. We are called upon to create in our society Shalom zones of compassion, love and respect—where neighbors love their neighbors as themselves. . . .

Elders closed the speech with an urgent appeal for involvement: "BMCR, I say again, you are the midwife through which God calls his church to deliver the Community of Shalom [Peace]. So if not you, who? If not now, when?"

In direct contrast to the metaphorical language employed in motivational speeches before congregations, Elders's style before the U.S. Senate was data-driven, detailed, tightly organized, and thorough. Her "Statement on Adolescent Pregnancy and Childbearing Before the U.S. Senate" is one such example. After overviewing statistical trends in adolescent childbearing, she discussed the consequences:

> The social and economic costs of premature parenthood are enormous. Adolescent childbearing has long been associated with reduced educational attainment and employment opportunities. In turn, poverty and AFDC dependency are more prevalent in families begun by adolescents, particularly those that are unmarried. In 1992, an estimated $34 billion was expended on AFDC, Medicaid, and food stamps for families begun by adolescents. Moreover, the children of adolescent parents are more likely to become adolescent parents themselves, perpetuating the cycle.

Following this, Elders compared the United States with other countries, documented successful interventions and federal programs, and ultimately discussed health-care reform, particularly the need to develop comprehensive health education and school-based health services. She asserted that "a sequential, age and developmentally appropriate approach to school health education would provide every child with a foundation of knowledge for risk reduction and health promoting behaviors." In her conclusion, she stated:

> The problems associated with adolescent childbearing are well documented, the continued high levels of adolescent pregnancy, abortion and births are a National embarrassment, and we know that we have done very little of real substance to address this issue. We know it is better for our young people to delay sexual activity and we should help them do so. We also know that when they do become sexually active they need contraceptives to protect them against pregnancy and STDs.

By its very nature, the position of surgeon general is controversial because many public health topics, such as sexually transmitted diseases, teenage pregnancy prevention, abortion, and HIV, are politicized topics. To many, Elders's candid and commonsense approach to health problems was decidedly *un*controversial. Her speeches, writes biographer Ann Gerhart, were "delivered in her ringing, unvarnished, plain English," and were well received by most audiences. Paula Wilson, writing for *USA Today* magazine, noted that Elders's messages held particular appeal for people in their twenties, the 1990s "Generation X," because "the nature of contemporary sexual relationships constitute[s] a life-threatening need to have access to contraceptives." Others, particularly conservatives, found her outspoken nature and blunt rhetoric on contentious issues to be threatening. According to Gerhart, Elders believes that her substance, more than her style, led to her termination as surgeon general. Nonetheless, she has no regrets about her actions because she never compromised her principles. She believes it would be worse to be an invisible surgeon general than to be a controversial one. Although some would say her actions were impolitic, most would agree that she was not ignored. As surgeon general, Elders opened the door for discussion about sensitive topics and was, perhaps, ahead of her time. Today, she lectures regularly at health organizations, clinics, and universities. As a testament to her appeal among today's college audiences, she often receives a standing ovations *before* she begins her speech. The *People* review of her autobiography expresses a sentiment that is likely embraced by many of her contemporary audiences: "Her nerve in the face of political opposition and her commonsense approach to health care may make readers wish that her voice was still audible in the Surgeon General's office."

INFORMATION SOURCES

Research Collections and Collected Speeches

There are no published collections of speeches available at this time. Transcripts of over 150 speeches delivered while Elders was surgeon general can be obtained from the National Library of Medicine, History of Medicine Division, 8600 Rockville Pike, Bethesda, Md. 20894. [*NLM*]. Some transcripts of speeches are available on the Internet at http://gos.sbc.edu/browse.html

Web Sites

Degan, Clara. "Dr. Jocelyn [*sic*] Elders Sparks Activism at Breast Cancer Action (BCA) Town Meeting." Available online at http://www.bcaction.org

Hubley, Doug. "Former U.S. Surgeon General Opens 148th Academic Year at Bates College." Available online at http://www.bates.edu

Hunter, D. Lyn. "Joycelyn Elders on Women in Leadership Positions." Available online at http://www.berkeley.edu

Levin, J. "Joycelyn Elders Speaks Out on Harm Reduction & Clean Needles: An Answer to Stemming the Tide of HIV and HCV." Available online at www.natap.org

Audiovisual Materials

Elders is featured in *Great Speeches: Today's Women*, vol. 1. Greenwood, Ind.: Educational Video Group, 1995.

Sojourner Truth Lecture. This is a one-hour tape/CD of Elders's talk when she became the thirteenth Sojourner Truth lecturer named by the Intercollegiate Department of Black Studies and the Claremont Colleges. It can be purchased from Pacifica Radio Archives at http://www.pacifica.org/products/index.html; https://area51.site5.com/%7Epacifica/catalog_e.php

Selected Critical Studies

Review of the book *Joycelyn Elders, M.D.: From Sharecropper's Daughter to Surgeon General of the United States of America. People*, November 4, 1996, p. 46.

Sharrell, Janine. "Elders Finds Herself a Campaign Target." (1996). Available online at http://www.cnn.com/ALLPOLITICS/1996/news/9610/09/elders/index.shtml

Sofalvi, Alan J. "Politics, Public Health and the Surgeon General of the United States Public Health Service: A Brief History." *American Journal of Health Studies* 13, no. 1 (1997): 27–32.

Wilson, Paula. "Rise and Fall of the Surgeon General." *USA Today* magazine, May 1997, pp. 58–60.

Selected Biographies

Current Biography Yearbook, vol. 55. Bronx, N.Y.: H. W. Wilson, 1994.

Elders, Joycelyn, and David Chanoff. *Joycelyn Elders, M.D.: From Sharecropper's Daughter to Surgeon General of the United States of America*. New York: William Morrow, 1996.

Gerhart, Ann. "Uninhibited, Unrepentant, and Unstoppable." *Biography* 1, no. 5 (May 1997): 83–86.

CHRONOLOGY OF MAJOR SPEECHES

See "Research Collections and Collected Speeches" for source code.

"Statement of M. Joycelyn Elders, M.D. Before the U.S. Senate Labor and Human Resources Committee" (confirmation testimony). Washington, D.C., July 23, 1993. *NLM*; also available online at http://gos.sbc.edu/browse.html

"Physician Activism: Prevention, Prevention, Prevention" (address to the American Medical Student Association). Philadelphia, October 15, 1993. *NLM*.

"Statement of M. Joycelyn Elders, M.D. Before the Association of Reproductive Health Professionals." Washington, D.C., October 20, 1993. *NLM*.

"Violence as a Public Health Issue" (address at the National Conference on Black on Black Crime and Youth Violence). Washington, D.C., January 6, 1994. *NLM*.

"Leading Us into the Future" (address before the National Family Planning and Reproductive Health Association). Washington, D.C., February 25, 1994. *NLM*.

"Remarks at the American Medical Association's National Conference on Family Violence." Washington, D.C., March 13, 1994. *NLM*.

"The Renaissance of Empowerment: The Tragedy of Not Growing Up—A Revival of Hope for Children" (address to the 27th annual meeting of the National Black Methodists for Church Renewal). Philadelphia, March 25, 1994. *NLM*.

"Remarks at Planned Parenthood of New York City" (accepting the Margaret Sanger Woman of Valor Award). New York City, May 2, 1994. *NLM*.

"Statement on Adolescent Pregnancy and Childbearing Before the U.S. Senate Subcommittee on Labor Appropriations." Washington, D.C., May 25, 1994. Available online at http://gos.sbc.edu/browse/html/

"Remarks Before the Prayer Breakfast at First Baptist Church." Warrenton, Va., July 31, 1994. *NLM*.

JERRY FALWELL (1933–)
Pastor, Thomas Road Baptist Church, Lynchburg, Virginia

PAUL STOB AND CHARLES CONRAD

For almost two decades Jerry Falwell's voice was a ubiquitous part of the U.S. political scene; his belief in the unity of religious doctrine and sociopolitical activism was perhaps the most important development during a momentous era of activism and moral revival. But since the dissolution of the Moral Majority in 1989, his national visibility has been more tenuous and more fleeting. When he led a moral crusade against Bill Clinton, claiming that a sitting president was immorality incarnate and even a murderer, or when he called the prophet Mohammed a "terrorist," his rhetoric brought him national and international attention. On the other hand, he repeatedly retreated into virtual obscurity, even among members of the evangelical community. In this essay we will examine Reverend Falwell's fluctuating visibility. We will suggest that it has resulted from two realities of religion and politics in contemporary America—the necessity of a credible devil figure and a rhetor's dependence on a viable, supportive institution.

Jerry Falwell's rhetoric thrives on devil figures. When he has a tangible, concrete opponent—someone or something whose immorality and power combine to threaten America with damnation—he is able to position himself as a righteous and worthy adversary of evil, one to whom the American media and the American people must pay attention. During the 1970s, Falwell successfully depicted a host of social actors in the role of devil figures—liberal politicians, abortionists, feminists, militant homosexuals, pornographers, and supporters of the welfare state. But with the election of a series of Republican presidents and the rightward shift of the Democratic Party, credible devil figures became harder to find. Simultaneously, other members of the religious right, who effectively exploited the twin secrets of Falwell's success—political-religious discourse and a dedicated media organization—

attracted the attention of the secular media and political actors. Ironically, the very success of his rhetorical action and the institutions he helped create forced Falwell to deal with a more complex rhetorical problem. Since the mid-1980s he has had to find a way to *motivate* his constituents in the face of apparent victory, *differentiate* himself from other spokespersons of the religious right, and *sustain* his national visibility. And he has had to so without the presence of viable devil figures, and without the support of the Moral Majority.

Jerry Falwell's mission began with a quintessential fundamentalist Protestant conversion experience. His father was a fairly successful entrepreneur but not very religious. When Jerry was fifteen, his father died, having sunk deeply into depression and alcoholism. His mother, however, was a woman of great faith and unwavering commitment to her family. Falwell credits her with sustaining the family after his father's death and being an extremely important influence in his life. As a teenager, Falwell was known for being rambunctious, even disorderly. But that changed in 1952 when, at the age of eighteen, he converted to Christianity. He had entered Liberty College with dreams of playing professional baseball or studying engineering at Virginia Tech. But after his conversion, he transferred to Baptist Bible College in Springfield, Missouri. One Sunday morning, Falwell had the opportunity to deliver a sermon before a local congregation. While delivering that sermon, he realized that his calling was the ministry.

Falwell graduated from Baptist Bible College with a strong dedication to the literal interpretation of the biblical word and biblical morality. In June 1956 he founded Thomas Road Baptist Church in his hometown of Lynchburg, Virginia. Immediately successful through his radio and television outreach, Falwell established quite a presence around Lynchburg. Through door-to-door canvassing, blanket mailings, public rallies, and prayer meetings, he and his church offered the local community a unique sense of cohesiveness. Thomas Road Baptist Church soon became the largest church in Lynchburg.

Falwell created Thomas Road as a stark contrast to "liberal" trends he saw among mainline Christian denominations during the 1960s. He preached religious conservatism in a time when mainline Christian churches seemed, at least to him, to be flouting God's Word. Falwell created Thomas Road Baptist Church to provide religious security, biblical certainty, and communal stability in a chaotic society. To expand his mission even further, in 1967 he founded Lynchburg Christian Academy, and in 1971, Liberty Baptist College, which later became Liberty University.

As his church's national reputation began to grow, so did Falwell's presence in the national spotlight. Until 1972, Falwell remained quiet on matters of public policy; his fervent belief in the separation of church and state made him shrink from the national political spotlight. But the 1973 *Roe v. Wade* decision made him rethink his reluctance to participate in national political discourse. His firmly held belief that public morality depends on personal morality, which in turn depends on religious belief, led him to condemn the Supreme Court's decision. To Falwell, it seemed that Christians and non-Christians alike were moving toward a morally bankrupt liberalism—moral sympathy for homosexuals, Chinese Communists, South African liberation forces, and anticapitalist economic doctrines. The "liberalization" of America signaled, according to Falwell, a move away from moral foundations, away from America's founding Truths, and toward damnation.

Roe v. Wade provided Falwell with the incentive and the mechanism to merge his theology and his sociopolitical beliefs into an integrated, discursive whole. A move away from moral Truths in national politics entailed a weakening of America's public morality, he believed, and any liberalization of sociopolitical policies entailed (and encouraged) moral degradation. When "true believers," true moral citizens, allow this to happen, Falwell said, they

will find themselves unable to live righteous lives. True believers must participate in and advocate national moral revival—the promotion of public and private virtue in accord with biblical Truths. America's public morality, Falwell proclaimed, must be infused with personal and social morality based on true Christian revelation.

However, for a number of reasons, Falwell's church and television ministry did not provide him with the sociopolitical influence he desired. The Moral Majority did that. Founded in 1979, the organization was based on four tenets: (1) being pro-life, opposing abortion and euthanasia; (2) being pro-family, supporting heterosexual unions for life; (3) being pro-moral, opposing pornography and drug trafficking; (4) being pro-American, supporting American principles, national defense, and the preservation of Israel. The Moral Majority gave Falwell the opportunity to keep himself in the national spotlight, a position from which he could address virtually any social, cultural, or political issue. He had the opportunity to appear around the country in a variety of contexts—on television, in lecture halls, in churches, and in debates—and deliver the same message to a host of different audiences. Consequently, his sermons sounded almost identical to his political orations; the two forms of discourse—religious and political—became inseparable.

Falwell's Moral Majority rhetoric was incredibly successful. During Ronald Reagan's presidency—an era of "moral revival," according to Falwell—a significant political constituency responded to his Moral Majority proclamations. Its chosen candidates won three consecutive presidential elections, as well as scores of congressional, state, and local contests. Thousands of laws that it supported were passed and implemented at every level of American government. In fact, Falwell credited the Moral Majority with establishing the modern religious right: "I feel that I have performed the task to which I was called in 1979. The religious right is solidly in place and, like the galvanizing of the black church as a political force a generation ago, the religious conservatives in America are now in for the duration." Then Vice President George H. W. Bush remarked before a meeting of Falwell's Liberty Federation: "America is in crying need of the moral vision you have brought to our political life." Thanks to the Moral Majority and similar organizations that it spawned, the religious right grew to be a mainstay in public discourse.

After a period of successful activism and advocacy, social movements and their organizations such as the Moral Majority tend either to achieve their goals and lose their motive force, or to break apart due to infighting among their constituents. Sometimes they do both—once the rhetorical battle is won and the need for unity declines, long-standing tensions within the movement erupt into open conflict. The success and visibility of the Moral Majority was a two-edged sword. It galvanized its opponents and attracted the constant attention of the secular media. This in turn meant that any conflicts within the movement or any indiscretions committed by its leaders were instant news. Dealing with one such event—the 1987 collapse of televangelist Jim Bakker's PTL Club amid accusations of sexual infidelity and an indictment for income tax fraud—would ensnare Falwell for years; and the movement's political success would lead to fragmentation.

When Bakker stepped down as head of the PTL, he selected Falwell to succeed him, a choice that proved to be organizationally fatal for both the PTL and the Moral Majority. Eventually Bakker was convicted of tax fraud and jailed, and Bakker's followers despised Falwell for mismanaging the ministry. Allegations and counterallegations over Falwell's performance as head of the PTL turned into a rhetorical "holy war" among Falwell, the Bakkers, Bakker's followers, and the remaining core constituency of the religious right. Two of Falwell's own organizations—the I Love America political action committee and the Old-Time Gospel Hour—were fined $6,000 each for buying and selling Bibles at inflated prices. Finally, in October 1987, after a tumultuous battle over control of the ministry, Falwell stepped down as head of the PTL. A month later he announced his resignation as head of the Moral Majority. In June 1989, the Moral Majority decided officially to call it quits, proclaiming its "mission accomplished."

The breakup of the Moral Majority left Falwell with a difficult rhetorical situation. For ten years the Moral Majority had provided him with an institution through which he could seamlessly integrate God's Word and his conservative politics into a balanced rhetorical whole. After declaring victory, he had no specific mission; after the demise of the Moral Majority, he had no mechanism. Perhaps more important, he had no enemy.

The most common, and most effective, strategy for motivating and unifying members of a rhetorical movement is to attack—a policy, a political adversary, or social conditions—and thereby sustain a balance between sociopolitical and religious discourses. For Falwell, a good "enemy" has to be implacably leading America—God's chosen land—toward sociopolitical immorality and Godlessness. An "enemy" who represents both immorality and religious destitution, therefore, gives Falwell the sense of urgency he needs to speak out polemically, to speak extremely in both substance and form, and, more important, to be heard nationally when he speaks out. But without an "enemy," Falwell has few chances to speak out in a way that people outside of his core constituency care about. Without the sense of urgency brought on by an "enemy," Falwell is left doing administrative discourse for his church or his lesser-known organizations, and he does not do that very well. Robbed of mission, mechanism, and adversary, for a time Falwell floundered.

During the 1988 presidential campaign, Falwell was on the political fringe. Pat Robertson, his religious right compatriot, was running for president, but the ongoing conflicts among the religious right encouraged little unity among its groups. Falwell supported George H. W. Bush, a politician whom few members of the religious right—true "Reaganites"—could endorse wholeheartedly. Bush simply did not represent the type of conservatism and national moral revival that the religious right had found in Reagan. During Bush's presidency, Falwell stayed out of the national political spotlight, choosing instead to focus his attention on Liberty University and Thomas Road Baptist Church, organizations he had neglected during his tenure as PTL director and during the demise of the Moral Majority.

When he stepped down as head of the Moral Majority, he told reporters: "I will not be stumping for candidates again. I will never work for a candidate as I did for Ronald Reagan. I will not lobby for legislation personally." During Bush's presidency, Falwell lacked a viable devil figure and had no institution to provide him with the visibility and support that the Moral Majority had provided. The lesser-known organizations that he controlled simply did not have enough financial stability to provide him with sustained national political visibility.

But in 1992, a perfect enemy entered the scene: William Jefferson Clinton. With Clinton in office, Falwell was able to energize and unite his constituency around a common enemy and once again occupy the national political spotlight. Falwell was also able to use his anti-Clinton crusade to invigorate his Liberty organizations, and encourage his constituents to join the campaign against the new devil figure. One such organization was Falwell's Liberty Broadcast Network— a formerly insignificant television ministry and political platform now gaining national visibility through its anti-Clinton polemics, polemics blaming Clinton for the bulk of America's sociopolitical immorality and "Godlessness." In 1994, Falwell aired on the Liberty channel *The Clinton Chronicles*, a videotape depicting Clinton as a sexual deviant, drug trafficker, conspirator planning a governmental takeover, and murderer. The tape opens with this narration:

> On January 20th, 1993, William Jefferson Clinton became the 42nd President of the United States. At the time, most Americans were not aware of the extent of Clinton's criminal background, nor were they aware of the media blackout which kept this information from the public. As state attorney general and later, governor, Bill Clinton in twelve years achieved absolute control over the political, legal, and financial systems of Arkansas. As president, he would attempt to do the same with the nation by bringing members of his inner circle with him to Washington. The Hijacking of America was under way and its impact on future generations would be incalculable.

Through his Liberty Network, Falwell sold ten thousand copies of the tape for $40 each. Not only was his financial viability coming back, but his revived national prominence allowed him to reintegrate his religious and political messages. Falwell once again had an audible voice in national political discourse.

In response to Falwell's videotape and a host of other allegations and verbal attacks from the religious right, Clinton lashed out, claiming his opponents distracted the nation from its true public business. This response, of course, enhanced Falwell's credibility with his constituents, and encouraged even more vocal attacks, eventually creating something of a national shouting match between the new president and the religious right. But calling Clinton a "devil" was able to sustain Falwell's visibility for only a short period of time. Anti-Clinton rhetoric soon became commonplace, especially in the friendly confines of cable television and talk radio. But the mainstream media and the national political audience found nothing unique or interesting in Falwell's attacks, and Falwell's broader audience soon stopped paying attention. Moreover, while the 30 percent or so of Americans who shared Falwell's view of Clinton became progressively more committed to their position, the bulk of Americans had a relatively favorable view of Clinton's job performance. Furthermore, when Clinton ran against Republican senator Bob Dole in 1996, Falwell found it difficult to assail Clinton as a devil and praise Dole as a national savior. The religious right knew that Bob Dole, just like George Bush, simply was no Ronald Reagan. Clinton won his second term, and the nation continued with its business.

But things change quickly in national political discourse. By 1998, the terms "sexual immorality" and "president" became virtually synonymous. For the religious right, and many others, Clinton fit the role of "sexual deviant president" perfectly, and Falwell once again had the means to motivate his constituents and unite his sociopolitical criticism with his religious messages. On February 1, 1998, Falwell told his congregation:

> This has been an embarrassing week for our nation. The world is laughing at us. Parents and grandparents have had great difficulty explaining to the children what is happening and what the media is talking about. Many Americans are

disgusted, depressed and have sadly lost all respect for their government. Regardless how the facts come out, no matter how the Bill Clinton–Ken Starr matter is resolved, the trashing of our national values, magnified through the lens of television has reached a new low.

As always Falwell tied private character to public virtue. With the president's private character at an all-time low, Falwell said, the whole nation suffers. In an editorial in *USA Today*, he wrote:

> Regardless what the polls say, the strength of our collective character, of our children and our families, is far more important (and permanent) than the strength of our economy. When our political leaders stand before God one day, He will not ask any of them how the economy fared on their watch. He will ask them if they were faithful stewards of their divine calling. We draw no moral strength as a nation, no bond of trust as a people, from a president who is unfaithful to his marital vows, abusive of an employer–employee trust, and dishonest with the public.

Clinton's behavior undermined the bonds of morality that unified religion and nation, Falwell concluded, and because of that, America, despite its economic prosperity, was in grave moral danger. By being "unfaithful to his marital vows," Clinton destroyed the sacred trust of the family, and in his role of national leader, he set an example of familial immorality for the rest of the nation.

For Falwell, private morality comes to fruition in the family, which in turn facilitates public morality and individual virtue. The most damnable aspect of Clinton's wrongdoings was the additional moral burden that his behavior forced upon decent American families, who, because of a highly visible national perversion, found it difficult to maintain private morality within their own homes. "I am angry because of the terrible injury that has been inflicted upon the children of this generation," Falwell fumed to his congregation. "The national moral bar has been dramatically lowered. The president's behavior puts America's parents and grandparents in a terrible position. . . . Our government has failed the families of America." President Clinton, Falwell believed, was a re-

flection of America's declining moral condition, which damaged the private virtue necessary to sustain public morality in accordance with God's Will. "I see the amoral passivity of this arrogant, materialistic, lawless, immoral nation as open defiance against Almighty God," Falwell proclaimed. With Clinton as morality's antithesis, Falwell was able to urge his audience to unite against a common foe and take serious action. Falwell's "true believers" could act positively—that is, *for* True Good—by donating time, prayer, or funds to Truth's cause—including Falwell's ministry. Or they could act negatively—that is, *against* the "enemy"—by voting against moral degradation and those who represent it.

In 2000, true believers voted *against* moral degradation and *for* George W. Bush. They enacted God's Word in a victory for Truth, Morality, and America. In early 2001, as Bush was preparing to take office, Falwell told his congregation, "The church is finally awakening to its 'salt' responsibilities. We are the conscience of the culture. We are the moral and spiritual preservation of the culture. . . . Our intensity of activism peaked in 2000. And God has rewarded us. He has blessed America." As he continued, Falwell spoke about the presidential election as evidence of God working in the world: "About 82% of . . . conservative Christians voted for George W. Bush. Without these 20 million evangelical votes, Al Gore would be president of the United States today. I can imagine very few more depressing thoughts. I want to stop right here and now and say thanks and congratulations to Bible-believing Christians nationwide."

Ironically, Bush's ascension to the presidency revived the first aspect of Falwell's recurring rhetorical problem—maintaining visibility in the face of victory. During the first part of the younger Bush's presidency, Falwell left the national political stage and focused his attention on Liberty University and Thomas Road Baptist Church, much as he had during the Reagan administration. But, on September 11, 2001, Falwell was given a new devil figure, and a new opportunity to gain national visibility. Only days after the terror attacks, while the nation was still unified through its shared anger and grief, Falwell told Pat Robertson's *The 700 Club*: "I really believe that the pagans and the abortionists and the feminists and the gays and the lesbians who are actively trying to make that an alternative lifestyle, the ACLU, People for the American Way—all of them who have tried to secularize America—I point the finger in their face and say, 'You helped this happen.' " As a result of the secularization and paganization of America—the land of God's chosen people—God permitted the terror attacks to happen, Falwell believed. "What we saw on Tuesday," he proclaimed, "as terrible as it is, could be minuscule if, in fact, God continues to lift the curtain and allow the enemies of America to give us probably what we deserve." In a true jeremiad, Falwell concluded: "If America does not repent and return to a genuine faith and dependence on Him, we may expect more tragedies, unfortunately."

While Falwell admitted that September 11 was an immense national tragedy, he also saw it as a point of renewal for the country, a wake-up call. "I rejoice in the new wave of patriotism sweeping our land. Flags are everywhere. Generosity is rampant. Thousands of prayer meetings are saturating the country." Falwell praised the "flags" and the "prayers" as symbols of the same discursive whole, symbols of the proper unification of religion and cultural politics. After 9-11, Falwell's sociopolitical–religious discourse thrived in the face of terror. "God's children must not fail our Lord, our nation or our president," Falwell proclaimed. "Let us build a protective hedge about President Bush and ceaselessly ask God to grant him the wisdom he will need for the awesome task ahead."

However, the magnitude of America's response to 9-11 revived the second aspect of Falwell's rhetorical problem—finding a way to stand out from like-minded rhetors. Falwell was only one voice in a chorus of moral outrage after 9-11. It took a year for him to separate himself from his peers. Speaking on the October 6, 2002, episode of *60 Minutes*, he called the prophet Mohammed a "terrorist." His comments set off a furious controversy, including fatal riots in India condemning Falwell and calling for his death. But they also differentiated him from mainstream conservatives while simultaneously throwing him into the glare of the national political spotlight. More important, Falwell's "war on terror" discourse, by uniting God's Will and Eternal Truth

with normative proclamations for foreign and domestic policy, satisfied his discursive need—the need to achieve national visibility by uniting religious ideology and sociopolitical rhetoric into a comprehensive whole.

For a third of a century, Jerry Falwell's rhetorical challenge has been to adapt his "worldly" rhetoric to the Divine Word in a way that will sustain his visibility and influence despite a constantly changing rhetorical situation. While his ideology of Christian fundamentalism has remained static and unshakable, the sociopolitical context within which Falwell acts as divinely appointed messenger repeatedly puts him in a bind. Because of his commitment to sociopolitical activism in the name of religion, he must maintain a proper balance between his language of worldly moral advocacy and God's Word, and to do so in a way that will distinguish his mission from the missions of like-minded Christian crusaders. To achieve his mission, he must remain visible on the national political scene. But the elements that are necessary for a distinctive visibility—credible devil figures and an effective organization—come and go, in part because of the success of his rhetoric. Jerry Falwell's career offers an important lesson for students of American oratory: moral crusades can be fought in many ways, but without devils and organizations, they languish.

INFORMATION SOURCES

Research Collection and Collected Speeches

Although Falwell is an active orator, his speeches are sometimes difficult to locate. Copies of his sermons at Thomas Road Baptist Church, dating from 1996 through the present, are available from the church's Web site.

American Rhetoric from Roosevelt to Reagan: A Collection of Speeches and Critical Essays [*ARRR*], ed. Halford Ross Ryan, 2nd ed. Prospect Heights, Ill.: Waveland Press, 1987.

Falwell, Jerry. *Moral Majority Report* [*MMR*]. Lynchburg, Va.: Thomas Road Baptist Church, "Interview with Jerry Falwell." *Penthouse*, March 1981, pp. 60–66.

Web Site

Thomas Road Baptist Church [*TRBC*]. Includes numerous sermons delivered by Falwell. http://www.trbc.org/christianresources/falwellsermons.php

Audiovisual Materials

Contemporary American Speeches. Alliance Video Productions. Greenwood, Ind.: Educational Video Group, 1988.

Great Speeches. Vol. 7. Alliance Video for Great Speeches. Roger Cook, executive producer and Susan Cook, director. Greenwood, Ind.: Great Speeches, 1985.

Selected Critical Studies

Brown, Ruth Murray. *For a "Christian America": A History of the Religious Right*. Amherst, N.Y.: Prometheus Books, 2002.

Brummett, Barry. "The Representative Anecdote as a Burkean Method, Applied to Evangelical Rhetoric." *Southern Speech Communication Journal* 50 (1984): 1–23.

Clabaugh, Gary. *Thunder on the Right*. Chicago: Nelson-Hall, 1980.

Conrad, Charles. "The Moral Majority as Romantic Form." *Quarterly Journal of Speech* 69 (1983): 159–70.

Daniels, Tom, Richard Jensen, and Allen Lichtenstein. "Resolving the Paradox in Politicized Christian Fundamentalism." *Western Journal of Speech Communication* 49 (1985): 248–66.

Harding, Susan Friend. *The Book of Jerry Falwell: Fundamentalist Language and Politics*. Princeton, N.J.: Princeton University Press, 2000.

Hart, Roderick. *The Political Pulpit*. West Lafayette, Ind.: Purdue University Press, 1981.

Leege, David. "Coalitions, Cues, Strategic Politics, and the Staying Power of the Religious Right." *PS: Political Science and Politics*, 25 (1992): 198–204.

McGee, Michael. "Secular Humanism." *Critical Studies in Mass Communication* 1 (1984): 1–33.

Miller, Alan, and John Hoffmann. "The Growing Divisiveness." *Social Forces* 78 (1999): 721–45.

Rozell, Mark, and Clyde Wilcox. "Second Coming: The Strategies of the New Christian Right." *Political Science Quarterly* 11 (1996): 271–94.

Shiels, Richard. "A Response." *Religion and Intellectual Life* 2 (1984): 23–27.

Simon, Merill. *Jerry Falwell and the Jews*. Middle Village, N.Y.: Jonathan David, 1999.

Smolla, Rodney A. *Jerry Falwell v. Larry Flynt: The First Amendment on Trial*. New York: St. Martin's Press, 1988.

Snowball, David. *Continuity and Change in the Rhetoric of the Moral Majority*. New York: Praeger, 1991.

Selected Biographies

D'Souza, Dinesh. *Falwell, Before the Millennium*. Chicago: Regnery Gateway, 1984.

Pingry, Patricia. *Jerry Falwell, Man of Vision*. Milwaukee: Ideals Publishing Corp., 1980.

CHRONOLOGY OF MAJOR SPEECHES

See "Research Collections and Collected Speeches" for source codes.

"America Was Built on Seven Great Principles." Multiple presentations. *MMR*, May 18, 1981, p. 8.

"Strengthening Families in the Nation." Atlanta, Ga., March 23, 1982. *ARRR*, pp. 250–64.

"Untitled Speech to the Republican National Convention Platform Committee." San Francisco, August 13, 1984. *MMR*, September 9, 1984, pp. 3, 8.

"A Cup of Cold Water." Lynchburg, Va., May 12, 1985. *TRBC*.

LOUIS ABDUL FARRAKHAN (1933–)
Nation of Islam Minister

MARK LAWRENCE McPHAIL

Persons of African descent in America have historically faced the rhetorical challenge of addressing and persuading two separate and unequal audiences: the Anglo-Americans who enslaved and dehumanized them, and their brothers and sisters who shared and endured the experience of racial oppression. In response to this rhetorical challenge, diverse and sometimes divergent persuasive strategies have emerged: assimilationist approaches that accept and embrace white views and values; integrationist orientations that attempt a reconciliation between Blacks and whites; and nationalist perspectives that affirm the Black culture and consciousness. The last of these strategic responses has often been the most provocative, since its affirmation of Blackness simultaneously advances a compelling critique of whiteness. No rhetor has embodied its controversial character more dramatically than the leader of the Nation of Islam, the Honorable Minister Louis Abdul Farrakhan.

Louis Abdul Farrakhan was born Louis Eugene Walcott on May 11, 1933, in the borough of the Bronx in New York City. His parents had emigrated from the Caribbean to New York, where his father worked as a schoolteacher and Baptist preacher, and his mother was a domestic worker. His father died when his son was only three, and Louis grew up in the Roxbury section of Boston, where he attended St. Cyprian Episcopal church and served as a choirboy. An honor student in high school, he participated in track and music, and despite having had a stuttering problem as a child, excelled in drama. He attended Winston-Salem Teachers College in North Carolina for two years, but then turned toward the entertainment industry. As a young man, he appeared on Ted Mack's *Original Amateur Hour* as an aspiring violinist, and during his twenties he performed in nightclubs, singing, dancing, and playing the guitar.

After one such performance in Chicago in 1955, Walcott was recruited to the Nation of Islam by Malcolm X. He changed his name to Louis X, and later to Louis Farrakhan. He served first as an understudy to Malcolm X at Temple No. 11 in Boston, and succeeded him as its minister when Malcolm left for Temple No. 7 in Harlem. During the 1960s, Farrakhan continued to pursue his interests in music and drama, writing and recording the Black Muslim anthem, "A White Man's Heaven Is a Black Man's Hell," and writing and directing two plays that were featured in Nation of Islam mosques across America. As minister of the Boston mosque, Farrakhan became an ardent spokesman for, and defender of, the teachings of Elijah Muhammad, founder of the Nation of Islam.

During the early 1960s, the Nation of Islam became divided over accusations that Elijah Muhammad had violated his own moral code by having illicit affairs with six of his female secretaries. Upon hearing that these accusations were true from Elijah Muhammad's son Wallace, Malcolm X expressed his criticism of the Nation's founder and contacted other ministers in the organization to inform them of Elijah Muhammad's transgressions. It was, according to Lawrence Mamiya, Louis Farrakhan and the commander of the Boston mosque's security force who reported that Malcolm was "spreading false rumors" about Elijah Muhammad. It was this event, and not his "chickens coming home to roost" comment about John F. Kennedy's assassination, that Malcolm believed led to his silencing. Malcolm X then broke with the Nation of Islam, and shortly afterward was himself assassinated. Subsequently, Farrakhan was named minister of the Harlem mosque, and later became the national spokesman for Elijah Muhammad.

As national spokesman for the Nation of Islam, Farrakhan had the responsibility for introducing Elijah Muhammad at the Nation of Islam's annual Savior's Day celebrations, and also served as a proxy for Muhammad at speaking engagements across the country. After the death of Elijah Muhammad in 1975, Farrakhan was called to Chicago by Elijah Muhammad's son W. Deen Muhammad, who began to restructure the organization by departing from his father's doctrines and moving toward the orthodox teachings of Islam. For the next two years Farrakhan traveled in Africa, and upon his return he denounced the revisionism of W. Deen Muhammad. In 1978 he publicly announced his departure from the organization, and soon began publishing *The Final Call*, the organ of a new Nation of Islam that remained true to the doctrine of Elijah Muhammad.

Farrakhan's rebuilding of the Nation of Islam was undoubtedly facilitated by his rhetorical skills. Over the next decade he traveled well over 250,000 miles a year on speaking engagements, and by the mid-1980s he drew crowds of up to 25,000. While he has continued to promote the original teachings of Elijah Muhammad, under his leadership the Nation of Islam has become more politically active, as evidenced by his vocal support of Jesse Jackson's 1984 presidential campaign. During this time, the Nation of Islam has grown dramatically. Experts estimate that as many as 300,000 people actively follow Farrakhan's teachings. Today Farrakhan lives with his wife, Khadijah, and their nine children and twenty-nine grandchildren in the home of his former teacher, Elijah Muhammad, in Chicago. There he continues to lead the Nation of Islam and speak on behalf of the philosophy of its founder.

BLACK NATIONALISM AND THE REDEFINING POWER OF RHETORIC

Dexter Gordon begins his discussion of nineteenth-century Black nationalism by noting the significance of the Million Man March for understanding "the identity, place, and role of 'black people' in America." He argues that the march "demonstrated the potential power of a black nationalist ideology to unify and mobilize blacks in the face of their material and symbolic alienation in the United States," and suggests that this potential was clearly expressed by Minister Louis Farrakhan: "In Farrakhan's words, 'we didn't come to Washington to petition the government for a way out of her, but to find a way out of our affliction.'" Gordon notes that Minister Farrakhan's message articulated an affirmation of Blackness which resisted and redefined the historical and contemporary characterizations of Black men as violent, undisciplined, and self-destructive. In contrast to this construction of Blackness, Farrakhan sought to call into being a "new" Black man, rooted in an African identity long denied, yet fully and unambiguously American, willing to take responsibility on both the material and the spiritual planes of existence. Gordon argues:

> Against the background of alienation and disenfranchisement, the Million Man March brought black men together in a powerful demonstration of solidarity and popular support. For people such as Farrakhan, the image of African Americans as a problem is not only inaccurate but racist. The march's background themes of atonement and restoration, then, framed Farrakhan's call for black men to return to the (black) family and take their rightful place in American society. To make this return, Farrakhan argued, blacks must assert their true identity, an identity based on their ances-

tral achievements. Accordingly, in Farrakhan's terms, blacks need a knowledge of their own history, and not from a white perspective.

Throughout the Black diaspora, persons of African descent not only have been denied personhood in white societies, but also have been disconnected from the African peoples with whom they claim common ancestry. Black nationalism has, from its beginnings, posed a critical stance toward the discourse of white supremacy and racism, and Black orators have persistently struggled with the need to re-create themselves and their diverse and often divergent audiences.

Two texts in particular illustrate Minister Farrakhan's discourse and his rhetorical efforts to challenge the status quo and thus re-create himself, his audience, and the rhetorical situation: the Million Man March address of October 1995, and the "World Press Conference" of September 16, 2001, presented in response to the attack on the World Trade Center and the Pentagon. Independently, each oration reveals the creative and re-creative impulses embodied in what Gordon describes as "a mature black nationalism."

Minister Farrakhan has been described in the popular press as a demagogue by some and a deliverer by others. While Michael Kramer refers to him as a "bigot" and a "racist," Manning Marable argues that Farrakhan cannot simply be dismissed as an anti-Semite, and that "a careful analysis of Farrakhan's public address reveals a strong commitment to an antiracist and anti-imperialist politics, which parallels the late social thought of Malcolm X." Responses to Louis Farrakhan are clearly paradoxical: where his followers see a deliverer, his critics see a demagogue. In response to this contradictory characterization of his persona, Minister Farrakhan's rhetorical response has been to re-create his own identity, reshape his audience's conception of self and other, and redefine the exigencies and constraints of American race relations. His Million Man March address illustrates the ways in which he attempts to accomplish each of these goals.

Analyzing the Million Man March speech, John Pauley II claims that Farrakhan invokes a "prophetic" ethos, a claim that resonates with those criticisms that attribute to him motives of self-promotion and self-aggrandizement. Similarly, John Arthos's depiction of Farrakhan as a "Shaman–Trickster" corresponds with popular criticisms of Farrakhan as deceptive and disingenuous. Yet Farrakhan explicitly denies attributions of prophetic status: "I am not a Prophet. I am not a Messenger," he explained in a speech delivered in 1985 in Washington, D.C. "But I am a warner. And I am a man in the mold of those men, calling you to account." Farrakhan claims no status other than that of a "man," and it is through the act of calling himself and his hearers to account that he fully invokes this sense of manhood in the Million Man March speech. Arthos's claim that Farrakhan attempts to misdirect his white listeners while "gettin ovah" with his Black listeners fails to acknowledge that Farrakhan directs his message of atonement to *both* audiences. To suggest that the theme of atonement is anything other than genuine, even as part of an elaborate cultural ritual of deception, is to fail to hear Minister Farrakhan's unambiguous message to his white audience: *I* have atoned; *we* have atoned; now *you* should atone.

When one reads Farrakhan's Million Man March address as a speech that attempts to re-create his audience, one dispenses with the need to impose interpretive claims upon it that are not readily apparent. For example, Farrakhan explicitly attends to his public persona, and does so early in the speech when he acknowledges that it "may certainly be so" that he is guilty of having a "defect" in his character. He then offers a brief but powerful apologia: "But let me say in truth, you can't point out wrong with malice. You can't point out wrong with hatred. So, we ask Muslims who, in our first stage, we pointed out the wrongs of America, but we didn't point it out with no love, we pointed it out with the pain of our hurt. The pain of our suffering. The bitterness of our life story. But, we have grown beyond our bitterness. We have transcended beyond our pain." Implicit in this explicit acknowledgment of past wrongs is the rhetorical shift which Farrakhan uses to reconstitute his white audience: a repudiation of the Nation of Islam's depiction of whites as "devils" and inherently evil, re-created to an under-

standing of whites as suffering from the "sickness" of "white supremacy." For this disease, he offers a cure: "Do you want a solution to the dilemma that America faces? Then don't look at our skin color, because racism will cause you to reject salvation if it comes in the skin of a black person." There is clearly no attempt by Farrakhan here to present himself as a prophet, nor to misdirect his white audience. The message is clear and direct: *I* have atoned. *We* have atoned. Now *you* should atone.

Popular writers engage in comparable criticism of Farrakhan. S. Craig Watkins argues that the media framed the Million Man March in a manner that gave priority to "the presence, leadership style, and racial politics of Louis Farrakhan." He contends that the media's characterization of Farrakhan framed the ways in which the March was reported, and suggests that the emphasis on Farrakhan served to reinforce popular conceptions of racial difference and identity: "The decision to peg the march on Farrakhan was crucial to the formation, tone, and ideological implications of the anticipatory narrative and played a decisive role in how the demonstration was perceived as a newsworthy event." This decision not only served to demonize Farrakhan and silence his larger constituency, but also functioned to construct the march as a demonstration of "reverse racism": "By emphasizing Farrakhan's relationship to the march, journalists focused much of their attention, and that of the public, on his polarizing racial politics." Watkins continues: "In addition, their framing judgments stigmatized the march as an expression of racism rather than a protest against racial inequality." The media's framing of Farrakhan, he concludes, undermined the possibility of positive racial dialogue, and reinforced the dominant culture's silencing of Black voices through its own silent disavowal of racial responsibility. Within the context of this narrative, Farrakhan cannot become a "new person" because he is framed as a "bad person." So, too, by implication, are the million men who supported him.

Similarly, Minister Farrakhan's response to the September 11 attack on the World Trade Center and the Pentagon challenges the depiction of him as a man of hatred and bigotry, and suggests that to many he has come to represent the hope that hate produced. The speech uncovers and contests some of our nation's most fundamental contradictions and ironies about race and justice, and suggests that in the case of Farrakhan, we cannot define who a man is solely by his past words and deeds, but must also look to what he embodies in the present, and the possibility of transformation that he offers for our future. Farrakhan not only presents a "new person" to his audiences, but also invites those audiences to participate in and identify with a reconstructed understanding of self, other, difference, and identity. Although Minister Farrakhan's press conference was largely ignored by the mainstream media, or reduced to sound bites or scrolling text on the bottom of the news broadcasts of some of the major networks, the significance of what he said and did on that day cannot be dismissed or ignored.

On September 16, 2001, Minister Farrakhan responded to the attacks on the World Trade Center and the Pentagon in a speech presented at the Nation of Islam's main temple in Chicago. In an unprecedented act, he opened Mosque Maryam to people of all races and religious denominations, and offered an address that clearly expressed the principles of a "mature" Black nationalism. In his speech, Farrakhan attempted to redefine himself and to reconstitute his audience across lines of racial difference and division, and presented a message that echoes many of the themes of the Million Man March address: atonement, a repudiation of violence, and acceptance of racial history and responsibility. Farrakhan's speech is unambiguous in its condemnation of the attacks on the Pentagon and the World Trade Center: "I, on behalf of all the members of the Nation of Islam and on behalf of many millions of Muslims here in America and throughout the world, lift our voices to condemn this vicious attack on the United States." Farrakhan encouraged the nation to seek "Divine guidance," invoked a rhetorical strategy that challenged the antagonistic interpretations of the attack, and offered an alternative strategy of response.

Farrakhan's redefinition of himself began with a reminder to his audience that he is himself a native New Yorker, and a concerned American citizen who, despite prior criticisms of his home, loves the country of his birth: "I was born in this country in New York City, and though the pain that Black people have suffered in America has caused me to be angry with the country of my birth, however, in my maturation, I know that, with all of America's problems, she's the greatest nation on this earth." Farrakhan next identified himself with his audience by establishing and then deconstructing George Bush's bipolar answer to the question the president had rhetorically posed: "Why do they hate us?"

> President Bush answered, saying they hate us because we're the beacon light of freedom. They hate us because we're good. They hate us because we are the land of opportunity. Pastors and preachers and Reverend Franklin Graham said that they hate us because we're Christians and they want us all to be Muslims.

Farrakhan then disrupted these paired oppositions, and all of the implications that they carry, when he explained that "no Muslim hates a Christian because he's a Christian." Through rhetorical reversal, he exposed the prejudicial and ethnocentric principles contained in the discourse of "they" and "us."

Farrakhan's first use of rhetorical reversal occurred when he shifted from the focus of the events of an "attack on America" to an "attack on people": "The perpetrators killed Black and White, Asian and Hispanic, Jews and Christians, Agnostics, Hindus, and Buddhists. This is why it was a crime against humanity." Farrakhan deconstructed racial and religious divisions in order to facilitate an understanding of the events of September 11 that appeals to an inclusive sense of identity. Once the attack was redefined, Farrakhan offered an explanation for the behavior of the hijackers that placed it within a context aligned with core American values—as a response to injustice: "Whenever any human being is deprived of justice, the mind becomes imbalanced. The greater the injustice, the greater the imbalance. In a democratic society and in a civilized nation, institutions are established for the redress of grievances, and it is the success of granting to those who seek redress of their grievance and having it done that returns balance to the human mind." Farrakhan again invoked the sickness motif that he had presented in his Million Man March address, but this time applied it to the victims of injustice instead of its perpetrators. This move further disrupted the "they" and "us" opposition by implying that both were implicated in a common pathology, a pathology that he next suggested was rooted in the moral incoherence of white racial ideology.

Farrakhan contended that this incoherence reveals itself most clearly in the profiling and stereotyping of Muslims as "terrorists," when prior to September 11, the most destructive act of terrorism committed on American soil was perpetrated by a white Christian male. He reminded his audience that in the aftermath of the Oklahoma City bombing, there was no widespread profiling of white Christian males, nor was the American system of justice intent on rooting out and destroying the terrorist militia organizations of which McVeigh was a proud member. "When Timothy McVeigh committed the worst act of terrorism on American soil, the first persons accused of this were members of the Nation of Islam and immigrant Muslims. Many followers of Islam were attacked, and then it was found that the perpetrator of this crime was a White American, a soldier who professed to be a Christian." Farrakhan's argument rejected the bipolar characterization of "terrorists" as "Muslim others" by rejecting the characterization of the "victims" as "White Christians." His juxtaposition of McVeigh and the hijackers called into question the implicit and unspoken characterization of difference invoked by politicians and priests in their responses to the September 11 attacks: that "they" hate "us" because we are *white*.

Through his speeches, Farrakhan seeks to disrupt the "ideology of innocence" that characterizes "white resistance to racial responsibility and the denial of white complicity in the continuing realities of racial division and discrimination." In his speech of September 16, 2001, he did so not by invoking the past injustices of racism but by appealing to his audience's understanding that we are *all* implicated in the events of September 11. This reframing of the attacks on the Pentagon and the World Trade Center redefined Farrakhan's persona from that of prophet of rage and repudiation to that of proponent of peace and reconciliation. It reveals his vision of an audience as one that can achieve unity despite deep and historically inscribed divisions of belief and ideology. And it offers a message based upon arguments and explanations that resist the simplistic separations of racial reasoning, and seek instead to cultivate a community of conscience. As he concluded in his speech of September 16:

> Let this terrible tragedy lead to a rebuilding of spiritual values that connect the children of Abraham—Muslim, Christian, and Jew—in a rebirth of moral and spiritual values that could lead to the making of a new world, a world that ultimately will beat swords into plowshares and spears into pruning hooks, not just for the cultivation of the earth, but for the cultivation of every living human being on this earth, so that never again will men be so depraved that they will do what was done on September 11, 2001. May God bless the citizens of America. May God guide the leadership of America in this very dark and troubling hour, as I greet you with peace, As Salaam Alaikaum (Peace Be Unto You).

This shift in Farrakhan's discourse may confirm Dexter Gordon's optimistic assessment of "the capacity of black nationalism to move beyond the leading role in the 'strategy of opposition' to guidance in a 'strategy of construction of a new order.' " It certainly indicates that Farrakhan has recognized the need for a more mature and inclusive rhetorical strategy, one that can contest division through unity, that appeals not to color but to conscience.

Yet some of Farrakhan's listeners still refuse to hear his message. Ken Hamblin of the *Denver Post*, for example, refers to Farrakhan as "a gullible and pitiful tool of radical Muslims like Osama bin Laden." Hamblin states that Minister Farrakhan "seldom has had a congenial word to spend on his America, his adopted nation," and comments on "how closely Farrakhan resembles bin Laden—since both of them, in my mind, are card-carrying crazy citizens of the Third World." Hamblin's comparison of Farrakhan to Bin Laden not only ignores the former's affirmation of his American identity and rejection of the acts of the attackers, but also reveals Hamblin's own underlying racial reasoning. Although Hamblin reports that Minister

Farrakhan spoke for one hundred minutes, he chooses one phrase to reduce Farrakhan to an anti-American demagogue. Had he considered the speech in its entirety, he could not reasonably reduce Farrakhan to "a voice of dissent that the nation can ill afford to let go unchallenged," nor deny that Minister Farrakhan explicitly criticized the events of September 11 as "an attack against humanity."

Hamblin's criticisms reveal the difficulties faced by Minister Farrakhan as he attempts to redefine himself and articulate a message that can reconstitute audiences that have so often defined themselves by race. Not only must Farrakhan redefine himself, but he must also realign his audience's understanding of both *blackness* and *whiteness*. As he did in his Million Man March speech, Farrakhan must reconstitute himself and his black audiences by recovery of the past, redefinition of self, and reconstruction of the future. In both the Million Man March address and the response to September 11, Farrakhan also had to reconstitute his white audiences, who may by virtue of their "sickness" be "unable to attend, and unable to respond," to his message. To a large degree, the challenge that Farrakhan faces is at work in all Black rhetoric that aims at social justice, racial reconciliation, and moral transformation.

In his seminal essay on Farrakhan's rhetoric, Stephen Goldzwig argues that the dismissal of what are prejudged by critics to be "questionable rhetorical tactics" undermines our understanding of the social and symbolic complexities of discourse such as Farrakhan's. Instead of reading such rhetoric prejudicially, Goldzwig argues, discursive practices must be understood situationally, and from this perspective he suggests that Farrakhan's rhetoric can be read as a fitting response to "intense, implacable, cultural warfare: its discursive goal actually may be to supplant the dominant cultural discourse." Farrakhan's oppositional stance, and the nonconventional language he uses to articulate it, illustrate a powerful indictment of the ideological and ethical assumptions and practices of a society that seeks to dismiss or minimize both his words and the worldview they represent.

Goldzwig concludes his analysis with an important and powerful insight into the rhetoric of those labeled "demagogues" by a society: "As consummate manipulators of the verbal symbol, their discourse is truly symbolic. It stands for what it is not. It is trick and chicanery and fluid motion; it is also a sometimes marred and sometimes marvelous portrait of ourselves." Goldzwig's final comment suggests that dominant discourses and institutions are implicated in the rhetorics of those who oppose them, and that the dismissal of oppositional rhetors as "demagogues" is sometimes more the result of a society's inability to look at its own underlying ethical inconsistencies and moral failings than of the essentially unethical or immoral character of those who criticize them. This is the "imperfection marked by urgency" that has confronted African American speakers for centuries, especially those espousing Black nationalism. Their voices speak loudly only because they have been silenced for so long; they threaten the society only because the society has threatened their existence; they call for its destruction only because their other means of redress have been destroyed.

In the aftermath of the Million Man March and in the wake of the tragedy of September 11, it is difficult to argue that Minister Farrakhan's rhetorical legacy can be reduced to a demagogic and irrational attack on white America. Nor can Farrakhan be dismissed as "paranoid," as his critics have repeatedly done in the past. Robert Singh offers a particularly harsh expression of this position: "The appropriate response to the leader of the NoI [Nation of Islam] is therefore one that entails recognizing the Farrakhan phenomenon for what it essentially is: a virulently bigoted, paranoid, and authoritarian expression of mass disillusionment not only with white America, but also with African Americans as well." Although Singh explicitly recognizes that "the Farrakhan phenomenon represents an expression and a function of the abiding American dilemma of race," and argues that this dilemma must be given "the fullest political attention and the most extensive, enlightened, and empathetic public candor," he ultimately dismisses Farrakhan as a demagogue. A more nuanced and empathetic account is offered by Robert Goldberg, who places the Farrakhan phenomenon squarely within the context of American race relations. "A history of racial oppression shadows America, and centuries of public and private incidents of humiliation still cause pain," he explains. "Louis Farrakhan's authority emerges from this context. His conspiracy theories cannot be dismissed simply as examples of the paranoid style, symbols of pathology that have no basis in reality." Indeed, the rhetoric and rise of Louis Farrakhan might just as easily be understood as a fitting response to a rhetorical situation marked by a symbolic pathology that may not be treated successfully through discourse.

Indeed, some critics believe that Farrakhan's reconstitution of self is well under way. Arthur Magida, one of Farrakhan's recent biographers, observed that Minister Farrakhan and his Nation's embrace of traditional Islamic teachings signals a major shift in their teachings and attitudes about race in America. Magida suggests that Farrakhan reflects a somewhat marred, and somewhat marvelous, portrait of our collective identity, and that he is criticized not so much because he is un-American as because of the double standard of justice that has always divided and distorted America's image of itself. He writes in *Prophet of Rage*, "If many reject the message he proclaims and the accusatory finger he aims, we ought to wonder about the impulses that cause the blaming and the pointing and question whether or not the target isn't all of us." Magida argues that Minister Farrakhan's "persona itself is symptomatic of our persistent, corrosive national difficulty and uncertainty about race and class," and that his most important message may be that we as Americans need "to reconcile the dualities swirling around race and class and faith in our *national* psyche; to rehabilitate the lives and the image of blacks that has currency not only among whites but also among blacks." If nothing else, Minister Farrakhan's rhetoric has been from its beginning committed to that rehabilitative mission.

Mattias Gardell offers a similar assessment of Farrakhan, as well as an insightful explanation of how Farrakhan's rhetoric might conceivably lead to a reconstitution of his audience. "Those who unequivocally condemn Minister Farrakhan and the Nation of Islam should pause to reflect on what they actually are attacking. Farrakhan is not so much a problem as he is a *symptom* of the problems presently tearing apart

American society." He also suggests that Minister Farrakhan's words and life hold an important message for the future of America: "Should observers focus less on the rhetoric of doom and study what actually is being done, a sober de-dramatization might replace the excited cries of condemnation," he writes. "I would argue that if left alone, the Nation of Islam will be of no danger to the present American society, and many of its detractors will most probably end up acknowledging the results as valuable." Such an acknowledgment would clearly indicate a transformed understanding by those who condemn Farrakhan of the importance of his message for facilitating racial change, transformation, and reconciliation.

Increasingly, since the Million Man March speech, these themes have been prominent in Farrakhan's discourse. In August 2001, for example, Farrakhan apologized through his lawyers to the British High Court, which had banned his entrance into the country since 1986. "In an ostensible change of heart, Mr. Farrakhan, who has prostate cancer, said he recognized that his remarks had been offensive. In place of his call to arms he is said to be 'preaching a new gospel' of self-reliance, discipline, and freedom from many of the perils that plague black America," explains Michael Hornsell, who suggests that Farrakhan's actions signal his attempt to construct a "new person," create a new relationship with his audience, and offer a new and perhaps more persuasive message. Those actions, however, continue to be received with skepticism. Hornsell continues: "That does not wash with the Board of Deputies of British Jews and other Jewish groups. One source said yesterday: 'When you look at his previous remarks, their meaning is inexcusable. A leopard does not change its spots.'"

Yet Americans of African descent have been committed to the belief that the community *can* change, whether by assimilating or integrating with white Americans, or seeking their own separate and distinct identities. All of these have been ways that Black people have tried to "change their spots," to reconstitute their sense of self, other, and situation. The question remains whether or not white Americans are capable of changing theirs. This continues to be a central preoccupation of the spiritual and rhetorical strivings that characterize the souls of Black folk, and Minister Louis Farrakhan's rhetoric embodies these strivings in their most vexing and perplexing forms. He is truly a "marred and marvelous portrait of ourselves," and his most recent rhetoric may suggest that he has matured into a man whose sense of self, other, and situation has become far more marvelous and much less marred. Finally, as Amy Alexander has written, "I accept Farrakhan as he is and, unlike some of his white detractors, do not view his Otherness as a source of fear. His most potent weapon to date has been his rhetoric." Perhaps Minister Farrakhan will turn that weapon into an instrument capable of sowing the seeds of a "new people," whose sense of self, other, and society might make of this old world, a new world.

INFORMATION SOURCES

Research Collections and Collected Speeches

Audiotapes and videotapes and transcripts of Farrakhan's speeches are in the Simon Wiesenthal Center in Los Angeles and The Final Call in Chicago. Video and audiotaped interviews and other archival materials may be obtained from the Schomburg Center for Research in Black Culture at the New York Public Library.

Eure, Joseph D., and Richard M. Jerome, eds. *Back Where We Belong: Selected Speeches by Minister Louis Farrakhan* [*BWB*]. Philadelphia: PC International Press, 1989.

Farrakhan, Louis. *Seven Speeches by Minister Louis Farrakhan* [*SS*]. Chicago: WKU and the Final Call, 1992.

Audiovisual Material

The Final Call [*FC*]. Audio and video copies of Minister Farrakhan's speeches can be obtained from Final Call, 734 W. 79th Street, Chicago, Ill. 60620, or online at http://www.finalcall.com

Selected Critical Studies

Alexander, Amy, ed. *The Farrakhan Factor: African American writers on Leadership, Nationhood and Minister Louis Farrakhan.* New York: Grove Press, 1998.

Arthos, John, Jr. "The Shaman–Trickster's Art of Misdirection: The Rhetoric of Farrakhan and the Million Men." *Quarterly Journal of Speech* 87 (2001): 41–60.

Barnes, Fred. "Farrakhan Frenzy: What's a Black Politician to Do?" *The New Republic*, October 1985, pp. 13–15.

Goldberg, Robert. "Jewish Devils and the War on Black America." In his *Enemies Within: The Culture of Conspiracy in Modern America.* New Haven, Conn.: Yale University Press, 2001.

Goldzwig, Steven R. "A Social Movement Perspective on Demagoguery: Achieving Symbolic Realignment." *Communication Studies* 40 (1989): 202–28.

Gordon, Dexter B. *Black Identity: Rhetoric, Ideology, and Nineteenth-Century Black Nationalism.* Carbondale: Southern Illinois University Press, 2003.

Hamblin, Ken. "Farrakhan a Dupe of Terrorists." *Denver Post*, November 18, 2001, p. E-04.

Hornsell, Michael. "Leader Who Inspires Love and Loathing." *The Times* (London), August 1, 2001.

Kramer, Michael. "Loud and Clear: Farrakhan's Anti-Semitism." *New York*, October 1985, pp. 22–23.

Marable, Manning. "In the Business of Prophet Making." *New Statesman*, December 1982, pp. 23–25.

McPhail, Mark. "Louis Abdul Farrakhan." In *African-American Orators: A Bio-Critical Soucebook*, ed. Richard Leeman. Westport, Conn.: Greenwood Press, 1996.

———. "Passionate Intensity: Louis Farrakhan and the Fallacies of Racial Reasoning." *Quarterly Journal of Speech* 84 (1998): 416–29.

Pauley, John L. II. "Reshaping Public Persona and the Prophetic Ethos: Louis Farrakhan at the Million Man March." *Western Journal of Communication* 62 (1998): 512–36.

Paulson, Michael. "Farrakhan's Nation of Islam Softening Stance." *Boston Globe*, March 4, 2000, p. B1.

Rosenblatt, Roger. "The Demagogue in the Crowd." *Time*, October 21, 1985, p. 102.

Singh, Robert. *The Farrakhan Phenomenon: Race, Reaction, and the Paranoid Style in American Politics.* Washington, D.C.: Georgetown University Press, 1997.

Smith, Robert C. *We Have No Leaders: African Americans in the Post-Civil Rights Era.* Albany: State University of New York Press, 1996.

Sullivan, Andrew. "Call to Harm: The Hateful Oratory of Minister Farrakhan. *The New Republic*, July 1990, pp. 13–15.

Watkins, S. Craig. "Framing Protest: News Media Frames of the Million Man March." *Critical Studies in Media Communication* 18 (2001): 83–101.

Selected Biographies

Gardell, Mattias. *In the Name of Elijah Muhammad: Louis Farrakhan and the Nation of Islam.* Durham, N.C.: Duke University Press, 1996.

Magida, Arthur. *Prophet of Rage: A Life of Louis Far-rakhan and His Nation*. New York: Basic Books, 1996.

CHRONOLOGY OF SPEECHES

See "Research Collections and Collected Speeches" for source codes.

"Congress of African People." Atlanta, Ga., September 1970. *SS*, pp. 123–36.

"Black Solidarity Day Address." New York City, November 2, 1970. *SS*, pp. 111–20.

"Minister Farrakhan on the Black Woman" (message at the East). Brooklyn, N.Y., January 1971. *SS*, pp. 13–39.

"Woe to the Hypocrites." n.p., n.d. *SS*, pp. 97–108.

"Warning to the Government of America." Washington, D.C., August 15, 1981. *FC*.

"Minister Farrakhan Speaks at Princeton University" ("What Is the Need for Black History?"). Princeton, N.J., 1984. *BWB*, pp. 47–79.

"P.O.W.E.R. at Last and Forever." Washington, D.C., July 22, 1985. *BWB*, pp. 143–67.

"Are Black People the Future World Rulers?" Chicago, April 12, 1987. *BWB*, pp. 225–55.

"Minster Farrakhan Challenges Black Men." Washington, D.C., October 16, 1995. CNN, at http://cnn.com/US/9510/megamarch/10-16/transcript/index.html

"World Press Conference from Mosque Maryam. The Honorable Minister Louis Farrakhan Responds to the ATTACK on AMERICA." September 16, 2001. *FC*.

GERALD RUDOLPH FORD (1913–)
Thirty-eighth President of the United States

HERMANN G. STELZNER, REVISED BY CHARLES F. OTTINGER

Gerald Rudolph Ford took the oath of office as president of the United States on August 9, 1974. The swearing in of the sixty-one-year-old vice president and former House minority leader took place in the East Room of the White House shortly after the departure of the man he succeeded, the impeached and disgraced Richard M. Nixon.

Many in the audience were Ford's friends in Congress, where he had served for twenty-five years as representative from Michigan's conservative Fifth District. His first speech after becoming president may have contained his most memorable utterance as holder of that office: "My fellow Americans, our long national nightmare is over."

Ford brought to the presidency talents developed in the House of Representatives: networking among colleagues, bargaining, negotiation, and other necessary political skills. He was regarded as a good mediator and counselor, and as being honest, loyal, straightforward, and friendly—in all, a decent man. He was a dependable but otherwise unremarkable professional politician who downplayed developing himself as a unique public persona.

Gerald Ford's ascendancy to the presidency was unique. He had been sworn in as vice president on December 6, 1973, succeeding Spiro Agnew, who had been forced to resign because of criminal charges stemming from his tenure as governor of Maryland. Ford insisted that his swearing-in ceremony take place in the Capitol, where he had previously hoped to become speaker of the House. In his address to those assembled he said, "I am a Ford, not a Lincoln," alluding to the latter's eloquence while ironically implying his own stylistic plainness, and defining himself by reference to two products central to the well-being of his home state of Michigan. Early in his political career, Ford reported that he "never thought of myself as a great orator," and nowhere in his public utterances is there recorded any strong aspiration to greater eloquence. Rather, he only asked his listeners to accept his modest communicative gifts for what they were, and himself for what he was.

The Watergate scandal, all-absorbing national crisis that it was at the time, has all too quickly receded in the minds of Americans. Michael

Schudson, in *Watergate in American Memory: How We Remember, Forget, and Reconstruct the Past*, notes a 1985 national survey asking what were the most important events of the past half-century, with these results:

World War II	29.3%
Vietnam	22.0%
Kennedy's Assassination	8.8%
Watergate	2.8% (14th place)

The Ford administration owed its very existence to Watergate, and Watergate in turn can be substantially traced to the wrenching trauma of the war in Vietnam. Schudson quotes journalist Sidney Blumenthal that "Watergate's 'underlying issue' was Vietnam." Schudson concludes, "Indeed, the investigation of Watergate itself in 1973 and 1974 can be judged a form of forgetting Vietnam."

These two crises were severe challenges, one in foreign affairs and the other in domestic, to the American civil religion, the national self-understanding of America as the "city on a hill," a shining beacon of "light to the nations." Vietnam and Watergate threw Americans' civil religion into doubt more than at any other time in the twentieth century. President Ford's task, from this perspective, was to restore and reconstruct America's foundational belief system, but there was little revival stirred from the bully pulpit of the Ford White House. Perhaps this was simply asking for too much.

FORD'S PROBLEMS AS PRESIDENTIAL PERSUADER

President Ford selected Nelson Rockefeller to be his vice president, and for the first time in the nation's history both the president and the vice president had not been elected to those offices, giving both officeholders the limited legitimacy of caretakers rather than the full authority attendant to a popular mandate.

In the wake of the climactic events of Vietnam that occurred during his term, such as the fall of Saigon to North Vietnamese forces on April 28, 1975, and Watergate as his presidency's precursor, Ford often mentioned the need for character and a restoration of values in his speeches, yet seemed unable to follow through with a rhetoric of moral urgency. He downplayed opportunities to deliver such messages, preferring metaphors of the marketplace and quotidian concerns.

Immediately after he took the oath of office on August 9, 1974, Ford said in his televised statement to the nation that his first duty was "to make an unprecedented compact with my countrymen. Not an inaugural speech, not a fireside chat, not a campaign speech, just a little straight talk among friends." Before a joint session of Congress on August 12, 1974, he returned to the automobile theme: "Only 8 months ago, when I last stood here, I told you I was a Ford, not a Lincoln. Tonight I say I am still a Ford, but I am not a Model T." After the 1976 presidential campaign, a note to President-elect Jimmy Carter began "Dear Jimmy," and was signed "Jerry Ford," not "President Gerald R. Ford."

Through his metaphors and self-representation Ford dissociated himself from Richard Nixon's "imperial presidency" and sought to restore a sense of decency, trust, and stability to government in a time of doubt. While Ford accomplished these rhetorical aims, he also consistently failed to inspire his hearers. His lack of charisma, the widespread disagreement over his pardon of former President Nixon, and the public disenchantment with the previous Republican administration resulted in Ford's inability to win his own full term as president in 1976.

Although he lost his bid for election, Ford re-

Gerald Ford's most famous public utterance came in his speech delivered after taking the oath of office for the presidency. Speaking on the White House lawn, Ford declared that the "long national nightmare is over." His speech is widely credited with helping heal a nation bitterly divided after the Watergate hearings.

---

alized that the public was grateful to have the presidency restored to an honest and unaffected man who served as an able caretaker of the office. The first sentence of President Jimmy Carter's 1977 Inaugural Address acknowledged this: "For myself and our nation, I want to thank my predecessor for all that he has done to heal our land."

Ford's contributions to the store of presidential eloquence are meager. His speeches were not models of invention and style. His delivery was not compelling. On balance, his platform appearances did not successfully communicate leadership qualities.

Prior to his formal announcement of candidacy in 1976, his staff prepared for him an assessment of his strengths and weaknesses as the Republican candidate. The report noted that as a campaigner and a speech maker, he needed improvement. He often mispronounced or stumbled over words, and confused the names of places where his campaign plane had touched down. These mistakes, forgivable in a lower-level office seeker, indicated the need for greater platform mastery from one who would be president.

When he had a text before him, Ford departed from it, adding adjectives, adverbs, and conjunctions that weakened the thrust of the prepared simple, declarative sentences. Audiences were not easily energized by lethargically delivered war and sports analogies. His staff warned him that he needed to discipline himself, especially on television, because when he got angry, he tended toward overkill. To counter the wooden qualities in his style, a professional comedy writer, Robert Orben, was hired to inject humor appropriate to Ford's manner.

Since Franklin D. Roosevelt, every president has used speechwriters to craft public statements. Ford was no exception, and his team was led by Robert Hartmann, a longtime employee. Ford clearly thought well of him, but others who worked with Hartmann believed that some of Ford's difficulties could be traced to Hartmann, whose personality was difficult and whose ways were fixed. Another problem was that Ford's ghostwriting team lacked depth of experience and a sense of commitment. More than the usual backbiting has been described in

public accounts. The problems were never surmounted.

Ford involved himself in the drafting of messages as issues required and his interest was engaged. For example, he insisted that a line in his 1976 State of the Union address—"1975 was not a year for summer soldiers and sunshine patriots," a direct reference to Thomas Paine's "The American Crisis"—remain despite staff objections.

The preparation of the 1976 State of the Union address illustrates his administration's sensitivity to evaluations of Ford's rhetorical efforts. His press secretary often reported to the press the hours that Ford himself had spent on it; the intense promotion of Ford's role in crafting the address was unusual. The address itself sounded better at the moment of utterance than when read in print, a reflection of media influence on invention and style. On balance, the speech was straightforward, optimistic, and energetic. Some evaluators rank it among Ford's best efforts.

Three rhetorical challenges particularly illustrate the rhetorical dimensions of Ford's presidency: the pardon of Richard M. Nixon, the war on inflation, and the 1976 campaign, marked by the struggle with Ronald Reagan for the Republican Party nomination and the general election campaign against Democrat Jimmy Carter.

Ford's first political test as president was to overcome the Nixon problem, a no-win issue for him. He chose to grant a "full, free and absolute pardon" to Nixon in order to "heal the wounds throughout the United States." The decision both cut short the potential aftermath of Watergate, which might have included an indictment and trial of former President Nixon, and aggravated old injuries. Ford's press secretary, Jerry ter Horst, promptly resigned to protest the decision.

Ford clearly hoped to close the book on Watergate, but the public and the press were angry and suspicious, as seen in the widespread public perception that he had "cut a deal" with former President Nixon before the pardon was granted. During the 1976 presidential campaign, Jimmy Carter exploited the pardon, consistently referring to the "Nixon–Ford administration."

After he assumed the presidency, Ford faced severe domestic problems: unemployment, energy (an issue that never captured his interest), and inflation, "Public Enemy No. 1," discussed through war metaphors that dominated his public speeches until his 1975 State of the Union address.

Citing the comic strip possum Pogo in his analysis of the inflation problem, Ford made the American people themselves the enemy—"We have met the enemy and he is us." To emphasize their personal involvement, Ford urged Americans to enlist in a WIN ("Whip Inflation Now") program and wear "WIN" buttons. Sylvia Porter, chair of the Citizens' Action Committee to Fight Inflation, was pleased when the program was discarded: "That wasn't our gimmick! You all know what happened—we were left with the job of building the airplane in the sky."

These tactics and tropes neither explained the problem nor mobilized the country. Given Ford's personal temperament and political caution, they were inappropriate to him, his audiences, and the times. The distance between Ford's imagery and his actions in support of the imagery raised questions about the authenticity of his analysis, and seemed more suited to the exhortations typical of the congressman Ford had been than to those of a national leader. The war metaphor demanded vigorous substantive action, which was not forthcoming. Asking the people to "plant WIN gardens" did not satisfy their need for action and leadership. Asked to accept the blame and the burden, citizens remained suspicious, dubious, and uncertain.

Before he could meet Jimmy Carter in the general election, Ford had to be nominated by the Republicans meeting in convention. Ronald Reagan challenged him vigorously in state primaries, testing the strength of his political ideology and his power base. The test continued on the convention floor until Ford earned the nomination by 57 votes more than the minimum of 1,130. As his running mate, Ford selected Robert Dole, a conservative acceptable to the Reagan camp. He invited Ronald and Nancy Reagan to share the stage with him when he delivered his acceptance speech. He came prepared with a well-polished text that he had practiced, videotaped, and evaluated. It contained no new ideas, but its language was direct, crisp, and energiz-

ing. Delivered flawlessly, it reached beyond the assembled Republicans. He identified himself with the broader audience: "You at home, listening tonight, you are the people who pay the taxes and obey the laws. You are the people who make the system work. You are the people who make America what it is. It is from your ranks that I come, and on your side that I stand." On that upbeat note, an unelected incumbent prepared for the 1976 presidential campaign.

Because Ford entered the campaign trailing Carter in the polls, he could not employ a "Rose Garden strategy," as it later came to be known (i.e., staying in the White House and goading Carter into mistakes). He actively entered the fray and managed to cut the distance between them.

Three debates modeled on the 1960 debates and sponsored by the League of Women Voters, the first to be held in a presidential general election since the 1960 Kennedy–Nixon debates, were scheduled: the first, on September 23 in Philadelphia, on domestic and economic issues; the second, on October 6 in San Francisco, on foreign policy and defense; the third, on October 22 in Williamsburg, Virginia, with an open agenda.

To many observers, Ford had a slight edge in the first debate; Carter was the stronger in the second and third. In the second debate, Ford, in response to a question, asserted, "There is no Soviet domination of Eastern Europe, and there never will be under a Ford administration." The self-inflicted wound was reflected in the polls, and efforts were made to cut the losses. For five days Ford insisted that no clarification was needed. Finally, on October 12, he agreed that he had erred, but the damage had been done. The gaffe again raised questions about his competence and seriously reduced his chances of overcoming Carter on Election Day.

On November 2, 1976, Carter defeated Ford by a margin of 49.9 percent to 47.9 percent of the votes cast. In the electoral college Carter garnered 297 votes; Ford, 241. The public's perceptions about Ford could not be changed, and Ford's rhetoric certainly contributed to its judgment. The public's criteria for public discourse had not been met.

INFORMATION SOURCES

Research Collections and Collected Speeches

The Gerald R. Ford Library, Ann Arbor, Michigan, contains extensive materials about his political career in the House of Representatives and in the White House. Some of his papers from after his presidency are also held at the library, but most are not currently open to scholars. Speech drafts and other preliminary documents can be accessed only in person. Many other documents, such as the papers of various aides to the president, public reaction mail, and formerly confidential memoranda, are summarized by topic on the Web site.

The Presidential Speeches and Public Statements series is particularly useful to rhetorical researchers. Secondary sources include oral histories, dissertations, and other aids associated with the presidential library system. Ford's speeches were prepared under the aegis of the Office of Editorial Staff, and speech sources are gathered in the Theis-Orben files. The Gerald R. Ford Foundation offers grants to support scholarly research based in part on the library's holdings.

Bitzer, Lloyd, and Theodore Reuter. *Carter vs. Ford: The "Counterfeit Debates" of 1976* [*CF*]. Madison: University of Wisconsin Press, 1980.

The Great Debates: Carter vs. Ford, 1976 [*TGD*], ed. Sidney Kraus. Bloomington: Indiana University Press, 1979.

Presidential Rhetoric, 1961–1980 [*PR*], ed. Theodore Windt, 2nd ed. Dubuque, Iowa: Kendall/Hunt, 1980.

Public Papers of the Presidents of the United States: Gerald R. Ford, 6 vols (1975–79) [*PPP*]. Washington, D.C.: Government Printing Office.

Web Sites

Gerald R. Ford Library and Museum [*GRFL*]. This Web site indexes many primary documents, such as the final drafts of speeches and some audio recordings of the speeches, that are available electronically at this University of Texas Web site. www.ford.utexas.edu

Theis-Orben files. A part of the Gerald R. Ford Library in Ann Arbor, Mich., these files include secondary files regarding speech preparation. www.fordlibrarymuseum.gov

Audiovisual Material

Audio recordings of some of Ford's presidential speeches may be accessed through the University of Texas Web site. www.ford.utexas.edu

Selected Critical Studies

Evans, Rowland, and Robert Novak. "Jerry Ford: The Eisenhower of the Seventies." *Atlantic Monthly*, August 1974, pp. 25–32.

Hahn, Dan F. "Corrupt Rhetoric: President Ford and the Mayaguez Affair." *Communication Quarterly* 28 (1980): 38–43.

Hart, Roderick P. *Verbal Style and the Presidency*. Orlando, Fla.: Academic Press, 1984.

Howell, David, Margaret-Mary Howell, and Robert Kronman. *Gentlemanly Attitudes: Jerry Ford and the Campaign of 1976*. Washington, D.C.: HKJV Publications, 1980.

President Ford: The Man and His Record. Washington, D.C.: Congressional Quarterly, 1974.

Stelzner, Hermann G. "Ford's War on Inflation: A Metaphor That Did Not Cross." *Communication Monographs* 44 (1977): 284–97.

Selected Biographies

Barber, James David. *The Presidential Character: Predicting Performance in the White House*, 2nd ed. Englewood Cliffs, N.J.: Prentice-Hall, 1977.

Casserly, John J. *The Ford White House: The Diary of a Speech Writer*. Boulder: Colorado Associated University Press, 1977.

Ford, Gerald R. *A Time to Heal*. New York: Harper & Row, 1979.

Greene, John Robert. *The Presidency of Gerald R. Ford*. Lawrence: University Press of Kansas, 1995.

Hartmann, Robert T. *Palace Politics : An Inside Account of the Ford Years*. New York: McGraw-Hill, 1980.

Nessen, Ron. *It Sure Looks Different from the Inside*. Chicago: Playboy Press, 1978.

Osborne, John. *White House Watch: The Ford Years*. Washington, D.C.: New Republic Books, 1977.

Reeves, Richard. *A Ford, Not a Lincoln*. New York: Harcourt Brace Jovanovich, 1975.

Vestal, Bud. *Jerry Ford, Up Close*. New York: Coward, McCann & Geoghegan, 1974.

Witcover, Jules. *Marathon: The Pursuit of the Presidency, 1972–1976*. New York: Viking Press, 1977.

CHRONOLOGY OF MAJOR SPEECHES

See "Research Collections and Collected Speeches" for source codes.

"Remarks on Taking the Oath of Office." Washington, D.C., August 9, 1974. *PPP*, 1974; *GRFL*.

"Address to Joint Session of Congress." Washington, D.C., August 12, 1974. *PPP*, 1974.

"Remarks on Signing a Proclamation Granting Pardon to Richard Nixon." Washington, D.C., September 8, 1974. *PPP*, 1974; *GRFL*.

"Address on the Economy Before a Joint Session of Congress." Washington, D.C., October 8, 1974. *PPP*, 1974.

"State of the Union Address." Washington, D.C., January 15, 1975. *PPP*; *GRFL*.

"Address Before the Conference on Security and Co-operation in Europe." Helsinki, Finland, August 1, 1975. *PPP*; *GRFL*.

"State of the Union Address." Washington, D.C., January 19, 1976. *PPP*; *GRFL*.

"Remarks in Philadelphia, Pennsylvania" (bicentennial celebration). July 4, 1976. *PPP*; *GRFL*.

"Republican Party Nomination Acceptance Address." Kansas City, Mo., August 19, 1976. *PPP*; *GRFL*.

"State of the Union Address." Washington, D.C., January 12, 1977. *PPP*; *GRFL*.

"Speech to the Republican National Convention." Philadelphia, August 1, 2000.

ALBERT ARNOLD GORE, JR. (1948–)
Vice President of the United States, U.S. Senator, Presidential Candidate

DAVID HOFFMAN

As an orator, Al Gore, Jr., displayed both extraordinary assets and extraordinary liabilities. There is little doubt that he was a bright star: a man of dignity, intelligence, and deep commitment who attained some soaring moments of oratory. There is also little doubt that Gore had a chronic image problem. At his best he is passionate and authoritative, yet for years he has been plagued by a reputation for being a wooden, patronizing serial exaggerator. Al Gore's public communication lay at the heart of both his successes and his failures.

Albert Arnold Gore, Jr., came from a political family. His parents were Albert Gore, Sr., a Democratic senator from Smith County in central Tennessee, and Pauline LaFon Gore. He was born in Washington D.C., on March 31, 1948, the second of two children. His sister, Nancy LeFon Gore (later Nancy Gore-Hunger), was ten years his elder. Gore's early life taught him about both politics and farm work. He split his time between an apartment on Washington's Embassy Row, where he lived with his parents while attending St. Albans Episcopal School for Boys, and the family farm in Possum Hollow, Tennessee, where his father sent him each summer with a long list of chores. Gore met his future wife, Mary Elizabeth Aitcheson, familiarly called "Tipper," at a senior dance at St. Albans in 1965. When Gore enrolled in Harvard University, Tipper followed him to Boston. After graduating from Harvard in 1969, Gore married, enlisted in the Army, and was assigned to Vietnam as a journalist. Later, he worked as an investigative journalist and attended Vanderbilt Law School. His political opportunity came in 1976, when Tennessee's 4th District seat, which his father had once held, opened up. He won his way into the House of Representatives easily, with a campaign in which he promised to bring down energy prices and close tax loopholes exploited by the wealthy. In the meantime, he and Tipper had started a family: Karenna, the first of four children, was born in 1973. She was followed by Kristin (1977), Sarah (1979), and Albert III (1982).

In the House, Gore developed a reputation as a hardworking, media-savvy policy expert, a man committed to both ideas and ideals. He staked out a political position as a "screaming moderate" who crusaded against corporate abuses, involving himself with everything from baby-food regulation to the Superfund, but also voted for a number of pro-life measures and was moderately hawkish in matters of foreign policy. He gained prominence as an expert in nuclear arms policy.

Gore won a Senate seat in 1984 when the Republican majority leader, Howard Baker of Tennessee, stepped aside in preparation for his presidential bid in 1988. The most notable crusade conducted by a Gore during Al's first year in the Senate was a campaign against "porn-rock" led by Tipper, cofounder of the Parents' Music Resource Center, that culminated in Senate hearings on the subject and a public tiff with musician Frank Zappa. Gore ran for president in 1988 and carried seven states in the primaries, but he was ultimately unsuccessful in obtaining the nomination. He easily won a second term in the Senate in 1990.

Between Gore's primary defeat and his reelection to the Senate, a near-tragedy struck his family. While leaving a baseball game at Baltimore Memorial Stadium, young Albert III was hit by a car and badly injured. For a month Al and Tipper watched over his recovery in the hospital. Also around this time, Tipper was diagnosed with clinical depression and began to undergo therapy. These experiences prompted a period of soul-searching for Gore that he negotiated by writing his environmental manifesto, *Earth in the Balance* (1992), a book in which all his idealism is on display as he calls for elimination of the internal combustion engine within twenty-five years and describes how the environment can become an organizing principle of politics.

Gore decided not to seek the presidency in 1992, saying that he was not willing to spend so much time away from his family so soon after his son's accident. But he was unexpectedly returned to presidential politics when Bill Clinton asked him to be his running mate. The two Democrats defeated incumbents George H. W. Bush and Dan Quayle.

In the early days of the administration, while Clinton's policies on gays in the military and health-care reform foundered, Gore scored a success with his initiative to reinvent government (REGO), shrinking the federal establishment to its smallest size since the Kennedy administration. Over the course of his term as vice president, Gore was influential, especially on matters of for-

eign policy and the environment. The Clinton–Gore administration remained popular enough to win a reelection in 1996. But Gore had his share of problems in office: a fund-raising scandal during his second term, and the revelation of Clinton's relationship with Monica Lewinsky and subsequent impeachment were a taxing ordeal. Still, it was a foregone conclusion that Vice President Gore would seek the presidency in 2000. After the defeat of his most significant primary opponent, Bill Bradley, Gore's campaign was energized by his naming of Senator Joseph Lieberman as his running mate, the first Jewish man to seek the vice presidency as a major party candidate. After accepting the Democratic nomination, the Gore–Lieberman ticket gained a strength that lasted until the election, despite Gore's having difficulty in living up to inflated expectations about how he would perform in the televised debates against his opponent, George W. Bush.

The election of 2000 was unique in American history. Watching it was like watching a flipped coin soar end over end through the air, only to land on its edge and refuse to fall either way. Gore won most of the east and west coasts, but lost most of the heartland and the South, including his home state of Tennessee, to Bush. He won 50.2 percent of the popular vote, but the outcome of the election was determined by the electoral vote count, in particular, the twenty-five electoral votes of Florida. The outcome in Florida was so close that a recount was automatically triggered under state law. After more than two weeks, Bush was declared the winner in Florida by 537 votes. Gore filed a lawsuit that challenged the election in Florida on the basis of voting irregularities and confusing ballots. The case went quickly to the Supreme Court, which voted 5–4 in favor of the Bush team's defense of the Florida outcome. Gore delivered his concession speech on December 13.

There was hope among some Democrats that Gore would make another try for the presidency in 2004. However, the former vice president announced in December 2002 that he would not run again, explaining that his candidacy would put the focus of the election on the past, and that the nation needed to have a debate about the future in 2004.

AL GORE: THE POPULIST PATRICIAN

Gore has delivered numerous addresses in the House and the Senate on legislative matters, but it is in campaign speeches, particularly his addresses to the Democratic National Convention (DNC) between 1992 and 2000, that the defining themes of his political oratory emerge. In these speeches Gore frequently cast himself as a defender of common people against the abuses of profit-driven corporations, powerful special interests, and their Republican allies. This stance is apparent in his 2000 DNC speech:

> Whether you're in a suburb or an inner city, whether you raise crops or drive hogs and cattle on a farm, drive a big rig on the interstate or drive e-commerce on the Internet, whether you're starting out to raise your own family or

votes and isolating right-wing Republicans in much the same way that Reagan was able to steal the center and isolate left-wing Democrats during the 1980s.

Gore's strategy of centrist populism is nowhere more evident than in his frequent use of family as an organizing theme in campaign speeches. In his 1996 DNC speech the family emerged as an organizing principle used to join a wide range of issues, such as product safety, the environment, violence on television, family and medical leave, education, the economy, health-care reform, gun control, and even smoking. In the 2000 presidential campaign, when Gore needed to increase his appeal to labor, family was again the vehicle. Simple references to the family changed to references to "working families," and a more labor-friendly message

---

At his best, Al Gore expresses complicated ideas in plain words, producing a political prose that is by turns both teacherly and journalistic: "Just as the false assumption that we are not connected to the earth has led to the ecological crisis, so the equally false assumption that we are not connected to each other has led to our social crisis."

—*Al Gore*, Earth in the Balance

> getting ready to retire after a lifetime of hard work, so often powerful forces and powerful interests stand in your way, and the odds seem stacked against you, even as you do what's right for you and your family.

Gore's rhetoric, especially in the 2000 campaign, has been called populist. The label is accurate in that Gore has seen himself as the champion of ordinary people against big business interests. Of course there are many kinds of populism, a term which simply designates a position that champions the cause of common people against any sort of elite. Gore's populism is a centrist populism, through which he and his New Democrat allies at the Council for Democratic Leadership have tried to move the Democratic platform to the very middle of the political spectrum, stealing moderate Republican

was grafted onto the series of issues already clustered around the family: "Together, let's make sure that our prosperity enriches not just the few, but all working families. Let's invest in health care, education, a secure retirement and middle-class tax cuts."

Gore's own experiences as a father and a brother have made seemingly unrelated subjects, such as the Republican agenda and tobacco regulation, into family matters, and have provided the basis for some of his most compelling and controversial moments of oratory. In his 1992 DNC speech, he deftly turned a moving story of his son's nearly fatal accident into an analogical indictment of the Bush–Quayle administration. Gore made a similar move in his 1996 DNC speech when he related the story, in graphic detail, of his sister Nancy's death from lung cancer, thus showing in the most explicit terms the impact of the tobacco industry on family life and justifying the need for tobacco regulation in terms of protecting families.

The environment has been another abiding theme in Gore's oratory. Gore has worked hard to make it into the same kind of center-populist issue as the family, but with somewhat less success. The threats posed by toxic chemicals, the hole in the ozone layer, and global warming are classed together with the danger of tobacco and other "invisible threats" posed by "powerful interests." In campaign speeches, such as the 1992 DNC speech, and in policy speeches specifically about the environment, such as his 1997 speech to the Kyoto Climate Change Conference in Japan, Gore treated the environment in essentially the same way that he does in *Earth in the Balance*, arguing for an essential connection between environmental and social problems:

> The task of saving the earth's environment must and will become the central organizing principle of the post-Cold War world. And just as the false assumption that we are not connected to the earth has led to the ecological crisis, so the equally false assumption that we are not connected to each other has led to our social crisis.

It is in the area of delivery that Gore's greatest liabilities, as well as some hidden strengths, lie. Critics complain that Gore is "stiff" or "wooden" and also "patronizing." These charges are founded more on his manner of speaking than upon the content of his speeches or their rhetorical style. The charge of stiffness is rooted in a body language that is almost always deliberate. Especially in contrast to his running mate Clinton, Gore gives the impression of never speaking a word or even raising an eyebrow without careful consideration. This unrelenting sense of purpose is reinforced by a speech pattern full of pregnant pauses. The overall effect gives some the impression that Gore is not really "being himself," and so perhaps cannot be trusted, and others have the impression that keeping his speech as slow and as simple as possible is condescending. The reality is probably closer to this: Gore is very serious about his political speeches, and so he habitually speaks in a manner that allows him

time to carefully consider what he is saying and how he is saying it.

Unable to completely shake his habitual pattern of speech, Gore has developed several strategies to live with, and even exploit, it. He realized early on that a reputation for stiffness was not incompatible with the image of the morally upright idealist he was cultivating, and rather than trying to divest himself of "stiffness," he joked about it. At the opening of his 1996 DNC speech, he performed the "Al Gore version of the macarena," a popular and highly kinetic dance of the time, by standing perfectly still and moving his eyes from side to side. This was just one of many instances of Gore mocking his own deliberate manner. In so doing he created an ironic distance between himself and his presentation style that invited listeners to take what he was saying as seriously as he did, even while they were given a space to laugh with him at the way he was saying it.

Leaving his manner of delivery aside and considering only his use of language, Gore, at his best, expresses complicated ideas in plain words, producing a political prose that is by turns both teacherly and journalistic. He avoids the use of arcane words for their own sake, and is careful to explain the technical terms that are necessary in his discussions of policy. Even though his sentences are generally more grammatically complex and varied than is usual in American political oratory, Gore avoids the frequent use of flashy rhetorical devices, such as antithesis and alliteration, that characterizes the oratory of John F. Kennedy, Jesse Jackson, and even George W. Bush in his prepared remarks.

Gore does make use of personal narratives, a rhetorical device common in American political oratory, calculated to produce audience involvement. In the wake of Reagan's success with personal stories, many politicians have turned to them, but few have done so with more vigor than Gore as he talked about his son's accident and his sister's death. Although the convention crowds were visibly moved on both occasions, critics questioned the tactic of playing upon personal tragedy for political gain. Perhaps in response to such criticisms, or perhaps because it had become standard form for presidential candidates, in 2000 Gore used several shorter stories of individuals in the audience to personalize his policy points.

Despite his reputation for being wooden, Gore did become known as a master of the peculiar kind of debate that candidates for high political office engage in on television. His success might be attributed, in part, to the way he was able to use his confrontational style to force opponents into "losing moments." One peculiarity of televised debate is that it is more often lost than won. In front of a large television audience with a limited ability to follow complex argumentation, it is rare for a candidate to clearly win a debate, because both sides typically have good principles and well-founded policies at first glance. It is more common for one candidate to lose a debate, and the other to win by default. This occurs when an inconsistency or weakness is dramatically exposed, as when Gerald Ford appeared to claim that eastern Europe was not occupied by the Soviet Union in his 1976 confrontation with Jimmy Carter, when Lloyd Bensen KO'd Dan Quayle with his "You're no Jack Kennedy" line in 1988, or when George H. W. Bush undercut himself by looking impatiently at his watch in a presidential debate in 1992.

Beginning in the 1988 presidential primaries, Gore developed a strategy to capitalize on the fact that televised debates are more "losable" than "winnable." He sought to find and expose his opponents' chief vulnerabilities in a dramatic way, using confrontation to force them into a "losing moment." He confronted Richard Gephardt with the charge of being inconsistent and changing his vote on a range of issues, including abortion, an issue on which he himself had changed his position. He confronted Michael Dukakis about being weak on defense and crime, the very issues that Bush would exploit to his advantage in the general election. Gore began to accumulate a reputation as a formidable debater as these moments were picked up by the media and were used in his own campaign advertising.

Gore was at his best in his 1993 debate with Ross Perot about the North American Free Trade Agreement (NAFTA) on CNN's *Larry King Live* show. If Gephardt's perceived weakness had been his policy shifts, and Dukakis' his softness on defense, Perot, who had been a Reform Party

candidate for president in 1992, was liable to lose his temper when rubbed the wrong way. Gore set about devising a strategy to exploit this trait. In the first few minutes of the debate he intentionally but subtly interrupted Perot several times, and then proceeded to give him a lecture on the Smoot–Hawley Tariff Act, an infamous piece of legislation that had raised tariffs to record high levels in 1930 and caused dramatic declines in international trade. The lesson was delivered in Gore's cool and patronizing manner, and concluded with Gore presenting a framed picture of "Mr. Smoot and Mr. Hawley" to Perot. Perot's composure was destroyed by the interruptions and the patronizing lecture, and he reacted with extreme indignation, accusing both Gore and the host, Larry King, of not giving him a fair chance to speak, hurting his own case in the process. To add injury to insult, Gore not only effectively responded to the points Perot managed to sputter, but he also presented evidence suggesting that Perot's business interests would benefit from the rejection of NAFTA.

Gore's debates with George W. Bush in 2000 yielded results that contrasted sharply with his outright defeat of Perot. By the time Gore confronted Bush, he had acquired a towering reputation as, in the words of James Fallows, "the most lethal debater in politics." But because televised debate is a psychological game of expectations, Gore's reputation worked against him. Few expected Bush to be able to compete with Gore in debate. Consequently, when Bush was able to hold his own, it registered as a psychological victory because he had exceeded expectations. A similar coup had taken place in Gore's 1992 confrontation with Dan Quayle, who also had benefited from low expectation.

Gore made a strong effort over the course of the three 2000 presidential debates. He made policy personal with the narratives of real American families. He repeated that he would put Social Security funds in a "lockbox" to ensure that the phrase made the news. He hammered Bush with questions about where the money for his tax cuts would come from. He even attempted to ruffle the Texas governor's feathers by walking to within a few inches of him and towering over him imposingly. But nothing quite succeeded.

The Bush team, knowing they could win by

merely fighting to a draw, had carefully studied Gore's long record and developed strategies of distraction and disruption to counter Gore's confrontational style of debating. The Republican spinners were able to frame the contest so that the focus was not who had prevailed on which issues, but rather on how Gore had conducted himself. Gore was condemned by this treatment to wander like Goldilocks from debate to debate, looking for the approach that was "just right." The verdict on the first debate was that Gore was too aggressive. In the second debate he was too soft. In the final debate he was about right, but too late. The consequence of these maneuvers was that media coverage of how Gore was doing distracted the audience from Gore's preferred sound bite about putting Social Security funds in a lockbox.

Knowing that Gore sometimes took interpretive liberties with his narratives and his reading of his opponents' records, the Bush team employed an army of fact-checkers to sift through Gore's statements. Unsurprisingly, they found a few flaws. In the first debate, Gore told the story of how a girl named Kailey Ellis, a high school student in Florida, "has to stand in her science class." The next day it came out that in fact Kailey now had a seat. Of course the school *was* overcrowded, and of course Kailey *did* have to stand in class in the past, but Gore's use of the present rather than the past tense qualified as a bona fide exaggeration which the press talked about for days, disrupting the positive effect not only of the story but of the entire debate for Gore.

The final outcome of Gore's debates with Bush was miles from what the Gore team might have hoped. Gore had a higher quota of incidents which could be viewed as "losing moments" than did Bush. Two occurred in the first debate. One was the Kailey Ellis story. The other was a series of loud sighs that escaped Gore while Bush was speaking. Since the average viewer could not find fault with the organizing principles or logic of either side, it was Gore who seemed to lose by "breaking the rules" in stretching the truth about Kailey and being uncivil with his sighs. It is difficult to understand why Gore sighed. The commonly presumed explanation, that Gore sighed unconsciously, seems unlikely. Judging by his record, Gore rarely does anything

unconsciously in public. One can only speculate that the sighs were intended to disconcert Bush as interruptions had disconcerted Perot. If they were, they were a giant miscalculation. The sighs served only to confirm the public perception that Gore was condescending.

Overall, Gore's oratorical successes outnumber his failures. Yet, undeniably, Gore still suffers from a bad reputation as a speaker, and one can ask what created his image problem. Doubtless, for a good part of the explanation, one need look no further than the occupational hazards of being vice president, particularly the vice president of a popular and charismatic president. The vice president is necessarily kept from appearing so commanding or charismatic as to overshadow the president, so in the public mind he becomes quintessentially a background figure. Because he appears in a subordinate role, many attribute an essentially subordinate nature to the vice president. At the beginning of the 2000 campaign, many questioned Gore's viability as an independent political entity.

Gore was also hurt by the simple fact that someone who is vice president for eight years necessarily accumulates a lengthy public record of statements that can be used against him. This is, no doubt, one of the reasons why looking for real and imagined exaggerations and lies in Gore's public statements became a national sport for the press corps at one stage of the election: Gore's critics had a mountain of public statements in which to hunt. Gore, like all politicians, has on occasion made statements that were inaccurate or that pushed the limits of plausible interpretation. His characterization of Dukakis' position on "Soviet client states" in Central America in a 1988 debate, for instance, appears to have been a purposeful mischaracterization. But many of his celebrated "lies and exaggerations," including his alleged statement that he "invented the Internet," are themselves rooted in inaccurate and politically motivated misreadings of what Gore did and said.

Gore also experienced some problems that had nothing to do with having been vice president. There was in him an odd blend of aristocrat and populist that many people had trouble accepting. Gore was a Washington insider who saw himself as a champion of the common person. But many common people didn't believe a Washington insider could be their champion. This is why the title "Prince Albert," given Gore in the *Doonesbury* comic strip, stuck. Gore's choice of product safety, the environment, and the arms race as pet issues, and his diligence in understanding them, further contributed to the problem by throwing into the mix the labels "idealist" and "intellectual." Gore did not particularly mind either designation, but every time he started talking about chlorofluorocarbons and ozone, he confirmed for some segments of the audience that "Prince Albert" did not live in quite the same world as everyone else.

Finally, Gore's greatest personal asset was the same quality that was perhaps his greatest political liability: the overwhelming sense of seriousness and purpose that he projected. Where Clinton made politics look like fun, even Gore's jokes were animated by a serious political purpose. Such seriousness made more than a few people suspicious of him. To them, Gore seemed untrustworthy exactly because he worked so hard to achieve. A man filled with such a strong ambition must be capable of doing or saying anything to get what he wanted, the reasoning went, and therefore cannot be trusted. Gore's most effective answer to these charges was, ironically, in his speech conceding the 2000 presidential race, where he showed himself to be both a true patriot and a decent human being when he put the interests of the country before his own ambition by accepting the Supreme Court decision that gave the election to Bush, despite his strong personal disagreement with it. "This is America," he said. "Just as we fight hard when the stakes are high, we close ranks and come together when the contest is done."

INFORMATION SOURCES

Research Collections and Collected Speeches

There are no archival or published collections of Gore's speeches at this time. There is a compendium of Gore quotations titled *The World According to Gore: An A-to-Z Compilation of His Opinions, Positions, and Public Statements*. Videos of some of Gore's convention speeches and candidate debates are on the C-SPAN and League of Women Voters' Web sites. Transcripts of many of Gore's campaign speeches, candidate debates, and vice presidential speeches are available through the Web sites of C-SPAN, the Commission on Presidential Debates, the Gore 2000 Campaign, and the National Archives.

Kauffmann, Joseph, ed. *The World According to Gore: An A-to-Z Compilation of His Opinions, Positions, and Public Statements*. Los Angeles: Renaissance Books, 1999.

Web Sites

Al Gore for President Campaign [*AGC*]. As of this writing, Gore's campaign Web site still provides transcripts of his convention speeches and many other presidential campaign speeches. www.al_gore-2004.org/gorespeeches

Commission on Presidential Debates [*CPD*]. This Web site includes transcripts of all Gore's presidential and vice presidential debates. www.debates.org

C-SPAN's Web site [*CS*] includes transcripts of the 2000 presidential debates as well as the 2000 convention speeches, political commercials, and material related to the postelection contest, including Gore's concession speech. www.c-span.org/

The National Archives [*NARA*]. Includes transcripts of various speeches Gore gave as vice president.

Audiovisual Materials

C-SPAN's Web site has videos of the 2000 presidential debates as well as the 2000 convention speeches, political commercials, and material related to the postelection contest, including Gore's concession speech. www.c-span.org/

The League of Women Voters' Web site includes two videos of the 1988 Democratic primary debates that featured Gore. www.lwv.org/media/debates/1988.html

Selected Critical Studies

Boehlert, Eric. "The Press vs. Al Gore." *Rolling Stone*, December 6, 2001, pp. 53–57.
Fallows, James. "An Acquired Taste." *The Atlantic*, July 2000, pp. 33–48.
Klein, Joe, and Jane Mayer. "The Anxiety of Influence." *The New Yorker*, November 22, 1999, pp. 70–79.
Lemann, Nicholas. "Gore Without a Script." *The New Yorker*, July 31, 2000, pp. 44–63.
Pomper, Gerald M. "The 2000 Presidential Election: Why Gore Lost." *Political Science Quarterly* 116 (2001): 201–23.
Simons, Herbert W. "Judging a Policy Proposal by the Company It Keeps: The Gore–Perot NAFTA Debate." *Quarterly Journal of Speech* 82, no. 3 (1996): 274–87.
Walman, Paul, and Kathleen Hall Jamieson. "Rhetor-

ical Convergence and Issue Knowledge in the 2000 Presidential Election." *Presidential Studies Quarterly* 33, no. 1 (March 2003): 145–63.

Selected Biographies

Turque, Bill. *Inventing Al Gore: A Biography*. Boston: Houghton Mifflin, 2000.

Zelnick, Bob. *Gore: A Political Life*. Washington, D.C.: Regnery, 1999.

CHRONOLOGY OF MAJOR SPEECHES

See "Research Collections and Collected Sources" for source codes.

"Remarks at the First Annual Family Reunion Conference." Nashville, Tenn., April 25, 1992. Available at www.familyreunion.org/

"Facing the Crisis of Spirit" (acceptance of vice presidential nomination at the 1992 Democratic National Convention). New York City, July 16, 1992. *Vital Speeches of the Day*, August 15, 1992, pp. 646–48.

"The Gore–Quayle–Stockdale Vice Presidential Debate." Atlanta, Ga., October 13, 1992. Available at *CPD*.

"NAFTA Debate: Gore vs. Perot." *Larry King Live*, November 9, 1993. Available at http://ggallarotti. web.wesleyan.edu/govt155/goreperot.htm

"The National Information Infrastructure: Information Conduits, Providers, Appliances and Consumers" (address to the Television Academy, University of California, Los Angeles). January 11, 1994. *Vital Speeches of the Day*, February 1, 1994, pp. 229–33.

"Cynicism or Faith: The Future of Democratic Society" (Harvard commencement address). Cambridge, Mass., June 9, 1994. *Vital Speeches of the Day*, August 15, 1994, pp. 645–49.

"The Rapid Growth of Human Population: Sustainable Economic Growth" (address to the National Press Club). Washington, D.C., August 25, 1994. *Vital Speeches of the Day*, October 1, 1994, pp. 741–45.

"Let's Continue the Journey" (acceptance of the vice presidential nomination at the 1996 Democratic National Convention). Chicago, August 27, 1996. *Vital Speeches of the Day*, September 15, 1996, pp. 712–14.

"The Gore–Kemp Vice Presidential Debate." St. Petersburg, Fla., October 9, 1996. Available at *CPD*.

"Remarks as Prepared for Delivery for Vice President Al Gore at the Kyoto Climate Change Conference." Kyoto, Japan, December 8, 1997. Available at *NARA*.

"Remarks as Prepared for Delivery by Vice President Al Gore at the World Economic Forum, Davos." Davos, Switzerland, January 29, 1999. Available at *NARA*.

"Democratic Primary Debate." Nashua, N.H., December 17, 1999. Available at *CS*.

"Democratic Primary Debate." New York City, February 21, 2000. Available at *CS*.

"Making America All It Can Be" (acceptance of the presidential nomination at the 2000 Democratic National Convention). Los Angeles, August 17, 2000. *Vital Speeches of the Day*, September 1, 2000, pp. 674–79. *CS*.

"First 2000 Gore–Bush Presidential Debate." Boston, October 3, 2000. Available at *CPD; CS*.

"Second 2000 Gore–Bush Presidential Debate." Winston-Salem, N.C., October 11, 2000. Available at *CPD; CS*.

"Speech at a Rally at Wayne State University." Detroit, Mich., October 14, 2000. Available at *AGC*.

"Third 2000 Gore–Bush Presidential Debate." St. Louis, Mo., October 17, 2000. Available at *CPD; CS*.

"Concession of the 2000 Presidential Election." Washington, D.C., December 13, 2000. *CS*.

"A Commentary on the War Against Terror: Our Larger Tasks" (address delivered to the Council on Foreign Relations). New York City, February 12, 2002. Transcript and video available at www.cfr.org/reg_issues.php?id=13|||5&puby=2002

WILLIAM FRANKLIN (BILLY) GRAHAM, JR. (1918–)
Christian Evangelist

HAL W. FULMER AND JENNIFER YOUNG ABBOTT

In 1949 William Franklin Graham, Jr. arrived in Los Angeles virtually unknown, just another of the nomadic evangelists who had crisscrossed the American landscape since the earliest days of the Republic. In a large tent on the corner of Washington Boulevard and Hill Street, this youthful minister of thirty preached a nightly message of people's sin, God's love, and Christ's sacrifice.

Eight weeks later, long after the original deadline for the conclusion of the revival, near physical exhaustion and having preached his entire repertoire of sermons, Billy Graham remained in Los Angeles—but now as a national figure whose revival was documented by such news magazines as *Time* and *Life*. A crowd estimated at greater than 9,000, the largest single gathering for a revival since the days of Billy Sunday, swelled his "canvas cathedral" at the final session on November 20. During the eight weeks of the revival, Graham preached to over 300,000 persons and delivered more than sixty sermons; more than 6,000 listeners came forward after the sermons to publicly affirm their responses to his oratory. Well-known athletes and media personalities came forward, at Graham's urging, to acknowledge their acceptance of his message. Within days, they were back on the platform with him, delivering their testimony of the events, setting a trend that continues today with the Graham crusades. As Graham biographer John Pollock notes of Graham's early Los Angeles days: "The people came because Graham preached with authority—and preached to the times." Graham's recollection of Los Angeles, forty-eight years later in his autobiography *Just as I Am*, accurately anticipated "that the phenomenon of the Los Angeles tent Campaign at Washington and Hill Streets would forever change the face of my ministry and my life."

In the following five decades, Graham became the best-known American evangelist of the twentieth century. He has preached the Christian message of sin and redemption to an estimated 100 million individuals who have heard him in person. How many people have heard these same messages via radio, television, and film is incalculable, although conservative estimates suggest a figure in the high hundreds of millions. Billy Graham probably has preached the Christian gospel more times and to more persons than any other religious figure in the history of Christianity. In 1990, *Life* magazine named him one of the "100 most important Americans" of the twentieth century.

Graham's rise to oratorical fame began with the early development of his religious beliefs and practices. His parents took the matter of religion seriously as members of the Associate Reformed Presbyterian Church, a rather formal and fundamentalist group that sang only psalms and had a strict observance of the Sabbath. For Graham, Sunday meant no comics, no baseball, and no frivolity. Activities, besides church attendance, included the reading of Scripture and religious tracts and listening to Charles Fuller's *Old-Fashioned Revival Hour* on the radio. Graham's father sternly enforced his son's religious observance; he once whipped Graham for fidgeting during a sermon and, on a later occasion, for chewing tobacco. According to Graham biographer Marshall Frady, Graham recalled of these days: "I didn't like Sundays then at all. I dreaded to see them come."

Graham's father, who apparently wanted to become a preacher but failed to receive "the call" from God, fervently hoped that his son would receive a God-inspired message to preach. For a Southern preacher of popular religion, the key element was knowing that God had personally "called" the person to the pulpit as an interpreter of the Almighty's will for the people. Together with Graham's mother, the elder Graham went about preparing his son for such a calling. By the age of ten, Graham had memorized the 107 articles of the Short Catechism of the Presbyterian faith. He was also required to participate in one sentence prayers and Scripture memorization. In addition, Graham's parents encouraged him to read history. Frady noted that Graham had read more than 100 historical volumes by the time he was fifteen years old. By high school graduation, he had read the *Decline and Fall of the Roman Empire*.

These familial beginnings planted seeds that later blossomed in Graham as an evangelist. From his earliest crusades, Graham's sermons reveal his devotion to historical example, reasoning from historical analogy, and using citations and quotations from historical figures. His memorization of the Shorter Catechism likely helped to develop his strongly authoritative mode of preaching, according to Stanley High in *Billy Graham: The Personal Story of the Man, His Message, and His Mission*. Graham's family context contributed to a dichotomized view of religion and its place in society. Within this view, values were unchanging, morality was of supreme significance, and activities were either good or evil. Strong and active family relationships were the cornerstone for the proper rearing of a child into a strong and active Christian faith. Time and again in his sermons across the decades, this vision of the "Christian family" is apparent in Graham's rhetoric.

In many ways, the religious devotion of Graham's parents reflected that of the Southern region in which they raised their son. Born in 1918 in Charlotte, North Carolina, Graham inhabited a South that was strongly devoted to evangelical Protestant forms of Christianity. Indeed, Graham's region embraced a religious gospel that was virtually unchanged from the Great Awakenings of the mid-eighteenth and early nineteenth centuries through the mid-twentieth century. That gospel was characterized by intense emotional conviction regarding wrongdoings, public confession and rebuke of this sinful way of life, and assured redemption. In brief, the religion of the South, from its earliest origins, has been marked by theological simplicity and emotional complexity. Revivals have been—and continue to be—central to evangelical religious practice in the South. These often protracted religious phenomena were commonplace throughout Graham's South. Indeed, High observed that the revival meetings of Graham's day were remarkably similar to those that had dominated the South for a century. Frady called these events "heaving moral melodramas" that "boomed like brush fires over the South in the summer."

Despite his family's lack of interest in most of the traveling revivals ("We were never among the more emotional of the Christian people," his mother recalled late in life), Graham attended these religious events while a youth. He heard a variety of national and regional revivalists, including Billy Sunday, and was converted to the Christian faith at a Mordecai Ham revival that took place on part of the Graham dairy farm in 1934. He rejected the intense public display of emotion at this initial conversion, recalling later: "I felt very little emotion. I shed no tears." However, he had an unswerving commitment to the certainty of redemption for the converted. According to Frady, Graham remembers thinking after the conversion, "Now, whatever I do, I cannot be unsaved."

Graham's oratorical career began at a Monroe, North Carolina, revival soon after his conversion. An Alabama evangelist named Jimmy Johnson asked Graham to offer a brief testimony about his recent conversion experience; according to Graham in his autobiography, it was "the first public utterance I had given of my faith." In 1950, he took his message to the airwaves, first with weekly radio broadcasts and later with weekly television shows. In 1957, between the May 15 and Labor Day, he held his first crusade in New York City. He preached ninety-seven sermons over the course of this 100-day period, and generally delivered at least two other speeches and talks every day of the crusade. In the tradition of the American evangelist, his early sermons often lasted over an hour, and his early crusades lasted for months at a time. With the New York City crusade, he began to televise his crusades nationally. The first of these were broadcast live each Saturday evening for fourteen weeks of the crusade. According to Curtis Mitchell's account of this crusade in *Billy Graham: Saint or Sinner*, over 96 *million* viewers watched these meetings and over 65,000 persons wrote or called to say they had made a "decision"—either a conversion experience or an experience of rededication to the Christian faith. Today, one-hour crusade "specials" are televised nightly for a week several times a year, generally within a few months following a crusade.

Graham's oratory has reflected the Southern revivalists who influenced him as a child. Frady recounts the comment of a fellow evangelist on Graham's theological education: "You know, he never did attend a theological school. He was just never instructed in all those excellent complications and equivocations. He more or less came straight up out of the grass into the pulpit. He's sort of God's own divine bumpkin." Lacking formal theological training, Graham preached the

spiration and examples from the oratory of others. Graham was fond of imitating the delivery of such national radio personalities as Walter Winchell and Drew Pearson; his sermons often borrowed heavily from those he had heard and enjoyed. Although he was known to occasionally scorn and even mock evangelists with exaggerated mimicry, he was also attracted to their oratorical abilities. One needs only to view the cinematic images of the early Graham crusades to see the remarkable resemblance between his own gestures and style and those of the revivalists with whom he grew up.

Yet, Graham's use of the mass media set him apart from pre-electronic evangelists and established him as a forerunner to the contemporary electronic church. His greatest talent may well

---

Billy Graham has delivered tens of thousands of sermons to millions of people in hundreds of locations. He preached to over 100,000 people in Yankee Stadium during his New York City crusade of 1957. His Los Angeles crusade of 1963 drew an officially recorded crowd of 134,254 to the Coliseum for a single sermon, an attendance record for that structure. Abroad, he preached to 120,000 at Wembley Stadium in the Greater London crusade in 1954. By the 1990s, his use of satellite technology enabled him to reach 100 million viewers for a single sermon originating in Hong Kong.

---

distinctive fundamental and evangelical religious faith that surrounded him in the South. Consequently, his theological leanings mirrored those of the South: a strong belief in the Bible as the literal word of God; a theologically unhindered view of man's sinfulness and God's redemptive grace through Jesus Christ; and the presentation and acceptance of this unchanging message in a manner marked by emotion.

Graham modeled his delivery after individuals he had admired in his youth rather than any specific training that he acquired. As Graham later recalled, "I never took a speech course in my life. I never read a book on speech. The way I speak in the pulpit is my natural form of speaking; except that before a big crowd, I speak a bit louder." Such a "natural" rhetoric draws its in-

have been his fusion of traditional American evangelism with modern American technology. In short, Graham took the crusade meeting from the revival tent of the nineteenth century and brought it into the living rooms of the twentieth century.

A SOUTHERN CLERICAL HERITAGE: THE ORATORY OF BILLY GRAHAM

Since the start of his oratorical career, Graham has consistently combined the discussion of the sacred with that of secular events, not unlike his forebears on the sawdust trail. In fact, a recurring characteristic of an evangelical Protestant preacher is the willingness to become involved with political matters. In its narrowest sense, *political* has usually meant involvement with some social issue, legislative activities, or electoral politics. Indeed, Graham has been actively involved with several political events and actors. He was a close friend of several presidents, especially Dwight Eisenhower, Lyndon Johnson, and Richard Nixon. He was the sole cleric with an active role in the inauguration of George H. W. Bush in January 1989, delivering both the invocation and the benediction. He was with Bush, at the president's invitation, the night American troops launched the ground phase of the Gulf War. He offered invocations at *both* the Democratic and the Republican National Conventions in 1992, and he delivered the invocation at Bill Clinton's inauguration in 1993.

Graham's involvement with political matters has plunged him into a variety of controversies. Many of his fellow Southerners denounced him in the 1950s for insisting on the racial integration of his crusades, even in the South. However, Graham received some of the sharpest criticism of his career when he campaigned on behalf of Richard Nixon and supported American involvement in the Vietnam War. He identified Nixon and American involvement in Vietnam with freedom, and he associated John F. Kennedy and Vietnam with communism. In his November 6, 1960, *Hour of Decision* radio sermon, Graham urged the audience to "cast your vote for Christ" and called the contest between Kennedy and Nixon "the most important election in American history. The future course of American history may well be decided this Tuesday. Go vote on Tuesday to preserve America's freedom for you and your children." The ballot box, Graham suggested, "is one of the greatest weapons in the hands of the free world" and protection against godless communism.

Despite the criticism that he received at times for his political involvement, Graham has continued to encourage fellow Christians to participate in the political process. He urges his listeners to be actively involved in the affairs of their world, from those of the neighborhood to those of the nation. He recommends that his listeners read widely about political and social matters, and he repeatedly suggests that Christians should practice good citizenship by voting for the candidates of their choice. Graham's oratory calls for Christians to be good citizens while rejecting the temptations and sins of a lost world; that is, he instructs Christians "to be in the world, but not of the world."

In addition to participating in political issues and events, Graham resembles his forebears through his use of world events in his messages. Traditional evangelical Protestant spokesmen have historically yoked politics to religion by interpreting clashes between nations and ideologies as representations of a greater clash between the good of God and the evil of Satan. In this latter effort, the realm of the secular is passed through a sacred medium, revealing a single cause for the world's ills: people's sin and separation from God. Graham has a long history of using secular events to bolster his sacred rhetoric and does, indeed, locate the source of political ills in humanity's rejection of God. Nowhere has this identification been more evident than in his early discourse about communism.

Graham's sharpest political rhetoric in the first half of his career concerned communism. In many respects, he echoed the sentiment of his time. These years saw the height of American fears about the Soviet Union, and Graham's oratory was entirely consistent with Communist-hating and Communist-hunting politicians. Graham separated from the purely political rhetors of his day by viewing communism as inspired by Satan to destroy Christian America. In *Religion in American Public Life*, James Reichley quotes Graham as thundering in 1949: "Communism is inspired, directed, and motivated by the Devil himself. America is at a crossroads. Will we turn to the left-wingers and atheists, or will we turn to the right and embrace the cross?"

For Graham, communism attacked godly principles and ideals once clearly possessed by America, but now in danger of being lost. The loss of these American–Christian virtues would signal the end of the country's power, prestige, and freedom. Such a loss was always impending; the apocalypse was always within the next moment of Graham's oratory. America stood "at the crossroads of decision," Graham said repeatedly. As each of Graham's radio sermons attested, he was "a man with God's message for these crisis days. For you, for the nation, this is the hour of decision." Graham envisioned America balancing constantly on the precipice of military disaster.

Consequently, in Graham's discourse, the battle between Communist Soviets and Christian Americans was cosmic warfare of the highest order. In a 1965 radio sermon, "The Ultimate Weapon," Graham implored:

> A war of ideologies is being waged throughout the world, a war of the secular against the spiritual. The actual fighting in the areas of combat are only material manifestations of the larger battles that rage in the hearts of men throughout the earth. Will it be a truth or a lie? Will we be motivated by materialistic philosophy or spiritual power? Will we be led by God or by Satan? The battle lines are clearly drawn. All men in every country are being asked to choose sides. Which will it be?

The evangelist saw the conflict between communism and Christianity as a battle to the death. Frady quoted Graham as declaring: "Either Communism must die or Christianity must die, because it is actually a battle between Christ and anti-Christ"—and, Graham declared, Satan was winning. According to William McLoughlin in *Billy Graham: Revivalist in a Secular Age*, Graham contended that more than a thousand social organizations were actually Communist-operated; that some of the country's best educators, politicians, and entertainers had become Communists; and that Joseph McCarthy's efforts to rescind the Fifth Amendment privileges for suspected Communists should be supported. In his 1965 "The Ultimate Weapon" sermon, Graham warned that America, along with the rest of the non-Communist world, was in serious trouble: "As we search the map of the world, we cannot find one point where the West is winning."

Even in the midst of such great fear appeals and seemingly unstoppable Soviet success, Graham offered a message of hope for the troubled times. Not surprisingly, he contended that the only certain way to save America from the beast was a national return to Christian principles. He was quite clear in his belief that God could triumph over Satan and Marx, if people would only become committed to a Christian faith and pray regularly: "It is inconceivable that Communism could penetrate the barrier of a praying nation whose security is moral and spiritual, not military." In his November 5, 1950, *Hour of Decision* radio sermon, Graham contended that "Faith,

more than fighting, can change the course of events today. Prayer can change the course of history. Such praying in other days has spared other nations."

For Graham, the American military and Christian religion existed symbiotically. On the one hand, the nation's faith in God resulted in military strength and success. An America committed to Christian principles enjoyed the protection of the Great Warrior Jehovah. In "Why God Allows Communism to Flourish" a sermon preached at Los Angeles on October 23, 1949, in the period following a national awareness that the Soviet Union now possessed atomic weapons, Graham defied the Soviet threat: "Let them shoot their rockets, their atomic bombs, send all their planes. Jesus will overcome and us with Him. Jesus will be on the throne and you and I with Him. Hallelujah." As Graham would note in a 1964 sermon titled "God and the Nations":

> If our nation at this hour would turn to the Word of God, if the men and women who make up our nation would put their trust in Jesus Christ, then I guarantee on the authority of God's Word that the enemies at our gates could be pushed back; God would intervene and put them to flight. . . . I am convinced that if our leaders would lead the American people in repentance of sin and in faith in Jesus Christ, God would do the fighting for us.

On the other hand, a strong military protected America's role as the chief Christian nation. In Graham's view, America was God's Chosen Nation, and its purpose was to serve as a base for evangelizing the world. In an untitled sermon delivered in Florida during World War II, Graham noted: "As we hear the tramp, tramp, tramp of soldiers, the roar of airplanes, and the thunder of cannon, and see men and women being slaughter[ed] about us, it should behoove us to carry this message of salvation, this one bright hope to a world sunk in the darkness of despair and sin." For Graham, American military strength was necessary for evangelical Christianity to flourish. A strong America meant opportunities to spread the Gospel unhindered; an America that was militarily weak hampered this task. In Graham's cosmology, Satan was working for the military downfall of America in an effort to halt the spread of Christianity. According to Frady, in 1947, two years prior to his Los Angeles crusade, Graham publicly acknowledged: "I am definitely in favor of building the strongest possible military force." In 1960, Graham was still calling for military strength. Frady quoted Graham as declaring, "Christianity needs a show of strength and force. . . . We must maintain the strongest military establishment on earth." Without such a military, America was potential prey for the godless nations of the globe, and Christianity was at risk.

Thus, for Graham, America's military might and its relationship with God were inseparable. Military conflicts were a physical manifestation of the never-ending struggle between God and Satan. Consequently, wars and conflicts were likely to continue until the Second Coming of Christ, when Jesus would conquer Satan, and thus end all warfare. On October 23, 1949, in Los Angeles, in a sermon titled "Why God Allows Communism to Flourish and Why God Allows Christians to Suffer," Graham suggested, "The next world war will occur in the next five years if Christ tarries. It will make the first two look like a little fist fight. This world war will sweep civilization into oblivion unless Christ comes and stops it. It's on the way." There was no end in sight for these conflicts, Graham proclaimed, in a 1971 sermon, "Something Is Happening in America":

> There are people today who would like to disarm the United States. They think we ought not to have a Defense Department. And they think that somehow all we have to do is lay down our arms, and everybody is going to hug each other and we're going to love each other. But the Bible teaches the very opposite. The Bible teaches that as long as human nature is as it is, we're going to have wars and rumors of wars till the end of time.

The sermon concluded, "We cannot have permanent peace until hearts are changed." Such hearts would not be changed until "man stands at Armageddon—which could happen in this century—with atomic bombs ready to burst, and God intervenes and Jesus Christ comes back to this world and sits on the throne and rules the world. Then we're going to have peace."

Given Graham's view of international warfare as an ongoing, epic battle between God and

Satan, it is not surprising that his rhetoric has, until recently, been distinctly hawkish. His oratory concerning Korea and Vietnam, for example, strongly favored American involvement in these wars. For Graham, Korea was the obvious battleground between communism and Christianity, Satan and God. Consequently, he challenged the Truman administration's policy of limited warfare and called for complete military victory. In *Billy Graham: Revivalist in a Secular Age*, McLoughlin quotes Graham's lament: "It is almost beyond belief that the American people will allow such a half-hearted war to drag on with an average now of nearly two thousand casualties every week." He was critical, as well, of the decision to relieve Douglas MacArthur as commander of the allied forces. In the aftermath of the formal stalemate, Graham bemoaned the American losses. McLoughlin quotes Graham: "During the last three years, we have lost tremendous prestige in the entire Far East. We have shown our moral weaknesses. We have shown that when pressed we could betray our friends and compromise with the enemy." Graham was concerned that America's reputation and moral epicenter had been damaged by not following St. Paul's admonition to "fight the good fight."

A dozen years later, Graham was faced with defining America's involvement in Vietnam. Once again, he characterized the war in Vietnam as a conflict between good and evil—a position initially accepted by a majority of Americans. According to this view, the United States had a moral obligation to protect democracy in the rice fields and jungles of Southeast Asia. In addition, Graham reminded his audience that because of sinful human nature, war was inevitable until the Second Coming of Christ. As he noted in 1968, according to Frady, "[U]ntil Christ comes again, we're going to have convulsions and wars. War is sinful, yes. But as long as you have human nature so wild as it is, you're going to have to use force." Christ himself understood this, according to Graham, and warned people of the warfare necessary to correct human nature. Frady quotes Graham as explaining in 1966:

> There are those who have tried to reduce Christ to the level of a genial and innocuous appeaser.

But Jesus said, "You are wrong—I have come as a fire-setter and a sword-wielder." There were thousands of people in Christ's day who could not understand what he meant when he said he would set fire to the earth. They were good-hearted, kind people who were anxious to have a better world. They were idealistic, but they were ignorant of the deep-seated disease of human nature. They looked at the world through rose-tinted glasses.

Graham's line of reasoning forestalled disagreement. To suggest that the conflict in Vietnam was unnecessary or could be resolved short of ultimate victory, Graham contended, was to reject the scriptural injunctions of Christ. In abbreviated form, this rhetoric claimed that those "good-hearted, kind people" with the "rose-tinted glasses" were not only unrealistic, they were unscriptural as well. Victory in Vietnam became a microcosm of the ultimate victory of Christ over Satan. To suggest any compromise short of complete victory would be anti-Christian.

Indeed, Graham criticized those who suggested compromise. He expressed concerns, yet again, with the Johnson administration's failures to pursue the goal of complete victory. Frady records Graham as protesting: "I don't think we should fight these long-drawn-out, half-hearted wars. It's like cutting a cat's tail off a half-inch at a time." He employed harsher words for protesters against the war, referring to them, according to Frady, as "a Satanic spiritual power of evil that is stirring up all the hatred and dissent in this country." He even attacked clergy who protested the war. In his 1966 sermon "Is God Then Dead?," Graham referred to "the spectacle of ministers and atheists marching comfortably together in anti-Vietnam demonstrations throughout the country." He responded to Martin Luther King Jr.'s attack on Vietnam, in particular, by claiming that such discussion was "an affront to the thousands of loyal Negro troops who are in Vietnam."

After Nixon's election, which he supported, Graham was increasingly attacked for not opposing the conflict and for not using his influence with the president to force an end to the fighting. By 1973, Graham issued a public proclamation stating that he deplored war and that he "regretted that this war has gone on so long and been such a divisive force in America. I hope and pray that there will be an early armistice." He also indicated his hope "for a rapid and just peace." By the end of America's involvement in Southeast Asia, Graham contended, as Frady notes, that he had always been careful not to be drawn into a discussion of the "moral implications of the Vietnam war."

Under normal circumstances, these rhetorical inconsistencies should have damaged Graham's credibility with his listeners. Certainly, his contradictions were noticed by the intellectual Left. But the masses, many of them equally confused about Vietnam, remained loyal to Graham and his organization. This puzzle raises the question of why Graham has been so successful as an orator. His harshest critics have attacked him for his disjointed speech structure and his simplistic theology. Even his kindest critics have acknowledged his tendency, especially in the early years, to talk too rapidly and gesture too wildly. Graham admits he is not a theologian and has acknowledged, repeatedly, that his public speaking skills have been learned through practice and imitation. If the critical standards are theological complexity and oratorical eloquence, Graham will certainly be found wanting. However, if Graham is judged by his ability to communicate effectively with vast numbers of listeners, then he is highly successful. By this standard, he is an outstanding communicator and, perhaps, the most successful Christian orator in American history.

Graham's early success as a national evangelist may be attributed partially to his attacks on communism. Graham reduced complex political matters to a simple theology: all troubles, from international war to personal anxieties, are the result of humanity's separation from God through sin. To escape the chaos of life's problems, one need only acknowledge one's sins and claim Christ's sacrifice for the forgiveness of these sins. This solution came with a tangible activity for Graham's listeners: leaving their seats and publicly professing their new lives as Christians. In return, God would grant an abiding sense of peace and order. In a time of great uncertainty and national fear, audiences found great appeal in Graham's suggestion simply to turn to God to successfully ride out the Red Storm. Graham offered an orderliness that transcended the personal and social chaos of the twentieth century. Thus, despite his use of fear appeals—most often the Communist threat—and the sense of urgency associated with Graham's oratory, his rhetoric was transcendentally comforting in its explanations, powerfully simple in its content, and tangibly interactive for his listeners.

In addition, Graham's rhetoric has offered the promise of an eternal life in Heaven, without pain, confusion, and fear. This view of an afterlife is consistent with those of other fundamentalist evangelists. What has made Graham's oratory comforting has been his long-standing tradition of focusing more attention on Heaven and less attention on Hell. Much of his oratory over the years has centered on the hope of salvation. The stereotypical "hellfire and brimstone" so commonly associated with evangelical fundamentalism is less a part of Graham's rhetoric. His message through the years has not played down the consequences of sin, but Graham's oratory has repeatedly been filled with hope rather than despair.

Indeed, Graham's rhetoric has grown more and more positive, moderate, and inclusive since 1949. The New Testament ethic of "Love thy neighbor," which contrasted sharply with the militancy of the Old Testament and often contended unsuccessfully for a place in Graham's early oratory, has become more prominent in his later years. With the passing of time and a global context that is markedly calmer, Graham's rhetoric has moved from that of warrior prophet to that of a gentler persona. His sermons are not as loud, nor as long, as they were in 1949. He no longer attacks the Communist ideology, having outlived the great adversary of his career. In fact, he has stated his regret over some of his more zealous statements, and he preached in the Soviet Union, China, and other Communist bloc countries in the 1980s. He even gave a major address in the Soviet Union on the subject of nuclear weaponry and the need for peaceful relations between the superpowers. By the time of the Gulf War in 1991, Graham urged Americans to love their enemies. A March 2, 1991, Associated Press news story, "Billy Graham: Prayers Answered in Quick War," quoted Graham as saying: "I don't think in any way that we ought to blame the Iraqi people or Islam. We ought to love them, because it was their leadership that led them into this disaster of war." Graham also suggested that the war ended quickly because "the Lord answered our prayers."

Yet, Graham's oratory has been successful because of the consistency of his core message over time. His message of sin, separation, sacrifice, and salvation has not changed in more than fifty years. Similar, too, are his stock phrases, reminding the audiences that "the Bible says" and "your friends will wait for you" when a listener makes his or her way to the crusade's altar at the end of the sermon. He encourages his listeners to "go to church next Sunday." There are no surprises with Graham's oratory.

Furthermore, Graham's televised events are highly predictable in their presentation. In fact, they are remarkable in their sameness from one crusade meeting to the next and from one year to the next—and even from previous revivalists' crusades to those of Graham. For his American audiences, Graham has retained the recognizable elements of an old-fashioned crusade: songs, testimony, Bible reading, preaching, altar calls, and a huge audience. This last element, the massive audience, has linked Graham to the the nation's best orators from earlier centuries. These orators frequently attracted live audiences in excess of tens, even hundreds, of thousands of people who gathered to listen. Even with his highly successful use of radio and television, Graham has continually attracted huge crowds. These live audiences help link him to an oratorical tradition not enjoyed by other, purely televangelistic, preachers.

Graham's familiarity and consistency are rhetorically important. With what some might consider old-fashioned activities, ideas, and quaint language for the twenty-first century, Graham reminds his listeners of America past, presenting a living retrospective of the country's idyllic view of its pride, power, and prestige. His events forge an unbroken link to distant American history, and Graham symbolizes a lost innocence and the audience's desire to regain that past.

To his international audiences, especially those in Third World countries and those countries freshly emerged from the Soviet bloc, Graham symbolizes what the future might be. His crusades suggest the power of freedom—the freedom to assemble in vast numbers and to express one's religion without liturgical and political constraints. While Graham preaches a message of spiritual freedom, his international listeners can easily traverse the distance between being free in the spirit and being politically empowered.

Graham's ability to reach both domestic and international audiences illuminates his success with adapting his message over time to particular audiences and contexts while retaining the core elements of an unchanging message. Perhaps his most impressive adaptation has been to a mass mediated audience. Over the years, Graham has evolved from using telephone lines to using satellites in relaying his sermons to distant sites. By the 1990s, his use of satellite technology enabled him to reach 100 million viewers for a single sermon preached in Hong Kong. Graham has successfully transported the critical elements of a crusade revival—particularly the ability to create an interpersonal connection with listeners—to a mass audience. As John Pollock observes in *Crusades: 20 Years with Billy Graham*, Graham avoids trying to reach a mass audience but instead "selects in his mind one unknown member of the audience and aims to reach the whole of that man—his intellect, his conscience, and his will." In this process, Graham maintains personal contact with his listener groups, including those present and those experiencing the event vicariously. Consequently, he speaks to all of his audiences, mediated and live, in ways that blend the two groups into a seamless whole.

When the same message is expressed year in and year out, crusade after crusade, the difficulty of offering it repeatedly in ways that breathe rhetorical life into it might be overlooked. Given the number of sermons delivered in his career, it would have been easy for Graham to stop adapting his message to new audiences and new contexts. It is easy to overlook the rhetorical power of an oratory that has remained so simple, adaptable, and consistent for more than fifty years. Much like the great baseball players he admired while growing up in North Carolina, there is a kind of effortless grace about Graham's oratory that disguises its difficulty and power. As T. E. Starr—a listener

at a October 1994 Atlanta crusade—remarked of Graham in an interview with Hal Fulmer, "Watching him preach is like watching Nolan Ryan pitch. You forget how old he is. You just marvel at what he's doing at his age."

Billy Graham's voice of thunder is gentler now than it was in 1949. That thunder is even comforting now, but it is no less powerful; and with the advent of mass media, it is heard in places far removed from its origin. According to Richard Ostling, Graham has often said, "I don't see anybody in Scripture retiring from preaching." In that case, it is likely that the thunder will continue to rumble, roll, and roar until Graham's voice is no longer heard in this world but, according to his faith, is still heard in the next.

INFORMATION SOURCES

Research Collections and Collected Speeches

The Billy Graham Center at Wheaton College in Wheaton, Illinois, has *Hour of Decision* audiotapes, as well as a scrapbook of assorted papers and clippings associated with Graham. The Billy Graham Evangelistic Association in Minneapolis offers for sale more than 250 of his radio sermons. Some of Graham's early sermons have been anthologized in *The Challenge: Sermons from Madison Square Garden*. In addition, Graham's sermons, especially in the 1950s and 1970s, were often reprinted verbatim in the leading newspapers of his crusade cities, and several sermons have been printed in *Christianity Today*.

Graham, Billy. *The Challenge: Sermons from Madison Square Garden* [*TC*]. Garden City, N.Y.: Doubleday, 1969.

Web Sites

Billy Graham Center. This page, which is the "archives" link from the Wheaton College Billy Graham Center Web site, includes links to the Center's archival collections as well as a link that provides information about Graham and guidance toward sites related to Graham. Bgc.gospelcom.net

Billy Graham Evangelistic Association [*BGEA*]. This is the primary Web site for Billy Graham's ongoing ministries. The site provides news about the Association's finances, spiritual beliefs, activities, and ministries, including Billy Graham's crusades as well as television and radio outreaches. It indexes and provides ordering information for more than 250 radio sermons. www.billygraham.org

Christianity Today. As the home page for this Christian magazine, this site provides a "search" feature that allows users to locate articles and editorials that the magazine has published about Graham. www.christianitytoday.com

Time magazine Heroes and Icons. This site, created in 1999, identifies Billy Graham as one of twenty people who "articulate the longings of the last 100 years. . . ." It includes a brief biography, issues of *Time* with Graham on the cover, and links to articles and letters about Graham. www.time.com

Audiovisual Materials

Balmer, Randall Herbert. *Crusade.* Cutting Edge/ WTTW Chicago, distributed by Turner Broadcasting and PBS Home Video, 1996. This video includes documentary footage of Graham and interviews with Graham's friends and critics.

Billy Graham Center, Wheaton College. Collection includes *Hour of Decision* audiotapes.

Billy Graham Evangelistic Association. Has produced more than 250 radio sermons. See Web site above.

Graham, Billy, and David Frost. *Billy Graham Talking with David Frost.* Alexandria, Va.: PBS Video, 1993. This video features an interview by David Frost with Graham.

Graham, Billy, and Bill Turpie. *Great Preachers. Series 1, Billy Graham.* Worcester, Pa.: Gateway Films/Vision Video, 1997. This video includes a sermon that Graham created for the broadcast and an interview with Bill Turpie about preaching.

Graves, Peter, and Randall Herbert Balmer. *Crusade: The Life of Billy Graham.* New York: A&E Home Video, 1993.

Selected Critical Studies

Apel, William D. "The Lost World of Billy Graham." *Review of Religious Research* 20 (Spring 1979): 138–49.

Fulmer, Hal W. "Billy Graham: Christian Evangelist." In *American Orators of the Twentieth Century: Critical Studies and Sources*, ed. Bernard K. Duffy and Halford R. Ryan. New York: Greenwood Press, 1987.

Mitchell, Curtis. *God in the Garden: The Story of the Billy Graham Crusade.* Garden City, N.Y.: Doubleday, 1957.

Selected Biographies

Arnold, Bob. "Billy Graham: Superstar." In *On Jordan's Stormy Banks: Religion in the South*, ed. Samuel S. Hill, Jr. Macon, Ga.: Mercer University Press, 1983.

Frady, Marshall. *Billy Graham: A Parable of American Righteousness.* Boston: Little, Brown, 1979.

Graham, Billy. *Just as I Am: The Autobiography of Billy Graham.* San Francisco: HarperSanFrancisco; Grand Rapids, Mich.: Zondervan Press, 1997.

High, Stanley. *Billy Graham: The Personal Story of the Man, His Message, and His Mission.* New York: McGraw-Hill, 1956.

Martin, William. "Billy Graham." In *Varieties of Southern Evangelicalism*, ed. David E. Harrell, Jr. Macon, Ga.: Mercer University Press, 1981.

———. *A Prophet with Honor: The Billy Graham Story.* New York: Morrow, 1991.

McLoughlin, William Gerald. *Billy Graham: Revivalist in a Secular Age.* New York: Ronald Press, 1960.

Mitchell, Curtis. *Billy Graham: Saint or Sinner.* Old Tappan, N.J.: F. H. Revell, 1979.

Pollock, John Charles. *Billy Graham: The Authorized Biography.* Grand Rapids, Mich.: Zondervan Press, 1966.

———. *Crusades: 20 Years with Billy Graham.* Minneapolis, Minn.: World Wide Publications, 1969.

Strober, Gerald S. *Graham: A Day in Billy's Life.* Garden City, N.Y.: Doubleday, 1976.

CHRONOLOGY OF MAJOR SPEECHES

See "Research Collections and Collected Speeches" for source codes.

"Our Bible" (radio sermon). 1951. *BGEA*, sermon 95.

"The Christian Answers to the World Dilemma" (opening sermon, New York City crusade). May 15, 1957. Reprinted in *New York Times*, May 16, 1957, pp. 22–23.

"The Ultimate Weapon" (radio sermon). 1965. *BGEA*, sermon 141.

"Why the Berlin Congress?" (address to the World Congress on Evangelism). Berlin, May 1966. Reprinted in *Christianity Today* 10 (1966): 3–7.

"Social Injustice" (radio sermon). 1967. *BGEA*, sermon 166.

"Come and Know God" (opening sermon, New York City Crusade). New York City, 1969. *TC.*

"The Other Death." New York City, 1969. *TC.*

"The Christian Faith and Peace in a Nuclear Age" (address to the Religious Workers for Saving the Sacred Gift of Life from Nuclear Catastrophe). Moscow, May 11, 1982. Reprinted in *Christianity Today* 26 (1982): 20–23.

"National Day of Prayer and Remembrance Sermon." Washington D.C., September 14, 2001. *BGEA.* Available at www.propheticroundtable.org.

ANITA FAYE HILL (1956–)
Law Professor, Author

VANESSA B. BEASLEY

Posterity will probably remember Anita Hill less for what she said than simply because she spoke. Reluctant to take the public spotlight, Hill nevertheless withstood its glare as a witness in the 1991 nationally televised confirmation hearings of Supreme Court nominee Clarence Thomas. Although her testimony lasted only one day, Hill was ostensibly the reason the televised hearings took place at all. She had worked for Thomas in various offices in the early 1980s, and when he was appointed by President George H. W. Bush to fill retiring Thurgood Marshall's seat on the Supreme Court, Hill came forth to allege to the Senate Judiciary Committee that Thomas had sexually harassed her while she was his employee. As news of such charges became public, members of the Senate Judiciary Committee faced increasing public pressure to investigate them, and the committee interrupted its regular confirmation process to hold additional hearings into the allegations. Suddenly news cameras from around the world filled the once quiet halls of the Russell Senate Office Building as reporters waited for what was sure to be a scintillating game of "he said/she said."

It was under these conditions that Anita Faye Hill, who by then had left government service to teach law at the University of Oklahoma, came to be nationally known as an orator. Beginning at 10:01 A.M. on October 11, 1991, Hill spoke and answered questions from committee members for almost nine hours. Her best-known oratory, then, was not a traditional speech or public address, but instead consisted of a brief opening statement followed by hours of responses to senators' questions. Nevertheless, both her words and her appearance that day remain noteworthy because they prompted an intense national debate—not just about Thomas's innocence or guilt, but also about gender inequity and sexual harassment in the United States. In the years since her testimony, Hill has returned to teaching, writing, and giving occasional public speeches. Because she is best known for her role in these hearings, however, this essay focuses primarily on that event, its immediate aftermath, and Hill's legacy.

HILL AS A RELUCTANT ORATOR

The thirteenth child of a farming family in Okmulgee County, Oklahoma, Hill has described her childhood as "one of a lot of hard work and not much money." As an undergraduate she attended Oklahoma State University and then went on to earn a law degree from Yale University. According to her testimony, she first met Clarence Thomas a year after her graduation from law school, when she was working at a private law firm in Washington, D.C. Thomas informed her that he was likely to receive a political appointment and asked if she would be interested in working for him. She answered that she would be, and subsequently followed him, as his assistant, when he was named assistant secretary of education for civil rights in the Department of Education and, later, chair of the Equal Employment Opportunity Commission (EEOC).

According to her October 11, 1991, testimony,

The impact of Hill's testimony before Congress is indisputable, such that the very fact of her speaking may ultimately have been of greater importance than the manner in which she spoke.

the harassment began while she worked at the Department of Education in 1981. Hill alleged that after she had repeatedly declined Thomas's invitations to go out socially and explained to him that "having a social relationship with a person who was supervising my work would be ill advised," he began to ask her out more often and "pressed" her as to why she continually declined. These conversations occurred in private, Hill testified, and were later followed by occasions on which "Judge Thomas began to use work situations to discuss sex" and used "vivid" language to speak about "acts he had seen in pornographic films," including bestiality, group sex, and rape scenes. Throughout these interactions, as well as those in which Thomas allegedly discussed his own sexual performance, Hill recounted, "I told him that I did not want to talk about these subjects." Over time, Hill recalled, Thomas's references to sexual matters "ended," and she came to believe that "our working relationship could be a proper, cordial, and professional one." Under these circumstances she followed him to the EEOC, where, after a brief respite during the first half of 1982, Hill claimed that Thomas once again began to initiate the same types of conversations. She testified that Thomas's comments became even more explicit throughout the fall and winter of 1982.

In 1983 Hill began to look for another job. "I was handicapped," she later testified, "because I feared that if he found out he might make it difficult for me to find other employment" and/or fire her. In February 1983, she was hospitalized for stomach pain, which she attributed to stress, and that spring she accepted a teaching position at Oral Roberts University, to begin in the fall. After her last day of work at the EEOC that summer, Thomas took her out to dinner. There, according to Hill's testimony, he told her "if I ever told anyone of his behavior it would ruin his career. This was not an apology, nor was it an explanation."

For the next nine years, Hill was largely silent about her experiences working with Thomas and shared the details only with her closest friends. Why, then, did she choose to speak out in 1991? As she explained at the end of her opening comments, she spoke up out of a sense of "duty," although one that was not without cost. Making

the decision to speak, she said, put her under a great deal of stress and strain, and she characterized "telling the world" as the "most difficult experience of my life." In fact, Hill admitted repeatedly that she had tried very hard to avoid being a public witness against Thomas. "This is exactly what I do not want," she told Senator Joseph Biden. "I don't like all of the attention I am getting," she told Senator Howell Heflin, adding later that "everything I knew how to do, I did" to prevent being a witness.

To some observers, Hill's body language underscored her reluctance. Nina Totenberg, the National Public Radio correspondent who broke the story about Hill's allegations, would later write that Hill was "trembling almost imperceptibly" as she walked to her seat in the Senate Caucus Room. Indeed, throughout her testimony, it was clear that Hill did not relish the attention she was receiving. After taking her seat at a table facing the senators, she read her opening remarks plainly and unenthusiastically as she spoke into the microphone on the table in front of her. Throughout the questioning, there were times when she seemed uncomfortable, frustrated, and even embarrassed. Instead of being an exemplar of an impassioned orator, voice booming with enthusiasm and activism, Hill appeared to be more of a hesitant figure, committed to telling her side of the story, to be sure, but cautious just the same.

Her reluctance would perhaps prove to be justified. Both on the day of the hearings and in the years that followed, many observers would publicly question Hill's motives for speaking out against Thomas. Over the course of the three days of hearings, for example, her motives would became just as much a topic of discussion as her initial allegations. Senator Heflin, for example, explored an almost comic line of questioning in which he asked Hill if she was a "scorned woman" or a "zealoting civil rights believer," or if she had a "militant attitude" or a "martyr complex." Throughout the remaining two days of the hearings, as Clarence Thomas and other witnesses spoke, both Hill's supporters and her detractors would be asked similar questions about her motives, her psyche, and what she might be trying to gain by speaking out now. In fact, over time, to many observers the hearings seemed to be more and more about Hill and less and less about Thomas. One of Thomas's main supporters, Senator John Danforth, reportedly attempted to call as a witness a psychiatrist who would testify that Hill suffered from a disorder characterized by romantic delusions. By October 13, speculation about Hill's motives and credibility forced Harvard Law professor Charles Ogletree, one of Hill's advisers, to report to the press that she had taken and passed a lie detector test. The Senate Judiciary Committee refused to enter this information into the record.

By the end of that third day, Senator Biden announced, to perhaps no one's surprise, that neither Professor Hill nor Senator Thomas was interested in testifying further. Without making any official statement of judgment regarding the allegations, the Senate confirmed Thomas as a Supreme Court justice by a vote of 52–48. The confirmation process may have been officially over, but throughout the United States, tempers—especially female tempers—flared at the Senate's perceived indifference to the issue of sexual harassment. Ultimately, then, even if Hill's reluctant rhetoric might not have seemed particularly spectacular or eloquent in and of itself, her speaking out unleashed a fury of rage and motivated countless others to speak out, too.

No one, and certainly not Anita Hill, could have predicted the tidal wave of political, social, and cultural changes that crashed to shore in the aftermath of her testimony and Thomas's confirmation. Some of these were foreshadowed by the protesters who stood on the steps of the Capitol as senators cast their votes for and against Thomas's confirmation in 1991, declaring, "We'll remember in November." And remember they did. The year 1992 quickly became dubbed the "Year of the Woman" as the number of women in Congress rose from twenty-eight to forty-two, with four new women being elected to the Senate. One of these new senators, Carol Moseley-Braun, ran a campaign that explicitly referenced the Hill–Thomas hearings in order to successfully unseat her opponent, one of the handful of Democrats who had voted to confirm Thomas.

Female voters were also widely given credit for Bill Clinton's successful bid for the presidency in 1992. The old guard, particularly the white male old guard so often epitomized by patrician leaders such as George H. W. Bush, just didn't seem to "get it," women throughout the land proclaimed. The old guard was quickly educated through legal action, and the number of sexual harassment lawsuits filed through the EEOC in 1992 was more than 70 percent higher than it was in 1990. Further, once cases were won, juries seemed more likely to give financial awards to victims of sexual harassment in a post-Anita Hill era, with some reports indicating that the total amount awarded in the United States almost quadrupled from 1991 to 1996.

In addition to obvious political and legal changes, the aftermath of the hearings brought signs of other types of social change and unrest. For one, the media coverage of the Hill–Thomas hearings presaged both the increased intensity and the increasingly melodramatic tone that would come to characterize the breathless, tabloid-like coverage of political scandals in the future. Perhaps more important, however, was the way in which the Hill–Thomas hearings charged racial politics in the United States. The fact that both Hill and Thomas were African American meant that the hearings were not merely about sexual politics but also about race. The hearings evoked stereotypes that were both racialized and sexualized, according to many observers, who noted that these stereotypes tended to work against both Hill and Thomas. When Thomas invoked a racialized image by complaining that the hearings had become a "high-tech lynching for uppity blacks," his comments suggested that there was a class dimension to the hearings as well. Located at the intersection of gender, race, and class, then, the hearings were in many ways a lightning rod that drew attention to the underbelly of U.S. politics, where such differences are not supposed to matter even when everyone knows that they do.

Anita Hill largely withdrew from the public spotlight after the hearings. She wrote in her autobiography, *Speaking Truth to Power*, that she was shocked by the response to her testimony and returned to Oklahoma "deeply wounded." It is not hard to imagine why. Shortly after she returned to her tenured position at the University of Oklahoma's College of Law, she encountered local activists, including a state representative, who sought, unsuccessfully, to have her fired. She also received death threats and endured a constant stream of reporters and news cameras wherever she went. In October 1992, one year after the hearings, she helped organize a conference at Georgetown University Law Center in which prominent scholars, jurists, and other public intellectuals responded to the hearings and their social significance. The conference proceedings resulted in a 1995 book titled *Race, Gender, and Power in America: The Legacy of the Hill–Thomas Hearings*, edited by Hill and Emma Coleman Jordan. Early in the book, Hill expresses her gratitude to "the group of African American women whose November 1991 ad in various papers around the country reminded the world that the Senate dismissal of me and my statement about Clarence Thomas' behavior had tragic and historical racial and gender dimensions."

Meanwhile, on a national level, Hill continued to be vilified while Thomas sat more comfortably, and quietly, on the bench. Perhaps predictably, given her testimony's success as a rallying cry to mobilize feminists and fight sexual harassment, Hill was skewered by critics on the right. One of the most notable examples was the 1993 best-selling book *The Real Anita Hill*, by David Brock. Brock, a journalist who had published an essay critical of Hill in *The Spectator* in 1992, used this book to launch a more full-scale attack on her credibility. He characterized her testimony as "false, incorrect and misleading," for example, while suggesting that she had much more of a leftist political agenda than had previously been acknowledged. In 2001, however, Brock admitted that many of the things he wrote in *The Real Anita Hill* were simply not true, and that he had repeatedly accepted false information concerning Hill from right-wing sources without checking its veracity.

Brock's admission underscores the extent to which Anita Hill had become a symbol rather than just a person by the end of the twentieth century. Repeatedly since the 1991 hearings, her name, her image, and her words have been appropriated by both the Right and the Left to argue about everything from gender equity and racial solidarity to media ethics and popular culture. Although she was a reluctant orator on that

October day, she is now remembered as one of the most important women in twentieth-century U.S. politics. In addition, in a recent survey of the top 100 speeches of the twentieth century, Anita Hill appears as one of the few women and one of the few minorities on this list, holding her own with such accomplished orators as Barbara Jordan and Jesse Jackson. On the merits of her style and delivery alone, Hill's somewhat meek presentation at the October 1991 hearings may at first appear to stand in stark contrast to such counterparts, especially when one considers Jordan's deep, forceful voice and Jackson's rhythmic, passionate delivery. Nevertheless, the impact of Hill's testimony is indisputable, such that the very fact of her speaking may ultimately have been of greater importance than the manner in which she spoke.

As of this writing, Hill teaches at Brandeis University's Heller School for Social Policy and Management. In her current position, according to university press releases, she is interested in "the connection, if any, between the rules we establish and the realities of our individual and collective lives." Such a statement seems especially appropriate given that Hill's initial moments in the public spotlight ultimately drew so much attention to the *dis*connection between the realities that women often face in the workplace and the rules that both men and women are supposed to follow there. In the years since 1991, she has made numerous public speeches, often at colleges and universities, to discuss topics such as sexual harassment, racism, and women's rights. On several of these occasions, as well as in her autobiography, Hill has told her audiences that there is transformative power in standing up for what one believes in. In a 1998 address at Ball State University, for example, Hill stated that "I spent my entire life trying to dress up, shielding myself from racism and sexism, only to find myself in Washington, D.C., in October. I learned I had nothing to hide. . . . Now, I'm not recommending that you go up against a U.S. Senate hearing. What I'm telling you is that when people as powerful as U.S. Senators try to destroy you, you can survive."

In an address given in February 2002 at Western New England College, Hill acknowledged that she still feels the "weight" of being the "embodiment" of the ongoing struggles for civil rights and women's rights, and that this position now brings her both privilege and responsibility. As she herself has commented on numerous occasions, she feels strongly that she did not choose sexual harassment as her issue; it chose her. If this is true, then Anita Faye Hill occupies a special place in the history of American oratory as one of the figures who perhaps never wanted to be part of this history. Nevertheless, in the years since her 1991 appearance before the Senate committee, Hill has apparently emerged as a victor instead of a victim of her circumstances. She was in the right place at the right time to speak out against sexual harassment and, intentionally or not, she thus mobilized American women and arguably changed the course of U.S. history.

INFORMATION SOURCES

Research Collections and Collected Speeches

Anita Hill is best known for her day of testimony in the 1991 confirmation hearings of Clarence Thomas. Although she went on to make numerous public appearances and speeches, these addresses were typically given on college and university campuses, and are not part of any larger published collection.

The Complete Transcripts of the Clarence Thomas–Anita Hill Hearings, October 11, 12, 13, 1991 [*CTAH*], ed. Anita Miller. Chicago: Academy Chicago Publishers, 1994.

Web Sites

There are no Web sites that provide systematic access to Anita Hill's speeches or other relevant materials.

Audiovisual Materials

No major collections of audiovisual resources pertaining to Anita Hill's speeches are available.

Selected Critical Studies

Armstrong, S. Ashley. "Arlen Specter and the Construction of Adversarial Discourse: Selective Representation in the Clarence Thomas–Anita Hill Hearings." *Argumentation & Advocacy* 32 (1995): 75–90.
Beasley, Vanessa B. "The Logic of Power in the Hill–

Thomas Hearings: A Rhetorical Analysis." *Political Communication* 11 (1994): 287–98.
Chrisman, Robert, and Robert L. Allen. *Court of Appeal: The Black Community Speaks Out on the Racial and Sexual Politics of Clarence Thomas vs. Anita Hill*. New York: Ballantine Books, 1992.
Hart, Roderick P. "Politics and the Virtual Event: An Overview of the Hill–Thomas Hearings." *Political Communication* 11 (1994): 263–76.
Hill, Anita Faye, and Emma Coleman Jordan, eds. *Race, Gender, and Power in America: The Legacy of the Hill–Thomas Hearings*. New York: Oxford University Press, 1995.
Lipari, Lisbeth. "As the World Turns: Drama, Rhetoric, and Press Coverage of the Hill–Thomas Hearings." *Political Communication* 11 (1994): 299–308.
Mayer, Jane, and Jill Abramson. *Strange Justice: The Selling of Clarence Thomas*. Boston: Houghton Mifflin, 1994.
Morrison, Toni, ed. *Race-ing Justice, En-gendering Power: Essays on Anita Hill, Clarence Thomas, and the Construction of Social Reality*. New York: Pantheon Books, 1992.
Regan, Allison. "Rhetoric and Political Process in the Hill–Thomas Hearings." *Political Communication* 11 (1994): 277–86.
Smitherman, Geneva, ed. *African-American Women Speak Out on Anita Hill–Clarence Thomas*. Detroit, Mich.: Wayne State University Press, 1995.

Selected Bibliography

Hill, Anita F. *Speaking Truth to Power*. New York: Anchor Books, 1998.

CHRONOLOGY OF MAJOR SPEECHES

See "Research Collections and Collected Speeches" for source code.

"Testimony of Anita F. Hill." October 11, 1991. *CTAH*, pp. 22–117.
"Speech at the National Women's Music Festival" (Ball State University). Muncie, Ind., June 28, 1998.
"Social Change and Workplace Realities" (Western New England College). Springfield, Mass., February 25, 2002. See the announcement of her speech at www.wnec.edu/communicator/news/2001/1217anitahill.html. Videotape available through Western New England College.

JESSE LOUIS JACKSON (1941–)
Civil Rights Leader, U.S. Presidential Candidate

DAVID B. McLENNAN

One of the most gifted and controversial speakers of his time, Jesse Jackson has delivered speeches that have unified diverse audiences and solidified his position as a major spokesperson for the civil rights movement after the tragic death of Martin Luther King, Jr. He has also delivered remarks that have divided his audiences and created major difficulties for him as a national African American leader. Throughout his career on national and international stages, Jackson has continuously evolved as a leader, and his oratory has reflected that change. From the dashiki-wearing social activist in Chicago to the tailored suit-attired presidential candidate, Jackson's personal and rhetorical persona is one that endears him to and often confounds both his supporters and his critics, and also makes him one of the most interesting figures of modern times.

Born Jesse Louis Burns on October 8, 1941, in Greenville, South Carolina, to Helen Burns, a single mother, Jackson was often ridiculed by his school classmates for being "a nobody with no daddy." These taunts during elementary school, along with other acts of discrimination that Jackson saw as a young person, helped create his empathy for the oppressed and became his motivation for effecting change. Jackson's mother later married Charles Jackson, and he adopted Jesse in 1957. A good athlete and student, Jackson graduated from Sterling High School in Greenville in 1959 and accepted a football scholarship to attend the University of Illinois, beginning in the fall of 1959. His decision to attend the University of Illinois was motivated in part by his desire to escape the South's racial atmosphere. He soon discovered that discrimination was pervasive; the racial climate in Illinois was not significantly different from what he had experienced in South Carolina. After two semesters at Illinois, Jackson transferred to North Carolina Agricultural & Technical College in Greensboro, North

Carolina, an African American institution. There he met Jacqueline Lavinia Brown, whom he married on December 31, 1962.

Jackson's stay in Greensboro was significant to his development politically and rhetorically, for he emerged as a leader of civil rights demonstrations during the turbulent spring of 1963. As a college senior, the popular Jackson was elected student body president, a position that he equated with being a civil rights leader. Greensboro during the 1960s was a hotbed of civil rights protests. Four African American freshmen from A&T staged their famous Woolworth's sit-in in February 1960, an event that precipitated other sit-in demonstrations throughout the South. Although Jackson was not in Greensboro during the Woolworth sit-ins, he learned from this event and encouraged his fellow students to stage similar protests during his year as student body president. On June 6, 1963, Jackson was arrested in Greensboro for "inciting to riot and disturb the peace and dignity of the state."

After graduating from North Carolina A&T in May 1964 with a degree in sociology, Jackson moved to Chicago, where he enrolled at Chicago Theological Seminary. Although a native of the South, Jackson has spent most of his adult life in Chicago and has based his political activism there. It was in Chicago that he gained regional and national notoriety for speaking out for improved economic conditions and quality housing for its poor citizens, and also where he first became a major figure in electoral politics.

One of the most significant events of Jackson's life occurred in March 1965. After watching a documentary on the civil rights movement, *Bloody Sunday*, on television, Jackson went to Selma, Alabama, where he met Dr. Martin Luther King Jr., who would influence his political beliefs and rhetorical style. Jackson asked King for a job with the Southern Christian Leadership Conference (SCLC). The next spring Jackson became head of the Chicago chapter of SCLC's Operation Breadbasket. Among his first actions in that position were launching an economic boycott and leading an open housing march.

On April 4, 1968, Martin Luther King, Jr. was assassinated in Memphis, Tennessee, while there to support a strike by sanitation workers. Jackson was at the Lorraine Hotel with Dr. King as the fatal shot was fired. There is some controversy about Jackson's whereabouts during the time immediately surrounding James Earl Ray's shooting of King. Jackson claimed on national television that he was the last person to talk to King and that he held the dying King in his arms, getting blood on his shirt. The other men at the Lorraine Hotel, including longtime King aides Hosea Williams and Andrew Young, disputed Jackson's claim, stating that he had been in the parking lot when King was shot, and that he had not come up to the balcony or gone to the hospital with King. Despite the controversy, Jackson's appearance on television the next day with his bloodied turtleneck, and the charismatic way in which he discussed King and the continuation of King's dream, elevated his image as a civil rights leader, especially for those outside the movement who might otherwise have favored Ralph Abernathy as King's successor.

Later that spring, Jackson left the seminary three courses short of finishing his degree (which he completed in the spring of 2000). In the late 1960s, he began his full-time association with the civil rights movement. During the 1970s and 1980s, Jackson became well known nationally through his involvement in political activism and for several controversial statements and actions. His fiery oratory contributed to his rise to national prominence, but also created some problems for Jackson both within the civil rights community and with other audiences.

In 1971, Jackson was suspended from the SCLC after its leaders claimed that he was using the organization to further his personal agenda. He then resigned from the SCLC and founded Operation People United to Save Humanity (PUSH), a community-building organization that he still leads. On the day he announced the founding of Operation PUSH, Jackson stood in front of a picture of Dr. King, promising to found "a rainbow coalition of blacks and white gathered together to push for a greater share of economic and political power for all poor people in America." During the 1970s Jackson became prominent for speaking out against racism, militarism, and class division in America. In many of these speeches, he began using the phrase "I am somebody," a phrase that became a symbol for Jackson and his message of self-improvement.

In 1976, Jackson founded PUSH-Excel, designed to motivate children and teens to succeed. For this program he traveled around the country, delivering speeches preaching personal responsibility and self-worth to students: "You're not a man because you can kill somebody. You are not a man because you can make a baby. . . . You're a man only if you can raise a baby, protect a baby and provide for a baby." Jackson's message of personal responsibility gained him credibility within the African American community, as well as within the white political establishment, where Jackson had been viewed with some suspicion.

As Jackson's prominence grew, so did his involvement in organized politics. In 1983, Jackson was involved in the election of the first African American mayor of Chicago, Harold Washington. One of the important ways in which he helped Washington was in convincing over 100,000 African Americans, including many young people, to register to vote. Jackson's message to members of the African American community and other disadvantaged groups was to exercise their political power at the ballot box.

In 1979, Jackson gained notoriety for two international trips. That year, President Jimmy Carter approved his trip to South Africa, where before large audiences he delivered several speeches denouncing apartheid, South Africa's political system that oppressed the rights and privileges of the black majority. Later that year Jackson toured the Middle East, where he met with and embraced the then-exiled Palestinian leader Yasir Arafat. Although Jackson's two trips gained him support within the African American community, the embrace of Arafat, considered a terrorist by the U.S. government, created problems for Jackson with moderates and conservatives within the United States.

Four years later, Jackson used his goodwill within the Arab world to broker the release of Lt. Robert Goodman, a U.S. Navy pilot shot down in Syria in 1983. Jackson met with Syrian President Hafez Assad and negotiated the release of Goodman on January 2, 1984. Although President Ronald Reagan considered Jackson's efforts to be in violation of diplomatic protocol for the U.S. government, Reagan welcomed Goodman back and praised Jackson's efforts, thus gaining Jackson additional attention.

By the early 1980s Jackson began moderating his political views and toning down his speeches, adopting the phrase "Rainbow Coalition" as symbolic of his position that all Americans can work together to improve the country. This phrase became institutionalized into the Rainbow Coalition, a national coalition formed in Washington, D.C., to reform the Democratic Party.

applied to Jews especially angered Jewish voters and those within the hierarchy of the Democratic Party, particularly when Jackson replied that he had "no recollection of it" when asked about his statement. Just two days before the New Hampshire primary Jackson reversed his position on the statement, and before an audience at a Manchester, New Hampshire, synagogue he apologized for the remarks. Although he attempted to address concerns about the motivations for his remark, the reference became an albatross to Jackson's campaign, especially after he received support from controversial Nation of Islam leader Louis Farrakhan.

Although many African American leaders did not support Jackson during his 1984 candidacy, many everyday African Americans were energized by his campaign. He received over 3 million votes in the primaries, with more than 2 million of those votes coming from newly registered voters. Jackson's unexpected showing in

---

Jesse Jackson received 3.5 million votes in the 1984 Democratic presidential primary, and over 7 million in his 1988 campaign. In 1988, he came in first or second in forty-six out of fifty-four contests.

The organization was an outgrowth of Jackson's historic decision in 1983 to enter the Democratic presidential race against leading Democratic candidates Walter Mondale and Gary Hart. He campaigned on a platform of social programs for the poor and the disabled, alleviation of taxes for the poor, increased voting rights, effective affirmative action initiatives for the hiring of women and minorities, and improved civil rights for marginalized groups, including people of color, the economically depressed, and homosexuals. Jackson also took stands on global issues, including more aid for African nations and more consideration of Arab nations and peoples. These last two positions again brought him to the center of controversy, especially after he called New York City "Hymie-town" and referred to New Yorkers as "Hymies" during a February 1984 interview with *Washington Post* reporter Milton Coleman. This use of an ethnic epithet

the primaries, although not strong enough to seriously challenge the nomination of Walter Mondale, did force the Democratic National Committee to recognize Jackson with an invitation to deliver a nationally televised speech during a prime-time session of the convention. The fifty-five-minute speech was immediately proclaimed a success, and the television audience, estimated to be 33 million, one of the largest of the convention. Of the speech, Florida governor Bob Graham later said, "If you are a human being and weren't affected by what you just heard, you may be beyond redemption." In a similar vein, Representative John Conyers claimed that "[Jackson] is to blacks what JFK is to Catholics." The speech had the effect of making Jackson a legitimate force within American politics, and for many, Jackson was anointed the "national spokesperson" for the African American community.

Jackson remained very visible on the national and international stages after his 1984 convention speech. In 1985 he met with the pope in the Vatican, led a mass demonstration of steelworkers in Pittsburgh, led another demonstration of farmers in Missouri, and headed an antiapartheid march of 100,000 people in London. He also hosted the popular television program *Saturday Night Live.* By the spring of 1987, a *New York Times* poll reported Jackson six points ahead of Massachusetts governor Michael Dukakis for the Democratic presidential nomination in 1988. Jackson soon announced his candidacy and achieved early success, winning the Michigan primary.

In early 1988, Jackson's ideas and rhetoric resonated with many Democrats. New York governor Mario Cuomo ascribed Jackson's popularity to his having "the single most identifiable and attractive message." Jackson eventually lost the nomination to Massachusetts governor Michael Dukakis, but he was again selected to speak during prime time at the Democratic National Convention, a speech he used to heal some of the wounds caused by a vigorous primary campaign. Although Democratic nominee Dukakis lost to Vice President George H.W. Bush in the general election, Jackson's work to register new voters and energize African Americans paid off four years later, when his support helped Governor Bill Clinton beat the incumbent Bush and become the first Democrat to occupy the White House in twelve years.

During the 1990s, Jackson used his enhanced stature for political and diplomatic purposes. Named one of the two "shadow senators" from Washington, D.C., in 1990, he argued for the district's statehood. In 1991 Jackson took a post-Gulf War trip to Iraq to urge Saddam Hussein to release hundreds of foreign nationals, and in 1997 he traveled to Kenya as President Clinton's "special envoy for democracy" and urged Kenyan president Daniel arap Moi to promote peaceful national elections. During the 1999 Kosovo war, Jackson negotiated the release of three U.S. POWs captured by Slobodan Milosevic's forces. Jackson was also instrumental in urging North Atlantic Treaty Organization (NATO) officials and Milosevic to "choose the bargaining table over the battlefield."

In recent years, Jackson has remained an activist and a controversial figure. In November 1999, he defended six Decatur, Illinois, high school students expelled for fighting. They were expelled for two years for brawling at a football game. Jackson attempted to have the school board reinstate the students. When those efforts failed, he organized a protest at Eisenhower High School, which led to his arrest on criminal trespassing charges. Later that month, Jackson received the Presidential Medal of Freedom from President Clinton for his work in world peace. Allegations of marital infidelity in 2001 tarnished Jackson's reputation as a moral spokesperson, especially after he acted as a confidant to President Bill Clinton and his wife, Hillary Rodham Clinton, during Clinton's impeachment hearings related to Clinton's affair with White House intern Monica Lewinsky.

During 2002 and 2003, Jackson was a vocal opponent of the U.S. military actions against Iraq. In a speech to over 300,000 antiwar protesters in London on February 15, 2003, he spoke out strongly against military action in Iraq, arguing that direct talks should be held between British Prime Minister Tony Blair and Iraqi leader Saddam Hussein, and that the war "is not too late to stop. . . . We must march until there is a declaration of peace and reconciliation."

Jackson's very public life remains enigmatic. Quite often, his social and political activism has produced positive results for the causes he advocates and has created the public perception that Jackson is a strong leader. At times, however, Jackson's activities have led to charges by his critics that he is more interested in promoting himself and finding the media spotlight than in making fundamental changes in society. William Raspberry, an African American *Washington Post* columnist, has described Jackson as "flitting from problem to problem" without focusing on one long enough to make significant changes: "Jackson, the nation's preeminent preacher, has the unquestioned ability to inspire audiences. But too often the inspiration departs with his entourage, leaving people and problems unchanged." Despite this type of criticism, Jackson has been, and continues to be, an influential figure on the American scene. Former *Washington Post* editor Ben Bradlee best summarized Jackson's effect on the twentieth century when he said: "In the last analysis, he remains a marvelously interesting cosmic man. I mean, a big figure in this century. He's going to disappoint, because he probably couldn't have lived up to the promise he inspired. But *goddamn*, he had a good whack at it."

JESSE JACKSON: THE ENIGMATIC RHETORICAL ACTIVIST

Jesse Jackson's rhetorical style is a reflection of his life as an activist and a minister, and also of his often enigmatic personality. Throughout his public life, Jackson has addressed a wide variety of audiences on a great many issues. He has spoken to Republican and Democratic Party leaders on civil rights and African American disenfranchisement; to university graduates on peace and medical reform; to teenagers on unwanted pregnancy; to the United Nations on nuclear disarmament; to labor union members on corporate responsibility; to international protest groups on antiwar activities; and to many others. Jackson has spoken to members of neighborhood churches and viewers of nationally televised political conventions. In most of the rhetorical situations he faces, Jackson demonstrates the ability to speak forcefully on issues even when audience members disagree with him. Although Jackson's audiences generally respond favorably to his speeches, his penchant for speaking directly on issues he cares deeply about creates some negative responses by certain audiences.

Throughout his career, Jackson has often been compared with Martin Luther King Jr., his mentor. Although the connection is natural, and in many of his speeches Jackson borrows from King, the the two speakers are not carbon copies of one another. Jesse Jackson's oratory can best be described as more grounded than King's loftier style. Although the two speakers differ slightly in their speaking styles, their speeches can be characterized as exhortative, in that they both use a variety of rational and emotional appeals designed to persuade their respective audiences to act on their policy recommendations. Even on ceremonial occasions, Jackson urges his audiences to do more than contemplate. His March 1991 speech on the twentieth anniversary of *Black Collegian* magazine is typical of his exhortative style. In this speech he begins by praising the magazine's commitment to African American education, but soon turns the speech into a sharp critique of the administrations of Ronald Reagan and George Bush. After discussing the policy effects of these two Republican presidents on the young African American audience, Jackson ends the speech by imploring the audience members to act for social change: "Register to vote, and vote. Use this weapon of empowerment to get full and fair representation, to define an agenda for this country." At the end of the speech, Jackson uses a variation on a common phrase that appears in many of his speeches to further motivate his audience: "Never surrender. As long as you keep fighting, hope is alive. You must keep hope alive for yourselves, for your brothers and sisters, and for future generations." The phrase "keep hope alive" is one of many that Jackson repeatedly employs in his speeches to exhort his audience.

As exhortations, Jackson's speeches are organized in a pattern similar to that of religious sermons. First, his speeches almost always discuss the past, providing historical context for the present situation. Here Jackson appeals to America's traditions and fundamental values, which enables him to move into the second section of his speeches, where he laments the nation's failure to live up to its ideals. After offering a strong critique of the current situation, Jackson ends his speeches by pointing the way toward a more just society. Typical of this approach is his 1984 speech before the Democratic National Convention, in which he stated: "We are reminded that we live in a great nation—and we do. But it can be greater still. The Rainbow is mandating a new definition of greatness. We must not measure greatness from the mansion down but from the manger up." This is vintage Jackson, in which he is the secular and religious prophet critiquing American society and offering a new vision through a Christian lens.

This organizational pattern used by Jackson is rooted in both religion and the African American protest tradition. In most of his speeches, he effectively employs this form of speaking, known as the jeremiad, to exhort his audiences. Named after the biblical prophet Jeremiah, the jeremiad has historical roots in American public discourse, having been employed by critics of public life from across the political spectrum. The standard form for the American political jeremiad involves three themes: reminding the audience that there is a special moral or spiritual standard that governs their lives; lamenting the ways in which individuals or the community have not lived up to those expectations; and exhorting the audience to return to that moral standard. Jackson's 1988 Democratic National Convention speech employs the jeremiad, as he echoes a theme common to many of his speeches: "We are a better nation than that. We can do better than that. . . . We meet tonight at a crossroad, a point of decision. Shall we expand, be inclusive, find unity and power, or suffer division and impotence?" Most of Jackson's speeches are political sermons in which he ends by promising redemption if his audience members rediscover the true interpretation of the American dream.

Within this basic organizational structure, Jackson's speeches are often very complex, sometimes meandering, orations filled with personal narratives, digressions, personal observations, apologies, and inspiring and entertaining passages. This is because Jackson rarely speaks from a prepared text, choosing instead to improvise as the occasion and the audience require. Political adviser for his 1984 and 1988 presidential campaigns Mark Steitz describes Jackson's speaking process thus: "When Jackson is speaking, he is concentrating very intensely on the audience. He is watching. He is not working; he very seldom reads a speech or uses a teleprompter." In further describing Jackson's extemporaneous approach, Steitz observes that Jackson creates a speech "exactly in the course of giving it. That's why he doesn't really have a speechwriter. Never has, never will." Commenting on his belief that speeches should be created spontaneously, Jackson recounted a story about a sermon he delivered early in his career: "When I first came back home from the seminary, I was asked to speak at church, and my grandmother and some of the older folk came up afterward. 'That was a nice speech, young man, very nice speech.' They meant the words were. Words came out nice. That's what it was . . . was a speech. But as you go on and begin to catch hold of it, you start hearing them say, 'Well, now. You spoke to my soul. You burned me this morning.' Got to do more than *speak*."

Jackson's spontaneity is effective because of the other defining qualities of his oratorical style. One obvious feature of his speeches is the strong sense of identification that Jackson creates between himself, the topic, and the audience through the use of historical and personal examples. In addition, Jackson typically creates the foundation for exhortation by using rational and emotional appeals to demonstrate the problem that needs resolution. Finally, as his speeches build toward his exhortative conclusion, Jackson uses language and delivery that reflect his personal background and create a memorable rhetorical spectacle for his audience.

One prominent feature of Jackson's speaking style is his use of historical examples to create identification between himself and his audience. Because Jackson is a spokesperson for African Americans and other historically disadvantaged groups, his use of historical examples to link these groups with the American dream is an effective and time-tested strategy. In most of his speeches, Jackson attempts to create a message of inclusion such that all people, even those who traditionally do not support him or his causes, might find common ground with his ideas. In speaking to the Republican National Committee meeting in Washington, D.C., on January 20, 1978, Jackson referenced prominent presidential elections to make his point about the importance of the African American vote: "Let me come back to the point of these seven million unregistered black voters. Only five presidents—Herbert Hoover (1928), Franklin Roosevelt (twice, 1932 and 1936), Eisenhower (1956), Johnson (1964), and Nixon (1972) have defeated their opponents by more than seven million votes." Later in the same speech, he directly addressed the Republican officials: "It is a mystery to me why Republicans have the attitude that blacks will not vote for them. Blacks vote as intelligently and as diversely as any other group." Although he was addressing an audience that generally disagrees with his goals and objectives, Jackson used historical examples to create a bond with his Republican audience interested in regaining the White House.

Similarly, Jackson uses historical examples with supportive audiences to demonstrate that he shares a common purpose with them. At the

1984 Democratic National Convention, he used historical examples to illustrate the point that his principles were aligned with those of the Democratic Party and its nominee, Walter Mondale, even after a divisive primary campaign: "From Fannie Lou Hamer in Atlantic City in 1964 to the Rainbow Coalition in San Francisco today; from the Atlantic to the Pacific, we have experienced pain, but progress, as we ended America's apartheid laws; got public accommodations; we secured voting rights; we obtained open housing; as young people we got the right to vote; we lost Malcolm, Martin, Medgar, Bobby, John and Viola." In an approach very reminiscent of Martin Luther King Jr., Jackson attempted to unify the Democratic Party for the general election by reminding the audience of past civil rights successes and invoking the names of past civil rights and Democratic heroes.

In addition to drawing on well-known historical examples to create identification with his audiences, Jackson often draws upon powerful American narratives and symbols. One such narrative is the "city on the hill," in which the United States is portrayed as a nation with a divinely appointed role in the world. This core narrative has been a part of the nation's religious and political discourse since John Winthrop originally designated Americans as the chosen people, the "city upon the hill," in the seventeenth century. Many orators concentrate on America as a chosen nation, blessed by God. Jackson, however, is one of the few speakers who has kept Winthrop's other message: that God may have chosen the nation as a lesson in how not to create a society. Jackson's rhetoric echoes Martin Luther King Jr.'s theme that a chosen nation has special responsibilities as well as special rewards. Failure to create a just society incurs the harsh judgment of a righteous God—what theologian Martin Marty calls "the prophetic mode" of the "nation under God" imagery. In "Liberation and Justice," a speech given to Operation PUSH on its tenth anniversary, Jackson stated: "This is a period of intense anxiety, fear, and doubt. The blood at the bottom of the American pool keeps coming to the surface. Centuries of crime and terror upon which the nation was built are beginning to show their effect and result. There is a crisis of

confidence and moral bankruptcy. All people and nations must live with the consequences of their choices. God is not mocked. Whatsoever a man soweth, that will he also reap."

Likewise, Jackson employs the "city on the hill" narrative to demonstrate common interests between audience members with different political beliefs, as he did during his May 24, 1983, address to the joint session of the Alabama legislature in Montgomery when he stated: "We knew this day would come because our faith has taught us that even though the road has been difficult, God didn't bring us this far to leave us. We knew this day would come because the arc of the universe is long, but bends toward justice. We knew this day would come, not because we're lucky, but because we're blessed. . . . Now that we're here together—because of God's investment in us and the stewardship that he has entrusted in us—we are obligated to give back to God a return on his investment."

By creating a sense of identification with his audiences through the use of historical examples, cultural narratives, and powerful symbols, Jackson is able to advance his arguments forcefully, even with unreceptive audiences. Jackson's central claims in his speeches are typically clear and straightforward, focusing on a single topic, such as self-respect or civil rights. It is Jackson's support for these claims, however, that gives his speeches their character. Jackson often intricately weaves rational and emotional appeals in a complex and effective manner that gives his speeches their exhortative force.

Jackson's command of current data endows his arguments with credibility for many audiences, even among those who are not typically Jackson supporters. His use of statistical proof in his 1984 address to the Democratic National Convention is representative: "Under President Reagan there are eight million people in poverty. Currently fifteen percent of our nation is in poverty, thirty-four million people. Of the thirty-four million people, twenty-three million are white; eleven million are black, Hispanic, Asian, or others. By the end of this year, there will be forty-one million people in poverty, more than at any time since the inadequate war on poverty began in 1965." In a similar vein, Jackson uses factual and statistical evidence to demonstrate support for other causes, as he did in a 1985 address to Operation PUSH members about the difficulties small farmers faced: "Between 1972 and 1975 the consumer price index for food went up forty-eight percent. However, the amount Americans were paying for food that actually went to farmers increased by only eight percent. Between 1973 and 1975, after-tax profits for food corporations rose by fifty-four percent—which, more than any other component, accounted for the rise in the nation's food bill. By the end of the 1970s, commodity prices went down, but the price that consumers paid in the store stayed high. That means that both farmers and consumers were getting the raw end of the deal."

While Jackson's many statistics and facts add credibility to his arguments, his true talent lies in his ability to use such data to evoke strong emotions within his audiences: fear, anger, compassion, and, at times, resentment. Jackson often uses facts to trigger an emotional response in his audience, as he did in his commencement speech at the University of Rhode Island in 1979: "The world's people pay a huge bill for the arms race—approximately $400 billion a year. At the same time, on any given school day, some 200 million children around the world are not in school, mostly because their families are too poor to send them or their country is too poor to provide classrooms for them to attend." Jackson typically employs statistics to document and illustrate the impersonal corporations and governments that earn and spend colossal sums of money while the common people—those within his audience—must do without. Jackson's attempt to sharply contrast the greedy bureaucracies with the deserving common person is effective in part because of his compelling employment of factual evidence, and the resentment his data evoke in his audiences.

Although they are often persuasive, Jackson's appeals to audience resentment can create problems for him. At times, Jackson has created a backlash by attacking certain segments of the public. Two such instances occurred in his 1984 *Washington Post* interview, in which he called New York "Hymie-town" and New Yorkers "Hymies," and in 1984, when he publicly criticized the Democratic Party and

its nominee for president, Walter Mondale, for not selecting him as Mondale's running mate, thereby suggesting that race was a factor. These examples demonstrate Jackson's enigmatic personality and provocative speaking style, but also illustrate his political instincts and ability to extract himself rhetorically from difficult situations.

In responding to criticism for previous statements, Jackson often relies on public apologies grounded in the notion of personal redemption. For example, in 1984, he countered his damaging "Hymie-town" remark with this statement of repentance in his Democratic National Convention speech:

> Throughout the campaign, I've tried to offer leadership to the Democratic Party and the nation. If, in my highest moments, I have done some good, offered some service, shed some light, healed some wounds, rekindled some hope, and stirred someone from apathy and indifference, or in any way along the way helped somebody, then this campaign has not been in vain. If, in my lowest moments, in word, deed, or attitude, through some error of temper, taste, or tone, I have caused anyone discomfort, created pain, or revived fears, that was not my truest self.

Similarly, in speaking to those gathered at Temple Adath Yeshurun in Manchester, New Hampshire, on February 26, 1984, Jackson delivered a more explicit message about personal redemption:

> This is the moment, like others throughout history, where our mettle is being tested. It was Nathan, a lowly prophet, who had the courage to tell David, a powerful king, that he was wrong. His mettle was tested. It was John F. Kennedy who admitted that he had made a mistake in the Bay of Pigs invasion. His mettle was being tested. I feel good tonight because I know that unearned suffering is redemptive. Suffering breeds character, character breeds faith, and in the end faith will not disappoint.

Although Jackson's comments about New York and its residents were not forgotten during the primary campaign, his apologies effectively defused the political backlash caused by his remarks to the reporter. More generally, his repentant appeals demonstrate Jackson's ability to combine secular apologies with religious language and thus evoke forgiveness from many in his audience.

Part of Jesse Jackson's success as a speaker and leader, particularly within the African American community, is due to his audience's knowledge of his personal history. Jackson often reminds his audiences of his humble upbringing and his personal struggles as a way of connecting with them, but also to underscore his messages. Throughout his career with Operation PUSH, Jackson has often spoken to children and others about self-respect, often opening his speeches with a call-and-response that has become a trademark:

> I am somebody.//I may be poor,//but I am
>   somebody.//I may be uneducated,//but I
>   am somebody.//I may be unskilled,//but
>   I am somebody.
> I may be on welfare,//I may be prema-
>   turely pregnant,//I may be on drugs,//I
>   may be victimized by racism,//but I am
>   somebody.
> Respect me. Protect me. Never neglect
>   me.//I am God's child.

While this passage has been criticized and even satirized by Jackson's critics, it demonstrates how Jackson creates an emotional bond with his audience by using appeals that identify with its experience. Each statement about being poor, uneducated, or victimized by racism evokes emotional responses from his audience by having them recall strong cultural narratives. In addition, Jackson embodies the response "I am somebody" because the audience understands his own story of overcoming personal hardships and poverty to become a prominent leader.

In addition to allusions to his own background, Jackson uses personal narratives in many of his speeches to create a visceral response from his audience. Personal narration was prominent in his 1984 Democratic National Convention speech: "When I was a child in Greenville, South Carolina, the Rev. James Hall used to preach a sermon, every so often, about Jesus. He would quote Jesus as saying, 'If I be lifted up, I'll draw men unto me.' When I was a child I didn't quite understand what he meant. But I understand it better now. If you raise up the truth, it's magnetic. It has a way of drawing people." Similarly, in a sermon delivered at Ebenezer Baptist Church in Atlanta on January 15, 1986, Jackson employed personal narrative to demonstrate his political lineage to Dr. Martin Luther King Jr.:

> I was privileged to be with a small band of warriors, apostles, and disciples on January 15, 1968, the last birthday Dr. King was alive. He showed us on that day how to celebrate his birthday by the way he celebrated his own birthday. . . . About 2 o'clock, someone came into the room with a birthday cake. We stopped for a moment, sliced the cake, blew out the candles, ate the cake, and kept on organizing the Poor People's Campaign. That's how he celebrated his own birthday.

Drawing upon his roots in the Black Pentecostal tradition, Jackson uses language in a way that has made his speeches both memorable and effective. Employing repetition and antithesis in a manner similar to Martin Luther King, Jackson often creates an optimistic vision for the future, as he did in his 1984 address to the Democratic National Convention in San Francisco:

> When I see a missing door, that's the slummy side. Train some youth to become a carpenter, that's the sunny side. When I see vulgar words and hieroglyphics of destitution on the walls, that's the slummy side. Train some youth to be a painter and artist, that's the sunny side. . . . Our time has come. Our faith, hope and dreams have prevailed. Our time has come. Weeping has endured for nights, but joy cometh in the morning. Our time has come. No grave can hold our body down. Our time has come! No lie can live forever. Our time has come! We must leave the racial battleground and come to the economic common ground and moral higher ground. America, our time has come!

Jackson frequently uses rhyme to underscore his antitheses and add cadence to the rhythm. Although it is criticized and parodied by some, the effect of his rhyme is to deliver short, memorable phrases, as he did in the 1984 Democratic National Convention speech. In the conclusion he told the audience to "put hope in their brains, not dope in their veins," and "choose the human race over the nuclear race." Jackson often uses such play on words to enhance the rhythm and engage the audience, as he did with the line

"Dream of preachers and priests who will prophesy and not just profiteer." Jackson's style emphasizes the juxtaposition of negative images with positive ones, and reflects the optimistic nature of his rhetoric as well as his theological belief in a model of redemption in which all people are welcome and valued.

Similarly, Jackson's use of the rainbow and quilt metaphors within many of his speeches reflects his attempt to create an inclusive message. Both describe Jackson's view of a pluralistic America and seek to demonstrate how all Americans can retain their ethnic or racial heritage while living together successfully. In using these two metaphors, Jackson rejects the traditional "melting pot" metaphor of American assimilation. As he spoke to the Democratic National Convention in 1988, he described the quilt as requiring many pieces, but "no one's patch is big enough." During his 1984 speech, he used the central theme of a rainbow. Early in the speech Jackson stated: "Our flag is red, white, and blue, but our nation is a rainbow—red, yellow, brown, black, and white, we are all precious in God's sight! . . . All of us count and all of us fit somewhere. We have proven that we can survive without each other, but we have not proven we can win and progress without each other. We must all come together! . . . We are much too intelligent; much too bound by our Judeo-Christian heritage; much too victimized by racism, sexism, militarism, and anti-Semitism; much too threatened as historical scapegoats, to go on divided from one another. . . . We must come together!" Throughout his career, but especially in 1988, Jackson's message took hold as his blend of peace, civil rights, and economic populism broadly appealed to audiences consisting of supporters from various economic, racial, and ethnic backgrounds.

One of the most energizing speakers of the latter half of the twentieth century, Jackson has a delivery that is a product of his religious background and his association with other African American speakers, most prominently, Dr. Martin Luther King, Jr. Jackson's delivery is actually an interplay between himself and the audience, as he appears to draw energy from listeners' responses. Much in the manner of King, Jackson often approaches the podium or pulpit in a slow,

purposeful manner, as he did in a September 1988 address at PUSH headquarters in Chicago, in a building that once housed a synagogue. Jackson biographer Marshall Frady writes that, speaking slowly at first, with very measured pronunciation of each phrase, Jackson began: "We are moving into the latter stages of this campaign now. Sometimes we may have . . . may have *narrow* choices. But we *do* have choices." Looking around to see the reactions of his audience, Jackson, as he often does, picked up his speaking rate and intensity as he received feedback: "But we are going on beyond November. The race goes not to the swift but to the patient and long-enduring, to those who persist and tire not. Going on *beyond* November!" Looking around the audience again and drawing on their reactions, Jackson ended with his most intense delivery: "The best is yet to come! We are going to outwork, outwalk, outtalk, outfast, and *outlast* them all. The best is yet to come! I may not be on this ticket, but I am still *on the scene*! I can't *wait* to get back up outta bed every morning. I don't need no alarm clock to wake me up—I'm driven by *purpose*."

Jackson's forceful delivery often electrifies secular audiences as well. His 1984 Democratic National Convention address demonstrated how a well-constructed and well-delivered address could pull together a diverse audience. At the opening of the speech, Jackson began slowly, with few gestures, and looked at his prepared text even when speaking phrases like "choose the *human race* over the *nuclear race*." Throughout the speech, he masterfully used pauses for emphasis, as in the following passage: "If in my high moments, I have done some good, offered some service, shed some light, healed some wounds, rekindled some hope or stirred someone from apathy and indifference, or in any way helped somebody [*pause*], this campaign has not been in vain." By the end of the speech, Jackson's delivery had quickened, his gestures had become more expansive, and his focus was distinctly on the audience. The immediate audience was energized and participative, and Jackson drew from that energy: "If we cut the military budget without cutting our defense, and we use that money to rebuild bridges and put steelworkers back to work, and use that money, and provide jobs for our citizens, and use that money to build schools, and train teachers and educate our children, and build hospitals, and train doctors and train nurses, the whole nation will come running to us." At this point in the speech, Jackson screamed the words with an infectious passion that had many in his audience on their feet and audibly responding to his statements. At the speech's conclusion, the conventioneers gave Jackson a prolonged ovation that reflected their appreciation for his message and delivery. Immediately after the speech, Florida governor Bob Graham stated about the speech, "If you are a human being and weren't affected by what you just heard, you may be beyond redemption." Other commentators proposed that it may have been the greatest oration delivered at a nominating convention since William Jennings Bryan's in 1896.

Jesse Jackson was, and remains, one of the most interesting and confounding political figures and public speakers in contemporary America. He asserts bold stands on issues that represent his activist roots, speaking on behalf of those people and causes he considers to be without a voice in society. In pursuit of that goal, he often seeks media attention and suffers the criticism of many, particularly those who do not support his positions. He makes daring arguments with emotional language that endear him to his supporters and strongly provoke those who oppose him. Employing a distinctive rhetorical style, Jackson creates a strong sense of identification with his audience through the use of religious and secular narratives and symbols, powerful appeals, imaginative language, and a forceful delivery. There are few who would dispute the claim that Jesse Jackson has been one of the most innovative and compelling orators of the twentieth century.

INFORMATION SOURCES

Research Collections and Collected Speeches

Although there are several collections of Jackson's speeches, in both video and text, there is no full archival collection of his materials, nor is there an exhaustive collection of his speeches. Speech texts since 1997 and other information may be obtained from the Rainbow/PUSH Coalition [RPC], 930 E. 50th Street, Chicago, Ill. 60615-2702. www.rainbowpush.org

Jackson, Jesse L. *Keep Hope Alive: Jesse Jackson's 1988 Presidential Campaign. A Collection of Major Speeches, Issue Papers, Photographs, and Campaign Analysis* [KHA], ed. Frank Clemente and Frank Watkins. Boston: South End Press, 1989.

———. *Straight from the Heart* [SFH], ed. Roger D. Hatch and Frank E. Watkins. Philadelphia: Fortress Press, 1987.

Audiovisual Material

Jesse Jackson: An Inventory of His Spoken Audio Recordings. [VVL.] East Lansing: Vincent Voice Library, Michigan State University. Eleven recordings.

Selected Critical Studies

Callahan, Linda F. "History: A Critical Scene Within Jesse Jackson's Rhetorical Vision." *Journal of Black Studies* 24, no. 1 (1993): 3–15.

Colton, Elizabeth O. *The Jackson Phenomenon: The Man, the Power, the Message.* New York: Doubleday, 1989.

Landess, Thomas H., and Richard M. Quinn. *Jesse Jackson & the Politics of Race.* Ottawa, Ill.: Jameson Books, 1985.

Makay, John. "An Analysis of Jesse Jackson's Convention Speech, 1988." In *African American Rhetoric: A Reader*, ed. Lyndrey A. Niles. Dubuque, Iowa: Kendall/Hunt, 1995.

McTighe, Michael J. "Jesse Jackson and the Dilemmas of a Prophet in Politics." *Journal of Church and State* 32, no. 3 (1990): 1–23.

Morris, Lorenzo, ed. *The Social and Political Implications of the 1984 Jesse Jackson Presidential Campaign.* New York: Praeger, 1990.

Niles, Lyndrey A., and Carlos Morrison. "Jesse Louis Jackson." In *African American Orators: A Bio-Critical Sourcebook*, ed. Richard W. Leeman. Westport, Conn.: Greenwood Press, 1996.

Reed, Adolph L. *The Jesse Jackson Phenomenon.* New Haven, Conn.: Yale University Press, 1986.

Solomon, Martha A., and Paul B. Stewart. "The Rainbow Coalition." In *Great Speeches for Criticism and Analysis*, ed. Lloyd Rohler and Roger Cook, 2nd ed. Greenwood, Ind.: Alistair Press, 1993.

Sullivan, Patricia A. "Signification and African American Rhetoric: A Case Study of Jesse Jackson's 'Common Ground and Common Sense' Speech." *Communication Quarterly* 41, no. 1 (1993): 1–15.

Selected Biographies

Frady, Marshall. *Jesse: The Life and Pilgrimage of Jesse Jackson.* New York: Random House, 1996.

McKissack, Patricia C. *Jesse Jackson: A Biography.* New York: Scholastic, 1989.

CHRONOLOGY OF MAJOR SPEECHES

See "Research Collections and Collected Speeches" for source codes.

"Political Votes, Economic Oats." Washington, D.C., January 20, 1978. *SFH*, pp. 23–36.

"A Pursuit of Peace: A More Excellent Way" (commencement speech at the University of Rhode Island). Kingston, R.I., May 27, 1979. *SFH*, pp. 215–23.

"Service and a New World Order" (speech to the First Annual Conference on Human Values). London, April 1, 1981. *SFH*, pp. 76–86.

"Liberation and Justice: A Call for Redefinition, Refocus, and Rededication" (speech to the tenth annual convention of Operation PUSH). Chicago, July 9, 1981. *SFH*, pp. 48–63.

"Dreaming New Dreams." Washington, D.C., August 27, 1983. *SFH*, pp. 19–22.

"The Call of Conscience: Redemption, Expansion, Healing, and Unity" (speech to the Democratic National Convention). San Francisco, July 17, 1984. *Vital Speeches of the Day*, November 15, 1984, pp. 77–81.

"Save the Family Farm and the Farm Family" (speech to the Saturday Morning Community Forum of Operation PUSH). Chicago, January 26, 1985. *SFH*, pp. 282–88.

"Common Ground and Common Sense" (address to the Democratic National Convention). Atlanta, Ga., July 20, 1988. *Vital Speeches of the Day*, August 15, 1988, pp. 649–53.

"Empower Your Dreams" (address to *Black Collegian* magazine's twentieth anniversary celebration). New York City, March 1991. *Black Collegian*, April 1991, p. 128.

"We Must Seek a New Moral Center" (address to the Democratic National Convention). Chicago, August 27, 1996. *Vital Speeches of the Day*, September 15, 1996, pp. 717–18.

"The Power of the Golden Rule" (commencement address at DePaul University). Chicago, June 10, 2000. *RPC*.

"Keeping Hope Alive" (address to the Democratic National Convention). Los Angeles, August 15, 2000. *Vital Speeches of the Day*, September 1, 2000, pp. 649–53.

"Full Circle: Dr. King's Agenda" (address at Rainbow/PUSH Coalition meeting). Washington, D.C., January 18, 2003. *RPC*.

"AntiWar Speech" (address delivered at antiwar rally in Hyde Park, London). London, February 15, 2003. *RPC*.

"Dignity Day: It's Healing Time." Greenville, S.C., May 17, 2003. *RPC*.

LYNDON BAINES JOHNSON (1908–1973)
Thirty-sixth President of the United States

DAVID ZAREFSKY

History has not been kind to Lyndon Baines Johnson. The achievements of his Great Society have fallen victim to the widespread belief during the 1980s and 1990s that "big government" does not work. After the Cold War ended, Vietnam was increasingly regarded as a tragic error prompted by blind adherence to ideology rather than to practical realities. As the issues in civil rights have become more complex and intractable, the massive achievements of the 1960s look in retrospect like a promise unfulfilled. The Johnson presidency does not appear to have presented occasions that would call forth decisive rhetorical moments. Even Democratic partisans frequently omit Johnson from the pantheon of past presidents whose words they cite to rally the party faithful.

Nor did President Johnson appear to put much stock in public address. He was almost completely uninvolved in the speechwriting process, usually reading whatever his writers prepared—often for the first time when he delivered the speech. His lack of practice may have been one of the causes of the artificial, wooden delivery that became characteristic of his public discourse. Most observers agree that his rhetorical skill was displayed in interpersonal encounters, face-to-face or over the telephone. As published transcripts of his telephone conversations have made clear, he was adept at sizing up the values and priorities of the person he sought to persuade and appealing to that person while persisting on his own course and refusing to take no for an answer. The dynamism of these informal conversations stands in stark contrast to his prepared speeches. Johnson disdained oratory; he thought that the presidential persona required a model of rectitude at odds with his own personality; and he was uncomfortable with and distrustful of the electronic media.

Nevertheless, the nature of the times made the president a public figure, and the exigencies of the Johnson presidency often called for public discourse. Moreover, public address had played a central role in Johnson's early life. His father served briefly in the Texas state legislature, and from an early age Johnson was familiar with the give-and-take of political discussion, legislative speaking, and campaign rallies. He was a successful politician at Southwest Texas State Teachers College (now Texas State University, San Marcos) through a combination of persuasion and political organization. He taught public speaking in a Houston high school, coaching a debate team to the state finals in 1931. As a congressman, he was an outspoken advocate of the New Deal. Because of the way he defined his role as Senate majority leader and vice president, Johnson had few occasions for oratory in those roles. In late 1963 he found himself in the throes of what has been called "the rhetorical presidency." Many of the key events of the 1960s were shaped by or reflected in Johnson's presidential discourse.

PRESIDENT JOHNSON AS PERSUADER

Johnson took office under irregular circumstances. For domestic and international reasons, it was necessary for him to demonstrate that the political system could endure even the shock of the Kennedy assassination. Replacing chaos with confidence required that people trust the new man at the helm, and Johnson's situation required him to find the right stance with respect to President Kennedy—revering him, of course, but not so completely subordinating himself to the late president that he was seen as having no substance of his own.

These imperatives shaped Johnson's first major

public address as president, his speech on November 27, 1963, to a joint session of Congress. The dominant motif of this speech was its stress on continuity. Johnson appealed for the tax cut and the civil rights bill on the grounds that they would be fitting memorials to the slain president. And the phrase "let us continue" revealed his intentions not only explicitly but also in the obvious allusion to Kennedy's Inaugural Address plea, "let us begin." Johnson had many choices about how to define "continuity"; he chose to regard it as enactment of the Kennedy legislative program. He thereby influenced the agenda of discussion and set the standard by which he later could be judged as having kept the faith. Moreover, by focusing on the sphere of politics in which he was most adept—congressional deliberation—Johnson managed subtly to suggest that he was a leader not utterly subordinate to Kennedy; after all, the thinker depended upon the doer to get the bills through.

The most pressing domestic issue when Johnson took office was civil rights. Inspired by the moral fervor of the protest demonstrations, Kennedy in 1963 had submitted a strong civil rights bill, which Johnson advised him to justify as a moral and constitutional obligation. But the bill was still languishing in committee at the time of Kennedy's death. Johnson quickly concluded that he must secure the passage of a bill at least as strong as Kennedy's. During the next few months, public address played but a slight role; the president relied instead on the interpersonal persuasion at which he was most gifted. He met with civil rights leaders and advised them which members of Congress to visit. And he concentrated his own attention on the Senate minority leader, Everett Dirksen of Illinois, whose support he needed to break the Southern filibuster. The Civil Rights Act passed Congress in June 1964 and was quickly signed into law. Johnson offered brief remarks on the occasion, as he tended to do when signing major bills. These remarks mixed bipartisan praise for Congress and recognition of significant achievements with reminders that much hard work remained and exhortations to press toward further improvement of the human condition.

Following passage of the Civil Rights Act, Johnson pursued two rhetorical objectives: to reconcile the South to the law and to shape the future direction of the civil rights movement. In speaking to Southerners, he employed a combination of rhetorical strategies. In one respect he met the issue head-on, telling his audiences that the law of the land had been passed by people of both parties and signed by him, and that he was determined to enforce it. At the same time, he sought to mute the significance of the issue, suggesting that outsiders were trying to agitate the South over civil rights in order to divide and subjugate the region but that a bright future lay ahead if only the racial controversy could be put to rest. This mix of appeals is evident in Johnson's October 1964 speech in New Orleans, in which he added an extemporaneous discussion of civil rights to his prepared remarks on other subjects.

Even with the Civil Rights Act in place, the moral force of the civil rights movement out-spoke the words of the civil rights anthem, "We Shall Overcome."

In the June 1965 commencement address at Howard University, Johnson tried to shape the civil rights movement's direction rather than merely responding to outside pressure. It was not enough, he said, "just to open the gates of opportunity. All our citizens must have the ability to walk through those gates." Accordingly, policies must be developed to recognize the handicapping legacy of discrimination and to compensate for it. In its recognition that unequal treatment may be necessary to achieve equal results, the Howard University address introduced the idea of affirmative action. Johnson, however, thought in terms of compensatory measures to equip individuals to compete on an equal basis in the race of life, not in terms of quotas or goals to be applied to the outcome of the race. Moreover, when the Howard speech attracted intense

---

Speaking at Howard University's commencement in 1965, Johnson made the case for additional civil rights legislation beyond the Voting Rights Act of 1964. It was not enough, he said, "just to open the gates of opportunity. All our citizens must have the ability to walk through those gates."

---

paced the efforts of the federal government. Again responding to events in the South, particularly to the violence that greeted voting-rights marchers in Selma, Alabama, Johnson spoke to a joint session of Congress in March 1965 to appeal for voting-rights legislation. This speech is sometimes identified as his most moving public address, conveying the natural eloquence that Johnson so often took care to shield. It was selected by experts as one of the top 100 American speeches of the twentieth century. Two points deserve special mention. First, the president linked the issues of civil rights, education, and poverty, drawing on the memory of his days as a teacher in rural Texas to describe the web of ignorance, poverty, and discrimination in which young children were caught. Second, the speech was notable because a Southern president built to a climax and then dramatically

criticism, largely on other grounds, Johnson retreated from the idea and seldom mentioned it again.

Johnson also tried to leapfrog the civil rights movement by proposing a third civil rights act that would, among other features, ban racial discrimination in housing. Originally requested in a presidential message in April 1966, the act finally passed Congress two years later, in the aftermath of the assassination of Dr. Martin Luther King.

Race riots from 1964 through 1967 posed a dilemma for Johnson's advocacy of civil rights. He recognized that despite the new laws, many of the riots were founded in legitimate grievances that needed to be addressed, yet he also knew that disregard for law and order cost him support for civil rights by moderate and conservative whites. He could not reward the rioters, but he could not castigate them either. He emphasized the need for order, called for renewed commitment to the goal of civil rights, and announced the appointment of a commission to study the causes and prevention of riots. Each of these approaches, however, was outflanked. Radicals condemned him for appealing for order as a pretext to preserve an immoral society rather than supporting the sweeping changes they thought were needed to remove the causes of riots. Conservatives, meanwhile, alleged that the administration actually had helped to create the climate for riots with an expansive rhetoric that raised false hopes and invited disappointment. And so long as riots continued, they found Johnson's efforts at social control insufficient. Ultimately it was Johnson's fate to seek to define the civil rights agenda at precisely the time when the old civil rights movement was coming apart and when white support for the cause of civil rights flagged notably.

Johnson inherited the civil rights issue, but the Great Society was his own creation. He began with the issue of poverty, declaring "unconditional war" on the enemy during his January 1964 State of the Union address. The war metaphor, consciously chosen, affected the nature of the program. It called for an omnibus effort, nationwide in scope, with maximum publicity and centralized administrative direction. Johnson formally proposed this program in a March 1964 message to Congress in which he deplored the "paradox of poverty amidst plenty." Despite the absence of organized pressure groups lobbying for the Economic Opportunity Act, within five months it became law.

The president next moved to set his entire domestic program in a broader framework and to try to find a term to describe it. Harking back to Franklin Roosevelt and Harry Truman, he had tried *better deal*, but that phrase had not attracted notice. The term *great society* surfaced in several Johnson speeches in the spring of 1964, particularly in the May commencement address at the University of Michigan. Johnson appealed to new themes and spoke especially about cities, countryside, and classrooms. Besides the War on Poverty, the key components of the Great Society were federal aid to education and medical care for the aged, each proposed to Congress in a special presidential message and each enacted

into law during 1965. But the Great Society also could be characterized by overarching themes: a concern for the quality of life as opposed to a purely materialistic sense of well-being, a balance between continuity and change, acknowledgment of the need for special efforts on behalf of those left behind, an active role for the federal government, and a confidence in the country's ability to achieve its goals. This last theme figured prominently in Johnson's 1965 Inaugural Address, in which he expansively boasted, "Is our world gone? We say farewell. Is a new world coming? We welcome it, and will bend it to the hopes of man." To the contemporary reader who has heard political leaders in both parties proclaim that the era of big government is over, this self-confidence appears as arrogance approaching hubris, but it reflected Johnson's genuine belief that the nation could accomplish whatever it set out to do.

In appealing for his domestic programs, Johnson consistently combined the articulation of a utopian vision—the abolition of poverty, conquest of disease, or attainment of "full educational opportunity"—with conservative appeals at the level of means: programs would not cost much, they would "make taxpayers out of taxeaters," save money in the long run, and benefit everybody. Particularly when such important social goals could be achieved without strain or sacrifice, support for the Johnson programs could be portrayed as a moral imperative. The success of the space program was often used as the premise for an argument that a nation that could conquer space surely could solve problems here on earth. The seeming ease of the effort, captured in the president's oratory, may itself have inflated expectations and led to frustration when all did not turn out for the best. Inflation, racial turmoil, and disappointments in Vietnam and in the cities jolted the national confidence in the future and threatened the Great Society. Nevertheless, Johnson got the last word. In his final economic message, in January 1969, he returned to the earlier themes of the Great Society, noting his accomplishments, setting forth the unfinished business for the next president, and even adding items, such as a guaranteed annual income, that he earlier had criticized.

Some of the same desire to control events that characterized domestic policy can be seen in foreign affairs: in Johnson's telephone diplomacy during the 1964 Panama crisis, in urging a new approach toward eastern Europe in 1966, in pursuing a summit meeting with Aleksei Kosygin of the Soviet Union in 1967, and in seeking a nuclear nonproliferation treaty in 1968. Still, for many, Johnson's foreign policy is synonymous with Vietnam. In this regard, it must be remembered that public opinion supported the president's policy on the war almost all the way through his administration. For many, Vietnam proved the Cold War assumptions that communism was an expansive force, that Communist advances anywhere were a threat everywhere, and that a strong stand against Communist aggression and subversion in other lands would deter attacks on our own. Vietnam stretched each of these assumptions to the breaking point, but opposition did not pass the 50 percent mark until March 1968—and of those who were opposed then, half wanted an even more hawkish course of action. One factor in the retention of public support was a series of presidential addresses that may seem sterile or irrelevant now but were powerfully persuasive in their day.

Johnson's primary goal was to stop aggression. But even that was only a prelude to a more positive and ambitious program: the economic development of all of Southeast Asia. In April 1965, he spelled out his objective in a speech at Johns Hopkins University, proposing a $1 billion economic development program once peace was restored to Vietnam. With this appeal, Johnson hoped to regain the support of those liberals who were dubious about his war aims and to induce the North Vietnamese to abandon an irrational war. Neither result came about, and in his disappointment Johnson made few other references to his hopes for the postwar development of Vietnam.

Besides, the war must be ended first. That required "saving" South Vietnam from communism in order to protect the Third World. Yet Johnson constantly portrayed himself as a man of restraint, refusing, for example, to call up the reserves or to seek a declaration of war. His explanation was that he was fearful of triggering secret treaties by which the Soviet Union and China would intervene, but it is more plausible that he feared that his domestic programs—on which his

claim to a place in history would rest—would become casualties of a national mobilization for war. The paradox of unconditional commitment to objectives and self-restraint as to means was reconciled through an unusual definition of victory. Johnson sought to persuade China and the Soviet Union that wars of national liberation fail. U.S. perseverance would be taken as a sign that communism could not triumph. Recognizing that sign, the major Communist powers would cease and desist, and then, in Johnson's view, the war would be won. It was this stance that served to lock the United States into a basically inflexible position, heavily dependent on the wishes of the South Vietnamese rather than in control of its own actions.

Events enabled Johnson to escalate the war, pursuing his military objective while proclaiming his action to be a limited response to a specific enemy provocation and repeating his desire for restraint. The perceived attack in the Gulf of Tonkin was a fortuitous event, enabling Johnson to justify military action while proclaiming his self-restraint. Even the nature of Johnson's public address on this occasion displayed his ambivalence: he announced the reprisals in a brief speech delivered twenty-four minutes before midnight, hardly the time likely to attract a large or attentive audience. What took place was defined by the president as aggression, forcing the United States to reply. The attacks would not intimidate the United States, but would strengthen its resolve. At the same time, Johnson described his response as limited in order to avoid the risk of wider conflict. Finally, he appealed for the swift and decisive passage of a congressional resolution of support, not because it was necessary in order to authorize action but in order to make clear to others the united determination of Americans.

Similarly, the shelling of a U.S. barracks at Pleiku, Vietnam, in February 1965 provided the occasion for a reprisal recommended earlier. And so began Operation Rolling Thunder, the sustained bombing of North Vietnam—without any public address. The commitment of major increments of U.S. troops was explained in July 1965 as a counter to the North Vietnamese infiltration of regular army units. This time, Johnson announced his action during a midday, midweek press conference, sandwiched between other announcements on unrelated subjects. In each of these escalations, the muted rhetorical response effectively portrayed Johnson as restrained even as he was stepping up the U.S. military involvement in the war.

The message of U.S. staying power in Vietnam was undermined by domestic dissent. How could the United States convince others that wars of liberation fail if it was unwilling to persevere? Johnson at first believed that dissenters were simply misinformed and that administration speakers could set them straight; for this reason he welcomed the national teach-ins in the spring of 1965. But when dissent continued, Johnson sought to co-opt the critics—with the Christmas 1965 bombing pause, for instance—and to compete with them for the headlines. When Senator J. William Fulbright (D-Ark.) held hearings on the war in February 1966, Johnson accepted a long-standing invitation to speak at Freedom House in New York, where he defended U.S. conduct in Vietnam as consistent with the cause of freedom. Still the opposition continued, and the president began to castigate his critics more directly. He thought that they were giving Hanoi the mistaken impression that the country was deeply divided, and thereby encouraging the enemy to prolong the war. In September 1967 it appeared that Johnson might prevail. In a speech in San Antonio, he set forth a framework for peace negotiations that most Americans thought reasonable, and when North Vietnam spurned this offer, public opinion rallied in support of the president. Seventy percent thought bombing of North Vietnam should continue. Administration speakers were confident that the long, difficult struggle would soon pay off.

Then came the Tet offensive, a blow far more serious psychologically than militarily. It cast doubt on the predictions of an end to the war and triggered an intense debate within the administration, which culminated in a dispute over what Johnson would say in a major speech on Vietnam scheduled for March 31, 1968. The hawks wanted a substantial increase in troop commitments and a fighting speech; the doves wanted a halt to the bombing and a cap on the U.S. troop presence. Speechwriter Harry McPherson developed two different drafts of the speech, a "war draft" and a "peace draft," not knowing which one the president would choose. Neither faction achieved its goals completely, but Johnson predominantly based the speech on the peace draft. The March 31 speech is a text in which one can find what one seeks. It can be read as a continuation of Johnson's policies in that it did announce a modest increase in troop levels and a bombing halt that was less generous than previous pauses had been. But it also can be taken as signaling a major change by placing a ceiling on troop levels and unilaterally halting even some bombing of North Vietnam without a prior commitment to reciprocity by the enemy. This latter interpretation, of course, was given added credence when North Vietnam, much to Johnson's surprise, agreed to open negotiations.

The most memorable aspect of the March 31 speech was the surprise peroration. Although virtually assured of renomination and having a good chance of reelection, the politician for whom Washington had been home for thirty-six years was heading back to Texas. He left in his presidential public addresses a record of his times. They were times of great and unpredictable change, of striving for mastery and control of events, of confidence in the country's ability to endure great problems.

Johnson sought consensus and induced Southerners to acquiesce in civil rights, businessmen in the Great Society, and—at least for a time—liberals in the Vietnam War. But Johnson also gained mastery over issues at precisely the wrong time. He dominated civil rights just when both blacks and whites weakened their commitment to integration. He championed the Great Society programs only to find the beginnings of national sentiment against big government. He followed the standard liberal course in Vietnam just when liberals were reappraising their basic assumptions about America's place in the world. And Johnson, master of flexibility when it came to tactics, proved to be overly rigid when it came to goals. Seeking to control the change he professed to welcome, his most basic commitments and values left him unable to master the challenge of change during the 1960s.

INFORMATION SOURCES

Research Collections and Collected Speeches

The best resource for research on the presidential rhetoric of Lyndon Johnson is the Lyndon Baines Johnson Library, University of Texas at Austin. The Johnson Library includes the White House central files, the president's appointment books and daily diaries, files of numerous aides, and presidential correspondence. It features an extensive collection of books and articles about Johnson and an excellent collection of oral histories by many of the principals of the Johnson administration. Finally, the library has a large collection of microfilms of theses and dissertations about Johnson, and numerous bibliographies and filing aids. As of this writing in 2004, the library's holdings are not available in digital form. However, texts of twenty-six speeches from 1963 to 1971 are available on-line from the library Web site http://www.lbjlib.utexas.edu

American Rhetoric from Roosevelt to Reagan: A Collection of Speeches and Critical Essays [*ARRR*], ed. Halford Ross Ryan. Prospect Heights, Ill.: Waveland Press, 1983.

Presidential Rhetoric [*PR*], ed. Theodore Windt. 3rd ed. Dubuque, Iowa: Kendall/Hunt, 1983.

Public Papers of the Presidents: Lyndon B. Johnson [*PP*], 10 vols. Washington, D.C.: Government Printing Office, 1965–70.

To Heal and to Build: The Programs of President Lyndon B. Johnson [*THB*], ed. James McGregor Burns. New York: McGraw-Hill, 1968.

Web Site

Lyndon B. Johnson Library and Museum. This site includes texts of presidential speeches as well some audio clips and an index to the Library's archival holdings. www.ljblib.utexas.edu

Audiovisual Material

Lyndon B. Johnson Library and Museum. This site includes audio clips of Johnson's November 27, 1963, eulogy of John F. Kennedy, his 1965 Inaugural Address, and the 1964 and 1965 State of the Union addresses. There are also an audio clip of his 1968 announcement not to run for reelection and clips of several conversations with national leaders. Available at www.lbjlib.utexas.edu

Selected Critical Studies

Ball, Moya Ann. *Vietnam-on-the-Potomac.* New York: Praeger, 1992.

Bass, Jeff D. "The Appeal to Efficiency as Narrative Closure: Lyndon Johnson and the Dominican Crisis, 1965." *Southern Speech Communication Journal* 50 (Winter 1985): 103–20.

Byrne, Richard. "Lyndon Agonistes." *The American Prospect* 15 (August 2004): 46–49.

Cherwitz, Richard A. "Lyndon Johnson and the 'Crisis' of Tonkin Gulf: A President's Justification for War." *Western Journal of Speech Communication* 41 (Spring 1978): 93–104.

Logue, Cal M., and John H. Patton. "From Ambiguity to Dogma: The Rhetorical Symbols of Lyndon B. Johnson on Vietnam." *Southern Speech Communication Journal* 47 (Spring 1982): 310–29.

Pauley, Garth. *The Modern Presidency and Civil Rights.* College Station: Texas A&M University Press, 2001.

Ritter, Kurt. "Lyndon B. Johnson's Voting Rights Address of March 15, 1965: Civil Rights Rhetoric in the Jeremiad Tradition." In *Great Speeches for Criticism and Analysis*, ed. Lloyd E. Rohler and Roger Cook, 4th ed. Greenwood, Ind.: Alistair Press, 2001.

Smith, F. Michael. "Rhetorical Implications of the 'Aggression' Thesis in the Johnson Administration's Vietnam Argumentation." *Central States Speech Journal* 23 (Winter 1972): 217–24.

Turner, Kathleen J. *Lyndon Johnson's Dual War: Vietnam and the Press.* Chicago: University of Chicago Press, 1985.

Zarefsky, David. "Civil Rights and Civil Conflict: Presidential Communication in Crisis." *Central States Speech Journal* 34 (Spring 1983): 59–66.

———. "The Great Society as a Rhetorical Proposition." *Quarterly Journal of Speech* 65 (December 1979): 364–78.

———. "Lyndon Johnson Redefines 'Equal Opportunity': The Beginnings of Affirmative Action." *Central States Speech Journal* 31 (Summer 1980): 85–94.

———. *President Johnson's War on Poverty: Rhetoric and History.* Tuscaloosa: University of Alabama Press, 1986.

———. "Subordinating the Civil Rights Issue: Lyndon Johnson in 1964." *Southern Speech Communication Journal* 48 (Winter 1983): 103–18.

Selected Biographies

Bernstein, Irving. *Guns or Butter: The Presidency of Lyndon Johnson.* New York: Oxford University Press, 1996.

Beschloss, Michael, ed. *Reaching for Glory: Lyndon Johnson's Secret White House Tapes, 1964–1965.* New York: Simon and Schuster, 2001.

———. *Taking Charge: The Johnson White House Tapes, 1963–1964.* New York: Simon and Schuster, 1997.

Bornet, Vaughn Davis. *The Presidency of Lyndon B. Johnson.* Lawrence: University Press of Kansas, 1983.

Califano, Joseph A. *The Triumph and Tragedy of Lyndon Johnson: The White House Years.* New York: Simon and Schuster, 1991.

Caro, Robert A. *The Years of Lyndon Johnson*, vol. 1: *The Path to Power.* New York: Knopf, 1982.

———. *The Years of Lyndon Johnson*, vol. 2: *Means of Ascent.* New York: Knopf, 1990.

———. *The Years of Lyndon Johnson*, vol. 3: *Master of the Senate.* New York: Knopf, 2002.

Dallek, Robert. *Flawed Giant: Lyndon Johnson and His Times, 1961–1973.* New York: Oxford University Press, 1998.

———. *Lone Star Rising: Lyndon Johnson and His Times, 1908–1960.* New York: Oxford University Press, 1991.

Divine, Robert A., ed. *Exploring the Johnson Years*, vol. 1. Austin: University of Texas Press, 1981.

———. *The Johnson Years*, vol. 2: *Vietnam, the Environment, and Science.* Lawrence: University Press of Kansas, 1987.

———. *The Johnson Years*, vol. 3: *LBJ at Home and Abroad.* Lawrence: University Press of Kansas, 1994.

Dugger, Ronnie. *The Politician: The Life and Times of Lyndon Johnson. The Drive for Power, from the Frontier to Master of the Senate.* New York: Norton, 1982.

Evans, Rowland, and Robert Novak. *Lyndon B. Johnson: The Exercise of Power.* New York: New American Library, 1966.

Goldman, Eric F. *The Tragedy of Lyndon Johnson.* New York: Knopf, 1969.

Goodman, Doris Kearns. *Lyndon Johnson and the American Dream.* New York: Harper & Row, 1976.

Henggeler, Paul R. *In His Steps: Lyndon Johnson and the Kennedy Mystique.* Chicago: Ivan R. Dee, 1991.

Johnson, Lyndon Baines. *The Vantage Point: Perspectives of the Presidency, 1963–1969.* New York: Holt, Rinehart, and Winston, 1971.

Miller, Merle. *Lyndon: An Oral Biography.* New York: Putnam, 1980.

Steinberg, Alfred. *Sam Johnson's Boy.* New York: Macmillan, 1968.

CHRONOLOGY OF MAJOR SPEECHES

See "Research Collections and Collected Speeches" for source codes.

"Address to Joint Session of Congress." Washington, D.C., November 27, 1963. *PP: 1963–1964*, vol. 1, pp. 8–10; *PR*, pp. 53–55.

"State of the Union Address." Washington, D.C., January 8, 1964. *PP: 1963–1964*, vol. 1, pp. 112–18; *PR*, pp. 56–61.

"Poverty Message to Congress." Washington, D.C., March 16, 1964. *PP: 1963–1964*, vol. 1, pp. 375–80.

"Great Society Speech." University of Michigan, Ann Arbor, May 22, 1964. *PP: 1963–1964*, vol. 1, pp. 704–7; *PR*, pp. 61–64.

"Tonkin Gulf Announcement." Washington, D.C., August 4, 1964. *PP: 1963–1964*, vol. 2, pp. 927–28; *PR*, pp. 65–66.

"Political Campaign Speech." New Orleans, La., October 9, 1964. *PP: 1963–1964*, vol. 2, pp. 1281–88.

"Inaugural Address." Washington, D.C., January 20, 1965. *PP: 1965*, vol. 1, pp. 71–74.

"Voting Rights Address." Washington, D.C., March 15, 1965. *PP: 1965*, vol. 1, pp. 281–87; *ARRR*, pp. 173–80; *PR*, pp. 66–72.

"Johns Hopkins University Address." Baltimore, Md., April 7, 1965. *PP: 1965*, vol. 1, pp. 394–99.

"Howard University Commencement Address." Washington, D.C., June 4, 1965. *PP: 1965*, vol. 2, pp. 635–40; *THB*, pp. 217–26.

"Announcement of Troop Increase." Washington, D.C., July 28, 1965. *PP: 1965*, vol. 2, pp. 794–803 (esp. p. 795); *PR*, pp. 80–85.

"Freedom House Speech." New York City, February 20, 1966. *PP: 1966*, vol. 1, pp. 208–15.

"Civil Rights Message to Congress." Washington, D.C., April 28, 1966. *PP: 1966*, vol. 1, pp. 461–69.

"Vietnam Policy Speech." San Antonio, Tex., September 29, 1967. *PP: 1967*, vol. 2, pp. 876–81; *PR*, pp. 93–98; *THB*, pp. 123–31.

"Renunciation Speech." Washington, D.C., March 31, 1968. *PP: 1968–1969*, vol. 1, pp. 469–76; *PR*, pp. 98–106; *THB*, pp. 455–64.

"Economic Message." Washington, D.C., January 16, 1969. *PP: 1968–1969*, vol. 2, pp. 1311–25.

SONIA JOHNSON (1936–)
Feminist Activist, Author, and Presidential Candidate

KAREN A. FOSS

Sonia Johnson's rhetoric is marked by a fearless integrity. From Mormon housewife to ERA supporter to radical feminist to presidential candidate, she has not been afraid to challenge herself and others by asking hard questions about the nature of the world. Johnson has been willing to make difficult choices, to change her mind, and to experiment with new rhetorical strategies as her perspective on the world has shifted. Her evolution offers a model of personal commitment, authenticity, and rhetorical creativity that defines a distinctive and radical edge of U.S. feminism.

Sonia Johnson was born on February 27, 1936 in Malad, Idaho, to Ida Howell Harris and Alvin Harris. The third of five children, she grew up in a family of devout fifth-generation members of the Church of Jesus Christ of Latter-day Saints. Her parents moved to Ferron, Utah, shortly after her birth, then to Preston, Idaho, and finally to Logan, Utah, where Johnson's father taught in a Mormon seminary. Johnson graduated from Logan High School and Utah State University in Logan, earning a B.A. degree in English from the latter. At Utah State she met Richard Johnson, a fellow student, whom she married a year after her graduation. They had four children, born in different locations as she followed her husband to teaching positions in Minnesota, California, New Jersey, Korea, Malaysia, and Africa. She completed M.A. and Ed.D. degrees at Rutgers University before the family settled permanently in Sterling, Virginia.

At the urging of a friend, Johnson and her husband began reading feminist literature, including information about the proposed Equal Rights Amendment (ERA) to the U.S. Constitution. The ERA, introduced in every session of Congress since 1923, would prohibit discrimination based on sex. On March 22, 1972, the amendment passed both houses of Congress for the first time and was sent to the states for ratification. Johnson entered the debate in its ratification stage, during which three-quarters of the states had to ratify the amendment by March 22, 1979. Although the Mormon Church opposed the amendment, Johnson saw the ERA and all political issues as quite separate from her religious commitment. When the stake president—the regional leader in charge of several wards within the church—came to discuss the reasons for the church's opposition, Johnson believed she finally would have the explanation she needed to understand the church's position. But not only did the president have no prepared remarks, suggesting to Johnson that the church had no legitimate reasons for its opposition, he made the mistake of reading the text of the amendment out loud. This was the first time Johnson had heard the text of the ERA, and its simplicity, combined with the president's ineptitude, produced an instantaneous and radical understanding of women's place in society.

Until that point, as she recounts in her speech "Living the Dream," delivered at the University of Alaska in 1990, Johnson had no need for women's movements:

> I know you had something called the women's movement going on here . . . but I didn't know what it was all about because, you know, I really didn't need it. I was having a wonderful life. I was doing exactly what I wanted to do. I was teaching poetry and literature at all these universities all over the world. And I had a marvelous husband and gorgeous children and these marvelous women to cook and clean for me, and I adored them. What would I want a women's movement for? It was clear that you didn't have this so you had to do something about it.

On the way home from the church meeting, Johnson declared to her husband that she was a feminist:

I'm a feminist. In fact, I'm a radical feminist. I didn't even know what that meant. But I was an English teacher and I knew it didn't mean wild-eyed crazy and off the wall, although you know, occasionally we are that, because it's kind of fun. I knew it came from the Latin word *rad* and it meant root—at the roots of things. And I knew that as I had been changed at the very roots of me, feminism, the rising of the women of the world, was changing the soul of the world and that the world would never be the same.

Johnson spent the next several years engaged in activism on behalf of the ERA. She was a founding member of Mormons for ERA, testified before the Senate subcommittee hearings on extending the ratification deadline for the ERA, and participated in marches and demonstrations for the ERA across the country. Her pro-ERA activities were increasingly problematic for the Mormon Church, however, and despite her continued

pated in acts of civil disobedience against the Republican Party, which had dropped the ERA from its platform in 1980, including chaining herself to the gates of Republican national headquarters, burning President Ronald Reagan in effigy, and scaling the White House gate. She was also one of eight women who fasted for forty-five days in the Illinois legislature in an effort—ultimately unsuccessful—to convince legislators that "women hunger[ed] for justice" and wanted to see the ERA passed as a symbol of justice.

Johnson ran as a candidate for president of the United States on the Citizens Party ticket in 1984, convinced that a feminist analysis of politics could create a shift of consciousness, whether or not she won. With her running mate, Richard Walton, Johnson traveled to almost every state in the union, advocating human rights, a major reduction of the U.S. military budget, restoration of social programs, laws governing equity in the

---

"If you always do what you've always done, you always get what you always got. So do something else. Do anything else!"

—*Sonia Johnson, "Living the Dream"*

---

affirmation of her allegiance to the church, she was summoned to a church court for trial on December 1, 1979. She was accused of doctrinal heresies and ultimately excommunicated, although she understood that her speaking out in favor of the ERA was the real issue. As she puts it, she was excommunicated for her "uppityness." A week after the trial, her husband asked for a divorce, and so she lost her two most important relationships—her marriage and her church—simultaneously. She began to support herself and her children with speaking engagements. "Living the Dream" is typical of her speeches in that she tells the story of coming to feminist consciousness, shares her shifts in thinking about patriarchy, and articulates her vision for women's world; it will be used as the exemplar of her rhetoric in this essay.

As the 1982 extended deadline for the ratification of the ERA approached, Johnson became even more committed to the cause. She partici-

workplace, and the abandonment of nuclear power projects. She became the first third-party presidential candidate to qualify for federal primary matching funds.

Johnson's fast on behalf of the ERA, coupled with her bid for the presidency, convinced her that working within the patriarchal system was not the way to achieve social change. She began to examine various institutions—from universities to newspapers to twelve-step programs to voting—finding all of them counter to women's interests. She abandoned participation in such institutions, no longer wishing to give the patriarchy any attention. Her examination of institutions also led to a questioning of relationships as institutionalized in patriarchy, which caused her to give up "coupled" relationships in the traditional sense. She also "divorced" her children—decided to have no further contact with them—believing that motherhood as constituted under patriarchy is a detrimental relationship for all concerned.

In addition to speaking out on feminist causes through speeches, protests, and campaigns, Johnson has presented her ideas through books. In both her speeches and her writings, she works through her positions with her audiences, shares how she came to a certain position, and discusses its implications for her feminist philosophy as a whole. Johnson's first book, *From Housewife to Heretic*, published in 1981, focuses on the process of her feminist awakening. In her 1987 book, *Going Out of Our Minds: The Metaphysics of Liberation*, she chronicles her efforts to disengage from the patriarchy, a process she continues in *Wildfire: Igniting a She/Volution* (1989). Her 1991 book, *The Ship That Sailed into the Living Room: Sex and Intimacy Reconsidered*, recounts her questioning of the institution of couples relationship under patriarchy.

SONIA JOHNSON: FROM RESISTANCE TO WOMEN'S WORLD

Sonia Johnson's rhetoric—her pronouncements in speeches, books, and articles—began in response to a patriarchal world. Her strategies, however, have undergone major transformations since her first rhetorical efforts on behalf of the ERA. During her days as an ERA activist, she focused her efforts on describing patriarchy as an oppressive system for women and the archetype upon which all other forms of oppression are modeled. Johnson devoted her efforts to changing patriarchy—to incorporating women's perspectives into the world in order to make it less oppressive for women.

Johnson's years of lobbying men, as well as her years as a mother, led her to two important realizations. First, change happens only if if someone chooses to change. She offers the following account of this realization in "Living the Dream":

> I had learned as a mother that you can't change anyone but yourself. I learned it in my own kitchen with my four children. I began to remember how I had these four human beings on this planet who had come right out of my womb—I had created them. . . . They were partly me, and we adored each other, we loved each other, we respected each other. . . . And I remember how I had never ever been able to make them do what I wanted from the moment they were born. They really wanted to . . . be-

cause they loved me. They tried very hard but they really couldn't do their lives the way I wanted them to.

If she could not get her children to do what she wanted, how could she expect men she did not even know to change at her request? Johnson concluded that it was not that women were not doing enough; rather, it was the strategy that was misguided: "We are so creative, so imaginative. Women thought of everything to try to change men. Women have been trying to get men to stop doing it for 5,000 years. I don't want to be hasty, but I think 5,000 years is long enough!"

A second realization was equally important—the current world suits men and, for the most part, they see no need to change it. In "Living the Dream," she describes how men's "eyes glazed over" when "I began to point out to them everything that was wrong with this world. It was a surprise to realize they thought they'd done a pretty spiffy job. That these are the people who on the whole thought this world was rather nifty. This is the way men do worlds. I realized we were asking the wrong people to change the world."

These realizations led Johnson to experiment with an entirely new set of strategies grounded in the need to "take our eyes off the guys." She decided to stop resisting—attending to what she did not want—and focusing instead on what she did want. Recalling the slogan "What if they gave a war and nobody came?," Johnson began to recognize that engaging the patriarchy by resisting it in fact maintained its power. She cites as an example *Roe v. Wade*, the 1973 Supreme Court decision that legalized abortion. In focusing on achieving a law within the patriarchal system, not only did women forget their own power—that for centuries women performed their own abortions and could do so again—but they created a situation in which they must continually lobby men and fight to keep the law from being overturned. Creating an alternative world independent of the male medical system would ensure the continuance of women's control over reproduction no matter what men's laws did.

For Johnson, taking the focus away from attempting to change men and attending instead to what women want was a critical rhetorical shift. She began to concentrate on what alternatives to patriarchy would look like, to create women's world: "I remember what my mother told me, 'Sonia, if you want it done right, do it yourself.'" And since she found nothing she liked about the present world, she had to figure out how to change it for herself: "And I looked out at the world men had done and I realized that there's not one single thing I would have done this way—not one single thing." In "Living the Dream," Johnson suggests that it is time for women to try an infinite number of things in order to create women's world: "If you always do what you've always done, you always get what you always got. So do something else. Do anything else!" This, for Johnson, is the best way to bring a new world into being.

Since her decision to stop paying attention to patriarchy, Johnson has concentrated on describing and realizing women's world. For her, it is a world "where my values are evident everywhere. Where there is peace and joy and love and plenty for everybody and kindness and beauty and fun and laughter. That's my world and I want it. So obviously the people who want it are the ones who have to build it." To this end, Johnson articulates three principles that serve as the foundation for her new standpoint and its accompanying rhetorical options: (1) a focus on changing the self rather than on changing others; (2) a focus on the present rather than the future; and (3) a focus on being rather than doing.

Johnson's first principle for realizing women's world is the notion of self-change rather than persuasion. Starting from the insight that she had never been able to get anyone to change in the direction she advocated, Johnson has continued to expand on this idea in her speeches and writings. She has come to realize that not only are efforts to change others ineffective, but they are harmful and disrespectful as well. To try to make others change, communicates to them that they are not capable of making their own life choices. In other words, it constructs them as victims, which only perpetuates the oppressive pattern of interaction that is central to patriarchy. A focus on changing the self, on the other hand—feeling, living, and acting out of one's own power rather than giving the power away to others—is antithetical to oppression because it empowers each

individual: "To be in your power means you no longer have to control anyone else. . . . I began to realize that to be in my power, I didn't look around for someone to make me feel a certain way. To be in your power means having your complete self at your disposal."

A rhetoric based on self-change places a great deal of responsibility on the rhetor. In Johnson's system, the rhetor is not simply the creator of a message designed to move others, but is totally responsible for her life and the world in which she lives. Johnson believes that to take responsibility for anyone or anything else diminishes the freedom and competence of the other—something she is no longer willing to do. She trusts that others are capable of managing their own lives, just as she is, and that all anyone needs is to be accepted as the expert on her own life, to be seen as someone who is doing the best she can at any moment. Johnson thus believes that when women are given the responsibility for their own lives, not only are there always an infinite number of choices available, but each woman makes the choices that are right for her. For Johnson, self-responsibility is power: "Power is always positive. . . . It is the generative, creative stuff of life." She wants a world in which women are in their power most of the time.

The second principle Johnson articulates is a focus on the present. For Johnson, the understanding, from atomic science, that time is not passing but simply surrounds us, like the ocean, was a major breakthrough. She realized that all the time that is and will ever be is here now, so only in the present can anything be created or changed: "Time isn't moving in there—it isn't a river going by pell-mell. It's not moving at all. . . . It's timeful—all time is there at once." In the present is where women's power is.

The power of the present also suggests yet another important implication of present time: the means are the ends. Whatever is happening in the present is creating its own future. When women's organizations sponsor "Take Back the Night" marches, they are creating a future in which women must continue to be afraid to walk alone at night. When women focus on sexual harassment policies in an organization, they create a world in which women will continue to be harassed by men. To create the desired world, then, requires a shift in focus from a future where things will be as imagined to a present in which the desired life is created and lived.

Finally, Johnson has adopted a third principle necessary for the creation of women's world: being, not doing. This idea is closely connected to Johnson's idea of the present as the only time in which to create a different world and to her notion of power. If the present is all that is available, being or living in the desired world is what will bring that world about. Doing, in contrast, implies working toward something in a future that is not yet here—something Johnson no longer believes. So she has stopped "doing" activities that are focused on the future. She believes that her only task is to live in "vibrant aliveness, enjoying, appreciating, and experiencing every moment" as a way to make the world in which she wants to live. She summarizes: "The purpose of life is to be fully ourselves—to be our authentic selves and to follow the desires of our hearts." When each person does this fully in her power, authentically, and with integrity, the world functions naturally and in accordance with women's values.

As with Johnson's other rhetorical options, being suggests an alternative approach to change. Johnson believes that patriarchy cannot exist in the presence of life, joy, and fearlessness, so when a woman is experiencing these feelings, she creates and holds a space in the cosmos where women's world is realized. As more and more women do this for longer and longer periods of time, women's reality becomes manifest across the planet.

Johnson's articulation and use of alternative rhetorical strategies results in a theory of change that looks quite different from traditional rhetorical models. First, rather than focusing on a situation that needs to be changed—the patriarchy— Johnson refuses to put her attention there any longer, believing this only maintains the situation in its power. Johnson shifts the focus of her rhetoric from an exigence—what needs to be fixed— to simply focusing on being fully herself, in harmony with all other creatures on the planet. Without an exigence to overcome, there is no need for strategies that will get others to change. Instead, self-change is the focus in Johnson's

rhetorical system, and beginning to live the desired changes is what will bring it about.

The audience looks quite different in Johnson's system than in most rhetorical theories. Traditionally, rhetorical strategies are chosen to get others to change in a particular direction, an approach that implicitly constructs the audience as generally less experienced, less informed, and less capable than the rhetor. Johnson inverts this perspective, making her audience members, rather than the rhetor, the experts on their own lives. Audience members are peers with the rhetor, and each woman is seen as competent, strong, and capable.

Johnson's speeches are enactments of her rhetorical choices. She describes her own process of discovery without asking others to adopt the same approach. She often starts to talk about "we women" and then switches to "I," joking that she often generalizes from a "sample of one," but is trying not to do that as much these days. She focuses on "present-ing" the world desired, using elaborate descriptions of how that world can be, rather than using persuasive strategies designed to bring it into being. Her use of humor enacts a playfulness that makes her world appealing to even the most skeptical of audiences. For instance, she began her "Living the Dream" speech with an account of an event that she says took place before her feminist awakening: "I wasn't a feminist yet. It was two or three weeks before the Mormons made me one." In general, she sees her rhetoric as widening and clearing a path of freedom, a space in which women's world can flourish: "If any of us is free, we are all more able to feel freedom."

Johnson now concentrates her efforts on simply living women's world, a world outside of patriarchy. She describes this life in *Out of This World: A Fictionalized True-Life Adventue*, written with Jade DeForest and published in 1993. She no longer writes or lectures, however, believing that each woman is capable of finding and following her own path to transformation.

So while Johnson began in the mainstream of second-wave feminism, her questioning examination of everything about her life, her motives, her goals, and the rhetorical strategies available to achieve those goals have taken her in truly radical directions. She has rejected strategies of resistance in favor of simply being and living the life she desires. This evolution, although more extreme than that of most feminists, is one that is increasingly of interest as feminists turn from persuasion to enactment and to invitation rather than manipulation.

INFORMATION SOURCES

Research Collections and Collected Speeches

Betty Bone Schiess Papers [*BBSP*], 1965–91. Division of Rare and Manuscript Collections, Cornell University Library, Ithaca, N.Y. Contains correspondence between Johnson and Schiess, one of the first women ordained to the priesthood in the Episcopal Church; materials related to a church service with Sonia Johnson, July 1980; and materials related to an appearance with Sonia Johnson on the *Today Show*, January 1981.

Margaret Miller Curtis Papers [*MMCP*], 1973–98. Special Collections, William Russell Pullen Library, Georgia State University, Atlanta, Ga. Contains correspondence between Curtis, a Georgia ERA activist, and Johnson (1980–88) (box 2); materials from a fund-raiser for Johnson (box 3); materials about Johnson's fast for the ERA; and photographs with Johnson (box 8).

Sonia Johnson and the ERA [*SJR*]. Special Collections and Archives, Utah State University Libraries, Logan, Utah. Contains correspondence from Johnson and news clippings about the ERA; news clippings about her excommunication (box 9); the press kit given to media on the evening of Johnson's excommunication trial (box 1); and Mormons for ERA newsletters (boxes 3–5).

Sonia Johnson Papers [*SJP*], 1958–82. Manuscripts Division, J. Willard Marriott Library, University of Utah, Salt Lake City (Ms. 287). Contains (1) materials about Johnson's excommunication, including family letters, letters from supporters to the Mormon Church, and documents about the Church's opposition to the amendment; and (2) materials related to Johnson's work on behalf of the ERA, including news clippings and manuscripts of Johnson's speeches.

Sonia Johnson Photograph Collection [*SJPC*], 1978–80. Special Collections, J. Willard Marriott Library, University of Utah, Salt Lake City. Contains approximately fifty photographs and slides of ERA demonstrations and Johnson's excommunication trial.

Web Site

Sonia Johnson Collection. J. Willard Marriott Library, University of Utah, Salt Lake City. This site includes links to the library's photo archive and an index to the special collections. www.lib.utah.edu

Audiovisual Materials

This list includes only audio/visual sources for Johnson's speeches not contained in the Sonia Johnson Papers [*SJP*].

Feminism: A World View. Speech presented on Pacifica Radio, Los Angeles, 1986. Audiocassette available from Pacifica Radio Archives, Los Angeles.

Interview and speech. Presented at the "Women in the Year 2000" conference, Portland, Ore., September 19–21, 1986. Videocassette available from Linn-Benton Community College Library, Portland, Ore.

Interview and speech. Presented on Minnesota Public Radio, St. Paul, Minn., January 19, 1980. Audiocassette available from St. Mary's University Library, Winona, Minn.

"Listen to Women for a Change." Presented at St. Cloud University, St. Cloud, Minn., 1984, as part of Johnson's presidential campaign. Videocassette available from St. Cloud State University, St. Cloud, Minn.

Speech. Presented as part of "Nothing to Hide," a series of presentations by noteworthy feminists and lesbians, Madison, Wis., April 23, 1988. Broadcast over the public access cable television station WYOU Community Television, Madison, Wis. Videocassette available from the University of Wisconsin, Madison, General Library System.

Speech. Presented at the Plenary Session of the Friends General Conference, Slippery Rock, Pa., June 30, 1985. Videocassette available from Friends Historical Library, Swarthmore College, Swarthmore, Pa.

"Women Changing the Future." Panel presentation by Sonia Johnson, Nellie Wong, and Madhu Kishwar. N.p., n.d. Audiocassette (#A7) available from the National Women's Studies Association, University of Maryland, College Park, Md.

Selected Critical Studies

Foss, Karen A., Sonja K. Foss, and Cindy L. Griffin. "Sonia Johnson." In their *Feminist Rhetorical Theories*. Thousand Oaks, Calif.: Sage, 1999.

Karl, Sarah L. "Changes in Religious Beliefs in Political Activists: Three Case Studies." Ph.D. dissertation, Rutgers University, 1988.

Pottmyer, Alice Allred. "Sonia Johnson: Mormonism's Feminist Heretic." In *Differing Visions: Dissenters in Mormon History*, ed. Roger D. Launius and Linda Thatcher. Urbana: University of Illinois Press, 1997.

Van Dyke, Annette J. "Feminist Curing Ceremonies: The Goddess in Contemporary Spiritual Traditions (Pueblo Indian; Afro-American; Celtic)." Ph.D. dissertation, University of Minnesota, 1987.

———. "From the Euro-American Mainstream: Sonia Johnson and Mary Daly." In her *The Search for a Woman Centered Spirituality*. New York: New York University Press, 1992.

Selected Biographies

Evans, Nancy H. "Sonia Johnson." In *Contemporary Authors: A Bio-Bibliographical Guide to Current Writers*, vol. 118, ed. Hal May. Detroit, Mich.: Gale, 1986.

Langlois, Karen S. "An Interview with Sonia Johnson." *Feminist Studies* 8 (Spring 1982): 7–17.

Pottmyer, Alice. "Sonia Johnson." In *Dictionary of Heresy Trials in American Christianity*, ed. George H. Shriver. Westport, Conn.: Greenwood, 1997.

"Sonia Johnson." In *Current Biography Yearbook 1985*, ed. Charles Moritz. New York: H. W. Wilson, 1986.

CHRONOLOGY OF MAJOR SPEECHES

See "Research Collections and Collected Speeches" for source codes.

"Statement in Support of the ERA" (statement before the U.S. Senate Subcommittee on Constitutional Rights). Washington, D.C., August 4, 1978. *SJP*, box 9, folder 1.

"Patriarchal Panic: Sexual Politics in the Mormon Church" (speech at the American Psychological Association meeting). New York City, September 1, 1979. *SJP*, box 24, folder 2.

"Off Our Pedestals, or the Chronicles of the Uppity Sisters" (speech at the Utah Women's Conference). October 1979. *SJP*, box 24, folder 3.

"Speech Presented to the World Conference of the U.N. Decade for Women. Copenhagen, Denmark, 1980. *SJP*, box 23, folder 26.

"Kalispell Address" (speech to the National Organization for Women, Montana State Convention). Kalispell, Mont., July 21, 1981. *SJP*, box 36, tape 2.

"The Last Great Western Patriarchy" (speech delivered as a member of the panel "ERA Referendum Strategies," to the Washington Institute for Women in Politics). Washington, D.C., February 10, 1982. *SJP*, box 24, folder 1.

"Going Further Out of Our Minds" (speech at the University of California, Santa Cruz). Santa Cruz, Calif., March 1988. Videocassette available from Karen A. Foss, University of New Mexico, Albuquerque.

"Living the Dream" (speech at the University of Alaska, Anchorage). March 1990. Videocassette available from Karen A. Foss, University of New Mexico, Albuquerque.

BARBARA CHARLINE JORDAN (1936–1996)
Texas State Senator, U.S. Representative

CARL R. BURGCHARDT

Barbara Charline Jordan's career is marked by distinctive milestones. Jordan was the first African American woman to be elected to the Texas Senate, to preside as governor for a day in Texas, to be elected to Congress from a Southern state, to serve on the House Judiciary Committee, to address a national political convention, and to deliver a commencement address at Harvard. Her perseverance and indomitable spirit vaulted her into national prominence and made her one of the most admired women in the United States. Yet she chose to forgo higher political office for a professorship, where her independent voice for fairness could be heard unimpeded by political exigencies and compromises.

Barbara Jordan was born in 1936 in Houston, Texas, a member of a poor but nurturing family. Before Jordan's birth, wrote Patricia Witherspoon, her mother had been "a respected orator in church circles," and her "father worked as a warehouse employee during her childhood and became a Baptist minister in 1949." It was only natural, then, that Jordan's first public performances occurred in church, where she recited poetry and sang, and her religious upbringing was a major influence on her values and beliefs.

Jordan's father stressed the importance of education. According to reporter David E. Rosenbaum, her father was not satisfied with less than perfect grades in school, and he was a stickler for correct language. Thus Jordan early developed "the precise diction that has become her hallmark."

Jordan attended a segregated public high school in Houston, where she developed into a talented orator. As a student she took top honors in local and state speaking events, as well as winning first place in the National Ushers Convention Oratorical Contest. Jordan's participation in these speech competitions convinced her of the importance of a captivating delivery, a skill at which she excelled.

Jordan continued her participation in forensics at Texas Southern University (TSU), where she led her debate team to success against both black and white competitors. After graduating magna cum laude from TSU in 1956 with a degree in political science, she pursued a law degree at Boston University. Law school proved challenging for Jordan, but she persisted. Most important, she noted in her autobiography, legal study honed her abilities to "think and read and understand and reason," capacities that she would display in future public speaking.

After receiving her LL.B. degree in 1959, Jordan practiced law in Houston out of her family's home. She soon became active in the local Democratic Party, working for John F. Kennedy's election in 1960. At first, Jordan labored behind the scenes to help organize a block-worker program. One evening, however, she was asked to fill in for an absent campaign speaker. Jordan's impromptu talk was such a success that the Harris County Democrats asked her to speak regularly. This experience thrilled Jordan and started her thinking about a political career of her own.

In 1962 and 1964, Jordan campaigned for the Texas House, but was defeated both times. In 1966, she was elected to the Texas Senate after the Supreme Court forced her district to be reapportioned. Jordan became the first black woman to be seated in the Texas State Senate and in 1968 was reelected to a four-year term. Jordan's effectiveness as a senator was demonstrated by the fact that about half of the bills she submitted became law. She concentrated on legislation concerning employment practices, the state minimum wage, and voting rights. Jordan was willing to work patiently and cooperatively for reform goals, although this approach was not without its critics. Nonetheless, she won the honor of outstanding freshman senator after completing her first year. In 1972, Jordan was elected president pro tempore of the Texas Senate. As a consequence, she was honored as governor for a day on June 10, 1972, which made her, however briefly, the first African American female governor in the United States.

In 1972, Jordan was elected overwhelmingly to the U.S. House of Representatives, which was another first: no woman had previously represented Texas in Congress. She was reelected in 1974 and 1976 by large margins. In Congress, Jordan advocated the rights of the poor, women, minorities, consumers, and the elderly; she opposed escalating military spending; and she sponsored an extension of the Voting Rights Act of 1965. Some African American legislators criticized her for not taking more militant stances on civil rights, but Jordan believed that pragmatic legislation would eventually provide equal opportunities for all Americans.

Jordan played a prominent role in Jimmy Carter's successful bid for the U.S. presidency in 1976. Afterward, the press and public speculated that she would be nominated for attorney general or another high-ranking post, but such an offer was not extended. After a period of contemplation, Jordan chose to leave politics altogether. In her autobiography, she reasoned that her national fame created an opportunity for her to address the public without the encumbrances of running for office: "I thought that my role now was to be one of the voices in the country defining where we were . . . [and] where we were going. . . . I felt I was more in an instructive role than a legislative role."

In 1979, Jordan accepted a professorship at the Lyndon B. Johnson School of Public Affairs at the University of Texas in Austin. According to Jordan, "The idea of playing a definitive role in educating young people to go into government was very attractive to me." After 1988, Jordan used a wheelchair or walker because of multiple sclerosis and other illnesses, but she continued an active career. In her words, reported Karen Zauber, "I felt I should treat the limitations as irrelevant and refuse to let them be an impediment." In addition to her teaching duties and membership on corporate boards, from 1991 to 1994 Jordan served as special counsel on ethics in government for Texas Governor Ann Richards. In 1994 she was appointed chair of the U.S. Commission on Immigration Reform. In this role, she helped craft a controversial report that advocated more stringent controls on illegal immigration. In January 1996, Barbara Jordan died from complications of pneumonia and leukemia.

Throughout her career, Jordan received numerous awards, distinctions, and honorary degrees. To name a few, in 1984 the International Platform Association named her "Best Living Orator." The National Women's Hall of Fame inducted her in 1990, and she was installed by

the second day, July 25. Prior to the speech, she was determined to be fair in her remarks about Nixon. She had studied the legal precedents and reviewed the testimony. Jordan had asked her assistant to prepare a chart that listed all of Nixon's suspect actions and matched them against criteria for impeachment obtained from historical precedents. Ultimately, Jordan decided to support impeachment, but she did not organize her statement until three hours before the committee was scheduled to reconvene on Thursday evening. When her turn came, she spoke extemporaneously from a four-page outline, using the chart that her assistant had assembled.

Jordan began the speech by noting that the Constitution originally excluded black women from full participation in society: "I was not included in that 'We the people.' . . . But through

---

The speech that brought Barbara Jordan to national attention, her speech on Nixon's impeachment before the House Judiciary Committee, was written only hours before its delivery. Although she had been gathering notes for the speech for some time, Jordan wrote the speech during the dinner break, giving her secretary parts of it to type as she completed them. The speech was delivered at approximately 9:00 P.M., and is considered by many to be an oratorical masterpiece.

---

the African American Hall of Fame in 1993. The following year, Bill Clinton awarded Jordan the Presidential Medal of Freedom. In 1995, she received the Sylvanus Thayer Award from West Point.

BARBARA JORDAN: VOICE FOR FAIRNESS

Barbara Jordan was thrust into the national spotlight in 1974 as a member of the House Judiciary Committee, which, during the spring and summer, conducted hearings concerning the possible impeachment of Richard Nixon. On the evening of July 24, the committee made its deliberations public. Each member was asked to make a fifteen-minute opening statement before a national television audience. As a junior member of the committee, Jordan did not speak until

the process of amendment, interpretation, and court decision, I have finally been included in 'We the people.'" Despite this original exclusion, Jordan stated, "My faith in the Constitution is whole. It is complete." She made a wise strategic decision to address the people of the United States rather than her committee colleagues, who were already well versed in the law and the facts of the Nixon case. In the body of the speech, Jordan systematically explained to the public how Nixon's actions fit reasonable standards for impeachment. The impeachment criteria were grounded in historical authority, including James Madison, Justice Story, and the North Carolina Ratification Convention. According to David Henry, Jordan arranged her speech "in a fashion strikingly similar to the dictates of the classical *stasis* system, which established standard lines of legal argumentation." Jordan concluded by declaring: "If the impeachment provision in the Constitution of the United States will not reach the offenses charged here, then perhaps that eighteenth-century Constitution should be abandoned to a twentieth-century paper shredder."

The reaction to her address was as immediate as it was positive. When Jordan left the Rayburn Building later that evening, she was cheered by an appreciative crowd. The press lauded her efforts the following day. R. W. Apple, Jr. opined in the *New York Times*: "In her booming voice, with her elegant articulations, she delivered a lecture in constitutional law." The didactic nature of her speech was not lost on the public. One man from Houston paid to display the following message on twenty-five billboards: "THANK YOU, BARBARA JORDAN, FOR EXPLAINING THE CONSTITUTION TO US." In addition, Jordan received scores of letters from admirers who praised her for being honest, eloquent, intelligent, cogent, logical, sincere, and dignified.

The positive reaction to Jordan's "We the People" speech made her a celebrity and attracted the attention of national Democratic Party leaders, who invited her, along with Senator John Glenn, to be a keynote speaker at the 1976 Democratic National Convention in New York. On July 12, Glenn delivered a sincere but dull speech to an inattentive audience at Madison Square Garden. Jordan's speech was preceded by a short film clip that traced her remarkable career. When Jordan finally appeared on the stage, she was cheered for three minutes. As she began to speak, the delegates immediately became silent and continued to give her their full attention, which is highly unusual for contemporary political conventions. Her twenty-five-minute oration was repeatedly interrupted by applause.

When Jordan gazed upon her audience, it was the first time an African American woman had addressed a Democratic National Convention, and she alluded to this fact: "There is something special about tonight. What is different? What is special? I, Barbara Jordan, am a keynote speaker. . . . [M]y presence here is one additional piece of evidence that the American dream need not forever be deferred." At that moment Jordan "embodied" the words she expressed. As Karlyn Kohrs Campbell and Kathleen Hall Jamieson put it: "She herself *was* the proof of the argument she was making."

In the body of the speech, Jordan warned about the dangers of the nation collapsing into competing "interest groups" and called for "national community." But Jordan did not stop with appeals for unity. In an unusual move, she criticized the past actions of her party. Although the Democrats had "made mistakes," these were "mistakes of the heart." At the same time, Jordan insisted that "the Democratic Party can lead the way" to greater "national community." According to Richard L. Johannesen et al., she criticized "her own party, but in such a moderate way as to freshen the speech without weakening her praise of party principles or generating negative audience reaction." Wayne N. Thompson argued that Jordan skillfully coupled generally accepted national values such as patriotism and traditional morality with values more specific to the Democratic Party such as "change and progress," "ethical equality," "equality of opportunity," and "rejection of authority."

When Jordan concluded her speech, cheers of "we want Barbara" reverberated throughout the hall. Her speech was so impressive that many urged Jimmy Carter to put Jordan on the ticket as his running mate. Jordan's keynote address proved to be successful outside the convention hall as well. *Time* magazine of July 26, 1976, reported that Jordan's speech would "take its place among Democratic convention oratorical classics," and Thompson noted that a public opinion poll revealed that more than half of the national audience reacted positively to the address.

The 1976 keynote address increased Jordan's fame and created a strong demand for her as a speaker. Jordan turned down most requests, but she was intrigued by an invitation to receive an honorary degree and be commencement speaker at Harvard, the school she had dreamed of attending while a student at Texas Southern University. Jordan agreed to appear in June 1977. She worked hard on topic selection, finally settling on a main theme of her political career: citizen involvement. Jordan argued that the people "want to be insiders on America" and appealed for "the reinclusion of the people in their government," which "would be a return of a right which we once considered unalienable." In sum, "What the people want is simple. They want an America as good as its promise."

Jordan's 1977 speech broke another barrier: she became the first African American woman to deliver a commencement address at Harvard. The immediate impact of the speech was positive; audience members approached her to obtain an autograph or a handshake. But the experience had an important, personal, long-term consequence: it crystallized her intention to leave politics and to become an impartial national voice.

In the 1970s and 1980s, Jordan gave several notable addresses on women's issues. On November 10, 1975, during the International Women's Year, she delivered a speech at the LBJ School of Public Affairs, University of Texas at Austin. Jordan argued that women must change their concept of themselves: "The problem remains that we fail to define ourselves in terms of whole human beings." The solution was to "act out the equality we say we feel." Women must exercise leadership to ensure "justice for everybody." She sounded much the same theme in a keynote speech delivered at the National Women's Conference in Houston on November 19, 1977: "We endorse personal and political freedom as a national right of human pride." During her February 11, 1988, speech to the Women and the Constitution Symposium in Atlanta, Jordan expressed doubt that the Equal Rights Amendment would be ratified, but she nonetheless believed that the future would have "as its centerpiece men and women working together—in our common humanity—trying to ensure at every turn that we live in peace and freedom, with order and civility."

In 1992, Jordan was again a keynote speaker at the Democratic National Convention. On July 13, she shared the platform with Senator Bill Bradley of New Jersey and Governor Zell Miller of Georgia. According to *Congressional Quarterly Weekly Report* of July 18, 1992, Senator Bradley delivered a "serious but uninspiring speech, often having trouble overcoming the buzz of conversation in the hall"; Governor Miller had some applause lines, but the delegates continued to be restless. Jordan, however,

"held their rapt attention" (p. 2094). As one *Wall Street Journal* reporter observed, "When she began to talk, the hall quieted, and save for the applause, it stayed quiet."

Jordan opened the speech by reminding her audience, "It was at this time; it was at this place; it was at this event, 16 years ago, I presented a keynote address to the Democratic National Convention." And, she added, "we won the presidency" in November 1976. She stated that the Democrats could reclaim the White House, but they would have to change their approach: "Why not change from a party with a reputation of tax and spend to one with a reputation of investment and growth?" Such an economic policy would provide educational and job opportunities to impoverished individuals. In order to create economic growth and reduce the deficit, however, "everybody must join in the sacrifice, not just a few." Significantly, she advised the convention, "The American electorate must be persuaded to trust us, the Democrats, to govern again." Jordan concluded by paraphrasing Franklin Roosevelt, who in his First Inaugural Address, delivered during the depths of the Depression, called for a leadership of frankness and vigor.

According to Leslie Barnes, the arrangement of ideas in the 1992 speech was virtually identical to that in the 1976 address. Jordan opened both speeches by referring to a positive historical event; she conceded that the party had made mistakes in the past; she argued that, despite the mistakes, the Democratic Party was still the one to assume leadership when the nation called for change; she explained how the party would bring about the needed change; she claimed that, in order to be successful, all American citizens must participate; and she concluded with a quotation from a national hero.

Daniel Henninger noted that Jordan received hearty applause for much of the speech, but only polite responses for other parts. She drew a warm ovation when she praised the presence of women candidates for Congress, but when she called for programs "which help us help ourselves," the applause was "tepid." The least-applauded sentence in the speech was her insistence that Democrats must admit their "complicity in the creation of the unconscionable deficit."

Jordan's speech received an uncertain reaction from delegates and virtual silence from Democratic officials, the press, and television commentators. Obviously, this address was not as celebrated as the 1976 keynote speech. Why did this happen? One reason is that the situation was no longer novel. In 1976 Jordan's appearance was unprecedented, but by 1992 many of the delegates had seen Jordan before and had heard a similar message. Moreover, Jordan had been out of Congress for thirteen years. Another reason for the subdued reaction is that the Democratic Party was more sensitive to criticism, even constructive criticism, because of the adversities of the Clinton candidacy. Although change was the central theme in Bill Clinton's presidential campaign, Jordan called for profound conversion within the Democratic Party itself, not just a partisan victory over the Republicans. While delegates were eager to cheer standard Democratic themes and welcomed the symbolism of an African American woman on the podium, they were less receptive to the honest criticism of Democratic failures.

No discussion of Jordan's oratory would be complete without considering her physical presence and resonant voice. Throughout her career, Jordan was self-conscious about her weight. At various times, journalists described her as "hulking," "massive," and "ample," although they also reported her charisma and great dignity. By far Jordan's most distinctive physical trait was her voice, however, which she considered her strongest oratorical feature. Patricia Lasher provides an excellent summary of Jordan's delivery skills:

> The sheer power of her rhetoric often caused otherwise inattentive legislators to sit up and listen. Her voice is that of a seasoned actress, an impassioned missionary, a righteous headmistress, a lecturing parent. It can sound arrogant, soothing, indignant, supportive, reproving or understanding, depending on her intent. She is a diva who provides her own chorus, often repeating key words and phrases with a rhythmic cadence that gives her speeches an evangelical quality.

Jordan emphasized points through inflection, pitch, varied rate, dramatic pauses, and rhetorical questions. Her exaggerated enunciation of words was a technique that held the attention of distracted delegates at chaotic political conventions.

A unifying theme in Jordan's rhetoric was "the people." Indeed, her indictment of Richard Nixon was grounded in the constitutional authority of the people. Her Harvard University commencement speech stressed the importance of citizen involvement in a democracy, as did her 1976 and 1992 keynote addresses. Another common thread of Jordan's discourse was her status as a female African American. Most of her speeches began with references to her race and gender. Yet, ironically, she stated repeatedly that she did not wish to become a symbol for blacks or women.

Rather than focusing exclusively on a particular group or cause, Jordan strove for balance and fairness. During her legislative career, she advocated the rights of the disadvantaged, but she also stressed the importance of individual drive, responsibility, and initiative. Her reform goals were not revolutionary, but simply asked for equal justice for all. Although Jordan condemned Richard Nixon in 1974, she agonized over her decision and struggled to weigh the facts of the case objectively. Her "We the People" speech is strongly analytical and exhibits thorough research and attention to detail. Jordan's two Democratic National Convention speeches promoted victory for her party, yet she offset praise with honest criticism of past faults and excesses. Because of her balanced, well-supported arguments, Lasher argued, Jordan "has come to represent uncompromising rectitude, moral authority, judicious reasoning and strength." In short, Barbara Charline Jordan became a determined voice for fairness in the United States.

INFORMATION SOURCES

Research Collections and Collected Speeches

Speech manuscripts, papers, personal memorabilia, and photographs are located in the Barbara Jordan Archives at Texas Southern University. A number of previously unpublished speeches from Jordan's papers have been collected by Sandra M. Parham in *Barbara C. Jordan: Selected Speeches.*

Congressional Quarterly Weekly Report [*CQ*], July 18, 1992.

Jordan, Barbara, and Shelby Hearon. *Barbara Jordan: A Self-Portrait* [*BJ*]. Garden City, N.Y.: Doubleday, 1979.

Parham, Sandra, ed. *Barbara C. Jordan: Selected*

Speeches [*BCJ*]. Washington, D.C.: Howard University Press, 1999.

Rohler, Lloyd E., and Roger Cook, eds. *Great Speeches for Criticism and Analysis* [*GS*], 3rd ed. Greenwood, Ind.: Alistair Press, 1988.

Web Sites

Armadillo: Barbara Jordan. Contains tributes to Jordan and links to newspaper articles about her life and political career. http://www.rice.edu/armadillo/Texas/jordan.html

Barbara Jordan Archives. Texas Southern University. http://www.tsu.edu/about/library/special.asp

Barbara Jordan National Forum on Public Policy [*BJN*]. Includes full texts and audio or video excerpts of several Jordan speeches, as well as a biography, a list of famous quotations, and links to other Jordan sites. http://www.utexas.edu/lbj/barbarajordanforum/aboutbj_speeches.htm

Inventory of Spoken Word Audio Recordings in the Vincent Voice Library, Michigan State University [*BJI*]. Contains chronology and voice recordings of six Jordan speeches from 1975 to 1977. http://www.lib.msu.edu/digital/vincent/findaids/JordanB.html

TxTell: Barbara Jordan [*TT*]. Consists of a concise biography, eulogies, links to related sites, and audio or video recordings of several Jordan speeches. http://txtell.lib.utexas.edu/stories/j0001-full.html

Audiovisual Materials

Barbara Jordan, Keynote Address [*BJK*]. Bowling Green, Ohio: Video Library, 1976.

Campaign '76: The Democratic National Convention. New York: CBS News Audio Resource Library, 1976.

Campaign '92: The Democrats [*CD*]. Greenwood, Ind.: Educational Video Group, 1992.

Great Speeches—Today's Women, Volume I [*GST*]. Greenwood, Ind.: Educational Video Group, 1995.

Great Speeches, Volume II [*GSII*]. Greenwood, Ind.: Educational Video Group, 1986.

Great Speeches, Volume IV [*GSIV*]. Greenwood, Ind.: Educational Video Group, 1987.

Interview with Barbara Jordan. Washington, D.C.: PBS Video, 1980. Interview with Ben J. Wattenberg.

The Legacy of Barbara Jordan: Four Speeches [*LBJ*]. Greenwood, Ind.: Educational Video Group, 1996.

A Profile of Barbara Jordan. New York: Encyclopedia Americana/CBS News Audio Resource Library, 1979. Interview with Dan Rather.

The Story of Barbara Jordan. Boston: WGBH Educational Foundation, 1997.

Summer of Judgment—the Impeachment Hearings.

LC Off-Air Taping Collection (Library of Congress). Washington, D.C.: PBS, 1984.

Women and the Constitution: The Challenge [*WC*]. West Lafayette, Ind.: Public Affairs Video Archives, 1988.

Selected Critical Studies

Barnes, Leslie. "Barbara Jordan, Then and Now: A Comparison of Jordan's 1976 and 1992 Keynote Addresses." Paper delivered at the Colorado Speech Communication Association Convention, Greeley, Colo., April 24, 1993.

Campbell, Karlyn Kohrs, and Kathleen Hall Jamieson. "Form and Genre in Political Criticism: An Introduction." In *Form and Genre: Shaping Rhetorical Action*, ed. Karlyn Kohrs Campbell and Kathleen Hall Jamieson. Falls Church, Va.: Speech Communication Association, n.d.

Henninger, Daniel. "A Woman of Substance." *Wall Street Journal*, July 15, 1993, p. A–12.

Henry, David. "Barbara Jordan." In *American Orators of the Twentieth Century*, ed. Bernard K. Duffy and Halford R. Ryan. New York: Greenwood, 1987.

Holmes, Barbara A. *A Private Woman in Public Spaces: Barbara Jordan's Speeches on Ethics, Public Religion, and Law*. Harrisburg, Pa.: Trinity Press International, 2000.

Johannesen, Richard L., R. R. Allen, and Wil A. Linkugel. "Democratic Convention Keynote Address: Barbara Jordan." In *Contemporary American Speeches*, 7th ed., ed. Richard L. Johannesen, R. R. Allen, and Wil A. Linkugel. Dubuque, Iowa: Kendall/Hunt, 1992.

Martin, Donald R., and Vicky Gordon Martin. "Barbara Jordan's Symbolic Use of Language in the Keynote Address to the National Women's Conference." *Southern Speech Communication Journal* 49 (1984): 319–30.

Rosenbaum, David. "Black Woman Keynoter." *New York Times*, July 13, 1976, p. 24.

Thompson, Wayne N. "Barbara Jordan's Keynote Address: The Juxtaposition of Contradictory Values." *Southern Speech Communication Journal* 44 (1979): 223–32.

Witherspoon, Patricia D. "'We the People': Barbara Jordan's Statement Before the House Judiciary Committee on the Impeachment of Richard M. Nixon." In *Great Speeches for Criticism and Analysis*, ed. Lloyd Rohler and Roger Cook. Greenwood, Ind.: Alistair Press, 1988.

Selected Biographies

Bryant, Ira B. *Barbara Charline Jordan: From the Ghetto to the Capitol*. Houston, Tex.: D. Armstrong, 1977.

Jordan, Barbara, and Shelby Hearon. *Barbara Jordan: A Self-Portrait*. Garden City, N.Y.: Doubleday, 1979.

Kennedy, Patricia Scileppi, and Gloria Hartmann O'Shields. "Barbara C. Jordan." In *We Shall Be Heard: Women Speakers in America*, ed. Patricia Scileppi Kennedy and Gloria Hartmann O'Shields. Dubuque, Iowa: Kendall/Hunt, 1983.

Lasher, Patricia. "Barbara Jordan." In *Texas Women: Interviews and Images*. Photos by Beverly Bentley. Austin, Tex.: Shoal Creek Publishers, 1980.

Rogers, Mary Beth. *Barbara Jordan: American Hero*. New York: Bantam Books, 1998.

Zauber, Karen. "Meet: Barbara Jordan." *NEA Today*, December 1992, p. 9.

CHRONOLOGY OF SPEECHES

See "Research Collections and Collected Speeches" for source codes.

"The Law, the Promise, and the Power." Houston, Tex., April 27, 1967. *BCJ*, pp. 33–38.

"Civil Liberties: Inoperative? Inaudible? Unintelligible? Expletive Deleted?" Washington, D.C., May 11, 1974. *BCJ*, pp. 43–48.

"Statement on the Articles of Impeachment" ("We the People"), Washington, D.C., July 25, 1974. *GS*, pp. 179–82 [transcribed from videotape]; *BJ*, pp. 186–92; *BCJ*, pp. 105–8; *GSII*; *LBJ*; *BJN*; *TT*.

"Moving on from Watergate." Austin, Tex., March 8, 1975. *BCJ*, pp. 9–13.

"International Women's Year Address." Austin, Tex., November 10, 1975. *BJ*, pp. 215–20.

"Democratic Convention Keynote Address" ("Who Then Will Speak for the Common Good?"). New York City, July 12, 1976. *GS*, pp. 76–79 [transcribed from videotape]; *BCJ*, pp. 97–100; *BJK*; *GSIV*; *LBJ*; *BJN*; *BJI*; *TT*.

"Commencement Address." Harvard University, June 16, 1977. *BJ*, pp. 260–66; *BCJ*, pp. 53–56.

"Women and the Constitution: The Challenge." Atlanta, Ga., February 11, 1988. *BCJ*, pp. 27–30; *WC*.

"Speech Seconding Lloyd Bentsen's Nomination for Vice President." Atlanta, Ga., July 21, 1988. *LBJ*; *BJI*.

"How Do We Live with Each Other's Deepest Differences?" Dayton, Ohio, June 28, 1990. *BCJ*, pp. 71–73.

"Council on Foundations Keynote Address." Chicago, April 21, 1991. *BCJ*, pp. 57–60.

"The Rebirth of Ethics—a Pervasive Challenge." San Antonio, Tex., May 5, 1992. *BCJ*, pp. 83–87.

"Keynote Address" ("Change: From What to What?"). New York City, July 13, 1992. *CQ*, pp. 2117–18 [unedited version]; *BCJ*, pp. 101–4; *CD*; *GST*; *LBJ*.

"Does the Idea of Civil Rights Remain a Good Idea as We Approach the Year 2000 A.D.?" Memphis, Tenn., September 10, 1992. *BCJ*, pp. 75–79.

"*E Pluribus Unum*: Myth or Reality? One from Many." Evanston, Ill., September 12, 1993. *BCJ*, pp. 63–69.

"Can We Govern Ourselves?" Tucson, Ariz., October 19, 1994. *BCJ*, pp. 49–51.

"National Archives Address." Washington, D.C., August 26, 1995. *BCJ*, pp. 23–25.

EDWARD MOORE KENNEDY (1932–)
U.S. *Senator*

WILLIAM D. PEDERSON

Ted Kennedy has been a U.S. senator for essentially his entire adult life. He has demonstrated leadership in that office through both his political and his rhetorical skills, emerging from the shadow of his two legendary older brothers to establish himself as an enduring political force in his own right. Most knowledgeable observers rank him as one of the most effective U.S. senators. A skilled debater, a competent legislator, and a charismatic political leader, Ted Kennedy is the foremost champion of the liberal wing of the Democratic Party and the second-ranking Democratic senator. His accomplishments reflect his unusual energy, stamina, and flexibility. At times he has possessed the potential to transform his party as well as the ability to capture the White House. Since he abandoned his presidential ambitions in 1980, he has concentrated on building a substantial legislative legacy in the Senate.

Oratory and political heritage played a key role in Kennedy's formative years as the son of an ambassador with presidential ambitions of his own, the grandson of a mayor renowned for Irish oratory, and the brother of the youthful president known for style, wit, and charisma. The youngest of the Kennedy brothers' political triumvirate, his drive to succeed was influenced by ethnic parents who struggled for acceptance in Brahmin Protestant Boston during an era when Irish Catholics were outsiders. He nervously lost his first school debate when he was eight years old, competing in a mock presidential debate during the 1940 election campaign. But he went on to win elective offices in elementary and junior high school.

Family patriarch Joseph Patrick Kennedy, a politically conservative wealthy businessman, was appointed by Franklin D. Roosevelt as the first chairman of the Securities and Exchange Commission. In 1936, the elder Kennedy published *I'm for Roosevelt*, and two years later was appointed by FDR as the first Irish American ambassador to Great Britain. That ambassadorship put Kennedy on equal, if not superior, footing with the Boston elite. He adopted an informal style that won approval of the press and the public, but his foreign policy of isolationism, anti-Semitic rhetoric, and personal criticism of the monarch and Winston Churchill conflicted with presidential policy. Eyeing a possible run for the presidency in 1940, before FDR decided to break the two-term tradition, Joseph Kennedy ranked fifth among hopefuls in a public opinion poll.

The drive to create a Kennedy political dynasty derived from the senior Kennedy's desire to accomplish through his sons what he himself could not. The three sons adopted their father's vision for their futures but, ironically, to secure their own political reputations they had to distance themselves from his. Despite this, all three proved they were indeed their father's sons with occasional lapses into reckless personal behavior that modeled his. Still, they became generational heroes, eclipsing their father and doing so on their own merits.

The Kennedy boys grew up playing to win. In high school, Ted Kennedy was in the drama club and on the debate team that beat Harvard University's freshman debaters. Public speaking and debate were areas in which he and his brother John excelled, and both used their rhetorical strength to great advantage throughout their political careers. Ted Kennedy was graduated from high school with honors in public speaking and a reputation as a poised and prepared debater who was particularly adept at refutation. At Harvard he majored in government and studied speech. His debate training resurfaced at the University of Virginia Law School, where he won the coveted moot court competition against future U.S. Senator John V. Tunney on April 17, 1959. Kennedy's lifelong emphasis on debate rather than law as an end unto itself suggests his ultimate interest in pursuing a career in politics.

It was the elder Kennedy's ambition to create a political dynasty, and son John's presidential victory in 1960, that cemented the Kennedy name in history. John Kennedy added to the legacy when he appointed his brother Robert as attorney general. Meanwhile, Ted Kennedy stumped for his first public office, seeking his brother John's old Senate seat. His youth and lack of experience were the central campaign issues hammered by his opposition. However, after an incredible display of the famous Kennedy energy through the grueling campaign, Ted Kennedy won the Democratic Party's convention endorsement over Edward McCormack, the well-respected Massachusetts attorney general and nephew of the powerful speaker of the U.S. House of Representatives. The most dramatic and critical event of that entire Senate campaign occurred during the primary, in the first televised debate between the candidates before a pro-McCormack crowd at South Boston High School, McCormack's alma mater. Kennedy advisers had shrewdly chosen that venue to counteract the possible portrayal of Ted Kennedy, from such a powerful family, as Goliath and the less well-connected McCormack as David.

From that one-hour confrontation emerged a pattern which has been repeated throughout Kennedy's political life: when he prepares for a public performance, Kennedy is virtually unbeatable. In the televised debate, he presented himself as a serious, sophisticated, and respectful candidate. He even shunned makeup. The highlight of the evening occurred during the final two-minute closing statement when the heavily made-up McCormack culminated his assault on his opponent with a miscalculated barb: "If his name were Edward Moore, with . . . [his] qualifications . . . [his] candidacy would be a joke, but nobody's laughing because his name is . . . Edward Moore Kennedy." Both candidates and close observers initially considered the debate a disaster for Kennedy, but by the next morning it was clear that he had won a backlash emotional victory against his overly aggressive opponent. Democrats gave him 69 percent of the primary vote.

Although he campaigned alone, the would-be senator relied on the advice, money, and techniques that had worked in John Kennedy's previous races. The president rehearsed his younger brother for an hour before Ted Kennedy made his

long Senate career. His ideological rhetoric is reflected in his maiden legislative speech in support of the Civil Rights Act of 1964. It was delivered fifteen months after he took his seat during the waning years of the "Old Senate," before the reforms of the early 1970s transformed it into a political institution that was more democratic with less centralized power. This delay in taking the floor followed the informal rules of the Old Senate, rules that his older brothers had chosen to break. John Kennedy delivered his first speech in the Senate after five months, and Robert Kennedy waited a mere month. The timing symbolized adherence to Senate tradition, suggesting that Ted Kennedy was more likely to become a member of the "gentlemen's club" in which he would earn his status as rhetorical champion for the oppressed and impoverished.

His first speech predicted his future relation-

"[My brother was] a good and decent man who saw wrong and tried to right it, saw suffering and tried to heal it, saw war and tried to stop it."

—*Edward M. Kennedy's eulogy of his assassinated brother, Robert F. Kennedy*

---

national television debut on NBC's influential *Meet the Press*. Like his presidential brother, Ted Kennedy stressed data more than argument in his presentations. And like President Kennedy, would-be Senator Kennedy appreciated the effective use of television to take his message directly to the masses. He bought more television time for the general election than his opponents combined while he tightened his grip on his brother's presidential coattails. In addition to success that can be attributed to his using the techniques and strategies proven effective by other Kennedy politicians, the youngest Kennedy brother also appeared to have a greater affinity for personal campaigning than either John or Robert Kennedy.

THE ORATORY OF A LIBERAL WORKHORSE SENATOR

The scope and depth of his rhetorical skills have broadened and matured during Kennedy's

ship with those denied civil rights: he sought to place the experience of African Americans within the context of discrimination suffered by other immigrant groups, including the Irish Americans: "My brother was the first President of the United States to state that segregation was morally wrong." That first speech template forecast the oratory style that would be his trademark: taking a very liberal position, acknowledging the difficulty in it, asserting that the benefits outweighed the difficulty, and concluding with an appeal to the better side of human nature. Apart from the rhetoric, the approach suggests that Kennedy had an early understanding of the legislative process, which involves making compromises and building coalitions. It is telling that presidential candidate and maverick Democratic Senator Wayne L. Morse, a former speech professor and law school dean at the University of Oregon, termed Kennedy's maiden effort a "truly great speech."

The 1963 assassination of President John Kennedy was the first in a series of tragic events that beset Ted Kennedy. His stature as an orator is apparent from the eulogy that he delivered at the funeral of his brother Robert, also assassinated in 1968. The eloquence and moving delivery reminded some of the great Athenian statesman Pericles, best remembered for his eulogy of the fallen heroes of the Peloponnesian War; others thought of General Henry Lee's still-quoted eulogy of George Washington. Kennedy captured the spirit of idealism and moral courage that his slain brother represented to many Americans. Although he did not write the text, he worked with Alan Walinsky and Milton Gwirtzman as they developed it. Kennedy decided to use a series of quotations from Robert's speeches as the basis for the eulogy. He stressed his brother's social conscience and the importance of private citizens becoming politically involved: "It is from numberless diverse acts of courage and belief that human history is shaped. Each time a man stands up for an ideal, or acts to improve the lot of others, or strikes out against injustice, he sends forth a tiny ripple of hope, and crossing each other from a million different centers of energy and daring those ripples build a current that can sweep down the mightiest wall of oppression and resistance." He did not idealize his brother, but characterized him "as a good and decent man who saw wrong and tried to right it, saw suffering and tried to heal it, saw war and tried to stop it." The eulogy concluded with two of Robert Kennedy's favorite lines from George Bernard Shaw: "Some men see things as they are and say why. I dream things that never were and say why not." By eulogizing his brother eloquently, Ted Kennedy left no doubt that he would uphold the torch of that fallen brother's progressive political legacy. In the process, he confirmed his stature as a noble and eloquent orator.

In the years that have followed, Ted Kennedy has also faced the deaths of Steve Smith, the brother-in-law who became a surrogate brother, and three young nephews, including John Kennedy Jr., who, he lamented, did not live long enough "to comb gray hair." His empathy for those who suffer tragic loss was apparent after September 11, 2001, when he personally called the family members of the nearly 100 Massachusetts residents who died on the planes hijacked from Boston's Logan Airport.

Death has brought profound grief to Kennedy, including the single event which most threatened his career and which would have ended the political life of almost any other senator. In July 1969, he was on Chappaquiddick Island for a cookout held for Senate staff secretaries. He left the party late with Mary Jo Kopechne and accidentally drove off a narrow road into the water. Kopechne drowned; Kennedy managed to swim to shore. He failed to report the accident to authorities immediately. That crisis prompted him later that month to deliver a seventeen-minute television address, the most criticized speech he has ever made. Ted Sorensen, John Kennedy's Senate and presidential speechwriter, and Milton Gwirtzman wrote most of the script, which amounted to a confession, an assumption of responsibility, and an appeal to Massachusetts voters for their support. His decision to confront the issue on television seems to have benefited him more than what he said or how he presented it.

Despite the fact that his most ideological opponents consider this episode as the defining moment in Kennedy's life, the public does not agree. In 1971 Kennedy finished third in a public poll seeking to identify the most admired man in the United States. In his public career since 1969, he has used his considerable rhetorical gift to help the poor, the sick, and the oppressed, raising his voice more often than anyone else in the Senate on behalf of those unable to speak for themselves.

After his tabloid headline divorce from his wife, Joan, and his equally high-profile second marriage to attorney Victoria Reggie in July 1992, Kennedy's life stabilized. He continues to be a responsible parent to his children and the pillar of his extended family. Despite his past failures, tragedies, and setbacks, Kennedy has demonstrated resilience, relying on a sense of humor and flexibility.

His ability to use humor, often self-deprecating humor, helps Kennedy to disarm opponents and establish rapport with audiences. A technique that he frequently employs is a humorous ad-lib remark that wins over a crowd. His enjoyment of the political arena and his instinct to combine work with play permits him to mock the artificiality of politics in the era of mass communications. Kennedy seems to enjoy toying with audiences, poking fun at the standard political speech and the endemic phoniness of political life. His Senate colleagues appear to appreciate his trademark "made for television" performances, for they know that following the public performance, Kennedy will deal with them not as an ideologue but as a practical politician willing and ready to reach across the partisan aisle to make friendships and reach legislative compromises. His typically magnanimous persona is contagious.

On the other hand, Kennedy is committed to carrying the political torch handed to him by his slain brothers, who represented progressive idealism in American government. His liberalism, directed at helping the less fortunate enjoy the benefits of a liberal society, translates into political noblesse oblige.

Some of Kennedy's most mature speeches were delivered in the 1970s and 1980s. His 1970 lecture at the College Historical Society Bicentenary, at Trinity College in Dublin, Ireland, drafted in collaboration with David Burke, drew from the conservative ideas of eighteenth-century political philosopher and parliamentarian Edmund Burke. In the nuclear age with governmental capacity to suppress political change, Kennedy presented Burke as an example for those who desire to be "moral but realistic, committed to their own nation but responsible for the condition of all men." His review of political protest in the United States, which indirectly hinted at the situation in Northern Ireland, rejected violence by governments as well as by oppressed minorities. Kennedy stated: "Change within Western nations will not come about through random acts of violence and disruption, for sheer violence cannot compel fundamental change. Rather it helps defeat those who are serious about change—the forces of humane moderation." His identification with Burke's ideals of moderation and skepticism in political life are consistent themes in his own rhetoric, a facet that many of his ideologically blinded critics overlook.

Two speeches delivered during his 1980 presidential primary campaign demonstrated Kennedy's ability to inspire audiences and the nation, even though he undermined his campaign from the start with overconfidence and lack of preparation. His interview in the fall of 1979 with journalist Roger Mudd and his postinterview reaction illustrate both the early difficulties Kennedy encountered in the campaign and his capacity to rebound personally and politically. He gave the initial televised interview at his Hyannisport home while his family and staff were unexpectedly absent. The program earned a Peabody Award for Excellence for Mudd, but a blurred reputation for Kennedy due to his responses to questions about Chappaquiddick and why he sought the presidency. He came across in the interview as a confused, inarticulate candidate.

Following the interview, Kennedy regrouped and redefined his campaign in what amounted to a reannouncement speech for the presidency that he delivered in January 1980 at Georgetown University. Once again he relied on the tradition of Edmund Burke and challenged President Jimmy Carter's politics as expressed in the recently delivered State of the Union message. "If the Vietnam war taught us anything, it is precisely when we do not debate our foreign policy, we may drift into deeper trouble," Kennedy countered. "If a president's policy is right, debate will strengthen the national consensus. If it is wrong, debate may save the country from catastrophe." By opposing the Carter doctrine in foreign policy and coming out in favor of wage and price controls along with gasoline rationing, Kennedy modified his style from that of a moderate forerunner to a liberal challenger. The speech was drafted by Carey Parker and Robert Shrum. Kennedy memorized and rehearsed it in the Georgetown hall where it was to be delivered.

The zenith of Kennedy's presidential campaign occurred at the Democratic National Convention as he delivered its most eloquent and emotional speech, proclaiming, "We kept the faith . . . the work goes on, the cause endures, the hope still lives, the dream shall never die." The first draft of that speech was by Shrum and Parker. Kennedy added to it, and Arthur M. Schlesinger and Ted Sorenson collaborated to polish it into final draft. Kennedy rehearsed the thirty-two-minute speech twice, using the teleprompter in his hotel and once more at the convention site. As he delivered the moving victory-in-defeat address, the audience interrupted his presentation with strong applause fifty-one times and at its close gave Kennedy a twenty-three-minute standing ovation. His refusal to raise Carter's hand on the podium at the end of the convention spoke volumes, conveying Kennedy's rejection of Carter's policies.

Kennedy's formidable public speaking and debating skills were recognized by Senator Sam Erwin early on. The former chairman of the Judiciary Committee and a leading constitutional expert in Congress, Erwin called upon Kennedy to present in a federal court the case against the president's use of the pocket veto. Lacking either a prepared text or notes, Kennedy prevailed in the arguments. Again in 1994 his considerable talent for debate was apparent during his Senate reelection campaign. He was challenged by the youthful, charismatic Mitt Romney, and polls in mid-September indicated that the race was a toss-up. Rejecting the advice of campaign staffers who opposed the idea, Kennedy agreed to a first debate at Faneuil Hall in Boston. When asked how he coped with his "personal failings," Kennedy quickly responded: "Every day of my life I try to be a better human being, a better father, a better son, a better husband. . . . And hopefully I am a better senator." After Romney accused Kennedy of a financial conflict with Washington, D.C., Mayor Marion Berry, Kennedy retorted: "Mr. Romney, the Kennedys are not in public service to make money. We have paid too high a price in our commitment to public service." The debate led to Kennedy's electoral victory with 57 percent of the vote.

The youngest Kennedy brother, who began his career in national politics as a thirty-two-year-old senator without experience, except what he had learned from his president brother, today is a political veteran. His performance in the Senate, the greatest institution in the United States for unlimited debate, has earned him the reputation of a legislative workhorse who derives enjoyment from his work. Kennedy has attained a rhetorical record based on fighting for liberal values, and his legislative accomplishments are virtually unmatched in the Congress. He also has built a reputation as a realist willing to build bipartisan coalitions necessary to enact legislation.

Ted Kennedy continues to perpetuate the progressive political legacy of the Kennedy family dynasty that was first envisioned by his ambitious father more than half a century ago. It was a goal that had painfully extracted "too high a price," as the senior senator from Massachusetts reminded the nation in his 1994 campaign debate.

INFORMATION SOURCES

Research Collections and Collected Speeches

There is no archival collection of Kennedy's speeches. However, many of his addresses and comments are available in a variety of published sources: *Congressional Digest*, *Congressional Record*, *Vital Speeches of the Day*, and the *New York Times*. One collection of speeches and written discourse, *Our Day and Generation*, is available.

Kennedy, Edward M. *Our Day and Generation: The Words of Edward M. Kennedy*, ed. Henry Steele Commager. New York: Simon and Schuster, 1979.

Web Site

Senator Kennedy official Web site. This site includes biographical information about Senator Kennedy, as well as speeches delivered on the floor of the Senate and elsewhere on a variety of issues. Many speeches are available in audio and video format. www.kennedy.senate.gov

Selected Critical Studies

Benoit, W. L. "Senator Edward M. Kennedy and the Chappaquiddick Tragedy." In *Oratorical Encounters*, ed. Halford R. Ryan. New York: Greenwood Press, 1988.

Butler, Sherry D. "The Apologia, 1971 Genre." *Southern Speech Communication Journal* 37 (1972): 281–89.

Devin, L. Patrick. "An Analysis of Kennedy's Communication in the 1980 Campaign." *Quarterly Journal of Speech* 69 (1982): 397–417.

Green, Thomas M., and William D. Pederson. "The Behavior of Lawyer-Presidents." *Presidential Studies Quarterly* 15 (1985): 343–52.

King, Robert L. "Transforming Scandal into Tragedy: A Rhetoric of Political Apology." *Quarterly Journal of Speech* 71 (1985): 289–301.

Kraus, Sidney, Timothy Meyer, and Maurice Shelby, Jr. "16 Months After Chappaquiddick: Effects of the Kennedy Broadcast." *Journalism Quarterly* 51 (1974): 431–40.

Ling, David L. "A Pentadic Analysis of Senator Edward Kennedy's Address." *Central States Speech Journal* 21 (1970): 81–86.

Newfield, Jack. "The Senate's Fighting Liberal: Kennedy at 70." *The Nation*, March 25, 2002, pp. 11–16.

Pederson, William D. " 'Presidential Senator' Ted Kennedy and a Character Test." In *The "Barberian" Presidency*, ed. William David Pederson. New York: Peter Lang, 1989.

Randolph, Eleanor. "The Best and the Worst of the U.S. Senate." *Washington Monthly* 13 (1982): 30–43.

Robinson, Michael S., and Philip M. Burgess. "The Edward M. Kennedy Speech: The Impact of a Prime Time Television Appeal." *Television Quarterly* 9 (1970): 29–39.

Scheele, Henry Z. "Evaluations by Experts and Laymen of Selected Political Speakers." *Southern Speech Journal* 33 (1968): 270–78.

Wayne, Stephen J., Cheryl Beil, and Jay Falk. "Public Perceptions About Ted Kennedy and the Presidency." *Presidential Studies Quarterly* 12 (1982): 84–90.

Selected Biographies

Burns, James M. *Edward Kennedy and the Camelot Legacy*. New York: Norton, 1976.

Clymer, Adam. *Edward M. Kennedy: A Biography*. New York: William Morrow, 1999.

Hersh, Burton. *The Shadow President: Ted Kennedy in Opposition*. South Royalton, Vt.: Steerforth Press, 1997.

Lerner, Max. *Ted and the Kennedy Legend: A Study in Character and Destiny*. New York: St. Martin's Press, 1980.

Lippman, Theo, Jr. *Senator Ted Kennedy: The Career Behind the Image*. New York: Norton, 1976.

McKenzie, Andrew M. "Senator Edward M. Kennedy and the 1970 Massachusetts Senatorial Campaign." Ph.D. dissertation, Ohio University, 1971.

CHRONOLOGY OF MAJOR SPEECHES

"McCormack–Kennedy Debate." Boston, August 27, 1962. In Murray B. Levin, *Kennedy Campaigning*. Boston: Beacon Press, 1966.

"Maiden U.S. Senate Speech." Washington, D.C., April 9, 1964. *Congressional Record*, April 9, 1964, p. 7573.

"Robert F. Kennedy Eulogy." New York City, June 8, 1968. *Congressional Record*, p. 16826; *Vital Speeches of the Day*, July 1, 1968, pp. 546–47.

"Chappaquiddick Apologia." Boston, July 25, 1969. *New York Times*, July 26, 1969, p. 10; also in James C. McCroskey, *An Introduction to Rhetorical Communication*, 2nd ed. Englewood Cliffs, N.J.: Prentice-Hall, 1972.

"Trinity College Lecture." Dublin, Ireland, March 3, 1970. *Congressional Record*, March 17, 1970, pp. 7775–77.

"Roger Mudd CBS Interview." November 4, 1979. In Murray B. Levin and T. A. Repak, *Edward Kennedy: The Myth of Leadership*. Boston: Houghton Mifflin, 1980.

"Georgetown University Address." Washington, D.C., January 28, 1980. Devin, "Analysis," p. 413; *Congressional Record*, January 29, 1980, p. 1092; *Vital Speeches of the Day*, February 15, 1980, pp. 260–63.

"Democratic National Convention Speech." New York City, August 12, 1980. *Congressional Quarterly*, August 16, 1980, pp. 2423–25; *Vital Speeches of the Day*, September 15, 1980, pp. 714–16. Available at www.historyplace.com/speeches/tedkennedy.htm

"The Changing Relation Between Politics and Public Policy." *Vital Speeches of the Day*, March 15, 1984, pp. 322–25.

"Is the Reagan Administration Policy Toward Nicaragua Sound?" *Congressional Digest*, November 1984, pp. 267+.

"Should Congress Act to Convey Line-Item Veto Authority to the President?" *Congressional Digest*, November 1985, pp. 266+.

"Should Congress Adopt Proposed Relaxation of Handgun Controls?" *Congressional Digest*, May 1986, pp. 139–41+.

"Where Was George?" (address to the Democratic National Convention). Atlanta, Ga., July 19, 1988. *Vital Speeches of the Day*, August 15, 1988, pp. 654–56.

"Should the Senate Approve the 'Americans with Disabilities Act of 1989'?" *Congressional Digest*, December 1989, pp. 294–96.

"Should Congress Place Limits on Entitlement Spending?" *Congressional Digest*, June/July 1992, pp. 181–83+.

"Should Congress Override the Veto of the Family and Medical Leave Act?" *Congressional Digest*, January 1993, pp. 24+.

"The Need for Gun Control Legislation." *Current History*, January 1994, p. 43.

"Should the Senate Approve the Mitchell Health Care Reform Plan?" *Congressional Digest*, October 1994, pp. 244+.

"What Democrats Should Fight For, Principle Is the Best Politics" (address to the National Press Club). Washington, D.C., January 11, 1995. *Vital Speeches of the Day*, February 1, 1995, pp. 232–35.

"Address to the Democratic National Convention." New York City, August 29, 1996. Available at http://www.pbs.org/newshour/convention96/floor_speeches/kennedy_8-29.html

"Tribute to John F. Kennedy, Jr." (eulogy at private memorial Mass). New York City, July 23, 1999. Available at www.historyplace.com.

"The New Frontier" (address to the Democratic National Convention). Los Angeles, August 15, 2000.

Vital Speeches of the Day, September 1, 2000, pp. 687–88.

"Should the Senate Approve Mental Health Equitable Treatment Act?" *Congressional Digest*, January 2002, pp. 24+.

JOHN FITZGERALD KENNEDY (1917–1963)
Thirty-fifth President of the United States

THEODORE O. WINDT, JR., REVISED BY STEVEN R. GOLDZWIG

John F. Kennedy was the first television president. It was through television that Americans initially realized his effectiveness as a political communicator, and that is the way most people remember him. His masterful performance in the first television debate with Richard Nixon turned the tide of the 1960 election. Through his nationally televised speeches, which he called "reports to the nation," he led the country from crisis to crisis: from foreign crises in Berlin and Cuba through domestic crises of steel price increases and racial integration. In the end, his assassination brought unprecedented television coverage of his funeral and burial, the murder of his assassin, and images of the country's collective grief.

Prior to the 1960 campaign, Kennedy was little known nationally as an effective speaker. Instead, his reputation rested on his war record as the hero of PT 109, his family's prominence and fortune, his successful campaigns for the House of Representatives (1946, 1948, 1950) and the U.S. Senate (1952, 1958), and his unsuccessful bid for the Democratic vice presidential nomination (1956). Above all it rested on his literary accomplishments. His senior thesis at Harvard had been published as *Why England Slept* and had become a best-seller. While recovering from critical spinal surgery, he wrote *Profiles in Courage*, which won the Pulitzer Prize in 1956. But during the 1960 campaign, and especially after he entered the White House, Kennedy became recognized first as an effective speaker and then as a president who could rise to eloquence.

KENNEDY AS A PRESIDENTIAL PERSUADER

John F. Kennedy was to live television what Franklin Roosevelt had been to live radio. But television offered greater flexibility than radio and new opportunities that the administration seized upon. It developed a variety of formats adapted to television to present the president and his message in the most favorable light. First, the president used conventional set speeches, the staple of presidential rhetoric, to speak directly to the nation without having his message filtered through the press. On nine separate occasions, Kennedy delivered a formal, prepared address limited to a single topic, usually an immediate issue or event to which he was reacting. This concentrated rhetorical approach was modeled after Harry Truman's "first brigade" uses of speeches rather than the broad review of policy that Roosevelt had favored. Second, Kennedy revolutionized press conferences by having them televised live and unedited. Often, his use of humor at the press conferences made him seem more human and more accessible, and it added to his rhetorical appeal. Of the seventy-two regular and special news conferences he held, no fewer than sixty-three were televised. In addition, his press conference of July 23, 1962, was carried live to Europe via Telestar; thus he became the first president able to reach out to Europeans in this fashion. Third, Kennedy invented conversations with news correspondents, the "rocking chair" interviews. On December 17,

1962, Kennedy sat in his rocking chair in the Oval Office, and answered questions from three reporters for an hour of prime time on all three national networks. Finally, the administration allowed a wide range of prerecorded television interviews, special tours of the White House, and documentaries of the president working in the White House. In using the new dimensions television offered, Kennedy explored and expanded the ways in which presidential rhetoric could be presented to the public. These efforts set precedents for subsequent presidents and pioneered methods in which presidential rhetoric and political television would merge, become inseparable, and eventually arise as a central and formidable force for the exercise of presidential power.

Kennedy's rhetorical dominance in the new televisual environment certainly could not have been predicted by his earlier speaking career. After

In accepting the Democratic nomination in 1960, Kennedy promised to usher in the era of the New Frontier, which he said was "not a set of promises" but a "set of challenges." During the campaign, he faced two major challenges: his religion and his underdog status.

Since 1928, when Al Smith, a Catholic, was defeated for the presidency, conventional political wisdom had held that a Catholic could not be elected president. In the West Virginia primary in 1960, Kennedy's Catholicism was a major issue with the dominant Protestant electorate, but he effectively dispatched it on his way to victory over Hubert Humphrey. Early in the 1960 general election campaign, however, a group calling themselves the National Conference of Citizens for Religious Freedom challenged Kennedy's fitness for the presidency because he was a Catholic. On September 12,

---

John F. Kennedy is best known for his idealistic eloquence, from his Inaugural Address ("Ask not what your country can do for you—ask what you can do for your country") to his declaration in West Berlin ("Ich bin ein Berliner"). In his address on civil rights, delivered on national television on June 11, 1963 he declared, "We are confronted primarily with a moral issue. It is as old as the Scriptures and as clear as the Constitution."

---

his election to the House in 1946, Kennedy gave little inkling of stirring oratory. Six years later, when he was elected to the Senate, he seemed content to deliver well-researched but not particularly memorable or eloquent addresses. As a result, many of his speeches were ignored or forgotten until he published them in *The Strategy of Peace*, which served as an introduction to Kennedy's foreign policy for opinion leaders in the 1960 campaign. Kennedy's national rhetorical prominence was first achieved at the 1956 Democratic National Convention, where he introduced Democratic presidential candidate Adlai Stevenson. The draft for this speech was written by Theodore Sorensen. Sorensen's draft helped shape the Kennedy "style," and Kennedy and Sorensen's close collaboration would become a hallmark in the evolution of Kennedy's public address.

Kennedy forcefully addressed the issue in a major speech before the Greater Houston Ministerial Association. He presented a rigorous defense of religious tolerance in U.S. politics and offered to resign should his religion ever interfere with his duties as president. The speech effectively put the religious issue to rest, and it was so persuasive that Democrats replayed portions of it throughout the campaign.

The rhetorical high point of the campaign was a series of four televised debates between Kennedy and his Republican opponent, Richard Nixon. More than 70 million Americans viewed the first, and most important, debate. Kennedy demonstrated that he had a grasp of the issues equal to that of Vice President Nixon, thus diminishing Nixon's claim to superior knowledge of government. Equally important was the contrast in the appearances of the two candidates. Nixon looked pale and wan in contrast to the sun-tanned, vigorous Kennedy. The consensus of those who saw the debate was that Kennedy won. Public opinion polls showed a shift in voters, es-pecially those undecided, toward Kennedy. Al-though the race remained close, the debates were a turning point in Kennedy's quest to shed his image as an underdog. The election of 1960 was the closest in popular vote in the twentieth cen-tury. Although Kennedy won 303 electoral col-lege votes, he defeated Nixon by only one-tenth of 1 percent of the popular vote. A mere 112,881 votes separated the two candidates. Thus, Kennedy gained the presidency but not a man-date from the people.

On January 20, 1961, John Kennedy deliv-ered one of the few truly memorable presiden-tial Inaugural Addresses in U.S. history. Al-though a number of people contributed to the final version, Ted Sorensen was the principal draftsman of the address. Sorensen had been with Kennedy during both his Senate years and the presidential campaign. As a speechwriter, he held a unique position. Not only was he the pri-mary writer of most of Kennedy's major speeches, he was also a close adviser, confidant, and at times alter ego. Seldom has a speech-writer had as much influence in an administra-tion as Sorensen had in Kennedy's.

Kennedy's reputation as a speaker of uncom-mon ability rests principally on his Inaugural Ad-dress. In substance and style, it is the best repre-sentative of his rhetoric. The speech is a mixture of idealistic musing and crisis alert. The first president to have been born in the twentieth cen-tury, Kennedy proclaimed that the torch of lead-ership had been passed to a new generation "born in this century, tempered by war, disciplined by a hard and bitter peace, proud of our ancient her-itage." In his most memorable and idealistic phrase, he called upon Americans to "ask not what your country can do for you—ask what you can do for your country." The idealism was coun-terbalanced by a mood of critical urgency. He de-scribed the world he faced in somber, but never-theless reassuring, words meant to help build confidence in his leadership: "In the long history of the world, only a few generations have been granted the role of defending freedom in its hours

of maximum danger. I do not shrink from the re-sponsibility—I welcome it." Thus the two major themes of his administration merge in his Inau-gural Address. The speech also bears the indeli-ble imprint of Kennedy's style. Successive para-graphs begin with parallelisms: "Let both sides explore," "Let both sides . . . formulate," "Let both sides seek." Rhythmic alliterations abound: "Bear any burden, pay any price." And finally, the most distinctive device marking the Kennedy style is the balanced and antithetical sentences or phrases: "Let us never negotiate out of fear. But let us never fear to negotiate." This grand style in which language elevates substance inspired a generation of Americans and led the poet Carl Sandburg to remark, "Around nearly every sen-tence of it could be written a thesis, so packed is it with implications."

The rhetorical euphoria of the inaugural ad-dress soon paled in the aftermath of the Bay of Pigs disaster. On April 17, 1961, some 1,400 anti-Castro Cubans landed at the Bay of Pigs in Cuba, intent on overthrowing Fidel Castro or joining other rebels in the interior of Cuba to fight a guerrilla war against Castro. It ended in abject failure, and the United States was soon implicated in the incursion for its training, trans-port, and support of the rebels. While some felt President Kennedy took complete responsibility for the Bay of Pigs fiasco, others implied that his bold, tough talk in response was actually a feeble attempt to mask a foreign policy misad-venture. In a major speech before the American Society of Newspaper Editors on April 20, Kennedy said there were three lessons to be learned from the venture. First, "the forces of communism are not to be underestimated, in Cuba or anywhere else in the world." Second, the United States "must take an even closer and more realistic look at the menace of external Communist intervention and domination in Cuba." Finally, the United States faced a "re-lentless struggle in every corner of the globe that goes far beyond the clash of armies or even nuclear armaments."

Alternating between ambivalence and tough talk, the president's subsequent foreign policy public address took a hard-line, conservative, anti-communist tone. This dominated Kennedy's rhet-oric and actions in foreign policy, especially toward the Soviet Union, during the next year and a half of his administration. One week after the address to newspaper editors, in an address to the American Newspaper Publishers Association on April 27, Kennedy seemed to deny responsibility for the Bay of Pigs, blaming instead the Communists, Castro, and the press. This speech tarnished the president's credibility; Kennedy castigated the press for printing stories in advance about the Cuban invasion and called for voluntary self-censorship in the interests of national security. His rather virulent anticommunism also led him to interpret Premier Nikita Khrushchev's demand for negotiations on Berlin and the two Germanys during their meetings in Vienna in June as a direct military challenge to a U.S. presence in West Berlin. The president's somber interpretation of his meetings with Khrushchev resulted in his apocalyptic address on the Berlin crisis on July 25. He cautioned that the United States "cannot and will not permit the Communists to drive us out of Berlin, either gradually or by force," and warned the Soviets that Americans "do not want to fight—but that we have fought before." He called for a doubling of the draft, major increases in the armed forces and reserves, and a rapid buildup and augmentation of the civil defense program, including public and private fallout shelters. This speech was so frightening to Americans that the fallout shelter industry boomed, and a nightmarish debate on the morality of defending one's fallout shelter from others poured forth from television and radio, public platforms and church pulpits. In the wake of the speech, the Berlin Wall was built, and the Soviets and the Americans resumed atmospheric testing of nuclear weapons. Eventually both sides relented and allowed the crisis to subside as they began discussions over the future of Germany and Berlin.

The strained relations between the United States and the Soviet Union hit their zenith in October 1962. Earlier that month, the president had learned that the Soviets had begun to deploy offensive missiles in Cuba. Kennedy issued an ultimatum demanding that Khrushchev remove the missiles or risk nuclear war. The president pursued three lines of argument traditionally associated with presidential crisis rhetoric. First, Kennedy portrayed the United States as an inno-

cent and virtuous nation desiring only peace, and portrayed the enemy as a thoroughly unscrupulous country bent on aggression and world domination. Second, he contended that the specific action—in this case, the placing of offensive missiles in Cuba—typified the essentially untrustworthy character of the enemy. Finally, he demanded unified support from the American people for the policy he announced, as a test of their character and loyalty as citizens.

The Soviets, given little advance notice of Kennedy's speech, were caught by surprise. The ultimatum worked, and within weeks the Soviets agreed to remove the missiles in exchange for a public pledge that the United States would not invade Cuba and for private assurances that obsolete U.S. missiles would be removed from Turkey. At the time and for some time after, Kennedy's speech and his handling of the Cuban missile crisis—though he ventured where no previous president had ever dared to go in risking nuclear war—were viewed by Americans as a triumphant victory for Kennedy and the major achievement of his administration. That opinion is not so widely held today.

During much of the first two years of his administration, Kennedy was politically defensive and rhetorically reactive. Instead of shaping the direction of public opinion, he found himself responding to emerging events. The same held true in his celebrated press conferences, which by their nature placed the president in a reactive position of responding to questions from reporters. Kennedy sought to give some focus to these conferences by beginning each with an opening statement. In addition, his aides sometimes planted questions that the president specifically wanted to answer. His most dramatic press conference occurred on April 11, 1962, and concerned the steel crisis. The day before, U.S. Steel and other corporations had announced an increase of $6.00 per ton in the price of steel, which the president believed violated his economic guidelines. In his opening statement at the press conference, Kennedy denounced the steel companies and used domestic crisis rhetoric to plead his case. He defined the issue as a clash between the president, who represents the public interest, and corporations, who represent private interests. He argued that he was supported by the majority of Americans (thereby drawing on the rhetorical power of the democratic maxim "majority rules"). Finally, he argued that the vast majority of Americans were willing to sacrifice to support the public interest, whereas the corporate executives acted only from the base motives of their "pursuit of private power and profit," which led them to "show utter contempt for the interests of 185 million Americans." This slashing attack, as well as additional actions by the administration, caused U.S. Steel and the other companies to quickly rescind the price increase. But as in other cases during the first two years, Kennedy's rhetoric was reactive, and the result was a return to the status quo.

In 1963, after the Cuban missile crisis and Democratic victories in the Senate off-term elections, Kennedy struck out in bold new directions on the two most critical issues facing the country: civil rights and the nuclear arms race. In both cases, the rhetorical change was dramatic.

Civil rights had been the most pressing domestic issue since the Supreme Court decision in *Brown v. Board of Education* (1954). In September 1962 the federal courts had ordered the University of Mississippi to admit James Meredith, a Black applicant. Some citizens of Mississippi resisted, and Kennedy federalized the Mississippi National Guard. On September 30, as rioting broke out on the campus, Kennedy reported to the nation on the situation. He described integration in narrow legal terms, implored the citizens of Mississippi to obey the courts' decisions, and called for a return to peace and tranquillity.

Less than a year later, however, when he was faced with a comparable situation, Kennedy reacted differently. On June 11, 1963, Governor George Wallace fulfilled a campaign pledge by blocking the entrance to the University of Alabama when several Black students, again under court order, sought to enroll. In his televised speech that evening, Kennedy defined civil rights not in the narrow legal sense of the year before but in stirring moral terms. In ringing and indignant eloquence, he declared: "We are confronted primarily with a moral issue. It is as old as the Scriptures and as clear as the Constitution." To redress this moral grievance, Kennedy introduced his first civil rights legislation, a bill intended to

eliminate racial discrimination in public accommodations. A year later, under President Lyndon Johnson, the bill became law and marked the first significant civil rights legislation since the Civil War. In addition, Kennedy endorsed, but did not attend, the historic March on Washington on August 28, 1963; later that day he met with leaders of the march to address his own and their concerns over passage of the civil rights bill. These acts and this rhetoric caused the civil rights movement to turn from reliance solely on judicial decisions to legislative action.

Kennedy exhibited this same boldness in his approach to the nuclear arms race. On June 10, 1963, he addressed graduates at the commencement exercises at American University in Washington, D.C., and arguably gave the best and most eloquent speech of his administration. As Richard Reeves has noted, Kennedy "gave the speech of his life trying to break the world's nuclear siege." His topic was world peace, not "a Pax Americana enforced on the world by American weapons of war" or "the peace of the grave or the security of the slave," but rather a "genuine peace" that "makes life on earth worth living." To pursue this vision of peace, Kennedy summoned Americans to reexamine their attitudes toward peace itself, toward the Soviet Union, and toward the Cold War. In the most moving section of the speech, he marshaled a compellingly simple logic as he declared plaintively: "And if we cannot end now our differences at least we can help make the world safe for diversity. For, in the final analysis, our most basic common link is that we all inhabit this small planet. We all breathe the same air. We all cherish our children's future. And we are all mortal." This address and subsequent negotiations in Moscow resulted in an end to atmospheric testing by the two nations, and the conclusion of the limited nuclear test ban treaty. The address marked a major change in U.S. foreign policy toward the Soviet Union from one of containment to one of détente, a policy on which presidents Nixon, Ford, and Carter were able to forge new initiatives with the Soviets. Many feel that Kennedy's address at American University will be remembered as one of the greatest diplomatic addresses in American history.

Kennedy's administration is difficult to assess because an assassin's bullet ended it all too quickly. Rhetorically, Kennedy brought innovations to the White House with his televised press conferences and other uses of television, but he rarely exploited the medium to lead the country through formal speeches. His rhetoric was one of idealism and crisis, all too often the latter. In point of fact, the televised crisis speeches often alarmed the nation. Nevertheless, Kennedy returned the grand style to presidential speeches, though his style in press conferences was laconic and cool. He used more diverse genres of presidential rhetoric than other recent presidents, but usually in reacting to events rather than in leading the nation. As others have indicated, John Kennedy's tragically brief administration was one of promise rather than of definitive performance. He affected the mood of the United States more than its policies. Thus, he is remembered more for his words than his deeds. Had Kennedy not been cut down by the assassin's bullet, and had he been able to enjoy a second term in office, the nation might have been able to come to a more definitive judgment on the significance of his presidency and the accomplishments of his administration. Speculation on these matters has yet to abate. The Kennedy myth and the Kennedy performance have been inextricably linked. New assessments and reassessments will continue, and the legacy of the Kennedy era and recurrent ruminations over its meaning and import seem certain to enliven and challenge the public political and cultural imagination well into our nation's future.

INFORMATION SOURCES

Research Collections and Collected Speeches

The John F. Kennedy Library in Boston has more than 32 million pages in its more than 150 collections. In addition to the collection of John Kennedy's papers, it holds those of Robert F. Kennedy and other members of the family, oral histories, and materials from the Democratic National Committee from 1960 to 1964.

Campaign Speeches of American Presidential Candidates, 1928–1972 [CS], comp. Aaron Singer. New York: Frederick Ungar, 1976.

Goldzwig, Steven R., and George N. Dionisopoulos.

In a "Perilous Hour": The Public Address of John F. Kennedy [IPH]. Westport, Conn.: Greenwood Press, 1995.

Kennedy, John F. *The Burden and the Glory* [BG], ed. Allan Nevins. New York: Harper & Row, 1964.

———. *A Compendium of Speeches, Statements and Remarks Delivered During His Service in the Congress of the United States* [CSS]. Washington, D.C.: Government Printing Office, 1964.

———. *The Joint Appearances of Senator John F. Kennedy and Vice President Richard Nixon: Presidential Campaign of 1960* [JA]. Washington, D.C.: Government Printing Office, 1961.

———. *Kennedy and the Press: The News Conferences* [KP], ed. Harold W. Chase and Allen H. Lerman. New York: Crowell, 1965.

———. *Public Papers of the Presidents of the United States: John F. Kennedy* [PP], 3 vols. Washington, D.C.: Government Printing Office, 1962–64.

———. *The Speeches of Senator John F. Kennedy: Presidential Campaign of 1960* [PC]. Washington, D.C.: Government Printing Office, 1961.

———. *To Turn the Tide* [TTT], ed. John W. Gardner. New York: Harper and Brothers, 1962.

Windt, Theodore, ed. *Presidential Rhetoric: 1961 to the Present* [PR], 3rd ed. Dubuque, Iowa: Kendall/Hunt, 1983.

Web Site

JFK Library Home Page. Includes oral histories, speeches, news conferences, and audiovisual materials. www.jklibrary.org

Selected Critical Studies

Bostdorff, Denise M., and Steven R. Goldzwig. "Idealism and Pragmatism in American Foreign Policy Rhetoric: The Case of John F. Kennedy and Vietnam." *Presidential Studies Quarterly* 24 (1994): 515–30.

Corbett, Edward P. J. "Analysis of the Style of John F. Kennedy's Inaugural Address." In his *Classical Rhetoric for the Modern Student*, 2nd ed. New York: Oxford University Press, 1971.

Godden, Richard, and Richard Maidment. "Anger, Language and Politics: John F. Kennedy and the Steel Crisis." *Presidential Studies Quarterly* 10 (1980): 317–31.

Goldzwig, Steven R., and George N. Dionisopoulos. "John F. Kennedy's Civil Rights Discourse: From 'Principled Bystander' to Public Advocate." *Communication Monographs* 56 (1989): 179–98.

Hahn, Dan F. "Ask Not What a Youngster Can Do for You: Kennedy's Inaugural Address." *Presidential Studies Quarterly* 12 (1982): 610–14.

Murphy, John M. "Domesticating Dissent: The Kennedys and the Freedom Rides." *Communication Monographs* 59 (1992): 61–78.

Spragens, William C. "Kennedy Era Speechwriting, Public Relations and Public Opinion." *Presidential Studies Quarterly* 14 (1984): 78–86.

Windt, Theodore Otto, Jr. "The Presidency and Speeches on International Crises: Repeating the Rhetorical Past." *Speaker and Gavel* 2 (1973): 6–14.

———. "Seeking Détente with Superpowers: John F. Kennedy at American University." In *Essays in Presidential Rhetoric*, ed. Theodore Windt and Beth Ingold. Dubuque, Iowa: Kendall/Hunt, 1983.

Selected Biographies

Burns, James MacGregor. *John Kennedy: A Political Profile.* New York: Harcourt, Brace, and World, 1961.

Dallek, Robert. *An Unfinished Life: John F. Kennedy, 1917–1963.* Boston: Little, Brown, 2003.

Fairlie, Henry. *The Kennedy Promise.* Garden City, N.Y.: Doubleday, 1973.

Giglio, James N. *The Presidency of John F. Kennedy.* Lawrence: University Press of Kansas, 1991.

Giglio, James N., and Stephen G. Rabe. *Debating the Kennedy Presidency.* Lanham, Md.: Rowman & Littlefield, 2003.

Hersh, Seymour M. *The Dark Side of Camelot.* Boston: Little, Brown, 1997.

Matthews, Christopher. *Kennedy and Nixon: The Rivalry That Shaped Postwar America.* New York: Simon and Schuster, 1996.

Paper, Lewis J. *The Promise and the Performance: The Leadership of John F. Kennedy.* New York: Crown, 1975.

Parmet, Herbert S. *Jack: The Struggles of John F. Kennedy.* New York: Dial, 1980.

———. *JFK: The Presidency of John F. Kennedy.* New York: Dial, 1983.

Paterson, Thomas G., ed. *Kennedy's Quest for Victory: American Foreign Policy, 1961–1963.* New York: Oxford University Press, 1989.

Pearce, Kimber Charles. *Rostow, Kennedy, and the Rhetoric of Foreign Aid.* East Lansing: Michigan State University Press, 2001.

Reeves, Richard. *President Kennedy: Profile of Power.* New York: Simon and Schuster, 1993.

Schlesinger, Arthur M., Jr. *A Thousand Days.* Boston: Houghton Mifflin, 1965.

Sorensen, Theodore C. *Kennedy.* New York: Harper & Row, 1965.

Stern, Mark. *Calculating Visions: Kennedy, Johnson and Civil Rights.* New Brunswick, N.J.: Rutgers University Press, 1992.

Sylvestri, Vito N. *Becoming JFK: A Profile in Communication.* Westport, Conn.: Praeger, 2000.

Walton, Richard J. *Cold War and Counterrevolution: The Foreign Policy of John F. Kennedy.* New York: Viking, 1972.

White, Mark J., ed. *Kennedy: The New Frontier Revisited.* Houndmills, U.K.: Macmillan, 1998.

CHRONOLOGY OF MAJOR SPEECHES

See "Research Collections and Collected Speeches" for source codes.

"Acceptance Speech to the Democratic National Convention." Los Angeles, July 15, 1960. *CS*, pp. 298–303.

"Address Before the Greater Houston Ministerial Association." Houston, Tex., September 12, 1960. *CS*, pp. 303–7; *PC*, pp. 206–18 (includes the question period that followed the formal speech.); *IPH*, pp. 151–54.

"The First Television Debate." Chicago, September 26, 1960. *JA*, pp. 78–92.

"Inaugural Address." Washington, D.C., January 20, 1961. *PR*, pp. 9–11; *PP*, pp. 1–3; *TTTT*, pp. 6–11; *IPH*, pp. 155–57.

"Address to the American Society of Newspaper Editors on the Bay of Pigs." Washington, D.C., April 20, 1961. *PR*, pp. 11–14; *PP*, pp. 304–6; *TTTT*, pp. 43–48; *IPH*, pp. 159–61.

"The Berlin Crisis." Washington, D.C., July 25, 1961. *PR*, pp. 24–30; *PP*, pp. 533–40; *TTTT*, pp. 188–98; *IPH*, pp. 164–70.

"Opening Statement at Press Conference on the Steel Crisis." Washington, D.C., April 11, 1962. *PR*, pp. 31–33; *PP*, pp. 315–17; *BG*, pp. 194–96; *KP*, pp. 223–28.

"The Cuban Missile Crisis." Washington D.C., October 22, 1962. *PR*, pp. 36–40; *PP*, pp. 806–9; *BG*, pp. 89–96; *IPH*, pp. 171–75.

"Commencement Address at American University." Washington, D.C., June 10, 1963. *PR*, pp. 40–46; *PP*, pp. 459–64; *BG*, pp. 53–58; *IPH*, pp. 181–87.

"Radio and Television Report on Civil Rights." Washington, D.C., June 11, 1963. *PR*, pp. 46–49; *PP*, pp. 468–71; *BG*, pp. 181–85; *IPH*, pp. 177–80.

ROBERT FRANCIS KENNEDY (1925–1968)
U.S. *Attorney General, and U.S. Senator from New York*

STEVEN R. GOLDZWIG AND PATRICIA A. SULLIVAN

Robert F. Kennedy was born in Brookline, Massachusetts on November 20, 1925. The seventh of nine children and the third son of Joseph P. and Rose Kennedy, he joined a family of great wealth that deemed political service a kind of preordained destiny. He would struggle to find and then pursue his own political career in a life overshadowed by his brother John, who became the thirty-fifth president of the United States. Robert served in the Navy from 1944 to 1946, and received an A.B. in government from Harvard University in 1948 and a law degree from the University of Virginia in 1951. He was admitted to the Massachusetts bar in 1951, and served as an attorney in the criminal division of the Department of Justice from 1951 to 1952. In 1946 Robert had assisted his brother John in his bid for a seat in Congress, and in 1952 he served as John's campaign manager in his successful run for the U.S. Senate.

In 1953, under the tutelage of Senator Joseph R. McCarthy, Kennedy served as assistant counsel for the Senate Permanent Subcommittee on Investigations; he worked for the Hoover Commission. From 1957 to 1960, he was chief counsel for the Senate Select Committee on Improper Activities in Labor or Management (also known as the McClellan Committee or, in popular parlance, the Rackets Committee). Here Robert investigated racketeering, challenging the Teamsters Union and its leaders, Dave Beck and Jimmy Hoffa, and later confronted corruption represented in the activities of underworld dons such as Sam Giancana. In 1960, he again took up duties as campaign manager, this time for John's successful presidential bid. After the election John, in a rather controversial move, appointed him attorney general, making him the youngest attorney general since the presidency of James Madison. As attorney general, Kennedy continued his pursuit of crime and corruption

until 1964, when he was elected a senator from New York. He campaigned for the presidency in 1968, but his bid was cut short by assassination at the hand of Sirhan Sirhan on June 4, 1968. Kennedy wrote several books, including *The Enemy Within* (1960), *Just Friends and Brave Enemies* (1962), *To Seek a Newer World* (1967), and *Thirteen Days: A Memoir of the Cuban Missile Crisis* (1969).

ROBERT F. KENNEDY: VOICE OF DISSENT

No brief chronological sketch could represent Kennedy's impact on politics in the 1960s and his influence in the larger American culture—during his lifetime and beyond. Robert F. Kennedy was not a gifted speaker. He labored over his speeches, and that labor was not easy for him. His delivery was marred by his Boston accent, nasal intonation, sometimes shrill and screechy voice, and lackluster, halting, and unenthusiastic delivery of a written text. Nevertheless, Kennedy proved to be a popular speaker. We might account for this puzzling set of affairs by suggesting that he and his audiences consciously or unconsciously latched themselves to the mythic coattails of his brother John. When he campaigned for president in 1968, he sometimes felt that the large crowds had not turned out for him, but to resurrect the memory of the slain president who had come to represent the hopeful dreams and vigorous visions of the "New Frontier" that had not been established. Kennedy was sometimes prone to discount his own unique contributions to oratory, to the nation, and to the world community. But this element of self-effacement was unfounded.

Although Kennedy had entered public life as a ruthless and impatient Communist hunter and racket buster during his early years of public service with Joseph McCarthy and on the McClellan Committee, during the latter part of his life he became known for his thirst for justice, his pursuit of human dignity, and his unparalleled compassion for the poor and dispossessed minorities— traits rare in modern politicians. Kennedy resolutely advocated the cause of blacks in the urban ghettos and migrant farmworkers in the fields, and created awareness of the plight of Native Americans sequestered as second-class citizens on the nation's Indian reservations. His affinity for the downtrodden was as genuine as his intermittent expressions of discomfort with the middle class. Thus the paradox of the scion of a wealthy family who was emotionally attached to the poor and championed their causes became much ballyhooed, and garnered Kennedy a noteworthy place in the pantheon of liberal politicians of the 1960s.

In 1955, at the behest of Joseph P. Kennedy, Supreme Court Justice William O. Douglas took Kennedy on a six-week tour through five Soviet Central Asian republics. The trip gave Kennedy an international platform for commentary and helped solidify his Cold War philosophy. Upon their return, Kennedy expressed the view that little was likely to change in U.S.-Soviet relations in the post-Stalinist era. His visit also convinced him that while the Communist system might have raised the people's standard of living, it was decidedly not the kind of social system that promoted human rights. Kennedy reported on his trip in a slide show presentation at Georgetown University on October 10, 1955. As Edwin O. Guthman and C. Richard Allen described the occasion, "it was his maiden speech." In the lecture, Kennedy spoke of his "impressions" during his travels. He concluded: "When we negotiate with Soviet Russia, we are dealing with a country in which the basic freedoms and rights, which we believe to be inalienable, are for its citizens, if at all, only terms prescribed by those in power in the Kremlin." Kennedy told his audience that he had encountered "secret police," "prison labor battalions," "slave labor camps," and a government where "all means of livelihood and all sources of income emanate from Moscow." In the Soviet system, "the right of a citizen to criticize the government does not exist." Other rights were described as circumscribed as well, including the rights to worship

and to enjoy a free press. Kennedy was wary of exporting technology and agricultural advice to the Soviets. Indeed, he decried entering into further agreements with the Russians that he felt might jeopardize the peace. His distrust was plainly evident: "All I ask is that before we take any more drastic steps . . . we receive something from the Soviet Union other than a smile and a promise—a smile that could be as crooked and a promise that could be as empty as they have been in the past."

In 1956, as chief counsel to the Senate Rackets Committee, Kennedy, upon exposing conflicts of interest and corruption in the military clothing procurement program, became intrigued by elements of organized crime that had surfaced in the investigation. His search for a new investigation led him to focus on the Teamsters Union, which had been investigated by Congress twice before, with no real results. On February 26, 1957, the Rackets Committee opened a two-year investigation of the Teamsters; the committee hearings were often televised, and they revealed a vigorous struggle between the chief counsel and James Hoffa. Although Hoffa escaped serious charges, the work Kennedy did for the McClellan Committee resulted in the Labor Reform Act of 1959, which strengthened federal laws against embezzlement of union funds, accepting bribes in labor–management relations, and other remedies against corruption.

On October 15, 1957, Kennedy delivered an interim report of his committee's findings before the Inland Daily Press Association in Chicago. He spoke of necessary changes in the law to prevent corrupt union leaders such as Dave Beck and Jimmy Hoffa from further eroding American labor and the American economy. He outlined a long list of abuses, including misuse of pension and welfare funds, diversions of union funds, abuses of trusteeship, misuses of the secret ballot, and acts of violence and intimidation. In the speech Kennedy lobbied for the need for reform. He told the journalists: "We need your help and support but also your ideas on what remedial action is necessary. If the press will share the committee's responsibility in this regard, we may later be able to consider the investigation a real step forward for American society."

Kennedy's attack against the mob bosses and corruption was undertaken in part because of his strong belief that, if it was left unchecked, an unsavory strain of union power was in a position to supplant that of the government. The links between labor and organized crime in the United States threatened to destroy national trust and subvert existing democratic institutions. Kennedy felt that existing political institutions had a responsibility to safeguard the nation from mob influence, weak law enforcement, and growing corruption. He strongly expressed those views in an unflinching address to the American Trucking Association on October 20, 1959. The Trucking Association was anything but a disinterested party. Kennedy viewed the "theft of millions of dollars" by corrupt union bosses as a betrayal of legitimate organized labor and, perhaps even more important, "only a symptom of other and more serious underlying problems." He was incensed that "[a] number of men in important union positions" had "come to regard unions as their own personal possessions." This development was a cause for alarm at a more profound level than many people realized. Kennedy warned: "Disaster is our destiny unless we reinstall the toughness, the moral idealism which has guided this nation during its history." This was a theme that was applied by John Kennedy in his bid for the presidency in 1960, a campaign that was managed by Robert. After the election, John appointed his brother attorney general. While some made charges of nepotism, Robert labored mightily to be worthy of a job he had tried to refuse.

As attorney general, Kennedy delivered his first major speech and earliest statement on civil rights on May 6, 1961, in the heart of the Deep South at the University of Georgia Law School. At the time, the Freedom Rides were making headlines. Kennedy made a special plea: "We know that it is law which enables man to live together, that creates order out of chaos. We know that the law is the glue that holds civilization together. And we know that if one man's rights are denied, the rights of all are endangered." To Kennedy's surprise and delight, the 1,600 students, faculty, administrators, and other audience members greeted his forthright address with a thirty-second standing ovation.

Thorny challenges lay ahead, including historic confrontations with Governor Ross Barnett over the admission of James Meredith to the University of Mississippi in 1962 and Governor George Wallace "standing in the schoolhouse door" at Tuscaloosa, Alabama, in 1963. John and Robert Kennedy also were forced to respond to Martin Luther King Jr.'s civil rights demonstrations in Birmingham, and they made secret arrangements for a peaceful March on Washington in 1963. But in November 1963, the world community was shocked with the news of a U.S. president's assassination.

Robert Kennedy was understandably shaken after the assassination of his brother John. In his grief, he was reluctant to fully reenter public life. After much coaxing he was finally persuaded to go to Scranton, Pennsylvania, on March 17, 1964, to address the Friendly Sons of St. Patrick of Lackawanna County. This speaking date would give him an opportunity to reflect on his Irish heritage, his brother's accomplishments, and, perhaps most important, his own future. Buoyed by his warm, enthusiastic reception, and challenged by the public task he had once again accepted, Kennedy delivered an address that outlined a brief history of Ireland and the quest for Irish freedom. The occasion also provided a platform to talk about "the greatest enemy of freedom today"— "communism." He concluded: "So on this St. Patrick's evening let me urge you one final time to recall the heritage of the Irish. Let us hold out our hands to those who struggle for freedom today—at home and abroad—as Ireland struggled for a thousand years. Let us not leave them to be 'sheep without a shepherd when the snow shuts out the sky.' Let us show them that we have not forgotten the constancy and the faith and the hope of the Irish." Kennedy's words also seemed to be addressed to himself. As Edwin O. Guthman and C. Richard Allen write, "the poignant outpouring of love for President Kennedy and much evidence that he stood well with the people in his own right" enabled Kennedy to make an "irrevocable decision. . . . Somehow, he would remain in public service."

Kennedy was often at his best when he dispensed with his prepared text. He was very good in press conferences and in question-and-answer sessions. He often engaged his audiences after delivering an address. He was direct, clear, and forceful, and at times he displayed an ability to employ humor as a means of defusing a volatile situation.

One of the most striking examples of Kennedy's facility with off-the-cuff remarks can be found in his address to the Democratic National Convention in Atlantic City, New Jersey, on August 27, 1964. On August 22, he had announced his intention to run for the U.S. Senate from New York. Kennedy had been asked by convention planners to introduce a filmed memorial to his slain brother. Introduced by Senator Henry Jackson, Kennedy strode to the lectern and bent toward the microphone, but before he could speak, the convention delegates broke into cheers and waves, and general pandemonium. Each time Kennedy tried to begin his speech, he was interrupted with more gales of applause and cheers. This lasted twenty-two minutes. When the audience calmed and Kennedy was able to subdue his own emotions, he dispensed with his prepared text. He thanked the delegates for their demonstration of support for him and for his beloved brother. In a moving speech Kennedy quoted from Shakespeare to memorialize his brother: "When he shall die/Take him and cut him out in little stars/And he will make the face of heaven so fine/That all the world will be in love with night/And pay no worship to the garish sun." And from Robert Frost he divined both individual and party destiny: "The woods are lovely, dark and deep/But I have promises to keep/And miles to go before I sleep,/And miles to go before I sleep." Kennedy was hopeful that Camelot would shine brightly again and deflect attention away from Lyndon Johnson. For Kennedy at the time, said one biographer, Johnson was nothing more than a "garish sun." Like his brother, Robert had miles to go before he, too, could sleep. Indeed, he resigned as attorney general on September 2, 1964, and went on to defeat Thomas B. Keating for U.S. senator from New York by a margin of 700,000 votes. Kennedy seemed a bit uncomfortable in the Senate, sometimes even bored; he had his sights on the presidency.

Revisionist accounts of Kennedy came to portray him as an ardent defender of the dispossessed, but his sense of justice and compassion had actually been honed in his youth. As

he grew older and more confident, he found that he could successfully wield power on behalf of his convictions. Whether his topic was free speech, urban renewal, human rights, or Vietnam, Kennedy was able to infuse his speeches with a reason, passion, and eloquence that overshadowed their sometimes screechy, uninspired delivery. He came to the defense of the young and the old, the powerless and the disenfranchised. Injustices at home and abroad became the subject of his ire and the target of his pointed words. Over time his delivery also improved.

Kennedy stumped for a number of congressional candidates in the midterm elections of 1966. On October 22, 1966, as he barnstormed the West, he stopped at the University of California at Berkeley, which had become a hotbed of civil dissent and unrest, especially over the Vietnam War. Paraphrasing the Socratic dictum that "the unexamined life is not worth living," Kennedy told those assembled that dissent was "the seminal spirit of American democracy." He indicated that there was "much to dissent from." In a series of powerful parallelisms, Kennedy chanted: "We dissent from the fact that millions are trapped in poverty while the nation grows rich. We dissent from the conditions and hatreds which deny a full life to our fellow citizens because of the color of their skin. We dissent from the monstrous absurdity of a world where nations stand poised to destroy one another, and men must kill their fellow men." Importantly, dissent was merely "self-indulgence" unless there was also an attempt to "solve the problems of our society." Kennedy left his listeners with a stark choice: "We can face our difficulties and strive to overcome them; or we can turn away, bringing repression, steadily increasing human pain and civil strife, and leaving a problem of far more terrifying and grievous dimensions to our children. Anyone who promises another course, who pledges a solution without cost or effort or difficulty, is deluding both himself and the people to whom he speaks."

Not willing to ask others to do what he did not do himself, Kennedy attacked joblessness and the related homelessness that decimated urban cores. Talk was backed up by action in a demonstration project he helped develop in the Bedford-

Stuyvesant section of Brooklyn, New York. This project would be different from the Johnson-sponsored programs, whose funding had been siphoned off by the Vietnam War. After considerable study, Kennedy determined that rebuilding the cities required a new and different impetus. Educational facilities, job training, jobs, housing, health care, and community services needed to be centrally located and accessible to all, including youth and senior citizens. Kennedy directed aides to look for successful models that he could locate in New York. He attached a Special Impact Program amendment to the Economic Opportunity Act of 1966 (Johnson's major poverty bill), securing $7 million for two years; it was specifically directed to "Bed-Stuy." Kennedy's forward-looking vision is perhaps best summed up in his December 10, 1966, speech, which was delivered on the occasion of launching the project: "To turn promise into performance, plan into reality . . . we must combine the best of community action with the best of the private enterprise system. Neither by itself is enough; but in their combination lies our hope for the future."

As attorney general, Kennedy would play a key role in foreign as well as domestic policy. President Kennedy relied on "Bobby," his closest adviser and confidant, to tell him the unvarnished truth. After the Bay of Pigs fiasco, the brothers grew closer; as time went on, they developed even greater mutual trust and respect. Robert's role in the Cuban missile crisis proved indispensable to the president and to the nation. When he struck out on his own as a senator, he traveled to a number of continents and capitals. One of his most memorable stops was in South Africa. While the government of South Africa was largely hostile to the trip, fearful that at best it was merely a publicity junket, Kennedy was granted a brief visit. In the fall of 1965 he was invited by Ian Robertson, president of the National Union of South African Students, to come to the University of Cape Town in the spring of 1966, to serve as the keynote speaker for the Annual Day of Reaffirmation of Academic and Human Freedom. The government bristled at the thought and subsequently banned Robertson from public meetings.

Fearing a challenge to its apartheid system, the government delayed Kennedy's visa, but on June 6, 1966, Kennedy was able to speak to the more than 1,500 assembled in the hall and to greet the 15,000 or so people who waited outside in the bitter cold to meet him. He was genuinely interested in what he might say to help the Africans rather than merely score political points with his New York constituency. He spoke forthrightly and, under the circumstances, courageously—appealing to mind and heart with a revolutionary call to pursue full citizenship for all: "This is a Day of Affirmation, a celebration of liberty. We stand here today in the name of freedom. . . . The first element of this individual liberty is the freedom of speech: the right to express and communicate ideas, to set oneself apart from the dumb beasts of the field and forest; to recall governments to their duties and obligations; above all, the right to affirm one's membership and allegiance to the body politic—to society—to the men with whom we share our land, our heritage, and our children's future." In perhaps the most eloquent and memorable segment of the address, Kennedy quoted Archimedes—"Give me a place to stand, and I will move the world"—then continued:

> It is from the numberless diverse acts of courage and belief that human history is shaped. Each time a man stands up for an ideal, or acts to improve the lot of others, or strikes out against injustice, he sends forth a tiny ripple of hope, and crossing each other from a million different centers of energy and daring those ripples build a current which can sweep down the mightiest walls of oppression and resistance.

When Kennedy finished this address, there was a brief moment of stunned silence, followed by an explosive round of sustained applause. Kennedy biographer Evan Thomas maintained that this speech "would be remembered as Kennedy's best." Words drawn from the Cape Town address are etched into the stone wall facing Kennedy's grave at Arlington National Cemetery. They stand in testament to the memory of the man and to his indomitable spirit. Ironically, after delivering the Cape Town address, Kennedy learned that James Meredith, who had survived the travails of his struggle to integrate the University of Mississippi some four years earlier, had been shot in the back while on a Freedom March from Memphis, Tennessee, to Jackson, Mississippi. At the time, it was unclear if Meredith would survive. Guthman and Allen report that Kennedy appeared "*really, really . . . terribly* upset."

Vietnam had rent the nation like no other previous foreign war. Nevertheless, a majority of liberal Democrats favored the war. Kennedy had defended the idea of dissent at Berkeley in October 1966. He increasingly also found himself defending the youth who had mounted protests over injustices at home and a war in a distant land. Many found the domestic injustice related to the machinations of the war. Not surprisingly, Kennedy, like the youthful protestors, often had his patriotism questioned, his motives impugned, and his patience sorely tested. He had grounds for identification with youth. On February 24, 1967, Kennedy addressed the Americans for Democratic Action. His topic was the "generation gap" that had been widely discussed as a sociological and practical problem. He attempted to explain not only why students opposed the war in Vietnam, but also why they felt alienated and distanced from many aspects of their government's policies. He decried "the insincerity" and the "absence of dialogue" that seemed to be gripping the nation, and declared that he could "understand why so many of our young people have turned from engagement to disengagement, from politics to passivity, from hope to nihilism, from SDS [Students for a Democratic Society] to LSD." But understanding was not enough. The young needed "to feel that change is possible; that they will be heard; that the cruelties and follies and injustices of the world will yield, however grudgingly, to the sweat and sacrifice they are so ready to give. If we cannot help open to them this sense of possibility, we will have only ourselves to blame for the disillusionment that will surely come. . . . [W]e will judge ourselves by the hope and direction we have left behind." Little wonder that youth felt they had found a defender and a voice. It was unparalleled in the annals of American politics. For some, it was simply astonishing. A mainstream politician was finding reason for, and perhaps even merit in, the counterculture.

There was a real and abiding animosity between Lyndon Johnson and Kennedy. Perhaps the biggest tension between them was over the Vietnam War. Johnson disliked Kennedy and tracked him quite closely. He firmly believed that Kennedy was, in historian Michael Beschloss's words, "search[ing] for some pretext on which to break with him and challenge his leadership." Vietnam provided just such an opportunity. Ironically, Johnson also "worr[ied] that Robert Kennedy's crowd would destroy him" if he were to abandon John Kennedy's commitment to Vietnam. Of course, Robert Kennedy's belated announcement of his candidacy in 1968 confirmed Johnson's worst suspicions. But during the 1966 off-year election, Kennedy had kept his distance from a critique of the war—after all, he had been party to many of the decisions that had decided the shape of the war, and many of those with whom he had worked were still in power. Vietnam was a Kennedy legacy; it would take some adroit political maneuvering to mount a meaningful dissent. In addition, Robert Kennedy told close advisers that he believed his dissent would more than likely infuriate Johnson and cause the president to escalate the war. Kennedy was well aware that Johnson relished J. Edgar Hoover's "secret" intelligence files on both his brother John and himself; he was wary that damaging information could be leaked at any time, creating irreparable political harm.

Nonetheless, Kennedy biographer Evan Thomas records that after a particularly vicious February 6, 1967, encounter with Johnson over Kennedy's alleged freelancing as a diplomat on Vietnam, Kennedy determined that the president would always assume the worst in regard to his actions, and therefore saw little profit in continuing to restrain his disagreements over the war. Kennedy was concerned about the escalation in bombing that had occurred in 1966, and he noted that U.S. casualties for the year had exceeded those of the South Vietnamese soldiers. Both the direction and the cost of the war in terms of men and matériel weighed on him heavily. As Kennedy and his advisers planned a major address in opposition to the present course of the war, a Louis Harris poll indicated that 70 percent of the American people supported the war and a mere 24 percent favored a halt in bombing. On March 2, 1967, Kennedy repaired to the Senate chamber to deliver a speech that would spell out his differences with the administration. Speaking of the "tangled and resistant . . . complexities" of the war that made "judgment difficult and uncertain," he nonetheless felt that the war's course "should be subject to a ceaseless and critical examination." Kennedy called for negotiations, a halt in bombing, international monitoring of any escalation, U.N. forces as replacements for U.S. troops in the transition to peace, and a final settlement that would allow the South Vietnamese to "govern their own future." These steps were offered, he said, "not as a fixed and frozen formula," but rather as "suggestions to be refined and revised" by the experts involved, shifting events, the responses of other nations, and the ardent desires of the people of Vietnam.

While the March 2 speech neither moved Johnson nor altered his Vietnam policies, it did launch Kennedy into a new phase in the public arena on a very contentious issue. More important, the address placed Kennedy in a position to challenge Johnson for the Democratic presidential nomination. On March 9, 1968, Kennedy announced his presidential candidacy. His challenge to Johnson and other potential candidates would be reinforced both by his strong advocacy for the poor and the dispossessed and by his opposition to the war. On March 18, 1968, Kennedy addressed students at the University of Kansas. He spoke of "recapturing America's moral vision" by acting to "erase material poverty" at home and ending the war abroad in order to secure "a decent respect

---

As the Vietnam War widened, Kennedy came to have serious misgivings about Johnson's conduct of the war. He publicly broke with the president for the first time in February 1966. The following year, he took responsibility for his role in the Kennedy administration's policy in Southeast Asia, urging Johnson to cease the bombing of North Vietnam and reduce the war effort. In his final Senate speech on Vietnam, Kennedy said, "Are we like the God of the Old Testament that we can decide, in Washington, D.C., what cities, what towns, what hamlets in Vietnam are going to be destroyed? . . . Do we have to accept that? . . . I do not think we have to. I think we can do something about it." On March 18, 1968, he announced his candidacy for the presidency.

Kennedy's fears about retaliation for his dissent on the Vietnam War proved well founded. After the March 2 speech Johnson convinced columnist Drew Pearson to publish a story that accused Kennedy of plotting to kill Fidel Castro; it charged that Kennedy's participation in that plot may have led to a decision by Castro to kill his brother John. To make matters worse, the Pearson article speculated that Kennedy might be experiencing more than "natural grief" associated with his brother's assassination, in that he might be living with the thought that he was responsible for the machinations that had led to his brother's death.

for the opinions of mankind." Kennedy's decision to campaign for the presidency was solidified on March 31, 1968, when Johnson announced that he would halt the bombing and call for peace negotiations with North Vietnam. A tired and deflated president also revealed that he would not seek reelection. A large boulder seemingly had been removed from Kennedy's path to the presidency, but Johnson's surprise announcement also seemed to dissolve one of Kennedy's most compelling campaign issues.

Just days after Johnson's announcement that he would not seek reelection, another national tragedy marred the social and political landscape. On

April 4, 1968, Martin Luther King, Jr. was assassinated in Memphis. Kennedy was campaigning in Indianapolis. His own personal loss was not far from his thoughts when he was forced to tell a shocked assembly that King had been killed by an assassin's bullet. Searching for words to heal the deep wound of the moment, Kennedy pleaded: "For those of you who are black and are tempted to be filled with hatred and distrust at the injustice of such an act, against all white people, I can only say that I feel in my own heart the same kind of feeling. I had a member of my family killed, but he was killed by a white man. But we have to make an effort in the United States, we have to make an effort to understand, to go beyond these rather difficult times." Sensing the division that this event would provoke, Kennedy reflected that "the vast majority of white people and the vast majority of black people in this country want to live together, want to improve the quality of our life, and want justice for all human beings who abide in our land." Kennedy urged his audience "to tame the savageness of man and make gentle the life of this world." He concluded: "Let us dedicate ourselves to that, and say a prayer for our country and for our people." It was a fitting response to an unfitting circumstance. The genuineness of the response seemed to have a calming effect on the audience. In a unique moment Kennedy was confronted with history, and his knowledge of history and literature aided him in a most perilous hour. That night there were riots in 110 cities, during which 39 people died and more than 2,500 were injured. As Edwin O. Guthman and C. Richard Allen observed: "Kennedy was the only white public official in America who could have addressed a crowd in a black neighborhood that tragic night and not encounter violence." This speech, which has been widely anthologized, was ranked seventeenth in a recent survey of the top 100 American speeches conducted by Stephen Lucas and Martin J. Medhurst.

Less well known but certainly as significant to the Kennedy legacy was the speech he delivered on April 5 in Cleveland. Kennedy, addressing a "time of shame and sorrow," used the themes of crisis and redemption to employ a rhetoric perhaps best associated with what John M. Murphy has identified as part of the Ameri-

can jeremiad tradition. In a telling analysis of how Kennedy, in Ernest Bormann's apt phrase, set about the process of "fetching good out of evil," Murphy does a masterful job of explicating the address. Journalist and Kennedy biographer Jack Newfield considered the Cleveland address RFK's best campaign speech and perhaps the finest of his career.

Kennedy continued to campaign for the presidency; his first primary was slated for May 7, in Indiana. Terming this primary's significance "my West Virginia," Kennedy defeated Hubert Humphrey's stand-in candidate Governor Roger Branigan, and Eugene McCarthy. A week later he won the Nebraska primary. He went on to defeat in Oregon. According to biographer Evan Thomas, this was the first defeat by any of Joseph P. Kennedy's sons since Jack lost his bid for the Harvard Board of Overseers. On June 1, Kennedy debated Eugene McCarthy in a nationally televised attempt to rebound from the Oregon loss and secure the all-important California primary. Kennedy defeated McCarthy in the South Dakota primary, held the same day as California's. When victory in California was assured, Evan Thomas reports, Kennedy called Kenneth O'Donnell and said: "You know, Kenny, I feel now for the first time that I've shaken off the shadow of my brother. I feel I made it on my own." On June 4, 1968, Kennedy delivered a victory speech in Los Angeles, at the Ambassador Hotel. The brief speech summarized the virulent turbulence and the great hope of the late 1960s. His words gave his audiences the sense that this period of inordinate tensions would pass, that unity was not only thinkable but on the immediate horizon: "I think we can end the divisions within the United States . . . the violence, the disenchantment with our society . . . the divisions, whether it's between blacks and whites, between the poor and the more affluent, or between age groups, or over the war in Vietnam—that we can start to work together again." Joy and hope quickly turned into shock and horror. After leaving the ballroom of the hotel, Kennedy tried to exit through the kitchen. Shots were fired. Robert Kennedy lay crumpled on the floor. He was rushed to Good Samaritan Hospital. On June 6, 1968, at age forty-two, Robert F.

Kennedy expired. A fruitful and promising public life had come to an end.

INFORMATION SOURCES

Research Collections and Collected Speeches

Robert F. Kennedy's speeches and papers are best accessed through the John F. Kennedy Presidential Library in Boston.

"An Honorable Profession": A Tribute to Robert F. Kennedy [*HP*], ed. Pierre Salinger et al. New York: Doubleday, 1968.

RFK: Collected Speeches [*CS*], ed. Edwin O. Guthman and C. Richard Allen. New York: Viking Press, 1993.

Robert Kennedy: In His Own Words [*OW*], ed. Edwin O. Guthman and Jeffrey Shulman. New York: Bantam Books, 1988.

Robert F. Kennedy: Apostle of Change [*AC*], ed. Douglas Ross. New York: Trident Press, 1968.

Web Sites

Arlington National Cemetery Memorial. www.arlingtoncemetery.org

Eulogy for Robert Kennedy by Edward M. Kennedy. www.jfklibrary.org

JFK Library Web site. Speeches by RFK. www.jfklibrary.org

Robert Kennedy Memorial. www.rfkmemorial.org

Selected Critical Studies

Anatol, Karl W., and John R. Bitner. "Kennedy on King: The Rhetoric of Control." *Today's Speech* 16 (1968): 31–34.

Cook, Roger. " 'To Tame the Savageness of Man': Robert Kennedy's Eulogy of Martin Luther King, Jr." In *Great Speeches for Criticism and Analysis*, ed. Lloyd E. Rohler and Roger Cook, 2nd ed. Greenwood, Ind.: Alistair Press, 1993.

Greene, Robert J. "The Kennedy–Keating 'Debate.' " *Today's Speech* 13 (1965): 12–13, 42.

Murphy, John M. "Crafting the Kennedy Legacy." *Rhetoric & Public Affairs* 3 (2000): 577–602.

———. "Domesticating Dissent: The Kennedys and the Freedom Rides." *Communication Monographs* 59 (1992): 61–78.

———. "Epideictic and Deliberative Strategies in Opposition to War: The Paradox of Honor and Expediency." *Communication Studies* 43 (1992): 65–78.

———. "The Light of Reason: Robert Kennedy's February 8, 1968 Address on Vietnam." In *Critiques of Contemporary Rhetoric*, ed. Karlyn Kohrs Campbell and Thomas R. Burkholder, 2nd ed. Belmont, Calif.: Wadsworth, 1997.

———. " 'A Time of Shame and Sorrow': Robert F. Kennedy and the American Jeremiad." *Quarterly Journal of Speech* 76 (1990): 401–14.

Rudolph, Harriet J. "Robert F. Kennedy at Stellenbosch University." *Communication Quarterly* 31 (1983): 205–11.

———. "Robert F. Kennedy's University of Capetown Address." *Central States Speech Journal* 33 (1982): 319–32.

Selected Biographies

Beran, Michael Knox. *The Last Patrician: Bobby Kennedy and the End of American* Aristocracy. New York: St. Martin's Press, 1998.

Heymann, C. David. *RFK: A Candid Biography of Robert F. Kennedy*. New York: Dutton, 1998.

Hilty, James W. *Robert Kennedy: Brother Protector*. Philadelphia: Temple University Press, 1997.

Kimball, Penn. *Bobby Kennedy and the New Politics*. Englewood Cliffs, N.J.: Prentice-Hall, 1968; New York: Morrow, 1988.

Palermo, Joseph A. *In His Own Right: The Political Odyssey of Senator Robert F. Kennedy*. New York: Columbia University Press, 2001.

Schlesinger, Arthur M., Jr. *Robert Kennedy and His Times*. Boston: Houghton Mifflin, 1978.

Shesol, Jeff. *Mutual Contempt: Lyndon Johnson, Robert Kennedy, and the Feud That Defined a Decade*. New York: Norton, 1997.

Steel, Ronald. *In Love with Night: The American Romance with Robert Kennedy*. New York: Simon and Schuster, 2000.

Thomas, Evan. *Robert Kennedy: His Life*. New York: Simon and Schuster, 2000.

Witcover, Jules. *85 Days: The Last Campaign of Robert Kennedy*. New York: Putnam, 1969; New York: Quill, 1988.

CHRONOLOGY OF MAJOR SPEECHES

See "Research Collections and Collected Speeches" for source codes.

"Lecture on Soviet Central Asia." Georgetown University, October 10, 1955. *CS*, pp. 11–19.

"Speech to the Inland Daily Press Association." Chicago, October 15, 1957. *CS*, pp. 24–32.

"Speech to the American Trucking Association." Washington, D.C., October 20, 1959. *CS*, pp. 33–38.

"Law Day Speech." University of Georgia Law School, Athens, Ga., May 6, 1961. *CS*, pp. 46–55.

"Speech to the Friendly Sons of St. Patrick of Lack-awanna County." Scranton, Pa., March 17, 1964. *CS*, pp. 103–10.

"Speech to the Democratic National Convention." Atlantic City, N.J., August 27, 1964. *HP*, pp. 4–6; *CS*, pp. 114–17.

"Day of Affirmation Speech." Cape Town, South Africa, June 6, 1966. *CS*, pp. 231–46.

"Speech at the University of California at Berkeley." October 22, 1966. *AC*, pp. 220–21; *CS*, pp. 139–48.

"Address Launching the Bedford-Stuyvesant Restoration Effort." Brooklyn, N.Y., December 10, 1966. *CS*, pp. 185–92.

"Address to the Americans for Democratic Action." Philadelphia, February 24, 1967. *AC*, pp. 272–73; *CS*, pp. 148–51.

"Speech to the U.S. Senate." Washington, D.C., March 2, 1967. *AC*, pp. 517–28; *CS*, pp. 231–46.

"Recapturing America's Moral Vision." Lawrence, Kan., March 18, 1968. *CS*, pp. 327–30.

"Statement on the Death of the Reverend Martin Luther King, Jr." Indianapolis, Ind., April 4, 1968. *HP*, pp. 7–8; *CS*, pp. 355–58.

"On the Mindless Menace of Violence." Cleveland, Ohio, April 5, 1968. *CS*, pp. 358–62.

"California Victory Speech." Los Angeles, June 4, 1968. *CS*, pp. 400–2.

JOHN F. KERRY (1942–)
U.S. Senator, Democratic Presidential Candidate

BERNARD K. DUFFY AND MARILYN DeLAURE

John Kerry was born to the purple. His father, Richard, the son of a well-to-do Boston merchant, grew up in prosperous Brookline, Massachusetts, attended Andover Academy, and graduated from Yale and Harvard Law School before entering the foreign service. Richard married Rosemary Forbes, whose family had deep roots in Massachusetts society and belonged to the Boston upper class. One of her forebears was John Winthrop, the first governor of the Massachusetts Bay Colony, who in 1630 proclaimed to his fellow Puritans: "We must consider that we shall be as a City upon a Hill, the eyes of all people are upon us." Ronald Reagan memorialized Winthrop's sentiment in speeches delivered during his presidency.

Kerry attended boarding school in Switzerland; the Fessenden School in West Newton, Massachusetts; and ultimately St. Paul's in Concord, New Hampshire all paid for by his great-aunt, Clara Winthrop. Such schools prepared students for admission to elite colleges and for social and political leadership. Kerry followed in his father's footsteps by attending Yale, and after his military service went on to take a law degree at Boston

College. He married Julia Thorne, the twin sister of his best friend at Yale. The Thorne family's influence on American history could be traced back to the eighteenth century. By comparison the Kerrys were recently arrived Americans. John's paternal grandfather, Fritz Kohn, a Czech Jew, immigrated to America in 1905. Several years earlier he had changed his name to Frederick Kerry and converted to Roman Catholicism in order to thwart anti-Semitism. Despite being only a third-generation American on his father's side, Kerry, both because of the conspicuous success of his father and grandfather and because of his mother's patrician lineage, enjoyed the privileges of good birth, and his schooling put him in the company of the scions of the American ruling class.

Biographer Douglas Brinkley thoroughly documents the development of Kerry's interest in politics and speaking early in his schooling. While he was at St. Paul's the events of the civil rights movement led him to craft a speech delivered to his classmates, titled "The Plight of the Negro." Later Kerry founded a debating society at St. Paul's and debated—on the affirmative—the recognition of the People's Republic of

China, then "Red China." He made clear his ambition to be a congressman or a senator, which put him at odds with some of his peers, for whom open ambition was perceived as a middle-class trait. Kerry also advocated for John F. Kennedy's election as president and, in a staged debate, took the role of his idol, Kennedy, while another St. Paul's student assumed the role of Richard Nixon. While dating Janet Auchincloss, the half-sister of Jacqueline Kennedy, Kerry had an unexpected opportunity in the summer of 1962 to meet and talk with President Kennedy at the Auchincloss summer home in Newport, Rhode Island, prior to sailing with Kennedy on Narragansett Bay. Kerry idolized Kennedy and began sounding like him, with a Boston accent thicker than the few years he had lived in Boston would predict. He particularly admired Kennedy's linguistic acumen and conscientiously sought to improve his own ability to speak and write.

Yale provided further opportunities for Kerry to practice his political oratory. He was a member of the debate team and was elected president of the Yale Political Union, which brought him into contact with government dignitaries invited to speak before the membership. He was also asked to speak at the Choate School on a topic of his choosing; he selected the Vietnam War. Kerry maintained that while he had originally supported precipitate withdrawal, he had since decided that winning the war or negotiating a peace would be a better solution. The Choate address was a success, and Kerry's confidence and reputation as a speaker grew. One of his classmates, Fred Smith, who later founded Federal Express, judged Kerry "a very, very powerful speaker, very articulate. He was a very visible figure on campus." His position at Yale led to his election to the secret society Skull and Bones (to which George H. W. Bush and George W. Bush also belong). In the same year as the Choate address, Kerry won the Ten Eyck Speech Prize at Yale for an address that counseled against the overextension of U.S. foreign commitments. He spoke of the "specter of Western imperialism." An even more important mark of Kerry's success as a speaker at Yale was his selection in 1966 to deliver the address for his graduating class. Writing and then rejecting a commencement address focusing prosaically on what the future held for

his classmates, he chose instead to criticize the Johnson administration's policy of foreign interventionism, essentially an amplification of his earlier prize-winning speech.

Before graduating from Yale, Kerry had committed to joining the Navy, and although his interest in military service had waned as his criticism of American foreign policy had grown, he nevertheless fulfilled his obligation. His first assignment after officer's candidate school was as the public affairs officer on the destroyer USS *Gridley*, bound for the Philippines. One of Kerry's regular duties was to educate the crew with a series of 800-word stories about World War II battles waged in the Pacific that corresponded to the ship's location along its route. According to Brinkley, Kerry read these stories "over the intercom in his best Edward R. Murrow stentorian tones."

After eight months on the *Gridley*, Kerry decided he wanted to see action in Vietnam. He volunteered for training as the captain of a Swift boat, the flat-hulled aluminum craft that patrolled the coastline of Vietnam. First assigned to coastline surveillance duty, Kerry soon asked to join the more adventurous Swift commanders who risked their lives drawing enemy fire along the Mekong Delta waterways. Paradoxically, Kerry not only lacked commitment to the war he was fighting, but was becoming increasingly critical of it. When his commanding officer finally offered him an opportunity for a river mission, Kerry was less than enthusiastic. He quickly grew frustrated with the Navy's risky but passive role for the Swift boats, wanting to engage the enemy hidden along the embankments rather than simply serve as a target for their fire. The river missions became increasingly aggressive and Kerry, in the midst of an ambush, suddenly ordered the patrol craft to head straight to the shore. There he jumped off the vessel and pursued, shot at, and killed a Vietcong insurgent who had an armed rocket launcher. He and his crew followed the Vietcong into the jungle, killing eight more in firefights. Kerry was recommended for the Navy Cross, but received the Silver Star for valor, a lesser award that did not require bureaucratic approval and could be given expeditiously. For other heroic action in Vietnam, he received the Bronze

Star, and for the wounds he received in combat, three Purple Hearts.

Because he had been wounded three times, Kerry was permitted to ask for reassignment to the United States. In 1969, he became the aide to Rear Admiral Walter F. Schlech, Jr., a fellow Silver Star winner who was based in Brooklyn, New York. Kerry's memory of the war and his encounters with veterans returning home, many suffering from post-traumatic stress disorder, increased his disillusionment with the Vietnam War. Somewhat indirectly, Kerry's sister involved him in ongoing antiwar protests by asking him to pilot a plane for Adam Walinsky, a former speechwriter for Robert F. Kennedy, who was touring New York State delivering antiwar speeches. The Vietnam moratorium of October 15, 1969, helped to convince Kerry that the United States needed to withdraw from Vietnam.

Kerry found a forum for his antiwar arguments by throwing his hat in the ring for the Democratic nomination for a congressional seat from Massachusetts. With the primaries close at hand, he decided to ask for an early discharge from the Navy, which was granted on January 3, 1970. Although Kerry seemed destined for a career in politics, his opposition to the war served as the touchstone for his first bid for political office. The Vietnam War had shaped his political conscience, and his early career in politics released the spring of antiwar sentiment coiled tightly during his tour of duty in Vietnam.

WAR ACTIVIST AND POLITICIAN

Accompanied by his fiancée, Julia Thorne, Kerry established a campaign headquarters in an apartment in Waltham, Massachusetts, from which to seek the Democratic nomination for the Third District congressional seat. At a citizens' caucus held at outside of Boston on February 22, 1970, he spoke eloquently about the need for a precipitate withdrawal from Vietnam. His reason for running, he explained to the caucus delegates, was rooted in his war experiences: "I want to tell them [the public] what it's like to walk amidst death in a country that wants only life and to have to shoot at people with whom we have no quarrel." The caucus was highly impressed with Kerry's speech—"stunned," his campaign chair said—but

after four votes it endorsed Father Robert F. Drinan, a well-known Jesuit activist, to run against the aging incumbent, Democrat Philip J. Philbin, who supported the war. Kerry withdrew from the race and later became the chair of Drinan's ultimately unsuccessful campaign. Kerry's three-month bid for the nomination and his support of Drinan attracted enough attention that fellow Yale alumnus Dick Cavett invited him to make an appearance on his television talk show.

Kerry joined the Vietnam Veterans Against the War (VVAW) and involved himself in a march to Valley Forge, Pennsylvania, part of Operation RAW (Rapid American Withdrawal). During the rally that followed in Valley Forge, Kerry spoke from the back of a pickup truck: "We are here to say that it is not patriotism to ask Americans to die for a mistake or that it is not patriotic to allow a president to talk about not being the first president to lose a war, and using us as pawns in that game." Members of the movement recognized in Kerry a native eloquence and forcefulness that would help them carry their message all the way to Capitol Hill. Kerry's effectiveness would eventually threaten Richard Nixon enough that Charles Colson, his legal counsel, suggested in a memorandum to another staffer: "Let's destroy the young demagogue before he becomes another Ralph Nader."

Kerry's famous speech to the Senate Foreign Relations Committee grew out of a rally in Washington that he had proposed to Vietnam veterans who attended meetings in Detroit called the "Winter Soldier Investigation." In Detroit, Kerry had listened to the members of the VVAW recount their terrible, mentally searing experiences in Vietnam. The organization rank and file saw Kerry, an articulate war hero, as an appropriate spokesman, one who would deflect Richard Nixon's public dismissal of antiwar protestors as college "bums."

The veterans' protest at the Washington Mall occurred as planned, and there was determination among the group to have Kerry testify before the Senate Foreign Relations Committee, but the means to achieve this end eluded everyone. Kerry attended a fund-raiser for the veterans hosted by senators Claiborne Pell and Philip Hart. Senate Foreign Relations Committee chair William Fulbright also attended. When Kerry spoke, Fulbright was so moved that he decided to have Kerry speak to the committee the next day. According to Gerald Nicosia, Kerry spent that evening "trying to assemble the various drafts of fund-raising speeches he had been using . . . into a powerful narrative of what it felt like to be a Vietnam veteran come home."

Kerry spent two hours testifying to the Foreign Relations Committee on April 21, 1971. The speech he gave on that occasion was the most important of his career. Had he never been heard of again, Kerry would have been remembered for this speech. He faced the committee dressed in his open-collared fatigues with his decorations and campaign ribbons pinned above his left pocket, looking more like a grunt soldier than an admiral's assistant. His ordinary appearance certainly did not predict the sophistication of his rhetorical appeals. Kerry exceeded the expectations of the VVAW members who

namese village of My Lai. In alleging that My Lai was an "isolated incident," the Nixon administration had further angered members of the VVAW, who knew better, and created an outpouring of sympathy for Calley, whom many Americans perceived as a victim.

Kerry detailed the war crimes with matter-of-fact coolness: "[The veterans] told stories [that] at times they had personally raped, cut off ears, cut off heads, taped wires from portable telephones to human genitals and turned up the power, cut off limbs, blown up bodies, randomly shot at civilians, razed villages in fashion reminiscent of Genghis Khan." Critics of this speech, then and now, have argued that Kerry himself did not witness these atrocities and that, moreover, he exaggerated them and thus mischaracterized the conduct of American soldiers in Vietnam. It must be remembered, however, that Kerry was recounting what veterans in De-

---

In his 1971 speech to the Senate Foreign Relations Committee, John Kerry asked memorably: "How do you ask a man to be the last man to die for a mistake?" With this question he answered Richard Nixon's declaration: "I'm not going to be the first President who loses a war."

---

were so confident in his ability to influence the Senate committee. He was the only member of the VVAW invited to speak, although he immediately told the senators that he represented thousands of Vietnam veterans who, if permitted, would tell a similar tale.

Kerry spoke extemporaneously and with a subdued earnestness about his own experiences and the testimony of other veterans at the "Winter Soldier Investigation" in Detroit. The veterans, he said, had recounted "war crimes committed in Southeast Asia, not isolated incidents but crimes committed on a day-to-day basis with the full awareness of officers at all levels of command." Charges of widespread war crimes were particularly explosive because of the sensationalized and highly debated case of Lt. William Calley, who had been court-martialed for ordering the massacre of civilians in the Viet-

troit said they did and saw in Vietnam. He would later admit, in an interview on Dick Cavett's show, that he himself had engaged in atrocities in Vietnam, since he regarded the killing of civilians in free-fire zones an atrocity.

The speech was far-ranging in its discussion of the war. Kerry took particular umbrage at Vice President Agnew's representation of war protestors as "criminal misfits," and praised their courage. As he understood it, the Vietnam War was a civil war in which the United States had no interest. He spoke of the search-and-destroy missions, the free-fire zones in which Vietnamese civilians were often shot, the disproportionate casualties among Blacks, the cheapening of the lives of the Vietnamese, and the deployment of weapons that would not be used in a European war. Calling for an immediate withdrawal from Vietnam, Kerry challenged

Richard Nixon's determination to "Vietnamize" the war, that is, slowly to turn the war over to the South Vietnamese.

Kerry counterpoised Richard Nixon's pledge not to be "the first President to lose a war" against a stinging question: "How do you ask a man to be the last man to die for a mistake?" And if the veterans returned home, the homecoming was often bitter: veterans suffered greater unemployment than any other class; Veterans Administration hospitals were understaffed, and some veterans died needlessly as a result; and more than half of those entering veterans hospitals spoke of suicide. The nation, Kerry said, had grown callous about the atrocities committed in Vietnam; it had "very coolly" accepted the My Lai massacre. Kerry bore witness that Calley was not alone in committing atrocities. Atrocities were committed against the enemy within the context of exculpatory propaganda that dehumanized the Vietnamese as "oriental human beings" while demanding an increased "body count."

Kerry's criticism of Richard Nixon and his administration emerged repeatedly in the speech. He lambasted the president for denying that the veterans protesting against the war were veterans. "We do not need their [the administration's] testimony. Our own scars and stumps of limbs are witnesses enough for others and for ourselves." Kerry's speech delivered on that day would, more than any other public utterance he had made to that date, express his political conscience and assure him of his ability as an orator to help shape American foreign policy. The situation would not and could not recur, but Kerry, who had represented himself as an ordinary soldier, seemed destined to become a politician extraordinary in his ability to debate the subjects of war and peace. He would not again truly be the voice for the nation's ears until the 2003–2004 presidential campaign. In the interim, Kerry attended law school at Boston College, became a highly effective prosecutor in the Middlesex district attorney's office, ran successfully for lieutenant governor of Massachusetts in 1982 and for the U.S. Senate in 1985. In the latter he took a seat on the Foreign Relations Committee, before which he had pled his case against Vietnam in 1972.

Kerry's interest in foreign policy and his war experiences have led him to make other memorable speeches about American military action. As a man deeply affected by war, he sees himself as one especially well positioned to speak about whether the United States should enter into war. In his Senate speeches concerning the resolutions authorizing Operation Desert Storm in 1991 and Operation Iraqi Freedom in 2003, he carefully weighed his decisions against the facts of the moment and a personal conscience formed by his memory of the Vietnam War.

On January 11, 1991, Kerry argued against a resolution to allow George H. W. Bush to convert Desert Shield to Desert Storm. He regarded the debate as "the most important . . . I have engaged in since I have been in the U.S. Senate." At President Bush's urging, the U.N. Security Council had agreed that force could be used unless Saddam Hussein withdrew from Kuwait by January 15, 1991. Kerry argued passionately that the president had given Congress little choice other than to enact the terms of the U.N. resolution. He laid the emotional basis for his speech by first addressing the awful repercussions of war—the catastrophic losses faced by individuals and their families. Drawing upon his experiences in Vietnam, he asked in a series of rhetorical questions: "Are we ready? Are we ready for the changes this war will bring—changes in sons and daughters who return from combat never the same, some not knowing their families and their families not even recognizing them. Are we ready? Are we ready for another generation of amputees, paraplegics, burn victims, and whatever the new desert war term will be for combat fatigue, shell shock or PTSD [post-traumatic stress disorder]?"

The logical development of the speech focused upon the acceptable criteria for going to war. Kerry maintained that the only legitimate reason to go to war in 1991—and later, in 2002—is a "broad consensus" of support for the war and an exhaustion of all other "peaceful alternatives." Much of Kerry's 1991 speech refuted arguments in favor of war. He expressed particular concern with the argument that the Senate should vote in favor of the resolution because the president's prestige and authority in international affairs would otherwise be compromised. "Are we supposed to go to war simply because one man—the President—makes a series of unilateral decisions that put us in a box—a box that makes the war . . . inevitable?" He said acerbically that Congress needed to remind itself that "we still elect our Presidents: We do not crown them." Kerry went so far as to argue that supporting the president in a fait accompli would destroy "the strength of the constitutional process."

Kerry also expressly criticized the president's idea that the Iraq crisis, properly resolved, could provide an opportunity for what Bush, in a speech on September 11, 1990, called "a new world order . . . freer from the threat of terror." The phrase, once uttered, became a locus for debate. Kerry believed that the war in Iraq, far from creating a new world order, would lead the United States to accept the role of an imperialist nation responsible for maintaining the peace. He questioned the strength and commitment of the multinational coalition stitched together by President Bush, noting that our "shadow battlefield allies" would, as in Vietnam, "mask" the truth that the United States would still bear the majority of the costs of war. "I see international cooperation," Kerry said, "yes, I see acquiescence to our position; I see bizarre new bedfellows and alliances, but I question if it adds up to a new world order."

In January 1991, one of the alternatives to war was waiting for the economic sanctions imposed upon Iraq to take full effect. Kerry argued that the sanctions, then in place for only six months, would in time seriously impede the Iraqi economy and thereby frustrate Saddam Hussein's ability to prosecute the war against Kuwait. He recognized that to refute the call for immediate military action, he needed to argue that the ends sought in war could be achieved by diplomacy and economic sanctions.

In addition to suggesting alternative actions short of war, Kerry argued that there would be an array of negative consequences if the United States committed to war without adequate justification. He worried that such a war would lead to "renewed terrorist attacks on America" and increased instability in the Middle East. Reminding senators of "the long-term danger of [Saddam Hussein's] arsenal of . . . nuclear, chemical, and biological weapons," Kerry urged circum-

spection. He presciently forecast that "the enmity that will build up will last beyond any of our lifetimes, the hatred that will fester will replace the weapons of today until that hatred is allied with the weapons of tomorrow and they will seek revenge." Such gravitas and judicious consideration of potential policy effects suggests that Kerry had modeled the tenor of his speech upon other deliberative speakers whom he had studied and admired. It comes as no surprise that, shortly after issuing this stern warning, he quoted England's greatest parliamentary orator, Edmund Burke, the conservative who counseled that a man should think carefully before "he dealt in blood." Kerry's prolix rhetoric reflected his need to find words equal to the importance of the decision before the Senate.

Though Kerry voted against the immediate launch of Operation Desert Storm in January 1991, he subsequently spoke out strongly, on several occasions, against Saddam Hussein, urging the Senate and the United Nations to respond decisively, and with force if necessary, to the Iraqi dictator's breach of U.N. weapons inspections mandates. In November 1997, he criticized the Bush administration's decision at the end of Desert Storm not to "utterly vanquish the Iraqi Government and armed forces," asserting that "Saddam Hussein remains the international outlaw he was when he invaded Kuwait." Kerry sketched a number of ominous possible outcomes should Saddam be left to develop weapons of mass destruction, concluding that if peaceful, diplomatic solutions failed, the United States and her allies should take military action. In the judicious and forceful tone that characterizes his deliberative utterances, Kerry declared: "As the world's only current superpower, we have the enormous responsibility not to exhibit arrogance, not to take any unwitting or unnecessary risks, and not to employ armed force casually. But at the same time it is our responsibility not to shy away from those confrontations that really matter in the long run."

Five years later, on October 9, 2002, Kerry spoke before the Senate to justify his decision to back a resolution authorizing President George W. Bush to use force against Iraq. In the wake of the September 11, 2001, terrorist attacks, public opinion and congressional actions had overwhelmingly supported Bush's war on terror. Kerry was one of seventy-seven senators who voted in October 2002 to give the president authority to invade Iraq; by contrast, the Senate vote authorizing Operation Desert Storm eleven years prior, which Kerry had opposed, was very close: 52 to 47. For his 2002 vote supporting the use of force against Iraq, Kerry received considerable criticism. He would spend a good part of his presidential campaign attempting to clarify his position on Iraq—criticizing the Bush administration while articulating a tough national defense plan.

Kerry opened his October 2002 speech to the Senate with a series of rhetorical questions that reminded his audience of Saddam Hussein's many brutal crimes, and then crystallized his position in a somewhat forced antithesis: "We should not go to war because these things are in his past but we should be prepared to go to war because of what they tell us about the future."

In the speech, Kerry detailed at some length Saddam's crimes against his own people, his weapons development programs, and his ousting of U.N. inspectors. He also criticized the past Bush and Clinton administrations for leaving the Iraqi dictator in power and failing to force him to comply with weapons inspections, "thus giving Saddam Hussein a free hand for four years to reconstitute his weapons of mass destruction programs." Kerry argued that President George W. Bush's decision to mobilize for war was ill-timed—that Bush should have forged an international coalition to disarm Iraq by capitalizing on the "unity of spirit" that existed after 9/11. He also chastised the Bush administration for "casting about in an unfocused, undisciplined, overly public internal debate for a rationale for war," thus confusing the American public, and for "engaging in hasty war talk," thus risking alienation of potential allies.

As he had done in his 1991 speech, Kerry weighed the situation at hand against carefully delineated criteria for going to war. He concluded that the threat to global security posed by Iraq's weapons development and refusal to admit inspectors did, in fact, sufficiently justify war. While he was voting in support of the president, Kerry carefully distinguished his reasoning from the administration's rhetoric. "Regime change," though

a policy Kerry supported, was not in his view an acceptable reason to embark upon war. Nor did intelligence suggest to Kerry that Iraq posed an "imminent and grave threat" to the United States, one that might justify a preemptive strike; in fact, Kerry was critical of Bush's "new strategic doctrine of preemption." Rather, the only discernible reason justifying military action was Saddam Hussein's thwarting of U.N. inspections and development of dangerous weapons systems. Praising a speech President Bush had delivered a few days earlier, and presumably hoping to commit the president to his statement, Kerry said: "This statement left no doubt that the casus belli for the United States will be Iraq's failure to rid itself of weapons of mass destruction." Even without Kerry's elaborate logical development, the use of terms such as "casus belli," the Latin for an act justifying war, tells the reader that this was not a speech meant to excite the emotions of the proletariat.

Kerry's speech teetered paradoxically between forcefulness and overqualification. There is no better example of this than when he tried hardest to put himself on the record. "Let there be no doubt or confusion as to where I stand," said Kerry. "I will support a multinational effort to disarm Iraq by force, if we have exhausted all other options. But I cannot—and will not—support a unilateral, U.S. war against Iraq unless the threat is imminent and no multilateral effort is possible." While seeming to express the very strongest commitment, the structure of the sentences embodied circumspection. Kerry, in fact, committed himself to little, except a willingness to review the need for war after the U.N. Security Council had contemplated another resolution to strengthen inspections of Iraq and, failing that, to have gathered our allies to fight "at our side." Such careful qualification and intellectualization, though appropriate in the Senate, does not populist campaign rhetoric make, and while Kerry talked tough about the war during the first months of the primary campaign, he toned down his criticism as he became the presumptive Democratic nominee for president.

In the 2002 Senate speech, Kerry attempted to further clarify his position on the war by noting that he would have rejected the Bush administration's first proposed resolution, which "granted exceedingly broad authority to the President to use force" and made no mention of working through the United Nations or building multilateral support for military action. The revised resolution, which Kerry endorsed, was much more limited in scope. Throughout this address, as in his other speeches on the topic, Kerry repeatedly stressed the importance of coalition building—using diplomacy to secure broad international consensus and to assemble a multilateral military alliance—as well as his firm conviction that war must be a last resort.

Kerry praised the Senate for asking questions and posing criticism, noting that this process of debate had significantly altered the administration's course of action regarding Iraq. The administration had been encouraged to scale back its demands, work through diplomatic bodies, appeal to Congress for approval, and refine its justifications for striking Iraq. Perhaps recalling his days as an antiwar activist, Kerry eloquently declared: "Criticism and questions do not reflect a lack of patriotism—they demonstrate the strength and core values of our American Democracy—they best protect our troops and our national security."

In his conclusion, Kerry highlighted his veteran status by making the point that the government must carefully seek a broad consensus before committing to war: "One of the lessons I learned fighting in a very different war at a very different time is that we need the consent of the American people for our mission to be legitimate and sustainable. I know what it means to fight in a war where that consent is lost, where allies are in short supply, conditions are hostile, and the mission is ill-defined. That's why I believe so strongly that before one American soldier steps foot on Iraqi soil, the American people need to know why."

Kerry's Senate speeches concerning the two Iraq wars, separated by more than a decade, reveal his studious approach to foreign policy deliberation. Even if one disagrees with Kerry's reasoning, one cannot easily fault the transparency of his reasoning. Admirable in itself, Kerry's proclivity for carefully delineated reasoning might be an impediment with less erudite audiences than the U.S. Senate. His magis-

terial approach to foreign policy argument provides a contrast to President Bush's public rhetoric on the same subject. While Kerry dons the rhetorical mantle of Edmund Burke and Daniel Webster to argue windily in the Senate, Bush couches his justification for the war in easily digestible sound bites—that Saddam's Iraq was part of an "axis of evil," a hub of terrorist activities, and an international threat; and, more recently, that regime change was incontrovertibly a good thing, whether or not there were weapons of mass destruction or conspiratorial involvement with international terrorists.

Kerry's political stump speeches are wholly different from the cerebral, dense, and orotund foreign policy speeches he delivers in the Senate chamber. They are cobbled-together epigrams attacking George Bush, praising Democrats and Democratic policies, and calling the public to action. Gone are the ear-filling sentences of Kerry's Senate speeches that sometimes run to more than sixty words, his carefully contemplated qualifications, Ivy League verbiage, and unhurried arguments. On the campaign trail, aided by media-savvy advisers including Robert Schrum, Kerry utters well-turned phrases crafted in appealing populist shorthand. Lofty Senate deliberation gives way to crisp and cleverly expressed, though undocumented, assessments of the current administration's failures and the Democrats' promise.

A speech Kerry delivered in Des Moines, Iowa, on November 15, 2003, well illustrates the tenor of his stump speeches. Kerry opened by mockingly referring to George Bush's speech announcing the end of major hostilities in Iraq given aboard the aircraft carrier USS *Abraham Lincoln* "in front of a sign saying 'Mission Accomplished,' " hoping, Kerry said, that "we wouldn't notice that our troops are dying in Iraq every day. . . . And we're here to say that tonight marks the beginning of the end of the Bush Presidency." Criticism of Bush's prosecution of the Iraq war was merely the opening salvo, although it also served as a metaphor for Bush's alleged false posturing.

Kerry turned from the war theme to accuse his political opponent of "coddling big oil, serving up tax giveaways for the wealthiest, and opening up doors for the lobbyists and for the polluters"—Bush's idea of "mission accomplished"—while critical national needs such as health care, education, employment, and security constitute "mission not accomplished." The speech was replete with hyperbole and ironic contrast; for example: "It is not enough to lay a wreath at Arlington Cemetery while [President Bush] cuts veterans' health care and 4,000 veterans are left on a hospital waiting list." There are well-planned verbal thrusts, all expressed in a vernacular style. "You know," Kerry said with folksy familiarity, "the real motto for this Administration should be 'no special interest left behind.'" Kerry also reminded the audience that he has war experience and the president has none. "He's overextended our troops, he can't find Saddam Hussein, he can't find Osama bin Laden.... I know about aircraft carriers for real. And if George Bush wants to make this election about national security, I have three words for him he'll understand: Bring. It. On." "Bring 'em on" was a phrase that George Bush had directed at insurgent forces in Iraq, and one that to his critics represented the president's ill-advised posturing and machismo.

The image of Kerry created by these blustery sentences seems out of character with the bookish Kerry who declined the company of his crew to read political history at night on the Swift boat in Vietnam or who in college debated, on the affirmative, the resolution that the rise in spectator sports had led to the decline of Western civilization—let alone the Kerry who spoke somberly of the casus belli in the Senate. Kerry the stump speaker is to Kerry the Senate orator what the trench fighter is to the duelist. However, the change of tone and ethos in Kerry's political campaign speeches is predicted by the genre. Stripped of their political viewpoint, stump speeches share the same traits, since they are all adaptations to the brief political encounters in which they are delivered and to the media that report them. Panache replaces finesse; unqualified denunciation and praise replace careful appraisal and measured judgment.

Kerry's nomination acceptance speech at the Democratic National Convention on the evening of July 29, 2004, was the grand finale of a carefully scripted and stage-managed four-day event that included praise of Kerry from every possible

quarter: Bill and Hillary Clinton, Ted Kennedy, Kerry's wife, Teresa Heinz, his daughters, his running mate, and various politicians who had also sought the nomination. Max Cleland, a Vietnam War triple amputee and former head of the Veterans Affairs Office, introduced Kerry as Kerry's Swift boat crew stood in a row on the platform. As Kerry entered the convention hall, loudspeakers blared Bruce Springsteen's "No Surrender" and an announcer intoned melodramatically: "This party has done everything it can and now this man is on his own!"

Bill Clinton had reminded the convention that Kerry had enlisted and subsequently volunteered for hazardous duty in Vietnam; "Take me" was the refrain Clinton used to represent Kerry's response to the call of duty. While eschewing "Take me" for his introduction, Kerry gratified his audience, which included 21.8 million television viewers, by opening with a military salute and the words: "I'm John Kerry and I'm reporting for duty." This was a fitting introduction for a speech whose focus was John Kerry's ability to lead, particularly as commander in chief of the Iraq war and the war on terrorism. Only secondarily was the speech about the domestic policy issues one would expect a Democratic candidate to discuss: improving health care, protecting civil rights, easing the middle-class tax burden, stemming the outsourcing of jobs, and protecting Social Security.

Kerry, a man criticized for aloofness and impersonality, used the speech to express his humanity and to reveal his character and commitments. Kerry's campaign manager and chief speechwriter had assured news reporters in advance that Kerry had penned the speech himself, in longhand on a yellow legal pad. Written in a conversational style, like Kerry's much shorter stump speeches, the address seemed like a forty-six-minute cinematic monologue, meant less to advance a plot than to reveal the character of the protagonist: the Vietnam veteran, who among a brave band of brothers was singled out, as if by destiny, to run for the American presidency. Some of its language was drawn from what might be called "the great American speech book"—the repository of sentiment-laden phrases and familiar shibboleths that politicians and their speechwriters endlessly recycle. Kerry spoke of America's new birth of freedom, the unfinished journey, the "greatest generation," the American dream, family values, Old Glory, the new horizon, the rising sun.

To assemble the lengthy procession of briefly encapsulated political ideas and images, Kerry's speech drew upon literary sources as well. Taking stock of his momentous acceptance of the nomination in his native city of Boston, Kerry wistfully recalled Thomas Wolfe's book title: " 'You can't go home again.' Tonight I am home. Home where my public life began. . . . Home where our nation's history was written in blood, idealism and hope. Home where my parents showed me the values of family, faith and country." The sentences tumbled out with the same lyrical repetition of "home where [my thought's escaping . . . where my music's playing . . . where my love lies waiting]" that had made Simon and Garfunkel's "Homeward Bound" a hit song in Kerry's youth. In style and substance, Kerry sought to reveal himself. He talked about his character-forming youth, including his firsthand witnessing of the Cold War as a child in Berlin, and his " 'greatest generation' parents" who "inspired me to serve."

The erstwhile soldier and prospective commander in chief, Kerry devoted more time to the war in Iraq and the war against terrorism than to any other issues. He responded not just to these exigencies but also to his own need to appear confident and certain. He acknowledged that there were those who "criticize me for seeing complexities." Republican political advertisements had shown him flat-footedly explaining apparently contradictory votes on a war funding measure, and his early campaign rhetoric had led friends to advise him to forgo elaborate explanation for plain speaking. In the acceptance speech, Kerry effectively crystallized his opposition to the war by appealing to what he described as "this nation's time-honored tradition": "The United States of America never goes to war because we want to, we only go to war because we have to." Although pundits later commented that such a tradition did not exist, Kerry's expression of such presumptive truths made him appear anything but equivocal.

Kerry represented himself as a man with a clear vision concerning the challenges of Iraq and terrorism. He even repeated that claim for emphasis: "I know what we have to do in Iraq. I know what we have to do in Iraq. We need a president who has the credibility to bring our allies to our side and share the burden, reduce the cost to American taxpayers, reduce the risk to American soldiers." And, as for terrorism, the answer was also simple: "rebuild our alliances, so we can get the terrorists before they get us." There were few specifics in his proposals. He called for a stronger military, for 40,000 additional troops, and for the development of new technologies, and promised to "fight a smarter, more effective war on terror." The purpose of the speech was not, however, to explain how to achieve the goals he established, but to persuade the public that he was capable of leadership. Kerry revealed this purpose clearly when he said: "Elections are about choices. . . . In the end it's not just policies and programs that matter. The president who sits at that desk must be guided by principle."

At times the speech devolved to the level of apparently unassailable, but also unmemorable, political catchphrases: "I know the reach of our power and I know the power of our ideals. We need to make America once again a beacon in the world. We need to be looked up to, not just feared." And there was the simple thematic refrain, printed on placards and eventually chanted by the audience as well: "America can do better. And help is on the way." Far more potent affirmations were those reflecting Kerry's deeply felt convictions based upon his personal struggles. Asserting in the rallying voice of American populism that "Our purpose is to reclaim our democracy itself," Kerry recalled the lesson learned from his protests against the Vietnam War: "We are here to affirm that when Americans stand up and speak their minds and say America can do better, that is not a challenge to patriotism, it is the heart and soul of patriotism."

Although Kerry was expectedly critical of the Bush administration, he was far less critical of George W. Bush than other presidential nominees have been of their political rivals. In his acceptance speech John F. Kennedy had counseled the public to "cut the cards" before Richard Nixon dealt them. Pundits immediately understood Kerry's reluctance to criticize President Bush as part of a strategy to avoid alienating undecided voters. There were brief, glancing indictments— not only of George Bush but also of Vice President Dick Cheney, Secretary of Defense Donald Rumsfeld, and Attorney General John Ashcroft— but Kerry's acceptance speech was far more diplomatic than his stump speeches. The most evocative criticism of the Bush administration was general, couched as Kerry's response to the charge that opponents of the Iraq war policy lack patriotism: "The flag doesn't belong to any president. It doesn't belong to an ideology. It doesn't belong to any party. It belongs to all the American people."

At several points in the speech, Kerry repeated this inspirational theme of a united America. He recalled that after 9/11, "There were no Democrats. There were no Republicans. There were only Americans. And how we wish it had stayed that way." Later, Kerry addressed President Bush directly, proposing genteel (if unlikely) rules of engagement for the upcoming battle: "In the weeks ahead let's be optimists, not just opponents. Let's build unity in the American family, not angry division. Let's honor this nation's diversity. Let's respect one another." Finally, he painted a unified vision in an attempt to transcend the deep and bitter division of the previous presidential election, calling on Americans "to reject the kind of politics calculated to divide race from race, region from region, group from group. Maybe some just see us divided into those red states and blue states, but I see us as one America—red, white and blue."

Kerry's conclusion returned to his Vietnam experiences and, curiously, found some of its ideas and phraseology in speeches delivered by Kerry's political hero, John Kennedy. He spoke of his gunboat crewmates and commented that in war, "No one cared where we went to school. No one cared about our race or our backgrounds." In a famous speech Kennedy delivered to respond to public anxieties about his Catholicism, the Democratic nominee had said of himself and his brother Joseph, who was killed in World War II, "No one suggested then that we might have a 'divided loyalty,' that we did not believe in liberty."

And Kerry, who told the convention delegates of the urgency of the moment and promised to "work my heart out," reflected: "But my fellow citizens, the outcome is in your hands more than mine," just as John Kennedy, who saw the perils and opportunities in the Cold War era, had said toward the end of his Inaugural Address: "In your hands, my fellow citizens, more than mine, will rest the final success or failure of our course." Such borrowing was more than homage to John F. Kennedy; it was part of the tactics of a man challenging an incumbent president. Kerry sought to appear presidential. Just as Kennedy had ended his pivotal campaign speech on the Catholic question by quoting the presidential oath of office, and thereby projecting himself into the role of the presidency, Kerry alternated between speaking to the national audience as one seeking their votes and as one who was already president.

Kerry's delivery, which had been carefully rehearsed, revealed more of the speaker than had often been the case. There was less of a disjunction between Kerry's provocative words and his nonverbal responses. His stony countenance was less impassive and his delivery, although not entirely relaxed, gave more evidence of genuine emotional response. Although the speech appeared rushed, presumably to stay within the confines of the allocated fifty minutes, his delivery gave a greater impression of spontaneity and candor. Kerry's speech sounded less like John F. Kennedy or Adlai Stevenson and more like the mature version of former Lt. John Kerry who spoke to the Senate Foreign Relations Committee in 1972.

John Kerry was defeated in his bid for the presidency, but his role as a voice protesting war in Vietnam, Operation Desert Storm, and Operation Iraqi Freedom will be among his lasting legacies. As a candidate for the presidency, his experiences in foreign policy debate and his affinity for political oratory in the tradition of John F. Kennedy helped him add substance to the most recent layer of American political rhetoric, although television campaigning served to erode many of the old-school oratorical qualities that formerly made Kerry's rhetoric distinctive.

INFORMATION SOURCES

Research Collections and Collected Speeches

There are no research or speech collections available for John Kerry. Many of his recent speeches are available on his Senate Web site: http://kerry.senate.gov/

Congressional Record [CR].

Jamieson, Kathleen M., comp. *Critical Anthology of Public Speeches* [*CAPS*]. Palo Alto, Calif.: Science Research Associates, 1978.

2004 Kerry–Edwards Democratic Presidential Election Ticket: Senator John Kerry and Senator John Edwards—Public Papers, Speeches, Work in Congress, Senate Roll Call Votes. CD-ROM. Progressive Management, 2004.

Selected Biographies

Brinkley, Douglas. *Tour of Duty: John Kerry and the Vietnam War.* New York: Morrow, 2004.

Kranish, Michael, Brian C. Mooney, and Nina J. Easton. *John F. Kerry: The Complete Biography by the Boston Globe Reporters Who Know Him Best.* New York: PublicAffairs, 2004.

Nicosia, Gerald. *Home to War: A History of the Vietnam Veterans' Movement.* New York: Crown, 2001.

CHRONOLOGY OF MAJOR SPEECHES

See "Research Collections and Collected Speeches" for source codes.

"Address Before the Senate Foreign Relations Committee." Washington, D.C., April 21, 1971. *CAPS*, pp. 9–12.

"Address in the U.S. Senate Concerning a Motion Authorizing the President to Initiate the Invasion of Iraq." Washington, D.C., January 11, 1991. *CR*, January 11, 1991, pp. 846–50.

"We Must Be Firm with Saddam Hussein" (address to the U.S. Senate). Washington, D.C., November 9, 1997. *CR*, November 9, 1997, pp. 12254–56.

"Address to the U.S. Senate Concerning a Resolution Authorizing the Use of U.S. Armed Forces Against Iraq." Washington, D.C., October 9, 2002. *CR*, October 9, 2002, pp. 10171–75.

"The Real Deal, Not the Raw Deal: Bring It On." Des Moines, Iowa, November 15, 2003. Project Vote Smart. http://www.vote-smart.org/index.htm

Nomination Acceptance Address (Democratic National Convention). Boston, July 29, 2004. http://www.presidentialrhetoric.com

---

MARTIN LUTHER KING, JR. (1929–1968)
Civil Rights Leader, President of Southern Christian Leadership Conference

MARILYN DeLAURE AND BERNARD K. DUFFY

Martin Luther King's historic speech on the steps of the Lincoln Memorial in 1963 is among the most memorable and inspirational in American history. Many public address scholars regard it as the best speech of the twentieth century, and few who have seen it have not been moved by its appeal, by King's charisma, and by the turbulent moment in American history the speech has come to represent. King's eloquent words and courageous deeds throughout the civil rights movement inspired victims of discrimination to demand equality, encouraged national politicians to dismantle pernicious Jim Crow laws, and goaded the federal government to pass legislation protecting the freedoms of all citizens. The effectiveness of King's oratory owed as much to his perceived authority and leadership as to his eloquence and wisdom. King's voice rang out in a song of justice for Black Americans. No other American in the twentieth century was as effective in touching the chords of the despair and longing of Blacks or the conscience and idealism of whites.

Martin Luther King was born Michael King on January 15, 1929, in Atlanta, Georgia; King's father later changed both their names to "Martin

Luther." His father and maternal grandfather were pastors of Baptist congregations, and King grew up listening to the themes and cadences of Black preaching. The middle of three children, he was a precocious and sensitive youth who skipped several grades in school. At age fifteen he enrolled at Atlanta's historically Black Morehouse College, where he majored in sociology and minored in English. Morehouse faculty, including Gladstone Lewis Chandler—a notably eloquent English professor who emphasized clarity of style and a rich, expansive vocabulary—and Benjamin Mays, the college president, influenced King deeply. In Mays, King saw a ministerial model, a moral leader engaged in social activism. At age seventeen, he decided to become a preacher, was ordained in 1947, and became assistant pastor of his father's church, Ebenezer Baptist.

After graduating college, King entered Crozer Seminary in Chester, Pennsylvania. During his time at Crozer, he attended a lecture on the life and teachings of Gandhi; he was deeply moved and inspired by Gandhi's method of nonviolent resistance, derived from Thoreau's essay on civil disobedience. Gandhi challenged British rule over India not with violence or hatred, but with *satyagraha*, the force of love and divine justice. Here King found a model for uniting religious faith and social activism: *satyagraha* was much like agape, the redemptive Christian love for all humankind that leads to the "beloved community."

King finished Crozer at the top of his class, won a $1,300 scholarship for graduate study, and decided to pursue a doctorate in theology at Boston University. There he continued to explore the relationship between pacifism and social justice, capitalism and racism, psychology and spiritual faith. His dissertation compared the theories of theologians Paul Tillich and Henry Nelson Wieman. More than thirty years later a King researcher discovered that King had plagiarized portions of his dissertation from another student's dissertation written three years earlier under the same adviser. While in Boston, King met (and ultimately married) Coretta Scott, a young student of vocal music at the New England Conservatory.

Upon completing his Ph.D. coursework, King accepted a post at Dexter Avenue Baptist Church in Montgomery, Alabama. He gave his first sermon to Dexter's largely middle-class Black congregation in May 1954; less than a month later, the U.S. Supreme Court handed down the *Brown v. Board of Education* decision, outlawing segregation in public schools. King continued to work on his dissertation into the fall, and joined a number of local civic groups. The following year, three weeks after Coretta gave birth to their first child, Yolanda, Rosa Parks, a respected young tailor's assistant, became an icon of the civil rights movement by refusing to relinquish her seat on the bus to a white man. Black passengers in Montgomery had long endured segregated public transportation and mistreatment by white drivers. Parks's arrest by local authorities outraged the Montgomery Black community, but also excited its leaders. Here was the first case of a Black being charged for violating the city's Jim Crow laws, which could be proved unconstitutional in the wake of the *Brown* decision. The next evening, nearly fifty ministers and civic leaders gathered at King's church to plan a bus boycott, to begin the following Monday. Organizers printed leaflets, pastors alerted their congregations, and the boycott began with nearly 100 percent participation.

The Montgomery Improvement Association (MIA), a group newly formed to direct the bus boycott, elected the unassuming but charismatic King its president. King's leadership and advocacy for the MIA thrust him into the public spotlight, and he now spoke as a civil rights organizer and social reformer. He preached the philosophy of nonviolent resistance he had explored intellectually as a divinity student, and confronted the practical rhetorical challenge of arousing an audience to action while simultaneously urging prudent moderation and pacifism. Even when his home was bombed and his life was threatened, King countered aggression with high-minded pacifism and instructed his people to respond with equal restraint. After nearly a year of protest, segregationist backlash, and litigation, the U.S. Supreme Court declared Alabama's laws requiring segregation on buses unconstitutional.

The following year, 1957, King joined A. Philip Randolph and Roy Wilkins of the NAACP in leading a prayer pilgrimage to Washington,

D.C., to mark the third anniversary of the *Brown* decision. There King delivered his first national address, "Give Us the Ballot." With the white South still stubbornly obstructing school desegregation, in August, King and other Black leaders met in Montgomery to form a group that would help coordinate the freedom struggle all across the South: the Southern Christian Leadership Conference (SCLC). King's fellow activists chose him to lead the SCLC, whose first project was a voter registration drive called the Crusade for Citizenship.

King continued to preach at Dexter for a few more years, keeping a busy schedule with speaking and organizing, writing a book about the Montgomery bus boycott, and traveling to Africa, Europe, and India. Early in 1960, he resigned his post at Dexter and returned home to Ebenezer Baptist Church as its assistant pastor, a post which

The year 1963 was a pivotal one for King. Beginning in February, the SCLC led Project C (for "confrontation") in Birmingham, Alabama, to force desegregation of all public facilities, including private businesses. King was jailed in April, when his fourth child, Bernice, was just weeks old. During his confinement, he wrote "Letter from a Birmingham Jail" in response to criticism by a group of eight white clergymen. In early May, Project C drew international attention as thousands of children joined the march for freedom, thousands of demonstrators were jailed, and many were injured when Police Chief Eugene "Bull" Connor turned fire hoses and vicious attack dogs against the demonstrators. The violent photographs and film footage, combined with the powerful rhetoric of King and other civil rights leaders, turned the tide in a state whose governor, George Wallace, had

---

Although "I Have a Dream" is the most famous of King's works, his "Letter from a Birmingham Jail" is the most widely reprinted, most widely read, and probably the most important written rhetorical document of the civil rights era. The letter is not merely a refutation of whites' arguments for gradualism and moderation; it is also a lengthy statement of King's civic–religious philosophy and a passionate justification of civil disobedience.

---

gave him more time for civil rights work. In April, King called a student conference at Shaw University in Raleigh, North Carolina. He was interested in creating a youth wing of the SCLC to coordinate the energies of students already involved in sit-in demonstrations at segregated lunch counters. The students eventually decided against joining SCLC, and instead formed the Student Nonviolent Coordinating Committee (SNCC); King served on SNCC's advisory committee. In October 1960, King joined students at a lunch counter sit-in in Atlanta, against the wishes of his father and established Black leaders, who preferred negotiation to public demonstrations. The following year, he joined the Freedom Riders as they protested segregated interstate bus terminals, and endured taunts and violence by the Ku Klux Klan, white mobs, and local police.

vowed in his 1963 Inaugural Address, "Segregation today . . . segregation tomorrow . . . segregation forever." On May 10, an agreement to desegregate Birmingham was reached.

That summer, President John F. Kennedy addressed the nation in a televised speech on civil rights, and submitted a bill to Congress that would outlaw segregation in interstate public facilities and allow federal enforcement of school integration. In hundreds of cities, demonstrators engaged in nonviolent, direct action campaigns to spark desegregation. On August 28, King helped lead the largest march to date on Washington, D.C., culminating in the rally at the Lincoln Memorial and his most famous speech, "I Have a Dream." Later that year, King was named *Time* magazine's Man of the Year. In November President John Kennedy was assassinated.

In 1964, King received the Nobel Peace Prize; he was, at age thirty-five, the youngest man ever to win the prestigious award. For King the ceremonies represented merely a brief interlude in the ongoing battle for civil rights. His acceptance speech, though philosophical and idealistic, also drew attention to the harsh realities of racism:

> I am mindful that only yesterday in Birmingham, Alabama, our children, crying out for brotherhood, were answered with fire hoses, snarling dogs and even death. I am mindful that only yesterday in Philadelphia, Mississippi, young people seeking to secure the right to vote were brutalized and murdered. And only yesterday more than 40 houses of worship in the State of Mississippi alone were bombed or burned because they offered a sanctuary to those who would not accept segregation.

The escalation of American involvement in Vietnam troubled King, who for some time had wrestled with whether or not to speak out on the war. His advisers were divided; some feared that criticizing the Johnson administration on foreign policy issues would weaken King's position as a civil rights leader. Already, the movement was threatening to pull apart at the seams as riots erupted in cities across the nation and more militant leaders, such as Malcolm X and Stokely Carmichael, and the idea of Black Power gained popularity.

Under King's leadership, the SCLC turned its efforts toward fighting economic injustice, through efforts such as Operation Breadbasket and demonstrations protesting housing discrimination in the North. King mounted a War on Slums in Chicago in 1966: he moved his entire family into a small inner-city flat for the summer, to experience firsthand the dire living conditions suffered by Northern Blacks crammed into ghettos. As he led marches and put pressure on the city government, King discovered an appalling deep-seated racism; he later remarked that the people of Mississippi ought to visit Chicago to "learn how to hate." While King's organizing work did eventually win some concessions from Mayor Richard Daley and local real estate agents, many saw Chicago as a failure; civil rights activist Bayard Rustin called it "a fiasco." King left the city depressed, with a newfound cynicism about the prospects of achieving a race-blind society.

Throughout 1967, King continued to broaden the scope of his call for nonviolence and justice. He spoke out more frequently and critically against the Vietnam War: his most famous speech on the subject—published under two titles, "A Time to Break Silence" and "Beyond Vietnam"—was delivered at Riverside Church in New York City on April 4. King also helped poor people fight for better working conditions. He was in Memphis, Tennessee, supporting local garbage collectors on strike, when he was shot and killed on April 4, 1968. The night before his assassination, King delivered his last speech, "I've Been to the Mountaintop," which seemed to foreshadow his death. King closed by saying, "I've been to the mountaintop. . . . And I've seen the promised land. I may not get there with you. But I want you to know tonight that we, as a people, will get to the promised land. And I'm happy, tonight. I'm not worried about anything. I'm not fearing any man. Mine eyes have seen the glory of the coming of the Lord."

KING'S RHETORIC OF NONVIOLENT CHANGE

Throughout his career as preacher and civil rights leader, King developed a number of central oratorical themes, evocatively embodied and dynamically delivered. He reinvented a new self-image for Black American citizens, encouraging them to engage in direct action to claim their just rights. Rhetorical critic Martha Solomon has argued that King also framed the civil rights project within a larger vision of the American dream: what he and his fellow activists sought was simply a completion of the covenant promised by the Declaration of Independence and the Constitution. King's rhetoric forged connections among various humanitarian causes: the same philosophy that anchored his fight for racial justice and equality also inspired him to speak out against poverty, discrimination in housing and labor, and war. Finally, King consistently upheld his method of nonviolent resistance, urging his people to "rise to the majestic heights of meeting physical force with soul force."

King's first speech to a national audience,

"Give Us the Ballot—We Will Transform the South," was delivered from the steps of the Lincoln Memorial as the keynote address for the Pilgrimage for Freedom on May 17, 1957. In this speech, King repeated many times over the demand "Give Us the Ballot," reasoning that if Blacks would simply be allowed to exercise their constitutional right to vote, they would be able to solve their problems by themselves. King's rhetoric of empowerment and self-reliance called not for special treatment or favors, but simply for access to full citizenship. Though his poetic style and use of metaphor were not as highly developed as they would be in his most famous speech, delivered six years later at the same place, a few phrases and themes in "Give Us the Ballot" do anticipate "I Have a Dream." Near the beginning, King described the 1954 Supreme Court *Brown v. Board of Education* decision as "a joyous daybreak to end the long night of enforced segregation" and "a great beacon light of hope." Near the end of the speech, he reminded his listeners that they must seek to win the friendship and understanding of white brothers, and work toward "an integration based on mutual respect."

King sought to forge such an integration based on respect within the labor movement in his speech "If the Negro Wins, Labor Wins," given on December 11, 1961, to the Fourth Constitutional Convention of the AFL–CIO. In this address, he illustrated the common interests shared by the labor and civil rights movements noting that "Negroes are almost entirely a working people," and hence "any crisis that lacerates you [is] a crisis from which we bleed." King assured the AFL–CIO that "labor has no firmer friend than the twenty million Negroes whose lives will be deeply affected by the new patterns of production," and called for an end to discrimination within organized labor, and for economic aid to civil rights organizing in the South. Again, toward the end of this speech, King used language that found its way into "I Have a Dream": he prophesied an American dream, yet unfulfilled, where "men will not argue that the color of a man's skin determines the content of his character," and the closing sentences of "Dream" are nearly identical to the peroration of "If the Negro Wins."

King's "Letter from a Birmingham Jail" is the most widely reprinted, most widely read, and probably the most important written rhetorical document of the civil rights era. The letter, ostensibly an apologia, a rhetorical response to the accusations of eight white Alabama clergymen, is not merely a refutation of their arguments for gradualism and moderation; it is also a lengthy statement of King's civic–religious philosophy and a passionate justification of civil disobedience, aimed at a much broader audience. Like the myth of Lincoln scribbling the Gettysburg Address on an envelope while en route to Gettysburg, the provocative story of King's letter enhances and reflects its perceived significance. While in solitary confinement, King reportedly began penning the letter on the margins of the newspaper that contained the clergy's editorial, and continued it on various scraps of paper smuggled in to him. The letter is dated April 16, 1963—during the time King was imprisoned—but the text was completed and edited at a later date, with assistance from King's colleagues and SCLC staff.

Though the letter is nominally addressed to the eight members of the clergy, they never received signed copies of the letter, which the SCLC circulated in a press release as part of a highly organized publicity campaign. Paradoxically, the news media paid little attention to the letter while the drama of the protest in Birmingham still ran high, but after the demonstrators triumphed over "Bull" Connor and his segregationist forces, the letter became a famous pronouncement of King's victory in Birmingham. Excerpts from the letter were published in the *New York Post Sunday Magazine* on May 19, 1963; a week later the American Friends Service Committee (Quakers) published 50,000 copies of the letter in pamphlet form, under the title *Tears of Love*, for national distribution at 10 cents a copy. Later that summer, the letter appeared in its entirety in a number of national media outlets.

King was later pressed to make audio and video recordings of the text; an audio recording of King reading and commenting on the letter is available at the King Center. "Letter from a Birmingham Jail" resembles King's speeches in both theme and style, and exhibits a number of his often used rhetorical devices, including metaphor, anaphora, and appeals to pathos. It exerts rhetorical force by highlighting the conditions of its writing: King opens with the words "While confined here in the Birmingham city jail," and near the end, he explains the lengthiness of the letter by asking, "What else is there to do when you are alone for days in the dull monotony of a narrow jail cell other than write long letters, think strange thoughts, and pray long prayers?" Readers can thus envision King composing this text in his dim cell, and this emphasis on the letter's genesis helps illustrate the "sublime courage" and commitment of demonstrators willing to endure "narrow jail cells," as he says in "I Have a Dream," in order to challenge unjust laws.

In the "Letter" King redefines the public image of civil rights activists. He asserts that he and his staff are not "outsiders," as the eight clergy accuse them of being; they were invited to Birmingham and, furthermore, King argues that all communities are interrelated and "injustice anywhere is a threat to justice everywhere." The activists are not reckless agitators; they have carefully and deliberately followed a four-step process of research, negotiation, self-purification, and direct action. They do not disrespect the law; in fact, those who break unjust laws openly and lovingly, and with willingness to accept the penalty, in reality express "the very highest respect for law."

The clergymen blamed King for bringing tension to Birmingham and condemned the activists for resorting to "extreme measures." In his letter King embraces these accusations and gives them redemptive meaning by referencing praiseworthy historical figures. He asserts that "constructive nonviolent tension . . . is necessary for growth," citing Socrates as an example of a gadfly who created tension to help improve Athens. Later, King recites a litany of people who were "extremists" in their time—Jesus, Martin Luther, Abraham Lincoln, Thomas Jefferson—thus dignifying and proudly accepting the label "extremist."

King's letter suggests the power of the words as he might have spoken them. In one of the most moving passages of the essay, King pours out a stream-of-consciousness narrative that expresses his multilayered emotions. Written in the second

person, the 325-word sentence is couched as a direct appeal to his audience. With each emotionally ascending clause, King urges the audience to experience vicariously the daily humiliation of segregation from the Black perspective:

> But when you have seen vicious mobs lynch your mothers and fathers at will and drown your sisters and brothers at whim; when you have seen hate-filled policemen curse, kick, brutalize and even kill your black brothers and sisters with impunity; . . . when you suddenly find your tongue twisted and your speech stammering as you seek to explain to your six-year-old daughter why she can't go to the public amusement park that has just been advertised on television . . . and see the depressing clouds of inferiority begin to form in her little mental sky . . . when you are forever fighting a degenerating sense of "nobodiness"; then you will understand why we find it difficult to wait.

King achieves in prose the rhetorical amplification and crescendo that characterize his oral delivery. Reading clause after clause of this seemingly endless sentence gives the audience some feeling of the wearing repetition and cumulative weight of the continual acts of discrimination endured by King and his people.

While "Letter from a Birmingham Jail" illustrates King's great rhetorical skills in written form, it also bears evidence of his liberal borrowing of ideas and even phrasing from other sources. In *Voice of Deliverance*, Keith Miller traces the source of several passages in "Letter" to sermons by H. H. Crane, speeches by U.S. senator and community service leader Harris Wofford, an essay by Morehouse professor George Kelsey, and the eloquent theologian Harry Emerson Fosdick's *Hope of the World*. King clearly took themes from others—sometimes quite liberally and without citation—in his speeches, sermons, and writings. Miller calls King's process "voice merging"; in a similar vein, Richard Lischer asserts that King crafted sermons by piecing together various "set pieces," some of his own making, some borrowed, and that King's "originality was originality of effect, not composition."

After Birmingham, King and other civil rights advocates sensed that the movement had laid the groundwork for a new national political agenda. Indeed, President Kennedy had been moved to make a televised address and introduce a civil rights bill to Congress on June 19. A. Philip Randolph and Bayard Rustin began to formulate plans for a massive march on Washington to press Congress to act. King, Randolph, and others met with Kennedy in late June to discuss the civil rights bill and projected march; the president feared that a demonstration could hurt the chances of the bill's passage, and cautioned the leaders that much was on the line. The Kennedy administration's approval ratings had fallen, and losing the fight in Congress could damage a number of other programs.

King spent much of the summer speaking coast to coast, riding the victory in Birmingham and pressing forth the cause. In a speech he delivered at the close of a Freedom Walk in Detroit in June 1963, King anticipated the more momentous March on Washington and also rehearsed many of the most potent passages of "I Have a Dream." He spoke emphatically about the importance of continued "determined pressure" to achieve the passage of Kennedy's civil rights bill: "In order to put this bill through, we've got to arouse the conscience of the nation, and we ought to march to Washington more than 100,000 . . . to engage in a nonviolent protest." In Detroit he said, as he would say in Washington, that 100 years after the Emancipation Proclamation, "the Negro in the United States still isn't free." As in Washington, he expressed his apprehension that the movement would lose its momentum. Sensitive to the dynamics of social movements, King cautioned against heeding "cries saying, 'Slow up and cool off.' " "There is," he joked, "always the danger if you cool off too much that you will end up in a deep freeze." The famous "dream" section, prefigured in his speech to the AFL–CIO, found even more concrete and poetic form in the Detroit address.

King's speech on the steps of the Lincoln Memorial represented the apotheosis of his oratory. He addressed a throng of more than 200,000 people of every race who had gathered to press for the passage of the historic legislation that would transform a nation rent by racial tensions and embarrassed by the bigotry and paternalism that had been institutionalized in much of the South but existed de facto in every corner of the country. King's memory is fixed by this important, though often uncritically mythologized, speech.

The speech inspired Americans already committed to racial justice and encouraged many others to support Blacks in their quest for legal, economic, and social equality. The substance of King's speech invited comparison with Lincoln's rhetoric on behalf of the rights of Blacks. In his Second Inaugural Address, Lincoln argued that slavery had caused the Civil War and that Blacks deserved the sweat from their own faces. Reflecting upon the Emancipation Proclamation, issued on January 1, 1863, King reminded his audience, in the first of many anaphoras (repetition of a word or phrase for rhetorical effect), that "One hundred years later, the Negro still is not free. . . . One hundred years later, the Negro lives on a lonely island of poverty in the midst of a vast ocean of material prosperity."

King expressed the dream of Black Americans in economic terms. His dream, he declared, was "deeply rooted in the American dream," and his metaphors reminded his audience of the economic consequences of racial discrimination. He asserted unabashedly that "We've come to our nation's Capital to cash a check" promising "the unalienable rights of life, liberty, and the pursuit of happiness" articulated in the Declaration of Independence. Historian Gary Wills has noted that, in his Gettysburg Address, Lincoln gave the nation a new political creed of racial equality by cannily using the authority of the Declaration of Independence, an antimonarchist document, to claim for emancipated slaves the economic rights of all men.

The signers of the Declaration understood the "pursuit of happiness" as a God-given natural right to prosper materially. They did not foresee that such a doctrine would be used as a basis for racial equality. In quoting the Declaration of Independence and speaking of a "promissory note to which every American was to fall heir," King appropriated Lincoln's radical reinterpretation of Jefferson's eloquent claim to human freedom and equality. Through his economic metaphor, King persuasively fused the philosophical and legal concepts of justice with the financial metaphor of the check or promissory note. Although he used the metaphor to "demand the riches of freedom and the security of justice," the transcendental dream also serves to remind his audience of the "shameful condition" it would replace. King insisted that it would be "fatal for the nation to overlook the urgency of the moment." He realized how easily social movements can be thwarted by partial and Pyrrhic victories. He warned against taking "the tranquilizing drug of gradualism," although Lincoln, whose authority he invoked, had advocated precisely such a policy concerning Black civil rights.

Many citizens, including those who supported civil rights for Black Americans, feared that the movement would grow more violent. King's persuasiveness among white Americans was predicated upon his support for nonviolent solutions, even in the face of the taunts and the brutality that civil rights protesters had experienced. King admonished his audience that "The whirlwinds of revolt will continue to shake the foundations of our nation until the bright day of justice emerges," but quickly added that Blacks must not commit "wrongful deeds." Many, including Malcolm X, did not agree with his Gandhian approach to protest, and King inclusively acknowledged this difference in outlook by noting the "marvelous new militancy which has engulfed the Negro community" while counseling Blacks to meet "physical force with soul force." Others, such as New York Congressman Adam Clayton Powell, envied King for the mantle of movement leadership that he had draped over his shoulders.

The effectiveness of King's message depended upon his audience's acceptance of him as the presumptive leader of the civil rights movement. The paragraph in which King acknowledged the divergence of viewpoints in the movement and the militancy of some of its members tellingly began with a pastoral declaration: "But there is something I must say to my people as they stand on the warm threshold that leads into the Palace of Justice." The tenor of the entire speech, whether judging the historical oppression of Blacks or predicting the "bright day of Justice emerging," cast King as a prophet not only for Blacks but also for whites in America "who have come to realize that their freedom is inextricably bound to our freedom."

Other metaphors and references in the speech reflect King's consciousness of time and space.

The speech is organized temporally, beginning with the social and political declarations of the nation's founders, proceeding to insist on the "fierce urgency of the moment," and concluding with King's expression of an as yet unrealized dream. The place from which he delivered the speech and the places from which his audience and fellow activists had come also figure prominently. King transformed the steps of the Lincoln Memorial into a place of revelation, presenting his inspired moral and civic prophecy. He brought a movement, whose roots were mainly in the Deep South, to the Washington Mall, the symbolic center of the nation. He referenced disparate parts of the nation by claiming, for example, that "a Negro in Mississippi cannot vote and a Negro in New York believes he has nothing for which to vote." In a spirit of benediction, he told his brethren to "go back" with renewed hope, not only to the Southern states that were the fiercest battleground of the civil rights movement, but also to "the slums and ghettos of our Northern Cities." In the conclusion he rhetorically constructed the geographical unification of the movement by proposing that the new freedom should ring from landmark promontories throughout the nation— "from the heightening Alleghenies of Pennsylvania . . . to every hill and molehill of Mississippi." The metaphors of unity that King used are distinctly musical. Not only did he embody freedom as a peal of bells, but he spoke of "transforming the jangling discords of our nation into a symphony of brotherhood." He drew his audience into a dream that is as much aural as visual.

King delivered his rhapsodic paean of economic freedom, social justice, and racial brotherhood as if from a musical score. His prologue was delivered slowly, confidently, deliberately, sometimes almost haltingly, though not without passion and force. The prophetic dream was expressed in an entirely different key, ascending in emotional and auditory leaps. King was tied to his text in roughly the opening two-thirds of his speech, but spoke with little reference to the text during the last third when he articulated his dream. Prophecy, if truly inspired, should not require a rehearsed text. In fact, King reported that he included the scintillating "I have a dream" section of the speech on an impulse: "I just felt I wanted to use it here. I don't know why. I hadn't thought about it before the speech." The difference in delivery between the planned and improvisational sections of the speech provides a casebook example of the relative virtues of extemporaneity.

King's delivery was a study in climax, wherein successive paragraphs built slowly to intermediary climaxes or crescendos, often achieved with quotations from or paraphrases of the Bible and King's thundering, sonorous delivery. At the conclusion of each of these intermediary climaxes, King reduced his volume and his rate of speech, then built again to another climax. The final crescendo of the speech was reached through a series of incrementally greater climaxes, most of which were created with the incorporation of Scripture—for example, the quotation from Isaiah: "I have a dream that one day every valley shall be exalted, every hill and mountain shall be made low." Many times throughout the speech, including those sections where crescendos were built, King made use of anaphora to help create climaxes in delivery and emotional evocation. Examples of anaphora include the eight-times repeated "I have a dream" and the six-times repeated "Let freedom ring from. . . ."

King rode the wave of audience response to the various climaxes in his speech. When the audience was at a pitch of emotion after the "I have a dream" sequence, he paused only briefly, and then made another ascent to the final emotional peak of the speech. The growing intensity of his delivery, exemplified in a series of emphatic declarations—"This is our hope," "This will be the day"—and the passionate timbre of his voice demonstrated that while he was a master of shaping audience response, King, the consummate performer, was also always an audience for his own potent message.

Some passages of King's oratory, particularly in the section that begins with the repeated drumbeat of "I have a dream," were inflected so uniquely and interpretively that King seemed almost to be singing rather than speaking. He performed every line dynamically, adding meaning and emotional gravity though oral emphasis and unexpected and unusually placed dramatic pauses. His delivery was reminiscent of the mu-

sical tradition of the blues. The lyricism of King's oratory was also punctuated by his quotations from song, including the counterpoise created by his quotation from "American the Beautiful"— "My country, 'tis of thee, sweet land of liberty" and his moving concluding quotation from a Black spiritual: "Free at Last! Free at last/ Thank God Almighty, we are free at last!" This six-second passage, which King delivered while slowly raising and panning his right arm in a final benediction to his audience, was as iconic an image of King as American painter Gilbert Stuart's unfinished portrait is of George Washington.

King's message of nonviolence and social justice advanced the civil rights movement but created a murderous rage among its most militant white opponents. Violence erupted in Birmingham only a few weeks later. A bomb planted by the Ku Klux Klan killed four young girls in the Sixteenth Street Baptist Church. King memorialized the dead girls in a subdued eulogy free of condemnation for the terrorists. His mildness in this private setting underscored the pacifism he preached before the masses. The broad emotional sweeps of his civic oratory contrasted with a compact and focused reflection on a loss borne most profoundly by four families and a community. King, who earned a reputation as a spellbinding orator and social activist, was first a compassionate pastor and spiritual leader.

The social and philosophical meaning that King wrested from the killing was muted with understatement. In his introduction, he recognized the historical significance of the event and the lives of these girls. "They entered the stage of history just a few years ago . . . they played their parts exceedingly well." Later, he expressed hope that "These tragic deaths may lead our nation to substitute an aristocracy of character for an aristocracy of color. . . . Indeed these tragic events may cause the white South to come to terms with its own conscience." While King's perspective on the girls and their death supported the cause of racial justice, it was consolatory rather than political, never straying from the intimate objectives of his eulogy. His approach was philosophical and spiritual, bringing perspective through the application of universal truths. He reflected that "There is an amazing democracy about death; it is not aristocracy for some people, but a democracy for all people. Kings die and beggars die; rich men and poor men die; old people die and young people die. Death comes to the innocent and it comes to the guilty. Death is the irreducible common denominator of all men." As he had begun with Shakespeare's insight that we are "merely players" upon the world's stage, King concluded by paraphrasing a soliloquy from Hamlet: "Good night, sweet princesses. Good night, those who symbolize a new day. And may the flight of angels take thee to thy eternal rest. God bless you." King met perfectly the requirements of occasion and audience. The sweetness of his words seemed to flow naturally from a contemplation of the young lives lost "between the walls of the church of God."

The Klan was not alone in perpetrating violence against Southern Blacks. In the Deep South the white establishment was recalcitrant in its denial of human and civil rights to Blacks. As with school desegregation, the cause of registering Black voters was not won by the stroke of a legislative pen. In Selma, Alabama, Blacks accounted for only 2 percent of registered voters. On behalf of the cause of Black voter registration, 600 Black men and women staged a march, and as they crossed the bridge spanning the Alabama River, state troopers attacked them brutally. These events of March 7, 1965, "Bloody Sunday," inspired King to lead another march following the same planned route as the first protest. On arriving at the state capitol, he delivered from its steps a powerful speech that condemned Governor George Wallace and the troopers, and predicted ultimate victory for Blacks. Nonviolent protest, oxymoronically "unsheathed from its scabbard," had confronted "the brutality of a dying order." He assured his audience and the nation that "We are on the move now," and in characteristic fashion repeated the phrase as a melodic refrain: "Yes, we are on the move and no wave of racism can stop us. We are on the move now. The burning of churches will not deter us. The bombing of our homes will not dissuade us. We are on the move now. The beating and killing of our clergymen and young people will not divert us. We are on the move now. . . . We are moving to the land

of freedom." The momentum developed in these sentences harmonized with the momentum of the march and the movement. Repetitions of phrase figured throughout the speech, as in a four-paragraph section in which marching is the driving figure: "Let us march on ballot boxes, march on ballot boxes until race-baiters disappear from the political arena. . . . Let us march on ballot boxes until the Wallaces of our nation tremble in silence." King seemed to follow Aristotle's stylistic advice to lend movement to speech by the use of animate metaphors.

King was brilliant in his ability to visualize his message for the audience and to involve them in the message. In the dramatic conclusion of the speech he answered a self-posed question "How long will it take" before it is not the day of the white man or the Black man, but "man as man?" Repeating the question again, "How long?" he answered, "Not long, because no lie can live forever. How long? Not long, because you shall reap what you sow. . . . How long? Not long, because the arc of the moral universe is long but it bends toward justice. How long? Not long, because." He then closed by reciting the first stanza of the "Battle Hymn of the Republic." Cadenced and potent, these authentic words of righteous indignation tumbled forth in successive waves, illustrating confidence, solidarity, and resolve.

Exactly one year before his untimely death, King delivered "A Time to Break Silence," a powerful address to the Clergy and Laymen Concerned About Vietnam who were assembled at Riverside Church in New York City. In April 1967, half a million U.S. troops were stationed in Vietnam, and more than 8,000 soldiers had been killed. In this speech, King called upon the government to stop immediately all bombing in North and South Vietnam, declare a unilateral cease-fire, and set a timetable for withdrawal of U.S. troops from the peninsula. He also urged his audience to "break the silence" and speak their conscience, no matter how difficult the task. But King's speech was about more than Vietnam—he framed this troubling war as a symptom of a larger, deeper malady afflicting the United States. King pointed to the hypocrisy of American involvement in a number of countries, and advocated a radical restructuring of foreign policy and public attitude: we must not frustrate political revolutions in other nations to protect our overseas investments; we must move from a "thing-oriented" society to a "people-oriented" one to redeem the soul of America.

Early on, King responded to charges that he should not mix dissent and civil rights. Vietnam and civil rights *were* connected, King asserted, because a disproportionate number of Blacks and poor were fighting and dying in the war. King bemoaned the "cruel irony" of "taking the black young men who had been crippled by our society and sending them eight thousand miles away to guarantee liberties in Southeast Asia which they had not found in southwest Georgia and East Harlem." The war was also inflicting damage on America's poor because it diverted resources from domestic programs to military operations. King explained, furthermore, that he was morally obligated to speak out as a Nobel Peace laureate charged to work for global peace, and as a champion of nonviolence. How, he asked, could he urge frustrated youth in the cities to resist turning to violence, without first speaking clearly to the government, the "greatest purveyor of violence in the world today"?

King took up the task of speaking for the voiceless, including the Vietnamese. The suffering people of South Vietnam must see us as "strange liberators," King noted, since we had frustrated their attempts at self-government, supported a vicious dictatorship, and methodically destroyed their farms, villages, and families. King also spoke for the National Liberation Front, or Vietcong, insisting that we must understand our enemy's point of view, and hear his questions and "know his assessment of ourselves" if we were to "see the basic weakness of our own condition," in order to grow and learn. By folding these other voices into his speech, King performed an imagined dialogue that broadened listeners' perspective on the war. The United States must move beyond its self-centered worldview, King insisted: "The Western arrogance of feeling that it has everything to teach others and nothing to learn from them is not just."

Throughout the speech, King developed a metaphor of the ailing American body politic. He described a deep malady of the American

spirit, caused by the "giant triplets of racism, materialism, and militarism" and sweeping us quickly toward our demise. The prognosis was grim. "If America's soul becomes totally poisoned," predicted King, "part of the autopsy must read Vietnam." Only swift and decisive treatment could forestall that collective death: we must learn to practice compassion and develop loyalties that transcend national boundaries. We must abandon negative anticommunism and war, and instead initiate a positive revolution for democracy. King saw "communism [as] a judgment against our failure to make democracy real and follow through on the revolutions that we initiated." Rather than fight communism with violence, we must fight poverty and injustice—those root conditions in which Communist movements typically arise.

Like his other speeches, "A Time to Break Silence" artfully situated a concrete, pragmatic task—ending the war in Vietnam—within a larger moral framework. In this case, King tied this specific end to the fate of the American democracy. "If we do not act," he warned, "we will surely be dragged down the long, dark and shameful corridors of time reserved for those who possess power without compassion, might without morality, and strength without sight." King's redemptive vision called for developing a global fellowship that transcends not only race and class, but also national boundaries. This speech clearly demonstrates King's commitment to unite the struggles of the dispossessed around the world.

Martin Luther King, Jr. played several roles in the civil rights movement. As organizer, King helped orchestrate demonstrations, including the Montgomery bus boycotts, Project C in Birmingham, and the 1963 March on Washington. He also put himself in physical peril, joining protests throughout the South, enduring threats and violence, and being repeatedly jailed. As spokesperson and diplomat, he met with leaders and elected officials—from city commissioners to U.S. presidents—to negotiate for legislative change. As a popular speaker, King traveled far and wide, publicizing the stories of the movement and raising money to help pay bail and legal fees for many imprisoned demonstrators. As orator, he motivated African Americans to engage in nonviolent action in their communities. He also articulated a moral vision to a broader national audience, linking the goals of the movement to the core values of American democracy and Christianity. King's speeches, sermons, interviews, and writings constitute the central rhetorical legacy of the civil rights era.

INFORMATION SOURCES

Research Collections and Collected Speeches

The King Center, in Atlanta, houses the King Library and Archives, the largest repository of primary sources related to King and the American civil rights movement in the world. Included in the archives are the organizational records of SCLC, SNCC, and several other civil rights groups; manuscript collections of King and other activists; audiovisual materials; and more than 200 oral histories of King's teachers, family, friends, and colleagues. Additionally, the Martin Luther King, Jr. Papers Project at Stanford University has published 4 of 14 projected volumes of the King papers (up to 1958).

Carson, Clayborne, and Peter Holloran, eds. *A Knock at Midnight: Inspiration from the Great Sermons of Reverend Martin Luther King, Jr.* New York: IPM/Warner Books, 1998.

Carson, Clayborne, and Kris Shepard, eds. *A Call to Conscience: The Landmark Speeches of Martin Luther King, Jr.* [*CC*]. New York: IPM/Warner Books, 2001.

Washington, James M., ed. *A Testament of Hope: The Essential Writings and Speeches of Martin Luther King, Jr.* [*TH*]. San Francisco: HarperSanFrancisco, 1991.

Web Sites

http://www.thekingcenter.org. This Web site indexes the King Center archives in Atlanta.

http://www.stanford.edu/group/King [*SU*]. The Martin Luther King, Jr. Papers Project at Stanford University has published 4 of 14 projected volumes of the King papers (up to 1958). Its Web site includes full texts and audio clips of several of King's speeches, and a comprehensive inventory of King's speeches, statements, and writings. There is also a good bibliography that includes audio and video source materials.

Selected Critical Studies

Bass, S. Jonathan. *Blessed Are the Peacemakers: Martin Luther King, Jr., Eight White Religious Leaders, and the "Letter from a Birmingham Jail."* Baton Rouge: Louisiana State University Press, 2001.

Calloway-Thomas, Carolyn, and John Louis Lucaites, eds. *Martin Luther King, Jr., and the Sermonic Power of Public Discourse.* Tuscaloosa: University of Alabama Press, 1993.

Dyson, Michael Eric. *I May Not Get There with You: The True Martin Luther King, Jr.* New York: Free Press, 2000.

Garrow, David J., ed. *Martin Luther King, Jr.: Civil Rights Leader, Theologian, Orator*, 3 vols. Brooklyn, N.Y.: Carlson, 1989.

Hansen, Drew D. *The Dream: Martin Luther King, Jr. and the Speech That Inspired a Nation.* New York: Ecco, 2003.

Lischer, Richard. *The Preacher King: Martin Luther King, Jr. and the Word That Moved America.* Oxford: Oxford University Press, 1995.

Miller, Keith. *Voice of Deliverance: The Language of Martin Luther King, Jr., and Its Sources.* New York: Free Press, 1992.

Selected Biographies

Branch, Taylor. *Parting the Waters: America in the King Years, 1954–63.* New York: Simon and Schuster, 1988.

———. *Pillar of Fire: America in the King Years, 1963–65.* New York: Simon and Schuster, 1998.

Garrow, David. *Bearing the Cross.* New York: Vintage Books, 1988.

King, Martin Luther, Jr. *The Autobiography of Martin Luther King, Jr.*, ed. Clayborne Carson. New York: IPM/Warner Books, 2001.

Oates, Stephen B. *Let the Trumpet Sound: The Life of Martin Luther King, Jr.* New York: Harper & Row, 1982.

CHRONOLOGY OF MAJOR SPEECHES

See "Research Collections and Collected Speeches" for source codes.

"Give Us the Ballot" (address at the Pilgrimage for Freedom). Washington, D.C., May 17, 1957. *CC*, pp. 43–45; *SU*.

"If the Negro Wins, Labor Wins" (address to the Fourth Constitutional Convention of the AFL–CIO). Bal Harbour, Fla., December 11, 1961. *TH*, pp. 201–7.

"Letter from a Birmingham Jail." Birmingham, Ala., April 16, 1963. *TH*, pp. 289–302; *SU*.

"I Have a Dream" (keynote address, March on Washington for civil rights). Washington, D.C., August 28, 1963. *CC*, pp. 75–87; *SU*.

"Eulogy for the Martyred Children" (sermon at funeral of girls killed in a church bombing). Birmingham, Ala., September 18, 1963. *CC*, pp. 89–99; *SU*.

"Nobel Prize Acceptance Speech." Oslo, Norway, December 10, 1964. *CC*, pp. 101–3; *SU*.

"Our God Is Marching On!" (address at conclusion of the Selma to Montgomery march). Montgomery, Ala., March 25, 1965. *CC*, pp. 111–17; *SU*.

"A Time to Break Silence"/"Beyond Vietnam" (address to Clergy and Laity Concerned About Viet-

nam). New York City, April 4, 1967. *CC*, pp. 139–64; *SU*.

"I've Been to the Mountaintop"/"I See the Promised Land" (sermon at Mason Temple). Memphis, Tenn., April 3, 1968. *CC*, pp. 207–23; *SU*.

LARRY KRAMER (1935–)
Gay Novelist and Playwright, Father of AIDS Activism

CHARLES E. MORRIS

At least once a century, Americans, against their "better" if tragically flawed judgment, are compelled by an irrepressible and irksome voice to account for their shameful complicity in catastrophic injustice. Such voices are sufficiently shrill and prophetic, which is also to say rare and memorable, to invite comparison. Larry Kramer's frontal assault on American homophobia, and its dire consequences in the closing decades of the twentieth century, can be aptly summarized in the words of slavery's most trenchant antagonist: "Tell a man whose house is on fire, to give a moderate alarm; tell him to moderately rescue his wife from the hands of the ravisher; tell the mother to gradually extricate her babe from the fire into which it has fallen;—but urge me not to use moderation in a cause like the present. I am in earnest—I will not equivocate—I will not excuse—I will not retreat a single inch—AND I WILL BE HEARD."

Like William Lloyd Garrison, Larry Kramer warned that oppression left to fester might cost the nation its life, if not its soul. Like William Lloyd Garrison, Larry Kramer determined that only unrelenting invective might expiate the murderous heart of the nation, whose bigotry, avarice, and indifference could be measured by the sufferings and deaths of thousands. In pitch and personality, neither man was long bearable, but neither man could be ignored. Our reckoning with slavery and AIDS, in their full magni-

tude, is attributable to these two similarly unendurable yet enduring voices.

As will become clear in this brief sketch, Kramer's rhetorical performances, by necessity, have not been exclusively, or even predominantly, oratorical. Oppressed minorities very often have learned through their attempts that access to privileged sites and occasions of oratory are barred, and that oral discourse must be one tactic among many rhetorical modes if social and political transformation is to be possible, perhaps especially in a mass-media world. For various reasons, therefore, homophobic and otherwise, oral rhetoric has historically played a comparatively limited role in gay American discourse. With that in mind, our attention to Kramer's significant rhetoric requires a broader scope, following that shrill voice from platform and street to the stage and through the pages of the satiric novel, the gay press, and the *New York Times*.

KRAMER AS CONSCIENCE, CASSANDRA, FIRE BELL, AND MEMORIAL

By 1981, the year the AIDS plague "officially" began, Kramer had already been cast to the margins of gay culture. Although he was a wealthy and Oscar-nominated screenwriter, he had the nerve to satirically portray—or to betray, as American gays largely interpreted it—the excesses that defined the post-Stonewall era. The anticapitalist, antipatriarchal, antihomophobic vision of the short-lived gay liberation movement of the early 1970s quickly succumbed, ironically paving the way for a solidified urban gay male culture largely characterized by its devotion to sex, beauty, youth, dancing, and drugs, a different but no less heady vision of sexual freedom for those who had been so long imprisoned in the closet.

In 1978, Kramer publicly responded to his liberated brethren in his novel *Faggots*, a minutely and graphically detailed—one might rightly say documentary—depiction of lovelorn Fred Lemish's four-day hedonistic odyssey through discos, bathhouses, and Fire Island parties in search of heartthrob Dinky Adams. Written in the tradition of Jonathan Swift and Evelyn Waugh, those rhetorical virtuosos of satirical fiction, *Faggots* placed Kramer's gay ideal of romance, commitment, and responsibility against a shallow and turbulent backdrop of promiscuous and anonymous sex, sado-masochism, tragic death, and, above all else, longing: "I'm tired of using my body as a faceless thing to lure another faceless thing, I want to love a Person!, I want to go out and live in that world with that Person, a person who loves me, we shouldn't *have* to be faithful, we should *want* to be faithful!"

Kramer's paean to love among men turned not the hearts but the stomachs of the gay community, which viewed *Faggots* as an embarrassing exposé, a sermon cloaked as a novel, that said more about the author's puritanical fear of sex and self-loathing than it did about liberated gay men; and, worse, it was a traitorous contribution to the oppressive homophobia of the straight world against which such open and proud gay "excess" functioned as robust resistance. Kramer was eviscerated in the gay press, and shunned on the street. More than its longevity—the novel has never gone out of print—however, *Faggots'* significance is now often judged by its awful prescience. Kramer would woefully say, as Ned Weeks did in Kramer's autobiographical play *The Destiny of Me*: "I wanted to be Moses but I could only be Cassandra." Like the woman whose prophecy of doom could not prevent the decimation of Troy, Kramer, without knowing of the impending AIDS epidemic, had warned his brethren that sex would destroy them. His warning was dismissed until it was too late.

Kramer's brief silence—an exile, really—in the wake of *Faggots* ended permanently with the emergence of the rare cancers and pneumonias mysteriously claiming gay men in 1981. Fear brought his soon-to-be signature ardor to what he already perceived as an emergent health crisis. Seeking the widest possible visibility and circulation of his message in a community without substantial political infrastructure or access to the broader public sphere, Kramer turned to the gay press. In his "A Personal Appeal," published in the *New York Native*, whose coverage of AIDS during the first decade of the epidemic dwarfed that of the likes of the *New York Times*, Kramer sought unity, vigilance, and funding—mobilization, in a word—from those at risk. It was the first alarm:

> It's difficult to write this without sounding alarmist or too emotional or just plain scared. . . . The men who have been stricken don't appear to have done anything that many New York gay men haven't done at one time or another. We're appalled that it is happening to them and terrified that it could happen to us. It's easy to become frightened that one of the many things we've done or taken over the past years may be all that it takes for a cancer to grow from a tiny something-or-other that got there who knows when doing who knows what. This is our disease and we must take care of each other and ourselves.

Given his reputation, Kramer did sound to most like an alarmist. If apathy had in part inspired this clarion call—early fund-raising totals were pitiful—however, then criticism would propel Kramer toward the discourse for which he is best known. A former lover, playwright Robert Chesley, offered, among dozens of editorials in the *New York Native*, the now famous rebuttal: "Read anything by Kramer closely. I think you'll find the subtext is always: the wages of gay sin are death."

Far from daunted, Kramer reckoned that earnestness and hyperbole in the form of rhetorical exhortation, whatever its personal repercussions, might be the only reasonable approach to the indifference that appeared as endemic as the growing disease: "I was also beginning to realize the usefulness of controversy. . . . It was, and is, controversy that helps an issue stay before the public, so that more people join in debate, in this process becoming, one hopes, politicized." If gay men balked as the Centers for Disease Control, the National Cancer Institute, the *New York Times* and the *Village Voice*, and New York Mayor Ed Koch employed various bureaucratic means of neglect—what Kramer would eventually and insistently term "genocide"—then he would fight all for the sake of their lives.

That fight manifested itself in brilliant organizational and rhetorical strategy. In 1982 Kramer and five others founded the Gay Men's Health Crisis (GMHC), which he understood to be "an advocacy group to spread information and fight in every way to help the living keep living." For him that meant publicity, agitation, and candor in sex recommendations. For his cohorts on the GMHC board of directors, some of whom were still closeted, such a boisterous approach seemed indecorous, risked reprisal, and promoted the unwanted message that sex was bad. Their desire was to become a respectable social services organization for the afflicted. Refusing to be chastened, Kramer again turned to the editorial as a means of mass persuasion, publishing "1,112 and Counting" in the *New York Native* shortly after the GMHC's contentious first year in existence. It is his most famous admonishment, targeting friend and foe alike; it set the pattern for Kramer's public discourse; it caused an irreconcilable rift in GMHC. Kramer would twice prove to be an ingenious catalyst for indispensable organizations that could not long sustain him.

The opening paragraph of "1,112 and Counting" captures well the spirit and vision of Kramer's activism:

> If this article doesn't scare the shit out of you, we're in real trouble. If this article doesn't rouse you to anger, fury, rage, and action, gay men have no future on this earth. Our continued existence depends on just how angry you can get. . . . I repeat: Our continued existence as gay men upon the face of this earth is at stake. Unless we fight for our lives, we shall die. In all the history of homosexuality we have never before been so close to death and extinction. Many of us are dying or already dead.

His incitement, a secular equivalent of the familiar fire-and-brimstone sermon, sought to shake his brethren free of their denial and apathy, and to reorient their approach to the ravaged gay world.

Fear, loathing, and shame—what Kramer's critics rightly observe to be the closet's legacy that so many had fought to escape—would constitute his means of "conversion." Statistics, typically so sterile, engendered pathos here, set as they were to the urgent rhythm of their awesome escalation:

> There are now 1,112 cases of serious Acquired Immune Deficiency Syndrome. When we first became worried, there were only 41. In only twenty-eight days, from January 13th to February 9th [1983], there were 164 new cases—and 73 more dead. The total death tally is now 418. Twenty percent of all cases were registered this January alone. There have been 195 dead in New York City from among 526 victims. Of all serious AIDS cases, 47.3 percent are in the New York metropolitan area.

Throughout his career, Kramer has embedded startling statistics within a causal logic meant to excoriate and arouse to action. By his account, the disease was spreading due to homophobia and racism in medicine, embodied in paltry research and publication, inadequate acquisition and dissemination of funds, and scandalous testing and treatment practices. The disease was also spreading due to government inaction; for instance, "Repeated attempts to meet with him [Mayor Koch] have been denied us. Repeated attempts to have him make a very necessary public announcement about this crisis and public health emergency have been refused by his staff. . . . No *human* being could otherwise continue to be so useless to his suffering constituents." And the list of the complicit, both straight and gay, became the refrain: "I am sick of closeted gay doctors." "I am sick of the *Advocate*." "I am sick of gay men who won't support gay charities." "I am sick of everyone in this community who tells me to stop creating a panic." "I am sick of guys who think that all being gay means is sex in the first place." The personal and pointed specificity of Kramer's disgust, designed to shame his audiences from their lethargy, closed with one additional inducement, an aggregate not of numbers but of names: those twenty friends Kramer had already lost. "1,112 and Counting" was Kramer's "J'Accuse!"

Much like Emile Zola, Kramer would consistently make polemical use of the public letter and editorial voice, available and optimal rhetorics that functioned to pressure the culpable by means of spectacle and witness. Imploring and exposing its addressees, his discourse blurred public and private to personify and scapegoat institutional power, to quicken time and timing, and to shift accountability from the abstract to the concrete. It sought to galvanize the community by making self-evident, in the broadest sense of proof and publicity, "crimes" that, harbored by silence and bureaucratic process, would become fugitive. Thus he published in 1984, again in the *New York Native*, "Equal to Murderers," vilifying by name the heads of the *New York Times*, the GMHC and the National Gay Task Force; the Department of health; and Mayor Koch:

> Because *The New York Times* is not reporting this vital news, because the city's Department of Health is not disseminating these appalling statistics, because the gay community's own organizations are too cowardly to speak out and speak up—all of this perpetuates the widespread ignorance that can make for continued contagion, infection, and—at the present rate of increase—a minimum of 64,000 cases in two years' time.

Similar letters, as well as op-ed pieces in various publications, criticized GMHC Executive Director Richard Dunne, GMHC Deputy Director of Policy Tim Sweeny, senior editor Richard Goldstein of the *Village Voice*, FDA Commissioner Frank Young, and President Ronald Reagan (all in 1987), Dr. Anthony Fauci of the National Institutes of Health (NIH) and the *New York Times* (1988), and the *Times* (again in 1993).

In each instance, Kramer castigated his targets: "How dare you"; "I call the decisions you are making acts of murder"; "I think every single person, *without exception*, who is making major decisions about AIDS, for this country, for this state, for this city, for the mainstream media—is second-rate"; "There's only one word to describe his [Reagan's] monumental disdain for the dead and dying: genocide." But more, Kramer meticulously provided information on experimental drug regimens ignored by the FDA and NIH, amplified and refuted medical reportage, and offered detailed procedural and policy initiatives to bolster communal advocacy, organizational efficiency, and quality of care. Such a deep moral and material investment in community differentiates Kramer's discourse from any cynical version of the diatribe.

Friends, colleagues, and neighbors were no less vulnerable to Kramer's incessant harangue. As Kramer viewed it, the exponential rise in the infection rate and death toll could not be stemmed by a hospice or (what he accused GMHC of having) a funereal mentality. The resignation of some meant the potential eradication of all. And so, again and again, he berated his own. Two instances are particularly memorable, not only for their audacity but also because with them we witness Kramer on the platform, spectacularly exhibiting in body and voice his rich capacity for oratorical performance. To fully appreciate Kramer in this rhetorical mode, one must envision his dramatic and often ungoverned gestures, his high-pitched, fevered rhythms mounting always, sometimes indiscriminately, to crescendo. His piercing wail and flailing limbs might be misunderstood as ranting, but, as the history of ranters bears out, such assumed chaos is in fact orchestrated, and its rhetorical effects calculated. Storms manifest their own gripping logic even as their violence seems to belie it.

In March 1987, Kramer substituted for Nora Ephron in the speaker series for New York's Gay and Lesbian Community Center. "I sometimes think we have a death wish," he admonished:

> I have never been able to understand why for six long years we have sat back and let ourselves literally be knocked off man by man—without fighting back. I have heard of denial, but this is more than denial; it *is* a death wish. I don't want to die. I cannot believe that you *want* to die. But what are we doing, *really*, to save our own lives? Two-thirds of you—I should say *us*, because I am in this, too—could be dead within five years. Two-thirds of us could be dead within five years.

Days later Kramer founded, in his living room, the AIDS Coalition to Unleash Power (ACT UP). By virtue of its guerrilla tactics of disruption and direct confrontation on the streets and in your face, ACT UP would, in the coming years, procure revolutionary changes in regulations and procedures regarding medical research, testing, and access, for the first time elevating the role of the patient-consumer in diagnosis and treatment.

In the summer of 1987, on the occasion of Gay Pride Weekend, Kramer defied celebratory expectation by echoing in Boston's Faneuil Hall a tradition long established by those radical voices that had rocked the "Cradle of Liberty." In a barrage of rhetorical questions, he upbraided his constituents for their insufficient knowledge of the disease and the medical establishment's inadequate response to it, for their unconscionable lack of commitment, for not acting grateful for the fact that they were still alive. "You are going to die and you are going to die very, very soon unless you get up off your fucking tushies and fight back! Unless you do—you will forgive me—you deserve to die."

Such rants often exhaust and alienate audiences. That Kramer wounded many, lost countless friends, and remains a pariah whom many consider an hysteric, or worse, should go without saying. But it is noteworthy that, despite the enmity he earned, Kramer has sometimes been grudgingly valued—even embraced by some of the very enemies against whom he had so savagely and unremittingly inveighed. Those unwilling to grant Kramer due credit for gains achieved by means of his lashing tongue are often found praising his plays, two of which were extraordinarily influential in making AIDS palpable, relevant, and unacceptable for a mass American audience.

On a brief stay in Europe after his divorce from GMHC in 1983, Kramer found renewed provocation at Dachau, which he discovered had been a site where Jews were slaughtered for years before the American government broke its callous and complicit silence. Over the next year and a half Kramer wrote and rewrote *The Normal Heart*, its title taken from W. H. Auden's political poem "September 1, 1939," and struggled to have it staged. Joseph Papp finally produced the play, which opened at the Public Theater on April 21, 1985.

More documentary than fiction, and in the radical tradition of agit-prop theater of the 1930s, *The Normal Heart* tells the thinly veiled story of GMHC's passionate founding and tumultuous growth, and the vexing prospects of love in a time of sexual abandon and devastating health crisis. Although there is no mistaking its political character—indeed, fact sheets were handed out with playbills, and the back wall of the set offered a handwritten, ongoing tally of the dead—*The Normal Heart* succeeded most in putting a human and unforgettable face on the "gay plague," perhaps the best weapon against homophobia. "I wrote it to make people cry: AIDS is the saddest thing I'll ever have to know. I also wrote it to be a love story, in honor of a man I loved who died. I wanted people to see on a stage two men who loved each other. I wanted people to see them kiss. I wanted people to see that gay men love and gay men suffering and gay men dying are just like everyone else." *The Normal Heart* would be produced more than 600 times around the world.

Kramer returned to the journey of Ned Weeks, his autobiographical stage persona, in *The Destiny of Me* (a title ultimately inspired by Walt Whitman), which was first performed by the Circle Repertory Company in October 1992. "Journey" is an apt term in several senses. As a companion play to *The Normal Heart*, it extends into Weeks's bleak medical future, finding him at the NIH seeking from his nemesis the experimental drugs that might extend his life. It also reaches backward into Weeks's unfolding past, exploring the long struggle with his family over his sexuality, and his own homophobia, en route to self-acceptance and pride, and the fortitude to engage the battle for his life and those of his gay comrades.

> This journey, from discovery through guilt to momentary joy and toward AIDS, has been my longest, most important journey, as important—no, more important—than my life with my parents, than my life as a writer, than my life as an activist. Indeed, my homosexuality, as unsatisfying as much as it was for so long, has been the single most important defining characteristic of my life.

Significantly, this family play successfully trod the path of Eugene O'Neill and Arthur Miller, achieving for gay men the familiar if tragic poignancy, and cultural currency, of *Long Day's Journey into Night* and *Death of a Salesman*. *The Destiny of Me* evoked empathy and compassion by rendering the lives of gay men discernible and meaningful for each of those—straight and gay—who encountered it, with a vision of social transformation and survival that might follow in its wake.

Throughout the 1990s Kramer continued to chastise those who embodied the institutional obstacles perpetuating the AIDS epidemic, and inciting those at risk to care enough to demand that their lives be valued enough to be saved. Distinctive, however, is Kramer's emergence as the voice of memory. His political use of the past sought to recollect for his community the recent history of the plague, too often forgotten by those whose lives were now extended by a "cocktail" of drugs and by a second generation of gay men living under the fatal illusion that the crisis had passed. Kramer's public memory also plumbed a pre-AIDS past in search of an alternative grounding for community, one that honored the dead and affirmed the living by excavating and exhibiting a gay American heritage.

Although the sheer scope and frequency of mourning would seem to diminish the prospects of the eulogy as a rhetorical genre, Kramer infused the eulogy with a militancy that powerfully transformed the memorial service into a political funeral. Again, Kramer's oratorical performance, his bodily imposition upon this most solemn of occasions, his shattering voice emanating from a pulpit in search of grief's dissipation and communal healing, must be recognized in order to fully comprehend his insurgency. Kramer correctly surmised that meaning, values, motivation—all those crucial communal bonds typically solidified in funeral oratory—could not be achieved by standard platitudes dispensed in the name of the deceased on behalf of the bereft. Instead, Kramer angrily performed the rites of the dead that might ensure a future for the living.

In his 1990 remembrance of Vito Russo, for instance, Kramer urged the bereaved to honor the influential activist and film critic through concerted action. Anything less would be construed not only as dishonorable, but as a sign of complicity in Russo's death.

Vito Russo devoted his life to fighting for us. And we let him die. Time and again he sacrificed his own career when he felt it was more important to protest or write an article or make a personal appeal that might help further the cause of gay rights or help for AIDS victims. That's right. I said victims. We are victims. Of our very own. We're killing each other.

Unlike the numerous political funerals held by ACT UP that utilized mourning as a weapon against national institutions, Kramer made his own community responsible for Russo's life and legacy. "If Vito meant anything to you, go out and emulate him. Do what he did. Get your hands dirty. Fight in his memory. If you don't know what I am talking about, learn." Similar injunctions echoed through the various events he attended that marked the ten-year anniversary of the epidemic. Kramer invoked the past as a grim, and intentionally motivational, reminder that no one had done enough, that too little had changed, that the community remained fragmented, that the dead might have perished in vain.

In 1997, memory served as means and ends in Kramer's public battles against gay literature and his alma mater. In May he published "Sex and Sensibility" in *The Advocate*, a screed that vilified fellow founder of GMHC and celebrated author Edmund White for his forthcoming novel *The Farewell Symphony*. Kramer lambasted White, and all gay authors, for creating a canon not akin to great Western literature but devoted instead to the depiction of sex, thus reinforcing it as the cornerstone of gay culture.

> Is it not incumbent, particularly in the time of a plague that has spread by our own callous indifference to ending it, that those of us who are read and listened to perceive of ourselves as fuller human beings and capable of writing about far more than just what sex we had night after night for 30 years? It is impossible for me to believe that this book embodies what AIDS really represents to Edmund or that this is the kind of tribute he wishes to leave all his dead friends and lovers.

Kramer's implication that a usable past is a political and cultural resource, one that inculcates values, bolsters identity, and forges a healthy community, is inherent in his accusations against White. It also led to his skirmish with Yale University the same summer. Wanting to bequeath substantial funds for an endowed chair of gay and lesbian studies, Kramer was outraged when Yale declined the offer. The specifics of his accusations against Yale, many of which were erroneous, are less important than his vision of underwriting a sex-free gay history for the next generation. "What is it that joins Michelangelo and Elton John and Herman Melville? Abraham Lincoln and George Washington? . . . Heterosexuals are not studied, dissected, adjudged, calibrated, compared by their sexual acts, by the peccadilloes of their genitalia."

Those questions constitute Kramer's most recent rhetorical mission, and likely his last project, begun in 1978, titled *The American People*. Kramer describes it as an epic history of America in novel form, "as reflected through disease, through illness," or what he calls "the perversion of sexual instincts," namely, homophobia. His personal and political impetus for *The American People* is reclamation in the face of homophobic erasure: "Most of the books I have been reading are history books. The main thing I'm learning from reading them is that we aren't in them. It's hard to believe so many books can be so filled with lies. Because we are not in these histories, in the eyes of most people, especially academics, we therefore don't exist."

Kramer molded one of the chapters into a public lecture he called "Our Gay President" when invited to speak to the Midwest GLBT Conference at the University of Wisconsin on February 22, 1999. Audacity functions best, perhaps, in performance. Its force is unmistakable when, for instance, even before an audience of like-minded Americans, one says, out loud in a quiet auditorium, "Abraham Lincoln was gay." In that address Kramer claimed to have secret documentary evidence that Abraham Lincoln and Joshua Speed, who had spent four years living together in Springfield during their formative days as bachelors, were lovers. "For years they shared a bed and their most private thoughts. They fell in love with each other and slept next to each other for four years." News of Kramer's lecture caused homophobic paroxysms not only in Springfield, where Lincoln tourism is economic and cultural ballast, but also among Lincoln scholars who

went public with their challenge to Kramer's defilement of Lincoln's sacred memory.

The controversy subsided without Kramer divulging the secret documents, and without historians waiting for that evidence before concluding, rather definitively and homophobically, that Lincoln could not have been gay. More important, however, Kramer's goal—indeed, the telos at stake in all his virulent discourse throughout decades as an activist—had been missed. Like Lincoln himself, Kramer willingly *innovated* in deploying usable symbolic resources, however unpalatable for some audiences, as a life-enhancing organizing principle in the present, and a moral vision for a sustainable future.

INFORMATION RESOURCES

Collected Speeches/Major Works

Kramer, Larry. *Faggots*. New York: Random House, 1978.

———. *Just Say No: A Play About a Farce*. New York: St. Martin's Press, 1989.

———. *The Normal Heart and The Destiny of Me*. New York: Grove Press, 2000.

———. *Reports from the Holocaust: The Making of an AIDS Activist* [*RH*], rev. ed. New York: St. Martin's Press, 1994.

Mass, Lawrence D. "Interview with a Writer." In *We Must Love One Another or Die: The Life and Legacies of Larry Kramer*, ed. Lawrence D. Mass. New York: St. Martin's Press, 1997.

Selected Critical Studies

Bergman, David. "Larry Kramer and the Rhetoric of AIDS." In his *Gaiety Transfigured: Gay Self-Representation in American Literature*. Madison: University of Wisconsin Press, 1991.

Dow, Bonnie J. "AIDS, Perspective by Incongruity, and Gay Identity in Larry Kramer's '1,112 and Counting.' " *Communication Studies* 45 (1994): 225–40.

Mass, Lawrence D., ed. *We Must Love One Another or Die: The Life and Legacies of Larry Kramer*. New York: St. Martin's Press, 1997.

Morris, Charles E., III. "My Old Kentucky Homo: Abraham Lincoln, Larry Kramer, and the Politics of Queer Memory." In *Framing Public Memory*, ed. Kendall R. Phillips. Tuscaloosa: University of Alabama Press, 2004.

Selected Biographies

Clendinen, Dudley, and Adam Nagourney. *Out for Good: The Struggle to Build a Gay Rights Movement in America. New York: Simon and Schuster, 1999.

Merla, Patrick. "A Normal Heart: The Larry Kramer Story." In *We Must Love One Another or Die: The Life and Legacies of Larry Kramer*, ed. Lawrence D. Mass. New York: St. Martin's Press, 1997.

Shilts, Randy. *And the Band Played On: Politics, People, and the AIDS Epidemic*. New York: St. Martin's Press, 1987.

CHRONOLOGY OF SELECTED RHETORICAL WORKS

Oratorical Works

"The Beginning of ACTing Up." New York City, March 10, 1987. *RH*, pp. 127–36.

"Message Queen." New York City, April 27, 1987. *RH*, pp. 145–48.

"I Can't Believe You Want to Die." Boston, June 9, 1987. *RH*, pp. 162–75.

"Before the President's Commission." Washington, D.C., September 9, 1987. *RH*, pp. 182–85.

"We Killed Vito." New York City, December 20, 1990. *RH*, pp. 369–72.

"No Sense of Urgency." New York City, November 22, 1991. *RH*, pp. 383–88.

"Our Gay President." Madison, Wis., February 22, 1999. Excerpted in *Capital Times* (Madison, Wis.), February 23, 1999, p. 2A.

Nonoratorical Works

Faggots. New York: Random House, 1978.

"A Personal Appeal." *New York Native*, August 24–September 6, 1981. *RH*, pp. 8–9.

"1,112 and Counting." *New York Native*, March 14–27, 1983. *RH*, pp. 33–50.

The Normal Heart. New York: New American Library, 1985.

"An Open Letter to Richard Dunne and Gay Men's Health Crisis." *New York Native*, January 26, 1987. *RH*, pp. 100–15.

"The Plague Years." *Newsday*, May 31, 1987. *RH*, pp. 149–58.

"An Open Letter to Dr. Anthony Fauci." *Village Voice*, May 31, 1988. *RH*, pp. 193–99.

The Destiny of Me. New York: Plume, 1993.

"Sex and Sensibility." *The Advocate*, May 27, 1997.

WINONA LaDUKE (1959–)
Native American Leader, Environmentalist, Vice-Presidential Candidate

DAYLE C. HARDY-SHORT AND C. BRANT SHORT

Like many political activists outside the mainstream in American history, Winona LaDuke uses public speaking as a fundamental means of gaining attention, developing credibility, and participating in the political process. Unlike many advocates, LaDuke represents multiple political constituencies, including Native Americans, environmentalists, and women. Her public speeches support a philosophy that links these three spheres into a unified vision of political activism. Although it is unlikely that LaDuke will ever hold elected office or be appointed to a governmental position, she emerged in the 1990s as one of the nation's leading advocates for social and political change. She achieved prominence in 1996 and again in 2000 when she served as the Green Party's vice presidential candidate (the party's presidential candidate was Ralph Nader). With a national platform, LaDuke used campaign speeches to address new audiences regarding the need for an alternative political paradigm. LaDuke is a masterful public speaker, modeling the standards for effective oratory in her campaign to bring issues of human rights and environmental justice to the forefront of contemporary political debate.

LaDuke was born in Los Angeles on August 18, 1959, to Betty Bernstein, an art student from New York, and Vincent LaDuke, an actor and member of the Anishinabeg Native American tribe (also known as the Ojibwe or Chippewa), which is located on the White Earth reservation in northern Minnesota at the headwaters of the Mississippi River. Her biographer Michael Silverstone states that her family had a significant influence on the development of her ideas. LaDuke's maternal grandmother, Helen Bernstein, had been active in supporting workers' rights and raising money to aid Hitler's European victims. Her mother had lived in Mexico for several years while an art student, and had worked with indigenous people. She became deeply interested in helping to improve conditions in the United States for African Americans and Native Americans. In Los Angeles, LaDuke's father, Vincent, started a magazine, *Many Smokes*, which reported on western tribal issues. Both parents participated in tribal activities and ceremonies, and took Winona with them. However, by the time she was five, her parents had separated, and Betty moved with Winona

national energy policy." At sixteen, LaDuke took pre-med classes at Barnard College in New York during a summer program; at the age of seventeen, she applied to, and was one of eight Native American students accepted at, Harvard. She was also accepted at Yale and Dartmouth, but chose to attend Harvard because of its location and "because they [her high school guidance counselor] told me I couldn't." After completing her degree at Harvard, she became a fellow at the Massachusetts Institute of Technology and earned a master's degree in rural development from Antioch College.

LaDuke started the White Earth Land Recovery Project, a nonprofit agency that focuses on efforts to regain ownership and control of the 837,000 acres of land ceded to the Ojibwa tribe in 1867 by U.S. treaty agreement; the Project

---

"The Earth is our Mother. It is our responsibility to care for our Mother, and in caring for our Mother, we care for ourselves. . . . [Our problem is that] decision-making is not made by those who are affected—people who live on the land—but by corporations with interests entirely different from that of the land and the people or women of the land."

—*Winona LaDuke, "Speech to the Non-Governmental Organization Forum," Huairou, China, 1995*

---

to Ashland, Oregon, where Betty soon married Peter Westigard, an entomologist. LaDuke reports that her stepfather was a strong influence on her, because he believed his work should be focused on helping others.

In an E-mail interview regarding her public speaking ("Responses"), LaDuke recalls working "pretty hard for three years" in high school, competing "in debate, oratory and humorous interpretation." LaDuke states that "my studies were absolutely the foundation of my research skills, and provided some formatting ideas for my subsequent work," and adds that she "did receive some state wide awards (second in Lincoln Douglas Debate) for my work." One topic she and her partner, Lynne Abernathy, debated was "Resolved: That the United States should have a

also focuses on cultural and sustainability projects on the reservation. LaDuke also serves as a program director for Honor the Earth, an organization that supports Native American environmental activism, and has been on the board of directors of Greenpeace. In 1994 *Time* magazine named LaDuke as one of America's top fifty leaders under the age of forty, and in 1998 *Ms.* magazine named her "Woman of the Year" for her political activism.

LaDuke's selection as the Green Party vice presidential candidate in 1996 and again in 2000 gave her added credibility as a national leader. Although she and Ralph Nader lost the presidential election, they gained significant vote totals in many states, and many analysts credited their ticket for Democratic candidate Al Gore's loss in several key states—and perhaps ulti-mately his loss of the election—during the 2000 presidential campaign.

WINONA LaDUKE'S ORATORY

As a high school speech and debate competi-tor, LaDuke learned the basics of argumentation and persuasion (*invention*), speech preparation (*arrangement*), audience analysis (*style*), and de-livery. She believes that her studies "were ab-solutely the foundation of my research skills, and provided some formatting ideas for my subse-quent work." Like many skilled debaters, LaDuke does not write out her speeches in essay form, but instead, as she explains in "Responses," "what I do is take a lot of my research material and look at it; I often end up taking article pieces or man-uscript pieces and cutting them into little pieces for my speech."

Although LaDuke utilizes deductive modes of argument in her speeches, she exhibits par-ticular skill in utilizing inductive methods to present compelling conclusions. She relies upon a wide variety of concrete research and under-stands the persuasive power of various forms of logical proof, including statistics, testimony, ex-amples, and analogies. For example, in her 1993 "Voices from White Earth" speech at Yale Uni-versity, she contrasted how indigenous peoples utilize sustainable practices with how capitalist culture views the acquisition of wealth. LaDuke reported that her reservation was a poor com-munity, and "people . . . comment on the 85 per-cent unemployment." What many people fail to understand is what tribal members do with their time, because they "have no way of valuing our cultural practices." She then explained that

[f]or instance, 85 percent of our people hunt, taking at least one or two deer annually, prob-ably in violation of federal game laws; 75 per-cent of our people hunt for small game and geese; 50 percent of our people fish by net; 50 percent of our people sugarbush and garden on our reservation. About the same percentage harvest wild rice, not for themselves; they har-vest it to sell. About half of our people produce handcrafts. There is no way to quantify this in America. It is called the "invisible economy" or the "domestic economy." Society views us

as unemployed Indians who need wage jobs. That is not how we view ourselves. Our work is about strengthening and restoring our tradi-tional economy.

In this passage, LaDuke presented one statistic that appears to make a particular statement about perceptions of unemployment—and per-haps by extension, the work ethic—and then added another set of statistics that offers an en-tirely different view of the situation. These par-ticular statistics allow her to draw the conclu-sion that sustainable practices look different depending upon the lens through which one views the meaning of "work." This example is typical of the way in which LaDuke utilizes log-ical evidence to make persuasive claims. She in-troduces an idea, presents a series of facts, and then draws a conclusion that often helps alter her audience's initial perception of the situation. Her speeches utilize a broad array of logical ev-idence and reveal that she conducts regular re-search in preparation for her presentations.

LaDuke builds her credibility (ethos) using each of the four ethical proofs that public speak-ers typically use: intelligence, goodwill, charac-ter, and dynamism. She blends her personal bi-ography with a political oration that enhances her ethos for given audiences. For example, in a speech at Santa Fe, New Mexico, during her 2000 Green Party vice presidential campaign, LaDuke explained in the introduction who she is and where she comes from before moving into the body of her speech, which focused primarily on the relationship between environmental is-sues and corporate behavior and responsibility. After beginning the speech in a traditional way by introducing herself in Ojibwe as part of a par-ticular clan and as from a particular place, she briefly acknowledged her friendships with spe-cific members of the audience and thanked the audience members for their support. Then she explained that she "would start by telling you a little about what brings me to this. Because I don't know that many of you." She began, "I'm a mother of three children. . . . As a mother, I'm motivated to do this kind of work because I can-not understand why I should be more concerned about how much sugar is in my child's breakfast cereal than I am how much PCBs is in my son's tissue. That is the reality of this day and age as a mother." Throughout much of the balance of the speech, she tied her personal experience to why she feels she must, and by extension why the audience members should, care about particular issues. She continued this process of self-disclosure later in the speech:

I come to this work because I work on a reservation in northwestern Minnesota. I spent most of my adult life working in different rural and reservation communities around this country. In doing so I came to the same questions as I worked here in the southwestern United States in '78 and '79 on uranium mining and coal strip mining issues. I came to wonder about and hear these questions being asked: Who gave these corporations these rights? Who gave them the rights to all our water? Who gave them the rights to contaminate that ground water? Who gave them the rights to all those minerals? Who signed all those leases? How did that happen that their rights came to supersede ours?

As she often does, LaDuke begins by describing her personal experience and how it has led her to ask questions about the injustice she sees around her. In one sense, she is reviewing her growth as a political activist, but in another sense, her experiences are shared vicariously by the audience members and, ideally, will lead them to the same questions—and conclusions—that she articulates. Thus her view of the world and her place in it is always grounded in personal experience and enhances her credibility with her audience. LaDuke appears to know what she is talking about because she has seen it firsthand and can weave those experiences into coherent patterns for audience members. Her public speeches are based solidly in her direct observations coupled with statistical information. For instance, later in the Santa Fe speech, LaDuke said, "You are a really smart looking bunch. So I do not need to tell you all the statistics. Let us remind ourselves however. We have cut most of the trees. Ninety-five percent of the old growth is gone. We are fighting over splinters that is left. . . . I am someone who was arrested once. I was arrested in 1995 in Los Angeles because I chained myself to the front of a phone book factory. In my gut I do not be-

lieve that a thousand-year-old tree should be turned into a phone book." Then she added, "I do not believe that we as people of conscience should have to spend our time in jail arguing over these things but sometimes that's what we have to do. You have to stand up and sometimes you have to get arrested. I fundamentally believe there are some trees we should just leave be." In this passage, LaDuke coupled a statistical claim with her personal experience in order to justify activism; however, she did not tell her audience members that they, too, were obliged to act. Rather, she presented herself as compelled to act and, by not blaming the audience members, she allowed them to make the choice to act—or not. Her credibility was centered in her willingness to act on her beliefs and her unwillingness to demand that audience members act in her stead.

In the use of emotional appeals, LaDuke develops pathetic (emotional) proofs that are grounded in logical proofs, personal examples, and examples relevant for her given audience. Her narratives tell stories that serve a dual function by engaging the emotions of her audience while at the same time confirming the premises of her arguments. She rarely uses personal narratives about individuals who suffer an injustice; instead, she prefers to speak about collective concerns, describing the suffering of a group of people in a specific time and place.

Mythos, the speaker's use of culturally shared narratives, is an essential dimension of LaDuke's oratory. Regardless of the demographic composition of her audience, LaDuke uses her Native American heritage as a key part of her speech preparation. She often turns to her native language and contrasts the meanings of Native words with the corresponding term in English. In "Honor the Earth," she noted that the Objiwa language is a language of verbs: "eight thousand verbs. That's a lot of verbs, eight thousand verbs. That's what I always say, though—I say that we're a people of action." In addition she uses Native history, prophecies, and culture to help her identify with a specific cause and contrast it with mainstream Western culture.

In terms of structuring her message, LaDuke uses well-developed introductions and conclusions that address the immediate audience, enhance her ethos, and set the thesis of the speech in clear terms. According to LaDuke, "I often work to make my speeches cyclical, returning to my original points somehow in the end and summary, which is more, I would say, of a Native approach, or a stylistic approach I would say is Native in this way." However, it is also common practice for debaters and public speakers who learn that to help one's audience remember the central point of the speech, the introduction and conclusion should be specifically linked, as well as linked to the main points in the speech.

An example of how LaDuke sees her style is highlighted in a speech to a national conference of architectural educators. In "Building with Reservations," she began with her tribal affiliation and her language, noting that "I always greet people in my language because I believe that cultural diversity is as beautiful as biodiversity, and this is reflected in language." She then turned to the immediate audience and expressed her honor to speak to such educators, then mentioned a controversial building project in the conference host city, Minneapolis. Noting that the road project would destroy a site sacred to the Mendota Dakota people, LaDuke challenged the audience directly: "I know that you are the people who design these projects, and maybe in my talking to you, you'll hear a little about what we go through in our community and that will help you in your thinking. I am fully aware of how little an American education teaches you about Native people."

In terms of style, LaDuke uses precise, direct, and clear language. She selects words to convey specific meanings and demonstrates her ability to communicate ideas to diverse audiences. Although she rarely uses figures of speech that are colorful, some figures do become part of her rhetorical style. For example, she regularly uses a hunting metaphor in her speeches. "The origins of this problem," she told the Non-Governmental Organization Forum, "lie with the predator/prey relationship that industrial society has developed with the Earth and, subsequently, the people of the Earth. This same relationship exists vis-à-vis women."

Rather than coining memorable metaphors and other colorful figures of speech, LaDuke

more often uses her Native language to engage her audience and at the same time make a larger point about cultural meaning. Speaking at the University of Wisconsin in 2001, she began her speech this way: "*Akiing* is the word for land in our language, and in the indigenous concept of land ownership, it is much more a concept that we belong to that land than the land belongs to us." This use of language allowed LaDuke to move easily into her topic, the cultural concept of land and ownership in North America.

LaDuke employs an extemporaneous style of delivery, speaking from a detailed outline with a common theme but creating sentences in an informal style. According to LaDuke, an extemporaneous style of delivery allows her to adapt her message more fully to each specific audience: "I prefer to use an outline and from there I embellish and am flexible about presenting what I want. I am also interested in spending a bit of time assessing my audience, knowing their demographics, knowledge, and a bit about what other experiences they have had recently with speakers and perhaps with Native subject matter."

Audiences find LaDuke's style of delivery direct, conversational, and inviting. Her eye contact is strong and varied, and she often responds to specific people in the audience because they remind her of an event, a memory, or some other means of identifying with her audience. LaDuke speaks from a lectern, referring occasionally to her notes but not moving from the central position of the lectern. Her gestures appear as natural extensions of her content, emphasizing a point, adding meaning, rarely distracting from the speech content. Her vocal quality is varied, with changes in rate, pitch, and volume as necessary to express meaning in her arguments, stories, and emotions. She often uses humor, especially when discussing complex and challenging issues, and conveys this through vocal changes, smiling, and gestures. As with many skilled orators, LaDuke's delivery is rarely considered apart from her arguments and appeals because her speaking style appears natural, genuine, and conversational.

LaDuke has crafted a rhetorical style in which her political passions—feminism, environmental sustainability, and indigenous culture—combine to create the form and content of her public oratory. Although she prepares unique speeches for different audiences, this particular style dominates her oratory, and audiences are asked to redefine their own existence through listening. Significantly, LaDuke resists classification as a speaker who is primarily a feminist, primarily a Native American activist, or primarily an environmentalist. While audience members may attend her speeches because of their affiliation with a particular political agenda, they will be asked to reconsider their own relationships in regard to all peoples and all living things. Through the connections she makes, LaDuke challenges her listeners to change their lives, not simply their political behavior. Speaking in Huairou, China, to the U.N. Non-Governmental Organization Forum in 1995, LaDuke addressed the women of the world. She honored the women in the audience and said, "The Earth is our Mother. It is our responsibility to care for our Mother, and in caring for our Mother, we care for ourselves." Later in the same speech, she addressed the inherent tension between wealth and poverty by pointing out that "decision-making is not made by those who are affected—people who live on the land—but by corporations with interests entirely different from that of the land and the people or women of the land." Shortly after enunciating that tension, LaDuke linked industrial society with sexism and other forms of domination when she stated:

> The origins of this problem lie with the predator/prey relationship that industrial society has developed with the Earth and subsequently, the people of the Earth. This same relationship exists vis-à-vis women. We collectively find that we are often in the role of the prey to a predator society whether through sexual discrimination, exploitation, sterilization, absence of control over our bodies, or being the subjects of repressive laws and legislation in which we have no voice.

In the conclusion of this speech, LaDuke challenged her audience to rethink the labels used in global political debates. She concluded that this is not a struggle between industrial and developing economic systems; instead, it is a "struggle to recover our status as Daughters of the Earth. In that is our strength and security, not in the predator, but in the security of our Mother, for our future generations. In that, we can ensure our security as the Mothers of Our Nations." In this brief passage LaDuke reconnected the values that guide her political agenda and in turn asked that her audience members redefine their own existence by rejecting global economics, embracing sustainable environmental and economic practices, and accepting the power of women to change the world. As such, her public speaking transcends the classical rhetorical goals of persuasion and attitude change, and asks for a transformation of the listener from observer to participant.

In a speech titled "Social Justice, Racism, and the Environmental Movement," delivered at the University of Colorado in 1993, LaDuke opened by announcing that "people who are not Indian need to change the way this country works. . . . I also believe that the issues that are brought up by the discussion are much deeper than the discussion itself of environmental racism." She then turned to a discussion of "indigenous ecological thinking" and its basic philosophical and practical dimensions. LaDuke sees her role as teaching a primarily white, young, and educated audience about a Native American worldview and its ability to redirect culture in a positive direction. To achieve this goal, she reconceptualizes the meaning of time for her audience by connecting indigenous philosophy with indigenous time: "I believe that traditional ecological knowledge, the knowledge of indigenous people who have inhabited ecosystems for thousands of years and both observed and been given, through gifts from the Creator and from spiritual practice, that that knowledge is superior to scientific knowledge. . . . I do not believe that the knowledge of scientists is yet at the state where it could match traditional ecological knowledge." In this section of the speech, LaDuke challenged her audience to reconsider their faith in science and its applied knowledge through the lens of time and spiritual practice. This seeing of time from another cultural perspective allows the audience to ask pointed questions of ecosystem management, a central question of many in her audience.

Later in the speech LaDuke presented a clear description of how her audience ought to view time and its place in their own understanding of history, politics, and culture. She concluded:

> I believe that this society also forwards a perception of linear thinking, in stark contrast to cyclical thinking. I believe that this has to do first of all with how you're taught time in this country on a time line. The time line usually begins around 1492 and continues from there on out, with a number of dates that are of importance to someone. . . . The consequence of linear thinking, permeating our consciousness in America, is that for instance there are values which go along with linear thinking, like the idea of progress, defined by indicators like "economic growth" and "technological advancement." You want to have progress. Where you want to be. So we have an underlying perception in the society that we need to have progress when we move along the time line.

LaDuke uses the public platform to transform her listeners from *citizens* into *activists*. Her vision of activism is broad; it demands a change in values, ideals, and worldview. Thus her goal is to change the whole person rather than merely a particular attitude or behavior. She accomplishes this rhetorical transformation in two ways. First, LaDuke links the three passions of her life—feminism and women's rights, environmental sustainability, and Native American culture—into a holistic, interconnected political vision for her audiences. She unifies the political, social, and cultural values of justice for women, justice for the environment, and justice for indigenous peoples into a single discourse. Although some observers might classify LaDuke as an environmental activist because of her Green Party affiliation or as a Native American advocate because of her leadership in the Anishinabeq tribe, a review of her speeches shows that her view of activism demands that all three concerns merge into one vision. Second, LaDuke enlarges the context of public action for her audience by challenging dominant cultural views of time and space. In regard to time, she integrates past, present, and future visions into her speeches and writings, but not necessarily in a particular chronological order. In this way LaDuke is able to show her audience that time is a human construct and that a cyclical view of time is an important alternative to linear time. In regard to space, she focuses much of her rhetoric on the Native American view of a collective, spiritual connection to place. At the same time, she identifies threats to the environment as a manifestation of a global economy that diminishes the importance of humans in particular places. In this manner, space is combined into a local/global juxtaposition; thus the behaviors of multinational corporations affect the behaviors of a family on an isolated, rural reservation. These two rhetorical strategies help LaDuke unify her audience regardless of their gender, race, age, or other demographic differences.

LaDuke continues the important work of an American political activist, helping to define an ideological stance that demands justice from those in power. Toward that end, the public speech becomes LaDuke's means of creating community, presenting a unified response, and empowering those who consider themselves victims of the prevailing political and economic system. Her audiences include Americans (and peoples around the world) who see injustice in terms of environmental degradation, sexism, and racism. Her rhetorical stance suggests common causes of these forms of injustice and provides a collective means of challenging such behaviors. Just as other advocates have sought a sense of identification as the primary purpose of rhetorical behavior, so LaDuke sees individual identity as the first step in changing the system. By connecting her causes into a unified ideological statement, she is able to show audiences that what affects one, affects the many. Moreover, by enlarging the context of justice to include all peoples in all times, LaDuke offers a powerful indictment of American progress and in turn provides an alternative vision of the status quo grounded in indigenous peoples' worldview. Her speeches affirm the inherent power of political oratory and suggest that any quest to understand American rhetorical history demands studying the voices of those at the margins of the established order. Like abolitionists, populists, suffragettes, and socialists, LaDuke has brought a sense of urgency and clarity into the contemporary political arena.

LaDuke considers public speaking central to her work as a political activist. As she writes in "Responses," "I am interested in encouraging political participation and action by people in terms of activism." In 1996, LaDuke reviewed the growing strength of Native American environmental groups, explaining that over 200 small, grassroots groups have emerged in recent years and many important victories have been achieved at this level. LaDuke's vision of many small groups coming together is expressed in her vision of a mighty river: "And like small tributaries joining together to form a mighty river, their force and power grows. This river will not be dammed." The vision of a mighty river resisting human efforts at control illuminates LaDuke's vision of political justice in the United States and beyond. Moreover, it affirms LaDuke's underlying goal as an orator: "I have to say, that I always hope and pray that what I may say will be good, and of consequence, because that's the responsibility of the speaker to society."

INFORMATION SOURCES

Research Collections and Collected Speeches

Many complete texts of LaDuke's speeches are available on the Internet, posted by organizations that sponsor her speeches as well as state and national Green Party Web sites. Several speeches are printed in *The Winona LaDuke Reader*, which also includes essays, fiction, and poetry produced by LaDuke. Videotapes of selected LaDuke speeches are also available.

LaDuke, Winona. *All Our Relations: Native Struggles for Land and Life*. Cambridge, Mass.: South End Press, 1999.

———. "Like Tributaries to a River." *Sierra*, November/December 1996, pp. 38–45.

———. "Responses to Questions Regarding Public Speaking." Personal E-mail. October 5, 2003.

———. *The Winona LaDuke Reader* [*WLR*]. Stillwater, Minn.: Voyageur Press, 2002.

Audiovisual Material

Videotapes of selected LaDuke speeches can be obtained from JusticeVision [*JV*], 1425 W. 12th St. #262, Los Angeles, CA, 90015 or http://justicevision.blogspot.com (or www.justicevision.com). For information about selection and pricing, go to http://www.justicevision.org

Selected Critical Studies

Docan, Anthony "Tony." "A Tale of Two Ideologies: Winona LaDuke's Vice Presidential Nomination Acceptance Speech." In *Rhetorical Criticism: Exploration and Practice*, ed. Sonja K. Foss, 3rd ed. Long Grove, Ill.: Waveland Press, 2004.

Salaita, Steven. "Digging Up the Bones of the Past: Colonial and Indigenous Interplay." In *Last Standing Woman*, ed. Winona LaDuke. Stillwater, Minn.: Voyageur Press, 1997. Also in *American Indian Culture Journal* 26 (2002): 21–43.

Selected Biographies

Baumgardner, Jennifer. "Kitchen Table Candidate." *Ms.*, April/May 2001, pp. 46–53.

Paul, Sonya, and Robert Parkinson. "Interview with Winona LaDuke." In *No Middle Ground: Women and Radical Protest*, ed. Kathleen M. Blee. New York: New York University Press, 1998.

Silverstone, Michael. *Winona LaDuke: Restoring Land and Culture in Native America*. New York: Feminist Press, 2001.

CHRONOLOGY OF MAJOR SPEECHES

See "Research Collections and Collected Speeches" for source codes.

"Social Justice, Racism, and the Environmental Movement" (speech at the University of Colorado). Boulder, Colo., September 28, 1993. Available at www.zmag.org

"Voices from White Earth: Gaa-waabaabiganikaag" (speech at Yale University). New Haven, Conn., October 1993. Available at www.schumachersociety.org

"Mothers of Our Nations: Indigenous Women Address the World" (speech to the Non-governmental Organization Forum). Huairou, China, September 1995. *WLR*, pp. 211–17.

"Deconstructing the American Paradigm: Indigenous Vision for the Millennium" (speech at the University of California). Berkeley, Calif., 1998. Available at *JV*, vol. 12.

"Building with Reservations" (speech to the Association of Collegiate Schools of Architecture National Conference). Minneapolis, Minn., 1999. *WLR*, pp. 44–53.

"Honor the Earth: Our Native American Legacy" (speech at the Ninth Annual Westheimer Peace Symposium at Wilmington College). Wilmington, Ohio, October 1999. *WLR*, pp. 172–80.

"Acceptance Speech, Green Party's Nomination for Vice President of the United States." Denver, Colo., June 24, 2000. *WLR*, pp. 267–72.

"Fighting the Bad Guys and Trying to Do the Right Thing: A Vision for Change." Santa Fe, N.M., August 28, 2000. Available at www.ratical.org

"Who Owns America? Minority Land and Community Security." Madison, Wis., June 2001. *WLR*, pp. 138–47.

"An Evening with Winona LaDuke." Berkeley, Calif., 2001. Videotape available at *JV*, vol. 12.

AUDRE GERALDINE LORDE (1934–1992)
Professor of English, Poet, Black Lesbian, and Socialist

LESTER C. OLSON

Audre Geraldine Lorde was a poet orator whose sensibility as a poet suffused her public speeches throughout her lifetime. She is better known today as a poet of international stature than as a public speaker, essayist, or pamphleteer, even though some of her speeches were brilliant, many have become classics in feminist scholarship, and most are the subject of ongoing controversies. Lorde's oratory focused upon the role of language in communicating social differences in ways that construct relations of power among groups. Her public speeches, the most important of which were collected in *Sister Outsider: Essays & Speeches by Audre Lorde* in 1984 and *A Burst of Light* in 1988, have an aphoristic, expansive quality resulting from her extensive use of metaphors, maxims, proverbs, narratives, and stories to affirm her perspective on the relationship among language, self, and society. Her speeches, like her essays and her poems, often examine human differences communicated within a sociopolitical system of power ranging across symbolic oppositions between white and Black, male and female, capitalist and socialist, heterosexual and homosexual, master and slave—oppositions that Lorde criticized as simplistic and as useful to dominant groups for exploiting subordinated communities. Her public speaking is a vital resource for communication scholars engaged in examining the role of language and action in transforming self and society in a diverse culture.

Lorde was born on February 18, 1934, in Harlem in New York City. Her parents, Linda Belmar and Frederic Byron Lorde, were immigrants from Grenada. In interviews, Audre mentioned that she grew up with West Indian parents who spoke patois at home, and whose accent and regard for language were factors in the qualities of her own speaking, such as the deliberate pace, cadence, and accent. Her parents tried to prevent her from learning patois or

speaking with a West Indian accent, because they wished to be private in their conversations and were concerned for the success of their children at a Catholic school run by nuns. Audre remarked in an interview that her parents were "very particular about how we talked, that we learned what was in the King's English."

In interviews, Lorde mentioned that her Catholic upbringing influenced her lifelong interest in rituals, though the substance of her own rituals changed significantly. She distinguished her spiritual life, however, from her Catholic upbringing. By "spirituality," she meant "that very deeply rooted consciousness that we are a part of something that didn't start with us, that came from before [us], and will continue after we have gone, but that our piece in it is essential and important." Regarding ritual, Lorde mentioned her love of incantations, which may be exemplified by her evocative poem "Call," with which she liked to conclude poetry readings. Her use of litany and choral as rhetorical resources also reflects her careful attention to ritual. By the conclusion of her life, she had engaged African cultures' views of spirituality, especially the history of Black goddesses.

As early as 1960, Lorde's poetry was recognized by accomplished writers such as Langston Hughes, a fellow member of the Harlem Writers Guild, who wrote to her about including her poetry in his anthology of "new Negro poets." During 1968, Lorde was a distinguished visiting professor at Atlanta University and, that summer, a poet-in-residence at Tougaloo College in Mississippi. That year she also received a National Endowment for the Arts grant to support her writing of poetry. In 1968, Lorde completed her first poetry collection, a now hard-to-find chapbook titled *The First Cities* that was published by the Poets Press in London and New York. It was followed in 1970 by her second poetry collection, titled *Cables to Rage*, published in London by Paul Breman. Ultimately she produced additional collections of poems including *From a Land Where Other People Live* (1973), *New York Head Shop and Museum* (1975), *Between Our Selves* (1976), *Coal* (1976), *The Black Unicorn* (1978), *Chosen Poems, Old and New* (1982), *Our Dead Behind Us* (1986), *Undersong* (1992), and *The Marvelous Arithmetics of Distance* (1993). In 1997, her *Collected Poems* was published by Norton, the most frequent publisher of her collections toward the end of her career. In addition to the poems mentioned elsewhere in this essay, her poetry may be exemplified by "Coal," "Blackstudies," "Afterimages," "Between Ourselves," "Outside," and "Who Said It Was Simple."

The content of Lorde's earliest poetry throughout the 1960s and early 1970s reflected her family life. She married Edwin Ashley Rollins in York City, especially Manhattan, Staten Island, and Brooklyn, where the extraordinary cultural diversity of people in the cosmopolitan, urban setting was doubtless an influence on her discourse. Lorde earned a B.A. with a double major in English and philosophy at Hunter College in 1959. During the late 1950s, she was an investigator for the Bureau of Child Welfare, and in the early 1960s, a young adult librarian at the Mount Vernon (New York) Public Library. In 1961, she earned a master's degree in library science from Columbia University. Beginning in 1970, initially as a lecturer and subsequently as an assistant professor, Lorde was on the faculty of the English department at John Jay College of Criminal Justice in Manhattan, where, among students of diverse backgrounds, she trained white police officers and FBI agents. In 1980, she departed for Hunter College, where in 1985 a poetry center was named in her honor and, in 1987, she was

---

"I am a poet. When I write prose, I am a poet writing prose. . . . when I say poet, I am speaking of a whole way of looking at life, of moving into it, of using it, of dealing with myself and my experience. I am not speaking of living itself, I am speaking of a use of my living."

1962, and they had two children, Elizabeth and Jonathan. They separated in 1970 and were formally divorced in 1975. Lorde's early poetry collections and radio broadcasts, such as *The Poet Speaks* on WGBH-FM in Boston (April 1970, December 1971), conveyed no obvious evidence of her lesbianism, which did not surface in her public work until her erotic poem "Meet," which was printed in 1977 in *Sinister Wisdom*. In *Zami: A New Spelling of My Name* (1982), Lorde explored her experiences as a Black lesbian in a book that she called a biomythography, which drew upon her 1953 trip to Mexico. Lorde's partner for almost two decades was Frances Louise Clayton, who helped to raise Lorde's children during most of the 1970s and 1980s and aided Lorde during her diagnosis and early confrontations with cancer.

For most of Lorde's life, she resided in New named Thomas Hunter Professor. Throughout this period she enjoyed her network of close friendships and professional colleagues engaged in the writing of poetry, history, and lesbian feminism through publication outlets such as the Women of Color/Kitchen Table Press, of which she was a founder, and Out & Out Books.

Lorde was diagnosed with breast cancer in 1978, shortly after her speech "The Uses of the Erotic." She had a mastectomy, a profoundly life-altering experience for her. Envisioning herself not as a victim suffering, but as a warrior battling her condition, she drew upon images of the Amazons of Dahomey, one-breasted women warriors, in her writings. Later she was diagnosed with liver cancer, treatments for which took her in 1984 to Germany, where she gave poetry readings and interviews. While in Berlin, Lorde became deeply involved with Gloria I.

Joseph, a scholar, writer, and social activist who became Lorde's partner and lived with her on St. Croix in the Virgin Islands. Lorde was a founder of Sisterhood in Support of Sisters in South Africa as well as the St. Croix Women's Coalition. While living in the Virgin Islands, she was given the honorific name Gambia Adisa, which means "Warrior: She Who Makes Her Meaning Known." She died there on November 11, 1992.

AUDRE LORDE: POET ORATOR FOR REVOLUTIONARY CHANGE

Lorde is well known for her contributions to the women's movement during the 1970s and 1980s, especially her courageous struggle with breast cancer as recorded in her *Cancer Journals* (1980). She addressed the topics of age, race, sex, sexual-

part of some group defined as other, deviant, inferior, or just plain wrong." In addition to using her public speeches, essays, and poems to resist externally imposed and reductive definitions of her differences from dominant groups, Lorde explicitly resisted the pressure "to pluck out some one aspect of myself and present this as the meaningful whole, eclipsing or denying the other parts of self"; in her view, "this is a destructive and fragmenting way to live." She affirmed, "My fullest concentration of energy is available to me only when I integrate all the parts of who I am, openly, allowing power from particular sources of my living to flow back and forth freely through all my different selves, without the restrictions of externally imposed definition."

Lorde's rhetoric demonstrated her complex

"When I call myself a feminist, I call myself a feminist because I recognize that the root of my vulnerability and my power lies in myself as a woman and because I am primarily focused upon changing the consciousness of myself and other women. That is the first level. I am of course also interested in changing the consciousness of anyone, and that includes men, who can use the work, who can use my energy, who can use what I put out. But my primary focus is my consciousness and the consciousness of women."

ity, and economic class in a wide range of forums and publication outlets. Themes in her speeches include silence and silencing; the habitual complicity of subordinated peoples with dominant groups; being an outsider as a position of both vulnerability and strength; the erotic as distinct from the pornographic in human relationships as well as commercial products; difference and anger as resources for collaboration and social change rather than divisiveness, capricious bias, and hatred; and survival in a hostile society. Whenever she spoke in public, she explicitly defined her own position as multiply marginal in her relationship to dominant groups. "As a forty-nine-year-old Black lesbian feminist socialist mother of two, including one boy, and a member of an interracial couple," Lorde remarked in 1980, "I usually find myself a

awareness of how privilege and oppression interact in each individual's life situation. Consequently, her rhetoric avoided the simplistic reduction of social tensions to the roles of oppressor and oppressed, noticing as she did so how social, political, economic, educational, and religious factors impinge upon lives in complicated ways that oftentimes have people operating within both roles, even if they are consciously mindful of only one of them. Evoking Paulo Freire's *The Pedagogy of the Oppressed*, Lorde commented, "The true focus of revolutionary change is never merely the oppressive situations which we seek to escape, but that piece of the oppressor which is planted deep within each of us, and which knows only the oppressors' tactics, the oppressors' relationships." As a consequence, her public speeches are extraordinarily complex, insightful, and instructive in their treatment of racism, sexism, heterosexism, ageism, and the like as they intersect and conflict. Her ideology situated her within a distinctive, though certainly not unique, strand of materialist feminist thought which held that "racism, sexism, and homophobia are inseparable," as she observed in 1979. She held that "there is no hierarchy of oppressions," which became the title of an essay in *Interracial Books for Children Bulletin* (September 1983).

Lorde wrote poetry from her childhood, and her poetry was published for almost two decades before her first recorded public speech. That speech, titled "The Transformation of Silence into Language and Action," was delivered as part of a panel discussion titled "Lesbians and Literature" at the Modern Language Association meeting in Chicago. It is perhaps her finest speech. Two of her other speeches, however, have been more frequently noted in scholarly literature. "Uses of the Erotic: The Erotic as Power," was delivered initially as part of a panel discussion titled "Power and Oppression" at the Fourth Berkshire Conference on the History of Women. "The Master's Tools Will Never Dismantle the Master's House" was delivered as part of a panel discussion, "The Personal and the Political," at New York University. These three orations are arguably the most important of her public speeches in terms of their technical sophistication in engaging dominant groups.

In Lorde's public address, she drew primarily on her feelings and experiences embodied in her own living as the most dependable resource for her rhetorical invention, because she believed that feeling was more fundamental than understanding for bringing about political change, and because she was deeply skeptical about the value of abstract, disembodied writings, which she designated "theory." Though Lorde was sometimes criticized for reproducing stereotypes of women as intuitive and emotional, she sought to integrate emotion with rational thought rather than artificially separating them. Her views of poetry are concisely summarized in "Poetry Is Not a Luxury," an essay published in *Chrysalis* (1977), for which Lorde served as poetry editor from 1976 until 1979. She described that essay as a transitional moment in her intellectual de-

velopment, which indeed it was, marking her movement into speeches, essays, pamphlets, and public letters, as well as her movement into what she characterized as "linear" modes of expression. Lorde characterized this change in her work as akin to learning a second language. Yet there are interconnections among her poetry, essays, and speeches, all of which were rooted in her life experiences and feelings, because of her practice of connecting the personal and the political, a very common feature of contemporary feminist practice. Consequently, it can be helpful for understanding Lorde's speeches to engage her poetry, as may be exemplified by the relationship between "A Litany for Survival" and "The Transformation of Silence into Language and Action," or that between "Power" and "The Uses of Anger: Women Responding to Racism," a difficult but important speech which she delivered to the National Women's Studies Association in June 1981. Ordinarily, her speeches include excerpts of her poetry and, on occasion, a complete poem.

Typically, Lorde's speeches reflected explicitly on language and symbolic practices. Lorde employed language tactically and strategically while being mindful of ideological inheritances of various sorts complicating communication among people of diverse backgrounds and commitments. One example of these qualities is her famous maxim: "The master's tools will never dismantle the master's house." The series of metaphors entailed—tools, dismantle, house— supply her maxim with an expansive and ambiguous quality. To Lorde, "the master's tools" designated techniques of domination through the exercise of political power, moral judgment, and social privilege. The "master" could be understood in relationships of domination over both the "mistress" and the "slave," focusing on sex, race, and the intersection of these embodied in Black women. More important, as a matter of adaptation to the immediate audience of feminists at the Second Sex conference, a white woman could be "mistress" in her relationship to the white "master" while being a "master" over "slaves" of either sex. Lorde's speech explored the ambiguities of the combined roles of white women in U.S. culture by evoking an understanding of their role as "mistress" to examine their analogous role as "master" across differences in race, class, and sexuality. The expression "the master's tools" underscored the actual tools for production of such material goods as "the master's house," the practices of domination employed by the master over the mistress and the slave, and, specifically in connection with sex differences, the male's sexual anatomy. In this last respect, the master's tool may have been seductive in a layered pun to heterosexual women of any race, age, or class who wanted to reside in the house as an intimate companion.

In general, Lorde was concerned about the seductiveness of power exercised for arbitrary domination over others, even among feminists who deplored its operations under patriarchy. A fundamental reason that using "the master's tools" would be self-defeating was that using those tools reproduced the practices and could transform the users of them into "masters." To Lorde, the practices of arbitrary domination needed to be transformed, not rehearsed. "The master's house" was likewise layered in its multiple meanings. It referred to the site for exercising power, judgment, and privilege as well as the products of these deeds. Unearned entitlement to "the master's house" was salient for Lorde, but "dismantling" the "master's house" referred to repudiating anyone's unearned privilege. In addition, "the master's house" designated the material and/or courtship interests that bound the mistress and/or slave to the master. Finally, "the master's house" implicitly distinguished the reformist approach of the "house" Black from the radical approach of the "field" Black. In this respect, one of "the master's tools" consisted in dividing members of subordinated communities by extending privileges to some through access to the interior of "the master's house" while exploiting most others in the field to support this dwelling. An opposition between "the master's house" and the master's field, though implicit in Lorde's maxim, was vital in challenging reformist feminists to adopt radical feminism. Lorde used an analogy between racism and sexism to shape insights about distinctive reformist and radical political commitments within feminism. As this sustained example may illustrate, Lorde's rhetoric is rich in its layers of meaning and technical sophistication.

Lorde's lively sense of humor and her ability to move adeptly through her audiences' defense mechanisms—which, she suggested, tended regularly to distort her messages—are perhaps more evident in the audio recordings of her live engagements with audiences at her poetry readings and interviews than in her orations. In a speech in 1980, for instance, Lorde reiterated two extreme distortions around human differences used to exclude work by women of color from the curriculum: "All too often, the excuse given is that the literatures of women of Color can only be taught by Colored women, or that they are too difficult to understand, or that classes cannot 'get into' them because they come out of experiences that are 'too different.'" She then amused her audience by incisively revealing the transparent hypocrisy of such excuses: "I have heard this argument presented by white women of otherwise quite clear intelligence, women who seem to have no trouble at all teaching and reviewing work that comes out of the vastly different experiences of Shakespeare, Molière, Dostoyevsky, and Aristophanes." Her extraordinary skill in leading discussion of sensitive topics is consistently evident in the question-and-answer periods which typically followed her speeches and readings.

Lorde was a perfectionist who extensively revised her ideas even after they had been published, altering them for later collections of poems, speeches, and essays. Because she also preserved numerous typed and handwritten drafts for each speech, essay, or poem, sometimes making the revisions on a copy of an earlier published version, the drafts are an invaluable resource for investigating her rhetorical invention, style, and organization, as well as changes in her sense of audience for the specific forum, genre, or publisher. A wide range of intellectual resources is in evidence in the preliminary drafts for her public address, through the explicit reference to a name or the concepts inaugurated by the person. Her preliminary drafts for speeches and essays often identified people and/or publications whose views or practices she overtly opposed. But these names ordinarily disappeared from the published versions of her remarks, possibly because Lorde was more concerned with the ideas or practices than the specific figure. A partial, but by no means complete, list of intellectual sources in evidence in her rhetorical invention and style would have to include W.E.B. Du Bois, Paulo Freire, and Adrienne Rich. Lorde spoke approvingly of the Black lesbian playwright Lorraine Hansbury and of Angelina Weld Grimké of the Harlem Renaissance.

To judge from the unpublished materials held at Spelman College, two of the most extensively revised speeches were "Uses of the Erotic" and "Learning from the 60s." For the former speech, there are multiple copies with taped and spliced paper text placed over earlier typed passages, as well as extensive handwritten inserts, not only on the fronts of pages, but sometimes spilling over onto the backs of pages. Lorde delivered the latter speech at Harvard University during Malcolm X Weekend in 1982. Her revisions reflected an endeavor to situate her political activism so that the speech, initially deliberative in its dominant thrust, eventually comported fully with the ceremonial character of the event as she called for future action to honor the famous Black leader's legacy. Yet honoring his legacy proved complex to Lorde. She sought explicitly to recognize and transform its specific shortcomings (in her view), such as the devaluation of women and other ramifications of his specific commitments within Islam in his early speeches. She emphasized how he changed his views with experience, asking that her audiences honor him by doing likewise.

Lorde's speeches in the late 1970s and early 1980s are more accessible to white scholars than her later speeches, because she consciously endeavored to reach them, especially white feminists. During the late 1970s and throughout the 1980s, Lorde struggled in public forums dominated by white women to engage feminism in order to transform it, despite its reformist politics and its ongoing legacies of racism, classism, and heterosexism. Yet her speeches were rife with evidences of her frustration, anger, and deepening skepticism about the prospects for change within the women's movement. In 1980, she remarked, "There is a pretense to a homogeneity of experience covered by the word *sisterhood* which does not in fact exist." Although Lorde expressly continued to welcome critical listening by persons from diverse backgrounds, her later speeches focused increasingly upon Black women. Three speeches toward the end of her life exemplify this trend: "I Am Your Sister: Black Women Organizing Across Sexualities," delivered in 1985 to the Black Women Rising Together Conference held at Medgar Evers College; "Sisterhood and Survival," a 1985 keynote speech at the conference "Black Women Writers and the Diaspora" held at Michigan State University; and her remarks at the I Am Your Sister Conference: Forging Global Connections Across Difference, held in Boston in October 1990 to honor Lorde for her lifetime achievements. Lorde commented that her speech at Medgar Evers College "came out very, very rapidly" and "just really flowed," requiring only minimal revision in its preparation because, she said, "I felt very strongly about what I was saying"—and presumably because this was the audience whom she knew the best and with whom she felt the most at home, even though, as Lorde often commented, both sexism and heterosexism within Black audiences posed difficulties for her discourse.

Lorde's rhetorical practices reflected her keen awareness of how institutions and organizations enable and disable discourses by women of color and lesbians, as well as often distorting the discourse as a consequence of a tendency to adapt to dominant groups' concerns and beliefs. In 1980, she commented, "I am responsible for educating teachers who dismiss my children's culture in school. Black and Third World people are expected to educate white people as to our humanity. Women are expected to educate men. Lesbians and gay men are expected to educate the heterosexual world." While superficially such educational projects seem to have merit, Lorde disclosed some deficiencies of such projects. "The oppressors maintain their position and evade responsibility for their own actions," she remarked, adding that for those who undertake the educating, "There is a constant drain of energy which might be better used in redefining ourselves and devising realistic scenarios for altering the present and constructing the future." In these respects, a certain meaning of "communication" is "pretense," because what is actually at stake is practicing, rehearsing, and perpetuating the underlying hierarchical dynamic between oppressor and oppressed, with the latter tending to the former's needs. Subsequently, this awareness was reflected in her publications and participation in organizations, sometimes as a founder.

With few exceptions, mainstream Black audiences have neglected Lorde's work. Yet, Lorde has become an icon of the women's movement. Her pictorial image has become a commodity, marketed on posters, T-shirts, buttons, and the like, symbolizing a strand of feminism committed to fair and equitable relationships across differences in race, sexuality, age, and class, among other social groupings. Her reputation among feminists and women's studies scholars continues to grow. Lesbian, transgender, and queer communities have likewise taken increased interest in Lorde over the years, sometimes coupling her image as a warrior against breast cancer with images of gay men battling the AIDS pandemic, at other times evoking her maxim "Your silence will not protect you" to counter the closeting of same-sexuality. Even so, Lorde's socialism, sex, and race have diminished her appeal to socially and economically conservative gay men and lesbians. Thus, her critical reception was as diverse as the extraordinary range of audiences she addressed, opinions ranging from heartfelt hostility to deep appreciation and gratitude for her work.

There are recurrent difficulties for scholars endeavoring to critically assess Lorde's discourse. She sometimes drew a stark contrast between Euro-American and African cultures in that she viewed Euro-American culture as linear and oriented toward problem-solving, whereas African cultures were holistic in their commitment to feeling through experience and deriving understanding from those feelings. Her commitment to the latter sensibility may explain, in part, why the organization of her speeches is often vexing to discern, since she resisted conventional linear, problem-solving sequences and preferred creative, open-ended, generative suggestions. As a related matter, Lorde's allusions to African goddesses, practices, and intellectual resources are sometimes a source of frustration and bewilderment to audiences. In addition, her speeches, essays, and interviews may be challenging for most readers and listeners because she dealt with sensitive and taboo topics ranging from rape and pornography to harassment, bias crimes, and other forms of abuse and violence. Finally, while concentrating on one aspect of bias as a topic in her speeches, it is easy for readers and listeners to unwittingly reproduce other varieties of bias, despite the best of intentions, simply because these biases continue to be endemic in U.S. culture. Regardless of these and other difficulties, Lorde was a brilliant thinker and speaker whose public address deserves careful study for its ramifications, not only for rhetoric scholars but also for anyone committed to social justice in all its complexity.

INFORMATION SOURCES

Research Collections and Collected Speeches

Most of Lorde's unpublished papers are held at two locations: the Lesbian Herstory Archives in Brooklyn, New York, and the Spelman College Archives in Atlanta. The Lesbian Herstory Archives is the single best resource for audio recordings of Lorde's speeches. The Spelman College Archives holds the most extensive collection of her papers and effects. In addition to several preliminary drafts for speeches, as well as folders pertaining to the forums for the public address, there is an immense body of unpublished correspondence as well as approximately sixty-three audio recordings, mostly interviews and poetry readings. Currently, Lorde's papers at Spelman are closed to all researchers except the authorized biographer, Alexis De Veaux. Lorde's most important speeches are printed in edited form in *Sister Outsider* and *A Burst of Light.*

Lorde, Audre. *A Burst of Light* [*BOL*]. Ithaca, N.Y.: Firebrand Books, 1988.

————. *Sister Outsider* [*SO*]. Trumansburg, N.Y.: Crossing Press, 1984.

Web Sites

There are currently no major Web sites appropriate to the study of Audre Lorde.

Audiovisual Materials

Lesbian Herstory Archives [*LHA*]. Brooklyn, N.Y.

Selected Critical Studies

Olson, Lester C. "Liabilities of Language: Audre Lorde Reclaiming Difference." *Quarterly Journal of Speech* 84 (1998): 448–70.

————. "On the Margins of Rhetoric: Audre Lorde Transforming Silence into Language and Action." *Quarterly Journal of Speech* 83 (1997): 49–70.

————. "The Personal, the Political, and Others:

Audre Lorde Denouncing 'The Second Sex Conference,'" followed by an exchange with Jessica Benjamin. *Philosophy and Rhetoric* 33, no. 3 (2000): 259–93.

Upton, Elaine Maria. "Audre Geraldine Lorde (1934–1992)." In *Contemporary Lesbian Writers of the United States: A Bio-Bibliographical Critical Sourcebook*, ed. Sandra Pollack and Denise D. Knight. Westport, Conn.: Greenwood, 1993.

CHRONOLOGY OF MAJOR SPEECHES

See "Research Collections and Collected Speeches" for source codes.

"The Transformation of Silence into Language and Action." Chicago, December 28, 1977. Published in *Sinister Wisdom* 6 (1978): 11–15; reprinted with revisions in Lorde's *The Cancer Journals* (San Francisco: Spinsters Ink, 1980), pp. 18–23, and with further revisions, in *SO*, pp. 40–44. Also in *Sinister Wisdom* 43/44 (Summer 1991): 40–45. None of the texts is identical to the audiotape, but the identical versions in *Sinister Wisdom* are the most accurate. Audiotape at *LHA*.

"Uses of the Erotic: The Erotic as Power." Mount Holyoke, Mass., August 15, 1978, and San Francisco, November 17, 1978. Reprinted initially as a pamphlet, *Uses of the Erotic: The Erotic as Power* (Brooklyn, N.Y.: Out & Out Books, 1978). An undated typeset version was distributed by the Lesbian Feminist Studies Clearinghouse. Reprinted in *Chrysalis* 9 (Fall 1979): 29–32; *Big Mama Rag* 7, no. 8 (September 1979): 11, 16; *Take Back the Night: Women on Pornography*, ed. Laura Lederer (New York: Morrow, 1980), pp. 295–300; *SO*, pp. 53–59; *Whole Earth Review* no. 63 (Summer 1989): 66–69; *Utne Reader* 24 (May/June 1991): 113–14. Broadcast on Pacifica Radio, March 1979. Audiotapes at *LHA* (Mount Holyoke version) as well as the GLBT Historical Society, San Francisco, and the Pacifica Radio Archives (San Francisco version). An unauthorized, shortened version, which Lorde once referred to as "a three-paragraph non-sequitur patchwork shred from it," was published by *Ms.* magazine.

"The Master's Tools Will Never Dismantle the Master's House." New York City, September 29, 1979. Printed with revisions in *This Bridge Called My Back: Writings by Radical Women of Color*, ed. Cherríe Moraga and Gloria Anzaldúa (Watertown, Mass.: Persephone Press, 1981; New York: Kitchen Table Press, 1983), pp. 98–101; *SO*, pp. 110–13. Audiotape at *LHA*.

"When Will the Ignorance End?" (keynote address to the National Third World Lesbian and Gay Conference). Washington D.C., October 13, 1979. Printed in *Off Our Backs* 9, no. 10 (November 1979): 8, 22; *Gay Insurgent* no. 6 (Summer 1980): 112–14.

"Age, Race, Class, and Sex: Women Redefining Difference" (address to the Copeland Colloquium at Amherst College). Amherst, Mass., April 2, 1980. *SO*, pp. 114–23. An undated typeset version was distributed by the Lesbian Feminist Studies Clearinghouse.

"The Uses of Anger: Women Responding to Racism" (keynote address at the National Women's Studies Association). Storrs, Conn., June 1, 1981. Printed in *Women's Studies Quarterly* 9, no. 3 (Fall 1981): 7–10; *SO*, pp. 124–33.

"Learning from the 60s." Cambridge, Mass., February 1982. *SO*, pp. 134–44; *The Rhetoric of Struggle: Public Address by African American Women*, ed. Robbie Jean Walker. New York: Garland, 1992, pp. 125–40.

"Difference and Survival" (address at the Honors Convocation, Hunter College). New York City, May 10, 1982. Printed in *Lesbians Rising: Lesbian Feminist Newspaper* (Hunter College) Spring 1982, pp. 8–9.

"Speech During the 'Litany of Commitment' Before the Civil Rights March/Martin Luther King 1963 Remembrance." Washington D.C., August 27, 1983.

"Sister Outsider" (speech at the University of Oregon). Eugene, Ore., November 12, 1984. Audiotape at Spelman College Archives.

"I Am Your Sister: Black Women Organizing Across Sexualities." Medgar Evers College, Brooklyn, N.Y., March 15–17, 1985. Printed in pamphlet titled *I Am Your Sister: Black Women Organizing Across Sexualities* (New York: Kitchen Table/Women of Color Press, 1985); *Practice: The Journal of Politics, Economics, Psychology, Sociology and Culture* 5, no. 1 (September 1987): 83–87; *BOL*, pp. 19–26.

"Sisterhood and Survival." Michigan State University, East Lansing, Mich., October 20, 1985. Printed in *The Black Scholar* 17, no. 2 (March/April 1986): 5–7.

"Turning the Beat Round" (address at the Hunter College Lesbian and Gay Community Center's Forum on Lesbian and Gay Parents of Color). New York City, October 1986. Printed in *Black/Out* 1, no. 3/4 (1987): 13–16; *Politics of the Heart: A Lesbian Parenting Anthology*, ed. Sandra Pollack and Jeanne Vaughn. Ithaca, N.Y.: Firebrand Books, 1987) *BOL*, pp. 39–48.

"A Question of Survival" (commencement speech at

Oberlin College). Oberlin, Ohio, May 29, 1989. Printed in *Gay Community News* 16, no. 46 (August 13–19, 1989): 5, 12. Videotape at Oberlin College Archives.

"Remarks to the 'I Am Your Sister Conference: Forg-

ing Global Connections Across Differences.' " Boston, October 5–8, 1990.

"Remarks at Albany, New York" (address on the occasion of Lorde's recognition as poet laureate of the State of New York). November 13, 1991.

WILMA MANKILLER (1945–)
Native American Activist and Former Principal Chief of the Cherokee Nation

CHRISTOPHER J. SKILES

Wilma Mankiller embodies the phrase "identity politics." In public life she vehemently advocates to increase awareness of both Native American and women's rights. For more than thirty years, she has helped initiate change at various levels— from congressional legislation, to community-help projects, to individual consciousness-raising about Native American and women's issues. A self-described Cherokee woman, she speaks regularly about issues from treaty rights to health care, from tribal self-determination to securing access to education for community members of all ages. Confident, purposive, and self-assured when addressing large audiences, congressional committees, or smaller, more intimate gatherings, Mankiller has a well-earned reputation for making members of her audience feel at ease. Her ability to establish rapport with audiences of all types, ranging from hostile and confrontational to genteel and friendly, suggests a mastery of public speaking that few orators achieve. Whether she is drawing on historical events, political theory, personal experience, or the lessons embedded in traditional Cherokee storytelling, Mankiller's oratory demonstrates the power of narrative as a means of persuasion. Indeed, her ability to weave together meaningful elements of narratives with straightforward arguments has helped her achieve an impressive body of political accomplishments.

Wilma Pearl Mankiller was born in the W.W. Hastings Indian Hospital on November 18, 1945, to Clare and Charley Mankiller. The sixth

of eleven children, she joined a Cherokee family long rooted in Tahlequah, Oklahoma. She has a particular fondness for her birthplace (especially her family's tract of land—Mankiller Flats), and after having lived all around the country, has moved back there. To Mankiller, her residence and the land at Mankiller Flats provide an ongoing, living connection not just to her direct past, but to the heritage of her culture and community, to her extended ancestry, and, perhaps most important, to the Earth. Indeed, Mankiller remains closely tied to her own past and that of her ancestors. She often talks about the physical connection she and her family feel to their main source of identity—their land.

It is not that the Mankillers have long owned their land. Although their connection to Mankiller Flats dates back only four generations, Mankiller and her family perceive this land as the palpable source of their spiritual being. The land in Oklahoma became Cherokee land in general, and Mankiller ancestral land in particular, only after the federal government forcefully removed the Cherokee nation from their lands in what is now the state of Georgia. Initiated by the U.S. Supreme Court's decision in *Cherokee Nation v. Georgia* in 1831 and finalized in 1839, the Trail of Tears (or, translated more directly from the Cherokee language, The Trail Where They Cried) constitutes for the Cherokee a continuing tragic memory. The forced migration of the Cherokee nation, in which tens of thousands of Cherokee suffered and thousands died, continues to evoke a collective mourning. Despite the tragic dimensions of the event, it is also a source of steadfast pride for many today, representing the ability of the Cherokee nation to endure inhumane treatment and not only to persevere, but also to rebuild in the face of adversity. The Trail of Tears left an indelible mark on the Cherokee people and still figures largely in discussions of contemporary tribal identity. Mankiller uses the Trail of Tears in her speeches as a historical analogy to contemporary political needs and obligations.

When she was nearly eleven, Mankiller and her family experienced their own removal. In the early 1950s, the U.S. Congress began a policy of terminating previously established treaties with Native American nations. Hoping that treaty termination would yield increased self-determination, a subset of these policies promised temporary housing and employment assistance to Indians agreeing to relocate to urban areas. Encouraged by the Bureau of Indian Affairs' promises, in 1956 Wilma's parents decided to move the family to San Francisco. The move had mixed results. Mankiller recalls confronting disdain and prejudice from many non-Indians, yet attributes her political awakening years later to her childhood experiences in the Hunter's Point district of San Francisco. Her relocation created detachment from her cultural identity as a Cherokee but provided her with multicultural experiences that developed sensibilities that later helped her to forge successful political alliances with members of many ethnic backgrounds. More important, however, Mankiller's participation in activities at the San Francisco Indian Center cultivated a greater understanding of, and appreciation for, the plight of Native Americans all around the country. Her experiences at the Indian Center in the late 1950s and 1960s planted the seeds of political discontent that germinated unexpectedly and furiously during the Indian occupation of Alcatraz Island in 1969.

Relocating to the San Francisco area did more than provide Mankiller with personal friendships and cultural connections to other Native Americans and members of other marginalized groups—it placed her in the heart of cultural protest during the tumultuous 1960s and early 1970s. The Black civil rights movement, and the

movements for women's rights and migratory workers' rights, found sympathetic audiences in the Bay Area. In the early 1960s, the burgeoning free speech movement at the University of California at Berkeley and San Francisco State University campuses had created a climate supportive of political and social protest. Living and working in San Francisco during the 1960s provided Mankiller with both the impetus to join political activists championing issues relevant to her own identity and opportunities to join forces with others channeling their discontent with the status quo into practical political action. In social activism Mankiller also found reasons to enroll at San Francisco State University. Her interest in Native American affairs inspired her to join the protests on Alcatraz Island, to become director of the Native American Youth Center in East Oakland, and to begin helping the Pit River Indians battle Pacific Gas and Electric over disputed land claims.

Many events influenced Mankiller's decision to return to Oklahoma in 1977, not the least of which was her increased activism in Native American affairs. Her father's death and a turbulent divorce from her husband also convinced her to seek a new beginning. She went to work for the Cherokee Nation of Oklahoma as an economic stimulus coordinator, responsible for helping members reintegrate into their communities upon completing university education programs. By 1981 she was in charge of the Cherokee Nation Community Development Department and helped initiate what became known as the Bell Community Project, which she directed. This program gained national recognition for successfully upgrading the infrastructure and quality of life for an isolated rural community. During this time she met Charlie Soap, a community activist whom she subsequently married.

The success of the Bell Community Project propelled Mankiller onto the center stage of Cherokee political life in 1983, when the incumbent chief, Ross Swimmer, asked her to run for deputy chief in the upcoming tribal election. Though the election generated considerable hostility and ill will from their opponents, Swimmer and Mankiller emerged successful. On August 14, 1983, Wilma Mankiller became the first woman to hold the office of deputy chief of the Cherokee Nation. Two years later, she made history again by ascending to the office of principal chief when Swimmer left the office to head the Bureau of Indian Affairs.

Mankiller was the first woman to function as the lead official of a major Native American nation. Her ability to successfully administer and oversee its resources—an enrolled population of more than 140,000 people, a budget that exceeded $75 million, and a land base of 7,000 square miles—was rewarded when her constituents elected her as principal chief in 1987, a position she held until 1995. By the time she left office, Mankiller had served for ten years as the highest political representative of the Cherokee Nation.

While serving as principal chief, Mankiller received a number of awards. In 1987 *Ms.* magazine named her Woman of the Year, and in 1988 San Francisco State University recognized her as Alumna of the Year. Her accomplishments have brought her honorary doctorates from eighteen educational institutions, including doctorates in humane letters from Yale University, Dartmouth College, and the University of Oklahoma. President Bill Clinton awarded her the Medal of Freedom, the highest federal commendation for civilians, in 1998 for her service to the people of the Cherokee Nation.

In her speeches, Mankiller displays a strong sensitivity toward others because of her own experience as a minority activist and her awareness of suffering, such as that of her own people. Her own battles with injuries from an accident and hereditary illness have also influenced her compassion and empathy toward all who suffer—whether from poverty, cultural dislocation, or physical illness. She has endured bouts with kidney disease and has undergone a kidney transplant. She was also in a devastating automobile injury that took the life of a close friend and left her physically impaired for years.

WILMA MANKILLER: A MESSENGER OF CHEROKEE PERSEVERANCE AND COMMUNITY STRENGTH

Mankiller uses powerful personal and cultural lessons in her oratory. Not only does she rely on narratives to help illustrate key themes and forge points of connection with her audiences, but she has lived through hardships similar to those presented in her messages. Mankiller utilizes a highly personal, very direct, and disarming manner of speaking when addressing others, and her speeches convey clear lessons about how to overcome adversity. Like many Native American orators, she strikes a balance between wanting to inform and entertain her audiences and the need to be assertive and direct. She demonstrates a remarkable confidence and comfort level when addressing audiences as varied as members of the Cherokee Nation, members of the Senate Committee on Indian Affairs, and college graduating classes. As an orator, Mankiller has a knack for reminding those listening to her that challenges that appear insurmountable can often be overcome by adopting simple truths, while challenges that appear simple often demand complex solutions.

Three characteristics stand out in Mankiller's public oratory. The first and most obvious to audiences is her personable style. Her ability to focus on her audience rather than on herself is quite remarkable. Mankiller's goal in speaking is less to provide information than to match her words to the needs of her audiences. This is not to say that she simply says what her audiences want to hear. On the contrary, the substance of her messages is often thought-provoking and unsettling, especially to non-Native audiences who may be unfamiliar with the historical tribulations of Native Americans, and of the Cherokee in particular. Nevertheless, Mankiller's delivery is relaxed and conversational—qualities that make listening to charges of racism and tales of tragedy less depressing. Commenting on Mankiller's style of leadership, noted women's rights activist Gloria Steinem said wisely: "Many leaders need to learn this new and ancient secret: one cannot raise a people's self-esteem by placing oneself above the people."

In her 1991 Inaugural Address as principal chief of the Cherokee Nation, Mankiller demonstrated that both her leadership and her speaking styles were collaborative. "I'm sure that Deputy Chief John Ketcher and I, and this Tribal Council feel the same degree of gratitude to you who have supported us during this past election, either by voting for us, saying prayers for us, or just being there when we needed you. During that time, I have received a lot of honors and recognition, much of it undeserved. Much of it should have gone to the employees, or the Tribal Council, or to the citizens of the Cherokee Nation." Not only did she refuse to take sole credit for the increasingly successful Cherokee Nation operations, although she was in many ways responsible, but she credited past and future accomplishments to the collective whole of the Cherokee Nation. "Today is a day for celebration, not just because we end one term of office and begin a new term. It's a time for celebration because the Cherokee Nation still has a strong, viable tribal government. Not only do we have a government that continued to exist, but we have a tribal government that is progressing and getting stronger. We have managed to move forward in a very affirmative way. Given our history of adversity, I think it is a testament to our

with us and help us launch this conference." With this opening sentence, she recognized the audience's importance in forging the communicative transaction to follow. The phrase "spending a little time" is brief, yet in the formal settings in which these words were uttered—an academic conference and a graduation ceremony—Mankiller's preference for dialogic communication is immediately obvious.

Mankiller also deflects attention from herself through her eagerness to entertain audience questions. In some contexts questioners occupy a position of power over those being questioned. Inverting the Socratic method, in which the teacher asks questions of the student, Mankiller consistently opens herself up to the audience, suggesting that their need for information should supersede her desire to lead them to what she believes they ought to care about. Whereas the Socratic

---

" 'It's hard to see the future with tears in your eyes.' . . . What [the Mohawk] mean by that is, don't always cry about the things that are happening around you and the things that have happened to you. Always look forward and think of the future generations in a good way."

—*Wilma Mankiller, keynote address at Lewis and Clark Conference*

---

tenacity, individually and collectively, that we have been able to keep the Cherokee government's voice alive since time immemorial."

Mankiller's collaborative communication style is evidenced in two other speeches she has delivered to an audience comprised primarily of non-Native Americans. While speaking at convocation ceremonies at Sweet Briar College on April 2, 1993, Mankiller began her speech, "Rebuilding the Cherokee Nation," by implying that she and her audience were about to engage in a dialogue: "Thank you very, very much for choosing to spend a little time with me tonight. I appreciate that. I'd like to introduce my husband, Charlie, who traveled with me from Oklahoma, who's here somewhere." In her 2002 keynote address at Penn State University's conference on the explorers Lewis and Clark, Mankiller used the same tactic: "Thank you all for coming out tonight to share a little time

method is used to demonstrate logical certitude, Mankiller's frequent use of question-and-answer periods at the end of her speeches displays a strong commitment to the needs of the audience as well as a habit of thought that leaves the speaker herself open to persuasion.

A second characteristic of Mankiller's public oratory is the use of Cherokee history and cultural teachings, either as subjects or, more usually, as frames for her presentations. While addressing an audience at Wartburg College in Waverly, Iowa, in 1992, Mankiller explained why she adopts this approach: "I don't change my focus very much. With Native people there's more focus on specific issues that we have in common . . . although my basic message is the same . . . it's a message of hope rather than focusing on all the problems and negative things, focusing on the positive things we see in our communities." Mankiller uses tragic historical stories to demonstrate the importance of persistence and to suggest the possibility of triumph. Emotionaly stirring, the stories are used to build confidence and solidarity. Mankiller's retelling at Sweet Briar College of the federal removal policy, which resulted in the Trail of Tears, is representative. That story, while tragic, also attests to the Cherokee spirit of perseverance: "Despite our best efforts and the efforts of our non-Indian friends removal did occur. In 1838 President Jackson ordered out U.S. Army Federal troops to the homes of Cherokee and rounded up Cherokees sort of like cattle. . . . By the time the last contingent of Cherokees arrived in Indian Territory in April of 1839, not really that long ago in the totality of history, a little more than 150 years ago, fully one-fourth of our entire tribe was dead." The suffering of forced removal, however, failed to diminish Cherokee optimism and initiative. Mankiller continued:

> Many people were dead, families were bitterly divided over the issue of removal itself, and yet almost immediately our people began to come together and rebuild a community. By the mid 1840s, [we had] . . . put together a new political system [and] signed a new constitution in 1839. We built beautiful institutions of government which still stand today as some of the oldest buildings in Oklahoma.

The quotations above demonstrate how out of negative conditions, positive actions and solutions emerged. Throughout this speech, Mankiller provided additional examples that demonstrated the Cherokee Nation's determination to rebuild itself following the Trail of Tears.

In a moving passage toward the end of the speech, Mankiller summed up her understanding of Cherokee character and implied that its tenacity and strength can be found in collective community action, Native and non-Native alike.

> I always tell college recruiters if you're going to go out in the more traditional communities and recruit college students, don't go out and tell them that if they get a college education that the college education will help them accumulate great personal wealth, or great personal acclaim, or help them get a BMW or whatever. Tell them that they can use their skills to help

their community, and help their family, and help their tribe, and you might get their attention. It's that sense of interdependence that I'd like to see us hang onto, and that is what we build on.

The third and final characteristic of Wilma Mankiller's public speeches is the consistency of her conclusions. Mankiller offers final words of hope that inspire her audiences to succeed in future endeavors. In contrast to the sorrowful and often tragic stories, anecdotes, and examples of her speeches, she seeks to end presentations on positive notes. Her ability to derive hope and encouragement out of the distressing and the pitiful reveals her ever-present optimism, and suggests even further why she has gained notoriety and favor among Native American and non-Native audiences alike. Illustrative of this tendency are Mankiller's concluding remarks in her 1992 keynote address at Penn State, which demonstrate the potency of her summations. Concluding with her favorite slogan, a Mohawk aphorism—"It's hard to see the future with tears in your eyes"—Mankiller invited her audience to help her and others work toward a positive and progressive future:

> What they mean by that is, don't always cry about the things that are happening around you and the things that have happened to you. Always look forward and think of the future generations in a good way. Our prayers in traditional Cherokee all begin with a similar process. They begin by saying "Let us remove negative thoughts from our mind and come together as one and focus on the task at hand." That is my favorite Cherokee prayer. And so, while many of you know the litany of statistics of poverty among our people, we also are a very hopeful people and we also are very positive. And so as you continue with this conference, I wish you well and hope you will come together as one in a very positive way and remove all the negative things from your mind so you can open a dialogue that begins with Lewis and Clark . . . that begins here at Penn State tonight.

Again, Mankiller's focus on collaboration and cooperation surfaces not just in her opening remarks, but in her concluding remarks as well. She recognizes the need to convey goodwill toward an audience. Despite the historical wrongdoings against Native people that often surface in her speeches, she does a remarkable job of initiating reconciliation and goodwill.

Wilma Mankiller has an ability to narrow cultural, ethnic, and gender differences by bridging the differences between speaker and audience. Despite using examples that highlight and exemplify the often perilous and destructive effects of identity differences, she harnesses the negativity of the past and appeals to basic human needs, desires, and experiences. Critics of Mankiller deride what they claim is her politics of division masquerading under the label of identity politics. Yet, as Mankiller's leadership and oratory make clear, confronting such differences can serve as rallying points that help build collective and collaborative efforts within various communities. Whether finding community within political and historical factions inside the Cherokee Nation, between the Cherokee Nation and its neighbors, or even between Native American and non-Native communities, Mankiller consistently makes one lesson clear: working together is the vehicle for achieving progressive change.

INFORMATION SOURCES

Reference Collections and Collected Speeches

There are no archival collections of Mankiller's work or collected speeches. Occasional Web sites carry speech texts and brief biographies of Mankiller, but no substantial collected materials are yet on the Web or in audiovisual form.

Mankiller, Wilma Pearl, and Michael Wallis. *Mankiller: A Chief and Her People.* New York: St. Martin's Press, 1993.

Selected Critical Studies

DeFrancisco, Victoria L., and Marvin Jensen. "Wilma Mankiller." In *Women's Voices in Our Time: State-* *ments by American Leaders*, ed. DeFrancisco and Jensen. Prospect Heights, Ill.: Waveland Press, 1994.

Duncan, Russell. "Risen from the Dead: American Indian Mythmakers." *American Studies in Denmark (Scandinavia)* 30 (1998): 50–59.

Janda, Sarah Eppler. "The Intersection of Feminism and Indianness in the Activism of LaDonna Harris and Wilma Mankiller." *Dissertation.* University of Oklahoma, 2002.

King, Janis L. "Justificatory Rhetoric for a Female Candidate: A Case Study of Wilma Mankiller." *Women's Studies in Communication* 13 (1990): 21–38.

Selected Biographies

Glassman, Bruce. *Wilma Mankiller: Chief of the Cherokee Nation.* New York: Blackbirch Press, 1992.

Johansen, Bruce E., and Donald A. Grinde. *The Encyclopedia of Native American Biography: Six Hundred Life Stories of Important People, from Powhatan to Wilma Mankiller.* New York: DaCapo Press, 1998.

Rand, Jacki Thompson. *Wilma Mankiller.* Austin, Tex.: Raintree Steck-Vaughn, 1993.

CHRONOLGY OF MAJOR SPEECHES

"Inaugural Speech as Deputy Chief of the Cherokee Nation." Tahlequah, Okla., August 14, 1983.

"Inaugural Address as the Principal Chief of the Cherokee Nation." Tahlequah, Okla., 1987.

"Inaugural Address as the Principal Chief of the Cherokee Nation." August 14, 1991. In *Women's Voices in Our Time: Statements by American Leaders*, ed. Victoria L. DeFrancisco and Marvin D. Jensen. Prospect Heights, Ill.: Waveland Press, 1994.

"Rebuilding the Cherokee Nation." Sweet Briar College, Sweet Briar, Va., April 2, 1993. Available at gos.sbc.edu

"Keynote Address" (Lewis and Clark, the Unheard Voices: A Conference). Pennsylvania State University, November 14, 2002. Available at lewisandclark.outreach.psu.edu

THURGOOD MARSHALL (1908–1993)
Lawyer, U.S. Supreme Court Justice

STEPHEN A. SMITH

Known as "Mr. Civil Rights," Thurgood Marshall was one of the heroes in the battles to secure the constitutional rights of Black Americans, and he had a leading role in that drama on the stage of public life for almost 60 years. Marshall is most remembered as the first African American justice of the U.S. Supreme Court, on which he served from 1967 to 1991, but his earlier career as a legal advocate for civil rights forever changed the nation far more than his opinions on the Supreme Court. "When I think of great American lawyers, I think of Thurgood Marshall, Abe Lincoln and Daniel Webster," said Georgetown law professor Thomas G. Krattenmaker. And Marshall, he told biographer Juan Williams, "is certainly the most important lawyer of the 20th century." As an attorney in private practice and later leading the NAACP Legal Defense Fund assault on segregation, Marshall fought and won hard legal cases throughout the South, culminating in the landmark *Brown v. Board of Education* and providing the rhetorical structure and the constitutional warrant for the political success of the civil rights movement.

Thurgood Marshall was born in Baltimore in 1908, a place and time that reflected the segregated praxis of American life, into his family that was securely among the middle class on the Black side of the color line. His mother, Norma Williams Marshall, was a teacher in the segregated elementary schools. A graduate of Coppin Normal who had completed additional graduate work at Morgan State and Columbia University, she emphasized the value of education and hoped that Thurgood would become a dentist, but it seems that he was adept with his own mouth in other ways. One neighbor recalled that Thurgood was "a jolly boy who always had something to say"; however, his jovial nature and quick wit were not always appreciated in school. Historian Richard Kluger wrote that Marshall's grade school principal often required him to remain after school and memorize portions of the Constitution as a consequence of his conduct, although his high school history teacher remembered him more charitably as "a good, earnest, argumentative student."

His father, Will Marshall, had been the first Black to serve on a grand jury in Baltimore, and he often took his son to the trial courts there. The elder Marshall was known for his "tendency to disputation," and that must have been infectious. Biographer Randall Bland reported that Thurgood later remarked, "He never told me to become a lawyer, but he turned me into one. He did it by teaching me to argue, by challenging my logic on every point, by making me prove every statement I made."

Graduating from high school with an admirable record in 1925, but barred from the University of Maryland and not quite qualified for an Ivy League institution, Marshall enrolled at Lincoln University, "the Black Princeton," at Oxford, Pennsylvania. There he first engaged the writings of W.E.B. Du Bois, Carter Woodson, and Langston Hughes, and he participated in an action to integrate the seating at the local movie theater. While he maintained a B average in his coursework for a Humanities degree, he worked to project an image of never studying and was suspended for a fraternity prank. Marshall was active in the Forensic Society and was an outstanding debater, leading the Lincoln squad to numerous victories over such schools as Bates, Bowdoin, and Colby. Biographers Michael Davis and Hunter Clark record that, in a letter to his father, he claimed, "If I were taking debate for credit, I would be the biggest honor student they ever had around here."

During his senior year at Lincoln, Marshall decided to attend law school, because he "loved speaking in public and thinking on his feet and dealing with people face to face," but again his choices were limited by law. Returning to Baltimore, he commuted by train to attend Howard Law School in Washington, D.C. There he came into his own, being mentored by Dean Charles Hamilton Houston, working with professors William Hastie and James Narbit preparing cases for the National Association for the Advancement of Colored People (NAACP), and attracting the attention of the organization's executive secretary, Walter White. The legal curriculum was enriched during his student days by lecture series including Justice Felix Frankfurter and Clarence Darrow as speakers, and he sometimes cut classes to watch such legal giants as John W. Davis argue cases before the Supreme Court.

After graduating as valedictorian in 1933, Marshall hung out his shingle in Baltimore and developed a broad, if not particularly lucrative, private practice. His personal qualities helped him to rise quickly to prominence in the community. As Rev. A. J. Payne recalled, "He showed his courage and tenacity, and the people liked him, the common people and the professional people both. . . . People in the community looked up to him. He was never arrogant and always accessible." He also helped reorganize the local NAACP, and he was retained to handle the civil rights cases of interest to Carl Murphy, the editor of the local newspaper, *Afro-American*. Murphy's daughter remembered him during that time: "He gave you the impression that he had taken the time to think over what he said. . . . He exuded confidence and seemed very solid—a born leader. His . . . size helped him give that impression, that and his outgoing personality. He was a bundle of energy—and never a stuffed shirt."

Marshall joined the NAACP field staff in 1936 as Assistant Counsel, and in 1938 he followed Houston as Counsel, becoming, at age thirty, the most important and most visible black attorney in the United States. He was Director-Counsel of the Legal Defense Fund from 1941 to 1961, planning and winning the legal assault on segregated America. In 1961, he was appointed by President Kennedy to the U.S. Court of Appeals for the Second Circuit, and in 1965, by President Johnson, as solicitor general of the United States, serving for two years as the government's advocate before the Supreme Court. In 1967, President Johnson nominated Marshall as the first Black associate justice of the Supreme Court, a position he held until he retired in 1991. He died on January 24, 1993.

THURGOOD MARSHALL AS CONSTITUTIONAL CRITIC

Marshall had memorized the Constitution as a schoolboy, but his entire adult life was spent giving meaning to the dry words of the text—in public speeches in the community, as an advocate at the bar, in his extrajudicial speeches to legal organizations, and in his opinions from the bench. He spoke from his own experiences, and he always held that the Constitution was a living document to be read and interpreted through the lens of real-life experiences.

As an attorney in private practice in Baltimore, Marshall was active in bringing the Constitution to life in the community. A. J. Payne recalled, "He spoke around at the churches a lot, and when he talked it would be about our rights." In 1934, working with Charles Houston from the NAACP national office, Marshall challenged the University of Maryland Law School's racial admission policies on behalf of Donald Murray. The victory in the state courts was the first such test of segregated education in a legal strategy that would occupy most of his public career as an attorney. It was a personal victory for Marshall, who had been barred from attending the school, and it was an important public victory as well. Juanita Jackson Mitchell, a local activist, later said of the case, "He brought us the Constitution like Moses brought the people the Ten Commandments."

Joining the NAACP field staff in 1936 and later heading the legal efforts for the national office and the Legal Defense Fund (LDF), Marshall continued to bring the Constitution to the people through public speaking while he argued its meaning and application in the courts. In 1940, for example, the first year of his twenty-one-year tenure as director-counsel of the LDF, he gave twenty-four public speeches, eighteen of which were in Baltimore and points south. During a three-week period in May of that year he spoke in Louisville, Kentucky; Dallas, Corpus Christi, and Houston, Texas; New Orleans, Louisiana; Mobile and Birmingham, Alabama; Atlanta, Georgia; and Asheville, North Carolina to mass meetings organized by state and local NAACP branches.

Marshall's legal strategy to secure rights relied on a parallel public campaign to recruit both lawyers and plaintiffs. In his book on Marshall's speeches, Mark Tushnet observes that his speeches during this period were meant to "push the members along a path he wanted them to follow, while their responses suggested some limits to the pace and direction of the litigation." In an extemporaneous speech to the National Bar Association, "Federal Civil Rights Statutes" (1940), Marshall urged Black attorneys to join the "struggle to obtain full citizenship rights for all American citizens" and to secure legal redress "through intelligent use of the federal [civil rights] statutes." Elaborating on the importance of the civil rights statutes in a speech titled "The Legal Attack to Secure Civil Rights," delivered to the NAACP Wartime Conference (1942), Marshall again drew public attention to the effective use of existing federal legislation—and the Fourteenth Amendment—in overcoming barriers to voting, serving on juries, equalizing teachers' salaries, and purchasing property despite restrictive covenants. Although the NAACP had not yet successfully challenged public school segregation, he stated his position that the Constitution and existing statutes could "be used to attack *every* form of discrimination against Negroes by public school systems." He reminded the delegates that they could "move no faster than the individuals who have been discriminated against," and that "the real job has to be done by the Negro population with whatever friends of the other races that are willing to join in."

Soon after the end of World War II, Marshall and the NAACP were ready to launch the legal assault on segregated education. In a speech to Black educators, "The Real Party of Interest Must Be the Child" (1945), Marshall seemed to reject Booker T. Washington's "Atlanta Compromise" and the arguments of W.E.B. Du Bois, contending, "There is little use in removing the barriers to economic security so as to place the Negro in fair competition with other citizens unless at the same time we make provision for educational facilities which will give our Negro youth the necessary educational background to stand their ground." Furthermore, Marshall be-

lieved that equal educational rights could not be achieved without equal political rights. When he accepted the Spingarn Medal, for his contribution to advancing the status of the Black population, at the NAACP Convention the following year, Marshall's speech, "The Essence of Democratic Government" (1946), reminded his audience and the nation that the victory over fascism abroad had not secured full freedom for the victors: "The body of America must throw off the disease of segregation and second-class citizenship or give up the spirit of democracy." He held that American citizens possessed certain rights merely by being born in a democracy, and he stressed the importance of political rights in both securing other freedoms and enjoying them.

Marshall presented eloquent testimony to the President's Commission on Civil Rights on April 17, 1947, calling for broad federal action to assure civil and political rights for all Americans, but there was only passing mention made of the fact that Blacks did not enjoy equal educational facilities. However, in June the NAACP Annual Conference unanimously adopted a resolution signaling a new position on the concept of separate-but-equal public education. That fall Marshall addressed the Texas State Conference of the NAACP and articulated the meaning of those resolutions in a speech titled "Complete Opposition to All Forms of Segregation" (1947). The resolution had declared, "Complete equality of educational opportunity cannot be obtained in a dual system of education," and Marshall told his audience, "It no longer takes courage to fight for mere equality in a separate school system." Blacks had been "fighting for equality of education in separate schools for more than eighty years," he said, but "segregation and discrimination are so tied up together that you can't tell one from the other." Segregation meant second-class citizenship, and it was time for a new strategy. The obvious conclusion, he said, was "that the only sane approach is a direct attack on segregation *per se.*"

The direct attack on segregated public schools soon came in five cases that would be remembered forever as *Brown v. Board of Education.* Each case was argued separately, allowing the NAACP team to develop different points in each, and Marshall was the legal strategist without peer. Marshall had litigated the case from South Carolina at the trial level, and lawyer Robert Carter said, "In the courtroom, Marshall was the consummate professional. I heard him make several splendid arguments before the Supreme Court. But perhaps the best courtroom performance I ever saw him give was his cross-examination . . . in *Briggs v. Elliott*." That performance both devastated the state's chief witness and exhilarated the Black audience in the courtroom. Nonetheless, to no one's surprise, he lost at the trial level in South Carolina.

Marshall was again responsible for the argument in *Briggs* when the cases came before the Supreme Court; South Carolina relied upon the venerable John W. Davis. Davis had been the Democratic presidential nominee in 1924, had served as U.S. solicitor general, had argued more than 140 cases before the Court, and was a mem-

appearance a continuation of dialogues they had had over the years. While the case was specifically *Briggs v. Elliott*, the subject was a long-standing one between Thurgood and the Court—the status of blacks and the role of the Constitution in defining, perhaps advancing, that status to one of full equality." In terms of delivery, he noted, "Thurgood spoke slowly, for him, on this occasion, making sure to articulate his words in an educated Southern way, rather than in the country style he often used." Richard Kluger, the foremost historian of the case, also commented on the effectiveness of Marshall's oral argument: "In some of his appearances before the Court, he was good; in others, he tended to be a bit on the dull side. On this day, he was at his best. He took the offensive from the start, and he held it throughout the argument."

In the mid-1950s, Marshall reportedly believed that Martin Luther King, Jr. was an "opportunist" and a "first rate rabble-rouser," but Marshall still agreed to prepare the legal brief for the Montgomery Improvement Association. Marshall's brief was successful, and the Supreme Court declared Montgomery's segregated bus system to be unconstitutional.

---

ber of a prominent Wall Street firm. Their arguments before the Supreme Court were high drama. Oral arguments in the cases consumed ten hours on December 9–11, 1952, and approximately 300 people packed the Supreme Court chamber, with another 400 lined up waiting to get in.

Each of the cases was important, but the rhetorical encounter between Davis and Marshall was the main act. Davis was confident, and his florid eloquence captured the attention of the justices as he presented his case almost uninterrupted. Marshall's presentation was equally compelling for different reasons. His colleague Jack Greenberg described it well: "He hovered imposingly over the lectern as he addressed the justices familiarly, but respectfully. He had been before the Court many times, and the justices knew him well and trusted him." Some of them, Greenberg said, "may well have considered this

Even after these historic arguments, the Supreme Court remained reluctant to reach a decision, and requested reargument the following year on a number of points. Greenberg reports that Marshall's performance during reargument was somewhat uninspiring, but the Court had been presented with reasons that would require it to decide whether segregation was constitutional. Changes in the composition of the Court, including the appointment of Earl Warren as chief justice, were fortuitous, and Marshall had "adopted a powerful rhetorical strategy," providing the Court with a plausible framework for overruling *Plessy v. Ferguson* and, more important, that overruling it was the right thing to do." On May 17, 1954, the Supreme Court unanimously declared that separate educational facilities were inherently unequal.

The momentous and historic victory in *Brown*,

the highlight in Marshall's career as a legal advocate, made him in great demand as a speaker and provided him with a much larger audience beyond the meetings of the NAACP. The opportunity to explain the meaning of *Brown* was welcome, and he accepted both traditional speaking engagements and numerous appearances on the new medium of television to tell the story. Yet, one of the most important speeches of this period was delivered at Jackson, Mississippi, to the NAACP State Conference. In his speech, "Emmett Till, Mississippi Justice, and the Rest of Us" (1955), Marshall confronted the horror of violence and placed the blame on all who tolerated it. Recapping the racial hatred and perverted justice in Mississippi, he asserted defiantly: "One thing we are certain of: Nothing that has occurred to date and indeed nothing more can happen which will prevent us from using every lawful means of attaining our rights. We will continue to put emphasis on the lawful means. In other words," he said for those who might not understand, "all of the White Citizens Councils, all of the state officials, and all other groups cannot intimidate American citizens who happen to have been born black."

Marshall's entire career had been devoted to achieving legal redress, and he was deeply committed to continuing the struggle through the instrument of law. The victory of the *Brown* decision and the outrage over the unpunished killing of Emmett Till, however, combined to bring forth a civil rights movement with an ambivalent attitude toward law and justice in the South. Marshall was upset by the confrontational approach employed in the Montgomery bus boycott and by other efforts to achieve change through civil disobedience. Davis and Clark report that he called Martin Luther King, Jr. an "opportunist" and a "first rate rabble-rouser," but King was allowed to address the NAACP convention in January 1956, and Marshall prepared the brief that spring for the Montgomery Improvement Association in the case whose decision declared the segregated bus system to be unconstitutional.

Continuing to wage the legal battle against segregation, Marshall was victorious in twenty-nine of the thirty-two Supreme Court cases on which he worked during his years with the

NAACP. He was appointed to the U.S. Court of Appeals by President Kennedy in 1961, serving in that position until he was appointed solicitor general in 1965 by President Johnson. None of his appellate opinions were overruled by the Supreme Court, and he had an impressive record as solicitor general, winning fourteen of the nineteen cases he argued for the government before the Supreme Court.

President Johnson nominated Marshall as associate justice of the Supreme Court in 1967, only thirteen years after his victory in *Brown*, and he served in that position for twenty-four years. As a member of the Court, Marshall limited his public speaking to legal groups, and most of these addresses dealt with the broad issues before the Court during his tenure.

The last major formal speech of Marshall's career was, perhaps, the most memorable, and it was certainly the most controversial. His address, "Reflections on the Bicentennial of the Constitution" (1987), delivered to about 150 attendees of the San Francisco Patent and Trademark Law Association annual seminar on Maui, Hawaii, on May 6, 1987, caught the nation's attention, drawing both harsh criticism and strong praise. The speech made the front page of the *Washington Post*, the *New York Times*, *USA Today*, and most major newspapers. Daniel Popeo of the Washington Legal Foundation called for Marshall's resignation; Eugene Thomas of the American Bar Association called the comments inappropriate; and Assistant Attorney General William Bradford Reynolds devoted a major speech to countering Marshall's views.

At first, Marshall had planned to avoid participation in the bicentennial celebration, even though it was being organized by former Chief Justice Warren Burger; however, in early 1986 he contacted an old friend, Prof. John Hope Franklin, for materials documenting the role of slavery in constitutional history and the ways in which it had been finessed by compromise. When Franklin complied with the request, Marshall replied, "Thanks so much for the material on the Bicentennial celebration or whatever else it is. You have given me just the material which will be used when the appropriate time arrives. As of now, everything is so hush hush around here. I don't know what is going on about the anniversary. I think I will wait to be asked to do something and let them have it."

As Marshall approached the lectern to address his audience more than a year later, there was no indication that it would be anything but another formulaic recitation of platitudes about the glory of the founding. He asked the audience to "recall the achievements of our Founders and the knowledge and experience that inspired them, the nature of the government they established, its origins, its character, and its ends, and the rights and privileges of citizenship, as well as its attendant responsibilities," slyly quoting from reports prepared by the Bicentennial Commission. Then he declared, "I cannot accept this invitation, for I do not believe that the meaning of the Constitution was forever 'fixed' at the Philadelphia Convention. Nor do I find the wisdom, foresight, and sense of justice exhibited by the framers particu-

mise which, under other circumstances, would not have been made." Marshall did not intend to let the celebrants off so easily, reminding them that "the effects of the framers' compromise have remained for generations. They arose from the contradiction between guaranteeing liberty and justice to all, and denying both to Negroes."

Indicating his views on both the official celebration and the appropriate way to read the Constitution, Marshall explained: "I plan to celebrate the bicentennial of the Constitution as a living document, including the Bill of Rights and the other amendments protecting individual freedoms and human rights." The Constitution was now much more than it had been 200 years earlier, and Thurgood Marshall—as a private attorney, as counsel for the NAACP Legal Defense Fund, as a judge on the Court of Appeals, as solicitor general, and as associate justice of

---

The first African American appointed to the U.S. Supreme Court, as a lawyer for the NAACP Thurgood Marshall had argued thirty-two cases before the Supreme Court. He had won twenty-nine of them.

---

larly profound. To the contrary," he said, "the government they devised was defective from the start, requiring several amendments, a civil war, and momentous social transformation to attain the system of constitutional government, and its respect for the individual freedoms and human rights, that we hold as fundamental today."

While Frederick Douglass had praised the Declaration of Independence and the Constitution in 1852, charging that the promises of the texts had been betrayed by prejudice in execution and interpretation, Marshall's faith was less in the original writing of the text and more in the political wrenching and judicial rendering of its subsequent life. Anticipating his critics, Marshall acknowledged that "when the unpleasant truth of the history of slavery in America is mentioned during this bicentennial year," it would be claimed that "the Constitution was a product of its times and embodied a compro-

the Supreme Court—had done much to make it so, to read the amended text as a document of freedom, to translate the promise of its ideas into the order of the day.

After twenty-four years on the Supreme Court, Thurgood Marshall resigned in 1991. Less than two years later he was buried in Arlington National Cemetery after services in the National Cathedral. In reflecting upon Marshall's contribution to the nation, Judge Irving R. Kaufmann said he "achieved national prominence as a staunch advocate of racial equality and social justice at a time when it was essential, but not fashionable, to be one." Through his honest oratory and the reason of his rhetoric, wrote biographer Carl Rowan, Thurgood Marshall "was able to sear the nation's conscience and move hearts formerly strangled by hoary intransigence. And because of him, we are all more free."

INFORMATION SOURCES

Research Collections and Collected Speeches

Records and papers pertaining to Thurgood Marshall's life and accomplishments are widely available and are housed in a variety of locations.

National Association for the Advancement of Colored People Collection [*NAACP*], Manuscript Division, Library of Congress, Washington, D.C. This collection includes manuscript and typescript copies of speeches by Marshall from 1940 to 1961 and press clippings relating to his speeches.

Papers of Thurgood Marshall [*PTM*], Manuscript Division, Library of Congress, Washington, D.C. This collection contains Marshall materials from the period 1949–91; however, the bulk of materials are from the years 1961–91, documenting Marshall's career as a judge of the Second Circuit Court of Appeals, solicitor general, and associate justice of the Supreme Court. It covers 231.6 linear feet and contains approximately 173,700 items in 580 boxes. A finding aid, prepared in 2001, is available online at http://www.loc.gov/rr/mss/

Smith, J. Clay, Jr., ed. *Supreme Justice: Speeches and Writings, Thurgood Marshall*. Philadelphia: University of Pennsylvania Press, 2003.

Tushnet, Mark V., ed. *Thurgood Marshall: His Speeches, Writings, Arguments, Opinions, and Reminiscences*. Chicago: Lawrence Hill Books, 2001.

Web Sites

Federal Bureau of Investigation [*FBI*], Department of Justice, Washington, D.C., has 1,394 pages of records from the headquarters and New York Office files relating to Marshall's activities with the NAACP and background investigations conducted in connection with his appointment as a federal judge and Supreme Court justice. Several of the reports contain comments on Marshall's courtroom demeanor and his public speeches to various groups. It is available online at http://foia.fbi.gov

Audiovisual Material

Columbia University [*CU*], Oral History Collection, New York City. Holdings include an extensive audiotaped interview with Marshall covering his life before appointment to the Supreme Court, conducted by Ed Erwin on February 15, 1977; two interviews focusing primarily on Marshall's work with the NAACP, conducted by Mark Tushnet on May 23 and August 2, 1989; and an interview regarding Marshall's work on cases of racial discrimination in the military, conducted by Thomas Buell, April 9, 1980.

Federal Judicial Center [*FJC*], Washington, D.C., holds twenty-seven hours of digital audiotape interviews with Marshall. Stephen Carter was the interviewer, and the taping was done in nineteen sessions in Marshall's chambers at the Supreme Court from March to November 1992. The interviews cover his whole career, although most of them focus on his work before he joined the Supreme Court.

National Archives and Records Administration [*NARA*], Washington, D.C., holds audiotapes of oral arguments before the Supreme Court dating from October 10, 1955. The collection is conveniently indexed, and researchers can make copies of the tapes for educational purposes. Marshall's presentations as director-counsel for the NAACP from 1955 to 1961 are available, as are his arguments for the government as solicitor general of the United States (1965–67).

Selected Critical Materials

Amsterdam, Anthony G. "Thurgood Marshall's Image of the Blue-Eyed Child in *Brown*." *New York University Law Review* 68, no. 2 (May 1993): 226–36.

Baugh, Joyce A. "Justice Thurgood Marshall: Advocate for Gender Justice." *Western Journal of Black Studies* 20, no. 4 (Winter 1996): 195–206.

Dickens, Milton, and Ruth E. Schwartz. "Oral Argument Before the Supreme Court: *Marshall v. Davis* in the School Segregation Cases." *Quarterly Journal of Speech* 57, no. 1 (February 1971): 32–42.

Goldman, Roger, and David Gallen. *Thurgood Marshall: Justice for All*. New York: Carroll & Graf, 1992.

Greenberg, Jack. *Crusaders in the Courts: How a Dedicated Band of Lawyers Fought for the Civil Rights Revolution*. New York: Basic Books, 1994.

Hines, Erma Waddy. "Thurgood Marshall's Speeches on Equality and Justice Under the Law, 1965–1967." Ph.D. dissertation, Louisiana State University, 1979.

Kennedy, Anthony M. "The Voice of Thurgood Marshall." *Stanford Law Review* 44 (Summer 1992): 1221–25.

Kluger, Richard. *Simple Justice: The History of Brown v. Board of Education and Black America's Struggle for Equality*, rev. and enl. ed. New York: Knopf, 2004.

Malakoff, Burton. "A Comparison of the Strategies in Three Oral Arguments Before the United States Supreme Court." Master's thesis, Pacific Lutheran University, 1976.

O'Connor, Sandra Day. "Thurgood Marshall: The Influence of a Raconteur." *Stanford Law Review* 44 (June 1992): 1217–20.

Parry-Giles, Trevor. "Character, the Constitution, and the Ideological Embodiment of 'Civil Rights' in the 1967 Nomination of Thurgood Marshall to the Supreme Court." *Quarterly Journal of Speech* 82, no. 4 (November 1996): 364–82.

Williams, Jayme Coleman. "A Rhetorical Analysis of Thurgood Marshall's Arguments Before the Supreme Court in the Public School Segregation Controversy." Master's thesis, Ohio State University, 1959.

Selected Biographies

Bland, Randall W. *Private Pressure on Public Law: The Legal Career of Justice Thurgood Marshall.* Lanham, Md.: University Press of America, 1993.

Davis, Michael D., and Hunter R. Clark. *Thurgood Marshall: Warrior at the Bar, Rebel on the Bench.* Secaucus, N.J.: Carol Publishing Group, 1994.

Rowan, Carl T. *Dream Makers, Dream Breakers: The World of Justice Thurgood Marshall.* Boston: Little, Brown, 1993.

Tushnet, Mark V. *Making Civil Rights Law: Thurgood Marshall and the Supreme Court, 1936–1961.* New York: Oxford University Press, 1994.

———. *Making Constitutional Law: Thurgood Marshall and the Supreme Court, 1961–1991.* New York: Oxford University Press, 1997.

Williams, Juan. *Thurgood Marshall: American Revolutionary.* New York: Times Books, 1998.

CHRONOLOGY OF MAJOR SPEECHES

See "Research Collections and Collected Speeches" for source codes.

"Federal Civil Rights Statutes" (National Bar Association Convention). Columbus, Ohio, August 3, 1940. *NAACP*, group II, box A533.

"The Legal Attack to Secure Civil Rights" (NAACP Wartime Conference). Chicago, July 13, 1942. *NAACP*, group II, box A534.

"The Real Party of Interest Must Be the Child" (Association of College and Secondary Schools for Negroes). Nashville, Tenn., December 6, 1945. *NAACP*, group II, box A534.

"The Essence of Democratic Government" (NAACP National Convention). 1946. *NAACP*, group II, box A534.

"Complete Opposition to All Forms of Segregation" (Texas State Conference of NAACP branches). Denison, Tex., September 5, 1947. *NAACP*, group II, box A535.

"Recent Supreme Court Decisions and the History of the Fourteenth Amendment" (Fisk University Institute on Race Relations). Nashville, Tenn., July 5, 1950. *NAACP*, group II, box A535.

"The Effect of Recent Supreme Court Decisions on the American Way of Life" (National Dental Association Convention). Chicago, August 8, 1951. *NAACP*, group II, box A535.

"The Bill of Rights for Negro Labor in America" (National Convention of the Congress of Industrial Organizations). Atlantic City, N.J., December 3, 1952. *NAACP*, group II, box A535.

"The Remaining Vestiges of Slavery" (National Urban League Conference). Philadelphia, September 8, 1953. *NAACP*, group II, box A536.

"Oral Argument Before the Supreme Court of the United States in *Briggs v. Elliott.*" Washington, D.C., 1954. In *Argument: The Oral Argument Before the Supreme Court in Brown v. Board of Education of Topeka, 1952–55,* ed. Leon Friedman. New York: Chelsea House, 1969.

"The Meaning of the Decisions: Bringing the Practice of Democracy in Line with Our Democratic Principles." (NAACP Annual Convention). Atlantic City, N.J., June 22, 1955. *NAACP*, group II, box A536.

"Towards the Final Phase of the Anti-Segregation Struggle" (American Teachers Association Meeting). Houston, Tex., July 24, 1955. *NAACP*, group II, box A536.

"Brainwashing with a Vengeance" (Virginia State Conference of the NAACP branches). Charlottesville, Va., October 9, 1955. *NAACP*, group II, box A536.

"Emmett Till, Mississippi Justice, and the Rest of Us" (Mississippi State Conference of NAACP branches). Jackson, Miss., November 6, 1955. *NAACP*, group II, box A536.

"The End of the Segregated Solid South" (South Carolina State Conference of NAACP branches). Columbia, S.C., November 27, 1955. *NAACP*, group II, box A536.

"The Real Task: Bringing Established Principles of Law into Everyday Practice in Local Communities" (AFL–CIO Convention). New York City, December 7, 1955. *NAACP*, group II, box A536.

"The Fifty Year Fight for Civil Rights" (Freedom Fund Report dinner). New York City, July 16, 1959. *PTM*, box 579, folder 16.

"Individual and Human Dignity" (Commencement address, Kalamazoo College). Kalamazoo, Mich., June 4, 1961. *PTM*, box 579, folder 16.

"Our Goal: World Peace Through Law" (Philippine Constitution Association). Manila, Philippines, February 8, 1968. *PTM*, box 579, folder 4.

"The Continuing Challenge of the Fourteenth Amendment" (University of Georgia Law School forum). Athens, Ga., September 30, 1968. *Georgia Law Review* 3 (1968): 1–10.

"Group Action in Pursuit of Justice" (James Madison lecture, New York University School of Law). New York City, April 17, 1969. *New York University Law Review*, 44 (1969): 661–72.

"Remarks on the Death Penalty" (Second Circuit ju-

dicial conference). Hershey, Pa., September 7, 1985. *Columbia Law Review*, 86 (1986): 1–8.

"Reflections on the Bicentennial of the Constitution" (San Francisco Patent and Trademark Law Association seminar). Maui, Hawaii, May 6, 1987. *PTM*, box 574, folder 11; *Harvard Law Review* 101 (November 1987): 1–5.

WILLIAM (BILL) PAUL McCARTNEY (1940-)
Founder and Former President of Promise Keepers

JENNIFER YOUNG ABBOTT

William (Bill) McCartney rose to fame first as the head football coach for the University of Colorado and later as the founder and president of the evangelical Christian men's group Promise Keepers. Although disparate, both football and Promise Keepers showcased McCartney's skills as a motivational speaker. As a football coach, McCartney helped to motivate the Colorado Buffaloes to win a national championship in 1990. As a spiritual "coach," he helped to inspire nearly 600,000 Christian men attend a Promise Keepers rally in Washington, D.C., in October 1997. McCartney adapted the speaking skills that he acquired while coaching football to his speaking engagements with Promise Keepers. Fiery and plainspoken, he charged his religious audience members with "winning" their society for Jesus Christ, and he offered a specific "game plan" to accomplish the task.

McCartney's football career began at Riverview High School in Michigan, where he showed prowess as a linebacker. His talent earned him a football scholarship to the University of Missouri. He graduated from college in 1962 with a degree in education, and soon after, he married Lynne Marie "Lyndi" Taussig, with whom he had four children. While raising his family, McCartney coached football and basketball at several Missouri and Michigan high schools, and in 1974 joined the football coaching staff at the University of Michigan. Eight years later, the University of Colorado hired him as its head football coach.

After a rocky start, McCartney coached his team to the Associated Press National Championship in 1990, as well as to three Big Eight Conference championships and several bowl appearances. He won numerous coaching awards, including the Big Eight Conference Coach of the Year in 1985, 1989, and 1990, and the National Coach of the Year in 1989.

Football was not McCartney's only passion, however. Influenced by his devoutly Roman Catholic father, William Patrick, McCartney fervently practiced Catholicism throughout his youth and early adulthood. In 1974, he experienced a spiritual "rebirth" at a Campus Crusade for Christ meeting in Brighton, Michigan, when he "accepted" Jesus Christ as his savior and became an evangelical Christian. McCartney continued to attend Catholic churches, however, until 1988, when he joined a Vineyard church—a nondenominational church associated with the Word of God Community and based in California.

McCartney's religious fervor spilled over into his coaching. McCartney regularly led his University of Colorado football players in prayer, Bible readings, and chapel services, and he appointed his Vineyard pastor, Rev. James Ryle, as the team's chaplain. McCartney was criticized for these actions, especially by the Colorado branch of the American Civil Liberties Union (ACLU), which in 1985 threatened to sue McCartney for forcing players to practice his religion. Faced with the lawsuit, McCartney made the activities voluntary, and the ACLU ended its legal action.

McCartney next aimed his religious advocacy at a broader audience. Beginning in 1988, he spoke against abortion at rallies sponsored by advocacy groups such as Right to Life and Operation Rescue. He also spoke against homosexuality at a press conference in 1992 while answering questions about his board membership with Colorado for Family Values, a conservative organization that sponsored a Colorado constitutional amendment to prohibit antidiscrimination laws directed at homosexuals. McCartney declared that homosexuality is an "abomination of almighty God"—a statement for which he was reprimanded by University of Colorado President Judith Albino because the press conference was affiliated with the university.

McCartney ultimately channeled his religious energy into Promise Keepers, the evangelical Christian men's organization that he founded in 1990. He conceived the idea for Promise Keepers during a trip to a Fellowship of Christian Athletes meeting in Pueblo, Colorado, with Dave Wardell, then Colorado chairman for the Fellowship. Having witnessed the large number of fatherless young men whom he had recruited to college football, McCartney focused Promise Keepers on helping men to make and keep commitments to their families, churches, communities, and each other. Each year since the group was founded, Promise Keepers has organized two-day conferences for men at football stadiums and coliseums throughout the United States. These conferences typically have consisted of singing, prayer, and speeches by Christian speakers. Since the earliest gatherings of the organization, McCartney has frequently closed the conferences as the keynote speaker—to great applause. As one *Denver Post* reporter recalled, "In his first Promise Keepers speech at Folsom Stadium in 1991, he received five standing ovations—in the rain."

Indeed, McCartney's motivational speaking abilities have accounted—at least in part—for his success as both a religious leader and a football coach. Several of his University of Colorado football players told a *Denver Post* reporter in 1994 that "his pep talks before Nebraska games should be taped and played before wars. He can rattle the walls during coaches' meetings." Even one of McCartney's critics, Alfred Ross, founder and executive director of the Center for Democracy Studies, described McCartney as a "world-class motivator."

Promise Keepers' growth during its early years reflected McCartney's ability to attract and inspire large numbers of men. Promise Keepers drew seventy men to its first gathering at Denver in 1990, and attracted larger numbers each year, culminating in 1.1 million men at twenty-two nationwide conferences in 1996. Promise Keepers grew so much during its first few years that McCartney retired from football at the close of the 1995 season in order to devote more time to the organization and his family. In 1997, Promise Keepers held its largest single public gathering. Nearly 600,000 men attended the "Stand in the Gap" rally on Independence Mall in Washington, D.C. That same year, Promise Keepers' budget reached $117 million, gathered primarily through donations, event fees, and sales of Promise Keepers merchandise. Since 1997, Promise Keepers' U.S. numbers have dwindled to 172,000 men and its budget has dropped to $27 million. However, the organization expanded overseas in 1999, and began targeting male teenagers in 2001 and male prisoners in 2003. McCartney resigned as Promise Keepers president on October 1, 2003, to care for his wife, who was suffering from emphysema.

"COACH MAC": MOTIVATOR

Referring to his football career during his speech at a 2000 Promise Keepers men's conference in Baton Rouge, Louisiana, McCartney reminisced, "I loved to coach." He added: "When I was seven years old, I knew that I was going to be a coach. . . . There was something in me that was designed to coach." Given McCartney's predisposition to coaching, it is not surprising that his speeches for Promise Keepers mimicked the speaking style, tone, and structure of pregame pep talks. Just as he strove to motivate his football players to win games, so McCartney sought to inspire his male Christian audience members to win over their friends, families, and coworkers to Jesus Christ. As the closing speaker at many Promise Keepers conferences, he sought to inspire the men to leave the events excited about their faith and committed to boldly sharing their spiritual beliefs with non-Christians. To this end, he spoke with passion and urgency, focusing his addresses on specific and practical "game plans" for the men to follow.

Like any good coach, McCartney motivated his listeners to act, and specifically to evangelize, by magnifying the significance of their task. In nearly every speech, he warned his audience of two impending crises—societal disintegration and racism—that would worsen if they failed to convert their friends and coworkers to Christianity. Most often, McCartney identified the increased number of divorces, fatherless children, and crime as evidence of a societal breakdown. He particularly identified fatherlessness as the "biggest single crisis facing our nation," claiming that it played a significant role in increased crime rates, male delinquency, and even homosexuality. He also identified racism as a crisis, especially as it was manifested within the Christian church and at Promise Keepers' own conferences. Referring to the Christian church in his 1992 speech in Boulder, Colorado, McCartney proclaimed that "we're still [racially] divided." He continued, "[W]e are all one family, . . . but we know that's not true. . . . [W]e have not treated each other all like family." Similar to an American Puritan jeremiad, in which the preacher warned audience members that conditions would worsen unless they repented their "sins" and lived righteously, McCartney, in his 1999 address, predicted that the impending crises would soon result in "total moral anarchy" unless members of Promise Keepers rededicated themselves to God.

McCartney attributed both societal disintegration and racism to Christian men's failure to boldly and consistently express their faith. In his 1997 speech in Honolulu, he used a passage from the book of Revelation to describe eight types of men. He emphasized the first kind of man—the cowardly man—as representative of current Christian men. Such men, according to McCartney, "refuse to stand up for the gospel. They are ashamed of the gospel of Jesus Christ at crunch time. They don't have a courageous heart for the living God. They're not sold out for the gospel of Jesus Christ." Consequently, Mc-

Cartney told his Cleveland, Ohio, audience in 2002, America was becoming increasingly secular: "It's on our watch, men. It's this brotherhood. It's happening right now. We're becoming a heathen nation right before our eyes. It's up to us. Don't you see?"

McCartney often adopted sentimental terms to describe Christian men's failure to express their faith. He equated the men's silence with apathy toward each other, their families, and fellow citizens. In his 2002 speech in Cleveland, he told the story of a pastor who dressed like a bum and stood outside of his church's front doors on Sunday morning to test the compassion of his congregation. Not one of the congregants stopped to help him. According to McCartney, this story "represents most churches. We don't carry each other's burdens." He then told the story of a funeral for an African American former football player that he had attended. McCartney wept during the service because—for the first time—he realized African Americans' "pain"—"what they really lived with." He concluded, "The church is not feeling each other's pain. We don't love each other." In both stories, McCartney specifically addressed white Christian men. White Christian men allowed societal disintegration and racism to worsen because of their indifference toward the people around them.

To solve the problem of Christian men's apathy, McCartney advocated that the men develop a total commitment to and burning passion for God. In his 1997 Honolulu address, he instructed his audience to become "red hot" for God and to be "on fire for the gospel of Jesus Christ." Just as McCartney's football players needed to play "all out" to win their games, so Christian men needed to be "sold out" to God in order to "win" their society to Christ. McCartney characterized being "sold out" as feverishly and courageously—even aggressively—declaring their allegiance to God and biblical "truth." In his 1993 speech in Boulder, Colorado, he even instructed his audience members to become warriors in their "stand for the truth."

McCartney presented sacrificial relationships between Christian men, including pastors and laymen as well as men of color, as integral to developing a "bold" faith and solving the problems of societal disintegration and racism. In his 1993 speech in Boulder, he implored: "We have to pray fervently for our pastors" and "stop criticizing them." He later added, "All of us got [*sic*] to go out of our way. Every one of us has got to take a burden for the shepherds [i.e., pastors] that are in our church." In 1992, McCartney declared: "The white man has got to reach out and grab the black man and grab the brown man and grab the yellow man and hug him and embrace him and love him and affirm him [in joy?] and go back with him and find out how we can be part of the solution."

Anecdotes were McCartney's favorite means to illustrate the power of intimate relationships and an uncompromising commitment to God. McCartney frequently told a story about hikers who wanted to climb a particular mountain in the Swiss Alps. It was possible to climb this mountain in one day and to descend the next day, but doing so required a complete commitment to the task. According to the proprietor of the "halfway house"—a restaurant situated halfway up the mountain—half of the hikers who reached the restaurant became comfortable in the warm and dry rest stop and chose not to continue to the summit. These men represented mediocrity—a word, according to McCartney, that "actually means halfway up the mountain." The men who continued to the summit were "sold out" to the task—the result, in part, of the encouragement of their close friends. McCartney explained that the men who continued to climb had buddies who "ma[de] sure that everybody [was] helped along the way." These friends mentally encouraged and physically aided the weaker men. Because the men "all ma[de] it up to the top" together, they enjoyed the "maximum experience" of the climb. McCartney instructed his audience that "you can't leave anybody behind. We can't leave anybody behind anymore." Christian men needed to support each other and commit themselves to winning their society to Jesus Christ.

If Christian men heeded McCartney's call, McCartney promised that God would bless them with spiritual revival. Again adopting the message of an American Puritan jeremiad, which offers spiritual blessings as reward for repentance and recommitment to God, he claimed in his 1999 speech that "revival is imminent, that moral anarchy is going to be set aside" if the men followed his instructions. In his 1996 address in Kansas City, Missouri, McCartney even promised, "If you will come together broken and empty and ask Him [God] to do what He wants to do, He will do it. Don't you see? Heaven waits on Earth."

McCartney's passionate delivery modeled his advocacy for bold, passionate faith. Like a coach addressing his players before a game, McCartney spoke dramatically, often very emotionally. For each of his main points, his voice built in volume and pitch, sounding either more sorrowful or angry. When he discussed Christian men's failures, for instance, his voice increasingly fluctuated, sounding more mournful—as though he might burst into tears. When McCartney instructed his audience to boldly express its faith in God, he spoke urgently, even angrily, nearly shouting at his audience to overcome its apathy. He used his body to make his delivery even more dramatic. As his points built in intensity, he grew flushed, jutted his neck toward the audience, gesticulated more passionately, and hunched down, bending his knees and leaning his body toward the audience. Through both his voice and his body, he embodied the commitment and zeal that he sought from his listeners.

McCartney's folksy style and appearance complemented his passionate delivery. He spoke plainly and colloquially, referring to his audience members as "guys" and frequently using contractions such as "ain't," "we're talking truth," and "can't nobody leave here without a brother." McCartney often used phrases to get his audience's attention, such as "Now hear me, men," or "You need to understand this now, men," and he commonly built each main point to a crescendo by repeating a rhetorical question, such as "Am I right?" "Did you pick up on that?" or "You got the picture?" Appropriate to his simple style, McCartney dressed casually for his speeches, nearly always wearing khaki pants, a T-shirt imprinted with the Promise Keepers insignia, and a warm-up jacket—similar to the apparel of a football coach on game day.

By speaking and dressing plainly, McCartney capitalized on his football persona. He approached his audience not as an imposing religious leader but as a motivating coach. He used language and drew on emotions that were reminiscent of a coach's pep talk. The settings for McCartney's speeches—football stadiums and coliseums—strengthened this resonance with a sports event. McCartney often accentuated his football persona by explicitly drawing on his football experience through analogies, such as when he referred to the Bible as a "playbook" and as the "rule book of life." He explicitly compared football coaches with pastors during his 1998 conference speech, and during his 2001 speech in Baltimore, he even compared a Promise Keepers conference with "what goes on in the locker room of an athletic contest when play is suspended." Both situations shared the dynamics of "relationships," "reassessment," and "resolve."

The organizational structure of McCartney's speeches further drew upon his speaking skills as a coach. McCartney typically structured his speeches around a problem or a need, such as Christian men's failure to boldly express their faith, their need to "master" God's "fundamentals," or the imminence of a societal breakdown. He then addressed the problem through a "game plan" of three or four specific ideas that audience members could immediately employ to help resolve the problem. McCartney focused his 1999 message, for example, on the need for Christian men to cure the "cancer" of apathy growing within the church by seeking a spiritual revival. He provided "three things" that his audience could do to make revival imminent: "draw near to God," which he described as developing a contrite heart; "draw near to God's word" by meeting once a week with other Christian men to read the Bible; and "draw near to God's work" by loving and attending to their own children and mentoring fatherless children.

One of McCartney's favorite organizational schemes focused on "taking inventory." As he explained in his 2002 speech in Cleveland, he adopted the structure from the University of Michigan head football coach Bo Schembechler (1969–1989), who periodically "took inventory" during his pep talks "to really get the attention of the team." "Taking inventory" consisted of three major points: "who we are,"

"where we are going," and "how we are going to get there."

In response to "who we are," McCartney regularly identified his predominantly Christian male audience as God's "chosen" people. Just as a football coach motivates his players by assuring them that they are the best athletes, McCartney praised his male Christian audience for being "handpicked" by God. He unified his listeners through their shared faith. In his 1992 message in Boulder, Colorado, he explained that regardless of race or denomination, "who we are" included all men who "love Jesus" and are "born of the Holy Spirit." McCartney distanced his audience from non-Christians, whom he described alternately as "spiritually lost," "wicked," or arrogant.

McCartney offered various responses to the second point, "where we are going," depending on the focus of his message. For example, in his 1992 speech that emphasized America's growing secularization, he declared that his audience would help to return the nation to its Christian roots by "going out" and "tak[ing] Jesus Christ to a world that's lost, to a Nation that's reversed a very good thing." In his 2002 Ohio address that highlighted Christian men's need to better love other people, McCartney reminded his audience members that they were bound for heavenly glory; they would spend eternity with God and, therefore, needed to share God's love more frequently while still on earth.

McCartney typically emphasized the third point, "how we are going to get there," by providing specific instructions to help Christian men develop a more committed and passionate faith in God and love for other people. Among his most frequent instructions were to read the Bible regularly, pray, and meet with other Christian men; to befriend Christians of other races; to "lead" their families spiritually; and to support their local pastors. McCartney occasionally demonstrated one or more of his instructions during or after his speeches. In 1993 in Boulder, Colorado, he modeled spiritual leadership of his family by praying out loud for his wife and sons, who joined McCartney on stage while he prayed for them. He later demonstrated support for pastors by asking the clergymen in the audience to walk to the front row so that the audience could identify and applaud them.

Underlying McCartney's instructions and three-point "game plan" was his assumption that societal improvement began with the individual. Rather than stress structural or institutional solutions, McCartney identified individual Christian men as society's saviors. If each man followed McCartney's instructions, their individual actions would together ameliorate the problems with the church and society. His focus on the individual was particularly evident through his frequent inclusion of sports and military figures in his speeches. He typically opened his speeches with a story about a sports or military figure's virtue or vice, such as his or her bravery, determination, or laziness. He then called on his audience to adopt (or reject) the characteristic in its own pursuit of an increased passion for God. For instance, McCartney began his 1999 address with the story of five-time Tour de France winner Lance Armstrong's victorious battle against testicular cancer. He stressed that Armstrong im-

stories or characters he referenced, most likely assuming that his Christian audience was already familiar with them. Second, McCartney presented himself as God's chosen spokesperson to Christian men. Between 1992 and 1995, he explicitly characterized his speeches as God's message to his audience. He explained in the introduction to each of these speeches that for several weeks or months before that speech, he had asked God to tell him what to say. McCartney stated in his 1993 speech in Boulder, Colorado, that he went "before the Lord faithfully, relentlessly, for weeks on end so that I don't speak a word of God to you that is not truly the heart of God. I submit to you that what you are about to hear now is God's heart to the men of this nation." After 1995, McCartney no longer mentioned his prayerful preparation for his speeches, but he continued to identify his messages as "the truth" or what "God has put on my heart."

Promise Keepers drew seventy men to its first gathering at Denver in 1990. In 1996, 1.1 million men attended twenty-two nationwide conferences.

---

proved because "he believed in his heart that he would ride again." This belief propelled Armstrong to seek treatment for his illness. McCartney instructed his audience members to commit themselves to healing the church's "cancer" by wholeheartedly seeking spiritual revival, just "like Armstrong went after [his own physical] healing."

McCartney justified his assessment of societal problems and solutions by grounding his messages in God's authority in two primary ways. First, he regularly invoked "God's word," the Bible, as definitive proof for his claims. He read and interpreted biblical stories and verses literally, without providing any historical context for or exegesis of the verses. He assumed that as "God's word," the biblical passages were timeless and, therefore, just as directly applicable to his audiences as to the historical audience to which they were originally addressed. In fact, McCartney rarely even explained the biblical

In 1997, McCartney adapted his typical oratorical methods for a unique speaking situation. On October 4, 1997, Promise Keepers hosted a huge rally, titled "Stand in the Gap: A Sacred Assembly," on Independence Mall in Washington, D.C. Leaders of Promise Keepers described the rally as a massive demonstration of Christian men's repentance for failing in their commitments to their families, churches, and communities. Nearly 600,000 participants, primarily men, attended the six-hour event, which consisted of speeches, songs, and prayers.

Yet, Christian men were not the sole rally attendees. C-SPAN televised the event live, and many news organizations covered the rally. In fact, McCartney and his fellow leaders of Promise Keepers actively sought news media coverage for the gathering. They hired two public relations firms and met with newspaper editors and journalists in the weeks and days prior to the rally. The rally also caught the attention of several feminist organizations, including the National Organization for Women, which accused Promise Keepers of hiding a conservative, patriarchal agenda behind its religious rhetoric. McCartney, the final speaker of the rally, had a challenging task. As the most widely recognized spokesperson for Promise Keepers, he needed not only to inspire the Christian audience members but also to neutralize accusations made by critics of the organization and to win public approval. Because of its uniqueness and widespread publicity, McCartney's "Stand in the Gap" speech has become his best-known address and is, therefore, worthy of closer examination.

McCartney's speech, titled "An Extraordinary Hope," illustrated his typical themes and methods as well as his adaptation to the unique situation. The speech followed his usual practice of addressing a problem, but it did not focus on the problems of societal degeneration or racism. Instead, McCartney tackled the (potential) problem of disunity and confusion among members of Promise Keepers. "It's my privilege to cast a vision. We need a precise plan," he said. "There can't be a guy who leaves here without knowing exactly what we're going to be doing so that the right hand will know what the left hand's doing." McCartney attempted to unify rally attendees so that they would leave as an organized movement. By doing so, he defused potential controversy by avoiding the controversial issues of racism and America's alleged "fall from grace," and presented Promise Keepers' plans in a positive light to the larger audience.

McCartney once again addressed the need for a vision by "taking inventory" of "who we are," "where we are going," and "how we are getting there." He defined "who we are" as a "brotherhood of believers." "Positionally," McCartney explained, "we are seated with Christ in Heaven, amen. Yet, practically, we are still here on earth but indwelled by God's Holy Spirit, amen! Every guy here has God's spirit in him." Unlike his previous speeches, which stressed the divinely "chosen" nature of his audience, here McCartney emphasized the unity and inclusiveness of Promise Keepers. "We are Baptists. We are Pentecostal. We are Methodist. We are Lutherans. We are Roman Catholics. We are independents. Anyone who names the name of Jesus, believes

in Jesus Christ as the son of the living God, loves Him with all his heart and has received Him in spirit, that's who we are." McCartney highlighted the organization's openness instead of explicitly distinguishing between members and "non-believers," who were likely in his immediate or television audience and would have substantiated some of the criticism of Promise Keepers. He did not even claim special status for himself. He never claimed to be God's spokesperson, and he never referenced his speech, himself, or Promise Keepers as delivering God's "message" or "truth." Instead, McCartney spoke as the president of Promise Keepers, who opened his organization to men from many religious denominations.

McCartney next addressed "where we are going" by, again, stressing the men's unity. Although Christian men previously had been alienated from each other by race and religious denomination, he said, "we're being reunited. And as we're reunited, we understand that this is unity with diversity. This is diversity without dissension. God is not a god of sameness. He is a god of oneness. Our destination is brotherhood in concert, true biblical oneness." Rather than proclaim that the rally attendees were bound for heavenly glory or destined to proselytize the nation, as he had in previous speeches, McCartney simply declared that his followers would become united—and were already doing so by gathering together on Independence Mall. He again avoided controversial issues and focused attention on Promise Keepers' inclusiveness and diversity.

As was typical, McCartney focused his third point, "how we will get there," on specific and practical ideas. He first offered instructions for his male audience members to follow to become more unified. He told the men to obey and aid their local pastor, and he told the pastors to "connect with the other pastors in their community. "We're asking you to meet once a week and not to compromise on this." To help the pastors preach and model "racial reconciliation and denominational reconciliation," McCartney asked them to attend a one-day pastoral conference in January.

Through his remaining suggestions, however, McCartney announced future Promise Keepers events and practices. These activities included the plan for church congregations across the country to meet at their state capitals on January 1, 2000, no longer charging audience members for two-day conferences, and going "global" as an organization in 2000. The speech, in other words, seemed more focused on ensuring future news coverage of the organization and further stressing Promise Keepers' inclusiveness than on providing a "vision" and "plan" for members or solving a particular problem, such as racism or societal degeneration. McCartney concluded the speech, once again, with a demonstration. Instead of demonstrating one of his instructions, however, he displayed Promise Keepers' unity by asking Ray Boltz to sing "I Pledge Allegiance to the Land," and inviting the audience members to sing along "to show that we are all together."

The reaction to McCartney's "Stand in the Gap" speech reflected his more general reception as a religious public speaker. Critics blasted McCartney as a charlatan who hid his fundamentalist agenda behind soft religious rhetoric. Christian supporters, on the other hand, praised the speech as inspirational. Nearly everyone who heard McCartney speak, however, agreed that he excelled as a motivational speaker—whether to good ends or ill. With McCartney's retirement from both football and Promise Keepers, it is doubtful he will rise to fame again as a public speaker, at least on a national scale. Nonetheless, McCartney will be remembered as an evangelical motivational orator who has inspired many like-minded speakers who are echoing his call to spiritual revival. Through his fiery, folksy style, identification of exigencies, and simple "game plans," McCartney has affected thousands of lives.

INFORMATION SOURCES

Research Collections and Collected Speeches

There are no archival collections or published collections of McCartney's speeches at this time. Transcripts of his speeches do not yet exist except for his speech at the 1997 "Stand in the Gap" rally, which is available through the online database Lexis-Nexis. Cassette, compact disc, and videotape copies of many of the speeches McCartney gave at Promise Keepers conferences from 1992 to 2003 are available for pur-

chase through Promise Keepers Web site (www. promisekeepers.org) and customer service department (1-800-456-7594). For each year, multiple copies of McCartney's speeches are available; however, they are often versions of the same speech. McCartney tended to deliver the same speech each conference year, at multiple locations and times.

Web Sites

National Organization for Women (NOW) [*PK*]. This site provides numerous links to texts produced by NOW for its campaign against Promise Keepers, including press releases, articles from the *National NOW Times*, and other texts. These texts are a helpful way of discovering the feminists' most prominent critiques of Promise Keepers. http://www.now.org

Promise Keepers official Web site [*LN*]. This site includes information about the history and purpose of the organization, news and images of its events, and links to related Web sites. In addition, the site is equipped to search through archived materials and contains McCartney's 1997 "Stand in the Gap" speech. www.promisekeepers.org

Audiovisual Materials

CBS. *Faith & Politics: The Christian Right.* New York: CBS, 1995. This video is available at libraries throughout the country.

The Changing Culture: The Men's Movement. Princeton, N.J.: Films for the Humanities & Sciences, 1998.

Dalton, Dan. *The Promise Keepers: A Dan Dalton Documentary.* Plymouth, Minn.: Simitar Entertainment, 1996.

Promise Keepers: Equality Bashers. New York: National Organization for Women, 1997. This video can be purchased for a nominal fee at 202-628-8669 or www.now.org/issues/right/promise/video.html

Promise Keepers: The Third Wave of the Religious Right. New York: Sterling Research Associates, 1996. Produced by the Center for Democracy Studies. This video can be purchased for a nominal fee at 212-423-9237.

Selected Critical Studies

Alsdurf, Phyllis E. "McCartney on the Rebound." *Christianity Today,* May 18, 1998, pp. 26–28, 30–32.

Brickner, Bryan W. *The Promise Keepers: Politics and Promises.* Lanham, Md.: Lexington Books, 1999.

Clatterbaugh, Kenneth. *Contemporary Perspectives on Masculinity: Men, Women, and Politics in Modern Society,* 2nd ed. Boulder, Colo.: Westview Press, 1997.

Claussen, Dane S., ed. *The Promise Keepers: Essays*

on *Masculinity and Christianity*. Jefferson, N.C.: McFarland, 2000.

———. *Standing on the Promises: The Promise Keepers and the Revival of Manhood*. Cleveland, Ohio: Pilgrim Press, 1999.

Hardisty, Jean. *Mobilizing Resentment: Conservative Resurgence from the John Birch Society to the Promise Keepers*. Boston: Beacon Press, 1999.

Kimmel, Michael. *Manhood in America: A Cultural History*. New York: Free Press, 1996.

Messner, Michael A. *Politics of Masculinities: Men in Movements*. Thousand Oaks, Calif.: Sage, 1997.

Van Leeuwen, Mary Stewart. "Servanthood or Soft Patriarchy? A Christian Feminist Looks at the Promise Keepers Movement." *Journal of Men's Studies* 5 (1997): 233–37.

Williams, Rhys H., ed. *Promise Keepers and the New Masculinity: Private Lives and Public Morality*. Lanham, Md.: Lexington Books, 2001.

Young, Jennifer. "Promise Keepers, Feminists, and the News Media: An Analysis of the Debate over the 'Stand in the Gap' Rally." Ph.D. dissertation, Pennsylvania State University, 2003.

Selected Biographies

Abraham, Ken. *Who Are the Promise Keepers? Understanding the Christian Men's Movement*. New York: Doubleday, 1997.

"Bill McCartney." *People, Weekly*, December 29, 1997–January 5, 1998, p. 100.

Hoffer, Richard, and Shelley Smith. "Putting His House in Order." *Sports Illustrated*, January 16, 1995, pp. 28–32.

McCartney, Bill, and Dave Diles. *From Ashes to Glory*. Nashville, Tenn.: Thomas Nelson, 1995.

McCartney, Bill, and David Halbrook. *Sold Out*. Nashville, Tenn.: Word Publishing, 1997.

Ostling, Richard N. "God, Football and the Game of His Life." *Time*, October 6, 1997, pp. 38–39.

CHRONOLOGY OF MAJOR SPEECHES

See "Research Collections and Collected Speeches" for source codes.

"Untitled" (address to Promise Keepers "What Makes a Man?" conference). Boulder, Colo., 1992. *PK*.

"Face to Face, Back to Back, Shoulder to Shoulder" (address to Promise Keepers "Face to Face" conference). Boulder, Colo., 1993. *PK*.

"A Man and His Relationships: Family, Church, Community and Brothers" (address to Promise Keepers "Seize the Moment" conference). Anaheim, Calif.: July 3, 1994. *PK*.

"The Power of a Promise Kept" (address to Promise Keepers "Raise the Standard" conference). Pontiac, Mich., April 29, 1995. *PK*.

"Broken Hearts Break Down Walls" (address to Promise Keepers "Break Down the Walls" conference). Kansas City, Mo., 1996. *PK*.

"An Overview: The Making of a Godly Man" (address to Promise Keepers "The Making of a Godly Man" conference). Honolulu, Hawaii, January 10, 1997. *PK*.

"An Extraordinary Hope" (address to Promise Keepers "Stand in the Gap" rally). Washington, D.C., October 4, 1997. Available at www.lexis-nexis.com/universe; *PK*.

"Untitled" (address to Promise Keepers clergy conference). n.p., 1998. *PK*.

"Understanding the Times" (address to Promise Keepers "Choose This Day" conference). n.p., 1999. *PK*.

"Character for the Journey: 'Brothers Going the Distance'" (address to Promise Keepers "Go the Distance" conference). Baton Rouge, La., 2000. *PK*.

"Extreme Privilege: 'Access to God'" (address to Promise Keepers "Turn the Tide: Living Out an Extreme Faith" conference). Baltimore, Md., 2001. *PK*.

"Kingdom Champions" (address to Promise Keepers "Storm the Gates" conference). Miami, Fla., 2002. *PK*.

"Untitled" (address to Promise Keepers "Storm the Gates" conference). Cleveland, Ohio, 2002. *PK*.

"Come Near to Me" (address to Promise Keepers clergy conference). Phoenix, Ariz., February 2003. *PK*.

RUSSELL MEANS (1939–)
American Indian Leader, Actor, Author, Musician, Artist

RANDALL A. LAKE AND CATHERINE H. PALCZEWSKI

For more than thirty winters, an Oglala Lakota from Porcupine, South Dakota, has been one of the most outspoken and controversial voices on behalf of American Indians (his preferred nomenclature, rather than "Native American") and indigenous peoples throughout the world. Russell Means's name is inextricably linked with almost all of the most famous Indian protests of this tumultuous period, including Alcatraz (1964), Mount Rushmore (1970, 1971), seizure of the *Mayflower II* on the 350th anniversary of the Pilgrims' landing at Plymouth Rock (1970), the Trail of Broken Treaties and occupation of the Bureau of Indian Affairs in Washington, D.C. (1972), the occupation of Gordon, Nebraska, stemming from the death of Raymond Yellow Thunder (1972), the Custer, South Dakota, courthouse melee over the murder of Wesley Bad Heart Bull (1973), the seventy-one-day standoff between the Independent Oglala Nation and the United States at Wounded Knee, South Dakota (1973), the International Indian Treaty Council in Geneva, Switzerland (1974–1977), the Longest Walk (1978), the Black Hills Alliance's "International Gathering for Survival" near Rapid City, South Dakota (1980), Yellow Thunder Camp in the Black Hills (1981–1982), and Columbus Quincentenary protests in Denver, the city that inaugurated Columbus Day (1991–1992, and subsequently).

Throughout this period, Means has been associated principally with the American Indian Movement, inaugurated in Minneapolis in 1968 to protest and monitor police brutality. After founding the American Indian Center in Cleveland, Ohio, in April 1969, Means first encountered AIM at a conference in San Francisco, and again at a protest against the National Council of Churches in Detroit later that year. As he recalled in his autobiography, those experiences changed his life: "at the age of thirty I became a full-time Indian." In 1970 he organized the

Cleveland AIM (CLAIM), the first chapter outside Minneapolis, and became AIM's first national coordinator the following year. Although he resigned from the latter position several times, first in 1980, before finally severing all ties in 1988, in 1991 he became executive director of the autonomous Colorado AIM, with which he continues to work closely.

In addition to protest, Means has pursued more conventional politics intermittently for many years. He has run, unsuccessfully, for tribal chairman on the Pine Ridge Reservation three times: 1974, when he lost to despised incumbent "Dickie" Wilson amid widespread fraud; 1984, when tribal officials removed Means's name from the primary ballot, citing his felony conviction in South Dakota; and 2002, when, following two primaries (the first of which was voided for irregularities) in which he was the top vote getter, he lost to the incumbent in the general election. For a time in 1984 he was pornographer Larry Flynt's running mate in a quixotic quest to wrest the Republican nomination for president from incumbent Ronald Reagan. In the mid-1980s, Means became enamored of the Libertarians, who, he likes to say, "are the first group of white people I ever met who think Indian"; in 1988 he came within three votes of capturing the Libertarian Party's presidential nomination. In 2002 Means campaigned for the New Mexico governorship first as a Libertarian and then as an independent; eventually he lost a lawsuit challenging state filing deadlines and was denied a place on the ballot.

In recent years, Means's notoriety has derived as much from his artistic as his political endeavors. His acting career began in *The Last of the Mohicans* (1992). Since then he has appeared in more than a dozen feature films, including Oliver Stone's *Natural Born Killers* (1994), Disney's *Pocahontas* (1995), *Wind River* (1998), *Thomas and the Magic Railroad*

(2000), *Cowboy Up* (2001), and *Black Cloud* (2004). Means also has acted in a host of television shows, from *Touched by an Angel* and *Walker, Texas Ranger* to *Nash Bridges* and HBO's *Curb Your Enthusiasm*. He has released two music CDs, *Electric Warrior* (1993)—the cover adorned with an Andy Warhol portrait of Means—and *The Radical* (1996); both blend a wide assortment of musical styles into what Means calls "rap-ajo." And he has painted a portrait series of adventurers Christobal Colon (Columbus), Carson, Crockett, and Boone; presidents Washington, Jackson, and Lincoln; generals Custer, Sheridan, and Cook; Colonel Chivington; and Father Serra. Means's status in popular culture is such that he now is a rather frequent subject in mainstream and alternative electronic media, ranging from network programs such as *The Today Show*, *Good Morning, America*, and *Larry King Live* to the American Indian Cable Network in southern California, to public radio, to Internet radio programs such as *Mysteries of the Mind*. In July 2000 Means began a weekly program on KILI, the radio station on Pine Ridge that he was instrumental in founding in 1983. He has been profiled and interviewed in mainstream and alternative print media, ranging from *The Progressive*, the *Los Angeles Times*, and the *San Francisco Chronicle* to *Easyriders*, *Cowboys and Indians*, *Emerging Markets* magazine, *Western Magazine* (in French), and *Indian Country Today*, for which he has been a guest columnist.

Each of these sometimes offbeat venues represents an opportunity for Means to deliver his message of Indian pride and self-determination. Traditionally, minority rhetors have enjoyed at best limited access to the dominant public sphere, and thus have had to be more inventive than more advantaged advocates. Means has proven to be most inventive, and persistent. Critical of even "enlightened" films such as *Dances with Wolves* (1990), which he calls "Lawrence of the Plains" because the Indians require a white savior, he has sought through acting to combat too-familiar stereotypes. His songs can be brutally caustic. For example, "Nixon's Dead Ass" bemoans: "the crook's resurrection," calls "Tricky Dick" a piece of "white trash," and declares that Means "ain't kissin'" the former president's posterior (*The Radical*, 1996).

Even Means's pictorial art communicates an unmistakable polemical message: his portrait series is titled "The Indian Killers." Thus, while this essay focuses on his public address—largely the portion that has been most accessible to and preserved by the mainstream—Russell Means's persuasive efforts are considerably more wide-ranging.

OYATE WACINYAPI, "WORKS"—AND SPEAKS—"FOR THE PEOPLE"

By his own account, Means's career as a public speaker began with oral book reports in junior high school in Vallejo, California. His report on *The Last of the Mohicans* was such "a piece of shit, boring and tedious," that he made up a story that "had those kids spellbound," and received an A. While majoring in accounting and computer programming at Iowa Technical College, in Ottumwa, in 1965, Means took a speech class, where he "usually got A's" for "impassioned" addresses about the plight of Indians; however, he received a C in the course because he moved and gestured too much, and had poor eye contact.

Means almost always speaks extemporaneously. He claims that his 1980 speech "The Same Old Song"—perhaps not coincidentally his most famous and often reprinted address—is the only one that was written down in advance. His style is conversational: its tone is direct and immediate, punctuated with exclamations such as "man," "duh!," and "I kid you not"; his syntax reflects the casualness of spontaneous speech; and aids to memory, such as repetition and recapitulation, are common. His speeches typically do not follow a linear inferential structure from premises to claim. Instead, they are organized thematically around a central, recurring idea that is amplified through diverse supporting materials that draw heavily upon Means's personal experiences and the social knowledge available to his audience as presumed facts. "Commentary #2," delivered about 1999, is exemplary. For more than half an hour, Means develops the idea that "colonialism" means "you are perfectly happy to be miserable." In support, he weaves together comments about reservation life, patriarchy, fear of everything from credit cards to police to God, road rage, crooked politicians and business leaders, and the pharmaceutical industry; he invokes Frantz Fanon, legal scholar Felix Cohen, an unnamed Muskogee medicine man whom he heard in Geneva, Luther Standing Bear ("another ancestor of mine"), an African cabbie from Los Angeles, Orwell's *1984*, Ben Franklin, and "some freedom-thinking person['s]" research on Ritalin. He invokes the authority of his own experiences. For example, he claims that the 1934 Indian Reorganization Act was the basis for the Bantu Development Act that established apartheid in South Africa: "I know; I read both." He also appeals to his listeners' experiences, asking, for instance, "Why do you hit the brakes every time you see a cop car?"

In short, Means's approach to public address reflects an oral culture. In "Free to be Responsible" (1995), he explains that "Indian people always talk in a circle. You always end up where you began. You have to listen very carefully, so you don't miss any of the spokes in the wheel that holds it together." In "Lessons from Native America: Knowing Who You Are" (1993), Means recalls that his "grandpa" John Feather used to take six-year-old Russell for walks in Greenwood, South Dakota, and tell "stories that didn't have an ending": "What I realized later was that he was really teaching me to analyze, to fire my own imagination, to come to conclusions of my own independently with logic." This mode of address, then, is both circuitous and empowering. While Means retains from those youthful days in Ottumwa the capacity for impassioned speech and dynamic delivery, including emphatic gestures, he can be soft-spoken as well, as in "Voice of Mother Earth" (1999). His eye contact has improved.

Two crucial ideas are interwoven throughout Means's oratory: the importance of Indian spiritual renewal and a call for Indian sovereignty and self-determination. From the earliest days of his involvement, Means has maintained that AIM was not a "revolutionary" movement but, as he said in an address at the Law Commune in 1973, "first a spiritual movement and second a liberation movement." In "Native American Spirituality," he explained to a radio audience at the time of his 1974 trial for involvement in Wounded Knee: "We only have things to liberate. And of course it begins with our spirituality because if we know who we are, why we are, where we're going and why we're going, then we are truly liberated and need no further dealings with outside forces." Understanding their traditions gives a people identity and direction, which make self-reliance possible. Thus, Means stresses that in order to survive, Native peoples must recover the wisdom of their ancestors.

Importantly, Means does not merely argue the need for spirituality. His speeches show the way, helping his listeners find their identity and direction within Indian traditions. Speech after speech seeks to educate its audience about Indian cultures and beliefs, even in unexpected contexts such as the technical forum of the law. His opening statement at the Wounded Knee trial promises:

"You cannot be everything to everyone. I do not propose to be used in such fashion by my enemies; I am not a 'leader.' I *am* an Oglala Lakota patriot. That's all I want or need to be. And I am very comfortable with who I am."

"The Same Old Song"

". . . although some men merely have jobs, I have a calling. Since I had joined AIM to serve my people, my work is much more than a vocation—it not only consumes my time and energy, it defines my identity."

Where White Men Fear to Tread

We will introduce evidence by our Holy Men commonly referred to as "Medicine Men," evidence from those people who will tell you the beauty of being a red man in the western hemisphere and how hard it is to maintain that beauty.

We will introduce evidence of how we've had to go underground in order to maintain our traditional religion, our traditional philosophy.

We are going to take you through a course of evidence and proof and testimony so that hopefully you can understand what the psyche of the American Indian is all about.

Shortly thereafter he delivers on this promise, explaining in small part:

It is our philosophy that because all living things come from one mother, our mother earth, then of course, we are all related and we have to—we have to treat one another with the same respect and reverence that we would our own blood relatives.

But the important thing in our philosophy is that we believe we're the weakest things on earth, that the two legged is the weakest thing on earth because we have no direction.

We have looked around us and . . . we saw that every living thing has direction and a role in life, every one of them, and only the two legged doesn't.

And so we built our civilization on what they could teach us, and this is our philosophy.

In a strategy that reverses the referents of "primitive" and "civilized," "inferior" and "superior," and in a tone both comic and acerbic, Means often characterizes white society as derivative. By presenting Indian traditions as prior to and the basis for white beliefs and achievements, he treats whites as trespassers, both geographically and culturally. In "Native American Spirituality," delivered in 1974, he draws upon the Indian belief that all life is a circle: "We knew spiritually that our mother was round centuries before Columbus decided to get lost a half a world off course, and we discovered him." Fourteen years later, in "The State of Native America," he employs this strategy of reversal at length:

Welcome to the Americas, my home, where the dust that you kick up as you walk is made up of the bones of my ancestors. Welcome. For

what you have appropriated and for what we have given to you, I will tell you.

Sixty percent of the world's foodstuffs comes from us. . . . We domesticated and developed, for instance, over ten thousand species of potatoes. So when the Europeans came over here, what did they take back? One species. So when the blight hit their potato crop, they had nothing to fall back on, and consequently, we got a lot of Kennedys coming over here. . . . And they call me primitive!

Sewage systems we gave to the Europeans. . . . I could go on and on and on.

Welcome to natural childbirth. The Lamaze method. A Frenchman comes over here, studies the Indian way of giving birth, goes back to France, writes it up, and you call it the Lamaze method.

Welcome to the Americas. Welcome. The finest medicines in the world developed here. Developed here! Welcome to the Americas. From quinine to penicillin. Welcome. Codeine.

Welcome to the Americas. But . . . instead of saying "thank you," we are still an "expendable people."

Finally, an example that recurs in Means's politically oriented talks, such as 1993's "Lessons from Native America: Knowing Who You Are":

Let's go into your history. I don't mind telling you about me. But I'm sick and tired of having to tell you about your own history. Let's go back into history and how the Constitution came about. It came from us, by the way, the Iroquois Confederacy specifically. . . . We gave you the idea of individual freedom through representative government. The Greeks, nobody, John Locke, Adam Smith, nobody knew about the freedom of the individual through representative government until we taught you all. The Constitution comes from us. That's already been acknowledged. It's fact.

Such appeals invite and enable Means's native audiences to recover their pride in being Indian. They invite and enable white audiences to experience shame. Yet, it is important to emphasize, the divide between "Indian" and "white" is cultural, not racial. In "The Same Old Song," while arguing that Marxism and capitalism are two sides of the same exploitative coin, he comments:

Those who ultimately advocate and defend the realities of European culture and its industrialism are my enemies. Those who resist it, who struggle against it, are my allies, the allies of American Indian people. And I don't give a damn what their skin color happens to be. Caucasian is the white term for the white race; *European* is an outlook I oppose.

In a closely related lecture, "Industrialism and American Indian Culture," presented before the E. F. Schumacher Society in 1981, argues for "natural" rather than "human" or "civil" rights, and claims that "the whole notion of race pride ultimately leads nowhere" because it masks the only difference that matters, the difference between the values and worldview of "tribal peoples, natural peoples," on the one hand, and "the European order," on the other:

> I reject the long-term utility of the concept of "Blackness" as emphatically as I reject the notions of White, Red, Yellow or Brown as explanatory of anything other than pigmentation and perhaps bone structure. Black is, in the long run, no more nor less than the genetic division of the American imperial pie, a negative force in the universe, a term based entirely in the civil rights context of demanding that the American power structure allow non-Whites to *join* it. The people I am interested in meeting, in reaching and in allying with are *Africans*.

Spiritual and cultural renewal is "liberating," enabling self-reliance and freedom from "outside forces." Thus, the second crucial thread running through Means's oratory is a demand for sovereignty and self-determination. Sovereignty is legalistic: tribal status as "domestic dependent nations" is unconstitutional, and the United States must recognize the authority of treaties (particularly the 1868 Fort Laramie Treaty as regards his own people) made between equally autonomous nations. As he contended in his 1973 address at the Law Commune, without treaty rights "we can no longer exist as a people." Self-determination is more bureaucratic: the "colonialism" of the "Bureau of Idiots Anonymous" and other federal agencies, and the "genocide" caused by the reservation system, must end. Also in his Law Commune address, delivered in the early days of the Independent Oglala Nation, Means argued that "we have to get rid of all nonIndian influences"

and promised that, if successful in his bid to be tribal chairman on Pine Ridge,

> I'm going to abolish my office, I'm going to abolish the tribal constitution, the Indian Reorganization Act, I'm going to abolish the Bureau of Indian Affairs, I'm going to abolish the public health system, I'm going to abolish the white ranchers that are on our land, and businessmen, and they're all going to have to walk off naked.

In the 1980s, Means began arguing that the colonialist system perfected on Indians was being applied throughout the country: "So what has happened? Now you're living on the biggest reservation in the world. It's called the United States of America. You've become dependent on government and you keep asking for more government" ("Welcome to the Reservation," 1992). In Means's view, government infringement of rights in the wake of the terrorist attacks of 9/11 "proves it even more"; in a lecture at California State University-Fresno in 2001, he wondered where the calls for Attorney General John Ashcroft's impeachment were.

The antidote to colonialism is "Freedom. You are free to be responsible. If you are a responsible person, then you need no laws" ("Free to be Responsible," 1995). During his gubernatorial campaign, Means argued that responsible people don't need a welfare state. In an appearance on the *Renaissance Radio Hour*, he argued that responsible people don't need government: "I come from an anarchist, matriarchal culture, where freedom of the individual is paramount. Duh! That's the Constitution of the United States!" Thus, much as he had promised to do on his reservation in 1973, as a gubernatorial candidate in 2001 Means urged the revival of the Sagebrush Rebellion by "people of the land" and promised that his first act as governor would be to give the U.S. Forest Service, the Bureau of Land Management, and other federal agencies one week to pack up and leave New Mexico. Apparently the universe is a circle, indeed.

Rhetoric such as the preceding makes it abundantly clear why Russell Means has been highly controversial from the day he became a "full-time Indian." During the heady days of AIM, he frightened and enraged much of white America, and was one of the federal government's most targeted "subversives." Over the years, he has defended himself in more than a dozen state and federal criminal trials. His sole conviction, stemming from what he describes as a "police riot" at the federal courthouse in Sioux Falls, South Dakota, in April 1974, cost him a year in prison. He has been shot at least five times, and stabbed at least once. Yet in the mid-1980s, in a move prefigured by his earlier critique of Marxism, he alienated his apparently natural political allies on the left (whom, according to his autobiography, "I despise"), as well as (his own creation) the International Indian Treaty Council, by denouncing the Sandinista revolution in Nicaragua for its treatment of Miskito and other indigenous peoples, endorsing the Reagan administration's CIA-backed Contra war and becoming the darling of the right-wing fringe, including the Unification Church. Although he is most comfortable in the Libertarian amalgam of left and right, his decision to snub the New Mexico party's endorsement four months after receiving its unanimous nomination for governor shocked party officials.

AIM, and Means, have stirred strong feelings in Indian communities. A series of bitter and well-publicized battles between, roughly speaking, Means and Colorado AIM on one side, and the Bellecourt brothers and the AIM "Grand Governing Council," based in Minneapolis, on the other, have carved deep divisions. Each side denies the other's authority and brands the other as a stooge for the FBI and CIA. Both sides have condemned the February 2004 conviction of Arlo Looking Cloud in the infamous 1975 slaying of AIM activist Anna Mae Aquash. Means, however, maintains that Vernon Bellecourt ordered her death. Also controversial in Indian country was Means's challenge to the jurisdiction of the Diné (Navajo) tribal courts in a case stemming from his 1997 arrest in Chinle, Arizona, for battery of his father-in-law. Many saw his challenge as a threat to the principle of tribal sovereignty.

Even Means's acting career has prompted sharp criticism that he has sold out to Hollywood and become precisely the kind of "hang-around-the-fort Indian," or "apple" (red on the outside but white on the inside), that he has de-

nounced for years. In particular, as the voice of Powhatan in *Pocahontas*, which in an interview with Will Swaim he defends as a beautiful story about a strong Indian woman, he was scorned roundly in some quarters. One scathing review is reproduced on the AIM Grand Governing Council's Web site: "Perhaps Means has turned into the biggest Red Delicious of them all, something of which the arch-conservative Walt Disney would greatly approve."

Yet, if Means's rhetoric bespeaks strong opinion, bluntness, outrage, even bellicosity, it also displays wit, intelligence, humanity, respectfulness, even humility. Unquestionably, it reveals an orator of uncommon presence and determination, with a vital message of hope. Vine Deloria Jr., a frequent critic, observed these qualities in an address that Means delivered on the Standing Rock Reservation in 1973. Paul Chaat Smith and Robert Allen Warrior recorded Deloria's comments in their history of the Indian movement:

> I came away from Means's speech with the feeling that Russell is a terribly important man to our tribe. He may be the greatest Lakota of this century and his ability to light the eyes that have been dimmed so long is probably more important for us than anything that anyone else can do. I think it is the pride in living that many Indians have lost and in the manner of clarity of Russell Means's speech many Indian people found that pride and also found a strength they did not know they had possessed.

More than thirty years ago, members of the American Indian Movement concluded that the key to survival was spiritual renewal. Today, Russell Means still strives to walk this road as he understands it, to encourage those of each of the four sacred colors who are receptive to walk it, and, through projects such as a total immersion school in Lakota culture, to enable future generations to walk it as well.

INFORMATION SOURCES

Research Collections and Collected Speeches

There are no archival collections or published collections of Mean's speeches at this time. Resources are scattered in media archives and university libraries across the country. The Robert L. Anderson American Indian Movement Papers, Center for

Southwest Research, General Library, University of New Mexico, contain miscellaneous materials pertaining to Means; see elibrary.unm.edu/ The largest repository, particularly of more recent audio, video, and print materials, is in the possession of Pearl Means, San Jose, New Mexico [*PM*], whose generosity made our research possible.

Native American Reader: Stories, Speeches and Poems, [*NAR*], ed. Jerry D. Blanche. Juneau, Alaska: Denali, 1990.

Web Sites

Alternative Radio [*AR*]. Boulder, Colo. Transcripts of four speeches may be purchased. www.alternative radio.com

American Indian Movement "Grand Governing Council" Web site. Some of Means's detractors in the Indian community, especially the Bellecourts, tell their side of the story here. This site also contains an extensive historical archive of declassified FBI, CIA, Department of Justice, and White House documents relating to AIM. www.aimovement.org

Libertarian Party Web site. This site contains miscellaneous material related to Means's involvement with the Libertarian Party. www.lp.org

Means's personal Web site [*RM*] contains biographical information; commentaries; lists of activities, appearances, and accomplishments; references to other materials about Means; and the texts of two speeches. www.russellmeans.com

Native America Calling [*NAC*]. Native American Public Telecommunications, Lincoln, Neb. Five appearances, with downloadable audio clips. http://www.nativecalling.org

Audiovisual Materials

Videocassettes, audiocassettes and downloadable audio and video clips are available from a variety of sources and are noted in the chronology of major speeches and statements. Several of the audiotapes have been produced by the Pacifica Tape Library.

Selected Critical Studies

Paystrup, Patricia. "Russell Means' Allopathic Cure for Environmental Degradation: Leave Europe's *Gaining* and Return to the Natural Order's *Being*." In *The Conference on the Discourse of Environmental Advocacy*, ed. Christine L. Oravec and James G. Cantrill. Salt Lake City: University of Utah Humanities Center, 1992.

Sanchez, John, and Mary E. Stuckey. "Communicating Culture Through Leadership: One View from Indian Country." *Communication Studies* 50 (1999): 103–15.

Selected Biographies

Means, Russell, with Marvin J. Wolf. *Where White Men Fear to Tread: The Autobiography of Russell Means*. New York: St. Martin's Press, 1995.

Smith, Paul Chaat, and Robert Allen Warrior. *Like a Hurricane: The Indian Movement from Alcatraz to Wounded Knee*. New York: New Press, 1996.

CHRONOLOGY OF MAJOR SPEECHES AND STATEMENTS

See "Research Collections and Collected Speeches" for source codes.

"Statement of Russell Means, National Coordinator, American Indian Movement." Kyle, S.D., June 17, 1973. In U.S. Congress, Senate, Subcommittee on Indian Affairs of the Committee on Interior and Insular Affairs. *Hearings on the Occupation of Wounded Knee*. 93rd Cong., 1st sess. Washington, D.C.: Government Printing Office, 1974.

Custer, S.D., Remarks. September 3, 1973. Ithaca, N.Y.: The Rest of the News, 1973. Audiocassette.

"Address at Law Commune." Cambridge, Mass., December 2, 1973. Broadcast on *The Drums: The Voice of Indian People*. Boston: WBUR. Rebroadcast as *Russell Means. Interview with David Barsamian*. Los Angeles: Pacifica Radio Archive, 1986. Audiocassette.

"Opening Statement." *U.S. v. Russell Means*. U.S. Dist. Ct., St. Paul, Minn., February 12, 1974. Transcript available from Earl G. Anderson & Associates.

Native American Spiritual Values. North Hollywood, Calif.: Pacifica Radio Archive, March 1974; Los Angeles: Pacifica Tape Library, March 1974; also as "Native American Spirituality." St. Paul: Minnesota Public Radio, April 4, 1974. Audiocassette.

Russell Means. Los Angeles: Pacifica Tape Library, 1976. Audiocassette.

"There Is Only One Color of Mankind That Is Not Allowed to Participate in the International Community. And That Color Is the Red." Presented at Discrimination Against the Indigenous Populations of the Americas. Conference of Non-Governmental Organizations of the United Nations. Geneva, Switzerland, September 1977. *NAR*, pp. 115–17.

"The Same Old Song" (Black Hills International Survival Gathering). Rapid City, S.D., July 1980. In *Marxism and Native Americans*, ed. Ward Churchill. Boston: South End Press, 1983. Variations of Means's most famous speech include (1) "Marxism Is a European Tradition," *Akwesasne Notes*, Fall 1980; (2) "For the World to Live, 'Europe' Must Die," *Mother Jones*, December 1980, pp. 24–38, also in *Great Speeches in American History*, ed. Richard J. Jensen, William H. Lyon, and Philip Reed Rulon. Edina, Minn.: Bellwether, 1990; (3) "For America to Live, Europe Must Die." In *Where White Men Fear to Tread*, pp. 545–54, and also *RM*.

"Industrialism and American Indian Culture" (Schumacher Lecture). Bristol University (U.K.), November 7, 1981. Available at www.schumacher.org.uk/lecture_archive.htm and in *The Schumacher Lectures*, vol. 2, ed. Satish Kumar. London: Blond & Briggs, 1984.

Nicaraugua's Other War (Eastern New Mexico University). Portales, N.M., April 7, 1986. Videocassette; *PM*.

"Native America" (University of Colorado). Denver, Colo., September 28, 1988. *AR*. Also available as "The State of Native America," in *NAR*, pp. 177–93.

"Statement of Russell Means, Indian Leader, Member, Oglala Sioux Tribe." Washington, D.C., January 30, 1989. In U.S. Congress, Senate, Special Committee on Investigations of the Select Committee on Indian Affairs. *Hearings on the Federal Government's Relationship with American Indians*. Washington, D.C.: Government Printing Office, 1989.

"Welcome to the Reservation" (Bowdoin College). Brunswick, Me., February 21, 1992. *AR*.

"For the World to Live, Columbus Must Die" (University of Colorado). Denver, Colo., April 27, 1992. *AR*.

"Lessons from Native America: Knowing Who You Are" (Boulder Public Library). Boulder, Colo., October 11, 1993. Also *Open* magazine, special ed., (1994); *AR*.

"Disney's Pocahontas." *Native America Calling*, June 27, 1995. *NAC*.

"Free to Be Responsible" (Diné College [formerly Navajo Community College]). Tsaile, Ariz., Fall 1995. *RM*.

"Interview with Will Swaim." *Life and Times*. Los Angeles: KCET, April 30, 1996. Videocassette.

"Voice of Mother Earth" (Presencia Taina and Long Island Native American Task Force, National Museum of the American Indian). New York City, March 27, 1999. Videocassette. *PM*.

"Indian in the Spotlight: Russell Means." *Native America Calling*, July 13, 1999. *NAC*.

"Plastic Shamans." *Native America Calling*, September 30, 1999. *NAC*.

"The History and Results of the Hatred of American Indians" (Equal Justice Society, College of Law, University of Nebraska). Lincoln, Neb., October 4, 1999. Videocassette. *PM*.

"The Murder of Anna Mae Pictou Aquash (Part I)." *Native America Calling*, November 3, 1999. *NAC*.

"Commentary #2." Produced by Helene Hagan. c. 1999. Audiocassette. *PM*.

"World Politics." 1999. CD. *PM*.

"Revolution!" (Libertarian Party National Convention). Anaheim, Calif., July 1, 2000. Available on *The Libertarian Alternative, with Russell Means, Parts I and II*. Produced by Mark Selzer. Videocassette. Excerpts available at www.lp.org/lpnews/0008/convention_means.html

Commentary. Porcupine, S.D., July 10, 24, 31, and August 14, 2000. Audiocassettes. *PM*.

"Columbus Day." *Native America Calling*, October 11, 2000. *NAC*.

"Interview with Brian Bull" (South Dakota Public Radio, University of South Dakota). Vermillion, S.D., October 24, 2000. Audiocassette. *PM*.

"Lecture" (Rice University). Fort Worth, Tex., April 20, 2001. Videocassette. *PM*.

"Remarks." World Radio Network. Hosted by Bill Morriss. June 28, 2001. Audiocassette. *PM*.

The Spiritual Legacy of the American Indian (New York Public Library Annex). New York City, August 2, 2001. Audiocassettes. *PM*.

"Remarks." *Renaissance Radio Hour*. Hosted by Leo and Deborah Knighton Tallarico. Santa Fe, N.M., September 3, 2001. Audiocassette. *PM*.

"Americans, What Are You Going to Do?" *Indian Country Today*, October 8, 2001. Available at www.indiancountry.com/?2328

"Remarks" (New Mexico gubernatorial campaign). Cloudcroft, N.M., September 22, 2001. Videocassette. *PM*.

"Lecture" (California State University–Fresno). October 30, 2001. Videocassette. *PM*.

The Columbus Legacy: A Visit with Russell Means. Free Speech TV, 2002. Videocassette. *PM*.

"Remarks." *The Tavis Smiley Show*. Albuquerque, N.M.: KUNM, November 26, 2003. Available at www.npr.org

HARVEY BERNARD MILK (1930–1978)
San Francisco Supervisor, Gay-Rights Activist

KAREN A. FOSS

Harvey Milk, the first gay supervisor in San Francisco, ran three campaigns before winning election in 1977, at a time when being out as a gay man was considered political suicide. Deliberately designed to disrupt the political scene, Milk's rhetoric simultaneously offered a new vision for what the city could be. That he was assassinated in 1978, after only eleven months in office, suggests the potential limits of his oppositional campaign strategies. Milk's rhetoric continues to stand as inspiration, template, and cautionary tale for individuals and groups moving from marginalization to mainstream.

Harvey Bernard Milk was born in Woodmere, New York, on May 22, 1930, to William and Minerva Karns Milk. His early years gave little indication of the political interests that ultimately came to dominate his life. After graduating from the New York State College for Teachers in 1951, he joined the Navy and fought in the Korean War. Upon his return, he taught high school, but moved on to a variety of jobs after he became bored with teaching. Eventually he took a position as a financial analyst on Wall Street and, at the same time, began to work on a friend's Broadway productions in his free time. When his partner took a job as stage manager for the San Francisco production of *Hair*, Milk moved with him to San Francisco, where he once again found work as a financial analyst. Milk's values increasingly were aligned with the counterculture, however, and he was fired for burning his BankAmericard during a demonstration against the Vietnam War. Milk returned to New York briefly to work in the theater, but in 1973, he moved back to San Francisco with his new partner, Scott Smith. They opened a camera store, called Castro Camera, on March 3, 1973.

Milk's decision to run for the Board of Supervisors in the summer of 1973 came from frustration over government's unresponsiveness to people's needs. Already disgusted by the government's lack of honesty in the Watergate scandal, Milk was upset about a special tax charged him as a small business owner. The last straw for Milk was when a teacher came into the camera store to borrow a projector because her district could not afford to buy one. Deciding he could make a difference, Milk ran for supervisor as a representative for all underrepresented groups in the city. He came in tenth out of thirty candidates—a solid showing for an unknown. Milk ran again for the Board of Supervisors in 1975, this time coming in seventh, trailing the six incumbents running for reelection. Because of his strong showing, the new mayor, George Moscone, appointed him to a seat on the Board of Permit Appeals.

Milk gave up that seat in 1976, only a few months into his term, to run for the Democratic nomination for the California State Assembly. He decided to run after learning that Art Agnos had been selected to be the Democratic candidate in advance of the primary election, technically the venue in which the candidate would be determined. Milk believed representatives should be selected by the people, and thus ran to challenge the political machine. He lost the election to Agnos by 4,000 votes.

Milk's third bid for the Board of Supervisors, in 1977, proved successful. His term was cut short when he and Mayor George Moscone were assassinated on November 27, 1978, by fellow supervisor Dan White. White had resigned his seat on the Board and then asked for it back; on the day of the killings, Moscone was to have announced that he had decided not to reappoint White to the seat. White was convicted of voluntary manslaughter and sentenced to five years in prison. He committed suicide on October 21, 1985, within a year of his release.

HARVEY MILK: UNOFFICIAL MAYOR OF CASTRO STREET

The rhetorical situation Harvey Milk faced in his bid for public office is at once typical and atypical of the novice politician. The exigence he faced and needed to address with his discourse was the desire to make a difference through holding office. In order to achieve this goal, Milk had to overcome several constraints that stood between him and his voting audience—that he was unknown in San Francisco, had no previous political experience, and was openly gay. His discourse, then, had to address not only the political exigence of running for office but the personal one of doing so as a gay man. Across his four campaigns, Milk consistently employed two pairs of oppositional strategies to manage these exigences: (1) antithesis and synthesis and (2) enactment and violation.

streets of San Francisco, holding "Milk for Supervisor" signs. These billboards made visible what had been a highly invisible group politically—gay men.

In his second campaign for supervisor, Milk continued his oxymoronic pairing, this time with gays and labor unions. The Teamsters Union had been attempting, without success, to implement a boycott of Coors beer in response to the brewer's refusal to sign a contract with the Teamsters. Milk convinced the gay bars in San Francisco to support the boycott—an action crucial to the boycott's success—and as a result received the endorsement of several labor unions. His ability to identify with blue-collar workers—often viewed as the antithesis of gay men—earned him strong support from labor during all of his campaigns.

Also in this campaign, Milk was given—or perhaps gave himself—the title "the unofficial

---

Harvey Milk's irreverence earned him considerable negative publicity. Milk knew, however, that even this kind of press kept his name before the public, as Randy Shilts recounts in his biography of Milk: "Sticks and stones may break my bones, but just spell my name right." Milk preferred to be noticeable and remembered on Election Day rather than appropriate and forgotten.

In terms of antithesis, Milk consistently paired opposing or contrasting ideas in such a way as to ensure that the contradictions remained evident. In his first campaign, he presented himself as an outsider, marginalized in every possible way because he was gay, Jewish, and a newcomer to San Francisco and to politics. Despite his outsider status, however, he also presented himself as capable of representing or standing for all of the outsider positions. In announcing his candidacy, Milk declared: "I stand for all those who feel that the government no longer understands the individual and no longer respects individual rights." His campaign slogan, "Milk Has Something for Everybody," captured his universal appeal—an appeal constructed on his outsider status. Milk also incorporated antithesis in his use of human billboards, in which rows of gay men lined the

mayor of Castro Street." The terms *unofficial* and *mayor* are strikingly antithetical and further suggest Milk's ability to present himself as someone capable of bringing together characteristically oppositional attributes. In this case, he preserved his outsider status—his unofficial status—while also suggesting his prominent role in the life of the Castro and of San Francisco. The synecdoche also suggested that there were two San Franciscos and two mayors.

Milk juxtaposed two additional antithetical categories—insider/outsider and human/machine—in his third campaign, the run for the democratic nomination for the Assembly. In this race, he reversed the meanings of insider and outsider in his campaign discourse. Typical is the description he offered in a May 27, 1976, column in the *Bay Area Reporter*, in which he presents himself as the political insider and his opponent, Art Agnos, as the outsider:

> He's been an observer, not a participant, and has never really experienced the daily fight for survival that most of us have to face. I'm not being accusatory here—in some respects, I may be envious. I'm a small business man and I'm well aware of the uncertainties of the economy, exactly what the "inflationary spiral" means when I'm forced to raise prices to my customers, and how taxes can eat into your earnings.

Milk similarly paired the antithetical terms of *human* and *machine* in the Assembly campaign, evident in his campaign slogan, "Milk Versus the Machine." In his announcement of his candidacy for the Assembly, he articulated his basic position that the political machine—and not the people of the state of California—had been making the decisions about who would run for office:

> The overriding issue is simply: do the people . . . that make up the Sixteenth Assembly District have the right of political self-determination—or, can the machine take that right away? Machines operate on oil and grease; they're dirty, dehumanizing, and too often unresponsive to any needs but those of the operators.

In Milk's final and successful bid for supervisor, antithesis is evident in that he took the title *incumbent* for himself, despite never having held office. Milk saw himself as the incumbent in terms of the things that mattered—knowledge of the city, involvement in and concern for the city, and experience with its daily challenges. Whether linking large concepts such as insider and outsider or creating specific oxymorons, such as the "unofficial mayor of Castro Street," Milk's campaigns were grounded in the juxtaposition of unlikely and paradoxical ideas.

With the incorporation of synthesis, Milk continued to work with the dualities that he often brought together in antithesis, then transcended the tension between them. In his first campaign, the creation of a coalition of "outsiders" is one example. Milk did not simply assert his outsider role, but offered himself as the candidate who would represent all marginalized groups. The op-

portunity for synthesis again presented itself when an ideologically conservative Arab Republican businessman took one of Milk's flyers, crossed out Milk's name, and inserted his own. Rather than expressing anger, Milk called a press conference and used it as an opportunity to point out that he must be doing a good job of bridging ideologies if someone whose politics were so different from his could use his campaign flyer without revision.

As another example, Milk developed a flyer that listed his position on thirteen city issues on the left side and the present Board of Supervisors' stance on each on the right side of the page. In the middle, complete with blank lines, was a column titled "Write in Your Position." Milk encouraged his audience to engage in synthesis after examining both his position and the position of the Board of Supervisors. He took the opportunities offered to move beyond dichotomies and to focus on what could be fashioned from their juxtaposition.

The strategies of antithesis and synthesis set the tone for Milk's rhetoric. Together, they demonstrate how his rhetoric functioned not only to disrupt the existing worldview by bringing opposites together in new juxtapositions but also to offer different visions for how the world could be. His disruptions of the norm and new ways of putting the world together became his basic rhetorical approach, and were evident as well in his second pair of strategies—enactment and violation.

Enactment was evident in that Milk consistently enacted or served as an example of his politics. He did what he believed in and what he said he was going to do. For the most part, this meant attending to and meeting basic human needs—those often ignored by the political mainstream. In Milk's address to the longshoremen during his first campaign, he set the stage for enactment in his description of his vision for San Francisco:

> San Francisco can start right now to become number one. . . . We can start overnight. We don't have to wait for budgets to be passed, surveys to be made, political wheelings and dealings . . . for it takes no money . . . it takes no compromising to give people their rights . . . it takes no money to respect the individual. It

takes no political deal to give people freedom. It takes no survey to remove repression.

Milk's campaign proposals were designed to enact his vision for the city, and he suggested uncomplicated and inexpensive ways to improve the quality of life for the inhabitants of San Francisco. Milk proposed, for example, that cars be banned from the heart of downtown; the Board of Supervisors, in contrast, supported a plan for more parking garages. Milk suggested that city officials be required to take public transportation to work; he believed it was the only way the city would get a better mass transit system. Although not able to implement his ideas for the city at the time, Milk remained committed to his pragmatic, populist platform throughout his campaigns and during his time in office.

By the time of his second campaign, Milk had worked to enact the vision he had for the city, starting with his own neighborhood, the Castro. As a local business owner in the Castro, he threw himself into efforts to make it a place where people talked to their neighbors about city issues. He organized the Castro Street fair and resurrected the Castro Village Association, both of which fit his image of what a neighborhood should be. And he registered over 2,000 new voters, in line with his vision of people directly impacting the political process.

Milk's decision to run for the California Assembly—his third campaign—also conveyed his commitment to enactment. When he learned that the Democratic candidate has been selected far in advance of the primary, he ran in order to provide a true alternative and to enact his vision of an open political system. And when he did win election to the Board of Supervisors, he did not abandon his concern with the basic rights and issues that make a city livable. He installed more than fifty new stop signs in his district and introduced a "pooper-scooper" ordinance that required pet owners to clean up after their animals. As Randy Shilts relates in his biography of Milk, "Harvey's political philosophy was never more complicated than the issue of dogshit; government should solve people's basic problems."

At the same time that Milk consistently enacted his worldview, he also made sure to do the unexpected in violating traditional political norms. In the first campaign, he refused to dress the part of a politician and instead wore his customary blue jeans and kept his hair long. His only concession was to tie it back in a ponytail. He also made outrageous comments throughout his campaigns—remarks that would be deadly for most politicians. Michael Wong, interviewed for David Lamble's audio documentary and ultimately a Milk supporter, described such a remark from his first encounter with Milk:

> I had heard from the so-called gay leaders—Jim Foster and the Alice B. Toklas Gay Democratic Club—that this guy was a nut. I was very wary of even talking to him. But in the course of the conversation, I was really impressed with the issues he brought up. . . . But halfway through this conversation, . . . Harvey told us that he thought . . . that some father who learned that he's homosexual will come out and shoot at him and he'll survive the shooting but that'll give him so much sympathetic publicity that he'll win on that. . . . And then I thought, Jim Foster was right—this guy is a nut.

Milk also talked about being gay at a time when doing so was a political taboo—another example of his strategy of violation. Not only did he admit he was gay, but he used gay supporters in very public ways—human billboards, for example—in the campaign. Joining gays and labor, as he did for the Coors beer boycott, violated not only expectations about gays but also about what political alliances were possible in the city.

In Milk's Assembly campaign, he continued his vocal discussions of gays and lesbians by constructing what would become known as his "Hope Speech." In the appeal to "hope" with which he concluded this speech, Milk used the disenfranchisement of gays and lesbians as the epitome of what it means to be left out of the mainstream:

> And the young gay people in the Altoona, Pennsylvanias and the Richmond, Minnesotas who are coming out. . . . The only thing they have to look forward to is hope. And you have to give them hope. . . . Without hope, not only gays, but the blacks, the seniors, the handi-

capped . . . will give up. And if you help elect . . . more gay people, that gives a green light to all who feel disenfranchised, a green light to move forward. It means hope to a nation that has given up, because a gay person makes it, the doors are open to everyone.

No matter what other issues he was addressing, Milk ended with this reference to gays and lesbians. Even when speaking on issues that had nothing to do with being gay, he made sure to talk about the fact that he was gay.

Milk's irreverence about and willingness to violate traditional political decorum earned him considerable negative publicity. Milk knew, however, that even this kind of press kept his name before the public, as Randy Shilts recounts in his biography: "Sticks and stones may break my bones, but just spell my name right." Milk preferred to be noticeable and remembered on Election Day rather than appropriate and forgotten.

When Milk became a city supervisor, he continued to be extremely vocal about the gay community and his allegiances—again contrary to existing political wisdom. Milk's speech "That's What American Is," is typical of the stance Milk took in terms of his gay identity: "I'm tired of the silence, so I'm going to talk about it. And I want you to talk about it." Milk demonstrated his commitment to talking about being gay by traveling the state and speaking out against Proposition 6, a ballot initiative introduced early in his tenure that would allow school boards to fire teachers who practiced, advocated, or accepted homosexuality. Enactment, then, paired with violation, constituted Milk's second set of rhetorical strategies. He continually violated political expectations at the same time he enacted what he believed in.

Milk's rhetorical strategies—antithesis and synthesis, enactment and violation—functioned simultaneously to embody and challenge the dualities that constructed the rhetorical situation Milk encountered in San Francisco as he sought political office. Beginning with his first campaign, however, he refused to accept the dichotomies that characterized politics—gay/straight, insider/outsider, appropriate/inappropriate. He consistently acknowledged the boundaries of the dominant worldview and stirred them up; he recognized the limits and at the same time crossed them. These

strategies allowed him to negotiate a rhetorical space characterized by "both-and" rather than "either-or." It is as if the juxtaposition of contrasting strategies literally pushed open the boundaries of the world so that Milk could pose different possibilities for it.

Milk's use of contradictory strategies also accomplished a "normalizing" of gay identity. He made his gay identity critical to, and at the same time just another part of, who he was. He was different from some people because he was gay; he was similar to many people in spite of being gay. In other words, Milk presented shifting and multiple framings of his identity at any one time, and invited others to similarly consider the various ways they negotiate and present multiple identities to others.

This does not mean, however, that everyone welcomed or appreciated the space that Milk's discursive tactics created for the city. Four campaigns in the space of five years offered very little time for the public to get used to his rhetorical approach. And because his rhetoric was built on the deliberate disruption of established ways of doing and being, there were those in Milk's audience who chose to focus on the disruptions his rhetoric caused rather than on the possibilities it contained. Dan White, of course, is the obvious example of this response to Milk's rhetoric, and his assassination of Milk suggests the extreme measures such rhetorical disruptions can provoke.

The rhetoric of Harvey Milk offers a look at a sustained effort to gain office by the use of oppositional tactics. Using antithesis and synthesis, enactment and violation, he gained entrance into San Francisco politics on his own terms at the same time that he became a voice for underrepresented groups, most notably gay men and lesbians. That he was one of the first openly gay politicians in the United States, combined with his near martyrdom following his assassination, assures his continued rhetorical importance.

INFORMATION SOURCES

Research Collections and Collected Speeches

The Harvey Milk Archives/Scott Smith Collection contains printed campaign materials, speech manuscripts, and photographs taken of and by Harvey Milk.

It is housed in the Special Collections of the San Francisco Public Library [*HMA*]. The Gay Lesbian Bisexual Transgender Historical Society in San Francisco maintains an archive of Milk artifacts, including his ponytail, which he cut off after the first campaign; his appointment book; and the pen with which he signed the first gay/lesbian antidiscrimination legislation. The Rare and Manuscript Collections at the Carl A. Kroch Library at Cornell University contain two folders with materials about and correspondence with Milk: the James Foster file (#7439) and the Firebrand Books file (#7670). No published collections devoted to Milk's speeches exist at this time.

Shilts, Randy. *The Mayor of Castro Street: The Life and Times of Harvey Milk* [*MCS*]. New York: St. Martin's Press, 1982. Includes Milk's "political will."

Web Sites

Although the biography of Harvey Milk is available on many Web sites, there is no substantial material related to his speeches or his work on any one Web site.

Audiovisual Materials

Harvey Milk Remembered. Audio documentary produced by David Lamble. San Francisco, 1979.

The Times of Harvey Milk. Film produced by Robert Epstein and Richard Schmiechen. San Francisco: Black Sands, 1984.

Selected Critical Studies

Foss, Karen A. "Harvey Milk." In *Reader's Guide to Lesbian and Gay Studies*, ed. Timothy F. Murphy. Chicago: Fitzroy Dearborn, 2000.

———. "Harvey Milk and the Queer Rhetorical Situation: A Rhetoric of Possibility." In *Queering Public Address*, ed. Charles E. Morris. Columbia: University of South Carolina Press, forthcoming.

———. "The Logic of Folly in the Political Campaigns of Harvey Milk." In *Queer Words, Queer Images: Communication and the Construction of Homosexuality*, ed. R. Jeffrey Ringer. New York: New York University Press, 1994.

Selected Biographies

Fenrich, R. Lane. "Harvey Milk and Gay Rights." In *American Reform and Reformers: A Biographical Dictionary*, ed. Randall M. Miller and Paul A. Cimbala. Westport, Conn.: Greenwood, 1996.

Foss, Karen A. "Harvey Milk." In *Encyclopedia of American Lesbian, Gay, Bisexual, and Transgender History and Culture*, vol. 2. New York: Scribner's, 2004.

———. "Harvey Milk: 'You Have to Give Them Hope.'" *Journal of the West* 27 (April 1988): 75–81.

Shilts, Randy. *The Mayor of Castro Street: The Life and Times of Harvey Milk*. New York: St. Martin's Press, 1982.

Weiss, Mike. *Double Play: The San Francisco City Hall Killings*. Reading, Mass.: Addison-Wesley, 1984.

CHRONOLOGY OF MAJOR SPEECHES

See "Research Collections and Collected Speeches" for source codes.

"A Populist Looks at the City" (address to the Joint International Longshoremen and Warehousemen's Union). San Francisco, September 10, 1973. *MCS*, pp. 349–52.

"Reactionary Beer" (address urging continuing boycott of Coors beer). undated. *HMA*.

"Statement of Harvey Milk: Candidate for the 16th Assembly District" (announcement of candidacy for the California Assembly). San Francisco, March 9, 1976. *HMA*.

"A City of Neighborhoods" (address to fund-raising dinner). San Francisco, January 10, 1978. *MCS*, pp. 353–58.

"The Hope Speech" (Milk's quintessential campaign and stump speech). San Diego, March 10, 1978. *MCS*, pp. 359–63.

"That's What America Is" (address to the Gay Freedom Day Parade). June 25, 1978. *MCS*, pp. 364–71.

RALPH NADER (1934–)
Consumer Advocate, Lawyer, Presidential Candidate

PATRICIA A. SULLIVAN AND STEVEN R. GOLDZWIG

Ralph Nader was born in Winsted, Connecticut on February 27, 1934, the son of immigrants from Lebanon. His parents succeeded in the United States, as did so many new arrivals from other countries. Nathra, Nader's father, arrived in the United States in 1912 with $20, a sixth-grade education, and limited knowledge of English. By working at a series of factory jobs, he saved enough money to return to Lebanon to seek a wife. In 1925 he married Rose Bouziane, a teacher, and although the match was arranged, the couple seemed compatible. As a child, Ralph was precocious and exhibited some of the personality traits that would mark him as a public figure. He placed enormous value on privacy, excelled as a student, and learned civics lessons from his parents. Nader's father had high expectations for the American system of government, and rejected hollow promises made by politicians. He believed that American values, including equality, representative democracy, and freedom of expression, required an engaged citizenry. Ralph was eight when his father began taking him to court to observe how lawyers presented cases and, as biographer Justin Martin noted, Nathra encouraged his son to see the arguments in court "as epic battles between the strong and the weak, rich and poor, just and unjust." The visits to court fostered a vision of the lawyer as advocate for those who were voiceless. From an early age, Ralph vowed, in Martin's words, to "represent underdogs, in keeping with the most sacred principles of democracy."

Nader graduated magna cum laude from Princeton in 1955 and received a law degree from Harvard in 1958. He was an outsider at both institutions. He attended Princeton because of its curriculum and emphasis on preparing students for positions in government and public service. Nader was a high achiever as an undergraduate and was admitted to the Woodrow Wil-

son School of Government during his sophomore year. He flourished academically, and his devotion to his studies set him apart from the sons of prominent fathers who partied, participated in sports, and received the "gentleman's C." Nader was a different type of outsider at Harvard Law School. Whereas he was a diligent student among casual students at Princeton, at Harvard he cut classes and showed contempt for the law school's philosophy. He objected to the elitist assumptions that shaped law school pedagogy. For Nader, the law was a tool to ensure social justice. His career path was beginning to take shape. Although he questioned instruction at the school, he understood that his ethos as an advocate would be enhanced if he had a degree from Harvard.

RALPH NADER: THE ORATORY OF A CONSUMER ADVOCATE

After Nader graduated from Harvard, he began a forty-year career as a consumer advocate. He uses his considerable power as a rhetorician to craft compelling arguments through oral and written communication. Consistently, Nader has been ahead of his time in arguing for consumer rights and questioning corporate power. More recently, he has criticized the influence of corporate power on government and education. Since 1965, Nader has presented himself as the David challenging the Goliath of corporate interests. Many of his admirers and detractors have referred to him as "relentless" and have expressed admiration for his political savvy. Over the years Nader has been popular on the lecture circuit, especially on college campuses, and the fees have supported his causes. Even in the mass media era of the sound bite, he continues to give long speeches. As an orator, he foregrounds clear themes as he weaves complicated narratives. His testimony before congressional hearings is systematic and detailed, and reflects his legal training. During his long career, Nader has cast himself as an outsider, a truth teller, a muckraker. His reputation as a tireless crusader enhances his ethos, and although he makes strong appeals to logos, or logic, grounded in facts, he also appeals to pathos by using anecdotes and playing the role of the outraged citizen. In presentations filled with facts, his sarcastic tone suggests "Do you believe this?" Additionally, he enhances his credibility and brings life to his speeches by including quotations from great orators such as Cicero, Martin Luther King Jr., and Daniel Webster.

From the vantage point of the twenty-first century, it may be difficult for observers to appreciate how radical Nader was in the 1960s. In a time of social ferment, he was not involved in the civil rights movement or the anti-Vietnam

phraseology. He spoke at length, laying down lawyerly verbal constructions that piled dependent clause upon dependent clause, but beneath the surface of his testimony there hummed a finely calibrated sense of outrage."

One of Nader's most important appearances was on March 22, 1966. A Senate subcommittee was convened to investigate whether Nader, a federal witness, had been harassed by General Motors (GM). General Motors had hired a private investigator to uncover "dirt" on Nader in order to damage his credibility as a critic of the company. According to Michael Salvador, Nader demonstrated rhetorical skills that would mark his public discourse throughout a long career of public service, and his speaking was marked by a "cunning integration of vivid storytelling and explicit rationality." During his testimony, Nader articulated a theme of corporate accountability that

---

In 1966, Ralph Nader articulated a philosophy that has remained unchanged throughout his career: "So much of what we do for and to ourselves is done through the large corporate institution directly and indirectly acting on other derivative institutions. The challenge is to bring corporate powers, privileges and de facto immunities into greater conformance with the public interest."

"Taming the Corporate Tiger"

War movement, but in his own movement for "body rights." As Martin explained, for Nader, "body rights" translated into "basic physical rights: against being maimed or killed." Although people now take attention to automobile safety for granted, the situation was quite different in 1964 when Nader began the crusade that resulted in publication of *Unsafe at Any Speed* (1965). On February 10, 1966, Nader testified, for the first of many times, before a congressional committee, and observers noted that he had a gift for giving such testimony. As he challenged the auto industry's commitment to safety and "body rights," a style emerged that would become familiar throughout his lengthy career. In Martin's words, "Nader was surprisingly self-assured. As he had in *Unsafe at Any Speed*, he interwove dry statistics with bursts of vivid

would echo in his speaking and writing in future years. He called on the public to hold corporate executives responsible for decision-making that led to "tremendous carnage, and because they are remote in time and space between their decision and the consequences of that decision, there is no accountability."

Through *Unsafe at Any Speed*, congressional testimony, speeches, and articles, Nader emerged as a charismatic advocate for consumer rights. His crusade against General Motors and its Corvair served as a template for his rhetorical approach to addressing other consumer issues. Nader declared victory when President Lyndon Johnson signed the National Traffic and Motor Vehicle Safety Act and Highway Safety Act in 1966.

Nader's campaign against GM addressed not only issues associated with safety and the environment, but also with privacy. In 1970, Nader's lawsuit against GM for invasion of privacy was settled. A central issue in the twenty-first century is technological invasion of privacy. On this issue, as with many other issues, Nader was ahead of his time. In 1971, he gave a speech at Dickinson College in which he addressed privacy issues in an information age. In "The Invasion of Privacy in Our Computerized Society," Nader said: "There is no way a complex society as a whole or in its constituent parts can intelligently plan for a just society without detailed information. What is needed are greater rights of participation, initiative and control by citizens so that more can be beneficiaries, not victims, of such information."

As Nader began a long career as a consumer advocate, he demonstrated consummate rhetorical skill in dramatizing the forces of good and evil—corporate interests versus the public interest. In "Taming the Corporate Tiger," a speech delivered before the National Press Club in 1966, Nader articulated a theme that he would return to over his long career. He argued for the need to curtail corporate power and protect consumer interests: "So much of what we do for and to ourselves is done through the large corporate institution directly and indirectly acting on other derivative institutions. The challenge is to bring corporate powers, privileges and de facto immunities into greater conformance with the public interest."

After his successful crusade against the auto industry, Nader identified other issues centering on "body rights." In his next public crusade, he took on the meat industry and loopholes in the Meat Inspection Act of 1906. Through congressional testimony, muckraking journalism, and speeches, he continued the pattern of combining vivid examples with factual information to illustrate that the meat industry was exploiting consumers. Shortly before President Lyndon Johnson signed the Wholesome Meat Act in 1967, Nader addressed the Consumer Assembly and noted that technology made it easier for the meat industry to make contaminated meat palatable for consumers: "Of course, here the wonders ingenious of modern chemistry come into play. A seasoning agent, preservatives and coloring agents do the job and the basic natural detection processes of the consumers are masked.

He is no longer able to taste, smell or see diseased or contaminated meat." In the speech, Nader addressed a range of consumer issues and demonstrated his power as an orator by drawing listeners in through his use of parallelism: "I don't think the credit problems in this country just affects a few corner pawn shops. I don't believe that the electric price-fixing conspiracy which bills consumers to the tune of hundreds of millions of dollars over the three decades of the conspiracy ending in 1961 simply was a result of a few fly-by-night electric firms. I don't think the lack of safety in automobiles is due to a few small garages who hand-make some hazardous automobiles."

In 1968 a *Newsweek* cover story featured an image of Nader as a knight who would save consumers from corporate abuses, and in the same year the first group of Nader's Raiders was formed. The Raiders were student volunteers who worked with Nader to expose government and corporate abuses. The years 1969–76 ushered in Nader's "golden age," his "most productive period" as a consumer advocate, in the words of one of his biographers. Nader's Raiders investigated the Federal Trade Commission, the Interstate Commerce Commission, the Food and Drug Administration, air pollution, airline safety, nursing homes, the medical profession, and other agencies in the public and private sectors.

During his "golden age," Nader founded the Public Interest Research Group (PIRG), the Center for the Study of Responsive Law, and Public Citizen. With the settlement from his lawsuit against GM, he started PIRG. Nader had been critical of the training he received at Harvard, and PIRG represented a counterpoint to the philosophy that informed the curriculum at prestigious law schools. Nader's vision of public interest law guided PIRG and the Center for the Study of Responsive Law. In "Ralph Nader Asks Students to Change," a speech delivered at Harvard Law School in 1972, he posed questions about values and challenged students to consider why they wanted to become lawyers: "Why are the most important problems so often treated in such a boring way, or so often believed to lack intellectual challenge? If you look, for example, at the written work done at the Law School a dozen years ago, you will see that the concentration was not in the areas where most people can be afflicted, affected, or helped by the legal system—areas like torts, urban development, housing, pollution, and industrial health and safety."

Nader was a popular speaker on college campuses and encouraged students to establish local PIRG chapters that would coordinate with the main organization in Washington. As was often the case, Nader moved on, but PIRG remained vital. In 1971 Nader founded Public Citizen, an umbrella organization that provided funding for a number of consumer advocacy groups, including the Health Research Group and the Litigation Group. Nader's vision of an active and engaged citizenry is reflected in a speech he gave in 1970 before the Conference on Property Tax Reform in Washington. He addressed myths that impeded property tax reform, but he placed the responsibility for change on citizens: "The combined force of courageous citizens in every locality, together with efforts by national organizations and authorities, will rapidly lead to a much more equitable property tax system with all that means for city and county services, education, small property owners, land use, the elderly and a more honest political structure."

During his "golden age," Nader received a number of overtures to run for elected office. He had a high profile and name recognition, and was scandal-free. Some supporters considered Nader a perfect choice to run against Nixon in 1972. He had his first brush with a third party, the New Party, courting him to run for the presidency. Nader refused the overtures and, as Martin observed, friends of Nader said he feared that a third-party candidate would draw votes from the Democratic candidate and ensure Nixon's victory.

Nader continued to work "on" rather than "in" government. During the 1970s he was unflappable. Defeats that others might have considered setbacks fueled Nader's commitment to consumer rights. During this period, Nader joined forces with the Union of Concerned Citizens in questioning the safety of nuclear power plants. In 1973 he founded Congress Watch, a group to lobby members of Congress on safety issues concerning nuclear power. He crusaded for an amendment of the 1966 Freedom of Information

Act. In his relentless pursuit to expose government corruption, he became aware of loopholes in the law. The legislation was amended in 1974, but Nader would continue to fight for access to government documents. Nader's name surfaced again as a possible presidential candidate in 1976, and potential Democratic candidates consulted with him. Nader had high hopes when Jimmy Carter was elected president in the wake of the Watergate scandal. After Carter took office in 1977, however, Nader was disappointed in his performance. He felt betrayed by Carter, although a number of Nader associates served in the administration. Whereas in 1968 Nader suggested there was a difference between the two major political parties in the United States, by 1977 he had concluded that the Democratic and Republican parties both served corporate rather than consumer interests.

Nader's "golden age" was over. He lobbied Congress to create a Consumer Protection Agency, and failed. As the Carter administration ended, Nader resigned as president of Public Citizen. During the administration of President Ronald Reagan, a favorable climate for business prevailed and business groups restored their images through highly effective rhetorical strategies. With Reagan in office, Nader had no influence in Washington.

Throughout the 1980s, Nader continued to give speeches and was known for his lengthy presentations. In "The Megacorporate World of Ronald Reagan," a speech given at the National Press Club in 1984, Nader identified rules for "the Teflon President" (e.g., avoid the details, cultivate amiability, avoid impromptu media events). He suggested that the "Reagan-corporatist revolution" should serve as a catalyst for renewed efforts to ensure consumer rights. He opened the speech by referring to a time in U.S. history when politicians served the public interest, and he quoted Thomas Jefferson as indicating "that the purpose of representative government was to curb 'the excesses of monied interests.'" The speech was fiery and fact-laden as Nader told the story of "Reagan's Darkness at Noon." He noted: "Subsidies, monopolistic licenses, protectionism, selective enforcement, lucrative contracts, loan guarantees, bailouts, and the free results of expensive research and development are among the dispensations of modern Uncle Sugar in Washington, D.C. Together these goodies make a bustling bazaar of corporate welfare and largess that requires nurturing and enlargement."

Early in the 1990s, Nader opened many presentations by asking, "America, what went wrong?" Analysis of his speeches reveals his inventional processes. In developing lengthy presentations, Nader organized his speeches around one theme—for example, democracy vs. plutocracy—and combined anecdotes with facts in making his case. Although he rambled in his speeches, the theme was clear, and he adopted the persona of a teacher who was determined to enlighten his audiences. In the "Concord Principles: An Agenda for a New Initiatory Democracy," he introduced a "new democracy toolbox" and offered it to candidates seeking the presidency in 1992. Generically, the document bore a resemblance to the Declaration of Independence. Just as the founders of the United States articulated a vision for a new nation, so did Nader's "Concord Principles." Nader longed for a time in the United States when the government served public rather than corporate interests. In sum, "The American people should assume reasonable control over the assets they have legally owned for many years so that their use reflects citizen priorities for a prosperous America, mindful of the needs and rights of present *and* future generations of Americans to pursue happiness within benign environments." He discussed the "Concord Principles" as part of his participation in the New Hampshire primary. As he advocated for national health insurance, campaign finance reform, and public ownership of the airwaves, he drew attention to everything that he believed had gone wrong in America. Political campaigns, financed by and captives of corporate interests, constituted one of those things that had gone wrong.

Two speeches in 1992 reflected Nader's vision for a new democracy. He was not on the ballot in the New Hampshire primary but, as he expressed in "The Citizen Agenda for '92: Dissolving the Plutocracy," a speech delivered at Harvard Law School on February 15, 1992, voters should write in his name for *None of the Above*. A *None of the Above* option would permit voters to express their dissatisfaction with

presidential campaigns. Nader often challenged his listeners by posing questions, and he said: "So what is the characterization of the presidential campaign anyway? Is it the novelty of the quadrennial period? Is it whatever the candidates think will play in Peoria? Is it the limited range of the candidates' backgrounds? Is it what conflicts with their campaign contributors' priorities? What really determines it? You'll notice I haven't raised the most important determinant, which should be what the citizens instruct them, urge them, to talk about." For Nader, the revisioning of political campaigns was another consumer issue. In drawing attention to the dominance of corporate interests—plutocracy vs. democracy—Nader's tone was sarcastic and outraged, the same tone he had used in identifying problems with General Motors and the automobile industry early in his career.

In 1992 at Harvard, Nader also called on listeners to exercise the civic power they were entitled to in a democracy. He addressed a range of issues, and wove together anecdotes and facts. The style that marked his earlier speeches was evident here. Although listeners might perceive Nader's ideas as disconnected, a thematic thread bound together all the ideas in his lengthy presentation. Plutocracy was responsible for all the problems Nader identified, from lack of access to health care to problems with education; it all came down to "grow [ing] up corporate." He was especially critical of corporate control of media, and emphasized: "And what is TV? It's ninety percent entertainment—including ads—ten percent redundant news, zero percent mobilization. But it is our property. We own the public airwaves." In this speech he also returned to an issue he had addressed earlier in his career, criticizing the pedagogy at Harvard Law School that encouraged students to "develop intellectual rigor in an intellectual cage" and, in turn, serve plutocracy rather than democracy.

During another speech in 1992, "The Decline of Democracy and the Concord Principles," delivered on May 9 at the University of San Francisco, Nader contrasted democracy with plutocracy, and challenged listeners to reflect on the following: "We have to ask ourselves how do we measure democracy before we determine if it's advancing or declining." He proceeded to tell the audience, using repetition and parallelism. In highlighting the "yardsticks" of democracy, Nader listed ways in which "a society is more democratic." He returned to his message about civic power and attacked an educational system in which "The very word 'civics' implies yawns" and students do not learn problem-solving skills that will help them become citizens. He combined extended illustrations (e.g., the elementary school teacher in Salt Lake City who encouraged her students to become socially engaged and wrote a book, *Kids in Action*) with factual information from sources such as the General Accounting Office.

Whereas Nader was not a "real" presidential candidate in 1992 and participated only in the New Hampshire primary, by 1996 he made a more serious run for the presidency. In the past, he had fought against many corporate abuses, but by this time he had formulated a message that defined his mission as a candidate. In "The Moral Courage to Stand Against Injustice," a speech delivered in Sacramento, California, on October 17, 1996, Nader said: "The present campaign [1996], led by TweedleDee and TweedleDum, Republican and Democrat, increasingly demonstrates that our political choices are becoming extraordinarily narrow, but even more important, that the narrowness of the choice itself reflects the increasing domination over both parties and our government of multinational corporations." Every problem Nader encountered, from access to members of Congress to access to members of the press, he attributed to the disintegration of democracy due to corporate influences. Although one might assume that Nader's vision of Washington would have improved during the years of the Clinton administration (1993–2001), such was not the case.

Just as Carter had disappointed Nader, so did President Bill Clinton and Vice President Al Gore. During these years, Nader became more convinced that the major political parties served corporate interests rather than the interests of the people, and he referred to President Clinton as "George Ronald Clinton." Nader was not consulted by members of the Clinton administration, and he was especially angry at the vice president because, as a senator, Gore had an excellent record on environmental issues. In this period, it was rare for Nader to testify before congressional committees. Earlier in his career he had cultivated a persona as an outsider, but in this time period he was truly an outsider. He became more concerned about the difficulty of getting media coverage for alternative political viewpoints and noted that large corporations own media outlets and those outlets serve corporate interests.

Nader believed that he had no voice in Washington, and he agreed to stand as a candidate for the Green Party in twenty-one state primaries. Even as an official candidate, he remained a political outsider. He did not join the Green Party or embrace its platform, and as Martin noted, in 1996 Nader "stood for president" instead of "running for president." He did not campaign, accept contributions, or place advertisements. Still, 580,627 people cast ballots for him, and he received 0.6 percent of the vote. During 1996, Nader called on audiences to reflect on social movement history in the United States. In his view, as he suggested in the speech "The Moral Courage to Stand Against Injustice" (1996), "any society that lets the profit-seeking mercantile value system dominate itself against other values of humanity—justice, opportunity, health, safety, respect for future generations, the intangibles of civilization—any society that allows the mercantile, the profit-seeking system to dominate gets into trouble." He challenged corporate greed and urged listeners to embrace values that defined the United States prior to the rise of corporate influence. He suggested that audiences derive inspiration for "moral courage" from social movements—abolitionism, suffrage, labor unions—that shaped U.S. history. As he narrated a history of social movements in the United States, he called on listeners to remember history and to continue the nation's story of activism. He blamed corporate influence on media messages for corrupting children's values. Nader used repetition and parallel structures to communicate that children do not learn moral courage from television: "They don't even know who the heroes were in our country any more. Their heroes are Chester Cheetah, Tony the Tiger, Power Rangers, Ninja Turtles. They don't inherit the stories from their ethnic background or their grandparents anymore. They don't inherit the stories that had the morals to them, from the books."

By 2000, Nader was even more passionate in challenging "autocratic governance," and he announced his candidacy for the presidency on February 21, 2000. As Martin observed, Nader was entering the race late, but he had led many consumer campaigns on shoestring budgets and tight time lines. His message was the same as in 1992 and 1996, but this time Nader was prepared to wage a serious campaign for the presidency and he mobilized his forces. He raised money, but as a proponent of campaign finance reform, he rejected political action committee money. He relied on small contributions from many donors. Whenever he faced serious barriers to getting his name on a state ballot, he mounted a legal challenge. In Washington, at the IFG/IMF World Bank Teach-in on April 14, 2000, he delivered "Challenging Autocratic Governance That Serves the Interests of Global Corporations." He emphasized that his

tics as usual, and he mocked Bush's photo opportunities and his label as a "compassionate conservative." He said sarcastically of Bush's label, "When you have to have an adjective you're in trouble as a movement." In defining a "different kind of campaign," Nader emphasized that citizens can defeat monied interests. In "The Central Contention of Politics Should be the Distribution of Power," a speech delivered on March 1, 2000, before the Los Angeles Press Club Conference, Nader said, "This campaign is going to be running *with* the people. Not parading *in front of* the people." In calling for civic engagement, he used repetition and argued: "We want to show more people in this country that citizen volunteer time, well-organized and directed, can overcome the money of the vested interests. There will be fundraisers and *time*-raisers because everybody in this country, no matter what their level of income or wealth is, possesses 24-hours-a-day. They can all participate with their time in political campaigns."

In 2000, Nader dismissed George Bush's portrayal of himself as a "compassionate conservative." Said Nader, "When you have to have an adjective you're in trouble as a movement."

---

remarks would be posted on the Internet because he did not expect coverage from mainstream corporate media. He argued that "corporate globalization" had destroyed democracy and used repetition to emphasize his point: "They [corporations] want to dominate governments. They want to dominate the workplace. They want to dominate the marketplace. They want to dominate the universities by corporatizing them. They want to dominate the very concept of childhood with their brazen commercial exploitation of small children."

Throughout the campaign in 2000, Nader challenged voters to recognize that they didn't need "to accept a choice between the bad and the worse." He cast himself as the outsider, the alternative, the anti-politician, and Bush and Gore (on some occasions he referred to Gush and Bore) as identical in their servitude to corporate interests. In the speech "Wasting Your Vote," presented in Santa Cruz, California, on August 23, 2000, he called for audience stamina in challenging poli-

Nader's themes were familiar to his audiences in 2000. Throughout his career, he had argued for civic engagement and social justice as the marks of a "deep democracy." When he accepted the nomination of the Green Party in Denver, Colorado, on June 25, 2000, he seemed to be teaching the civics lessons that he had learned from his parents. He narrated a history of social justice movements in the United States, and called on listeners to return to a time before "the unfortunate resurgence of big business influence, generating its unique brand of wreckage, propaganda and ultimatums on American labor, consumers, taxpayers, and most generically, American voters. Big business has been colliding with American democracy and American democracy has been losing." In vivid language, he invited listeners to demand solutions to a host of problems identified in the speech, and emphasized: "A collective understanding must distinguish people's yardsticks to measure the quality of the economy from corporate yardsticks."

Although Nader's themes were familiar to audiences in 2000, there is no question that this campaign was different from his campaigns in 1992 and 1996. This time he was an official candidate who was campaigning, fund-raising, staging rallies, and running televised advertisements. In "Wasting Your Vote," Nader posed questions about his opponents, and explained why they did not debate "real" issues: "Do you think Bush or Gore would debate about who is tougher on corporate crime? Do you think they will accuse each other of being soft on corporate crime? Of course not. Because they are beholden to the corporate government in Washington, D.C."

To what extent was Nader's candidacy responsible for the outcome of the 2000 presidential election? Would Gore have defeated Bush if Nader had not been in the race? Nader's role as a "spoiler" in the 2000 presidential debate will be debated for years. He received 2.7 percent of the vote nationally, and 1.6 percent in Florida, the state that sealed George Bush's win over Al Gore by 537 votes. Scholars also may debate whether Nader's rhetoric enhanced or hindered his campaign. Christine Harold proposed that Nader's rhetoric is problematic because it "frames him as the only pure, authentic candidate." Her analysis of Nader's rhetoric has implications for third-party candidates: "Consequently, it can be argued that the goals of the Green Party were ill served precisely because Nader and his followers were not contaminated *enough*. Instead of ardently (and vainly) protecting a pure, unadulterated space from which to launch their attacks on a corrupt system, the Greens might have had more success by *embracing* their role as a viral corrupting agent—a kind of green virus—actively forcing a reconfiguration of the American political system."

Nader continues to advocate a democratic toolbox and a new democracy. His quest for consumer rights, and all his causes, at least metaphorically, involve "body rights, basic rights that we have as human beings in a democracy." He is highly visible as a speaker, writer, and consumer advocate, and it is reasonable to assume that he may once again seek the presidency and run *with* the people rather than parade *in front of* them.

INFORMATION SOURCES

Research Collections and Collected Speeches

There are no archival collections or published collections of speeches at this time. *The Ralph Nader Reader*, with a useful foreword by Barbara Ehrenreich, is organized thematically, and includes speeches and articles from 1966 to 2000. Rat Haus Reality Press maintains a Web site that includes some speeches by Nader as presidential candidate and some press reports covering campaigns.

Nader, Ralph. *The Ralph Nader Reader* [*RNR*]. New York: Seven Stories Press, 2000.

Web Sites

The Nader Page. History, opinions and editorials, In the Public Interest, correspondence, testimony, news releases, books, biographical, information. http://www.nader.org

Official Campaign Site for Ralph Nader's Presidential Campaign in 2004. http://www.votenader.com

"Public Interest," weekly newspaper column. http://www.nader.org/public_interest.html

Ralph Nader—Challenging Autocratic Governance/ Expanding Democratic Participation. Transcripts of past and recent speeches. http://www.ratical.org/co-globalize/RalphNader

Rat Haus Reality Press [*RAT*]. Includes texts of speeches from Nader's 1992, 1996, and 2000 presidential campaigns, plus press accounts. www.ratical.org

Selected Critical Studies

Harold, Christine L. "The Green Virus: Purity and Contamination in Ralph Nader's 2000 Presidential Election." *Rhetoric and Public Affairs* 4 (2001): 581–603.

Salvador, Michael. "The Rhetorical Genesis of Ralph Nader: A Functional Exploration of Narrative and Argument in Public Discourse." *Southern Communication Journal* 59 (1994): 227–39.

Stein, Harry H. "American Muckraking of Technology Since 1900." *Journalism Quarterly* 67 (1990): 401–9.

Selected Biographies

DiCanio, Margaret B. *Encyclopedia of American Activism: 1960 to the Present*. Santa Barbara, Calif.: ABC-CLIO, 1998.

Martin, Justin. *Nader: Crusader, Spoiler, Icon*. Cambridge, Mass.: Perseus, 2002.

May, Martha. "Ralph Nader and Consumer Politics." In *American Reform and Reformers: A Biographical Dictionary*, ed. Randall M. Miller and Paul A. Cimbala. Westport, Conn.: Greenwood, 1996.

McCarry, Charles. *Citizen Nader.* New York: Saturday Review Press, 1972.

CHRONOLOGY OF MAJOR SPEECHES

See "Research Collections and Collected Speeches" for source codes.

"Congressional Testimony: Hearings Before the Subcommittee on Executive Reorganization." In *Federal Role in Traffic Safety.* Washington, D.C.: Government Printing Office, March 22, 1966.

"Taming the Corporate Tiger" (speech to the National Press Club). Washington, D.C., December 21, 1966. *RNR,* pp. 133–44.

"Keynote Address Presented to the Consumer Assembly." November 2, 1967. *RNR,* pp. 251–60.

"Remarks Before the Conference on Property Tax Reform." Washington, D.C., December 12, 1970. *RNR,* pp. 186–94.

"Remarks Before the Public Affairs Symposium on the Invasion of Privacy in Our Computerized Society" (speech at Dickinson College). Carlisle, Pa., February 7, 1971. *RNR,* pp. 419–24.

"Speech to the Harvard Law School." Cambridge, Mass., February 26, 1972. *RNR,* pp. 379–87.

"The Megacorporate World of Ronald Reagan" (speech to the National Press Club). Washington, D.C., June 6, 1984. *RNR,* pp. 80–91.

"The Citizen Agenda for '92: Dissolving the Plutocracy." Cambridge, Mass., January 15, 1992. *RAT.*

"The Concord Principles: An Agenda for a New Initiatory Democracy." Concord, N.H., February 1, 1992. *RNR,* pp. 40–51.

"The Decline of Democracy and the Concord Principles" (speech at University of San Francisco). May 9, 1992. *RAT.*

"The Moral Courage to Stand Against Injustice." Sacramento, Calif., October 17, 1996. *RAT.*

"The Central Contention of Politics Should Be the Distribution of Power" (Los Angeles Press Club press conference). March 1, 2000. *RAT.*

"Challenging the Autocratic Governance That Serves the Interests of Global Corporations" (IFG IMF/World Bank Teach-in). Washington, D.C., April 14, 2000. *RAT.*

"Acceptance Statement of Ralph Nader for the Association of State Green Parties Nomination for President of the United States." Denver, Colo., June 25, 2000. *RAT.*

"Wasting Your Vote." Santa Cruz, Calif., August 23, 2000. *RAT.*

RICHARD MILHOUS NIXON (1913–1994)
Thirty-seventh President of the United States

CELESTE M. CONDIT AND SHANNON HOLLAND

The career of Richard M. Nixon demonstrates both the great potentials and the severe limitations of public oratory. Raised in a family where voluble political argument was common, he refined his speaking skills in debate and intramural political contests during his school years. The competitive experience shaped his public discourse, making the primary focus of his oratory to win, using whatever strategies were available. After graduating from Duke Law School in 1937, Nixon honed these skills throughout his career, evolving from what critics have called a rough and immature extremist into an effective presidential orator.

Nixon's first major political battle was the campaign against Jerry Voorhis for California's Twelfth District congressional seat in 1946. Here, he established the major theme of his political life: anticommunism. Its emotional application led to his victory and gave him the House Un-American Activities Committee as a platform from which he emerged as a national figure by exposing Alger Hiss as a Communist espionage agent. He used the same harsh anticommunist appeals successfully in his next major race, against Helen Gahagan Douglas, for the U.S. Senate in 1950. He was soon selected by Dwight D. Eisenhower as the Republican vice presidential candidate, and the ticket won in 1952 and 1956, propelling Nixon to the Republican nomination for the presidency in 1960. After losing this close race to John F. Kennedy, he ran for governor of California in 1962, a contest he also lost. Always "Mr. Republican," he continued to work diligently for the party and to learn to use the medium of television more effectively. He emerged again in 1968 as the Republican presidential nominee, winning the presidency after a bitter campaign, only to face the divisive issue of the Vietnam War. During his first term, he laid the groundwork for several international achievements but, facing a hostile Congress and a divided nation, he was unsuccessful in achieving many of his domestic goals. He was reelected over George McGovern in 1972; however, this election occasioned the Watergate break-in. As a consequence of his participation in the Watergate cover-up, he was compelled to resign from office after losing the confidence of his party and the American public.

NIXON AS A POLITICAL PERSUADER

Nixon's most natural speaking milieu was probably that of his many political campaigns, where the rules of the game emphasized personal victory. Trained in the art of competitive debate, Nixon constructed his speeches carefully, thoroughly preparing background materials. Furthermore, he adopted an antagonistic position toward his opponents and relied on the strategy of attack, mostly through claims that they supported, represented, or indirectly served international communism. His use of aggressive attack strategies began in his first political campaign. After joining the Navy at the end of World War II, Nixon returned from active duty and entered his first political race in 1946. Seeking a victory in the Twelfth Congressional District election over Democratic incumbent Jerry Voorhis, Nixon portrayed himself as the hard-nosed conservative determined to rid the government of Communist sympathizers. At the time, the Republican Party desperately sought a new campaign strategy that could end its sixteen years of minority party status. The solution was to reinvent the Red Scare. For Nixon, this strategy suited his aggressive political persona perfectly. Not only did he campaign vigorously against communism in general, but he also accused Voorhis of personally supporting communism.

Although the allegations were entirely unfounded, Nixon's discourse sparked anxiety among the voting public. His unyielding attack appealed to many Americans unnerved by the ongoing threat of the Soviet Union. The linchpin of this election was the Nixon–Voorhis debates. Voorhis agreed to participate in public debates with Nixon, allowed Nixon to speak first and last, and agreed there would be no set topic. In the debates against the amateur Voorhis, Nixon used his argumentative skills to decimate his opponent and establish his own political ethos. As Voorhis blundered through the question-and-answer periods, Nixon launched vicious attacks on Voorhis's Communist connections. Unable to match Nixon's aptitude in the debate arena, Voorhis was politically incapacitated. On Election Day, Nixon seized the seat of the five-time-elected incumbent by a margin of 15,000 votes.

In his victorious campaign against Voorhis, Nixon discovered the potency of his aggressive anticommunist position; in his second campaign, he deployed the same strategies. In the Senate race of 1950, Nixon campaigned head-to-head with Helen Gahagan Douglas, a woman who had won the seat in 1944 and quickly established a reputation as an independent thinker and liberal. Implying her association with communism, Nixon immediately dubbed Douglas "The Pink Lady" for her record of consistently voting in support of welfare programs and her alleged collusion with Alger Hiss. Again, Nixon relied on personal attacks. Unlike Voorhis, however, Douglas retaliated, making counterclaims about Nixon's participation in Communist plots. Particularly, she censured his relationship with Representative Vito Marcantonio of New York, a known Communist. Quickly, the race deteriorated into a contest of name-calling, accusations, and personal indictments. Nonetheless, Nixon's aggressive strategies panned out, and the election culminated in his victory by a margin of 680,000 votes.

Nixon's victories over Voorhis and Douglas centered on his ability, through innuendo and guilt by association tactics, to link his opponents with Communist interests. In his memoirs, Nixon indicated that his claims were perhaps overstated, although he relied on his favorite excuse—that others were doing the same. Often biographers and critics have described his tactics as vicious, emotional, and unwarranted. Nonetheless, those tactics were successful, and through their use, Nixon established a reputation as an avid anticommunist and skilled political figure; this persona landed him the Republican vice presidential candidacy in 1952.

By 1952, Dwight D. Eisenhower was revered by the American people for his military accomplishments in World War II; however, politically, his liberal tendency isolated him from the conservative base of the Republican Party. In order for Eisenhower to gain Republican support for his presidential campaign, he needed to select a vice presidential candidate who could bridge the gap between the conservatives and Eisenhower's liberal platform. Nixon seemed to be the perfect choice. Known for his tough anticommunist stance and aggressive campaign strategies, Nixon was young, an excellent orator, and an experienced political figure in both

cratic nominee Adlai Stevenson, arguing that Stevenson was a Communist appeaser connected to mobsters from the Capone organization. He promised to "nail down those lies" Stevenson was telling, clean up the government, and maintain an uncompromising stance toward communism domestically and abroad. Although his strategies were highly effective in mobilizing popular and conservative support for the Republican ticket, the persona made him highly vulnerable to counterattack. Ironically, at the same time Nixon was proclaiming that he would "clean up Washington," the *New York Post* featured the headline "Secret Nixon Fund." The story revealed that Nixon had received $18,000 from wealthy Californians to cover his campaign expenses.

Angered by Nixon's attack campaign, the Democrats launched a counterattack to regain support and taint the public's perception of Nixon as a clean politician. The accusations that

Although often criticized for its simple narrative and bald emotional appeals, Richard Nixon's Checkers speech not only was effective at keeping him on the Republican ticket, but also is widely considered the first landmark televised speech.

the House and the Senate. His youth appealed to younger voters, thus balancing Eisenhower's maturity. Nixon was the solution for mending the divide between the liberal and conservative wings in the Republican Party.

In the election of 1952, Nixon's strategic attacks on the Democratic Party in general (and on Adlai Stevenson in particular) united the Republican Party and gained support from the American people. As the vice presidential candidate, Nixon was assigned the hatchet job of partisan attack. His themes were corruption, communism, and Korea, and he campaigned vigorously. The political chaos caused by corruption within the Truman administration became a focal point of Nixon's campaign. During his whistle-stop campaigns, he attacked the Truman administration, advancing suspicion of corruption in the executive branch. Furthermore, Nixon aggressively challenged Demo-

Nixon received funds as political bribes and allegations that Nixon used the fund for personal reasons were unsubstantiated; however, the scandal was an embarrassment to both Nixon and Eisenhower. Nixon's campaign had emphasized the need to "clean up Washington," and now he was being charged with corruption and unscrupulous conduct. The event provoked so much controversy that Eisenhower considered dropping Nixon from the ticket. For Nixon, a response was essential. Before the largest national television audience to that date, he replied to those attacks with the "Checkers" speech of September 23, 1952, which he called "My Side of the Story." The speech was one of the most successful public orations in U.S. history, resulting in over 2 million supportive telegrams, telephone calls, and letters; it was the salvation of Nixon's career.

Although the critics have agreed that Nixon's

speech failed to use sound argument or evidence to address the major issue, they have generally nominated it as a paradigm of the development and use of ethos. In "Checkers," Nixon presented personal narratives reflecting his modest upbringing and his commitment to the common people. He projected sincerity and homeyness, using a vernacular diction that was characteristic of his style at that time. Other hallmarks, including the personalization of the event, the use of innuendo, and the predisposition toward the attack, were also evident. Nixon's preparation of the speech was typical of this early speaking style. He wrote multiple draft outlines, drawing material from minor impromptu speeches he had given in the days before the event. He delivered the speech extemporaneously, which allowed him to project sincerity. In his decision to speak directly to the people rather than through the news media, the speech represented Nixon's continual, eventually almost obsessive, distrust of the press. Ultimately the speech vindicated Nixon the man, but perhaps at the cost of making him seem too simple, immature, and "unpresidential."

In the presidential campaign of 1956, Nixon sought a new image as a vice president and presented more positive themes in his campaign: "peace, prosperity, and progress." By this time he had fully mastered his powerful baritone voice, dynamism, and general competence as a platform orator. In 1960, this new Nixon ran on his own, facing a new type of campaign dominated by the mass media. The nationally televised Republican National Convention featured much skilled oratory, evoking a positive response to Republicanism in general. Nixon's speech provided the ultimate performance of the convention. He had learned to project sincerity and maturity through the new medium. The seasoned fighter continued his stump oratory throughout the country, giving more than 180 prepared speeches and as many informal speeches; however, four televised debates with his opponent, John Kennedy, captured the most public interest and presented him directly to the largest number of people—10 million for each debate.

Most commentators judged Kennedy the winner in the crucial first debate. Many commentators have posited that because television highlights appearance over substance, Kennedy's victory could

be attributed to his superior physical presence in the debate. Political scholars suggest that Kennedy's countenance and physical control during the debates impressed the audience more than a sweating and ill Richard Nixon. Accentuating this claim, scholars also note that many radio audiences preferred Nixon to Kennedy. The radio audience probably consisted of rural and older voters predisposed to favor Nixon because they were more conservative, and they were perhaps influenced by Nixon's superior vocal qualities. More voters watched the televised debate; hence, Nixon's loss in the first debate is more likely accounted for by the fact that television demanded a different type of image than earlier media. Because television is a medium that stimulates the audience through sight and sound, the partisan, attack-oriented Nixon fulfilled the demands of television less naturally than the more confident Kennedy. In any case, the debates are credited with changing a small margin of votes, a factor perhaps significant in Nixon's narrow loss. However, they taught Nixon more lessons about the new medium, and he was able to apply them diligently in later campaigns.

Nixon's heart was probably not in his gubernatorial contest in 1962, but his efforts at rebuilding the party were both sincere and well calculated to gain him the Republican Party's 1968 nomination for the presidency. In 1960, Nixon had attempted to appeal to small-town America through close personal identification on the stump in all fifty states. In 1968, Nixon and his staff worked hard to find new ways to use television to appeal to a broader audience in a less personal style. His speechwriting had changed dramatically from the early days. Although he would always take primary responsibility for major addresses (in campaigns and in the presidency), he now had a large, sophisticated, and skilled speechwriting staff that he relied on heavily. The staff included, at various periods, Patrick Buchanan, William Safire, Ray Price, and more than a dozen other writers, researchers, and editors. The staff was extremely sensitive to television as a medium. At one point, they reviewed many television tapes of Nixon, concluding that he was best in spontaneous question-and-answer formats. The "man in the arena" campaign commercial evolved from these conclusions. In addition, in 1968 the Republicans handled the televising of their convention far more skillfully than the Democrats (who were plagued by controversial demonstrations in Chicago), and Nixon's acceptance speech was extremely successful.

By 1972, Nixon's strategy and style had evolved even further from the partisan slugger who was just a common man. Not only did Nixon rely on others to write his speeches, he also relied on them to deliver them. He campaigned very little in person, sending a dozen surrogates to speak for him around the nation. He appeared on radio and television late in the campaign, and adopted a presidential image throughout. In this campaign, Nixon integrated his traditional strategies of attack into the requirements of television. In a series of television advertise-

reinvigorated his "peace and prosperity" campaign to secure voters in the center. His tactics were effective. On Election Day, Nixon gained 61 percent of the popular vote, outpolling McGovern in the electoral college 521 to 17, one of the largest margins in history.

The change in Nixon's campaign strategies is an example of both the evolution of the orator (from vicious partisan to national leader) and the evolution of campaigning between two different periods (that of platform public address and televised public address). Also, Nixon's campaign is uniquely interesting because it produced a highly controversial presidency. Nixon's major concern as president was foreign policy. Although his summit meetings with the Soviets and his diplomatic initiatives with China and the Middle East

---

As president, Nixon's first major speech on Vietnam, the "Vietnamization" address of November 3, 1969, was his most controversial address. The speech was highly effective, earning Nixon a 77 percent public approval rating for his handling of Vietnam. It was well designed to appeal to Nixon's "silent majority," and the clear, simple style allowed him to create a public understanding of difficult matters in a way that led to acceptance of his policy. Critics, however, have noted that Nixon applied his standard political tactics of polarizing the audience and characterizing some of the nation's citizens as extremists, thereby pitting the country against itself.

---

ments, he deployed a two-pronged strategy. First, McGovern's social views made him an easy target for attacks. Nixon depicted McGovern as an irresponsible liberal dedicated to defense cuts, the legalization of marijuana, an antiwar stance, and welfare hikes. Through his ads, Nixon created the impression that McGovern was outside the center of his own party and not responsive to middle Americans. Second, and in contrast to McGovern, Nixon projected a more personal side of himself, presenting footage of White House events such as state dinners, meetings with international leaders, and work in the Oval Office. Although he maintained his image as "Mr. Republican," Nixon constructed a softer side of himself, emphasizing his connection with hardworking Americans. He also

have received the most foreign policy attention, his oratory on the Vietnam War—bridging the domestic and the international realms—has received the most attention from rhetorical critics. As president, Nixon's first major speech on Vietnam, the "Vietnamization" address of November 3, 1969, was his most controversial address, and it has spawned an enduring debate about the nature and purposes of rhetorical criticism. Most critics agree that the speech was highly effective; it garnered a 77 percent public approval rating for Nixon's handling of Vietnam. It was well designed to appeal to the "silent majority," the middle audience that Nixon clearly targeted. The style was clear and simple, allowing him to create a public understanding of difficult matters in a way that led to acceptance of his policy. Critics, however, have noted that Nixon applied his standard political tactics of polarizing the audience and casting some of the nation's citizens as an unacceptable extremist group, thereby pitting the country against itself. The speech relied on weak logic, including a heavy dependence on either-or fallacies. Thus, the speech was similar to many of his other partisan efforts, effective in gaining what he wanted—in this case, majority public support to carry on the war until he could negotiate a graceful exit—but at the price of divisiveness.

The later speeches on the Vietnam War, particularly the April 30, 1970, address defending the invasion of Cambodia and the May 8, 1972, speech announcing the mining of Haiphong Harbor, relied on fairly similar strategies but received less dramatic public response. In the Vietnam speeches, Nixon emphasized the need to protect allies and achieve a "just" peace without shame to the United States. He vilified and blamed the enemy for the failure of negotiations. He suggested his willingness to make the hard decision to continue the fighting, and he provided historical descriptions to buttress his interpretations. In the long run, these speeches were perhaps most firmly supported by the clever policy they announced. Pulling out Americans while maintaining an anticommunist stance through material support satisfied the most central demands of the major national factions.

Nixon's most eloquent statement of his goals for peace and freedom came not from his Vietnam War speeches but in his First Inaugural Address. This address has been attacked by critics as mediocre and as having attempted, but failed, to achieve greatness. While it is true that several of Nixon's phrases—"we will be as strong as we need to be as long as [we] need to be" and "I know the heart of America is good"—seem to fall short of the sonorous heights of John F. Kennedy's inaugural address, the speech compensates for these weaknesses in sentence construction by offering Americans a fresh dose of high ideals. Nixon began by calling attention to the "orderly transfer of power" that would allow Americans to "celebrate the unity that keeps us free." He asked Americans to turn away from merely material concerns to "build a great cathedral of spirit." He offered every American the

path to greatness through the simple tasks of "helping, caring, and doing." Most forcefully, he applied Archibald MacLeish's depiction of the earth from space—"small and blue and beautiful in that eternal silence where it floats"—as a compelling metaphor for the necessity of peace. Nixon's Inaugural Address, although spoken in the words of a common man, not a poet, was loftily delivered and offered Americans the broadest vision they had heard in a long time. Enhanced as it was by the majestic setting, the public response was extremely positive. The negative response of the critics is traceable to the fact that they judged the man who delivered the phrases as incompetent of keeping such promises. Even when transcending in words the partisan style of his past, the partisan slugger's ethos continued to limit his larger effectiveness.

Although domestic issues did not draw most of his interest, Nixon delivered many important speeches on these issues, and generally they were well crafted. For instance, his clear and forceful "Energy Emergency" speech on November 7, 1973, called for balanced responses to a complex situation. Comparing it with President Jimmy Carter's far less effective efforts on similar topics, for example, demonstrates Nixon's great skill in using the rhetorical power of the presidency to gain public support and action.

Nixon's greatest rhetorical challenge, however, was presented by the Watergate incident, and in that case not even his seasoned and artful skill was adequate to surmount the obstacles. The long ordeal of Watergate began for the public on June 17, 1972, when political spies, acting on the authority of the Committee to Re-elect the President, were caught breaking into the Democratic Party's Watergate office. In the next two years, revelations of improper wiretaps, break-ins, and political dirty tricks would add to the Watergate story. In addition to Nixon's self-admitted general responsibility for these acts, the crucial blow to his public confidence was the revelation, through tapes made in the White House, that Nixon participated actively in the cover-up of these activities.

Nixon made what he calls his first formal address on Watergate on April 30, 1973. In his memoirs, he admits that for the sake of simplicity, he chose to claim falsely that he had not been personally involved in the cover-up. He announced the resignation of his top advisers, insisted on his determination to get to the truth and bring the guilty to justice, and tried to explain the events. He concluded by urging the country to forget Watergate and get on with the "vital work to be done" for the country. The speech was well designed in most respects. Unfortunately, it followed too well his long-established speaking patterns, relying on ethos and neglecting evidence. In this case, and increasingly throughout the year, counterevidence presented in other media, often with admittedly partisan frenzy, thoroughly impugned his character. Gradually, he was forced to recognize this.

Nixon's adaptation is evident in the "Watergate Investigation" speech of August 15, 1973. The address repeated much of his earlier strategies but also emphasized a higher principle in the president's actions. If the facts had been other than they were, this might have been recorded as a truly great speech. Nixon clearly and forcefully elaborated the principle of confidentiality. Moreover, he argued eloquently for the need to "clean up politics" because Americans needed to "show a renewed respect for the mutual constraints that are the mark of a free and civilized society."

The facts, however, once again betrayed Nixon's words. At the time of this speech, he was already at an all-time low in the polls, and because it could not counter with evidence of innocence, this speech did little to change the public's opinion. The man did not exemplify his words. The words that were taken as a true sign of his character were those finally revealed in his last major Watergate policy address on April 29, 1974. After losing a Supreme Court test, Nixon finally admitted that it was necessary to waive executive privilege, since executive privilege protects the actions of a president in the national interest, not the personal interest of someone who wishes to win or maintain the presidency. In this final speech, Nixon skillfully tried to recharacterize what the nation would hear in the tapes that were to be released. He carefully contextualized damaging phrases and emphasized those lines that might redeem him. The nation, however, would see the full transcript of the tapes, which revealed a profane, extremely partisan, ethically lax person, a man who operated without the restraint necessary for a civilized society. The Congress and the public, and, most important, the Republican Party leaders, denied Nixon their confidence.

The denouement came with Nixon's resignation speech of August 8, 1974, and the White House farewell of August 9, 1974. The resignation speech was dignified and appropriate; once defeated, the partisan exhibited good grace in leaving the arena. The speech has been criticized as failing to meet the demands of the genre of apologia, but it did not really attempt to provide an apology. Nixon explained the reason for his resignation as a loss of a political base that would allow him to govern effectively, and then provided a fairly standard presidential farewell address. The address does not provide a fully satisfactory response to the situation, but Nixon's situation had long gone beyond the ability of oratory to "make all come right," as he himself noted in his memoirs. Only the sad and maudlin personal farewell to the White House staff remained. This was an address appropriately full of pathos, one that should not have been made available to the public. Nixon—the common man, the personal partisan, the emotional orator—reappeared here; the man who rose to the presidency with the rise of television was its captive even in his private farewell.

In the years following his presidency, Nixon delivered few public speeches. After his resignation, he disappeared from the public sight for several years. In the mid-1980s, he reentered politics as a diplomatic representative of the United States. He traveled to countries in Europe, Asia, Africa, and the Middle East. In 1986, he visited Mikhail Gorbachev. During this time Nixon helped bridge U.S. relations with other nations by coordinating dialogues between the Reagan administration and foreign leaders. In 1989, he visited China for the sixth time, expressing outrage over the Tiananmen Square killings, and in 1991, after meeting Boris Yeltsin, he became an outspoken opponent of extending aid to Gorbachev's regime in the Soviet Union. In the last years of his life, he wrote several books, including his memoirs, and he counseled the Bush and Clinton administrations on foreign policy. Despite his reemergence in politics, he was largely unable to rehabilitate his image in the public sphere.

There is no doubt that Richard M. Nixon was one of the most skillful modern-day American political rhetors. He learned to adapt to the changing media and roles. Unfortunately, in the end, his discourse and its effectiveness were shackled by the partisan nature of the creature who constructed and delivered the rhetorical creation.

INFORMATION SOURCES

Research Collections and Collected Speeches

Many of Nixon's private papers were donated to the National Archives. On July 19, 1990, the Nixon Library and Birthplace officially opened. Public documents and transcripts of Nixon's speeches can be obtained at 18001 Yorba Linda Boulevard, Yorba Linda, CA 92886 or via the Web site. This library's site includes information and speeches delivered during and after Nixon's presidency. Also, three months before his death on January 20, 1994, Nixon announced the creation of the Nixon Center, an organization dedicated to exploring ways to increase national security. The Nixon Center is independent of the Nixon Library and is a nonpartisan institution that gathers research material on foreign policy issues. This information can be found at 1615 L Street, NW, Suite 1250, Washington, DC 20036 or at the Web site. Additional documents and speeches from Nixon's presidency can be found in *Public Papers of the Presidents* and *Weekly Compilation of Presidential Documents.*

Andrews, James R., and David Zarefsky. *Contemporary American Voices: Significant Speeches in American History, 1945–Present* [*CAV*]. New York: Longman, 1992.

Bremer, Howard F., ed. *Richard M. Nixon, 1913: Chronology, Documents, Bibliographical Aids* [*RMN*]. Dobbs Ferry, N.Y.: Oceana Publications, 1975.

Podell, Janet, and Steven Anzovin, eds. *Speeches of the American Presidents* [*SAP*], 2nd ed. Bronx, N.Y.: H.W. Wilson, 2001.

Singer, Aaron, comp. *Campaign Speeches of American Presidential Candidates: 1928–1972* [*CPAPC*]. New York: Fredrick Ungar, 1976.

Web Sites

Center for the Study of the Presidency. http://www.thepresidency.org

Nixon Center [*NC*]. http://www.nixoncenter.org

Nixon Library and Birthplace Foundation [*NLB*]. http://www.nixonfoundation.org and http://www.nixonlibrary.org

Watergate Info [*WI*]. http://www.watergate.info

Audiovisual Materials

Greatest Presidential Speeches of the 20th Century. Renton, Wash.: CounterTop Software, 2001.

Great TV News Stories: The Great Debates—John F. Kennedy vs. Richard M. Nixon. Orlando Park, Ill.: MPI Home Video, 1994.

Nixon, Richard M. *In the Arena: A Memoir of Victory, Defeat, and Renewal.* New York: Simon and Schuster Audio, 1990.

Selected Critical Studies

Baskerville, Barnet. "The New Nixon." *Quarterly Journal of Speech* 43 (1957): 38–43.

Campbell, Karlyn Khors. "Richard M. Nixon and Vietnamization: The President's Address on the War." In her *Critiques of Contemporary Rhetoric.* Belmont, Calif.: Wadsworth, 1972.

Harrell, Jackson, B.L. Ware, and W.A. Linkugel. "Failure of Apology in American Politics: Nixon on Watergate." *Communication Monographs* 42 (1975): 245–61.

Harris, Barbara Ann. "The Inaugural of Richard M. Nixon: A Reply to Robert L. Scott." *Western Journal of Speech Communication* 34 (1970): 231–34.

Hart, Roderick P. "Absolutism and Situation: Prolegomena to a Rhetorical Biography of Richard M. Nixon." *Communication Monographs* 43 (1976): 204–28.

Johnson, Thomas J. *The Rehabilitation of Richard Nixon: The Media's Effect on Collective Memory.* New York: Garland, 1995.

Newman, R.P. "Under the Veneer: Nixon's Vietnam Speech of November 3, 1969." *Quarterly Journal of Speech* 56 (1970): 168–78.

Reeves, Richard. *President Nixon: Alone in the White House.* New York: Simon and Schuster, 2001.

Schudson, Michael. *Watergate in American Memory: How We Remember, Forget, and Reconstruct the Past.* New York: Basic Books, 1992.

Scott, Robert L. "Rhetoric That Postures: An Intrinsic Reading of Richard M. Nixon's Inaugural Address." *Western Journal of Speech Communication* 34 (1970): 46–52.

Summers, Anthony, and Robbyn Swan. *The Arrogance of Power: The Secret World of Richard Nixon.* New York: Viking, 2000.

Witcher, Russ. *After Watergate: Nixon and the Newsweeklies.* Lanham, Md.: University Press of America, 2000.

Selected Biographies

Ambrose, Stephen E. *Nixon: The Education of a Politician, 1913–1962.* New York: Simon and Schuster, 1987.

———. *Nixon: Ruin and Recovery, 1973–1990.* New York: Simon and Schuster, 1991.

———. *Nixon: The Triumph of a Politician, 1962–1972.* New York: Simon and Schuster, 1990.

Gellman, Irwin F. *The Contender: Richard Nixon. The Congress Years, 1946–1952.* New York: Free Press, 1999.

Parmet, Herbert S. *Richard Nixon and His America.* Boston: Little, Brown, 1990.

CHRONOLOGY OF MAJOR SPEECHES

See "Research Collections and Collected Speeches" for source codes.

"The Fund Crisis Speech" (Checkers). Los Angeles, September 23, 1952. *NLB.*

"The Need for Leadership." Greensboro, N.C., August 17, 1960. *WI.*

"First Nixon–Kennedy Debate." Chicago, September 26, 1960. *WI.*

"Acceptance of the Republican Nomination for President." Miami Beach, Fla., August 8, 1968. *WI.*

"First Inaugural Address." Washington, D.C., January 20, 1969. *WI.*

"Vietnamization" (The Silent Majority). Washington, D.C., November 3, 1969. *CAV*, pp. 240–47.

"Address to the Nation on the Situation in Southeast Asia." Washington, D.C., April 30, 1970. http://www.pbs.org

"Address to the Nation on the Situation in Southeast Asia." Washington, D.C., May 8, 1972. *NLB.*

"Nixon's Second Inaugural Address." Washington, D.C., January 20, 1973. *WI.*

"Address to the Nation Announcing Conclusion of an Agreement on Ending the War and Restoring Peace in Vietnam" (Peace with Honor). Washington, D.C., January 23, 1973. *NLB.*

"The Watergate Case." Washington, D.C., April 30, 1973. *SAP*, pp. 687–91.

"Address to the Nation About Policies to Deal with the Energy Shortages." Washington, D.C., November 7, 1973. *NLB.*

"Resignation Speech." Washington, D.C., August 8, 1974. *WI.*

"Remarks on Departure from the White House" (farewell speech). Washington, D.C., August 9, 1974. *WI.*

SAMUEL AUGUSTUS NUNN (1935–)
U.S. Senator 1973–97, Cochair of Nuclear Threat Initiative

EDWARD M. PANETTA

Sam Nunn served in the U.S. Senate for twenty-four years (1973–97). He was raised in the small town of Perry, Georgia, in a family with political interests. His father served as mayor of Perry and his great-uncle was a legendary political figure, long-term chair of the House Armed Services Committee, Carl Vinson. Nunn attended the Georgia Institute of Technology, Emory University, and the Emory Law School, where he graduated with distinction in 1962. Following his graduation from law school he was hired to work for Carl Vinson at the House Armed Services Committee. This experience, in part, stimulated his lifelong interest in foreign affairs. He entered political life in 1968 when he was elected to the Georgia House of Representatives. He was elected to the U.S. Senate in 1972. Nunn attributes his 1972 victory partly to his performances in a series of televised debates against the incumbent congressman, David Gambrell. During his years in Washington, Nunn served on many Senate committees including the Armed Services Committee, the Permanent Subcommittee on Investigations, and the Subcommittee on Intelligence.

In 1985 Senator Nunn was one of the cofounders of the Democratic Leadership Conference (DLC), an organization devoted to moving the Democratic Party to a politically centrist position. One important issue Nunn championed through the DLC was a commitment to a national service program. The 1989 DLC text *Citizenship and National Service* articulates a rationale for service in the country. In 1989 Nunn sponsored congressional legislation for national service. While the Nunn–McCurdy plan, a proposal to convert student loans to entitlements, was not enacted, it did serve as the precursor to President Clinton's National and Community Service Act (1993). The Nunn–McCurdy legislation was provocative and drew sharp political criticism from both the Left and the Right.

Among Nunn's most salient legislative accomplishments was the passage of the Panama Canal Treaty, upon which he expended considerable effort. The Panama Canal Treaty debate was a two-year exchange, and as the vote approached in March 1978, Nunn played an important role in its passage. Nunn and Herman Tallmadge, the senior senator from Georgia, proposed a reservation to the treaty that made it palatable to Senate moderates and conservatives. The Nunn–Tallmadge reservation asserted that treaty ratification would not preclude the

changes became manifest when troops were deployed in Panama and the Persian Gulf. Interestingly, Nunn's reform position was antithetical to that of Carl Vinson, who blunted such efforts for decades while serving in the House. During the 1980s Nunn was embroiled in the high-profile confirmation hearings of Secretary of Defense nominee John Tower. In opposing George H. W. Bush's nomination of the former Texas senator, Nunn cast one of the most difficult and controversial votes of his tenure in Washington. The pivotal issue was the role the Senate should play in the nomination process. Amid accusations of alcohol abuse and claims of sexual harassment, Senate Democrats voted to reject the nomination. In the Tower controversy Nunn asserted the prerogatives of Congress. In deliberations concerning troop withdrawal from Korea (1977), the ABM treaty (1987), the SALT II Treaty (1979), and gays in the military (1993),

---

"It's very puzzling to me how someone could give up on the embargo after five months when nobody that I know of predicted that it was going to last less than nine months to a year."

Sam Nunn, opposing President Bush's decision to attack Iraq in 1991

United States from developing an agreement to deploy troops in Panama after 1999.

During the 1980s Nunn was best known as an authority on the value of various weapon systems. He addressed the viability of the MX missile and the need to sustain support for the ABM treaty. In fact, his floor speeches on the utility of the ABM treaty in March 1987 played a significant role in halting President Reagan's effort to reinterpret the treaty. As a result of the ABM battle, senators added an amendment to the INF Treaty stipulating that succeeding presidents could not repudiate treaty interpretations presented to the Senate during the ratification process.

When discussing the highlights of his Senate career, Nunn identifies the Department of Defense Reorganization Act. Written with Barry Goldwater (R–Ariz.), the act was considered by some a landmark law. The statute established clear lines of authority at the Pentagon, and those

as in the Tower confirmation hearings, Nunn defied presidents, both Democratic and Republican, in order to preserve the importance of congressional decision-making.

With the demise of the Soviet Union, Nunn joined with Richard Lugar to craft the Nunn–Lugar Cooperative Threat Reduction Program, providing assistance to Russia and former Soviet republics to dismantle nuclear weapons. This legislation was finally passed without the support of President George H. W. Bush and many in Congress who were more concerned with domestic issues. After several failed efforts, Nunn and Lugar pushed through a compromise $500 million package to dismantle the Soviet nuclear arsenal and provide humanitarian aid. In recognition of their efforts both senators were nominated for the Nobel Peace Prize in 2000 and 2001.

In 1991 Nunn broke ranks with his perceived

conservative Southern Democratic roots, and with President George H.W. Bush, to vote against the use of military force in the Persian Gulf. He based his opposition on the claim that the embargo was effective and would erode Iraq's ability to respond with military force over time. Nunn's hesitancy to deploy troops was shaped by his interpretation of Civil War history. It was his belief that decisions made in a state of emotion often failed to calculate the long-term implications of military deployment. As Nunn himself later noted, the Persian Gulf controversy effectively eliminated his prospects for the 1992 Democratic nomination for president. With Bill Clinton's arrival in Washington, Nunn again found himself at odds with a president; the issue was whether homosexuals should serve in the military. Nunn stood against the president because he believed that Clinton's proposal would compromise the safety of enlisted personnel and affect national security.

Since leaving the Senate in 1996, Nunn has remained active in public service. For a while he was cochair of the Concord Coalition, a group devoted to implementing a program of fiscal restraint at the federal level. He also served as cochairman of the Center for Strategic and International Studies board of trustees and of the Nuclear Threat Initiative (NTI) with Ted Turner. The NTI was established to respond to two public policy challenges at the beginning of the twenty-first century. First, NTI urges Americans to recognize nuclear, biological, and chemical weapons as the greatest threats to the world's peace and security. Second, NTI seeks to resolve the persistent gap between the reality of the threat these weapons pose and the global, official response of the responsible parties. To close this gap, NTI has undertaken several initiatives, including the establishment of pilot projects and models that states could adopt. Additionally, the NTI works to promote dialogue involving governmental and nongovernmental parties and to increase public awareness of the gaps between threat and response policies.

SAM NUNN: THE ORATORY OF A CONSERVATIVE SOUTHERN DEMOCRAT

A vanishing breed in our political culture, the conservative Southern Democrat is character-

ized by a deliberate and measured approach to public policy concerns rather than a commitment to a particular ideological agenda. Such conservatism embraces incrementalism in place of revolutionary politics and, at times, inaction in place of reform politics.

Nunn has delivered a variety of important deliberative speeches since the 1960s. While one can find a plethora of ceremonial addresses in the Selected Archives of Georgia Tech and Emory collection, his policy arguments define Nunn's rhetorical character. The public policy area in which Nunn initially established his reputation—military affairs—grew out of a series of speeches on military preparedness. His September 11, 1976, address to the New York Militia Association outlined a clear vision of the Soviet threat and the need for a stronger military in Europe. Although he was a recognized expert on military preparedness, Nunn exhibited an interest in a variety of legislative issues while serving in the Senate. He was very involved in issues related to the Senate's sustaining its authority as a legislative body, as illustrated by his March 3, 1989, speech on the nomination of John Tower to serve as secretary of defense. Additionally, he advocated the development of a national service program, and in a February 26, 1990, speech called for an extension of the National Park Service in Georgia.

Nunn delivered classical deliberative addresses that responded to international, national, and regional exigencies. As such, the speeches were usually problem-solution addresses. His November 13, 1991, address on Soviet defense conversion painstakingly outlined the serious consequences associated with inaction regarding the dismantling of Soviet weapons. Nunn made the audience painfully aware of the consequences of Soviet military secrets and hardware ending up in the hands of people bent on using weapons of mass destruction. He delivered this chilling account a full decade before 9/11 and its impact on foreign policy rhetoric in the United States.

When describing both public policy problems and the range of potential solutions, Nunn regularly used history to make his claims salient with the audience. As a Southerner, he was apt to call upon Civil War history to make a point when needed. In his September 11, 1976, address he referred to the "recent unpleasantness known as the Civil War" and called upon the words of Nathan Bedford Forrest—"who git thar furstest with the mostest"—when outlining a prescription for enhanced military force in Europe. During the homosexuals in the military debate, some advocates of lifting the ban on service made the argument that no such restriction had been imposed on the military prior to 1982. Refuting that argument in his speech of January 27, 1993, Nunn detailed the administrative sanctions associated with homosexual behavior in the U.S. military. The speech argued that prior to World War II, military commanders had the right to separate individuals from service based upon "inaptness or undesirable habits or traits of character." Nunn went on to chronicle a series of administrative decisions, beginning in 1944 and culminating in 1982, that documented an established military policy that excluded homosexuals from active military service.

Historical references abound in Nunn's speeches. In a September 4, 1989, speech delivered before the International Institute for Strategic Studies, Nunn argued for support for Russia based upon a reading of European, Russian, and world history. Russia, he maintained, could easily slip back into an authoritarian state. To avoid this slippage, NATO and the United States needed to implement a set of policies to assure the Russian transition to democracy. The failure to learn from history before making policy decisions was often repeated in his speeches. The February 1991 address on intervention in the Persian Gulf was predicated on the claim that the United States often intervened without thinking about long-term consequences, and a link was drawn between the Persian Gulf crisis and President Reagan's disastrous decision to deploy troops in Lebanon in 1982.

Beyond the use of historical events, Nunn's speeches made frequent references to evidence that framed his policy positions. Throughout the John Tower nomination controversy, the weight of the evidence was described as controlling Nunn's final vote. John Tower, a senator from Texas, had served as the chair of the Armed Services Committee and also had played an important role in the negotiation of the INF arms control accord with the Russians. For Nunn, this set of experiences presumptively made Tower a strong candidate for this cabinet post. Nunn expected to support the nomination when it reached the Armed Services Committee in 1989. However, the FBI background report on Tower compelled Nunn to change his position and vote against the nomination. The FBI report isolated three issues and provided evidence in support of each. First, there was an apparent conflict of interest. Tower served as a consultant to defense contractors, and Department of Defense regulations precluded his oversight of financial matters related to those companies. Second, there was evidence that the candidate had a drinking problem. Third, the report found cases of indiscreet conduct toward women. In the end, following "the most thorough review of any nominee to come before the Committee," Nunn spoke forcefully against the appointment. He delivered a series of speeches and editorials in the following days that called for the rejection of the nominee. According to Nunn, this was perhaps the most painful decision he made during his Senate tenure. As a result of his public statements on this matter, the normally low-key and bipartisan Nunn was labeled "Nunnpartisan" by supporters of Tower.

During the effort to pass the Soviet Defense Conversion and Demilitarization Act, Nunn relied heavily on evidence from a variety of authorities to support passage of the act. In the United States, at that time, there was a growing lack of interest in policy initiatives focused on the Soviet Union. The Cold War was over, and Americans wanted to put that chapter in history behind them. The desire to reach closure on Soviet relations and a flagging domestic economy led Americans to look inward during the early 1990s. Against this backdrop, Nunn crafted a speech that integrated evidence from a wide variety of sources to make an argument on behalf of demilitarization. First, quoting Russian leaders, Nunn argued that the risk of a Russian civil war turning nuclear was a real one. He read from a commentary by Igor Malashenko describing the possibility of such a war, and buttressed the quotation by stating: "That is a direct quotation from a top Soviet aide." Nunn went on to refer to a speech by President George H. W. Bush calling for the exploration of a policy to dismantle Soviet weapons. Nunn affirmed the need to dismantle Soviet weapons by reminding the audience that some Russians and former Soviets were willing to sell both weapons and secrets to the highest bidders; evidence of this was provided by Canadian and U.S. nonproliferation experts. At the end of the speech two articles from the *New York Times* and the *Los Angeles Times* were inserted into the record.

Analysis of the solutions that Nunn offers to a variety of public policy concerns reveals a well worn path. As might be expected, this conservative rhetor presents incremental solutions to exigencies. In the Persian Gulf crisis, Nunn championed the use of sanctions to undermine Saddam Hussein. For Nunn, without a vital interest in immediately attacking Iraq, the Bush administration and the country were best served by letting sanctions run their course. In his January 10, 1991, speech Nunn stated: "None of the intelligence experts or other experts who testified felt the embargo was really going to have any effect before April or May of 1991 and almost all of them said it would take at least a year. . . . It's very puzzling to me how someone could give up on the embargo after five months when nobody that I know of predicted that it was going to last less than nine months to a year, and most people said a year to eighteen months from the time of inception, which was August of last year." This position indicated his commitment to working through levels of solutions fully before moving on to larger or more drastic measures.

In 1992, when Bill Clinton was elected president, it was clear that the Department of Defense policy prohibiting homosexuals from serving in the military would be amended. For many on the political Left, this was an opportunity to open military service to homosexuals. Against this political groundswell within his own party, Nunn once again trod the path of incrementalism. In his January 27, 1993, floor speech, he called for more study on the subject and suggested that the administration hear from those who serve in the military. Second, he cautioned against swift political action and called upon

decision-makers to think through a series of unresolved matters. As in most of his political debates, Nunn's arguments reflected a concern with the long-term implications of policy change and counseled against abrupt policy shifts.

Nunn's commitment to incrementalism was also apparent in the expression of his own policy suggestions. In the case of the Nunn–Lugar amendment, he framed the plan as a modest proposal. The initial $1 billion decommissioning request was juxtaposed against the $4 trillion spent on the arms race in Europe in the period following World War II. On November 13, 1991, he stated: "I am confident that the American people are perceptive enough and smart enough to realize that taking $1 billion—up to $1 billion, at the Administration's discretion—out of the Defense budget would not be too high a price to pay to help destroy thousands and thousands of Soviet nuclear weapons."

Opposition to big government solutions was yet another conservative marker of Nunn's rhetoric. Although he did not adhere to the archetypal Republican position that all government was potentially bad or evil, Nunn did perceive the role of government as a facilitator rather than a savior. In his February 1, 1996, speech to the National Prayer Breakfast, he affirmed that government policies can help with domestic issues, but it cannot fundamentally alter values. In both domestic and foreign policy there was an ongoing commitment to limited governmental responses. Indeed, many of Nunn's greatest legislative accomplishments were associated with efforts to streamline government. The Nunn–Goldwater Reform Act of 1986 and similar legislative initiatives in 1992 and 1994 all worked to increase the efficiency of the Department of Defense. The underlying goal, as articulated in Nunn's March 6, 1986, speech was to improve the decision-making capabilities of people. By streamlining government, the legislature would have greater control over policy and military personnel could make better decisions.

Beyond exhibiting a commitment to incrementalism, Sam Nunn's most controversial speeches always made explicit references to constitutional obligations as rationales for policy positions. When Nunn found himself in conflict with a sitting president, he would invariably identify a constitutional rationale for his opposition. In the case of homosexuals in the military, he referred to Article I, Section 9, of the Constitution. His stand on the Persian Gulf crisis was grounded in his obligations as found in Article I, Section 8, of the Constitution. During the Tower confirmation hearings he again made use of a constitutional argument, but in a more philosophical fashion: "The Constitution reflects the firm conviction of the Founding Fathers that the investiture of individuals in positions of great governmental authority is not the exclusive domain of the President." When forced to oppose a sitting president, this conservative Southerner looked for a foundational principle—either constitutional or philosophical—upon which he could base his policy argument.

As a speaker who addressed some of the most important public issues of the twentieth century, Nunn delivered speeches that were usually organized in a problem-solution scheme. Depending upon the particular issue, there was frequently an emphasis on either the problem or a set of solutions. Most of the speeches exhibited an asymmetrical structure; they examined the problem or the solution but rarely discussed both at equal length.

Nunn often utilized repetitive sentence structure as a device to organize his thoughts and sustain audience interest. In a July 2, 1992, speech, for instance, he used variations on "The fundamental question is not what is best for the Navy or Marine Corps or Air Force. The question is what is best for America" seventeen times. This language allowed Nunn to work through a series of arguments highlighting the redundancy and duplication among the branches of the military. Through repetition, he could detail the problems that required a program to reform the Pentagon just six years after the Nunn–Goldwater reforms were implemented in 1992.

In addition to repetitive structure, Sam Nunn's speeches often contained a storytelling device that shaped the development of his argument. When discussing the types of solutions that needed to be implemented in post-Soviet Russia in his September 4, 1989, speech, he used a traffic light analogy to distinguish appropriate from inappropriate political steps: "As for our policy toward the Soviet Union, NATO's strategy must distinguish between those areas where we move ahead and those where we stand firm. We should keep in mind the signals on a traffic light: red, for those Soviet proposals to which we must say 'no'; yellow, for those which call for moving slowly with care and caution; and green, for those which we should press forward with vigor." In the speech Nunn proceeded to assess a series of policy options for which the traffic light colors oriented the listeners toward prioritizing the array of solutions.

Nunn remains an accomplished public speaker. Ken Askew, a noted professional speechwriter who worked for Nunn in the 1980s, describes Nunn's ability to add extemporaneous comments to a prepared text and deliver an effective speech. In some cases the nature of his issues led to speeches that were both detailed and informative. His long-standing area of expertise, military preparedness, could require Nunn to highlight technical, tactical, and procedural issues. While intellectually interesting, such material is not often entertaining. Given his almost universally recognized expertise, however, Nunn was a speaker listened to by both peers and critics for his opinions on military matters.

Although Nunn left the Senate after twenty-four years, he did not abandon the public arena. Currently, he serves as cochair of the Nuclear Threat Initiative (NTI) and continues to deliver speeches that are influential on nuclear doctrine. The rhetorical pattern he polished while a legislator is still on display while he represents a nonprofit organization. The NTI is interested in making progress in reducing the current dangers associated with nuclear proliferation. It is committed to facilitating policies that build nuclear transparency and improving methods of verification and security. Ted Turner, the other cochair of NTI, is committed to the elimination of nuclear weapons, yet the agency models its policy agenda on the incremental approach championed by Nunn. NTI suggests policy actions, but only after serious study and evaluation of the relevant evidence. The actions suggested are usually predicated on developing a working coalition between government and nongovernmental agencies. NTI's initiatives often advocate nongovernmental solutions, such as educational initiatives in the United States and training programs in Russia that seek to reduce risk associated with weapons of mass destruction. A conservative orator in the Southern tradition of constitutional principles and incremental reform, Sam Nunn remains an active speaker on military and global affairs.

INFORMATION SOURCES

Research Collections and Collected Speeches

Following his retirement from the Senate in 1996, Nunn donated his files to Emory University, and they are cataloged in the Selected Archives at Georgia Tech and Emory [SAGE]. Currently, much of the collection is restricted, as many of the materials relate to constituent matters, classified documents, and other sensitive materials. Scholars do have access to Nunn's speeches, radio and television broadcasts, and newsletters. Some of the materials are digitized and available at the SAGE Web site. Speeches delivered in the Senate are available in the *Congressional Record.*

Web Site

[SAGE]. Some speeches, broadcasts, and newsletters have been digitized and are available at this Web site. http://sage.library.emory.edu/collection-0800.html

Selected Critical Studies

Askew, Ken. "Confessions of a Wounded Speechwriter." *Executive Speeches*, August 2003, pp. 33–41.

Blumenthal, Sidney. "The Mystique of Sam Nunn." *New Republic*, March 4, 1991, pp. 23–27.

Judis, John. "Nunn of the Above." *New Republic*, October 30, 1995, pp. 16–19.

Murphy, John. "Epideictic and Deliberative Strategies in Opposition to War: The Paradox of Honor and Expediency." *Communication Studies* 43 (1992): 65–78.

Shipp, Bill. "Sam Nunn: Sam the Prophet." *Georgia Trend*, March 1, 2002, pp. 16–20.

CHRONOLOGY OF MAJOR SPEECHES

See "Research Collections and Collected Sources" for source code.

"Gearing Up to Deter Combat in Europe" (address to the New York Militia Association). New York City, September 11, 1976. *Vital Speeches of the Day*, November 1, 1976, pp. 49–53.

"Introduction of DOD Reorganization Bill" (Senate address). Washington, D.C., March 6, 1986. *SAGE*.

"Floor Statement of Senator Sam Nunn on the Nomination of Senator John Tower to Be Secretary of Defense." Washington, D.C., March 2, 1989. *SAGE*.

"Senator Nunn Replies: We Are Not Being Unfair." Washington, D.C., March 3, 1989. *SAGE*.

"Challenges to NATO in the 1990s" (address to the International Institute for Strategic Studies). London, September 4, 1989. *Vital Speeches of the Day*, December 15, 1989, pp. 135–41.

"Floor Statement of Senator Sam Nunn on the National and Community Services Act." Washington, D.C., February 26, 1990. *SAGE*.

"The Persian Gulf Crisis." Washington, D.C., January 10, 1991. *SAGE*; *Vital Speeches of the Day*, February 1, 1991, pp. 238–42.

"Soviet Defense Conversion and Demilitarization." Washington, D.C., November 13, 1991. *SAGE*; *Congressional Record*, November 13, 1991, pp. S16486–89.

"The Defense Department Must Thoroughly Overhaul the Services' Roles and Missions." Washington, D.C., July 2, 1992. *SAGE*; *Vital Speeches of the Day*, August 1, 1992, pp. 617–25.

"Hearings on the Department of Defense Policy Excluding Homosexuals from Service in the Armed Forces." Washington, D.C., January 27, 1993. *SAGE*; *Congressional Record*, January 27, 1993, pp. S755–57.

"Intellectual Honesty, Moral and Ethical Behavior" (address to the National Prayer Breakfast). Washington, D.C., February 1, 1996. *Vital Speeches of the Day*, March 15, 1996, pp. 326–30.

"Statement of Sam Nunn on the Announcement of the Nuclear Threat Initiative." Atlanta, Ga., January 8, 2001. Available at http://www.nti.org

"Moving Away from Doomsday and Other Dangers" (address to National Press Club). Washington, D.C., March 29, 2001. *Vital Speeches of the Day*, May 1, 2001, pp. 424–29.

SANDRA DAY O'CONNOR (1930–)
Associate Justice of the U.S. Supreme Court

JANICE SCHUETZ

Sandra Day O'Connor debuted on the national public stage at the time of her confirmation hearings for the U.S. Supreme Court in 1981. In one sense her debut seemed more like a cameo appearance than the prologue to a long career on the legal public stage. Before she came to the attention of President Ronald Reagan, her public acting was confined to small roles in the Arizona legal system as a public defender and state appeals court judge. Until her nomination for the Supreme Court, her most distinguished roles were as an appointed and then an elected member of the Arizona state legislature, and as a citizen involved in Phoenix Republican politics and community organizations. In her twenty-two years of playing the lead female role on the U.S. Supreme Court, the public has learned a great deal about this leading lady from her legal opinions and her public speaking. O'Connor's primary scripts are her written opinions in hundreds of cases that have come before the Court, but her secondary scripts consist of invited public lectures and special occasion speeches.

O'Connor's personal story resembles the dramatic saga of a cowgirl in the Old West. Born in 1930, she was the first child of Ada Mae and Harry "Mo" Day. Because her parents resided on a remote 340-square-mile ranch in southeastern New Mexico far from a public school, she went to El Paso, Texas, to live with her maternal grandmother and attend private schools there, but she spent weekends and summers on her family ranch. At the ranch, her mother taught her to cook and organize family events, and her father showed her how to use a .22 rifle, mend fences, brand cattle, and ride horses. In her autobiography, *Lazy B*, she wrote, "It is possible to survive and make a living in that formidable terrain [at the Lazy B Ranch]. The Day family did it for years, but it was never easy. It takes planning, patience, skill and endurance."

O'Connor recalled that "the family had lively discussions about politics, world events, economics, and ranch problems. Everyone joined in. . . . Then all of us sat in the living room reading and talking until time for bed. Before going to bed, all of us walked outside to look at the sky." In "Life and the Law: A Personal Journey," a speech she delivered at the Singapore Academy of Law in 2002, O'Connor proudly told her international audience: "I'm the first cowgirl to serve on the United States Supreme Court." She noted that "the value system we learned out on the ranch was simple and unsophisticated. What counted there was competence and to do whatever was required to keep the ranch in good working order. Verbal skills were less important than the ability to know and understand how things worked in the physical world." The values O'Connor learned on the ranch emerge in her work on the Court. She has gained a reputation for issuing pragmatic opinions that emphasize planning, fact-based content, and deductive reasoning.

By all accounts, O'Connor was a gifted student from grade school through law school. In an interview with Prudence Mackintosh, O'Connor's childhood friend Hondey Hill McAlmon recalled that O'Connor "was terrific at impromptu speaking. . . . She was never loud or awkward, I was never jealous of her, but I do remember feeling a little inferior. She really could do everything well." O'Connor skipped two grades, and at the age of sixteen enrolled at Stanford University, where she majored in economics. She spent only six years earning both an undergraduate degree and a law degree. She credited her skills in logic to a business law course, and has complimented her law professors for using the Socratic method of questioning and their analysis of cases. In an address titled "Fiftieth Anniversary Remarks," delivered at her alma mater in March 1997,

O'Connor concluded that her writing and research on the law journal were her most valued law school experiences.

O'Connor was one of only four women to graduate in law from Stanford in 1956. After her appointment to the Court, she became a symbol of the achievement of women in the legal profession. She often presented her personal experiences as evidence for the conclusion that the current generation of women lawyers and judges had overcome significant obstacles in order to be taken seriously by their profession. After finishing law school, she married lawyer John J. O'Connor. In her speech to the Singapore Academy of Law, she recalled that although she thought it would be easy to get a job after law school, her experience ran contrary to her belief. For example, after one job interview, secured through the good offices of a friend's father, she impressed the interviewer, but was offered only a position as a legal secretary. In "Portia's Progress," delivered on October 29, 1991, at the New York University Law School, O'Connor placed herself within the historical struggle of women to receive recognition in the legal profession. She noted that even now "women lawyers have difficulty managing both a household and a career," a reference to her struggle to raise three sons and develop a career as a young lawyer in Phoenix. It was difficult for her to secure the kind of position that men with similar credentials were obtaining.

Prior to her appointment to the U.S. Supreme Court, O'Connor gained more substantive experience in politics than in law. After graduating from law school, she was briefly a public defender in California. Then she accompanied her husband, now a military draftee, to Germany and worked there as a contract lawyer for the military. When the O'Connors returned to Phoenix, she took a position as a public defender, raised her three sons, became active in the Republican Party, volunteered at the YMCA and the historical society, and served on various boards and commissions. In 1965, O'Connor became an assistant state attorney general, and shortly after was appointed to fill a state Senate vacancy. She was reelected, and her legislative colleagues elected her Senate majority leader in 1973–74. Her political work had two important consequences. First, O'Connor gained status in the Republican Party and came to the attention of Senator Barry Goldwater, who later recommended her to President Ronald Reagan as a Supreme Court nominee. Second, her legislative experience solidified her political position that states hold sovereign rights with which the federal government should not interfere. O'Connor made this position clear in "Our Judicial Federalism," delivered at Case Western Reserve University School of Law in November 1984. In that speech she declared that "federal courts must give deference to state court findings," and state courts should "emphasize the substantial degree of control they have over our dual judicial system."

Unlike her male predecessors serving on the Supreme Court, O'Connor lacked substantial judicial experience. She became a judge of the Maricopa County Superior Court in Phoenix in 1975 and served until 1979. Democratic Governor Bruce Babbitt appointed her to fill a vacancy on the Arizona Court of Appeals in 1979, and there she worked with a three-member hearing panel. She wrote twenty-nine brief opinions based on other courts' precedents. During her confirmation hearings, some U.S. senators tried to force O'Connor to disclose her judicial philosophy, but she avoided stating a clear position on abortion, the death penalty, and the rights of the accused. Since members of both parties on the Senate Judiciary Committee believed the time was right for a woman to serve on the Court, her responses did not seem to matter as much as the fact that she was a competent woman. As a result, she gained confirmation with a unanimous vote. Even today O'Connor takes pride in her selection as the first woman to serve on the U.S. Supreme Court. She believes her rise to the Court was a significant moment for American women. In a 2002 interview with Katie Couric for NBC's *Dateline*, O'Connor remarked, "The minute I was confirmed on the Court, states across the country started putting more women on [the bench] than had ever been the case on their supreme courts. It made a difference in the acceptance of young women as lawyers. It opened doors for them."

O'Connor never apologized for the fact that her legal credentials did not measure up to those of her predecessors. Instead she turned what was an apparent negative into a positive. After serving many years on the Court, O'Connor acknowledged that she began at the bottom and learned good lessons to allow her reach a high judicial position. In the "Fifth Annual Sandra Day O'Connor Medal of Honor" speech at Seton Hall University School of Law, given on November 26, 1996, O'Connor noted that "starting at the bottom and working hard while you are there can have its present consolations and benefits as well." In addition to presenting her legal credentials in a positive light, she repeatedly emphasized that her community and political experiences empowered her to be an effective justice. In the Seton Hall address she urged lawyers and law students to "become involved in the community," do "volunteer work," and become an "elected or appointed representative in some community agency or institution." Clearly, she hoped others would follow a career path to the judiciary similar to hers, not by the traditional route of acquiring legal distinction but through her public and political service. On July 1, 2005 Associate Justice O'Connor informed the president of her intent to retire, effective upon the selection and confirmation of her successor.

SUPREME COURT ORATORY: LEGAL WRITING AND PUBLIC LECTURES

Sandra Day O'Connor's public speaking roles stem from her judicial career. By tradition, judges do not publicly campaign for legislation they may later rule on in their courtroom, nor do they publicly commit to specific policies, lest such positions affect future judicial decisions. O'Connor's speeches are typical of Supreme Court speaking, focusing on legal lessons and principles. In a very pronounced fashion, they feature the same legal perspective, method of decision-making, and deductive argumentation as her legal writing. Typically delivered in law school settings, this genre of speech is designed to share her view of the law's meaning and its proper interpretation with a knowledgeable and sophisticated audience.

O'Connor's legal philosophy is prominently featured in her written opinions and public speeches. Robert W. Van Sickel, in *Not a Particularly Different Voice*, argues that O'Connor's legal writing has several distinctive features. He concludes that she is a centrist, adopts a pragmatic approach toward law and legal practice, joins coalitions that support the majority position in the Court, and maintains conservative positions on individual, state, and administrative rights. O'Connor has published nearly 500 majority, dissent, and concurring opinions during her more than twenty years on the Supreme Court.

One frequently cited example of O'Connor's centrist position appeared in her 1989 concurring opinion in *Webster v. Reproductive Health Services*, a case that decided whether the state of Missouri could use public employees and facilities to perform nontherapeutic abortions. The Court upheld the Missouri ban on the use of public facilities. O'Connor voted with the Court's conservatives, who wrote that the state should make childbirth a more attractive option than abortion by limiting the facilities where an abortion could take place. However, she did not fully side with those conservatives who wanted to end abortion rights completely, but neither did she agree with liberals who supported the use of public facilities for abortions. Instead, O'Connor took a middle position that a woman's right to an abortion must be protected, but also held that a woman's right to choose needed to be balanced with the state's compelling interest to limit abortions in public facilities. She thus concluded that those public facilities should not be used for abortions and emphasized the right of the state to limit access to abortion in cases where the law did not place an "undue burden on the health of the woman."

O'Connor's position in *Webster* mirrors the states' rights argument in her speeches. For example, she enunciated the right of the state to delimit the application of federal laws in "Our Judicial Federalism," a speech given at the Case Western Reserve University School of Law on November 13, 1984. She concluded that "judicial federalism must acknowledge the primary role of the state courts in our federal system of government." The federal system, she said, "guarantees state courts a large measure of autonomy in the application of federal law." She claimed that "our judicial federalism can and will work. But the marriage between our state and federal courts, like any other marriage, requires an equal partner to respect the other, to make a special effort to get along with the other, and to recognize the proper sphere of the other partner." Just as O'Connor's written opinion in *Webster* upheld the State of Missouri's autonomy to make its own laws as long as these laws did not violate the precedent established in *Roe v. Wade*, the legal perspective presented in "Our Judicial Federalism" portrayed the states as equal partners with the federal government.

O'Connor's opinions demonstrate a situational, case-by-case approach grounded in judicial history, legislative intent, and textual rules. When these features are inconsistent or unclear, she opts for compromise. In *Justice Sandra Day O'Connor* Nancy Maveety argues that O'Connor engages in "discursive commentary" on legal opinions, situates cases within the community, and often articulates a compromise position. O'Connor's 1990 opinion in *Cruzan v. Director, Missouri Department of Health* (1990) is representative. After doctors determined that Cruzan was brain dead, the family insisted that she be allowed to die, but the Court claimed the state had the right to keep her alive. O'Connor wrote a compromise, concurring majority opinion that situated Cruzan's case in personal and legislative history, but she then used the opinion as a justification for advocating that citizens should take charge of their end-of-life concerns. She reasoned that competent individuals have a right to make the decision themselves, but if the individual lacks competence, then family members must let the state decide. In this compromise opinion, O'Connor called attention to the medical realities of the right to die, and argued that all individuals need to create living wills and appoint surrogate medical decision-makers.

Several of O'Connor's speeches resemble the decision-making process she used in *Cruzan*. In "Conference on Compelling Government Interests," delivered at the Albany School of Law on September 26, 1991, she called attention to the importance of history and tradition. "It is our duty," she said, "to apply analysis of the immediate and distant past to questions of the present. . . . History is of course relevant in interpreting constitutional or statutory language." She argued that the language of a law makes clear what the meaning of a case is in the historical context. She explained that legal decisions inhere "in the Constitution itself" and that weighing competing interests "as if put on scales" may not work because morality is not the same as the public interest. She concluded that the Court "has encouraged the development of experimentation" and "accommodation of competing interests." For her the Court has the right to find out what the law is, balance the competing rights of the state and the individual, and make recommendations about how citizens should act in the future.

O'Connor's legal arguments typically begin with relevant history and statutes, follow with a statement of facts, proceed in a deductive chain of reasoning, and culminate in a definitive decision based upon precedents. Her 2000 decision in *Kiel v. Florida Board of Regents* exemplified this kind of reasoning. This case sought to overturn a Florida State University decision to dismiss faculty and staff because of age. A class action lawsuit filed by university employees asked the Supreme Court to overrule the state of Florida's decision. O'Connor's meticulous deductive arguments evolved in the following sequence of reasoning: (1) a descriptive statement of the provisions of the 1967 Age Discrimination in Employment Act (the statute); (2) a listing of the facts; (3) a statement of relevant precedents about age discrimination; (4) a statement of her premise (the federal government lacks the power to overrule state decisions); and (5) a conclusion that Florida's decision to discriminate based on age must be upheld because Congress cannot abrogate the states' sovereign immunity to lawsuits.

O'Connor's arguments in lectures often proceed in the same deductive fashion. "The Judiciary Act of 1789 and the American Judicial Tradition," an address given at the University of Cincinnati School of Law on September 29, 1989, is representative. In that speech, O'Connor constructed a deductive chain of reasoning that located the federal system's judicial independence in the 1789 statute: (1) the Judiciary Act established the Supreme Court, set the number of justices, established the office of attorney general, and created the network of federal and state courts; (2) the Judiciary Act emerged from historical lessons learned by the framers of the Constitution from the French and American revolutions; (3) Court precedents proved the Judiciary Act worked well to "balance our commitment to change" with the "rule of law"; (4) the opinions of previous Supreme Court justices show the independence of the judiciary and the tradition of judicial restraint; (5) [therefore] "the Act initiated and made possible the American judicial tradition, with its judicial independence, commitment to considered democratic governance, and adherence to the rule of law."

In addition to the speeches that address legal issues and legal decision-making, O'Connor often adopts the role of a historical interpreter and spokesperson for women legal professionals. Unlike many other public speakers, who derive much of their status from their ability to persuade audiences orally, the speeches of judges are not typically published on the Internet, nor are their addresses reprinted in anthologies. As is true of most other justices, O'Connor's speeches most often appear in the law journals of the institutions where she has spoken. These are speeches usually read from a written manuscript and presented

tional issues are of interest to many of her audiences. In her speech "The Anniversary of Abraham Lincoln's Gettysburg Address," delivered in Gettysburg, Pennsylvania, on November 19, 1996, O'Connor positioned herself as a historian and interpreted the subject of habeas corpus in relation to President Abraham Lincoln's actions in the Civil War. She concluded that in the tradition of habeas corpus, "Lincoln preserved liberty by not trampling on others' rights." She developed the theme by answering several questions—What does habeas corpus mean? How did the principle evolve? When has it been tested? How should it be interpreted? Who has applied it correctly? Similarly, in "The Judiciary Act of 1789 and the American Judicial Tradition," O'Connor adopted the role of historian by interpreting the importance of the Judiciary Act to the American tradition of law.

In "Portia's Progress" (1991), Justice O'Connor's most controversial address, she took issue with feminist legal theorists who have argued that women practice law in a more caring and community-oriented way than men. That perspective, she argued, reinvents the Victorian myth of "True Womanhood," and "again sets up the polarity between feminine virtues of homemaking and masculine virtues of bread winning." This feminist approach, she continued, "threatens" to "establish new categories of 'women's work' to which women are confined and from which men are excluded."

---

as a deductive and fact-based argument. Although they are formally structured and delivered to an audience familiar with the mechanism of law, O'Connor still works to adapt the technical legal content to her live audience. For example, she relates to her audience by using motivational appeals and testimony from legal heroes. In each speech she constructs an explicit theme that addresses an issue of interest to the audience, and she clearly and carefully develops that theme through a problem–solution or cause–effect organizational pattern. Three themes are common in her speeches: constitutional issues, professional responsibility, and women as legal professionals.

Because she is an associate justice of the Supreme Court, O'Connor's views on constitu-

She emphasized that "the legal system plays a special role in how we preserve what we most value as a nation and how we strive to become the nation that we aspire to be." She explained how the framers of the Constitution created the Judiciary Act of 1789 to remedy the problems of earlier governments and the effect was a "unique legal tradition." She taught audiences about the history and meaning of the Judiciary Act, claiming the act permits judges to right "some injustices and strive to right others." But her role was not just that of a historian; she also exhorted her audience to "be proud" of "our successes" and to understand the ways that this act has enabled the nation to establish "its place in the world as the land of freedom and opportunity."

A second theme for O'Connor is professional

legal responsibility. She often assumes the role of moral custodian and urges law school students to pay more attention to morality and professional responsibilities than to pragmatic and material goals. In the "Fifth Annual Sandra Day O'Connor Medal of Honor Speech," she argued that "lawyers must do even more than know the law and the art of practicing it"; they must "develop a consciousness of their moral and social responsibilities to their clients, to the courts in which they appear, to the attorneys and clients on the other side of an issue and to others who are affected by the lawyers' conduct." The problem, she said, is that "merely learning and studying the code of professional responsibility is clearly insufficient to satisfy your ethical duties as a lawyer." Such guideposts "do not address the broader aspect of what a good lawyer should do to live up to the ideals of the legal profession." She offered pragmatic solutions, urging law students to "aim high. . . . strive for excellence, work hard while you are there [at the bottom]." In "Professionalism," a lecture given at the University of Oregon School of Law in May 1998, O'Connor warned lawyers that they are the object of "public derision," and they "suffer from stress related diseases." She faulted the words that lawyers use to talk about their legal practice. Instead of using the language of "attack," "demolish," and "shoot down," she said, lawyers should employ language that expresses problem-solving, helping, and caring. When addressing this theme, O'Connor adopted the role of moral guardian by emphasizing that "a great lawyer is always mindful of the moral and social aspects of the attorney's power and position as an officer of the court." She told the future lawyers that they could enhance the quality of their experiences and improve their public images if they would "dedicate even more . . . time and resources to public service" and show responsibility to their communities.

O'Connor's third speaking theme centers on women and law. In these speeches, she portrays herself as a symbol of women's achievement in law, one whose personal experience demonstrates the historical changes in women's legal opportunities. "Portia's Progress" is her most controversial and most often cited speech. O'Connor began by relating legal facts and cases that excluded women in New York—including Clara Shortridge Foltz, Belva Lockwood, and Myra Bradwell—from the practice of law. She claimed that "a revolution has occurred" in the last hundred years that had resulted in women becoming "well represented in law." She denied that today's women lack opportunities available to men. She refuted feminist legal theorists who have argued that women practice law in a more caring and community-oriented way than men. That perspective, she argued, reinvents the Victorian myth of "True Womanhood" and is therefore "a question that is both dangerous and unanswerable" because "it again sets up the polarity between feminine virtues of homemaking and masculine virtues of bread winning." This feminist approach, she continued, "threatens" to "establish new categories of 'women's work' to which women are confined and from which men are excluded." Calling upon her personal experience as proof, she held that women can have both "a rich and fulfilling career" and a "supportive family life." This speech, in ways similar to her legal opinions, adopted a compromise position that women can have "both family and career."

In most of her speeches, O'Connor presents testimony from legal heroes and draws conclusions about the principles and practices of law. Frequently, she echoes the words of previous Supreme Court justices who are her legal heroes. This strategy calls attention to her knowledge of legal history and positively associates herself with conservative and pragmatic judicial positions. To emphasize her judicial allegiances, O'Connor often appropriates the words of justices John Marshall, Oliver Wendell Holmes, Louis Brandeis, William Howard Taft, and Felix Frankfurter in her speech titles and content. Oliver Wendell Holmes's phrase "the life of the law" often appears in her speeches, as well as his observation that "there is a difference between what law is and what law ought to be." She frequently concludes her speeches with quotations from esteemed Supreme Court judges of the past.

In her speeches, O'Connor advocates ideas with precision more often than with eloquence. A few passages, however, have created quotable phrases. In "Legal Education and Social Responsibility," a speech delivered on October 24, 1984, at the Fordham Law School, she employed analogy and parallel structure to illuminate the true measure of a good lawyer: "Just as bricks and mortar do not a great law school make, so too the traditional teaching of only substantive and procedural courses do not a good lawyer make." In her February 8, 1999, speech for the dedication of the Western Justice Center Foundation's Friends Building, she used vivid metaphor to instruct her audience that "we must find ways to mend the tears in our social fabric." Descriptive metaphor was again the literary figure used in "Portia's Progress," as she warned her audience that "you must reopen the velvet curtain between work and home that was drawn closed in the Victorian era."

O'Connor has sometimes duplicated, and other times extended, her primary role as a jurist writing legal opinions into her secondary role as public speaker. In her speeches, she typically duplicates the legal principles and deductive argumentation that mark her written opinions. Using precise deductive logic grounded in history, often expressed through phrases borrowed from judicial icons, she advances her theme of pragmatic action. Although Sandra Day O'Connor frequently acknowledges her status as the first woman justice of the U.S. Supreme Court, she has not embraced a distinctly feminist approach to law. Her speeches as well as her written judicial opinions show her to be a conservative pragmatist and a compromiser whose speeches mirror her writing.

INFORMATION SOURCES

Research Collections and Collected Speeches

No archival collections or published collections of Sandra Day O'Connor's speeches exist at this time. Some of her speeches are published on Internet sites or in law journals. All of her legal opinions are published in the *U.S. Supreme Court Reporter.* A videotape with several excerpts of O'Connor's speeches, "Justice Profile: Sandra Day O'Connor," is available in VHS from http://c-span.org (order no. 161056).

Selected Critical Studies

Brown, Judith, Wendy E. Parmet, and M. E. O'Connell. "The Rugged Feminism of Sandra Day O'Connor." *Indiana Law Review* 32 (1999): 1218–19.

Davis, Sue. "The Voice of Sandra Day O'Connor." *Judicature* 77 (November–December 1993): 134–39.

Lazarus, Edward. "The Geography of Justice." *U.S. News & World Report*, July 7, 1997, pp. 20–27.

Maveety, Nancy. *Justice Sandra Day O'Connor: Strategist on the Supreme Court.* Lanham, Md.: Rowman & Littlefield, 1996.

Van Sickel, Robert W. *Not a Particularly Different Voice: The Jurisprudence of Sandra Day O'Connor.* New York: Peter Lang, 1998, 2002.

Selected Biographies

Bentley, Judith. *Justice Sandra Day O'Connor.* New York: Julian Messner, 1983.

Couric, Katie. "Her Honor: Supreme Court Justice Sandra Day O'Connor." *Dateline NBC*, January 25, 2002. Transcript.

Hamilton, Marci. "Justice Sandra Day O'Connor's Twenty Years on the Supreme Court." www.find law.com/scripts/hamilton

Mackintosh, Prudence. "Sandra Day O'Connor: First Woman on Our Highest Court." *McCalls*, October 1982, pp. 12–17.

O'Connor, Sandra Day, and H. Alan Day. *Lazy B: Growing Up on a Cattle Ranch in the American Southwest.* New York: Random House, 2002.

Wohl, Alexander. "First Lady of the Law: Sandra Day O'Connor." *Biography*, October 1998, pp. 88–95.

CHRONOLOGY OF MAJOR SPEECHES

"Professional Competence and Social Responsibility: Fulfilling the Vanderbilt Vision." Vanderbilt University School of Law; Nashville, Tenn., September 24, 1982. *Vanderbilt Law Review* 36 (January 1983): 1–8.

"Our Judicial Federalism" (third Summer Canary Lecture). Case Western Reserve University School of Law; Cleveland, Ohio, November 13, 1984. *Case Western Reserve Law Review* 35 (1984–85): 1–12.

"Legal Education and Social Responsibility." Fordham Law School; New York City, October 24, 1984. *Fordham Law Review* 52 (March 1985): 559–62.

"Swinford Lecture" (Kentucky Bar Association). 1985. *Kentucky Bench & Bar*, Summer 1985, pp. 20–23, 50–52.

"Women in the Constitution" (Conference on Women and the Constitution). Atlanta, Ga., February 2, 1988. Available on VHS from http://c-span.org (order no. 1485).

"The Judiciary Act of 1789 and the American Judicial Tradition" (William Howard Taft Lecture, University of Cincinnati College of Law). Cincinnati, Ohio, September 29, 1989. *University of Cincinnati Law Review* 59 (1990): 1–13.

"Conference on Compelling Government Interests"

(Albany Law School). Albany, N.Y., September 26, 1991. *Albany Law Review* 55 (1992): 535–47.

"Portia's Progress" (Madison Lecture, New York University School of Law). New York City, October 29, 1991. *New York University Law Review* 66 (December 1991): 1546–57.

"19th Amendment 75th Anniversary" (League of Women Voters). Phoenix, Ariz., August 12, 1995. Available on VHS from http://c-span.org (order no. 67705).

"The Life of the Law: Principles of Logic and Experience from the United States" (Thomas E. Fairchild Lecture, University of Wisconsin). Madison, Wis., October 20, 1995. *Wisconsin Law Review* 1:1–9.

"The Anniversary of Abraham Lincoln's Gettysburg Address." Gettysburg, Pa., November 19, 1996. www.gdg.org

"Fifth Annual Sandra Day O'Connor Medal of Honor" (Women's Forum, Seton Hall University School of Law). South Orange, N.J., November 26, 1996. *Seton Hall Law Review* 27 (1997): 83–87.

"Fiftieth Anniversary Remarks." Stanford University Law School; Palo Alto, Calif., May 1997. *Stanford Law Review* 50 (1997): 1–8.

"Professionalism" (William W. Knight Law Center; University of Oregon). Eugene, Ore., May 1998. *Oregon Law Review* 78 (1999): 385–91.

"On the Occasion of the Dedication" (dedication of the Friends Building, Western Justice Center Foundation). Pasadena, Calif., February 8, 1999. Available at www.westernjustice.org/dedication.htm

"Life and the Law: A Personal Journey" (annual lecture, Singapore Academy of Law). Singapore, 2002. Available at www.sal.org.sg

H. ROSS PEROT (1930–)
Billionaire, Independent and Reform Party Presidential Candidate

VALERIE A. ENDRESS AND MARI BOOR TONN

What Americans love most of all is a maverick, an untamed cowpoke, willing to ride in and clean up the town.
—Morley Safer, CBS News

From the very start, millions of Americans saw 1992 and 1996 presidential candidate H. Ross Perot as a walking oxymoron—a billionaire populist, an extraordinary ordinary person, a larger-than-life "little guy," views succinctly captured in the T-shirt slogan of one Perot supporter in 1992: "He's just like us only richer." Although his two presidential bids were cloaked in controversy and upheaval, the very presence of this firebrand businessman reanimated the belief of some Americans in the value of grassroots democracy. And for many, his rhetoric symbolized a plainspoken honesty and a respect for the citizenry they believed had been sorely lacking in contemporary presidential campaigns.

Henry Ross Perot was born June 27, 1930, in Texarkana, Texas, to Ross and Lulu May Ray Perot. With his older sister Bette, he spent his childhood on the isolated East Texas prairie, where the family lived in modest circumstances, but comparatively well, during the Great Depression. Perot describes his life on the prairie as isolated but idyllic, reflecting the moments depicted in a Norman Rockwell painting. The homespun tales Perot tells of his youth are also ones of enterprise and achievement. Beginning at age seven, he claims to have worked at numerous jobs, including breaking horses; selling Christmas cards, magazines, and garden seeds; buying and selling bridles and saddles; buying and selling horses and calves; delivering newspapers; and collecting for classified ads.

His small stature prevented him from excelling in sports, but Perot developed a competitive edge and a proclivity for confrontation in other pursuits. He was only an average student, but a star on his high school and junior college debate teams. As president of the student council at Texarkana Junior College, Perot frequently locked horns with classmates and members of the school's administration. As one of his peers described him, at the time "He [was] the sort of person you just love. Other times you could kill him." As Perot himself once admitted, it was during this period that his reputation as an agitator took hold. "As a young man, I wanted to be a pearl," said Perot. "Unfortunately, my lot in life is to be a grain of sand that irritates the oyster."

In 1949, Perot accepted an appointment to the U.S. Naval Academy, where he rose to class president, chairman of the honor committee, and battalion commander. Following his graduation in 1953, he served his required tour of duty aboard a destroyer and an aircraft carrier at sea. In 1956, he married Margot Birmingham, a teacher from Greensburg, Pennsylvania, whom he met while at the Naval Academy. They had five children: Ross Jr., Nancy, Suzanne, Carolyn, and Katherine. The year following the Perot's marriage, he resigned his commission and entered the private sector as a salesperson for IBM's data-processing division in Dallas. In 1962, with the help of a $1,000 loan from his wife, he established his own data-processing company, Electronic Data Systems (EDS). The rapid success of the company under his command prompted *Fortune* magazine to put the billionaire entrepreneur on its cover in 1968, dubbing Perot the "fastest, richest Texan." In 1984, General Motors (GM) purchased EDS for $2.5 billion and, as the major stockholder, Perot gained a seat on the GM board. He resigned his position and sold his stock just two years later, following a series of well-publicized conflicts with the CEO of GM, Roger Smith. With the profits from the GM buyout, he and eight associates founded Perot Systems, a worldwide computer service company, in 1988.

As the Texas executive's wealth grew, so did his desire for public service and, perhaps, for the public spotlight. Beginning in 1969, Perot embarked upon a second career as a freelance diplomat when he engaged in a lobbying campaign for the release of American POWs in Vietnam. For his efforts, Perot received the Medal for Distinguished Public Service, the highest civilian award

presented by the Department of Defense. In 1978, when two EDS executives were arrested and held captive by Iranian authorities, Perot and a team of EDS volunteers participated in a much publicized and successful rescue mission. In 1980, Ronald Reagan appointed Perot to the little-known but powerful Foreign Intelligence Advisory Board, a group of presidential appointees whose approval is required for all U.S. covert operations.

During the remainder of the Reagan administration, however, Perot focused more of his attention homeward and on domestic issues. At the request of the Texas governor's office, Perot spearheaded a project to curtail the trafficking of illicit drugs in the state. He also led an initiative to improve the quality of education in the Texas public school system. Both of his efforts resulted in the passage of comprehensive legislative reforms. He also built his public service reputation outside the political arena, particularly as a philanthropist.

In 1988, with his national profile higher than ever, Perot embarked upon a brief but remarkably successful speaking tour, arranged by an independent publicist, that would set the stage for his first presidential run. Although the Texan's speeches on this 1988 circuit reflected both the style and the form of campaign stump rhetoric, his sole purpose, he insisted, was to advance a policy agenda. Yet following President George H. W. Bush's commitment of American troops to the Persian Gulf a few months later, Perot reappeared on the public platform and sounded increasingly like a surfacing candidate. His attacks on the president intensified as he challenged Bush's constitutional power to commit troops, and as he blamed his fellow Texan for ignoring the budget deficit, citing "gross excess spending" in the Oval Office and "mismanagement in our country" as the culprits.

On February 21, 1992, Perot embarked on his first of two consecutive runs for the Oval Office. The curtain rose on this nonpolitician's unconventional first bid for the nation's highest elective office in an equally unconventional way. On *Larry King Live*, he told his genial host and his viewing audience that he would agree to run for president if volunteers registered him in all fifty states. "I'll promise you this," he said, "between now and the convention we'll get both parties' heads straight. . . . If enough people want me, I'll be their hero." At times during the summer, the undeclared candidate polled higher than the two major party candidates. After abruptly withdrawing from consideration in mid-July, Perot officially entered the race eleven days before his October appearance in the presidential debates, the first such debates featuring three presidential candidates. Despite the upheaval of his on-off-and-on-again campaign and the poor performance of his running mate, retired Admiral James Stockdale, in the vice-presidential debate, when the polls closed on Election Day, the maverick candidate had received 19 percent of the popular vote. That showing was more than any third-party candidate had received since Theodore Roosevelt campaigned on the Bull Moose ticket in 1916.

Following the 1992 presidential race, Perot initially focused his attention on his nonprofit, nonpartisan organization, United We Stand America. Soon, however, he had gained a national platform by opposing the controversial North American Free Trade Agreement (NAFTA), which he had criticized during the 1992 campaign. By mid-1993, Perot had given more speeches on this single issue than he had delivered from his entire topical repertoire during the 1992 campaign. He rejoined the talk show circuit, appeared before Congress to testify on the issue, aired lengthy informational segments about it, and with Pat Choate wrote a *New York Times* best-selling book on the topic. *U.S. News & World Report* featured the Texan on its cover with the following statement: "Ross Perot may be the most important force in American politics." In November, however, Perot's petulant performance in a televised debate against Vice President Al Gore severely damaged both Perot and anti-NAFTA efforts. Almost overnight, Perot's favorable ratings in Gallup polls fell precipitously from 66 percent to 29 percent, and his unfavorable ratings climbed 12 percent. Support for NAFTA grew from 34 percent to 57 percent, and the legislation passed eight days later with the support of previously undecided members of Congress.

Within months, Perot announced he was organizing the Reform Party, a vehicle by which in 1996 he launched his second bid for the Oval Office as its official nominee. But the fledgling party failed to galvanize the kind of interest in it

or in Perot that he had enjoyed in 1992. Voters registering intent to vote for Perot languished in single-digit percentages, poll numbers cited by the Commission on Presidential Debates (CPD) to justify their decision to exclude him, as a nonviable candidate, from the televised debates. His exclusion by the CPD generated some controversy among certain voters and analysts who argued that inclusion of the political provocateur would render the electoral process more honest and the debates more relevant to the political interests of many average citizens. But Perot's preoccupation with his exclusion from the presidential debates, at the expense of articulating other issues, failed to build the needed momentum. In 1996, Perot received 8 percent of the popular vote, less than half of his 1992 showing.

H. Ross Perot continues as head of Perot Systems. Moreover, the Perot family ranks among the country's leading philanthropists, having donated more than $100 million to charitable and civil causes.

H. ROSS PEROT: THE POLITICAL PROVOCATEUR

In no small measure, the vibrancy of Ross Perot's first insurgent presidential campaign symbolized the escalating cynicism of U.S. voters toward traditional politics. This crisis of confidence peaked just as the Texas billionaire entered the 1992 campaign, when a Gallup poll reported fewer than one in four Americans rating government in positive terms and a meager 2 percent expressing unalloyed trust in the institution. Unlike the feelings of cynicism that persisted during the Vietnam and Watergate areas, the alienated voter of the 1990s defied easy categorization, representing no particular party, ideology, single issue, or demographic profile. As several focus group participants put the matter during the 1992 presidential debates, many Americans withdrew from politics because they felt powerless to influence a system held captive by mounting bureaucracy, monied lobbyists, and media and political agenda-setting. For many, H. Ross Perot shimmered as an alternative.

As illustrated in his rhetoric and responses by many citizens to it, Perot possessed a keen ear for hearing the anger of middle-class America toward their leaders in Washington. Moreover, his small-town Texas roots rendered him fluent in the vernacular that gave voice to that anger in ways that many ordinary citizens understood and appreciated. Following in a long tradition of prairie populists, Perot spoke the language of revolt and reform that reflected, but also united, the unexpressed sentiments of millions of citizens. For a number of months in 1992, his popularity grew as he mounted his populist attack, focusing on the leadership in Washington and their penchant for top-down governance. It was a system, he said, marked by "mud wrestling" and "finger pointing," an institution that takes "10 years to solve a 10 minute problem," one paralyzed by "gridlock," given to "meandering and wandering," and filled with "empty talk."

But Perot's rhetoric went beyond verbalizing the widespread frustration of the common people with the country's president and congressional leaders. Rather, Perot also continually pointed not just to the wisdom of unelected citizens, the common people, but also to their naïveté and negligence in assuming some responsibility for the nation's circumstances. Speeches given during his 1988 speaking tour contain these twin features. During his first appearance, a speech to the National Press Club in Washington, D.C., he sketched the framework for what would become the central issue in his 1992 presidential platform: the spiraling budget deficit. In his trademark plainspoken, commonsensical, and invective style, Perot lambasted elected politicians for ignoring the budget deficit and treating the subject "like a crazy aunt we keep in the basement." He also branded his audience of reporters the "dwarfs" and "wimps" of the 1988 campaign, castigating them for allowing the politicians to "get away with murder" as citizens continue to live in "this fantasy land beyond [their] means." To a Harvard audience the following month, Perot declared, "Our country is diseased with just doing enough to get by." As proof, he condemned the country's public school system, the decline of manufacturing, the rising trade deficit, and the blight of drug use in America. Yet, as was a motif in his rhetoric, Perot dispersed responsibility for the nation's dire straits beyond the traditional targets of out-of-touch or self-interested politicians by chastising the voting public for failing to demand more from the

1988 presidential campaign: "They [politicians] sounded like Lawrence Welk—'Wonderful, wonderful, wonderful'—and we bought it."

Besides his notable lack of elective experience, Perot positioned himself as different from major party candidates in at least three respects. First, unlike candidates whose chief claim was their unique qualifications to lead the country, Perot contended he was somewhat "incidental to the whole process" of democracy, and even encouraged voters to "drop him" if a more fitting candidate emerged. Second, although Perot often lampooned the Washington establishment, his rhetoric still avoided certain usual trappings of a negative campaign. He assured his audiences that "the people in Washington are good people" who were constrained by a "bad system" difficult to change. In a campaign marked by continual charges of draft-dodging, pot-smoking, and marital infidelity, Perot pledged to remain "issues-oriented and not personality-oriented," to operate above the fray of personal attack. Third, the Texas billionaire enacted his concern over the corrosive influence of money on politics by personally funding his entire first campaign.

Ironically, Perot as an "of the people" symbol was nourished by his eschewal of conventional whistle-stop campaigning in favor of the free media of the talk show circuit. His conspicuous presence in this electronic front-porch campaign and his absence from more traditional forums burnished his appealing image as an unconventional, antisystem maverick. In the months following his promise to run if drafted by a committed cadre of volunteers, he appeared frequently on programs such as *This Week with David Brinkley*, *The MacNeil/Leher NewsHour*, *ABC News 20/20*, *Talking with David Frost*, *Evans and Novak*, *Donahue*, and *60 Minutes*. Until Perot's performances in the October 1992 presidential debates, his thirty-three appearances on talk show and call-in programs were the mainstay of his public exposure.

In his talk show rhetoric, Perot explicitly acknowledged the public's capacity for political intelligence, a theme central to his espoused philosophy of government. Significantly, his talk was composed of features that facilitated the exercise of practical wisdom. Indeed, the types of questions asked and comments made by citizens on the call-in shows, and Perot's responses to them, help to explain much of his initial "commonsense" appeal. Although the issues were virtually indistinguishable from those raised by journalists, the approach was distinct, as ordinary citizens often shared the folk wisdom of their everyday observations. In turn, Perot invited his audiences to pass judgment on political issues with the same critical tools they had used as private citizens in navigating the challenges of their everyday lives. In a segment on the talk show *Donahue*, for example, Perot constructed a hypothetical narrative to evaluate President George H. W. Bush's decisions leading to the Gulf War through the same perspective his audience would use to judge a next-door neighbor:

> I knock on my neighbor's door. I say, "We need to borrow your son and daughter to go to the Middle East." Say, "What for?" I say, "We've got this dude over there with [gold faucets in his bathroom and] 70 wives. . . . And we made a deal with Saddam Hussein—he could take the northern part of this country, then he took the whole thing. Now we're all upset. And by the way, we spent ten years giving [Hussein] all the money, all the power and what have you he needed." And I think you'd probably hit me in the face at this point. You're not going to send people over to fight and die for emirs and kings.

In exchanges such as this, Perot engaged in a type of "folk criticism," in which people borrow experiences from one realm of life and shift them to another to pass judgments and solve problems. Indeed, among the most distinctive features of Perot's rhetoric was his couching of political issues in the metaphors of down-home, everyday life: sports, illness, family relationships, and domestic chores such as car repair, cooking, and housework. He argued that the political system had broken down because such wisdom had become elusive to the career politicians. In one of his appearances, for example, Perot compared the income-tax system to "an old inner tube that's been patched by every special interest in the country." "In plain Texas talk," he said, "it's time to take out the trash and clean out the barn."

As important, the call-in show format likewise enabled Perot to directly admonish cynical naysayers to assume responsibility and "look in the mirror. We're the owners of this country. We don't act like the owners." Although Perot was short on studied positions on the issues, he was devoted to the notion of the civic community. Reminiscent of John Dewey and his "creative democracy," Perot envisioned a partnership with the citizenry that would blur traditional boundaries between leaders and the led. "You're going to have to stay in the ring after Election Day," he often told his followers. "I don't care how gifted [any political official] is . . . he has got to have your organized visible support to make this system work." He exhorted audiences to become "buried [in] the local, state, and national level." Otherwise, he warned, "You'll never get your schools cleaned up unless you're willing to put your shoulder to the wheel, know who's on the school board, attend PTA meetings, etc., etc." This bottom-up communitarian perspective on democracy became the hallmark of his run for the presidency in 1992, and one that resonated deeply with significant portions of the electorate.

Consistent with his emphasis on a grassroots philosophy of political engagement, Perot offered little in the way of specific proposals on key campaign issues during his first presidential bid, saying, "I don't have positions on those things. I haven't thought about them." As he was fond of telling his supporters, "Everybody wants a position on everything from frogs to mosquitoes to the deficit." Rather, Perot portrayed his brand of leadership as soliciting creative ideas for reforming education, health care, the tax system, and other innovations. The ideas generated were to be "kicked around," experimented with in "pilot projects," and "de-bugged." Perot even proposed an electronic town hall, whereby he and Congress, after brainstorming together, would present drafts to the public for feedback. He also floated the prospect of a toll-free number to enable citizens to register their concerns and suggestions directly with the executive branch. Many citizens praised the Texan for these and other ideas to include them more fully in the political process, and applauded his refusal to treat them, in his words, "as objects to be programmed during the campaign with commercials and media events and fear messages and personal attacks."

The basic themes and folksy approach of Perot's rhetoric changed little following the 1992 campaign, but responses to his feisty, combative style underwent a sharp shift. As he had when discussing the trade deficit and NAFTA in 1992, Perot directed his anti-NAFTA rhetoric in 1993 toward middle-class Americans and their pocketbooks. He argued that the agreement would send American jobs to Mexico and that entire industries would be lost to enterprises overseas, reprising his 1992 characterization of factories moving abroad as a "giant sucking sound," a colorful phrase that has since entered the cultural lexicon as shorthand for various types of job migration. Also, in classic Perot fashion, he ridiculed Washington and the Clinton administration for hoodwinking the American public. "Washington said that there were 700,000 jobs created. That's hot air that would make a helium balloon go to its maximum altitude," Perot said. "If you want to have some fun, call. Ask where all those people are working." But ironically, the privileging of "internal evidence" to render judgments that had been the magic of Perot's rhetoric in 1992 worked against him in the 1993 NAFTA Gore–Perot debate televised on Perot's longtime turf, *Larry King Live*. There, communication critic Herbert Simons argues, Perot's continual interruptions of his opponent, constant complaining about procedures, and repeated ad hominem attacks shifted the burden of proof of trustworthiness from the reputedly wooden and long-winded vice president to Perot, a figure who once had embodied political trustworthiness for millions of Americans. During his weeks of hiatus from the race in 1992, both major parties had courted the popular Perot and his devoted followers at the Texan's behest. Only a bit more than a year later, "Congressional opponents of NAFTA," writes Simon, "began distancing themselves from Perot immediately following the debate."

Thus, in the final analysis, Perot's political inexperience in his two presidential bids proved to be double-edged. On the one hand, legions of Americans in 1992 saw his foremost credential for the nation's highest political post to be his very lack of elective experience. And because he personified positive change in the electoral process for so many of the voters, his major party opponents granted him nearly total immunity from attack in the televised presidential debates. As Clinton strategist George Stephanopoulos re-

counted, "Perot chang[ed] the entire dynamic of the race. Still, you couldn't very well go after him for his easy answers to hard problems—not if you wanted to compete for his voters on Election Day." As an additional advantage, the various formats for some of the debates proved to be particularly well suited to Perot's sharp one-liners and folksy style; one format even replicated the town hall style of the talk show. Moreover, Perot benefited from lower expectations for him than for his seasoned political rivals. Many citizens in focus groups, responding to his first debate performance, expressed surprise that the political neophyte held his own against political veterans. And postdebate media evaluations concurred that the messenger of change outperformed Bush in all three appearances, and ran neck-and-neck with the charismatic Clinton. Finally, Perot's transporting of certain boardroom techniques into the campaign proved to be strokes of genius. His most powerful advertising vehicle was his infomercials, unsophisticated thirty-minute sales pitches that would become one of the most enduring and talked-about images of the 1992 presidential race. Even some skeptics praised Perot's innovative format, complete with detailed charts and graphs, as a welcome change from the patronizing tone of the sound bite slogans and orchestrated film footage of typical campaign advertisements. As one California citizen stated, "I've got to admit that I'm not for Ross Perot. But his [infomercial] presentation the other night, as simplistic as it was, of our nation's economic problems . . . I thought was outstanding. And I'm frankly getting tired of Americans being treated like we're a bunch of idiots [who] can't figure out what's going on."

On the less positive side, Perot's experience as an incredibly successful business entrepreneur and not as a politician may have led to disadvantages in dealing with the traditions, conventions, and demands of both political campaigns and political life more generally. Unaccustomed to the scrutiny and criticism that are staples of election campaigns and legislative debate, Perot became preoccupied with challenges by the major party candidates and sitting politicians to his unconventional proposals and vague remedies—and, even more acutely, with the escalating number of critical media stories occasioned by his rising political profile. His testy, counterproductive performance in the NAFTA debate was emblematic, fueling concerns that Perot lacked both the political temperament and the political skill for compromise so crucial for forging political alliances across differences and avoiding the partisan "gridlock" Perot himself had long decried. So, too, Perot's mantra of deficit reduction and his businessman approach in 1992 struck some observers, including a number of focus group participants in 1992, as ignoring myriad issues beyond the economic ones that presidents are forced to tackle. Also, as a longtime CEO more schooled in giving professional advice than taking it, Perot clashed frequently with his professional staff over control of his 1992 campaign, resulting in the highly publicized resignation of Ed Rollins, Perot's high-profile strategist. This internecine strife was replicated in the divisive battle over who would become the Reform Party's nominee. Possibly even more damaging to his formal organization and his grassroots volunteers was his abrupt withdrawal from the race in early summer, only to officially reenter eleven days before the debates. His last-minute choice for a running mate—retired Admiral James Stockdale, who, like Perot, lacked elective experience—proved disastrous. Stockdale's disorientation shocked most viewers, either prompting or renewing concerns over Perot's fundamental judgment and calling into question whether anyone honest and intelligent possessed the requisite skills to run the country.

Still, despite failing to garner a single electoral vote in either presidential election, Perot's influence on the political process has been significant and enduring in many respects. Even some citizens who did not believe that Perot possessed presidential fiber claimed, in 1992, that they appreciated the provocative role he played in the campaign, and notably envisioned various roles for him outside the Oval Office: a political adviser, a cabinet member, or other advisory roles. Echoing Perot's own characterization of his political role years earlier, a citizen from Washington state opined, "To me, he's like the perfect foil, the little piece of sand in the oyster that makes the pearl, the irritant, the catalyst [who] has succeeded in getting a lot of issues talked about in ways that I don't ever remember hearing them talked about in elections before." And although the cause-and-

effect relationship is difficult to prove, 1992 Election Day results intimate that Perot's presence may have influenced some 13 million citizens to exercise their right to vote for the first time, even though over half of those initiates cast ballots for a major party candidate rather than the political maverick who had demanded their participation. Moreover, Perot extended the horizons of political talk and advertising through his innovative use of "new media" and his use of infomercials. Perhaps most important, Perot understood how to tap the concerns of Americans in a manner unprecedented in contemporary campaign history. His candidacy represented something more than the electorate's disillusionment with the traditional two-party system: he demonstrated that energizing the power of the political middle through mutual accountability is not merely an ideal; it is possible. As one New Hampshire citizen so aptly expressed it, Perot's place in history will be "the guy . . . [who] slapped the American people and said, 'You are going to have to start taking responsibility.' "

Although Perot maintained a relatively low profile in the 2000 presidential election, his planned release of his latest book venture, *America the Broken: How to Reform and Revive the Greatest Democracy Ever Known*, offers some indication that he will remain a political player. Many of the core issues raised by Perot over a decade ago continue to preoccupy or bedevil the political establishment. With the federal deficit again an issue on the table, national health care yet unresolved, the continued decline of both industry and white-collar jobs, and renewed concern over weapons of mass destruction overseas, Perot may be able once again to make his message relevant to a new group of disaffected citizens.

INFORMATION SOURCES

Research Collections and Collected Speeches

There are no archival collections or published collected speeches of Perot at this time. Talk show transcripts of Perot's 1992 campaign may be obtained from network sources. The debate transcripts are archived on a variety of database and Internet sites, including the Commission on Presidential Debates (www.debates. org) and C-SPAN (www.c-span.org).

Adler, Bill, and Bill Adler Jr., eds. *Ross Perot: An American Maverick Speaks Out*. Secaucus, N.J.: Carol Publishing Group, 1994.

Chiu, Tony. *Ross Perot in His Own Words.* New York: Warner Books, 1992.

Perot, Ross. *Intensive Care: We Must Save Medicare and Medicaid Now.* New York: HarperPerennial, 1995.

———. *Not for Sale at Any Price: How We Can Save America for Our Children.* New York: Hyperion, 1993.

———. *United We Stand: How We Can Take Back Our Country.* New York: Hyperion, 1992.

Perot, Ross, with Pat Choate. *Save Your Job, Save Our Country: Why NAFTA Must Be Stopped—Now!* New York: Hyperion, 1993.

Robinson, James W., ed. *Ross Perot Speaks Out: Issue by Issue, What He Says About Our Nation: Its Problems and Its Promise.* Rocklin, Calif.: Prima, 1992.

Web Sites

On the Issues. This Web site provides full quotations from Perot on a wide variety of issues. www.issues2000.org

Reform Party, USA. Includes a history of the Reform Party. The archived news material goes back only to 1998. www.reformparty.org

United We Stand America. Includes transcripts of appearances on television talk shows as well as Perot's radio programs from 1995. www.uwsa.com

Audiovisual Materials

Vincent Voice Library, Michigan State University [*VVL*]. Five sound recordings of speeches by Perot are available digitally.

Selected Critical Studies

Ajemian, Peter. "Did the Media Serve Us Well? A Critic's View of Coverage of Ross Perot's 1992 Presidential Campaign." Occasional paper, John W. McCormack Institute of Public Affairs. Boston, Mass.: December 1995.

Atkeson, Lonna R., James A. McCann, Ronald B. Rapoport, and Walter J. Stone. "Citizens for Perot: Assessing Patterns of Alienation and Activism." In *Broken Contract*, ed. Stephen C. Craig. Boulder, Colo.: Westview Press, 1996.

Feigert, Frank B. "The Ross Perot Candidacy and Its Significance." In *America's Choice: The Election of 1992*, ed. William Crotty. Guilford, Conn.: Dushkin Publishing Group, 1993.

Jelen, Ted G. *Ross for Boss: The Perot Phenomenon and Beyond.* Albany: State University of New York Press, 2001.

McCann, James A., Ronald B. Rapoport, and Walter Stone. "Heeding the Call: An Assessment of Mobilization into H. Ross Perot's 1992 Presidential Campaign." *American Journal of Political Science* 43, no. 1 (1999): 1–28.

Menendez, Albert J. *The Perot Voters and the Future of American Politics.* Amherst, N.Y.: Prometheus Books, 1996.

Simons, Herbert W. "Judging a Policy Proposal by the Company It Keeps: The Gore–Perot NAFTA Debate." *Quarterly Journal of Speech* 82, no. 3 (1996): 274–87.

Tonn, Mari Boor. "Flirting with Perot: Voter Ambivalence About the Third Candidate." In *The 1992 Presidential Debates in Focus*, ed. Diana B. Carlin and Mitchell S. McKinney. Westport, Conn.: Praeger, 1994.

Tonn, Mari Boor, and Valerie A. Endress. "Looking Under the Hood and Tinkering with Voter Cynicism: Ross Perot and 'Perspective by Incongruity.'" *Rhetoric & Public Affairs* 4, no. 2 (2001): 281–308.

Zaller, John, with Mark Hunt. "The Rise and Fall of Candidate Perot: Unmediated Versus Mediated Politics—Part I." *Political Communication* 11, no. 4 (1994): 357–90.

———. "The Rise and Fall of Candidate Perot: The Outsider Versus the Political System—Part II." *Political Communication* 12, no. 1 (1995): 97–123.

Selected Biographies

Adler, Bill, and Bill Adler Jr., eds. *Ross Perot: An American Maverick Speaks Out.* Secaucus, N.J.: Carol Publishing Group, 1994.

Gross, Ken. *Ross Perot: The Man Behind the Myth.* New York: Random House, 1992.

Posner, Gerald. *Citizen Perot: His Life and Times.* New York: Random House, 1996.

CHRONOLOGY OF MAJOR SPEECHES

See "Research Collections and Collected Speeches" for source code.

"Speech at Harvard University." Cambridge, Mass., 1988.

"Speech to the National Press Club." Washington, D.C., 1988.

"Announcement of Candidacy on *Larry King Live.*" February 21, 1992.

"Campaign Speech." Lansing, Mich., July 1992. *VVL.*

"Presidential Debates." 1992.

"NAFTA Debate on *Larry King Live.*" November 8, 1993.

"Speech to the Reform Party Convention." Long Beach, Calif., August 11, 1996. Available at usinfo.state.gov.

"On the Nation's Economic Situation." September 8, 1996. Available at www.historychannel.com

"Concession Speech." November 5, 1996. Available at cgi.usatoday.com

COLIN LUTHER POWELL (1937–)
Secretary of State, General of the U.S. Army

RICHARD W. LEEMAN

In many regards, perhaps more so than with most other speakers, the oratory of Colin Powell appears to reflect who he is as a person. His is a discourse that sounds the themes of pride, hope, strength, determination, and the value of hard work. Whether he is speaking to high school students at his alma mater in the Bronx or the World Summit on Sustainable Development, Powell's oratory is focused on problem-solving. What problems do "we" face? How can "we" solve them? What can "you," the audience, do about them? Occasionally his speaking style soars and he demonstrates a capacity for what is traditionally called eloquence, but generally he prefers the direct and clear over the flowery and poetic. Like his life, his public speaking is businesslike; one always has a sense that his speech is prefatory to some sleeve-rolling, let's-get-down-to-work time.

Colin Luther Powell was born in Harlem, New York City, on April 5, 1937, to Luther and Maud Ariel Powell. His parents were Jamaican immigrants who worked in the apparel industry, his father as a shipping clerk and his mother as a seamstress. With his older sister, Marilyn, he was part of a tight-knit family that stressed hard work and education. In school, Powell performed well enough, even if he did not excel academically. He was a respected employee at his summer and part-time jobs, and in 1958 he graduated from the City College of New York with a B.S. in Geology. In college, academics had not interested him nearly as much as the Reserve Officers Training Corps (ROTC). In addition to straight-A work in his ROTC classes, he joined the elite Pershing Rifles, became the company commander in his senior year, and graduated at the top of his ROTC class with the rank of cadet colonel.

After boot camp at Fort Benning, Georgia, Powell worked infantry assignments in Germany and then stateside in Massachusetts, where he met Alma Vivian Johnson, an audiologist and graduate student at Emerson College from Birmingham, Alabama. They were married on August 25, 1962, after Powell received orders to go to Vietnam to serve as a U.S. military adviser to the Army of South Vietnam. During his initial tour in Vietnam, the first of the Powells' three children, Michael, was born. Powell received the Purple Heart for a foot injury from stepping on a punji-stick trap. Despite the wound, he finished his tour. After a series of stateside assignments, in 1968 Powell, now a major, was assigned a second tour of duty in Vietnam. While on a reconnaissance flight his helicopter crashed, and he made four trips to pull fellow soldiers out of the smoldering wreckage. For that action he received the Soldier's Medal, as well as the Bronze Star for his overall service in Vietnam.

Back in the United States, Powell continued his education, earning an M.B.A. from Georgetown University in 1971, and then becoming a White House fellow in 1972. Throughout the 1970s and early 1980s, he was primarily assigned to positions in the Pentagon. In 1983 he became the senior military assistant to Secretary of Defense Caspar Weinberger. He was named the commanding general of the Fifth Corps, stationed in Frankfurt, Germany, in 1986; only after President Reagan himself called, did Powell accept yet another desk assignment in 1987 as deputy national security adviser. In December 1987, Powell was named national security adviser. As director of the National Security Council, he was involved with the Nicaraguan contras, nuclear arms negotiations with the Soviet Union, and the naval escort of tankers through the Persian Gulf. After one more brief military posting, Powell became the chairman of the Joint Chiefs of Staff on October 1, 1989.

In that position, Powell is best remembered for his roles in the U.S. military effort in Nicaragua that removed Manuel Noriega from power, the Persian Gulf War, and the management of the military realignment at the end of the Cold War. At the end of his four-year term as chairman, and after thirty-five years in the military, Powell retired in 1993. At first he was occupied with writing his autobiography and touring the country as a public speaker. In 1994, President Clinton drafted him to be part of a three-person team, with former President Jimmy Carter and Senator Sam Nunn, to negotiate a peaceful end to military rule in Haiti. During 1995, there was considerable speculation that Powell would run for president, but that fall he announced a decision not to seek the presidency. He was a featured speaker at the Republican National Convention in 1996, and in 1997 was named chairman of America's Promise, a national organization designed to motivate and channel voluntarism among youth. He spoke again at the Republican National Convention in 2000, following rumors that he had been considered as a candidate for vice president. He was named secretary of state by President George W. Bush, in which position he was involved in many issues, particularly the Serbian–Bosnian crisis, the continuing violence in the Middle East, and the war in Afghanistan. He resigned as secretary of state shortly after President Bush's reelection.

COLIN POWELL: THE ORATORY OF A GENERAL

Powell's oratorical style never strays very far from the identity of the speaker himself. His is a problem-solving style of discourse, uniformly well organized and employing relatively plain language. Whether speaking as chairman of the Joint Chiefs of Staff, chairman of America's Promise, or secretary of state, Powell places a premium on clarity, argument, and evidence. His oratory sounds like a general's, although in the mode of Dwight D. Eisenhower or George Marshall, not Douglas MacArthur.

Broadly, Powell's speeches can be grouped into two types: policy speeches and ceremonial speeches. In his various official capacities, Powell delivered numerous speeches advancing and defending governmental policy, such as his April 18, 2002, Jerusalem speech on Middle East peace. Powell has also had many opportunities to deliver ceremonial speeches, such as commencement ad-

dresses and Memorial Day speeches, that have spoken to the broad concerns of the audience rather than specific policy issues associated with his office. Some speeches, such as his Republican National Convention addresses, have blended both types of messages rather equally, but usually one message or the other has been predominant.

Certain characteristics of Powell's content and style are constant across these two speech types. First, his speeches almost always focus on solving a problem. Second, in developing his solutions, Powell typically looks to history, experience, and traditional values. Finally, whether he is discussing the problem, the solution, or both, his speeches always display a keen awareness of the audience and the occasion.

As problem-solving oratory, Powell's speeches are tightly organized. His Louisville, Kentucky, speech on terrorism, delivered on November 20, 2001, is typical. He opened the speech by locating his central theme in the occasion: "The McConnell Center [at the University of Louisville] is all about leadership and . . . I am here today to talk to you about American leadership in today's world." Powell then developed three major areas illustrating American leadership: fighting terrorism and al-Qaida, constructing economic and security agreements, and pursuing peace in the Middle East. The development was clear and logical. He began with the issue that was most on people's minds in the fall of 2001: terrorism. He then proceeded to discuss those efforts that strengthen world ties and will, he asserted, make the world safer from terrorism. Last, he addressed the major continuing threat to peace in the world, the Arab–Israeli conflict.

Within each of these major portions of the speech, Powell organized further. In the first section, on terrorism, he surveyed the most recent developments in Afghanistan, discussed the nature of terrorists, and then turned to the future of Afghanistan. In the section on trade and security agreements, he examined the value of such agreements in relationship to Russia, China, and Africa, and then argued on behalf of fast-track trade legislation to speed the creation of additional such pacts. The final section, on Mideast peace, was organized around what Powell called two "fundamental truths," and he developed each of them in turn: that the "Israelis must be able to live free from terror," and that "the Palestinians must also be secure and in control of their individual lives and collective security." Each truth was to be enacted through change: the former meant that the culture of hatred toward Israelis must cease, and the latter meant that Israeli occupation and settlement activity must be halted. Powell concluded the section by reaffirming American commitment to the peace process as framed by the Madrid and Oslo conferences and the 1994 Israeli–Jordanian peace treaty.

Throughout the speech Powell used clear transition statements to delineate his structure: "While the fight against the terrorists is our top priority, it is not our only priority"; "It is also a time of danger and a time of challenges requiring American leadership, and nowhere are the challenges greater than in the Middle East"; "President Bush and I are convinced that the Arab–Israeli conflict can be resolved, but that will only happen if all of us, especially Israelis and Palestinians, face up to some fundamental truths." The transitions are typical of those Powell uses; they do not simply announce a new section of the speech, they summarize the critical point he is prepared to advance: that there are other important priorities to discuss, that nowhere are the challenges greater than in the Middle East, that the Arabs and Israelis must accept certain fundamental truths. Powell's speeches always proceed clearly through the construction of reasons and arguments.

Within his tight organizational structure, Powell's oratorical approach to solving problems is a rational one. He first identifies the problem and any knowledge that might aid in solving that problem, and then enumerates the steps of the solution. While describing the problem and specifying the solution are both important, there is a sense in which the key task seems to lie in identifying the lessons learned elsewhere and properly applying them to the problem at hand. Throughout Powell's speeches, there is a distilling of the lessons learned, some recent and some very old.

Clear-sighted lessons are important in Powell's speech "U.S. Foreign Policy in a Changing World," delivered to the Town Hall of California in Los Angeles on March 23, 1990. The first lesson Powell drew from world events was a les-

son of firmness. In a typical blending of past and present, he identified the source of American success in winning the Cold War: "Almost a half a century ago, George Kennan advocated a policy of containment. If we held firm, he said, the inherent weaknesses of communism would bring it down. We held firm. And the walls of communism are coming down."

Amid the welter of changes accompanying the end of the Cold War, Powell summarized the critical importance of discerning the true lesson from the false: "As Clausewitz said, 'Beware the vividness of transient events.' Amidst these incredible changes, we have to identify the principal factors that affect our interests and sort them out from the cascade of more glamorous but essentially transient events." Powell "sorted out" three such factors. First, America must understand that "yes, the Soviet army is going home" as it withdrew from Eastern Europe, "but it is not disbanding," he warned. Second, Powell noted that while current U.S.–Soviet relations were friendly, "we have no way of knowing what is in store for the Soviet Union." Third, he observed that "the world has not ceased being a place where America's interests are sometimes threatened." Drawing upon these truths, Powell returned to George Kennan's lesson: "These three factors remind us of the importance of the strength that brought the Free World this victory in the first place."

Other lessons followed. For example, Powell noted that "superpower status imposes responsibilities on us. Our outlook must be global and it must encompass the strong alliances that are critical to the future peace of the world." In solving U.S. budget problems, "we must find the balance between our superpower base force requirements and what the American people are willing to pay." Americans should also realize that the end of the Cold War had shifted their strategic task. Now, Powell said, "the task is keeping democracy alive, not fighting and containing communism. Now the task is helping the dozens of democracies that are just being born." Within these changing tasks, however, the lesson of military strength and resolve remained constant: "No one is better fitted for these tasks than America and her allies. If we stay strong and lead, the world will follow. Of that I am sure."

Many of Powell's lessons are drawn from history, and especially from the history that he himself has witnessed. That is especially true of speeches he delivered as chairman of the Joint Chiefs of Staff, chairman of America's Promise, and his ceremonial speeches. In his 1990 West Point commencement speech, for example, he contrasted the Cold War world of the newly commissioned "Second Lieutenant Powell" of thirty-two years earlier with the post-Cold War world confronting the newly commissioned graduates he was addressing. In his Harvard commencement speech of June 10, 1993, Powell made reference to General George Marshall's 1947 commencement speech delivered at Harvard, which announced the Marshall Plan for rebuilding war-torn Europe. "In perhaps the most famous speech ever delivered here," Powell told the audience, Marshall "committed America's wealth and leadership to the task of rebuilding Europe and ensuring its peace and prosperity." Again, Powell drew a lesson from that work: "There could be no going back after that. . . . We had to be *of* this world, not just *in* it." Powell used that lesson to justify maintaining a strong U.S. military posture in the post-Cold War world.

In his most recent speeches as secretary of state, Powell deemphasized the use of lessons, as his speeches more often focused on describing recent events and enunciating policy. Still, Powell occasionally drew on lessons learned, but usually from the more contemporary diplomatic past. In his speech at Louisville, he grounded his call for Arab–Israeli negotiations by citing his experience at the 1991 Madrid conference, at which Arabs and Israelis "took the opportunity to launch an historic process of negotiations," an opportunity once again present post September 11. Later in the speech he applied a different lesson, learned through a life lived in common sense: "One thing I've learned in my life is that treating individuals with respect and dignity was the surest path to understanding. Both sides need to treat the other with respect. Humiliation and lack of respect are just another path to confrontation."

In many cases, the lessons Powell learns from history or personal experience can be labeled "traditional." His Fisk University commencement speech, delivered on May 4, 1992, in Nashville,

Tennessee, is representative of the values he displayed throughout his speeches. For example, Powell fervently articulated the belief that America is the land of opportunity: "America is the only country in the world that strives incessantly to make the dream of America the reality of America." He acknowledged the limitations, as documented by the Rodney King beating and trial, and the subsequent rioting in Los Angeles, but went on to avow that "if I didn't believe in the depths of my heart that we could work it out, I wouldn't be able to call myself an American." The solution to these problems again lay in traditional values such as hard work. "Believe in yourself," Powell told graduates, "for there is nothing—NOTHING—you cannot accomplish by hard work and commitment." You must also believe in America, he told them, for "I've traveled around this world and I've seen a hundred countries and I've got to tell you there is no better place or system on earth than that which we enjoy here in America." Third, he said, "find strength in your diversity. . . . Let it be someone else's problem, but never yours. Never hide behind it or use it as an excuse for not doing your best." Finally, he told them, remember to "raise strong families." In language as traditional as the values he espoused, Powell insisted that "the worst kind of poverty is not economic poverty, it is a poverty of *values*. It is the poverty of *caring*. It is the poverty of *love*." Hard work, determination, confidence, family, and America: these are the values that Powell learned and profited by in his own life, and they are the values that he preached throughout his speeches.

These "traditional" values are traditional across ethnic lines in America; they are also the same values one can read in the speeches of Mary McLeod Bethune, Marian Wright Edelman, Martin Luther King Jr., and a host of other African American orators. In his speeches, Powell often sounds another "traditional" theme that is particularly strong in African American rhetoric: remembering where you came from. This theme can be found in almost any speech Powell delivers to a predominantly Black audience. In his August 10, 1991, speech to the national convention of the Tuskegee Airmen in Detroit, Powell recalled the military contributions of African Americans from the Revolutionary War through the 54th Massachusetts in the Civil War, from the Buffalo Soldiers of the West to the Tuskegee Airmen of World War II. "I never forget for a day, or for an hour, or for a minute," he told his audience, "that I climbed to my position on the backs of the courageous African American men and women who came before me." In fact, Powell used almost identical language to make the same observation in his commencement speeches at Fisk University in 1992 and at Howard University in 1994. In the Howard speech as well as that given at Fisk, Powell explained the responsibility that goes with the memory: "They would say to me now, 'Well done. And now let others climb up on your shoulders.'" He told the Howard graduating class that they faced the dual responsibility of achieving for themselves and helping those who come after: "You can now continue climbing to reach the top of the mountain, while reaching down and back to help those less fortunate." "You face great expectations," Powell challenged the students; "much has been given to you and much is expected from you."

While most of Powell's speeches can be characterized as businesslike, discussing problems and solutions using a relatively plain style, he is capable of achieving eloquence. Sometimes eloquent appeals are placed in the introductions of his speeches, but his rhetorical flourishes are more usually found in his conclusions. Speaking at the Vietnam Veterans Memorial in Washington, D.C., on the first Memorial Day following the Persian Gulf War, Powell used the occasion to commemorate particularly the veterans of the Vietnam War. Employing the parallel structure of antithesis and the metaphorical construction of personification, Powell asserted the veterans' honor:

> The parades and celebrations [such as those that followed the Gulf War] are not needed to restore our honor as Vietnam veterans because we never lost our honor. They're not to clear up the matter of our valor because our valor was never in question. Two hundred and thirty-six Medals of Honor say our valor was never in question. Fifty-eight thousand, one hundred and seventy-five names on this Wall say our valor and the value of our service were never in question.

Echoing the words of Jefferson's Declaration of Independence and the history of American arms, Powell concluded his memorial to the American soldier.

> My friends, Americans have placed their lives, their fortunes, and their sacred honor in harm's way from Concord Bridge to Gettysburg, from Normandy to Pork Chop Hill, from the A Shau Valley to the Valley of the Euphrates. And today, we are proud of all who served. Today, we remember all who gave their lives for our beloved America. Today—we remember. Thank you.

As secretary of state, Powell's speeches also came to employ some traditional eloquence when enunciating key elements of policy. In his Louisville speech, for example, parallel structure, vivid metaphor, and alliteration were used to condemn the terrorists:

> These murderers did not act on behalf of Muslims or on behalf of the poor and downtrodden of the world, or on behalf of Palestinians. . . . No, these criminals have no religion, and they have no human cause. Their goal, and the goal of all like them, is to divide and embitter people. They are evil merchants of death and destruction.

Later in that speech, Powell combined antithesis and metaphor to enunciate one of the fundamental truths: "No one can claim a commitment to peace while feeding a culture of hatred." Similarly, in his Jerusalem speech Powell employed the classic figure of chiasmus to declare the relationship of peace and security, and the compelling need for both sides of the Arab–Israeli conflict to commit themselves to the cause of peace: "There can be no peace without security, but there can also be no security without peace."

Until 2003, Powell's best-known, and most important, speeches were the two nationally televised speeches he delivered to the Republican National Convention. His speech of July 31, 1996, delivered in San Diego, announced his affiliation with the Republican Party and provided an opportunity for him to express his vision for the party's future. His July 31, 2000, speech, given in Philadelphia, was primarily an exposition on education, but it presaged his appointment as secretary of state.

After a few introductory remarks, his 1996 speech began with Powell recounting his parents' experiences as immigrants to America, a story he had frequently told in previous ceremonial speeches. Among the traditional lessons imparted by his parents was their firm belief in America and the American dream. The Republican Party, Powell declared, represents that vision of America that "rests on values . . . that are the conscience of a society. Values which must be lived, not just preached." Those values, beginning in the home and with the family, would be strengthened by a party that created economic wealth for all, reduced the burden of taxes, and prevented government from interfering with and impeding family life and economic growth.

After committing himself to the civil libertarian and fiscal conservatism traditionally associated with the Republican Party, Powell enunciated a social policy that emphasized fairness and equality. "We must be firm [in cutting government]," he declared, "but we must also be fair." Less government meant less government for all. Indeed, "corporate welfare, and welfare for the wealthy must be first in line for elimination. All of us—all of us, my friends—all of us must be willing to do with less from government." Powell then moved on to address the issue of equality: "A nation as great and diverse as America deserves leadership that opens its arms not only to those who have already reaped the rewards of the American dream, but to those who strive to struggle each day against daunting odds to make that dream come true." He called upon the Republican Party especially to be inclusive and support equality for all: "It is our party, the party of Lincoln, that must always stand for equal rights and fair opportunity for all." Powell concluded this section of the speech with a series of "I became a Republican because" statements that reiterated his commitment to less but fairer government. In the section that repeated his belief in the party's inclusivity, Powell declared his commitment to choice in the matter of abortion and the continuation of affirmative action.

The speech began its conclusion with an extended endorsement of Robert Dole's candidacy for president, with Powell providing personal testimony regarding the senator. He began by contrasting his own New York City upbringing with Dole's Kansas childhood, declaring that although Dole's "story began half a continent away . . . it is a story with common threads. It is one shared

in many ways by millions of Americans from every state, from every generation, and from every race and creed." As national security adviser and chairman of the Joint Chiefs of Staff, Powell had worked closely with Dole and found him to be a man of competence, strength, and integrity, committed to the American dream and the values that Powell had woven throughout the body of the speech. After strongly endorsing Dole, Powell concluded the speech by asking that the coming campaign be a vigorous debate of the parties' political differences, but one conducted with "civility" and, as "we stand on the eve of a new century," a commitment to those traditional principles of "freedom, democracy, and the free enterprise system" that has been the promise of America.

Powell returned to the Republican National Convention in 2000, speaking on the night devoted to education and George W. Bush's pledge to "leave no child behind." Grounding the introduction in his experience as chairman of America's Promise, Powell reaffirmed the values traditionally associated with America and the promise of today's youth, but also noted the "poverty, failing communities, [and] people who've lost hope" that he had seen "in my travels." Many youth, he asserted, were being lost to poverty, drugs, crime, and despair. In addition, "the issue of race still casts a shadow over our society." How, then, to solve this problem? The solution begins, he said, by "teaching children to value life." Although he did not repeat the story of his childhood, one could hear its strains as he declared that the solution "begins in the home with caring, loving parents and family members who pass on the virtues of past generations, who live good lives which serve as models for their children." Where such families do not exist, neighbors, communities, schools, and government must be committed to filling the need.

Focusing on education, Powell said that many schools are succeeding, and working hard to produce well-educated youth. Others, however, are failing, and government must do better to provide a quality education for its children. Powell endorsed educational "innovation," including reduced educational bureaucracy, standardized testing, charter schools, the testing of teachers, and prudent experimentation with school vouchers.

His speech then illustrated the enactment of these reforms by their success in Texas under Governor Bush. Despite concentrating on education and education reforms, Powell's speech included a call for inclusion more sharply worded than that in the 1996 speech. George Bush, he observed, had noted in a campaign speech "that 'the party of Lincoln has not always carried the mantle of Lincoln.'" "The party," Powell asserted, "must listen to and speak with all leaders of the Black community, regardless of political affiliation or philosophy." In this speech he more strongly hinted at the racism of some when they oppose affirmative action:

> We must understand the cynicism that exists in the Black community. The kind of cynicism that is created when, for example, some in our party miss no opportunity to roundly and loudly condemn affirmative action that helped a few thousand black kids get an education, but hardly a whimper is heard from them over affirmative action for lobbyists who load our federal tax codes with preferences for special interests.

In the speech's conclusion Powell returned to the themes of the American dream and of inclusion. He claimed that America stood at a unique time in history—full of power and wealth but with no ideological enemy to consume that power and wealth.

> The world is watching to see if all this power and wealth is just for the well-to-do, the comfortable, the privileged. Or are we a nation that can make our dream real for all Americans, so that all share in what we have been given by a generous God? . . . That is the challenge. This is the time. And in Governor George Bush we have the leader.

With the exception of the final endorsement, it was a conclusion that could have as easily been delivered at the Democratic National Convention.

Undoubtedly, the apex—or nadir—of Powell's oratory was his February 5, 2003, speech to the U.N. Security Council in which he forcefully argued the U.S. case against Saddam Hussein and Iraq, and for a military response to the situation. Since discredited and apologized for by Powell himself, that speech brought to bear all the strengths of his oratorical skills. It was,

for example, well organized, clearly laying out the administration's brief against Iraq. The speech subtly intertwined two primary themes. First, there was a logical, legal case against Iraq. Powell repeatedly enunciated the central point of this argument: Iraq had violated Resolution 1441. It was, he declared, in "material breach," and therefore the "serious consequences" provided for in the resolution were justified. At several junctures, Powell implied that the United Nations, and by extension the United States, did not need to prove the existence of weapons of mass destruction. Iraq had violated international law in 1990, and had repeatedly done so since, because it had not lived up to the punishments that had been imposed upon it in 1991. Those violations justified a military response. As he declared in his conclusion, "My colleagues, we have an obligation to our citizens. We have an obligation to this body to see that our resolutions are complied with." Resolution 1441 had provided for "serious consequences," and Iraq's violation of it thus justified resort to those serious consequences.

In support of this legal brief, Powell wove a second major theme: the psychological need to prevent a dictator or terrorists from acquiring and using weapons of mass destruction. This theme constituted the bulk of the speech, and it was this element of the speech that since then has attracted the most attention because weapons of mass destruction were not found in Iraq and because important portions of the evidence for such weapons was suspect. Powell argued that Saddam was intent upon building weapons of mass destruction, that those weapons were dangerous and life-threatening, and that if Saddam himself did not use them, then his terrorist allies would. Referring to Iraq testing chemical agents on prisoners, Powell alleged that "one eyewitness saw prisoners tied down to beds, experiments conducted on them, blood oozing around the victims' mouths, and autopsies performed to confirm the effects on the prisoners." While linking the al-Zarqawi terrorist network to the Iraqi government, Powell declared:

> The network is teaching its operatives how to produce ricin and other poisons. Let me remind you how ricin works. Less than a pinch—imag-

ine a pinch of salt—less than a pinch of ricin, eating just this amount in your food, would cause shock, followed by circulatory failure. Death comes within seventy-two hours and there is no antidote. There is no cure. It is fatal.

Clearly, terrorists who even contemplated the use of such a poison, and a dictatorial regime even remotely interested in abetting that network, are forces to be feared. Powell asked, "Should we take the risk that [Saddam] will not someday use these weapons at a time and a place and a manner of his choosing?" Through multiple psychological appeals to fear, he sought to motivate his audience to endorse the use of military force that his legal brief legitimated.

Powell's speech to the United Nations will long be noted for its use of evidence. Although some of the evidence has subsequently been attacked, and many have now dismissed the threat of weapons of mass destruction, Powell's extensive use of evidence will long be studied by communication scholars. To begin, one notes the sheer volume and variety of evidence used. Using Powerpoint as well as audio recordings, the speech employed multiple media in a way we have come to expect in a corporate or courtroom setting, but have rarely experienced in politics. Three times his speech included recorded conversations between Iraqi soldiers, twice it included videotapes of simulations, and ten satellite photographs were used. He cited U.N. reports, reports from Iraqi defectors, and "human sources," as well as intelligence reports from Britain and the United States. Wherever possible, he used the United Nations' own findings. "Dr. Blix," he said, talking of the Iraqi document supplied in December 2002, "pronounced the 12,200-page declaration 'rich in volume' but 'poor in information and practically devoid of new evidence.'" "UNSCOM estimates," he said, and "UNSCOM also gained forensic evidence," and "UNMOVIC told this Council."

When he could not conclusively use the source's expertise to resolve the matter, Powell skillfully blended logic and his own credibility. For example, he noted that there was an ongoing dispute as to whether aluminum tubes being purchased by Iraq were to be used in production of enriched uranium for nuclear weapons, or were to serve as rocket bodies for multiple rocket

launchers. "Most U.S. experts" thought that the tubes were designed to produce fissile material. "Other experts"—and the Iraqis—argued that the tubes were for conventional weaponry only. "I am no expert on centrifuge tubes," Powell admitted, and by doing so identified himself with most in his audience, "but this is an old army trooper. I can tell you a couple of things." Combining referent power as an "old army trooper" with "common sense" shared by all, Powell wondered why Iraq would purchase rocket tubes manufactured to a higher specification than the U.S. military does, if all it wanted to do was blow the rocket into shrapnel. Why did the Iraqis keep working to further refine the specifications beyond the minimum needed for conventional weaponry? "Maybe Iraqis just manufacture their conventional weapons to a higher standard than we do," Powell observed ironically, again asking his audience to identify with his commonsense approach, "but I don't think so."

Finally, Powell's February 5 speech is notable for its use of informality even as it avoided trivializing the subject. Just as he had informally appealed to his listeners through his reference to being an "old army trooper," so Powell regularly addressed his audience as "my friends" or "my colleagues." Throughout his speech, he adopted a conversational tone, often posing questions. "With Iraq's well-documented history on biological and chemical weapons, why should any of us give Iraq the benefit of the doubt?" he asked. After listening to the audiotapes of intercepted Iraqi conversations, Powell posed questions to his audience: "Why does he repeat it that way?" and "What is their concern?" "Note what he says," Powell directed the audience. At one point, in recounting an audiotaped Iraqi conversation, he referred to one of the Iraqi soldiers as "the other guy," as he portrayed the conversation as an informal, candid exchange between two soldiers. Repeatedly, Powell addressed his audience as conversational partners, equals who, like Powell, were examining the evidence in order to decide the correct course of action. Counterbalanced with precise organization and careful reporting of voluminous evidence, this conversational ethos supplied the speech with an important sense of sincerity while avoiding an attitude of condescension that such informality could have produced. The result was a masterful employment of the persona Powell brought to the speech, that of a reasonable, experienced public servant who was interested in arriving at the right decision, and one who treated others as coparticipants in the democratic process. Although much of his evidence has since been discounted and the "weapons of mass destruction" have been found to be nonexistent, it is a telling point of his persona that Powell has apologized for his speech. The speech itself has been dismissed, but among most audiences his ethos remains strong.

Despite his speech to the United Nations, Powell has been, and still is, generally well received as a public speaker. Newspapers characterized his 1996 convention speech as "straightforward" and "powerful." Reactions by the convention audience were generally enthusiastic, although his prochoice and affirmative action endorsements were

his speech of endorsing the students' right to disagree, noting that it is a fundamental American principle and right.

His speeches to the Republican National Convention and the United Nations were vintage Colin Powell. They were well organized, with an emphasis on defining problems and identifying solutions. He grounded those speeches in his personal experience and in core, shared values. With more plain speaking than rhetorical flourish, he included moments of eloquence where needed. Powell's approach to all his oratory seems to reflect his approach to life: it is direct, efficient, and very goal-oriented, and he routinely seems to achieve an identity of speaker and speech. With any Powell speech, one comes away with the impression that what one sees and hears is what one gets. He is an orator who seems comfortable with who he has become as

---

"I never forget for a day, or for an hour, or for a minute, that I climbed to my position on the backs of the courageous African American men and women who came before me. . . . They would say to me now, 'Well done. And now let others climb up on your shoulders.'"

Colin Powell, Commencement Speech at Howard University

---

met with a mixture of "strong applause" and "scattered boos." His 2000 convention address gained more uniform approval, despite the more strongly stated stand on affirmative action. Some observers credited this to a more tightly orchestrated convention in 2000, but certainly the audience's expectations, shaped by Powell's 1996 speech, played a part as well. CNN reported that Powell's 2000 address was "an electrifying social policy speech," and the *Christian Science Monitor* termed it "a rousing speech . . . that often seemed only incidentally Republican." Prior to becoming secretary of state, probably the harshest response Powell received to a speech occurred at Harvard University, when some of the graduating students in the audience stood and turned their backs to him in response to the Pentagon's "Don't ask, don't tell" policy regarding gays in the military. Even then, however, Powell made a point in

a person, and who is similarly comfortable with his oratorical style and choices.

INFORMATION SOURCES

Research Collections and Collected Speeches

There are no archival collections or published collections of speeches at this time. Transcripts, audio clips, and video clips of Powell's speech to the United Nations and his two Republican National Convention speeches are widely available. Transcripts of speeches delivered while Powell was chairman of the Joint Chiefs of Staff can be obtained from the Office of the Chairman, Public Affairs, 9999 Joint Staff, Pentagon, Washington D.C., 20318 [*PAP*]. Many of his speeches as secretary of state are reprinted in the *Department of State Bulletin* [*DSB*].

Web Sites

America's Promise. This Web site includes a history of the organization and Powell's role as founder. It also has transcripts of several speeches he delivered in that role. www.americaspromise.org

Department of State. The State Department Web site includes the transcripts of numerous speeches and press conferences, as well as official statements. www.state.gov

Audiovisual Material

"Speech to the 1996 Republican National Convention." Great Speeches Video Series. Cataloged at www.evgonline.com

Selected Critical Studies

Booker, Simeon. "Colin L. Powell: Black General at the Summit of U.S. Power." *Ebony*, July 1988, pp. 136–82.

Brown, Luther. "Powell Ascends to Center of Political Prominence." *Black Enterprise*, February 1988, p. 36.

Brown, Marshall. "Powell Reaches the Pinnacle of Pentagon Power." *Black Enterprise*, October 1989, p. 22.

Selected Biographies

Means, Howard. *Colin Powell*. New York: Donald I. Fine, 1992.

Powell, Colin L., with Joseph E. Persico. *My American Journey*. New York: Random House, 1995.

Roth, David. *Sacred Honor: A Biography of Colin Powell*. San Francisco: HarperSanFrancisco, 1993.

CHRONOLOGY OF MAJOR SPEECHES

See "Research Collections and Collected Speeches" for source codes.

"U.S. Foreign Policy in a Time of Transition" (address to the National Press Club). Washington, D.C., October 27, 1988. *DSB*, January 1989, pp. 30–32.

"Economics and National Security" (address to the Economic Club of Detroit). Detroit, Mich., December 12, 1988. *PAP*; *Vital Speeches of the Day*, January 15, 1989, pp. 194–97.

"U.S. Foreign Policy in a Changing World" (address to the Town Hall of California). Los Angeles, March 23, 1990. *PAP*; *Vital Speeches of the Day*, May 1, 1990, pp. 418–21.

"Commencement Address." U.S. Military Academy, West Point, N.Y., May 31, 1990. *PAP*; Office of Public Affairs, U.S. Military Academy, West Point, N.Y., 10996.

"Remarks to Morris High School." Bronx, N.Y., April 15, 1991. *PAP*.

"Remarks to the Association for a Better New York." New York City, April 16, 1991. *PAP*.

"Memorial Day Speech" (address at the ceremony at the Vietnam Veterans Memorial). Washington, D.C., May 27, 1991. *PAP*.

"Remarks at the 20th Annual National Convention of the Tuskegee Airmen." Detroit, Mich., August 10, 1991. *PAP*.

"Commencement Address" (Fisk University). Nashville, Tenn., May 4, 1992. *PAP*.

"Remarks Introducing President Bill Clinton at the Memorial Day Ceremonies." Washington, D.C., May 31, 1993. *PAP*.

"Commencement Address" (Harvard University). Cambridge, Mass., June 10, 1993. *PAP*.

"Remarks at the Groundbreaking Ceremony for the Vietnam Women's Memorial." Washington, D.C., July 29, 1993. *PAP*.

"Commencement Address" (Howard University). Washington, D.C., May 14, 1994. Available through the Public Relations Office, Howard University, Washington, D.C., 20059.

"Address to the Republican National Convention." San Diego, July 31, 1996. Videotape: *Public Speaking: An Audience-Centered Approach*. New York: Macmillan. Audio version available at www.pbs.org

"Address to the Republican National Convention." Philadelphia, July 31, 2000.

"Address at McConnell Center, University of Louisville." Louisville, Ky., November 20, 2001. *DSB*.

"Address on Middle East Peace." Jerusalem, April 18, 2002. *DSB*.

"Remarks at World Summit on Sustainable Development." Johannesburg, South Africa, September 4, 2002. *DSB*.

"Speech to the United Nations." New York City, February 5, 2003. *DSB*.

RONALD WILSON REAGAN (1911–2004)
Fortieth President of the United States

RONALD H. CARPENTER AND WINDY Y. LAWRENCE

He is called the Great Communicator. Long after his second term as president of the United States, Ronald Reagan's personal popularity and public approval of his leadership remain largely undiminished. How his communication helped him attain that stature warrants description, and an apt beginning for that account is the ending of his life. On June 11, 2004, during the Washington National Cathedral state funeral for the deceased president, Supreme Court Justice Sandra Day O'Connor repeated words first uttered in 1630 during a sermon by John Winthrop—and subsequently favored by Ronald Reagan during the 1980s and even after his presidency: "We must consider that we shall be as a city upon a hill," for "the eyes of all people are upon us." She thereby underscored a prominent theme that resonated well with Americans for over three centuries, became a hallmark of Reagan's presidential discourse, and thus offers a context for understanding and appreciating rhetorical sources of effectiveness that culminated in the sobriquet "great communicator." Dwight Eisenhower exemplifies the immensely popular military hero who in the public mind did no presidential wrong; other Americans also capitalized politically on earlier, heroic images to attain the presidency and function effectively therein. But Ronald Reagan drew upon no such rhetorical resource initially (although he consistently lauded other Americans' heroism and behaved heroically himself when shot by a would-be assassin). This American orator was elected and reelected, and remained esteemed to substantial degree because of his abilities as a communicator.

Reagan's communication prowess evolved from experiences preceding his formal entry into politics as governor of California from 1967 to 1974. After growing up in Illinois and attending Eureka College (where he played football), he was a sports announcer on radio from 1932 to 1937 and a Hollywood actor from 1937 to 1966

(in films such as *Brother Rat, Knute Rockne, All American,* and *Bedtime for Bonzo*). More significant were his years of important experience as a platform speaker. Beginning in 1954, with his role as host of the *G.E. Theatre* on television, he contributed extensively for almost ten years to the public relations program of General Electric by speaking at business conventions, Chamber of Commerce meetings, and club luncheons. Then, on the evening of October 27, 1964, as cochairman of the California Citizens for Goldwater–Miller Committee, Reagan delivered a thirty-minute nationally broadcast speech titled "A Time for Choosing" and supporting Republican presidential candidate Barry Goldwater. Heralded as one of the most successful televised political broadcasts since Richard Nixon's 1952 "Checkers" speech, the address established Reagan as a favored candidate for the governorship of California, which he later won. Reagan, however, chose not to announce his candidacy officially until January 1966. Instead, for nine months prior to his announcement, he embarked on a speaking tour throughout California and the nation, delivering various versions of his Goldwater address, which he referred to as "the Speech."

In a letter to Lorraine and Elwood Wagner in 1992, Reagan explained that this oratorical coup derived from a speaking engagement that had a profound effect on him:

Now I come to the "speech." I was still in show business and had no thought of getting into politics. Not being able to sing or dance, when I did personal appearances I made speeches. I wrote them myself and was out on the circuit much of the time. During campaign years I went out on the speaking tour in behalf of people I believed should be elected. "The Speech" as you termed it was one I'd been delivering for appearances at fund-raisers for presidential candidate Barry Goldwater. Here in California the

Republican Party was split down the middle. The Republican leadership asked me if I would make my speech (and it was mine, written by me) on national radio if they bought the time on NBC. I said yes and did the speech. It was pretty successful and raised $8.5 million for the Goldwater campaign. . . . I told them if they'd make it possible to accept all the speaking invitations I was getting in California I'd come back and tell them who should be running for governor and I'd campaign for him. After a few months I discovered the people wanted me to be the candidate. . . . I was a victim of "the speech." It was entirely mine.

And "it" constituted a rhetorical milestone on his road to the presidency by epitomizing how "a Big forth." But the public understood his stance because he excelled at articulating these themes as prominent symbols of hopes and fears to which Americans were emotionally tied. Thus, for a wide range of issues, speaking on the banquet circuit for General Electric was a "proving ground" to test ideational content of his future political agenda as president—but he had to be elected first. To understand more fully his successful campaign and his presidential communication thereafter, one first might contemplate briefly the societal evolution of the United States from the latter nineteenth century to the 1960s, 1970s, and 1980s sound stage upon which Ronald Reagan began to act and star in his most important role until his death in 2004

As president, Ronald Reagan was highly regarded for his ability to effectively deliver other writers' words. The popular belief was that his acting experience had prepared him to excel at having others write his speeches for him. Yet he was an active editor of his speeches, and as governor of California had been disinclined to use speechwriters at all. He recalled that as president of the Screen Actors Guild and spokesman for General Electric, he had always written his own speeches:

"Nancy gives me h–ll because [as governor] I won't get a speechwriter and just go along with someone's canned product, but I've been on the mashed potato circuit so long doing my own I just can't be comfortable with someone else's words."

Brother or paternalistic government" seriously endangered more limiting leadership whereby "problems would all be solved if the federal government would return to the states and communities some of the sources of taxation the federal government has usurped for itself."

Consistent attacks on big government became "the Speech" on free enterprise from which Reagan never varied significantly over the years. Moreover, "it" offered the foundation for what later was called "Reaganomics." As James A. Baker III recalled in his oral history, everyone knew where Reagan "stood on a strong defense, peace through strength, free-market economics, supply-side economics, opportunity, and so from old age and the ravages of Alzheimer's disease.

TOWARD GREAT PRESIDENTIAL COMMUNICATION

Americans once were a vocal people. They often spoke in Grange halls or town meetings, and nineteenth-century higher education often helped many of them become competent and confident communicators. Colleges and universities taught rhetoric as the art of writing and speaking for important situations in which people participated. Moreover, rhetoric taught for writing and speaking was read and heard often (notably the Scriptures). Before the Civil War, one

American in four was a townsman, but nine of ten Americans soon lived in cities and urban sprawls. After tiring trips home in rush-hour traffic, they were unlikely to go out again and participate in discourse. Some read mass circulation magazines and daily newspapers that proliferated with their congregating in these new environments; more, however, became viewers and listeners in a vast communication mosaic of pervasive and persuasive electronic mass media. Writers and speakers turned into readers and listeners (with more of the latter). Indeed, seemingly accepting President Richard Nixon's characterization of them as his "great silent majority," many Americans now began their speeches by saying with complete conviction, "Unaccustomed as I am to public speaking." Nevertheless, despite their personal communication ineptness, many Americans were not content simply to lead, as Henry David Thoreau wrote, "lives of quiet desperation"—but accordingly bestowed political leadership on more adept communicators who did say well what they wanted said well. In short, they longed for that surrogate spokesperson, the "citizen orator," articulating well our "American dream."

Watergate briefly altered Americans' expectations for their presidents, however. After the trauma of President Richard Nixon's resignation, what Americans wanted most in the White House was honesty. Jimmy Carter fulfilled that expectation in 1976 with television commercials, including those with the candidate in farmer's garb as a virtuous man of the soil, underscoring his basic campaign promise that he would "never lie" to us. For virtue and honesty in the White House, voters overlooked Carter's communication liabilities such as unnatural pause patterns and tendencies toward slips of the tongue. His ineptness as "citizen orator" for the nation became more apparent and detrimental, however. During the 1980 presidential campaign, Jimmy Carter as an inarticulate incumbent contrasted starkly with challenger Ronald Reagan, whose communication skills were preferred in the presidency to dispel voters' fears for the present and articulate their hopes for the future. After all, in 1979 Carter's nationwide television address pessimistically pronounced that "a majority of our people believe that the next five years will be worse than the past five years." In a

survey at that time, Americans were asked questions about the quality of their lives on a scale of 1 to 10, with 10 representing the "best possible life." In 1979, Americans deemed themselves below the halfway step on their "ladder of life" (4.7 on a scale of 10). Evincing nostalgia, they deemed their lives five years earlier to have been better (5.7); and when they looked to the future five years later on the "ladder of life," they anticipated falling farther down the ladder (4.6). Americans seriously questioned what the future held for them; they answered in voting booths by voting for Ronald Reagan.

Winning the presidency in 1980 required a skillful media campaign strategy of "packaging the presidency" for voters. Gerald Rafshoon and political consultants recommended that Reagan project a persona of strength contrasting with Carter's perceived weakness and indecisiveness. The polling firm of Decision/Making/Information, headed by Richard Wirthlin, conducted a national study that tested six themes and their resonance with voters. The strategists made several important findings upon which they predicated their broad political campaign. First, Americans were tired of "slick" television advertisements and preferred that a candidate speak openly and plainly to them. Accordingly, the campaign produced more close-up ads of Reagan speaking directly to the camera than any other presidential candidate since 1960. This stratagem proved to be a gold mine of opportunity because the former actor excelled in front of the camera. The consultants also confirmed that voters were weary of the pessimism pervading the Carter years and were ready for Reagan's "can do," upbeat themes: "Don't let anybody tell you that inflation can't be controlled. It can be, by making some tough decisions to control federal spending," and "As President, I'm ready to make those decisions." Aligned with this "can do" theme, pollsters found leadership, competence, strength, and decisiveness to be important attributes for Reagan to project. He responded by incorporating these tested qualities into campaign discourse that many times repeated this question to American voters: "Ask yourself, are you better off now than you were four years ago?" A rhetorical question, one containing its own answer, this tendentious query encapsulated the fears and frustrations concerning the faltering economy under Carter's administration. But Reagan's winning the White House in 1980 could not be counted as irrefutable evidence of his being a great communicator if Jimmy Carter's losing the election could be explained by the ineptness of his persuasiveness as president.

During the presidential campaign and the Reagan presidency, several suasory themes recurred consistently in Reagan's discourse. For example, his First Inaugural Address identified the praiseworthy people prevailing in any neighborhood infused with an American civil religion. They were "extraordinary 'ordinary' Americans who never make the headlines and will never be interviewed." They were "men and women who raise our food, patrol our streets, man our mines and factories, teach our children, keep our homes, and heal us when we are sick—professionals, industrialists, shopkeepers, clerks, cabbies, and truck drivers." And all of them shared, he said on January 25, 1984, a "vision of a better life." The president also consistently identified a domestic threat to American well-being, in that "government is not the solution to our problem" but *is* "the problem." Or, as he said on October 13, 1982, "the problem isn't who is to blame; it's what to blame." Any current economic problems therefore were results of government growing unnecessarily and spending money extravagantly.

A solution resided in restoration of a proud heritage that Reagan's 1984 State of the Union address lauded, when "faith, work, family, neighborhood, freedom, and peace are not just words," but rather "what American means, definitions of what makes us a good and loving people." Or, on July 27, 1981, "I ask you to trust yourselves. That's what America is all about." That "can do" Americanism would manifest itself, whether with economic shrewdness or physical heroism. Barbara Proctor, for instance, "rose from a ghetto to build a multimillion-dollar advertising agency in Chicago"; and similar praise was heaped upon "Secret Service agent Tim McCarthy, who placed his body between mine and the man with the gun."

The neighborly Americans whom Reagan persuaded can be described in other ways. Although Reagan obviously was a prominent person, his discourse also displayed a "Second Persona." Audiences often listen for "cues" that tell them how they are to view the world, and oratory often describes overtly—or implies tacitly—personae who may be models of what speakers would have their listeners become. An audience thereby persuaded becomes a collectively unified "people" because they are cognizant of—and respond favorably to—those particularly potent words, or "ideographs," that historically have governed their social reality. Indeed, those people also may acquire a "fantasy" fostering desires to participate in a dream of a future social reality. Reagan's pollster, Richard Wirthlin, recommended "symbolizing the past and future greatness of America" by radiating "inspirational confidence," for a president can "pull a nation together while directing its people toward fulfillment of the American dream." Reagan thereby invited Americans to make a covenant with civil religion that promised a better future of individual success if they worked hard, valued their families, and helped their neighbors.

People praised by Reagan were not just contemporary Americans, however, but also those hardy individuals of 350 years earlier: Puritans who adhered to a collective vision of their mission in a New World Eden and the resultant millennium to follow. John Winthrop (1588–1649) was founding governor of the Massachusetts Bay Colony almost continuously from 1630 to 1649. His famous sermon "The Modell of Christian Charity," which he wrote in 1630 and possibly delivered aboard the *Arabella* as it was carrying Puritans to America, articulated a moral code for the godly society that would prevail for them. When predicting that "wee shall bee as a Citty upon a hill, the eyes of all people . . . upon us," Winthrop promulgated a civil religion that nurtured American exceptionalism as a "chosen people" who achieved their "manifest destiny" across the continent and then undertook imperial diplomacy, if not armed action, on behalf of freedom and democracy around the world, beginning in the last years of the nineteenth century and continuing thereafter.

Puritan preachers often cast their sermons in the form of a jeremiad that warned people of impending doom if they strayed from values of their religious covenant that assured achieving the millennium in the New World. Dire consequences awaited those who failed to take the right side in struggles between good and evil at pivotal points when the nation was tested and the souls of its citizens were tried. This seventeenth-century Puritan view of "apocalypticism" persisted to become a contemporary, mainstream Americanism for people unhappy with their present and nervous about their future. To be articulated persuasively, however, an "American dream" must be threatened by an apocalyptic "evil" in order for presidential discourse to resonate with this pervasive view of what a gloomy future might hold for people who strayed from their cherished values. What could be a more evil threat to the American millennium than Russian communism?

While campaigning in 1964 for Barry Goldwater, Reagan had emerged as a prominent spokesman not only for Republicans but also for an anti-Soviet stance predicated upon American strength to thwart communism. Particularly in platform speeches to conservative groups, Reagan was emphatic, if not strident, about the threat of communism to the United States. Later, as president, on television to national audiences, he urged military strength to counter communism. Nevertheless, because public opinion polls showed many Americans in a nuclear age inclined toward improved relations with the Soviet Union, "common sense" warranted that Reagan meet amiably with Soviet Premier Gorbachev in Geneva. In the main, however, the president did so only with Americans firmly believing that he would deal with Soviet "savagery" from a position of military strength. Thus was born rhetorically the alliterative "Evil Empire" of the Soviet Union. Potential nuclear war conducted with missiles left the world essentially with "zero option," and the immensity of the threat posed by the "Evil Empire" of Russia could be countered only by a means as epic as an American "Star Wars" defense system in outer space.

Presidential orators who appeal effectively to basic values and adjust to changing public opinion are not unique, however. To appreciate more fully one's success as a citizen orator, a helpful orientation is the exception principle, whereby the factors of interest are not those that the orator utilizes in common with other communicators but those by which the speaker differs from them, quantitatively or qualitatively. From this frame of reference, *what* Reagan said often was not exceptional; as candidate and then as president, he succeeded in large measure because of *how* his content was communicated. When classical theorists parsed the principles of persuasive discourse, they organized their commentaries into canons of rhetoric. One was what Roman rhetorical theorists called *actio*, the canon of delivery, or how orators manage voice and body for effective discourse. For a communication context in which many Americans are inarticulate, one who speaks well has an advantage, particularly when using the mass medium of television, which conjoins visual imagery with the auditory impress of spoken words.

While attesting to the primacy of oral speech, Father Walter J. Ong's epigram epitomizes the power that evolves from "orality" even when it is in the form of natural or conversational expression: "Sight isolates, sound incorporates." After all, sound exists only when it is going out of existence. When a public speaker utters the word "permanence," by the time " 'nence" appears, "perma" is gone. Thus, to understand the utterance, a listener must participate in a sensory union with the speaker *and* other audience members to close the gaps between successive sounds. If the speaker asks an audience to read a handout, each reader enters into his or her own private reading world and the unity of an audience is shattered, to be reestablished only when oral speech begins again. Whereas clarity and distinctness of vision require a "taking apart," listening demands sensory endeavors of "putting together" and "unifying" successive sounds that nurture a "communal sense."

For presidential discourse on television, Reagan's prowess with orality was perhaps unequaled. Only rare lapses marred his extemporizing or reading from scripts. During the first television debate with Walter Mondale in 1984, for instance, dysfluencies occurred in some answers, and the president's meandering and stumbling through his concluding illustration were disconcerting. In the second debate, though, he bounced back to customary performance levels perfected during years of practice on Hollywood sets and in television studios. Observers of presidential discourse for the most part acclaim Reagan's mastery of voice and body while speaking. Conducive to his admirable performance (*actio*) were a particularly well-modulated baritone voice capable of controlled variation between restrained forcefulness and an almost hushed whisper, sustained eye contact, well-timed gestures, physical poise, and a superb sense of when to pause for clarity, emphasis, and emotional affect. From a perspective of dramatic acting, only Reagan as candidate could carry off so well the conclusion of his acceptance address to the Republican National Convention in 1980: "I'll confess that I've been a little afraid to suggest what I'm going to suggest, [beat] I'm more afraid not to. [beat] Can we begin our crusade joined together in a moment of silent prayer?" Add his well-timed, characteristic nod of the head with clenched teeth and pursed lips between some words, whereby an impression of determination was reinforced. In combination with physical poise that bespoke both unflappable stature and the coolness so suitable for television, Reagan's rhetoric of voice and body warranted acclaim for performance (*actio*) and the controlled flexibility and polished delivery of his lines. Indeed, for the vocal aspects of skillful delivery, no other president, save Franklin Roosevelt, matched Ronald Reagan.

Television demands favorable visual impress, however, and Ronald Reagan had another asset not surpassed by presidents before him (and unlikely after him). Valuable experience was acquired on Hollywood sound stages, where the skill necessary to converse with a camera was mastered. When two characters in a film scene are conversing (such as Humphrey Bogart and Ingrid Bergman in *Casablanca*), an "establishing shot" first shows two of them. Then, "continuity editing" creates a pattern called "shot and reverse shot," whereby the camera focuses full-face on the person talking, as if that camera is within the listener in the scene, paying attention to lines directed at him or her. When Reagan acted in Hollywood, that listener often was *not* physically present. Since the same scene often had to be shot several times to achieve the director's desired product, the presumed "listener" often left the sound stage. Thus, the actor's lines were delivered again and again, but

facing a camera instead of another actor. Reagan thereby learned how to "converse" with cameras. Critics have noted that he viewed his live speeches for General Electric as "theatrical" events. Nevertheless, as Marshall McLuhan has observed, television is a "cool" medium requiring a correspondingly cool, subdued delivery. Yes, Franklin Roosevelt could be soothing during fireside chats on radio, but his eloquent lines that are remembered were spoken before people present to him. In those settings he often was strident, almost shouting "the only thing we have to fear is fear itself" or "this generation of Americans has a rendezvous with destiny." For television, "strident" does not play well. Some presidents become actors in their jobs, but Reagan's job as actor helped him become president.

Hollywood lingered in Reagan's sense of apt communication. For sardonic humor, he could repeat dialogue from the hard-nosed detective Dirty Harry (played by Clint Eastwood) and proclaim to those who would increase taxes, "Go ahead, make my day." But for high drama during the Cold War with Russia, Reagan wrote his own script for a scene shot on location in Berlin on June 12, 1987—when he emphatically called upon Russian Premier Gorbachev to "tear down this wall!"

Although Reagan clearly mastered the delivery necessary for television, similar acclaim is not warranted for his command of the classical canon of rhetoric called *lexis* (by the Greeks) or *elocutio* (by the Romans), that is, how word choice and word order stylistically achieve eloquent sentences that survive as epigrams, if not axioms by which to live one's life. Other presidents assured their places in posterity with eminently quotable, memorable phrases and sentences, such as Abraham Lincoln's "government of the people, by the people, for the people" and John Kennedy's "Ask not what your country can do for you—ask what you can do for your country." No comparable eloquence came from Reagan, who in terms of this canon has been labeled "less than great." We notice and remember his quip about sending a film hero, Rambo, to solve a problem or an on-mike slip during a voice check prior to a radio address: "I'm pleased to tell you today that I've signed legislation that will outlaw Russia forever. We begin bombing in five minutes." Reagan does not deserve esteem for classically eloquent style. For him, the more conversational his delivery and language were, the more he was suited to television.

Reagan was not eloquent in the traditional sense partly because of his consistent striving for homespun, everyday language that did not call attention to itself. This preferred verbal style of his presidency reveals itself through a computer-based analysis (DICTION) that demonstrates how he eschewed eloquence, if not poetic references, in favor of content expressed in a conversational mode. This president clearly was committed to a time-honored "oral tradition" based upon television speeches favoring spontaneous-sounding conversation. Thus, characteristic contractions such as "we're," "it's," "we've," and "we'll" transform what could be elevated discourse into idiomatic expression. Moreover, Reagan was particularly fond of a conversational and stylistically inept "well" or "now" to begin sentences, as in his First Inaugural Address and the 1984 State of the Union address: "Well, I believe we the Americans of today are ready to act" and "Now, I believe there is. . . ." Those colloquial interjections are verbal filler to accompany nods of the head with pursed lips; they are not the lofty, elevated expressions that find their way onto monuments. Consider what is lost in Reagan's Second Inaugural by saying, "Well, with heart and hand, let us stand as one today."

Other shortcomings appear even when eloquent style *seemed* to be the goal. To create a particularly memorable line, Martin Luther King, Jr. began successive sentences with the same words, a stylistic device known as *anaphora* or *epanaphora*, and emphasized by repetition the optimistic "I have a dream . . . I have a dream . . . I have a dream." But to amplify "the will and moral courage of free men and women," Reagan said, "It is a weapon our adversaries in today's world do not have. It is a weapon that we as Americans do have." Discounting grammar by which plural "will and moral courage" become a singular "it," the words "it is" are unworthy of emphasis. Or, while describing a "Star Wars" defense system in space during his Second Inaugural, the president said, "It wouldn't kill people, it would destroy weapons. It wouldn't militarize space, it would help demilitarize the ar-

senals of earth. It would render nuclear weapons obsolete." The exemplary surrogate spokesman for Great Britain, Winston Churchill, reinforced key words in "We shall fight on the beaches, we shall fight on the landing grounds, we shall fight in the fields and in the streets, we shall fight in the hills." We learn what is repeated for us, and through an abortive attempt to stylize, Reagan would have Americans learn a word devoid of rhetorically potent connotation, *it*. In one view, delivery (*actio*) minus style (*elocutio*) might suggest a less-than-great communicator, but this presidential orator had other rhetorical assets from which to draw.

If eloquent epigrams are lacking, what are their substitutes in terms of specific wording that contributes to being a "great communicator" as president? A reminder from research in communication merits reconsideration: for persuasiveness via discourse, rhetorical sensitivity is a sine qua non. Although speakers may opt to "tell it like it is," the *rhetorically sensitive person* appreciates that ideas can be communicated in *multi-form ways*. Thus, to deal effectively with the "perceptional world of the Other," persuaders will be adaptive and select wordings that are particularly likely for "it" to achieve desired *e*ffect and *a*ffect. Reagan's 1978 personal correspondence with William Loeb, publisher of the *Manchester Union Leader* attests to how he personally adapted and honed the wording of the same essential message that he preached over and over to different audiences who had not previously heard his presentation:

> You know when you take a speech on the road and use the same theme to audience after audience (and I've had that experience in years past) it is possible to achieve a great freedom from notes. You can also hone and polish the original draft. In this job, though [as Governor of California], it seems as if I'm always having to come up with a new speech on a new subject. The night before I left California I addressed a national convention of construction engineers. In Washington, two nights before New Hampshire it was the Touchdown Club, and by the end of the week the Alfalfa Club and the American Conservative Union. Nancy gives me h–ll because I won't get a speechwriter and just go along with someone's canned product, but I've been on the mashed

potato circuit so long doing my own I just can't be comfortable with someone else's words.

When Reagan was speaking on behalf of General Electric, each banquet or convention audience was a new one hearing the same old message. As president of the United States, however, he was addressing mass audiences at one time and some thematic material could recur, but each speech essentially had to be a new one.

During his eight years as president, Reagan spoke nearly 4 million words of prepared text. His words had to be crafted into nearly 2,500 sets of remarks. During a typical month, he delivered twenty formal speeches, gave five weekly radio talks, and appeared at three press conferences (each of which began with a prepared set of remarks). Of necessity, the speechwriting department of the Executive Office of the President was engaged. The speechwriting staff admired each other's "first-rate" craftsmanship in the fulfillment of Reagan's desire to use the "bully pulpit" of the presidency. As good servants, they not only conformed to the president's verbal predilections, they came to anticipate what he would want to say. As Reagan recalled in 1992 when writing to Lorraine and Elwood Wagner, "After I was elected governor and later as president I found out you no longer had time to write your own speeches. So I worked with the speechwriters and gave them copies of my previous speeches so they could learn my style and it's been that way since."

But Reagan *also* had "first rate" *technological* help. Like other presidents before him, he relied on polls and public opinion research, but his presidency had the unique advantage of Richard Wirthlin's research tool called PINS (Political INformation System). The resultant "quantifiably safe rhetoric" of Reagan's July 17, 1980, acceptance address to the Republican National Convention in Detroit was ascertained *beforehand* by "war-gaming" to determine which specific words would be the most effective (at the cost of $1.5 million in campaign funds paid to Wirthlin). With technology called PulseLine, focus groups from 30 to 100 members would react to initial drafts of what might be Reagan's speeches. They were asked to turn dials in specific directions—in "real time," as a speech was presented—to indicate what they liked or disliked. The result, assisted by computers, was an EKG-like chart show-ing the precise moments in various versions of a speech when words did or did not resonate well with people. For Reagan's pivotal 1980 acceptance address, Wirthlin's prior research indicated that the following words evoked positive responses: work, family, freedom, peace, and strong America/ neighborhood (numerically, in the address as delivered, those value-laden or emotive words occurred, respectively, eleven, eight, six, five, and five times). For rhetorical sensitivity, how much more "safe" could rhetoric be?

Despite his speechwriters' craftsmanship (and Wirthlin's technological assistance), Reagan's personal imprint upon his speeches cannot be ignored. Evidence resides in his longhand emendations to texts of what he finally would say, such as his "Address to the Nation on Events in Lebanon and Grenada," October 27, 1983. At 5:30 P.M. on the previous day, he received a draft from Ben Elliott (other writers for this address were David Gergen and Allan Myers). After the bombing of the U.S. Marine barracks at the Beirut airport in Lebanon, in which "more than 200 of the sleeping men were killed," a presidential address was required to explain what Reagan called "one hideous, insane attack" (as well as unfolding events in Grenada, which "needed our help"). His personal longhand emendations upon that draft copy demonstrate Reagan's rhetorical sensitivity. In the first paragraphs, sequential stages in the *chronology* of the event were heightened with longhand insertions such as "this was not the end of the horror," "there is another factor," "for several years," and "only a year ago." And Reagan made the passage more conversational by adding, "Well, it is as I described it." The length of the passage increased from 243 words to 282 words to achieve the president's characteristic narrative form. Later in the speechwriters' draft, Reagan added an anecdote: "A Lebanese mother told one of our ambassadors her little girl had only attended school two of the last eight years. Now because of our presence there her daughter could live a normal life."

The president's predilection for narrative clearly had resonated with his advisers and the White House speechwriting staff. They appreciated this rhetorical preference on his part and accordingly supplied Reagan with precisely the kind of anecdotes that he preferred using in discourse, and the speech about the terrorist bombing of the Marine barracks in Lebanon demonstrates how well the president was promptly served by his aides. Just the previous day, October 26, 1983, speechwriter and adviser Anthony R. Dolan wrote a memorandum to the other writers on the staff: Robert C. McFarlane as well as Gergen, Elliott, and Myer. The stated subject of the memorandum was emphasized: "*Very Important Passage in TV Address.*" Moreover, Dolan's opening remark in the memo was an imperative: "Urge inclusion of this anecdote. It says it all." What Dolan wrote to come out of Reagan's mouth appears below:

> I know of course that no words from me can ever fully describe or do justice to the unselfish devotion of the young men who were and are today part of our Marine contingent in Beirut. I will attempt no such words.
>
> But I do think something that happened to the commandant of our Marine Corps, General Paul Kelley, while he was visiting our critically injured Marines in an Air Force Hospital, says more than any of us could ever hope to say about the gallantry and heroism of these young men who serve so willingly so that others might have a chance at peace and freedom in their own lives and in the life of their country.
>
> I will let General Kelley's words describe the incident. He spoke of a "young Marine with more tubes going in and out of his body than I have ever seen in one body.
>
> "He could not see very well. He reached up and grabbed my four stars, just to make sure I was who I said I was. He held my hand with a firm grip. He was making signals and we realized he wanted to tell me something. We put a pad of paper in his hand . . . he wrote 'Semper fi.' " Well, if you've been a Marine or if like myself you're an admirer of the Marines, you know those words are a battle cry, a greeting and a legend in the Marine Corps. They're Marine shorthand for the motto of the corps— "Semper Fidelis"—"always faithful."
>
> General Kelley has a reputation for being a very sophisticated General and a very tough Marine. But he cried when he saw those words, and who can blame him? That Marine and all those others like him, living and dead,

have been faithful to their ideals, they have given willingly of themselves so that a nearly defenseless people in a region of great strategic importance to the free world will have a chance someday to live lives free of murder and mayhem and terrorism. I think that young Marine and all of his comrades have given every one of us something to live up to. They were not afraid to stand for their country or, no matter how difficult and slow the journey might be, to give to others that last best hope of a better future. We cannot and will not dishonor them now and the sacrifices they have made by failing to remain as faithful to the cause of freedom and the pursuit of peace as they have been.

In his own handwriting on the memorandum, Reagan crossed out Dolan's opening paragraph. He preferred to get more directly to the anecdote itself, beginning, "May I share something with you I think you'd like to know? It's something that happened to the Commandant of our Marine Corps. . . ." The remainder of the story supplied by Dolan was used unchanged in the final draft. Thus, technological assistance afforded by Wirthlin's PINS was supplemented by Dolan's rhetorical sensitivity complementing that of the president. Nevertheless, an imperative to include anecdotal narrative was complemented still further in this speech about the tragic event in Lebanon with other, more subtle longhand insertions by the president that demonstrate his personal rhetorical sensitivity.

If Americans, as a "chosen people," are so exceptional, a reference to the "multinational" force—of which U.S. Marines were a part—was deleted, as if to say Americans were the *only* force restoring order in that troubled part of the world. By the fifth page of the emended draft, Reagan had deleted his speechwriters' reference to the Marines' barracks as "not an ideal location." After all, what commander in chief would place his armed forces unnecessarily at risk? The speechwriters' draft also described how "we ordered the battleship *New Jersey* offshore. The presence of its big 16-inch guns silenced those who once fired down on us from the hills." The president's longhand insertions made sure that Americans knew of *his* martial expertise because "without even firing them [,] it's [*sic*] 16-

inch guns" silenced those people "from the hills." He added, "And that may very well be the reason we suddenly had a cease-fire." On the same page, the speechwriting team would have had the president ask the rhetorical question "Would the terrorists have launched their suicide attack against the multinational force if it were not doing its job?" Reagan's emendation, inserted immediately preceding that sentence, defused his potential political detractors with "The answer to those who ask if we're serving any purpose in being there, let me answer with a question." And to demonstrate *his* timely, complete control of the situation, a longhand insertion noted: "Little attention has been paid to the fact that we have had special envoys there working literally around the clock to bring the warring factions together." Then, from its former place, he moved a sentence at the bottom of the page *up* thirteen lines to add that "this coming Monday in Geneva, President Gemayal of Lebanon plans to sit down with other factions from his country to see if national reconciliation can be achieved." And the speechwriters' "plans to" was changed in longhand to a more decisive "will."

America as savior of the world persisted in Reagan's deletions of his speechwriters' references later in the draft to "urge others to join us" and "I call on the world community. . . ." Indeed, by the time of the next draft on October 27, Reagan heightened exceptionalism further with "We will insure that the multinational peacekeeping forces—our Marines—are given the greatest possible protection," as if we indeed were the *only* force for stability in the world. No other alternative was likely when an optimistic Reagan deleted the negative suggestion from his speechwriters that "The radicals, the rejectionists, the violent will have won. The message will be clear that relying on the Soviet Union pays off because you cannot rely on the United States." Negative suggestion also was avoided later when he deleted "Our industries would quickly shut down without raw resources from abroad." Furthermore, he was optimistically willing to take credit for peace between Lebanon and Israel by inserting "that's another accomplishment of this past year." He also heightened the sacrifices by Marines, who were not just "brave men" but "brave young men." And

American nobility was emphasized further when the speechwriters would have had him say "We are there protecting our own interests." For other parts of the world (if not for some Americans), "our interests" might suggest ignoble mercenary goals, political advantage, or access to Middle East oil. With the most subtle of rhetorical sensitivity, the president deleted "interests." Thus, with finesse favoring family and neighborhood, we were only protecting "our own."

Reagan's emendations also emphasized his seeming omnipotence. A sterile, third-person recounting by speechwriters was carefully prefaced with his insertion "I know." A presence of "700 Cuban military and paramilitary forces" in Grenada became the more dangerously potent "hundreds" of them. Speechwriters would have had Reagan say "There is not just one response to these threats, there are many." The president deleted the line, for his was *the* way. And after recounting the ordeal of that Marine wounded in Beirut, Reagan returned to civil religion to close with his prayer in longhand: "I would like to ask you all—wherever you may be in this blessed land—to pray for these wounded young men and to pray for the bereaved familys [*sic*] of those who gave their lives. I will not ask you to pray for the dead because they are safe in God's loving arms and beyond need of our prayers." Thanks to someone—either a speechwriter remembering Wirthlin's research about "safe" words to use or Reagan himself—at the last minute before delivery the prayer was changed to end with "pray for the bereaved families of those who gave their lives for our *freedom*" [italics added].

In the final appraisal of Reagan as citizen orator, one last question may be asked: What determines greatness as a communicator in a president? The answer may reside to large extent in timing per se. Republicans and many Americans had long been awaiting a return to earlier values of a "civil religion," the seeds of which had been sown by John Winthrop and our Puritan ancestors in New England. Republicans had cultivated those early crops starting in the late 1940s and early 1950s by bemoaning the loss of China to communism, for a "China myth" held that Democrats under President Harry Truman destroyed what some noteworthy Republicans had worked diligently for during decades: nurturing the growth of Christianity in Asia. Dwight Eisenhower was not the Republican president to achieve that goal, but Ronald Reagan had been rehearsing for the role with a broader, more epic script about restoration for several years, finally was cast for it in 1980, and starred in the part for two terms as president of the United States.

On August 17, 1992, as a private citizen once more, Ronald Reagan addressed the Republican National Convention to urge the reelection of George H. W. Bush to a second term as president. Reagan was in large measure autobiographical, and recounted monumental events that took place throughout his life generally and during his presidency specifically, including a testimonial to his own oratorical triumphs when he proclaimed again that America faced a pivotal "time for choosing" during the quest of this nation to come still "closer to that shining city upon a hill." And Justice Sandra Day O'Connor corroborated that testimony when her eulogy of the former president repeated his view of America as aspiring to that "city on a hill." She thereby unequivocally corroborated the deceased president's adoption of—and effective adaptation to—a civil religion of family values undergirding the American dream.

In conclusion, some presidents are good communicators primarily because their rhetorical imperatives to restore values from the past are timely; other presidents are good communicators because of their timely visions of a future for which people should strive. A citizen orator who comfortably could wear the mantle of a "great communicator," however, is sufficiently synchronized politically to both past *and* future, such as a Puritan "city on the hill" and a millennial "American dream." If ever a president seemed to conjoin—through communication prowess—the timeliness of the past and future *within* the present, Ronald Reagan was he.

INFORMATION SOURCES

Research Collections and Collected Speeches

Ronald Reagan's presidential speeches, press conferences, interviews, and other oral discourse is in *Public Papers of the President: Ronald Reagan, 1981–1989*. Much of his presidential, gubernatorial, and private correspondence is at the Ronald Reagan Presidential Library, 40 Presidential Drive, Simi Val-

ley CA 93065. Innumerable critical essays have been written about Reagan's public speaking. The *Index to Journal in Communication Studies Through 1990* (Washington, D.C.: National Communication Association, 1992) lists sixty-three critical essays about Ronald Reagan.

Reagan, Ronald. *Public Papers of the President: Ronald Reagan, 1981–1989* [*PPP*]. Washington D.C.: Government Printing Office, 1981–91.

Web Sites

Ronald Reagan Presidential Library Official Web Site. Photos, texts, and other resources are on this source. www.reagan.utexas.edu

Ronald Reagan: The Heritage Foundation Remembers. A variety of Reagan's speech texts as well as some audio clips are on the Heritage Foundation's Web site honoring the former president. www.reagansheritage.org

Audiovisual Materials

ABC New Presents Ronald Reagan: An American Legend. ABC News, 2004. DVD.

Ronald Reagan. NBC News, 2004. DVD.

Ronald Reagan: The Great Communicator. MPI Home Video, 2004. DVD.

Ronald Reagan: A Legacy Remembered. History Channel, 2002. DVD.

Ronald Reagan: The Many Lives. CEL Communications with the A&E Network, 1991.

Salute to Reagan: A President's Greatest Moments. Time-Life Video, 2001. DVD.

Selected Critical Sources

Carpenter, Ronald H. "Ronald Reagan." In *American Orators of the Twentieth Century: Critical Studies and Sources*, ed. Bernard K. Duffy and Halford R. Ryan. New York: Greenwood Press, 1987.

———. "Ronald Reagan and the Presidential Imperative to Stylize: A–E = < GC." *Speaker and Gavel* 20 (1982–83): 1–6.

Dalleck, Robert. *Ronald Reagan: The Politics of Symbolism.* Cambridge, Mass.: Harvard University Press, 1984.

Denton, Robert. E. *The Primetime Presidency of Ronald Reagan: The Era of the Television Presidency.* New York: Praeger, 1988.

Erickson, Paul D. *Reagan Speaks*. New York: New York University Press, 1985.

Goodnight, G. Thomas. "Ronald Reagan and the American Dream: A Study of Rhetoric Out of Time." In *The Presidency and Rhetorical Leadership*, ed. Leroy G. Dorsey. College Station: Texas A&M University Press, 2002.

Hall, Wynton C. "The Invention of 'Quantifiably Safe

Rhetoric': Richard Wirthlin and Ronald Reagan's Instrumental Use of Public Opinion Research in Presidential Discourse." *Western Journal of Communication* 66 (Summer 2002): 319–46.

Hart, Roderick P. "The Great Communicator and Beyond." In his *Verbal Style and the Presidency: A Computer-Based Analysis*. Orlando, Fla.: Academic Press, 1984.

Houck, Davis W., and Amos Kiewe, eds. *Actor, Ideologue, Politician: The Public Speeches of Ronald Reagan*. Westport, Conn.: Greenwood Press, 1993.

Ingold, Beth A. J. "Ideology, Rhetoric, and the Shooting Down of KAL 007." In *Essays in Presidential Rhetoric*, ed. Theodore Windt and Beth Ingold, 2nd ed. Dubuque, Iowa: Kendall/Hunt, 1987.

Ivie, Robert L. "Speaking 'Common Sense' About the Soviet Threat: Reagan's Rhetorical Stance." *Western Journal of Speech Communication* 48 (Winter 1984): 39–50.

Jamieson, Kathleen Hall. "1980: I'm Qualified to Be President and You're Not." In her *Packaging the Presidency: A History and Criticism of Presidential Campaign Advertising*. New York: Oxford University Press, 1984.

Kiewe, Amos, and Davis W. Houck. *A Shining City on a Hill: Ronald Reagan's Economic Rhetoric, 1951–1989*. New York: Praeger, 1991.

Muir, William K., Jr. *The Bully Pulpit: The Presidential Leadership of Ronald Reagan*. San Francisco: ICS Press, 1992.

———. "Ronald Reagan's Bully Pulpit: Creating a Rhetoric of Values." In *Presidential Speechwriting: From the New Deal to the Reagan Revolution and Beyond*, ed. Kurt Ritter and Martin J. Medhurst. College Station: Texas A&M University Press, 2003.

Ritter, Kurt W. "Ronald Reagan and 'The Speech': The Rhetoric of Public Relations Politics." *Western Journal of Speech Communication* 32 (Winter 1968): 50–58.

———. "Ronald Reagan's 1960s Southern Rhetoric: Courting Conservatives for the GOP." *Southern Communication Journal* 64 (Summer 1999): 333–45.

Ritter, Kurt W., and David Henry. *Ronald Reagan: The Great Communicator*. New York: Greenwood, 1992.

Scheele, Henry Z. "Ronald Reagan's 1980 Acceptance Address: A Focus on American Values." *Western Journal of Speech Communication* 48 (Winter 1984): 51–61.

Smith, Craig Allen. "MisteReagan's Neighborhood: Rhetoric and National Unity." *Southern Speech Communication Journal* 52 (Spring 1987): 219–39.

Stuckey, Mary E. *Getting into the Game: The Pre-Presidential Rhetoric of Ronald Reagan*. New York: Praeger, 1989.

Weiler, Michael, and W. Barnett Pearce, eds. *Reagan and Public Discourse in America*. Tuscaloosa: University of Alabama Press, 1992.

Selected Biographies

Morris, Edmund. *Dutch: A Memoir of Ronald Reagan*. New York: Random House, 1999.

Reagan: A Life in Letters, ed. Kiron K. Skinner, Annelise Anderson, and Martin Anderson. New York: Free Press, 2003.

Reagan, Ronald. *An American Life*. New York: Simon and Schuster, 1990.

Strober, Deborah Hart, and Gerald S. Strober. *Reagan: The Man and His Presidency. The Oral History of an Era*. Boston: Houghton Mifflin, 1998.

CHRONOLOGY OF MAJOR SPEECHES

See "Research Collections and Collected Speeches" for source code.

"A Time for Choosing" (televised address for Goldwater presidential campaign). San Francisco, October 27, 1964. *Los Angeles Times*, October 27, 1964, pt. IV, p. 11.

"Inaugural Address." Washington, D.C., January 20, 1981. *PPP, 1981*, pp. 1–4.

"Remarks to Members of the National Press Club on Arms Reduction and Nuclear Weapons" ("Zero Options" speech). Washington, D.C., November 18, 1981. *PPP, 1981*, pp. 1062–67.

"Remarks at the Annual Convention of the National Association of Evangelicals" ("Evil Empire" speech). Orlando, Fla., March 8, 1983. *PPP, 1983*, vol. 1, pp. 359–64.

"Address to the Nation on the Soviet Attack on a Korean Civilian Airliner" (KAL 007). Washington, D.C., September 5, 1983. *PPP, 1983*, vol. 2, pp. 1227–30.

"Address to the Nation on Events in Lebanon and Grenada." Washington, D.C., October 27, 1983. *Weekly Compilation of Presidential Documents*, vol. 19. Washington, D.C.: GPO, 1983.

"Address to the Nation Announcing the Reagan–Bush Candidacies for Reelection." Washington, D.C., January 29, 1984. *PPP, 1984*, vol. 1, pp. 109–10.

"Remarks at a Ceremony Commemorating the 40th Anniversary of the Normandy Invasion, D-Day." Point du Hoc, France, June 6, 1984. *PPP, 1984*, vol. 1, pp. 817–20.

"Remarks at a United States–France Ceremony Commemorating the 40th Anniversary of the Normandy

Invasion, D-Day." Omaha Beach, France, June 6, 1984. *PPP, 1984*, vol. 1, pp. 821–23.

"Remarks Accepting the Presidential Nomination at the Republican National Convention in Dallas." Dallas, Tex., August 23, 1984. *PPP, 1984*, vol. 2, pp. 1174–81.

"Second Inaugural Address." Washington, D.C., January 21, 1985. *PPP, 1985*, p. 1.

"Address at Bitburg, Germany." Bitburg, Germany, May 5, 1985. *New York Times*, May 6, 1985, part I, p. 10.

"Address to the Nation on the Explosion of the Space Shuttle *Challenger*." Washington, D.C., January 28, 1986. *PPP, 1986*, vol. 1, pp. 94–95.

"Remarks on East–West Relations at the Brandenburg Gate" ("Berlin Wall"). West Berlin, Germany, June 12, 1987. *PPP, 1987*, vol. 1, pp. 634–38.

"Farewell Address to the Nation." Washington, D.C., January 11, 1989. *PPP, 1988–89*, vol. 2, pp. 1718–23.

"Address to the Republican National Convention." Houston, Tex., August 17, 1992. *Ronald Reagan: The Heritage Foundation Remembers*. www.reagansheritage.org

---

JANET RENO (1938–)
U.S. Attorney General

JANICE SCHUETZ

Janet Reno's appointment as the first female U.S. Attorney General immediately placed her in the media spotlight. In that position she led the world's largest law office with more than 125,000 employees for nearly eight years and served as the federal government's chief law enforcement officer. Not only was Reno the first woman to hold that office, she was one of the most prolific public communicators in the administration of President Bill Clinton. When she spoke, she commanded the attention of public audiences with authority and tried "to do the right thing." Reno was the target of public ridicule because she stood more than six feet tall, dressed simply, spoke frankly, and took unpopular positions. A close analysis of her public speeches, however, reveals that Reno's oratory was neither dogmatic nor pedestrian, but showed personal respect and concern for her audiences and promoted positive human values.

Janet Reno's family figured prominently in the personal experiences that she used in her speeches. She was born on July 21, 1938, to parents who were journalists for the *Miami Herald*. In her May 20, 2001, commencement address at Cornell University, Reno told her audience that her father was an immigrant from Denmark and "he taught me that your word is your bond and if you're not care-

ful and you're not accurate, then a newspaper reporter is going to get after you, so you might as well be candid and honest in everything you do." As a public advocate she attempted to put her father's advice into practice. Reno also acknowledged her mother's influence. In another commencement address, delivered at Boston College on May 19, 1997, she told graduates that when she was eight years old, her mother announced to the family that she was going to build a house. Although she had no training for that task, she was willing to learn. Reno said, "She went to the brick mason, she went to the electrician, she talked to them about how to build a house. She came home and over the next two years she dug the foundation with her own hands with a pick and shovel, laid the blocks, [and] put in the wiring and the plumbing. . . . And that house was a symbol to me that you can do anything you really want to if you work hard enough at it, and if it's the right thing to do." Reno's parents, both liberal Democrats, encouraged her to express her ideas in writing and speaking, and she did both at an early age. In 1952, Reno, with the help of her father, published her first article in the *Miami Herald*, a story about her nine months in Europe as a thirteen-year-old. In high school, Reno learned competitive speaking through the National Forensic League, was a member of the debating society, and won the state championship in extemporaneous speaking.

Reno was educated at two distinguished Ivy League universities, Cornell and Harvard, where she developed confidence in her intellectual abilities and became a leader in student government. To help pay her tuition, Reno's father found her a job in the Dade County (Florida) Sheriffs Department the summer before she entered college. She graduated from Cornell in 1960 with a degree in chemistry. In her 2001 commencement address at her alma mater, Reno reflected on her experience: "Cornell taught me not to be afraid of big ideas. I had a philosophy professor the first year, and I'd go up and start chewing on his ear about some big idea, and it was touching later to hear that he thought that I wasn't off base, that I might make something of myself." At Cornell, Reno was president of the Women's Student Government Association, a position that biographer Paul Anderson, in *Janet Reno: Do the Right Thing*, claims gave Reno the opportunity to introduce former President Harry Truman to the student body.

Reno graduated from Harvard Law School in 1964, one of sixteen women in her class. When she returned to Harvard to deliver the commencement address in June 1993, she said the law school provided "the best educational experience I ever had. Those classes that I often anticipated with trepidation really taught me how to think. And I believe the way I approach problems—taking them apart and putting them back [together] again—is due to the training I got from some extraordinary professors." These skills served her well in her legal career, playing a prominent role in her work as a public problem-solver. During her tenure as U.S. attorney general, she frequently spoke about the need for problem-solving and communication skills. In her commencement address at Florida State University, given on April 30, 1999, Reno expressed the need "to solve the problems of the world. . . . To become better peacemakers and problem-solvers, the first thing we've got to learn to do is to communicate . . . with small, old words. We've got to learn to talk to people, and look at them when we talk, and we have got to learn to listen." Reno put this advice into practice through the form and content of her public speeches.

After she graduated from law school, Reno's career developed in both politics and law. Reno started to practice law at the bottom of the legal ladder. She took a job at the small firm of Brigham & Brigham, working in real estate law and occasionally appearing in court. After four years at Brigham, she joined with a friend, Gerald Lewis, to set up a general practice in wills, real estate, and business law. During her early years of legal practice she became actively involved with the Democratic Party, and in 1970 ran unsuccessfully for the Florida House of Representatives from Dade County. Reno's political involvement eventually led to her appointment in 1971 as the staff director of the Judiciary Committee of the Florida House of Representatives. In that role she helped write Florida's no-fault divorce law and drafted constitutional amendments to reform the state's courts. Her judicial reform bill eliminated municipal courts and replaced them with county and state circuit courts. After Reno lost a campaign for a state legislative position in 1972, she served as a member of the Dade County State Attorney's Office from 1973 to 1976. In 1978 she was appointed Florida attorney general and served five consecutive elected terms in that position. Her job as Florida attorney general was difficult: she was confronted with race riots, Cuban immigration problems, drug trafficking, unenforced child support laws, and high rates of juvenile crime. In a crime-ridden state, she gained a reputation as a successful crime fighter concerned with the rights of victims.

Reno's years at the helm of Florida law enforcement produced successes as well as failures. Some of her greatest successes were reforming Florida's juvenile justice system, forcing the state's deadbeat dads to pay child support, prosecuting sexual abuse cases, creating community policing, and establishing separate courts for drug offenders. As attorney general of Florida, she was an activist who sought and accomplished policy changes. This activism won both allies and enemies in politics as well as the media. Her reputation as an activist brought Reno to the attention of President Bill Clinton. The president had eagerly sought a woman for the job of U.S. attorney general; his first two choices, Zoe E. Baird and Kimba Wood, removed themselves from consideration after they admitted employing illegal immigrants as nannies to care for their children. While Reno's political and legal experiences in Florida helped her to be a successful public advocate and a knowledgeable law enforcement official, no state experience could prepare her for the political and legal firestorms and the media criticism that she would endure during her eight years in the Clinton administration.

CONTROVERSY AND APPEAL: DEFENDING THE LAW

During Reno's confirmation hearing, Senator Carol Mosely-Braun told her: "This hearing demonstrates in my mind that the best qualified man for the job is very often a woman, and you have demonstrated that very clearly." Reno was the first woman appointed U.S. attorney general, and she also held that position the longest time. The job put her in charge of the U.S. Department of Justice and made her responsible for enforcing the laws of the United States regarding the environment, civil rights, elections, taxation, and antitrust. Reno had oversight of the Federal Bureau of Investigation (FBI), the Drug Enforcement Administration (DEA), the Bureau of Alcohol, Tobacco and Firearms (ATF), the Immigration and Naturalization Service (INS), and the Bureau of Prisons. Her position gave her enormous responsibility for supervision and leadership as well as significant opportunities for public advocacy. During Reno's eight-year tenure in the position, she advanced several controversial policies, gave hundreds of speeches, and became a familiar media figure.

Some of Reno's controversial policies, and the oratorical defense of those policies, probably had more to do with her reputation while in office than any of her other rhetorical efforts. Two policies received extensive public attention and engendered much public criticism—the decision to allow the FBI to enter the Waco compound of the Branch Davidians and the seizing of Elian Gonzales from his Miami relatives. Both policies were advanced and defended in a series of short public statements delivered over a period of time. Her approach to this type of public advocacy demonstrated her style of leadership.

Reno began her term as attorney general with the firestorm of controversy that ensued when she approved the FBI raid that led to the deaths of David Koresh and seventy-four of his religious followers at the Branch Davidian compound in Waco, Texas. In February 1993, a shootout at the compound had resulted in the deaths of four federal law enforcement officers. At that time, and for fifty-one days afterward, two federal agencies—the ATF and the FBI—surrounded the compound while agency leaders tried to negotiate a truce with Koresh and his followers. According to journalist Carol Moore, the negotiations had stalled when Reno took office. After being briefed by FBI agents on the scene on April 19, 1993, barely five weeks after taking office, Reno gave the order for the agents to use military tanks to shoot tear gas into the compound to force out the Branch Davidians. Her initial response, delivered that day in a press conference, was, "We had information that babies were being beaten." In a hearing before the House Judiciary Committee on April 28, 1993, however, Reno retracted this statement, saying her earlier information was incorrect: "I can't tell you that a child was being beaten. (After the compound burst into flames that killed Koresh and his followers, Reno said, "I was responsible, the buck stops here. . . . I made the decision, and I will live with it.") Reno also indicated to the Judiciary Committee that the FBI had assured her that they would not fire incendiary devices into the compound unless the law enforcement officers were fired on first. She told the lawmakers, "I was concerned about intentional or accidental explosions and ordered that additional resources be provided to ensure that there was an adequate emergency response" available if a fire occurred, and that the FBI would use tear gas only to try to get Koresh's followers to come out.

Reno defended her decision on Waco to congressional hearings in 1995 and again in 1999. The hearings in 1999 vindicated Reno, finding that she had never been told that the FBI planned to fire incendiary devices into the compound. Yet, in a 2001 PBS interview, after Reno had left office, Jim Lehrer asked her, "What was your darkest day?" She responded: "It was Waco. . . . It's obvious what went wrong, but one will never know what the right answer was, because one doesn't know what Koresh would have done two weeks later without any provocation, so we just have to learn." Reno's decision and subsequent explanations of her policy enraged conservative religious and political groups, who blamed her for the incident.

In 2000, seven years after the burning of the compound in Waco, Reno's decision to return young Elian Gonzalez to his Cuban father created another public firestorm. Her policy pronouncements about the child and his return to his biological father took place in a series of short public statements over a period of several weeks. In November 1999, six-year-old Elian Gonzalez was rescued on a Florida beach from an overturned Cuban refugee boat, following an accident in which his mother died. The authorities placed the child in the custody of a great-uncle, Lazaro Gonzalez, a Cuban refugee living in Miami. In her "Elian Gonzalez statement," presented at a Washington press conference on April 13, 2000, Reno declared that she was going to negotiate the return of the child to his father in Cuba. In this statement, she framed her policy as one might in a family court. The attorney general told a national audience: "Juan Miguel Gonzales has been separated from his son for four long months, his bond with Elian has never been severed. I know that because I met with Mr. Gonzalez—a man who helped raise Elian and make him into the fine boy he is today. . . . I heard his pleas in his own words. He loves his son and he wants him back." She told the media that she had consulted with experts who concluded it was in the best interests of the child to be returned to his father. She claimed that an orderly transfer was needed to "respect the rule of law."

Reno, however, could not convince the boy's Miami relatives that the child should be returned to his father, and a tug-of-war ensued between the Miami relatives and federal law enforcement officials. Despite Reno's effort to mediate the conflict, court injunctions filed by the relatives of the child and public demonstrations in the Little Havana neighborhood of Miami fueled the conflict. In her April 22, 2000, press conference statement, "Elian Returned," Reno announced that she had ordered officials from the INS to enter the home of the great-uncle, take Elian, and return him to his father. When the

federal agents seized the child in the dark of night, the media broadcast the event live on television. After the child was safely retrieved, Reno argued that "we tried every way we could to encourage Lazaro Gonzalez to voluntarily hand over the child to his father. . . . The Miami relatives rejected our efforts. . . . This was in the end about a little boy who lost his mother and has not seen his father in more than five months. I hope, with time and support, Elian and his father will have the opportunity to be a strong family again." Although many in the Miami Cuban community and some conservatives in Congress expressed outrage at Reno's proclamations and actions in the case, the day after the event, journalist Lars-Erik Nelson reported that Reno's office was "filled to overflowing with flowers from ordinary Americans," and someone flew a plane over Miami trailing a banner saying, "America Loves Janet Reno."

Reno's defense of the Justice Department's policies regarding Waco and Elian Gonzalez infuriated the political Right and resulted in their strident condemnation of her. Her public defense also certified her credibility as a forthright leader, because Reno spoke and acted in ways consistent with her promises to the public. She justified her decisions in line with the promise she had made shortly after she was nominated in her "Remarks to the Justice Department." Speaking in Washington on March 20, 1993, Reno announced: "While I am attorney general, we will address each issue with one question, 'What's the right thing to do?'" Then she warned, "Remember that sometimes doing the right thing is politically unpopular." The degree to which she made unpopular political decisions about Waco and about Elian Gonzalez became clear in the relentless vilification she received from the Web sites of conservative groups, including Judicial Watch, the Landmark Legal Foundation, and the National Rifle Association. For example, the founder of Judicial Watch, Richard Melton, called Reno's Justice Department "a legal thunderdome—a world of arbitrary rules, soap-operatic infighting, peculiar liaisons, and isolated eruptions of decency"—and demanded the "impeachment of Reno."

The most common public addresses Reno delivered as attorney general were invited presentations to the legal agencies she directed, universities and law schools, and community groups. The content of these speeches often received less media attention than did Reno's image and demeanor. During her years as U.S. attorney general, Reno delivered an average of two speeches per week. The frequency of her speaking engagements may be one of the reasons why her speeches often repeated the same principles, restated her favorite phrases and stories, and followed a hub-and-spoke pattern of organization with a central theme extending into multiple points about problems and solutions. Despite these consistent features of her public addresses, Reno spoke about a wide range of topics, ranging from women's rights to crime fighting, and from juvenile delinquency to alternative means of settling disputes. In "Gender Equity in America," a speech delivered at the Women's Center Conference in Toledo, Ohio, on January 29, 1994, she enunciated principles similar to those found in many of her speeches as attorney general: "We have to continue and renew our commitment to vigorous enforcement of civil rights laws. . . . We have to achieve equity in other areas. . . . We have to make sure that people understand the obligation of parenting. . . . We have to focus on housing for our women and children. . . . We can make an investment in full-service schools that reach out to the community. . . . We can give our children a future while at the same time giving the children an opportunity to grow in a safe, constructive way. . . . We have to make a difference in developing a health care package that will provide coverage for all Americans. . . . We have to all work together."

Reno organized most of her speeches in a hub-spoke configuration. In "Gender Equity in America," for example, she started with the general theme of social justice for women and related various subtopics to that theme. She anchored the theme at the hub, then offered problems and solutions as spokes that emanated from this central principle. Typically, the spokes consisted of policy claims supported by personal experience and statistical proof. In this speech, she offered personal experience as evidence for the claim that parents have an obligation to make life better for their children. She remarked, "I have never been married. I did not have children. I just understood

it intellectually . . . until about nine years ago when a friend died, leaving me as the legal guardian of her fifteen-year-old twins, a boy and a girl. I have learned a lot about raising children in these last nine years." In her speeches, Reno elaborated the particular spoke by using an extemporaneous delivery that related ideas in stages. She often began by complimenting the members of her audience. Then she enunciated a single theme and related it to the interests of the particular group she was addressing. She would next proceed to discuss a series of policy or value claims, supporting each conclusion with examples and statistics.

In "Juvenile Justice at the Crossroads," a speech to the Office of Juvenile Justice and Delinquency Prevention's national conference in Baltimore, on December 13, 1996, Reno praised her audience, saying, "My thanks to you all. . . . There are so many dedicated people in this room who I think are the heroes and the heroines of this nation, people who care about children, care about giving them a future, care about holding them accountable, care about making sure that they can live up to their fullest potential." She reiterated her theme, "Caring can make a difference for our children"; located it at the center of the speech; then constructed a series of spokes in the form of policy and value claims: "We've got to have current information. . . . We have got to talk about this issue based on fact, not politics. . . . We can't say we've done the job and go home. . . . We can form community courts. . . . [We] can use common sense and go back to the people and their problems and start to solve them. . . . [We] can develop aftercare programs in this community. . . . We can show what we can do when we organize together and use all of the resources involved. . . . . [We] have to listen to our young people . . . who want so much to contribute to this nation, who want so much to grow up to be somebody, to make a difference." Like many of her speeches, this address featured evidence drawn from Reno's personal experience as well as national statistics about juvenile crime. Reno infused the speech with inclusive pronouns, such as "we," "us," and "our," thus defining the audience as integral to the context and the solution of the problem. Despite the first-person, inclusive pronouns, Reno never scolded her audience as having caused the problem, instead telling them that she valued the efforts they had made in the past and the good work she was confident they would do in the future.

Reno addressed some agency groups repeatedly on the issue of crime detection and prevention, including the American Bar Association, the National Sheriffs Association, and the Drug Enforcement Administration. In these speeches, she encouraged the law enforcement officials she addressed, telling them to continue to do their jobs and serve their communities, cheered their accomplishments, and vowed her support for their work. These speeches, too, employed the hub-and-spoke organization. In her keynote address to the Drug Enforcement Administration, delivered on February 5, 1997, in Baltimore, Reno praised her audience: "I just appreciate what you do day in and day out. . . . I just appreciate your efforts on the part of the American people and I want you to know that." Then she presented her theme: "It is time to develop [drug] enforcement and prevention strategies together before we have this demon totally out of control." She focused first on drug users, who were "replacing crack and cocaine as the drug of choice" with "high purity heroin" and "snorting." A long list of evils related to drug use followed, including the costs "to combat drug-related crime," the loss of childhood, the high emergency room costs, the spread of AIDS, the deaths, and the breakup of families. Reno offered the solution that "by working together, the people and federal agencies can succeed." She included the audience in her solutions by repeating the pronoun "we." Reno argued, "We can reduce the distribution and consumption," and "We [must] locate our limited resources very carefully." Or, again, "We must have the tools to do the education, prevention, and treatment," and "We cannot afford to be complacent. She concluded, "We will succeed here this week and in the weeks and months and years to come if we can raise some measure of national consciousness as to the current threat posed by heroin." Reno's motivational statements called attention to the audience's abilities and accomplishments while expressing her appreciation for their work.

Reno also used a motivational approach in her commencement addresses at high schools, universities, and law schools. Her commencement address at Wayne State University School of Law, given on May 16, 1998, exemplified her cheerleader-like approach to public audiences. She began her speech exuding enthusiasm for law and lawyers: "I love the law after 35 years of practice, and I love good lawyers. . . . I can tell you that there are wonderful lawyers across the land doing great work for the people they serve." After complimenting her audience, she announced her theme—a legal education prepares students for great opportunities. This thematic hub then evolved into spokes emphasizing the qualities and benefits of legal education. Reno told the graduates that law school "builds good citizens," "makes men and women think more clearly, communicate more effectively, analyze diverse viewpoints, negotiate productively and spot and solve problems." She listed careers available to law graduates, including business, teaching, the arts, charity work, and banking. She added that "one [lawyer] I know of even raises llamas," and another was a baseball manager. She identified three positive emblems for the work of lawyers—"protector," "problem solver," and "peacemaker." Reno then exhorted the students to live the law in a righteous way by repeating one of her favorite phrases, borrowed from an engraving in the Justice Department Building: "The common law is derived from the will of mankind, issuing from the people, framed by mutual confidence, and sanctioned by the light of reason." She told the law students to live out this principle by "becoming public defenders, working for humanity, being community advocates for children, speaking out against hatred and bigotry." She ended by showing respect for her audience. "I think," she said, "this nation will be in good hands with you, and wish you Godspeed and great success." Like her other commencement address, this one exuded warmth, respect, and enthusiasm for the values she shared with her audience.

Reno addressed audiences of different genders, ages, and backgrounds. She even visited grade schools on a regular basis and spoke to the students about learning and citizenship, and the children and their teachers celebrated her visits. The media, however, presented Reno in a very different light: They often ridiculed her appearance—her short haircut, her unfashionable glasses, her towering size, her manlike toughness, and even the tremors she experienced from Parkinson's disease. Her physical characteristics made her the victim of comic diminishment, a phenomenon that Barbara Garlick explains as "demeaning jokes and biting satire" used by detractors to reduce the power and influence of women leaders. During her eight years in office, Jay Leno and David Letterman repeatedly made fun of Reno's appearance, but the most memorable media portrayals were Will Ferrell's performances on *Saturday Night Live*. In some skits, Ferrell caricatured Reno as a sexually aggressive socialite making advances toward President Clinton, and in others he portrayed her as a feisty politician with disdain for the president. Reno endured the ridicule with grace. She frequently told her commencement audiences, "Learn to laugh at yourself." Even when the media viciously ridiculed her

alty," and "faithfulness." In this commencement address, Reno recalled her recent appearance on *Saturday Night Live*, saying it "was the perfect way to end eight years of public service. Because it is very important that we laugh at ourselves every now and then and realize that we are not all that we are cracked up to be sometimes, that we are only mortal and that there is much more to be done in this world."

Janet Reno's oratorical legacy will be found more in her principled defense of her department's policies than in the media's or her opponents' vilification. Her direct enunciation of legal principles and plainspoken defense of controversial policies mark her as a public speaker willing to assume responsibility for her decisions and the deep-seated beliefs that guided her policies. In part, her direct way of speaking sparked firestorms that surrounded her tenure as U.S. at-

---

Janet Reno spent seven years in private law practice and thirty years as a prosecutor and as attorney general for the state of Florida and later the United States. She told an audience at Wayne State School of Law, "I love the law after 35 years of practice, and I love good lawyers. . . . I can tell you that there are wonderful lawyers across the land doing great work for the people they serve."

---

appearance and demeanor, she was able to laugh at herself with others. After she left office in January 2001, Reno appeared in a *Saturday Night Live* skit. This cameo appearance demonstrated her good will toward those who mocked her and showed the public that she could laugh at herself.

When Cornell President Hunter Rawlings introduced Reno for her commencement address, he enunciated her legacy as a public figure. He said it was not her controversial policies nor the media's ridicule of her, but the issues that she stood for and the relationships that she developed while in office, that won her recognition in the National Women's Hall of Fame in Seneca Falls, New York. Rawlings identified Reno's "personal honesty," "undaunted independence," and "integrity and professionalism" as "the hallmarks of her administration," and recognized Reno for her virtues of "personal support," "loy-

torney general, but her plain manner of speaking that related principles to policies, and personable style that helped her connect with many of her audiences, also served her well.

INFORMATION SOURCES

Research Collections and Collected Speeches

There are no archival collections or speech anthologies available. Some speeches can be found in congressional hearing records.

Web Sites

Department of Justice Web site [*DJW*]. This Web site includes transcripts of Reno's speeches, news conferences, public statements, and testimony at hearings from 1996 to 2001. www.usdoj.gov

Audiovisual Materials

C-SPAN. A few of Reno's speeches are available on video from C-SPAN. www.c-span.org

Selected Critical Studies

Dennis, Edward S. G. "Evaluation of the Handling of the Branch Davidian Stand-off in Waco, Texas." Washington, D.C.: U.S. Department of Justice, October 8, 1993.

DeYoung, Karen, and April Witt. "Mediators Seek Elian Accord: Initial Optimism Fades as Miami Kin, Father Trade Offers." *Washington Post*, April 22, 2000, p. A1.

Garlick, Barbara. "Radical Hens and Vociferous Ladies: Representation and Class in the Mid-Nineteenth Century." In *Stereotypes of Women in Power*, ed. Barbara Garlick, Suzanne Dixon, and Pauline Allen. New York: Greenwood, 1992.

Gibbs, N., and M. Duffy. "The Elian Grab." *Time*, May 1, 2000, pp. 24–31.

Melton, Richard. "Impeach Reno." *Judicial Watch*, July 15, 2000. www.judicialwatch.org

Moore, Carol. *The Davidian Massacre*. Franklin, Tenn.: Legacy Publications, 1995.

Olson, Theodore B. "The Most Political Justice Department Ever." *American Spectator* 33 (September 2000): 22–26.

Selected Biographies

Anderson, Paul. *Janet Reno: Doing the Right Thing*. New York: John Wiley, 1994.

Isikoff, Michael, and David von Drehle. "Prosecutor Wins High Marks Battling Miami Vice." *Washington Post*, February 12, 1993, p. A23.

"Janet Reno." www.wic.org

Lehrer, Jim. "Exit Interview: Janet Reno." January 18, 2001. Online NewsHour, transcript. www.pbs.org

Mayer, Jane. "Janet Reno: Alone." *The New Yorker*, June 1, 1997, pp. 40–45.

Moody, Liza. "Why Janet Reno Fascinates, Confounds, and Even Terrifies America." *Washington Post*, January 25, 1998, p. W6.

CHRONOLOGY OF MAJOR SPEECHES

See "Research Collections and Collected Speeches" for source code.

"Nomination of Janet Reno to Be Attorney General of the United States." March 9–10, 1993. U.S. Senate, Hearings Before the Committee on the Judiciary, 103rd Cong., Sess. 1.

"Remarks to the Justice Department." Washington, D.C., March 20, 1993. *DJW*.

"Reno Says, 'I Made the Decision.' " *Washington Post*, April 20, 1993, p. A9.

"Commencement Address" (Harvard Law School). Cambridge, Mass., June 1993. *DJW*.

"Robert Kennedy 25th Anniversary Memorial Mass." Washington, D.C., June 6, 1993. Available on video at www.c-span.org (order no. 4254).

"Gender Equity in America" (Women's Center Conference). Toledo, Ohio, January 29, 1994. *University of Toledo Law Review* 25 (1994): 869–74.

"Address Delivered at the Celebration of the Seventy-fifth Anniversary of Women at Fordham Law School." New York City, May 19, 1994. *Fordham Law Review* 63 (1994): 5–15.

"Summit on Youth Violence" (International Association of Chiefs of Police). Arlington, Va., April 25, 1996. *DJW*.

"Juvenile Justice at the Crossroads" (Office of Juvenile Justice and Delinquency Prevention National Conference). Baltimore, Md., December 13, 1996. *DJW*.

"Keynote Address to the Drug Enforcement Administration." Baltimore, Md., February 5, 1997. *DJW*.

"Commencement Address at Boston College." Chestnut Hill, Mass., May 19, 1997. *DJW*.

"Lawyers as Problem Solvers" (keynote address to American Association of Law Schools). New Orleans La., January 8, 1998. *Journal of Legal Education* 13 (1999): 5–13.

"Alternative Dispute Resolution and Negotiation" (American Judicature Society). Chicago, February 5, 1998. *DJW*.

"Commencement Address" (Wayne State University Law School). Detroit, Mich., May 16, 1998. *DJW*.

"Shaping the Future" (address to the American Arab Anti-Discrimination Committee). Arlington, Va., June 12, 1998. *DJW*.

"Commencement Address" (Florida State University). Tallahassee, Fla., April 30, 1999. *DJW*.

"Elian Gonzales Statement." April 13, 2000. www.CNN.com

"Elian Returned." CNN News. April 22, 2000. Available at www.CNN.com

"National Commission on the Future of DNA Evidence" (John F. Kennedy School of Government, Harvard University). Cambridge, Mass., November 20, 2000. *DJW*.

"Justice Issues" (National Council on Crime). Miami, Fla., January 3, 2001. Available at www.c-span.org (order no. 162940).

"Commencement Address" (Cornell University). Ithaca, N.Y., May 20, 2001. *DJW*.

DONALD H. RUMSFELD (1932–)
U.S. Secretary of Defense

GORDON STABLES

Donald Rumsfeld provides one of the most compelling sources of American public discourse in the early twenty-first century. From his position as secretary of defense, Rumsfeld became one of the most pronounced voices of the American response to the terrorist attacks of September 11, 2001, and the subsequent war on terrorism. He had previously held a number of prominent positions, including a previous term as secretary of defense (1975–77), White House chief of staff for President Gerald Ford, U.S. ambassador to NATO, a four-term U.S. congressman, and chief executive officer of two Fortune 500 companies, but it was during his second stint as secretary of defense that his role as the public face of America's new war catapulted him onto the short list of orators whose public commentary plays a distinctive role in the conduct of U.S. foreign policy. Rumsfeld emerged as the rare cabinet official to speak with a voice both heard and appreciated by the American public. In many ways, the complexity of opinions expressed by and about Rumsfeld reflects the range of feelings about the course of the post-9/11 period.

A history of national American politics in the last three decades of the twentieth century would likely include passing references to Rumsfeld as a minor player in some of the most prominent events. He resigned from Congress in 1969 to join Richard Nixon's cabinet as Director of Economic Opportunity, but left the chaotic American political scene in 1973 to serve as ambassador to NATO. He returned to Washington to lead the transition period of President Ford and then served as Ford's chief of staff before becoming the nation's youngest defense secretary in 1977. Many viewed Rumsfeld as one of the most formidable figures in federal government. His mastery of the political process appeared to be leading toward an eventual run at the presidency, a

move consistent with his efforts to have his chief Republican rival, George H. W. Bush, nominated to the politically dangerous position of director of the Central Intelligence Agency.

After the defeat of the Ford–Dole Republican ticket in 1976, Rumsfeld left national office and played only minor roles in the Reagan administration. He periodically accepted special assignments, such as serving as the special presidential envoy to the Middle East in 1983–84 and as the chair of the U.S. Ballistic Missile Threat Commission in 1998, but he made his living as a prominent member of the business community. Rumsfeld spent the bulk of the next quarter-century as an important figure in corporate America. He served as chief executive officer (CEO), president, and then chairman of G. D. Searle and then as the chairman and CEO of the General Instrument Corporation. His role as a corporate leader was occasionally punctuated by appearances on the political scene, as when he briefly launched a campaign for the presidency in 1988 and when he served as a chair of Bob Dole for President in 1996.

When Rumsfeld joined the administration of President George W. Bush in January 2001, he was an unlikely choice as a public face of the administration. He was now the oldest person to occupy the position of secretary of defense, and the administration was full of prominent officials with extensive foreign policy backgrounds, such as Vice President Richard Cheney and Secretary of State Colin Powell. Rumsfeld's efforts appeared to be focused primarily on transforming the way the Defense Department operated. His plans to reform the foundation of Pentagon operations threatened many military officials and contractors, and in the summer of 2001 it appeared that Rumsfeld might be one of the first cabinet secretaries to leave the administration.

The terrorist attacks of September 11, 2001, immediately elevated Rumsfeld's importance. In those first frightening and terrible hours, he represented the spirit of American resilience as he assisted wounded at the Pentagon and later held the first of many press conferences that would become a primary means of explaining the new war to the nation. David Montgomery of the *Washington Post* noted this phenomenon and gave Rumsfeld the title "Articulator in Chief of this perilous national effort" (2001). "The Rummy Show," as his briefings were dubbed, featured his frank style and ability to dominate the traditionally aggressive Washington press corps. They captivated the nation and earned him respect among journalists and congressional leaders, even as his forthright and confrontational style frustrated political opponents. Eliot Cohen, a professor of strategic studies at Johns Hopkins University's Nitze School of

dam Hussein from power, Rumsfeld initially towered over his critics. After the formal end of hostilities, however, the difficulties associated with the management of Iraq threatened his aura of invulnerability. As the costs of war, both human and financial, mounted, Rumsfeld became a central target for those frustrated by the continuing difficulties. The leak of a Rumsfeld memo in October 2003 signaled his effort not only to define the course of the war but also to reassert his position within the administration.

The canon of Donald Rumsfeld's political rhetoric includes a wide range of public commentary. Whatever the form, his unique commentary about military operations in Afghanistan and Iraq was consumed by an eager nation. The defense secretary who initially appeared to be an anachronism among the youth of the Bush administration would become not only a media darling who evoked memories of the most television-savvy po-

---

Later in the day on September 11, 2001, after helping Pentagon workers escape the smoking building, Secretary Rumsfeld offered some of the first official commentary about what had changed and what would remain the same. Speaking from the wounded Pentagon, Rumsfeld defiantly declared, "The Pentagon is functioning. It will be in business tomorrow."

Advanced International Studies, noted how the war transformed Rumsfeld's weaknesses into strengths. In a time of war, his disagreeable brusqueness appeared as refreshing honesty; his uncomfortably hard edge became the kind of resolution required of a leader; his willingness to badger his generals was not an absence of diplomacy but a firm hand on the reins. In a reflection of their significance, Rumsfeld's briefings were lampooned on the long-running comedy program *Saturday Night Live*. The traditionally liberal *SNL* often portrayed Rumsfeld as cool and self-assured, while the press corps was mocked as a cadre of inadequate foils.

Rumsfeld's dominance of the media continued in the early days of the 2003 war against Iraq. Popularly understood to have designed the risky, but dramatically successful, plan to remove Sad-

litical figures but also the public face most associated with the frustrations of the long war against terror.

THE PUBLIC DISCOURSE OF DONALD RUMSFELD

The unique circumstances that made Donald Rumsfeld a prominent American orator are deeply embedded in why Rumsfeld, perhaps more than any other national figure, appeared capable of expressing a particular mood within post-9/11 America. Understanding how Rumsfeld managed the Defense Department helps explain how he was able to rise to such prominence after the terrorist attacks. His discourse places a high value on exploring and explaining change. In his public speeches and comments, Rumsfeld engaged the instability of the current moment, and in doing so, he offered a more coherent perspective than many of his contemporaries. This commentary examines how he defined and attempted to manage the complexity of change in two primary areas: the management of the Defense Department and the current historical period.

Rumsfeld had no plans to spend his second term as defense secretary merely extending past policies and practices. He spent his first eight months in office extolling the virtue of reforming the Defense Department. At his official welcoming ceremony, held at the Pentagon on January 26, 2001, Rumsfeld pledged to the assembled members of the military: "We will make the system work, work so you can serve with pride and know that service to our nation is a sacred calling." His call for reform was not merely the empty platitudes of an incoming bureaucrat; Rumsfeld had very clear designs for making the Pentagon function more effectively. He generated a great deal of resistance from military officers by considering radical reforms that would fundamentally overhaul how the nation procured weapons, planned for their employment, and ultimately utilized them.

The controversy over the future of the Army's self-propelled howitzer, the Crusader, provided a very public opportunity for Rumsfeld to display his vision of Pentagon operations. Testifying before the Senate Armed Services Committee on May 16, 2002, he defended the decision to terminate the weapons system because it was "originally designed in a different strategic concept." Rumsfeld explained that the system was a product of a traditional way of preparing for war. To continue with this type of program would be a return to a type of planning that embraced the certainty of a model of warfare, a risk Rumsfeld determined the United States could not afford.

The procurement decision surrounding the Crusader became highly politicized and publicly pitted Rumsfeld against Army Secretary Thomas White. This confrontation displayed the abrasive Rumsfeld: "Some individuals in the Army were way in the dickens out of line. Someone with an overactive thyroid seemed to get his hands in his mouth ahead of his brain. And that happens in life." This would not be the only occasion when Rumsfeld would publicly belittle those who resisted his philosophy of change. Indeed, a prominent element of his public persona is the frequency and candor with which he rebukes his opponents.

This controversy was part of a broader struggle to redefine the very nature of Pentagon operations. In September 2001, Rumsfeld gave what was planned as a major speech calling for extensive changes within the department. An opening event of the department's Acquisition and Logistics Excellence Week, Rumsfeld's presentation was titled "Bureaucracy to Battlefield." It stated in no uncertain terms that the inability of the Pentagon to function efficiently was one of the most pressing national security problems: "The topic today is an adversary that poses a threat, a serious threat to the security of the United States of America." Drawing upon the legacy of the Cold War, Rumsfeld invoked the central tenets of the Soviet Union as he personified Pentagon bureaucracy as "one of the last bastions of central planning" that "stifles free thought and crushes new ideas." He emphasized the importance of removing the administrative limitations placed upon the American military. For America to retain its prominence in the future, it would need to change the way its military functioned. He described a zero-sum relationship between excessive bureaucracy and the ability to wage wars: "Every dollar squandered on waste is one denied to the warfighter." He carefully and specifically elevated the seriousness of this challenge and visualized the importance of reform, declaring that modernization remained "a matter of life and death, ultimately, every American's. A new idea ignored may be the next threat overlooked. A person employed in a redundant task is one who could be countering terrorism or nuclear proliferation."

His speech was designed to raise the importance of his reform program within the Pentagon, the Congress, and the nation. Even as he spoke of the importance of new ideas and new threats, the massive power of the American military was unable to stop a small group of terrorists from turning commercial airliners into weapons of mass destruction. Rumsfeld made his call for change at the Pentagon on September 10, 2001, but massive changes to that site and the composition of the entire nation lay just hours ahead—changes that would accentuate Rumsfeld's emphasis on innovation.

The significance of 9/11 for American society was dramatic, and historians will be examining the specific contours for decades. In the way that defense policy was designed, 9/11 suddenly enhanced the significance of threats to American national security and demanded a speedy response. This urgent need for action reinforced Rumsfeld's insistence on change. Testifying before the House Armed Services Committee on February 5, 2003, he extolled the value of creatively encouraging Pentagon employees. Citing the need to develop an "entrepreneurial approach," he spoke of the need for a "climate where people have freedom and flexibility to take risks and try new things." Rather than interpreting the post-9/11 uncertainties as a justification for restraint, Rumsfeld argued that transformation became "an even more urgent priority" because only by breathing creativity into the nature of military planning could the United States effectively pursue preemption and ensure American security. Similarly, in the speech before the National Defense University on January 31, 2002, he described the war on terrorism as "a transformational event that cries out for us to rethink our activities and put that new thinking into action."

At the heart of this rethinking would be an undertaking to redefine the nature of risk. Rumsfeld encouraged new and flexible defense planning by extolling the benefits of creativity and innovation. He believed that past declarations of military policy, such as the plans to allow for fighting two wars at one time, balanced risks in an inherently conservative approach that discouraged change. Rumsfeld argued instead for a mode of thinking that would shift the priorities inherent in the way military policy would be developed. Defense planners would embrace change by conceptualizing American vulnerabilities instead of specific enemies. America's enemies would remain prominent in defense planning, but Rumsfeld demanded a perspective that could look beyond the need to focus on a single specific adversary or threat. This theme of why action could be less risky than inaction surfaced when he testified before the Senate Armed Services Committee regarding Iraq on September 19, 2002. Describing the importance of early action against Saddam Hussein, Rumsfeld noted that had European governments in the 1930s employed a similar calculus, millions of lives could have been saved.

The American military response against Afghanistan provided Rumsfeld with a specific context to explain the importance of transformation. In a speech at the National Defense University on January 31, 2002, he explored the changes in military practice demonstrated by recent battles. He organized his comments around the late 2001 battle to weaken the Taliban in the city of Mazar-e Sharif. Rumsfeld argued this was a "transformational battle" because it blended modern military equipment with historical military tactics. American Special Forces were supported not only by precision-guided munitions but also by allied Afghan fighters who rode into battle on horseback. The contrasting styles of combat led Rumsfeld to seize on this battle as a representative example that validated his philosophy of changing the U.S. military.

> That day, on the plains of Afghanistan, the 19th century met the 21st century—and defeated a dangerous and determined adversary—a remarkable achievement. . . . But this is what transformation is about. Here we are in 2002, fighting [in] the first of the 21st century, and the horse cavalry was back—and being used in previously unimaginable ways. It shows that a revolution in military affairs is about more than building new high-tech weapons. . . . It is also about new ways of thinking . . . and new ways of fighting.

In this context, Rumsfeld clearly emphasized the ability of the military to respond to unpredictable challenges. This embrace of creativity was a direct repudiation of the traditional military emphasis on weapons procurement: planning for the next war through advance weapons purchases. Rumsfeld rejected the constraints that this procurement-driven policy imposed on the Pentagon. The significance of Rumsfeld's perspective on change went beyond defense planning. September 11 signaled an end to the amorphous post–Cold War era, and an anxious nation looked for a new framework to understand the suddenly dangerous world. Rumsfeld was fond of explaining the importance of change in the international political system before September 11, but his potentially clichéd commentary about change seemed all too appropriate in the now highly uncertain times. At a celebration of Armed Forces Day at Andrews Air Force Base in May 2001, Rumsfeld played the role of historian, noting that

> a great deal has changed in the last 25 years. It was a different world then, a world of confrontation and struggle between the state Ronald Reagan called "the Evil Empire" and the nation Thomas Jefferson promised would become an "empire for liberty." . . . I suspect that future generations will look back at this time and judge that it was a time of transition—transition from the old, familiar, well-understood threats to new challenges from sources much less understood.

Grounding his perspective on the Cold War that defined the goals of so much of American policy, Rumsfeld expressed this sense of uncertainty about the future. He had similarly noted this tension during his comments at his official welcoming ceremony in January 2001: "We enjoy peace amid paradox. Yes, we're safer now from the threat of massive nuclear war than at any point since the dawn of the atomic age, and yet we're more vulnerable now to suitcase bombs, the cyber-terrorist, the raw and random violence of the outlaw regime." This narrative of clearly defined past challenges and ambiguous, yet deadly, future threats provided a clear template for Rumsfeld's post-9/11 views.

In the immediate aftermath of the attacks, Rumsfeld, flanked by the chairman of the Joint Chiefs of Staff and the ranking members of the Senate Armed Services Committee, gave the first of many press briefings that attempted to explain what happened and how America would respond. With the president forced to traverse the nation by air, waiting for clearance to land and make a lengthy statement, Rumsfeld offered some of the first official commentary about what had changed and what would remain the same. Speaking from the wounded Pentagon, Rumsfeld defiantly declared, "The Pentagon is functioning. It will be in business tomorrow." Although the briefing was short, especially when compared with the later sessions, Rumsfeld remained firmly in control of publicly judging the appropriateness of certain topics. Stating that the current moment was not the proper time to discuss who might have masterminded the attack, Rumsfeld bluntly described the essence of what had occurred, without concern for formalities. When asked if the attacks constituted an act of war, he responded: "There is no question but that the attack against the United States of America today was a vicious, well-coordinated, massive attack against the United States of America. What words the lawyers will use to characterize it is for them." Rumsfeld captured the sensibility of the moment in a manner that resonated with many Americans. The formal naming of what had transpired was a question left for those without more pressing matters to attend to, not for someone who had helped the wounded out of the burning Pentagon. Rumsfeld again helped to set an "appropriate" agenda for media coverage of the attack and America's response, but he nonetheless implied his feelings: "I have no intentions of discussing today what comes next, but make no mistake about it, your armed forces are ready."

In the days that followed, President Bush and other national figures, including New York mayor Rudy Giuliani, filled a leadership void created by the tragedy, but Rumsfeld was an unmistakable part of the moment. His comments expressed the sense of loss that so many Americans felt, and he also became the voice of the impending American retaliation. In addition to describing the change that was occurring within the Pentagon, Rumsfeld prominently grounded his views in the changes taking place in the international arena.

President Bush provided the broad outline of American policy, but it was senior officials such as Rumsfeld who delivered the explanations of how these new policies would be implemented. In an editorial written for the *New York Times*, and published September 27, 2001, Rumsfeld described "A New Kind of War." He cautioned that "this will be a war like none other our nation has faced" and warned it might be most easily explained in reference to what it was not. This war would not involve a conflict of formal alliances with a predefined scope. This war would not have fixed rules of engagement. In summary, "The vocabulary of this war will be different."

In addition to defining the importance of change in U.S. defense planning, Rumsfeld was often called upon to provide interpretations of other important elements of this new vocabulary of war. Rumsfeld's direct approach to explaining important events and concepts helped to further his public popularity. Although other prominent officials might shy away from providing direct explanations, Rumsfeld embraced the role of unofficial national historian of the current moment and explained the importance of the war's opening battle, how long the war would last, who America's enemies were, and what victory would look like.

The seemingly basic question of determining if this was, in fact, a war was one important area where Rumsfeld demonstrated his unique style and public importance. At that initial postattack press conference, Rumsfeld located the essence of answering this question when he deferred the question of a formal declaration of war. For Rumsfeld, developing a means of response was far more important than quibbling over the legal nature of the actions. This would not be the last time he was asked such a question, but Rumsfeld's answers rarely changed. He would remain far more interested in explaining what had happened and what Americans could expect, than in worrying about the legal nature of the situation.

Rumsfeld took part in the effort to explain what had taken place at the September 12, 2002, funeral service for unidentified victims of the attack on the Pentagon. On that day, he declared that those who perished died on a "battlefield that tells us a great deal about the war we are in." Embracing the symbolic value of the Pentagon, he acknowledged it as a representative of American military power and emphasized the use of power to "right wrong" and "help achieve a more perfect day when nations might live in peace." Rumsfeld explained this new war in language that returned to traditional narratives that describe Americans as fundamentally peace-loving people. This emphasis on peacefulness and compassion informed Rumsfeld's view of how September 11 should be remembered. Speaking at a memorial ceremony at the Pentagon exactly

one year after the attacks, he offered both a way to understand the horrible day and the resolve to aggressively pursue those responsible: "The terrorists wanted September 11th to be a day when innocents died. Instead it was a day when heroes were born. The terrorists wanted September 11th to be a day when hatred reigned. Instead it was a day when we witnessed love beyond measure." Employing a formal style and parallel structure uncommon to much of his public commentary, Rumsfeld explained the 9/11 terrorist attack in terms of a new beginning to the best parts of the national character. The attack, he said, could be understood as a time when a "sleeping patriotism was awakened" and an embattled, but resolute, nation began a new conflict.

Rumsfeld was often called upon to predict how this conflict would end, and he remained careful to avoid tying success to a particular nation or battle. His comments such as those at the anniversary memorial at the Pentagon emphasized: "We will win, no matter how long or hard or difficult or costly it is." In this long-term view of the conflict, Rumsfeld consistently avoided placing too much emphasis on the individual status of specific people. In his September 19, 2002, testimony before the Senate Armed Services Committee, he clearly indicated that the inability to locate Osama bin Laden (or UBL, as he often shortened it) was not a measure of the overall success of military operations. While some critics have noted that President Bush erred in his early emphasis on capturing bin Laden, Rumsfeld clearly described the larger al-Qaeda organization as the central threat in an interview on *Fox News Sunday* on September 16, 2001. Although calling bin Laden a "prime suspect," Rumsfeld provided a cautionary note about the possible barriers to killing him: "Well, my goodness. If that were doable—it isn't a matter of him, it's a matter of his network. If he were not there, there would be 15 or 20 or 30 other people who would step in and take care of those pieces." Focusing on the broader conflict remained a prominent Rumsfeld trait. While testifying before the Senate Armed Forces Committee on July 31, 2002, Rumsfeld was called upon to explain the progress of the war in Afghanistan. He kept a clear focus on Afghanistan as an early stage in a much longer conflict. The war on terror might have begun in Afghanistan, but "It will not end until terrorist networks have been rooted out, wherever they exist."

The war on terrorism reached a new front in the spring of 2003, and Rumsfeld was again at the forefront of efforts to describe the war with Iraq. On March 20 he opened a highly anticipated press briefing by describing what could be expected from the conflict:

> Coalition forces hit a senior Iraqi leadership compound last evening. . . . That was the first. It will likely not be the last. The days of the Saddam Hussein regime are numbered. . . . What will follow will not be a repeat of any other conflict. It will be of a force and scope and scale . . . beyond what has been seen before. The Iraqi soldiers and officers must ask themselves whether they want to die fighting for a doomed regime or do they want to survive, help the Iraqi people in the liberation of their country and play a role in a new, free Iraq.

Even at this early stage Rumsfeld began speaking of the new Iraq that would follow the Saddam Hussein regime. He earned additional public accolades for his role in developing the war plan, though some felt that he provided an overly optimistic determination of the conflict's success. Three weeks later, on the April 23 edition of NBC's *Meet the Press*, Rumsfeld noted the cooperative spirit of Iraqis liberated by American forces:

> An awful lot of Iraqis are being cooperative . . . in city after city across the country, people are coming up and telling us where the Baath Party members are that are causing the problem, where these Fedayeen Saddam terrorists are. And that's a good thing. And they're also volunteering to restore order in cities where there has been disorder. In some cases there's actually joint patrols going on with local people, with U.S. and coalition military, out policing the area and restoring order.

As the violence against American forces continued, Rumsfeld's vision was increasingly challenged. As much as he was able to define the scope and pace of change in prior American military plans, his vision of change in this instance undermined confidence in his leadership. Rumsfeld also provoked controversy for his creative nomenclature of the European nations willing to support the Iraq war as "New Europe," as opposed to the more confrontational, traditional European allies, dubbed "Old Europe." Rumsfeld was the voice of the nation in the immediate 9/11 period, but by the middle of 2003 his view of change appeared strained to many observers. His inability to prevent or successfully manage the Abu Ghraib prison abuse scandal in 2004 further weakened Rumsfeld publicly and increased the calls for his resignation. It seemed that Rumsfeld's invulnerable aura had been shattered. *Newsweek*'s Evan Thomas argued that his broad cultural changes at the Pentagon "paved the road to Abu Ghraib," and somewhat sarcastically noted, "Apparently, even the almighty Rumsfeld could not control everything that happens in the vast American gulag that has sprung up since 9/11."

Rumsfeld can therefore be better appreciated by recognizing the central role he has played in defining the new era of American security policy. Any thorough understanding of this role, however, must also account for the unique way in which Rumsfeld frequently incorporated the personification of himself as the visible reminder of change. Rumsfeld's sense of humor is often noted in descriptions of his personal style as a speaker, but it is rarely observed that the humor is often directed inward, often at his stature as a seasoned public servant. This specific brand of humor is an important component of Rumsfeld's public commentary, helping to define which subjects are ripe for humor and which are deadly serious.

In a speech commemorating Armed Forces Day on May 18, 2001, Rumsfeld opened by comparing this occasion with the last time he was able to celebrate Armed Forces Day as the defense secretary, twenty-five years earlier:

> Back then, designer jeans were the rage, and "Charlie's Angels" was the top-rated show on TV. Today designer jeans are back, "Charlie's Angels" are back, and so am I. [Laughter.] And what a pleasure it is, as well as a surprise. Bob Dole, my friend here, remembers "Charlie's Angels" and designer jeans. We served together in the House some 35 years ago, I think.

Rumsfeld's humor is not accidental, nor is it unrelated to his emphasis on the changing nature of current times. He playfully noted the return of *Charlie's Angels* even as he contrasted the Soviet threat with the current, more diverse challenges. Merging personal humor and policy preferences, Rumsfeld routinely attempts to place the current moment in a larger historical perspective. When he once again described the importance of the battle at Mazar-e Sharif, this time at the May 29, 2002, Air Force Academy commencement ceremony, he joked: "When President Bush called me back to the Pentagon after a quarter century, and asked us to come up with a new defense strategy, he knew I was an old-timer. But I'll bet he didn't imagine for a second we would bring back the cavalry!" Rumsfeld's self-deprecating humor provides an easy transition to the importance of policy change. Blending his own status as elder public servant with the task of transformation, Rumsfeld comfortably describes the importance of appropriating the best of many different historical epochs and perspectives to best prepare for future threats.

Rumsfeld's willingness to engage in humorous banter is balanced by his seeming sovereignty over very serious subjects. It is widely noted that Rumsfeld possesses a unique ability to maintain order when dealing with a potentially chaotic scene while briefing the Pentagon press pool, but by appreciating this tension between levity and gravity, a great deal of his appeal can be better appreciated. Even though he is hailed as a plainspeaking public official, Rumsfeld is very willing to declare certain subjects off-limits to his inquisitive audience. Attaching a life-and-death quality to the preservation of state secrets, he will quickly depart from lighthearted banter when the topic violates his conceptions of public matter.

In late October 2003 a memo written by Rumsfeld that questioned the future of American policy in Iraq became public. Rumsfeld expressed concern about the ability of American institutions, specifically the Defense Department, to keep pace with the ever-changing global war on terror. For many, the debate surrounding the intentionality of the leak was secondary to the challenge Rumsfeld faced in his quest to dictate the terms of the American campaign. Mounting public concern about the direction of the policy and the rising number of American casualties was easily directed at Rums-

feld's prominent position. Despite the challenge, Rumsfeld continued to serve as one of the most prominent members of the Bush administration. As future historians survey the earliest part of the twenty-first century, it seems likely that Donald Rumsfeld will be understood as both a major actor and an important voice of change.

INFORMATION SOURCES

Research Collections and Collected Speeches

The largest collection of Rumsfeld's public statements in his second tenure as defense secretary is at the Department of Defense's official site, DefenseLink. It is continuously updated and provides a wealth of public commentary. Transcripts of some public appearances may not appear on DefenseLink. The U.S. Mission to NATO site provides useful secondary sources of information.

Web Sites

North Atlantic Treaty Organisation [*NATO*]. The NATO Web site archives speeches delivered to this organization, including those by Rumsfeld. www.nato.int

U.S. Department of Defense [*DOD*]. DefenseLink. www.defenselink.mil

U.S. Mission to NATO [*NM*]. http://nato.usmission.gov

Selected Critical Studies

Cohen, Eliot A. "A Tale of Two Secretaries." *Foreign Affairs* 81, no. 3 (May/June 2002): 20–32.

Hersh, Seymour M. "Offense and Defense: The Battle Between Donald Rumsfeld and the Pentagon." *The New Yorker*, April 7, 2003, pp. 43–45.

Keegan, John. "The Radical at the Pentagon." *Vanity Fair*, February 2003, pp. 126–27.

Kurtz, Howard. "Rumsfeld, America's New Rock Star." *Washington Post*, December 13, 2001. Web only. www.WashingtonPost.com

Loeb, Vernon. "Rumsfeld's Flying Circus: When It Comes to Going Fast, Far and Frequently, the Defense Secretary Is Way Out Front." *Washington Post* (final ed.), May 3, 2003, p. C1.

Montgomery, David. "The Best Defense: Donald Rumsfeld's Overwhelming Show of Force on the Public Relations Front." *Washington Post*, December 12, 2001, p. C1.

Nordlinger, Jay. "Rumsfeld Rules: The Defense Secretary Is a Blast from the Past Who Is the Man of the Hour." *The National Review*, December 31, 2001, p. 24.

Purdum, Todd S. "Rumsfeld's Imperious Style Turns Combative." *New York Times*, March 30, 2003, p. B10.

Purdy, Matthew. "After the War, New Stature for Rumsfeld." *New York Times*, April 20, 2003, p. A1.

Rose, Gideon. "A Memo That Speaks Volumes: Rumsfeld's Leaked Note Points to His Strengths—and His Serious Shortcomings." *Los Angeles Times*, October 31, 2003, p. B17.

Rosett, Claudia. "Keep On Rockin' in the Free World: Why Don Rumsfeld Became a Star." *Wall Street Journal*, December 31, 2001, p. A7.

Schmitt, Eric, and Douglas Jehl. "Troubles in Iraq Dim Rumsfeld's Star, but He Fights Back." *New York Times* (late ed.–final), September 9, 2003, p. A13.

Thomas, Evan. "No Good Defense." *Newsweek*, May 17, 2004, pp. 24–30.

———. "Rumsfeld's War." *Newsweek*, September 16, 2002, p. 20.

Selected Biographies

Decter, Midge. *Rumsfeld: A Personal Portrait*. New York: ReganBooks, 2003.

"The Honorable Donald Rumsfeld." *DOD*.

Krames, Jefferey A. *The Rumsfeld Way: Leadership Wisdom of a Battle-Hardened Maverick*. New York: McGraw-Hill, 2002.

Mann, James. "Young Rumsfeld." *Atlantic Monthly*, November 2003, p. 89.

"The Straight Talker. Profile: Donald Rumsfeld." *The Telegraph* (London). March 16, 2003, p. 27

CHRONOLOGY OF MAJOR SPEECHES

See "Research Collections and Collected Speeches" for source codes.

"Remarks as Delivered by Secretary of Defense Donald H. Rumsfeld at Armed Forces Day." Andrews Air Force Base, Md., May 18, 2001. *DOD*.

"DOD Acquisition and Logistics Excellence Week Kickoff—Bureaucracy to Battlefield Remarks as Delivered by Secretary of Defense Donald H. Rumsfeld." Arlington, Va., September 10, 2001. *DOD*.

"Briefing by Rumsfeld, Shelton on Terrorist Attacks." Arlington, Va., September 11, 2001. *NATO*.

"Defense Briefing with Secretary of Defense Donald Rumsfeld on the Attack on the Pentagon Yesterday." Arlington, Va., September 12, 2001. *NATO*.

"Department of Defense News Briefing." Arlington, Va., September 20, 2001. *NATO*.

"A New Kind of War." *New York Times*, September 27, 2001. *DOD*.

"Remarks as Delivered by Secretary of Defense Donald Rumsfeld and General Richard Myers, Chairman, Joint Chiefs of Staff" (Pentagon ceremony for remembrance). Washington, D.C., December 11, 2001. *DOD*.

"Secretary Rumsfeld Speaks on '21st Century' Transformation of the U.S. Armed Forces" (speech at the National Defense University). Washington, D.C., January 31, 2002. *DOD*.

"Defense Department Town Hall Meeting with Secretary of Defense Donald H. Rumsfeld." Arlington, Va., March 7, 2002. *DOD*.

"Transcript of Testimony by Secretary of Defense Donald H. Rumsfeld on Homeland Security Before Senate Appropriations Committee." Washington, D.C., May 7, 2002. *DOD*.

"Secretary of Defense Donald H. Rumsfeld at United States Air Force Academy Commencement Ceremony." Colorado Springs, Colo., May 29, 2002. *DOD*.

"Transforming the Military." *Foreign Affairs*, May/June 2002, pp. 20–24.

"Prepared Testimony of U.S. Secretary of Defense Donald H. Rumsfeld Before the Senate Armed Services Committee on Progress in Afghanistan." Washington, D.C., July 31, 2002. *DOD*.

"Remarks by Secretary of Defense Donald H. Rumsfeld at the Pentagon Memorial Ceremony." Arlington, Va., September 11, 2002. *DOD*.

"Remarks at Arlington National Cemetery Funeral Service for the Unidentified Victims of the Attack on the Pentagon." Arlington, Va., September 12, 2002. *DOD*.

"Testimony of U.S. Secretary of Defense Donald H. Rumsfeld Before the Senate Armed Services Committee Regarding Iraq." Washington, D.C., September 19, 2002. *DOD*.

"Secretary Rumsfeld Briefs at the Foreign Press Center." Washington, D.C., January 22, 2003. *DOD*.

"Remarks by Secretary of Defense Donald H. Rumsfeld for the House Armed Services Committee" (FY2004 defense budget testimony). Washington, D.C., February 5, 2003. *DOD*.

"DOD News Briefing—Secretary Rumsfeld and Gen. Myers." Washington, D.C., March 20, 2003. *DOD*.

"Remarks as Delivered by Secretary of Defense Donald H. Rumsfeld." (speech before the Council on Foreign Relations). New York, N.Y., May 27, 2003. *DOD*.

"Remarks as Delivered by Secretary of Defense Donald H. Rumsfeld" (speech at the Marshall Center tenth anniversary). Garmisch, Germany, June 11, 2003. Available at http://www.marshallcenter.org

"Testimony of Defense Secretary Donald H. Rumsfeld, Senate Armed Services Committee" (testimony on Iraq). Washington, D.C., July 9, 2003. *DOD*.

"Remarks as Prepared for Delivery by Secretary of Defense Donald H. Rumsfeld" (Message to the Iraqi people). September 5, 2003. *DOD*.

ANTONIN SCALIA (1936–)
U.S. Supreme Court Justice

CATHERINE LANGFORD

Appointed to the U.S. Supreme Court by Ronald Reagan to fill the associate justice position left vacant by William Rehnquist's appointment as chief justice, Scalia was unanimously confirmed by the Senate in 1986. After graduating magna cum laude from Harvard in 1960, he had practiced law with a private firm in Cleveland for seven years before resigning to teach at the University of Virginia in 1967. He then served in various capacities in the Nixon and Ford administrations. When the Republicans lost the White House, Scalia returned to teaching—this time at the University of Chicago Law School. He remained at Chicago Law until Reagan appointed him to the U.S. Court of Appeals for the District of Columbia in 1982.

Of his years prior to the High Court, judicial scholar Christopher E. Smith states that Scalia "became known as an advocate of deregulation and increased power for the executive branch, two ideas reflecting his criticism of the exercises of authority by the Democrat-controlled Congress." Scalia's criticisms of congressional action were in line with the political perspective of Ronald Reagan, who sought to appoint conservative judges who would leave a lasting mark on the judicial branch long after Reagan left the presidency. Reagan's efforts were successful; many constitutional scholars have commented upon the "conservative turn" of the modern Court. Yet Scalia's decision-making, Richard A. Brisbin, Jr. argues, reflects more of a knee-jerk reaction against the Warren and Burger Courts, which furthered New Deal legislative aims, rather than a consistent conservative ideology in cases deciding questions of "criminal procedural due process, abortion rights, free speech, free exercise of religion, the Establishment Clause, and the Equal Protection Clause." Regardless, in Scalia, Reagan found an articulate advocate of conservative ideology and judicial interpretation, and a justice willing to overturn New Deal judicial decisions.

A vocal advocate of textualist interpretation and judicial restraint, Scalia is one of the most visible and controversial justices on the Supreme Court today. Cartoonist Ruben Bolling frequently posts sketches about Scalia in his "Tom the Dancing Bug" cartoon, characterizing Scalia as "the crusading judge who travels the land doling out tough justice." In the spring of 2003 Scalia made headlines for refusing to allow his speech of acceptance for the Citadel of Free Speech Award to be recorded and for asserting support, in a speech at John Carroll University, of the government's constitutional right to decrease individual rights during times of war. That summer Scalia was widely criticized for claiming that the Supreme Court had "signed on to the so-called homosexual agenda" and that "the Court has taken sides in the culture war" in his *Lawrence v. Texas* dissenting opinion.

Considered one of the most intellectual among the current justices, Scalia is known for his sharp questioning during oral arguments and the caustic tone of his judicial opinions. His method of constitutional interpretation, textualism, is widely discussed in law review articles, and his opinions create much dialogue in the popular press as well as in legal publications.

ANTONIN SCALIA: VOICE OF JUDICIAL CONSERVATISM

As an American orator, Justice Antonin Scalia strangely is simultaneously present and absent in the public sphere. He frequently speaks to bar associations, foundations, institutions, think tanks, civic organizations, religious groups, and schoolchildren, and at law school commencement ceremonies. Yet he refuses to allow his speeches to be taped, so little record of his speaking engagements exists. From the spring of 2000 until the of fall 2003, the Supreme Court's Web site had posted twenty-six speeches by Chief Justice William Rehnquist, ten speeches by Justice Stephen Breyer, one speech by Justice Sandra Day O'Connor, four speeches by Justice Ruth Bader Ginsburg, and one speech by Justice Anthony Kennedy. No speeches by Antonin Scalia have been published on the Web site. Yet Scalia is one of the most speech-giving justices on the Court. David Savage, reports in the *Los Angeles Times* that "Scalia is one of the most talkative, but least seen, of the nine Supreme Court justices."

Five of Scalia's speeches have become part of public record: his 1989 Sibley Lecture to the University of Georgia School of Law; his Tanner Lecture in March 1995, later published as "Common-Law Courts in a Civil-Law System: The Role of United States Federal Courts in Interpreting the Constitution and Laws," in Scalia's *A Matter of Interpretation: Federal Courts and*

According to Scalia, a central tenet of American jurisprudence is that the Constitution should be interpreted as a statute. In other words, the Constitution's meaning was fixed at the time of its adoption by the American people. Moreover, justices should not take the lawmaking process into their own hands—since in a democracy the government is to be ruled by the people. The Constitution, meant to be fixed and rigid, was not intended to respond to the changing needs of society. The founders intended, and the practice of the American people—until recently—supported, that changing moral values are reflected by adopting new statutory law or throwing out old statutory law, and not by reinterpretation of the Constitution as statute.

In his 1989 Sibley Lecture, Scalia highlighted the symbolism of the Constitution, the founders'

"Men may intend what they will; but it is only the laws that they enact which bind us."

Antonin Scalia, the Sibley Lecture

---

the Law; his remarks at the Catholic University of America on October 18, 1996, titled "A Theory of Constitutional Interpretation"; his 1997 Wriston Lecture to the Manhattan Institute for Policy Research on November 17, 1997, titled "On Interpreting the Constitution"; and his remarks to the Pew Forum on Religion and Public Life at the University of Chicago Divinity School, titled "God's Justice and Ours." An examination of these speeches illustrates the consistency of Scalia's message. Following the political consultant's creed that consistency of message is important to achieving one's political aims, in speeches spanning fifteen years Scalia has articulated a single recurring message centered on the themes of constitutional interpretation, judicial deference, and the democratic process. In his *Los Angeles Times* article, David Savage observes that Justice Scalia "delivers the same speech over and over. But, as he has told

purposes in establishing a written constitution, and the difference between the U.S. Constitution and the constitution of another nation—the Union of Soviet Socialist Republics. His purpose was to reinforce his argument that the Constitution should not be altered easily, that it means what it means even if that meaning is not what the personal predilections of a justice believe it ought to mean.

He began by noting the distinctive nature of the Constitution: "When statutes are amended you take the old one, throw it out, and insert the new one. . . . Not so with the venerated document that is our United States Constitution. . . . We append all of the amendments at the end. That is how reluctant we are to touch that venerable document, that symbol of our nation." Scalia acknowledged the inherent difference between statutory and constitutional law—that constitutional law is meant to be more enduring and less easily altered than laws created by the legislature.

Next Scalia addressed one of the criticisms of originalist and textualist interpretations of the law—their reliance upon the original meaning of the Constitution. He argued that the Constitution has been in effect for 200 years—much longer than any other nation. Therefore, Scalia believed, the ideals of the Founders, captured in the specific enumerations that the Founders chose to include in the articles and the amendments of the Constitution, should be followed.

Scalia offered a speech by Benjamin Franklin, given at the signing of the Constitution, as evidence that although one might not agree with the entire document, one should nevertheless seek to perpetuate the ideals secured in the Constitution for the sake of better future judgment. This point is, in fact, a subtle chastisement of judicial legislation—judges believing that they should be able to alter the constitutional text through a Supreme Court opinion. Quoting Franklin, Scalia stated, "For having lived long I have experienced many instances of being obligated by better information or fuller consideration to change opinions even on important subjects which I once thought right but found to be otherwise."

If his audience accepts Scalia's premises that the Constitution is enduring and not easily changed, and that we may learn that what we think is right in the present is not, in fact, the best option for the future, they will also allow that judges should not use personal predilections to determine judicial outcomes. The Court, Scalia believes, is not different from society as a whole, and therefore justices will bring "compromises of principles" and "misperceptions of liberty" to the bench. Therefore, society should rely upon the constitutional text as crafted by the Founding Fathers.

In March 1995 Scalia delivered a presentation to which four prominent scholars responded. The entire panel discussion was later published in Scalia's book *A Matter of Interpretation*. His remarks, "Common-Law Courts in a Civil-Law System: The Role of United States Federal Courts in Interpreting the Constitution and Laws," set forth Scalia's arguments against a "living" Constitution and in favor of "reasonable" textual interpretation. Through "Common-Law Courts" Scalia argued that constitutional interpretation is a science that has been neglected. Yet he failed to operationalize the process of textual interpretation, criticizing more expansive readings of the Constitution without offering guidelines for interpreting the text.

Scalia began: "The following essay attempts to explain the current neglected state of the science of construing legal texts, and offers a few suggestions for improvements." Projecting a dichotomous relationship between the "science" of law as opposed to the "art" of law (reminiscent of Socrates' split between rhetoric as an art and dialectic as a science in Plato's *Gorgias*), Scalia differentiated between different types of law. Common law, Scalia said, is an art (and the judge is king) in which the creative crafting of law is more important than the "right" result. On the other hand, statutory law and constitutional law are a science (and the law is king) in which the neutral principles of the law determine the necessary legal outcome. The underlying focus of this argument is that statutory and constitutional law should have predictable outcomes and, thereby, perpetuate the stability of the legal system.

Scalia's characterization of statutory and constitutional law as "science" implies that their interpretation should be objective, predictable, and replicable. For law to be objective, the judge has to be a neutral party applying pertinent legal principles to the case at hand. Law is predictable because the end result of a case can be foreseen; a judge does not create new legal principles but applies existing ones. Lower courts, moreover, should be able to follow previous decisions and reach similar results in similar cases, thus replicating legal decisions and reasoning. Law that is objective, predictable, and replicable values expertise and procedure, and devalues opinion and normative decisions.

Thus Scalia's characterization of law as a science leaves us with a legal system that gives agency to the law rather than to the lawmaker or the judge. Yet Scalia tells us that in actuality little attention has been given as to how the science of law should be performed. Frequently judges try to use legislative intent to understand what the law is, rather than relying upon the language of the text itself. Scalia rejected this practice: "Men may intend what they will; but it is only the laws that they enact which bind us." Congress little knows or participates in a dynamic democratic process of passing laws. Few legislators write statutes or are involved in the committee process; few members of Congress are on the floor during debate; and rarely do all representatives vote in favor of a bill that is passed. Judges should let the law guide them, and base decisions on the statutory text. Therefore, the rule of law and the lack of clear and consistent legislative intent create a space for Scalia's solution to the practice of legal decision-making: textualism.

Scalia first attempted to define textualism strictly, and then moved to a broader conception. "[W]hen the text of a statute is clear, that is the end of the matter," he stated. Yet Scalia did not characterize himself as a strict constructionist: "A text should not be construed strictly, and it should not be construed leniently; it should be construed reasonably, to contain all that it fairly means." While one may at first be reminded of Goldilocks searching for a bed to sleep in, Scalia is simply trying to escape an either or fallacy and to craft a textualism that can be responsive to shifting communal needs. Interpretation should be neither strict nor loose; it should be "reasonable." But what does "reasonable" mean, and how should "reasonable" be applied? For Scalia, "reasonable" meant that "words have a limited range of meaning, and no interpretation that goes beyond that range is permissible." Supporting his point with the Due Process Clause, Scalia contended that the death penalty is constitutional because the Constitution ensures a *process*, not a *result*. A person can be denied life, but only after due process.

Scalia's remarks at the Catholic University were a warning to the community in which Scalia called the people back to the "traditional" strict interpretation of the Constitution. He began his speech, "A Theory of Constitutional Interpretation," by asking, "What is the object of the enterprise [that the Supreme Court engages in]?" No agreement exists as to how justices should interpret the Constitution. Scalia quickly declared himself to be a textualist, and one concerned with what the text of the Consti-

tution meant at the time of its adoption, not what the founders intended it to mean. He urged the people to alter their government "at the ballot box," rather than seek redress in the courts.

According to Scalia, many justices have historically agreed with him that the Constitution is limited in meaning, and that if one wants to change that meaning, one must adopt a constitutional amendment. Citing the Nineteenth Amendment as an example, he argued:

> As you know, there was a national campaign of "suffragettes" to get this constitutional amendment adopted, a very big deal to get a constitutional amendment adopted. Why? Why did they go through all the trouble? If people then thought the way people think now, there would have been no need. There was an equal protection clause, right there in the Constitution in 1920. As an abstract matter, what in the world could be a greater denial of equal protection in a democracy than denial of the franchise? And so why didn't these people just come before the court and say, "This is a denial of equal protection"? Because they didn't think that way.

Abortion and the death penalty served as examples of the errors in judicial decision-making, sites where the justices had constructed their own version of what the Constitution "ought" to mean. Instead of permitting abortion or prohibiting the death penalty through an altered meaning of the Constitution, Scalia claimed that changes should be made by democratically elected representatives.

Scalia denied that his version of constitutional interpretation leaves the United States with a rigid system of government. Rather, by leaving the outcome to the people at the ballot box, America is assured a "flexible" system. Judges were not meant to establish "evolving standards of decency." "I am so out of touch with the American people," Scalia declared. "I don't even try to be in touch. . . . If you want someone who's in touch with what are the evolving standards of decency that reflect a maturing society, ask the Congress." His job was to interpret what the document actually says, not what it ought to say. The Constitution is not an "empty vessel," waiting to be filled with whatever the justices think it should be, Scalia maintained. He concluded that if America did not heed his warning to return to a limited view of what the Constitution can do, our democracy would be weakened.

Scalia began his Manhattan Institute speech with the end of a story:

> But the burden of this story is that the fox knows many things. And the hedgehog knows only one thing. But it is a big thing. I am the hedgehog. What I want to talk to you about tonight is what I will bend anybody's ear about, what I go to law schools to talk about, what I speak to any assembly of intelligent people from high school age onward about, and that is what in the world we think we're doing when we interpret the Constitution of the United States.

He chastised those who advance the concept of a "living" Constitution, insisted that the Bill of Rights was "a closed set" of rights, and cited the example of the death penalty as the problem with "evolving" approaches to constitutional interpretation. He reiterated, as he does in most speeches, that his approach to constitutional interpretation is flexible—that the people can have whatever government they desire, so long as they institute that government through democratic processes.

The misconception that the Constitution is a "living" document does not reside only within "liberal" camps. In this speech Scalia criticized "conservatives" for their desire to alter the meaning of the Constitution to suit their needs. In addition to abortion and the death penalty, he cited homosexual conduct, product liability, and how to rear one's children as subjects about which the Constitution is silent. "Due process of law never meant you've got the right answer. It meant the process was fair," Scalia declared. In other words, the process, not the result, is guaranteed. Again he pointed to the adoption of the Nineteenth Amendment as an example of America's altered conception of constitutional meaning.

One's understanding of constitutional interpretation directly affects how one understands democratic practice. Rather than work to achieve popular support of the majority, groups need only to achieve five votes out of nine to effect social change. The loss of democratic processes "is a great sadness" to Scalia. Also, judicial legislating is a threefold problem for him. First, it

makes the Constitution mean whatever legislators want it to mean, which suggests that it does not mean much of anything. Second, there are no criteria by which to interpret the Constitution if it has situationally variable meanings. Third, it opens the Supreme Court up to the pressures placed on other political branches. These three points detract from the prestige of the Court and open it to political attack.

Scalia's speech to the Pew Forum on Religion and Public Life, given at the University of Chicago Divinity School, is perhaps his most surprising speech. In his remarks Scalia contended that he has no moral struggles with upholding the death penalty, regardless of his Catholicism. What was surprising, however, was his argument that the state is the "minister of God" in administering His justice.

Scalia began his discussion about constitutional interpretation by distinguishing between personal belief and professional action. He emphasized that, regardless of his religious beliefs against capital punishment, his actions reflect the constitutionality of capital punishment. For Scalia the death penalty can be administered because the Constitution says it can. "That statement would not be true if I subscribed to the conventional fallacy that the Constitution is a 'living document'—that is, a text that means from age to age whatever the society (or perhaps the Court) thinks it ought to mean." Justices who reject the constitutionality of capital punishment should resign, Scalia argued.

Scalia is a strong supporter of the death penalty because he believes the state is the administrator of justice for God. He has even criticized Pope John Paul II for his opposition to the death penalty, a somewhat surprising move for a conservative Catholic. Quoting the Book of Romans, he claimed that the United States was established upon the concept of God as represented in the Christian Bible, as reflected in our practices and traditions. A cultural belief in God is reflected in the "In God We Trust" stamped on our money, the "under God" in our Pledge of Allegiance, and the prayers that open the Supreme Court session.

One must pause and consider carefully what Scalia was saying, and to whom, in his speech to the Pew Forum. Scalia was speaking before a group of religious intellectuals, people who had gathered together to consider the relationship between religion, politics, and public life. Therefore, it was predictable that Scalia should quote Scripture and argue that the Christian viewpoint asserted in Romans is a heritage of the American people. Clearly, Scalia would not have the liberty to state in one of his Supreme Court opinions that the state is the "minister of God"—such would violate the First Amendment's Establishment Clause. Therefore, when considering a "moral" question, Scalia referred to whether the "traditions" of the American people support or condemn the issue at hand.

Last, Scalia considered whether society has evolved. He concluded that we have not. In fact, he argued that the increased capacity for destruction, murder, and death that technology has brought actually increases the need for the death penalty. People can harm others in more cruel and destructive ways than the Founders ever could have imagined. Therefore, he disagrees with the edict of the Catholic Church that the death penalty is not morally acceptable. For Scalia, the practice of capital punishment is more necessary now than ever.

In general, Scalia's speeches reflect his belief in limited constitutional meaning, judicial deference to the legislature, and the desirability of democratic processes. Constitutional meaning should be restricted to the meaning at the time of the founding or of an amendment's adoption. Judicial deference refers to the belief that there are certain issues that can be considered by the Supreme Court and there are issues that cannot. The latter are issues which should instead be decided by the elected representatives of the people. The democratic process requires that social norms and governmental freedoms and regulations should be determined by the people, not by the judiciary. Scalia's judicial opinions consistently uphold these values, and his abortion opinions provide a representative example of these three values.

Scalia's abortion decisions reflect his belief that the Constitution does not mention abortion. In *Hodgson v. Minnesota*, Scalia stated, "One will search in vain the document we are supposed to be construing for text that provides the basis for the argument over these distinctions;

and will find in our society's tradition regarding abortion no hint that the distinctions are constitutionally relevant, much less any indication how a constitutional argument about them ought to be resolved." In *Ohio v. Akron Center for Reproductive Health*, Scalia maintained, "The Constitution contains no right to an abortion . . . it cannot be logically deduced from the text of the Constitution." Because the text of the Constitution does not expressly set forth protections guarding a right to abortion, the states may legislate on abortion as they see fit. "The States may, if they wish, permit abortion on demand, but the Constitution does not *require* them to do so," Scalia asserted in *Planned Parenthood v. Casey*, the Court's most important abortion decision since *Roe v. Wade*. Thus, Scalia established a chain of reasoning that supports his values: since the Constitution does not mention abortion, the judiciary should defer to the legislatures, allowing the popularly elected representatives to decide whether the people of their state want abortion legalized or not.

In addition to the content of Scalia's opinions, the form of his opinions rejects the conception that the Constitution "speaks to" abortion. Most of Scalia's abortion opinions are extremely short. If Scalia were to construct arguments discussing previous case history, a woman's "right to choose," or the constitutionality of state laws policing abortion, he would undermine his entire argument. His argument can be limited to declaring that the Court should not adjudicate abortion—and it does not take much prose to assert such an argument. Form supports content in this case.

His *Casey* dissent also serves as a good exemplar of Scalia's judicial voice, which is typically hostile, condescending, and superior. According to Scalia, the majority opinion was "rhetoric rather than reality"; the opinion, a "verbal shell game [that] will conceal raw judicial policy choices"; its use of precedent, "contrived"; and its portrayal of *Roe*, as "nothing less than Orwellian." Frequently engaging in ad hominem arguments, Scalia attacked other justices' decision-making and reasoning. This abrasive language was typical of a Scalia dissent; other justices opted for less confrontational language.

In both his speeches and his judicial opinions, Scalia rejects the belief that the Constitution can respond to all social needs. He also refuses to accept a "living Constitution"—the belief that the Constitution should be interpreted in light of modern social needs and standards. Scalia believes instead that the purpose of a written constitution is to incorporate clarity and stability into the American system of government. In speech after speech and opinion after opinion, he affirms the same message: that the Constitution has limited meaning and that legislatures should respond to the shifting needs of the people.

INFORMATION SOURCES

Research Collections and Collected Speeches

There are no archival collections or speech anthologies at this time. Scalia's contemporary lectures are, however, widely available on the Web. The Supreme Court's Web page provides some audiotapes of oral arguments before the Court, as well as transcripts of speeches by other justices.

Scalia, Antonin. *A Matter of Interpretation: Federal Courts and the Law.* Princeton, N.J.: Princeton University Press, 1997.

———. "Originalism: The Lesser Evil." *University of Chicago Law Review* 57 (1989): 849–65.

———. "The Rule of Law as a Law of Rules." *University of Chicago Law Review* 56 (1989): 1175–88.

Web Site

U.S. Supreme Court. Transcripts of speeches by other justices as well as audio of oral arguments. www.supremecourtus.gov

Selected Critical Studies

Bolling, Ruben. "Tom the Dancing Bug." http://archive.salon.com

"Justice Scalia Bans Media from Free Speech Ceremony." *Online NewsHour.* www.pbs.org

Savage, David G. "Some 'Mystified' by Award to Scalia for Free Speech." *Los Angeles Times*, March 18, 2003. p. A28.

Selected Biographies

Brisbin, Richard A., Jr. *Justice Antonin Scalia and the Conservative Revival.* Baltimore, Md.: Johns Hopkins University Press, 1997.

Friedelbaum, Stanley H. *The Rehnquist Court: In Pursuit of Judicial Conservatism.* Westport, Conn.: Greenwood Press, 1994.

Savage, David G. *Turning Right: The Making of the Rehnquist Supreme Court.* New York: John Wiley, 1992.

Schultz, David A., and Christopher E. Smith. *The Jurisprudential Vision of Justice Antonin Scalia.* Lanham, Md.: Rowman & Littlefield, 1996.

Smith, Christopher E. *Justice Antonin Scalia and the Supreme Court's Conservative Moment.* Westport, Conn.: Praeger, 1993.

CHRONOLOGY OF MAJOR SPEECHES

"1989 Sibley Lecture to the University of Georgia School of Law." Athens, Ga., 1989. Available at www.uga.edu

"Tanner Lecture at Princeton University." Princeton, N.J., March 8 and 9, 1995. Available at www.tannerlectures.utah.edu

"A Theory of Constitutional Interpretation" (remarks at the Catholic University of America). Washington, D.C., October 18, 1996. Available at www.courttv.com

"On Interpreting the Constitution" (Wriston Lecture at the Manhattan Institute for Policy Research). New York City, November 17, 1997. Available at www.manhattan-institute.org

"God's Justice and Ours" (remarks at the Pew Forum on Religion and Public Life at the University of Chicago Divinity School). Chicago, January 25, 2002. Available in original form at www.pewforum.org; written adaptation available at www.firstthings.com

AL SHARPTON (1954–)
Baptist Minister, Civil Rights Activist, U.S. Presidential Candidate

DANIEL A. GRANO

During a career of well-publicized mistakes, successes, and transformations, Al Sharpton has used his speaking talents to pursue activist and political ambitions. A primary ambition has been legitimacy: "I've been indicted. I've been stabbed. And . . . I've been sued. I have every base covered being a great civil-rights leader." Engaging yet controversial, Sharpton is most recognized as an aggressive civil rights activist and political candidate. Holding him to the mistakes of his past, critics have called Sharpton a "firebrand," "a walking sound bite," a "con artist," an "ambulance chaser," and a racial divider. Despite this, he has emerged as an important civil rights leader and a voice of reform that the Democratic Party cannot ignore. Sharpton still struggles for perceived legitimacy between two conflicting images: to some he lives up to the negative labels of his critics, while to others he is a vital spokesperson for social and political consciousness. Whatever perception holds, Sharpton's speaking talents have made him an important figure for the communities he serves most closely.

Sharpton began his speaking career early. Born on October 3, 1954, in Brooklyn, New York, he started preaching at the age of four. By age ten, he was ordained as a Pentecostal minister and was touring with Mahalia Jackson as the "Wonderboy" preacher. That same year, 1964, he preached to 10,000 people at the World's Fair in New York. During the same time period, however, Sharpton's father, Alfred Sr., began an affair with his wife's daughter from a previous marriage, had a child with her, and abandoned Sharpton and his mother. Sharpton went from a middle-class life in Queens to the public housing projects in Brooklyn, and the experience resonates in several of his speeches. Moving to the projects did not bother Sharpton as much as see-

ing other residents accept their condition as inevitable; having lived in Hollis, Queens, he knew there were better possibilities.

As a ten-year-old, Sharpton had become enamored with Adam Clayton Powell's style and sense of drama. Powell had been a successful civil rights leader in Harlem during the Depression, and at this time was an influential member of Congress. Sharpton met his hero when Powell visited Abyssinian Baptist church in Harlem. He was elated when Powell knew him by reputation as "the Wonderboy preacher from my good friend F.D. Washington's church, Alfred Sharpton!"

Since his boyhood, Sharpton met civil rights leaders, celebrities, and "father figures" who had a tangible influence on his own activism and speaking. In 1969 Jesse Jackson appointed Sharpton, then fourteen years old, youth director of the New York chapter of Operation BreadBasket, an organization that used boycotts to fight racial discrimination in hiring. While in his teens, Sharpton established a friendship with the singer James Brown, eventually became his business manager and agent, and met his wife, Kathy Jordan Sharpton, who was a backup singer for Brown. In the 1970s and early 1980s, Sharpton worked with boxing promoter Don King and became further involved in African American politics and entertainment. Sharpton's talent for political theater is evidence of these and other influences.

Sharpton used that talent to first make his way into the nation's consciousness in the 1980s. In 1985, after Bernard Goetz shot four African American teenagers on a New York subway, Sharpton staged a series of demonstrations, sit-ins, and protests, gaining media attention for his flamboyant style. In 1986, he demonstrated to raise public consciousness of the circumstances surrounding the death of a Black teen who was killed after being chased and beaten by a white mob in the outer Queens neighborhood of Howard Beach. Sharpton considers the Howard Beach incident the moment when he "arrived as an activist."

In the 1980s Sharpton's reputation became tarnished when he took up the case of Tawana Brawley, a fifteen-year-old Black girl who claimed that she had been kidnapped and sexually assaulted by a group of white men. Supporting Brawley, Sharpton and his associates blamed Steven Pagones, a former Dutchess County prosecutor, for defaming her. A seven-month investigation by a New York State grand jury concluded that Brawley had fabricated the abduction and rape, and in 1998 Sharpton was ordered to pay $65,000 to Pagones. Some of Sharpton's supporters have asked him to apologize, but he has steadfastly refused. Many in the

motivated by rage at the pervasiveness of racism in New York City and around the nation. After the stabbing, Sharpton wanted to be more substantial, organized, and practical. He shifted focus from local activism to electoral politics, and made changes not only in his speaking style but also in his dress, now wearing conservative suits rather than the flamboyant ones he had preferred.

In 1992, Sharpton ran for the U.S. Senate in the New York Democratic primary and won 15 percent of the vote; he ran again in 1994 and won 26 percent of the vote. His most successful political campaign was the 1997 run for mayor of New York City, in which he won a surprising 32 percent of the vote. But in what many consider the finest moment in this transformation, Sharpton, wanting to prove his allegiance

---

"We come with different religions, different political ideologies, different races, because we come . . . to underscore that in this capital city they are perpetrating one of the greatest untruths in world history. Across town, a man who lost the election is being sworn in to preside over these United States. . . . Too many people died, too many cold nights in jail, too many people lost their careers [to let this inauguration pass without protest]."

Al Sharpton, Protesting the 2001 inauguration of George W. Bush

---

African American community still believe that Brawley may have been telling the truth, and Sharpton maintains he is right for believing the story of a teenage girl and not compromising by bowing to mainstream opinion. The Brawley case defines Sharpton in the minds of critics and comes up in almost every mainstream article and interview concerning him. Conversely, his continued support of Brawley has solidified his reputation as a leader in some parts of the African American community.

In 1991, while protesting in Bensonhurst, New York, Sharpton was attacked and stabbed in the chest, the incident served as a defining moment in Sharpton's life. He decided that he had been too flippant in the past and had responded, without careful deliberation, to too many phone calls and incidents. He had been

to the nonviolent teachings of Martin Luther King Jr., asked for leniency at his assailant's hearing, then visited his would-be assassin in jail, and forgave him. Sharpton said after the visit, "The day I walked out of that jail prepared me for the rest of my life."

If Sharpton has "reinvented" himself, he has also stayed with his roots as a civil rights activist and preacher, maintaining a talent for rousing speeches that raise consciousness of racial inequality. Sharpton maintains his original communal ties through the National Action Network (NAN), which he founded in 1991 and headquartered in Harlem. NAN serves the local community as a "House of Justice" with a full-time crisis unit that takes calls. Sharpton's ambition extends beyond these local interests, however. He wants to lead the progressive movement in the same way that Jesse Jackson did in the 1980s, and he wants to live up to the civil rights legacy of Martin Luther King, Jr. In *Go and Tell Pharaoh*, Sharpton sees his ambition to change the "broad socioeconomic conditions" of society in the same way he did when he was a little boy: as a "calling" consistent with his religious background.

AL SHARPTON'S SEARCH FOR LEGITIMACY

Early in his career, Sharpton gained a reputation for identifying and publicizing racial conflicts as he began his search for legitimacy as a leader within the civil rights tradition. His efforts were praiseworthy to some, and suspicious to others, since as much as he seemed to raise awareness of issues important to African American and other minority communities, it also was possible that his speaking style would cause further divisiveness. Of his activism in the mid-to-late 1980s, when Sharpton first made his way onto the national stage, he admits in *Go and Tell Pharaoh* that he was "outraged" by Bernard Goetz, Howard Beach, and other incidents. While he and others were successful at showing the nation "the ugly face of northern racism," he was "still in many ways just reacting" and "putting out fires." During this period Sharpton's efforts to publicize racial inequality aroused establishment critics to brand him an "ambulance chaser" a "con artist," and a "rabble-rouser." These labels have been hurtful to Sharpton, who saw his stylistic choices as necessary: "I was speaking for people who didn't normally have a voice, I was speaking from neighborhoods that didn't normally gain attention, I had to be dramatic, I had to be loud."

After the 1991 stabbing incident, Sharpton made changes to gain more mainstream appeal, but the sense of political theater he learned from his boyhood associations has not been lost. Nor has he lost his outrage at racial injustice. As a result, his speaking still fluctuates between the bellicose style of an aggressive grassroots activist and the measured tones of a man who wants to create societal change through electoral politics.

In addition to the Tawana Brawley case, perceptions of Sharpton as a racially divisive speaker still affect mainstream perceptions of his legitimacy. This is especially true of Sharpton's perceived roles in conflicts between the African American and Jewish communities in New York City. The 1991 riots in the Crown Heights section of Brooklyn are a primary example. On August 19, 1991, a station wagon driven by a member of the Hasidic Lubavitcher sect ran a red light, collided with another car, and jumped a curb, striking two African American children. Seven-year-old Gavin Cato was killed in the accident, and his seven-year-old cousin, Angela Cato, was seriously injured. Preexisting tensions in Crown Heights erupted into four nights of violence. Sharpton has been blamed for taking the role of demagogue after the accident. Speaking at Gavin Cato's funeral, he said of the Hasidic community, "They don't want peace, they want quiet." His speech displayed more outrage than measured reflection:

> [T]he world will tell us he was killed by accident. Yes, it was a social accident. . . . It's an accident to allow an apartheid ambulance service in the middle of Crown Heights. It is an accident to think that we will keep crying and never stand up and call for justice. . . . What type of city do we have that would lie on our children and allow politics to rise above the blood of innocent babies? . . . The issue is not anti-Semitism; the issue is apartheid. . . . All we want to say is what Jesus said: if you offend one of these little ones, you got to pay for it. No compromise, no meetings. . . . Pay for your deeds. . . .

The apartheid reference played on perceptions by some Crown Heights African Americans that members of the Lubavitcher sect, who established their world headquarters there in 1940, had set up an apartheid situation where they received preferential treatment from police and city authorities.

This, and another incident in 1995 have led to criticisms that Sharpton is anti-Semitic. The 1995 incident involved the Jewish owner of Freddy's Fashion Mart, who he believed was trying to drive out an African American owner of a local record store by raising his rent. Sharpton called for a boycott of Freddy's Fashion Mart in his September 1995 radio address on the National Action Network, saying, "We will not stand by and allow them to move this brother so that some white interloper can expand his business on 125th Street." Sharpton admitted in his book *Al on America* that it was wrong to call the man a "white interloper": "I should not have used the word 'white' because that made the whole thing racial." However, Sharpton also refuses to accept blame for the actions of a man who, after the address, went into Freddy's and shot several employees, then set fire to the store. Sharpton claims the man was actually one of his critics, and acted on his own. In *Al on America*, Sharpton addresses charges of anti-Semitism levied against him and other African American leaders, maintaining that his efforts in Crown Heights and at Freddy's Fashion Mart did not cause any violence, and that there is a racial double standard when considering the lack of uproar over anti-Semitic comments by white leaders in America. Though he is increasingly able to overcome his divisive image, Sharpton has had a difficult time shaking it completely.

Considering the criticism surrounding him, it is not surprising that many underestimated Sharpton's legitimacy as a candidate for the Democratic nomination in the 1997 New York City mayoral race. In that race, Sharpton's speeches reflected recurring themes from his activist past, and previewed newer themes and capabilities that he would take to a national stage in the 2004 presidential campaign. Voicing his aspiration to run for mayor in a 1996 speech at Canaan Baptist Church, Sharpton once again raised consciousness of racial inequality, and added the substantive comments of a legitimate political candidate: "Anytime you have police brutality at the highest level it's been in 30 years, and the mayor tells you crime is going down, as if the crimes committed by police are not crimes too. . . . We need someone in office who will fight crime whether the perpetrators are wearing blue jeans or blue uniforms. Crime is crime." By now, Sharpton could speak credibly of years of activism against racial, including police, brutality as he attempted to transform his local activities into political legitimacy.

Sharpton also offered evidence that his "sound-bite" reputation could be of great benefit in televised debates, where cameras and time constraints make memorable, quick jabs neces-

sary and effective. In a debate between the Democratic candidates for mayor on February 19, 1997, Sharpton matched humor with substantive policy positions—opposing tuition vouchers, promising to fight police abuse, criticizing tax breaks for corporations—and had the best line in the debate. Concerning the incumbent Rudolph Giuliani's record of hiring minorities, Sharpton said: "This administration is like the Rocky Mountains. The higher up you go, the whiter it gets." Sharpton's ability to criticize politicians' minority policies in debates would become central during the 2004 presidential race as well.

Sharpton's work on racial profiling and police brutality continued to bolster his legitimacy. In 1999, he met with Attorney General Janet Reno and President Clinton to lay the groundwork for an executive order directing federal law enforcement agencies to collect race, gender, and ethnic data on citizens they question and arrest. Sharpton's work on racial profiling came to bear more publicly in the Amadou Diallo case. In February 1999, four New York City police officers shot and killed Diallo during a routine "stop-and-frisk." Diallo's race raised the suspicion that profiling was behind the decision to stop him, and the number of bullets fired at him, forty-one in total, became a symbol of police brutality. Sharpton established a peaceful leadership role when, after all four officers were acquitted, he spoke outside the courthouse in Albany: "Let not one brick be thrown, not one bottle be thrown. . . . Those that believe in Amadou should not betray his memory by acting like those who killed him." This shift from outrage to a nonviolent message is more indicative of the Al Sharpton who forgave his 1991 attacker than of the figure who spoke at Gavin Cato's funeral after the Crown Heights incident.

It was also more in keeping with the legacy of Martin Luther King Jr., to whose leadership and credibility Sharpton aspires. Indeed, in a significant number of his speeches, Sharpton attempts to connect the legitimacy of his own leadership with historic civil rights struggles. In a 2000 National Action Network speech commemorating the "real soldiers" of Memorial Day, for example, Sharpton said the soldiers to be remembered were the soldiers who had fought for, not against, civil rights: "If we are going to deal with Memorial Day, we can't remember those soldiers that stood at the door in Birmingham and blocked schoolhouses from us." Rather, he said, "If we are going to talk about soldiers, let's talk about those soldiers who went on the battlefield for freedom, justice, empowerment, and fairness." Sharpton went on to list "real" soldiers within the context of the civil rights struggle: Medgar Evers, Sojourner Truth, and Fannie Lou Hamer.

The strategy was similar at Sharpton's 2001 speech at Stanton Park in Washington, D.C., protesting the inauguration of George W. Bush. Sharpton opened with a unifying message: "We come with different religions, different political ideologies, different races, because we come . . . to underscore that in this capital city they are perpetrating one of the greatest untruths in world history. Across town, a man who lost the election is being sworn in to preside over these United States." Linking the present protest with past sacrifices, Sharpton said, "Too many people died, too many cold nights in jail, too many people lost their careers." Toward the end of the speech, he reinforced the connection between his leadership role and the protection of historical civil rights progress, saying, "We have taken an oath today that the blood of Goodman, Chaney, and Schwerner was not shed in vain . . . that Martin Luther King will not be erased from the annals of history . . . that we will turn this nation around."

Considering his ambition to carry the legacy of King, it seems fitting that Sharpton spoke at a 2003 antiviolence rally in Crown Heights, Brooklyn, where in 1991 he had been accused of agitating racial divisiveness. He spoke at the rally to express his sorrow over the death of his longtime friend Councilman James Davis, who had been shot while Sharpton was on a peace mission in Africa. "I was in Africa a few days ago, trying to convince the Motherland, especially the warring factions in Liberia, that there are other ways to settle disputes rather than using violence, not realizing that in my own backyard in New York City, violence was tearing apart my people." Sharpton spoke against the use of violence to settle political scores, adding: "Brother Davis' untimely death should

be a great lesson to us all that there is a need to review how politics is played in this town."

Sharpton's message of reform has become more substantive later in his career. Reflecting his renewed focus on creating societal change through the political process, several of Sharpton's speeches, such as his 2003 speech at Crown Heights, are aimed at broad social-political reform. As part of this effort, Sharpton ran for the 2004 Democratic presidential nomination. His purpose was to direct a critical reform message at the Democratic Party, calling for a return to its ideological roots, and to state its obligations to minority communities.

As a speaker during the 2004 Democratic presidential primaries, Sharpton's growing maturity as a political orator was evidenced by substantive policy proposals and a more measured style. He also maintained the strategy of constructing his own legitimacy by connecting his efforts to the civil rights movement. In his closing remarks at the 2004 Brown–Black Democratic Presidential Candidates Debate in Des Moines, Iowa, Sharpton said: "Martin Luther King's mission was to change America. . . . He changed America because he confronted what was wrong. . . . To honor Dr. King is not to take silence, and not to tell those who dissent in our party to be quiet. . . . I will not be silent because it would be a disservice to the memory of Dr. King." Continuing to revisit civil rights struggles, Sharpton was now able to call upon the speaking talents and themes he had developed since his youth to create a substantive criticism of the Democratic Party and of America. As in the 1997 New York City mayoral race, Sharpton was most effective during televised debates, where his talents for making memorable utterances and for thinking on his feet enlivened the primaries.

Over his entire career Sharpton's attempts at constructing legitimacy have centered on his activist past. Sharpton has tried to convey the fundamental idea that he, more than any other member of the Democratic Party since Jesse Jackson, has had experience as a civil rights activist and has made the real sacrifices of a leader in the movement, including going to jail and being stabbed. At the 2003 Democratic National Committee debate in Des Moines, Iowa, Sharpton said: "I don't just quote Dr. King, I started my career as a young organizer in a movement he started." Sharpton feels both entitled and obliged to raise issues of race and racism in the dialogue of the Democratic Party and the nation.

In the Democratic National Committee debate Sharpton expressed concern that the party was trying to become "Republican-like" and increasingly took the African American vote for granted. In memorable closing remarks at the 2004 Democratic primary debate sponsored by the Black Caucus Institute and Fox News in Detroit, Sharpton repeated a line he used often in the primaries, saying that the Democrats were elephants wearing donkey jackets. He then added: "I intend to slap this donkey, the Democratic Party, until this donkey kicks George Bush out of the White House next November!" At the 2003 CNBC/Wall Street Journal Democratic debate in New York City, Sharpton again used humor to get a reform message across to the Democrats. Addressing General Wesley Clark, a Democratic presidential candidate who had joined the party shortly before the primaries, Sharpton said: "[A]s the only New Yorker, I want to welcome General Wesley Clark to New York, and I want to welcome him to our list of candidates. And don't be defensive about just joining the party. . . . It's better to be a new Democrat that's a real Democrat than a lot of old Democrats up here that have been acting like Republicans all along."

Sharpton connected this perceived move to the political right with a criticism of the Democratic Party's commitment to African American voters. At the 2003 Congressional Black Caucus Democratic presidential candidates debate in Baltimore, he got his message across by using an interpersonal metaphor to discuss the Democratic Party's failures concerning the African American community:

> I think we need to take the Democratic Party home to our daddies and discuss marriage or a break-up. I think that it's time. And I think it's time to do that based on issues. When I look around this country and see where we see double-digit unemployment in black communities, where we see that we're four times more likely to go to jail for the same crime, and we cannot get the Democrats to deal with it. You know, the only thing I never got over

in life is I took a young lady to a dance when I was in high school and she left with somebody else. And that's what the Democrats, some, have done to the black community. We helped take you to the dance and you leave with right wingers, you leave with people that you say are swing voters, you leave with people that are antithetical to our history and antithetical to our interests. I am saying in 2004, if we take you to the party, you're going home with us or we're not taking you to the party.

Finally, Sharpton demonstrated an ability to adjust his party reform message to a labor audience at the 2003 AFL–CIO Working Families Presidential Forum in Chicago. Saying that the Democratic Party must stand up for its core— labor and minorities—instead of treating them like special interests, Sharpton legitimated his candidacy on the basis of his activist past: "Since my pre-teenage years, I have fought in the area of corporate accountability and civil rights." He added that forty years after King's "I Have a Dream" speech, we still see gaps between rich and poor, and still live in a country that will not deal equally with labor. Criticizing the Democrats for moving away from progressive politics, Sharpton wryly let the audience in on the "secret" that he was the conservative on stage: "I'm fighting to conserve Roe versus Wade, to conserve affirmative action, to conserve workers' rights to organize. . . . We must conserve what we've won in the last fifty years."

Adding to a reform message built on humor and civil rights commitments, Sharpton once again displayed his talent for raising racial consciousness in biting critiques of his fellow Democrats. The most prominent and publicized example came when Sharpton attacked Howard Dean during the 2004 Black–Brown Democratic presidential debate in Des Moines for "lecturing" about race during the primaries, yet not hiring any minorities for senior policy positions during his time as governor of Vermont. After being criticized for "blowing up" a racial debate by the only other minority candidate in the Democratic primary, Carol Moseley Braun, Sharpton claimed moral authority: based on his activism against police brutality and racial discrimination, his effort to hold Dean accountable was justified. The most memorable lines of this exchange came when Sharpton criticized Dean for talking about his endorsements rather than his record on the issue: "I think you only need co-signers if your credit is bad."

Though he has tried to "reinvent" himself as a more measured politician, Sharpton has not left his past as an activist for racial consciousness behind. This was evident throughout the 2004 Democratic primaries, whether he was talking about inequality in trade policy, criticizing the Confederate battle flag as a symbol of racism, or protesting the war with Iraq. As an orator in the 2004 campaign, Sharpton had substantially increased his ability to make complex and effective comments on policy issues. In part, this was due to his utilization of metaphor and analogy to frame issues. Two examples make this point.

First, during the 2004 primary Sharpton described America as being in a state of "nonmilitary civil war." At the 2003 Congressional Black Caucus Democratic presidential candidates debate in Baltimore, for example, he used the metaphor to describe why he was running for president: "We are witnessing a nonmilitary civil war. It started with the recount in Florida, it went to the redistricting in Texas, now it's the recount in California . . . we need to fight back. I'm a man of action. And unlike Schwarzenegger, I never had a stunt man do my hard work." Through the figure of the nonmilitary civil war Sharpton tied together major themes from his speaking career to make significant policy commentary. The Florida recount and Texas redistricting cases referenced Sharpton's ongoing work with minority voter disenfranchisement, again raising consciousness of racial inequality, and his self-reference as a man of action served to reinforce his legitimacy as a career activist.

Sharpton also successfully used a medical analogy to criticize the Bush administration's claims that the economy was recovering. During the Brown–Black debate in Des Moines, he compared Bush's claims of economic recovery to a hospital setting where the doctors and nurses have a cold, get over the cold, and call it a recovery. "But the sick people are still sick," Sharpton quipped. "So you've got some of the

managers of America recovering, but those that are ill are just as sick as they ever was." Sharpton concluded: "Recovery is not for the staff. Recovery is for the patients. The patients, Mr. Bush, are still sick." The analogy between medical and economic "recovery" allowed Sharpton to highlight race and class inequalities he claimed persist in the economy's improvement. The analogy also worked as an overall race/class criticism of the Bush administration's economic policies. Throughout the Democratic primaries, for example, Sharpton claimed that Bush had not provided a tax "cut" for the nation but a tax "shift" that benefited the wealthy. Both of these examples illustrate Sharpton's ability to combine his well-known flamboyance and memorable phrasing with substantive policy commentary.

By combining the rhetorical skills of his activist past with an increasingly effective reform message, Sharpton may be acquiring the legitimacy he desires as a political candidate and civil rights leader. Both his detractors and his supporters have been less apt to question his intelligence and speaking ability than to criticize some of the decisions he has made in his past. While some of those decisions, such as his advocacy in the Tawana Brawley case, still partially undermine Sharpton's hopes for mainstream legitimacy, he has carefully reconstructed his image through speech and appears to have a real chance of improving his reputation as his mistakes from the mid-1980s recede further into the background. Al Sharpton has become a speaker who can call upon a life of civil rights activism and utilize the stylistic talents of a "boy wonder" preacher to craft social and political criticisms.

Depending on one's sympathies, Sharpton is either a racially divisive figure or a vital leader who brings a racial consciousness to politics. Either way, he is not likely to ignore his "call" to leadership. As he himself concluded in the 2004 Brown–Black debate:

> we still have institutional discrimination in this country, which is worse than blatant discrimination. What is hurting us is that [fifty] years ago we had to watch out for people with white sheets, now they have on pinstriped suits. And they discriminate against our advancement, they discriminate against our achievement, and

we're called divisive if we bring it up. We're divisive if we don't bring it up. Our fathers had to fight Jim Crow, we've got to fight James Crow, Jr., Esquire, and we need to take on that fight.

INFORMATION SOURCES

Research Collections and Collected Speeches

Al Sharpton's speeches have not been collected in a single location; rather, researchers can obtain some full texts of speeches online and through library databases such as LexisNexis. Some speech fragments are in various media sources.

Web Sites

George Washington University's *Democracy in Action*. This section of George Washington University's Web site has biographical information and links to articles and interviews pertaining to Sharpton. http://www.gwu.edu?~action/2004/sharpton.html

Project Vote Smart [*VS*]. This site includes a collection of full texts of some of Sharpton's speeches and public statements from the 2004 presidential campaign. www.vote-smart.org

Selected Critical Studies

Gourevitch, Philip. "The Crown Heights Riot and Its Aftermath." *Commentary*, January 1993, pp. 29–34.

Mandery, Evan J. *The Campaign: Rudy Giuliani, Ruth Messinger, Al Sharpton, and the Race to Be Mayor of New York City*. Boulder, Colo.: Westview Press, 1999.

"Race Relations. Al Sharpton Tamed." *The Economist*, February 14, 1998, p. 31.

Scherer, Ron. "Echoes of the Brawley Case: Accused Becomes the Accuser." *Christian Science Monitor*, July 13, 1998, p. 3.

Sherman, Scott. "He Has a Dream." *The Nation*, April 2001, pp. 11–18.

Toobin, Jeffrey. "The Unasked Question: Why the Diallo Case Missed the Point." *The New Yorker*, March 2000, "Annals of Law sec.," p. 38.

White, Jack E. "Big Al's Finest Hour." *Time*, March 6, 2000, pp. 28–30.

Selected Biographies

Sharpton, Al, and Karen Hunter. *Al On America*. New York: Dafina Books, 2002.

Sharpton, Al, and Anthony Walton. *Go and Tell Pharaoh: The Autobiography of the Reverend Al Sharpton*. New York: Doubleday, 1996.

CHRONOLOGY OF MAJOR SPEECHES

See "Research Collections and Collected Speeches" for source code.

"Democratic Presidential Debate." Columbia, S.C., May 3, 2003. Transcript available at www.lexis.com; *VS*.

"Human Rights Campaign Forum with the Democratic Candidates for President of the United States." Washington, D.C., July 15, 2003. Available at www.lexis.com; *VS*.

"AFL–CIO Working Families Presidential Forum." Chicago, August 5, 2003. Available at www.lexis.com; *VS*.

"Congressional Black Caucus Democratic Presidential Candidates Debate." Baltimore, Md., September 9, 2003. Available at www.lexis.com; *VS*.

"CNBC/Wall Street Journal Democratic Candidates Debate." New York City, September 25, 2003. Available at www.lexis.com; *VS*.

"Democratic National Committee, Arizona Democratic Party, and CNN Sponsored Presidential Debate." Phoenix, Ariz., October 9, 2003. Available at www.lexis.com; *VS*.

"Democratic Presidential Candidates Debate Sponsored by the Congressional Black Caucus Institute and Fox News Channel." Detroit, Mich., October 26, 2003. Available at www.lexis.com; *VS*.

"America Rocks the Vote Democratic Presidential Candidates Forum." Boston, November 4, 2003. Available at www.lexis.com; *VS*.

"Democratic National Committee Debate." Des Moines, Iowa, November 24, 2003. Available at www.lexis.com; *VS*.

"Democratic Presidential Debate in Durham, N.H." December 9, 2003. Available at www.lexis.com; *VS*.

"Brown–Black Democratic Presidential Candidates Debate." Des Moines, Iowa, January 11, 2004. Available at www.lexis.com; *VS*.

"The Union Leader and ABC News Democratic Presidential Candidates Debate." Manchester, N.H., January 22, 2004. Available at www.lexis.com; *VS*.

"Democratic Presidential Candidates Debate Sponsored by the Young Democrats of South Carolina and Furman University." Greenville, S.C., January 29, 2004. Available at www.lexis.com; *VS*.

"Wisconsin Presidential Candidates Debate." Milwaukee, Wis., February 15, 2004. Available at www.lexis.com; *VS*.

"Speech to the Democratic National Convention." New York City, July 28, 2004. Available at www.dems2004.org; www.nytimes.com

GLORIA STEINEM (1934–)
Founder of Ms Magazine, Feminist Activist

LISA SHAWN HOGAN

Gloria Steinem's life has been filled with irony and—some might say—contradictions. Having overcome a paralyzing fear of public speaking, she has spent the period from the 1970s on addressing audiences from college campuses to the U.S. Congress. Although her motto is "Express, don't persuade," most of her speeches—even on ceremonial occasions—have argued vigorously for women's rights. Outside observers have long viewed Steinem as a confident, even aggressive, public advocate. In 1992, however, she published a personal memoir, *Revolution from Within*, detailing her battles against anxiety and low self-esteem. The contradictions of Steinem's personal life reflect, in a sense, the complexities of the feminist cause with which she has been identified.

Steinem's unconventional upbringing taught her independence and empathy—values that she brought to the feminist cause. Born on March 25, 1934, in Toledo, Ohio to a mentally unstable mother and a financially irresponsible father, Steinem learned early to depend on herself. Her father, Leo, was a restless entrepreneur whose business schemes often left the family near poverty. When she was a young girl, Steinem's family owned a struggling summer resort in Michigan and traveled to California or Florida every winter to escape the cold weather. In grade school Steinem attended school sporadically; some years she hardly went at all. After her parents separated in 1944, she was forced to take care of her mother. She spent her teenage years back in Toledo, where she was a lackluster student. Working two jobs to support her mother and herself left little time for schoolwork, but Steinem was a curious student and an avid reader.

Despite her average high school grades and SAT scores, Steinem's high school guidance counselor recognized her potential and helped her with her college applications. In 1952 she was accepted to Smith College, a prestigious private women's college in Northampton, Massachusetts. Smith strove for geographic and economic diversity, so Steinem's working-class background worked to her advantage. Steinem proved to be an excellent student at Smith. She was elected to Phi Beta Kappa and graduated magna cum laude in 1956 with a degree in government. After graduation Steinem discovered that she was pregnant. Convinced that motherhood would destroy her independence (not to mention her reputation), she contemplated suicide and eventually obtained an abortion—an event that would influence her attitude toward reproductive rights over the next thirty years. Soon after her graduation, Steinem accepted a two-year fellowship to study in India, where she traveled around the country with followers of the late Mahatma Gandhi.

In the late 1950s and early 1960s, Steinem was a struggling freelance journalist. Even today she considers herself first and foremost a journalist, despite the fact that she spends most of her time speaking. In 1963, Steinem published her famous exposé of the New York Playboy Club, "A Bunny's Tale," in *Show* magazine. The article revealed the exploitation of the Bunnies and detailed the day-to-day humiliations of the job. Nevertheless, she believed that the article damaged her reputation as a serious journalist and stereotyped her as a former Bunny.

In 1971 Steinem helped found *Ms* magazine, and she has contributed articles to the magazine ever since. In 1983 she published *Outrageous Acts and Everyday Rebellions*, which consisted primarily of articles reprinted from *Ms*. The book became an instant best-seller and was followed in 1992 by the publication of her memoir, *Revolution from Within*. In 1994 she published *Moving Beyond Words*, which addressed a number of personal and political issues, including eating disorders, women and aging, and Steinem's personal struggles to keep *Ms* magazine afloat in the 1970s. Steinem's books have sold well, although some experts criticized *Revolution from Within* for its psychological advice to women.

In the late 1960s, Steinem began her career as a professional lecturer, speaking on women's rights and civil rights across the country. Her most controversial speeches were delivered early in her career, when she often talked about politics and advocated controversial reforms. In the 1970s, Steinem's speeches often provoked controversy and heated debates. In the 1980s and 1990s, however, she delivered mostly commencement addresses, and her views sounded more mainstream. Today, at the age of seventy-one, Steinem continues to lecture and give commencement addresses around the country. Appearing at approximately five events a month, she speaks on a broad array of feminist issues. Now, however, she places more emphasis on electoral politics than social protest, and instead of advocating revolution, she encourages young women to vote.

GLORIA STEINEM: CELEBRATING FEMINIST VALUES

Although Gloria Steinem prefers to think of herself as a writer, she has difficulty turning down invitations to deliver public speeches, especially opportunities to speak to young women. She earns up to $12,000 for a single speech. She prepares her addresses without the aid of speechwriters and typically speaks extemporaneously from roughly sketched notes. Tailoring her messages to the immediate concerns of her audiences, she delivers speeches that are often sprinkled with local stories and familiar examples.

Steinem's intelligence, quick wit, and pointed retorts appeal to audiences and the media alike. As biographer Carolyn Heilbrun observed, Steinem speaks quietly, gently, and with a certain graciousness. Biographer Syndey Ladensohn Stern described her as "unfailingly courteous," and another observer characterized her style as "feminine mildness." Steinem refuses to talk down to her audience, but she also scorns intellectual posturing and jargon. As she explained it in *Outrageous Acts and Everyday Rebellions*, "[a]cademic and other generalized language often

obfuscates, distances, and removes insight and information." Steinem's style is clear, direct, and unpedantic. Yet, because of her feminist views, she has often been seen as a controversial figure and her speeches have sometimes provoked heated debate.

Although audience members describe Steinem as eloquent and poised, she had to work hard to overcome a fear of public speaking. Early in her career, she called "standing up to give a whole speech unaided" the "stuff of nightmares." She once told a reporter from the *Washington Post* that she sometimes felt in a "catatonic state" before taking the stage to deliver a speech. Her fears have abated over the years, although she still has occasional bouts of anxiety. As she now explains her attitude toward public speaking, "You do not die from it, however awful it feels."

In May 1970 Steinem appeared before the Senate Subcommittee on Constitutional Amendments, testifying in support of the Equal Rights Amendment. Reading from a manuscript, she refuted the "out-dated myths" used to prove the inferiority of women. Steinem also articulated a variety of other themes that would become the mainstays of her public speeches: women are not biologically inferior to men, women are mistreated in the workforce, and child rearing is not solely a woman's job. Concluding her testimony with a fierce attack on President Nixon, Steinem maintained that a "masculine mystique" had corrupted the entire Nixon administration, and she urged Congress to support a peaceful end to the hostilities in Vietnam. Not surprisingly, some thought Steinem's partisan attack on the president detracted from her credibility as an advocate of the ERA.

In 1970 Steinem delivered the first of her many commencement addresses. Speaking at Vassar College in Poughkeepsie, New York, she defined feminism as a broad, humanistic movement, and she called for the elimination of all forms of oppression, whether rooted in gender, race, or class. She invited men to join the movement and suggested that feminism would liberate both sexes. She assured the men in her audience that she did not "want to prove the superiority of one sex to another." "That," she concluded, "would only be repeating the masculine mistake." Instead, she urged her audience to envision an alternative society without prescribed gender roles. Using a line that she would repeat for decades, Steinem concluded that the "first problem for all of us, men and women, is not to learn but to unlearn." In her speech at Vassar, Steinem also lamented women's unequal treatment in the workforce and urged the graduates to support economic reforms. "The truth is," she observed, "that a woman with a college education working full-time makes less than a black man with a high school degree." She also noted that women were "only 6 percent of all the people in the country receiving $10,000 a year or more." Finally, Steinem blamed the country's social problems on the "masculine mystique" and urged her audience to create a "human, compassionate alternative" to violence and war. Again denouncing the Nixon administration's policies in Vietnam, she concluded that Nixon's "manhood somehow depends on the subjugation of other people."

Some audience members praised Steinem's polemical commencement address; others considered it inappropriate. At Smith, many parents and alumnae walked out during the address, and afterward some wrote angry letters to the school newspaper. To make matters worse, Steinem had sent the president of Smith College an advance draft of the speech but delivered a much more polemical version. Although Steinem insisted that she departed only slightly from the original draft, the administration of the college claimed they had been duped. Whatever the case, Steinem clearly had violated traditional conventions of commencement speeches, yet she made no effort to apologize or to appease her critics.

On May 12, 1972, Steinem delivered a very different sort of speech to a skeptical audience at the U.S. Naval Academy. Steinem and civil rights activist Dorothy Pitman were invited to speak to more than 4,000 midshipmen and an ad-

---

Gloria Steinem was one of the first modern feminists to include men in her definition of feminism. She defines feminism as "the belief in the whole social, political and economic equality of women and men. Obviously, women and men can and should be feminists."

Steinem's commencement address at Smith College in 1971, "The Politics of Women," proved even more controversial. Using the platform to deliver a provocative political speech, Steinem called for equal pay for women in the workforce, invoked a feminist version of history (what she called a "gynecocracy"), called for sisterhood among women of all ages and races, and attacked racism and sexism in all realms of social, political, and economic life. Going beyond these general principles, she defined illegal abortions as "our number one health problem" and urged liberalization of antiabortion laws. She even attacked the Smith curriculum, suggesting that the historians, political scientists, and religious scholars on the faculty perpetuated sexist and racist views. Steinem concluded the speech with her familiar depiction of President Nixon as a warmonger caught up in the "masculine mystique."

ditional 2,000 civilians. Lecturing her audience on the role of women in history, Steinem challenged the history that the cadets had learned in their classes with a feminist interpretation of the past. Women, she claimed provocatively, had ruled the world from 12000 to 8000 B.C., and the modern idea of patriarchy was a relatively new phenomenon. It was only a matter of time, she insisted, before women's leadership would be recognized and restored. Although speaking to a predominantly male audience—and a naval one at that—Steinem voiced pacifist sentiments as she lamented the country's involvement in the Vietnam War, and she even poked fun at the midshipmen, calling them part of a "jockocracy." Pointing to women's inequality in the workforce, Steinem implied that the men in her audience, were to blame as part of the masculine mystique. She concluded that the women's movement was not about reform, but instead called for a "revolution." Not surprisingly, the audience responded with occasional jeers and hostile remarks during the question-answer period that followed the speech. Steinem later admitted to a reporter from the *Washington Post* that the experience had been grueling.

Not all of Steinem's early speeches were controversial. In a 1973 commencement address at Simmons College, a private women's school in Boston, her tone was less combative and her characteristic humor and wit were more evident. Speaking to a friendly audience, she seemed relaxed and joked easily with the graduates. Identifying with her listeners, Steinem frequently referred to the graduates as "sisters" and "partners" in a common struggle. She again cited statistics to prove discrimination against women in the workforce, and although she again defined her goal as "revolution," her ideas were not very radical. Steinem's "humanistic revolution" really amounted to little more than equal pay for equal work. In a plea for unity, Steinem assured the males in the audience that feminism was not antimale. To the contrary, she insisted, the ultimate goal of feminism was to "humanize the roles for both of us" and to "liberate individuality."

As Steinem reached middle age, she became less of a provocateur and more of a sage. In her commencement addresses in the 1980s, she typically encouraged graduates to learn from both her successes and her mistakes, and she became more reflective and philosophical, often elaborating on the theme "What I know now that I wish I'd known then." With the country no longer divided over the Vietnam War, Steinem generally avoided controversial and provocative issues, and instead dispensed common-sense advice and expressed optimism about the future, consistent with the conventions of the commencement address. Rather than provoke audiences, Steinem now sprinkled her commencement speeches with humorous anecdotes and professed her love of graduation ceremonies. She noted the progress of feminism in the past twenty years, and she envisioned the global spread of feminism in the future.

Steinem's 1987 commencement address at Tufts University in Medford, Massachusetts,

typified the lighter tone of her addresses in the 1980s. She began with a humorous salutation:

> Faculty with tenure. Faculty without tenure. Parents and families of graduates. Stepparents and chosen family of graduates—and anyone else who helped pay the bills. Friends and lovers of graduates (you know who you are). Also students who will someday graduate, and people who just stopped by to watch because, like me, they are commencement junkies. Staff members who house, feed and maintain all of the above, as well as prepare for the ceremony. And most of all, graduates, co-conspirators and subversives—Those who were born before June 1, 1965, and those born after.

Recalling her own college commencement some thirty years earlier, Steinem admitted that she did not "remember *one single thing* my own commencement speaker said." At the time, she confessed, she was more concerned with "how my friends would get on with my family, and vice versa; about how I was going to pack four years of possessions into one car; and about how I was *not* going to get married to the very tempting man I was then engaged to." With self-deprecating humor, Steinem recalled how, as a young girl, she thought her fame would come as a dancer, not as a political activist. She disclosed that her greatest ambition as a young woman was "to dance her way out of Toledo, Ohio, and into the hearts of Americans." Yet Steinem still sounded political themes at her address at Tufts. She no longer attacked the president or criticized American foreign policy, but she did urge her audience to invest in social change. Urging her listeners to recognize politics in their own lives, Steinem declared: "Anytime one human being is habitually powerful over another, or one group over another, not because of talent or experience, but because of race, or sex, or class, *that's politics*." Politics, she concluded, "is not just what goes on in the electoral system or in Washington."

By the mid-1980s Steinem could point to a number of positive changes that feminism had brought about over the preceding decade. In a commencement address at Wheaton College in 1986, for example, she recalled just a few of the achievements for which feminists could take credit: there were more university classes in women's studies, Black studies, and Native American history; more women were calling themselves feminists (she cited a *Newsweek* poll claiming that 60 percent of women embraced the label); more women worked in traditionally male professions; and marriages had become much more equal. "Yes, marriage is far more equal now," Steinem observed. "You are less likely to lose your name, your credit rating, your legal residence, and other civil rights, and even less likely to be doing the housework all alone." This, she proclaimed, was the "good news." Still, much work remained to be done in what she termed the "second stage" of the feminist struggle. Shifting to family issues, she emphasized the problems of unequal parenting, domestic violence, and the lack of affordable day care. Steinem referred to herself as a leader of the "Revolutionary Feminist Government in Exile," but in fact she had become the voice of mainstream feminism.

In her later years, Steinem expanded her notion of "sisterhood" to a global scale. In her commencement address at Wheaton, a well-known Christian liberal arts college, she lamented that "women do not even examine the policies of other countries toward their sisters," and observed that the topic of women in developing countries was apparently "off-limits," even among feminists. Recognizing the limited perspective of most college students, she urged young women to empathize with "all of the women of the Middle East who cannot leave their countries, perhaps even their houses, without patriarchal permission," as well as those "women political prisoners whose spirit is broken by being forced to bear the children of their torturers." Using pathos to build empathy for abused and oppressed women around the world, Steinem urged her audience to become involved politically, not just in their own communities but as citizens of the world. As in most commencement speeches, Steinem's ultimate message was one of hope. Invoking the memory of Martin Luther King Jr., Steinem concluded her commencement address at Wheaton with the metaphor of a "dream": "You have a dream. You are one of the first generations that have not had the dream taken away. The reality is

very different, but with the dream you have the possibility of changing reality. . . . It is the future. It is you."

By the 1990s, Steinem had become a seasoned public speaker. Having produced two best-selling books, she was also a respected and popular writer. Seemingly uncomfortable with her "star" status, she sometimes rejected the formality of platform speaking in favor of more casual discussions. In a lecture at Salem (Massachusetts) State University in 1993, for example, she asked for her audience's help in "overcoming this old-fashioned structure of you looking at each other's backs and me looking back at you." Rejecting what she called the "hierarchal structure" of the speech situation, she invited audience members to stand up and make "organizing announcements of any upcoming trouble-making meetings you think this group should know about." Then she added, "If you'd rather not say it yourself, pass me a note. I'm leaving early in the morning, I'll read anything." Steinem took the same approach at Hobart and William Smith colleges in 1996. "I want us generally to really learn from each other," she said, "and turn this into what every meeting should be, which is an organizing meeting."

Steinem's most recent speeches have been more philosophical and reflective than the controversial speeches of her early days. Speaking again at Hobart and William Smith colleges in 1998, Steinem sounded like a transcendentalist philosopher as she celebrated the "laws of connectedness" that unite women of all races, ages, and backgrounds. Attempting to empower the graduates while revealing her connection to them, she reflected on how seemingly insignificant acts of nature create monumental changes. The "flap of a butterfly's wing," she argued, "can change the weather hundreds of miles away. Think of the power that it gives each of us in each of our actions, in each of our choices." Steinem concluded her speech by celebrating that connection as she congratulated the graduates: "Good luck. We'll be together no matter where you are."

Yet, while Steinem may have become more of a philosopher than a rebel in recent years, her speeches still have a feminist political edge. In her lecture at Salem State University, for example, she continued her lifelong effort to rewrite history from a feminist perspective, proclaiming that it is "endlessly, endlessly interesting to look at history whole instead of half." She lamented that "the female half of the world, whatever our race or ethnicity or sexuality or class," has been "treated with great invisibility" in conventional histories. She took the opportunity on this occasion to celebrate Joan of Arc—a woman who, Steinem claimed, had been killed for exercising male power. Steinem offered an even more radical interpretation of women in history as she celebrated the notorious witches in Salem as "freedom fighters."

On September 3, 2000, at the age of sixty-six, Steinem shocked supporters and detractors alike when she married David Bale, an antiapartheid activist whom she met at a Voters for Choice benefit. Bale died of cancer in December 2003. As she reaches her seventy-first birthday, Steinem continues to advocate reproductive freedom, workplace equality, and changes in the family structure to allow for equal parenting. She has devoted increasingly more time to exposing abuses against women throughout the developing world, including such difficult topics as genital mutilation. She also has continued to rewrite history from a feminist perspective, most recently in a *Ms* magazine article titled "Remember Our Power." Reminding her readers that patriarchy is a relatively recent phenomenon, Steinem insisted that "[t]here was another way." Sounding like a Zen philosopher, she called for "balance: between females and males, between each person, and the community between nature and humans."

In a commencement address at Webster University in 1978, Steinem confided: "One initial problem for me was learning to speak in public. That's a great problem, I think, for women in general." Obviously, Steinem overcame that problem, and her example has been an inspiration to countless other women. Yet her contributions reach well beyond the inspiration she has provided to individual women. As biographer Carolyn Heilbrun concluded, her name is so closely identified with the changes that feminism has brought to American life that "she is, like the mythical Kilroy of World War II, essential and ubiquitous: Steinem was here."

INFORMATION SOURCES

Research Collections and Collected Speeches

Gloria Steinem's papers are housed at Smith College in Northampton, Massachusetts. They are part of a special collection titled Agents of Social Change, and include the largest collection of audiovisual materials. More information on the collection, including contact information, is at http://www.smith.edu/libraries/libs/ssc/exhibit/steinem.html

Steinem, Gloria. "I Was a Playboy Bunny," reprint of "A Bunny's Tale." In her *Outrageous Acts and Everyday Rebellions*, 2nd ed. New York: Holt, 1995.

———. "Remember Our Power." *Ms*, Summer 2003. Available at http://www.msmagazine.com

Web Sites

A&E Biography. http://search.biography.com/print_record.pl?id=19738. This Web site has short biographies of celebrities and famous activists, including Steinem. Visitors to the site can order VHS or DVD recordings of the network program *Biography*.

Glass Ceiling Biographies. http://www.theglassceiling.com/biographies/bio32.htm. This Web site has biographical information on Steinem, emphasizing how even famous women face a glass ceiling that impedes their progress in the professional world. There is also a list of further readings on Steinem.

National Women's History Project. http://www.nwhp.org/tlp/biographies/steinem/steinem_bio.html. This Web site lists the key accomplishments in Steinem's life and includes a detailed bibliography of her writings.

Women in American History. http://search.eb.com/women/articles/Steinem_Gloria.html. In addition to obtaining some basic biographical information, visitors to this site can hear a speech, "Reproductive Freedom," delivered by Steinem at a National Organization for Women rally in 1986.

Audiovisual Materials

Gloria Steinem: Ms America. New York: A&E Home Video, 1995. Videocassette available at www.biography.com and at 169 libraries.

Gloria Steinem: A Woman's Progress. Princeton, N.J.: Films for the Humanities, 1994. Videocassette available at 71 libraries.

Greatest Speeches of All Time. Includes Steinem's speech "The End of the Vietnam War." Los Angeles: NewStar, 1998. Audiocassette available at 62 libraries.

Great Speeches of the 20th Century: Dreams and Realities. Includes Steinem's speech "On Releasing the Watergate Tapes." Los Angeles: Rhino/World Beat, 1994. Videocassette available at 77 libraries.

Intimate Portrait: Gloria Steinem. New York: Lifetime Productions, 1998. Videocassette available at 24 libraries.

Papers of Gloria Steinem [*PGS*]. Smith College, Northampton, Mass. This is the largest collection of audiovisual materials on Steinem.

Critical Study

Perkins, Sally. "The Myth of the Matriarchy: Annulling Patriarchy Through the Regeneration of Time." *Communication Studies* 42 (1991): 371–82.

Selected Biographies

Heilbrun, Carolyn G. *The Education of a Woman: The Life of Gloria Steinem.* New York: Dial, 1995.

Steinem, Gloria. *Moving Beyond Words.* New York: Simon and Schuster, 1994.

———. *Outrageous Acts and Everyday Rebellions*, 2nd ed. New York: Holt, 1995.

———. *Revolution from Within: A Book of Self-Esteem.* Boston: Little, Brown, 1992.

Stern, Sydney Ladensohn. *Gloria Steinem: Her Passions, Politics, and Mystique.* Secaucus, N.J.: Carol Publishing Group, 1997.

CHRONOLOGY OF MAJOR SPEECHES

See "Research Collections and Collected Sources" for source code.

"Testimony Before the Senate Hearings on the Equal Rights Amendment." Washington, D.C., May 6, 1970. In *American Rhetorical Discourse*, 2nd ed., ed. Ronald Reid. Prospect Heights, Ill.: Waveland Press, 1995.

"Living the Revolution." Vassar College, Poughkeepsie, N.Y., 1970. *PGS.*

"Commencement Address." Smith College, Northampton, Mass., May 1971. Available at http://smith.alumnae.net/homepages/Classes/1971/gloria.html

"Speech at the U.S. Naval Academy." Annapolis, Md., May 12, 1972. In *Critical Anthology of Public Speeches*, comp. Kathleen M. Jamieson. Palo Alto Calif.: Science Research Associates, 1978.

"Commencement Address" (Simons College). Boston, 1973. *PGS.*

"Lecture" (College of Marin). Kentfield, Calif., October 1974. *PGS.*

"Lecture" (Webster College). St. Louis, Mo., 1978. *PGS.*

"Commencement Address" (Wheaton College). Wheaton, Ill., May 31, 1986. *PGS.*

"Commencement Address" (Bryn Mawr College). Bryn Mawr, Pa., 1988. *PGS.*

"Commencement Address" (Tufts University). Medford, Mass., May 17, 1987. Available at http://gos.sbc.edu/ and in *Contemporary American Public Discourse*, 3rd ed., ed. Halford Ross Ryan. Prospect Heights, Ill.: Waveland Press, 1992.

"Scholars, Witches and Other Freedom Fighters" (Salem State University). Salem, Mass., March 1993. Available at http://gos.sbc.edu/

"Commencement Address" (Wellesley College). Wellesley, Mass., May 28, 1993. Available at http://www.wellesley.edu/

"Education from the Inside Out" (Hobart and William Smith Colleges). Geneva, N.Y., February 19, 1996. Available at http://www.hws.edu/news/speakers/transcripts/steinemblackwell.asp

"Commencement Address" (Hobart and William Smith Colleges). Geneva, N.Y., June 14, 1998. Available at http://www.hws.edu/news/speakers/transcripts/steinemcomm1998.asp

GEORGE CORLEY WALLACE (1919–1998)
Four-Term Governor of Alabama

ANDREW KING

George Corley Wallace, four times governor of Alabama, produced two kinds of rhetoric. During the 1960s he was associated with demagogic anti-integration oratory; after being paralyzed by a would-be assassin's bullet during his presidential campaign of 1972, he was transformed into a "remorseful, colorblind civil rights sympathizer." Wallace's early rhetoric was fiery and unabashedly racist; his later speeches, inclusive and repentant. Oddly, the man whose rhetoric aroused our most ignoble fears became a symbol of racial healing and redemption. His political legacy, that "of the harbinger of the conservative groundswell that shaped recent American politics," is generally forgotten by liberals and unacknowledged by conservatives.

Wallace first came to national attention in 1963 when he concluded his First Inaugural Address as the Democratic governor of Alabama with the words "and so I say, segregation now, segregation tomorrow and segregation forever!" In the same speech he promised to stand in the schoolhouse door to prevent federally mandated integration of public schools in the state. In June 1963 he attempted to bar the admission of two Black students to the University of Alabama by "temporarily" blocking an entrance to the administration building. Nineteen years later, elected to a fourth term as governor of Alabama with substantial Black support, Wallace appointed a record number of African Americans to governmental positions and carried out an ambitious populist program. The story of the two decades between these events reveals as much about the transformation of the American South as it does about Wallace.

Wallace presided over a period of almost revolutionary change. When he came to office, Alabama's state politics was still dominated by an alliance of the Big Mules (Birmingham industrialists) and planters from the Black Belt counties. These two groups were vastly overrepresented at the polling booth, one farmer having the voting power of three to five urbanites. Both groups represented constituencies dedicated to slowing the pace of social and cultural change. Long before the end of Wallace's last term, however, this powerful alliance was defunct. Suburban growth and loss of population in the Black Belt counties, federally mandated reapportionment, the growth of an influential urban voting population, the 1965 Voting Rights Act, and federal court decisions on civil rights combined to change the political landscape. This is not to say that these changes resulted in a progressive and prosperous Alabama. Wallace and other governors simply made too many bad decisions. He made no move to change the unfair property tax system that his predecessors had sought to reform. While allowing massive resistance to bring about forced busing and the destruction of neighborhood schools, Wallace's gubernatorial support accelerated the founding and growth of private academies as more affluent parents snatched their children from the public schools. Using his wife, who had been diagnosed with cancer, to succeed him as governor while attempting to change the laws on gubernatorial succession damaged the image of the state. The growth of the great University of Alabama Medical Center in Birmingham and the space industry in Huntsville were financed by federal monies and driven by federal programs.

Late in his political life Wallace increased vocational-technical schools, expanded colleges, and wooed industry to the state with tax breaks and aggressive promotion, but he had missed the period of great economic opportunity, the 1960s and early 1970s, when population and resources made a rapid North/South shift. While other Southern states such as North Carolina, Georgia, and Florida were making their great leap forward, Alabama made only modest gains in closing the wide economic gap between itself and states in the North and the West. And by the 1980s, Alabama again began to fall behind the rest of the nation in teacher salaries, business expansion, and educational attainment.

It is tempting to say that the key to George Wallace's racism, fatalism, and populism can be found in Clio, Alabama, a rural town in Barbour County on the edge of the Black Belt. But the tiny family farm on which Wallace was born has long been absorbed into the huge mechanized factory farms of the "New South." The farm, purchased by Wallace's grandfather, the country doctor George Oscar Wallace, was not a successful enterprise. Wallace said of it, "The roof leaked. There was no electricity and there were no indoor sanitary facilities." The county had a long history of racial unrest. Not long after the expulsion of Native Americans from Alabama, Scotch–Irish Presbyterians took up land. Other immigrants from Tennessee and Georgia followed them, and finally the large planters came to clear vast tracts of land, dominating the area until the Civil War. Reconstruction temporarily enfranchised Blacks and built alliances between Republican whites and the freedmen, but the fragile populism was broken by racial demagoguery, and one-party rule was firmly established a decade before the close of the nineteenth century.

A good student with a deep interest in Southern history, Wallace quarterbacked his high school football team, and as a bantamweight won the Alabama Golden Gloves and went to the Southeastern Conference finals. After graduating from the University of Alabama Law School, he served in the Air Force from 1942 to 1945. Following his discharge, Wallace was appointed an assistant state's attorney. Subsequently, he was elected to two terms in the state legislature. He was judge of the Third Judicial Circuit of Alabama in 1953, and in 1957 went to Washington to testify against the Civil Rights Bill then pending in Congress. At that time he received national attention in a well-publicized clash with Emanuel Celler of New York.

GEORGE WALLACE: SEGREGATIONIST AND POPULIST

In 1958 Wallace ran for governor, opening his campaign with a salvo against the federal gov-

ernment: as a judge he had closed his court's records to civil rights investigations and he soon hoped to include voting records in his court order. Wallace lost the Democratic nomination to John Paterson, a strong supporter of segregation who had been endorsed by the Ku Klux Klan. Abandoning many of his moderate and progressive stands, Wallace became openly defiant of the U.S. Commission on Civil Rights investigation of Black voting rights. By the time he left his judicial post in 1959, Wallace had developed the segregationist and populist themes that would dominate his rhetoric for the next fifteen years. In stump speeches he began to refer to the South as "the Confederate States of America."

Wallace won the governorship of Alabama in 1962 on a platform of protecting segregation and populist issues. Within a few months he kept his pledge to stand in the schoolhouse door by blocking the enrollment of two Black students at the University of Alabama. His protest was wholly symbolic, for he quickly withdrew upon the arrival of the federalized National Guard. On the eve of the tremendous confrontation in Birmingham, Martin Luther King, Jr. called Wallace "perhaps the most dangerous racist in America today. I am not sure that he believes all the poison that he preaches, but he is artful enough to convince others that he does." Other confrontations at Huntsville, Anniston, and Mobile made Wallace the leading symbol of massive resistance to racial integration at all levels.

Wallace began his national odyssey of speaking tours in his first term as governor. He spent a great deal of time out of the state, adjusting his message to each particular audience: speaking about constitutional matters at Harvard and the forgotten white working class in Milwaukee. Wallace's presidential campaign in 1964 was memorable but poorly organized. At the Democratic National Convention he mounted a ferocious attack on the civil rights plank to which the platform committee did not even bother to respond.

Because Wallace was ineligible under state law for reelection, his first wife, Lurleen, ran for and won the governorship, only to die in office in 1968. In that year, Wallace became a successful third-party presidential candidate, winning 13 percent of the vote and five Southern states outright. As the nominee of the American Independent Party, he had drawn support largely from white Southerners and Northern blue-collar workers alienated by the cultural changes of the 1960s and the spending priorities of the Johnson administration.

In 1970 Wallace won the governorship again in an easy victory. In 1972, while campaigning for the Democratic presidential nomination, he was shot and permanently paralyzed below the waist in an assassination attempt at Laurel, Maryland. No longer bound by the state law prohibiting successive terms, Wallace won the governorship again in 1976 and again campaigned for the presidential nomination. His rhetoric was skewed away from race and more toward class grievances. He was a knight championing the working classes, denouncing the alliance of elitist intellectuals, arrogant federal bureaucrats, the Supreme Court, and

Medical School in Birmingham. He met with John Lewis, a veteran of hundreds of civil rights marches. Wallace asked Lewis for forgiveness, and the two men prayed together. No photographer or journalist was present. Later Wallace went to Martin Luther King Jr.'s Dexter Avenue Church in Montgomery and took part in a ceremony of healing and forgiveness. He shared the platform with Rev. Ralph Abernathy, Coretta Scott King spoke well of him, and a renewed and transformed Wallace was elected in 1983 with an astonishing 90 percent of the African American vote. Although he appointed African Americans to office at every level, his final term was lackluster, and Wallace was often too ill to do much work. His energy was gone, and he was often absent from the capital.

George Wallace's legacy is a mixed one. Howell Raines of the *New York Times* once noted: "He was the first politician of his generation to

---

George Wallace's most famous spoken line exemplifies his marriage of race appeals and populism. He declared at his first gubernatorial inaugural in 1962: "I draw the line in the dust and toss the gauntlet before the feet of tyranny, and so I say, segregation now, segregation tomorrow and segregation forever."

---

the dependent poor. In Wallace's mind the poor had become especially undeserving after two decades of being alternately romanticized and corrupted by their liberal patrons. But his message had lost its fire, and Wallace appeared to have lost his zeal and his driving purpose. He was often late for appearances, and some were canceled due to his poor health. After losing the Florida and North Carolina primaries by wide margins to fellow Southerner Jimmy Carter, he bowed out of the race with a fulsome endorsement. Dan T. Carter, his major biographer, noted, "Even when he did lash out, he seemed to have lost his touch." Wallace finally admitted that his presidential bids had always been a Don Quixote operation, and that however he reinvented himself, he would never be free of the taint of his segregationist past.

During 1978 Wallace began his quest for forgiveness. He became a consultant for the rehabilitation center of the University of Alabama

exploit the antipathy toward Washington that became a prime force in politics from coast to coast." He may also have exploited a reaction to the secular society that has become global. The rise of religious fundamentalism in the growth areas of the world; the ubiquity of ethnic struggle in the former Soviet Union, the Middle East, Asia, and Africa; and the deep sense of powerlessness that grips the former colonial world have brought to the fore tribal rhetorics that echo Wallace's early themes.

Wallace's rhetorical strategy during the 1960s and early 1970s was quintessential. He informed his audiences that even if he could not win the fight against segregation at any particular locale, he still might be able to delay the process long enough for a wave of antifederal reaction to sweep through the nation. Anyone who heard Wallace speak, as this writer did at several points during his career, might conclude that the governor was obsessed with two subjects: race relations and the South's colonial status in regard to the nation. But the same listener would also conclude that Wallace had not thought deeply about the two subjects until the final years of his career. He repeated the same stock phrases that had been uttered in the South since time out of mind. His stump speaking and lecture circuit oratory was not about analysis of intractable problems; rather, it sought to use these problems to create fear and resentment in large numbers of Americans. Although Wallace is often seen as a source of modern conservatism, he did not talk about empowering the audience to solve its problems, as Goldwater and Reagan did. He used the problems to demonstrate the powerlessness of the audience. His answer was less about local communal control than visceral suspicion of the federal government. The issue of communism allowed Wallace to knit together his images of sinister social engineering by federal bureaucrats with spineless defense of American interests abroad.

This writer witnessed a Wallace speech in Indianapolis in 1967 in which he threatened to drive over "any silver spooned brats who will lie down in front of our car" and to "turn the Vietnam War over to experts who know how to win it." Nearly everything Wallace said that afternoon brought down the house. People stamped their feet, clapped their hands wildly, and shouted like worshippers at a tent meeting: "Go tell 'em, Governor!" and "Hit 'em, George! Hit 'em again!" In March of that year, at the University of Minnesota, he overcame a few initial catcalls and jeers and within twenty minutes received the first of several standing ovations. These cheers occurred on one of the most radical campuses in the nation, a place where Hubert Humphrey was being denounced as Johnson's bagman. Within a few minutes Wallace had convinced the angry students that they were all victims of a sinister conspiracy of power-mad senators, generals, and bureaucrats. Wallace's image of a ruthless, power-mad government that ignored antiwar demonstrators as easily as it ignored the working- and middle-class taxpayers struck a chord in the youthful audience. He was a master at making people feel powerless.

Wallace made thousands of speeches during his forty-year career in politics. This writer heard him during three of his four decades. Wallace used stock themes throughout: race relations, local versus federal power, workers (producers) versus consumers, the hypocrisy of reformers and what he was the first to call "the liberal elite," "family," and what he referred to as "the integrity of neighborhoods." He was at his most creative when under attack by hecklers. His humorous answers appeared spontaneous, but they were part of a large and colorful repertoire. He was especially effective on campuses with "liberal" reputations because he so contradicted expectations. Students who had expected a fiery demagogue encountered a soft-spoken and humorous speaker who gave them truisms about constitutional rights and told charming stories about his humble beginnings.

Wallace's most famous speech is his 1963 Inaugural Address, an address that contained all the themes of his career before he was struck down by the would-be assassin's bullet. In his Inaugural Address he denounced the duplicity of the North. Comparing the Northern treatment of the South during Reconstruction to the American treatment of Europe following World War II, Wallace painted a picture of the North as an alien occupier, carrying out the old family romance of Northern oppression a century later: "There were no governmental hand-outs, no Marshall Plan aid, no coddling to make sure that our people would not suffer; instead the South was set upon by the vulturous carpet bagger and federal troops." These words, that could be read the next day in the *New York Times* as well as throughout the South, appeared in only slightly altered form in all four of his presidential campaigns.

According to political scientist Dan T. Carter, Wallace created code to talk about the politics of race, class envy, and fear of displacement that mainstream politicians such as Nixon and Agnew developed into a conservative idiom. This idiom spoke not of race but of private property, community control, neighborhood schools and union seniority. Wallace linked the fiscal conservatives of the boardroom with blue-collar whites and middle-class suburbanites whose homes and businesses ringed the inner cities. Although Wallace never gained national office, his success inspired

Richard Nixon's Southern strategy and ultimately created the huge conservative tide upon which Ronald Reagan gained the presidency. In this way, Wallace's oratory had a profound and enduring impact on political discourse, even if its heirs seldom acknowledge it.

INFORMATION SOURCES

Research Collections and Collected Speeches

The main archive for Wallace's collected speeches is at the University of Alabama Library. Other collections are at the Alabama Department of Archives and History, the Montgomery Library at Auburn University, the Special Collections at Emory Library of Emory University, and at the Archival and Manuscript section of the Birmingham Public Library. No useful collection of published speeches exists. A few books on public address contain scattered speeches, often condensed or heavily edited.

Wallace, George C. *Stand Up for America*. Garden City, N.Y.: Doubleday, 1976.

Web Site

University of Alabama archives Web page [*UAA*]. http://www.lib.ua.edu

Selected Critical Studies

Carlson, Jody. *George C. Wallace and the Politics of Powerlessness*. New Brunswick, N.J.: Transaction Books, 1981.

Carter, Dan. *The Politics of Rage: George Wallace, the Origins of the New Conservatism, and the Transformation of American Politics*, 2nd ed. Baton Rouge: Louisiana State University Press, 2000.

Clark, E. Culpepper. *The Schoolhouse Door: Segregation's Last Stand at the University of Alabama*. New York: Oxford University Press, 1993.

Clark, Wayne Addison. "An Analysis of the Relationship Between Anti-Communism and Segregationist Thought in the Deep South, 1948–1964." Ph.D. dissertation, University of North Carolina, 1976.

Fadley, Lawrence Dean. "George Wallace: Agitator Rhetorician. A Rhetorical Criticism of George Corley Wallace's 1968 Presidential Campaign." Ph.D. dissertation, University of Pittsburgh, 1974.

Grossman, Edward A. "Harvard Looks Back on Governor Wallace's Visit." *Harvard Alumni Bulletin* 66 (November 23, 1963): 3–5.

Makay, John Joseph. "The Speaking of Governor George C. Wallace in the 1964 Primary." Ph.D. dissertation, Purdue University, 1969.

McGill, Ralph. "George Wallace: Tradition of Demagoguery." *West Los Angeles Times Magazine*, December 16, 1967, pp. 8–11.

Permaloff, Anne, and Carl Grafton. *Political Power in Alabama: The More Things Change . . .* Athens: University of Georgia Press, 1995.

Robinson, Michael, and Clifford Zukin. "Television and the Wallace Vote." *Journal of Communication* 26 (Spring 1976): 79–83.

Saxon, John D. "Contemporary Southern Oratory: A Rhetoric of Hope Not Desperation." *Southern Speech Communication Journal* 40 (1975): 262–74.

Warnick, Barbara. "The Rhetoric of Conservative Resistance." *Southern Speech Communication Journal* 42 (1977): 256–73.

Selected Biographies

Canfield, James Lewis. *A Case of Third Party Activism: The George Wallace Campaign Worker and the American Independent Party*. Washington, D.C.: University Press of America, 1984.

Dorman, Michael. *The George Wallace Myth*. New York: Bantam Books, 1976.

Jones, Bill. *The Wallace Story*. Northport, Ala.: American Southern, 1966.

Wallace, George, Jr. (as told to James Gregory). *The Wallaces of Alabama: My Family*. Chicago: Follett, 1975.

CHRONOLOGY OF MAJOR SPEECHES

See "Research Collections and Collected Speeches" for source code.

"A Plan for Progress" (gubernatorial campaign address delivered at Montgomery City Hall). Montgomery, Ala., March 10, 1962. *UAA*.

"First Inaugural Address." Montgomery, Ala., January 14, 1963. *UAA*.

"The Real Story in Alabama" (speech at Harvard University). Cambridge, Mass., November 4, 1963. *UAA*.

"The Civil Rights Bill and Involuntary Servitude in 1964" (speech at the University of California Los Angeles). Los Angeles, January 9, 1964. *UAA*.

"Address to the National Press Club." Washington, D.C., June 4, 1964. *UAA*.

"Stand Up for America." Cleveland, Ohio, June 11, 1964. *UAA*.

"Address to the Alabama Education Association." Birmingham, Ala., March 18, 1965. *UAA*.

"Trust the People" (presidential campaign announcement). Montgomery, Ala., November 12, 1975. *UAA*.

ALYCE FAYE WATTLETON (1943–)
Nurse, Public Health Official, Planned Parenthood President

LORRAINE D. JACKSON

Throughout her tenure as the president of the Planned Parenthood Federation of America (PPFA) from 1978 to 1992, Alyce Faye Wattleton emerged as a leading spokesperson for the pro-choice movement. She redefined the abortion controversy from a moral question into an issue about personal choice and control. Her messages focused on reproductive planning and health and on the rights of women as autonomous decision-makers. Wattleton's leadership ability, talent for debate, and public speaking skills gained respect from supporters and adversaries alike. Lois Romano, writing in *Glamour*, remarked that "even pro-life activists concede she is everything you don't want in an opponent—articulate, strikingly telegenic, bright, and most importantly, messianic on this subject."

Faye Wattleton, as she prefers to be called, was born in St. Louis, Missouri, on July 8, 1943. Her father, George Wattleton, worked in a factory, and her mother, Ozie, was a minister in the fundamentalist Church of God. In an interview with Nancy Rubin for *Savvy Woman*, Wattleton discussed her childhood experiences: "I was raised by my parents to believe that it was my obligation to help those with less than I had. Although we were materially poor, the value of my family life was that there was a sense of achievement." Her drive to achieve was apparent at an early age. She entered Ohio State University at the age of sixteen, with the goal of becoming a missionary nurse, and graduated in 1964 with a bachelor's degree in nursing. In 1966, after working for two years as an instructor for new mothers, Faye entered Columbia University in New York. While working toward an M.S. in maternal and infant care, she completed an internship at Harlem Hospital. During that time, she was particularly affected by the suffering that faced disadvantaged women, many of whom tried to terminate pregnancies themselves in the absence of safe, legal abortions. For example,

Wattleton saw a seventeen-year-old die of kidney failure after the girl's mother injected a combination of Lysol and bleach into her daughter's uterus. Incidents such as these had a profound effect upon Wattleton's development.

After completing her M.S., Wattleton moved to Dayton, Ohio, where she became assistant director of the Montgomery County Combined Public Health District. Once again, she was confronted by frightened young women, botched abortions, and neglected children. As a result of these experiences, Wattleton turned her attention to becoming a different type of missionary. While in Dayton, she served on the board of directors for Planned Parenthood of Miami Valley; two years later she was asked to serve as executive director, a position she held for seven years. Prevention became an important focus. When asked by a reporter for *USA Today* why she joined Planned Parenthood, she replied, "Is it better to continue trying to save these children and those people who are injured and vulnerable, or to work for a world in which these conditions don't occur?"

The 1970s brought new personal and professional responsibilities for Wattleton. In 1973 she married social worker Franklin Gordon. Two years later, while pregnant with her daughter Felicia, she was elected chair of PPFA's National Executive Director's Council. In January 1978, she was chosen from among over 200 applicants to assume the presidency of PPFA, a position previously held only by white men. Wattleton became the first African American, the first woman, and the youngest president in the history of the organization. She set out to change the organization's image from one of conservatism to one of advocacy for women's reproductive freedom. During her first year, antiabortion extremists increased their firebombing attacks on abortion clinics, and Wattleton herself received death threats.

The 1980s were marked by continued struggles. In legal assaults on Planned Parenthood's services, the Reagan administration was cutting funding for family-planning services, requiring parental consent for contraceptives for teenagers, and imposing a "gag rule" that prevented federally funded clinics from counseling women on abortion, even if withholding such information endangered the woman's health. The Reagan administration also attempted to restrict access to reproductive services by forbidding foreign recipients of general family-planning funds to offer abortion counseling, referrals, or abortions, even when the abortion-related efforts were funded separately by private funds. Perhaps the most damaging legal attack for the pro-choice movement occurred in July 1989, when the Supreme Court's *Webster* ruling referred the issue of abortion to the state legislatures. Although this did not reverse *Roe v. Wade*, it meant that a woman's right to an abortion would have to be argued state by state. During this time, in her efforts to counter these legal rulings, Wattleton made public appearances on television and radio shows to debate right-to-lifers, established an Action Fund to increase lobbying efforts against the anti-choice movement, and mobilized high-profile pro-choice celebrities.

During President George H. W. Bush's term, she continued to fight the erosion of women's reproductive rights by challenging women to become involved in the political process and to protect their reproductive freedom. She explained to reporter Elizabeth Kolbert, writing for *Vogue*: "I think the pro-choice movement has done a good job of articulating the dangers . . . but how can you make people feel that those dangers imminently affect them? I don't know, except for women to start dying and filling up the hospital wards. I say to women all day long, 'you have a special responsibility.' I don't know how much plainer that can be."

Wattleton resigned from Planned Parenthood in 1992. Under her leadership, the organization's budget tripled to approximately $380 million. In 1993, she was honored by Planned Parenthood with its Margaret Sanger Award, and also inducted into the National Women's Hall of Fame. In 1996, she published her autobiography, *Life on the Line*. Today, she serves as president of the nonprofit Center for Gender Equality, sits on the boards of directors of numerous organizations, and continues to speak to various groups about women's equality, health care, and civil rights issues.

FAYE WATTLETON: SETTING THE AGENDA FOR WOMEN'S HEALTH

Faye Wattleton's competence is evidenced by her ability to adapt her message appropriately. On some occasions, her arguments are marked by emphatic, metaphorical examples and language; at other times, emphasis is placed on neutral language and well-informed, carefully reasoned arguments. Her ability to remain confident, focused, and unwavering in the face of powerful opposition is impressive. Additionally, her substantive messages are complemented by her elegance. Standing almost six feet tall, Wattleton has beauty, style, and poise that capture the attention of the media, and through her oratory she has developed into an influential political force. Today, she remains an articulate role model for women.

The themes of Wattleton's speeches have been influenced by external political, social, and legal events. In a speech titled "The End of the Reagan Era: The State of Worldwide Reproductive Rights," delivered in 1988 to the Commonwealth Club in San Francisco, Wattleton outlined the need for and status of family-planning efforts throughout the world. The speech demonstrated both the family-planning successes in developing countries such as Thailand and the necessity for efforts to be expanded in places such as sub-Saharan Africa, where it is not uncommon for women to have eight to ten unplanned children in their lifetime. After comparing the infant mortality rates of various countries, Wattleton explained that with adequate access to family planning, many unplanned pregnancies and maternal deaths would be preventable. Moreover, she explored the suffering that accompanies being unable to plan and support a family.

Statistical evidence reinforced Wattleton's main point as she illuminated the irony of the Reagan administration's anti-abortion effort. The "crippling restrictions" imposed on family-planning programs abroad, she argued, undermined the programs that provided contraceptives and prevented unwanted pregnancies—and, ultimately, abortions. Through her skillful use of logical appeals and dramatic metaphors she depicted the gravity of the situation: "Three and a half to four million people we serve are hanging by a thread. . . . if Planned Parenthood's program is de-funded, there will be 400,000 additional unwanted pregnancies, 70,000 additional abortions, and over 1,200 deaths from abortions." Both directly and through metaphors, she indicted the Reagan administration for violating human rights: "Many millions of people who suffer these horrors have been turned into political hostages by our own federal government," she noted, then warned that Planned Parenthood would pursue legal action.

Through careful word choice, Wattleton attempted to discredit her opponents and their policies. In one passage, she charged that "these regulations . . . are nothing more than transparent attempts to pay off the Administration's debt to a handful of anti-family-planning extremists, whose lust for sexual repression remains unfulfilled." As in the majority of her speeches, she did not refer to the opposition as "pro-life," but instead used descriptors such as "anti-family-planning extremists" or "anti-abortionists."

Ultimately, the purpose of this speech was to lead the members of her audience to lobby their public officials. She compelled the audience to feel compassion for young pregnant women and, more importantly, "to speak out for those who are too weak, too young, too far away—or just too desperate and dispirited—to make their voices heard." The speech concluded with an affirmation of teamwork: "If we are willing to work together on behalf of common sense and common human decency, we cannot help but win the many other struggles before us."

Wattleton strove to win the battle for reproductive freedom by mobilizing grassroots support. In a 1989 speech, "March and Rally for Women's Equality/Women's Lives," delivered in Washington, D.C., she employed a poignant metaphor to magnify the restrictions on freedom: "And as a woman, I know that the power of the government to control women's reproduction is more frightening than any other tyranny, more binding than any other prison." In this speech, she also used repetition to empha-

size the importance of privacy: "In a pluralistic nation, private morality must be just that—private! . . . Let privacy be the bedrock of our freedom!" She concluded with an emphatic reference to specific individuals: "And to the Bushes, the Thornburghs [U.S. attorney general], and the Falwells [a leader of the religious Right] of the world, it is we who say 'Read our lips. No more back alleys!' "

Wattleton's impassioned delivery and provocative content are also evidenced in her speech "Remarks at Central Park Rally," made on Earth Day in 1990, characterized by several stylistic and poetic devices. The ancient Greeks coined the word *ecphrasis* to describe a stylistic device whereby speakers use vivid descriptions to make a thought "stand out" in the minds of listeners. Wattleton declared vividly: "200,000 women die every year from sharp sticks, from drinking bleach, from horrifying means of abortion." She also contrasted President Bush's words with her own in the following rhetorical question: "What could be *less* kind or gentle—what could be more cruel and illogical—than trying to reduce abortion by curbing contraception?" Wattleton also incorporated rhyme into this speech, asserting: "It is high time our government created a foreign policy that responds to *compassion for distress—not a compulsion to oppress*." Once again, her purpose was to motivate her audience to participate in political processes, and she ended her Earth Day speech with a specific plea for action to benefit "all the Earth's people."

In "Guaranteeing the Promise of Roe," delivered in 1991 to the Family Planning Advocates of New York State, Wattleton commended her audience for working to defeat abortion-restrictive bills. At the same time, she discussed the difficulties still facing reproductive freedom: parental notification policies and the gag rule that prevented practitioner/patient discussion of abortion as an option. Her style was personal as she talked about her own teenage daughter. Through personal references she stressed the importance of voluntary communication in families while rejecting the compulsory communication associated with parental notification. Her goal in this speech was to revitalize and reinforce the concerns of an audience who already agreed on the need for reproductive liberation. Again, her proficiency was apparent. She commonly employed "military" metaphors such as "Our opponents won't give up . . . we can expect major battles to continue . . . I know I can count on you to be my partners in this fight" in order to energize her audience. Her inventive use of rhyme and alliteration added notable form to her points: "By forbidding practitioners to provide complete, accurate health information, the gag rule turns *doctors* into *indoctrinators*, and *patients* into *pawns*."

In her speech "African-American Reproductive Choices," delivered to the National Medical Association Council on the Concerns of Women Physicians on July 28, 1991, Wattleton attempted to increase active involvement of and support from health professionals. She first asserted that botched abortions particularly affected minority women: "Before 1973, 80% of deaths from illegal abortions occurred to minority women! The mortality rate from illegal abortion for minority women was twelve times the rate for white women!" Resuming her criticism of the gag rule, she made convincing use of analogy:

> If *your* pregnant patient asks about abortion, even if continuing the pregnancy threatens her health, the government has decreed what you must tell her—"The project does not consider abortion an appropriate method of family planning." Imagine a gag rule applied to other areas of medical care: "You have emphysema, Ms. Smith, but the government subsidized tobacco industry doesn't think that stopping smoking is an appropriate matter for discussion in a federal clinic." This is larger than "abortion." This is censorship. This is government mind control. This is government propaganda in physicians' examining rooms.

In addition to the use of analogy, this excerpt also employs *anaphora*, a scheme of repetition in which successive sentences begin with or incorporate the same language. Again, Wattleton's use of repetition lent emphasis to her assertions.

Wattleton adapted this speech to a primarily female audience by making specific references to issues of gender inequality: "This debate is about controlling women by controlling our fertility! I am aware of *no proposals* in this country aimed at regulating *men's* fertility." In her conclusion, she urged women to join her in the struggle for reproductive freedom by becoming involved in political processes.

Two speeches from 1992, "Planned Parenthood and Pro-Choice: Sexual and Reproductive Freedom" and "Sacred Rights: Preserving Our Reproductive Freedom," provide representative examples of Wattleton's advocacy of reproductive freedom. Although both speeches are similar in content and purpose, the latter is worthy of particular attention because it required special audience analysis and adaptation. In this speech, delivered at Marble Collegiate Church in New York City, Wattleton developed the argument that fundamental rights of the individual, including religious freedom, need to be protected from intrusive government involvement. Initially, she did not mention "abortion" directly but instead referred to autonomous decision-making: "The freedom to practice the religion of our choice and serve the God of our beliefs is inextricably tied to our right to think and speak for ourselves, without the government telling us what to do." Wattleton also made a personal reference to her mother's occupation as a fundamentalist Protestant preacher and went on to say: "We don't quite agree on many issues! But we respect each other's convictions, and we feel no need to impose them on each other." This admission appeared near the beginning of her speech and was important because it established common ground with the audience by decreasing polarization on the abortion issue while emphasizing similarities and issues of respect. In this speech, Wattleton recounted anecdotes rather than arguing from statistical evidence and focused on personal choice and reproductive freedom. The following passage depicted her beliefs:

> Like religion, questions of reproductive choice are deeply *personal*. . . . No one group has a monopoly on *truth*. No one group has a lock on morals and ethics for all time. The promise of the First Amendment is that Americans need *never* fear that they will be *governed* by a *religious* doctrine! . . . A government that can mandate *prayer in the schools* is a government that can mandate *which prayers* we say! How would Christian Fundamentalists like it if government forced their children, to recite daily hymns to the Krishna or the Earth Goddess? A government that can compel women to *have*

children is a government that can force them *not to* have children.

In a later passage of this speech, Wattleton addressed the firebombings of abortion clinics that were carried out for religious reasons:

> In the *Bray* case before the court, the Bush administration and the terrorist mobs of Operation Rescue have entered into an unholy alliance. They say that a law enacted in 1871 to protect blacks against the Ku Klux Klan does *not* protect women against the attacks of Operation Rescue. In other words, as an African American, I am protected from mob violence, but as a woman, I enjoy no such protection! . . . The flames of intolerance still burn brightly in our nation.

By comparing Operation Rescue to the Ku Klux Klan, Wattleton portrayed extremists as violent and intolerant. Later, she asked rhetorically: "And isn't true Christianity based on compassion and tolerance?" This juxtaposition, along with her poise and reason, defined Wattleton's strategies of influence. Near the end of this speech, Wattleton mentioned abortion directly and offered a rejoinder:

> I have no quarrel with those who oppose abortion and contraception and try to *convince* others of their views. That's what religious liberty and free speech are all about. But the danger is translating *personal morality* into *public law*, imposing a single standard of morality by force of law—the kind of tyranny, denial of choices, and choking off of dissent, that the founders of this nation were *escaping* when they first came to these shores.

In closing this speech, Wattleton enjoined her audience to support and preserve individual freedoms.

Two speeches delivered by Wattleton after her resignation from Planned Parenthood and after Bill Clinton was elected president are noteworthy. In both the 1993 speech "Equality, Liberty, and Justice: Women's Unfinished Agenda" and "The Future of Women's Health," delivered in 1994, abortion-related themes were diminished and emphasis was placed upon broader feminist issues. In the former speech, she stated, "There is a bigger issue of which we must not lose sight.

The big picture is that *reproductive health care* is at the center of women's struggle to achieve social, economic, and political equality." In the latter speech, Wattleton acknowledged political changes, but suggested that women's health needs continued to be a priority:

> Some things have changed now that Bill Clinton is in the White House. But as Will Rogers warned us, "Even if you're on the right track, you'll get run over if you just sit there." Because reproductive rights and reproductive health are inextricably joined, this will be the arena in which the political struggle in the health care debate will be most intense. Even beyond the politically charged issue of abortion, women's health has not been given the priority it deserves.

"The Future of Women's Health" was delivered at Salem College in March 1994 and drew heavily upon recent research affecting women's health. This speech represented a shift in Wattleton's use of persuasive appeals. In order to adapt to her college-educated audience, she relied on research evidence instead of emphatic, metaphorical language. Wattleton explained that prior to 1993, the Food and Drug Administration did not publish guidelines recognizing that women and men may have different hormonal responses to drugs. She warned that AIDS is expected to become one of the five leading causes of death among women aged fifteen to forty-four, and more research is needed that explores women and AIDS. Wattleton wanted to see more efforts centered on screening for ovarian cancer. She also noted major studies of heart disease that found women were less likely to be treated as aggressively as men, even though heart disease is a leading killer of women. Wattleton also cited research indicating that women's and men's wishes regarding the termination of treatment are not given equal respect.

Underlying all of these health controversies were issues of gender bias and discrimination. Reporting the number of women and men in various elected positions, Wattleton noted that between 1776 and 1992, men outnumbered women 1,733 to 16 in the U.S. Senate, and four of those women were elected in November 1992. Wattleton went on to cite research indicating that society tends to stifle young girls' sense of power for the sake of acceptance and approval, and that gender bias in schools and society accounts for a measurable loss of self-esteem in adolescent girls.

In a reflective narrative, Wattleton explained how her own background represented an enriching departure from cultural and gender norms and, in simple diction, explained her perception of her mission: "The richness of my career is a blessing beyond all my expectations. I have been praised—and vilified, but whatever I faced, it was not intimidating, because I stood for what I believed was right. I am the daughter of a woman. I stood for women. I stood for the future of my child—a woman." The speech concluded with quotations by the founder of Planned Parenthood, Margaret Sanger, and abolitionist Soujourner Truth that promoted empowerment. Like these women, Faye Wattleton is, and will continue to be, recognized for her courage and dedication to helping women.

An uncommon kind of power is unleashed when a passionately determined, competent orator leads a cause. Faye Wattleton's oratory is characterized by deeply held convictions, confidence, and commitment. Her speeches are often marked by stirring accounts of injustice and inequality, and she consistently challenges her audience to take specific action to promote personal choice. Although she is primarily known for her pro-choice message regarding abortion, her speeches touch on broader, yet related, themes. Through skillful oratory, Wattleton has provided leadership on several consequential issues involving the role of the government and personal autonomy, gender equality, and other equally vital matters relating to equality and women's health.

INFORMATION SOURCES

Research Collections and Collected Speeches

Speech texts are available from the Planned Parenthood Federation, 810 7th Avenue, 12th Floor, New York NY 10019. I thank Ellen Schorr and Alywnn Wilbur for their assistance.

Selected Critical Studies

Kolbert, Elizabeth. "Faye Unfazed." *Vogue* 182 (January 1992): 140–46.

Romano, Lois. "Faye: The Leader Women are Waiting For? *Glamour* 88 (February 1990): 194–99.

Rubin, Nancy. "The Politics of Parenthood." *Savvy Woman* 10 (October 1989): 80–108.

Selected Biographies

Current Biography Yearbook. vol. 51. Bronx, N.Y.: H.W. Wilson, 1990.

Hine, Darlene, ed. *Black Women in America: An Historical Encyclopedia.* Brooklyn, N.Y.: Carlson, 1993.

Wattleton, Faye. *Life on the Line.* New York: Ballantine Books, 1996.

CHRONOLOGY OF MAJOR SPEECHES

"The End of the Reagan Era: The State of Worldwide Reproductive Rights" (speech to the Commonwealth Club). San Francisco, January 21, 1988.

"March and Rally for Women's Equality/Women's Lives." Washington, D.C., April 9, 1989.

"Remarks by Faye Wattleton: Earth Day Central Park Rally." New York City, April 22, 1990.

"Guaranteeing the Promise of *Roe*" (speech to the Family Planning Advocates of New York State). Albany, N.Y., January 28, 1991.

"African-American Reproductive Choices" (speech to the National Medical Association Council on the Concerns of Women Physicians). Indianapolis, Ind., July 28, 1991.

"Sacred Rights: Preserving Our Reproductive Freedom" (speech at the Marble Collegiate Church). New York City, February 4, 1992.

"Planned Parenthood and Pro-Choice: Sexual and Reproductive Freedom" (speech to the Columbus Metropolitan Club and Planned Parenthood of Central Ohio). Columbus, Ohio, March 9, 1992.

"Equality, Liberty, and Justice: Women's Unfinished Agenda" (speech at the Jewish Community Center of Norwalk). Norwalk, Conn., May 6, 1993.

"The Future of Women's Health" (speech at Salem College). Winston-Salem, N.C., March 23, 1994.

CHRISTINE TODD WHITMAN (1946–)
Governor of New Jersey, U.S. Environmental Protection Agency Administrator

KRISTINA HORN SHEELER

The oratory of Christine Todd Whitman reflects her roots growing up in a politically active, affluent Republican family in the 1950s and 1960s. This upbringing shaped her fiscally conservative, socially inclusive stance premised on a connection with people. Balance, listening, and partnerships for meeting common goals characterize Whitman's rhetoric. At times her oratory shines with a narrative structure that inductively drives her purpose. More often, she is businesslike, straightforward, adapting skillfully to her audience—whether fellow political leaders, corporate CEOs, or constituents across the state or country.

Born Christine Temple Todd in New York City, Whitman grew up in Hunterdon County, New Jersey. Her parents, Eleanor Schley Todd and Webster Todd, owned the construction business that built Rockefeller Center and Radio City Music Hall. At fifty, Webster Todd retired to politics, becoming the state campaign director for Dwight Eisenhower, a state and national Republican Party leader, and eventually President Eisenhower's economic emissary to NATO. Eleanor Schley Todd served as president of the New Jersey Federation of Republican Women, a state and national party leader, and vice chairperson of the Republican Party; she was a regular official at the Republican National Convention, and was hailed as a possible gubernatorial candidate. The youngest of four siblings, Christine Whitman attended her first Republican National Convention in 1956, and presented President Eisenhower with a golf tee holder as he left the stage. She later worked for the Rockefeller campaign in 1964 and 1968, and still calls herself a "Rockefeller Republican" (from which her moderate Republicanism stems).

After graduating in 1968 from Wheaton College in Massachusetts, with a degree in government, Whitman held various staff positions, including assistant in the U.S. Office of Equal Opportunity, where she officially began her political career. In 1969 she designed what she called a "listening tour" as an outreach worker for the Republican National Committee, during which she traveled around the country to learn why so many young people, especially African Americans, were not attracted to the Republican Party. Listening and inclusiveness became two themes of her oratory.

In 1974, Christine Temple Todd married John Whitman, whom she had asked to escort her to President Nixon's second inaugural ball in 1972. His family has Republican ties as well; Charles Whitman, his grandfather, was a governor of New York, and his father had been a New York State judge. John Whitman is a financier and, with Steve Forbes and Larry Kudlow, served as one of Whitman's earliest economic advisers.

Whitman's political résumé includes one elective office before becoming governor. She was elected to the Somerset County Board of Freeholders in 1982 and served two terms. In 1988, New Jersey's Republican Governor Tom Kean appointed her to a cabinet-level position with the state Board of Public Utilities, through which she developed a political network enabling her 1990 Senate run against Democratic incumbent Bill Bradley. While Whitman's race against Bradley was viewed as unwinnable, Bradley didn't anticipate the disapproval he would receive following Democratic Governor Jim Florio's tax increase. As a result, Whitman capitalized on negative feelings against the Democrats, and Bradley in particular (he won by only 59,000 votes statewide), thereby solidifying her image as a formidable political opponent and a possible gubernatorial candidate.

Taxes were again part of Whitman's campaign strategy in 1992 when she defeated incumbent Governor Florio—the first time an incumbent governor was defeated in New Jersey—to become the first woman governor of the state. Reelected in 1996, she contemplated another Senate run in 2000, but bowed out. Whitman completed her second gubernatorial term in January 2001, when she was selected as administrator of the Environmental Protection Agency under President George W. Bush, a position she held until her resignation in June 2003.

Immediately upon her election, as governor, Whitman was hailed as a Republican superstar, and her promise in her first inaugural to cut taxes retroactively brought her national media attention. As the only female Republican governor at

CHRISTIE WHITMAN: THE ORATORY OF MODERATE REPUBLICANISM

Christie Whitman became the exemplar of moderate Republicanism during the 1990s. Her gubernatorial rhetoric struck a balance between fiscal conservatism and social inclusiveness, economic growth and environmental protection. Her speeches regularly featured themes of listening, partnerships, and responsibility for the future. Whether she was delivering a policy or a ceremonial address, her remarks were purposeful and well organized toward solving problems and creating change for the better. Her goals included, as governor, making New Jersey a better place "to live, work and raise a family" and, as EPA administrator, leaving "our air cleaner, our water purer, and our land better protected." Whitman frequently employed an inductive style, reasoning from examples, which peaked

> "There is a revolution sweeping America today, begun not in Washington, D.C., but in the states. . . . The American people are seeking freedom in a new revolution that began before I ever came to office. . . . They rejected tyranny. . . . [T]hey have chosen freedom."
>
> *Christine Whitman, "State of the Union Response"*

the time, she was in high demand during the 1994 midterm elections. Eighteen of the twenty-two candidates for whom she campaigned, won. In 1995 she was the first woman and the first governor to deliver the response to a presidential State of the Union address. Bob Dole was said to have placed Whitman on his "short list" of potential running mates in the 1996 election, though her stances on abortion and gay rights may have made her unelectable to more conservative members of her party. Her environmental initiatives as governor added to her image as the steward of New Jersey's open spaces, paving the way for her environmental rhetoric as EPA administrator. Yet her tendency toward moderation and balance—her moderate Republicanism, as it was known—may have been both her allure and her shortcoming.

during her 2000 State of the State address, in which she wove four narratives throughout her speech in an eloquent, confident manner. As EPA administrator, her inductive style was evident, but measured. Enforcing environmental policy required succinctness rather than the ceremony of an inaugural or State of the State address. Not necessarily remembered for her eloquent oratory (though she was presented with the public speaking merit badge by the Boy Scouts of America in 1996), Whitman was a speaker attuned to her audience who may have been much more at home in the governor's office of her beloved New Jersey than in the confines of her Beltway office in the cabinet of President George W. Bush.

Whitman's First Inaugural Address on January 18, 1994, in Trenton, New Jersey, set the thematic tone of her oratory in a well-organized fashion. The speech was arranged around what she called "a crisis of confidence" in government's ability "to deliver services efficiently, to lend a helping hand when it is needed and to get out of the way when it is not." In particular, the governor stated three "worries" to serve as main points of her speech: "We worry about the ability of our economy to generate jobs and restore prosperity. . . . the ability of our schools to deliver the quality education our children deserve at a price their parents can afford. . . . the ability of our criminal justice system to prevent crime, and to deliver justice and safety." The state faced these three problems at Whitman's inauguration, issues left behind by the outgoing Democratic administration of Governor Jim Florio.

Whitman completed the problem–solution structure of her speech by articulating her plans to regain the people's confidence in government. First, she pledged to "trust and listen to the people . . . for as long as I am governor." Whitman's plans for economic growth included tax cuts, budget cuts to streamline government, and incentives to small businesses; she vowed to "reinvent government" to assure it provided "efficient, cost-effective service." Significantly, Whitman had announced her plans to cut taxes retroactively to January 1, 1994, seventeen days earlier, something she and her staff managed to keep from the media until the Inaugural Address. Next, when discussing government's responsibility to educate its diverse citizenry and protect them from crime, Whitman employed a metaphor she used frequently during her terms as governor, defining the citizens as "one family" working "together" with government to "make New Jersey first." Thus the address clearly outlines her results-oriented focus and the themes of listening, working together, fiscal conservatism, and social inclusiveness that were the touchstones of her oratory.

Whitman's organizational structure can be explained a second way: future orientation. When taking office as governor for the first time, she sought to distinguish herself from the previous Democratic administration; thus, the problem–solution format worked well to contrast her goals with the previous administration's failures. When

Whitman had a couple of years of experience, she wanted to build on those successes; thus, the theme became one of "where we have been and where we are going," a statement that served to preview her purpose in her 1997 State of the State address.

The 1997 State of the State address, delivered on January 14, was significant for two reasons. First, Whitman's oratorical style began to blossom. Whitman reasoned inductively, capitalizing on examples made visible by reference to those in her audience. Many political speakers refer to individuals sitting conveniently in the audience, and Whitman was no exception. However, her overall use of specific examples worked to give substance to her inductive structure, add a personal tone to her remarks, and enhance her credibility by illustrating partnerships with people with real faces and real names. To exemplify the conclusion that small business growth stimulates the economy and creates jobs, necessitating "a new system in the Department of Commerce and Economic Development," Whitman used the extended example of Mark Terranova, an accountant at Ohm Laboratories who had been working on a temporary basis until Ohm expanded its North Brunswick plant, giving Mark a full-time, permanent job:

> When asked why they chose to expand in our state, Ohm's president, Arun Heble, said, "New Jersey has been very good to us. . . . [T]he atmosphere is very business friendly." Mark Terranova and Arun Heble are with us today in the gallery, representing the tens of thousands of New Jerseyans who are using their energy and talent to build New Jersey's future. . . . In a Dun and Bradstreet study released just last week, New Jersey ranked in the top ten of the 50 states in attracting jobs from other states. . . . But despite these successes . . . [w]e need to do more to foster and encourage that growth. That is why we are establishing a new system in the Department of Commerce and Economic Development.

Similar extended examples were abundant in the 1997 address. To justify expanding Urban Coordinating Council neighborhoods by six, Whitman shared the example of Monica Jones, who "learned her carpentry skills through our Women in Trades program" and was "literally helping to reconstruct her own neighborhood." It was just one "partnership" that "made a difference in the life of one particular young woman—and her neighborhood." And to highlight her commitment to distance education, Whitman employed a real-time example to show the audience "how this really works. I've asked three students from the Trenton schools, Devina Clayton, Ashley Johnson, and Ezequiel Rosado, to join us on a field trip today to learn about the Jersey shore. Let's go to Liberty Science Center, and meet Dr. Emlyn Koster." The address continued with a distance learning demonstration to justify increased spending on children, made visible thanks to modern technology.

The 1997 State of the State address was significant for a second reason: Whitman's image as an environmental steward began to develop, paving the road for her selection as President Bush's EPA administrator four years later. In fact, Whitman quoted Shelley Metzenbaum of the EPA on the partnership that New Jersey developed with the Environmental Protection Agency, which had put "New Jersey in the forefront nationally in our efforts to keep our state clean and green." Whitman discussed the Green Acres program to preserve thousands of acres of open space; the Sussex Branch Trail, almost twenty miles for biking, walking, and fishing; and her proposal "to create a vital economic sector for environmentally progressive companies" that would encourage "environmentally friendly businesses [to] expand or locate in New Jersey," thus illustrating balance between business/economic interests and environmental protection.

Whitman continued her future orientation with her Second Inaugural, delivered at the new Performing Arts Center in Newark on January 20, 1998. In a speech fitting to the location and audience, she spoke of the "renaissance" many New Jersey cities were undergoing on the eve of "a new millennium." She revisited the hope she had possessed upon taking her first oath of office and the improvements already made in employment, public safety, education, and the environment, which made families "proud to call the Garden State home." And she asked: "How do we continue this momentum?" Whitman answered the question with her vision for New Jersey's future and announced the main

points of her Second Inaugural: "a vision for rebuilding our cities, preserving our open space, and enriching our sense of personal responsibility." Her vision for New Jersey's open space would be remembered as the legacy of her administration, according to Ralph Siegel, writing for the Associated Press in an article on Whitman's EPA appointment three years later. Whitman's goal in her 1998 inaugural was to "preserve another 300,000 acres during the next four years. Our ultimate goal will be to preserve 1 million acres in the coming decade." To make this goal a reality, Whitman pledged to work with the legislature "to establish a permanent, stable source of funding—this year" in order to win "the open space race."

A representative example of Whitman's developing gubernatorial oratory at the height of her style is the 2000 State of the State address, delivered on January 11, which focused on four themes: the economy, education, the environment, and the elderly. However, rather than being a recited list of policy initiatives, each topic was woven as a narrative affecting one of four children to whom Whitman referred by name, four children who were born ten days earlier, on January 1, 2000, the first day of the new millennium. This address, complete with pictures of the babies, is one of many during Whitman's tenure that can be accessed via the Internet.

Whitman's pride in New Jersey was clear. She began the 2000 State of the State by introducing the newborns "who exemplify the potential within all the children we bring into the world."

> They are John Kueny of Mount Laurel, Steven Decker of Frelinghuysen, Patti Ann Van Meter of Neptune, and Yordy Hernandez of Paterson. John, Steven, Patti Ann, and Yordy were all born ten days ago, on January 1 of a new year, a new century, a new millennium. As these newest faces join New Jersey's one family, I am proud to say that the state of the state is bright, bold, and brimming with promise.

After bringing these children into the New Jersey family with her often-used metaphor, Whitman listed many specifics these children looked forward to as a result of her first four years in office: more and better-paying jobs, lower taxes, safer streets, and more green space on which to play. In other words, she looked back at where she had been, and then turned to the future with her statement of main points: "As I enter the second half of my second term as governor, I want to continue strengthening New Jersey in four key areas: expanding the economy, improving education, protecting the environment, and serving the elderly—the four E's [sic], if you will."

Four newborns and four Es set up the narrative structure guiding the speech. Whitman then detailed specific examples of the Es. When discussing the economy, she listed the high salaries of the high-tech industry cultivated by the state and discussed Lucent Technologies as an example. She maintained her inductive structure, reasoning by example, but added to it the narrative of one of the four children born on January 1. "Someday little John Kueny will reap the benefits of these investments, whether it's learning in a wired classroom, owning or working at a technology company, or using a product home-grown in the Garden State." The narrative of John Kueny, along with the extended examples, made it clear that New Jersey must continue its commitment to economic growth and justified the New Jersey Jobs for a New Economy program that Whitman proposed.

As Whitman concluded the address, the narrative structure brought everything full circle, with a final nod to her consistent goals for New Jersey and her pledge to continue working until her second (and last) term expired:

> It [this ambitious agenda] is one that builds on our record and locks in our achievements. It is an agenda that gives John the hope of a prosperous high-tech career in a new economy. It enriches the quality of the schools that Yordy will enter in a few short years. It gives Patti Ann's grandmother the promise of a more secure and independent life as she ages. It protects the environment where Steven will live, play, and go to school. Let us be guided by these four E's. Let us be inspired by these four precious faces. Let us rededicate ourselves to making this state—our home—the very best place in which to live, work, and raise a family.

As these examples demonstrate, Whitman's gubernatorial speeches were well organized, focused on results and the future. She articulated

and developed her main points using an inductive approach, reasoning by example, which eventually blossomed into the narrative achievement of her 2000 State of the State address. Her examples demonstrated a resonance with the audience and occasion, and she frequently employed the metaphor of the New Jersey family to unify the diversity of the state.

In her speeches as administrator of the Environmental Protection Agency, Whitman was rarely so developed in her narrative style. Her speeches were ones of policy through and through, and she was careful to credit the Bush administration for policy proposals, which gave her oratory a measured style. Though employing examples, her speeches were brief and came from her experiences as governor, providing relevant points of comparison, as if to say, "It worked in New Jersey; it can work in this situation, too." The examples bolstered her credibility and demonstrated an attention to the audience and occasion before she articulated environmental policy.

Whitman often attributed her approach at the EPA to a campaign promise of George W. Bush: "Government should be citizen-centered, results-oriented, and, wherever possible, market-based. Government should be guided not by process but by performance." Whitman's first major speech as EPA administrator defined this approach for her administration, just as her 1994 Inaugural had done for her gubernatorial rhetoric. The themes did not change, just the job title. Partnership was the priority. However, partnership was the issue on which she would receive the most criticism as EPA administrator: the partnership between business and the environment, letting the market drive environmental protection.

To define her approach to partnerships, Whitman admonished what she called the "command and control" mentality of Washington, using it as a contrast to her course. Her speech to the Business Council in Washington, D.C., on February 22, 2001, her first major speech as EPA administrator, is representative of her EPA oratory.

> It's time to leave the command and control model behind. It's time to start seeking and building energetic partnerships for environmental progress. I come to Washington from one of America's fifty statehouses. My boss, as

you know, has followed a similar career path. . . . My experience has convinced me that more good gets done—and gets done more effectively and efficiently—when Washington builds partnerships.

From there, Whitman illustrated her specific gubernatorial successes when Washington allowed her to determine how New Jersey could best meet the environmental goals the Garden State shared with Washington. Specifically, she discussed the National Environmental Performance Partnership System (NEPPS), in which New Jersey was selected to participate.

> As governor, I loved NEPPS for two simple reasons. First, because it acknowledged that I was an ally of the EPA in our shared goal of improving New Jersey's environment. Second, it allowed me to develop the means by which we would meet the goals Washington set. . . . NEPPS can serve as a model for how EPA should conduct most of its business with the states. . . . I look forward to building partnerships that reach across traditional boundaries, so that every voice and every concern can be given a fair opportunity to participate and be heard.

This passage defined Whitman's environmental leadership: allowing businesses the opportunity to determine how best to comply with federal environmental regulations rather than being quick to jump to punishment, fines, and a control-oriented model. The governor as EPA administrator discussed brownfield cleanup, emissions reduction, and global warming—the environmental issues that she outlined again and again in her policy speeches, using the language of partnerships—and concluded in this way:

> Taken all together, these priorities of process and policy at the EPA are designed to achieve one major goal—to leave America's environment cleaner when we're done than it was when we started. . . . I will be asking questions like these: Is our air cleaner; is our water purer; is our land being restored? Those are the true measures of whether EPA is meeting its mission. It's a mission I believe we share, and one I believe we can work together to achieve.

While clearly prioritizing partnerships and returning control to the businesses and localities affected by environmental policy, Whitman set forth the themes of her EPA administration based on her experiences as New Jersey governor working with, rather than being controlled by, Washington. Her focus on results, not process, required Whitman, in partnership with localities, to identify common ground with her audience. Then the localities, according to Whitman, would determine how best to meet those ends. She often explained that a "one-size-fits-all" solution does not exist. She also encouraged those in attendance to share their ideas with her on how the EPA could work more flexibly to enable localities to meet shared goals.

Just two years into her EPA term, Whitman's oratory took a noted turn, represented in her speech to the Georgetown University College Republicans on January 13, 2003. By this time the Bush administration, and Whitman in particular, had been the target of much criticism from Democrats and, in particular, environmental groups for allowing businesses the opportunity to determine how best to meet environmental goals. Thus, much of the oratory of her final six months as EPA administrator was in a defensive mode, justifying her market-based, performance-oriented approach.

Her speech to the Georgetown College Republicans began with a bit of humor underscoring their common bond as Republicans and demonstrating her attention to audience. Whitman then stated the purpose of her speech: "to set things straight." She explained that she took "strong exception to those characterizations" that the Bush administration did not care about the environment. "They're not accurate. They're not true. And they do a disservice to the American people and to our shared goal of environmental progress." The shared goal of all Americans, the Bush administration, and Whitman herself was "to leave America's air cleaner, its water purer, and its land better protected than it was when we took office. We have made real progress in meeting that goal. Let me tell you about it." This goal, stated over and over again throughout her EPA oratory, served as the preview of main points. Whitman's speech then detailed how the Bush administration, and her office in particular, had improved the air, water, and land through a market-based approach during her two years in office.

Similarly, on February 20, 2003, to students at Princeton University, the alma mater of her father and brother, Whitman attempted to set the record straight on one of the most contentious elements of her environmental policy: new source review. Her office was seen as relaxing clean air standards that she had fought for as governor while getting older plants to improve emissions levels. However, she called the Clean Air Act an example of Washington's "command and control" mentality, arguing that "it has brought diminishing returns." Thus, in Whitman's mind, it was time to "amend the Clean Air Act to meet the challenges of the 21st century":

> One way is to address the pollution emitted by older manufacturing facilities and coal-burning power plants, which the current Clean Air Act does not adequately address. President Bush has proposed two new solutions to address this challenge. The first is to reform what are called the New Source Review rules that govern upgrades to any facility that emits certain pollutants. The second is to require mandatory reductions in the three most noxious pollutants emitted by America's older power plants.

Whitman went on to explain the "confusion" and to counter objections to these plans. In particular, regarding New Source Review, she stated:

> New Source Review—or NSR—[is] a program that was designed to require manufacturing facilities and power plants to modernize their pollution controls when upgrading their facilities beyond routine maintenance. It sounds good in theory. But it hasn't worked that well in practice. The unintended result of NSR has actually been to discourage many of these facilities from making any upgrades to their plants because they cannot afford the expense of upgrading their entire facility.

As a result, Whitman and the EPA adjusted New Source Review rules to encourage older plants to modernize, if only incrementally.

Part of the problem was that this legislation appeared to be counter to Whitman's environmental policy as governor. According to a Sierra Club statement issued in response to Whitman's EPA resignation in June 2003, Whitman "did

the best she could," but "she wasn't given the power to do the job of cracking down on polluters." The Sierra Club statement acknowledged that Whitman, while New Jersey governor, "worked for clean air, supporting strong New Source Review protections to cut power plant pollution. Yet last year the Bush Administration weakened the Clean Air Act by gutting the New Source Review protections." Perhaps the kindest evaluation of Whitman's performance as EPA administrator was printed in the *Christian Science Monitor*. According to Philip Class, president of the National Environmental Trust, "I think Governor Whitman is exactly what she bills herself—a moderate Republican who cares very much about protecting the environment. Her first choice will always be to see if the market can do the job, but she's also shown herself willing, when that won't work, to take stronger measures." In hindsight, the criticism of Whitman's EPA direction, the turn in her oratory to a defensive posture during the last six months of her term, and her difficulty in selling her message of balance and moderation challenged her effectiveness as the leader of the EPA. Her resignation may have been the best option.

For the most part, Whitman's oratory was straightforward and direct, whether she was countering opposition, speaking on an occasion of ceremony, or outlining policy. Yet she did employ two stylistic devices frequently for particular effect. Whitman's first and most consistent stylistic device across her rhetoric was her use of metaphor. Two clusters of metaphors characterize her rhetoric: the metaphor of the family to unify the diverse citizens of New Jersey and metaphors related to gardening/farming, signaling growth fitting for her future orientation. The gardening metaphor had a particular resonance with her position as governor of the Garden State and later EPA administrator. In her oratory, Whitman frequently used words such as blossom, seeds, plant, and common ground, choices which also show an awareness of the audience and the occasion. For example, in her first State of the State address in 1995 she discussed planting the "seeds" that would spur the economy. In her 1997 budget address she promised to "cultivate a Garden State in which good jobs grow in a healthy environment." In remarks to the Farm Bureau in March 2001, in her capacity as EPA administrator, she discussed the seeds that had been planted three decades ago that represented a commitment to the environment that was now "in full bloom." And at the U.S. Conference of Mayors on April 5, 2001, she looked forward to seeing brownfield "success stories blossom all over America." These are only a few examples of gardening metaphors that are commonplace in Whitman's oratory.

Frequent use of anaphora, the sequential repetition of words or phrases, worked to create a cadence in Whitman's oratory that was appropriate for calling out her purpose at the beginning of a speech or driving home her goal at the end. It was particularly fitting during her January 24, 1995, Republican response to President Clinton's State of the Union address, as a way of carrying on the momentum of the "Republican revolution" following the 1994 midterm election. The example illustrates the drive and power created through the use of anaphora and comes from the conclusion of her speech to the nationwide audience as the representative of the Republican Party. It had served as the closing to her first State of the State address to the citizens of New Jersey two weeks earlier.

> By the time President Clinton makes his next State of the Union address: We will have lower taxes. We will have more efficient government. We will have a stronger America. We will have more faith in our politics, more pride in our states and communities, and more confidence in ourselves. We will go forward together, as one family with many faces, building a future with opportunity. A future with security. A future based on mutual respect and responsibility. And most of all, a future filled with hope, for our children and our children's children.

Whitman's 1995 response to President Clinton's State of the Union address illustrated an appeal that Whitman frequently employed in her oratory, an appeal to the Founding Fathers, the American Revolution, and values such as liberty and freedom that have a particular salience within the context of her location in Trenton, New Jersey, and specifically within the context of the "Republican Revolution" during the 1994 midterm election. At the beginning of the speech,

Whitman recalled the story of George Washington crossing the Delaware River in 1776 and noted that the Battle of Trenton "was a turning point" in the Revolution. Similarly, "There is a revolution sweeping America today, begun not in Washington, D.C., but in the states. . . . The American people are seeking freedom in a new revolution that began before I ever came to office. . . . They rejected tyranny. . . . [T]hey have chosen freedom."

Whitman's 1995 Republican response was probably the most nationally recognized of her addresses, occurring as it did during her days as a Republican superstar when nearly anything she touched turned to gold. Since that time her national star has waned, yet she will be remembered in New Jersey for her efforts in open space preservation. As an orator, Whitman was straightforward, focused on solving problems and creating change for the future. Her speeches were well organized and relied on examples to bolster her argumentation and credibility. Whitman's tendency toward balance fit with her moderate Republican upbringing, but it may have created a no-win situation for her in her capacity as administrator of the Environmental Protection Agency. Even though her oratory demonstrated a strong awareness of audience and occasion, her attempts to form partnerships between environmental protection and business interests did not win favor with environmental groups. Nor were business interests completely in her corner. Thematically, listening and balance defined her oratory, but may not have succeeded in making Christine Todd Whitman a popular national politician.

INFORMATION SOURCES

Research Collections and Collected Speeches

Transcripts of speeches delivered while Whitman was New Jersey governor can be obtained from the New Jersey State Archives (225 W. State St., PO Box 307, Trenton, NJ 08625-0307). To date, only a portion of her records have been transferred to the archives. Transcripts of Whitman's speeches as Environmental Protection Agency administrator have been archived by that agency.

Earnshaw, Doris, and Maria Elena Raymond, eds. *American Women Speak: Voices of American Women in Public Life*. Davis, Calif.: Alta Vista Press, 1995.

Nomination of Christine Todd Whitman. Hearing before the Committee on Environment and Public Works, United States Senate, One Hundred Seventh Congress, First Session, on the Nomination of Hon. Christine Todd Whitman to Be Administrator. U.S. Environmental Protection Agency, January 17, 2001. Washington, D.C.: Government Printing Office, 2001. Available online at http://purl.access. gpo.gov/GPO/LPS10672

Web Sites

Environmental Protection Agency [*EPA*]. Includes speeches, official statements, and press conferences. www.epa.gov

New Jersey State Archives [*NJA*]. www.njarchives. org/links/archives.html

Selected Critical Studies

Christensen, Peter. *Shenanigans: Christine Whitman and the Great New Jersey Pension Fracas.* Philadelphia, Pa: Xlibris, 1998.

Gonzalez, Juan. *Fallout: The Environmental Consequences of the World Trade Center Collapse.* New York: New Press, 2002.

Maugh, Casey Malone. "The Construction of Caretaker as Political Style: A Rhetorical Analysis of Christine Todd Whitman." M.A. thesis, Colorado State University, 2002.

Sheeler, Kristina Horn. "Christine Todd Whitman and the Ideology of the New Jersey Governorship." In *Navigating Boundaries: The Rhetoric of Women Governors,* ed. Brenda DeVore Marshall and Molly A. Mayhead. Westport, Conn.: Praeger, 2000.

———. "Women's Public Discourse and the Gendering of Leadership Culture: Ann Richards and Christine Todd Whitman Negotiate the Governorship." Ph.D. dissertation, Indiana University, 2000.

Selected Biographies

Aron, Michael. *Governor's Race: A TV Reporter's Chronicle of the 1993 Florio/Whitman Campaign.* New Brunswick, N.J.: Rutgers University Press, 1994.

Beard, Patricia. *Growing Up Republican: Christie Whitman, the Politics of Character.* New York: HarperCollins, 1996.

Felix, Antonia. *Christie Todd Whitman: The People's Choice.* New York: Kensington, 1996.

Gulotta, Charles. *Extraordinary Women in Politics.* New York: Children's Press, 1998.

McClure, Sandy. *Christie Whitman for the People: A Political Biography.* Amherst, N.Y.: Prometheus Books, 1996.

Weissman, Art. *Christine Todd Whitman: The Making of a National Political Player.* New York: Carol Publishing Group, 1996.

CHRONOLOGY OF MAJOR SPEECHES

See "Research Collections and Collected Speeches" for source codes.

"Inaugural Address." Trenton, N.J., January 18, 1994. *NJA.*

"The First State of the State Speech." Trenton, N.J., January 10, 1995. *NJA.*

"State of the Union Response." Trenton, N.J., January 24, 1995. *NJA.*

"Address of Governor Christine Todd Whitman to the New Jersey State Legislature Concerning the State of the State." Trenton, N.J., January 11, 1996. *NJA.*

"Address to the Republican National Convention." San Diego, August 15, 1996. Videotape available on *Republican Acceptance Speeches.* West Lafayette, Ind.: Purdue University, Public Affairs Video Archives, *Republican National Committee.* C-SPAN Archives, 1996. See http://www.pava.purdue.edu

"Address of Governor Christine Todd Whitman to a Joint Session of the New Jersey State Legislature Concerning the State of the State." Trenton, N.J., January 14, 1997. *NJA.*

"Budget Address." Trenton, N.J., January 29, 1997. *NJA.*

"Address of Governor Christine Todd Whitman to a Joint Session of the New Jersey State Legislature Concerning the State of the State." Trenton, N.J., January 13, 1998. *NJA.*

"Second Inaugural Address." Newark, N.J., January 20, 1998. *NJA.*

"Governor Christine Todd Whitman's State of the State Address." Trenton, N.J., January 12, 1999. *NJA.*

"Governor Christine Todd Whitman's State of the State Address." Trenton, N.J., January 11, 2000. *NJA.*

"Governor Christine Todd Whitman's State of the State Address." Trenton, N.J., January 9, 2001. *NJA.*

"Remarks of Governor Christine Todd Whitman, Administrator of the U.S. Environmental Protection Agency, at the Business Council." Washington, D.C., February 22, 2001. *EPA.*

"Remarks of Governor Christine Todd Whitman, Administrator of the Environmental Protection Agency, to the Iowa, Michigan, and Missouri Farm Bureau Federations." Washington, D.C., March 21, 2001. *EPA.*

"Remarks of Governor Christine Todd Whitman, Administrator of the U.S. Environmental Protection Agency, at the United States Conference of Mayors National Summit on Investment in the New American City." Washington, D.C., April 5, 2001. *EPA*.

"Talking Points for Governor Christine Todd Whitman, Administrator of the U.S. Environmental Pro-

tection Agency, to the Georgetown University College Republicans." Washington, D.C., January 13, 2003. *EPA*.

"Remarks of Governor Christine Todd Whitman, Administrator of the U.S. Environmental Protection Agency, at Princeton University." Princeton, N.J., February 20, 2003. *EPA*.

MALCOLM X (1925–1965)
Spokesman for Black Liberation and Human Rights

THOMAS W. BENSON

Malcolm X was killed because he spoke his truth. It must be seen as a central fact of the history of American oratory that the two most eloquent Black speakers of the twentieth century—Malcolm X and Martin Luther King Jr.—were assassinated. Their messages and their methods differed. King was a messenger for redemption and reconciliation through nonviolence, whereas for most of his short career Malcolm X was perceived as an agitator for rebellion through potentially violent self-defense. King held a doctorate from Boston University; Malcolm had educated himself in prison. King was the leader of a national movement of direct action that changed the laws, customs, and attitudes of a nation; Malcolm was an influence on, but not a direct participant in, the civil rights movement. King was awarded the Nobel Peace Prize; Malcolm was often seen as a thrilling but curious anomaly, threatening a fantasy of Armageddon. And yet Malcolm has come to be regarded as a unique and essential contributor to the rhetoric that defines America's racial agony, and as a defining voice in the debate over racial identity that followed the civil rights movement. He was an original American spokesman with deep roots in its radical traditions, and it is partly a measure of his achievement that almost every serious discussion of American racism must come to terms with Malcolm's uncompromising challenge.

MALCOLM X AS PILGRIM AND PREACHER

Malcolm's life is the story of a series of conversions, to which he gave witness in his rhetoric as a process of change impelled by a consistent motive—to break the bonds of racism.

Malcolm X was born Malcolm Little on May 19, 1925, in Omaha, Nebraska. Before his twenty-first birthday he was in prison, serving an eight-to-ten-year sentence for burglary that came at the end of a cycle of dope dealing, burglary, and hustling in Harlem and Boston under the name "Detroit Red." In prison he began his self-education by voracious reading of the classics and a painstaking copying of the dictionary. Malcolm experienced a mystical conversion while reading a letter from his brother Reginald that described Elijah Muhammad's Lost-Found Nation of Islam. After his release from prison in 1952, Malcolm devoted his life to the Nation of Islam, rapidly becoming a minister, organizing mosques in Boston and Philadelphia, and then assuming leadership of Mosque No. 7 in Harlem. He was the Lost-Found Nation's most effective spokesman and was generally regarded as Elijah Muhammad's heir apparent.

From the Harlem mosque Malcolm—who had dropped his "slave name" of Little in accordance with the Nation of Islam's practice and assumed the name Malcolm X—undertook leadership of a congregation of highly disciplined and family-centered converts who lived by a rigorous code of upright conduct. He also became a street-corner preacher who walked unafraid throughout the ghetto, speaking a compelling message of dignity and a cynical rejection of white hypocrisy. He was widely noticed by the white press and mass media, and was a frequent speaker on radio and television and at white colleges and universities, where he effectively raised the specter of Black revolution—sometimes in debates with more moderate Black leaders, whom he delighted in confounding with his brilliance as a debater.

In 1964, Malcolm broke with Elijah Muhammad and undertook a pilgrimage to Mecca, from which he returned as a Sunni Muslim with the revelatory news that whites must no longer be regarded as the devil. He founded a religious and a political organization, the Muslim Mosque, Inc.,

ing took place while he was a minister for Elijah Muhammad, a large percentage of the texts available for study are from his last year.

Malcolm's speeches during his years with the Nation of Islam are marked by two chief features. As a minister, Malcolm preached the theology of Elijah Muhammad, a tale that identified the white race as the devil and predicted the imminent destruction of the white world. The Black Muslims claimed that they were devout Muslims, but in addition they had a unique doctrine that Elijah Muhammad traced to his teacher, Wallace D. Fard: that a great man-made mother ship shaped like a wheel and accompanied by 1,500 smaller ships would destroy the earth with bombs, and that only Blacks who had separated from the white race and joined the Muslims would survive.

Malcolm X is widely known for his sharp presentation of the choices that faced America generally and his African American audience specifically. In the "Ballot or the Bullet," he charged white America to deliver voting rights to Blacks, or there would be violent consequences. In another speech, from which his salient phrase still resonates in contemporary American culture, he told—and threatened—that equal rights must be attained "by any means necessary."

---

and the Organization of African-American Unity, and adopted a Muslim name, El-hajj Malik Elshabazz. On February 21, 1965, while preaching to his followers, he was assassinated. Later in 1965, Grove Press published *The Autobiography of Malcolm X*, which brought the story and the rhetoric of Malcolm before a worldwide audience.

Malcolm's career as an orator was brief. He assumed leadership of Harlem Mosque No. 7 in 1954, broke with Elijah Muhammad in March 1964, and was killed less than a year later. An assessment of his rhetoric is further complicated by the unfamiliarity of his message to many Americans, by the range of topics he spoke about, by the changes in his views that developed after he left the Black Muslims, and by the changes in Malcolm's reputation from 1954 to the present. Although most of his public speak-

Malcolm also preached the lesson of Black nationalism, and he did so with a direct appeal to the American experience that was in startling contrast to the supernatural doctrines of the Lost-Found Nation. On this theme, Malcolm spoke compellingly, underscoring in direct language the fact of American racism; excoriating the hypocrisy of America's unfulfilled promise of freedom, justice, and equality; and threatening that Blacks who were denied their rights were increasingly ready to fight in their own self-defense. This message was persuasive to many Americans of different views. To many Black Americans impatient with the deferral of justice, Malcolm's cynicism about whites and the simple clarity of Black nationalism were both appealing and sensible. To a generation of idealistic white college students, Malcolm's accusations of white hypocrisy seemed painful but just. To those white Americans still unwilling to acknowledge the rights of Black Americans, Malcolm's threats of violence fit their own worst fears.

In a debate with James Farmer of the Congress of Racial Equality at Cornell University in 1962, Malcolm argued that if the United States would not permit Blacks to return to Africa or give them freedom in America, it should give Blacks a separate section of the United States for their own sovereign state. His defense of the proposition illustrates his matter-of-factness about the history of racism:

> Some of you may say, Well, why should you give us part of this country? The Honorable Elijah Muhammad says that for four hundred years we contributed our slave labor to make the country what it is. If you were to take the individual salary or allowances of each person in this audience it would amount to nothing individually, but when you take it collectively all in one pot you have a heavy load. Just the weekly wage. And if you realize that from anybody who could collect all of the wages from the persons in this audience right here for one month, why they would be so wealthy they couldn't walk. And if you see that, then you can imagine the result of millions of black people working for nothing for 310 years. And that is the contribution that we made to America. Not Jackie Robinson, not Marian Anderson, not George Washington Carver, that's not our contribution; our contribution to American society is 310 years of free slave labor for which we have not been paid one dime. We who are Muslims, followers of the Honorable Elijah Muhammad, don't think that an integrated cup of coffee is sufficient payment for 310 years of slave labor.

After his break from Elijah Muhammad, Malcolm's views changed, but he did not become an integrationist. As a speaker, he faced the difficulties of reconsidering his own religious and political commitments and finding a way to present them so as not to appear completely inconsistent with his former views. Perhaps Malcolm's greatest rhetorical work, and the work in which he fashioned his solution to this problem, was not a speech but the eloquent *Autobiography*, whose prose rings with the cadences of Malcolm's voice and which makes principled change a central theme of Malcolm's life.

The most widely known speech of Malcolm's last year is "The Ballot or the Bullet," delivered with slight variations as his standard speech. In this speech, Malcolm redefined Black nationalism. No longer calling for a return to Africa or for a separate state in the New World, Malcolm said that "the political philosophy of Black nationalism means that the black man should control the politics and the politicians in his own community, no more." In interviews given during his last days, Malcolm acknowledged that he had formerly been dogmatic in his usage of *Black nationalism*, since the phrase focused on skin color rather than actions.

In "The Ballot or the Bullet," Malcolm rejected the phrase *civil rights* in favor of *human rights*, since the struggle for civil rights confined Blacks

> to the jurisdiction of Uncle Sam. No one from the outside world can speak out in your behalf as long as your struggle is a civil-rights struggle. Civil rights comes within the domestic affairs of this country. All of our African brothers and our Asian brothers and our Latin-American brothers cannot open their mouths and interfere in the domestic affairs of the United States. And as long as it's civil rights, this comes under the jurisdiction of Uncle Sam. But the United Nations has what's known as the charter of human rights, it has a committee that deals in human rights.... When you expand the civil-rights struggle to the level of human rights, you can then take the case of the black man in this country before the nations of the U.N. You can take it before the General Assembly. You can take Uncle Sam before a world court.

Malcolm's career as a speaker was not only brief, it was also clearly unfinished, cut off in the midst of a search that in its courage and integrity was as much a part of his rhetorical appeal as the particulars of his evolving political and religious views.

Malcolm's changing and unfinished rhetoric and his immense appeal as a speaker and writer have invited a variety of strongly differing interpretations of Malcolm's message and the meaning of his life. Molefi Asante positions Malcolm as a precursor of Afrocentrism, arguing that Malcolm "was pre-eminently a cultural spokesperson, a cultured person, an analyst and theorist of culture, a revolutionary cultural scientist." George Breitman claims that Malcolm was moving toward international socialism. He writes that Malcolm was, at the end of his life, "a revolutionary internationalist on the way to becoming a liberator of his people, . . . a pro-socialist in the last year of his life, but not yet a Marxist." Michael Eric Dyson portrays Malcolm as conveying essentially a moral authority: "Malcolm's moral authority finally consisted in telling the truth about our nation as best he could. He damned its moral hypocrisy and insincerity in trying to aid the people it had harmed for so long, a fact that created seething pockets of rage within the corporate black psyche. Malcolm blessed our rage by releasing it." Dyson writes that although "it seemed that, as an opponent of racial essentialism, homophobia, and ethnic bigotry, I was in direct conflict with Malcolm's values. . . . Malcolm was a complex figure, that his thought evolved, and that his moral vision was transformed over the course of a complicated, heroic life." And so Dyson wants "to make Malcolm available to the wider audience that he deserves without making him a puppet for moderate, mainstream purposes, and without freighting him with the early bigotries and blindnesses he grew to discard." Archie Epps writes that at the very end of his life, searching for a new way,

> Malcolm X sounded . . . very like a bland liberal, perhaps for the first time in his public career. In the end, it had all overwhelmed Malcolm X. . . . But most of what he drew from Negro history and American society were archaic and cruel ideas, useless things to calm a raging race war. The Negro did wish to be stirred up by a vigorous and courageous voice. But being a practical people, he also valued a good sense of direction. The Negro also wished desperately for a full racial pride. This was the only relevant legacy left by Malcolm X. But paradox appeared even here. Malcolm X left the Negro not only racial pride, but a certain arrogance that has now become the facade of an essentially rhetorical black nationalism.

Continuing developments in the accessibility of Malcolm's rhetorical legacy indicate that in the years to come there will be new and perhaps revisionist studies of his words. In the spring of 2002, the scholarly world and Malcolm's family were surprised by an announcement that many of Malcolm's papers were to be sold at public auction. If that auction had taken place, his papers would almost certainly have been dispersed into private collections, and many of them would have disappeared from public view, perhaps forever. Two of Malcolm's six daughters, Ilyasah Shabazz and Malaak Shabazz, acting in their roles as the administrators of the estate of Betty Shabazz, Malcolm's widow, worked to cancel the auction and then entered into an agreement with the Schomburg Center for Research in Black Culture, a research unit of the New York Public Library, to place all the papers in the center, where they are to be made available to scholars. Access to these materials, which include diaries, photographs, and drafts of speeches and radio addresses, will almost certainly enrich and add nuance to the understanding of Malcolm's craft and his quest to change himself and his society.

Malcolm's dignity, his sincerity, and his unique ability to combine a vividly evoked street-level experience of American racism with a world perspective framing his demand for freedom, justice, and equality create a unique place for him in the history of American oratory.

INFORMATION SOURCES

Research Collections and Collected Speeches

The Schomburg Center for Research in Black Culture holds a large collection of Malcolm X's papers, photographs, diaries, and other archival materials deposited by his family. The Schomburg Center, a division of the New York Public Library, is located at 515 Malcolm X Boulevard, New York, NY 10037-1801; (212) 491-2200. The special collections department of the Robert W. Woodruff Library at Emory University in Atlanta owns a small collection of original documents pertaining to Malcolm X.

Bosmajian, Haig A., and Hamida Bosmajian, comps. *The Rhetoric of the Civil Rights Movement* [*RCRM*]. New York: Random House, 1969.

Breitman, George, ed. *Malcolm X Speaks: Selected Speeches and Statements* [*MXS*], 2nd ed. New York: Pathfinder, 1989.

Carson, Clayborne, David J. Garrow, Gerald Gill, Vincent Harding, and Darlene Clark Hine, eds. *The Eyes on the Prize Civil Rights Reader.* New York: Penguin, 1991.

Clarke, John Henrik, ed. *Malcolm X: The Man and His Times* [*MHT*]. New York: Macmillan, 1969.

Davis, Lenwood G., comp. *Malcolm X: A Selected Bibliography.* Westport, Conn.: Greenwood Press, 1984.

Epps, Archie, ed. *Malcolm X: Speeches at Harvard* [*SAH*]. New York: Paragon House, 1991.

Golden, James L., and Richard D. Rieke. *The Rhetoric of Black Americans* [*RBA*]. Columbus, Ohio: Charles E. Merrill, 1971.

Hill, Roy L., ed. *The Rhetoric of Racial Revolt* [*RRR*]. Denver, Colo.: Golden Bell Press, 1964.

Karim, Imam Benjamin, ed. *The End of White World Supremacy: Four Speeches by Malcolm X* [*EWWS*]. New York: Arcade, 1971.

Lomax, Louis. *When the Word Is Given* [*WWG*]. New York: New American Library, 1964.

Malcolm X. *By Any Means Necessary*, 2nd ed. New York: Pathfinder Press, 1992.

Perry, Bruce, ed. *Malcolm X: The Last Speeches* [*TLS*]. New York: Pathfinder Press, 1989.

Reporting Civil Rights, 2 vols. New York: Library of America, 2003.

Smith, Arthur L., and Stephen Robb, eds. *The Voice of Black Rhetoric* [*VBR*]. Boston: Allyn and Bacon, 1971.

Web Sites

Freedom of Information Act record of FBI files based on investigation of Malcolm X. http://foia.fbi.gov

Malcolm X: A Research Site. Africana Studies Program, University of Toledo. www.brothermalcolm.net

Schomburg Center. www.nypl.org

Audiovisual Materials

Malcolm X. Directed by Spike Lee. Warner Brothers, 1992.

Malcolm X: Make It Plain. Produced and directed by Orlando Bagwell. PBS Video, 1994.

The Speeches of Malcolm X. MCI Home Video, 1997.

Selected Critical Studies

Asante, Molefi Kete. *Malcolm X as Cultural Hero and Other Afrocentric Essays.* Trenton, N.J.: Africa World Press, 1993.

Benson, Thomas W. "Rhetoric and Autobiography: The Case of Malcolm X." *Quarterly Journal of Speech* 60 (1974): 1–13.

Branham, Robert. " 'I Was Gone on Debating': Malcolm X's Prison Debates and Public Confrontations." *Argumentation and Advocacy* 31 (1995): 117–37.

Breitman, George. *The Last Year of Malcolm X: The Evolution of a Revolutionary.* New York: Merit, 1967.

Campbell, Finley C. "Voices of Thunder, Voices of Rage: A Symbolic Analysis of a Selection from Malcolm X's Speech, 'Message to the Grass Roots.' " *Speech Teacher* 19 (1970): 101–10.

Dyson, Michael Eric. *Making Malcolm: The Myth and Meaning of Malcolm X.* New York: Oxford University Press, 1995.

Eakin, Paul John. "Malcolm X and the Limits of Autobiography." *Criticism* 3 (1976): 230–42.

Houck, Davis. " 'By Any Means Necessary': Re-Reading Malcolm X's Mecca Conversion." *Communication Studies* 44 (1993): 285–98.

Illo, Joseph. "The Rhetoric of Malcolm X." In *Language, Communication, and Rhetoric in Black America*, ed. Arthur L. Smith [Molefi Kete Asante]. New York: Harper & Row, 1972.

Lucaites, John, and Celeste Condit. "Reconstructing Equality: Culturetypal and Counter-Cultural Rhetorics in the Martyred Black Vision." *Communication Monographs* 57 (1990): 5–24.

Mullen, Robert W. *Rhetorical Strategies of Black Americans.* Washington, D.C.: University Press of America, 1980.

Rich, Andrea L., and Arthur L. Smith [Molefi Kete Asante]. *Rhetoric of Revolution: Samuel Adams, Emma Goldman, Malcolm X.* Durham, N.C.: Moore, 1971.

Scott, Robert L., and Wayne Brockriede. *The Rhetoric of Black Power.* New York: Harper & Row, 1969.

Smith, Arthur L. *The Rhetoric of Black Revolution.* Boston: Allyn and Bacon, 1969.

Terrill, Robert. "Colonizing the Borderlands: Shifting Circumference in the Rhetoric of Malcolm X." *Quarterly Journal of Speech* 86 (2000): 67–85.

Selected Biographies

Essien-Udom, E. U. *Black Nationalism: A Search for an Identity in America.* Chicago: University of Chicago Press, 1962.

Franklin, John Hope. *From Slavery to Freedom: A History of Negro Americans,* 3rd ed., rev. and enl. New York: Alfred A. Knopf, 1967.

Goldman, Peter. *The Death and Life of Malcolm X.* New York: Harper & Row, 1973.

Malcolm X, with Alex Haley. *The Autobiography of Malcolm X.* New York: Grove Press, 1965.

Myers, Walter Dean. *Malcolm X: By Any Means Necessary.* New York: Scholastic, 1993.

Wolfenstein, Eugene Victor. *The Victims of Democracy: Malcolm X and the Black Revolution.* Berkeley: University of California Press, 1981.

CHRONOLOGY OF MAJOR SPEECHES

See "Research Collections and Collected Speeches" for source codes.

"Unity." New York City, "early spring" 1960. *WWG*, pp. 128–35.

"Speech at Yale University." New Haven, Conn., October 1960. *WWG*, pp. 153–67.

"Speech at the Harvard Law School Forum." Cambridge, Mass., March 24, 1961. *SAH*, pp. 115–31.

"University Speech" (delivered with variations on university campuses). 1961–62. *WWG*, pp. 136–46.

"Speech at Queens College." Flushing, N.Y., n.d. *WWG*, pp. 147–52.

"Debate at Cornell University Between James Farmer and Malcolm X." Ithaca, N.Y., March 7, 1962. *RCRM*, pp. 59–88; *RBA*, pp. 422–39.

"Black Man's History" (speech at Mosque #7). New York City, December 1962. *EWWS*, pp. 23–66.

"The Ballot or the Bullet" (speech at Cory Methodist Church). Cleveland, Ohio, April 3, 1964. *MXS*, pp. 23–44; *VBR*, pp. 214–35.

"Black Revolution." New York City, April 8, 1964. *MXS*, pp. 45–57; *VBR*, pp. 235–50.

"Appeal to African Summit Conference." Cairo, Egypt, July 17, 1964. *MXS*, pp. 72–77. [J. H. Clarke, in *MHT*, pp. 288–93, identifies this text as a speech, but Breitman refers to it as a memorandum presented to the conference.]

"Prospects for Freedom in 1965." New York City, January 7, 1965. *MXS*, pp. 147–56; *VBR*, pp. 250–63.

"There's a Worldwide Revolution Going On" (speech at the Audubon Ballroom). New York City, February 15, 1965. *TLS*, pp. 111–49.

"Not Just an American Problem, but a World Problem" (speech at Cora Hill Methodist Church). Rochester, N.Y., February 16, 1965. *TLS*, pp. 151–81.

Bibliographic Essay

ALAN RAZEE

At the end of each essay in this book is a section headed "Information Sources" that lists pertinent books and articles about each speaker and where texts of the speaker's most important public addresses can be found. This essay provides a corresponding outline of the general information sources available to students and critics of oratory, including both print and Internet sources.

Although this book surveys American oratory from roughly 1960 to the present, focusing particularly on recent speakers, several important academic works that helped shape an approach to studying oratory were published before 1960. Early collections of speech texts, such as A. Craig Baird's *American Public Addresses, 1740–1952* (1956) established a pattern for subsequent anthologies by augmenting the speech texts with chapters instructing students in the purposes and methods of speech criticism. A classic standard source for the criticism of speeches is *A History and Criticism of American Public Address*, published in three volumes by William Norwood Brigance (who edited the first two volumes in 1943) and Marie Hochmuth (Nichols) (who edited the third volume in 1955). Although it is a historical work on the most important American orators up to the middle of the 20th century, serious students of contemporary public address will still find it useful. *Landmark Essays on American Public Address* (1993), edited by Martin Medhurst, retrospectively assembles some of the most influential essays on the state, nature, and practice of public address scholarship. A useful companion to Medhurst's collection is Thomas Benson's edited volume *American Rhetoric: Context and Criticism* (1989). Benson's collection offers critical analyses of a number of texts from every period of American history—including the contemporary era.

These early works on American oratory established goals, objectives, and methods still found in more recent works discussed below. Succeeding books on contemporary American oratory fall into one of three categories: (1) anthologies of public speeches—often contextualized with prefatory remarks; (2) reference works with biographical and contextual information about significant speakers and speeches; and (3) analytical and critical studies of particular speeches, speakers, genres of oratory, or speech-making processes and effects.

ANTHOLOGIES OF HISTORICALLY
IMPORTANT SPEECHES

Of the anthologies of speech texts available, in print and on the Internet, many of the broadest collections are college-level textbooks. Ronald Reid's *American Rhetorical Discourse* (1994) is a collection of 100 speeches drawn from American history and presented in chronological order. Section 14, the final section of the book, contains speeches from the post–World War II era. A similar extensive collection of speech texts is James Andrews and David Zarefsky's textbook *Contemporary American Voices: Significant Speeches in American History, 1945– Present* (1992). After an introductory chapter on the study of contemporary speeches, the book presents a large number of speeches, organized by theme, with short introductions that contextualize each speech. *Contemporary American Voices* contains speeches up to the early 1990s, and it is a companion volume to Andrews and Zarefsky's other anthology of speeches, covering the period from 1640 to 1945.

Anthologies geared to nonstudent audiences are also available. These anthologies often take a theme or type of speech as their organizing principle. Representative of these books is Davis Lott's collection of Inaugural Addresses, *The Presidents Speak: The Inaugural Addresses of the American Presidents from George Washington to George W. Bush* (2002), in which each speech text is introduced with information on its historic and political context. Also included in this category is *"We Want Our Freedom": Rhetoric of the Civil Rights Movement* (2002), by Stuart Towns. Towns has compiled an anthology of speeches, with introductory remarks, about civil rights issues from throughout American history up to the 1960s; more than half of the speech texts in this book are from the 1960s. *The Rhetoric of Struggle: Public Address by African American Women* (1992), edited by Robbie Walker, blends interests in African American oratory and women's oratory into a single volume. This anthology features introductions that contextualize each address. The speeches are arranged chronologically up to Barbara Jordan's 1976 keynote address at the Democratic National Convention. Walker also includes a section on the analysis and criticism of African American women's oratory, using standard rhetorical approaches of criticism adapted to the unique qualities of African American women's oratory. Daniel O'Neill's *Speeches by Black Americans* (1971) is an older anthology that reviews the history of black oratory, but the collection does include some speeches from the 1960s.

An excellent source of speeches, especially those that might be difficult to come by in typical anthologies, is the series Representative American Speeches, part of the Reference Shelf series of booklets and publications that offer collections of statements by officials and experts on a variety of current topics. This series of annually published books, from 1937 to the present, has had a number of successive editors. Each book gathers speeches and organizes them by various themes; the 2003 issue, for example, presents speeches under the headings of war and foreign policy, homeland security, freedom of speech, the welfare of children, and the spirit of adventure.

While print is the traditional medium for collections of speeches, the Internet has proven to be a valuable and adaptable source of speech texts. *American*

Rhetoric, for example, is one of the most extensive collections of public address texts on the Internet. Organized and maintained by Michael E. Eidenmuller of the University of Texas at Tyler, this Web site includes a database of thousands of full texts of speeches, sermons, legal proceedings, lectures, debates, interviews, and other recorded media events, some in streaming audio and video. Other features of the Web site include an index and a partial database of the 100 most significant American political speeches of the twentieth century; a text and audio database of a number of Hollywood movie speeches; and links to topical collections of speeches, notes on relevant subjects, journals, and exercises.

The American Memory section of the Library of Congress Web site is also valuable. It is a large database of discursive and visual texts and artifacts, collections, and exhibits pertaining to the American experience. One can search within the database for the texts of numerous speeches and rhetorical texts.

Some television networks have compiled collections of significant public speeches. The History Channel has collected a number of text and audio speeches under four headings: "Politics and Government"; "Science and Technology"; "Arts, Entertainment, and Culture"; and "War and Diplomacy." *Great American Speeches: Eighty Years of Political Oratory*, part of the Public Broadcasting System (PBS) site, contains text versions of speeches and is linked to a videotape of speeches that can be purchased.

C-SPAN, a not-for-profit consortium of cable television companies, has compiled on its Web site a large collection of videos from the previous three months, organized by topical category (e.g., economy, defense, international, judiciary, science and technology, state and local). The Vanderbilt Television News Archive on the Internet contains text transcripts of television news programs from the major networks, from 1968 to the present, including over 30,000 individual broadcasts from ABC, NBC, CBS, and CNN, as well as ABC's *Nightline*. Transcripts of news events can also be found at Federal News Service.

There are a number of academic Web sites as well. The *Douglass Archive of American Public Address*, organized and maintained by Northwestern University, contains texts of speeches from throughout American history. The Web site *History and Politics Out Loud*, a project maintained by the University of Michigan and sponsored by the National Endowment for the Humanities, has more than 100 audio recordings of speeches. The Vincent Voice Library, affiliated with Michigan State University Library, is a large collection available at the library. It is currently being digitized and made available on the Internet, though availability still varies.

Some academic Web sites focus their attention on significant documents in U.S. history and law, and they often include texts of speeches. *The Avalon Project* is a Web site housed at the Yale Law School and contains written transcripts of documents, including speeches, from throughout the world but focusing mainly on American texts. Similarly, the University of Oklahoma College of Law has compiled and posted *A Chronology of U.S. Historical Documents* that includes written documents from throughout history, the vast majority of them American.

Commercial Internet sites with free or purchasable speech texts include *The History Place*, a section of which, "Great Speeches Collection," contains transcripts of a number of historic American speeches. Similarly, Webcorp operates "Historic Audio Archives," a collection of speeches and sound clips (in .wav format) of American oratory, including presidential rhetoric.

As with print sources, some Internet collections anthologize speeches of a particular theme or group. "Public Papers of the Presidents" is part of the *American Presidency Project* at the University of California, Santa Barbara. It includes an extensive collection of papers of the presidents, among them speeches and statements. Another Web site, *From Revolution to Reconstruction*, in the section "Presidents" has a very inclusive collection of speeches from every U.S. president, including Inaugural Addresses and State of the Union addresses. Though this site is a personal Web project, organized and maintained by students at the University of Groningen in the Netherlands and supervised by Dr. George M. Welling, it is a very complete Web source, culled from Internet sources affiliated with Radio Free Europe. A Web site devoted to Supreme Court proceedings is the U.S. Supreme Court's, *Oyez: U.S. Supreme Court Multimedia*, which contains audio recordings of Supreme Court arguments.

Some Internet sources specialize in social movement and cultural texts. Nobel laureate acceptance speeches are available at the Nobel e-museum. The University of California at Berkeley (UCB) library has made available *Online Audio and Video Recordings: UC Berkeley Lectures and Events*. This site contains audio and video recordings of speeches, lectures, and programs at UC Berkeley. The UC Berkeley library also maintains the *Pacifica Radio/UC Berkeley Social Activism Sound Recording Project*. This site collects recordings of speaking events associated with the Free Speech Movement and the Black Panthers in Berkeley in the 1960s. The *Harvard Law School Forum* contains audio recordings of speeches, lectures, and programs at Harvard Law School. The monthly publication *Vital Speeches of the Day* has an Internet site where the texts of every speech it has published from 1934 to the present are available for a nominal charge. Sweet Briar College maintains a textual collection of speeches by women at *Gifts of Speech: Women's Speeches from Around the World*.

The *Great Speeches* video series, available from Glencoe, a division of McGraw-Hill, has eighteen videotapes with American speeches from the twentieth and twenty-first centuries. Unfortunately, the series is organized neither topically nor chronologically. *Great American Speeches: 80 Years of Political Oratory*, from Pieri & Spring Productions, is linked to the PBS Web site described earlier.

The strength of these Internet sources is their accessibility and breadth, rather than their depth and sophistication. The Internet is useful as a first source for American oratory, but researchers must also consult critical studies and histories available only in print. Though most Internet sites lack scholarly source material, a notable exception is *PresidentialRhetoric.com*, an academic Web site organized and maintained by Martin Medhurst at Baylor University and Paul Stob at the University of Wisconsin at Madison. It contains summaries of scholarship, information, and links regarding every American president, and a thorough collection of texts of recent presidential speeches—primarily those of George W. Bush. Texas A&M University's Program in Presidential Rhetoric also maintains a speech archive and information about scholarly activity regarding presidential rhetoric.

CRITICAL REFERENCE SOURCES

American Voices is part of a collection of reference works on public address published by Greenwood Press. The books in this series provide contextual information on significant American speeches and orators, including biographical and cultural context, and descriptions of rhetorical strategies used by orators in their speeches. Companion volumes to the present work are Bernard Duffy and Halford Ryan's *American Orators of the Twentieth Century: Critical Studies and Sources* (1987) and *American Orators Before 1900: Critical Studies and Sources* (1987), which describes a large number of speech makers from throughout the twentieth century. Collectively these works describe the careers of more than 150 American speakers, discussing their major speeches and providing students and critics with major themes that can be pursued in their own research and writing.

Several other books have focused on specific groups of orators. Halford Ryan edited a book specifically on presidents as orators. *U.S. Presidents as Orators: A Bio-Critical Sourcebook* (1995), is an encyclopedic volume of oratorical entries on individual presidents. This work covers all presidents from George Washington but gives special attention to twentieth-century presidents up through Bill Clinton. A second book by Ryan, *The Inaugural Addresses of Twentieth Century American Presidents* (1993), is an edited work of essays on each inaugural address from George Washington up through George H.W. Bush. The entries offer historical context and provide information needed to understand the content and delivery of each speech: the inaugural's content, composition, delivery, and public reaction. Richard Leeman's *African American Orators: A Bio-Critical Sourcebook* (1996) considers the rhetoric of Black Americans, and the rhetoric of American women is addressed in Karlyn Kohrs Campbell's *Women Public Speakers in the United States, 1925–1993: A Bio-Critical Sourcebook* (1994), which is a companion to her volume encompassing speakers between the years 1800 and 1925.

ANALYTICAL AND CRITICAL SOURCES

A general history of American public address is outlined in *America in Controversy: History of American Public Address*, edited by DeWitte Holland (1973). This book contains essays on the history of significant issues in American history and the public address they engendered. It is an older source and, hence, includes issues only up to the 1970s, though its later sections have information on contemporary issues such as isolationism vs. internationalism, Black empowerment, freedom of speech in the 1960s, and the peace movement and Vietnam War. The Great American Orators series published by Greenwood and advised by Bernard Duffy and Halford Ryan comprises books on thirty-two individual speakers.

For the beginning student of contemporary American oratory, there are a number of textbooks that provide instruction in and examples of analysis of public address and rhetorical criticism. Karlyn Kohrs Campbell and Thomas Burkholder's *Critiques of Contemporary Rhetoric* (1997) is a college-level textbook on rhetorical criticism that includes texts and critiques of contemporary speakers—mostly American—including Nelson Mandela's speech before a joint session of Congress in 1990. Likewise, *Contemporary American Speeches* (2000), by Richard Johannesen, R. R. Allen, Wil A. Linkugel, and Ferald J. Bryan, contains a large number of contemporary speeches and offers instruction in the analysis and criticism of those speeches within informative, factual, value, policy, and evocative frameworks. *Contemporary American Public Discourse: A Collection of Speeches and Critical Essays* (1992), edited by Halford Ryan, presents descriptive and critical essays of twentieth-century orators—mostly from the post-1960s period.

Although it is not a textbook, Dennis Cali has collected generic studies of public address in his edited volume *Generic Criticism of American Public Address* (1996). Stuart Towns, in *Public Address in the Twentieth-Century South: The Evolution of a Region* (1999), has not taken a generic approach but has examined significant public address in the American South. This book is an analysis of twentieth-century public address, organized into themes and topics that address mainly racial issues in the South, such as civil rights, white supremacy and its resistance, and Southern demagogues.

The study of American public address is, to a large extent, the study of political oratory, and no political oratory has received as much attention as presidential speeches. The generic conventions of presidential oratory are examined in Karlyn Kohrs Campbell and Kathleen Hall Jamieson's *Deeds Done in Words: Presidential Rhetoric and the Genres of Governance* (1990). They examine genres of public address such as inaugural addresses, veto messages, war speeches, and farewell addresses from George Washington to Ronald Reagan. Dante Germino's *Inaugural Addresses of American Presidents: The Public Philosophy and Rhetoric* (1984) is an analysis and criticism of inaugural addresses.

Further analysis and criticism of presidential oratory are in Theodore Windt and Beth Ingold's *Essays in Presidential Rhetoric* (1987), which brings together significant essays in the study of presidential rhetoric. Windt and Ingold start with an introduction to the study of presidential rhetoric, followed by four essays that present four themes in presidential public address that frame the book. The remaining essays are specific studies of the oratory and rhetoric of each president from John Kennedy to Ronald Reagan. In the same vein, *The Presidency and Rhetorical Leadership* (2002), edited by Leroy Dorsey, contains essays on individual presidents and the specific rhetorical strategies they employed. Most of the essays are on historical figures who predate the subjects of *American Voices*, although Ronald Reagan and Bill Clinton are included in Dorsey's volume. This book is a compilation of papers presented at an annual conference on presidential rhetoric at Texas A&M University, and is one in the series of books on presidential rhetoric produced by Texas A&M University Press. Other titles in the series focus on the rhetoric of specific presidents.

Kurt Ritter and Martin Medhurst shift the focus of presidential oratory from individual speeches and speakers to the larger processes of speech production intrinsic to each president's administration. Their book, *Presidential Speechwriting: From the New Deal to the Reagan Revolution and Beyond* (2003), contains an introductory chapter on scholarship in presidential speech making, and then, in successive chapters, explores speechwriting for individual presidents from Franklin Roosevelt to Ronald Reagan. Other scholars of presidential public address have explored the relationship between presidential public address and cultural change in twentieth-

and twenty-first-century American political culture. This line of inquiry, articulated by Jeffrey Tulis as the "rhetorical presidency," is expanded in Tulis's *The Rhetorical Presidency* (1987). Tulis explores the role of rhetoric and oratory as a tool of presidential governance—how presidents shape popular opinion through direct appeals to the electorate in addition to (or even in place of) addressing the legislative branch of government. In short, it concerns the role of popularity and the need to address the public continuously as uniquely twentieth-century elements of presidential governance. Martin Medhurst's edited volume, *Beyond the Rhetorical Presidency*, newly updated in a 2004 edition, is a collection of essays further analyzing the rhetorical presidency and extending the work originally developed by Tulis.

The role of public address as part of larger dialogues on significant social and cultural issues is the subject of a number of books. In *Presidents and Protesters: Political Rhetoric in the 1960s* (1990), Theodore Windt first provides studies of the public address of individual presidents as they responded rhetorically to a number of issues in the 1960s; a second section examines protest rhetoric that responded to the original political rhetoric. Justin Gustainis, in *American Rhetoric and the Vietnam War* (1993), takes a similar approach by examining pro-war rhetoric, then antiwar rhetoric, and finally the role of the media on the rhetoric of the Vietnam War. Although it is an older source, critics may still find *The Agitator in American Society* (1968), by Charles Lomas, useful because it offers introductory essays on the nature of agitation and the role of the critic in examining agitation oratory, then presents speech texts with introductory essays that contextualize those speeches. Most of the speeches in this book date from before the 1960s, but there are three that were given in the 1960s: two on civil rights and one on the internal Communist threat. The theoretical material may be of most interest to critics of contemporary oratory. In a similar vein is Halford Ryan's *Oratorical Encounters: Selected Studies and Sources of Twentieth-Century Political Accusations and Apologies* (1988), an edited volume of case studies examining speeches of defense (*apologia*) as responses to speeches of accusation (*kategoria*).

A number of academic journals publish critical analyses of contemporary public address. *Quarterly Journal of Speech* and *Critical Studies in Media Communication* publish essays that cover a range of contemporary communication phenomena, while *Rhetoric & Public Affairs*, *Presidential Studies Quarterly*, and *Political Communication* are more likely to publish essays on specifically political topics. Other journals include *Exetasis* and *Rhetoric Society Quarterly*.

Citations: Books

Andrews, James R., and David Zarefsky. *Contemporary American Voices: Significant Speeches in American History, 1945–Present*. New York: Longman, 1992.

Benson, Larry D. *Analysis of Political Rhetoric: A Bibliography of Journal Literature*. Monticello, Ill.: Vance Bibliographies, 1990.

Benson, Thomas W., ed. *American Rhetoric: Context and Criticism*. Carbondale: Southern Illinois University Press, 1989.

Brigance, William Norwood, ed. *A History and Criticism of American Public Address*, 2 vols. New York: McGraw-Hill, 1943.

Cali, Dennis. *Generic Criticism of American Public Address*. Dubuque, Iowa: Kendall/Hunt, 1996.

Campbell, Karlyn Kohrs, ed. *Women Public Speakers in the United States, 1925–1993: A Bio-Critical Sourcebook*. Westport, Conn.: Greenwood Press, 1994.

Campbell, Karlyn Kohrs, and Kathleen Hall Jamieson. *Deeds Done in Words: Presidential Rhetoric and the Genres of Governance*. Chicago: University of Chicago Press, 1990.

Campbell, Karlyn Kohrs, and Thomas R. Burkholder. *Critiques of Contemporary Rhetoric*, 2nd ed. Belmont, Calif.: Wadsworth, 1997.

Dorsey, Leroy G., ed. *The Presidency and Rhetorical Leadership*. College Station: Texas A&M University Press, 2002.

Duffy, Bernard K., and Halford R. Ryan, eds. *American Orators Before 1900: Critical Studies and Sources*. New York: Greenwood Press, 1987.

———. *American Orators of the Twentieth Century: Critical Studies and Sources*. New York: Greenwood Press, 1987.

Germino, Dante. *Inaugural Addresses of American Presidents: The Public Philosophy and Rhetoric*. Lanham, Md.: University Press of America, 1984.

Gustainis, J. Justin. *American Rhetoric and the Vietnam War*. Westport, Conn.: Praeger, 1993.

Hochmuth, Marie Kathryn, ed. *A History and Criticism of American Public Address*, vol. 3. New York: McGraw-Hill, 1955.

Holland, DeWitte, ed. *America in Controversy: History of American Public Address*. Dubuque, Iowa: William C. Brown, 1973.

Johannesen, Richard L., R. R. Allen, Wil A. Linkugel, and Ferald J. Bryan, comps. *Contemporary American Speeches*, 9th ed. Dubuque, Iowa: Kendall/Hunt, 2000.

Leeman, Richard W., ed. *African American Orators: A Bio-Critical Sourcebook*. Westport, Conn.: Greenwood Press, 1996.

Lomas, Charles W. *The Agitator in American Society*. Englewood Cliffs, N.J.: Prentice-Hall, 1968.

Lott, Davis Newton, comp. *The Presidents Speak: The Inaugural Addresses of the American Presidents from George Washington to George W. Bush*, 4th ed. Los Angeles: Olive Grove, 2002.

Medhurst, Martin J., ed. *Beyond the Rhetorical Presidency*. College Station: Texas A&M University Press, 2004.

———. *Landmark Essays on American Public Address*. Davis, Calif.: Hermagoras Press, 1993.

O'Neill, Daniel J., ed. and comp. *Speeches by Black Americans*. Encino, Calif.: Dickenson, 1971.

Reid, Ronald F., ed. *American Rhetorical Discourse*, 2nd ed. Prospect Heights, Ill.: Waveland Press, 1995.

Representative American Speeches. New York: H.W. Wilson Company.

Ritter, Kurt, and Martin J. Medhurst, eds. *Presidential Speechwriting: From the New Deal to the Reagan Revolution and Beyond*. College Station: Texas A&M University Press, 2003.

Ryan, Halford Ross, ed. *Contemporary American Public Discourse: A Collection of Speeches and Critical Essays*, 3rd ed. Prospect Heights, Ill.: Waveland Press, 1992.

———. *The Inaugural Addresses of Twentieth-Century American Presidents.* Westport, Conn.: Praeger, 1993.

———. *Oratorical Encounters: Selected Studies and Sources of Twentieth-Century Political Accusations and Apologies.* New York: Greenwood Press, 1988.

———. *U.S. Presidents as Orators: A Bio-Critical Sourcebook.* Westport, Conn.: Greenwood Press, 1995.

Towns, W. Stuart. *Public Address in the Twentieth-Century South: The Evolution of a Region.* Westport, Conn.: Praeger, 1999.

———, comp. *"We Want Our Freedom": Rhetoric of the Civil Rights Movement.* Westport, Conn.: Praeger, 2002.

Tulis, Jeffrey K. *The Rhetorical Presidency.* Princeton, N.J.: Princeton University Press, 1987.

Walker, Robbie Jean, ed. *The Rhetoric of Struggle: Public Address by African American Women.* New York: Garland, 1992.

Windt, Theodore Otto, Jr. *Presidents and Protesters: Political Rhetoric in the 1960s.* Tuscaloosa: University of Alabama Press, 1990.

Windt, Theodore, and Beth Ingold. *Essays in Presidential Rhetoric*, 2nd ed. Dubuque, Iowa: Kendall/Hunt, 1987.

Citations: Journals

Central States Communication Journal
Communication Quarterly
Critical Studies in Media Communication
Exetasis
Political Communication
Presidential Studies Quarterly
Quarterly Journal of Speech
Rhetoric & Public Affairs
Rhetoric Society Quarterly
Southern Communication Journal
Western Journal of Communication

Citations: Web Pages

The "American Memory" section of the Library of Congress Web site. http://memory.loc.gov

American Rhetoric. http://www.americanrhetoric.com. Organized and maintained by Michael Eidenmuller of the University of Texas at Tyler.

Avalon Project. Yale Law School. http://www.yale.edu/lawweb/avalon/avalon.htm.

C-SPAN. www.c-span.org

Douglass Archive of American Public Address, Northwestern University. http://douglassarchives.org

Federal News Service. http://www.fnsg.com

From Revolution to Reconstruction. Section titled "Presidents." http://odur.let.rug.nl/~usa

Great American Speeches: Eighty Years of Political Oratory, part of the Public Broadcasting System (PBS) site. http://www.pbs.org/greatspeeches

Harvard Law School Forum. Harvard Law School. http://www.law.harvard.edu/students/orgs/forum/audio.html

History and Politics Out Loud. http://www.hpol.org

The History Channel. http://www.historychannel.com/speeches

The History Place. "Great Speeches Collection." http://www.historyplace.com/speeches/previous.htm

New Deal Network Web site. Section "New Deal Document Library." http://newdeal.feri.org/texts

Nobel e-museum. http://www.nobel.se/

Oyez: U.S. Supreme Court Multimedia. http://www.oyez.org

PresidentialRhetoric.com. Organized and maintained by Martin Medhurst at Baylor University and Paul Stob at the University of Wisconsin at Madison. http://www.presidentialrhetoric.com

Program in Presidential Rhetoric. Texas A&M University. http://www.tamu.edu/comm/pres/pres.html

"Public Papers of the Presidents." Part of the *American Presidency Project* at the University of California at Santa Barbara. http://www.presidency.ucsb.edu

Sweet Briar College. *Gifts of Speech: Women's Speeches from Around the World*. http://gos.sbc.edu

University of California Berkeley library. *Online Audio and Video Recordings: UC Berkeley Lectures and Events*. http://lib.berkeley.edu/MRC/audiofiles.html

University of California Berkeley library. *Pacifica Radio/UC Berkeley Social Activism Sound Recording Project*. http://www.lib.berkeley.edu/MRC/pacifica.html

University of Oklahoma College of Law. *A Chronology of U.S. Historical Documents*. http://www.law.ou.edu/hist

Vanderbilt Television News Archive. http://tvnews.vanderbilt.edu

Vincent Voice Library. Michigan State University Library. http://www.lib.msu.edu/vincent

Vital Speeches of the Day. http://www.votd.com

Citations: Videotapes

Great American Speeches: 80 Years of Political Oratory. Written and produced by Parker Payson. Princeton, N.J.: Pieri & Spring Productions Films for the Humanities & Sciences, 1997.

Great Speeches video series. Available from Glencoe, a division of McGraw-Hill.

Index

ABM treaty, 347

abortion issues: Ashcroft's views on, 4; and Catholic Church, 100–101; Elders on, 143, 145, 147; partial-birth abortions, 4; Reagan administration and, 435–36; reproductive freedom advocacy, 434–39; Scalia on, 410, 412; supreme court decisions on: *Ohio v. Akron Center for Reproductive Health,* 412; *Planned Parenthood v. Casey,* 412; *Planned Parenthood* v. *John Ashcroft,* 4; *Roe v. Wade,* 3, 4, 150, 213, 356, 435–37; *Webster v. Reproductive Health Services,* 355–56, 435

Abu Ghraib, 404

ACLU (American Civil Liberties Union), 307–8

actio, 382, 383

ACT UP, 273–74, 275

affirmative action: Ashcroft's opposition to, 3

Afghanistan, 401, 403–4

"African-American Reproductive Choices" (Wattleton), 437

age discrimination, 2

Agnew, Spiro, 17, 18

agrarian myth, 105–6

AIDS: antidiscrimination laws, 9; Larry Kramer's activism, 270–75

AIDS Coalition to Unleash Power. *See* ACT UP

AIM (American Indian Movement), 71, 318, 321

Alexander, Amy, 162

Al on America (Sharpton), 417

Al-Qaeda, 34, 76; training manual, 4–5

ALRA (California Agricultural Labor Relations Act), 63

Al-Zarqawi terrorist network, 374–75

"America, what went wrong?" (Nader), 334

American Civil Liberties Union. *See* ACLU

American Friends Service Committee, 262

American Indian issues: American Indian Movement (AIM), 71, 318, 321; Russell Means, 316–21. *See also* Native American issues

American Indian Movement. *See* AIM

analogy, 437

anaphora, 101, 263, 384, 447

Andrews Air Force Base speech (Rumsfeld), 402

"Angela Davis Speaks" (Davis), 111

"Anniversary of Abraham Lincoln's Gettysburg Address, The" (O'Connor), 357

anthrax threat, 107

anti-communist position, 238, 240, 282, 339–40; Billy Graham, 180–81, 182, 183–84; Lyndon Johnson, 207; Ronald Reagan, 382

anti-Semitism, 416–17

antithesis, 101, 328

apartheid, 193, 242

Aristotle, xiv

Ashcroft, John D., **1–8**; on abortion, 3, 4; legal interpretations, 3; memoirs, 1–2; religious beliefs, 1–2, 4, 5–6; rhetorical style, 4, 5; speechwriters, 5

Association of Reproductive Health Professionals speech (Elders), 143, 145

Athenian democracy, xiv

Autobiography of Malcolm X, The, 450, 451

"axis of evil," 5, 34

"The Ballot or the Bullet" (Malcolm X), 451

Bay Area Reporter (Milk), 325–26

"Beacon" imagery, 14

Bell Community Project, 294

Billy Graham: Saint or Sinner, 178–79

Billy Graham: The Personal Story of the Man, His Message, and His Mission (High), 178

Birch, Elizabeth M., **8–15**; addressing the Christian Coalition, 9–12; Democratic National Convention speech, 12–13; Human Rights Campaign (HRC), 8, 9, 13–15; response to September 11 attack, 13–14; rhetorical style, 10, 11, 13, 14

Black, Edwin, xii–xiii

"Black Family in America, The" (Edelman), 137

Black Methodists for Church Renewal (BMCR) speech (Elders), 146–47

Black Muslims for Church Renewal. *See* BMCR

Black nationalism, 157, 450–51

Black Panthers, 47, 72

Black Power: The Politics of Liberation (Carmichael), 48–50, 51–52

"Black Women in the Academy: Defending Our Name" (Davis), 117–18

"Bloody Sunday," 267

BMCR (Black Muslims for Church Renewal), 146–47

Bob Jones University speech (Ashcroft), 4, 5

boycotts, 63–64, 66

Branch Davidian compound, 392–93

Brawley, Tawana, 415

breast cancer, 286, 287

Briggs v. Elliott, 302

Brock, David, 190

Brown, Jerry, 54

Brown v. Board of Education, 235, 259–60, 262, 301–3

Buchanan, Patrick J., **16–22**; oratorical style, 16–17, 18, 19; presidential campaigns, 18–19; religious faith, 16, 20; speechwriter, 17–18, 341

"Building with Reservations" (LaDuke), 281

"Bureaucracy to Battlefield" (Rumsfeld), 400

Bush, George Herbert Walker, **22–31**; debates, 30; Gulf War rationale, 29; Inaugural Address, 27–28; Iran-Contra scandal, 25; presidential campaign, 24; rhetorical style, 24–25; speechwriters, 24, 26–27

Bush, George Walker, xi, xiv, xv, xix, **31–39**; acceptance speech, 37; press conferences, 36; religion as source of strength, 36; rhetorical style, 36, 37–38; speechwriters, 36; war on terror rhetoric, 32–37

Bush at War (Woodward), 33

Byrd, Robert Carlyle, **39–46**; Clarence Thomas hearings, 42–43; line item veto addresses, 43–44; opposition to preemptive strike, 44; oratorical style, 40, 43; Senate election, 41

California Agricultural Labor Relations Act (ALRA), 63

"Cambodia Incursion" (Nixon), 18

Cancer Journals (Lorde), 285

Carmichael, Stokely (Kwame Touré), **46–53**; *Black Power: The Politics of Liberation,* 48–50, 51–52; opposing nonviolent self-sacrifice, 47; rhetorical style, 48–52

Carter, James Earl "Jimmy," **53–61**; background, 53–54; Cuba, 58–59; doctrine, 318, 319; Inaugural Address, 55; morality position, 53–54, 56, 60; Panama Canal, 56, 57–58; pragmatic realism,

54–56, 58, 60; rhetorical style, 54, 55–56, 57, 59; speechwriters, 57; *Volk,* 54–55, 56

Catholic Church: influence on Buchanan, 16, 20; nonviolence model, 64; on social justice, 65, 68

CDF (Children's Defense Fund), 135–36, 139

censorship, 123

Central Intelligence Agency, 23, 24

Cesar Chavez: Autobiography of La Causa, 62

Cesar Chavez: The Rhetoric of Non-violence, 62, 65

Chavez, Cesar Estrada, **61–70**; background, 61–62; boycotts, 63–64, 66; religious faith, 64; rhetorical style, 62, 64–69

"Checkers" (Nixon), 340–41

chemical weapons elimination, 28

Cherokee Nation, 293–98

Cherokee Nation v. Georgia, 293

Children's Defense Fund. *See* CDF

Children's issues, 133–40, 146, 394–95

Child Watch Visitation Program, 139

Christian Coalition: Birch address to, 9–12

Christian evangelists: Billy Graham, 177–86; William McCartney, 307–14

church and state, separation of, 100–101, 123–24

Churchill, Ward L., **70–77**; association with Black Panthers, 72; and COINTELPRO, 71–76; commentaries on September 11 attack, 71, 75–76; on genocide, 71, 72, 73–74

Church of God in Christ speech (Clinton, W. J.), 89

Cicero, xii, xxiii

"City on the hill" narrative (Jackson), 198

"City upon a hill" (Reagan), 378, 388, 391

civil rights: *Black Power: The Politics of Liberation* (Carmichael), 48–50, 51–52; censorship, 123; *Cesar Chavez: Autobiography of La Causa,* 62; *Cesar Chavez: The Rhetoric of Non-violence,* 62, 65; children's issues, 133–40; "city on the hill" narrative (Jackson), 198; Commonwealth Club speech (Chavez), 67; constitutional rights, 120–25; Democratic National Convention speech (Chavez), 66; Democratic National Convention speech (Jackson), 197, 198, 199, 200; "El Plan de Delano" (Chavez), 64; "Give Us the Ballot" (King), 260, 262; "I have a dream" (King), 260, 264–66; JFK on, 235, 260, 263–64; King's role in movement, 268–69; legislation, 204–6, 226, 235, 260, 264, 394; "Letter from a Birmingham Jail" (King), 65, 262–63; Lincoln Memorial speech (King), 258, 264–66; Montgomery bus boycott, 259, 260; *The Pitfalls of Liberalism* (Carmichael), 50–51; racism, 112–18, 268–69, 414–18; RFK on, 240; *The Rhetorical Career of Cesar Chavez,* 64; *Sexual McCarthyism: Clinton, Starr, and the Emerging Constitutional Crisis*

(Dershowitz), 120, 122; *Shouting Fire: Civil Liberties in a Turbulent Age* (Dershowitz), 120, 121–22; *Soledad Brother* (Jackson), 113; "Statement on Conclusion of a Fast for Nonviolence" (Chavez), 64; *Stokely Speaks* (Carmichael), 48; *Supreme Injustice: How the High Court Hijacked Election 2000* (Dershowitz), 120; Temple Adath Yeshurun speech (Jackson), 199; Thurgood Marshall on, 299–304; UFW's Seventh Constitutional Convention speech (Chavez), 67; *Why Terrorism Works: Understanding the Threat* (Dershowitz), 120; "Wrath of Grapes Speech" (Chavez), 67–68. *See also* age discrimination; American Civil Liberties Union; gay and lesbian issues; Native American issues; nonviolent resistance; social justice; women's issues

Civil Rights Act, 204–5, 226

Clark, Russell, 2

Clinton, Hillary Diane Rodham, **77–84**; background, 77–78; health care reform, 78, 79–80; rhetorical style, 77, 79–82; women's rights, 80–82

Clinton, William Jefferson, **84–97**; Falwell's crusade against, 152–53; impeachment and Senate trial, 92–93, 124; presidential campaign, 86, 88–89; rhetorical style, 86–94; speechwriters, 90–91, 92

COFO (Council of Federated Organizations), 47

COINTELPRO, 71–76

Colby, William, 23

Cold War, 235, 382, 401–2

Commonwealth Club speech (Chavez), 67

communism, 111–12. *See also* anti-communist position

"Concord Principles: An Agenda for a New Initiatory Democracy" (Nader), 334

"Conference on Compelling Government Interests" (O'Connor), 356

confirmation hearings: Clarence Thomas, 42–43, 187–90; Janet Reno, 392; John Ashcroft, 3; John Tower, 347; Ronnie White, 3

Congress of Racial Equality. *See* CORE

Constitution: First Amendment rights, 120–22; O'Connor's views on, 357; role of religion in, 123–24; Scalia's interpretation, 408–13; Thurgood as critic of, 300–304; "We the People" speech (Jordan), 219–20, 222

consumer advocate, 330–37

Contreras, Rufino, 67

Coolidge, Calvin, xvii

CORE (Congress of Racial Equality), 46

Council of Federated Organizations. See *COFO*

criminal justice system issues, 120–25

"Crisis of Confidence" (Carter), 56

Cruzan v. Director, Missouri Department of Health, 356

Cuba: Bay of Pigs, 233–34; Carter's position, 58–59; missile crisis, 235

Cuomo, Mario Matthew, **97–103**; background, 97–98; criticism of Ronald Reagan, 99–100; legal "crusades," 98; oratorical style, 99–103

Daschle, Thomas Andrew, **104–11**; agrarian myth, 105–6; background, 104–5; oratorical style, 104–10

Davis, Angela Yvonne, **111–19**; background, 111–12; rhetorical style, 111, 118

death penalty, 411

debates, 173, 225–26, 248, 419, 451. *See also* presidential debates

Declaration of Independence, 123, 264

"Decline of Democracy and the Concord Principles, The" (Nader), 334–35

deliberative functions, 108

Democratic Leadership Conference (DLC), 346

Democratic National Committee debate, 419

Democratic National Convention speeches: Birch, 12–13; Chavez, 66; Clinton, 87–89, 91; Cuomo, 98–100, 102; Dukakis (1988), 25; Gore, 171–72; Jackson, 197, 198, 199, 200; Jordan, 220–22; Kennedy, E. M., 228–29; Kennedy, R. F., 241; Kerry, xv, 255–57

"Den of Thieves" (Buchanan), 19–20

De Oratore, xii

Dershowitz, Alan, **119–26**; background, 120; due process, 124–25; First Amendment rights, 120–22; separation of church and state, 123–24

Desert Shield. *See* Gulf War

Desert Storm. *See* Gulf War

Destiny of Me, The (Kramer), 274–75

disease prevention, 143–47. *See also* Health care reform

DLC (Democratic Leadership Conference), 346

"Doing Time" (Churchill), 67–68

Dolan, Anthony R., 386

Dole, Elizabeth Hanford, **126–33**; background, 126–28; religious beliefs, 128; rhetorical style, 126, 128–32; speechwriters, 128

domestic partnerships, 14

Douglas, Helen Gahagan, 339

Drug Enforcement Administration address (Reno), 395

due process, 124–25

Dukakis, Michael Stanley, 25, 26

Earth in the Balance (Gore), 170, 171, 172

"Earth is our Mother, The" (LaDuke), 282

economic disparities, 99–100

Edelman, Marian Wright, **133–41**; background, 133–34; "Leave No Child Behind," 135–36, 137; "Prayer," 136, 139; rhetorical style, 136–40

Edwards, John, xiv

Elders, Joycelyn, **141–48**; background, 142–43; preventitive care, 144–47

Ellul, Jacques, xvi

"El Plan de Delano" (Chavez), 64

enactment, 328

"End of the Reagan Era: The State of Worldwide Reproductive Rights, The" (Wattleton), 435

environmental issues: Kyoto Climate Change Conference, 172; and Native Americans, 108, 277–83; White Earth Land Recovery Project, 278; Whitman on, 443, 444–47. *See also* LaDuke, Winona

Environmental Protection Agency, 444–47

EPA (Environmental Protection Agency), 444–47

epanaphora, 384

epideictic oratory, 107, 108

"Equality, Liberty, and Justice: Women's Unfinished Agenda" (Wattleton), 438

"Equal to Murderers" (Kramer), 273

ERA (Equal Rights Amendment), 211–13, 423

ethos, 172

evil, 5, 34, 382

"evil empire," 5

extemporaneous speaking, 87

"Extraordinary Hope, An" (McCartney), 313–14

"Facing Our Common Foe: Women and the Struggle Against Racism," 114

Faggots (Kramer), 271

Falwell, Jerry, **149–55**; conversion, 149–50; crusade against Clinton, 152–53; *Hustler* magazine suit, 121; Moral Majority, 149–52; response to September 11 attack, 153–54; rhetorical style, 149, 150

"Families First Agenda" (Daschle), 108

Families in Peril: An Agenda for Social Change (Edelman), 136

Family values, 13

Farm labor reform, 62–69

Farrakhan, Louis Abdul, **155–64**; background, 156; criticism of, 158; Million Man March, 157–58; redefining himself, 159–63; response to September 11 attack, 158–61; rhetorical style, 156, 161–63

fasting, 64, 65

"Federal Government in the Indian Nation: Indian Education," 108

Fellows, James, 57

feminism: Audre Lorde on, 287–91; Equal Rights Amendment, 211–13, 423; and femininity, 128–30; Gloria Steinem's talks on, 422–27; and women's health, 438–39

"Fifth Annual Sandra Day O'Connor Medal of Honor Speech" (O'Connor), 357

First Amendment rights, 120–22. *See also* Constitution

First Baptist Church speech (Elders), 145–46

First Cities, The (Lorde), 285

Flint, Larry, 121, 316

Ford, Gerald Rudolph, **164–69**; rhetorical challenges, 166; speechwriters, 166; watergate response, 164–66

"Forgotten Children, The" (Edelman), 137

Fortune 500 Forum speech (Cuomo), 101

Fosdick, Harry Emerson, 263

Fourth World Conference on Women (Clinton, H. R.), 79–80

"Freedom From Fear" (Bush), 33

From Housewife to Heretic (Johnson), 213

"Future of Women's Health, The" (Wattleton), 438

Gandhi, Mohandas, 62, 259, 422

Gardell, Mattias, 162

Gavora, Jessica, 5

gay and lesbian issues: AIDS activism, 270–76; Audre Lorde and, 291; Harvey Milk and, 324–28; KGBT movement, 8–15; "Lesbians and Literature" panel discussion, 288; military service, 350

Gay Men's Health Crisis. *See* GMHC

"Gender Equity in America" (Reno), 394

genocide, 71, 72, 73–74

Georgetown University speech (Edelman), 136, 139

Gerson, Michael, 37

Gettysburg Address (Lincoln), xiii

"Give Us the Ballot" (King), 260, 262

"Global Health Council" (Carter), 59

GMHC (Gay Men's Health Crisis), 272, 273–74

"God and the Nations" (Graham), 181

Going Out of Our Minds: The Metaphysics of Liberation (Johnson), 213

Goldberg, Robert, 161

Gonzalez, Elian, 392, 393

Gorden, Dexter, 157, 160

Gore, Albert Arnold Jr., **169–76**; background, 169–70; 2000 campaign, 170–71; debates, 173–74; environmental issues, 172; populist rhetoric, 171–75

Gore v. Bush, 122, 170

Gorgias, xvi

Gourevitch, Michael, xix

Government as Good as Its People, A (Carter), 54

Graham, William Franklin Jr. "Billy," **177–86**; anticommunist position, 180–81, 182, 183–84; background, 177–78; oratorical style, 179–85; Vietnam War position, 182–83

Great Society, 206, 208

Green Party campaign speeches: LaDuke, 279–80; Nader, 335–37

Gregory v. Ashcroft, 2

"Guaranteeing the Promise of Roe" (Wattleton), 436–37

Gulf of Tonkin resolution, 44

Gulf War: Perot's criticism of, 364. *See also* Iraq War

habeas corpus, 357

Habitat for Humanity, 58

Hart, Roderick, xxi

Hartmann, Robert, 166

Harvard commencement speech, 220–21

Hasidic Lubavitcher sect, 416

"Health Care: We Can Make A Difference" (Clinton, H. R.), 79–80

Health care reform: Clinton's plan, 78, 79–80, 89; connections between health and poverty, 116–17; Daschle on, 108; preventive care, 143–47; women's agenda, 287, 435–39

Hill, Anita Faye, 42, **187–91**

"History of Racism" (Malcolm X), 451

Hodgson v. Minnesota, 412

Hoffa, Jimmy, 239

Hoffman, Abbie, 120–22

Holmes, Oliver Wendell, 121

Hope of the World (Fosdick), 263

"Hope Speech" (Milk), 327–28

Human Rights Campaign (HRC), 8, 9, 13–15

Hussein, Saddam, 29, 35

Hustler v. Falwell, 121

"Hymie-town," 194, 199

Hyperbole, 58

"I have a dream" (King), 260, 264–66

"I have a scream" (Dean), xv

"Imagining the Future" (Davis), 113

Immigrants, 102, 372–73

"Immigration Address" (Cuomo), 99, 102

impeachment hearings, 92–93, 124, 219–20

"In a Pig's Eye" (Churchill), 72, 74, 75

Inaugural Address: Governor Cuomo, 101

Inaugural Address, Presidential, xvii; Bush, G. H. W., xviii, 27–28; Bush, G. W., 32; Carter, 55; Clinton, 89, 91; Kennedy, 233; Lincoln, xviii; Reagan, 381; Wilson, xviii

Indians are Us? (Churchill), 71

"Industrialism and American Indian Culture" (Means), 320

Iran-Contra scandal, 25

Iraq War, 404; Bush's rationale for, 29; Jackson's opposition to, 195; Kerry's speech's on, 251–54; link to war on terror, 35–36; opposition to, 44; Powell's support of, 374–76. *See also* Gulf War

It Takes a Village: And Other Lessons Children Teach Us (Clinton, H. R.), 81

Jackson, George, 113

Jackson, Jesse Louis, **192–203**; background, 192–93; King's influence, 192–93, 200; rhetorical style, 196–202

Jamieson, Kathleen Hall, xix

jeremaid, 197

Johnson, Lyndon Baines, **203–10**; domestic programs, 203–6; rhetorical style, 203–4; speechwriters, 203; Vietnam War, 207–8

Johnson, Sonia, **211–17**; background, 211–12; ERA, 211–13; rhetorical style, 213–16

Jordan, Barbara Charline, **217–24**; background, 217–19; rhetorical style, 219–22; "We the People," 219–20, 222

"Judiciary Act of 1789 and the American Judicial Tradition, The," 356, 357

juvenile crime, 394–95

"Juvenile Justice at the Crossroads" (Reno), 394–95

Kennedy, Edward Moore, **224–31**; background, 225; debates, 225–26; rhetorical style, 226–29

Kennedy, John Fitzgerald, **231–37**; civil rights, 235, 260, 263–64; foreign policy, 233–35; Inaugural Address, 233; rhetorical style, 231–36; speechwriters, 232

Kennedy, Robert F., **238–47**; response to King's assassination, 245; Vietnam War position, 243–44

Kerry, John F., **247–58**; background, 247–48; presidential campaign, 255–57; Senate speech's on Iraq, 251–54; Vietnam War, 248–51

Kiel v. Florida Board of Regents, 356

King, Martin Luther Jr., xvii, **258–70**, 384; and Al Sharpton, 415, 417, 418, 419; background, 258–60; and Bill Clinton, 89, 91; and Cesar Chavez, 65; compared to Malcolm X, 261, 265, 449; Gandhi's influence, 259; and Jesse Jackson, 192–93, 200; Montgomery bus boycott, 259, 260; Nobel Peace Prize, 261; nonviolent resistance, 259–69; rhetorical style, 261–69; Robert Kennedy's response to death of, 245; role in civil rights movement, 268–69; on Vietnam War, 261, 267–68

Koresh, David, 392–93
Kramer, Larry, **270–77**; ACT UP, 273–74, 275; Gay Men's Health Crisis (GMHC), 272, 273–74
Ku Klux Klan, 40, 134, 266
Kyoto Climate Change Conference, 172

"Labor Day" speech (Carter), 56
Labor Reform Act, 239
LaDuke, Winona, **277–84**; background, 277–78; Green Party campaign speech, 279–80; rhetorical style, 279–83
LDF (Legal Defense Fund), 300
"Leadership and Social Change," 138
"Learning from the 60s" (Lorde), 290
"Leave No Child Behind," 135–36, 137, 373–74
Legal Defense Fund. *See* LDF
"Legal Education and Social Responsibility" (O'Connor), 358
lesbian, gay, bisexual, and transgender (LGBT) movement, 8–15; link with Christian Coalition, 10–12
"Lessons from Native America: Knowing Who You Are" (Means), 318, 319
"Letter from a Birmingham Jail" (King), 65, 262–63
"Let Us All Rise Together" (Davis), 113, 117
Levy, Jacques, 62
Lewis and Clark Conference speech (Mankiller), 296, 297–98
Libertarian Party, 316
"Life in Occupied America" (Churchill), 75
"Lifting as we climb" (Davis), 117
"Light" imagery, 14
Lincoln, Abraham, xiii, xviii, xix, 276
Lincoln Memorial speech (King), 258, 264–66
Living History (Clinton), 80–81
"Living the Dream" (Johnson, S.), 211–12, 213
Long, Huey, xviii
Looking Forward (Bush, G.H.W.), 23, 29
Lorde, Audre Geraldine, **285–93**; background, 285–86; rhetorical style, 287–91

Magida, Arthur, 162
Makeba, Miriam, 47
Malcolm X, **449–54**; background, 449–50; compared to Martin Luther King, 261, 265, 449
Manhattan Institute speech (Scalia), 411
Mankiller, Wilma, **293–98**; background, 293–94; Lewis and Clark Conference, 296, 297–98
Marshall, Thurgood, **299–307**; background, 299–300; constitutional interpretation, 300–304; Mr. Civil Rights, 299–304

"Master's Tools Will Never Dismantle the Master's House, The" (Lorde), 288–89
Matter of Interpretation, A (Scalia), 408–9
McCarthy, Joseph, 122, 238
McCartney, William Paul (Bill), **307–15**; background, 307–8
McClellan Committee, 239
McGovern, George, 342
Means, Russell, **316–23**; Wounded Knee trial, 318–19
Measure of Our Success, The (Edelman), 133–34
media coverage: influence of Hill-Thomas hearings, 189; network organizations, xvii. *See also* press conferences
Meredith, James, 47, 235, 240, 242–43
metaphor, 263, 264 265, 268, 446–47
MIA (Montgomery Improvement Association), 259, 302
migrant farm workers, 62–69
Milk, Harvey Bernard, 8–9, **324–29**; background, 324; rhetorical style, 328
"Milk Versus the Machine" (Milk), 326
Miller, Keith, 263
Million Man March, 157–58
Montgomery bus boycott, 259, 260
Montgomery Improvement Association. *See* MIA
"Moral Equivalent of War, The" (Carter), 56
morality position: Jerry Faldwell, 150–54; Jimmy Carter, 54–55, 56, 60; Mario Cuomo, 100–101
Moral Majority, 149–52
Moscone, George, 324
Ms magazine, 422; "Woman of the Year," 278, 295
Muhammad, Elijah, 156–57, 450
Muslims: Farrakhan's talks on, 159–60; Malcolm X, 450–52; Stokely Carmichael, 48–50
My Life (Clinton, W. J.), 92–93

NAACP, 300–301
NAACP Legal Defense and Education Fund, 134–35, 299
Nader, Ralph, **330–38**; background, 330; "body rights," 331–32; criticism of Reagan, 333–34; nuclear power safety, 333; presidential candidate, 335–37; rhetorical style, 330–31
NAFTA (North American Free Trade Agreement), 173, 362, 365
NAG (Nonviolent Action Group), 46
NAN (National Action Network), 415–16
Narratives: "city on the hill" (Jackson), 198; of ordinary citizens, 107–9; self-disclosing, 128–29, 172, 200
National Action Network. *See* NAN
National Defense University speech (Rumsfeld), 401

National Farm Workers, 62

National Prayer Breakfast speech (Dole), 128–29

National Religious Broadcasters Convention speech (Ashcroft), 5

Nation of Islam, 156–63, 450

Native American Activists. See Churchill, Ward L.; LaDuke, Winona; Mankiller, Wilma; Means, Russell

Native American issues: Cherokee Nation, 293–98; Churchill on, 70–76; EPA anecdote, 108; Winona LaDuke on, 277–84. See also American Indian issues

"Native American Spirituality" (Means), 318, 319

"New Foreign Policy" (Carter), 56

New Republic, The (Carmichael), 50

Newton, Huey P., 72

New York Review of Books, The (Carmichael), 48–52

New York's Gay and Lesbian Community Center speech (Kramer), 273

Nixon, Richard Milhous, **338–46**; "Checkers" speech, 340–41; speechwriters, 17–18, 341; Vietnam War, 342–43; Watergate, 165, 219–20, 343–44

Nobel Peace Prize, 58, 59, 261, 347

Nonviolent Action Group. See NAG

nonviolent resistance: Carmichael's opposition to, 47; farmworkers use of, 64, 65, 66; and Martin Luther King, 259–69; vs. violence, 76

Noonan, Peggy, 91–92

Noriega, Manuel, 29, 369

Normal Heart, The (Kramer), 274

North American Free Trade Agreement. See NAFTA

Nuclear power, safety issues, 333

Nuclear Threat Initiative (NTI), 348, 351–52

Nuclear weapons: arms race, 235; threat reduction, 347–48, 351–52

Nunn, Samuel Augustus, **346–52**; background, 346; nuclear weapons, 347–48, 351–52

O'Connor, Sandra Day, **353–60**; background, 353–654; centrist position, 355; eulogy of Ronald Reagan, 378, 388; oratorical style, 369–70; states rights, 354, 355, 356; woman and law, 358

Oklahoma City bombing, 160

"1,112 and Counting" (Kramer), 272–73

On My Honor: The Beliefs That Shape My Life (Ashcroft), 2

Open Housing Act of 1968, 23

"Open Letter and Speech to the Christian Coalition" (Birch), 9–12

Operation People United to Save Humanity. See PUSH

Operation Rescue, 438

Oratory, xi–xxiii

"Ordered liberty" metaphor (Ashcroft), 6

"Our Gay President," 276

Out of This World: A Fictionalized True-Life Adventure (Johnson), 215

"Pacifism and Pathology in the American Left" (Churchill), 76

Panama: Bush's incursion, 29

Panama Canal Treaty, 56, 57–58, 347

parallel structure, 24

Paranoid Style in American Politics, The (Hofstadter), 4

partial-birth abortions, 4

partisan zealotry, 1

pathos, 263

patriarchy, 213–16

PATRIOT Act, 2, 3, 5

Peltier, Leonard, 71, 74

Pericles, xii, xiv

Perot, H. Ross, **360–67**; background, 360–61; criticism of Gulf War, 364; NAFTA position, 362, 365; presidential campaigns, 361–66; rhetorical style, 362–64

Persian Gulf crisis, 348, 350

"Personal Appeal, A" (Kramer), 271

Pesticides, danger of, 67–68

Pew Forum on Religion and Public Life speech (Scalia), 411

"Physician Activism: Prevention, Prevention, Prevention" (Elders), 144–45

PINS (Political INformation System), 385, 386

PIRG (Public Interest Research Group), 332–33

Pitfalls of Liberalism, The (Carmichael), 50–51

Plame, Valerie, 35

Planned Parenthood Federation of America. See PPFA

Planned Parenthood speech (Elders), 145

Planned Parenthood v. Casey, 412

Planned Parenthood v. John Ashcroft, 4

Plessy v. Ferguson, 302

political decisions: influenced by religious beliefs, 100–101

Politican Information System. See PINS

"Portia's Progress" (O'Connor), 357, 358

poverty: children and, 133–40; and health care, 116–17, 144–47

Powell, Adam Clayton, 414

Powell, Colin Luther, **368–77**; background, 368; Republican National Convention speeches, 372–74; United Nations address, 374–76

power brokers, 54–55

PPFA (Planned Parenthood Federation of America), 434–35. *See also* abortion issues

pragmatic realism, 54–56, 58, 60

"Prayer" (Edelman), 136, 139

preemptive strike doctrine, 44

presidential campaigns: 1952, 340–41; 1956, 341; 1960, 232–33; 1968, 339, 341–42; 1972, 339, 342; 1976, 54–55, 167; 1980, 22–23, 56, 380–81; 1984, 25, 382; 1988, 26–27; 1992, 18–20, 29–30, 86, 88–89, 361–66, 365–66; 1996, 20, 91, 129–30, 278–79, 335–36, 362; 2000, 20–21, 106, 121, 122, 153, 170–71, 173–75, 278–79, 336–37, 373–74; 2004, 37, 255–57, 418–20

presidential debates, xxii; Bush / Gore, xx, 173–74; Carter / Ford, 167; Clinton / Bush, xvii, 30; Kennedy / Nixon, 232–33, 341; Reagan / Carter, xv; Reagan / Mondale, 382

press conferences: Bush, G.H.W., 27; Bush, George W., 36; Kennedy, 231–32

Price, Ray, 341

pro-choice movement, 435

Promise Keepers, 307–14

Prophet of Rage (Magida), 162

"Protect Children from Unjust Policies" (Edelman), 135

PTL Club, 151

Public Citizen, 333

Public Interest Research Group. *See* PIRG

PUSH (Operation People United to Save Humanity), 193

Quakers. *See* American Friends Service Committee

Race, Gender, and Power in America: The Legacy of the Hill-Thomas Hearings (Hill), 190

racism, 112–18, 414–18, 450–52; profiling, 417

rainbow metaphors, 194, 201

Reagan, Ronald Wilson, xv, xix, **378–90**; anti-abortion effort, 435; background, 378; communication skills, 379–88; criticism of, 99–100, 107, 116–17, 333–34; eulogy by Sandra Day O'Connor, 378, 388; rhetorical style, 382–86; speechwriters, 379, 385–87; "the Speech," 378–79

Real Anita Hill, The (Brock), 190

"Rebuilding the Cherokee Nation" (Mankiller), 296

Reed, Ralph, 10

"Reflections on the Bicentennial of the Constitution" (Marshall), 303–4

Reform Party Nomination Acceptance Speech (Buchanan), 21

religion: advocacy of William McCartney, 307–14; and political decisions, 100–101; as source of strength, 36

Religious Right, 149–54; Ashcroft on, 1; Falwell, J. as member of, 149–154. *See also* Christian Coalition

"Remarks at Central Park Rally" (Wattleton), 436

Reno, Janet, **390–97**; background, 390–91; oratorical style, 396

repetition, 437

Republican National Convention speeches: Buchanan, 18–19; Bush, G.H.W., 25–26, 29; Bush, G. W., 37; Dole, E., 126, 129–30; Powell, 372–74; Reagan, 383, 385, 388

rhetoric, xiv, xxiii

Rhetorical Career of Cesar Chavez, The, 64

"Rhetorical presidency," xvi

rhetorical questions, 21

rhetorical reversal, 159

rhyme, 200–201

ridicule, 20

right to die, 356

Roe v. Wade, 3, 4, 150, 213, 356, 436–37

Roosevelt, Franklin, xi

Rumsfeld, Donald H., **398–406**; background, 398; response to September 11 attack, 399, 401, 402–3; sense of humor, 404–5

"Rush to War Ignores U.S. Constitution" (Byrd), 44

Russo, Vito, 275

"Sacred Rights: Preserving Our Reproductive Freedom" (Wattleton), 437–38

Safire, William, 341

SALT II Treaty, 347

sarcasm, 20

"Save America's Treasures" (Clinton, H. R.), 81–82

Scalia, Antonin, **407–13**; background, 407; Constitutional interpretation, 408–13

"Scalp bounty," 73–74

SCLC (Southern Christian Leadership Conference), 192–93, 260, 261

SDS (Students for a Democratic Society), 71

segregation, 259, 260, 429–31

September 11 attack, xi–xii; Ashcroft's response, 4–5; Bush's response, 33; Churchill's commentaries on, 71, 75–76; Daschle's remarks about, 107; Dershowitz's comments on, 124–25; Falwell's response, 153–54; Farrakhan's response, 158–61; Rumsfeld's response, 399, 401

"Sex and Sensibility" (Kramer), 275

sexism: sexual harassment, 187–91, 214–15; violence against African American women, 112–18

Sexual McCarthyism: Clinton, Starr, and the

Emerging Constitutional Crisis (Dershowitz), 120, 122

"shadows" metaphor, 14

Sharpton, Al, **414–21**; anti-Semitic charges, 416–17; background, 414–15; King's influence on, 415, 417, 418, 419; presidential campaign, 418–20

Ship That Sailed into the Living Room: Sex and Intimacy Reconsidered, The (Johnson), 213

Shouting Fire: Civil Liberties in a Turbulent Age (Dershowitz), 120, 121–22

Sibley Lecture (Scalia), 408–9

"Sick and Tired of Being Sick and Tired" (Davis), 116–17

"Silent Majority" (Nixon), 18

Sixteenth Street Baptist Church bombing, 266–67

Smith, Rick, 128

SNCC (Student Nonviolent Coordinating Committee), 46, 47, 260

social action: Clinton's call for, 89–90

social Darwinism, 101

social issues: church and state, separation of, 100–101, 123–24; death penalty, 411; segregation, 429–31; violence, 145–46. *See also* abortion issues; feminism; health care reform

social justice: economic disparities under Reagan, 99–100; farm labor reforms, 62–69; for Native Americans, 71–76

"Social Justice, Racism, and the Environmental Movement" (LaDuke), 282–83

Soledad Brother (Jackson), 113

"Something is Happening in America" (Graham), 182

Sorensen, Theodore, 232

Southern Christian Leadership Conference. *See* SCLC

Southern Democrats, 348–49, 430–33

Speaking Truth to Power (Hill), 189

"Speech, The" (Reagan), 378–79

speechwriters, use of, xv; Agnew, 17, 18; Ashcroft, 5; Buchanan, 16–18; Bush, George W., 37; Carter, 57; Clinton, 90–91, 92; Dole, 128; Ford, 166; Kennedy, 232; Nixon, 17–18, 341; Reagan, 379, 385–87

spirituality values: Christian Coalition, 11; LGBT, 11

"spiritual" speeches, 318, 319; Carter, 55

"Spoken Word, The" (Byrd), 43

"Stand in the Gap: A Sacred Assembly" (McCartney), 312–13

Starr, Kenneth, 92–93

Stasis system, 219–20

"Statement on Adolescent Pregnancy and Childbearing" (Elders), 147

"Statement on Conclusion of a Fast for Nonviolence" (Chavez), 64

State of America's Children, The (Edelman), 137, 138

State of the State address: Ashcroft, 3; Whitman, 442–44, 447

State of the Union address: Clinton, 89, 90, 92, 93; Ford, 166; George H. W. Bush, 28; George W. Bush, 35, 36; Reagan, 381

"State of the Union Response" (Whitman), 441, 447

"State of the Workforce" (Dole), 128–29

state's rights, 354, 355, 356

statutory law, 408

Steinem, Gloria, **422–28**; background, 422–23

stem cell research, xvi, 32

Stokely Speaks (Carmichael), 48

Strategic Defense Initiative, 28

Strategy of Peace, The (Kennedy), 232

strategy of violation, 327

strikes: farmworkers, 65

Stewart, Martha, 120

Student Nonviolent Coordinating Committee. *See* SNCC

Students for a Democratic Society. *See* SDS

stylistic devices and features: *actio*, 382, 383; analogy, 437; anaphora, 101, 263, 384, 437, 447; antithesis, 101, 328; deliberative functions, 108; enactment, 328; epanaphora, 384; epideictic oratory, 107, 108; ethos, 172; extemporaneously speaking, 87, 88; hyperbole, 58; imagery, 14; jeremaid, 197; metaphor, 101–2, 263, 264 265, 268, 446–47; parallel structure, 24; pathos, 263; repetition, 437; rhyme, 200–201; ridicule, 20; sarcasm, 20; *stasis* system, 219–20; synthesis, 328; violation, 328

Supreme court decisions: *Briggs v. Elliott,* 302; *Brown v. Board of Education,* 235, 259–60, 262, 301–3; *Cherokee Nation v. Georgia,* 293; *Cruzan v. Director, Missouri Department of Health,* 356; *Gore v. Bush,* 122, 170; *Gregory v. Ashcroft,* 2; *Hodgson v. Minnesota,* 412; *Hustler v. Falwell,* 121; *Kiel v. Florida Board of Regents,* 356; *Planned Parenthood v. Casey,* 412; *Planned Parenthood v. John Ashcroft,* 4; *Plessy v. Ferguson,* 302; *Roe v. Wade,* 3, 4, 150, 213, 356, 436–37; *Webster v. Reproductive Health Services,* 355–56, 435

Supreme Injustice: How the High Court Hijacked Election 2000 (Dershowitz), 120

Sweet Briar College speech (Mankiller), 297

"Tale of Two Cities, A" (Cuomo), 99

Teamsters Union, 63, 239

television, xix–xxiii
"Television News Coverage" (Agnew), 17, 18, 21
Temple Adath Yeshurun speech (Jackson), 199
terrorists. *See* Al-Zarqawi terrorist network; September 11 attack; War on Terrorism
"Theory of Constitutional Interpretation, A" (Scalia), 410–11
Thomas, Clarence: confirmation hearings, 42–43, 187–90
Thomas, Helen, 36
Till, Emmett, 303
Tilting the Playing Field (Gavora), 5
"Time for Choosing, A" (Reagan), 378–79
"Time to Break Silence, A" (King), 267–68
torture, 124–25, 404
Trail of Tears, 293–94, 297–98
"Transformation of Silence into Language and Action, The" (Lorde), 288
Tufts University commencement address (Steinem), 425
Tulane University commencement address (Edelman), 139
Tulis, Jeffrey, xvi
Touré, Kwame. *See* Carmichael, Stokely (Kwame Touré)
Tymchuk, Kerry, 128

UFW's Seventh Constitutional Convention speech (Chavez), 67
"Ultimate Weapon, The" (Graham), 181
United Farm Workers (UFW), 62–63
United Nations: ambassador, 23
United Nations, addresses to: Bush, G.H.W., 28; Clinton, H. R., 80–81; Powell, 374–76
University of Cape Town speech (Kennedy R. F.), 242
University of Michigan commencement speech (Clinton, H. R.), 80
University of Notre Dame speech (Cuomo), 99, 100–101, 102
Unsafe at Any Speed (Nader), 331–32
Uranium purchases, 35
Urban Research Institute Immigration Address (Cuomo), 99, 102
"U.S. Foreign Policy in a Changing World" (Powell), 370
"Uses of the Erotic" (Lorde), 288, 290
"USS Abraham Lincoln speech" (Bush), xv, 36, 37, 254

vernacular style, xx
veto: line item, 43–44; pocket, 229

"Vietnamization" (Nixon), 342–43
Vietnam Veterans Against the War (VVAW), 249–51
Vietnam War: Billy Graham on, 182–83; "Cambodia Incursion" speech, 18; Johnson's policies, 207–8; Kerry's experiences of, 248–51; King on, 267–68; Nixon's policies, 342–43; Robert Kennedy on, 243–44
"Violence as a Public Health Issue (Elders), 145–46
Voice of Deliverance (Miller), 263
"Voices from White Earth" (LaDuke), 279
Volk, 54–55, 56
Voorhis, Jerry, 339
VVAW (Vietnam Veterans Against the War), 249–51

Waldman, Michael, 90–91, 92
Wallace, George Corley, **429–33**; background, 429–30; condemned by King, 267; transformation of, 429
War on Terrorism: Ashcroft on, 4–6; Bush on, 32–37; constitutionality of torture, 124–25; Rumsfeld on, 401–4
Warren, Earl, 42
Watergate incident, 165, 219–20, 343–44
Wattleton, Alyce Faye, **434–39**; background, 434; rhetorical style, 437
weapons of mass destruction, 35, 374–76
Weaver, Richard, xii, xiii
Webster, Daniel, xii, xiii
Webster v. Reproductive Health Services, 355–56, 435
"We Do Not Consent" (Davis), 115
"We have no king but Jesus" (Ashcroft), 1
"We the people" (Jordan), 219–20, 222
Wheaton commencement address (Steinem), 426
Whip Inflation Now. *See* WIN
White, Ronnie, 3
White, Thomas, 400
White Earth Land Recovery Project, 278
"White Man's Heaven Is a Black Man's Hell, A" (Farrakhan), 156
Whitman, Christine Todd, **440–49**; background, 440; elective offices, 440–44; environmental goals, 443, 444–47; rhetorical style, 446–47
"Why do they hate us?" (Farrakhan), 159
Why Terrorism Works: Understanding the Threat (Dershowitz), 120
Wildfire: Igniting a She/Volution (Johnson), 213
Will, Mari Maseng, 128
Wilson, Joseph, 35
Wilson, Woodrow, xvi
Winthrop, John, 378, 381
WIN (Whip Inflation Now), 167

Wirthlin, Richard, 385, 386

"Woman of the Year" (*Ms* magazine), 278, 295

women's issues: breast cancer, 287; children's issues, 133–40, 146, 394–95; ERA, 211–13; fight against violence and oppression, 112–18; Fourth World Conference on Women, 80–82; health agenda, 287, 435–39; patriarchy, 213–16; Reno on, 394; reproductive rights, 434–39; sexual harassment, 187–91; women and law, 358. *See also* feminism

Woodward, Bob, 33

Wounded Knee trial, 318–19

"Wrath of Grapes Speech" (Chavez), 67–68

Yarborough, Ralph, 23

About the Editors and Contributors

JENNIFER YOUNG ABBOTT, Byron K. Trippet assistant professor of speech at Wabash College, teaches courses in contemporary rhetorical theory and criticism. Her research interests include the news media, gender, and social movements (including the New Christian Right). She completed a dissertation on Promise Keepers, titled "Promise Keepers, Feminists, and the News Media: An Analysis of the Debate over the 'Stand in the Gap' Rally."

KARRIN VASBY ANDERSON, assistant professor of speech communication at Colorado State University, teaches courses in political communication, gender and communication, and public speaking. Her research on gender and political leadership has appeared in journals such as *Rhetoric & Public Affairs* and *Women's Studies in Communication*. She received the 2003 Feminist Scholarship Award from the Organization for Research on Women and Communication for an essay on Hillary Rodham Clinton's rhetoric. She currently is writing a book on gender, metaphor, and political identity.

VANESSA B. BEASLEY, assistant professor of communication at Southern Methodist University, teaches courses in political communication, communication theory, and communication research. She is the author of *You, the People: American National Identity in Presidential Rhetoric*. Her research has been published in *Quarterly Journal of Speech*, *Rhetoric & Public Affairs*, *Communication Monographs*, *Political Communication*, and elsewhere. In 2000, Beasley was named the Outstanding New Teacher by the Southern States Communication Association.

THOMAS W. BENSON, the Edwin Erle Sparks professor of rhetoric at Penn State University, teaches rhetorical criticism. He is the author of *Writing JFK: Presidential Rhetoric and the Press in the Bay of Pigs Crisis* and of two books on the films of Frederick Wiseman, *Reality Fictions* and *Documentary Dilemmas* (with Carolyn Anderson), as well as the editor of a number of other books and many essays. He has served as editor of *Quarterly Journal of Speech*, *Communication Quarterly*, and *Review of Communication*.

JASON EDWARD BLACK is a rhetorical critic and communication instructor at the University of Maryland. His studies involve the intersection of American nationalism and cultural studies. Black has researched the LGBT community, as well as animal rights and American Indian rights. His work can be found in *Communication Quarterly*, *American Indian Quarterly*, *Ohio Speech Journal*, and several books.

CARL R. BURGCHARDT, professor of speech communication at Colorado State University, teaches courses in public speaking, the history of American public address, and critical methodology. He has published articles in *Quarterly Journal of Speech* and written a rhetorical biography of Robert M. LaFollette Sr. He has also edited several editions of *Readings in Rhetorical Criticism*.

RONALD H. CARPENTER is professor of English and communication studies at the University of Florida, where he teaches speechwriting and rhetorical criticism. He is the sole author of several books, as well as of numerous book chapters and research articles in scholarly journals. He has received a Golden Anniversary Monograph Prize for Outstanding Scholarship from the National Communication Association, as well as the Douglas Ehninger Distinguished Rhetorical Scholar Award.

CELESTE M. CONDIT, distinguished research professor of speech communication at the University of Georgia, teaches courses in rhetorical criticism. She is the former coeditor of *Critical Studies in Media Communication*, and the author or coauthor of *Decoding Abortion Rhetoric: Communicating Social Change*, *Crafting Equality: America's Anglo–African Word*, and *The Meanings of the Gene: Public Debates About Human Heredity*. She is an NCA Distinguished Scholar.

CHARLES CONRAD, professor of communication at Texas A&M University, teaches courses in organizational communication, organizational rhetoric, and communication, power, and politics. He currently is editor of *Management Communication Quarterly*. His essays on rhetorical theory and criticism have appeared in *Quarterly Journal of Speech*, *Rhetoric & Public Affairs*, *Central States Speech Journal*, and *Southern Communication Journal*. He currently is working on a book-length project on the impact of organizational rhetoric on health care policy formation.

MARILYN DeLAURE, assistant professor of communication studies at California Polytechnic State University at San Luis Obispo, teaches rhetorical criticism, media criticism, and persuasion. Her work on rhetoric as embodied performance has appeared in theater and anthropology journals, and in *Text and Performance Quarterly*. She also wrote an essay on the Abusters Media Foundation for the edited volume *Confronting Consumption*.

R. JOHN DeSANTO, emeritus professor of mass communication in the Minnesota State University system, is currently an adjunct professor of communication studies at the University of North Carolina at Charlotte. He teaches media law, ethics, and public relations. He has been a senior Fulbright professor in Nigeria and a special consultant to the U.S. Information Service AMPART program for African counties.

BERNARD K. DUFFY, professor of communication studies at California Poly-technic State University at San Luis Obispo, teaches courses in rhetorical theory and the history of American public address. He is the coeditor of two reference works on American orators, coauthor (with Martin Jacobi) of a book on rhetorical theorist Richard Weaver, and coauthor (with Ronald Carpenter) of a book on the rhetoric of Douglas MacArthur. He is also coeditor (with Lorraine Jackson) of a book on health communication research, and the coadviser for the Great American Orator series published by Greenwood Press.

VALERIE A. ENDRESS, assistant professor of communication at Rhode Island College, teaches courses in political communication, presidential and campaign rhetoric, communication and civic engagement, and public address. She has written essays and conducted research on gender in public address, Vietnam rhetoric and more generalized treatments on the rhetoric of war, H. Ross Perot (with Mari Boor Tonn), and the relationship between composition theory and rhetorical pedagogy.

KAREN A. FOSS, professor of communication and journalism and a presidential teaching fellow at the University of New Mexico, has chaired both the Communication and Journalism and the Women's Studies departments. Her research and teaching interests include rhetorical theory and criticism, feminist perspectives on communication, and social movements and social change. She is the coauthor of *Contemporary Perspectives on Rhetoric*, *Women Speak*, *Feminist Rhetorical Theories*, and *Inviting Transformation*.

HAL W. FULMER is associate provost and dean of the College of Communication and Fine Arts at Troy University, where he holds the rank of professor of communication. His principal research has focused on Southern political and religious rhetoric. He has published his work in *Southern Communication Journal*, *Western States Communication Journal*, and *Rhetoric Society Quarterly*. He is the coauthor of a text on public relations and of a forthcoming book on the success industries. He was a contributor to two previous reference works on American public address published by Greenwood Press.

STEVEN R. GOLDZWIG, professor of communication studies at Marquette University, teaches courses in argumentation, persuasion, politics, and ethics. He is the coauthor (with George N. Dionisopoulos) of *"In a Perilous Hour": The Public Address of John F. Kennedy*, and is coeditor (with Patricia A. Sullivan) of *New Approaches to Rhetoric*. He is currently working on a book-length study of Harry S. Truman's 1948 whistle-stop campaign.

DANIEL A. GRANO, assistant professor of communication studies at the University of North Carolina at Charlotte, teaches courses in rhetorical theory, political communication, persuasion, and sports culture. He is a rhetorical critic interested primarily in ethics. His research has been published in *Critical Studies in Mass Communication* and *Southern Communication Journal*.

CINDY L. GRIFFIN, professor of speech communication at Colorado State University, teaches courses in rhetorical theory and women and communication. She is the author of *Invitation to Public Speaking* and coeditor of *Feminist Rhetorical Theories: A Reader*. Her articles on women and rhetoric have appeared in a variety of journals, including *Quarterly Journal of Speech*, *Communication Monographs*, *Western Journal of Communication*, and *Women's Studies in Communication*.

NICHOLA GUTGOLD, assistant professor of communication arts and sciences at the Pennsylvania State University and Berks-Lehigh Valley College, and codirector of Communication Across the Curriculum, teaches courses in public speaking, speechwriting, and political communication. She is coauthor (with Molly Meijer Wertheimer) of a rhetorical biography of Elizabeth Dole. Her research has appeared in journals such as *Communication Teacher*, *Iowa Journal of Communication*, *Women and Language*, and *Pennsylvania Speech Communication Annual*.

JOHN C. HAMMERBACK, professor emeritus in the department of communication at California State University at Hayward, teaches courses on the theory, analysis, and practice of human communication. His research has recently focused on communication that changes the character of audiences. His authored or coauthored scholarship includes four books and some forty essays in journals and books, and a CD-ROM. He received California State University at Hayward's Professor of the Year award in 2002; his address upon accepting the honor, "Embodying Our Message, Teaching Our Students," appears in *Vital Speeches of the Day*.

DAYLE C. HARDY-SHORT, associate professor of speech communication at Northern Arizona University, teaches courses in rhetorical criticism, rhetorical theory, rhetorical history, and the rhetoric of environmental politics. She is coeditor of *Proceedings of the Fifth Biennial Conference on Communication and Environment* and has published in many professional journals.

HARRY HELLENBRAND, provost of California State University at Northridge and professor of English, teaches English and American literatures from colonial times to the present. He has written a book on Thomas Jefferson, *The Unfinished Revolution*, as well as articles and essays on the American Revolutionary period, American Romanticism, African American literature, and higher education.

DAVID HOFFMAN, assistant professor in the School of Public Affairs at Baruch College of the City University of New York, has taught courses in public sector communication and advocacy, leadership studies, film studies, rhetorical theory, and persuasion. A former president of the American Society for the History of Rhetoric, he has published on argumentation and ancient Greek rhetoric and culture.

LISA SHAWN HOGAN teaches women's studies and communication arts and sciences at the Pennsylvania State University. She has published in *Southern Journal of Communication*, *Rhetoric & Public Affairs*, *Gender Issues*, *Review of Communication*, and *Women's Studies: An Interdisciplinary Journal*.

SHANNON HOLLAND is a doctoral student in speech communication at the University of Georgia.

LORRAINE D. JACKSON, associate professor of communication studies at California Polytechnic at San Luis Obispo, teaches courses in health communication, gender and communication, and communication theory. Her research interests include improving doctor–patient communication and the study of effective health campaigns. She is coeditor (with Bernard K. Duffy) of *Health Communication Research: A Guide to Developments and Directions.*

RICHARD J. JENSEN is emeritus professor of communication at the University of Nevada, Las Vegas. Dr. Jensen is the author or coauthor of nine books, including *The Rhetorical Career of Cesar Chavez* and *The Words of Cesar Chavez.* He has authored or coauthored more than fifty articles and book chapters, and has made more than sixty professional presentations. Dr. Jensen has been active in regional and national professional associations.

ANDREW KING is Hopkins professor of communication at Lousiana State University. He teaches courses in British, American, and political rhetoric. He is the author of *Communication and Power*, *Black Salt*, and *Postmodern Political Communication* and has edited *Great American Critics* with Jim Kuypers.

RANDALL A. LAKE, associate professor in the Annenberg School for Communication at the University of Southern California, teaches courses in contemporary rhetorical theory and criticism, argumentation, and movements for social change. He has written extensively about social controversies, including Native American protest, and particularly about the rhetorical construction of identities among dominant and subaltern groups. He has received the National Communication Association's Golden Anniversary Monograph Award and the American Forensic Association's Daniel Rohrer Award for outstanding scholarship. Currently, he is the editor of *Argumentation and Advocacy: The Journal of the American Forensic Association.*

CATHERINE LANGFORD is a doctoral student in the Department of Communication Arts and Sciences at the Pennsylvania State University. She teaches courses in legal rhetoric, rhetorical theory, and public speaking.

WINDY Y. LAWRENCE, assistant professor of speech communication at the University of Houston–Downtown, teaches courses in political rhetoric and public address.

RICHARD W. LEEMAN, professor of communication studies at the University of North Carolina at Charlotte, teaches courses in rhetorical theory, political communication, and African American oratory. He is the editor of *African-American Orators: A BioCritical Sourcebook.* He is also the author of *The Rhetoric of Terrorism and Counterterrorism* and *"Do Everything" Reform: The Oratory of Frances E. Willard.* He is coauthor (with Bill Hill) of *The Art and Practice of Argumentation and Debate.*

DAVID B. McLENNAN, associate professor at Peace College, teaches courses in political communication. His research interests include presidential rhetoric, image revitalization, strategies of political figures, and women's leadership.

MARK LAWRENCE McPHAIL is professor of interdisciplinary studies in the Western College Program at Miami University in Oxford, Ohio. He is the author of *Zen in the Art of Rhetoric: An Inquiry into Coherence* and *The Rhetoric of Racism Revisited: Reparations or Separation?* His scholarship has been published in *Quarterly Journal of Speech*, *Critical Studies in Mass Communication*, and *Howard Journal of Communications*; his creative work has appeared in *Dark Horse* magazine and *American Literary Review*. His research interests include rhetorical theory and epistemology, language and race relations, and visual communication.

CHARLES E. MORRIS, assistant professor of communication studies at Vanderbilt University, is coeditor, with Stephen Howard Browne, of *Readings on the Rhetoric of Social Protest*. His essays have appeared in *Quarterly Journal of Speech*, *Women's Studies in Communication*, and *Free Speech Yearbook*. For his work on queer rhetorical history, he has received the Karl Wallace Memorial Award and the Golden Anniversary Monograph Award from the National Communication Association.

TROY A. MURPHY, associate professor of communication in the Department of Humanities at the University of Michigan–Dearborn, teaches courses in twentieth-century public argument and the rhetoric of social movements. He has published articles in such journals as *Communication Review*, *Communication Education*, *Communication Quarterly*, and *Great Plains Quarterly*. In 1999, he received the National Communication Association's Gerald R. Miller Outstanding Dissertation Award.

SINA K. NAZEMI, product manager for Microsoft CRM, was head page in the U.S. Senate in 1998, serving the members of the 105th Congress. He also has worked as a consultant with the World Bank in Washington, D.C.

LESTER C. OLSON, associate professor and chancellor's distinguished teacher in the Department of Communication at the University of Pittsburgh, teaches courses on rhetorical criticism, rhetoric and human rights, and visual rhetoric. He is the author of *Emblems of American Community in the Revolutionary Era: A Study in Rhetorical Iconology* and *Benjamin Franklin's Vision of American Community: A Study in Rhetorical Iconology*. His essays concerning Audre Lorde's public speeches have appeared in *Quarterly Journal of Speech* and *Philosophy and Rhetoric*. He has received the NCA's Karl Wallace Memorial Award and the Winans-Wichelns Award.

CHARLES F. OTTINGER, adjunct professor of communication at Monmouth University and the College of New Jersey, teaches courses in argumentation and debate, as well as other areas. He also teaches philosophy to adult students and has a private practice in philosophical counseling.

CATHERINE H. PALCZEWSKI, professor of communication studies and director of debate at the University of Northern Iowa, teaches courses in argumentation and rhetoric. Keynoter at the 2001 Alta NCA/AFA Summer Argumentation Conference and winner of the AFA Daniel Rohrer Award for outstanding scholarship, she focuses her writings on how marginalized groups can gain access to the dominant public sphere.

EDWARD M. PANETTA, associate professor of speech communication and director of debate at the University of Georgia, teaches courses in argumentation and political communication. His published work looks at the nature of contemporary argument controversies and the practice of intercollegiate debate.

SHAWN PARRY-GILES is an associate professor of communication, director of the Center for Political Communication and Civic Leadership, and affiliate associate professor of women's studies at the University of Maryland. Her research and teaching center on the study of rhetoric and politics. Her work appears in *Quarterly Journal of Speech* and *Rhetoric & Public Affairs*, among other academic journals. Parry-Giles is the author of *The Rhetorical Presidency, Propaganda, and the Cold War, 1945–1955* and coauthor of *Constructing Clinton: Hyperreality and Presidential Image-Making in Postmodern Politics*.

WILLIAM D. PEDERSON is professor of political science, the American studies chair in liberal arts, and director of the International Lincoln Center at Louisiana State University in Shreveport. His most recent books are *Leaders of the Pack: Polls and Case Studies of Great Supreme Court Justices* and *Franklin D. Roosevelt and Abraham Lincoln: Competing Perspectives on Two Great Presidencies*.

ALAN RAZEE has been a lecturer in communication studies at California Polytechnic State University at San Luis Obispo, and California State University at Fresno. He conducts research on the rhetoric of environmental advocacy and on environmental controversies in the western United States.

JANICE SCHUETZ, professor of communication at the University of New Mexico, teaches courses in public communication, rhetorical theory, and persuasion. She has written or edited eight books and more than sixty articles. She also works as a speech consultant for political campaigns and as a legal consultant for civil and criminal trial lawyers.

KRISTINA HORN SHEELER, assistant professor of communication studies at Indiana University Purdue University Indianapolis (IUPUI), teaches courses in political rhetoric, and gender and communication. She publishes on the topic of women and leadership, and in 2003 received a research grant from IUPUI to support travel to interview women political figures around the country. She is the coauthor (with Karrin Vasby Anderson) of a book on female political figures titled *Governing Codes: Gender, Metaphor, and Political Identity*.

C. BRANT SHORT, associate professor of speech communication at Northern Arizona University, teaches courses in rhetorical history and criticism, and environmental discourse. He is author of *Ronald Reagan and the Public Lands* (1989), editor of a volume examining politics in the intermountain West (1989), and coeditor (with Dayle Hardy-Short) of proceedings of the 1999 Conference on Communication and Environment.

CHRISTOPHER J. SKILES, assistant director of forensics and lecturer in communication studies at California Polytechnic State University at San Luis Obispo, examines both the rhetorical dimensions and the rhetorical functions of public argument in the area of Native American studies. His published work has appeared in *Journal of Communication Inquiry* and *Argument at Century's End: Reflecting on the Past and Envisioning the Future.* His dissertation research examines identity claims and public memory in the formation of the Native American Graves Protection and Repatriation Act of 1990.

CRAIG R. SMITH is a professor in the Communication Studies Department and director of the Center for First Amendment Studies at California State University at Long Beach. He served as a full-time speechwriter for President Gerald Ford and as a consulting writer for many political leaders, including George H. W. Bush. He has written over a dozen books and fifty scholarly articles. His latest book on oratory is *The Quest for Charisma.*

STEPHEN A. SMITH, professor of communication at the University of Arkansas, teaches courses in political communication and freedom of speech. He is the editor of two books on Bill Clinton. He served as chief of staff for Clinton when he was attorney general of Arkansas, and as executive assistant when Clinton was governor of Arkansas.

GORDON STABLES, director of debate and clinical assistant professor of communication at the Annenberg School for Communication at the University of Southern California, studies mediated representations of warfare. He had published articles examining the representation of gendered violence in the Kosovo conflict in *Critical Studies in Media Communication,* and the emerging phenomenon of American public diplomacy in the Middle East in *Controversia.*

HERMANN G. STELZNER (deceased) was professor emeritus at University of Massachusetts, Amherst. He was editor of *Communication Quarterly* and the *Quarterly Journal of Speech.*

PAUL STOB is a doctoral student at the University of Wisconsin at Madison, and teaches courses in public speaking, communication theory, and communication technology skills. His research interests include legal rhetoric and the rhetoric of classical American philosophy, particularly the work of William James and John Dewey.

PATRICIA A. SULLIVAN, professor of communication at the State University of New York at New Paltz, teaches courses on rhetorical criticism, political communication, gender and communication, and communication and dissenting voices. She coauthored (with Lynn H. Turner) *From the Margins to the Center: Contemporary Women and Political Communication*, and coedited (with Carole Levin) *Political Rhetoric, Power, and Renaissance Women*, as well as (with Steven R. Goldzwig) *New Approaches to Rhetoric*. Her scholarly articles have appeared in journals including *Quarterly Journal of Speech* and *Women and Politics*.

ROBERT E. TERRILL, associate professor of communication and culture at Indiana University at Bloomington, teaches courses in rhetoric and public address. He is the author of *Malcolm X: Inventing Radical Judgment*. His work has appeared in *Quarterly Journal of Speech*, *Critical Studies in Media Communication*, and *Southern Journal of Communication*.

MARI BOOR TONN, associate professor of communication at the University of Maryland at College Park, teaches courses in rhetorical criticism, public address, rhetorical theory, and feminist criticism. She has written essays on female labor union leaders including Mary Harris "Mother" Jones and Elizabeth Gurley Flynn; on political figures such as Ann Richards (with Bonnie J. Dow), H. Ross Perot (with Valerie A. Endress), and Colin Powell; and on social controversies, including the rhetoric surrounding abortion.

MARY ANNE TRASCIATTI, assistant professor of speech communication and rhetorical studies at Hofstra University, teaches courses in rhetorical theory, persuasion, public address, and political communication. Her work has been published in the journals *Critical Studies in Media Communication* and *Advances in the History of Rhetoric*. She is coeditor (with Jerome Delamater) of an interdisciplinary volume on the cultural and political legacy of the Sacco–Vanzetti case, and she is completing a manuscript on the rhetoric of American citizenship during World War I and the 1920s.

RICHARD E. VATZ, professor of communication studies at Towson University, has taught courses involving presidential rhetoric for thirty years. He is coauthor of a book on Thomas Szasz and psychiatric rhetoric; has published more than 250 articles and reviews in professional journals and newspapers; and has provided scores of convention papers and extensive commentary on politics for CBS Radio News and for Baltimore and Washington television and radio stations. He has won five universitywide teaching awards at Towson, as well as Towson University's 2004 President's Award for Distinguished Service to the University.

BETH WAGGENSPACK, associate professor of communication and director of the undergraduate program at Virginia Tech, teaches courses in rhetorical theory, history, and criticism, and in the rhetoric of American first ladies and social movements. She has written numerous book chapters on Eleanor Roosevelt, Helen Herron Taft, Elizabeth Cady Stanton, Marian Wright Edelman, and Lucy Stone. In addition, she conducts research on the impact of communication on families and adoption.

THEODORE O. WINDT, JR. (deceased) was professor of political rhetoric at the University of Pittsburgh. He was the author of *The Rhetoric of Peaceful Co-Existence: A Criticism of Selected American Speeches by Nikita Khrushchev*, *The Cold War as Rhetoric: The Beginnings, 1945–1950*, and *Rhetoric as Human Adventure: A Short Biography of Everett Lee Hunt*, editor of *Presidential Rhetoric: 1961 to the Present* and coeditor of *Essays in Presidential Rhetoric*. He was a weekly commentator on presidential politics for KDKA-TV in Pittsburgh, a professional political consultant and speech writer, and a consultant to the ABC-TV News department, New York City.

DAVID ZAREFSKY is Owen L. Coon professor of communication studies at Northwestern University, where he formerly was dean of the School of Speech. He teaches and conducts research in American public discourse, argumentation, and rhetorical criticism. He is the author of *President Johnson's War on Poverty: Rhetoric and History* and several articles on the rhetoric of the Johnson presidency, as well as a book and numerous articles on the Lincoln–Douglas debates of 1858. He has served as president of the National Communication Association, the Central States Communication Association, and the Rhetoric Society of America.